TEXAS CIVIL PROCEDURE
TRIAL & APPEAL

CASES AND MATERIALS

2019
EDITION

RICHARD E. FLINT
L. WAYNE SCOTT
PROFESSORS OF LAW
ST. MARY'S UNIVERSITY SCHOOL OF LAW

IMPRIMATUR PRESS

8111 LBJ FREEWAY, SUITE 1325
DALLAS, TEXAS 75251
TELEPHONE (214) 366-1155
FACSIMILE (214) 879-9939
800-811-6725
EMAIL: BOOKS@IMPRIMATURPRESS.COM
www.ImprimaturPress.com

Printed in the United States of America

ISBN 978-1-60503-130-9

These materials are prepared for classroom use. It is not a substitute for specific legal research. The cases and laws are discussed generally and the author's comments should not be relied on for the basis of a legal opinion or course of action, without careful review of applicable authorities including those cases decided since the publication of this book.

TABLE OF CONTENTS

CHAPTER 1.
DISPOSITION WITHOUT TRIAL

CHAPTER 2.
THE JURY TRIAL AND THE SELECTION OF JURORS

CHAPTER 3.
PREPARATION OF THE JURY CHARGE AND RECEIPT OF THE VERDICT

CHAPTER 4.
NO EVIDENCE REVIEW AND TAKING THE CASE AWAY FROM THE JURY

CHAPTER 5.
NON-JURY TRIALS

CHAPTER 6.
PRECLUSION: RES JUDICATA AND COLLATERAL ESTOPPEL

CHAPTER 7.
THE COURT OF APPEALS

CHAPTER 8.
PROCEEDINGS TO THE SUPREME COURT

CHAPTER 9.
ORIGINAL JURISDICTION OF APPELLATE COURTS

APPENDIX

Chapter 1.
Disposition Without Trial

INTRODUCTION

JOSKE
v.
IRVINE

91 Tex. 574, 44 S.W. 1059
(1898)

Franklin & Cobbs, for plaintiff in error.
C. K. Breneman, for defendant in error.

DENMAN, J.

Joe Shely, an officer of the city of San Antonio, arrested James Irvine without a warrant, and confined him nearly 24 hours in the city prison. Irvine sued Alexander Joske to recover damages, claiming that such arrest was unlawful and directed by him. The arrest was not sought to be justified under any statute or charter provision, but under a city ordinance authorizing the arrest of suspicious characters without warrant. The trial court having instructed the jury that the arrest was unlawful, verdict and judgment were for plaintiff for $250, which having been affirmed by the court of civil appeals, Joske has brought the case to this court upon writ of error.

Said charge is assigned as error. The court of civil appeals overruled the assignment on the ground that the city charter did not authorize the council to pass such an ordinance. We were inclined to hold otherwise at the time of granting the application for writ of error, but do not feel called upon to determine the question, for the reason that we do not consider there is any evidence in the record of the existence of such an ordinance. The only testimony on the subject is that of Shely, as follows: 'I made the affidavit against Irvine. The warrant issued on the ground of suspicious character. Under the city ordinance we have a right to do so during investigation. * * * I have a right, as an officer acting in the discharge of his duty, to arrest anybody whom I think has committed an offense against the state or city. I thought this man had committed an offense from his own actions. I did not see him commit any offense. I had authority to arrest Mr. Irvine, and take him to the city jail and confine him there, without a warrant and without any complaint against him. I made complaint against him the next morning. I couldn't make it until the next morning, because the recorder was not there.' His evidence further shows that he arrested Irvine in the evening, but did not make the affidavit until the next morning.

We construe the first portion of his testimony above quoted as tending only to establish an ordinance authorizing the making of an affidavit against one as a suspicious character in order to hold him during an investigation of his case. It does not tend to show the existence of an ordinance authorizing a person's arrest without a warrant on the ground that the officer considers him a suspicious character. The latter portion of his testimony, above quoted, is merely the opinion of the officer as to his authority, and does not purport to state even the substance of an ordinance. It does not even appear to have been based upon an ordinance. It may have been his construction of the statutes and charter authorizing the city officers to arrest without warrant in certain cases. The existence and contents of the ordinance were facts to be established by proof. The proof did not bear upon those issues, but, assuming them to be established, Shely merely gave his opinion as to the authority conferred upon him thereby. This was only his opinion upon a question of law. Such an opinion could not establish the fact-the ordinance-upon which it was based. Since there was no evidence of an ordinance justifying the arrest without warrant, and since it cannot be justified either under the general statutes or any provision of the city charter, the trial court did not err in giving said charge. We are therefore of opinion that the record shows that plaintiff's arrest was unlawful.

But more must be shown to hold Joske liable therefor. Upon this subject the court charged the jury: 'If you believe from the testimony that the defendant, Alexander Joske, requested or directed the officer Joe Shely to arrest and confine said plaintiff in jail, then you are instructed that plaintiff is entitled to recover of defendant, Joske.' Joske, by proper assignment, urges that the giving of this charge was error, for the reason that there was no evidence tending to show that he 'requested or directed' the arrest. Irvine was driving a delivery wagon for Joske Bros., of which Alexander Joske was a member, and in the performance of his duties started out with a number of packages for delivery to various customers of the firm in the city of San Antonio. He returned at night, and informed the stableman that some of the packages, the value of which seems to have been about $30, had been stoled from his wagon, and then, without informing Joske, went to his room. Very soon afterwards Alexander Joske and the stableman appeared at the room, and from that time Irvine's version of Joske's connection with his arrest, as given on his direct examination, is as follows: 'Mr. Joske called out, did I live there; called out my name, Jim Irvine. I answered, 'Yes, sir;' and he jumped up, and in a very angry way asked what I did with those goods and what I had done with the money. I said, 'Mr. Joske, I lost them.' He asked me where, and I told him where they had been stolen from my wagon. I don't know whether he believed my statement or not, but any way he went off, and came back with two police officers, and they questioned me regarding the packages which had been lost, and I told them all I knew about it; that they had been lost or stolen out of the wagon, and told them the place. Some of the police officers said, 'You had better come along with us.' Captain Roberts asked me to go along, and I did so. I had my coat on, and we went to the stable, and Mr. Joske asked the stableman what was my condition when I came in, and he said, 'He was drunk.' Mr. Joske also requested Captain Roberts to ask the stableman as to my condition when I came in, and the man answered that I was drunk. I told him that I was not. Then he took me to the store, and went inside, and looked over this delivery sheet. Then we went outside the store again, and Mr. Joske and the officers had a talk, and then Frank Roberts, captain of the police, told me I could go; and in the meantime Mr. Joske said, 'You come to my office in the morning, but don't take your horse and wagon along.' He discharged me right there. I said, 'All right.' So I went home, and the next morning I showed up at the office at his request. I had some change of theirs that I had out the day before. I went up to the shipping clerk, who was the man I did my business with, and I balanced up my account with the exception of $3 that the house owed me for work, which I retained. Then I waited till Mr. Joske came, and he called me into his office, and said: 'Tell me what you did with those goods, and I will make it as easy for you as possible; I won't hurt you,'—or words to that effect. Well, of course it made me feel right angry with Mr. Joske to think I had stolen the goods. I answered: 'Good Lord, Mr. Joske, you don't think for a moment I stole those goods, do you?' He said: 'What did you do with them? What was done with the money?' I said: 'They were stolen out of my wagon; that is all I can tell you about it.' Then he went to the shipping clerk, and asked: 'Has this man any C. O. D. money?' And the clerk said: 'Yes, sir; he has got three dollars.' Then he didn't say another word, but was very angry, and jumped to the telephone, and rang up police headquarters, and said: 'Send an officer here at once.' I waited till the officer came, and when he did come Mr. Joske met him, and talked with him, and then called me over to one side, and, with the officer, he asked me about those goods being lost, and I told him just what I have already said,—that they were stolen out of my wagon. Then the officer said: 'Mr. Joske says you have three dollars of his money.' I said that I had retained three dollars for wages which he owed me. He said I ought to pay Mr. Joske that money, and I said I would not do so until the law compelled me, because Mr. Joske had discharged me the night before without allowing me to make any explanation, or settle up with him for the goods lost or stolen, and that I intended to keep the money. He then told me there was a law compelling me to pay it, and that I had better pay it. I said that at that rate I would pay him, but that I didn't have enough in my pocket to pay him then, but that I could get it in two minutes; that I could go to my room and get it. He took me along, and we went in his buggy, and as we were going along I noticed that it was about twelve o'clock, and I thought my boarding house was nearest to the store,—nearer than my room,-and I would go there. I was pretty sure I could catch the man I roomed with, and that would save my going to my room, and we did so, and I asked him for a couple of dollars, and he let me have it, and we came back to Joske's,—Detective Shely and myself,—and Mr. Shely remarked to Mr. Joske that 'this man didn't go to his room for the money, but went to another man for it.' 'Well,' he says, 'I will make an affidavit against him, anyhow.' They talked together a little while, and I stayed in Mr. Shely's buggy, and he came back and I said, 'What is it?' And Mr. Shely said, 'You have got to go with me; you have got to go to jail.' They put me in jail, and kept me there all that evening and until ten o'clock the next morning.' Joe Shely, witness for defendant, Joske, testified as to the circumstances attending the arrest as follows: 'I was assistant city detective at that time. * * * I was called to Mr. Joske's store, * * * and found Mr. Joske and Mr. Irvine arguing and contending in a very boisterous way. Mr. Irvine seemed to be angry. I had a conversation with him and Mr. Joske, in which Mr. Joske desired Irvine to tell him what he had done with certain goods that he had taken out the day previous, and he refused to give an accounting, and seemed to be in various ways very aggressive towards Mr. Joske. When I came up and commenced to talk to him he addressed me in the same manner. * * * I told him that he couldn't abuse me; that I proposed to have him give an account of these things. He said he didn't have to. I told him he might have to, and then I told him who I was. He may not have known at the time that I was an officer. * * * Well, he studied a little bit, and then there was something said about the three dollars of Mr. Joske's money. I asked him what right he had to appropriate that money to his own use. He said he was going to keep it until Mr. Joske paid him for his work. * * * I asked him what he had done with the money, and he said he had it in his room on Blum street, and I asked him to go up there with me. He got in the buggy with me, and we went around to the Menger, around the corner of Crockett and Alamo Plaza. * * * Irvine was not arrested then. He went with me voluntarily to get Mr. Joske's money. We went around there, and Irvine got out, and went into a restaurant. I got out of the buggy and followed him. I saw him talking to a man, and presently he came out. I saw him and the man together, and the man passed him something; and he came out, and got into the buggy with me, and we started back to go up Blum street, and he said we would go on back. I said, 'Well, let's go up to your room.' He said, 'No; that he had the money.' I said, 'You said you had the money at your room.' 'Well,' he says, 'I have got the money now to give to him.' I then told him that I wanted to know what he had done with those goods, or give an account of the things he had the evening before. He said he didn't have to. I told him that he would have to give an account of those things or go to his room, or that I would arrest him, and for him to take his choice. I told him that I wanted an explanation; that I demanded it as an officer; and he positively refused to give an explanation; and I drove back to Mr. Joske's, and called Mr. Joske out, and told him that I was going to put Irvine in jail. I brought him down, and put him in jail, and made an affidavit against him. In the first place, before I went away from there, Irvine challenged me to arrest him. That was in the store, in the presence of Mr. Joske and some of his clerks. He challenged me to arrest him, and defied me to do it. I told him I didn't want to arrest him, and Mr. Joske said he did not want to have him arrested at all, but what he wanted was an explanation or some satisfaction as to where his goods had gone to, and when I came back there Mr. Joske never advised me to arrest him or anything of that kind. I did it on my own responsibility. I told Irvine that I was an officer in the discharge of my duty, and that Mr. Joske had just turned the case over to me, and it was my duty to investigate it, and that I wanted him to tell me all about it. He refused positively to do so, and defied me to arrest him and put him in jail. I took him down, and advised with Capt. Druse, my chief. The captain advised me to go ahead, and whatever I did he knew would be right. He said, 'You are acquainted with the case, and you know the law and you know your business.' When I drove back to Mr. Joske's I called him out. He did not direct me to arrest Irvine in any way at all. Mr. Joske had nothing at all to do with the arrest of the man; never advised me to arrest him; just turned the case over to me, and wanted it investigated. * * * I could get from Irvine no explanation whatever in reference to the goods until after I put him in jail. After he had been in jail a while he sent for me, and told me where he was playing cards,-where he got drunk,—and I went up there and got information. I found out where the articles were lost. He told me that he had been drunk, and everything, and they corroborated what he had told me after he had been in jail three or four hours. The next morning after I came back, I went before the recorder and had the case dismissed.' Frank Roberts, captain of police, testified for defendant that when he was investigating the case on the evening the goods were lost, as detailed in Irvine's testimony above, 'Joske did not in any way direct me to arrest or imprison said Irvine; in fact, he told me not to do so. * * * By all sorts of examination I tried to ascertain from him the whereabouts of the missing property, and threatened to put him in jail if he did not tell; but from his dazed condition, and from his actions, I became satisfied that he did not know where the goods were.' Alexander Joske testified in his own behalf to all the circumstances connected with the several transactions referred to in the testimony above, his testimony agreeing substantially with that of Capt. Roberts and Shely. He also testified that he had no intention of having Irvine arrested, and told both Roberts and Shely that he did not wish to have him arrested, but that he merely sent for them in order to have them, as officers, trace up and recover his property. He also denied that he made the remark testified to by Irvine, to the effect that he was going to file a complaint against Irvine. He further testified that he never recovered the goods, and that he did not go to the police court. W. O. Hilgers, whom we understand to have been an employee of Joske Bros., testified as to the conversation between Shely and Joske, as Shely was about to leave the store the last time, as follows: 'Mr. Joske said: 'I don't want anything to do with the arrest. I just want my goods that belonged to me. I positively do not want anything to do with the arrest.' The above is all the testimony that we understand is material to the question under consideration.

The question for our determination may be stated thus: Is it a legitimate inference from this testimony that Joske 'requested or directed' the arrest? Or, in other words, should the trial court have instructed the jury that they could not so find therefrom? If so, it is our duty to set aside the verdict; if not, we have no power to do so. It is important, before proceeding to an examination of the evidence, to determine the rule of law by which the trial court should have been governed in deciding whether he would so instruct; for we are governed by the same rule in passing upon the question above stated. In 1870, BULLER, J., laid down the since much quoted and often misunderstood proposition that 'whether there be any evidence is a question for the judge; whether sufficient evidence, is for the jury.' *Company of Carpenters v. Hayward*, 1 Doug. 375. The correctness of this proposition is generally admitted, but great difficulty has been experienced in determining the exact legal meaning of the phrase 'any evidence.' In 1868, WILLIS, J., in *Ryder v. Wombwell,* L. R. 4 Exch. 32, said: 'It was formerly considered necessary in all cases to leave the question to the jury if there was any evidence, even a scintilla, in support of the case; but it is now settled that the question for the judge (subject, of course, to review) is, as stated by MAULE, J., in *Jewell v. Parr*, 13 C. B. 916, not whether there is literally no evidence, but whether there is none that ought reasonably to satisfy the jury that the fact sought to be proved is established;' and held that plaintiff could not recover of a minor for a goblet valued at £15, and a pair of ornamental stud buttons valued at £25, the former being, within the knowledge of plaintiff at time of sale, intended by the minor as a present to a third person, there being no evidence offered by plaintiff that such articles were necessaries in the particular case, and set aside the verdict and judgment in favor of plaintiff and entered a nonsuit. In *Wittkowsky v. Wasson*, 71 N. C. 454, the court, in speaking of the meaning of the phrase 'any evidence,' say: 'Did it mean the slightest scintilla of evidence, or such only as that from which a jury might reasonably infer the existence of the alleged fact? The latter view has been adopted in this state and in England, and, so far as my researches have extended, in other states generally.' In *Hyatt v. Johnston*, 91 Pa. St. 200, it is said: 'Since the scintilla doctrine has been exploded, both in England and in this country, the preliminary question of law for the court is, not whether there is literally no evidence, or a mere scintilla, but whether there is any that ought reasonably to satisfy the jury that the fact sought to be proved is established. If there is evidence from which the jury can properly find the question for the party on whom the burden of proof rests, it should be submitted; if not, if should be withdrawn from the jury.' In *Baulec v. Railroad Co.*, 59 N. Y. 356, the court said, quoting from *Toomey v. Railway Co.*, 3 C. B. (N. S.) 149, that 'it is not enough to authorize the submission of a question, as one of fact, to a jury, that there is 'some evidence.' A scintilla of evidence, or a mere surmise that there may have been negligence on the part of the defendants, would not justify the judge in leaving the case to the jury'; and held that a single act of casual neglect, though admissible as evidence, as held by this court in *Cunningham v. Railway Co.*, 88 Tex. 534, 31 S. W. 629, was not sufficient to authorize a jury to find that an employé was incompetent, and that the retention of such employé in its service, after having investigated the facts connected with such act, would not authorize a finding that the company was guilty of negligence in continuing to employ him.

This court in *Lee v. Railway Co.*, 89 Tex. 588, 36 S. W. 65, said: 'To authorize the court to take the question from the jury, the evidence must be of such a character that there is no room for ordinary minds to differ as to the conclusion to be drawn from it.' In *Mynning v. Railroad Co.*, 64 Mich. 93, 31 N. W. 147, the rule is stated thus: 'If the circumstances are such that reasonable minds might draw different conclusions respecting the plaintiff's fault, he is entitled to go to the jury upon the facts. The judge takes the case from the jury only when it is susceptible of but one just opinion.' The supreme court of the United States have approved the rule announced in *Ryder v. Wombwell, supra. Railway Co. v. Munson*, 14 Wall. 442; *Commissioners v. Clark*, 94 U. S. 278; *Griggs v. Houston*, 104 U. S. 553.

From a careful examination of the cases, it appears (1) that it is the duty of the court to instruct a verdict, though there be slight testimony, if its probative force be so weak that it only raises a mere surmise or suspicion of the existence of the fact sought to be established, such testimony, in legal contemplation, falling short of being 'any evidence'; and (2) that it is the duty of the court to determine whether the testimony has more than that degree of probative force. If it so determines, the law presumes that the jury could not 'reasonably infer the existence of the alleged fact,' and 'that there is no room for ordinary minds to differ as to the conclusion to be drawn from it.' The broad and wise policy of the law, formed in and descending to us through the crucibles of time, does not permit the citizen to be deprived of his property, his liberty, or his life upon mere surmise or suspicion, and places upon a trained judiciary the grave responsibility of determining as a question of law whether the testimony establishes more. 'There is, no doubt, a possibility, in all cases where the judges have to determine whether there is evidence on which the jury may reasonably find a fact, that the judges may differ in opinion, and it is possible that the majority may be wrong. Indeed, whenever a decision of the court below on such a point is reversed, the majority must have been so either in the court above or the court below. This is an infirmity which must affect all tribunals.' *Ryder v. Wombwell, supra.*

We are, then, called upon to determine whether the testimony in this case does more than to create a mere surmise or suspicion that Joske 'requested or directed' Irvine's arrest. We think it does not, if it can be said to go that far. It shows clearly that Joske was urging the officers to ferret out and recover, if possible, his goods, which Irvine had received and had not returned, and that both he and the officers were endeavoring to ascertain from Irvine the circumstances attending their loss, so that they might be traced. This Joske had a clear legal right to do, and we are of opinion that from the mere exercise of this right the law will not permit the inference to be drawn that he 'requested or directed' the arrest, though it be conceded that but for its exercise the arrest would never have been made. It would be against reason to hold that the mere fact that a citizen has called upon the officer of the law to search for and recover his lost or stolen property will authorize the inference that he 'requested or directed' the arrest subsequently made. *Newell*, Mal. Pros. p. 108, § 7, and authorities cited; Tayl. Ev. § 118, and authorities cited. The evidence would probably justify a finding that the arrest was made in Joske's presence, though it would be difficult to conclude therefrom that Shely did not fully determine upon and in legal contemplation make the arrest at the time Irvine refused to go to his room, or give any explanation as to the circumstances under which the goods were lost. It would be a grave question whether any statement made by Irvine after that time would be admissible against him if on trial for a criminal offense. But if it be conceded that the evidence warrants the inference that the arrest was not made until they returned to the store, and Shely had the conversation with Joske, still we are of opinion that nothing is shown to have occurred there that would warrant the inference that Joske 'requested or directed' Shely to make the arrest. The conversation, as detailed by Shely, Joske, and Hilgers, shows the contrary, and that Shely made the arrest on his own responsibility, against Joske's request; and it is difficult to perceive just how Joske could have prevented the arrest at that time if he had seen fit to go beyond the exercise of his clear legal right to remain passive. But, if it be conceded that the jury had the right to lay out of the case the testimony of all these witnesses, then we are left without information as to the conversation, except that Irvine says that Joske said, 'I will make an affidavit against him anyhow.' We are of the opinion that this remark does not tend to show that Joske 'requested or directed' Shely to then make the arrest, but, on the contrary, if taken as true, it indicates a purpose on Joske's part to proceed in the mode prescribed by law, by making an affidavit, and thus placing the matter before the courts. If this purpose had been carried out, this suit for an illegal arrest could not have been maintained, though one for malicious prosecution may have been, under certain circumstances not necessary to mention here. *Mullen v. Brown*, 138 Mass. 114. Would the mere fact that Shely made the arrest immediately after leaving Joske warrant the conclusion that the latter 'requested or directed' him to make it? We think not. The whole case shows that Joske was pressing both the officers and Irvine to aid him in the recovery of his goods. This he had the legal right to do. There are no circumstances tending to show any collusion between Joske and the officers, or that he had or attempted to exercise any authority or control over them in the performance of what they supposed to be their duties, or that he, while ostensibly trying to recover his goods, was covertly seeking to procure Irvine's arrest. There is no direct testimony that Joske 'requested or directed' the arrest, and we are of the opinion that such fact cannot be reasonably inferred from the circumstances. 'An inference is a deduction which the reason of the jury makes from the facts proved.' 1 Rice, Ev. § 36. If the jury cannot reasonably make the deduction, the law does not authorize it. Upon the whole case, we are of opinion that the probative force of the testimony does not go beyond the point of creating a mere surmise or suspicion that Joske 'requested or directed' the arrest, and that, therefore, under the principles above discussed, there is not, in legal contemplation, 'any evidence' of that fact. It results that it was error for the court to give the charge complained of, for which the judgments of the court of civil appeals and the trial court will be reversed, and the cause remanded.

Note

The *Joske* decision was revisited in *City of Keller v. Wilson,* 168 S.W.3d 802 (Tex. 2005): The "scintilla" rule has been modified by the broader "meager circumstantial evidence" test, which allows the appellate court greater review power over fact findings based on circumstantial evidence.

In claims or defenses supported only by meager circumstantial evidence, the evidence does not rise above a scintilla (and thus is legally insufficient) if jurors would have to guess whether a vital fact exists. When the circumstances are equally consistent with either of two facts, neither fact may be inferred. In such cases, the courts must view each piece of circumstantial evidence, not in isolation, but in light of all the known circumstances. Thus, when the circumstantial evidence of a vital fact is meager, a reviewing court must consider not just favorable but all the circumstantial evidence and competing inferences as well.

1. *Traditional Motion for Summary Judgment*

Note

Texas summary judgment practice had been stable for many years. However, in 1997, the Texas Supreme Court amended TEX. R. CIV. PROC. 166a, by adding section i. to provide for a "no-evidence" summary judgment. In studying this chapter, the "traditional" summary judgment practice, which is still in place, will be examined first. This represents the procedures that will be used in all but "no-evidence" summary judgments. Attention will then turn to the "no-evidence" summary judgment practice, introduced in 1997. It will be necessary to contrast and compare the two types of summary judgment practice.

a. *The Frame Work of Summary Judgment Practice*

Notice. Under Tex. R. 166a(c), "Except on leave of court, with notice to the other party, the motion and any supporting affidavits shall be filed and served at least twenty-one days before the time specified for hearing." Notice of the date of the hearing should be included in the summary judgment notice. The non-movant waives the notice requirement by appearing at the hearing, without filing a motion for continuance. The notice require can also be waived by agreement.

Reply. Under Tex. R. Civ. P. 166a(c) "Except on leave of court, the adverse party, not later than seven days prior to the day of hearing may file and serve opposing affidavits or other written response."

Hearing. Under Tex. R. Civ. P. 166a(c) "No oral testimony shall be received at the hearing."

Judgment. Under Tex. R. Civ. P. 166b(e), the trial court may enter judgment on the entire case, or a part of the case. "If . . . judgment is not rendered upon the whole case or for all the relief asked and a trial is necessary, [the trial court] . . . shall . . . make an order specifying the facts that appear without substantial controversy, including the extent to which the amount of damages or other relief is not in controversy, and directing such further proceedings in the action as are just. Upon the trial of the action the facts so specified shall be deemed established, and the trial shall be conducted according."

Appeal. A summary judgment which disposes of all issues and parties is subject to a final appeal. One that does not dispose of all issues and parties is interlocutory, and not appealable. However, it is important to remember the decision in *Mafrige v. Ross,* 866 S.W.2d 590 (Tex. 1993), which held that the inclusion of "Mother Hubbard" language or its equivalent in an order granting summary judgment makes an otherwise partial summary judgment final for appeal purposes. If a summary judgment order appears to be final, as evidenced by the inclusion of language purporting to dispose of all claims or parties, the judgment should be treated as final for purposes of appeal.

Casso v Brand, 776 S.W.2d 551, 558 (Tex. 1989). This case describes the difference between the traditional summary judgment practice in Texas and the federal practice which recognizes the concept of a "no-evidence" summary judgment motion (now incorporated into the TEX. R. CIV. P. 166a(i). In 1989, in this case, the Texas Supreme Court held that Texas does not have to, and did not, adopt the more liberal summary judgment standard in public figure defamation actions used in fed court. The case gives a preview of the changes brought about by the 1997 amendment. It also demonstrates the flexibility available in traditional motion for summary judgment cases.

Texas (in all but Rule 166a(i) cases). In Texas, summary judgment are used only to eliminate patently unmeritorious claims and untenable defenses. The burden of proof is never shifted to the non-movant, unless, and until the movant has established its entitlement to a summary judgment on the issues expressly presented to the trial court by conclusively proving all essential elements of its cause of action or defense as a matter of law. The Texas law is favorable to maintaining the action in court, and is, thus, favorable to plaintiffs.

Federal. Summary judgments in federal court are based on a different presumption and point of view. In federal court, under R56(c) the entry of summary judgment is proper, after adequate time for discovery and upon motion, against a party who fails to make a showing sufficient to establish the existence of an element essential to that party's case, and on which that party will bear the burden of proof at trial. *Celotex v. Catrett,* 477 U. S.

317, 324 (1986) (the federal standard places the burden of presenting competent evidence at the summary judgment hearing on the party who bears the burden of proof at trial). The federal law makes it difficult for the plaintiff to keep a case in court, and thus is favorable to defendants.

WFAA-TV, Inc. v. McLemore, 978 S.W.2d 568 (Tex. 1998), represents the product of *Casso v. Brand.* In an action by a public figure, a libel defendant is entitled to summary judgment under TEX. R. CIV. P. 166a(c), if it can negate actual malice, as a matter of law. A libel defendant can negate actual malice by presenting evidence that shows he or she did not publish the alleged defamatory statement with actual knowledge of any falsity, or with reckless disregard for the truth.

b. *The Legal Basis for a Conventional Motion for Summary Judgment*

Notes

1. The Texas summary judgment practice is designed to eliminate patently unmeritorious claims and untenable defenses while preserving the right to a jury trial on disputed fact issues. In order to be entitled to a summary judgment the movant needs to establish his entitlement to the summary judgment on the issues expressly presented to the trial court by conclusively establishing all essential elements of his cause of action or defense as a matter of law. It is only after this showing that a non-movant is required to come forward with competent evidence to avoid the summary judgment. A plaintiff meets this burden by producing evidence which conclusively establishes each element of his cause of action. This is identical to the burden he must establish if he moved for an instructed verdict during the trial of the case. *See Ortega-Carter v. American Int'l Adjustment Co.*, 834 S.W.2d 439 (Tex. App.—Dallas 1992, writ denied). In *Randall's Food Mkts. v. Davis*, 891 S.W.2d 640 (Tex. 1995) the Court succinctly stated the requirements for a defendant to establish a motion for summary judgment as follows:

> To prevail on a motion for summary judgment, a movant must establish that there is no genuine issue as to any material fact and that he or she is entitled to judgment as a matter of law. TEX. R. CIV. P. 166a(c). A defendant who conclusively negates at least one of the essential elements of a cause of action is entitled to summary judgment as to that cause of action. *Wornick Co. v. Casas*, 856 S.W.2d 732, 733 (Tex. 1993); *Gibbs v. General Motors Corp.*, 450 S.W.2d 827, 828 (Tex. 1970). Likewise, a defendant who conclusively establishes each element of an affirmative defense is entitled to summary judgment. In reviewing a summary judgment, we must accept as true evidence in favor of the non-movant, indulging every reasonable inference and resolving all doubts in his or her favor. *El Chico Corp. v. Poole*, 732 S.W.2d 306, 315 (Tex. 1987).

2. On appeal from the granting of a motion for summary judgment, the standard of review and the presumptions favor reversal. In *Gibbs v. General Motors Corp.*, 450 S.W.2d 827 (Tex. 1970) the court set out the standard for review in summary judgment cases in the following language:

> [T]he question on appeal, as well as in the trial court is not whether the summary judgment proof raises fact issues with reference to the essential elements of a plaintiff's claim or cause of action, but is whether the summary judgment proof establishes as a matter of law that there is not genuine issue of act as to one or more of the essential elements of the plaintiff's cause of action.

c. *The Burden upon the Movant for a Summary Judgment*

WALKER
v.
HARRIS
924 S.W.2d 375
(Tex. 1996)

Kenna M. Seiler, John M. Causey, Conroe, for Petitioners.
Lawrence Rothenberg, Houston, for Respondents.

ENOCH, JUSTICE.

This wrongful death action involves the duty of care a lessor owes to persons injured on the leased property by the criminal acts of third parties. The trial court granted summary judgment for the lessors, but the court of appeals reversed. 1995 WL 477560. We hold that the lessors, Deborah and William Walker, owed no legal duty to the decedent, Ronald Harris. We reverse the judgment of the court of appeals and render judgment that Harris's parents, Joyce and Donald Harris, take nothing.

The Walkers owned and operated two of ten separate fourplex apartment units in Brookshire, Texas. In 1990, Ronald Harris attended a party at one of the apartments and was stabbed to death by Andre Steffon Lasker somewhere near one of the Walkers' fourplexes. The parties dispute whether either Ronald Harris or Andre Lasker were invited guests at the party; neither Harris nor Lasker were the Walkers' tenants. The Harrises sued the Walkers for negligence, alleging that the Walkers knew or should have known that the area where the fourplex was located was known for criminal activity. They sought over $2,000,000 in actual damages based on the Walkers' alleged (1) negligent failure to warn the public, including Harris, of this condition, and (2) negligent failure to provide adequate security, including lighting, access control devices, or security guards. The Harrises also sought an unspecified amount of exemplary damages.

The Walkers sought summary judgment, arguing that a property owner generally has no duty to prevent the criminal acts of third parties. They asserted that although property owners may owe a duty to protect individuals from the criminal acts of third parties when the owners know or have reason to know that the third parties present an unreasonable risk of harm to those individuals, they did not owe such a duty because Harris's stabbing was not foreseeable. The Walkers also argued that Lasker's intentional acts were a superseding and proximate cause of Harris's harm. Without stating its reasons, the trial court granted the Walkers' motion for summary judgment. The court of appeals reversed and remanded, holding that a genuine issue of material fact existed regarding the adequacy of the security provided by the Walkers. 1995 WL 477560 *2.

I

To obtain a summary judgment, a defendant must either negate at least one element of the plaintiff's theory of recovery, *"Moore" Burger, Inc. v. Phillips Petroleum Co.*, 492 S.W.2d 934, 936 (Tex. 1972), or plead and conclusively prove each element of an affirmative defense. *City of Houston v. Clear Creek Basin Auth.*, 589 S.W.2d 671, 678 (Tex. 1979). After the defendant produces evidence entitling it to summary judgment, the burden shifts to the plaintiff to present evidence creating a fact issue. *"Moore" Burger*, 492 S.W.2d at 936-37. We take all evidence favorable to the nonmovant as true and indulge every reasonable inference in the nonmovant's favor. *Nixon v. Mr. Property Management Co.*, 690 S.W.2d 546, 549 (Tex. 1985).

II

The existence of a duty is a question of law for the court to decide from the facts surrounding the occurrence in question. *Centeq Realty, Inc. v. Siegler*, 899 S.W.2d 195, 197 (Tex. 1995); *Greater Houston Transp. Co. v. Phillips*, 801 S.W.2d 523, 525 (Tex. 1990). As a general rule, a person has no legal duty to protect another from the criminal acts of a third person or control the conduct of another. *Centeq*, 899 S.W.2d at 197; *Phillips*, 801 S.W.2d at 525; *Otis Eng'g Corp. v. Clark*, 668 S.W.2d 307, 309 (Tex. 1983). Similarly, a landowner has no duty to prevent criminal acts of third parties who are not under the landowner's supervision or control. *Exxon Corp. v. Tidwell*, 867 S.W.2d 19, 21 (Tex. 1993); *El Chico Corp. v. Poole*, 732 S.W.2d 306, 313 (Tex.

1987). This general no-duty rule, however, is not absolute. *See, e.g., Exxon*, 867 S.W.2d at 21 (lessor who retains control over the security and safety of the premises owes a duty to a tenant's employee to use ordinary care to protect the employee if the lessor knows or has reason to know of an unreasonable and foreseeable risk of harm from the criminal acts of third parties); *Nixon*, 690 S.W.2d at 549 (apartment management owed a duty under an ordinance to a minor raped in vacant apartment to protect against such foreseeable criminal acts).

We need not decide and express no opinion on whether this case falls within any exception to the general no-duty rule. Whatever duty a lessor may have to protect persons injured on the leased premises against the criminal acts of third parties, that duty does not arise in the absence of a foreseeable risk of harm. Accordingly, the Walkers are entitled to summary judgment if they established as a matter of law that violent criminal acts like the stabbing were not foreseeable.

Foreseeability requires only that the general danger, not the exact sequence of events that produced the harm, be foreseeable. *Lofton v. Texas Brine Corp.*, 777 S.W.2d 384, 387 (Tex. 1989); *Nixon*, 690 S.W.2d at 550-51. In this case, the general danger the Walkers had to foresee was the danger of injury from violent crime on the premises. We have held that evidence of specific previous crimes on or near the premises may raise a fact issue on the foreseeability of criminal activity. *Nixon*, 690 S.W.2d at 550. The Harrises did not bring forth any summary judgment evidence raising a fact issue on foreseeability.

The summary judgment evidence relied on by both the Walkers and the Harrises, principally the deposition testimony of the Brookshire Police Chief, indicates that the neighborhood where the fourplexes are located is an area of low to moderate crime, that the residential neighborhood across the street from the apartments has "very little crime," and that the amount of crime at the fourplexes is "average" for apartments. The record further indicates that police were never called to the property for a violent crime, except for Ronald Harris's stabbing. The only other calls to the units were for matters such as domestic or neighbor disturbances. The summary judgment evidence also indicates that there were four prior incidents of vandalism and one instance when a refrigerator was taken from a vacant apartment. No one was ever burglarized. This summary judgment evidence establishes that the Walkers had no reason to foresee the likelihood of violent criminal activity at their fourplexes.

We hold that the Walkers established that the violent criminal act of Ronald Harris's stabbing was not foreseeable as a matter of law. Accordingly, the Walkers negated the duty element of the Harrises' cause of action and were entitled to summary judgment. We reverse the judgment of the court of appeals and render judgment that the Harrises take nothing.

d. *The Summary Judgment Procedure is a Form of Non-Jury Trial*

Note

From time to time a significant primary holding from a case will be presented as a "Abbreviated Case". An "Abbreviated Case" is a short summary of a case that decides an important point that is printed in this book in outline form to reduce the length of the book. <u>These notes are as important as "full" cases,</u> but add nothing significant other than the primary holding or holdings. The following short summary of the *Goswami* case is an example of an "Abbreviated Case".

GOSWAMI
v.
METROPOLITAN SAVINGS AND LOAN ASSOCIATION

751 S.W.2d 487
(Tex. 1988)

A summary judgment proceeding is a trial within the meaning of TEX.R.CIV.P. 63.

Under Rule 63, in the absence of a sufficient showing of surprise by the opposing party, the failure to obtain leave of court when filing a late pleading may be cured by the trial court's action in considering the amended pleading. Thus, when the record is silent, it will be presumed that the trial court considered a late filed pleading, when it ruled upon the motion for summary judgment.

Notes

1. In *Roark v. Stallworth Oil & Gas*, 813 S.W.2d 493 (Tex. 1991) the Court held that an unplead affirmative defense may also serve as the basis for a summary judgment when it is raised in the summary judgment motion, and the opposing party does not object to the lack of a rule 94 pleading in either its written response or before the rendition of judgment. The Court continued:

> [U]nder our rules, unplead claims or defenses that are tried by express or implied consent of the parties are treated as if they had been raised by the pleadings. The party who allows an issue to be tried by consent and who fails to raise the lack of a pleading before submission of the case cannot later raise the pleading deficiency for the first time on appeal. There is no valid reason why these rules should not apply to issues raised in the motion for summary judgment. If the non-movant does not object to a variance between the motion for summary judgment and the movant's pleadings, it would advance no compelling interest of the parties or of our legal system to reverse a summary judgment simply because of a pleading defect.

2. *Lewis v. Blake*, 876 S.W.2d 314 (Tex. 1994): When a motion for summary judgment is served by mail, does TEX. R. CIV. P. 21a add three days to the 21-day notice period of the hearing prescribe by Rule 166a(c)? The effect of Rule 21a is to require that a summary judgment motion served by mail be served at least 24 days before the hearing. The phrase "at least" in Rule 166a(c) means that no fewer than 24 days must intervene between the day the motion is mailed, and the day of hearing. In other words, the hearing cannot be held before the 24th day after the day the motion is mailed.

Rule 4 applies to any period of time prescribed by the rules of procedure, and Rule 166a is one of those rules. Applying Rule 4 to Rule 166a(c), the day of service is not to be included in computing the minimum 21-day notice for hearing, and the day of hearing is. Thus, the hearing on a motion for summary judgment may be set as early as the 21st day after the motion is served, or the 24th day if the motion is served by mail.

3. *Martin v. Martin, Martin & Richards, Inc.,* 989 S.W.2d 357 (Tex. 1998). Although TEX. R. CIV. P. 166a(c) calls for a hearing on a motion for summary judgment, not every hearing called for under every rule of civil procedure necessarily requires an oral hearing. Unless required by the express language or the context of the particular rule, the term "hearing" does not necessarily contemplate either a personal appearance before the court or an oral presentation to the court. An oral hearing on a motion for summary judgment may be helpful to the parties and the court, just as oral argument is often helpful on appeal, but since oral testimony cannot be adduced in support of, or in opposition to, a motion for summary judgment, an oral hearing is not mandatory.

Notice of hearing or submission of a summary judgment motion is required, although it is not jurisdictional. The hearing date determines the time for response to the motion; without notice of hearing, the respondent cannot know when the response is due. The district court erred in granting defendant's motion for summary judgment without notice to Gary. The error was harmless, however, because the court fully considered Gary's response and reconfirmed its ruling.

4. *Dow Chemical Company v. Bright*, 89 S.W.3d 602 (Tex. 2002): When both sides have moved for summary judgment and one motion is granted and one denied, the court shall determine all questions presented and render the judgment the trial court should have rendered. *See also City of Garland v. Dallas Morning News*, 22 S.W.3d 351, 356 (Tex. 2000).

e. *Summary Judgment Evidence*

UNITED BLOOD SERVICES
v.
LONGORIA
938 S.W.2d 29
(Tex. 1997)

PER CURIAM.

In this summary judgment case, we decide whether the trial court abused its discretion by rejecting the nonmovant's expert testimony. The court of appeals held that it did. 907 S.W.2d 605. Because we conclude that the court of appeals improperly substituted its opinion for that of the trial court on a matter committed to the trial court's discretion, we reverse the judgment of the court of appeals and render judgment that Plaintiffs take nothing.

Shortly after her birth in 1982, San Juanita Longoria contracted acquired immune deficiency syndrome (AIDS) and cytomegalovirus (CMV) following a transfusion of blood supplied by United Blood Services (UBS). After her death at age four, her parents sued UBS and the hospital where she received the transfusion. The trial court first granted summary judgment in favor of the hospital and UBS based on undisputed expert testimony that in 1982 the medical community did not know that AIDS was a blood-borne disease and no procedures were available for routine testing of blood for exposure to the AIDS virus. The court of appeals reversed, holding that the Longorias had raised a fact issue about the failure to screen for CMV, for which testing was available, and which testing might have eliminated donors at high risk for AIDS. *Longoria v. McAllen Methodist Hosp.*, 771 S.W.2d 663, 665 (Tex. App.—Corpus Christi 1989, writ denied).

On remand, UBS offered additional expert testimony on CMV testing, and also challenged the qualifications of Melvin Kramer, the Longorias' expert witness, to testify on the standard of care for the blood-banking industry. UBS pointed out that Kramer is not a doctor of medicine or osteopathy, has previously conceded that he did not consider himself an expert in blood banking, hematology, or immunology, never worked for a blood bank, never took any courses on blood banking, never published any articles related to blood banks, and obtained his Ph.D. by correspondence course from Pacific Western University, which is not accredited by any nationally recognized accrediting agency. The trial court again granted UBS's motion for summary judgment.

The court of appeals again reversed, pointing out that Kramer holds degrees in bacteriology, anthropology, and public health, and "through self education and reading the relevant medical literature in epidemiology, Kramer has further developed an expertise concerning the standard of care in the collection of blood." 907 S.W.2d at 613. The court noted, however, "we express no opinion concerning the ultimate admissibility of Kramer's testimony at trial, when the basis for his qualification as an expert may be more fully tested by UBS and subjected to closer scrutiny by the trial court." *Id.* at 613 n. 5.

Texas Rule of Civil Procedure 166a(f) requires that in summary judgment proceedings, supporting and opposing affidavits "shall set forth such facts as would be admissible in evidence, and shall show affirmatively that the affiant is competent to testify to the matters stated therein." When a party relies on expert testimony, this requirement includes proof of the expert's qualifications. Contrary to the court of appeals' notation, no difference obtains between the standards for evidence that would be admissible in a summary judgment proceeding and those applicable at a regular trial. *See Hidalgo v. Surety Savings & Loan Ass'n*, 462 S.W.2d 540, 545 (Tex. 1971).

Whether a witness is qualified to offer expert testimony is a matter committed to the trial court's discretion. *Broders v. Heise*, 924 S.W.2d 148 (Tex. 1996). The trial court must determine if the putative expert has "knowledge, skill, experience, training, or education" that would "assist the trier of fact." *See* TEX.R. CIV. EVID. 702. The burden of establishing an expert's qualifications is on the offering party. *Broders*, 924 S.W.2d at 151. We gauge abuse of discretion by whether the trial court acted without reference to any guiding rules or principles. *E.I. du Pont de Nemours and Co. v. Robinson*, 923 S.W.2d 549, 558 (Tex. 1995).

The trial court did not clearly abuse its discretion by rejecting Kramer's testimony. UBS's objections, which were, for the most part, based on facts conclusively established by the Longorias' responses to requests for admissions, demonstrate that Kramer did not have the particular knowledge, skill, experience, training, or education to testify to the relevant standard of care in this case. *See Broders*, 924 S.W.2d at 153 ("What is required is that the offering party establish that the expert has 'knowledge, skill, experience, training, or education' regarding the specific issue before the court which would qualify the expert to give an opinion on that particular subject.") (Emphasis added). While properly citing the correct standard of review, the court of appeals improperly substituted its opinion for that of the trial court's. *See Du Pont*, 923 S.W.2d at 558.

Accordingly, pursuant to Texas Rule of Appellate Procedure 170, without hearing oral argument, the Court reverses the judgment of the court of appeals and renders judgment that Plaintiffs take nothing.

Notes

1. *Earle v. Ratliff,* 998 S.W.2d 882 (Tex. 1999), holds that a summary judgment may be based on the affidavit of an interested expert witness if the basis for the expert's opinion is explained in the affidavit. In this medical malpractice case, the trial court entered summary judgment for the Dr. Earle. The plaintiff, Ratliff claims that Earle was negligent in performing the 1993 surgery. In his affidavit supporting his motion for summary judgment, Earle states that he did not breach the applicable standard of care in performing the 1993 surgery. "Both in 1991 and 1993," Earle's affidavit states, "use of Steffe pedicle screws and plates met the standard of care." The plaintiff offered the affidavit of their expert, Mooney. Mooney's affidavit states with respect to the 1993 surgery: "Considering the degree of spinal instability created by Mr. Ratliff's first surgery, and the fact that Mr. Ratliff's first set of AcroMed screws and plates resulted in hardware failure with loosening, the insertion of another device was medically unwarranted." In reversing the trial court's grant of summary judgment for Dr. Earl, the Supreme Court noted that "Mooney's statement raises the question whether, given Ratliff's failure to improve following the first surgical implantation and his increased spinal instability, a second implant was warranted. Earle's affidavit and other summary judgment evidence do not address this issue. *Summary judgment can be granted on the affidavit of an interested expert witness, like Earle, but the affidavit must not be conclusory. An expert's simple ipse dixit is insufficient to establish a matter; rather, the expert must explain the basis of his statements to link his conclusions to the facts.* Earle's affidavit does not explain why implantation of additional devices in the 1993 surgery was medically warranted, given Ratliff's history; the affidavit states only the conclusion that Earle met the applicable standard of care."

2. In a companion case to *Earle v. Ratliff*, the Supreme Court in *Burrow v. Arce*, 997 S.W.2d 229 (Tex. 1999), restated the applicable rule: "An expert's opinion testimony can defeat a claim as a matter of law, even if the expert is an interested witness, such as the defendant. But *it is the basis of the witness's opinion, and not the witness's qualifications or his bare opinions alone, that can settle an issue as a matter of law; a claim will not stand or fall on the mere ipse dixit of a credentialed witness. Conclusory statements made by an expert witness are insufficient to support summary judgment.*

3. *Little v. Texas Department of Criminal Justice*, 148 S.W.3d 374 (Tex. 2004): ". . . [W]hen testimony is contradictory, credibility is for the fact finder to decide. *Jones v. Tarrant Util. Co.*, 638 S.W.2d 862, 866 (Tex. 1982)."

4. *Seim v. Allstate Texas Lloyds*, 551 S.W.3d 161 (Tex. 2018): Rulings on a motion for summary judgment and objections to summary judgment evidence are not alternatives; nor are they concomitants. Neither implies a ruling—or any particular ruling—on the other. In short, a trial court's ruling on an objection to summary judgment evidence is not implicit in its ruling on the motion for summary judgment; a ruling on the objection is simply not "capable of being understood" from the ruling on the motion for summary judgment.

CATHEY
v.
BOOTH
900 S.W.2d 339
(Tex. 1995)

Michael E. Starr, Douglas R. McSwane, Jr., Tyler, Monte F. James, and J. Kevin Oncken, Austin, for petitioners.

David B. Griffith and Robert D. Bennett, Gilmer, for respondents.

PER CURIAM.

The Texas Tort Claims Act requires a claimant to provide a governmental unit with formal, written notice of a claim against it within six months of the incident giving rise to the claim; however, the formal notice requirements do not apply if the governmental unit has actual notice of the claim. TEX. CIV. PRAC. & REM. CODE § 101.101. In this cause, we consider whether a hospital may receive actual notice of a claim against it from its own medical records. We conclude that, for a hospital to have actual notice, it must have knowledge of (1) a death or injury; (2) its alleged fault producing or contributing to the death or injury; and (3) the identity of the parties involved. Because the records at issue in this case do not convey to the hospital its possible culpability, we reverse the judgment of the court of appeals as to any remaining claims against Wood County Central Hospital and render judgment that the Booths take nothing from the Hospital.

Glenda Booth was admitted to Wood County Central Hospital with labor pains on August 1, 1990, following a course of prenatal care by Dr. George Cathey. Glenda and Jerry Booth's child was delivered stillborn on that day.

The Booths sued Dr. Cathey and the Hospital, alleging that their negligence resulted in the stillbirth of the Booths' child and in physical pain and mental anguish to the Booths. The Booths allege that the doctor and the Hospital were negligent in failing to diagnose and treat Glenda Booth's condition as a high risk pregnancy and in failing to diagnose and treat Glenda Booth for gestational diabetes.

The trial court granted summary judgment in favor of Dr. Cathey and the Hospital on all claims. The court of appeals affirmed as to the Booths' claims for the mental anguish that they suffered as a result of the negligent treatment of the fetus. Otherwise, the court of appeals reversed and remanded for a new trial. 893 S.W.2d 715, 720.

To prevail on a motion for summary judgment, a movant must establish that there is no genuine issue as to any material fact and that the movant is entitled to judgment as a matter of law. TEX. R. CIV. P. 166a(c). A defendant who conclusively negates at least one of the essential elements of each of the plaintiff's causes of action or who conclusively establishes all of the elements of an affirmative defense is entitled to summary judgment. *Wornick Co. v. Casas*, 856 S.W.2d 732, 733 (Tex. 1993); *Montgomery v. Kennedy*, 669 S.W.2d 309, 310-11 (Tex. 1984). In reviewing a summary judgment, we must accept as true evidence in favor of the nonmovant, indulging every reasonable inference and resolving all doubts in the nonmovant's favor. *Nixon v. Mr. Property Management Co.*, 690 S.W.2d 546, 548-49 (Tex. 1985).

Section 101.101(c) of the Tort Claims Act provides that the formal notice requirements of section 101.101(a) "do not apply if the governmental unit has actual notice that death has occurred, that the claimant has received some injury, or that the claimant's property has been damaged." TEX. CIV. PRAC. & REM. CODE § 101.101(c). It is undisputed that the Booths failed to provide the Hospital with formal, written notice of their claims against it pursuant to section 101.101(a). The Booths assert, however, that the Hospital received actual notice of their claims. The Booths argue that section 101.101(c) requires only that a governmental unit have knowledge that a death, an injury, or property damage has occurred. We disagree.

The purpose of the notice requirement is to ensure prompt reporting of claims in order to enable governmental units to gather information necessary to guard against unfounded claims, settle claims, and prepare for trial. *See City of Houston v. Torres*, 621 S.W.2d 588, 591 (Tex. 1981). The interpretation of section 101.101(c) urged by the Booths would eviscerate the purpose of the statute, as it would impute actual notice to a hospital from the knowledge that a patient received treatment at its facility or died after receiving treatment. For a hospital, such an interpretation would be the equivalent of having no notice requirement at all because the hospital would be required to investigate the standard of care provided to each and every patient that received treatment.

We hold that actual notice to a governmental unit requires knowledge of (1) a death, injury, or property damage; (2) the governmental unit's alleged fault producing or contributing to the death, injury, or property damage; and (3) the identity of the parties involved. Our holding preserves the purpose of the notice statute, and is consistent with the holdings of the majority of the courts of appeals. *See Parrish v. Brooks*, 856 S.W.2d 522, 525 (Tex. App.—Texarkana 1993, writ denied); *Bourne v. Nueces County Hosp. Dist.*, 749 S.W.2d 630, 632-33 (Tex. App.—Corpus Christi 1988, writ denied); *Tarrant County Hosp. Dist. v. Ray*, 712 S.W.2d 271, 274 (Tex. App.—Fort Worth 1986, writ ref'd n.r.e.). To the extent that *Texas Dep't of Mental Health & Mental Retardation v. Petty*, 817 S.W.2d 707, 717 (Tex. App.—Austin 1991), aff'd on other grounds, 848 S.W.2d 680 (Tex. 1992), is inconsistent with this opinion, we disapprove it.

As summary judgment proof, Wood County Central Hospital presented the affidavit of its administrator, Marion Stanberry, who stated that prior to its receipt of a letter dated July 7, 1992, the Hospital had no knowledge of any alleged injuries of Glenda or Jerry Booth or of any alleged fault of the Hospital with respect to such injuries.

The summary judgment evidence provided by the Booths does not raise a fact issue that Wood County Central Hospital had actual notice of any alleged culpability on its part producing or contributing to any injury to Glenda or Jerry Booth. The only evidence presented by the Booths concerning the Hospital's knowledge of its culpability is an affidavit from Dean Cromartie, an obstetrician who reviewed Glenda Booth's medical records and determined that Dr. Cathey and the Hospital were negligent in their treatment of Glenda Booth. Dr. Cromartie explained that the Cesarean section was not performed on Glenda Booth until more than half an hour after the time that it was called for. Even if the Hospital was aware of the information in its medical records relied upon by Dr. Cromartie in forming his opinion, we hold that, as a matter of law, this information failed to adequately convey to the Hospital its possible culpability for mental and physical injuries to Glenda and Jerry Booth. *Cf. Dinh v. Harris County Hosp. Dist.*, 896 S.W.2d 248, 252-53 (Tex. App.—Houston [1st Dist.] 1995, writ dism'd w.o.j.).

Wood County Central Hospital and Dr. Cathey also argue that the judgment of the court of appeals should be reversed because the Booths failed to plead a cause of action for damages independent of the stillbirth. The Booths' pleadings contain allegations that Dr. Cathey and the Hospital were negligent in their treatment of Glenda Booth and allegations that such treatment resulted in physical and mental injuries to Glenda and Jerry Booth. A mother "may recover mental anguish damages suffered as a result of her injury which was proximately caused by [a doctor's or a hospital's negligence] and which includes the loss of her fetus." *Krishnan v. Sepulveda*, ______ S.W.2d _____, _____ [1995 WL 358844] (Tex. 1995). However, a father may not recover mental anguish damages from either the treating physician or the hospital because neither owes a duty to him. *Id.* at _____.

Accordingly, a majority of the Court grants the applications for writ of error, and, without hearing oral argument, affirms in part and reverses in part the judgment of the court of appeals. TEX. R. APP. P. 170. The Court renders judgment that the Booths take nothing from Wood County Central Hospital and that Jerry Booth take nothing from Dr. George Cathey. With regard to the claims asserted by Glenda Booth against Dr. George Cathey, the Court affirms the judgment of the court of appeals, which remanded those claims for trial.

Notes

1. *Texas Department of Criminal Justice v. Simons,* 140 S.W.3d 338 (Tex. 2004): Simons, an inmate incarcerated at the Terrell Unit of the TDCJ, was injured while working with a tractor, digging a post hole. The TDJC immediately investigated the accident. Simons did not mention the matter again to TDCJ prior to filing suit on 8/28/1996, two days before the two year statute of limitations would have run. Nearly five years later, on 8/20/2001, TDCJ filed a plea to the jurisdiction, arguing that, because it had not received notice of Simons's claim within six months of the incident, as required by section 101.101, its immunity from suit was not waived under the Tort Claims Act, and therefore the court lacked subject matter jurisdiction over the suit. In *Cathey v. Booth*, 900 S.W.2d 339, 341 (Tex. 1995) (per curiam), the Supreme Court construed section 101.101 of the

Texas Tort Claims Act to provide that a governmental unit is entitled to receive formal, written notice of a claim against it within six months of the incident from which the claim arises, unless it has actual notice of the claim, including knowledge of its "alleged fault producing or contributing to the death, injury, or property damage". The trial court denied the plea, and TDCJ appealed. The court of appeals reversed and remanded. The Supreme Court held that the appeal should be dismissed. It is not necessary to determine whether TDCJ established that it lacked actual notice of Simons's claim. A claimant's failure to comply with § 101.101 does not deprive the trial court of subject matter jurisdiction. While compliance is no less mandatory, and a governmental unit is entitled to dismissal of the action for lack of notice, that right cannot properly be asserted in a plea to the jurisdiction from which an interlocutory appeal is allowed. Since notice under § 101.101 is not jurisdictional, an interlocutory appeal from the denial of a plea to the jurisdiction based on lack of such notice is not allowed.

2. *Life Ins. Co. of Virginia v. Gar-Dal*, 570 S.W.2d 378 (Tex. 1978): Although attaching the original document is the better practice, TEX. R. CIV. P. 166-A(e), TEX.R.CIV.P., in requiring the attachment of "sworn or certified copies of documents," does not require that originals be attached to summary judgment affidavits. The photocopy of the note attached to the affidavit under these circumstances (stating that the plaintiff was the owner and holder of the note and that the copy of was an accurate copy of the original) was a "sworn copy" within the meaning of Rule 166-A(e) and that, therefore, it was proper summary judgment evidence.

Further, this was, if anything, a defect of form, and defects of form are waived if not pointed out to the trial court before summary judgment is rendered.

Finally, conclusions in an affidavit (here, that all offsets and payments had not been credited to the note) are insufficient to raise an issue of fact (here, that plaintiff failed to credit all offsets and payments to the note).

RYLAND GROUP, INC.
v.
HOOD

924 S.W.2d 120 (Tex. 1996)

Chris E. Ryman, Michael O. Whitmire, Houston, for Petitioner.
K. Michael Mayes, Mark D. Haas, Conroe, for Respondents.

PER CURIAM.

This is a summary judgment case based on the statute of repose. In 1976, Ryland completed and sold a home. Later, Theresa Hood rented the home from its current owner. On June 8, 1991, the second story deck collapsed, seriously injuring Hood and her guests. Hood and her guests sued Ryland alleging that Ryland negligently used untreated lumber as the "runner board" for the deck that had completely rotted and deteriorated. Ryland moved for summary judgment asserting that the statute of repose barred Respondents' action because they did not file suit within the ten year statutory period prescribed by the statute of repose. Respondents raised fraudulent concealment and willful misconduct as affirmative defenses to the statute of repose in their response to Ryland's motion for summary judgment. They offered the affidavit of their expert, James Manning, a long-time contractor, as their only summary judgment proof to raise a fact issue. Ryland filed a reply alleging that Respondents did not prove their affirmative defenses. The trial court rendered summary judgment for Ryland.

The court of appeals reversed and remanded. 911 S.W.2d 931. The court of appeals concluded that: (1) Ryland conclusively established as a matter of law that the statute of repose, TEX. CIV. PRAC. & REM. CODE § 16.009, applies to this case; and (2) Manning's affidavit did not raise a fact issue about fraudulent concealment; however, (3) Manning's affidavit did raise a fact issue about whether Ryland's use of untreated lumber amounted to willful and intentional misconduct. Ryland argues that the court of appeals incorrectly reversed its summary judgment because: (1) Ryland conclusively established that § 16.009 bars the suit; and (2) Respondents did not satisfy their burden for raising a fact issue on willful misconduct. We agree and reverse the court of appeals.

The standards for reviewing a motion for summary judgment are well established. The movant has the burden of showing that there is no genuine material fact issue and that it is entitled to judgment as a matter of law.

Nixon v. Mr. Property Management Co. Inc., 690 S.W.2d 546, 548 (Tex. 1985). When a defendant moves for summary judgment based on an affirmative defense, such as the statute of repose, the defendant, as movant, bears the burden of proving each essential element of that defense. *See City of Houston v. Clear Creek Basin Authority*, 589 S.W.2d 671, 678 (Tex. 1979); *Swilley v. Hughes*, 488 S.W.2d 64, 67 (Tex. 1972). A non-movant asserting fraudulent concealment has the burden "to come forward with proof raising an issue of fact with respect to" that claim. *See American Petrofina, Inc. v. Allen*, 887 S.W.2d 829 (Tex. 1994), *citing Nichols v. Smith*, 507 S.W.2d 518, 521 (Tex. 1974)(once defendant established its statute of limitations defense as a matter of law, plaintiff had burden to prove a fact issue about fraudulent concealment to defeat summary judgment).

The statute of repose requires a party to sue:

> . . . a person who constructs or repairs an improvement to real property not later than ten years after the substantial completion of the improvement in an action arising out of a defective or unsafe condition of the real property or a deficiency in the construction or repair of the improvement.

See TEX. CIV. PRAC. & REM. CODE § 16.009(a). The statute, however, does not bar an action "based on willful misconduct or fraudulent concealment in connection with the performance of the construction." TEX. CIV. PRAC. & REM. CODE § 16.009(e)(3); *Texas Gas Exploration Corp. v. Fluor Corp.*, 828 S.W.2d 28, 32 (Tex. App.—Texarkana 1991, writ denied).

Ryland conclusively established that Respondents' damages occurred outside the statute's ten year limitation period. Respondents do not dispute that the statute of repose applies. Consequently, Ryland met its summary judgment burden to prove as a matter of law that section 16.009 applies because Respondents did not file suit within the ten year statutory period. *See Swilley*, 488 S.W.2d at 67. The question is whether Respondents in turn presented enough proof to raise a fact issue on their affirmative defenses—fraudulent concealment and willful misconduct, to defeat Ryland's right to summary judgment. *See Brownlee v. Brownlee*, 665 S.W.2d 111, 112 (Tex. 1984).

Respondent's only summary judgment evidence was James Manning's affidavit. The relevant standard for an expert's affidavit opposing a motion for summary judgment is whether it presents some probative evidence of the facts at issue. *Trapnell v. John Hogan Interests, Inc.*, 809 S.W.2d 606, 611 (Tex. App.—Corpus Christi 1991, writ denied). Conclusory affidavits are not enough to raise fact issues. *Brownlee*, 665 S.W.2d at 112. They are not credible, nor susceptible to being readily controverted. *See* TEX. R. CIV. P. 166a(c).

Rule 166a(f) requires that "supporting and opposing affidavits shall be made on personal knowledge, shall set forth such facts as would be admissible in evidence, and shall show affirmatively that the affiant is competent to testify to the matters stated therein." TEX. R. CIV. P. 166a(f); *Humphreys v. Caldwell*, 888 S.W.2d 469, 470 (Tex. 1994)(affidavit lacking testimony that statements were unequivocally based on personal knowledge was legally insufficient). An interested witness' affidavit which recites that the affiant "estimates," or "believes" certain facts to be true will not support summary judgment. *See Lightfoot v. Weissgarber*, 763 S.W.2d 624, 628 (Tex. App.—San Antonio 1989, writ denied)(holding testimony based on affiant's best knowledge and belief does not meet Rule 166a(e)'s strict requirements); *Ardila v. Saavedra*, 808 S.W.2d 645, 647 (Tex. App.—Corpus Christi 1991, no writ). Such language does not positively and unqualifiedly represent that the "facts" disclosed are true. *Brownlee*, 665 S.W.2d at 112.

In his affidavit, Manning testified that he examined the deck and exterior of the house where the deck had been attached. He stated he was of the opinion that Ryland should have treated the runner board. The court of appeals concluded that "Manning's affidavit makes no claim, nor offers any evidence that Ryland had actual knowledge of the use of untreated wood, much less that they purposely concealed that knowledge." 911 S.W.2d at 935, *citing Baskin v. Mortgage & Trust, Inc.*, 837 S.W.2d 743, 746 (Tex. App.—Houston [14th Dist.] 1992, writ denied)(holding one cannot fraudulently conceal facts of which one has no actual knowledge). Yet, based on the same affidavit, the court of appeals concluded that Hood raised a fact issue about willful misconduct. 911 S.W.2d at 935. Manning's affidavit asserts:

> To use untreated lumber for a deck support in new construction, when treated lumber is specified, amounts to intentional or willful misconduct by the builder.

If Manning's affidavit cannot raise a fact issue that Ryland had actual knowledge of the untreated lumber, how can use of such be intentional? It cannot.

Moreover, Respondents provide no summary judgment evidence that the parties ever specified or contracted for the use of treated wood. Manning's affidavit further states:

> It is my understanding that neither the builder nor the subsequent deck renovator notified the inspectors, appraisers, owners, tenants, or any other party with an interest in the home of the use of the untreated wood. This failure to notify amounts to a concealment of a known violation of the specifications and industry practice. (emphasis added).

We should not equate Manning's "understanding" to personal knowledge about whether Ryland notified anyone about the use of untreated wood. *See Humphreys*, 888 S.W.2d at 470. Manning's opinion that Ryland's "failure to notify amounts to concealment or a known violation of the specifications and industry practice," is conclusory. Therefore, his affidavit does not raise a fact issue on willful misconduct. *See Brownlee*, 665 S.W.2d at 112.

Accordingly, the Court grants petitioner's application for writ of error, and under Texas Rule of Appellate Procedure 170, without hearing oral argument, we reverse the judgment of the court of appeals and render judgment that Respondents take nothing.

Notes

1. A legal conclusion in an affidavit is insufficient to raise an issue of fact in response to a motion for summary judgment or to establish the existence of a fact in support of a motion for summary judgment.

2. *McConathy v. McConathy,* 869 S.W.2d. 341 (Tex. 1994). Deposition excerpts used as summary judgment evidence need not be authenticated by a court reporter's certificate as well as an original affidavit certifying the authenticity of the copied excerpts.

3. The petition filed by the plaintiff, even if sworn to, is not summary judgment proof. *Hidalgo v. Surely Savings & Loan Ass'n*, 462 S.W.2d 540 (Tex. 1971). This does not mean that there cannot be summary judgments on the basis of pleading where, for example, the pleadings fail to state a cause of action. This is discussed below in subsection g.

4. *Campbell v Ft. Worth Bank & Trust Co.,* 705 S.W.2d 400 (Tex. App.—1986, n.r.e.). A summary judgment affidavit stating "To the best of my knowledge. . . ." is insufficient as summary judgment proof. Affidavits must be made upon personal knowledge. The statements in plaintiff's affidavit based upon the "best of his knowledge" constitutes no evidence at all.

5. *The requirements for an affidavit.* In *Acme Brick v Temple Associates, Inc.*, 816 S.W.2d 440 (Tex. App.—Waco 1991, writ denied), the document purporting to be an affidavit was signed by the person named in the statement; however, the signature appeared above and not below the statement in the jurat that the amount was just and correct. The court held that the document was, indeed, an affidavit. They described the requirements for an affidavit.

Statement in Writing. An affidavit is a statement, in writing, of a fact or facts signed by the party making it, sworn to before an officer authorized to administer oaths, & officially certified to by the officer under his seal of office.

Contents (Caption, Title, Venue, Body, Signature, and Jurat). An affidavit includes the caption or title, the venue, the signature of the affiant, the jurat & the body of the instrument.

The Jurat. The jurat of an affidavit is a certificate by a competent officer that the writing was sworn to by the person who signed it. No particular terminology is required to render a document an affidavit because it is the substance & not the form of an affidavit that is significant.

The Signature. An affiant's signature which is placed below the jurat for the purpose of subscribing to the instrument meets the object of the law. Thus, when Pamela Byas placed her signature on the document in question, she did so for the purpose of subscribing to the instrument. The law does not direct or guide where the necessary signature is to be located. Thus, the document constituted a valid affidavit.

6. *Lujan v. Navistar, Inc.*, 544 S.W.3d 824 (Tex. 2018): The court reiterates that it reviews the rendition of summary judgments de novo. But we review a trial court's decision to exclude evidence for an abuse of discretion. Rule 166a obligates Texas trial courts to distinguish genuine fact issues, which must proceed toward trial, from non-genuine fact issues, which should not survive summary judgment. Application of the sham affidavit rule is merely one way in which trial courts have gone about discharging that obligation. We affirm this approach today. Under Rule 166a(c), a trial court may conclude that a party does not raise a genuine fact issue by submitting sworn testimony that materially conflicts with the same witness's prior sworn testimony, unless there is a sufficient explanation for the conflict. We emphasize that this rule does not contravene the longstanding principle that the trial court is "not to weigh the evidence or determine its credibility, and thus try the case on the affidavits." *Gulbenkian*, 252 S.W.2d at 931. Rather, the sham affidavit rule is a tool that may be used to distinguish genuine fact issues from non-genuine fact issues in service of the "underlying purpose of Rule 166a [to] eliminat[e] . . . patently unmeritorious claims or untenable defenses . . . ." *Id.* By recognizing the rule today, we do not hold in conflict with *Randall* that depositions control over affidavits. Instead, we hold that when one contradicts the other and appears to the trial court to be a sham designed to avoid summary judgment, the trial court may require a sufficient explanation and may grant summary judgment in the absence of one.

7. *Mansions in the Forest, L.P. v. Montgomery County,* 365 S.W.3d 314 (Tex. 2012): Montgomery County filed a condemnation action against portions of three properties owned by The Mansions and asked the court to appoint special commissioners to assess the fair market value of the condemned land and determine the diminution in value of the remainder. After the County deposited into the court's registry the amount found by the commissioners to be the fair market value of the condemned land and any damages caused by the seizure, the trial court issued a writ of possession; and the Mansions filed objections to the amount of the award. The County then moved for summary judgment on the issue of damages. In response, the Mansions filed Matthew Hiles's purported affidavit asserting that the commissioners should have awarded at least $800,000. Although the County objected to the affidavit on the grounds that it was untimely and conclusory, it did not object to the lack of a jurat. The trial court sustained the County's objections, excluded Hiles's purported affidavit, and granted summary judgment in the County's favor. The court of appeals affirmed, holding that the County's argument that the trial court properly excluded Hiles's affidavit because it lacked a jurat raised a defect of substance, rather than of form and therefore could be raised for the first time on appeal. ***Held*:** An "affidavit" is defined by the Texas Government Code as "a statement in writing of a fact or facts signed by the party making it, sworn to before an officer authorized to administer oaths, and officially certified to by the officer under his seal of office." Although the Government Code requires that a written statement must be sworn to qualify as an affidavit, it does not require that the statement contain a jurat — a clause stating that the statement was sworn to before an authorized officer. Nor does Rule 166a. However, for a written statement that lacks a jurat to qualify as an "affidavit" under the Government Code definition, "other evidence must show that it was sworn to before an authorized officer." There is no such evidence in this record; and the County failed to object to its absence. The County therefore waived error under Texas Rule of Appellate Procedure 33.1(a), which requires (1) a party to complain to the trial court by a timely request, objection, or motion; and (2) the trial court to rule or refuse to rule on the request, objection, or motion. These general requirements for the preservation of error serve "important prudential considerations," *i.e.*, affording the trial court an opportunity to rule before an appeal, thus maximizing correct decision-making, and affording the opposing party a chance to correct the error before an appeal. The Court therefore disapproves of the courts of appeals' extension of its hold in *Perkins v. Crittenden,* 462 S.W.2d 565, 568 (Tex. 1970), that "the jurat is an integral part of [Rule 166a(f)] which particularly refers to 'sworn or certified copies ... referred to in an affidavit,'" to affidavits filed in opposition to a motion for summary judgment. The Court thus distinguishes the defect in filing unsworn or uncertified copies, which is not waivable, from the defect in filing an unsworn affidavit, which is waivable.

8. *In re E.I. DuPont de Nemours and Company*, 136 S.W.3d 218 (Tex. 2004): The plaintiffs contends that Connor's affidavit is not probative, because it is not based on personal knowledge. For an affidavit to have probative value, an affiant must swear that the facts, presented in the affidavit, reflect his/her personal knowledge. Connor swore that his statements were based on his "personal knowledge of the facts stated in the affidavit." Even though Connor later explained that his determinations were "[b]ased on [his] review of the DuPont human resources database for the legal department," an affiant's acknowledgment of the sources, from which he gathered his knowledge, does not violate the personal knowledge requirement. Therefore, Connor's affidavit satisfies the personal knowledge requirement.

9. *Fort Brown Villas III Condominium Association, Inc. v. Gillenwater*, 285 S.W.3d 879 (Tex. 2009): Texas Rule of Civil Procedure 193.6, which provides for the exclusion of evidence, due to an untimely response to a discovery request, applies in a summary judgment proceeding. Under Rule 193.6, discovery that is not timely disclosed, and witnesses that are not timely identified, are inadmissible as evidence. A party who fails to timely designate an expert has the burden of establishing good cause, or a lack of unfair surprise or prejudice, before the trial court may admit the evidence. A trial court's exclusion of an expert who has not been properly designated can be overturned only upon a finding of abuse of discretion. Before the no-evidence motion for summary judgment was introduced to Texas trial practice, courts did not apply evidentiary sanctions and exclusions for failure to timely designate an expert witness in a summary judgment proceeding. However, in 1997, the no-evidence summary judgment motion was introduced to the Texas Rules of Civil Procedure as Rule 166a(i), and in 1999, pretrial discovery rules were amended to include evidentiary exclusions under Rule 193.6. The new discovery rules establish a date certain for the completion of discovery, which depends on the discovery plan level, and not on the trial date. Under the new rules, there is no longer a concern that discovery will be incomplete at the summary judgment stage. Combined with the no-evidence motion for summary judgment rule, the "hard deadline" established by the pretrial discovery rules ensures that the evidence presented at the summary judgment stage and at the trial stage remains the same. Accordingly, the 193.6 exclusionary rule applies equally to both proceedings.

f. *The Traditional Summary Judgment Motion and Response*

HOUSTON
v.
CLEAR CREEK BASIN AUTH.
589 S.W.2d 671
(Tex. 1979)

Robert M. Collie, Jr., City Atty., Fulbright & Jaworski, David J. Beck, Houston, for petitioner.
Kronzer, Abraham & Watkins, Robert E. Ballard, Houston, for respondent.

SPEARS, JUSTICE.

Respondent Clear Creek Basin Authority, a statutory governmental entity existing under article 8280-311 (1965), sued the City of Houston for injunctive relief and statutory penalties, alleging the unlawful discharge of waste waters by treatment plants operated by the City in violation of chapter 26 of the Texas Water Code. The trial court granted summary judgment for the City of Houston, but the court of civil appeals reversed and remanded. 573 S.W.2d 839.

* * *

Clear Creek's suit alleges numerous violations of waste control orders of the Texas Water Quality Board and a common law nuisance as a result of the discharge of sewage into waters which ultimately flow into Galveston Bay. The Attorney General of Texas, on behalf of the Texas Water Quality Control Board and the State of Texas, intervened as a necessary party-plaintiff pursuant to the requirement of the Texas Water Code.

Clear Creek alleged in its first amended original petition that the City of Houston had committed numerous violations at 31 different locations. Defendant City admitted that four of these plants discharging effluent are situated within the territorial boundaries of Clear Creek Basin Authority set forth in section 2 of Article 8280-311, supra, and that these four plants exceeded the terms of the City's permit from the Water Quality Control Board during the periods of 1974 and 1976. The remaining plants were located upstream and outside of Clear Creek's territorial jurisdiction.

The City of Houston filed a motion for summary judgment, alleging three grounds: 1. The matters upon which Clear Creek bases its claims for relief fall within the primary jurisdiction of the Texas Water Quality Board; Clear Creek has failed to exhaust its administrative remedies; and that neither the Texas Water Quality Board nor the Texas Department of Water Resources has authorized the bringing of this action; 2. As a matter of law, Clear Creek cannot obtain relief for violations of the Texas Water Code which occur outside the territorial jurisdiction of the Authority; and 3. The action represents an attempt by Clear Creek to perform a function or service which the City of Houston is authorized to perform without the written consent of the governing body of the City of Houston, all in violation of Article 8280-311, sec. 5. Clear Creek filed this response to the motion:

I.

The only issue before this Court is a question of law: can a downstream victim of pollution sue an upstream polluter?

II.

The City has admitted that its sewer plants exceed the parameters of its permits on a regular basis. See Answers to Admissions and Interrogatories.

III.

The City's effluent is flushed into Clear Lake on a daily basis and causes pollution there. See deposition testimony of Sidney H. Tanner and Affidavits on file.

There is no Verbatim record of the hearing on the motion, but the trial court's judgment recites that at the hearing, Clear Creek withdrew its common law cause of action in open court and announced its desire to proceed only on the basis of its claims under chapter 26 of the Texas Water Code. It further recites that the City of Houston withdrew paragraphs 1 and 3 of its motion for summary judgment and desired to proceed to hearing only on paragraph 2 challenging Clear Creek's right to sue for violations outside its jurisdictional boundaries. In this context, the trial court granted the City's motion for summary judgment.

In the meantime, and apart from the summary judgment proceeding, the City of Houston and the state Attorney General worked out a settlement agreement between them to which Clear Creek was not a party. The settlement agreement was incorporated in the trial court's final judgment but was made expressly contingent upon the judgment that Clear Creek take nothing being upheld on appeal. The settlement provided for an agreed injunction judgment obligating the City to construct and place into operation some $500,000,000 worth of additional waste water treatment plants, sludge disposal plants, and sewage diversion lines with a reporting schedule to the Texas Department of Water Resources and to the trial court.

The court of civil appeals, in reversing and remanding the cause for trial, held that a fact issue existed as to the alleged violations occurring within Clear Creek's territorial boundaries. The court reasoned that even if the admitted fact of those violations was not presented to the trial court at the hearing on summary judgment, this part of Clear Creek's cause of action was not waived because there was no written agreement of waiver filed under rule 11. The court said that the City had not carried its burden and was not entitled to a summary judgment despite Clear Creek's failure to specify the reasons why the motion should not be granted.

Petitioner City of Houston asserts nine points of error. The first alleged error is that the judgment of the court of civil appeals is erroneous for the reason that it is contrary to the requirement of rule 166-A, that "(I)ssues not expressly presented to the trial court by written motion, answer or other response, shall not be considered on appeal as grounds for reversal." The remaining points claim that Clear Creek waived and abandoned any fact issue and that it is estopped from asserting any complaints of violations occurring within the geographical boundaries of the Clear Creek Basin Authority.

The first question is whether the 1978 amendment to rule 166-A(c), providing that issues not expressly presented to the trial court may not be considered on appeal as grounds for reversal, precludes the court of civil appeals from reversing the summary judgment when the non-movant agreed to the submission to the trial court of a single issue of law. We hold that because the parties agreed on the submission of only one issue to the trial court and its ruling on that issue constituted the basis of the granting of the motion for summary judgment, Clear Creek is precluded from later urging on appeal the issue not presented, i.e., the violations of the four plants located within Clear Creek's boundaries.

A history of the summary judgment rule, rule 166-A, reflects that the high hopes of increasing judicial efficiency advanced by the proponents of the rule did not materialize. While no summary judgment rule was included in the initial promulgation of the rules of civil procedure in 1940, after considerable urging by legal scholars and commentators and by the Texas Civil Judicial Council, rule 166-A was adopted by this court, effective March 1, 1950. Pittsford and Russell, *Summary Judgment In Texas: A Selective Survey*, 14 HOUS. L. REV. 854 (1977). Despite predictions of success by its supporters, the rule has been fraught with misunderstanding. One prominent writer observed in 1961 that a poll of district judges throughout the state reflected many were skeptical about the efficacy of the rule because of frequent reversals by appellate courts. McDonald, *The Effective Use of Summary Judgment*, 15 SW. L.J. 365, 373-4 (1961). In 1977, a survey concluded that fewer than two percent of the civil cases disposed of in Texas in the six preceding years were decided by summary judgment. *See Pittsford and Russell, supra* at 854. Another survey of the cases decided by this court between 1968 and 1976 reflected that when a summary judgment was granted in the trial court, seventy percent of those cases were reversed and remanded for trial. Sheehan, *Summary Judgment: Let the Movant Beware*, 8 ST. MARY'S L.J. 253, 254 (1976).

Attempts within the bar to clarify summary judgment practice began to gain momentum in the early 1970's. After several unsuccessful attempts at revision, the Committee on the Administration of Justice of the State Bar of Texas voted in March of 1976 to recommend changes in rule 166-A that would require the non-movant to provide some assistance to the trial judge in narrowing the issues to be decided. That proposal was then considered by the Supreme Court Advisory Committee in March of 1977, and after several changes, was recommended to this court for adoption. The proposal recommended significant change in section (c), primarily by requiring the non-movant to "define specifically in writing" the controverted issues and defects in the movant's proof that would defeat the motion. The recorded minutes of the Advisory Committee reflect a prevailing sentiment to change the rule, to make summary judgments a more useful procedure in judicial administration, to require non-movant to specify his opposition to the motion, and to prevent the non-movant from "laying behind the log" within his objections until appeal.

A comparison of section of the rule as it existed before January 1, 1978, and as amended demonstrates the significance of the change in the mechanics of the summary judgment procedure. The new rule adopts the objectives of the Advisory Committee, but goes even further by precluding from consideration on appeal grounds not raised in the trial court in opposition to a summary judgment motion. The pre-1978 summary judgment rule had a chilling effect on the willingness of trial courts to utilize the intended benefits of the procedure. *See* McDonald, *The Effective Use of Summary Judgment*, 15 SW.L.J. 365, 375-382 (1961). The new rule attempts to encourage the trial court to utilize the summary judgment in appropriate cases.

Prior to January 1, 1978, section . . . read: . . . Motion and Proceedings Thereon. The motion for summary judgment shall state the specific grounds therefor. The motion shall be served at least ten days before the time specified for the hearing. The adverse party prior to the day of hearing may serve opposing affidavits. No oral testimony shall be received at the hearing. The judgment sought shall be rendered forthwith if the pleadings, depositions, answers to interrogatories, and admissions on file, together with the affidavits, if any, show that, except as to the amount of damages, there is no genuine issue as to any material fact and that the moving party is entitled to a judgment as a matter of law. Section now reads: Motion and Proceedings Thereon. The motion for summary judgment shall state the specific grounds therefor. Except on leave of court, the motion shall be served at least twenty-one days before the time specified for the hearing. Except on leave of court, the adverse party, not later than seven days prior to the day of hearing may serve opposing affidavits or other written response. No oral testimony shall be received at the hearing. The judgment sought shall be rendered forthwith if the pleadings, depositions, answers to interrogatories, admissions and affidavits, if any, on file at the time of the hearing, or filed thereafter and before judgment with permission of the court, show that, except as to the amount of damages, there is no genuine issue as to any material fact and the moving party is entitled to judgment as a matter of law on the issues as expressly set out in the motion or in an answer or any other response. Issues not expressly presented to the trial court by written motion, answer or other response shall not be considered on appeal as grounds for reversal. A summary judgment may be based on uncontroverted testimonial evidence of an interested witness, or of an expert witness as to subject matter concerning which the trier of fact must be guided solely by the opinion testimony of experts, if the evidence is clear, positive and direct, otherwise credible and free from contradictions and inconsistencies, and could have been readily controverted. (emphasis added) A concomitant change to section (e) of the rule added this sentence: Defects in the form of affidavits or attachments will not be grounds for reversal unless specifically pointed out by objection by an opposing party with opportunity, but refusal, to amend.

Responding to the criticism that a non-movant could "lay behind the log" in the trial court and urge deficiencies for the first time on appeal, the new section specifically prohibits this tactic by clearly requiring: . . . Issues not expressly presented to the trial court by written motion, answer or other response shall not be considered on appeal as grounds for reversal. (emphasis added)

The word "written" modifies not only the word "motion," but also the words "answer" and "other response." The "issues" required by the rule to be "expressly presented" are those pointed out to the trial court in written motions, written answers or written responses to the motion. The term "answer" in the context of the rule refers to an answer to the motion, not an answer generally filed in response to a petition. *Feller v. Southwestern Bell Tel. Co.*, 581 S.W.2d 775 (Tex. Civ. App. Houston (14th Dist.) 1979, no writ). The movant must also expressly set out his grounds in writing: . . . The judgment sought shall be rendered forthwith if . . . and the moving party is entitled to judgment as a matter of law on the issues as expressly set out in the motion or in an answer or any other response.

Thus, both the reasons for the summary judgment and the objections to it must be in writing and before the trial judge at the hearing. The appellate court which must later decide whether the issue was actually presented to and considered by the trial judge will then be able to examine the transcript and make its determination. To permit "issues" to be presented orally would encourage parties to request that a court reporter record summary judgment hearings, a practice neither necessary nor appropriate to the purposes of such a hearing. *Richards v. Allen*, 402 S.W.2d 158, 161 (Tex. 1966); rule 166-A(c).

If the issues are to be further restricted or expanded by the parties beyond those "expressly presented" by the written motion, the answer to the motion, or any other written response, the change must meet the requirements of rule 11 which provides: No agreement between attorneys or parties touching any suit pending will be enforced unless it be in writing, signed and filed with the papers as a part of the record, Or unless it be made in open court and entered of record.

The City of Houston contends that the parties orally agreed in open court at the hearing on the motion to narrow the issue to a single question of law does Clear Creek have standing under the code to sue for pollution originating outside its territorial boundaries? The City further maintains that if that agreement must comply with rule 11, the recitations in the judgment satisfy the requirements of the rule.

We agree that the parties in open court should be able to narrow the issues presented to the trial court provided the agreement is reduced to writing, signed, and filed with papers or "entered of record." If a party represents to the court that he waives a ground or objection that he has previously asserted in a written motion or response and agrees that a certain issue is the only issue before the court, rule 11 is satisfied if the oral waiver or agreement made in open court is described in the judgment or an order of the court. Rule 11 expressly approves this procedure.

The trial court's judgment reflects that the parties by agreement expressly presented only one issue to the court, and the requirements of rule 11 were met when the agreement was reflected in the judgment. Counsel for the City announced in open court that he was withdrawing grounds 1 and 3 of its motion for summary judgment. Clear Creek agreed to withdraw its common law cause of action, and the City of Houston agreed not to object to its revival if the case were remanded for a new trial. The only issue then remaining to be determined at the hearing on the motion for summary judgment, taking into consideration the motion, the written response, and the open-court representations of counsel recited in the judgment, was the second ground asserted by the City's motion the standing of Clear Creek to file a suit under the Texas Water Code for violations which occur upstream and Outside the jurisdictional boundaries of the Clear Creek Basin Authority. No other issues were presented to the trial court by either party, and he ruled on no others.

Clear Creek next argues that its pleadings on file in the case adequately assert its claim of violations by the four plants located within its territorial boundaries, that its response to the City's motion for summary judgment does not supersede Clear Creek's previous pleadings, and that it should not have to replead in its response to the motion what it had already pled.

Pleadings do not constitute summary judgment proof. *Hidalgo v. Sur. Sav. & Loan Ass'n*, 462 S.W.2d 540 (Tex. 1971). The new rule requires that contentions be expressly presented in the written motion or in a written answer or response to the motion, and pleadings are not to be considered in determining whether fact issues are expressly presented in summary judgment motions. The terms "answer" and "response" as used in the context of the rule clearly refer to the motion and not to the pleadings generally. *Feller v. Southwestern Bell Tel. Co., supra*. To hold otherwise would be to perpetuate the evil the rule change was designed to eliminate. The written answer or response to the motion must fairly apprise the movant and the court of the issues the non-movant contends should defeat the motion.

We are not to be understood, however, as shifting the burden of proof that exists in summary judgment proceedings. The trial court may not grant a summary judgment by default for lack of an answer or response to the motion by the non-movant when the movant's summary judgment proof is legally insufficient. The movant still must establish his entitlement to a summary judgment on the issues expressly presented to the trial court by conclusively proving all essential elements of his cause of action or defense as a matter of law. *See Swilley v. Hughes*, 488 S.W.2d 64, 67 (Tex. 1972). Summary judgments must stand on their own merits, and the non-movant's failure to answer or respond cannot supply by default the summary judgment proof necessary to establish the movant's right.

While it would be prudent and helpful to the trial court for the non-movant always to file an answer or response, the non-movant needs no answer or response to the motion to contend on appeal that the grounds expressly presented to the trial court by the movant's motion are insufficient As a matter of law to support summary judgment. The non-movant, however, may not raise any Other issues as grounds for reversal. Under the new rule, the non-movant may not urge on appeal as reason for reversal of the summary judgment any and every New ground that he can think of, nor can he resurrect grounds that he abandoned at the hearing.

With the exception of an attack on the legal sufficiency of the grounds expressly raised by the movant in his motion for summary judgment, the non-movant must expressly present to the trial court any reasons seeking to avoid movant's entitlement, such as those set out in rules 93 and 94, and he must present summary judgment proof when necessary to establish a fact issue. No longer must the movant negate all possible issues of law and fact that Could be raised by the non-movant in the trial court but were not. *See, e. g., "Moore" Burger Inc. v. Phillips Petroleum Co.*, 492 S.W.2d 934 (Tex. 1972); *Doyle v. USAA*, 482 S.W.2d 849 (Tex. 1972); *Hidalgo v. Sur. Sav. & Loan Ass'n*, 462 S.W.2d 540 (Tex. 1971); *Womack v. Allstate Ins. Co.*, 156 Tex. 467, 296 S.W.2d 233 (1957). In cases such as *Torres v. Western Cas. & Sur. Co.*, 457 S.W.2d 50 (Tex. 1970) (existence of good cause for late filing of worker's compensation claim), *and Gardner v. Martin*, 162 Tex. 156, 345 S.W.2d 274 (1961) (failure of movant to attach certified copies of prior case to establish res judicata), the non-movant must now, in a written answer or response to the motion, expressly present to the trial court those issues that would defeat the movant's right to a summary judgment and failing to do so, may not later assign them as error on appeal.

Having held that Clear Creek is not entitled to defeat the summary judgment by raising a fact issue for the first time on appeal which was not expressly presented to the trial court, we now determine if the City of Houston is entitled to its summary judgment as a matter of law for the reason asserted in its motion. Specifically, the question is whether under the Texas Water Code, Clear Creek Basin Authority can sue to enforce the Code provisions prohibiting unauthorized discharges of polluting waste into the waters of the state when those discharges occur upstream and Outside the territorial jurisdiction of the Clear Creek Basin Authority. As we have said, this issue was the only question before the trial court.

* * *

[After reviewing the various statutes the Court holds] that a local government may not bring a statutory action for civil penalties and injunctive relief pursuant to § 26.124 of the Texas Water Code for discharges that occur outside its geographical boundaries.

* * *

The judgment of the court of civil appeals is reversed, and the judgment of the trial court is affirmed.

McCONNELL
v.
SOUTHSIDE INDEP. SCH. DIST.

858 S.W.2d 337
(Tex. 1993)

James M. Heidelberg, Stacy C. Ferguson, San Antonio, for petitioner.
John T. Fleming, Austin, for respondents.

HIGHTOWER, JUSTICE.

This case presents the question whether grounds for summary judgment must be expressly presented in the motion for summary judgment itself or whether such grounds may be presented in either a brief filed contemporaneously with the motion or in the summary judgment evidence. We conclude that grounds for summary judgment must be expressly presented in the summary judgment motion itself. Consequently, we reverse the judgment of the court of appeals and remand this cause to the trial court for further proceedings consistent with this opinion.

John S. McConnell (McConnell) sued Southside Independent School District (Southside) after Southside failed to renew his contract of employment. Southside moved for summary judgment, stating in its motion only that there were "no genuine issues as to any material facts". Southside also filed a twelve page brief in support of the motion in which it expressly presented the grounds allegedly establishing its entitlement to summary judgment. McConnell filed a written exception to the motion, arguing that the motion was defective in that it failed to present any grounds. The trial court overruled McConnell's exception and rendered summary judgment for Southside. The court of appeals affirmed, holding that "Rule 166a allows a summary judgment movant to set out the specific grounds for summary judgment in a brief served on all parties contemporaneously with the motion itself." 814 S.W.2d 247.

I.

McConnell argues that the specific grounds for summary judgment must be expressly presented in the motion for summary judgment itself and not in a brief filed contemporaneously with the motion or in the summary judgment evidence. We agree.

Motion For Summary Judgment

The first sentence of Rule 166a(c), added in 1971, plainly provides: "The motion for summary judgment shall state the specific grounds therefor." TEX. R. CIV. P. 166a(c). Several cases have paraphrased this requirement as follows:

The motion for summary judgment must itself state specific grounds on which judgment is sought . . . . The motion for summary judgment must stand or fall on the grounds it specifically and expressly sets forth . . . . There is authority to the effect that a summary judgment cannot be sustained on a ground not specifically set forth in the motion. *Westbrook Const. Co. v. Fidelity Bank of Dallas*, 813 S.W.2d 752, 754-55 (Tex. App.—Fort Worth 1991, writ denied) (emphasis added). *See, e.g., Roark v. Stallworth Oil and Gas, Inc.*, 813 S.W.2d 492, 494-95 (Tex. 1991) ("[A]n unpleaded affirmative defense may also serve as the basis for a summary judgment when it is raised in the summary judgment motion . . . ."); *410/West Ave. Ltd. v. Texas Trust Savings Bank, F.S.B.*, 810 S.W.2d 422, 424 (Tex. App.—San Antonio 1991, no writ) ("Motions for summary judgment 'stand or fall on the grounds specifically set forth in the motions.' "); *Hall v. Harris County Water Control & Improvement Dist.*, 683 S.W.2d 863, 867 (Tex. App.—Houston [14th Dist.] 1984, no writ). Consequently, a literal reading of Rule 166a and these authorities indicate that the motion itself must state the grounds.

Other cases have considered the same language of Rule 166a when the motion for summary judgment presented no grounds. In *Boney v. Harris*, 557 S.W.2d 376 (Tex. Civ. App.—Houston [1st Dist.] 1977, no writ), the motion for summary judgment stated only that the defendant's answer was "insufficient in law to constitute a defense . . . ." *Id.* at 378. The court held that such a motion failed to satisfy the requirements of Rule 166a(c). *Id.* In another case in which the motion presented absolutely no grounds, the court held: The motion, however, does not state any grounds, specific or otherwise, upon which it is based, and, as a result, it is not in compliance with Rule 166-A as amended. *Moody v. Temple National Bank*, 545 S.W.2d 289, 290 (Tex. Civ. App.—Austin 1977, no writ). *See also Mallory v. Dorothy Prinzhorn Real Estate, Inc.*, 535 S.W.2d 371, 372 (Tex. Civ. App.—Eastland 1976, no writ) (motion stating that "original answer is insufficient to raise a controverted fact issue" insufficient under rule 166a(c)).

* * *

All such rules [of procedure] can be applied under the rubric of literal construction to defeat their own purposes unless those purposes govern and define the rules. The underlying principles must control. 858 S.W.2d 344, 347 (Hecht, J., dissenting). The Texas Rules of Civil Procedure including Rule 166a should be clearly understandable and be applied in a predictable and consistent manner. In an attempt to avoid the effect of Rule 166a(c), the dissent would do a great disservice to the litigants whom we serve by rewriting the unambiguous text of Rule 166a In light of the dissent's perceptions concerning Rule 166a(c)'s "underlying purpose and principles." This approach would inject an element of uncertainty into every rule, no matter how clearly stated.

Consistent with the precise language of Rule 166a(c), we hold that a motion for summary judgment must itself expressly present the grounds upon which it is made. A motion must stand or fall on the grounds expressly presented in the motion. In determining whether grounds are expressly presented, reliance may not be placed on briefs or summary judgment evidence.

Non-Movant's Answer or Response

Likewise, issues a non-movant contends avoid the movant's entitlement to summary judgment must be expressly presented by written answer to the motion or by other written response to the motion and are not expressly presented by mere reference to summary judgment evidence. *See City of Houston v. Clear Creek Basin Authority*, 589 S.W.2d 671, 678 (Tex. 1979) ("the non-movant must expressly present to the trial court any reasons seeking to avoid movant's entitlement . . . .").

The summary judgment pleading rules we announce today are consistent with the express language of Rule 166a requiring that the motion for summary judgment state the specific grounds therefor and further the purpose of Rule 166a to provide adequate information for opposing the motion, and to define the issues. *See Weaver v. Stewart*, 825 S.W.2d 183, 184-85 (Tex. App.—Houston [14th Dist.] 1992, writ denied) ("[Rule 166a] is important because it provides the opposing party with notice of all matters expected to be asserted in arguing the motion."). Carving exceptions to this simple requirement that the motion for summary judgment state the specific grounds frustrates the purpose of Rule 166a(c). Eventually the exceptions would consume the rule, and inject uncertainty into summary judgment proceedings concerning what issues were presented for consideration. Furthermore, it is certainly not unduly burdensome to require the movant to state the specific grounds in the motion for summary judgment. These rules also permit the trial court to consider a brief in support of a motion for summary judgment as guidance in making its determination whether the summary judgment evidence demonstrates that the moving party is "entitled to judgment," *see* TEX. R. CIV. P. 166a(c), but not in determining whether summary judgment grounds and issues are expressly presented. Finally, these rules further the policy of seeking clarity and simplicity in summary judgment practice. *See, e.g., Black v. Victoria Lloyds Ins. Co.*, 797 S.W.2d 20, 27 (Tex. 1990) ("[T]he motion [for summary judgment] must identify or address the cause of action or defense and its elements." (emphasis added)).

II.

A corollary question concerns whether a burden exists to except or object to a defective motion for summary judgment or response. In certain situations, we conclude that such a burden exists.

Motion Presenting No Grounds

When the grounds for summary judgment are not expressly presented in the motion for summary judgment itself, any confusion may and should be resolved by exception in the trial court. However, summary judgments must stand or fall on their own merits, and the non-movant's failure to except or respond cannot supply by default the grounds for summary judgment or the summary judgment proof necessary to establish the movant's right—the movant's right is not established and the movant must still assert grounds in the motion for summary judgment itself and establish its entitlement to summary judgment. *See Clear Creek*, 589 S.W.2d at 678. While it would be prudent and helpful to the trial court for the non-movant always to file an [exception,] answer or response, the non-movant needs no [exception], answer or response to the motion to contend on appeal that the grounds expressly presented to the trial court by the movant's motion are insufficient as a matter of law to support the summary judgment. *Id.* (emphasis in original). Even if the non-movant fails to except or respond, if the grounds for summary judgment are not expressly presented in the motion for summary judgment itself, the motion is legally insufficient as a matter of law. Consequently, we conclude that Rule 166a does not require a non-movant to except in this situation.

Motion Presenting Only Certain Grounds

When the motion for summary judgment clearly presents certain grounds but not others, a non-movant is not required to except. This distinction was recognized and correctly resolved in *Roberts v. Southwest Texas Methodist Hospital*, when the court held: When a motion for summary judgment asserts grounds A and B, it cannot be upheld on grounds C and D, which were not asserted, even if the summary judgment proof supports them and the responding party did not except to the motion. 811 S.W.2d at 146. Why should a non-movant be required to except to a motion expressly presenting certain grounds and not others? The only effect of such a rule would be to alert the movant to additional unasserted grounds for summary judgment. Consequently, we conclude that Rule 166a does not require a non-movant to except in this situation.

Grounds Unclear from Motion

An exception is required should a non-movant wish to complain on appeal that the grounds relied on by the movant were unclear or ambiguous. *See Lochabay v. Southwestern Bell Media, Inc.*, 828 S.W.2d 167, 170 n. 2 (Tex. App.—Austin 1992, no writ) ("Lochabay did not except to the motion for summary judgment, as he was required to do if he wished to claim lack of specificity."). Prudent trial practice dictates that such an exception should be lodged to ensure that the parties, as well as the trial court, are focused on the same grounds. This prevents the non-movant from having to argue on appeal each and every ground vaguely referred to in the motion. The practical effect of failure to except is that the non-movant loses his right to have the grounds for summary judgment narrowly focused, thereby running the risk of having an appellate court determine the grounds it believes were expressly presented in the summary judgment. Even in this situation, however, "[a]n appellate court cannot 'read between the lines, infer or glean from the pleadings or the proof' any grounds for granting the summary judgment other than those grounds expressly set forth before the trial court [In the motion for summary judgment]." *Clark v. First National Bank of Highlands*, 794 S.W.2d 953, 956 (Tex. App.—Houston [1st Dist.] 1990, no writ) (*quoting Great-Ness Professional Serv., Inc. v. First Nat'l Bank of Louisville*, 704 S.W.2d 916, 918 (Tex. App.—Houston [14th Dist.] 1986, no writ)).

Non-Movant's Answer or Response

With one exception, the above rules apply equally to a non-movant's response. The non-movant must expressly present to the trial court, by written answer or response, any issues defeating the movant's entitlement. *Clear Creek*, 589 S.W.2d at 678 ("The written answer or response to the motion must fairly apprise the movant and the court of the issues the non-movant contends should defeat the motion."). If it is clear what issues the non-movant contends should defeat the movant's entitlement, the movant should be able to reply only to these issues. *See* TEX. R. CIV. P. 166a ("Issues not expressly presented to the trial court by written motion, answer or other response shall not be considered on appeal as grounds for reversal."). Any confusion regarding what issues are expressly presented by the non-movant can also be resolved by exception. However, summary judgments must stand or fall on their own merits, and the non-movant's failure to answer or respond cannot supply by default the summary judgment proof necessary to establish the movant's right. *Clear Creek*, 589 S.W.2d at 678. If a non-movant fails to present any issues in its response or answer, the movant's right is not established and the movant must still establish its entitlement to summary judgment. The effect of such a failure is that the non-movant is limited on appeal to arguing the legal sufficiency of the grounds presented by the movant. *Id.* at 678.

III.

The summary judgment pleading rules we announce today are simple, equitable, and prevent the confusion that results when parties fail to expressly present grounds and issues entitling or defeating entitlement to summary judgment. They also prevent parties from arguing that grounds and issues were presented in lengthy briefs or voluminous summary judgment evidence. Finally, these rules ultimately prevent the controversies that result when appellate courts are forced to ascertain whether grounds and issues were expressly presented to the trial court.

Because Southside's motion for summary judgment stated no grounds and because McConnell properly excepted to this defect, the court of appeals erred in affirming the trial court's rendition of summary judgment for Southside. For these reasons, we reverse the judgment of the court of appeals and remand this cause to the trial court for further proceedings consistent with this opinion.

GONZALEZ, J., concurring.

HECHT, JUSTICE, dissenting.

* * * I do not join in the plurality opinion's extensive discussions of various other subjects, all obiter dicta, which are in some respects wrong and in all respects completely unnecessary to a decision of the dispute before us. * * *

CORNYN, J., joins in this dissenting opinion.

ENOCH, JUSTICE, dissenting.

I agree with the Court that the plain words of Rule 166a of the Texas Rules of Civil Procedure establish a bright line rule. The grounds for the granting of a motion for summary judgment must be stated in the motion. However, I would not address any of the other issues, nor can I agree that in this case the failure to include the grounds in the motion itself is harmful. The evidence in the record establishes that neither the court nor the non-movant was unaware, confused or mislead as to the specific grounds being relied upon by the movant. Therefore, I would affirm the judgment of the court of appeals.

PHILLIPS, C.J., joins in this dissenting opinion.

Note

Johnson v. Brewer & Pritchard, P.C., 73 S.W.3d. 193 (2002): As recognized in *McConnell,* "When the motion for summary judgment clearly presents certain grounds but not others, a non-movant is not required to except. This distinction was recognized and correctly resolved in *Roberts v. Southwest Texas Methodist, Hospital,* 811 S.W.2d 141 (Tex. 1991), when the court held: 'When a motion for summary judgment asserts grounds A and B, it cannot be upheld on grounds C and D, which were not asserted, even if the summary judgment proof supports them and the responding party did not except to the motion.' " 858 S.W.2d at 342. The court also reiterated that a court cannot grant summary judgment on grounds that were not presented in the summary judgment motion.

RHONE-POULENC, INC.
v.
STEEL
997 S.W.2d 217
(Tex. 1999)

The trial court's case management orders did not shift the burden of proof from the movant, Rhône-Poulenc, to the nonmovants, the Steels, in a summary judgment proceeding under Rule166a(c) of the Texas Rules of Civil Procedure. Because Rule 166a(c) requires a summary judgment movant to prove it is entitled to judgment as a matter of law, the orders did not shift the burden from Rhône to the Steels. Rhône's summary judgment evidence did not meet Rule 166a(c)'s burden.

A defendant moving for summary judgment on the affirmative defense of limitations has the burden to conclusively establish that defense. When the plaintiff pleads the discovery rule as an exception to limitations, the defendant must negate that exception as well.

Summary judgments must stand on their own merits. Accordingly, on appeal, the nonmovant need not have answered or responded to the motion to contend that the movant's summary judgment proof is insufficient as a matter of law to support summary judgment. When reviewing a summary judgment, the appellate court takes as true all evidence favorable to the nonmovant, and indulges every reasonable inference and resolve any doubts in the nonmovant's favor. On appeal, the movant still bears the burden of showing that there is no genuine issue of material fact and that the movant is entitled to judgment as a matter of law.

Because September 19, 1992 fell on a Saturday, the Steels' lawsuit, filed on September 21, 1992, the first Monday after September 19, 1992, was, under Texas Rule of Civil Procedure 4, within two years from September 19, 1990.

CARPENTER
v.
CIMARRON HYDROCARBONS CORPORATION

98 S.W.3d 682
(Tex. 2002)

A motion for leave to file a late summary-judgment response should be granted when the nonmovant establishes good cause by showing that the failure to timely respond (1) was not intentional or the result of conscious indifference, but the result of accident or mistake, and (2) that allowing the late response will occasion no undue delay, or otherwise injure the party seeking summary judgment. Because Cimarron did not establish good cause, the trial court did not abuse its discretion in denying Cimarron leave to file a late response.

Any error in denying it had to be brought up (preserved and briefed) on appeal. The *Craddock v. Sunshine Bus Lines*, 133 S.W.2d 124 (Tex. 1939) standard does not apply to Cimarron's motion for new trial, because the rules of procedure provided Cimarron an opportunity, before judgment was rendered, to obtain a continuance or leave to file an untimely response. (Although the trial court denied that relief to the plaintiff here, its decision is not contested in this appeal. Accordingly, the Court does not consider whether the trial court abused its discretion in denying plaintiff's continuance motion.).

g. *Summary Judgment on the Pleadings*

TEXAS NATIONAL CORPORATION
v.
UNITED SYSTEMS INTERNATIONAL

493 S.W.2d 738
(Tex. 1973)

While, as with any other judgment, pleadings are required to support a summary judgment, pleadings, even if sworn to, are not summary judgment proof. A motion for summary judgment must be supported by its own summary judgment proof, unless the case is one properly decided on pleadings alone.

NATIVIDAD
v.
ALEXSIS

875 S.W.2d 695
(Tex. 1994)

A summary judgment based on a pleading deficiency is proper if a party has had an opportunity by special exception to amend and fails to do so, or files a further defective pleading. A review of the pleadings in such case is de novo, with the reviewing court taking all allegations, facts, and inferences in the pleadings as true and viewing them in a light most favorable to the pleader. The reviewing court will affirm the summary judgment only if the pleadings are legally insufficient.

Notes

1. In the *Natividad* case the court stated that it was reviewing the pleadings in the summary judgment case de novo. The phrase "de novo review" can be used several ways. First, it may refer to an appeal from the justice court to the county court. Unless there is a statute (as in some minor criminal cases) for a substantial evidence review of the record in justice court, the trial in county court is de novo. This means that the trial begins anew, as if there had been no trial court in the justice court. The judgment of the justice court is meaningless in deciding the case in the county court.

The phrase "de novo review," however, can be used in other ways. The second, and primary, use for the phrase concerns questions of law. A trial court's ruling on evidentiary issues are subject to review on a abuse of discretion standard. A trial court's review on factual issues is subject to a factual sufficiency review. In those situations, the appellate court can reverse the trial court, but cannot substitute their decision for that of the trial court. However, on issues of law the appellate court is in as good a position as the trial court to determine the issue. This includes cross-motions for summary judgment, legal sufficiency issues, and ordinary issues of law. In these situations, the appellate court may substitute its judgment for that of the lower court, and render the judgment which the law requires.

2 *City of Garland v. Dallas Morning News*, 22 S.W.2d 351 (Tex. 2000) (Plurality Opinion by Justice Baker, joined by Justices Hankinson, O'Neill, and Gonzales; Concurring Opinion by Justice Enoch, joined by Chief Justice Phillips and Justice Abbott; Dissenting Opinion by Justice Owen, joined by Justice Hecht.) On cross-motions for summary judgment, each party bears the burden of establishing that it is entitled to judgment as a matter of law. When the trial court grants one motion and denies the other, the reviewing court should determine all questions presented. The reviewing court should render the judgment that the trial court should have rendered, including rendering judgment for the other movant.

3. *Friesenhahn v. Ryan,* 960 S.W.2d 656 (Tex. 1998). Before a court may grant a "no cause of action" summary judgment on the pleadings, it must give the parties an adequate opportunity to plead a viable cause of action. This is akin to the use of special exceptions to challenge the sufficiency of a pleading. When the trial court sustains special exceptions, it must give the pleader an opportunity to amend the pleading. If a party refuses to amend, or the amended pleading fails to state a cause of action, then summary judgment may be granted. The same is true when a summary judgment is used to challenge the opponent's pleadings. Summary judgment is proper when the opponent refuses to, or cannot amend the pleadings to state a legal cause of action or defense. But, whether special exceptions or summary judgments are involved, the opponent must be given a reasonable period of time to amend the pleadings.

4. *Haase v. Glazne*, 62 S.W.3d 795 (Tex. 2001): Summary judgment may be granted when a party is ordered to replead and fails to do so.

5. *Chavez v. Kansas City Southern Ry. Co.,* 520 S.W.3d 898 (Tex. 2017): **Summary Judgment. Rebuttable Presumption Does Not Relieve Movant of Proving the Underlying Facts**. At trial, a presumption operates to establish a fact until rebutted, but not in summary judgment proceedings. Assuming without deciding that an attorney retained for litigation is presumed to possess express authority to enter into a settlement agreement on behalf of the client, the presumption may be rebutted with evidence to the contrary. But a summary judgment movant may not use a presumption to shift, to the non-movant, the burden of raising a fact issue of rebuttal.

2. *No Evidence Summary Judgment Practice*

HIGHT
v.
DUBLIN VETERINARY CLINIC
22 S.W.3d 614
(Tex. App.—Eastland 2000, pet. denied)

Brad Jackson, Jackson & Matthews, Dallas, for appellant.

Christopher J. Pruitt, Donald A. Ferrill, Brown, Thompson, Pruitt & Peterson, Fort Worth, Gale Warren, Law Office of Gale Warren, Stephenville, for appellee.

JIM R. WRIGHT, JUSTICE.

The trial court granted appellees' no-evidence motions for summary judgment. Because we find that the trial court properly granted the motions, we affirm.

Background Facts

This case arises from the death of a Boer goat named Pancho. In their second amended original petition, appellants alleged that they were in the business of owning, breeding, and selling goats; that they placed Pancho with the Edwards "at their breeding facility for the purpose of standing him at stud, collecting, storing and selling his semen"; that an employee of the Edwards spoke with and explained to Carter's wife that "Pancho's horns [were] growing into his head, and we need to do something about it"; that Carter consented to what he considered a "tip[ping]" of Pancho's horns; that Pancho was anesthetized at the Dublin Veterinary Clinic and dehorned; that approximately 15 to 20 minutes after the dehorning procedure was completed, Pancho died; that Vet appellees sent tissue samples from Pancho to the Texas Veterinary Medical Diagnostic Laboratory and the tests showed that Pancho died of acute pulmonary congestion and edema; and that Vet appellees then burned Pancho's body without their consent.

Procedural Facts

Appellants sued the Clinic for negligence, breach of contract, and breach of warranty. Appellants also sued the Edwards for violations of the Texas Deceptive Trade Practices Act, TEX. BUS. & COM. CODE ANN. ch. 17 (Vernon 1987 & Pamph.Supp.2000) (DTPA). In response to appellees' no-evidence motions for summary judgment, appellants filed responses which included the affidavits of appellants and their expert witness, Dr. David Fazzino. The Clinic then filed a reply to appellants' responses and asserted objections to appellants' affidavits. The Edwards did not file a reply nor did they assert any objections. The trial court sustained the Clinic's objections to the affidavit of Dr. Fazzino, striking it in its entirety. The court then granted appellees' motions for summary judgment. Appellants filed a motion for new trial which was overruled by operation of law.

Issues on Appeal

Appellants argue that the trial court erred in granting the Clinic's motion for summary judgment because (a) the trial court improperly struck Dr. David Fazzino's affidavit; (b) the Clinic's motion for summary judgment is not supported by any competent summary judgment evidence; (c) genuine issues of material fact existed on appellants' negligence claims; (d) the doctrine of res ipsa loquitur applies herein precluding summary judgment; (e) appellants were entitled to a spoliation presumption; (f) genuine issues of material fact existed on appellants' breach of contract and implied warranty claims; and (g) appellants were entitled to recover for the loss of income resulting from Pancho's death. In addition, appellants argue that the trial court erred in granting the Edwards' motion for summary judgment because (a) their motion does not comply with TEX. R. CIV. P. 166a(i); (b) the Edwards' motion for summary judgment is not supported by competent summary judgment evidence; (c) a genuine issue of material fact existed on appellants' negligence claims; (d) the doctrine of res ipsa loquitur applies herein precluding summary judgment; (e) appellants were entitled to a spoliation presumption; (f) genuine issues of material fact existed on appellants' breach of contract and implied warranty claims; (g) genuine issues of material fact existed on appellants' DTPA claims; and (h) appellants are entitled to recover for the loss of income resulting from Pancho's death.

No-evidence summary judgments are relatively new to Texas jurisprudence. In 1997, the rule pertaining to summary judgments, TEX. R. CIV. P. 166a, was amended to provide a procedure whereby a party might obtain a summary judgment based upon the proposition that there was no evidence of one or more of the essential elements of a claim or defense relied upon by the opposite party. That rule, Rule 166a(i), provides as follows:

> After adequate time for discovery, a party without presenting summary judgment evidence may move for summary judgment on the ground that there is no evidence of one or more essential elements of a claim or defense on which an adverse party would have the burden of proof at trial. The motion must state the elements as to which there is no evidence. The court must grant the motion unless the respondent produces summary judgment evidence raising a genuine issue of material fact.

Frequently, the cases reviewing no-evidence summary judgments do so as though they were pretrial directed verdicts. Accordingly, the standard of review applied was one in which the court considered the evidence in the light most favorable to the non-movant and disregarded all contrary evidence. *See, e.g., Bosque Asset Corp. v. Greenberg*, 19 S.W.3d 514 Tex. App.—Eastland, 2000); *Grant v. Southwestern Electric Power Company*, 20 S.W.3d 764 (Tex. App.—Texarkana, 2000); *Denton v. Big Spring Hospital Corporation*, 998 S.W.2d 294 (Tex. App.—Eastland 1999 no pet'n); *Moore v. K Mart Corporation*, 981 S.W.2d 266 (Tex. App.—San Antonio 1998, *review denied*); *Jackson v. Fiesta Mart, Inc.*, 979 S.W.2d 68 (Tex. App.—Austin 1998, no pet'n); Judge David Hittner and Lynn Liberato, *Summary Judgments in Texas*, 34 HOUS. L .REV. 1303 (1998).

We now believe that the better approach is to review no-evidence motions for summary judgments in the same manner any other Rule 166a summary judgment is reviewed. We see no reason to engage in analogies when we already have in place a standard by which to review motions for summary judgments. In reviewing any Rule 166a summary judgment, we hold that, including a no-evidence summary judgment under that rule, we must accept as true evidence in favor of the non-movant and indulge every reasonable inference and resolve all doubts in favor of the non-movant. *El Chico Corporation v. Poole*, 732 S.W.2d 306 (Tex. 1987). An exercise of this standard would not involve any consideration of any summary judgment evidence offered by the proponent of the motion. Rule 166a(a) and (b) provide that the movant may proceed with or without supporting affidavits. (Emphasis added) To the contrary, Rule 166a(i) provides that "a party without presenting summary judgment evidence may move for summary judgment." (Emphasis added) Therefore, summary judgment evidence proffered by the movant is not to be considered in determining a no-evidence summary judgment. We point out that the Waco Court of Appeals held in *Grimes v. Andrews*, 997 S.W.2d 877 (Tex. App.—Waco 1999, no pet'n), that, in cases where a moving party attaches summary judgment evidence, the review would be conducted as though the motion for summary judgment was a traditional one.

In summary, we hold that, in reviewing a no-evidence summary judgment, we will not consider summary judgment evidence propounded by the movant and that we will accept as true evidence in favor of the non-movant, indulging every reasonable inference and resolving all doubts in favor of the non-movant.

The question then becomes whether the summary judgment evidence presented by the non-movant, when so considered, is some evidence which raises a material issue of fact. The trial court properly granted the no-evidence summary judgment if appellants failed to bring forth more than a mere scintilla of probative evidence to raise a genuine issue of material fact as to an essential element of appellants' claims. Less than a mere scintilla of evidence exists when the evidence is "so weak as to do no more than create a mere surmise or suspicion" of a fact, so that the legal effect is that there is no evidence. *Kindred v. Con/Chem, Inc.*, 650 S.W.2d 61, 63 (Tex. 1983). More than a mere scintilla of evidence exists when the evidence rises to a level that would enable reasonable and fair-minded people to differ in their conclusions. *Merrell Dow Pharmaceuticals, Inc. v. Havner*, 953 S.W.2d 706 (Tex. 1997).

We now examine appellants' issues in accordance with these standards.

* * *

Appellants further argue that the Edwards' no-evidence motion for summary judgment did not comply with Rule 166a(i). Specifically, appellants urge that the Edwards' motion was conclusory and, therefore, would not support summary judgment. As evidence of the motion's general and conclusory nature, appellants point to the Edwards' challenge of every element of their DTPA claim, urging that there can be no question of appellants' consumer status. Also, the motion lists a violation of TEX. INS. CODE ANN. art. 21.21 (Vernon 1981 & Supp. 2000) as an element with no evidentiary support, and appellants argue that there is no pleading which possibly suggests a claim under that provision. Appellants further argue that they were not allowed adequate time for discovery.

The Edwards' motion also states, however, that, in order for appellants to prevail in a negligence cause of action, they must establish by evidence of probative force the following elements: (1) a duty owed by the Edwards to appellants; (2) a breach of that duty; and (3) proximate causation resulting in compensable damages to appellants. The motion then states that, "[a]fter adequate time for discovery, [appellants] cannot provide evidence to support any of the aforementioned elements of negligence."

Under Rule 166a(i), a party:

> [M]ay move for summary judgment on the ground that there is no evidence of one or more essential elements of a claim or a defense on which an adverse party would have the burden of proof at trial.

Rule 166a(i) "requires the movant to specify the essential element or elements of a claim or defense to which there is no evidence." * * * *Lampasas v. Spring Center, Inc.*, 988 S.W.2d 428, 436 (Tex. App.—Houston [14th Dist.] 1999, no pet'n). In *Lampasas*, the movant's no-evidence motion for summary judgment stated that there was no evidence of any duty, breach, or causation. The court held that the motion provided notice to the non-movant that "he must come forward with some evidence on these challenged elements, or his negligent causes of action would fail." *Lampasas v. Spring Center, Inc., supra* at 436. The Edwards' motion meets the requirements of Rule 166a(i).

We also hold that there has been more than "adequate time for discovery" in this case. Pancho died on July 5, 1995, and the lawsuit was filed on July 7, 1997. Appellants did not begin discovery as to the Edwards until September 10, 1998. Appellants filed a motion for continuance on October 28, 1998, for the purpose of conducting discovery, and the trial court granted their motion. Dr. Fazzino's affidavit was taken on December 1, 1998. The summary judgment proceeding was held on January 6, 1999, approximately 18 months after the suit was filed, and approximately three and one-half years after Pancho's death. Appellants' argument is overruled.

Appellants also insist that both the Clinic's and the Edwards' no-evidence motions for summary judgment are not supported by competent summary judgment evidence. Rule 166a(i) does not permit summary judgment proof from the movants. Because appellants failed to produce summary judgment evidence raising a genuine issue of material fact on their negligence claim, we overrule appellants' first three contentions.

* * *

Appellants argue that genuine issues of material fact existed on appellants' breach of contract and implied warranty claims against both the Clinic and the Edwards. Appellants' second amended original petition alleges that each appellee: [F]ailed to perform the work for which the [appellee] was engaged by [appellants] in a good and workmanlike manner, thereby materially breaching their contract with [appellants] and resulting in their damages as set forth below.

The damages claimed by appellants include the value of Pancho and the loss of income generated by Pancho. In their motions for no-evidence summary judgment, the Clinic and the Edwards asserted that appellants had no evidence of the existence of a contractual duty and breach of that duty.

Although the principles of contract and tort causes of action are well settled, the distinction between the two is not always clear. We must look to the substance of the cause of action and not the manner in which it is pleaded. *Jim Walter Homes, Inc. v. Reed*, 711 S.W.2d 617, 617-18 (Tex. 1986).

The acts of a party may breach duties in tort or contract alone or simultaneously in both. The nature of the injury suffered usually determines the existence of a cause of action in tort. Tort obligations are generally "obligations that are imposed by law—apart from and independent of promises made and therefore apart from the manifested intention of the parties—to avoid injury to others." *Clary Corporation v. Smith*, 949 S.W.2d 452, 463 (Tex. App.—Fort Worth 1997, *pet'n den'd*), *quoting Southwestern Bell Telephone Company v. DeLanney*, 809 S.W.2d 493, 494 (Tex. 1991). If appellees' conduct would give rise to liability independent of whether a contract existed between the parties, then appellants' claim sounds in tort. *Clary Corporation v. Smith, supra.* The duty that appellants alleged the Clinic and the Edwards breached in this case was one imposed by law, not contract. If appellees had breached this duty, their "breach would give rise to liability independent of whether a contract existed between [appellants] and [appellees]." *Clary Corporation v. Smith, supra* at 463. We hold appellants' claim sounds in tort, not contract.

Moreover, without an express agreement in the record, we decline to recognize an implied warranty for veterinarian services. *See Dennis v. Allison*, 698 S.W.2d 94 (Tex.1985) (declining to recognize an implied warranty in connection with medical services when a patient was sexually assaulted and beaten by her psychiatrist); *Downing v. Gully, supra* (adopting the standard applied to physicians and surgeons in medical malpractice cases in a veterinary negligence case). Having already discussed appellants' negligence claims, appellants' argument is overruled.

* * *

Appellants contend that the trial court erred in granting the Edwards' motion for summary judgment on their DTPA claim. Appellants assert that the Edwards "represented themselves as a reputable and established service company which was capable of caring for Pancho and standing him at stud, collecting, storing and selling his semen, and providing reproductive services." Appellants argue that, since Pancho died while in the Edwards' custody and care, they were not capable of caring for Pancho as represented. In addition, appellants state that evidence existed that the Edwards "took an unconscionable course of action." We disagree.

In reviewing the record before us, we have found no evidence of any false, misleading, or deceptive act or practice enumerated in Section 17.46 of the DTPA. We have also been unable to find any evidence of unconscionability. Section 17.45(5) defines an unconscionable action or course of action as "an act or practice which, to a consumer's detriment, takes advantage of the lack of knowledge, ability, experience, or capacity of the consumer to a grossly unfair degree."

The Edwards provided routine boarding and care for Pancho at their breeding facility. Appellants offer no evidence that the Edwards were incompetent in providing genetic services or routine boarding and care. Additionally, appellants offer no evidence of any representation made by the Edwards which encompasses the performance of veterinary care, surgical treatment, or postoperative treatment. The Edwards informed Hight of the problem with Pancho's horns after almost one year of caring for him, and there is evidence in the record that Pancho's horns were growing into the back of his neck. This information was not false, misleading, or deceptive and does not constitute an unconscionable action by the Edwards. Appellants' final contention is overruled.

The judgment of the trial court is affirmed.

Note

Johnson v. Brewer & Pritchard, P.C., 73 S.W.3d 193 (Tex. 2002): A respondent to a motion under TEX. R. CIV. P. 166A (i) need not marshal evidence, but may point out evidence that raises a fact issue on the challenged elements. Here, whether plaintiffs adequately pointed out evidence relating to challenged elements of the conspiracy cause of action is a close question. But, the summary judgment response [detailed in the opinion] met the minimum requirements of Rule 166a(i).

BINUR
v.
JACOBO
135 S.W.3d 646
(Tex. 2004)

JUSTICE OWEN delivered the opinion of the Court.

The issues in this medical malpractice suit have narrowed as the case has proceeded. Although the plaintiff Donna Jacobo originally asserted a number of counts of negligence against the defendant Nir Binur, a physician, Jacobo has since confined her complaints to her contention that Binur failed to obtain her informed consent to the surgical removal of both her breasts. She contends that Binur told her that she would definitely develop breast cancer and that this was the reason she consented to a prophylactic bilateral mastectomy.

After a trial in which a jury was unable to agree on a verdict and a mistrial was declared, the trial court granted summary judgment in Binur's favor. Jacobo appealed, and a divided court of appeals reversed and remanded, concluding that fact issues exist. We hold that although Jacobo might have pursued a claim against Binur for negligence in reaching his prognosis, an erroneous prognosis that is the basis for recommending surgery cannot be the basis of a cause of action for lack of informed consent. Because informed consent is the only claim Jacobo has pursued, we reverse the court of appeals' judgment and render judgment for Binur.

The summary judgment record includes affidavits, excerpts from testimony adduced at trial, and documentary evidence. The record reflects that fourteen years before Donna Jacobo underwent the mastectomy at issue in this case, she had a lump removed from her breast that proved to be benign, and that she had another benign lump removed seven years later. In the summer before her mastectomy, her mother died of breast cancer. Three months after her mother's death, Donna Jacobo detected another lump in her breast. She consulted her primary care physician, who examined her and ordered a mammogram. Jacobo's breasts had fibrocystic tissue, which made it more difficult to interpret the mammogram. Jacobo's physician referred her to a general surgeon, Dr. John Schmidt. Schmidt reviewed Jacobo's mammogram, and she told him about her prior lumpectomies, her mother's death, and the fact that her maternal grandmother had survived breast cancer.

After this initial consultation, Dr. Schmidt reported in a note to Jacobo's primary care physician that Schmidt's diagnosis was: "(1) Probable fibrocystic disease (2) Very [underscored three times] strong risk of developing breast ca[ncer]." Schmidt's recommended treatment was: "(1) Re-examine in 3 mos. (2) Strongly [underscored twice] consider referral to plastic surgeon for possible sub[cutaneous] mastectomy & implants." Donna Jacobo's affidavit states that at her initial consultation with Dr. Schmidt, he recommended a bilateral mastectomy, but she "decided against the proposed surgical removal of my breasts." She explained, "I felt that this was a rather extreme mode of treatment for preventing a disease that I did not have—especially in light of the fact that my previous lumps had been benign."

Dr. Schmidt referred Jacobo to Binur, a plastic surgeon. Binur, like Schmidt, recommended that Jacobo undergo a mastectomy. Jacobo's affidavit states, "When I questioned Dr. Binur about my risk of developing breast cancer, he told me that it wasn't a question of *if* I required it, but more of a question of *when* it would happen. Essentially, he told me that it was a certainty that I would develop the disease." Binur disputes that he told Jacobo that it was certain she would develop breast cancer, but in our review, we accept all that Jacobo said as true.

After meeting with Binur, Jacobo returned to see Dr. Schmidt and told him that she had decided to proceed with the surgery. Before surgery, Jacobo signed a written consent form that identified both Schmidt and Binur in the blank for "PHYSICIAN'S/SURGEON'S NAME." She consented to a "Bilateral simple mastectomy, tissue expanders." All parties and experts agree that two distinct procedures were performed on Jacobo during this surgery. The first was the bilateral mastectomy, and the second was partial breast reconstruction with the insertion of tissue expanders. It is also undisputed that Dr. Schmidt performed the mastectomy with the assistance of Binur, although the extent of Binur's participation and the legal duty he owed to Jacobo as a result is disputed. Binur performed the reconstruction procedure, which is no longer at issue in this case.

Binur continued to treat Jacobo after this initial surgery, and she alleged that as a result, she experienced pain, deformity, and other ill-effects. We will not detail her further treatment by Binur since it is no longer part of Jacobo's claim. We note only that Binur performed three more surgical procedures and that Jacobo then consulted other surgeons and had three additional surgical procedures to remedy Binur's alleged negligence in reconstructing her breasts.

Jacobo sued Schmidt and Binur. The trial court granted summary judgment in Schmidt's favor and severed the suit against him. The remaining claims against Binur proceeded to a jury trial. Both Binur and Schmidt, as well as experts for Jacobo and Binur, testified. Before the case was submitted to the jury, Jacobo waived her claims against Binur pertaining to his treatment of her after the mastectomy and her claim that Binur was negligent in performing the reconstruction procedure when the mastectomy was performed. The only claims she pursued were those related to Binur's role in the mastectomy. As noted above, at the conclusion of the evidence, the jury was unable to reach a verdict, and the trial court declared a mistrial.

Binur then moved for summary judgment under Texas Rules of Civil Procedure 166a(b) and 166a(i). Binur contended that as a matter of law he was not negligent and that he owed no duty to Jacobo to obtain her informed consent for the mastectomy. He also contended that if he owed a duty, informed consent was properly obtained. Finally, he contended that any failure to obtain informed consent was not a proximate cause of injury or damages to Jacobo. The trial court granted this motion, reciting in the judgment that: 1) Binur was not negligent as a matter of law; 2) he had no duty to obtain informed consent for the mastectomy; 3) informed consent to the mastectomy was properly obtained; and 4) any alleged act or omission of Binur was not a proximate cause of any injury or damages to Jacobo.

Jacobo appealed, arguing that the information Binur had given her "was not medically accurate" and had caused her to consent to surgery for "a disease that she did not have." She contended that because Binur "played a primary role in the pre-operative, information-giving, consent obtaining portion of the surgery," he had a duty to properly inform her and obtain her informed consent. Jacobo's briefing also focused on the extent of Binur's participation as Schmidt's assistant during the mastectomy. She argued that Binur was a "co-surgeon" and therefore that he, as well as Schmidt, was required to obtain informed consent, which he had not done. At the conclusion of her brief, Jacobo suggested to the court of appeals that its holding should be as follows: "An assistant surgeon has the duty of obtaining a patient's informed consent only when the surgeon has an established doctor-patient relationship with the patient and voluntarily injects himself into the process by prescribing, recommending and/or performing the procedure."

The court of appeals concluded that although the duty to obtain a patient's informed consent does not extend to an assistant surgeon, there was conflicting summary judgment evidence "about whether Dr. Binur was an operating surgeon during the mastectomy with a direct obligation to the patient or a doctor whose only role was to assist during the procedure." The court of appeals also concluded that there was evidence that Binur breached a duty to obtain informed consent because "Dr. Binur essentially told [Jacobo] that there was no risk that the mastectomy was unnecessary because it was a certainty that she would develop breast cancer." Therefore, the court determined that a fact question existed on whether "Dr. Binur failed to disclose the risk that the mastectomy might have been unnecessary." With regard to proximate cause, the court of appeals concluded that based on Jacobo's affidavit, there was a fact question of "whether a reasonable person would have refused the mastectomy had she been accurately informed of the risk that the procedure might be unnecessary."

Before we turn to the substantive issues raised by this appeal, we first address the court of appeals' decision that it would treat Binur's summary judgment motion as presenting only a motion under Rule 166a(b) and that it would disregard his "no evidence" contentions, brought under Rule 166a(i), because Binur presented summary judgment evidence.

Texas Rule of Civil Procedure 166a does not prohibit a party from combining in a single motion a request for summary judgment that utilizes the procedures under either subsection (a) or (b), with a request for summary judgment that utilizes subsection (i) and asserts that there is "no evidence of one or more essential elements of a claim or defense." The fact that evidence may be attached to a motion that proceeds under subsection (a) or (b) does not foreclose a party from also asserting that there is no evidence with regard to a particular element. Similarly, if a motion brought solely under subsection (i) attaches evidence, that evidence should not be considered unless it creates a fact question, but such a motion should not be disregarded or treated as a motion under subsection (a) or (b). We disapprove of decisions that hold or imply that, if a party attaches evidence to a motion for summary judgment, any request for summary judgment under Rule 166a(i) will be disregarded.

Some Texas courts have declared that when a party seeks summary judgment under subsection (a) or (b), and also under subsection (i), the better practice is to file two separate motions, or at least to include headings that clearly delineate and segregate the part of a motion relying on subsection (a) or (b) from the part that relies on subsection (i). We agree that using headings to clearly delineate the basis for summary judgment under subsection (a) or (b) from the basis for summary judgment under subsection (i) would be helpful to the bench and bar, but the rule does not require it. If a motion clearly sets forth its grounds and otherwise meets Rule 166a's requirements, it is sufficient. Here, Binur's motion for summary judgment asserted that there was no evidence of proximate cause. The court of appeals erred in concluding that this ground could be disregarded because evidence was attached to the motion.

* * *

We hold that the trial court did not err in granting summary judgment. We therefore reverse the judgment of the court of appeals and render judgment for Binur. We do not reach or consider any of the court of appeals' determinations regarding assisting and "operating" surgeons or the duty to obtain informed consent because of our disposition of other issues raised by the parties.

Notes

1. In *Hight* the court recognizes a disagreement about the standard of review. The Texas Supreme Court has resolved any conflict in *King Ranch, Inc. v. Chapman*, 118 S.W.3d 742 (Tex. 2003). In addressing this issue the court stated:

> "Because King Ranch's summary judgment motion was, in part, a no-evidence motion, we consider the evidence in the light most favorable to the non-movant. *Wal-Mart Stores, Inc. v. Rodriguez*, 92 S.W.3d 502, 506 (Tex. 2002); *Johnson v. Brewer & Pritchard, P.C.*, 73 S.W.3d 193, 208 (Tex. 2002). A no-evidence summary judgment is essentially a pretrial directed verdict, and we apply the same legal sufficiency standard in reviewing a no-evidence summary judgment as we apply in reviewing a directed verdict. *See, e.g., Valero Mktg. & Supply Co. v. Kalama Int'l*, 51 S.W.3d 345, 350 (Tex. App.—Houston [1st Dist.] 2001, no pet.); *Blackburn v. Columbia Med. Ctr. Of Arlington Subsidiary*, 58 S.W.3d 263, 270 (Tex. App.—Fort Worth 2001, pet. denied); *Mansfield v. C.F. Bent Tree Apartment, L.P.*, 37 S.W.3d 145, 149 (Tex. App.—Austin 2001, no pet.); *Espalin v. Children's Med. Ctr.*, 27 S.W.3d 675, 683 (Tex. App.—Dallas 2000, no pet.); *Barraza v. Eureka Co.*, 25 S.W.3d 225, 231 (Tex. App.—El Paso 2000, pet. denied); *Moore v. K Mart Corp.*, 981 S.W.2d 266, 269 (Tex. App.—San Antonio 1998, pet. denied).
>
> Accordingly, we review the evidence in the light most favorable to the non-movant, disregarding all contrary evidence and inferences. *Merrell Dow Pharms., Inc. v. Havner*, 953 S.W.2d 706, 711 (Tex. 1997). "A no evidence point will be sustained when (a) there is a complete absence of evidence of a vital fact, (b) the court is barred by rules of law or of evidence from giving weight to the only evidence offered to prove a vital fact, (c) the evidence offered to prove a vital fact is no more than a mere scintilla, or (d) the evidence conclusively establishes the opposite of the vital fact." *Id.* (*citing* Robert W. Calvert, "*No Evidence*" and "*Insufficient Evidence*" Points of Error, 38 TEX. L.REV. 361, 362-63 (1960)). Thus, a no-evidence summary judgment is improperly granted if the respondent brings forth more than a scintilla of probative evidence to raise a genuine issue of material fact. TEX.R. CIV. P. 166a(i); *Wal-Mart*, 92 S.W.3d at 506. Less than a scintilla of evidence exists when the evidence is "so weak as to do no more than create a mere surmise or suspicion" of a fact. *Kindred v. Con/Chem, Inc.*, 650 S.W.2d 61, 63 (Tex. 1983). More than a scintilla of evidence exists when the evidence "rises to a level that would enable reasonable and fair-minded people to differ in their conclusions." *Merrell Dow Pharms.*, 953 S.W.2d at 711. With this standard in mind, we turn to the claims made and the evidence adduced in this case."

2. In *Moore v. K Mart Corporation,* 981 S.W.2d 266 (Tex. App.—San Antonio 1998, review denied) the court discussed the meanings of the terms material fact and genuine as they are used in Rule 166a(i) as follows:

> Having set forth the standard we must apply in reviewing a no-evidence summary judgment, we must further understand the meaning of the terms "genuine" and "material fact," as they are used in rule 166a(i). For clarification of these terms, we turn to federal law. *See* Judge David Hittner and Lynne Liberato, *No-Evidence Summary Judgments Under the New Rule*, in STATE BAR OF TEXAS PROF. DEV. PROGRAM, 20 ADVANCED CIVIL TRIAL COURSE D, D-5 (1997).
>
> Materiality is a criterion for categorizing factual disputes in relation to the legal elements of the claim. *Anderson v. Liberty Lobby, Inc.*, 477 U.S. 242, 249, 106 S.Ct. 2505, 91 L.Ed.2d 202 (1986). The materiality determination rests on the substantive law, and only those facts identified by the substantive law to be critical are considered material. *See id.* Stated differently, "[o]nly disputes over facts that might affect the outcome of the suit under the governing law will properly preclude the entry of summary judgment." *Id.*
>
> A material fact issue is genuine if the evidence is such that a reasonable jury could find the fact in favor of the non-moving party. *Anderson*, 477 U.S. at 249, 106 S.Ct. 2505; *Matsushita Electric Industrial Co., Ltd. v. Zenith Radio Corp.*, 475 U.S. 574, 588, 106 S.Ct. 1348, 89 L.Ed.2d 538 (1986). If the

evidence simply shows that some metaphysical doubt as to the fact exists, or if the evidence is not significantly probative, the material fact issue is not "genuine." *Anderson*, 477 U.S. at 250-51, 106 S.Ct. 2505.

3. For additional guidance in this area *see* David F. Johnson, "*The No Evidence Motion for Summary Judgment in Texas*", 52, BAYLOR L. REV. 929 (2000); Sarah B. Duncan, *"No-Evidence Motions for Summary Judgment: Harmonizing Rule 166A(1) and Its Comment*", 41 S. TEX. L. REV. 873 (2000).

4. In *Dow Chemical Company v. Francis*, 46 S.W.3d 237 (Tex. 2001) the Court made the following observations concerning a no evidence motion for summary judgment:

> A fraud cause of action requires: (1) a material misrepresentation, (2) that was either known to be false when made or was asserted without knowledge of its truth, (3) which was intended to be acted upon, (4) which was relied upon, and (5) which caused injury. *Formosa Plastics Corp. U.S.A. v. Presidio Eng'rs and Contractors, Inc.*, 960 S.W.2d 41, 47 (Tex.1998). The trial court rendered summary judgment on the fraud claim without specifying the grounds. Because Dow and Hegyesi filed a no-evidence summary-judgment motion challenging each of these elements, if Francis failed to raise a "genuine issue of material fact" about any of these elements, the summary judgment for Dow and Hegyesi should stand. TEX. R. CIV. P. 166a(i). Here, the court of appeals reversed the summary judgment after determining that Francis raised a fact issue concerning a material misrepresentation, but failed to consider Dow and Hegyesi's alternative ground for summary judgment—that Francis presented no evidence of damages. "When a trial court's order granting summary judgment does not specify the ground or grounds relied on for its ruling, summary judgment will be affirmed on appeal if any of the theories advanced are meritorious." *Carr v. Brasher*, 776 S.W.2d 567, 569 (Tex.1989). We therefore conclude that the court of appeals erred in not considering this alternative ground.

5. *Misc. Docket No. 97-9139*, Aug. 15, 1997, Tex.S.Ct. (PER CURIAM Opinion)(Dissenting Opinion by JUSTICE SPECTOR; Dissenting Opinion by JUSTICE BAKER). LWS 3433 (pp. 11).

> "1. Rule 166a of the Texas Rules of Civil Procedure, amended by Order in Misc. Docket No. 97-9067, dated April 16, 1997, 60 Tex. Bar. J. 534 (June 1997), with only the comment changed to reflect public comments received, is attached; 2. The amendments take effect September 1, 1997, and apply to all motions for summary judgment filed on or after that date; 3. *The comment appended to these changes, unlike other notes and comments in the rules, is intended to inform the construction and application of the rule*; and, 4. The Clerk is directed to file an original of this order with the Secretary of State forthwith, and to cause a copy of this Order to be mailed to each registered member of the State Bar of Texas by publication in the TEXAS BAR JOURNAL."
>
> "Comment to 1997 change: This comment is intended to inform the construction and application of the rule. Paragraph (i) authorizes a motion for summary judgment based on the assertion that, after adequate opportunity for discovery, there is no evidence to support one or more specified elements of an adverse party's claim or defense. A discovery period set by pretrial order should be adequate opportunity for discovery unless there is a showing to the contrary, and ordinarily a motion under paragraph (i) would be permitted after the period but not before. The motion must be specific in challenging the evidentiary support for an element of a claim or defense; paragraph (i) does not authorize conclusory motions or general no-evidence challenges to an opponent's case. Paragraph (i) does not apply to ordinary motions for summary judgment under paragraphs (a) or (b), in which the movant must prove it is entitled to judgment by establishing each element of its own claim or defense as a matter of law or by negating an element of the respondent's claim or defense as a matter of law. To defeat a motion made under paragraph (i), the respondent is not required to marshal its proof; its response need only point out evidence that raises a fact issue on the challenged elements. The existing rules continue to govern the general requirements of summary judgment practice. A motion under paragraph (i) is subject to sanctions provided by existing law (TEX. CIV. PRAC. & REM. CODE sections 9.001-10.006) and rules (TEX. R. CIV. P. 13). The denial of a motion under paragraph (i) is no more reviewable by appeal or mandamus than the denial of a motion under paragraph (c)."
>
> JUSTICE SPECTOR dissents, adopting JUSTICE BAKER'S dissent, and adding "I write separately, however, because, unlike JUSTICE BAKER, I do not agree with the basic concept underlying Rule

166a(i). . . ." She anticipates an increase in discovery and a serious risk that meritorious lawsuits will be summarily dismissed.

JUSTICE BAKER dissents: "I agree with the basic concept of a no evidence motion for summary judgment. However, * * * I am concerned that the Court ignores its own Supreme Court Advisory Committee's recommendations and promulgates a rule of its own choosing. In doing so, the Court eliminates the balance, fairness and safeguards the Committee's recommendations provide. Consequently, I respectfully dissent."

6. *Wal Mart Stores, Inc. v. Rodriguez*, 92 S.W.3d 502 (Tex. 2002): "*Wal-Mart Stores, Inc. v. Rodriguez*: In reviewing a no-evidence summary judgment, we examine the record in the light most favorable to the nonmovant, looking to see if Rodriguez presented more than a scintilla of evidence raising a genuine issue of material fact on the element of willful detention."

7. *Fort Worth Osteopathic Hospital, Inc. v. Reese*, 148 S.W.3d 94 (Tex. 2004): To succeed in a motion for summary judgment under Rule 166a(c), a movant must establish that there is no genuine issue of material fact so that the movant is entitled to judgment as a matter of law. TEX. R. CIV. P. 166a(c). In deciding whether there is a disputed issue of material fact, every doubt must be resolved in favor of the nonmovant and evidence favorable to the nonmovant must be taken as true. Under Rule 166a(i), a movant must establish that "[a]fter adequate time for discovery . . . there is no evidence of one or more essential elements of a claim or defense on which an adverse party would have the burden of proof at trial." To defeat a Rule 166a(i) summary judgment motion, the nonmovant must produce summary judgment evidence raising a genuine issue of material fact. A genuine issue of material fact exists if the nonmovant produces more than a scintilla of evidence establishing the existence of the challenged element.

8. In *Mack Trucks, Inc. v. Tamez*, --- S.W.3d ----, 2006 WL 3040534 (Tex.): A summary judgment motion pursuant to TEX. R. CIV. P. 166a(i) is essentially a motion for a pretrial directed verdict. Once such a motion is filed, the burden shifts to the nonmoving party to present evidence raising an issue of material fact as to the elements specified in the motion. The evidence presented by the motion and response is reviewed in the light most favorable to the party against whom the summary judgment was rendered, crediting evidence favorable to that party if reasonable jurors could, and disregarding contrary evidence unless reasonable jurors could not.

9. *Timpte Industries, Inc. v. Gish*, 286 S.W.3d 306 (Tex. 2009): A trial court cannot grant a summary judgment motion on grounds not presented in the motion. The motion must be specific in challenging the evidentiary support for an element of a claim or defense; TEX.R.CIV.P.166a(i) does not authorize conclusory motions or general no-evidence challenges to an opponent's case. The underlying purpose of this requirement is to provide the opposing party with adequate information for opposing the motion, and to define the issues for the purpose of summary judgment. This purpose may be analogized to that of the "fair notice" pleading requirements of TEX R.CIV. P. 45(b) and 47(a).

3. *Appeals from Summary Judgments*

Note

North East ISD v. Aldridge, 400 S.W.2d 893 (Tex. 1966): When a judgment, not intrinsically interlocutory in character, is rendered and entered in a case regularly set for a conventional trial on the merits, no order for a separate trial of issues having been entered pursuant to R 174. . ., it will be presumed for appeal purposes that the Court intended to, and did, dispose of all parties legally before it and of all issues made by the pleadings between such parties." However, it will not be presumed that a judgment dismissing a plaintiff's suit on non suit, plea to the jurisdiction, plea in abatement, for want of prosecution, etc., also disposed of the issues in an independent cross-action.

The problem can be eliminated entirely by a careful drafting of judgments to conform to the pleadings or by inclusion in judgments of a simple statement that all relief not expressly granted is denied. [Such a statement, "that all relief not expressly granted is denied, is referred to as a "Mother Hubbard Clause."]

LEHMANN
v.
HAR-CON CORPORATION

39 S.W.3d 191
(Tex. 2001)

In *Mafrige v. Ross*, 866 S.W.2d 590 (Tex. 1993), the Supreme Court held that a summary judgment is final if it contains language purporting to dispose of all claims and parties. Held: The inclusion of a Mother Hubbard clause—"all relief not granted is denied", or essentially those words—does not indicate that a judgment rendered without a conventional trial is final for purposes of appeal. *Mafrige* is overruled to the extent it states otherwise.

In cases in which only one final and appealable judgment can be rendered, a judgment issued without a conventional trial is final for purposes of appeal if, and only if, either it actually disposes of all claims and parties then before the court, regardless of its language, or it states with unmistakable clarity that it is a final judgment as to all claims and all parties. In making this determination, the Court does not consider cases where more than one final and appealable judgment can be rendered, as in probate and receivership proceedings. Nor does it consider a judgment's finality for purposes other than appeal, such as issue and claim preclusion.

The finality of the judgment must be determined without the benefit of any presumption. A judgment that finally disposes of all remaining parties and claims, based on the record in the case, is final, regardless of its language.

The language of an order or judgment cannot make it interlocutory when, in fact, on the record, it is a final disposition of the case. But the language of an order or judgment can make it final, even though it should have been interlocutory, if that language expressly disposes of all claims and all parties. The intent to finally dispose of the case must be unequivocally expressed in the words of the order itself.

Note

Farm Bureau Cty Mut. Ins. Co. v. Rogers, 455 S.W.3d 161 (Tex. 2015): In this declaratory-judgment action involving insurance coverage, the court of appeals held that the trial court's order denying the insurer's summary-judgment motion is not final because the insured did not file a cross-motion for summary judgment. The issue is whether a trial court's order issued without a full trial and containing a "Mother Hubbard" clause—that is, a statement that relief not expressly granted is denied—is final for appeal purposes. The Supreme Court HOLDS that the order is not final, but because it did not resolve the parties' competing attorney fees requests.

In *Lehmann*, we held that "a judgment issued without a conventional trial is final for purposes of appeal if and only if either [1] it actually disposes of all claims and parties then before the court, regardless of its language, or [2] it states with unmistakable clarity that it is a final judgment as to all claims and all parties." *Lehmann*, 39 S.W.3d at 192-93. We explained that "[a]n order does not dispose of all claims and all parties merely because it is entitled 'final', or because the word 'final' appears elsewhere in the order, *or even because it awards costs*." *Id.* at 205 (emphasis added). "Rather, there must be some other clear indication that the trial court intended the order to completely dispose of the entire case." *Id.* Attempting to resolve decades of confusion, we held that "the inclusion of a Mother Hubbard clause—by which we mean the statement, 'all relief not granted is denied', or essentially those words—does not indicate that a judgment rendered without a conventional trial is final for purposes of appeal." *Id.* at 203-04. Mother Hubbard clauses are problematic because they are open to interpretation. *Id.* at 204. Sometimes a Mother Hubbard clause "mean[s] only that the relief requested *in the motion*—not all the relief requested by anyone in the case—and not granted by the order is denied," and sometimes it "may also have no intended meaning at all, having been inserted for no other reason than that it appears in a form book or resides on a word processor." *Id.* We thus rejected the notion that a Mother Hubbard clause gives "any indicia of finality in any order not issued after a conventional trial." *Id.*

After *Lehmann*, we confirmed that the disposition of a claim for court costs does not dispose of a claim for attorney's fees, even when doing so would also dispose of all parties and claims. *See McNally v. Guevara*, 52 S.W.3d 195, 196 (Tex. 2001). In *McNally*, the defendants filed a motion for summary judgment but failed to request summary judgment on their counterclaim for attorney's fees. Although the trial court's order granted the motion and taxed court costs against the plaintiff, we concluded that "[n]othing in the trial court's judgment, other than its award of costs to the defendants, suggests that it intended to deny the defendants' claim for attorney fees. The award of costs, by itself, does not make the judgment final." *Id.* Consistent with our statement in *Lehmann*, we held that the resolution of a claim for court costs did not dispose of a claim for attorney's fees and did not serve as an indicium of finality. *See id.*; *Lehmann*, 39 S.W.3d at 205.

In re ELIZONDO

544 S.W.3d 824
(Tex. 2018)

Robert B. Gilbreath, Hawkins Parnell Thackston & Young LLP, Ryan C. Hale, Thackston & Young LLP, Dallas, TX, R. Kelly Donaldson, R. Scott Wolfrom, Vincent Serafino Geary Waddell Jenevein, P.C., Houston, TX, for Relators.

Orlando Cuello, Porter, TX, pro se.

Maria De Jesus Gamez, Porter, TX, pro se.

Rhonda L. Allen, Linda Johnson White, Nicole Killgore, Allen Killgore & White, P.C., Karalynn C. Cromeens, The Cromeens Law Firm PLLC, Houston, TX, for Real Parties in Interest Orlando Cuello, Maria De Jesus Gamez, M & O Homebuilders, Inc. and Texas Homebuilders, LLC.

Elizabeth G. Bloch, Husch Blackwell LLP, Austin, TX, for Amicus Curiae State Bar of Texas Appellate Section.

PER CURIAM.

This is a mandamus action. After its plenary power had expired, the trial court issued an amended order omitting a *Lehmann*-like finality phrase that it had included in its original order. *See generally Lehmann v. Har-Con Corp.*, 39 S.W.3d 191, 205-06 (Tex. 2001) (discussing finality phrases). The court of appeals directed the trial court to vacate the amended order. Here, the relator seeks a writ directing the court of appeals to vacate its opinion. For seventeen years, we have relied on *Lehmann* to mitigate the mischief and chaos that can arise when the prospect of appeal rears its head long after the parties believed a judgment to be final. We see no need to reduce *Lehmann*'s ambit, and we deny Elizondo's petition for writ of mandamus. *See* TEX. R. APP. P. 52.8(d).

Paul Elizondo, Cynthia Elizondo, and Eagle Fabricators, Inc. (collectively, Elizondo) hired M & O Homebuilders, Inc., Orlando Cuello, Maria De Jesus Gamez, and Texas Homebuilders, LLC (collectively, the Builders) to build a home. A cost dispute arose. Elizondo sued the Builders, asserting breach of contract, fraud, negligence, and other claims. Elizondo placed a lien on the Builders' property on the theory that the Builders had improved it using funds intended for his home. For good measure, he also applied for a temporary injunction to prevent the Builders from selling the property until the underlying litigation ended. The trial court granted the temporary injunction.

The Builders argued the lien was invalid and they filed a motion to remove it. The Builders drafted and submitted an order titled "Order on Defendants' Summary Motion to Remove Invalid Lien." The trial court signed the order, which included at the bottom of its first and only page a finality phrase that stated: "This judgment is final, disposes of all claims and all parties, and is appealable. All relief not granted herein is denied." The order left lots of relief not granted—namely, all other relief Elizondo sought against the Builders. Thirty days elapsed, marking the end of the trial court's plenary power. *See* TEX. R. CIV. P. 329b(d). Several weeks later, Elizondo noticed the original order had disposed of his entire case. He requested an amended order, which the trial court issued, this time omitting the finality phrase.

The Builders sought mandamus relief in the court of appeals, requesting a writ directing the trial court to vacate the amended order. The Builders argued that the original order was final, and that the amended order was void since the trial court issued it after the court's plenary power had expired. *See id.* ("The trial court . . . has plenary power to grant a new trial or to vacate, modify, correct, or reform the judgment within thirty days after the judgment is signed."). Elizondo argued that the original order was not final, and that even if it was, the finality phrase constituted a clerical error the likes of which a trial court can modify even after its plenary power expires. *See id.* 329b(f) (clarifying that "the [trial] court may at any time correct a *clerical* error in the *record* of a judgment and render judgment nunc pro tunc under Rule 316" (emphasis added)).

A divided panel conditionally granted the writ in favor of the Builders. * * *

Elizondo seeks a writ of mandamus directing the court of appeals to vacate its opinion. He argues that the original order was not final, and that even if it was, the trial court's inclusion of the finality phrase was a clerical error. Elizondo cites *Lehmann*'s statement that "whether a judicial decree is a final judgment must be determined from its language and the record in the case." *See Lehmann*, 39 S.W.3d at 195. In Elizondo's view, the record in this case makes clear that the trial court did not intend to render a final judgment. Elizondo also argues that the original order is ambiguous because although its title refers to removing a lien, its body includes a finality phrase. In the alternative, Elizondo asks the Court to clarify that *Lehmann* does not apply to the trial court's original order. He argues that applying *Lehmann* to the original order leads to the absurd result that Elizondo loses all of his claims against the Builders. Furthermore, he argues, that result will incentivize attorneys to sneak finality language into orders that are otherwise routine.

In response, the Builders argue that the original order was final under *Lehmann*, which means that the amended order improperly sought to correct judicial error rather than clerical error. The Builders concede that *Lehmann* allows a court of appeals to look at the record, but only "[t]o determine whether an order disposes of all pending claims and parties." *Id.* at 205. In other words, according to the Builders, a reviewing court may not look at the record where, as here, the order includes a finality phrase. They further contend that the original order was not ambiguous on its face, and that Elizondo's argument to the contrary depends on the record. True, the order granted more relief than the Builders requested, but the Builders urge that *Lehmann* specifically contemplates that possibility. The windfall the Builders' received was reversible, but it was not interlocutory. *See id.* at 206 ("An express adjudication of all parties and claims in a case is not interlocutory merely because the record does not afford a legal basis for the adjudication. In those circumstances, the order must be appealed and reversed."). Thus, the Builders argue, the court of appeals correctly held that the trial court's original order was a final judgment.

We conclude that the court of appeals correctly applied *Lehmann*. Elizondo had thirty days to examine the one-page order and notice that it included a finality phrase. Even if he disagreed that the order was final, he should have treated it as though it was. *See id.* at 196 ("A party who is uncertain whether a judgment is final must err on the side of appealing or risk losing the right to appeal."). Had he examined the order within the thirty-day window, he could have sought an amended order or pursued an appeal. Since Elizondo waited more than thirty days to contend that the order improperly disposed of his other claims, he has lost them. Though jarring for Elizondo, this outcome reflects *Lehmann*'s reasoning and comports with this Court's subsequent application of *Lehmann*'s finality tests.

Our decision in *In re Daredia* offers guidance. *See* 317 S.W.3d 247 (Tex. 2010) (orig. proceeding) (per curiam). In that case, American Express sued a corporation and an individual to recover about $750,000 due on multiple credit-card accounts. The individual answered, but the corporation did not. American Express drafted a default judgment against the corporation, which the trial court signed. The judgment included a finality phrase. The time for appeal expired, and when American Express attempted to continue its case against the individual, the individual argued the judgment was final as to all of American Express's claims—not only those against the corporation, but also those against him. The court of appeals held that the judgment was ambiguous, and thus interlocutory. This Court reversed in a per curiam opinion reasoning that "[t]he court of appeals' holding that the [order's] failure to mention [the individual] creates an ambiguity" contradicted *Lehmann*. *Id.* at 249. The order in *Daredia* was "unequivocal, and therefore effective." *Id.*

Daredia's reasoning decides this case, too. Although the order in *Daredia* bore the title "Default Judgment," the argument that the difference in title matters overlooks the crucial trait the orders share: neither mentions the claims of which it disposes. *See id* at 248-49. If anything, the original order in this case is *more* susceptible to *Lehmann*'s analysis because it at least mentions Elizondo; the order in *Daredia* did not name the individual. *See id.* at 248. And although in *Daredia* the party who authored the order suffered the harm, *Daredia*'s reasoning depended on the finality language rather than on which party the order benefited. *See id.* at 249.

The court of appeals was correct that *Lehmann* instructs reviewing courts to look at the record "only if the order [i]s not clear and unequivocal." *See Homebuilders*, 516 S.W.3d at 106. *Lehmann* said:

> "[W]hether a judicial decree is a final judgment must be determined from its language *and* the record in the case." *Lehmann*, 39 S.W.3d at 195 (emphasis added).

"[W]hen there has not been a conventional trial on the merits, an order or judgment is not final for purposes of appeal unless it actually disposes of every pending claim and party *or* unless it clearly and unequivocally states that it finally disposes of all claims and all parties." *Id.* at 205 (emphasis added).

"To determine *whether* an order *disposes of all pending claims and parties*, it may of course be necessary for the appellate court to look to the record in the case." *Id.* at 205-06 (emphasis added).

Elizondo relies on the first sentence. The Builders rely on the second and third, and those sentences more accurately convey *Lehmann*'s holding. While the first sentence appears in *Lehmann*'s discussion of finality's history, *id.* at 195, the second and third sentences appear within the body of *Lehmann*'s analysis, *Id.* at 205-06. By implication, the second and third sentences mean that a reviewing court confronting an order that includes a finality phrase cannot look at the record. Instead, it must take the order at face value. That makes sense. If it were otherwise, finality phrases would serve no purpose. That is, if both of *Lehmann*'s tests allow a reviewing court to look at the record, then a reviewing court may always look at the record. That would distill *Lehmann*'s joint tests into a simple rule: when there has not been a conventional trial on the merits, a court must look to the record to determine whether the judgment is final. That is not *Lehmann*'s rule. Had it lacked the finality phrase, the original order in this case would not have disposed of all claims and parties. However, since the original order included a finality phrase, it was clear and unequivocal.

Elizondo urges the Court to conclude that the original order is ambiguous. He contrasts the finality phrase with the original order's title, which addressed the summary removal of a lien—a proceeding he argues is not intended to be final or appealable. *See* TEX. PROP. CODE § 53.160(e). The trouble is that the title and the finality phrase admit of only one construction: the order (correctly) removes a lien and (incorrectly) disposes of Elizondo's other claims. Elizondo's ambiguity argument also errs in attempting to create an ambiguity from language that *Lehmann* describes as clear and unequivocal. *See Lehmann*, 39 S.W.3d at 206. The order may lack a basis in law, but it is not ambiguous. Rather, the order clearly purports to dispose of all claims and all parties. Error is not the same as ambiguity.

Nor did the court of appeals reach an absurd result. Elizondo contends that *Lehmann* embraced the absurdity doctrine as a limit without explicitly referring to it. Even if that were true, the absurdity doctrine does not decide this case. The reason is that the doctrine is merely a presumption against absurdity, and presumptions must yield to clear and unequivocal language. But even accepting Elizondo's view of *Lehmann*, the outcome here was not absurd. Elizondo argues that the order could not reasonably be read as final, and that it would therefore be absurd to conclude that it was final. To the contrary, the absurd thing would be to hold that a clear and unequivocal finality phrase does not trigger *Lehmann*'s directive that "[a] party who is uncertain whether a judgment is final must err on the side of appealing." *Id.* at 196. Elizondo also urges that the court of appeals' opinion generates absurdity by encouraging unscrupulous attorneys to sneak finality phrases into commonplace orders. The *Lehmann* rule actually helps on this front. No rule, alas, can altogether prevent unethical attorneys from acting unethically, but *Lehmann* discourages trickery by making it easier to spot.

In the dissent's view, the majority erred in reading the finality phrase as an indication of intent. *Homebuilders*, 516 S.W.3d at 112 (KEYES, J., dissenting). Yet *Lehmann*'s test holds that an order is final if it "states" that it is—not if the court intends it to be. *Lehmann*, 39 S.W.3d at 205. The dissent's second line of attack is that "[n]either *Lehmann* nor *Daredia* expands the power of . . . finality language to establish the finality of a judgment beyond the summary judgment or default judgment context." *Homebuilders*, 516 S.W.3d at 115. However, "when there has not been a conventional trial on the merits," *Lehmann*'s two-pronged test applies to "an order *or* judgment." *Lehmann*, 39 S.W.3d at 205 (emphasis added). Thus, *Lehmann* and its progeny apply beyond summary and default judgments. Finally, the dissent points to *Lehmann*'s qualification that an "order that adjudicates only the plaintiff's claims against the defendant does not adjudicate a counterclaim, cross-claim, or third party claim." *Homebuilders*, 516 S.W.3d at 115 (quoting *Lehmann*, 39 S.W.3d at 205). However, the only claims that either order adjudicated were Elizondo's. The original order removed the lien that Elizondo had placed on the Builders' property, but it also denied all other relief.

Our conclusion that the original order was final also decides the issue whether the amended order was void as an attempt to correct judicial error. A trial court may correct clerical errors in a judgment even after its plenary power has expired. *See* TEX. R. CIV. P. 329b(d), (f). But it must correct judicial errors within thirty days of judgment or not at all. *See Escobar v. Escobar*, 711 S.W.2d 230, 231 (Tex. 1986) ("After the trial court loses its jurisdiction over a judgment, it can correct only *clerical* errors in the judgment by judgment nunc pro tunc." (emphasis added)).

The trial court's inclusion of the finality phrase in the original order constituted judicial error. It is settled that "only errors made in entering a judgment are clerical; an error in rendition is judicial." *Daredia*, 317 S.W.3d at 249 (citing *Escobar*, 711 S.W.2d at 231). Here, as in *Daredia*, the trial court signed an order that one of the parties submitted. *See Daredia*, 317 S.W.3d at 249. As such, the finality phrase was part of the judgment that the trial court rendered. *See id.* ("[P]rovisions alleged to have been inserted by mistake of the attorney nevertheless become a part of the court's judgment and therefore are judicial errors when thus rendered in writing by the court." (quoting *Dikeman v. Snell*, 490 S.W.2d 183, 185-86 (Tex.1973))). Since the amended order sought to correct judicial error after the trial court's plenary power had expired, the amended order was void.

In sum, we conclude that the original order's finality phrase was clear, unequivocal, and neither ambiguous nor absurd. The court of appeals correctly reasoned that the finality phrase rendered the record irrelevant to determining whether the order was final. Consequently, the original order was final—"erroneous, but final." *Lehmann*, 39 S.W.3d at 200. The trial court's amended order was an attempt to correct judicial error beyond the period of that court's plenary power. The amended order was therefore void. Elizondo should have raised the error while the trial court still had plenary power over the case. Alternatively, Elizondo should have appealed. Having done neither, he has lost his claims. We emphasize that parties may avoid this result by following *Lehmann*'s admonition to "err on the side of appealing or risk losing the right to appeal." *Id.* at 196.

When a trial court issues an order or judgment without a conventional trial on the merits, *Lehmann* remains the rule for identifying whether the order or judgment is final. It is a rigid rule, but that is why it is useful. Although no rule can altogether prevent parties from using finality as a sword, the requirement of clear and unequivocal language makes offensive blows easy to spot. Blunting *Lehmann*'s blade would neither cushion finality's cuts nor reduce their number. Accordingly, we deny Elizondo's petition for writ of mandamus. *See* TEX. R. APP. P. 52.8(d).

Notes

1. *Jacobs v. Satterwhite*, 65 S.W.3d 653 (Tex. 2001): In this action for professional negligence and for breach of contract, D moved for summary judgment only on the professional negligence claim. P responded that he was asserting only a breach of contract claim. The trial court entered summary judgment, without stating the grounds. P appealed the summary judgment on the ground that his sole cause of action against D was the breach of contract claim, which was not addressed in the motion for summary judgment. Held: Reversed and remanded as to the contract claim. If a defendant moves for summary judgment on only one of multiple claims asserted by the plaintiff, but the trial court renders judgment that the plaintiff take nothing on all claims asserted, the judgment is final-erroneous, but final. Here, the trial court's judgment was a final judgment encompassing both the breach-of-contract and the professional negligence claims; but because the breach-of-contract claim was not addressed in D's motion, summary judgment on that claim was erroneous. P did not assign error on appeal concerning the negligence claim, and thus waived that claim.

2. *King Ranch, Inc. v. Chapman*, 118 S.W.3d 742 (Tex. 2003): The Chapman heirs assert that after granting King Ranch's summary judgment motion, a subsequent order granting summary judgment to other defendants effectively "ungranted" the first motion because the second order contained a "Mother Hubbard" clause. The Court reject this contention noting that there was not indication that the trial court intended to set aside the first order, and the later judgment does not automatically set aside an earlier interlocutory judgment.

3. *In the Interest of S.M.R., et al*, 434 S.W.3d 576 (Tex. 2014): A trial court's "approval of a settlement does not necessarily constitute rendition of judgment," because rendition of judgment requires a "present act" to "decide the issues." When parties dictate a settlement agreement on the record (creating an enforceable agreement under Rule 11), and the trial court approves it on the record, such a settlement agreement does not constitute an agreed judgment, unless the words used by the trial court ... clearly indicate the intent to render judgment at the time the words are expressed."

Note

1. *Bandera Electric Cooperative, Inc. v. Gilchrist*, 946 S.W.2d 336 (Tex. 1997): "The inclusion of Mother Hubbard language or its equivalent in an order granting summary judgment makes an otherwise partial summary judgment final for appellate purposes. In those situations where the summary judgment order grants more relief than requested, it is not proper for the court to reverse and remand the entire case as such would cause needless relitigation of decided issues." In such a situation, the court should reverse and remand that portion of the case for which relief was not sought in the motion for summary judgments and perform its ordinary review of the granting of the relief sought in the motion for summary judgment.

2. *Argonaut Insurance Co. v. Baker,* 87 S.W.3d 526 (Tex. 2002): "When both parties move for summary judgment and one motion is granted and one denied, the appellate court should determine all questions presented and render the judgment that the trial court should have rendered. *City of Garland v. Dallas Morning News*, 22 S.W.3d 351, 356 (Tex. 2000). Here, both parties rely on statutory provisions to support their entitlement to summary judgment. In general, matters of statutory construction are questions of law."

4. *Offer of Settlement*

Revised Rule 167 of the Texas Rules of Civil Procedure provides:

167. OFFER OF SETTLEMENT; AWARD OF LITIGATION COSTS

167.1. Generally. Certain litigation costs may be awarded against a party who rejects an offer made substantially in accordance with this rule to settle a claim for monetary damages—including a counterclaim, cross-claim, or third-party claim—except in:

(a) a class action;
(b) a shareholder's derivative action;
(c) an action by or against the State, a unit of state government, or a political subdivision of the State;
(d) an action brought under the Family Code;
(e) an action to collect workers' compensation benefits under title 5, subtitle A of the Labor Code; or
(f) an action filed in a justice of the peace court or small claims court.

167.2. Settlement Offer.

(a) Defendant's declaration a prerequisite; deadline. A settlement offer under this rule may not be made until a defendant—a party against whom a claim for monetary damages is made—files a declaration invoking this rule. When a defendant files such a declaration, an offer or offers may be made under this rule to settle only those claims by and against that defendant. The declaration must be filed no later than 45 days before the case is set for conventional trial on the merits.

(b) Requirements of an offer. A settlement offer must:

(1) be in writing;

(2) state that it is made under Rule 167 and Chapter 42 of the Texas Civil Practice and Remedies Code;

(3) identify the party or parties making the offer and the party or parties to whom the offer is made;

(4) state the terms by which all monetary claims—including any attorney fees, interest, and costs that would be recoverable up to the time of the offer—between the offeror or offerors on the one hand and the offeree or offerees on the other may be settled;

(5) state a deadline—no sooner than 14 days after the offer is served—by which the offer must be accepted;

(6) be served on all parties to whom the offer is made.

(c) Conditions of offer. An offer may be made subject to reasonable conditions, including the execution of appropriate releases, indemnities, and other documents. An offeree may object to a condition by written notice served on the offeror before the deadline stated in the offer. A condition to which no such objection is made is presumed to have been reasonable. Rejection of an offer made subject to a condition determined by the trial court to have been unreasonable cannot be the basis for an award of litigation costs under this rule.

(d) Non-monetary and excepted claims not included. An offer must not include non-monetary claims and other claims to which this rule does not apply.

(e) Time limitations. An offer may not be made:

(1) before a defendant's declaration is filed;

(2) within 60 days after the appearance in the case of the offeror or offeree, whichever is later;

(3) within 14 days before the date the case is set for a conventional trial on the merits, except that an offer may be made within that period if it is in response to, and within seven days of, a prior offer.

(f) Successive offers. A party may make an offer after having made or rejected a prior offer. A rejection of an offer is subject to imposition of litigation costs under this rule only if the offer is more favorable to the offeree than any prior offer.

167.3. Withdrawal, Acceptance, and Rejection of Offer.

(a) Withdrawal of offer. An offer can be withdrawn before it is accepted. Withdrawal is effective when written notice of the withdrawal is served on the offeree. Once an unaccepted offer has been withdrawn, it cannot be accepted or be the basis for awarding litigation costs under this rule.

(b) Acceptance of offer. An offer that has not been withdrawn can be accepted only by written notice served on the offeror by the deadline stated in the offer. When an offer is accepted, the offeror or offeree may file the offer and acceptance and may move the court to enforce the settlement.

(c) Rejection of offer. An offer that is not withdrawn or accepted is rejected. An offer may also be rejected by written notice served on the offeror by the deadline stated in the offer.

(d) Objection to offer made before an offeror's joinder or designation of responsible third party. An offer made before an offeror joins another party or designates a responsible third party may not be the basis for awarding litigation costs under this rule against an offeree who files an objection to the offer within 15 days after service of the offeror's pleading or designation.

167.4. Awarding Litigation Costs.

(a) Generally. If a settlement offer made under this rule is rejected, and the judgment to be awarded on the monetary claims covered by the offer is significantly less favorable to the offeree than was the offer, the court must award the offeror litigation costs against the offeree from the time the offer was rejected to the time of judgment.

(b) "Significantly less favorable" defined. A judgment award on monetary claims is significantly less favorable than an offer to settle those claims if:

(1) the offeree is a claimant and the judgment would be less than 80 percent of the offer; or

(2) the offeree is a defendant and the judgment would be more than 120 percent of the offer.

(c) Litigation costs. Litigation costs are the expenditures actually made and the obligations actually incurred—directly in relation to the claims covered by a settlement offer under this rule—for the following:

(1) court costs;

(2) reasonable fees for not more than two testifying expert witnesses; and

(3) reasonable attorney fees.

(d) Limits on litigation costs. The litigation costs that may be awarded under this rule must not exceed the following amount:

(1) the sum of the non-economic damages, the exemplary or additional damages, and one-half of the economic damages to be awarded to the claimant in the judgment; minus

(2) the amount of any statutory or contractual liens in connection with the occurrences or incidents giving rise to the claim.

(e) No double recovery permitted. A party who is entitled to recover attorney fees and costs under another law may not recover those same attorney fees and costs as litigation costs under this rule.

(f) Limitation on attorney fees and costs recovered by a party against whom litigation costs are awarded. A party against whom litigation costs are awarded may not recover attorney fees and costs under another law incurred after the date the party rejected the settlement offer made the basis of the award.

(g) Litigation costs to be awarded to defendant as a setoff. Litigation costs awarded to a defendant must be made a setoff to the claimant's judgment against the defendant.

167.5. Procedures.

(a) Modification of time limits. On motion, and for good cause shown, the court may—by written order made before commencement of trial on the merits—modify the time limits for filing a declaration under Rule 167.2(a) or for making an offer.

(b) Discovery permitted. On motion, and for good cause shown, a party against whom litigation costs are to be awarded may conduct discovery to ascertain the reasonableness of the costs requested. If the court determines the costs to be reasonable, it must order the party requesting discovery to pay all attorney fees and expenses incurred by other parties in responding to such discovery.

(c) Hearing required. The court must, upon request, conduct a hearing on a request for an award of litigation costs, at which the affected parties may present evidence.

167.6. Evidence Not Admissible. Evidence relating to an offer made under this rule is not admissible except for purposes of enforcing a settlement agreement or obtaining litigation costs. The provisions of this rule may not be made known to the jury by any means.

167.7. Other Settlement Offers Not Affected. This rule does not apply to any offer made in a mediation or arbitration proceeding. A settlement offer not made under this rule, or made in an action to which this rule does not apply, cannot be the basis for awarding litigation costs under this rule. This rule does not limit or affect a party's right to make a settlement offer that does not comply with this rule, or in an action to which this rule does not apply.

Note

Amedisys, Inc. v. Kingwood Home Health Care, LLC, 437 S.W.3d 507 (Tex. 2014): The settlement offer was made under Rule 167, which allows for recovery of litigation costs if the offer is more favorable than ultimate judgment. Plaintiff accepted the offer; Defendant contended that acceptance was ineffective because it omitted a material term and refused to pay. Held: The effectiveness of settlement was to be examined under common-law, not Rule 167. In this case, it is found, as a matter of law, that Plaintiff accepted the offer, despite variation in language regarding potential claims.

In re COMPLETERX, LTD.

366 S.W.3d 318
(Tex. App.—Tyler, 2012, orig. proceeding)

Katherine L.I. Hacker, Jonathan J. Ross, Susman Godfrey LLP, Houston, Suyash Agrawal, Susman Godfrey LLP, New York, NY, for Relator.

Rex A. Nichols, Jr., Nichols & Nichols P.C., Longview, for Real Party in Interest.

WORTHEN, CHIEF JUSTICE.

Good Shepherd Hospital sued Relator, CompleteRx, Ltd., for an accounting. CompleteRx made an offer of settlement to Good Shepherd pursuant to Texas Rule of Civil Procedure 167. On Good Shepherd's motion, the trial court entered an order modifying the deadline for Good Shepherd to respond to the offer.

In this original mandamus proceeding, CompleteRx challenges the trial court's December 8, 2011 order modifying the deadline for responding to the offer. We agree with CompleteRx that the trial court clearly abused its discretion in rendering the order. We also agree that CompleteRx does not have an adequate remedy at law. Accordingly, we conditionally grant the requested mandamus relief.

FACTUAL AND PROCEDURAL BACKGROUND

Between October 1, 2005, and March 1, 2010, Good Shepherd and CompleteRx had a pharmacy management agreement whereby CompleteRx managed Good Shepherd's pharmacy. During that time, CompleteRx administered prescription drugs to patients and then billed Good Shepherd for those drugs. Following termination of the agreement, Good Shepherd audited the sale of prescription drugs for a one year period and determined that CompleteRx had substantially overcharged it. Good Shepherd extrapolated the amount of the overcharges over the period of the agreement and concluded that the total overcharges by CompleteRx could be "hundreds of thousands of dollars." On January 19, 2011, Good Shepherd sued CompleteRx for an accounting. The parties agree that the statute of limitations has run for any overcharges from the inception of the agreement through January 18, 2007.

After filing an answer and counterclaim, CompleteRx audited its financial records pertaining to the agreement between the two entities from January 1, 2008, through February 28, 2010. From this audit, CompleteRx determined that on the $37.2 million in transactions during this period, it had overcharged Good Shepherd approximately $37,000.00. CompleteRx shared these results with Good Shepherd.

On October 21, 2011, Good Shepherd filed a motion to appoint an auditor pursuant to Texas Rule of Civil Procedure 172. Six days later, at a hearing on Good Shepherd's motion, CompleteRx agreed to have the court appoint an auditor. However, counsel for Good Shepherd and CompleteRx disagreed about whether the auditor's fee should be taxed against the losing party if the case did not settle. On November 8, the trial court notified the parties of its appointment of Robert Bailes of Tyler as auditor. On November 11, CompleteRx filed a declaration invoking Texas Rule of Civil Procedure 167 and Chapter 42 of the Texas Civil Practice and Remedies Code. On November 15, pursuant to Rule 167 and Chapter 42, CompleteRx offered to settle the case for $70,000.00. The offer specified that Good Shepherd must accept it no later than 5:00 p.m. on December 1, 2011.

Good Shepherd responded by filing a motion for modification of time limits on the same day the offer was made asking the court to delay the deadline for responding to CompleteRx's Rule 167 offer until after the auditor had submitted his final report. CompleteRx opposed the motion. Following a hearing on November 22, 2011, the trial court signed an order granting Good Shepherd's motion. The order provided that "Rule 167 shall not be effectively invoked or an offer made until such time as the agreed auditor files his final report," or alternatively, that Good Shepherd would have until fourteen days following the filing of the auditor's final report to respond to CompleteRx's offer of settlement. CompleteRx then filed this mandamus proceeding and a motion for temporary relief. We granted the motion and stayed the trial court's order pending our disposition in this proceeding.

AVAILABILITY OF MANDAMUS

To be entitled to mandamus relief, CompleteRx must meet two requirements. First, it must show that the trial court clearly abused its discretion. *In re Prudential Ins. Co. of Am.,* 148 S.W.3d 124, 135 (Tex. 2004) (orig. proceeding). Second, it must show that it has no adequate remedy by appeal. *Id.* at 135-36.

A trial court abuses its discretion if it reaches a decision so arbitrary and unreasonable as to amount to a clear and prejudicial error of law or if it clearly fails to correctly analyze or apply the law. *In re Cerberus Capital Mgmt., L.P.,* 164 S.W.3d 379, 382 (Tex. 2005) (orig. proceeding). The test for abuse of discretion is whether the court acted without reference to any guiding rules and principles. *Downer v. Aquamarine Operators, Inc.,* 701 S.W.2d 238, 241-42 (Tex. 1985). (orig. proceeding). The reviewing court may not substitute its judgment for that of the trial court on matters within the trial court's discretion. *See Walker v. Packer,* 827 S.W.2d 833, 839-40 (Tex. 1992) (orig. proceeding). The trial court's ruling should be set aside only if it was arbitrary or unreasonable. *See Cire v. Cummings,* 134 S.W.3d 835, 839 (Tex. 2004).

Review of a trial court's determination of the legal principles controlling its ruling is much less deferential. *Walker,* 827 S.W.2d at 840. A trial court has no discretion in determining what the law is or applying the law to the facts. *Id.* Thus, a clear failure by the trial court to analyze or apply the law correctly will constitute an abuse of discretion. *Id.*

Whether a clear abuse of discretion can be adequately remedied by appeal depends on a careful analysis of the costs and benefits of appellate review. *See In re McAllen Med. Ctr., Inc.,* 275 S.W.3d 458, 464 (Tex. 2008) (orig. proceeding). As this balance depends heavily on circumstances, it must be guided by analysis of principles rather than simple rules that treat cases as categories. *Id.* Appeal is not an adequate remedy when the trial court's abuse of discretion thwarts legislative intent for speedier resolution of lawsuits. *See In re United Servs. Auto Ass'n,* 307 S.W.3d 299, 314 (Tex. 2010) (orig. proceeding).

HISTORY OF RULE 167

In 2003, our legislature determined that our state faced "a general environment of excessive litigation." House Comm. on Civil Practices, Bill Analysis, Tex. H.B. 4, 78th Leg., R.S., at 1 (2003) [hereinafter *Analysis*].

Reformers in the legislature argued that the civil justice system should provide appropriate incentives to litigants to avoid unnecessary expense and shorten the time lawsuits stay in the system. *Part Two: Detailed Analysis of the Civil Justice Reforms,* 36 TEX. TECH L.REV. 51, 66 (2005) [hereinafter *Reforms*]. They also contended that some lawsuits unnecessarily involved lengthy discovery and pretrial maneuvering because one or both parties failed to realistically evaluate the lawsuit early in the litigation process to determine the possibility of settlement. *Id.*

One legislative solution to this crisis was to reduce the cost of litigation through cost shifting of litigation costs in some cases. *Analysis, supra,* at 1. To accomplish this, the legislature adopted an offer of settlement statute as part of H.B. 4, which includes the following provisions:

> (a) If a settlement offer is made and rejected and the judgment to be rendered will be significantly less favorable to the rejecting party than was the settlement offer, the offering party shall recover litigation costs from the rejecting party.
>
> (b) A judgment will be significantly less favorable to the rejecting party than is the settlement offer if:
>
> (1) the rejecting party is a claimant and the award will be less than 80 percent of the rejected offer; or
>
> (2) the rejecting party is a defendant and the award will be more than 120 percent of the rejected offer.
>
> (c) The litigation costs that may be recovered by the offering party under this section are limited to those litigation costs incurred by the offering party after the date the rejecting party rejected the settlement offer.

TEX. PRAC. & REM. ANN.CODE ANN. § 42.004(a)-(c) (West Supp. 2011).

The offer of settlement statute was designed to provide an incentive for litigants to make and accept reasonable settlement offers early. *Reforms, supra,* at 66; *see also* Professor Elaine Carlson, *Offer of Settlement,* STATE BAR OF TEX. LITIGATION SECTION REPORT 6 (Fall 2003) (stating that Chapter 42 of the Texas Civil Practice and Remedies Code "provides for shifting of certain 'litigation costs' when an offer to settle is rejected and the ultimate judgment is less favorable to the offeree"). Fee shifting is common in a majority of our states and has been a part of federal practice since 1938 under Federal Rule of Civil Procedure 68. Carlson, *supra,* at 6.

When the legislature created this offer of settlement mechanism, it also directed the Texas Supreme Court to promulgate rules providing the procedural details for its implementation. Specifically, the legislature directed as follows:

> (a) The supreme court shall promulgate rules implementing this chapter. The rules must be limited to settlement offers made under this chapter. The rules must be in effect on January 1, 2004.
>
> (b) The rules promulgated by the supreme court must provide:
>
> (1) the date by which a defendant or defendants must file the declaration required by Section 42.002(c);
>
> (2) the date before which a party may not make a settlement offer;
>
> (3) the date after which a party may not make a settlement offer; and
>
> (4) procedures for;
>
> (A) making an initial settlement offer;
>
> (B) making successive settlement offers;
>
> (C) withdrawing a settlement offer;
>
> (D) accepting a settlement offer;
>
> (E) rejecting a settlement offer; and
>
> (F) modifying the deadline for making, withdrawing, accepting, or rejecting a settlement offer.

TEX. CIV. PRAC. & REM.CODE ANN. § 42.005(a)-(b) (West 2008). In response, the supreme court, through its advisory committee, worked on a proposed offer of judgment/settlement rule for one and one-half years before adopting Texas Rule of Civil Procedure 167 prior to the January 1, 2004 deadline set by the legislature. *See* Carlson, *supra,* at 6. Texas Rule of Civil Procedure 167.2(a) specifies how the settlement offer provision is to be invoked:

> (a) *Defendant's declaration a prerequisite; deadline.* A settlement offer under this rule may not be made until a defendant—a party against whom a claim for monetary damages is made—files a declaration invoking this rule. When a defendant files such a declaration, an offer or offers may be made under this rule to settle only those claims by and against that defendant. The declaration must be filed no later than 45 days before the case is set for conventional trial on the merits.

TEX.R. CIV. P. 167.2(a).

The supreme court also placed the following time limitations on when the offer can be made:

> (e) *Time limitations.* An offer may not be made:
> (1) before a defendant's declaration is filed;
> (2) within 60 days after the appearance in the case of the offeror or offeree, whichever is later;
> (3) within 14 days before the date the case is set for a conventional trial on the merits, except that an offer may be made within that period if it is in response to, and within seven days of, a prior offer.

TEX.R. CIV. P. 167.2(e). But the supreme court specified that only two of these time limitations can be modified by the trial court:

> (a) *Modification of time limits.* On motion, and for good cause shown, the court may—by written order made before commencement of trial on the merits—modify the time limits for filing a declaration under rule 167.2(a) or for making an offer.

TEX.R. CIV. P. 167.5(a).

Notably, the statute requires that the rule provide a procedure for "modifying the deadline for making, withdrawing, accepting or rejecting a settlement offer." *Reforms, supra,* at 75 (citing TEX. CIV. PRAC. & REM.CODE ANN. § 42.005(b)(4)(F)). However, Texas Rule of Civil Procedure 167.2(a)—the implementing rule—only provides a procedure for modifying the deadline for the defendant's filing of the initial declaration and for "making" an offer. *Id.* at 75-76 (citing TEX.R. CIV. P. 167.2(a)). "The rule seems to omit an associated mechanism for 'withdrawing, accepting or rejecting a settlement offer.' " *Id.* at 76.

ABUSE OF DISCRETION

CompleteRx contends that the trial court had no authority to modify the time limit for Good Shepherd to respond to the settlement offer and clearly abused its discretion by doing so.

When construing rules of procedure, we apply the same rules of construction that govern the interpretation of statutes. *In re Christus Spohn Hosp. Kleberg,* 222 S.W.3d 434, 437 (Tex. 007) (orig. proceeding). When a rule of procedure is clear and unambiguous, we construe the rule's language according to its plain or literal meaning. *Id.* Rule 167.5(a) clearly states that the trial court can modify the time limits for the defendant to file a declaration under Rule 167.2(a) or for making an offer of settlement. *See* TEX.R. CIV. P. 167.5(a). The rule makes no provision for the trial court to modify any other time limits in the offer of settlement statute. *See id.*

Good Shepherd concedes that Rule 167.5 does not explicitly refer to an extension of the deadline for responding to offers. It contends, however, that the legislature intended for the offeree be able to modify the deadline for accepting or rejecting a settlement offer. *See* TEX. CIV. PRAC. & REM. CODE ANN. § 42.005(b)(4)(F) (West 2008) (rules promulgated by supreme court implementing Texas Civil Practice and Remedies Code Chapter 42 to include procedure for "modifying, the deadline for making, withdrawing, accepting, or rejecting a settlement offer"). Therefore, Good Shepherd argues that we must harmonize Texas Rule of Civil Procedure 167.5(a) with Texas Civil Practice and Remedies Code Section 42.005(b)(4)(F).

It is well established that when a conflict arises between a statute and a rule of procedure, we must harmonize the statute and the rule if possible. *See La Sara Grain Co. v. First Nat'l Bank of Mercedes,* 673 S.W.2d 558, 565 (Tex. 1984) (holding that courts are to construe statutes so as to harmonize with other relevant laws, if possible"). Ultimately, however, the statute prevails unless the rule has been adopted subsequent to the statute and repeals the statute as provided by Texas Government Code Section 22.004. *Jackson v. State Office of Admin. Hearings,* 351 S.W.3d 290, 298 (Tex. 2011). But this case does not involve a conflict between a procedural statute and a procedural rule. *Cf. M.R.R. v. State,* 903 S.W.2d 49, 52 (Tex. App.—San Antonio 1995, no pet.) (harmonizing statute and rule where statute required appellate court to consider statement of facts and rule of procedure prohibited court from considering late statement of facts absent timely motion for extension). Instead, it is a legislative directive to the supreme court.

The legislature specifically authorized the supreme court to promulgate procedural rules to implement Chapter 42 of the civil practice and remedies code. *See* TEX. CIV. PRAC. & REM.CODE ANN. § 42.005(a), (b)(4); *see also* TEX. GOV'T CODE ANN. § 22.004(a) (West Supp. 2011). Good Shepherd urges that the supreme court did not fully comply with Section 42.005 and that reading Rule 167 and Section 42.005 together will comply with the legislature's intent. However, the rules of construction do not authorize us to, in effect, modify the rule so that it addresses modification of the deadline for accepting or rejecting an offer. *See Christus Spohn,* 222 S.W.3d at 437 (requiring construction of unambiguous procedural rule according to its plain or literal meaning).

Good Shepherd also contends that even if we consider only the express language of Rule 167, we must uphold the trial court's order. Specifically, the trial court's order provides, in part, that "Rule 167 shall not be effectively invoked or an offer made until such time as the agreed auditor files his final report." This order was signed approximately one month after CompleteRx filed its declaration invoking Rule 167. Good Shepherd points out that Rule 167 permits a trial court to modify the deadline for effective invocation of Rule 167 and the making of an initial offer. Therefore, it contends, the trial court acted within its authority in modifying the deadline for invoking Rule 167, even though that modification effectively extended the time for Good Shepherd to respond to the offer. It is true that Rule 167 authorizes the trial court to modify the time limits for filing a declaration under Rule 167.2. However, we see nothing in the rule that permits a trial court to modify that time limit as to defendant that has filed a declaration.

Rule 167.5(a) is clear as to which time limits the trial court has the authority to modify in the offer of settlement statute. There is no authorization for the trial court to extend the time limit for an offeree to accept or reject a settlement offer. Nor is there any authorization for to relax the mandates of the rule would be tantamount to amending established rules of procedure. *Metro Dairy Queen Stores v. Dominguez,* 883 S.W.2d 322, 324 (Tex. App.—El Paso 1994, no pet.). This rulemaking power is invested solely in the Supreme Court of Texas. *Id.; see also* TEX. GOV'T CODE ANN. § 22.004(a)-(b) (supreme court has full rulemaking power in practice and procedure in civil actions; rules and amendments remain in effect "unless and until disapproved by the legislature"). Accordingly, we hold the trial court clearly abused its discretion when it granted Good Shepherd's motion for modification of time limits.

INADEQUATE REMEDY BY APPEAL

CompleteRx was entitled to invoke the Texas offer of settlement statute (Chapter 42) and Texas Rule of Civil Procedure 167. Therefore, it was entitled to shift the cost of the court-appointed auditor to Good Shepherd if settlement was not reached as outlined in the statute and the rule.

Two criteria should be met in order for a defendant to put any significant pressure, or risk, on the plaintiff by invoking Rule 167. Cliff Harrison, "*Texas Hold 'Em: Offer of Settlement Under Rule 167: Putting More Chips on the Table, Earlier in the Game*" 70 TEX. B.J. 936, 938 (2007). First, the case should be one of reasonably clear liability, such that the plaintiff has a good chance of recovering something at trial. *Id.* Second, the settlement offer should be reasonable, or, if anything, slightly more than reasonable." *Id.* After all, the higher the offer, the easier it should be for the defense to obtain a judgment of less than eighty percent of the offer, if rejected. *Id.*

Here, CompleteRx performed an internal audit of transactions occurring during the final twenty-six months of the agreement. The audit showed that CompleteRx had overcharged Good Shepherd $37,000.00 out of $37.2 million dollars in transactions over this twenty-six month period. Because approximately one year of the agreement was not addressed in its audit, CompleteRx made an offer of $70,000.00 to Good Shepherd to settle the case. This shifted the risk to Good Shepherd as contemplated under Chapter 42 and Rule 167. The trial court's order permitting Good Shepherd to delay its acceptance or rejection of CompleteRx's offer of settlement until after the court-appointed auditor completed his work took away the benefit of the statute for CompleteRx, i.e., requiring Good Shepherd to pay the entire cost of the court-appointed auditor if its own audit was correct. Because CompleteRx has no other way to take advantage of the statute, the trial court's order thwarted the legislature's intent. Accordingly, we hold that remedy by appeal is inadequate.

DISPOSITION

Having concluded that the trial court clearly abused its discretion by granting Good Shepherd's motion to modify the time limit to respond to CompleteRx's offer of settlement and that CompleteRx does not have an adequate remedy at law, we ***conditionally grant mandamus relief***. We trust that the trial court will promptly vacate its order granting Good Shepherd's motion for modification of time limits pursuant to Texas Rule of Civil Procedure 167.5 signed December 8, 2011. The writ will issue only if the trial court fails to comply with the court's opinion and order ***within ten days*** after the date of the opinion and order. The trial court shall furnish this court, within the time for compliance with the court's opinion and order, a certified copy of its order evidencing such compliance. Our stay of the trial court's order is lifted.

Note

Note Investment Group, Inc. v. Associates First Capital Corp., ___ S.W.3d ___ , 2015 WL 5604682 (Tex. App.—Beaumont 2015, no pet.): A Rule 167 settlement offer may include unplead claims.

CHAPTER 2.
THE JURY TRIAL AND THE SELECTION OF JURORS

1. *Right to Trial by Jury*

Notes

1. Article I, Section 15 of the Texas Constitution provides:

The right of trial by jury shall remain inviolate. The Legislature shall pass such laws as may be needed to regulate the same, and to maintain its purity and efficiency. Provided, that the Legislature may provide for the temporary commitment, for observation and/or treatment, of mentally ill persons not charged with a criminal offense, for a period of time not to exceed ninety (90) days, by order of the County Court without the necessity of a trial by jury.

2. Article V. Section 10 of the Texas Constitution provides:

In the trial of all causes in the District Courts, the plaintiff or defendant shall, upon application made in open court, have the right of trial by jury; but no jury shall be empanelled in any civil case unless demanded by a party to the case, and a jury fee be paid by the party demanding a jury, for such sum, and with such exceptions as may be prescribed by the Legislature.

TEXAS
v.
CREDIT BUREAU OF LAREDO
530 S.W.2d 288
(Tex. 1975)

John Hill, Atty. Gen., Joe K. Longley, Asst. Atty. Gen., Austin, for petitioner.

Stone & Stone, Emerson Stone, Jr., Jacksonville, Salmanson & Smith, Allen E. Smith, Austin, for respondent.

POPE, JUSTICE.

The question presented is whether the Texas Constitution gives a right to trial by jury in this suit for civil penalties brought pursuant to the Texas Deceptive Trade Practices Act. TEX. REV. CIV. STAT. ANN. art. 5069, § 10.01 Et seq. (1971). The trial court denied the defendants' request for a jury and after trial rendered judgment against defendants, Miller and Credit Bureau, for civil penalties in the amount of $35,000. The court of civil appeals reversed the judgment of the trial court and remanded the cause for a jury trial. 515 S.W.2d 706. We affirm the judgment of the court of civil appeals.

On April 11, 1972, the State of Texas brought an action against Edward Miller, individually and d/b/a Credit Bureau of Laredo, Inc. to enjoin certain allegedly deceptive practices conducted in violation of article 5069, section 10.02. Credit Bureau was sending to a number of debtors notices which simulated legal process and official action by public officials. The notice forms were styled 'Certificate of Assignment,' 'Preliminary Law Suit Listing for Civil Court,' 'Notice to Appeal,' 'Notice of Impending Execution,' and 'Seven Day Official Notification.' The suit was resolved on April 20, 1972, by an agreed injunction, the terms of which prohibited Miller and Credit Bureau from continuing the deceptive collection practices.

Credit Bureau thereafter made some changes in its debt collection forms, but the State believed that the revised forms were still deceptive and in violation of the injunction. On the trial of this case, the evidence revealed that Credit Bureau was continuing to mail forms which the injunction apparently was designed to prohibit. After the injunction was issued, Credit Bureau ordered 13,500 'Seven Day Notifications'; 6,000 'Notices of Impending Law Suit'; 5,000 'Preparatory Listings For Civil Court'; and 5,000 'Final Notices Before Suit.' On March 8, 1973, the State filed its petition for civil penalties against Credit Bureau in the same court that had issued the injunction. The State sought assessment of penalties of $10,000 for each of seven separate violations. Credit Bureau answered and requested a jury. The trial court denied the jury request, conducted a trial, and rendered judgment that the injunction had been violated, in each of the seven instances, assessing civil penalties of $35,000 against Miller and Credit Bureau, jointly and severally.

* * *

Whether the defendants were entitled to a jury requires our first deciding the nature of this suit. The State urges that its right to recover penalties is occasioned by Credit Bureau's violation of an injunction and that the action is one for civil contempt in which there is no right to trial by jury. It is our opinion that the penalty section of the Deceptive Trade Practices Act, article 5069, section 10.08 shows that the suit is one for civil penalties and not contempt. * * * We must next determine whether an action to enforce civil penalties under the Deceptive Trade Practices Act is one to which the right to a trial by jury attaches. Since the Act is silent about the right to a jury, we must determine whether the Texas Constitution fixes the right. The Texas Constitution contains two separate provisions regarding the right of trial by jury. The first is Article I, Section 15, found in the Bill of Rights of the Constitution; the second is Article V, Section 10, contained in the Judiciary Article.

Bill of Rights Jury Article

Article I, Section 15, contains a jury provision similar to that found in the United States Constitution and every other state constitution. It states simply that 'the right of trial by jury shall remain inviolate . . . .' In our opinion the Bill of Rights Article preserved the right to a trial by jury in a suit for the collection of civil penalties. It is well-established that the Bill of Rights provision continues the right to a jury in all actions where that right existed at the time the Constitution was adopted. *White v. White*, 108 Tex. 570, 196 S.W. 508 (1917); *Hatten v. City of Houston*, 373 S.W.2d 525 (Tex. Civ. App. 1963, writ ref'd n.r.e.); *Hickman v. Smith*, 238 S.W.2d 838 (Tex. Civ. App. 1951, writ ref'd). This interpretation is uniformly given to similar provisions in other jurisdictions. 47 AM. JUR. 2D, Jury § 29 at 649 (1969).

Texas, by successive constitutions both as a Republic and as a State, has protected the right to a trial by jury in those cases where a jury would have been proper at common law. TEX. CONST. art. I, § 15 (1876); TEX. CONST. art. I, § 12 (1868); TEX. CONST. art. I, § 12 (1866); TEX. CONST. art. I, § 12 (1861); TEX. CONST. art. I, § 12 (1845); Const. of the Republic of Texas, Declaration of Rights, #9 (1836); *See White v. White, supra*; *Grigsby v. Reib*, 105 Tex. 597, 153 S.W. 1124 (1913); *Cockrill v. Cox*, 65 Tex. 669 (1886); 47 AM. JUR. 2D, Jury § 17 (1969).

At common law, suits for civil penalties were tried as actions for debt, and actions for debt were triable before a jury. 47 AM. JUR. 2D, Jury §§ 17, 36 (1969); 1 CHITTY, PLEADINGS 263 (3d ed. 1819); 50 C.J.S. JURIES § 10 (1947); 3 WENDELL'S BLACKSTONE'S COMMENTARIES 161-162 (1847). In *Hepner v. United States*, 213 U.S. 103, 29 S.Ct. 474, 53 L.Ed. 720 (1909), the United States brought suit to recover the penalty provided for the violation of the Alien Immigration Act. The court reviewed and cited a number of precedents holding that actions for penalties are recoverable in civil actions and held 'the defendant was, of course, entitled to have a jury summoned in this case.' *United States v. Hindman*, 179 F.Supp. 926 (D.N.J. 1960), held that the defendants were entitled to a jury in a suit brought against them by the United States for civil penalties for violation of the Federal Trade Commission Act, a statute very similar to the Texas Deceptive Trade Practices Act, article 5069, section 10.01 Et seq. *See also*, *Damsky v. Zavatt*, 289 F.2d 46 (2d Cir. 1961); *Connolly v. United States*, 149 F.2d 666 (9th Cir. 1945); *Atchison, Topeka & Santa Fe Ry. v. United States*, 178 F. 12 (8th Cir. 1910); *United States v. Friedland*, 94 F.Supp. 721 (D.Conn. 1950); *United States v. Jepson*, 90 F.Supp. 983 (D.N.J. 1950); 5 MOORE'S FEDERAL PRACTICE, § 38.31(1), 232-233 (2d ed. 1974). The right to a trial by jury is not limited to the precise form of action in which civil penalties were enforceable at common law. The right exists when 'the action involves rights and remedies of the sort typically enforced in an action at law.' *Curtis v. Loether*, 415 U.S. 189, 94 S.Ct. 1005, 39 L.Ed.2d 260 (1974); 5 MOORE'S FEDERAL PRACTICE, § 38.11(7), 128 (2d ed. 1974).

Judiciary Jury Article

We also hold that Article V, Section 10, of the Constitution extends the right to a jury to Credit Bureau in this case. Some decisions have mistakenly treated the Bill of Rights and the Judiciary Articles as identical in meaning, that is, as protecting the right of trial by jury only as it existed at common law or by statutes in effect at the time of the adoption of the Constitution. *Hickman v. Smith*, 238 S.W.2d 838 (Tex. Civ. App. 1951, writ ref'd).

In *Cockrill v. Cox*, 65 Tex. 669 (1886), the court correctly wrote that the present Judiciary Article protecting the right to a jury was added by the Constitution of 1845 because the Bill of Rights Article contained in the Constitution of the Republic did not extend to causes in equity. TEX. CONST. art. IV, § 16 (1845). In other words, the Judiciary Article was intended to broaden the right to a jury afforded by Article I, Section 15. *Tolle v. Tolle*, 101 Tex. 33, 104 S.W. 1049, 1050 (1907); *Hatten v. City of Houston*, 373 S.W.2d 525, 531-535 (Tex. Civ. App. 1963, writ ref'd n.r.e.); *Walsh v. Spencer*, 275 S.W.2d 220 (Tex. Civ. App. 1955, no writ). Subsequent constitutions extended the right to a jury to 'all cases of law or equity.' TEX. CONST. art. V, § 16 (1868); TEX. CONST. art. IV, § 20 (1866); TEX. CONST. art. IV, § 16 (1861); TEX. CONST. art. IV, § 16 (1845). It was the present Constitution of 1876 which changed the words of the earlier constitutions from 'all cases of law or equity' to its present form, 'trial of all causes.'

The term 'cause' is defined in BLACK, LAW DICTIONARY (4th ed. 1951), as 'a suit, litigation, or action. Any question, civil or criminal, litigated or contested before a court of justice.' The United States Supreme Court in *Ex parte Milligan*, 71 U.S. 2, 112, 18 L.Ed. 281 (1866), stated that in any legal sense, 'action,' 'suit' and 'cause' are convertible terms. The court then defined the terms to mean any legal process which a party institutes to obtain his demand or by which he seeks his right. This broad meaning of the word, 'cause,' comports with the interpretation given by other courts and legal writers in the period when our present Constitution was drafted. *See also, Fish v. Farwell*, 160 Ill. 236, 43 N.E. 367 (1895); *Gibson v. Sidney*, 50 Neb. 12, 69 N.W. 314 (1896); *Baltimore & O.R. Co. v. Larwill*, 83 Ohio St. 108, 93 N.E. 619 (1910); ABBOTT, DICTIONARY OF TERMS & PHRASES USED IN AMERICAN OR ENGLISH JURISPRUDENCE 193 (1879); BOUVIERS, LAW DICTIONARY 211 (1859); 1 C.J., ACTIONS § 26(c) (1914); 1 RULING CASE LAW, ACTIONS § 3 (1914).

Special circumstances justify our former holdings that not all adversary proceedings qualify as a 'cause' under the Judiciary Article. These cases have been isolated upon a case-by-case determination. Harris, *Jury Trial in Civil Cases—A Problem in Constitutional Interpretation*, 7 SW. L.J. 1, 7-13 (1953); 7 TEX. L. REV. 663 (1928). They include such proceedings as civil contempt proceedings, *Ex parte Allison*, 99 Tex. 455, 90 S.W. 870 (1906); *Crow v. State*, 24 Tex. 12 (1859); *Johnson v. State*, 267 S.W. 1057, 1062 (Tex. Civ. App. 1925, writ ref'd); election contests, *Hammond v. Ashe*, 103 Tex. 503, 131 S.W. 539 (1910); habeas corpus proceedings for the custody of minor children, *Burckhalter v. Conyer*, 9 S.W.2d 1029 (Tex. Com. App. 1928, jdgmt adopted); *Pittman v. Byars*, 112 S.W. 102 (Tex. Civ. App. 1908, no writ); suit for removal of a sheriff, *Davis v. State*, 35 Tex. 118 (1872); appeals in administrative proceedings, *State v. De Silva*, 105 Tex. 95, 145 S.W. 330 (1912); *Texas Liquor Control Board v. Jones*, 112 S.W.2d 227 (Tex. Civ. App. 1937, no writ), and others. In each of the above instances, there is some special reason that a jury has been held unsuitable, but no sound reason exists for the denial of a jury in this case. We hold that Credit Bureau was entitled to a trial by jury to determine whether it committed the violations of the injunction with which it was charged, and if so to determine the amount of civil penalties which should be assessed against it.

* * * We affirm the judgment of the court of civil appeals which reversed the judgment of the trial court and remanded the cause to the trial court.

Notes

1. The Supreme Court has held that there is no constitutional right to trial by jury under Article I, section 15 of the Texas Constitution before the imposition of mandatory disciplinary sanctions against an attorney for conviction of an intentional crime, so long as the disbarred attorney's conviction was obtained in a court of competent jurisdiction by constitutionally adequate procedures. *See In re Humphreys*, 880 S.W.2d 402 (Tex. 1994). In that case the Court noted:

> Trial by jury cannot be claimed in an inquiry that is non-judicial in its character, or with respect to proceedings before an administrative board." *Middleton v. Texas Power & Light Co.*, 108 Tex. 96, 185 S.W. 556, 561-62 (1916). Even if the right to a jury is denied before an administrative agency, the dispositive question is whether a trial *de novo* and the corresponding right to a jury trial is constitutionally required upon judicial review of the agency's decision. *See Cockrill v. Cox*, 65 Tex. 669, 674 (1886) ("The right of jury trial remains inviolate, though denied in the court of first instance [in civil cases], if the right to appeal and the jury trial on appeal are secured.") (bracketed language in original).

2. Furthermore, the Supreme Court in *Texas Ass'n Bus. v. Texas Air Control Bd.*, 852 S.W.2d 440 (Tex. 1993), held that Article I, section 15 of our Constitution does not give the right to a jury trial in appeals from administrative adjudications under the Texas environmental statutes regulating air and water quality. The issue of whether there was a right to trial by jury in such cases under Article V, section 10 of the Constitution, was not raised by the parties. The Court noted:

> In *Credit Bureau*, we concluded that a suit for civil penalties for violation of an injunction issued pursuant to the Texas Deceptive Trade Practices Act was analogous to the common law action for debt, tried to a jury at the time our constitution was adopted. 530 S.W.2d at 293. Thus, we held that the right to a jury trial for that action remained inviolate. . . . [however] we conclude that these [administrative] agencies' assessments of environmental penalties are not actions, or analogous actions, to those tried to a jury at the time the constitution of 1876 was adopted. To hold that these environmental statutes and regulations promulgated in the late 1960s merely parrot common law and statutory rights triable to a jury in 1876 would turn a blind eye to the emergence of the modern administrative state and its profound impact on our legal and social order. In the late 19th century, ours was primarily a sparsely-populated agrarian society. By contrast, concentrated industrial activity and its by-products, including the wide-spread emission of pollutants, with their resulting potential for significant damage to our natural resources are phenomena of relatively recent origin. In response to such phenomena, regulatory schemes, such as those challenged here, were designed to balance mounting environmental concerns with our state's economic vitality. In 1876 no governmental schemes akin to these existed. Thus, we conclude that the contested proceedings are not analogous to any action tried to a jury in 1876. Accordingly, we hold that no right to a jury trial attaches to appeals from administrative adjudications under the environmental statutes and regulations at issue here.

3. *DiGiuseppe v. Lawler*,--- S.W.3d ----, 52 Tex. Sup. Ct. J. 29, 2008 WL 4605951 (Tex. 2008): When contested fact issues must be resolved before a court can determine the expediency, necessity, or propriety of equitable relief, a party is entitled to have a jury resolve the disputed fact issues.

2. *Waiver of the Right to a Jury Trial*

a. *Jury Fee and Demand*

Read Rule 216 Texas Rules of Civil Procedure.

HUDDLE
v.
HUDDLE
696 S.W.2d 895
(Tex. 1985)

Jay Floyd, Austin, for petitioner.
H.J. Bernard, Houston, for respondent.

PER CURIAM.

This is an appeal from a probate court order. Our question is whether the probate court erred in denying a request for a jury trial. The court of appeals held the denial was in error. 687 S.W.2d 58 (Tex. App.—Houston [14th Dist.] 1985). We hold the trial court did not abuse its discretion and reverse the judgment of the court of appeals.

This cause was set for trial for July 13, 1983. The jury fee had been paid on June 30 but the jury request was not made until July 12. The trial court denied the jury request because the request was not made earlier. A motion for a continuance was not made following the denial of the jury request.

Rule 216, TEX. R. CIV. P., provides that the demand for a jury be made and the necessary fee paid "on or before appearance day or, if thereafter, a reasonable time before the date set for trial of the cause on the non-jury docket, but not less than ten days in advance." The court of appeals held the time limitations contained in Rule 216 apply only to the time that the jury fee must be deposited with the clerk. 687 S.W.2d at 60. We disagree. The time limitations apply with equal force to the application for jury trial and the payment of the jury fee. In *Texas Oil & Gas Corporation v. Vela*, 429 S.W.2d 866 (Tex. 1968), this court held that a demand for a jury trial made ten days in advance of the date set for trial of the cause on the non-jury docket is not necessarily timely as a matter of law. 249 S.W.2d at 877.

The judgment of the court of appeals conflicts with Rule 216, TEX. R. CIV. P., and this court's opinion in *Vela*. Accordingly, we grant Jack A. Huddle's motion for rehearing, grant the application for writ of error and, without hearing oral argument, reverse the judgment of the court of appeals and remand the cause to that court for consideration of Lois Huddle's remaining points of error. TEX. R. CIV. P. 483.

Note

1. TEX. GOV'T. CODE § 51.604. Jury Fee provides:

> (a) The district clerk shall collect a $30 jury fee for each civil case in which a person applies for a jury trial. The clerk of a county court or statutory county court shall collect a $22 jury fee for each civil case in which a person applies for a jury trial. The clerk shall note the payment of the fee on the court's docket.
>
> (b) The fee required by this section must be paid by the person applying for a jury trial not later than the 10th day before the jury trial is scheduled to begin.
>
> (c) The fee required by this section includes the jury fee required by Rule 216, Texas Rules of Civil Procedure, and any other jury fee allowed by law or rule.

2. In *Universal Printing Co., Inc. v. Premier Victorian Homes, Inc*, 73 S.W.3d 283 (Tex. App.—Houston [1st Dist.], 2001) pet. denied, the court address the apparent conflict between the preceding statute and rule 216 in the following language:

> The homeowners assert section 51.604 and rule 216 conflict, and that a statute prevails over a rule. However, we conclude the statute and rule are not inconsistent; instead, they supplement one another. Based on a plain reading of the statute and rule, rule 216 requires that a $10 jury fee be paid "not less than thirty days in advance" before "the date set for trial." Section 51.604, on the other hand, addresses additional revenue-enhancing or administrative-type fees that a district clerk shall charge in relation to the jury fee, and states those additional fees must be paid "no later than the 10th day before the jury trial is scheduled to begin." Sub-section (c) specifically states that the $30 jury fee *includes the [$10] jury fee required by rule 216.* Section 51.604 increases revenue to the clerk's office, but does not supplant the 30-day deadline imposed by rule 216.
>
> We note that the $30 fee provision of section 51.604, sub-section (a), is separate from the 10-day deadline provision, sub-section (b). Also, sub-section (c) harmonizes the statutory fee and rule 216 fee by prohibiting the clerk from charging a $30 section 51.604 fee *and* a $10 rule 216 fee. Thus, to ensure a jury here, the homeowners were required to pay as follows: at least $10 as the jury fee, no later than 30 days before trial was set (pursuant to rule 216); and the remaining $20, no later than 10 days before trial was scheduled (pursuant to section 51.604). Because, as the trial court implicitly found, the homeowners did not pay rule 216's $10 jury fee 30 days in advance of trial, they did not timely pay the jury fee.

HALSELL
v.
DEHOYOS

810 S.W.2d 371
(Tex. 1991)

Craig L. Austin, Jim B. Halsell, San Antonio, for petitioner.
Evelyn M. Martinez, San Antonio, for respondents.

PER CURIAM.

In this cause, we consider whether the continuance of a trial setting affects the timeliness of a jury request. The court of appeals held that it does not, and therefore upheld the trial court's denial of Petitioner's jury request. We disagree, and therefore reverse.

Esther and George Dehoyos brought this suit against Jim B. Halsell for wrongful eviction and conversion. On the Dehoyoses' motion, the trial court set the case on the non-jury docket for final trial on the merits on September 8, 1989. Halsell filed a jury request, and paid the proper fee, on August 15, 1989.

The trial court called the case as scheduled on September 8, 1989. Thereafter, by order of September 14, 1989, the court struck Halsell's request for a jury trial on the ground that it was not timely filed. By the same order, however, the court also reset the case on the non-jury docket for final trial on the merits on October 13, 1989.

Under our rules, a request for a jury trial must be filed "a reasonable time before the date set for trial of the cause on the non-jury docket, but not less than thirty days in advance." TEX. R. CIV. P. 216. A request in advance of the thirty-day deadline is presumed to have been made a reasonable time before trial. *See Wittie v. Skees*, 786 S.W.2d 464, 466 (Tex. App.—Houston [14th Dist.] 1990, writ denied). The adverse party may rebut that presumption by showing that the granting of a jury trial would operate to injure the adverse party, disrupt the court's docket, or impede the ordinary handling of the court's business. *Id.*

At the time the trial court struck Halsell's request for a jury trial, the request was timely as to the October 13, 1989, trial setting. The record contains no indication that the granting of the jury trial would have injured the Dehoyoses or caused undue disruption to the trial court. Thus, the untimely jury demand became timely when the trial court reset the case for October 13. The trial court therefore erred in denying Halsell's request for a jury trial.

A refusal to grant a jury trial is harmless error only if the record shows that no material issues of fact exist and an instructed verdict would have been justified. *See Olson v. Texas Commerce Bank*, 715 S.W.2d 764, 767 (Tex. App.—Houston [1st Dist.] 1986, writ ref'd n.r.e.). Here, the record reflects the existence of several material fact issues: chiefly, whether the Dehoyoses abandoned their apartment, and the extent of the Dehoyoses' damages.

We conclude that the trial court's refusal to grant a jury trial amounted to harmful error. We therefore grant Petitioner's application for writ of error and pursuant to Texas Rule of Appellate Procedure 170, without hearing oral argument, a majority of the court reverses the judgment of the court of appeals and remands this cause to the trial court for a jury trial.

CORNYN, J., not sitting.

Note

JUSTICE O'CONNOR has written in *Whiteford v. Baugher,* 818 S.W.2d 423, 425 (Tex. App.—Houston [1st Dist] 1991, writ denied):

> "Before *Halsell*, many decisions of the courts of appeals held that if a party made a request for a jury more than 30 days before trial, but after the case was certified for trial on the non-jury docket, the request was not timely, and the party was not entitled to a jury trial. Since *Halsell*, a request for a jury trial that is made 30 days before the trial is timely, even if it is made after the case is certified for trial. If the case is re-set, the final trial date is the one that controls the 30 day deadline."

MERCEDES-BENZ CREDIT CORPORATION
v.
RHYNE

925 S.W.2d 664
(Tex. 1996)

Karen L. Watkins, Shannon H. Ratliff, Jeff Bohm, Austin, Rebecca A. Leigh, Mitchell J. Buchman, Houston, Richard Kelley, for Petitioner.

Raymond L. Thomas, Francisco J. Rodriguez, McAllen, Luther H. Soules, II, Vincent Lee Marable, Wharton, Robinson C. Ramsey, Sara S. Murray, San Antonio, James P. Wallace, Austin, for Respondents.

SPECTOR, JUSTICE.

In this case of first impression, we consider whether a trial court abuses its discretion by denying a jury trial to a litigant who had relied on the court's order issued a year before the trial date setting the case on the jury docket. The court of appeals affirmed the trial court's denial. *See* _____ S.W.2d _____, _____. We hold that the trial court abused its discretion, and we therefore reverse the judgment of the court of appeals and remand the case to the trial court.

I

This case arose when the Mercedes-Benz Credit Corporation repossessed two trucks from Norman A. Rhyne, sold them, and then sued Rhyne for the deficiency between the sale price and the money it said Rhyne owed on the trucks. Rhyne counterclaimed for violations of the Deceptive Trade Practices Act, wrongful repossession, usury, conversion, and breach of contract. After a bench trial, the court rendered judgment that Mercedes take nothing on its deficiency claim. It also rendered judgment that Rhyne take the following: $1.95 million in actual damages; $1.95 million in enhanced DTPA damages or, in the alternative, exemplary damages; and attorney's fees. The court of appeals affirmed, holding in part that the trial court did not abuse its discretion by denying Mercedes a jury trial. *See id.* at _____. We granted the application for writ of error to consider points of error concerning breach of the peace, wrongful repossession, waiver, default, written assurance of performance, unconscionability, conversion, and the legal sufficiency of the damage award. Because we dispose of this case on the jury trial question, we do not reach the merits of those issues, and the Court neither approves nor disapproves of the opinion of the court of appeals.

II

Mercedes argues that the trial court abused its discretion by denying it a jury trial. The record reveals that Rhyne filed a request for a jury trial but never paid the jury fee. On February 19, 1991, the trial court signed an order declaring that "[i]t is hereby ORDERED that the above entitled and numbered cause is set for trial on the merits before a jury on February 3, 1992." Order Setting Trial at 1, *Mercedes-Benz Credit Corp. v. Rhyne* (No. C-3175-89-A) (emphasis added). Thereafter, the trial court never modified or withdrew its order setting the case for trial before a jury. Neither party, however, had paid the jury fee. On Friday, January 31, 1992, the final business day before the trial setting, Mercedes discovered that Rhyne had never paid the jury fee and that he no longer wanted a jury. Mercedes then made its own jury demand and paid the $10 jury fee the next business day. On that day, the trial court on whose jury docket the case had been set transferred the case to a new court. Four days later, the new trial court held a pretrial hearing, denied Mercedes's jury request, and proceeded with a bench trial.

The United States and Texas Constitutions guarantee the right to trial by jury. *See* U.S. CONST. art. III, § 2; TEX. CONST. art. I, § 15. We review the trial court's denial of a jury demand for an abuse of discretion. *See State v. Wood Oil Distrib. Inc.*, 751 S.W.2d 863, 865 (Tex. 1988). In conducting an abuse of discretion review, we examine the entire record. *See Simon v. York Crane & Rigging Co.*, 739 S.W.2d 793, 795 (Tex. 1987). We only find an abuse of discretion when the trial court's decision is arbitrary, unreasonable, and without reference to guiding principles. *See Downer v. Aquamarine Operators, Inc.*, 701 S.W.2d 238, 241-41 (Tex. 1985), *cert. denied*, 476 U.S. 1159, 106 S.Ct. 2279, 90 L.Ed.2d 721 (1986).

Mercedes argues that two sets of events lead to the conclusion that the trial court abused its discretion by denying Mercedes's request for a jury trial. First, Mercedes contends that Rhyne's conduct during the pretrial stage of the litigation created the reasonable expectation that Rhyne had paid the jury fee. Rhyne had expressed his intent to have issues resolved by a "panel of [his] peers" in interrogatory responses filed within thirty days of the trial setting, and he also emphasized his intent to try his counterclaims to a jury in correspondence he sent to Mercedes before trial. We do not, however, believe that Rhyne's conduct controls the outcome of this case. Only when a party demands a jury and pays the fee can the opposing party rely on those actions. *See* TEX. R. CIV. P. 220. In such a case, the trial court may not remove the case from the jury docket over the objections of the opposing party. *See* TEX. R. CIV. P. 216, 220. Mercedes could not rely on Rhyne's actions because Rhyne never paid his jury fee.

Second, Mercedes argues that the trial court abused its discretion by disregarding its own order setting the case on the jury docket for a jury trial. Rule 216 of the Texas Rules of Civil Procedure, which provides the requirements for a party to assure its right to a jury trial, normally furnishes the guidelines under which a trial court must act. That rule calls upon parties to make a jury request and pay the jury fee "a reasonable time before the date set for trial of the cause on the non-jury docket, but not less than thirty days in advance." TEX. R. CIV. P. 216(a) (emphasis added). In this case, neither party paid the jury fee more than thirty days before the trial setting. But Rule 216 does not speak to this case, in which the trial court set the case on the jury docket and issued an order announcing that it had done so. A trial court clerk, not the court itself, usually performs the ministerial duty of placing a case on the jury docket. *See* O'CONNOR'S TEXAS RULES CIVIL TRIALS 352 (1996) ("Generally, the court does not enter an order on a request for a jury trial."). When the trial court took the uncommon step of signing the order setting the case for a jury trial, the court was not free to later ignore that order.

We agree with Mercedes that the trial court's disregard of its own order in this case was arbitrary and capricious and therefore an abuse of discretion. The trial court issued a written order a year before trial stating that the case would be tried before a jury. The trial court's order remained unmodified and unchallenged throughout all of the pretrial proceedings. In such a situation, Mercedes was entitled, as a matter of law, to rely on the trial court's order setting the case for a jury trial. For the trial court to vacate or change its order, it must have given the parties a reasonable time to comply with Rule 216 requirements for making a jury demand and paying the fee.

Rhyne relies on *Higginbotham v. Collateral Protection, Incorporated*, 859 S.W.2d 487 (Tex. App.—Houston [1st Dist.] 1993, writ denied), for support, but that case is distinguishable for two reasons. First, the trial court in *Higginbotham* signed an order "that did not identify the trial as a jury trial, but merely said that the case was set preferentially." *Id.* at 488 (citation omitted). Second, the court of appeals in *Higginbotham*, although holding that the trial court did not abuse its discretion in denying the jury request, also held that because of "mistakes on the part of the court and its personnel" the trial court did abuse its discretion by denying a motion for continuance that immediately followed the jury request. *Id.* at 489. As the dissent pointed out, the majority's decision to hold that the trial court abused its discretion on the continuance motion was no different than a decision that the trial court abused its discretion on the jury trial question. *See id.* at 491 (SMITH, J., dissenting) ("Appellants' motion for a continuance primarily addresses the topic of why they are entitled to a jury trial rather than why a continuance should be granted.").

Because we hold that the trial court's denial of Mercedes's request for a jury trial was an abuse of discretion, we next determine whether the court's error was harmful and requires reversal. The wrongful denial of a jury trial is harmful when the case contains material fact questions. *See Halsell v. Dehoyos*, 810 S.W.2d 371,

372 (Tex. 1991). The dispute between Rhyne and Mercedes is replete with material fact questions. Therefore, the denial of the jury trial was harmful error and requires reversal.

III

We hold that the trial court abused its discretion and committed harmful error by ignoring its own order and denying Mercedes a jury trial. We therefore reverse the judgment of the court of appeals and remand this case to the trial court for a new trial before a jury.

In re The PRUDENTIAL INSURANCE CO. OF AMERICA
148 S.W.3d 124
(Tex. 2004)

Jury Trial May Be Waived By Contractual Agreement Made In Advance Of Dispute Or Litigation.

The parties to a commercial lease agreed to waive trial by jury in any future lawsuit involving the lease. When the tenant and its guarantors later sued for rescission and damages, they, nevertheless, demanded a jury trial. The trial court denied the landlord's motion to quash the demand. *Held:* Writ of mandamus will issue. A contractual waiver of the right to a jury trial, made in advance of litigation, is valid and enforceable.

Mandamus. Appellate Remedy Is "Adequate" When Any Benefits To Mandamus Review Are Outweighed By The Detriments.

Mandamus relief is available only when there is no adequate remedy on appeal. The operative word, "adequate", has no comprehensive definition; it is simply a proxy for the careful balance of jurisprudential considerations that determine when appellate courts will use original mandamus proceedings to review the actions of lower courts. Mandamus review of significant rulings in exceptional cases may be essential to preserve important substantive and procedural rights from impairment or loss, allow the appellate courts to give needed and helpful direction to the law that would otherwise prove elusive in appeals from final judgments, and spare private parties and the public the time and money utterly wasted enduring eventual reversal of improperly conducted proceedings. An appellate remedy is "adequate" when any benefits to mandamus review are outweighed by the detriments. When the benefits outweigh the detriments, appellate courts must consider whether the appellate remedy is adequate. Trial to a jury followed by appeal, if one were even allowed, defeats the reasons for agreeing to waive a jury in the first place.

b. ***Failure to Appear for Trial***

Read Rules 220 and 243 Texas Rules of Civil Procedure.

BRADLEY MOTORS
v.
MACKEY
878 S.W.2d 140
(Tex. 1994)

Ronald D. Nickum, Amarillo, for petitioner.
Laurence Alan Bransgrove, Amarillo, for respondent.

PER CURIAM.

This is a suit brought under the Texas Deceptive Trade Practices—Consumer Protection Act by Bradley Motors against David Mackey. Bradley Motors claimed that Mackey misrepresented his intentions to transfer title of a "trade-in" automobile. Mackey filed an answer as well as a counterclaim. Mackey also requested a trial by jury and paid the required jury fee. When the case was called for trial as scheduled, Bradley Motors announced ready for trial, but neither Mackey nor his counsel appeared. Bradley Motors waived trial by jury, presented testimony and exhibits to the court, and made a record. The trial court rendered judgment for Bradley

Motors on its unliquidated damages claims, including actual damages and attorney's fees. The court also ordered that Mackey take nothing on his counterclaim. Holding that Mackey had not waived his right to a jury trial on the issue of damages, the court of appeals reversed the trial court judgment. 871 S.W.2d 243. We reverse the judgment of the court of appeals.

The primary question presented is whether Mackey, who had filed an answer and properly requested a jury trial, waived his right to a jury trial on Bradley Motors' unliquidated damages claim by not appearing for trial. Since Mackey had answered but failed to appear for trial, the judgment in this case was a post-answer default judgment. In such a situation, a trial court may not render judgment on the pleadings and the plaintiff is required to offer evidence and prove all aspects of his case. *See Stoner v. Thompson*, 578 S.W.2d 679 (Tex. 1979). The issue here is whether the trial court erred in hearing evidence of Bradley Motors' unliquidated damages and rendering a judgment. The two rules which are relevant are TEX. R. CIV. P. 243 and TEX. R. CIV. P. 220. Rule 243, which deals with default judgments, states: If the cause of action is unliquidated or be not proved by an instrument in writing, the court shall hear evidence as to damages and shall render judgment therefor, unless the defendant shall demand and be entitled to a trial by jury in which case the judgment by default shall be noted, a writ of inquiry awarded, and the cause entered on the jury docket. TEX. R. CIV. P. 243. Rule 220, which deals with withdrawing a case from a jury docket, states: When any party has paid the fee for a jury trial, he shall not be permitted to withdraw the cause from the jury docket over the objection of the parties adversely interested. If so permitted, the court in its discretion may by an order permit him to withdraw also his jury fee deposit. Failure of a party to appear for trial shall be deemed a waiver by him of the right to trial by jury. TEX. R. CIV. P. 220 (emphasis added). We have found no court of appeals decision other than the present one that has addressed this issue and held that a party who has properly requested a jury trial but fails to appear at trial has not waived the right to a jury trial on unliquidated damages. *See, e.g., Hanners v. State Bar of Texas*, 860 S.W.2d 903, 911 (Tex. App.—Dallas 1993, no writ) (*citing Moldanado v. Puente*, 694 S.W.2d 86, 89 (Tex. App.—San Antonio 1985, no writ)); *Chavco Investment Co., Inc. v. Pybus*, 613 S.W.2d 806, 809 (Tex. Civ. App.—Houston [14th Dist.] 1981, writ ref'd n.r.e.); *Lopez v. Soliz*, 619 S.W.2d 12, 13 (Tex. Civ. App.—Corpus Christi 1981, no writ); *Hall v. C-F Employees Credit Union*, 536 S.W.2d 266, 267 (Tex. Civ. App.—Texarkana 1976, no writ); *Chandler v. Chandler*, 536 S.W.2d 260, 262 (Tex. Civ. App.—Corpus Christi 1976, error dism'd); *Crabbe v. Hord*, 536 S.W.2d 409, 415 (Tex. Civ. App.—Fort Worth 1976, writ ref'd n.r.e.); *Carruth v. Shelter Air Systems, Inc.*, 531 S.W.2d 913, 915 (Tex. Civ. App.—Houston [1st Dist.] 1975, no writ). We agree that Rule 220 controls Rule 243, so that a party who fails to appear at trial after filing an answer waives the right to a jury trial.

Pursuant to TEX. R. APP. P. 170, a majority of this court grants petitioner's application for writ of error and, without hearing oral argument, reverses the judgment of remand by the court of appeals on the issue of damages. We agree with the court of appeals, however, that the trial court erred by granting more relief than was requested by Bradley Motors in its petition, a conclusion Bradley Motors does not challenge in this Court. Therefore, we reform the trial court judgment to reduce the actual damages to $500.00, to delete the declaratory judgment that the contract between Mackey and Bradley Motors was binding, to delete the validation of the assignment of a retail installment sales contract by Bradley Motors, to delete the declaration that no grounds exist to rescind the contract between Mackey and Bradley Motors, and to delete the order that the State of Texas (a non-party) reissue title to an identified automobile. All other provisions remain as in the trial court judgment. As reformed, we render judgment in accordance with the trial court judgment.

3. *Setting Case for Trial and Notice of Setting*

Read Rule 21a, 245 & 246 TRCP.

MANSFIELD STATE BANK
v.
COHN
573 S.W.2d 181
(Tex. 1978)

Day & Day, Marshall J. Day, Joe Day, Jr., and Lewis D. Wall, III, Fort Worth, for petitioner. Strother, Davis, Stanton & Levy, Linda S. Aland, Dallas, for respondent.

DENTON, JUSTICE.

The issue presented in this case is whether the defendant, Maurice J. Cohn, was given adequate notice of a trial setting. Suit was filed by Mansfield State Bank against Cohn and two corporations of which he was president, seeking recovery on a promissory note. After a general denial was filed on behalf of all of the defendants, the action against Cohn was severed and later set for trial. The trial court rendered judgment for the bank against Cohn. The court of civil appeals reversed and remanded, holding that notice of the trial setting which was sent to Cohn by the bank's counsel was insufficient to apprise Cohn that the case had been set for trial. 562 S.W.2d 923. We reverse the judgment of the court of civil appeals and affirm the judgment of the trial court.

Mansfield State Bank brought this suit against two corporations and their president, Maurice J. Cohn, on a promissory note and guaranty agreement. Cohn had executed the promissory note and guaranty thereof in his capacity as president of the two corporations. Cohn was also sued in his individual capacity under TEX. TAX.-GEN. ANN. art. 12.14 (1969), since Cohn had knowledge that the corporate charters of both corporations had been forfeited prior to incurring the debts. All of the defendants answered by general denial. In September, 1976, summary judgment against the two corporations was granted to the bank, and the action against Cohn individually was severed for trial. At about the same time, Cohn's attorney of record filed a motion requesting leave to withdraw as counsel for Cohn.

In October, 1976, counsel for the bank sent by certified mail two letters to both Cohn and his counsel of record. The first letter said:

* * *

> Dear Mr. Cohn:
>
> It is my understanding that Mr. Dilts has withdrawn as counsel in this cause, and therefore, I am writing you direct. You will please find enclosed a copy of our standard setting letter notifying you that the Bank's suit against you has been set for trial for the week of November 1, 1976. I have purposely set this case a month in advance to give you adequate time to retain new local counsel should you deem that desirable.

The second letter was addressed to the district clerk with reference to "Mansfield State Bank v. Maurice J. Cohn, No. 141-40245-76," and read as follows:

> Please set the above numbered and styled cause on the non-jury docket for the week of November 1, 1976.
>
> This request is made in good faith in the belief that Plaintiff will be ready for trial at the time requested. All of Plaintiff's pleadings are now in order or will be at least seven days prior to trial date.
>
> There are no special exceptions or other pre-trial matters which should be presented to the Court in advance of trial. All necessary ad litem appointments have been made. All other attorneys in this cause are being mailed a copy of the request for setting on this date.

The return receipt shows, and Cohn does not deny, that he received these letters. The November 1 trial date was passed, however, because the attorney's motion for leave to withdraw as Cohn's counsel was still pending. That motion for leave to withdraw was granted on November 2, 1976, and Cohn received a copy of the order permitting withdrawal. The withdrawing attorney also wrote a letter to Cohn on November 8, informing Cohn that the motion for leave to withdraw had been granted and that the case was not set for trial at that time. On November 11, the bank's counsel sent the district clerk another request for trial setting identical to the previous one sent to the district clerk, except that the requested trial date was December 27, 1976. Cohn was sent a copy of this letter by certified mail; the return receipt shows, and Cohn does not deny, that he received the letter on November 15. Pursuant to the request letter, the district clerk placed the cause on the trial court's docket for the week of December 27. No further notice of the setting was requested by or sent to Cohn. The case came on to be heard on December 27, but Cohn made no appearance. After the bank presented evidence, testimony, and argument, the trial court rendered judgment that the bank recover against Cohn on the promissory note. Interest and attorney's fees were also awarded to the bank.

On January 19, 1977, three weeks after rendition of judgment, Cohn filed a motion to set aside the judgment. He alleged that the letter sent to the district clerk, of which he received a copy, indicated that it was merely a Request for a trial setting rather than an actual setting of the case. Therefore, he did not receive adequate notice of the trial setting. After a hearing, the trial court denied Cohn's motion to set aside the judgment.

On appeal by writ of error, the court of civil appeals reversed and remanded for new trial. The court held that no evidence supported the award of attorney's fees, which holding the bank does not here attack. With respect to Cohn's contention that he had not received adequate notice of the trial setting, the court held:

> (T)his court recognizes that persons unrepresented by counsel may not realize that the letter requesting a setting in a non-jury case is their only notice that the case is actually being set for trial. Such failure to receive notice of the actual trial date is a denial of due process for a litigant not represented by counsel.

562 S.W.2d at 925. The bank now contends that adequate notice of the trial setting was sent to Cohn under the applicable rules, and that there is no basis for differentiation between litigants represented by counsel and litigants representing themselves.

In *Plains Growers, Inc. v. Jordan*, 519 S.W.2d 633 (Tex. 1974), this Court held that no rule required notice to the parties of a trial setting made at the regular call of the docket. Where there is no statute or rule to the contrary, "parties over whom the court has properly obtained jurisdiction are expected to keep themselves informed of the time a case is set for trial and are not entitled to notice of the trial other than the setting of the case on the docket." In response to that case, Rule 245 was amended and Rule 330(b) was repealed so that Rule 245 is now fully applicable to all district courts and requires ten days notice of a trial setting. The basis of the dissenting writer's disagreement with the outcome in *Plains Growers* has been eliminated by Rule 245 as amended. See *Morris v. Morris*, 554 S.W.2d 792 (Tex. Civ. App.—San Antonio 1977, no writ). Rule 245 now provides:

> The court may set contested cases on motion of any party, or on the court's own motion, with reasonable notice of not less than 10 days to the parties, or by agreement of the parties. Noncontested cases may be tried or disposed of at any time whether set or not, and may be set at any time for any other time. With respect to a party who had no notice of setting of a contested case for trial, the provisions of Rule 329b governing motions for new trial and finality of judgments shall operate from the time of receipt of notice of rendition of the judgment; provided that the original motion for new trial shall in any event be filed within 90 days from the rendition of judgment.

Thus, ten days' notice of a trial setting is now required by Rule 245 where the case is set on the motion of one party or on the court's own motion.

Pursuant to Rule 817, local rules of civil procedure have been adopted in Tarrant County, where this case was tried. Rule 1 of the Tarrant County rules provides:

> Jury and Non-Jury Settings
>
> (a) On the first Monday in each calendar month the judge of each district court shall set for trial during the calendar month following the month in which a request for setting is made, all contested jury and non-jury cases for which setting has been requested by one of the parties. (b) *Either at or before the time the written request for setting is made to the District Clerk, a copy thereof must be served upon all counsel of record and upon all parties not represented by counsel.*

(Emphasis added). Rule 1 of the local rules and TEX.R.CIV.P. 245 have both been satisfied in this case. Notice was received by Cohn on November 15 for a trial setting on December 27. This is obviously more than ten days notice, in compliance with Rule 245. Also, a copy of the request for setting was sent to Cohn, a party not represented by counsel, at the time the request for setting was made to the district clerk, in accordance with local rule 1. No further notice is required by the local rules, and the form requesting setting which was sent to Cohn by the bank was the same form set out by local rule 1 as a suggested form. We therefore hold that Cohn received proper notice of the trial setting in accordance with both the local rules and the Texas Rules of Civil Procedure.

The bank also asserts that the court of civil appeals erred in holding that the "failure to receive notice of the actual trial date is a denial of due process for a litigant not represented by counsel." We agree with the bank that no basis exists for differentiating between litigants represented by counsel and litigants not represented by counsel in determining whether rules of procedure must be followed. With respect to a Criminal case, the United States Supreme Court has said:

> The right of self-representation is not a license to abuse the dignity of the courtroom. Neither is it a license not to comply with the relevant rules of procedural and substantive law. *Faretta v. California*, 422 U.S. 806, 835 n. 46, 95 S.Ct. 2525, 2541, 45 L.Ed.2d 562 (1975). There cannot be two sets of procedural rules, one for litigants with counsel and the other for litigants representing themselves. Litigants who represent themselves must comply with the applicable procedural rules, or else they would be given an unfair advantage over litigants represented by counsel. *Stein v. Lewisville Independent School District*, 481 S.W.2d 436 (Tex. Civ. App.—Fort Worth 1972, writ ref'd n. r. e.), cert. denied, 414 U.S. 948, 94 S.Ct. 272, 38 L.Ed.2d 203 (1973).

We also regard the letter requesting a trial setting, a copy of which was sent to Cohn, as sufficient notice of the trial setting. The letter asked the district clerk to set the cause on the nonjury docket for the week of December 27. It is reasonable to assume that if a trial setting is requested from the district clerk, a litigant is put on notice that trial may be on that requested date. Furthermore, in connection with the bank's first requested trial setting on November 1, the bank sent Cohn another letter stating that the case had been set for trial by the standard setting letter on the requested date. After this November 1 trial date was passed, Cohn should have known, upon receipt of the second setting letter, that the case would actually be set for trial on the requested date. Even though he was a litigant not represented by counsel, Cohn is bound by a proper setting of the case as if he were represented. This should be true especially in this case since the evidence shows that Cohn is himself an attorney living in New York. We hold that the notice of the setting for trial was sufficient.

The judgment of the court of civil appeals, as to the principal debt and interest thereon, is reversed and the judgment of the trial court in favor of the bank is affirmed. The portion of the court of civil appeals' judgment which denies the bank attorney's fees is not attacked, and is affirmed.

Dissenting opinion by DANIEL, J., in which STEAKLEY, J., joins (omitted).

Notes

1. The Texas Supreme Court reversed this case on other grounds, but held that the court of appeals correctly found that *Norman* did not show error on the face of the record on its claim that it had no notice of the trial setting that led to the default judgment against it. *Norman Communications v. Texas Eastman Co.*, 955 S.W.2d 269 (Tex. 1997).

2. In *Stum v. Stum*, 845 S.W.2d 407 (Tex. App.—Ft. Worth 1992, no writ) the first notice of a trial setting received was an unsigned order setting the case for trial sent to the appellants' attorney of record by telephonic document transfer shortly before his withdrawal. The court noted that a photocopy of this unsigned order, sent by letter to appellants by their withdrawn attorney, was in writing and was given more than forty-five days before trial. Thus, the court concluded that this first notice met the time requirements of rule 245. The court also noted that this first notice was also properly served on appellants as it was sent to their attorney of record by telephonic document transfer pursuant to Rule 21a of the Texas Rules of Civil Procedure. In discussing the issue of notice the court stated:

Appellants argue that they believed that this order, because it was unsigned, was a mere proposal. However, the letter accompanying the order informed them that if there were no objections, the order would be entered, and it was entered twelve days later. Further, their attorney positively testified that he passed the information on to them before he withdrew from representing them.

The Texas Supreme Court has held that a copy of a letter merely requesting a trial setting, sent to a pro se litigant, is sufficient notice of the trial setting. *Mansfield State Bank v. Cohn*, 573 S.W.2d 181, 185 (Tex. 1978). This copied request, meeting the county's local rules and the state's procedural rules, put the litigant on notice that "trial may be on that requested date." *Id.* at 184-85. Thus, the court found that the letter was sufficient notice of the trial setting. *Id.* at 185.

In our case, the order setting the case for trial, albeit unsigned, is at least as much notice as a letter of request, especially considering the letter informing appellants that the order would be entered. This and appellee's attorney's confirmation of the setting at the motion to compel hearing should have alleviated any doubt appellants retained as to when they were going to trial. Further, appellants testified that they complied with the substance of the temporary injunction order in which the court set the case for trial. This discredits their assertion that they believed the order was a mere proposal. Finally, appellant Cynthia Stum's telephone conversation with the court before the trial met the local rule's de minimis requirement that appellants be informed that they need to appear for the trial set for that day.

Not only did appellants receive as much notice as the litigants in *Mansfield*, they received notice that met the due process requirements that appellants have notice of the trial setting. Since *Peralta*, the Texas Supreme Court has twice held that when the record establishes that a litigant "had no actual or constructive notice" of a trial setting, a motion for new trial should be granted pursuant to *Peralta*. *Lopez v. Lopez*, 757 S.W.2d 721, 723 (Tex. 1988) (per curiam); *LBL Oil Co. v. International Power Servs.*, 777 S.W.2d 390, 391 (Tex. 1989) (per curiam). The converse of this rule is that when the record establishes that a litigant had actual or constructive notice, *Peralta* does not require the granting of a new trial. In this case, the record reflects that appellants had actual or constructive notice of the trial setting; thus, *Peralta* does not require the granting of a new trial.

3. In *Bruneio v. Bruneio*, 890 S.W.2d 150 (Tex. App.—Corpus Christ 1994, no writ) the court addressed the interrelationship between Rules 245 and 246. The court stated:

Although Maria concedes that Anthony never received notice of the trial setting, she points to the relevant Texas Rules of Civil Procedure governing notice of trial settings as showing that Anthony waived his right to notice by not properly requesting it. Texas Rule of Civil Procedure 245 provides that: The court may set contested cases on written request of any party, or on the court's own motion, with reasonable notice of not less than forty-five days to the parties of a first setting for trial, or by agreement of the parties; provided, however, that when a case previously has been set for trial, the Court may reset said contested case to a later date on any reasonable notice to the parties or by agreement of the parties. * * * Texas Rule of Civil Procedure 246 provides that: The clerk shall keep a record in his office of all cases set for trial, and it shall be his duty to inform any non-resident attorney of the date of setting of any case upon request by mail from such attorney, accompanied by a return envelope properly addressed and stamped. Failure of the clerk to furnish such information on proper request shall be sufficient ground for continuance or for a new trial when it appears to the court that such failure has prevented the attorney from preparing or presenting his claim or defense. Maria argues that Rule 246 is the operative rule requiring that Anthony first have provided a proper request and a stamped return-addressed envelope to the clerk in order to be entitled to receive notice of the trial setting. We disagree.

We note that Rule 246 does not define what it means by a "non-resident attorney"—a non-resident of the state, non-resident of the county, or non-resident of the city in which the courthouse is located? *See Armentrout v. Murdock*, 779 S.W.2d 119, 123 (Tex. App.—Houston [1st Dist.] 1989, no writ) ("non-resident" as applying to Houston, Harris County, attorneys who appeared in a lawsuit in neighboring Galveston County). Accordingly, we believe that the term "non-resident" was intended not so much as a limiting or defining term as merely a descriptive term for those attorneys who may be expected to request mailed notice. This interpretation would be consistent with the idea that Rule 246 does not change or qualify the requirements of Rule 245 concerning due process notice to the parties, but that it merely provides an additional vehicle for notice to any of the various attorneys who may be working on the case and want direct notification of its setting. Under the provisions of Rule 246, non-resident counsel thus has a more direct means of keeping up with the status of the case rather than relying entirely on the attorney in charge to keep him informed or constantly checking with the clerk to determine whether the case has been set. Accordingly, Rule 246 should not be read to qualify the notice requirements of Rule 245, but to expand the requirements of notice to include non-resident attorneys who would not otherwise be entitled to direct notification of the setting under Rule 245 as the attorney in charge.

4. *Continuance*

Read Rules 251-254 Texas Rules of Civil Procedure.

FRITSCH
v.
J. M. ENGLISH TRUCK LINE, INC.
151 Tex. 168, 246 S.W.2d 856
(1952)

Morris, Underwood & Oldham, Houston, Graves, Dougherty & Greenhill, Austin, for petitioner.
Dyess & Dyess, Houston, for respondent.

CALVERT, Justice.

The only question in this case decided by the Court of Civil Appeals and argued in this Court is this: Did the trial court abuse its discretion in overruling defendant's motion for continuance? The Court of Civil Appeals has held that it did and on that ground alone has reversed the trial court's judgment for plaintiff, which judgment was based upon a jury's answers to special issues, and has remanded the cause for retrial. 243 S.W.2d 464.

The application for writ of error by a single point of error challenges the correctness of the ruling of the Court of Civil Appeals. Defendant has not favored us with an answer or reply to the application. In oral argument, advanced on the submission of the cause, defendant's counsel not only contended that the Court of Civil Appeals had ruled correctly on the continuance question but contended also, for the first time, that this Court has no jurisdiction of the case and therefore should not have granted the application in the first instance. In the application for writ of error jurisdiction of this Court was said to attach under section 2 of Article 1728, V.A.C.S., in that the holding of the Court of Civil Appeals in this case was in conflict on a question of law with prior holdings of this Court and of other Courts of Civil Appeals. Two of the cases with which the holdings here was said to be in conflict so as to confer jurisdiction upon this Court, and with which we think it is conflict, are *Hensley's Adm'rs v. Lytle*, 5 Tex. 497, 55 Am.Dec. 741 and *Campbell v. McCoy*, 3 Tex. Civ. App. 298, 23 S.W.2d 34 (no writ history).

The witness whose absence was made the basis of the motion for continuance was one O. E. Greenhaw, who was not an officer nor an employee of the defendant, and, so far as the record reflects, was in no way connected with nor obligated to the defendant. Plaintiff does not contend that the testimony of this witness was not material to the defendant's case; he contends only that the defendant did not establish the use of such diligence to procure the attendance of the witness nor to obtain his testimony as to require the granting of the motion for continuance. To properly evaluate the rival contentions of the parties on this issue it becomes necessary to review the sequence of events leading up to the filing of the motion for continuance.

Plaintiff's suit was one for damages for personal injuries alleged by him to have been received on November 8, 1947. His suit was filed on November 3, 1949, almost two years later.

The record reflects, largely through an unchallenged pleading sworn to by plaintiff's counsel and controverting the defendant's motion for new trial, that at plaintiff's request the case had been set for trial on November 20, 1950, at which time plaintiff announced ready for trial but the defendant announced that it was not ready; that the parties then joined in a motion requesting that the case be passed and be given a preferential setting for the week of December 11th, which motion was granted; that on Friday, December 8th, the docket of those cases set for the week of the 11th was called for the purpose of determining which cases would be ready for trial, and on such call both parties to this cause announced ready without qualification; that accordingly the case was listed as the 15th case on the docket ready for trial when reached by any of the district courts of Harris County during the following week; that when the case was reached for trial on Tuesday morning, December 12th, defendant filed its motion to withdraw its announcement of ready and for continuance based on the absence of Greenhaw and two other witnesses, which motion was overruled by the presiding judge on the ground that defendant had failed to use diligence in procuring the attendance of the witnesses. Two of the witnesses later appeared and testified on the trial and any right to a continuance by virtue of their absence went out of the case. Rule 252, T.R.C.P., formerly Article 2168 of the statutes, reads as follows: 'If the ground of such application be the want of testimony, the party applying therefor shall make affidavit that such testimony is material, showing the materiality thereof, and that he has used due diligence to procure such testimony, stating such diligence, and the cause of failure, if known; that such testimony cannot be procured from any other source; and, if it be for the absence of a witness, he shall state the name and residence of the witness, and what he expects to prove by him; and also state that the continuance is not sought for delay only, but that justice may be done; provided that, on a first application for a continuance, it shall not be necessary to show that the absent testimony cannot be procured from any other source.'

From the very language of the rule it will be noted that the only difference between a first and a subsequent motion is that the first motion is not required 'to show that the absent testimony cannot be procured from any other source.' This fact is brought into much sharper focus by a review of the history of Rule 252. * * * In matters not therefore whether the motion in this case be regarded as a first or a second motion; the requirement of the rule that there be a showing of diligence to procure the testimony applies to the one as well as to the other. The rule requires that the party seeking the continuance make affidavit 'that he has used due diligence to procure such testimony, stating such diligence,' and Rule 251, T.R.C.P., directs that a continuance shall not be granted 'except for sufficient cause'. Of course the absence of a material witness is 'sufficient cause', but only if proper diligence has been used to procure the testimony of the witness.

Defendant's motion was in substantial compliance with the requirements of Rule 252, and contained an allegation that each of the three witnesses was out of the county but that each was expected back in the county by Friday, December 15th. When Greenhaw failed to appear by noon of Thursday the 14th the Court recessed the trial until the morning of the 15th to give defendant additional time to obtain the presence of the witness.

With respect to the witness Greenhaw, the motion set out, in the words of the Rule, that the defendant had used due diligence to procure the testimony of said witness, and by way of stating such diligence as required by the Rule, set out that on December 6th the witness had 'orally agreed to appear as a witness in behalf of the defendant' when called, and that counsel relied upon this promise, but, as an added precaution had a subpoena issued for him on December 7th. The motion further alleged that the witness was out of the county and unavailable.

There is nothing in the rules on continuance requiring the granting of a first motion merely because it is in statutory form and is not controverted by affidavit of the opposite party. Surely it will not be gainsaid that a trial court, in determining the existence of diligence, may examine the allegations of diligence contained in the motion in the light of the record before it. Moreover, a trial court will not be required to grant a motion for continuance, at the risk of committing error in overruling it, when the allegations in the motion examined in the light of the record show beyond cavil a complete lack of diligence as measured by other rules regulating procedure in the trial of cases.

In addition to the sworn allegations of the motion for continuance, the trial judge in this case had before him a record showing that the suit grew out of an injury which occurred three years before; that the suit was filed more than a year before; that the case had been set for trial some two weeks before, at which time it had been passed on the joint motion of the parties and had been given a preferential setting with the definite understanding that the parties would get ready for trial; that four days before presenting his motion the defendant had made a definite and unqualified announcement of ready for trial; that no subpoena for the witness had been issued by the clerk and placed in the hands of the sheriff until December 7th and that no effort had been made to take the deposition of the witness. Except for the statement that the witness had orally agreed to appear as a witness when called, the motion did not seek to excuse the failure of defendant to place the witness under subpoena for the November 20th setting, nor to excuse the failure to place him under subpoena for the December 11th preferential setting promptly upon the making thereof, nor to excuse the failure to take his deposition at some time prior to the November setting or thereafter and prior to the December setting as provided for in Rule 186, T.R.C.P.

Rules 176 et seq., authorizing the placing of witnesses residing in the county of suit under subpoena to compel their attendance until discharged by the court or the party summoning them and Rules 186 et seq. authorizing the taking of depositions, if utilized, offer parties to civil suits ready and fairly certain means of procuring the testimony of resident witnesses. More than that, if resorted to with promptitude and pursued with diligence, they offer parties absolute protection against being forced to trial by arbitrary and unreasonable action of a trial court without the benefit of the testimony of material witnesses. If parties choose to forego their rights under these rules and resort to other and less effective and less certain means of procuring the testimony of material witnesses they must be held to do so at their own risk and with foreknowledge that they may be put to trial without the benefit of the testimony. * * *

The case of *Hensley's Adm'rs v. Lytle* is squarely in point. In that case the motion for continuance, to quote from the opinion, was 'founded on an affidavit of the absence of a material witness, who had not been subpoenaed, but who, the affidavit stated, lived so near the court-house that he could be called in at any time, and who was known by the affiant to be willing and determined, if practicable, to attend the trial, but who had left the state since the last term of the court with the intention and expectation of returning in time to be in attendance at the trial, but had been unavoidably detained abroad.' The motion was overruled by the trial court. In an opinion by Justice Wheeler, this court said: 'It (the affidavit) admits the witness had not been subpoenaed, but seeks to excuse the non-observance of this ordinary diligence by setting forth the circumstances which had induced the belief on the part of the affiant that the witness would be present at the trial. The facts stated, however, in our opinion do not constitute that diligence which the law requires. It has provided parties with the process of the court by subpoena, and in case of its non-observance, attachment to enforce the attendance of witnesses; and where a party has omitted to employ the means provided by the law when practicable, the omission will in general be fatal to his application. If he elects to employ other means than those provided by law, it will be at his peril. Accordingly, it is held that where a party neglects to subpoena a witness and relies on his promise to attend, his non-attendance will not be a cause of continuance.' The court recognized certain exceptions to the rule which are not material here.

That the defendant in this case at the eleventh hour asked the issuance of a subpoena which could not be served because the witness had left the county, can not be in ease of his want of diligence nor alter his position for the better. * * * Testimony taken on the motion for new trial showed that the written statement of the witness had been taken a year before the filing of the suit and two years before the subpoena was issued. The materiality of the testimony of the witness had long been known to the defendant. The trial court did not abuse its discretion in overruling defendant's motion for continuance.

The judgment of the Court of Civil Appeals is reversed. From defendant's brief in the Court of Civil Appeals it appears that he had before that court thirty-two points of error, thirty-one of which the court, in its opinion, states it had not considered. Among the thirty-one points are at least fifteen of which this court has no jurisdiction since they assert that the answers of the jury to certain issues are so contrary to the greater weight and preponderance of the testimony as to be clearly wrong. Accordingly, we remand the cause to the Court of Civil Appeals for further consideration consistent with this opinion. *Wood v. Kane Boiler Works*, Tex. Sup., 238 S.W.2d 172; *Ritchie v. American Surety Co.*, 145 Tex. 422, 198 S.W.2d 85.

VILLEGAS
v.
CARTER
711 S.W.2d 624
(Tex. 1986)

Jose Montes, Jr., El Paso, for petitioner.
Edwards, Belk, Hunter and Kerr, J. Crawford Kerr, El Paso, for respondents.

SPEARS, JUSTICE.

This case involves the trial court's discretion to deny a motion for continuance after allowing the attorney to withdraw two days before trial. As a result of the denial, the petitioner Villegas appeared pro se and prosecuted his case unsuccessfully. In an unpublished opinion, the court of appeals affirmed the judgment. We reverse the court of appeals judgment and remand to the trial court for a new trial.

In June, 1982, Jaime Lara Villegas bought a home in El Paso from Wilmot and Alicia Carter. Villegas assumed a first lien and executed a second lien for approximately $38,000. He defaulted in July 1983, and the Carters accelerated the note. Villegas and the Carters then worked out an agreement, with Villegas executing a new note for $47,000 that included accrued interest, expenses, and a higher interest rate. In January 1984, the Carters' trustee informed Villegas that he owed $1,350 in delinquent payments. Villegas paid the Carters $5,000 on March 2nd to cure the default, pay the attorney's fees, and provide a credit on future payments. On April 9th the Carters' trustee posted the property for foreclosure. On June 5th, the trustee sold the property at public auction back to the Carters.

Villegas filed suit in county court on June 25, 1984, alleging that: (1) the second promissory note was void for usury; (2) the sale was for an inordinately low amount; (3) he had not received notice of the foreclosure sale; and (4) there were other irregularities in the public sale of the property. He was represented by Paula Thomas and Miguel Cervantes. The court set the cause for trial on October 25, 1984. On October 3rd, Thomas moved to withdraw as counsel, and the motion was granted that day. Cervantes moved to withdraw as counsel on October 5th, alleging irreconcilable differences. The court granted his motion to withdraw on October 23rd.

Two days later, Villegas appeared for trial without an attorney and told the court that he wanted time to get an attorney; that he first learned about Cervantes' attempt to withdraw only six days before at his deposition; that Cervantes would not turn over his file and important evidence to him although Cervantes had not presented him with a bill; that he wanted to hire a new attorney, Jose Montez, Jr., but that Montez would not take the case until he could see the file, look over the facts, and determine the fee; and that Montez had called Cervantes to obtain the file but that Cervantes would not return his call.

The court refused Villegas' request for a continuance to obtain an attorney and his papers. The case was then tried to the court. The court denied Villegas' claim and awarded the Carters restitution of their property and a deficiency judgment of $19,700.

TEX. R. CIV. P. Rule 253 provides:

> [A]bsence of counsel will not be good cause for a continuance or postponement of the cause when called for trial, except it be allowed in the discretion of the court, upon cause shown or upon matters within the knowledge or information of judge to be stated on the record.

The granting or denial of a motion for continuance is within the trial court's sound discretion. *State v. Crank*, 666 S.W.2d 91, 94 (Tex. 1984); *Hernandez v. Heldenfels*, 374 S.W.2d 196, 202 (Tex. 1963). The trial court's action will not be disturbed unless the record discloses a clear abuse of discretion. When the ground for the continuance is the withdrawal of counsel, movants must show that the failure to be represented at trial was not due to their own fault or negligence. *State v. Crank*, 666 S.W.2d at 94. Generally, when movants fail to comply with TEX. R. CIV. P. 251's requirement that the motion for continuance be "supported by affidavit," we presume that the trial court did not abuse its discretion in denying the motion. *Garcia v. Tex. Emp. Ins. Ass'n*, 622 S.W.2d 626, 630 (Tex. App.—Amarillo 1981, writ ref'd n.r.e.). It would be unrealistic, however, to apply this presumption to lay movants who without fault have their attorney withdrawn. *Robinson v. Risinger*, 548 S.W.2d 762, 765 (Tex. Civ. App.—Tyler, 1977, writ ref'd n.r.e.).

The right to counsel is a valuable right; its unwarranted denial is reversible error. *See State v. Crank*, 666 S.W.2d at 94; *Stefanov v. Ceips*, 395 S.W.2d 663, 665 (Tex. Civ. App.—Amarillo, 1965, no writ). Therefore, when a trial court allows an attorney to voluntarily withdraw, it must give the party time to secure new counsel and time for the new counsel to investigate the case and prepare for trial. *Lowe v. City of Arlington*, 453 S.W.2d 379, 382 (Tex. Civ. App.—Fort Worth 1970, writ ref'd n.r.e.); *Stefanov v. Ceips*, 395 S.W.2d at 665; *Leija v. Concha*, 39 S.W.2d 948, 950 (Tex. Civ. App.—El Paso 1931, no writ). *See Robinson v. Risinger*, 548 S.W.2d 762 (Tex. Civ. App.—Tyler 1977, writ ref'd n.r.e.). Before a trial court allows an attorney to withdraw, it should see that the attorney has complied with the Code of Professional Responsibility: [A] lawyer should not withdraw from employment until he has taken reasonable steps to avoid foreseeable prejudice to the rights of his client, including giving due notice to his client, allowing time for employment of other counsel, delivering to the client all papers and property to which the client is entitled and complying with applicable laws and rules. Supreme Court of Texas, Rules Governing the State Bar of Texas art. XII, s 8 (Code of Professional Responsibility) DR 2-110(A)(2); *Smith v. State*, 490 S.W.2d 902, 909-910 (Tex. Civ. App.—Corpus Christi 1972, writ ref'd n.r.e.).

In this case, the trial court abused its discretion because the evidence shows that Villegas was not negligent or at fault in causing his attorney's withdrawal. The court granted Villegas' attorney's motion to voluntarily withdraw two days before trial—too short a time for Villegas to find a new attorney and for that new attorney to investigate the case and prepare for trial. In addition, Villegas could not obtain a new attorney or present his case because the former attorney refused to turn over Villegas' files with his papers and evidence. The attorney did not give Villegas time to employ new counsel or deliver to Villegas the papers and property to which Villegas was entitled. In short, Villegas' attorney did not take reasonable steps to avoid foreseeable prejudice to the client.

The trial court should either have denied the attorney's motion to withdraw or granted the party's motion for continuance; it did neither. Therefore, we reverse the court of appeals judgment and remand for a new trial.

Note

Brown v. Gage, 519 S.W.2d 190 (Tex. App.—Ft Worth 1975, no writ). If the use of due diligence is not alleged, the application is not "statutory" [in compliance with the Rule] even though the facts stated may show diligence. But, it is also not enough to allege that diligence was used, the party must also set out the diligence that has been used. Mere conclusions are not enough.

HUMPHREY
v.
AHLSCHLAGER

778 S.W.2d 480
(Tex. App.—Dallas 1989, no writ)

Facts: This is a suit on a note. In a single point of error, Humphrey contends that the trial court abused its discretion in overruling his fourth motion for continuance. We disagree and affirm the trial court's judgment. The defendant filed four motions for continuance. The last was denied.

Issue: Did the defendant establish the materiality of the testimony of the absent party? No. The requisites for an application for continuance are set forth in rule 252 of the Texas Rules of Civil Procedure, which states, in part, "If the ground of such application be the want of testimony, the party applying therefor shall (1) make affidavit that such testimony is material, (2) showing the materiality thereof, and (3) that he has used due diligence to procure such testimony, (4) stating such diligence . . . ."

Summary: To obtain a continuance on the basis of an absent party, the party must comply with rule 252 of the Texas Rules of Civil Procedure, which states, in part, "If the ground of such application be the want of testimony, the party applying therefor shall (1) make affidavit that such testimony is material, (2) showing the materiality thereof, and (3) that he has used due diligence to procure such testimony, (4) stating such diligence. In showing due diligence, the party must show why the testimony could not be procured by deposition, and must show the nature of the testimony of the witness that makes the testimony material."

Notes

1. In *Reyna v. Reyna*, 738 S.W.2d 772(Tex. App.—Austin 1987, no writ), the court in discussing the availability of a continuance following an announcement of ready noted:

> Generally, a motion for continuance must be filed before an unconditional announcement of "ready" since such an announcement waives the right to seek subsequently a delay based upon any facts which are, or with proper diligence should have been, known at the time. *See* 3 MCDONALD, TEXAS CIVIL PRACTICE s 10.29, at 82 (rev. ed. 1970); *see also Cameron County Water Improvement Dist. No. 1 v. Cameron County Water Improvement Dist. No. 15*, 134 S.W.2d 491 (Tex. Civ. App. 1939, no writ); *Wood v. Fulton Property Co.*, 92 S.W.2d 549 (Tex. Civ. App. 1936, no writ). This general rule is, of course, subject to exception when an unforeseeable event arises through no fault of the movant. *See, e.g., McAden v. Soil Improvement Corporation*, 394 S.W.2d 662 (Tex. Civ. App. 1965, no writ) (counsel absent because of service in the U.S. Army). However, this exception does not apply here because appellant's attorney had at least ten days notice of each trial setting, *see* TEX. R. CIV. P. ANN. 245 (1976), but failed to take any of the necessary steps to avoid a conflict (e.g., withdrawing his unconditional announcement of "ready," seeking a continuance from the court in Harris County, or retaining local counsel to try the case should a conflict arise). We conclude the trial court's denial of the continuance was consistent with the applicable rules of law.

2. The legislature has codified the availability of the right to continuance for its own members. Section 30.003 of the Texas Civil Practices and Remedies Code Provides:

> (a) This section applies to any criminal or civil suit, including matters of probate, and to any matters ancillary to the suit that require action by or the attendance of an attorney, including appeals but excluding temporary restraining orders.
>
> (b) Except as provided by Subsections (c) and (c-1), at any time within 30 days of a date when the legislature is to be in session, at any time during a legislative session, or when the legislature sits as a constitutional convention, the court on application shall continue a case in which a party applying for the continuance or the attorney for that party is a member or member-elect of the legislature and will be or is attending a legislative session. The court shall continue the case until 30 days after the date on which the legislature adjourns.
>
> (c) Except as provided by Subsection (c-1), if the attorney for a party to the case is a member or member-elect of the legislature who was employed on or after the 30th day before the date on which the suit is set for trial, the continuance is discretionary with the court.
>
> (c-1) If the attorney for a party to any criminal case is a member or member-elect of the legislature who was employed on or after the 15th day before the date on which the suit is set for trial, the continuance is discretionary with the court.
>
> (d) The party seeking the continuance must file with the court an affidavit stating the grounds for the continuance. The affidavit is proof of the necessity for a continuance. The affidavit need not be corroborated.
>
> (e) If the member of the legislature is an attorney for a party, the affidavit must contain a declaration that it is the attorney's intention to participate actively in the preparation or presentation of the case and that the attorney has not taken the case for the purpose of obtaining a continuance under this section.
>
> (f) The continuance provided by Subsection (b) is one of right and may not be charged against the party receiving it on any subsequent application for continuance.
>
> (g) If the attorney for a party seeking a continuance under this section is a member or member-elect of the legislature, the attorney shall file a copy of the application for a continuance with the Texas

Ethics Commission. The copy must be sent to the commission not later than the third business day after the date on which the attorney files the application with the court.

Rule 254 of the Texas Rules of Civil Procedures states:

> In all civil actions, including matters of probate, and in all matters ancillary to such suits which require action by or the attendance of an attorney, including appeals but excluding temporary restraining orders, at any time within thirty days of a date when the legislature is to be in session, or at any time the legislature is in session, or when the legislature sits as a Constitutional Convention, it shall be mandatory that the court continue the cause if it shall appear to the court, by affidavit, that any party applying for continuance, or any attorney for any party to the cause, is a member of either branch of the legislature, and will be or is in actual attendance on a session of the same. If the member of the legislature is an attorney for a party to the cause, his affidavit shall contain a declaration that it is his intention to participate actively in the preparation and/or presentation of the case. Where a party to any cause, or an attorney for any party to a cause, is a member of the legislature, his affidavit need not be corroborated. On the filing of such affidavit, the court shall continue the cause until thirty days after adjournment of the legislature and the affidavit shall be proof of the necessity for the continuance, and the continuance shall be deemed one of right and shall not be charged against the movant upon any subsequent application for continuance. The right to a continuance shall be mandatory, except only where the attorney was employed within ten days of the date the suit is set for trial, the right to continuance shall be discretionary.

In re FORD MOTOR COMPANY

165 S.W.3d 315
(Tex 2005)

Michael W. Eady, Thompson, Coe, Cousins & Irons, L.L.P., Jose Santiago Solis, Harlingen, Craig A. Morgan, Austin, and Jaime A. Saenz, Rodriguez, Colvin Chaney & Saenz, L.L.P., Brownsville, for Relator.

Michael Matthew Guerra, Mikal C. Watts, John Gregory Escamilla, Watts Law Firm, L.L.P., McAllen, Thomas O. Matlock Jr., College Station, TX, for Real Party.

J. Michael Myers, Ball & Weed, P.C., San Antonio, for other.

PER CURIAM.

On May 28, 2004, Robin Fuentes, her husband, and her two children were involved in a car accident. Fuentes suffered serious injuries that rendered her a quadriplegic. Less than three months later, the Fuentes family sued Ford Motor Company, Goodyear Tire & Rubber Company, and the tire repair shop that installed tires on the pick-up truck for damages arising from an alleged tire failure that caused the truck to roll over. The case was set for trial to commence on May 16, 2005, less than nine months after it was filed. On April 1, 2005, Ford filed a motion for legislative continuance under Section 30.003 of the Texas Civil Practice and Remedies Code. On April 21, 2005, the trial court held a hearing on the motion. Four days later, the trial court denied the motion and set the case for trial on May 31, 2005. The court of appeals denied Ford's petition for writ of mandamus, and on May 13, 2005, Ford filed its petition with this Court.

To be entitled to mandamus relief, Ford must show that the trial court committed a clear abuse of discretion and that it has no adequate remedy by appeal. *In re Prudential Ins. Co. of Am.*, 148 S.W.3d 124, 135-36 (Tex. 2004); *Walker v. Packer*, 827 S.W.2d 833, 839 (Tex. 1992). A trial court abuses its discretion if "it reaches a decision so arbitrary and unreasonable as to amount to a clear and prejudicial error of law" or if it clearly fails to correctly analyze or apply the law. *Walker*, 827 S.W.2d at 839, 840 (*quoting Johnson v. Fourth Court of Appeals*, 700 S.W.2d 916, 917 (Tex. 1985)). Although this Court has acknowledged that the second requirement for mandamus relief "has no comprehensive definition," we have explained that determining whether a party has an adequate remedy by appeal requires a "careful balance of jurisprudential considerations" that "implicate both public and private interests." *In re Prudential*, 148 S.W.3d at 136. "When the benefits [of mandamus review] outweigh the detriments, appellate courts must consider whether the appellate remedy is adequate." *Id.*

Section 30.003 of the Texas Civil Practice and Remedies Code provides that a court shall grant a motion for continuance if an attorney representing a party is a member of the legislature and will be attending a legislative session. . . . The statute provides that when a lawyer-legislator is retained more than thirty days before the date a civil case is set for trial, a trial court lacks discretion to deny a properly requested motion for legislative continuance. *Id.* § 30.003(b), (c); *see also Waites v. Sondock*, 561 S.W.2d 772, 776 (Tex. 1977); *Collier v. Poe*, 732 S.W.2d 332, 343, 346 (Tex. Crim. App.—1987) (analyzing previous version of statute).

In *Waites v. Sondock*, this Court recognized a constitutional limitation on the mandatory nature of the legislative continuance. 561 S.W.2d at 776. In *Waites*, a mother initiated a contempt proceeding to compel her former husband to comply with a child support order. *Id.* at 772. The husband's lawyer filed a motion for legislative continuance with supporting affidavit, which the mother opposed. She argued that the child support payments were "critical to her ability to feed and support her children." *Id.* at 774. This Court held that requiring mandatory continuances when the party opposing the continuance "faces irreparable harm from the delay in enforcing existing rights" violates the due process clause of the Fourteenth Amendment of the United States Constitution and Article I, Sections 13 (open courts) and 19 (due process) of the Texas Constitution. *Id.* at 773. However, the Court emphasized the limited nature of its holding: "a legislative continuance is mandatory except in those cases in which the party opposing the continuance alleges that a substantial existing right will be defeated or abridged by delay." *Id.* at 776. When a party opposes a legislative continuance in such circumstances, the trial court must conduct a hearing on the allegations and deny the motion if the allegations are shown to be meritorious. *Id.* Subsequently, the Court of Criminal Appeals and several lower courts of appeals have addressed the scope of the *Waites* exception to mandatory legislative continuances, but we have not. *See, e.g., Collier*, 732 S.W.2d at 344 (holding that the *Waites* exception cannot be invoked by the prosecutor in a criminal proceeding); *In re Starr Produce Co.*, 988 S.W.2d 808, 811-12 (Tex. App.—San Antonio 1999, orig. proceeding) (holding that loss of attorney's services because of his inability to continue representation through the new trial date did not create the type of irreparable harm described in *Waites*); *Amoco Prod. Co. v. Salyer*, 814 S.W.2d 211, 213 (Tex. App.—Corpus Christi 1991, orig. proceeding) (holding that the harm caused by lost business opportunities did not "rise to the level of a due process violation"); *Condovest Corp. v. John Street Builders, Inc.*, 662 S.W.2d 138, 141 (Tex. App.—Austin 1983, no writ) (concluding that inability to convey title to real property was "clearly a substantial right" protected by the *Waites* exception).

Ford's motion for a legislative continuance meets the requirements of the statute. Representative Jim Solis's affidavit states that he is a member of the Texas House of Representatives, that the session extends from January 11, 2005 through May 31, 2005, and that he will be attending the legislative session. *See* TEX. CIV. PRAC. & REM.CODE § 30.003(d), (e). Solis also stated that he represents Ford and intends to participate actively in the preparation and presentation of the case. *See id.* Finally, the affidavit also declares that Solis did not take this case for the purpose of obtaining a continuance under Section 30.003 of the Texas Civil Practice & Remedies Code. *See id.* Because Ford's motion was filed more than thirty days before the scheduled trial date and met the statutory requirements, the trial court was without discretion to deny the motion unless Fuentes established her entitlement to an exception. *See id.* § 30.003(b), (c), (f); *Waites*, 561 S.W.2d at 776.

Fuentes opposed the motion, essentially contending that because her participation in a comprehensive rehabilitation services program with the Texas Department of Assistive and Rehabilitation Services will conclude soon, any continuance will prevent access to needed medical care. Fuentes argues that she has an "existing right to rehabilitation and medical care" that constitutes a "substantial existing right" under our decision in *Waites*. Additionally, Fuentes argues that granting the continuance in this case violates her rights to access the court system. To support these contentions, Fuentes attached the affidavits of her husband, Robert Fuentes, and Dr. Joe Gonzales.

Robert Fuentes's affidavit explains that his wife has been a quadriplegic since the accident and requires constant medical attention and therapy. He also states that he and his wife recently received a letter from the Texas Department of Assistive and Rehabilitative Services explaining that the temporary funding provided for her treatment will soon expire. The letter is attached to the affidavit. Finally, Robert Fuentes explains that he is not qualified to provide the treatment that his wife requires. He does not indicate when the current funding ends, whether other funding arrangements have been made, or whether other funding sources are available.

In his affidavit, Dr. Gonzales states that he is familiar with the condition of Fuentes and the current funding source of her medical treatment. He explains that "prompt, consistent, and continued rehabilitation is essential to maximize recovery for persons with spinal injuries." He further opines that "if [Fuentes] discontinues her treatment, which will happen in the near future unless she obtains additional funding, she will be permanently and irrevocably harmed." He does not indicate specifically when the current funding ends or whether additional funding has been obtained.

In this case, the trial court made nine specific findings in its order denying Ford's motion for legislative continuance, apparently based on the exception this Court described in *Waites*:

> I. Ford Motor Company retained Representative Jim Solis on or about April 1, 2005, approximately 45 days before the May 16, 2005 trial, and he has averred that he intends to play a substantial role in the case and that he is not appearing for the purpose of delay.
>
> II. Ford Motor Company moved for a continuance on the same date Rep. Solis appeared in this case.
>
> III. Robin Fuentes sustained disabling back injuries in the incident made the basis of this suit, which injuries require access to round the clock medical care and rehabilitative therapy.
>
> IV. Robin Fuentes presently has a right and access to medical and rehabilitative services to aid in the treatment for, and rehabilitation from, her injuries.
>
> V. Robin Fuentes also has Due Process rights under the United States and Texas constitutions, and she has a right to seek redress for her injuries pursuant to Texas Constitution Art. I, Section 13.
>
> VI. Robin Fuentes' access to such medical treatment and rehabilitative therapy will be jeopardized should this case be continued from its present trial setting.
>
> VII. Robin Fuentes will be irreparably harmed if her access to medical care and rehabilitative therapy is discontinued.
>
> VIII. Robin Fuentes' constitutional right to redress and to Due Process will be violated if the Court grant [sic] a continuance based on Rep. Jim Solis' legislative service.
>
> IX. The Court has considered the contents of the court's file, including the affidavit of Robert Fuentes, the affidavit of Dr. Joe Gonzales, and correspondence from the Texas Department of Assistive and Rehabilitative Services.

Fuentes claims that the *Waites* exception applies because she has a right to "access to medical and rehabilitative services to aid in the treatment for, and rehabilitation from, her injuries." But she does not have a right to have Ford pay for those services unless or until mandate to that effect issues after trial, judgment, and possible appeals. Although we sympathize with the disabling injuries from which Fuentes suffers, relief from a mandatory legislative continuance requires a higher showing than the record in this case makes. She has no substantial existing right to access to medical care that is enforceable against Ford. Her claims against Ford arise from alleged defects of a pick-up truck, not for improperly denying her access to medical care. If she succeeds in obtaining a favorable final judgment against Ford, then she will have an existing right that could be subject to the *Waites* exception. Until then, she has a right to access the court system to pursue her claims against Ford. *See Sax v. Votteler*, 648 S.W.2d 661, 665-66 (Tex. 1983). Continuing this case, which has been pending only a few months, in accordance with the Legislature's "determination that the interests of the people of the State will be best served by the attendance of legislator-attorneys at legislative sessions" does not violate the due process clause of the Fourteenth Amendment of the United States Constitution or Article I, Sections 13 (open courts) and 19 (due process) of the Texas Constitution. *Waites v. Sondock*, 561 S.W.2d 772, 774 (Tex. 1977). Because the constitutional exception in *Waites* does not apply, the trial court had no discretion to deny the motion for continuance.

We recognize that some tension exists between Article II, Section 1 of the Texas Constitution, which divides the powers of the government into three distinct branches, and a legislative enactment that makes mandatory what is typically left to judicial discretion. *Gov't Servs. Ins. Underwriters v. Jones*, 368 S.W.2d 560, 564-67 (Tex. 1963). But the tension is not all on one side. Given the relative infrequency of legislative sessions in Texas and the key roles played by members who are attorneys, a serious constitutional crisis could arise if a court in a remote part of the state could force a legislator to trial the moment a legislative session ends, as the trial court planned to do here. Enforcing legislative continuances is also consistent with the constitutional protection afforded legislators to attend legislative sessions. Except in cases of treason, felony, or breach of the peace, the Texas Constitution itself protects legislators from arrest while traveling to or attending such sessions. Tex. Const. art. III, § 14. As that provision shows, the legislative privilege is not absolute, but trial courts construing the *Waites* exception must require a higher showing of impairment of an opposing party's constitutional rights than the trial court did here.

As our sister court summarized, a mandatory legislative continuance "usually serves a dual purpose of encouraging good men and women to sacrifice their time in the interest of good government and of protecting a party to a law suit whose attorney may be serving in the Legislature." *Collier v. Poe*, 732 S.W.2d 332, 334 (Tex. Crim. App.—1987). Without such a device, a lawyer-legislator could be forced to decide between fulfilling the duty owed to a client and the duty owed to constituents to participate in a legislative session. The consequences of that decision—possibly nonparticipation in a legislative session—could not be remedied on appeal. To give full effect to the Legislature's policy decision regarding legislative continuances, we conclude that a party has no adequate remedy by appeal when a trial court abuses its discretion by denying a motion for legislative continuance. *See In re Prudential Ins. Co. of Am.*, 148 S.W.3d 124, 136-37 (Tex. 2004).

Pursuant to Texas Rule of Appellate Procedure 52.8(c), we issue this opinion without hearing oral argument and conditionally grant a writ of mandamus directing the 139th Judicial District Court of Hidalgo County, Texas, to grant the motion for legislative continuance. That writ will issue only if the district court fails to act in accordance with this opinion.

5. *Jury Selection*

a. *Qualifications and Exemptions*

1. Section 62.102 of the **Texas Government Code** provides:

A person is disqualified to serve as a petit juror unless the person:

(1) is at least 18 years of age;
(2) is a citizen of the United States;
(3) is a resident of this state and of the county in which the person is to serve as a juror;
(4) is qualified under the constitution and laws to vote in the county in which the person is to serve as a juror;
(5) is of sound mind and good moral character;
(6) is able to read and write;
(7) has not served as a petit juror for six days during the preceding three months in the county court or during the preceding six months in the district court;
(8) has not been convicted of misdemeanor theft or a felony; and
(9) is not under indictment or other legal accusation for misdemeanor theft or a felony.

2. Section 62.106 of the Texas Government Code provides:

(a) A person qualified to serve as a petit juror may establish an exemption from jury service if the person:

(1) is over 70 years of age;
(2) has legal custody of a child younger than 10 years of age and the person's service on the jury requires leaving the child without adequate supervision;
(3) is a student of a public or private secondary school;
(4) is a person enrolled and in actual attendance at an institution of higher education;
(5) is an officer or an employee of the senate, the house of representatives, or any department, commission, board, office, or other agency in the legislative branch of state government;
(6) is summoned for service in a county with a population of at least 200,000, unless that county uses a jury plan under Section 62.011 and the period authorized under Section 62.011(b)(5) exceeds two years, and the person has served as a petit juror in the county during the 24-month period preceding the date the person is to appear for jury service;
(7) is the primary caretaker of a person who is an invalid unable to care for himself; or
(8) except as provided by Subsection (b), is summoned for service in a county with a population of at least 250,000 and the person has served as a petit juror in the county during the three-year period preceding the date the person is to appear for jury service.

(9) is a member of the United States military forces serving on active duty and deployed to a location away from the person's home station and out of the person's county of residence.

(b) Subsection (a)(8) does not apply if the jury wheel in the county has been reconstituted after the date the person served as a petit juror.

Read Rules 230 & 292 Texas Rules of Civil Procedure.

PALMER WELL SERVS.
v.
MACK TRUCKS

776 S.W.2d 575
(Tex. 1989)

Randall L. Rouse, Odessa, for petitioner.
Gail Kuhne, Brad Crawford, Lubbock, for respondent.

PER CURIAM.

Conflict with Rule 292 of the Rules of Civil Procedure and Section 62.102 of the Government Code, regarding the qualifications of jurors and the requisites of verdicts, prompts this court's examination of this case.

Suit was filed to recover for personal injuries suffered by petitioner, Paul Quinonez, as a result of an explosion and fire of a hot oil treatment unit and truck. Quinonez was employed by petitioner Palmer Well Services, Inc. (Petitioners will be referred to collectively as "Palmer"). The trial was to jury which rendered a 10-2, take-nothing verdict against the plaintiffs. Palmer filed a motion for new trial alleging the discovery, after the verdict, of a felony indictment pending against one juror. The trial court overruled the motion for new trial.

The court of appeals held that the juror should have been excluded from the panel because of the pending felony indictment and that due diligence was not lacking in failing to discover that fact earlier. However, the court of appeals held that Palmer was required to demonstrate that the unqualified juror's presence on the jury was a material factor which was reasonably calculated to, and probably did, cause the rendition of an improper judgment. The court of appeals held that Palmer failed to establish the requisite material injury needed to sustain this burden and affirmed the trial court.[1] For the reasons expressed, the court of appeals' judgment is reversed and this cause is remanded for new trial.

The only facts pertinent to this appeal regard one of the jurors, Mr. Ira Anderson. Anderson was one of the majority of 10 jurors that rendered the take-nothing verdict. During voir dire, the trial judge queried the panel as to their qualifications to serve. Conflicting evidence exists regarding whether Anderson had gone to the restroom, or remained silent when the panel was asked about pending indictments or legal accusations for a misdemeanor or felony.

Palmer contends that the verdict was not rendered by the requisite number of qualified jurors. In all but one instance, where the jury is originally composed of twelve jurors, a minimum of ten members of the original jury must concur in the verdict. TEX. R. CIV. P. 292. All individuals are competent to serve as petit jurors unless disqualified by statute. TEX. GOV'T CODE ANN. § 62.101 (Vernon 1988). The general qualifications permitting jury service are set forth by statute in Texas Government Code § 62.102. That statute disqualifies a person to

---

[1] TEX.R.CIV.P. 327(a) provides that when a motion for new trial is sought on the ground that a juror gave an erroneous or incorrect answer on voir dire examination, the court may grant a new trial if such erroneous or incorrect answer "be material, and if it reasonably appears from the evidence both on the hearing of the motion and the trial of the case and from the record as a whole that injury probably resulted to the complaining party." TEX.R.CIV.P. 327(a). Also pertinent is TEX.R.APP.P. 81(b)(1) which provides in part: No judgment shall be reversed on appeal and a new trial ordered in any cause on the ground that the trial court has committed an error of law in the course of the trial, unless the appellate court shall be of the opinion that error complained of amounted to such a denial of the rights of the appellant as was reasonably calculated to cause, and probably did cause, rendition of an improper judgment in the case . . . .

serve as a petit juror if he is "under indictment or other legal accusation of misdemeanor or felony theft, or any other felony." *Id.* § 62.102(8).

Respondent, Mack Trucks Inc. (Mack Trucks) concedes that Anderson was under indictment for a felony and does not argue that Palmer lacked due diligence in failing to discover that fact. Mack Trucks argues, however, that Palmer was in no way prejudiced or injured by the inclusion of Anderson on the jury. Relying on *De Leon v. Longoria*, 4 S.W.2d 222 (Tex. Civ. App.—San Antonio 1928, writ dism'd), and *Mendoza v. Varon*, 563 S.W.2d 646, 648 (Tex. Civ. App.—Dallas 1978, writ ref'd. n.r.e.), Mack Trucks asserts that showing the absence of a qualification or establishing a ground for disqualification of a juror does not render a jury verdict invalid nor require the jury verdict to be set aside. The cases of *De Leon* and *Mendoza*, however, are factually distinguishable from the instant case. In *De Leon*, although the pending felony indictment and due diligence were stipulated by the parties, a sufficient number of jurors remained that could have rendered a binding verdict. *See De Leon*, 4 S.W.2d 222, 224-225. In *Mendoza*, the parties discovered the pending felony indictment during the course of the trial and agreed to allow that juror to remain empanelled and participate in the verdict. *See Mendoza*, 563 S.W.2d at 648. Because of the agreement to continue, the parties waived their right to complain of the disqualification of the juror. *Id.*

Palmer's plight with regard to the claim that Anderson was disqualified as a juror is distinct from either *De Leon* or *Mendoza*. First, the discovery of the pending felony indictment was not made until after the verdict was rendered. Second, the failure to discover the pending felony indictment was not due to Palmer's lack of diligence. Finally, if the rules and statutes governing the qualifications of jurors and the requisites of verdicts are to have any effect, litigants similarly situated to Palmer must be held to have suffered material injury as a matter of law. Therefore, because this is not an instance in which a verdict could have been rendered by less than ten jurors, as a matter of law Palmer was materially injured by the rendition of an unfavorable verdict by less than the requisite number of qualified jurors.

For the foregoing reasons, a majority of this court grants the application for writ of error, and without hearing oral argument, reverses the judgment of the court of appeals and remands this case to the trial court for new trial.

McDANIEL
v.
YARBROUGH

898 S.W.2d 251
(Tex. 1995)

Edmund L. Cogburn, George A. Rustay, P. Randall Crump, Houston, for petitioners.
Kathleen Hopkins Alsina, Vance J. Christopher, Houston, for respondent.

GAMMAGE, JUSTICE.

The primary question this case presents is whether the trial court abused its discretion by dismissing a juror as "disabled from sitting" when she asserted she was unable to return to the courthouse because of inclement weather. The court of appeals affirmed the trial court judgment, holding there was no abuse of discretion in determining that the juror was disabled from sitting on the jury. 866 S.W.2d 665. We conclude that a weather-induced delay is not a "disability" and hold that the trial court abused its discretion in dismissing the juror. Consequently, we reverse the judgment of the court of appeals and remand the cause to the trial court for a new trial.

B.J. and Pamela McDaniel brought suit against Tom Yarbrough for damages arising out of an automobile collision. The case was tried before a jury from March 2 through March 5, 1992. Twelve jurors were selected, impaneled, and sworn on March 2. The jury heard opening statements and evidence on March 3. On the afternoon of March 3, the trial judge determined that juror Robert David Hogan, a minister, would be permitted to officiate a funeral service the following morning, and at the conclusion of the day's proceedings announced that trial would recess until the following afternoon to allow Hogan to conduct the funeral. The judge instructed the jury panel to reconvene at 1:00 p.m. on March 4.

Upon reassembling the court the next day, the judge announced that juror Shirley Seals had notified the court that because of heavy flooding she would be unable to return that afternoon. The trial court, *sua sponte*, dismissed Seals from further participation and ordered that the trial proceed with eleven jurors. The judge overruled the McDaniels' objection to Seal's dismissal. The trial continued with eleven jurors. On March 5, the jury returned a 10-1 verdict finding Yarbrough 70% negligent, but awarding zero damages to the McDaniels. The court of appeals affirmed, holding that the trial judge did not abuse his discretion in dismissing Seals from sitting on the jury as disabled when she was temporarily unable to return to the courthouse because of heavy rain. The court of appeals concluded that a "mental or physical disability is not the only type of disability that will justify a dismissal of a juror," and held that a temporary delay because of the weather is a "disability."

I.

Yarbrough first asserts the McDaniels failed to preserve their complaint of the trial court's dismissal of Seals. To preserve error, an objection must state the specific grounds for the desired ruling if those grounds are not apparent from the context of the objection. TEX. R. APP. P. 52(a). An objection is sufficient to preserve error for appeal if it allows the trial judge to make an informed ruling and the other party to remedy the defect, if he can. *McKinney v. Nat'l Union Fire Ins. Co.*, 772 S.W.2d 72, 74 (Tex. 1991). In this case, the McDaniels' objection to improper dismissal of Seals was raised with the trial court and the grounds for the McDaniels' objection were apparent from the context of the record. Upon dismissing Seals, the trial judge stated: Let the record reflect that Shirley Seals, Juror No. 7 on the panel, has reported to the Court that because of the weather she is unable to get back, so we could resume the trial in this case. And pursuant to the provisions of Rule 292, the Court on its own motion has decided to go ahead and proceed with 11 jurors. The trial court, on its own motion, dismissed Seals "pursuant to the provisions of Rule 292." The McDaniels' attorney immediately objected to the trial court's decision to dismiss Seals. The McDaniels' objection gave sufficient notice to the trial court that Seals was not "disabled from sitting" within the context of Rule 292. The objection suggested the proper remedy was not disqualification, but a further recess to allow the juror to return.

II.

The Texas Constitution and Texas Rules of Civil Procedure require that a district court jury consist of twelve members unless not more than three jurors die or "be disabled from sitting." *See* TEX. CONST. art. V, § 13; TEX. R. CIV. P. 292.

In *Houston & Texas Central Ry. Co. v. Waller*, 56 Tex. 331 (1882), this Court set out guiding principles for defining "disabled from sitting" under the Texas Constitution.[2] While trial courts have broad discretion in determining whether a juror is "disabled from sitting" when there is evidence of constitutional disqualification, a trial court may not ignore the constraints established in *Waller*. The *Waller* opinion equates "disabled from sitting" with an actual physical or mental incapacity: [W]ithout deeming it proper to attempt to define fully the meaning of the expression used in the constitution, we are satisfied that the causes which disable the juror from sitting, and justify the extreme course of allowing, over a party's objection, a verdict to be rendered by the remainder of the jury, must be of a nature more directly showing his physical or mental incapacity than mere mental distress occasioned by the sickness of others, and the feeling that duty to the sick demanded his presence elsewhere. Extreme cases of the kind, however strongly they may appear to the court to release the juror, do not belong to the class provided for by the constitution or statute. *Id.* at 337-38.

No evidence of record suggests that Seals became "disabled from sitting" within the constitutional meaning as explained in *Waller*. She was not mentally incompetent or sick, nor did she have some other physical or mental incapacity. On the contrary, she was temporarily detained by flooding caused by heavy rain, which is at most a transient physical barrier. Her dismissal from the jury as "disabled" was improper.

---

[2] *Waller* was decided over one-hundred years ago, before various procedural changes. For example, when *Waller* was decided, jury decisions had to be unanimous, but civil cases today may be determined by a 10-2 verdict. TEX.R.CIV.P. 292; *see Waller*, 56 Tex. at 336. Moreover, alternate jurors now may, prior to the time the jury retires to consider its verdict, replace jurors who become unable to perform their duties. TEX.GOV'T CODE ANN. § 62.020(1988). Such procedural modifications, however, do not alter the definition of "disabled from sitting" set forth in *Waller*. Although a unanimous verdict is no longer required and alternate jurors are available, a jury still must consist of twelve members unless not more than three jurors "die or be disabled from sitting." TEX.R.CIV.P. 292.

III.

The test for abuse of discretion is whether the trial court acted without reference to any guiding rules and principles or whether the act was arbitrary and unreasonable. *Downer v. Aquamarine Operators, Inc.*, 701 S.W.2d 238, 241-42 (Tex. 1985). In this case, the trial judge delayed the trial by one-half day to accommodate one juror, but refused to give similar accommodation to another juror who was temporarily delayed by flooding. By recessing in the morning to accommodate Hogan, the trial judge's decision may have affected Seals' inability to appear at the courthouse in the afternoon. As a matter of law, the circumstances did not give rise to a question of disability under the constitution or Rule 292. A clear failure by a trial court to analyze or apply the law correctly is an abuse of discretion. *Walker v. Packer*, 827 S.W.2d 833, 840 (Tex. 1992).

Denial of the constitutional right to trial by jury constitutes reversible error. *See Heflin v. Wilson*, 297 S.W.2d 864, 866 (Tex. Civ. App.—Beaumont 1956, writ ref'd). Depriving the McDaniels of a full jury of twelve members, absent an exception authorized by the constitution or applicable rules, is a denial of the right to jury trial guaranteed by the Texas Constitution. The trial court abused its discretion in dismissing Seals as "disabled from sitting" because it was clear error to apply that provision in the absence of some physical or mental disability.

For the foregoing reasons, we reverse the judgments of the court of appeals and the trial court and remand this cause to the trial court for further proceedings consistent with this opinion.

GONZALEZ, J., dissenting.

The Court today misconstrues precedent in reversing and remanding for new trial a case in which an eleven-member jury found that the plaintiffs had no damages. The Court reaches this conclusion by holding that the trial court erred in excusing a juror who was physically unable to return to the courthouse. Because I think that the trial court did not err, much less deprive the McDaniels of a constitutional right, I would affirm the judgment of the court of appeals.

In this case, on March 4, 1992, the twelfth juror, Shirley Seals, notified the trial court after a morning's recess that she was unable to reach the courthouse to report for jury duty because of heavy flooding in Houston, Texas. On this particular day, the flooding of White Oak Bayou near downtown Houston, where the courthouse is located, was widely reported in the media. Interstate 10 was closed to traffic from downtown to several miles west, due to flooding which trapped hundreds of vehicles in ten feet of water. Given these travel conditions, the trial court certainly would have understood Juror Seals' assertion that she could not make it to the courthouse to be an honest statement of inability. Moreover, no one could have known how long the flooding which prevented her attendance would continue. By contrast, the facts known to the trial court were quite different when it recessed the trial the morning of March 4th for Juror Hogan to officiate a funeral. As the court of appeals noted, the trial court had advance warning of the exact amount of time—one morning—necessary to recess in order to accommodate Juror Hogan's conflict. 866 S.W.2d 665, 670. In temporarily recessing one time, the trial court did not establish a rule in favor of continuances. Because the information about the two jurors' inability to attend the proceedings differed significantly, the trial court's decision to grant the morning recess for Juror Hogan did not control its later decision to excuse Juror Seals. When all the jurors but one were present and ready to resume proceedings the afternoon of March 4th, the most efficient course was to excuse the twelfth juror and get on with the trial. There is no basis for the McDaniels' suggestion that the trial court did not care whether Juror Seals attended the trial or that it valued her presence less than that of any other juror.

In my opinion, the trial court did not err in excusing Juror Seals and continuing the trial with eleven jurors. This decision was within its discretion. *See Southern Pac. Transp. Co. v. Peralez*, 546 S.W.2d 88, 97 (Tex. Civ. App.—Corpus Christi 1976, writ ref'd n.r.e.) (finding no abuse of discretion in a trial court excusing a juror whose ill family member caused her worry and made her "unable to serve as a juror"). The Court itself errs by failing to employ the correct standard to review a trial court's management of proceedings within the courtroom—to determine whether the lower court acted without reference to any guiding principles. *Morrow v. H.E.B., Inc.*, 714 S.W.2d 297, 298 (Tex. 1986); *Brandon v. Schroeder*, 172 S.W.2d 488, 491 (Tex. 1943). Under an abuse of discretion standard of review, an appellate court may not substitute its judgment for that of the trial court even if it would have reached a contrary result. *See Beaumont Bank, N.A. v. Buller*, 806 S.W.2d 223,

226 (Tex. 1991). The Court justifies its overreaching review by asserting that its opinion corrects an error of constitutional magnitude. I disagree.

Article V, Section 13 of the Texas Constitution states: Grand and petit juries in the District court shall be composed of twelve men . . . . In trials of civil cases . . . nine members of the jury, concurring, may render a verdict . . . . When, pending the trial of any case, one or more jurors not exceeding three, may die, or be disabled from sitting, the remainder of the jury shall have the power to render the verdict. Rule 292 of the Texas Rules of Civil Procedure substantially repeats the constitutional provision, as follows: A verdict may be rendered in any cause by the concurrence . . . of the same ten members of an original jury of twelve . . . . However, where as many as three jurors die or be disabled from sitting and there are only nine of the jurors remaining of the original jury of twelve, those remaining may render and return a verdict. Juror Seals was unable to reach the courthouse in the city of Houston due to "some of the worst flooding in its history." 866 S.W.2d at 670 n. 1. The issue is whether Juror Seals was thus "disabled from sitting" within the meaning of Article V, Section 13 and Rule 292. For the reasons discussed below, I conclude that she was. Consequently, the trial and verdict rendered by the eleven-member jury fulfilled the McDaniels' constitutional right to trial by jury. The Court's holding to the contrary is based on a mistaken application of a case decided in 1882, *Houston & Central Ry. v. Waller*, 56 Tex. 331.

In *Waller*, the trial court excused a juror on the ground that the distress occasioned by a sick child disabled him from sitting on the jury. *Id.* at 337. The *Waller* Court held that the trial court committed reversible error when it excused the juror for "mere distress of mind." *Id.* This was Waller's sole holding with regard to Article V, Section 13. The case stated that a juror who suffered physical prostration or a loss of mental powers would meet Article V, Section 13's requirement of "disabled from sitting." *Id.* A line of cases following *Waller* assumed that the "disabled from sitting" provision refers solely to a juror's physiological or psychological condition. *See, e.g., Daniels v. Southwestern Transp.*, 621 S.W.2d 188, 191 (Tex. Civ. App.—Texarkana 1981, no writ) (excusing a juror with a heart ailment); *Dickson v. J. Weingarten, Inc.*, 498 S.W.2d 388, 391 (Tex. Civ. App.—Houston [14th Dist.] 1973, no writ) (stating that a juror may be legally "disabled from sitting" due to illness, mental disability, misconduct, or drunkenness); *Marvin Drug Co. v. Couch*, 134 S.W.2d 356, 362 (Tex. Civ. App.—Dallas 1939, writ dism'd judgmt. cor.) (dismissing a juror because the trial judge determined he was not of sound mind); *Sunset Wood Co. v. Broadnax*, 136 S.W. 487, 488 (Tex. Civ. App.—San Antonio 1911, writ ref'd) (excusing a juror who became insane); *Routledge v. Elmendorf*, 116 S.W. 156, 160-61 (Tex. Civ. App.—San Antonio 1909, writ ref'd) (rather than waiting for a drunken juror to become sober, excusing him because his drunkenness made him incapable of understanding the trial).

However, *Waller* did not specify all the conditions or circumstances that would render a juror "disabled from sitting." *See Waller*, 56 Tex. at 337. The opinion instead articulated the following test for determining when a juror can be excused: [T]he causes which disable the juror from sitting, and justify the extreme course of allowing . . . a verdict to be rendered by the remainder of the jury, must be of a nature more directly showing his physical or mental incapacity than mere mental distress . . . . *Id.* at 337-38 (emphasis added). This test did not foreclose a construction of "physical . . . incapacity" that contemplates a trial judge excusing a juror who is physically incapable of getting herself to the courtroom. *See, e.g., Remuda Oil & Gas Co. v. Nobles*, 613 S.W.2d 312, 314 (Tex. Civ. App.—Fort Worth 1981, no writ) (holding that the trial court did not abuse its discretion in excusing an elderly juror who was unable to drive in icy road conditions). It is not *Waller* but this Court today that "equates 'disabled from sitting' with an actual physical or mental incapacity." _____ S.W.2d at _____. *Waller* does not compel this narrow construction of the Constitution.

Article V, Section 13 and Rule 292 allow a juror to be excused for "illness, mental disability, misconduct, drunkenness or other facts." *Berry Property Management, Inc. v. Bliskey*, 850 S.W.2d 644, 652-53 (Tex. App.—Corpus Christi 1993, writ dism'd by agr.) (holding that the trial court did not abuse its discretion in dismissing a juror for pro-defendant bias which arose during trial); *see Peralez*, 546 S.W.2d at 97 (finding no error in the trial court excusing a juror unable to serve because she was worried about an ill family member). Early in this century, courts began to recognize that *Waller's* dicta suggesting a narrow construction of "disabled from sitting" infringes on trial courts' discretion to manage trials and juries. *See, e.g., Schebester v. Stewart*, 37 S.W.2d 781, 783 (Tex. Civ. App.—Fort Worth 1930, writ dism'd) (excusing a juror who showed signs of physical illness after receiving news that a family member was very sick); *Barker v. Ash*, 194 S.W. 465, 466-67 (Tex. Civ. App.—Dallas 1917, writ denied) (excusing a juror whose child was seriously ill on the ground that the juror was incapable of giving his best attention to the case), discussed in *Recent Case*, 10 TEX. L. REV. 117, 117-18 (1932) (*comparing Barker to Waller*, and approving the result in *Barker*).

The term "disabled" in Article V, Section 13 is not a mere euphemism for a "handicapped" or a "crippled" juror who cannot fulfill her role despite bodily presence in the jury box. "Disabled" encompasses physical or mental incapacity, but also any other condition or circumstance that renders a person incapable of fulfilling the function of a juror. Inability to physically attend the proceedings is one circumstance that will make a juror incapable of fulfilling her function. The statutory exemptions from jury service reflect a recognition that other conditions and circumstances make persons incapable of effectively performing a juror's function. *See* TEX. GOV'T CODE §§ 62.105-06. Also, if a juror dies, Article V, Section 13 allows the remainder of the jury to render a verdict. This provision, like the "disabled from sitting" provision, illustrates a pragmatic aspect of the right to jury trial under the Constitution. For practical reasons, in civil cases Article V, Section 13 authorizes a trial to continue even if some exigency renders a juror physically unable to attend proceedings. As the commentators to Article V, Section 13 concluded: Prior to the present constitution, if a regular juror died, or became ill, or for any other reason was unable to serve, it necessitated a retrial. In view of the fact that retrials were expensive . . . it was felt imperative to prevent delay and additional costs that a trial could continue without the juror. TEX. CONST. art. V, § 13 interp. commentary (Vernon 1993) (emphasis added).

Waller was decided when a procedural statute required unanimous jury verdicts. When enacted, Article V, Section 13 approved verdicts based on the concurrence of at least nine jurors' votes. *See* TEX. CONST. art. V, Section 13, reprinted in 8 H.P.N. GAMMELL, LAWS OF TEXAS 779, 804 (1878). Article V, Section 13 also authorized the Legislature to specify if less than all the members of the jury could render a verdict. *See id.* (stating that "the Legislature may change or modify the rule authorizing less than the whole number of the jury to render a verdict"). In 1876, the Legislature passed a statute in accordance with this constitutional provision that required jury verdicts to be unanimous. *See Bowen v. Davis*, 48 Tex. 101, 102 (1877) (*citing* Act of Aug. 1, 1876, 15th Leg., R.S., ch. 76, s 19, 1876 TEX. GEN. LAWS 78, 82, reprinted in 8 H.P.N. GAMMELL, LAWS OF TEXAS 835, 918 (1878)). This statute was in effect at the time of *Waller*. *See Waller*, 56 Tex. at 336. Thus, given the unanimity requirement imposed by statute, the *Waller* Court's trouble with the trial court's dismissal of a juror was that it potentially affected the outcome of the entire trial. Had the juror in *Waller* remained on the panel and voted against the plaintiff, the one vote would have precluded a verdict for the plaintiff. In short, because of the unanimous verdict requirement, the presence or absence of a single juror could be dispositive. In 1973, this Court, pursuant to its rulemaking power under TEX. GOV'T CODE § 22.004, changed the requirement of juror unanimity to allow ten-to-two jury verdicts. *See* TEX. R. CIV. P. 291-92 historical notes (Vernon 1977). Therefore, the rules of procedure no longer require that "all members of the jury" concur in the verdict. *See* TEX. R. CIV. P. 291-292.

I conclude that this change made the concerns animating *Waller* obsolete. The Constitution and the rules of procedure are now in accord that "a less than unanimous verdict" suffices. Because unanimity among the jurors is no longer required, one single vote cannot be dispositive. In the present case, if Juror Seals had been present on the panel, her vote could not affect the outcome of the plaintiffs' trial. The Court makes a considerable leap when it equates the McDaniels' eleven-member jury with "denial of the constitutional right to trial by jury." _____ S.W.2d at _____. Under the present rules of procedure permitting judgments rendered upon ten-to-two verdicts, and in the absence of a statute requiring juror unanimity, I cannot agree with the Court's *Waller*-era holding that an eleven-member jury is equivalent to no jury at all.

One could speculate about the result if Juror Seals had not been excused. She might have decided that the McDaniels were entitled to greater than zero damages, and she might have persuaded two other jurors to her point of view. In this scenario no valid verdict could have been rendered. *See* TEX. R. CIV. P. 292. However, to constitute reversible error, this Court must find that the McDaniels' alleged denial of their rights was reasonably calculated to cause and probably did cause rendition of an improper judgment. TEX. R. APP. P. 81(b)(1). Speculation about what Juror Seals might have concluded and persuaded other jurors of in this trial does not meet the standard.

For the forgoing reasons, I would hold that the trial court did not infringe upon the McDaniels' constitutional right to jury trial by excusing Juror Seals from the panel and rendering judgment based on an eleven-member jury verdict. I would affirm the judgment of the court of appeals.

PHILLIPS, C.J., and HECHT and ENOCH, JJ., join in this dissenting opinion.

IN THE INTEREST OF M.G.N. AND A.C.N., MINOR CHILDREN

441 S.W.3d 246
(Tex. 2014)

Oscar L. Cantu, Jr., Law Offices of Oscar Cantu, San Antonio, TX, for Petitioner Monica Noyes.

James N. Higdon, Higdon Hardy & Zuflacht LLP, San Antonio, TX, for Respondent George C. Noyes.

PER CURIAM.

Our constitution permits trial courts to proceed with fewer than twelve jurors if the trial court finds that up to three jurors are constitutionally disabled. Our statutes allow trial courts to substitute qualified alternate jurors for regular jurors who become statutorily disqualified—a different standard altogether. This case tests both principles. Here, the trial court substituted an alternate for a regular juror whom it found to be disqualified. Subsequently, the trial court found that one of the twelve jurors had become disabled and proceeded with the remaining eleven. The court of appeals reversed, concluding that the dismissal of the disqualified juror ultimately led to an eleven-member jury in violation of the constitutional right to a jury trial. We conclude the court of appeals failed to properly examine the two dismissals under their appropriate standards: whether the substitution for an alternate was proper due to a statutory disqualification and whether continuing with eleven jurors was proper due to a constitutional disability. Accordingly, we reverse the court of appeals' judgment and remand to that court for further proceedings consistent with this opinion.

This is a child custody dispute. George Carl Noyes and Monica Noyes were divorced in May 2007. The final divorce decree appointed them joint managing conservators of their two children. In 2010, each party sought to be designated sole managing conservator, and both agreed to a jury trial.

Following voir dire, the trial court empaneled twelve jurors and retained one alternate. During cross-examination of George at trial, Monica's counsel asked him a series of questions concerning his former employer, Tim Smoot. The inquiries insinuated that George was at least partly responsible for Smoot's alleged business troubles, and Smoot was said to have accused George of "running his business into the ground." At the recess following this cross-examination, Joel Turney, a juror, alerted a court deputy to the fact that he personally knew Smoot. Before continuing with trial, and outside the presence of the other jurors, the trial court questioned Juror Turney about his connection to Smoot. Juror Turney disclosed he had transacted business with Smoot for many years and believed the insinuations by Monica's counsel were misleading because the juror knew Smoot was solvent. The trial court asked Juror Turney whether, in light of this personal knowledge, he could deliberate as a fair and impartial juror. Juror Turney admitted he was inclined to share his knowledge with the other jurors "unless you tell me I can't bring up things that were not brought up between the lawyers." The trial court instructed Juror Turney to withhold this information from the other jurors.

Following this hearing, Monica's counsel requested Juror Turney be excused, and George's counsel objected. The trial court dismissed Juror Turney, replaced him with the lone alternate juror, and proceeded with the trial. The court reasoned that because there was an alternate juror available, "there [was] no reason to take the risk here of impartiality . . . or of extra information going into the jury room."

A second juror issue arose on the morning of the seventh day of trial when juror George Park left a message with the clerk indicating he was ill and unable to attend the proceedings. Before resuming trial for the day, the trial court called Juror Park and, along with counsel for both parties, questioned him about the nature of his illness. Juror Park was not able to definitively state when he thought he would convalesce sufficiently to return to service. Recalling its assurance to the jurors that they would be done with trial by that day and noting that Juror Park's return date was uncertain, the court held that the trial would proceed with eleven jurors. George's counsel moved for a mistrial, which the trial court denied. The eleven-member jury returned a unanimous verdict denying both parties' requests for sole managing conservatorship.

George appealed, arguing that the trial court violated his constitutional right to a jury trial, as the eleven-person jury fell short of constitutional and statutory strictures. The court of appeals agreed, and reversed and remanded for new trial, citing the Texas Constitution's requirement that a jury must consist of twelve members unless not more than three of them die or become "disabled from sitting." TEX. CONST. art. V, § 13. Such disability, the court reasoned, must be in the nature of an actual physical or mental incapacity—mere inconvenience or delay does not suffice. 401 S.W.3d 677, 679. While Juror Turney concededly "posed a risk of impartiality and of extra information going into the jury room," potential contamination from a tendentious juror is not a constitutional disability requiring dismissal. *Id.* at 680. When the trial court dismissed the second juror—Juror Park—due to illness, only eleven jurors remained. Therefore, the court of appeals concluded the dismissal of Juror Turney when he was not constitutionally disabled ultimately resulted in an eleven-member jury and violated George's constitutional right to a jury trial.

Monica petitioned this Court for review, claiming the court of appeals misconstrued the Texas Constitution and our precedent. The construction of the constitution and statutes are questions of law we review de novo. *Fin. Comm'n of Tex. v. Norwood*, 418 S.W.3d 566, 585 (Tex. 2013); *Nathan v. Whittington*, 408 S.W.3d 870, 872 (Tex. 2013).

The parties invite us to consider whether a juror's potential bias may render her constitutionally "disabled from sitting." But we need not reach that question in resolving this matter, as the issue is considerably more straightforward. In brief, a court need not find a juror constitutionally disabled in order to substitute an alternate when doing so does not lead to numerical diminution of a twelve-member jury.

The relevant jury requirements in this proceeding are found in both the Texas Constitution and in the Texas Rules of Civil Procedure. TEX. CONST. art. V, § 13; TEX. R. CIV. P. 292. The constitution specifies that grand and petit juries in the district courts shall be composed of twelve members. TEX. CONST. art. V, § 13. As few as nine jurors may render a verdict if, during trial, as many as three jurors "die, or become disabled from sitting." *Id.* The Rules of Civil Procedure have similar language allowing as few as nine remaining jurors to return and render a verdict if "as many as three jurors die or be disabled from sitting." TEX. R. CIV. P. 292. Thus, if a trial court's dismissal of a juror results in fewer than twelve jurors, the dismissal must either be based on the juror's constitutional disability or the trial court must declare a mistrial if there was no constitutional disability.

In an effort to improve efficiency by reducing mistrials, the Legislature implemented a system of alternate jurors. These alternate jurors are "drawn and selected in the same manner as regular jurors." TEX. GOV'T CODE § 62.020(c). In practice, this means that an alternate juror must have the same qualifications as a regular juror, be subjected to the same challenges, swear the same oath, and otherwise be considered equivalent to a regular juror. The plain language of this statute allows an alternate juror to substitute for a regular juror by a different and lesser standard than constitutional disability: when a regular juror is "unable or disqualified to perform their duties." *Id.* § 62.020(d); *see also Schlafly v. Schlafly*, 33 S.W.3d 863 (Tex. App.—Houston [14th Dist.] 2000, pet. denied). A juror is deemed disqualified if he "has a bias or prejudice in favor of or against a party in the case." TEX. GOV'T CODE § 62.105(4). Taking the statute and constitution together, a trial court may substitute a regular juror with an alternate if the regular juror is unable to fulfill or is disqualified from fulfilling his duties, but a trial court may only dismiss a juror and proceed with fewer than twelve jurors if the dismissed juror is constitutionally disabled.

Here, the court of appeals conflated these provisions and held that the trial court wrongly proceeded with fewer than twelve jurors even though Juror Turney was not constitutionally disabled. Because the trial court substituted an alternate juror for Juror Turney, under the statute the trial court only needed to find that Juror Turney was disqualified from fulfilling his duties and that the alternate was qualified to serve. TEX. GOV'T CODE § 62.020(c)-(d); *Schlafly*, 33 S.W.3d at 863. The parties do not brief those issues here, and we do not address them. If the court of appeals concludes the trial court did not abuse its discretion in substituting the alternate juror for Juror Turney, it must then assess whether the trial court abused its discretion in proceeding with eleven jurors after finding Juror Park constitutionally disabled. *See, e.g., McDaniel v. Yarbrough*, 898 S.W.2d 251 (Tex. 1995) (juror not disabled due to severe flooding that made travel to the courthouse difficult); *Houston & T.C. Ry. Co. v. Waller*, 56 Tex. 331, 337 (1882) ("If a juror becomes so sick as to be unable to sit longer, he is plainly disabled from sitting."). Accordingly, pursuant to Texas Rule of Appellate Procedure 59.1, we grant the petition for review and, without hearing oral argument, reverse the court of appeals' judgment and remand for that court to consider the remaining issues in a manner consistent with this opinion.

Note

Yanes v. Sowards 996 S.W.2d 849 (Tex. 1999): The trial court did not abuse its discretion by dismissing a juror whose grandfather was ill and not expected to live, and proceeding with only eleven jurors. If the death or serious illness of a family member renders a juror unable to discharge his responsibilities, trial may proceed with fewer than twelve jurors. The Court distinguishes *McDaniel v. Yarbrough*, 898 S.W.2d 251 (Tex. 1995) on the ground that the flood caused a temporary detention of the juror, which did not affect the juror's mental capacity to understand or concentrate at trial. The Court also distinguishes *Houston & Texas Central Ry. Co. v. Waller,* 56 Tex. 331 (1882) (juror received note from spouse informing him that child was sick, and urging him to come home if he could), on the ground that in that case it was a sense of parental duty that caused the juror to want to be excused. There was no inquiry as to what the knowledge of his child's sickness would have on his mental capacity to fully and fairly perform his jury duty.

b. *Voir Dire Examination*

Read rule 226a Texas Rules of Civil Procedure.

BABCOCK
v.
NORTHWEST MEMORIAL HOSP.

767 S.W.2d 705
(Tex. 1989)

Kevin Dubose and Jim M. Perdue, Perdue, Turner & Berry, Ray Hensarling, Houston, Tex., for petitioners.
Sam W. Cruse, Jr., Andrews & Kurth, Dion C. Raymos, Ryan & Smith, and John Roberson, John Landa, Jr. and Suzan Cardwell, Hill Parker, Franklin, Cardwell & Jones, Houston, Tex., for respondents.

MAUZY, JUSTICE.

The court's opinion of December 14, 1988 is withdrawn and the following is substituted therefor.

This cause concerns the propriety of a trial court's refusal to allow attorneys to question the venire panel about the alleged "lawsuit crisis." Artaruth Babcock and husband, Gifford Babcock, sued respondents, Northwest Memorial Hospital, Dr. E.E. Kearns and Dr. Fred DeFrancesco for damages arising out of alleged medical malpractice. During voir dire, the trial judge refused to allow the Babcocks to question the jury panel about the alleged "lawsuit crisis." The trial court rendered judgment in favor of the defendants in accordance with the jury's verdict. The court of appeals affirmed the judgment of the trial court. 751 S.W.2d 277. We reverse the judgment of the court of appeals and remand the cause to the trial court.

Artaruth Babcock broke her pelvis and was hospitalized. During her hospitalization, Mrs. Babcock developed blisters on her heels which allegedly ultimately resulted in the amputation of both her legs. Mrs. Babcock and her husband sued the hospital and her doctors alleging negligence in their care of Mrs. Babcock.

The trial court granted two pre-trial motions in limine. The first motion in limine prohibited "[a]ny mention of the alleged 'liability insurance crisis,' 'medical malpractice crisis', or any similar mention of or questions to potential jurors regarding the current state of affairs in the liability insurance industry." The second motion in limine prohibited "calling the jury's attention to any advertisements either on radio, television, in newspapers or magazines which speak of malpractice crisis and are paid for by and credited to insurance companies." During voir dire, a member of the jury panel stated that he had read articles and advertisements discussing the alleged liability crisis, and his concern for the effect of jury awards on insurance premiums might impede his ability to be impartial. After that juror was struck for cause, the Babcocks renewed their request for permission to question the entire jury panel about the alleged "lawsuit crisis." The trial court again denied the request. The following exchange took place before the bench: COUNSEL FOR BABCOCKS: Your Honor, while everybody is still up here and on the record, I would like to bring—bring out the Court's ruling on my motion—on their Motion in Limine. It's my understanding that the Court has precluded me from asking questions as to whether the jury has heard or read about, not necessarily the insurance crisis, but the liability crisis and the lawsuit crisis. This man obviously is very influenced by it and I think his answer that he was concerned about malpractice, the insurance premiums specifically, I think that that brings forth the need and the necessity for a fair trial that the Plaintiff be allowed to go into this in a little more depth with all the rest of the jurors. THE COURT: All right. Let the record show that [motion] was made, carefully considered, and the same ruling is in effect. Otherwise, it would open the door completely to both sides to go into that, which would completely prejudice the jury. We couldn't get a fair trial.

After the jury was selected, the Babcocks for the third time objected to the trial court's refusal to allow questions concerning the alleged "lawsuit crisis" and asked for an opportunity later in the day to include the questions they would have asked the jurors in the record. The objection was overruled and the request denied. After trial, the trial court rendered judgment in favor of the respondents. The Babcocks' motion for new trial included an affidavit which delineated the questions they would have asked during voir dire about the "lawsuit crisis."

The Babcocks appealed to the court of appeals claiming the trial court abused its discretion by prohibiting voir dire questions about the alleged "lawsuit crisis." The court of appeals, affirming the trial court's judgment, held that since the Babcocks did not timely advance the specific questions they wanted to ask, they could not complain on appeal that the trial court abused its discretion in refusing to allow the questions.

At issue in this cause is whether the trial court abused its discretion by prohibiting voir dire examination inquiring about the "lawsuit crisis" or "liability insurance crisis" and whether the Babcocks properly preserved error.

We disagree with the court of appeals' conclusion that the Babcocks failed to timely advance their proposed questions and thus failed to preserve error. Rule 52(a) of the Rules of Appellate Procedure states: In order to preserve a complaint for appellate review, a party must have presented to the trial court a timely request, objection or motion, stating the specific grounds for the ruling he desired the court to make if the specific grounds were not apparent from the context. It is also necessary for the complaining party to obtain a ruling upon the party's request, objection or motion. If the trial judge refuses to rule, an objection to the court's refusal to rule is sufficient to preserve the complaint. It is not necessary to formally except to rulings or orders of the trial court.

The record reflects that the Babcocks adequately apprised the trial court of the nature of their inquiry twice during trial after having originally objected to the trial court's grant of the respondents' motions in limine. During voir dire, the matter arose when a prospective juror expressed doubt about his ability to be impartial because of his concern about the effect of judgments on insurance premiums. Apart from the rest of the panel, the juror was questioned about his concerns for malpractice premiums. The juror answered affirmatively when asked if he had read advertisements about the difficulty of obtaining insurance because of jury verdicts. He stated he believed the assertions made in the advertisements and would be concerned about insurance premiums. After that juror was struck for cause, the Babcocks again requested permission to question the remaining prospective jurors about the "lawsuit crisis." The trial judge denied this request.

The Babcocks made a final objection at the conclusion of the voir dire examination, before any evidence was admitted. The Babcocks re-urged their objection and, while they acknowledged that the trial court's ruling had already been made, they requested an opportunity later in the day to enter in the record the questions they would have asked. The trial judge responded, "[l]et the record show that this matter's already been ruled on twice, that this request that's made is carefully considered by this court and denied."

We hold that the Babcocks properly preserved error in accordance with TEX. R. APP. P. 52(a). They presented a timely request to the trial court, stating the specific grounds for the ruling they desired, and obtained a ruling from the court.

The court of appeals held that it was not compelled to find an abuse of discretion by the trial court because the specific questions were not before the trial court at the time of its decision and the offer of such questions by the Babcocks was not timely. This holding is inconsistent with the language of rule 52(a).

Rule 52(a) requires that specific grounds for a ruling be stated if the specific grounds are not apparent from the context. TEX. R. APP. P. 52(a). There is no requirement to place specific questions in the record if the nature of the questions is apparent from the context. In this case, the language of the motions in limine and the recorded voir dire of the excused juror makes it obvious what questions the Babcocks wanted to ask. Furthermore, the

Babcocks attempted to place their proposed questions into the record, but their request was denied by the trial court.

We now reach the Babcocks' contention that the trial court abused its discretion by refusing to allow them to question the jurors about the alleged "lawsuit crisis." In Texas, the right to a fair and impartial trial is guaranteed by the Constitution and by statute. *See* TEX. CONST. art. I, § 15; TEX. GOV'T CODE ANN. § 62.105 (Vernon 1987). It is widely recognized that Texas courts permit a broad range of inquiries on voir dire. *Texas Employers Ins. Ass'n v. Loesch*, 538 S.W.2d 435, 440 (Tex. Civ. App.—Waco 1976, writ ref'd n.r.e.); *Green v. Ligon*, 190 S.W.2d 742 (Tex. Civ. App.—Fort Worth 1945, writ ref'd n.r.e.). At the time of trial, tort reform and the debate concerning the alleged "liability insurance crisis" and "lawsuit crisis" were the subject of much media attention. No one can deny the media blitz spurred by the controversy over tort reform during the 1987 legislative session. Advertisements proclaiming a "lawsuit crisis" asserted that personal injury lawsuits had created an economic crisis and that excessive jury awards resulted in higher premiums.

Media coverage of the alleged "lawsuit crisis" has unquestionably created the potential for bias and prejudice on both sides of the personal injury docket. As stated in *Green*, "[i]f counsel has reason to believe that a juror is directly or indirectly interested in the result of the trial to be had, he has a right to question the juror touching that interest." *Green*, 190 S.W.2d at 747.

In a recent opinion, the Second Court of Appeals, when confronted with the same issue, held that the plaintiffs had a right to question the jury to determine if anyone was prejudiced against plaintiffs' rights by such advertising. *National County Mut. Fire Ins. Co. v. Howard*, 749 S.W.2d 618, 621 (Tex. App.—Fort Worth 1988, writ denied). The defendants in *Howard* alleged error by the trial court because the plaintiffs were allowed to question prospective jurors about certain advertisements on tort reform. They contended that such questioning interjected liability insurance into the case. *Id.* at 620. The court of appeals held that such questions were necessary to ask and that the questions in no way indicated the defendants were insured. *Id.* at 621.

Similarly, the respondents in this case contend that allowing such questions would interject insurance into the case. We are unpersuaded by this argument. The mere mention of insurance is not necessarily grounds for reversal. *St. Louis S.W. Ry. Co. v. Gregory*, 387 S.W.2d 27, 33 (Tex. 1965); *Dennis v. Hulse*, 362 S.W.2d 308, 309 (Tex. 1962). When the Babcocks requested to ask the prospective jurors questions about the "liability crisis" and the "lawsuit crisis," they specifically stated they did not want to question the jury about insurance. The proposed voir dire questions that were subsequently filed with the trial court avoid any mention of insurance.

The test for abuse of discretion is whether the trial court acted without reference to any guiding rules and principles or whether the act was arbitrary and unreasonable. *Downer v. Aquamarine Operators, Inc.*, 701 S.W.2d 238, 241-42 (Tex. 1985). Both the Fourteenth Court of Appeals and the Second Court of Appeals have concluded that litigants have a right to question prospective jurors about their exposure to media coverage of the "lawsuit crisis." 751 S.W.2d at 278; *Howard*, 749 S.W.2d at 621. This right is based on the fundamental right to trial by a fair and impartial jury. We hold that the trial court abused its discretion by refusing to allow the Babcocks to question the jurors about the alleged "lawsuit crisis."

A broad latitude should be allowed to a litigant during voir dire examination. This will enable the litigant to discover any bias or prejudice by the potential jurors so that peremptory challenges may be intelligently exercised. *Lubbock Bus Co. v. Pearson*, 277 S.W.2d 186, 190 (Tex. Civ. App.—San Antonio 1955, writ ref'd n.r.e.). Although we recognize that voir dire examination is largely within the sound discretion of the trial judge, *Loesch*, 538 S.W.2d at 440, a court abuses its discretion when its denial of the right to ask a proper question prevents determination of whether grounds exist to challenge for cause or denies intelligent use of peremptory challenges. *Dickson v. Burlington N.R.R.*, 730 S.W.2d 82, 85 (Tex. App.—Fort Worth 1987, writ ref'd n.r.e.).

In the instant case, the Babcocks were denied the opportunity to intelligently exercise challenges. The trial court's refusal to allow questions directed at exposing bias or prejudice resulting from the controversy over tort reform denied the Babcocks the right to trial by a fair and impartial jury.

Respondents contend that the trial court's refusal to allow the questions was harmless error. We disagree. The trial court's actions, which resulted in the denial of the Babcocks' constitutional right to trial by a fair and impartial jury, was harmful. *Texas & Pac. Ry. v. Van Zandt*, 159 Tex. 178, 182, 317 S.W.2d 528, 531 (1958). Therefore, we hold that the trial court's refusal to allow questions during voir dire addressing the alleged "liability insurance crisis" and "lawsuit crisis" was an abuse of discretion and was reasonably calculated to cause and probably did cause the rendition of an improper judgment. TEX. R. APP. P. 81(b).

The judgment of the court of appeals is reversed and the cause is remanded to the trial court.

HYUNDAI MOTOR CO.
v.
VASQUEZ
189 S.W.3d 743
(Tex. 2006)

Brendan K. McBride, David M. Prichard, Kevin M. Young, Prichard Hawkins & Young, LLP, Thomas H. Crofts Jr., Crofts & Callaway, P.C., San Antonio, David E. Keltner, Jose Henry Brantley & Keltner, Fort Worth, for Petitioners.

Michael A. Caddell, Cynthia Bodendieck Chapman, James Juranek, Caddell & Chapman, Houston, Ricardo G. Cedillo, L. J. Strieber, Davis Cedillo & Mendoza, Inc., San Antonio, Ezequiel Reyna Jr., Law Offices of Ezequiel Reyna, Jr., Weslaco, for Respondents.

Harvey G. Brown Jr., Wright Brown & Close, LLP, Houston, Vincent S. Walkowiak, O. Rey Rodriguez, Fulbright & Jaworski L.L.P., Dallas, TX, Hugh F. Young Jr., Reston, VA, Brent M. Rosenthal, Baron & Budd, P.C., Dallas, G. Alan Waldrop, Locke, Liddell & Sapp LLP, Austin, for Amicus Curiae.

JUSTICE BLAND delivered the opinion of the Court, in which JUSTICE HECHT, JUSTICE O'NEILL, JUSTICE BRISTER, JUSTICE WILLETT, and JUSTICE CAYCE joined.[1]

CHIEF JUSTICE JEFFERSON and JUSTICE GREEN are recused.

In this case, we decide whether a trial court abuses its discretion in refusing to allow a voir dire question from counsel that previews relevant evidence and inquires of prospective jurors whether such evidence is outcome determinative. We hold that it does not. The court of appeals held that it does. Accordingly, we reverse and remand.

I. Background

Four-year-old Amber Vasquez died in a low-speed neighborhood traffic collision, after the passenger-side airbag in her aunt's Hyundai Accent deployed with enough force to catch Amber's chin and break her neck. The driver of the other car had turned unexpectedly in front of the Hyundai, and the force of the collision threw Amber forward in her seat. It is undisputed that Amber was not buckled into her front-seat seat belt at the time of the accident.

Amber's parents, Victor and Brenda Vasquez, sued Hyundai Motor Company and Hyundai Motor America, Inc. (together "Hyundai"), contending that Hyundai had placed the airbag incorrectly, and that the airbag had deployed with too much force in this low-impact accident. Hyundai responded that the airbag that killed Amber was not defective because a child wearing a seat belt—as state law requires—or sitting in the back seat—as the car's warnings cautioned—would not have been injured by its deployment.

In placing Amber unbuckled in the front seat, Amber's aunt, Valerie Suarez, disregarded airbag warnings on both sunvisors, a hangtag from the rearview mirror, a decal on the dashboard, and a notification in the owner's manual. Suarez ignored the warnings because she planned a short neighborhood trip and believed that the airbags would deploy only at higher speeds. Hyundai conceded that it knew some occupants would ignore the airbag warnings about placing children unbuckled in the front seat, but maintained the risk was outweighed by the benefits of the airbag to all others. Hyundai named Suarez and the driver of the other car as responsible third parties.

---

[1] The Honorable John Cayce, Chief Justice, Second District Court of Appeals, and the Honorable Jane Bland, Justice, First District Court of Appeals, sitting by commission of the Honorable Rick Perry, Governor of Texas, pursuant to Tex. Gov't Code § 22.005.

The trial judge dismissed two jury panels before seating the jury in the case from a third. During the first voir dire, Amber's counsel asked jurors whether the fact that Amber was not wearing her seat belt would determine their verdict. After numerous jurors indicated that the lack of a seat belt would determine their verdict, the trial court dismissed the jury panel. During the second voir dire, the trial judge questioned the jurors along similar lines, with slightly fewer, but nonetheless significant, affirmative responses. The court again dismissed the panel.

Before the third voir dire, the trial judge discussed with counsel her concern that the previous jury panels had misunderstood the inquiry about placing a child in the front seat without a buckled seat belt to be one about the weight they could give to particular evidence in the case rather than whether they could fairly consider all of the evidence presented. As a result, during the third general voir dire, in response to counsel's request to ask general questions "about belting, seat belting, and seat belting habits much akin to what I did the last time I did general voir dire," the trial court responded, "I am going to let you ask those questions." Thereafter, the trial court allowed counsel to ask "general questions about belting" and to inquire about jurors' personal seat belt habits, but she did not allow disclosure that Amber was not wearing one at the time of the accident. Counsel asked questions about whether the jurors buckled their seat belts on short trips, before leaving the garage, before exiting a driveway, and before leaving a parking spot. At the conclusion of the third voir dire, the trial court excused 3 of the first 28 jurors for cause and seated a 12 member jury and one alternate.

The jury heard evidence for three weeks and returned a verdict in favor of Hyundai. It found no design defect and assessed liability for Amber's death to the two drivers (75 percent to Suarez, and 25 percent to the other driver). The trial court rendered a take-nothing judgment.

The Vasquezes appealed, contending the trial court erred in disallowing voir dire inquiry into whether the jurors would be "predisposed, regardless of the evidence," against the Vasquezes because "there is no seat belt in use," to a point that "[the jurors] could not be fair and impartial." Hyundai responded that the proposed voir dire inquiry is improper in that it asks jurors about the weight they would place on a particular piece of relevant evidence, and thus the trial court properly refused to allow it. A panel of the Fourth Court of Appeals affirmed the trial court's judgment. Upon rehearing en banc, however, the court of appeals reversed, holding that the trial court had abused its discretion in disallowing the inquiry because the proposed question focuses "on the ability of the jurors to be fair." This Court granted Hyundai's petition for review.

II. The Purpose of Voir Dire

The Bill of Rights in the Texas Constitution guarantees litigants a right to trial by a fair and impartial jury and authorizes the Legislature to pass laws "to maintain its purity and efficiency." The Legislature thus has authority to pass laws establishing those qualified to serve, consistent with the right to a jury trial. To that end, the Legislature has established general juror qualifications relating to age, citizenship, literacy, sanity, and moral character. The Legislature also has established bases for juror disqualification, including those relating to witnesses, relatives, and interested parties. Among these bases, the Legislature has disqualified from jury service anyone who "has a bias or prejudice in favor of or against a party in the case."

Voir dire examination protects the right to an impartial jury by exposing possible improper juror biases that form the basis for statutory disqualification. Thus, the primary purpose of voir dire is to inquire about specific views that would prevent or substantially impair jurors from performing their duty in accordance with their instructions and oath.

In addition, this Court recognizes that trial courts should allow "broad latitude" to counsel "to discover any bias or prejudice by the potential jurors so that peremptory challenges may be intelligently exercised." "A peremptory challenge, commonly referred to as a 'strike,' is defined by rule 232 as one 'made to a juror without assigning any reason therefor.' " Peremptory challenges allow parties to reject jurors they perceive to be unsympathetic to their position. The long-established practice of voir dire inquiry for use in exercising peremptory challenges acknowledges the subjectivity inherent in jury selection voir dire does not lend itself to formulaic management. * * *

Peremptory strikes are not intended, however, to permit a party to "select" a favorable jury. Counsel's latitude in voir dire, while broad, is constrained by reasonable trial court control. Such control is necessary because, "[t]hough the motive of a peremptory challenge may be to protect a private interest, the objective of jury selection proceedings is to determine representation on a governmental body." Thus, the exercise of jury strikes is not solely a private endeavor: "[W]hen private litigants participate in the selection of jurors, they serve an important function within the government and act with its substantial assistance."

III. Voir Dire Inquiry Regarding Facts in a Case

Voir dire inquiry into potential juror bias and prejudice thus is proper to determine whether jurors are disqualified by statute and to seek information that allows counsel to intelligently exercise their peremptory strikes. * * *

Although a juror may be statutorily disqualified because of a bias or prejudice against a type of claim or a general inability to follow the court's instructions regarding the law, this Court has refused to hold that statements that reflect a juror's judgment about the facts of a case as presented, rather than an external unfair bias or prejudice, amount to a disqualifying bias. In *Cortez v. HCCI-San Antonio, Inc.*, 159 S.W.3d 87, 94 (Tex. 2005) an attorney summarized the evidence during voir dire, and then inquired of the jurors whether either party was "starting out ahead." The Court held that such inquiries are improper, and that a trial court should not disqualify a juror based on an answer to an inquiry that seeks "an opinion about the evidence."

Cortez thus adopted the general rule that it is improper to ask prospective jurors what their verdict would be if certain facts were proved. Fair and impartial jurors reach a verdict based on the evidence, and not on bias or prejudice. Voir dire inquiries to jurors should address the latter, not their opinions about the former. *Cortez* involved a general summary of all the evidence, and thus we did not review whether a voir dire question addressed to the weight a juror would give a relevant piece of the evidence could be objectionable. Such an inquiry, however, raises similar concerns.

First, an inquiry about the weight jurors will give relevant evidence should not become a proxy for inquiries into jurors' attitudes, because the former is a determination that falls within their province as jurors. Just as excluding jurors who weigh summarized facts in a particular way infringes upon the right to trial by a fair and impartial jury, so too does excluding jurors who reveal whether they would give specific evidence great or little weight. In both cases, questions that attempt to elicit such information can represent an effort to skew the jury by pre-testing their opinions about relevant evidence. And, when all of the parties to the case engage in such questioning, the effort is aimed at guessing the verdict, not at seating a fair jury.

Second, inquiring whether jurors can be fair after isolating a relevant fact confuses jurors as much as an inquiry that previews all the facts. Lawyers properly instruct jurors that voir dire is not evidence, yet jurors must answer whether they can fairly listen to all of the evidence based only upon the facts that counsel have revealed. In responding, jurors are unable to consider other relevant facts that might alter their responses, rendering their responses unreliable. This confusion may explain in part why jurors' voir dire reactions to the evidence have not been proven to be predictors of jury verdicts: experience tells that, whatever jurors' stated opinions about particular evidence may be at the outset, they can shift upon hearing other evidence.

Third, previewing jurors' votes piecemeal is not consistent with the jurisprudence of our sister court. In *Standefer v. State*, the Court of Criminal Appeals held it improper to ask jurors whether they would presume guilt if one fact was proved and no others. 59 S.W.3d 177, 183 (Tex. Crim. App. 2001) (holding it was improper to ask jurors "[w]ould you presume someone guilty if he or she refused a breath test on their refusal alone?"). * * *

Finally, the Court's decision in *Babcock v. Northwest Memorial Hospital* does not dictate that a trial judge must accept questions that seek to assess jurors' opinions about the weight they will place on particular evidence. In that case, we held that counsel could question jurors about bias or prejudice resulting from a societal influence outside the case—namely, tort reform. In contrast, a question that asks jurors to judge the weight to be given an operative fact will not reveal whether jurors have potential external biases or prejudices that improperly skew their view of case facts.

Statements during voir dire are not evidence, but given its broad scope in Texas civil cases, it is not unusual for jurors to hear the salient facts of the case during the voir dire. If the voir dire includes a preview of the evidence, we hold that a trial court does not abuse its discretion in refusing to allow questions that seek to determine the weight to be given (or not to be given) a particular fact or set of relevant facts. If the trial judge permits questions about the weight jurors would give relevant case facts, then the jurors' responses to such questions are not disqualifying, because while such responses reveal a fact-specific opinion, one cannot conclude they reveal an improper subject-matter bias.

IV. Trial Court Discretion

One of the primary rules of voir dire in Texas civil cases has long been that trial courts have broad discretion in conducting it. * * *

It can be a close question whether a juror's response indicates a prejudice due to personal animus or bias, rather than a fair judgment of the previewed evidence. Similarly, it can be a close question whether a voir dire inquiry focuses on the former or the latter, as the question presented for a ruling in this case reflects. Determining whether jurors' answers assume or ignore the evidence disclosed to them turns on the courtroom context, and perhaps the looks on their faces. So, too, does the import of counsel's questions, and whether as phrased they seek external information or a preview of a potential verdict. The trial judge is in a better position to evaluate the reasonableness of both aspects—the question and the answer.

We observed in *Cortez* that trial judges have discretion to clarify whether a juror's response is the result of confusion, misunderstanding, or mistake. Similarly, the trial judge must have discretion to exclude questions that seek to gauge the weight a juror will place on specific evidence. In *Cortez*, we held improper both (1) a juror's disqualification based on answers that previewed the juror's vote, and (2) the actual questions that sought the same. Depending on the circumstances, a trial judge may choose to hear jurors' responses before deciding whether an inquiry pries into potential prejudices or potential verdicts, but if the question reaches for the latter, a trial court does not abuse its discretion in refusing to allow it. If the trial court allows a question that seeks a juror's view about the weight to give relevant evidence, then the juror's response, without more, is not disqualifying.

Permitting disclosures about the evidence the jury will hear during the case increases the potential for discovering external biases, but inquiries to jurors after doing so should not spill over into attempts to preview the verdict based on the facts as represented to the jurors. Balancing these competing concerns depends on the facts in a case and on the inquiries posited to the jury. The trial judge is in a better position to achieve the proper balance.

V. The Question

The Vasquezes contend the trial court erred in refusing to allow the following inquiry to the jurors:

> THE COURT: What is the type of question you need to ask other than what has already been asked about their own individual use of seat belts or not seat belts?
>
> [PLAINTIFFS' COUNSEL]: Your Honor, I need to know whether or not they would be predisposed regardless of the evidence to—their preconceived notion is that if there is no seat belt in use, no matter what else the evidence is, that they could not be fair and impartial.
>
> THE COURT: And that's the type of question you are asking to ask?
>
> [PLAINTIFFS' COUNSEL]: That's the kind of question I need to ask . . . .

After Hyundai's objection that the question would "pretest these jurors about the facts of this case," the trial judge stated:

> THE COURT: All right. I'm going to sustain the objection. We are not going to go any further into seat belts . . . .

The court of appeals held that the trial court abused its discretion in excluding the inquiry, agreeing with the Vasquezes that the proposed question "clearly focuses on the ability of the jurors to be fair," because, upon learning that Amber was not wearing a seat belt, jurors should not be so biased that they could not consider the remaining evidence in the case. Here, however, the trial court reasonably could have determined that the question seeks to gauge the jurors' verdicts and therefore we disagree with the court of appeals.

* * *

The substance of a question, not its form, determines whether it probes for prejudices or previews a probable verdict. The trial court in this case reasonably could have concluded that the substance of the proposed question did not present a basis for disqualifying a juror for cause, and instead sought to test the weight jurors would place on the relevant fact that Amber was not wearing a seat belt at the time of the accident. Thus, the trial judge did not abuse her discretion in refusing to allow it.

VI. Further Questions

At the conclusion of the general questioning of the panel, the trial judge asked counsel to state the additional questions he sought to ask the jurors about seat belts. The Vasquezes proffered the above question. In sustaining Hyundai's objection, however, the trial judge also ruled: "We are not going to go any further into seat belts." In so ruling, the trial judge reversed an earlier decision to allow further follow up about seat belt usage during the time allotted to counsel to question jurors individually at the bench. In sustaining an objection to an improper voir dire question, a trial court should not foreclose all inquiry about a relevant topic. The Vasquezes' complaint as to this part of the trial court's ruling, however, is not preserved.

A trial court may not foreclose a proper line of questioning, presuming that the actual questions posed are proper. In some instances, an area of inquiry may be proper, but not the particular question asked. In such circumstances, a trial court may exercise its discretion to reject the form of the question. If it is necessary to discuss the facts in the case to probe for potential biases, counsel must frame corresponding inquiries to avoid jury confusion and ensure that the question does not seek to preview the verdict. When the trial court determines that a proffered question's substance is confusing or seeks to elicit a pre-commitment from the jury, counsel should propose a different question or specific area of inquiry to preserve error on the desired line of inquiry; absent such an effort, the trial court is not required to formulate the question.

Thus, to preserve a complaint that a trial court improperly restricted voir dire, a party must timely alert the trial court as to the specific manner in which it intends to pursue the inquiry. Such a requirement provides the trial court with an opportunity to cure any error, obviating the need for later appellate review, and further allows an appellate court to examine the trial court's decision in context to determine whether error exists, and if so, whether harm resulted. In *Babcock*, we held that litigants need not present a list of each intended voir dire question, but parties must nonetheless "adequately apprise[ ] the trial court of the nature of their inquiry." A timely, specific presentation to the trial court of the manner of an inquiry is important because it is difficult to evaluate after a trial whether the trial court's denial of an inquiry caused a biased juror to be seated on the jury or to evaluate what additional information a party could have adduced for the exercise of peremptory strikes. Thus, the Court traditionally has adhered strictly to the principle that voir dire objections must be timely and plainly presented.

* * *

The Texas Constitution guarantees a trial by a fair and impartial jury, and our courts use voir dire to achieve that goal. Voir dire inquiries that explore external biases and unfair prejudices further the effort, but those that test jurors' possible verdicts based on case-specific relevant evidence detract from it. The distinction between the two in some cases is a fine one. Thus, we vest trial judges with the discretion to decide whether an inquiry constitutes the former or the latter; as appellate courts, we should defer to their judgment. We hold that the trial court did not abuse its discretion. We therefore reverse the judgment of the court of appeals and remand the case to that court to consider the Vasquezes' remaining issues on appeal.

JUSTICE WAINWRIGHT filed a dissenting opinion, in which JUSTICE JOHNSON joined. [omitted].

JUSTICE MEDINA, joined by JUSTICE WAINWRIGHT and JUSTICE JOHNSON, dissenting.

We can all agree that (1) litigants are entitled to fair and impartial jurors, (2) voir dire should not be used as an exercise to preview the verdict, and (3) trial courts must necessarily have broad discretion when conducting voir dire. That said, I do not agree that a trial court can totally divorce the legitimate search for bias and prejudice during voir dire from all material facts in the case. I also disagree with the Court's statement of the issue in this case because this case is not simply about the weight prospective jurors may attach to certain evidence but whether such jurors can follow their oath and the court's instructions. I believe that the issue is whether the trial court abused its discretion when it cut off questioning about seat belts; specifically questions about whether members of the venire would fairly consider all the evidence in the product liability and wrongful death suit, knowing that the decedent was not wearing her seat belt at the time of the accident.

The trial court here summarily dismissed two jury panels after approximately 60% of the first panel, and 35% of the second, initially indicated that they would not listen to any other evidence in the case upon learning that Amber was not wearing a seat belt at the time of the accident. Before beginning a third voir dire, the trial court devised a new format for questioning the panel, requiring that specific questions about seat belt attitudes be asked only during individual questioning of prospective jurors, and not to the panel as a whole, as had been done previously. When the time came to ask these questions individually, however, the trial court abandoned its plan, forbidding any further questions about seat belts. The Court agrees that this was error, but concludes that the error was not appropriately preserved for our review. I disagree and therefore respectfully dissent.

Notes

1. In *McCoy v. Wal-Mart Stores, Inc.*, 59 S.W.3d 793, (Tex. Civ.—Texarkana 2002, no pet.) the court discussed court limitations on lawyers voir dire as follows:

> Attorneys have a duty to appropriately budget their time for voir dire questioning within the reasonable limits set by the trial court. *Whitaker v. State*, 653 S.W.2d 781, 781 (Tex.Crim.App.1983); *Torres*, 4 S.W.3d at 836; *Thacker v. State*, 889 S.W.2d 380, 391 (Tex.App.—Houston [14th Dist.] 1994, pet. ref'd). . . .
>
> * * *
>
> We recognize that voir dire questioning is possibly the most important part of any jury trial and that the parties in any given case should be afforded full opportunity to examine the jury panel with no more interference from the trial court than necessary. We also recognize that not all lawyers approach voir dire questioning the same way, nor should they. Our system is capable of accommodating a variety of strategies in selecting a jury, and the innovative advocate should not be punished for not doing it the same way an opponent does, or even the same way the trial court would. However, counsel should always be realistic and give due respect to the court, opposing counsel, the venire members, and other litigants. With our dockets over-burdened and the courts constantly pressured to keep the cases moving, the trial courts must be given considerable latitude in controlling voir dire examinations, so that the time allotted for this important part of the trial is put to its best use. Voir dire questioning is typically done while other parties and their counsel wait their turn. In a rural jurisdiction, such as the one where this case was tried, it is not uncommon for a single jury panel to sit through the voir dire of multiple cases in a single day.
>
> We recognize that justice should never be sacrificed for the sake of expediency. The parameters set for voir dire questioning should always be fair and reasonable, and take into consideration the complexity and uniqueness of each case. These boundaries should also be flexible, subject to exceptions as justice and the circumstances require.
>
> Because voir dire questioning is such an important part of the proceeding, counsel should plan for it well in advance and be prepared to elicit from the venire members all necessary information within the parameters set by the court. The prudent lawyer will recognize that this may require some adjustment of the voir dire questioning from what that lawyer would prefer to what must be done within the time allotted.
>
> In this case, it appears there was an initial misunderstanding on the part of McCoy's counsel as to the procedure to be followed by the trial court in ruling on challenges for cause. However, ten minutes into his voir dire questioning, the trial court warned that he would not be able to complete his questioning in the thirty minutes allotted if he persisted in the approach he was taking. Counsel should have heeded the trial court's warning and adjusted his voir dire examination to accommodate the court's parameters. Had he done so, he could have asked the questions that his own unfortunate choice precluded him from asking. This was not a complex case, nor was it so unique as to require extraordinary consideration in voir dire questioning. Defense counsel had no difficulty complying with the thirty minutes allotted. We perceive no reason why McCoy's counsel could not also comply.

2. *In the Interest of M.S.*, 115 S.W.3d 534 (Tex. 2003): In this action to terminate parental rights, Strickland's attorney's failed to ensure that a stenographic record was made for portions of her trial—voir dire, the jury charge conference, and closing argument. TEX. R. APP. P. 13.1 requires the presence of a court reporter, "unless excused by agreement of the parties." The record here does not indicate that the parties agreed to the absence of the court reporter, but neither does Strickland contend that either party objected to the court report-

er's absence. ***Held:*** Counsel's failure to ensure recording of voir dire, the charge conference, and closing arguments, does not constitute ineffective assistance of counsel, without a showing of harm, and Strickland has not shown that she was harmed by the lack of a complete record. Therefore counsel's failure, in this case, to ensure that the entire proceedings were recorded, does not constitute ineffective assistance of counsel.

3. *Murff v. Pass*, 249 S.W.3d 407 (Tex. 2008): In this health care liability case, following a confusing line of questioning about the burden of proof, a venireperson stated that he would hold the plaintiff to a clear and convincing standard of proof. Additional venirepersons raised their hands, indicating that they agreed. Believing that the panel members were confused, and after informing the venire of the proper standard, the trial court refused to disqualify these venirepersons. The court of appeals held that the venirepersons were disqualified as a matter of law, and reversed and remanded the case for a new trial. ***Held:*** Reversed and rendered, in accordance with the jury verdict. The trial court did not abuse its discretion in refusing to disqualify the challenged jurors. A person is disqualified from serving on a jury if the person has a bias or prejudice in favor of or against a party or claim, or if the person is unable or unwilling to follow the trial court's instructions. Such bias, prejudice, or inability to follow the court's instructions may not be discernible from a single statement or response to a general question. Statements of partiality may be the result of inappropriate leading questions, confusion, misunderstanding, ignorance of the law, or merely loose words spoken in warm debate, and do not necessarily establish disqualification. When a venireperson expresses bias or confusion, the trial court has the discretion to stop the line of questioning in order to clarify that person's response. Trial judges, because they are in the best position to evaluate the sincerity and attitude of individual panel members, are given wide latitude in both conducting voir dire proceedings, and in determining whether a panel member is impermissibly partial. The reviewing court must consider the entire examination in reviewing whether a trial court abused its discretion in deciding that a juror was or was not disqualified.

4. **Tex. Gov't Code** § 62.0132. Written Jury Summons Questionnaire.

(a) The Office of Court Administration of the Texas Judicial System shall develop and maintain a questionnaire to accompany a written jury summons.

(b) A written jury summons must include:

(1) a copy of the questionnaire developed under this section; or

(2) the electronic address of the court's Internet website from which the questionnaire developed under this section may be easily printed.

(c) The questionnaire must require a person to provide biographical and demographic information that is relevant to service as a jury member, including the person's:

(1) name, sex, race, and age;

(2) residence address and mailing address;

(3) education level, occupation, and place of employment;

(4) marital status and the name, occupation, and place of employment of the person's spouse; and

(5) citizenship status and county of residence.

(d) Except as provided by this subsection, a person who has received a written jury summons shall complete and submit a jury summons questionnaire when the person reports for jury duty. If the district and criminal district judges of a county adopt a plan for an electronic jury selection method under Section 62.011, the county may allow a person to complete and submit a jury summons questionnaire on the court's Internet website as authorized under Section 62.0111(b)(5).

(e) In developing and maintaining the questionnaire required by this section, the Office of Court Administration of the Texas Judicial System shall solicit and consider the opinions of the members of the judiciary, district clerks, and attorneys.

(f) Except as provided by Subsection (g), information contained in a completed questionnaire is confidential and is not subject to Chapter 552.

(g) The information contained in a completed questionnaire may be disclosed to:

(1) a judge assigned to hear a cause of action in which the respondent to the questionnaire is a potential juror;

(2) court personnel;

(3) a litigant and a litigant's attorney in a cause of action in which the respondent to the questionnaire is a potential juror; and

(4) other than information provided that is related to Section 62.102(8) or (9), the voter registrar of a county in connection with any matter of voter registration or the administration of elections.

(h) The questionnaire must notify a person that if the person states that the person is not a citizen, the person will no longer be eligible to vote if the person fails to provide proof of citizenship.

CARR
v.
SMITH

22 S.W.3d 128
(Tex. App.—Fort Worth 2000, review denied)

Sue Walker, Law Office of Sue Walker, Michael T. Watson, Watson & Parker, P.C., Fort Worth, for appellant.

Jordan M. Parker, Evelyn R. Leopold, Cantey & Hanger, L.L.P., Fort Worth, for appellee.

TERRIE LIVINGSTON, JUSTICE.

Marion and Thomas Carr, appellants, sued Gregory H. Smith, D.O. and Scott Allen, M.D. for medical malpractice. The only issues appellants present for review after their two-week jury trial relate to the propriety of the jury shuffle granted by the trial court on Allen's motion. We reverse.

Procedural Background

About a month before trial, one of the defendants, Scott Allen, M.D., filed a motion to use a confidential juror questionnaire form during voir dire. The proposed questionnaire contained 54 questions and included specific questions regarding juror personal information, education, employment, and beliefs. It also included inquiries into juror history or involvement with litigation and medical treatment. Appellants filed a response to Allen's motion indicating their approval of the submission of the 54 questions so long as the questionnaire included an additional nine questions they proposed. Although there is no order showing the court granted Allen's motion, the questionnaire, with all 63 questions, was submitted to the 60 panel members to fill out while they were in the central jury room.

The panel members were segregated in the central jury room, by jury numbers one through 60. Once segregated, they were sworn and all counsel had an opportunity to view the panel members in their seated order. Counsel for appellants and paralegal for appellee viewed the panel. All counsel received the standard jury information cards. The panel members filled out the questionnaires and all counsel received copies to review overnight before starting trial the next day. The next morning Allen's counsel requested a rule 223 jury shuffle. Appellants objected. They argued that the request came too late because voir dire had already begun when all counsel received and had the opportunity to review the extensive juror questionnaire. *See* TEX. R. CIV. P. 23. The court overruled their objection and shuffled the jury. Sometime during the hotly contested trial, appellants non-suited Allen. The jury ultimately returned a verdict in favor of Smith, the appellee. Appellants' subsequent motion for mistrial was denied, and their motion for new trial claiming the trial court erred by granting Allen's request for a jury shuffle was overruled by operation of law.

* * *

When Does Voir Dire Begin?

The answer to this question is controlled by the application and interpretation of rule 223 of the Texas Rules of Civil Procedure. That rule states:

> [T]he trial judge . . . upon the demand *prior to voir dire examination by any party or attorney in the case* . . . shall cause the names of all members of such assigned jury panel . . . to be . . . shuffled . . . .

TEX. R. CIV. P. 223 (emphasis added). Here, the trial court overruled appellants' objection and granted Allen's shuffle. Apparently, counsel for appellee made no objection and, although present at the hearing on the objection, made no comments and voiced no complaints. At the time Allen requested the shuffle, the venire panel had been sworn and segregated in the jury pool room, had completed juror information cards, and had turned in their responses to the questionnaire. Appellants argue the dissemination and subsequent review of the fact-specific questionnaire constitute the beginning of voir dire whereas appellee contends voir dire does not commence until the venire panel is brought into the court where they will be serving, is viewed there by counsel, and verbal questioning by counsel and the court has begun. Appellee also argues that the use of juror information cards and questionnaires that provide basic juror information does not constitute the beginning of voir dire. [*Id.*]

* * *

Here, . . . we are dealing with a detailed thirteen-page questionnaire of 63 questions. And these questions go far beyond name, rank, and serial number. For example, question 30 asks each juror whether the juror or any family member has had any training or education in the legal field, the medical field, or specifically any X-Ray, MRI or CT training. Question 35 directs the jurors to disclose whether they have, or any family member has had, any of the back or disk surgeries listed. While all these questions are appropriate, they are detailed, specially-tailored inquiries into the jurors' life experiences and prejudices directly related to the underlying claim. Because of these distinctions and because Garza is a criminal case dealing with a criminal statute, we are not bound by it and do not apply it to this case. Instead, we look to civil precedent to determine the propriety of a granted jury shuffle, whether harm need be shown, and what remedy, if any, may be appropriate.

As appellants note, there is no constitutional or fundamental right to a jury shuffle, it being a creature of statutory and common law. But, appellants continue, the right to trial by jury is a fundamental and constitutional right. *See* U.S. CONST. amend VII; TEX. CONST. art. I, § 15. And, they say this right assumes the right to a fair and impartial jury that has been selected in accord with the procedural rules and safeguards imposed by the legislature. *See Jackson v. Golden Eagle Archery, Inc.*, 974 S.W.2d 952, 958 (Tex.App.—Beaumont 1998, pet. granted). Appellants argue that to allow a jury to proceed after an untimely shuffle has been granted destroys the randomness inherent in the original jury panel list and of the renumbered list after a timely requested shuffle. We agree.

To grant a shuffle after parties and counsel have had the opportunity to review substantive responses based upon written questions, as opposed to oral questions in the courtroom, makes no sense. The distinction between oral and written questioning is virtually meaningless, especially where each party has already had the opportunity to view the panel. The distinction between the type of information solicited in a standard jury form card and that of a detailed, case specific questionnaire should be the focus of the inquiry, not whether the questions are asked verbally or in writing. After the venire panel has been sworn and once substantive inquiry begins and responses have been observed or made available to the parties or their counsel, whether verbally or in writing, voir dire has begun. Again, the critical focus is on whether substantive inquiry has begun with case specific questions, not necessarily the number of questions or who drafted them, as the dissent erroneously states. We therefore hold the trial court erred when it granted Allen's untimely demand for a shuffle. We sustain appellants' first and second issues and overrule appellee's first reply issue.

* * *

Conclusion

Because we have determined that appellants properly preserved their objection to the shuffle, the shuffle was untimely granted, and the trial court should have either granted appellants' motion for mistrial or new trial, we reverse the judgment of the trial court and remand the case to the trial court for a new trial.

c. *Challenges for Cause*

Rule 228. "Challenge for Cause" Defined

A challenge for cause is an objection made to a juror, alleging some fact which by law disqualifies him to serve as a juror in the case or in any case, or which in the opinion of the court, renders him an unfit person to sit on the jury. Upon such challenge the examination is not confined to the answers of the juror, but other evidence may be heard for or against the challenge.

Rule 229. Challenge for Cause

When twenty-four or more jurors, if in the district court, or twelve or more, if in the county court, are drawn, and the lists of their names delivered to the parties, if either party desires to challenge any juror for cause, the challenge shall then be made. The name of a juror challenged and set aside for cause shall be erased from such lists.

Notes

1. Section 62.105 of the Texas Government Code provides:

A person is disqualified to serve as a petit juror in a particular case if he:

(1) is a witness in the case;

(2) is interested, directly or indirectly, in the subject matter of the case;

(3) is related by consanguinity or affinity within the third degree, as determined under Article 5996h, Revised Statutes, to a party in the case;

(4) has a bias or prejudice in favor of or against a party in the case; or

(5) has served as a petit juror in a former trial of the same case or in another case involving the same questions of fact.

2. The Supreme Court has given the lower courts some assistance in determining when bias or prejudice exists. It has defined the terms in the following language:

> Bias, in its usual meaning, is an inclination toward one side of an issue rather than to the other, but to disqualify, it must appear that the state of mind of the juror leads to the natural inference that he will not or did not act with impartiality. Prejudice is more easily defined for it means prejudgment, and consequently embraces bias; the converse is not true.

Compton v. Henrie, 364 S.W.2d 179, 182 (Tex. 1963).

3. It should be noted that the harmless error rule is relaxed in the case of errors by the trial court in determining challenges for cause. Our system of jury selection is designed to provide a jury composed of persons who are not biased or prejudiced. The object is an impartial jury. However, the refusal of the trial court to excuse an unqualified juror does not necessarily constitute reversible error. *See Hallett v. Houston Northwest Medical Center*, 689 S.W.2d 888 (Tex. 1985). The *Hallett* court noted:

> [H]arm occurs only if the party uses all of his peremptory challenges and is . . . prevented from striking other objectionable jurors from the list because he has no additional peremptory challenges. It is at this point that any harmful error occurs, i.e., when the court is made aware that objectionable jurors will be chosen. Thus, it is incumbent upon the complaining party to inform the trial court at that time of the error. Once informed, the court is able to determine if the party was in fact forced to take objectionable jurors.

Id. at 890.

4. Rev. Civ. Stat. Art 5996h was amended in 1991 to adopt the civil law method for determination of consanguinity under the nepotism rules. That statute has since been incorporated into TEX. GOV'T CODE §§ 573.021-.025. The civil law method reckons kinship by degree of removal. The affected statutes are: CIVIL PRAC & REM CODE § 72.001 (limited liability for injury to a relative of the second degree in an auto accident); GOVT. CODE § 62.105 (disqualification of petit juror for relation within the 3rd degree to a party); GOVT. CODE § 82.066 (an attorney may not appear in a case if related in the 1st degree to a judge); CODE CRIM. PROC § 30.01 (disqualification of judge within 3rd degree of relation to a party); CODE CRIM. PROC § 30.16 (challenge for cause allowed for a juror related within 3rd degree of a party to the case).

Consanguinity. Two persons are related by consanguinity if one is a descendent of the other or if they share a common ancestor. An adopted child is the same as a natural child for this purpose.

Individuals within the 3rd degree of consanguinity are:

1) parent or child (relatives in the 1st degree);

2) brother, sister, grandparent, or grandchild (relatives in the second degree);

3) great-grandparent, great-grandchild, aunt who is sister of a parent of the individual, uncle who is a brother of a parent of the individual, nephew who is a child of a brother or sister of the individual, or niece who is a child of a brother or sister of the individual (relatives in the third degree).

Affinity. Two persons are related by affinity if they are married or if their spouse is related by consanguinity to the other person. Divorce or death terminates the relationships by affinity unless there is a child of the marriage living, then it continues.

Two individuals are related by affinity if

a) they are married to each other;

b) the spouse of one of the individuals is related by consanguinity to the other individual.

Death or divorce ends relationships by affinity created by that marriage unless a child of that marriage is living, in which case the marriage is considered to continue as long as a child of that marriage lives.

BROWN
v.
PITTSBURGH CORNING CORPORATION

909 S.W.2d 101
(Tex. App—Houston [14th Dist] 1995, writ denied)

Richard N. Countiss, Houston, for appellants.
David L. Tolin, Michael Rose, Lyn Stevens, Houston, for appellee.

ANDERSON, JUSTICE.

This is an asbestos case. Appellants, collectively referred to as the "Workers," filed suit against Pittsburgh Corning Corporation to recover damages for personal injury and death caused by exposure to asbestos products manufactured by the corporation. A jury failed to find the company's products were defective or that the company was negligent. Consistent with that verdict, the trial court entered a take-nothing judgment. The Workers bring one point of error. They contend that jury panelist Charles Lee Young, whom they challenged for cause, was disqualified as a matter of law from serving on the jury, and that the trial court committed error by overruling their challenge to panelist Young. They further contend that error forced them to exercise a peremptory challenge on Young, which prevented them from striking one of two other jurors who were objectionable to the Workers, and those two jurors were seated on the panel. Pittsburgh Corning contends the Workers failed to properly preserve error on the disqualification issue in accordance with *Hallett v. Houston Northwest Medical Ctr.*, 689 S.W.2d 888, 890 (Tex. 1985), thus waiving error by the trial court in overruling the challenge to panelist Young. We agree, and affirm the judgment of the trial court.

In order to preserve error where the trial court overrules a challenge for cause to a prospective juror, a party must give notice to the trial court of two things prior to exercising any peremptory challenges: (1) the party must inform the trial court that it will exhaust all peremptory challenges; and (2), the party must inform the trial court that after exercising all its peremptory challenges, specific objectionable jurors will remain on the jury list.[3] *Hallett*, 689 S.W.2d at 890. The Texas Supreme Court specifically stated "[a] complaining party waives any error by not timely bringing such error to the attention of the trial court prior to making his peremptory chal-

[3] The notification required by *Hallett* has been simplified as follows: a party must show that because it has used its peremptory challenges on jurors A and B who should have been struck for cause, the peremptory challenges used on jurors A and B are no longer available to strike jurors Y and Z whom the party wanted to strike and would have been able to strike had the court properly struck jurors A and B for cause. Sullemon v. U.S. Fidelity and Guar. *Co.*, 734 S.W.2d 10, 13 (Tex. App.—Dallas 1987, no writ). While this rule is simple to state, it is strictly applied on appeal. *In* White v. Dennison, 752 S.W.2d 714, 719 (Tex. App.—Dallas 1988, writ denied) the appellant failed to advise the trial court of specific objectionable jurors who would remain on the jury list after he exercised his peremptory challenges. Because White notified the trial court of only one of the two things required by *Hallett* to preserve trial court error, the court held White waived any error by the trial court in its refusal to discharge the challenged juror.

lenges." *Id.* at 890. Three recent courts of appeals have held that a party exercises its peremptory challenges when it delivers the list of challenges to the court. *Ortiz v. Ford Motor Credit Co.*, 859 S.W.2d 73, 75 (Tex. App.—Corpus Christi 1993, writ denied); *Lopez v. Southern Pacific Transp. Co.*, 847 S.W.2d 330, 333 (Tex. App.—El Paso 1993, no writ); *Beavers v. Northrop Worldwide Aircraft*, 821 S.W.2d 669, 681 (Tex. App.—Amarillo 1991, writ denied). The entire focus of an analysis of an asserted trial court error on appeal regarding the overruling of a challenge for cause to a prospective juror is the timing of appellant's delivery of the *Hallett* notice to the trial court versus the exercise of appellant's peremptory challenges.

Whether the Workers gave the trial court the *Hallett* notice regarding prospective juror Young before exercising their peremptory strike is intensely debated by the parties in this cause. The record shows the following events transpired at trial:

> [Counsel has just finished questioning the final prospective juror.]
>
> THE COURT: Sir, would you step outside and come back in with the rest of the jurors when I call everyone back in?
>
> A PROSPECTIVE JUROR: Sure, your honor.
>
> THE COURT: Thank you. And, Deputy Martel, if you'd tell the jurors that we're running about fifteen minutes behind.
>
> DEPUTY MARTEL: Yes, sir.
>
> THE COURT: Off the—do you have anything?
>
> MR. WILLIAMS [COUNSEL FOR PLAINTIFFS/APPELLANTS]: No motion, Judge.
>
> THE COURT: In that case, off the record.
>
> (Whereupon, a brief recess was taken after which the following proceedings were had out of the presence and hearing of the venire panel.)
>
> MR. WILLIAMS: Judge, on behalf of all the Plaintiffs, I need to point out that because of the Court's failure to grant our Motion to Excuse for Cause juror number eight, Mr. Duessel and juror number 17, Mr. Young, that we were forced then to take two objections of both jurors, being juror we had to use our preemptory [sic] strikes on number eight and 17, and were not then allowed preemptory [sic] strikes to use on juror number nine, Mr. Paternuster, who is objectionable because he's an IRS agent which we find those people are objectionable because of their views towards damages. And also we were prevented from striking juror number 31, Mr. Schorre, S-c-h-o-r-r-e. Mr. Schorre is objectionable because he works for a large corporation, Tenneco, and because he's a Lutheran, which affects the views toward damages and because of Mr.—because working for large corporations, he has more visibility or more in common with the large corporation than he would with our working Plaintiffs. Thank you, your honor.
>
> THE COURT: All right. With due respect, I'm sorry—
>
> MR. TOLIN [DEFENSE COUNSEL]: Excuse me, Your Honor, my notes reflect that the requests to have number eight examined before the Court were withdrawn and that Mr. Williams did not register a Motion to Strike for Cause as to juror number eight. And if I'm correct about that, then I except to any record made on the basis of number eight.
>
> MR. WILLIAMS: You may be right.
>
> THE COURT: You are correct. He did withdraw the request and didn't call Mr. Duessel up as for challenge for cause. With due respect, the motions—your motion, as I understand it, is denied. I do have a problem though. You marked somewhere between 36 and 37 as your persons. You're objecting to 36 or 37.
>
> MR. WILLIAMS: No, your Honor. That is—I've marked that as—that's the end of where we were going.
>
> THE COURT: I just wanted to make sure I knew how to count.
>
> MR. WILLIAMS: My six are written at the bottom. I think I did six strikes.

THE COURT: Thank you very much.

[At this point, the court took care of another motion. That discussion is omitted.]

THE COURT: Off the record for just a moment.

(Whereupon, a discussion was held off the record and the following proceedings were had in the presence and hearing of the venire panel.)

THE COURT: Counsel, please be seated. Before we go on the record.

(Whereupon, a discussion was held off the record.)

THE COURT: Now, ladies and gentlemen . . . [the court goes on to talk to the jury about how some will be selected and some will not; the jury list is then read and the jurors selected.]

The Workers' contend it is obvious from the above recitation counsel was holding and reading from his list when he informed the trial court of the objectionable jurors and the strikes he had to use. He called the various jurors by name and list number. The Workers suggest this is not information he would have memorized, and thus it is a reasonable inference from the record that he was reading from his strike list.

Pittsburgh Corning responds by arguing the italicized text portions above indicate the plaintiff's list of peremptory challenges had been delivered to the court prior to any attempt to preserve error. They suggest the more compelling inference is counsel was referring to his notes at the time, because the trial judge could not have asked about markings on the strike list if the list had not been tendered to the court. Moreover, Pittsburgh Corning contends Mr. Williams would not have responded, "I think I did six strikes," if he were holding the list. They posit the only permissible inference is the plaintiff's strike list was tendered during or immediately following the brief recess taken by the trial court at the conclusion of the voir dire examination. However, the record plainly states, ". . . a brief recess was taken after which the following proceedings were had out of the presence and hearing of the venire panel." It does not say the peremptory strike lists were tendered at that time.

It would be inappropriate for this court to draw inferences from the record as to when the peremptory strike lists were tendered to the trial court. The exact moment is not pinpointed in the record. TEX. R. APP. P. 50(d) places the burden on the appellant, or other party seeking review, to see that a sufficient record is presented to show error requiring reversal.

In *Beavers*, the Amarillo Court of Appeals, in an opinion by Judge Boyd, determined that the record demonstrated appellants had exercised their strikes prior to attempting to preserve error regarding the court's overruling of two challenges for cause, which sequence fails the *Hallett* test. Thus, the court held that, under Rule 50(d), no error was preserved for appellate review. However, especially persuasive for our decision is the court's alternative determination in *Beavers* that "Even if the record could not be construed to indicate when the list was delivered, no error has been preserved." (emphasis added). 821 S.W.2d at 681. That is precisely the situation in the case sub judice.

Similarly, in *Born v. Virginia City Dance Hall & Saloon*, 857 S.W.2d 951, 955 (Tex. App.—Houston [14th Dist.] 1993, writ denied), this court applied Rule 50(d) and held that because appellants had failed to bring forward a record demonstrating where appellants advised the trial court that its refusal to strike disqualified jurors forced appellants to take objectionable jurors after using all of their peremptory challenges, appellants failed to preserve the complaint for appeal.

We read *Beavers* and *Born* as clear guides for our decision. Under Rule 50(d), when the record on appeal does not reveal that the *Hallett* notice was timely given, nothing is preserved for review. A party cannot wait until the trial is finished, then seek to reverse an unfavorable verdict by complaining of an error which the trial court could have corrected had it been timely informed of the error. *Hallett*, 689 S.W.2d at 890. In order to preserve error a timely, specific objection must be made. TEX. R. APP. P. 52(a). A "timely" objection is one interposed at a point in the proceedings which gives the trial court the opportunity to cure any alleged error. *Beall v. Ditmore*, 867 S.W.2d 791, 795 (Tex. App.—El Paso 1993, writ denied). That point in time cannot be definitively determined from the record before this court.

We overrule appellant's single point of error and affirm the judgment of the trial court.

SEARS, J., dissenting.
HUDSON, J., concurring.

Notes

1. *Shepherd v. Ledford* consolidated with *Transamerica Natural Gas Corporation v. Fuentes* (Nos. 96-0994 & No. 96-1243 [1 opinion]), 962 S.W.2d 28 (Tex. 1998). A prospective juror who admits bias or prejudice is disqualified to serve as a juror. When a trial court refuses to disqualify a juror for bias or prejudice, the complaining party must show that the error was harmful. To do this, the party, before exercising its peremptory challenges, must advise the trial court that the court's denial of the challenges for cause would force the party to exhaust its peremptory challenges and, that after exercising its peremptory challenges, specific objectionable jurors would still remain on the panel.

2. Judges, as well as jurors may be accused of bias. Consider *Dow Chemical Company v. Francis,* 46 S.W.3d 284 (Tex. 2001): "Judicial rulings alone almost never constitute a valid basis for a bias or partiality motion," and opinions the judge forms during a trial do not necessitate recusal "unless they display a deep-seated favoritism or antagonism that would make fair judgment impossible. Thus, judicial remarks during the course of a trial that are critical or disapproving of, or even hostile to, counsel, the parties, or their cases, ordinarily do not support a bias or partiality challenge." *Liteky v. United States*, 510 U.S. 540, 555 (1994); *see also, e.g., Matassarin v. Lynch*, 174 F.3d 549, 571 (5th Cir. 1999); *Hollywood Fantasy Corp. v. Gabor*, 151 F.3d 203, 216 n.6 (5th Cir. 1998); *United States v. Landerman*, 109 F.3d 1053, 1066 (5th Cir. 1997). Further, "[n]ot establishing bias or partiality . . . are expressions of impatience, dissatisfaction, annoyance, and even anger . . . . A judge's ordinary efforts at courtroom administration—even a stern and short-tempered judge's ordinary efforts at courtroom administration—remain immune." *Liteky*, 510 U.S. at 555-56. In short, a trial court has the inherent power to control the disposition of cases "with economy of time and effort for itself, for counsel, and for litigants." *Landis v. North Am. Co.*, 299 U.S. 248, 254 (1936).

3. *State v. Wilemon,* 393 S.W.2d 816 (Tex. 1965): To preserve error, an objection to a trial court's alleged improper conduct or comment must be made when it occurs, unless the conduct or comment cannot be rendered harmless by proper instruction.

4. *Murff v. Pass*, 249 S.W.3d 407 (Tex. 2008): In this health care liability case, following a confusing line of questioning about the burden of proof, a venireperson stated that he would hold the plaintiff to a clear and convincing standard of proof. Additional venirepersons raised their hands, indicating that they agreed. Believing that the panel members were confused, and after informing the venire of the proper standard, the trial court refused to disqualify these venirepersons. The court of appeals held that the venirepersons were disqualified as a matter of law, and reversed and remanded the case for a new trial. Held: Reversed and rendered, in accordance with the jury verdict. The trial court did not abuse its discretion in refusing to disqualify the challenged jurors. A person is disqualified from serving on a jury if the person has a bias or prejudice in favor of or against a party or claim, or if the person is unable or unwilling to follow the trial court's instructions. Such bias, prejudice, or inability to follow the court's instructions may not be discernible from a single statement or response to a general question. Statements of partiality may be the result of inappropriate leading questions, confusion, misunderstanding, ignorance of the law, or merely loose words spoken in warm debate, and do not necessarily establish disqualification. When a venireperson expresses bias or confusion, the trial court has the discretion to stop the line of questioning in order to clarify that person's response. Trial judges, because they are in the best position to evaluate the sincerity and attitude of individual panel members, are given wide latitude in both conducting voir dire proceedings, and in determining whether a panel member is impermissibly partial. The reviewing court must consider the entire examination in reviewing whether a trial court abused its discretion in deciding that a juror was or was not disqualified.

d. *Peremptory Challenges*

Rule 233. Number of Peremptory Challenges

Except as provided below, each party to a civil action is entitled to six peremptory challenges in a case tried in the district court, and to three in the county court.

Alignment of the Parties. In multiple party cases, it shall be the duty of the trial judge to decide whether any of the litigants aligned on the same side of the docket are antagonistic with respect to any issue to be submitted to the jury, before the exercise of peremptory challenges.

Definition of Side. The term "side" as used in this rule is not synonymous with "party," "litigant," or "person." Rather, "side" means one or more litigants who have common interests on the matters with which the jury is concerned.

Motion to Equalize. In multiple party cases, upon motion of any litigant made prior to the exercise of peremptory challenges, it shall be the duty of the trial judge to equalize the number of peremptory challenges so that no litigant or side is given unfair advantage as a result of the alignment of the litigants and the award of peremptory challenges to each litigant or side. In determining how the challenges should be allocated the court shall consider any matter brought to the attention of the trial judge concerning the ends of justice and the elimination of an unfair advantage.

Notes

1. Peremptory challenges are a mechanism by which parties to a lawsuit are permitted to strike a certain number of prospective jurors from the jury panel without showing cause.

2. TEX. R. CIV. P. 233. "Except as provided below, each party to a civil action is entitled to *six* peremptory challenges in a case tried in the district court, and to *three* in the county court."

3. Rule 233 also provides for the alignment of parties to determine whether litigants upon the same "side" of the docket are antagonistic with respect to any issue to be submitted to the jury. The term "side" means one or more litigants who have common interests on the matters with which the jury is concerned.

4. In multiple party cases, upon motion of any litigant made prior to the exercise of peremptory challenges, it shall be the duty of the trial judge to equalize the number of peremptory challenges so that no litigant or side is given unfair advantage as a result of the alignment of the litigants and the award of peremptory challenges to each litigant or side.

5. To complain on appeal of improper apportionment of strikes, the complaining party must have made a motion to equalize. However, it is not necessary to identify an unacceptable jury that the party is forced to take (as it is when a challenge for cause is sustained).

6. *King v Maldonado,* 552 S.W.2d 940 (Tex. Civ. App.—Corpus Christi 1977, n.r.e.). Within reasonable limits, the trial judge has discretion to allocate different numbers to different parties. Mathematical equality is not required. Equalization means an allocation so that no party is given an unequal advantage because of the number of peremptory challenges allowed that party.

7. *Patterson Dental Co. v Dunn,* 592 S.W.2d 914 (Tex. 1979). Proportionalizing the strikes may be accomplished by increasing the number allotted a sole party on one side, by decreasing the number allotted the multiple parties on the other side, or by both. The question of whether antagonism exists is determined prior to the exercise of the strikes by the parties. To make the determination of whether the trial was materially unfair, the entire record must be examined, and the presence of error is to be viewed from the perspective of the trial judge as of the time he makes his determination. However, when the trial is contested and the evidence is sharply conflicting, the error results in a materially unfair trial without showing more.

GARCIA
v.
CENTRAL POWER & LIGHT CO.

704 S.W.2d 734
(Tex. 1986)

Dan Pozza, Pasqual & Pozza, San Antonio, for petitioners.

Darrell L. Barger, Hunt, Hermansen, McKibben & Barger, Ronald B. Brin, Brin & Brin, Richard E. Flint, Richard E. Flint, P.C., Corpus Christi, Gay C. Brinson, Jr., Vinson & Elkins, Houston, Cecil D. Redford, Corpus Christi, for respondents.

HILL, CHIEF JUSTICE.

This is a wrongful death suit brought by the surviving beneficiaries of David Garcia for actual damages against Sargent & Lundy, Mid-West Conveyor, Inc., and H.B. Zachry Company and for exemplary damages against Central Power & Light Company. After a trial to a jury, a take-nothing judgment was rendered against the Garcias. In their sole issue on appeal, the Garcias argued the trial court's allowance of peremptory challenges was erroneous. The court of appeals disagreed and affirmed the trial court's judgment. 703 S.W.2d 696. We reverse the judgments of the courts below and remand this cause for trial.

David Garcia was employed by CP & L as a helper in the coal-handling section of the Coleto Creek Power Station in Goliad County, Texas. On February 5, 1982, Garcia was assigned to work on a bulldozer in the area of the coal reclaim pile. His job was to bulldoze coal toward the center of the reclaim pile so that the coal would fall down the feeder grates onto an underground conveyor belt that carried the coal to the plant for fuel. Garcia was bulldozing near the reclaim pile when he called the control room and stated that he saw something on the "reclaim." Garcia then apparently got off his bulldozer and entered the cut out place in the coal pile. His body was subsequently found buried in the coal pile, and he died shortly thereafter.

The Garcias filed suit against CP & L alleging gross negligence because of its alleged failure to provide a safe working place for its employees. The Garcias also brought suit for joint and several liability against Sargent & Lundy (the design engineer of the power station), Mid-West (the supplier of the power station's coal-handling conveyor system), and Zachry (the general contractor of the power station), alleging specific acts of negligence and/or products liability with reference to their respective responsibilities for the design and construction of the Coleto Creek Power Station and its coal-handling system.

Mid-West and Sargent & Lundy both filed cross-actions against each other, CP & L, and Zachry, affirmatively pleading the doctrine of comparative fault, and sought indemnity and/or contribution from such cross-defendants in the event Mid-West and Sargent & Lundy were found liable for the accident. CP & L also filed a cross-action against Sargent & Lundy and Mid-West, seeking indemnity and/or contribution from these two defendants if CP & L was found liable. In addition, each cross-defendant answered by way of denial to the respective cross-actions asserted against them. The trial court sustained Zachry's plea of privilege to be sued in Bexar County in response to the Garcias' original petition, and, when the Garcias filed a second petition again naming Zachry as a defendant, the trial court sustained Zachry's plea in abatement. However, Zachry remained a defendant as a result of the cross-actions filed by Sargent & Lundy and Mid-West.

The cause eventually proceeded to trial and the trial court allocated, without objection, six peremptory challenges to the Garcia family, and a total of ten peremptory challenges to the four defendants. However, after the voir dire examination, the Garcias moved to allocate the peremptory challenges six and six as opposed to six and ten because the attorneys' representations during voir dire indicated that there was no antagonism among the defendants as a matter of law. TEX. R. CIV. P. 233. Alternatively, the Garcias argued that if antagonism did exist, it was so slight that it would be an abuse of discretion to award defendants ten peremptory challenges compared to the Garcias' six. The trial court overruled the Garcias' motion.

Trial was to a jury which answered twenty-three special issues. By a ten-to-two verdict, the jury found that Garcia was 100% negligent, and the trial court accordingly rendered a take-nothing judgment against the Garcias.

The Garcias' sole complaint on appeal was the overruling of their motion to allocate the same number of peremptory challenges to each side based on their assertion that there was no antagonism between the respective defendants as a matter of law. The court of appeals affirmed the trial court's ruling, stating that antagonism was present because of the cross-actions between the defendants and because the jury was asked to allocate causation among each of the four defendants.

In allocating peremptory challenges when multiple litigants are involved on one side of a lawsuit, a trial court must determine whether any of those litigants on the same side are antagonistic with respect to an issue of fact that the jury will decide. *Patterson Dental Co. v. Dunn*, 592 S.W.2d 914, 918 (Tex. 1979). In this case, the trial court conducted a pre-trial hearing immediately before the voir dire examination. At this pre-trial hearing, the defendants informed the court that they were united in asserting that Garcia was 100% contributorily negligent and requested that they be allocated twelve or fourteen strikes. Although recognizing that some antagonism might exist among the defendants because a comparative causation issue would be submitted to the jury, the Garcias contended at that time that eight or nine peremptory challenges would be sufficient. The trial court thereupon awarded the defendants a total of ten peremptory challenges and granted the Garcia's six peremptory challenges. A voir dire examination followed.

During the voir dire examination, the defendants asserted Garcia's contributory negligence as the sole cause of his death, and also made affirmative exculpatory representations about their co-defendants. For example, the attorney for CP & L stated: "They are claiming that some of the defendants who designed this plant did not design it properly. Well, you're gonna hear testimony about that, and I think you will see that the plant was designed properly." Later, that same attorney stated: Sargent and Lundy designed the plant, and the plant was designed properly. H.B. Zachry built the plant, and they built it in accordance with the design, and Mid-West Conveyors, they supplied the conveyor system out there, and what we are telling you that there is nothing wrong with the design. Mr. Garcia was properly trained, and he knew about it. He just made a mistake . . . . The attorney for Sargent & Lundy then stated: "With regard to CP & L, that is a household word down here in this part of the country. They are an extremely competent organization." The attorney for Zachry also spoke on behalf of CP & L: "We, also, think, however, that the evidence is gonna show that David Garcia had good training about the dangers of this coal pile in several ways . . . . The evidence is probably gonna show that David Garcia really did have some very meaningful type of training." Lastly, the Zachry attorney summed up the case on behalf of all the defendants: So it is our position, really, not just on our own behalf that this suit has no merit against H.B. Zachry, but I think after you have heard all the evidence, really, and as sad as it may be, that this suit does not really have any merit against any of the people that were sued in the case.

The existence of antagonism is a question of law. *Patterson*, 592 S.W.2d at 919. If no antagonism exists, each side must receive the same number of strikes. We hold that, as a matter of law, no antagonism existed among the defendants.

The defendants contend, however, that in addition to the Garcias' admission of antagonism prior to voir dire, the pleadings themselves established several sources of antagonism. Both Mid-West and Sargent & Lundy pled that the accident was caused solely by the other defendants. Further, Sargent & Lundy, Mid-West, and CP & L asserted cross-actions against each other and Zachry affirmatively seeking indemnity and contribution. Zachry remained in the suit only because of the cross-actions filed by Sargent & Lundy and Mid-West. Moreover, the Garcias' allegations against Mid-West included claims of product liability. Thus, the defendants contend that antagonism existed as a matter of law because the comparative liability of all the defendants was accordingly submitted to the jury. *See Duncan v. Cessna Aircraft Company*, 665 S.W.2d 414, 427 (Tex. 1984).

The defendants did indeed file cross-claims and allege that other defendants were the sole cause of the plaintiff's injuries. Prior opinions of this court have held that such pleadings were sufficient to establish antagonism. *E.g., Shell Chemical Company v. Lamb*, 493 S.W.2d 742 (Tex. 1973); *Tamburello v. Welch*, 392 S.W.2d 114 (Tex. 1965). However, in *Patterson*, this court made it clear that in determining whether antagonism exists, the trial court must consider the pleadings, information disclosed by pretrial discovery, information and representations made during voir dire of the jury panel, and any other information brought to the attention of the trial court before the exercise of the strikes by the parties. 592 S.W.2d at 919. In this case, the pleadings, viewed in isolation, support a finding of antagonism. However, as we noted in *Patterson*, the pleadings are not the only factor. *Id.* The existence of antagonism must be finally determined after voir dire and prior to the exercise of the strikes of the parties. Here, the affirmative exculpatory representations made by the defendants during voir dire overcame any antagonism evidenced by the pleadings and established that no antagonism existed between the defendants.

Once it is determined that the trial court committed error in allocating peremptory challenges, the next step is to determine if the error resulted in a trial that was materially unfair, thus requiring reversal. *Id.* at 920. Normally, the determination of whether a trial was materially unfair requires that the entire record, including the statement of facts, be examined by the reviewing court. *Id.* at 921. When the trial is hotly contested and the evidence sharply conflicting, the error results in a materially unfair trial without showing more. *Id.*

In this case, there were no motions for summary judgment filed. At trial, there were only two motions for an instructed verdict, and both were by Mid-West concerning the strict product liability claim against them. The jury heard from eighteen witnesses. The Garcias brought two experts to testify that the safety training of CP & L was inadequate and the design of the plant was also defective. The defendants countered with expert witnesses of their own to testify that the design of the plant was proper. The Garcias also brought forward many witnesses to testify about the lack of warnings given by CP & L to employees regarding the hazards of the coal pile. CP & L countered with witnesses of their own who testified that employees were indeed warned of the dangers of the coal pile. The jury was then asked twenty-three special issues many of which contained several parts. As to these issues, not only did none of the defendants take a position opposite to the others they continued to make affirmative exculpatory statements about their co-defendants in jury argument. Given these circumstances, and the ten-to-two verdict, we hold that this was a hotly contested trial which resulted in a materially unfair trial as a matter of law. We accordingly reverse the judgment of the courts below and remand this cause for trial.

Note

In *Lopez v. Foremost Paving*, 709 S.W.2d 643 (Tex. 1986) the Court followed *Garcia*, and reiterated that the harmless error rule had been relaxed in cases where a trial court had committed error in awarding peremptory strikes. A complaining party, assuming that he has properly preserved his error, is only required to show that the trial was material unfair. The *Lopez* Court identified several factors which might lead to the conclusion that a materially unfair trial occurred. The Court stated:

> Two other significant factors are that defendants used their ostensibly antagonistic positions unfairly by having one defendant call a witness to establish the adequacy of the temporary striping, asking a few perfunctory introductory questions, and then quickly turning the witness over to the co-defendant for "cross-examination" by leading questions. In *D.G. Counsel v. Bankers Comm. Life Ins. Co.*, 558 S.W.2d 487, 488-89 (Tex. Civ. App.—Beaumont 1977, writ ref'd n.r.e.), the court held the fact that one party would call a witness and then the other purportedly antagonistic party would "cross-examine" established the material unfairness. Second, defendants collaborated on the exercise of their strikes and did not have any double strikes. Lastly, defendants neither presented motions for summary judgment nor ever requested an instructed verdict.

e. *Constitutional Limitations on the Use of Peremptory Challenges*

GOODE
v.
SHOUKFEH
943 S.W.2d 441
(Tex. 1996)

Jury Selection. Three Step Process To Resolve Claim That Peremptory Challenges Motivated By Race. Facts: This is a personal injury case. James Goode died from complications following knee-replacement surgery performed at Methodist Hospital of Lubbock. Orlin Goode, as independent executor of the estate of James Goode, brought a medical malpractice case against Shoukfeh, a cardiologist who treated James for a pulmonary embolism several days after his surgery. Following voir dire of the prospective jury panel, Shoukfeh peremptorily challenged six venire members. Goode, an African-American, objected to four of these challenges, allegedly impermissibly motivated by race under *Edmonson v. Leesville Concrete Co.,* 500 U.S. 614 (1991). The challenged jurors included three African-Americans (jurors 7, 26, and 28) and one Hispanic (juror 9).

The trial court conducted a hearing on Goode's *Edmonson* challenge, which Goode's counsel began by stating that: (1) the four challenged jurors were members of a racial minority; (2) no sufficient, racially neutral reason justified these challenges; and (3) Goode would put forth evidence of his claims, if the court so desired. The court declined this offer of evidence, and instead called upon Shoukfeh's counsel to reply. Shoukfeh's counsel offered explanations for striking the four jurors in question. Juror 7 knew and had worked with either James Goode's widow or one of his children. Juror 26 was once a nurse at Methodist Hospital, and Shoukfeh's counsel expressed concern with "the reasons that she left employ there." The objection to juror 28 was that she made an "unequivocal statement . . . that she had a problem sitting in judgment" and also that she failed to disclose her prior jury service on her jury information card. Finally, juror 9 was a single mother of four who listed her occupation as "house mother," which counsel for Shoukfeh took to mean unemployed, and Shoukfeh's counsel stated that he was concerned that her service on the jury would affect her ability to take care of four children. Shoukfeh's counsel also claimed that juror 9 would be "more of a plaintiff's juror," because she appeared to be a welfare recipient. Goode questioned Hund and Moss, Shoukfeh's attorneys, and sought their voire dire notes. Both asserted the work-product privilege in refusing to disclose their notes to Goode. The trial court sustained the privilege claims, and refused to conduct an *in camera* inspection of the notes. The court then overruled Goode's *Edmonson objections.* The case was tried to a jury, and judgment was entered on their verdict that Goode take nothing. The court of appeals affirmed. 915 S.W.2d 666. *Held:* Affirmed.

Issue: How is an Edmonson challenge resolved?

Holding: A three-step process is utilized in resolving an *Edmonson* objection to peremptory challenges:

(1) *At the first step of the process, the opponent of the peremptory challenge must establish a prima facie case of racial discrimination.* Once a party offers a race-neutral explanation for the peremptory challenge and the trial court has ruled on the ultimate question of intentional discrimination, the preliminary issue of a prima facie case is moot.

(2) *During the second step of the process, the burden shifts to the party who has exercised the strike to come forward with a race-neutral explanation.* The appellate court does not consider whether the explanation is persuasive, or even plausible. The issue for the trial court and the appellate court, at this juncture, is the facial validity of the explanation. A neutral explanation means that the challenge was based on something other than the juror's race. Unless a discriminatory intent is inherent in the explanation, the reason offered will be deemed race-neutral for purposes of the analysis at step two.

(3) *At the third step in the process, the issue of whether the race-neutral explanation should be believed is purely a question of fact for the trial court.* I.e., whether the explanations offered for exercising peremptory challenges are credible is a fact question to be resolved by the trial court, under an abuse of discretion standard. Where there are two permissible views of the evidence, the factfinder's choice between them cannot be clearly erroneous. The trial court's decision will be reviewed by an abuse of discretion standard of review by which trial court rulings of this nature historically have been judged in civil cases." However, a reviewing court will not be bound by a finding of no discrimination, under either the Texas abuse of discretion standard or the clearly erroneous standard, if the justification offered for striking a potential juror is simply too incredible to be accepted.

Issue: Are Voir Dire Notes of the opponent discoverable?

Holding: Maybe.

Voir Dire Notes: An *Edmonson* movant has the right to examine the voir dire notes of the opponent's attorney, [if] when the attorney relies upon these notes while giving sworn or unsworn testimony in the *Edmonson* hearing. Absent such reliance, the voir dire notes are privileged work product, and the movant may not examine them.

Issue: What procedures are followed in determining an *Edmonson* challenge?

Holding: The following procedures should be used when an *Edmonson* challenge is made, that peremptory challenges have been exercised on the basis of race:

(1) At a minimum, the proceedings should be held in open court. Unsworn statements of counsel may be offered to explain why the peremptory challenges were exercised. The juror information cards may be made a part of the record by inclusion in the transcript, or by a former tender into evidence. To the extent that any party wishes to include other information or matters in the record, the rules of evidence and procedure apply.

(2) Because the party challenging the peremptory strikes has the ultimate burden of persuasion, the trial court should provide the party challenging the strikes under *Edmonson a reasonable opportunity to rebut the race-neutral explanations.*

(3) The trial court should provide the party asserting objections under *Edmonson* with a reasonable opportunity to conduct cross-examination.

DAVIS
v.
FISK ELECTRIC COMPANY
268 S.W.3d 508
(Tex. 2008)

Renuka V. Jain, Renuka V. Jain & Associates, P.C., Sugarland, TX, for Petitioner.

J. Cary Gray, Looper Reed & McGraw, P.C., Kyle Wayne Sanders, Looper Reed Mark & McGraw, Richard P. Hogan Jr., Jennifer Bruch Hogan, Hogan & Hogan, L.L.P., Houston, TX, for Respondents.

Virginia K. Hoelscher, Brown McCarroll, L.L.P., Austin, Allecia Lindsey-Pottinger, Houston, TX, for Amicus Curiae.

CHIEF JUSTICE JEFFERSON delivered the opinion of the Court, joined by JUSTICE HECHT, JUSTICE O'NEILL, JUSTICE WAINWRIGHT, JUSTICE MEDINA, JUSTICE GREEN, JUSTICE JOHNSON, and JUSTICE WILLETT.

Our rules generally permit each party in a civil action to exercise six peremptory strikes, which are challenges "made to a juror without assigning any reason therefor." TEX. R. CIV. P. 232, 233. But peremptories exercised for an improper reason, like race or gender, are unconstitutional. In this case, the African American petitioner asserted that he was terminated based on his race. The respondents used peremptory challenges at trial to exclude five of six African Americans from the venire but contend that their reasons for doing so had nothing to do with the potential jurors' race. The stated reasons, however, when viewed in conjunction with the 83% removal rate and a comparative juror analysis, defy neutral explanation. Because we conclude that at least two of the strikes were based on race, we reverse in part the court of appeals' judgment and remand the case for a new trial.

I
Factual Background

Donald Davis, an African American, worked for Fisk Electric Company as an assistant project manager. In February 2001, Fisk was awarded the contract to install cables at Goodson Middle School, in the Cypress Fairbanks School District. After problems arose on the Goodson project, Fisk terminated Davis. Davis asserts that his termination was based on his race, as evidenced in part by his supervisor's alleged use of the "n-word" when planning Davis's termination.

Davis sued Fisk, claiming violations of 42 U.S.C. § 1981 and the Texas Labor Code. Fisk denied liability. The case was called for trial, and at the conclusion of voir dire, Fisk peremptorily struck six venire members, five of whom were African American and all of whom were minorities. Davis objected, *citing Batson v. Kentucky*, 476 U.S. 79, 106 S.Ct. 1712, 90 L.Ed.2d 69 (1986), and the trial court, after a hearing, overruled the objection. The jury returned a defense verdict, the trial court signed a take-nothing judgment, and the court of appeals affirmed. 187 S.W.3d 570, 577. We granted Davis's petition for review to apply the United States Supreme Court's most recent guidance on peremptory challenges that are allegedly race-based. 50 Tex. Sup.Ct. J. 446 (Feb. 23, 2007).

II
Batson Challenge

Davis raises a single complaint: that Fisk struck prospective jurors based on race, in violation of Batson. We last wrote on *Batson* challenges in *Goode v. Shoukfeh*, 943 S.W.2d 441 (Tex. 1997), and in the intervening years, the landscape has evolved. Significantly, after the trial in this case, the Supreme Court decided *Miller-El v. Dretke*, 545 U.S. 231, 125 S.Ct. 2317, 162 L.Ed.2d 196 (2005) ("Miller-El II"), a case in which the Court concluded that a habeas petitioner was entitled to relief because prosecutors in his criminal trial peremptorily struck potential jurors based on race. Although Miller-El II is a criminal case, it involves many of the same factors at issue here, and we examine it in some detail.

* * *

[The United States Supreme Court] [n]oting that a Batson challenge requires an examination of " 'all relevant circumstances,' " the Court examined five factors in determining that jury selection in Miller-El's criminal trial violated the Equal Protection Clause. *Miller-El II*, 545 U.S. at 240, 125 S.Ct. 2317 (*quoting Batson*, 476 U.S. at 96-97, 106 S.Ct. 1712). The first involved an analysis of the statistical data pertaining to the prosecution's peremptory strikes. The Court noted that prosecutors used peremptory strikes to exclude 91% of the eligible African-American venire members-a percentage too great to attribute merely to "[h]appenstance." *Id.* at 241, 125 S.Ct. 2317.

The Court then conducted a comparative juror analysis, noting that "[m]ore powerful than these bare statistics, however, are side-by-side comparisons of some black venire panelists who were struck and white panelists who were allowed to serve." *Id.* The Court explained that "[i]f a prosecutor's proffered reason for striking a black panelist applies just as well to an otherwise-similar nonblack who is permitted to serve, that is evidence tending to prove purposeful discrimination to be considered at Batson's third step." *Id.* In conducting this analysis, the Court rejected the notion that struck venire members must be compared only to jurors who are identical in all respects (save race): "A per se rule that a defendant cannot win a Batson claim unless there is an exactly identical white juror would leave Batson inoperable; potential jurors are not products of a set of cookie cutters." *Id.* at 247 n. 6, 125 S.Ct. 2317. * * *

A third factor the Court considered was the prosecution's use of the jury shuffle, a practice unique to Texas, and one that the Court held could "indicate decisions probably based on race." *Id.* at 253, 125 S.Ct. 2317. The *Miller-El* jury was shuffled some eight times, at the request of both the prosecution (three times) and the defense (five times). *Miller-El II*, 545 U.S. at 255 n. 14, 125 S.Ct. 2317. The Court noted that " 'the prosecution's decision to seek a jury shuffle when a predominant number of African-Americans were seated in the front of the panel, along with its decision to delay a formal objection to the defense's shuffle until after the racial composition was revealed, raise a suspicion that the State sought to exclude African-Americans from the jury.' " *Id.* at 254, 125 S.Ct. 2317 (*quoting Miller-El I*, 537 U.S. at 346, 123 S.Ct. 1029). This was amplified by testimony that the Dallas County District Attorney's Office had previously admitted to using the shuffle to manipulate the racial makeup of juries. *Id.* The Court concluded:

> The State notes in its brief that there might be racially neutral reasons for shuffling the jury, and we suppose there might be. But no racially neutral reason has ever been offered in this case, and nothing stops the suspicion of discriminatory intent from rising to an inference.

Id. at 254-55, 125 S.Ct. 2317 (citation omitted).

A fourth factor the Court relied on was the "contrasting voir dire questions posed respectively to black and nonblack panel members." *Id.* at 255, 125 S.Ct. 2317. Prosecutors gave black panel members a vivid, graphic account of the death penalty before asking about the member's feelings on the subject, while it gave nonblacks a "bland description." *Id.* While the State conceded that disparate questioning occurred, it asserted that the disparity was based on panel members' differing views of the death penalty-those who expressed ambivalence received the "graphic script," while those who did not received the watered-down version. *Id.* at 256-57, 125 S.Ct. 2317. Based on the record, however, the Court concluded that black venire members were more likely to receive the graphic script regardless of their expressions of ambivalence, and the State's explanation failed for four of the eight black panel members who received that script. Id. at 258, 125 S.Ct. 2317. Additionally, four out of five nonblacks who were given the graphic script were not those who had expressed ambivalence but were instead unambiguously in favor of, or vehemently opposed to, the death penalty. *Id.* at 259, 125 S.Ct.

2317. The Court also noted that the State disparately used manipulative questioning regarding minimum punishments. *Id.* at 261, 125 S.Ct. 2317. The State conceded that practice but argued that it was premised on opposition to or ambivalence regarding the death penalty, rather than race. *Id.* at 261-62, 125 S.Ct. 2317. The Court disagreed, noting that "only 27% of nonblacks questioned on the subject who expressed these views were subjected to the trick question, as against 100% of black members. Once again, the implication of race in the prosecutors' choice of questioning cannot be explained away." *Id.* at 263, 125 S.Ct. 2317.

Finally, the Court considered the Dallas County District Attorney's Office's history of "systematically excluding blacks from juries." *Id.* Specifically, the defense presented evidence that the DA's office had adopted a formal policy to exclude minorities from jury service, and that policy was summarized in a " 'manual entitled 'Jury Selection in a Criminal Case' [sometimes known as the Sparling Manual]' " that was distributed to prosecutors. *Id.* (*quoting Miller-El I*, 537 U.S. at 335, 123 S.Ct. 1029). Although the manual was written in 1968, the evidence showed it was available to at least one of *Miller-El*'s prosecutors. *Id.* The Court also observed that prosecutors had noted the race of each prospective juror on their juror cards. *Id.*

Considering the totality of the circumstances, the Court held:

> It blinks reality to deny that the State struck Fields and Warren, included in [the] 91% [of black venire members who were struck], because they were black. The strikes correlate with no fact as well as they correlate with race, and they occurred during a selection infected by shuffling and disparate questioning that race explains better than any race-neutral reason advanced by the State. The State's pretextual positions confirm Miller-El's claim, and the prosecutors' own notes proclaim that the Sparling Manual's emphasis on race was on their minds when they considered every potential juror.

Id. at 266, 125 S.Ct. 2317. Holding that the state court's conclusion about the prosecutors' strikes of those two jurors was wrong "to a clear and convincing degree," the Court reversed the court of appeals' judgment and remanded the case for entry of judgment for Miller-El, "together with orders of appropriate relief." *Id.*

III

Batson Procedure

With this context in mind, we turn to the Batson challenge at issue in this case, * * *

In contrast to the federal system, which employs a "clearly erroneous" standard of review, we review a trial court's Batson ruling for abuse of discretion. *Goode*, 943 S.W.2d at 446 (noting that "[a] trial court abuses its discretion if its decision 'is arbitrary, unreasonable, and without reference to guiding principles' " and observing that standard is "similar, although not identical to," federal "clearly erroneous" standard); * * * We now turn to an analysis of "all relevant circumstances."

***

V

Analysis

A

Statistical Disparity

Here, as in *Miller-El*, the statistics are "remarkable." *Miller-El II*, 545 U.S. at 240, 125 S.Ct. 2317 (noting that prosecutors used peremptory strikes to exclude 91% of eligible black venire members). Jurors were chosen from the first twenty-eight members of the venire. At the conclusion of the parties' questioning, four panelists were struck for cause or by agreement, and the parties then submitted their peremptory challenges. Fisk struck five of the six African Americans (83%) but only one (5.5%) of the eligible nonblack prospective jurors, and "[h]appenstance is unlikely to produce this disparity." *Miller-El I*, 537 U.S. at 342, 123 S.Ct. 1029.

B

Comparative Juror Analysis

Beyond the raw statistics, a comparative juror analysis is similarly troubling. Fisk struck Juror No. 12, Patrick Daigle, and provided the following explanation:

> Of all the jurors, juror No. 12, who initially I thought would be good a good [sic] juror for us, reacted that corporations should be punished with the use of punitive damages. He was the most clear on that subject. In addition, I attempted to draw out of him a discussion from him about his involvement in this management-employee committee thing at Continental, something that would make me think he recognized that many of the discrimination claims that they deal with-I know he said he didn't have any personal involvement with race discrimination cases; but he seemed to be too ready to believe that Continental has discriminatory employment practices; which, you know, I could be totally wrong about this, Your Honor; but my belief is that I tend to have a high degree of skepticism about that, about Continental and the fact that he didn't have that same skepticism caused me to believe they we should exercise a challenge on him.

The trial court then immediately overruled Davis's Batson objection to the strike.

Davis's counsel conducted the only questioning on punitive damages, and, as is evident from the colloquy, Daigle never verbally responded to the questions about punitive damages. Fisk nonetheless asserted in the trial court that Daigle nonverbally "reacted that corporations should be punished with the use of punitive damages." Fisk did not elaborate on the type of nonverbal conduct that Daigle manifested, other than to say Daigle was "most clear" on the subject. Davis's counsel objected that "the nonverbal cues that Defense Counsel has cited throughout are not supported by the record" and also noted that Fisk never attempted to question Daigle about any alleged "nonverbal cues."

Last term, the Supreme Court decided a Batson case involving nonverbal conduct. In *Snyder v. Louisiana*, the Court held that the prosecution improperly struck a potential juror. *Snyder*, 552 U.S. at ----, 128 S.Ct. 1203. The prosecution gave two reasons for its strike, one of which was that Brooks, the potential juror, looked "very nervous" throughout the questioning. *Id.* at ----, 128 S.Ct. 1203. The Court noted that the "record [did] not show that the trial judge actually made a determination concerning Mr. Brooks' demeanor." *Id.* at ----, 128 S.Ct. 1203. Absent such a finding, the Court concluded that it could not "presume that the trial judge credited the prosecutor's assertion that Mr. Brooks was nervous." *Id.* Thus, while "deference [to the trial court] is especially appropriate where a trial judge has made a finding that an attorney credibly relied on demeanor in exercising a strike," *id.* at ----, 128 S.Ct. 1203, here there was no such finding, and we cannot presume the trial court credited Fisk's explanation.

* * *

On appeal, Fisk cites Daigle's voir dire responses about past personal experiences with discrimination as a basis for the strike. This reason-never advanced in the trial court-may not now be used to justify the strike. *See, e.g., Miller-El II*, 545 U.S. at 252, 125 S.Ct. 2317 (noting that, "when illegitimate grounds like race are in issue, a prosecutor simply has got to state his reasons as best he can and stand or fall on the plausibility of the reasons he gives"); *see also id.* (noting that reason given during *Batson* hearing but after State's initial reasons were shown to be incorrect "reeks of afterthought" and showed "pretextual timing"). On balance, we conclude that Fisk's reasons for striking Daigle "cannot reasonably be accepted." *Miller-El II*, 545 U.S. at 247, 125 S.Ct. 2317 (*citing Miller-El I*, 537 U.S. at 339, 123 S.Ct. 1029 (noting that the credibility of reasons given can be measured by "how reasonable, or how improbable, the explanations are; and by whether the proffered rationale has some basis in accepted trial strategy")).

***

VI
Conclusion

Despite its laudable goal, *Batson* has been difficult to enforce. In *Miller-El II*, decided a year after this case was tried, the Supreme Court noted that *Batson's* "individualized focus came with a weakness of its own owing to its very emphasis on the particular reasons a prosecutor might give." *Miller-El II*, 545 U.S. at 239-40, 125 S.Ct. 2317.

If any facially neutral reason sufficed to answer a *Batson* challenge, then *Batson* would not amount to much more than *Swain*. Some stated reasons are false, and although some false reasons are shown up within the four corners of a given case, sometimes a court may not be sure unless it looks beyond the case at hand. Hence, *Batson's* explanation that a defendant may rely on 'all relevant circumstances' to raise an inference of purposeful discrimination. *Id.* at 240, 125 S.Ct. 2317 (*quoting Batson*, 476 U.S. at 96-97, 106 S.Ct. 1712). Miller-El I' s "totality of the circumstances" analysis places a heavy burden on trial courts, and we acknowledge that some of the factors that Court examined-most especially the comparative juror analysis-are perhaps more easily reviewed on appeal, with the benefit of a transcript from which such comparisons may most accurately be drawn. But without Miller-El II' s searching inquiry into the basis of the challenged strikes, Batson would become a "mere exercise in thinking up any rational basis." *Id.* at 252, 125 S.Ct. 2317.

Unlike *Miller-El II*, there is no evidence here of a historical pattern of excluding blacks from juries. But *Miller-El II* made it clear that the five factors it considered were neither exhaustive nor mandatory; courts must consider "all relevant circumstances" when reviewing *Batson* challenges. *Miller-El II*, 545 U.S. at 240, 125 S.Ct. 2317 (*quoting Batson*, 476 U.S. at 96-97, 106 S.Ct. 1712); *see also Snyder*, 552 U.S. at ----, 128 S.Ct. 1203 ("In *Miller-El v. Dretke*, the Court made it clear that in considering a Batson objection, or in reviewing a ruling claimed to be Batson error, all of the circumstances . . . must be consulted."). And here, the relevant circumstances include many of those pertinent in Miller-El II, including a statistical disparity and unequal treatment of comparable jurors.

We acknowledge that peremptory strikes, often based on instinct rather than reason, can be difficult to justify. *Miller-El II*, 545 U.S. at 252, 125 S.Ct. 2317. The trial lawyer's failure to do so here does not suggest personal racial animosity on his part. *See, e.g.*, Antony Page, *Batson's Blind Spot: Unconscious Stereotyping and the Peremptory Challenge*, 85 B.U. L.REV. 155, 160-61, 184 (2005) (noting that "research has compellingly demonstrated the existence of unconscious race- and gender-based stereotyping"). A zealous advocate will seek jurors favorably inclined to his client's position, and race may even serve as a rough proxy for partiality. *See, e.g., Batson v. Kentucky*, 476 U.S. 79, 139, 106 S.Ct. 1712, 90 L.Ed.2d 69 (1986) (REHNQUIST, J., dissenting) (noting that factors like race are often a "proxy" for potential juror bias). But whatever the strategic advantages of that practice, the Constitution forbids it.

The concurrence suggests that we ascribe sinister motives to Fisk's counsel. The question presented, however, is not whether this particular advocate harbors ill will, but whether the record explains, on neutral grounds, a statistically significant exclusion of black jurors. It is not enough, under the Supreme Court precedent we examine here, that the lawyer be pure of heart. We assume that he is. Our holding depends not on the personal sentiments of the advocate but on the state of the record. *Miller-El II* and *Snyder* emphasize that *Batson's* promise cannot be fulfilled if its requirements may be satisfied merely by ticking off a race-neutral explanation from a checklist.

After examining the totality of the circumstances, we conclude that race explains Fisk's strikes of Daigle and Pickett better than any other reason, and the trial court abused its discretion in failing to sustain Davis's *Batson* challenge. *Miller-El II*, 545 U.S. at 266, 125 S.Ct. 2317; *Powers*, 813 S.W.2d at 491. We reverse in part the court of appeals' judgment and remand the case to the trial court for a new trial. TEX.R.APP. P. 60.2(d).

JUSTICE BRISTER, joined by JUSTICE MEDINA as to Part III, concurring.

I disagree with the Court's conclusion that defense counsel's peremptory strikes were racially motivated. Neutral reasons were given for them but were not properly preserved, in part because the rules changed during this appeal. The difference between not having neutral reasons and merely not preserving them is no technicality; charges of discrimination (like discrimination itself) can have far-reaching effects, including use in future trials.

If we are to blame rather than just decide, we ought to be more even-handed. The plaintiff's strikes here were even more "remarkable" than the defendant's, as plaintiff's counsel used all six of her peremptory strikes (100 percent) to exclude white males. In Harris County, where this case was tried, every racial group is a minority. The Court's extra effort to censure one counsel after disregarding his explanations on procedural grounds is simply too one-sided.

I agree that peremptory strikes provide an opportunity for discrimination. But they also provide an opportunity to accuse an opponent of discrimination and get a new trial if the first one turns out badly. As these strikes have outlived their original purpose, it is time we did something about them. Rather than using this case as an opportunity to disparage one attorney, I would use it as an opportunity to discontinue a practice inherently based on stereotypes. As the Court misses that opportunity, I concur only in the judgment.

* * *

There is no constitutional right to peremptory strikes. Indeed, recent cases suggest the opposite may be true, as several justices have already concluded. The Equal Protection Clause protects citizens from arbitrary and capricious state action. In 1991 peremptory challenges were declared to be "state action"; they have always been recognized as "arbitrary and capricious" by their very nature. As JUSTICE SCALIA has written, "[t]o affirm that the Equal Protection Clause applies to strikes of individual jurors is effectively to abolish the peremptory challenge."

A majority of this Court could curb peremptory strikes today, as they stem entirely from our Rules of Civil Procedure. The reason we hesitate to do so is that lawyers are tenaciously protective of them, believing they can use these strikes to mold a favorable jury. Study after study has shown this belief to be unfounded. But even if it were true, that reason is not enough: "Peremptory strikes are not intended . . . to permit a party to 'select' a favorable jury."

All these problems-discriminating against minorities, disrupting trial, and discarding perfectly good jurors-are particularly acute in Texas. Whether because of the state's diversity, the generous allowance of peremptory strikes, or something else, Batson challenges are far more frequent here than anywhere else. A recent Westlaw search for state court cases citing to *Batson* yields:

- 4 cases from Idaho,
- 17 from Alaska,
- 43 from Colorado,
- 58 from Oklahoma.
- 74 from Minnesota
- 90 from Florida,
- 181 from Pennsylvania,
- 342 from Illinois,
- 676 from California, and
- 1,364 cases from Texas.

More than any other state, we in Texas must consider whether peremptory strikes are worth the price they impose.

Notes

1. *Powers v. Palacios,* 813 S.W.2d 489 (Tex. 1991). A private litigant in a civil case may not use a peremptory challenge to exclude a juror on account of race. Such an exclusion violates the equal protection rights of the challenged juror.

2. *Jones v. Martin K. Eby Construction Co., Inc.***,** 841 S.W.2d 426 (Tex. App.—Dallas 199 , writ denied). Any error in the improper exercise of peremptory challenges on the basis of race is waived by the failure to make a timely objection. A contemporaneous objection, or similar timely complaint, is required to preserve any error for appellate review.

6. *Disqualification, Recusal, and Assignment of Judges*

TEX. CONST. Art 5

Sec. 11. No judge shall sit in any case wherein the judge may be interested, or where either of the parties may be connected with the judge, either by affinity or consanguinity, within such a degree as may be prescribed by law, or when the judge shall have been counsel in the case. When the Supreme Court, the Court of Criminal Appeals, the Court of Appeals, or any member of any of those courts shall be thus disqualified to hear and determine any case or cases in said court, the same shall be certified to the Governor of the State, who shall immediately commission the requisite number of persons learned in the law for the trial and determination of such cause or causes. When a judge of the District Court is disqualified by any of the causes above stated, the parties may, by consent, appoint a proper person to try said case; or upon their failing to do so, a competent person may be appointed to try the same in the county where it is pending, in such manner as may be prescribed by law. And the District Judges may exchange districts, or hold courts for each other when they may deem it expedient, and shall do so when required by law. This disqualification of judges of inferior tribunals shall be remedied and vacancies in their offices filled as may be prescribed by law.

TEX. GOV'T CODE

§ 74.053. Objection to Judge Assigned to a Trial Court

(a) When a judge is assigned to a trial court under this chapter:

(1) the order of assignment must state whether the judge is an active, former, retired, or senior judge; and

(2) the presiding judge shall, if it is reasonable and practicable and if time permits, give notice of the assignment to each attorney representing a party to the case that is to be heard in whole or part by the assigned judge.

(b) If a party to a civil case files a timely objection to the assignment, the judge shall not hear the case. Except as provided by Subsection (d), each party to the case is only entitled to one objection under this section for that case.

(c) An objection under this section must be filed not later than the seventh day after the date the party receives actual notice of the assignment or before the date the first hearing or trial, including pretrial hearings, commences, whichever date occurs earlier. The presiding judge may extend the time to file an objection under this section on written motion by a party who demonstrates good cause.

(d) An assigned judge or justice who was defeated in the last primary or general election for which the judge or justice was a candidate for the judicial office held by the judge or justice may not sit in a case if either party objects to the judge or justice.

(e) An active judge assigned under this chapter is not subject to an objection.

(f) For purposes of this section, notice of an assignment may be given and an objection to an assignment may be filed by electronic mail.

(g) In this section, "party" includes multiple parties aligned in a case as determined by the presiding judge.

Rule 18a. Recusal and Disqualification of Judges

(a) *Motion; Form and Contents.* A party in a case in any trial court other than a statutory probate court or justice court may seek to recuse or disqualify a judge who is sitting in the case by filing a motion with the clerk of the court in which the case is pending. The motion:

(1) must be verified;

(2) must assert one or more of the grounds listed in Rule 18b;

(3) must not be based solely on the judge's rulings in the case; and

(4) must state with detail and particularity facts that:

(A) are within the affiant's personal knowledge, except that facts may be stated on information and belief if the basis for that belief is specifically stated;

(B) would be admissible in evidence; and

(C) if proven, would be sufficient to justify recusal or disqualification.

(b) *Time for Filing Motion.*

(1) Motion to Recuse. A motion to recuse:

(A) must be filed as soon as practicable after the movant knows of the ground stated in the motion; and

(B) must not be filed after the tenth day before the date set for trial or other hearing unless, before that day, the movant neither knew nor reasonably should have known:

(i) that the judge whose recusal is sought would preside at the trial or hearing; or

(ii) that the ground stated in the motion existed.

(2) Motion to Disqualify. A motion to disqualify should be filed as soon as practicable after the movant knows of the ground stated in the motion.

(c) *Response to Motion.*

(1) By Another Party. Any other party in the case may, but need not, file a response to the motion. Any response must be filed before the motion is heard.

(2) By the Respondent Judge. The judge whose recusal or disqualification is sought should not file a response to the motion.

(d) *Service of Motion or Response.* A party who files a motion or response must serve a copy on every other party. The method of service must be the same as the method of filing, if possible.

(e) *Duty of the Clerk.*

(1) Delivery of a Motion or Response. When a motion or response is filed, the clerk of the court must immediately deliver a copy to the respondent judge and to the presiding judge of the administrative judicial region in which the court is located ("the regional presiding judge").

(2) Delivery of Order of Recusal or Referral. When a respondent judge signs and files an order of recusal or referral, the clerk of the court must immediately deliver a copy to the regional presiding judge.

(f) *Duties of the Respondent Judge; Failure to Comply.*

(1) Responding to the Motion. Regardless of whether the motion complies with this rule, the respondent judge, within three business days after the motion is filed, must either:

(A) sign and file with the clerk an order of recusal or disqualification; or

(B) sign and file with the clerk an order referring the motion to the regional presiding judge.

(2) Restrictions on Further Action.

(A) Motion Filed Before Evidence Offered at Trial. If a motion is filed before evidence has been offered at trial, the respondent judge must take no further action in the case until the motion has been decided, except for good cause stated in writing or on the record.

(B) Motion Filed After Evidence Offered at Trial. If a motion is filed after evidence has been offered at trial, the respondent judge may proceed, subject to stay by the regional presiding judge.

(3) Failure to Comply. If the respondent judge fails to comply with a duty imposed by this rule, the movant may notify the regional presiding judge.

(g) *Duties of Regional Presiding Judge.*

(1) Motion. The regional presiding judge must rule on a referred motion or assign a judge to rule. If a party files a motion to recuse or disqualify the regional presiding judge, the regional presiding judge may still assign a judge to rule on the original, referred motion. Alternatively, the regional presiding judge may sign and file with the clerk an order referring the second motion to the Chief Justice for consideration.

(2) Order. The ruling must be by written order.

(3) Summary Denial for Noncompliance.

(A) Motion to Recuse. A motion to recuse that does not comply with this rule may be denied without an oral hearing. The order must state the nature of the noncompliance. Even if the motion is amended to correct the stated noncompliance, the motion will count for purposes of determining whether a tertiary recusal motion has been filed under the Civil Practice and Remedies Code.

(B) Motion to Disqualify. A motion to disqualify may not be denied on the ground that it was not filed or served in compliance with this rule.

(4) Interim Orders. The regional presiding judge or judge assigned to decide the motion may issue interim or ancillary orders in the pending case as justice may require.

(5) Discovery. Except by order of the regional presiding judge or the judge assigned to decide the motion, a subpoena or discovery request may not issue to the respondent judge and may be disregarded unless accompanied by the order.

(6) Hearing.

(A) Time. The motion must be heard as soon as practicable and may be heard immediately after it is referred to the regional presiding judge or an assigned judge.

(B) Notice. Notice of the hearing must be given to all parties in the case.

(C) By Telephone. The hearing may be conducted by telephone on the record. Documents submitted by facsimile or email, otherwise admissible under the rules of evidence, may be considered.

(7) Reassignment of Case if Motion Granted. If the motion is granted, the regional presiding judge must transfer the case to another court or assign another judge to the case.

(h) *Sanctions.* After notice and hearing, the judge who hears the motion may order the party or attorney who filed the motion, or both, to pay the reasonable attorney fees and expenses incurred by other parties if the judge determines that the motion was:

(1) groundless and filed in bad faith or for the purpose of harassment, or

(2) clearly brought for unnecessary delay and without sufficient cause.

(i) *Chief Justice.* The Chief Justice of the Supreme Court of Texas may assign judges and issue any orders permitted by this rule or pursuant to statute.

(j) *Appellate Review.*

(1) Order on Motion to Recuse.

(A) Denying Motion. An order denying a motion to recuse may be reviewed only for abuse of discretion on appeal from the final judgment.

(B) Granting Motion. An order granting a motion to recuse is final and cannot be reviewed by appeal, mandamus, or otherwise.

(2) Order on Motion to Disqualify. An order granting or denying a motion to disqualify may be reviewed by mandamus and may be appealed in accordance with other law.

Rule 18b. Grounds for Recusal and Disqualification of Judges

(a) *Grounds for Disqualification.* A judge must disqualify in any proceeding in which:

(1) the judge has served as a lawyer in the matter in controversy, or a lawyer with whom the judge previously practiced law served during such association as a lawyer concerning the matter;

(2) the judge knows that, individually or as a fiduciary, the judge has an interest in the subject matter in controversy; or

(3) either of the parties may be related to the judge by affinity or consanguinity within the third degree.

(b) *Grounds for Recusal.* A judge must recuse in any proceeding in which:

(1) the judge's impartiality might reasonably be questioned;

(2) the judge has a personal bias or prejudice concerning the subject matter or a party;

(3) the judge has personal knowledge of disputed evidentiary facts concerning the proceeding;

(4) the judge or a lawyer with whom the judge previously practiced law has been a material witness concerning the proceeding;

(5) the judge participated as counsel, adviser, or material witness in the matter in controversy, or expressed an opinion concerning the merits of it, while acting as an attorney in government service;

(6) the judge knows that the judge, individually or as a fiduciary, or the judge's spouse or minor child residing in the judge's household, has a financial interest in the subject matter in controversy or in a party to the proceeding, or any other interest that could be substantially affected by the outcome of the proceeding;

(7) the judge or the judge's spouse, or a person within the third degree of relationship to either of them, or the spouse of such a person:

(A) is a party to the proceeding or an officer, director, or trustee of a party;

(B) is known by the judge to have an interest that could be substantially affected by the outcome of the proceeding; or

(C) is to the judge's knowledge likely to be a material witness in the proceeding.

(8) the judge or the judge's spouse, or a person within the first degree of relationship to either of them, or the spouse of such a person, is acting as a lawyer in the proceeding.

(c) *Financial Interests.* A judge should inform himself or herself about personal and fiduciary financial interests, and make a reasonable effort to inform himself or herself about the personal financial interests of his or her spouse and minor children residing in the household.

(d) *Terminology and Standards.* In this rule:

(1) "proceeding" includes pretrial, trial, or other stages of litigation;

(2) the degree of relationship is calculated according to the civil law system;

(3) "fiduciary" includes such relationships as executor, administrator, trustee, and guardian;

(4) "financial interest" means ownership of a legal or equitable interest, however small, or a relationship as director, adviser, or other active participant in the affairs of a party, except that:

(A) ownership in a mutual or common investment fund that holds securities is not a "financial interest" in such securities unless the judge participates in the management of the fund;

(B) an office in an educational, religious, charitable, fraternal, or civic organization is not a "financial interest" in securities held by the organization;

(C) the proprietary interest of a policyholder in a mutual insurance company, of a depositor in a mutual savings association, or a similar proprietary interest, is a "financial interest" in the organization only if the outcome of the proceeding could substantially affect the value of the interest;

(D) ownership of government securities is a "financial interest" in the issuer only if the outcome of the proceeding could substantially affect the value of the securities;

(E) an interest as a taxpayer or utility ratepayer, or any similar interest, is not a "financial interest" unless the outcome of the proceeding could substantially affect the liability of the judge or a person related to him within the third degree more than other judges.

(e) *Waiving a Ground for Recusal.* The parties to a proceeding may waive any ground for recusal after it is fully disclosed on the record.

(f) *Discovery and Divestiture.* If a judge does not discover that the judge is recused under subparagraphs (b)(6) or (b)(7)(B) until after the judge has devoted substantial time to the matter, the judge is not required to recuse himself or herself if the judge or the person related to the judge divests himself or herself of the interest that would otherwise require recusal.

In re UNION PACIFIC RESOURCES COMPANY

969 S.W.2d 427
(Tex. 1998)

Carlos Villarreal, Tom Hermansen, Corpus Christi, for Relator.

William R. Edwards, III, John Blaise Gsanger, William R. Edwards, Corpus Christi, Fred Davis, Bryan, for Respondent.

PHILLIPS, CHIEF JUSTICE, delivered the opinion of the Court, in which HECHT, ENOCH, SPECTOR, OWEN, BAKER, ABBOTT and HANKINSON, JUSTICES, join.

In this case, the court of appeals conditionally issued a writ of mandamus compelling the trial court to vacate its order denying a recusal motion. *Monroe v. Blackmon*, 946 S.W.2d 533 (Tex. App.—Corpus Christi 1997). Because the complaining party has an adequate remedy by appeal, mandamus was improper. We therefore conditionally grant the petition for writ of mandamus. We express no opinion regarding whether the trial court abused its discretion in denying the recusal motion.

Jeffrey Lee Monroe and Gena Jo Monroe sued Union Pacific Resources Company and other defendants for personal injury damages. The Monroes moved to recuse the trial judge, the Honorable Max Bennett. The Monroes alleged, as grounds for recusal, that Carlos Villareal, a partner in the law firm representing Union Pacific in the underlying lawsuit, was currently representing Judge Bennett, in his official capacity, in an unrelated lawsuit. The Monroes alleged that Judge Bennett's impartiality might reasonably be questioned because of the attorney-client relationship with Mr. Villareal. Judge Bennett declined to recuse himself. Pursuant to Texas Rule of Civil Procedure 18a(d) Judge Bennett forwarded the motion to recuse to the presiding judge for the administrative judicial district. The presiding judge appointed the Honorable Robert Blackmon, Nueces County district judge, to hear the recusal motion. After a hearing at which Judge Bennett appeared and testified, Judge Blackmon granted the motion ordering Judge Bennett's recusal. Judge Bennett then wrote to Judge Blackmon requesting a rehearing on the recusal matter. In response to Judge Bennett's request, Judge Blackmon held another hearing and reversed his ruling. In response to this second ruling, the Monroes petitioned the court of appeals for writ of mandamus to direct Judge Blackmon to vacate his order and grant the motion for recusal. The court of appeals sitting en banc divided evenly on the petition, and the Chief Justice of this Court assigned the Honorable Alfonso Chapa, Retired Chief Justice of the Fourth Court of Appeals, to the case. *See* TEX. GOV'T CODE § 74.003(b); TEX.R.APP. P. 41.2(b). With Justice Chapa sitting, the court of appeals conditionally granted the Monroes' petition for writ of mandamus. Union Pacific then sought mandamus relief from this Court.

Judges may be removed from a particular case either because they are constitutionally disqualified, TEX. CONST. art. V, § 11, because they are subject to a statutory strike, TEX. GOV'T CODE § 74.053(d), or because they are recused under rules promulgated by this Court. TEX.R. CIV. P. 18a, 18b; TEX.R.APP. P. 16. The grounds and procedures for each type of removal are fundamentally different. *See generally* Kilgarlin & Bruch, *Disqualification and Recusal of Judges*, 17 St. Mary's L.J. 599 (1986). When a judge continues to sit in violation of a constitutional proscription, mandamus is available to compel the judge's mandatory disqualification without a showing that the relator lacks an adequate remedy by appeal. *Cf. Mitchell Energy Corp. v. Ashworth*, 943 S.W.2d 436, 437 (Tex. 1997) (addressing the mandatory disqualification of assigned judges under TEX.

GOV'T CODE § 74.053(d)). This makes sense, because any orders or judgments rendered by a judge who is constitutionally disqualified are void and without effect. *See, e.g., Buckholts Indep. Sch. Dist. v. Glaser*, 632 S.W.2d 146, 148 (Tex. 1982); *Fry v. Tucker*, 146 Tex. 18, 202 S.W.2d 218, 221 (1947). Likewise, on timely objection, the disqualification of an assigned judge who is not a retired judge is mandatory under section 74.053(d) of the Texas Government Code and any orders entered by a trial judge in a case in which he is disqualified are void. *See Mitchell Energy Corp.*, 943 S.W.2d at 440-441; *Fry*, 202 S.W.2d at 221. Therefore, the objecting party is also entitled to mandamus relief without a showing that there is no adequate remedy by appeal. *See Dunn v. Street*, 938 S.W.2d 33, 34-35 (Tex. 1997); *Flores v. Banner*, 932 S.W.2d 500, 501 (Tex. 1996).

In contrast, the erroneous denial of a recusal motion does not void or nullify the presiding judge's subsequent acts. While a judgment rendered in such circumstances may be reversed on appeal, it is not fundamental error and can be waived if not raised by proper motion. *See Buckholts Indep. Sch. Dist.*, 632 S.W.2d at 148; *Gulf Maritime Warehouse Co. v. Towers*, 858 S.W.2d 556, 559 (Tex. App.—Beaumont 1993, writ denied); *Aguilar v. Anderson*, 855 S.W.2d 799, 809-810 (Tex. App.—El Paso 1993, writ denied); *AmSav Group, Inc. v. Amer. Sav. & Loan Ass'n*, 796 S.W.2d 482, 485 (Tex. App.—Houston [14th Dist.] 1990, writ denied). Recognizing this distinction, our Rules of Civil Procedure expressly provide for appellate review from a final judgment after denial of a recusal motion. *See* TEX.R. CIV. P. 18a(f); *Thomas v. Walker*, 860 S.W.2d 579, 581 (Tex. App.—Waco 1993, orig. proceeding). If the appellate court determines that the judge presiding over the recusal hearing abused his or her discretion in denying the motion and the trial judge should have been recused, the appellate court can reverse the trial court's judgment and remand for a new trial before a different judge. This procedure is no different than the correction of any trial court error through the normal appellate process. As we have observed, "an appellate remedy is not inadequate merely because it may involve more expense or delay than obtaining an extraordinary writ . . . . [T]he 'delay in getting questions decided through the appellate process . . . will not justify intervention by appellate courts through the extraordinary writ of mandamus.' " *Walker v. Packer*, 827 S.W.2d 833, 842 (Tex. 1992) (*quoting Iley v. Hughes*, 158 Tex. 362, 311 S.W.2d 648, 652 (1958)).

The court of appeals abused its discretion by issuing writ of mandamus when the complaining party has an adequate remedy by appeal. *See* TEX.R. CIV. P. 18a(f); *see also Thomas v. Walker*, 860 S.W.2d at 581. We therefore conditionally grant the petition for writ of mandamus and direct the court of appeals to withdraw its order conditionally granting writ of mandamus against the trial court. TEX. GOV'T CODE § 22.002(a).

GONZALEZ, JUSTICE, did not participate in the decision.

HECHT, JUSTICE, concurring.

I concur fully in the Court's opinion and write separately to add two brief observations. First: The rule that appeal affords an adequate remedy for an erroneous denial of a motion to recuse cannot be without exceptions. In other contexts we have noted that mandamus may be appropriate when a judge has flagrantly refused to follow procedural rules, *see Deloitte & Touche v. Fourteenth Court of Appeals*, 951 S.W.2d 394, 398 (Tex. 1997), or when the ruling is almost certain to require a reversal of the final judgment on appeal, *see Walker v. Packer*, 827 S.W.2d 833, 841, 843 (Tex. 1992). I do not read the Court's opinion to preclude mandamus relief in such extraordinary cases.

Second: Plaintiff's motion for recusal in this case asserted that Judge Bennett's impartiality might reasonably be questioned because he was being represented by defendant's counsel in a mandamus proceeding. In many circumstances, obviously, a lawyer's representation of a judge can raise reasonable doubts about the judge's ability to be impartial in a case involving the lawyer. *See* ABA Comm. on Ethics and Professional Responsibility, Informal Op. 1477 (1981). But the relationship between judge and lawyer is of less concern, it seems to me, when it involves no more than the lawyer's representation of the judge as a respondent in a mandamus proceeding. Because the nature of the relationship is important, it may be necessary for the judge to testify concerning the facts, as Judge Bennett did. But the need for a judge to testify concerning facts pertaining to a recusal motion does not justify the judge's offering testimony on the more general matter of the existence of any perceived impartiality. Judges should not inject themselves too far into recusal hearings. Not that Judge Bennett did, I should add; but other judges might. While no judge likes to think of being perceived as partial, a hearing on a motion to recuse is simply not a trial of the judge's character and should not be treated as such. The less a judge is involved in recusal proceedings, voluntarily or involuntarily, the better.

Note

Freedom Communications, Inc. v. Coronado, 372 S.W.3d 621 (Tex. 2012): Juan Antonio Coronado, Francisco Solis Ramirez, Roberto Rivera III, and Ruben Contreras (collectively, "Coronado") sued Peter Zavaletta, Freedom Communications, and former Cameron County District Attorney Yolanda DeLeon for defamation and invasion of privacy arising out of an advertisement placed by Zaveletta in conjunction with his race for district attorney in two Freedom Communications publications. The advertisement alleged that DeLeon failed to prosecute Coronado for alleged child abuse. Freedom Communications moved for summary judgment on the ground that the advertisement was accurate, true, and non-actionable under the United States and Texas Constitutions and Texas statutory and common law. The trial judge, Abel Limas, denied the motion; and Freedom Communications filed an interlocutory appeal. The court of appeals affirmed. Thereafter, Limas entered into a plea agreement in which he pleaded guilty to federal racketeering charges and admitted taking $8000 in cash in part to rule in favor of the plaintiffs in this case on Freedom Communications' motion for summary judgment. On petition for review, Freedom Communications included a copy of the plea agreement and asked that it be considered in deciding the merits of its appeal. ***Held*:** A court must take judicial notice of another court's records if a party provides proof of the records. Here, the plea agreement establishes that Limas, by accepting the bribe, became "interested" in the case and was therefore disqualified under article V, section 11 of the Texas Constitution; as a result, the summary judgment order is void. Therefore, neither the court of appeals nor the supreme court is vested with jurisdiction to decide the merits of Freedom Communications' appeal. The summary judgment order is vacated and the case is remanded to the trial court.

***In re* PERRITT**

992 S.W.2d 444
(Tex. 1999)

John B. Gessner, Gessner & Flores, Dallas, John David Crisp, Crisp, Jordan & Boyd, Texarkana, John H. Barr, Burt Barr & Associates, Christopher M. Weil, Weil & Petrocchi, Dallas, Paul W. Nye, Chaves, Gonzales & Hoblit, Corpus Christi, for relators.

John R. Mercy, Atchley, Russell, Waldrop & Hlavinka, Lynn A. Grisham, Waltman & Grisham, Bryan, for respondent.

PER CURIAM.

In this original mandamus proceeding, we decide whether a judge designated by the presiding judge of the administrative judicial district to hear a recusal motion under Texas Rule of Civil Procedure 18a is also an assigned judge subject to objection and mandatory disqualification under section 74.053(b) of the Texas Government Code. We hold that the assigned judge was subject to section 74.053(b) and conditionally grant the writ.

Billy Wayne and Ann Perritt own and operate a Golden Corral restaurant franchise. They, along with Golden Corral Corporation and Golden Corral Franchising Systems, Inc., were named as defendants in the underlying litigation. The real parties in interest to this proceeding are diners who claim they became ill after eating at the Perritts' restaurant.

The Perritts moved to recuse the trial judge, who referred the matter to the Presiding Judge of the First Administrative Judicial Region, Judge Pat McDowell. Judge McDowell, in turn, designated the Honorable Bill Stephens, a former judge subject to assignment under section 74.054(a)(2) of the Government Code, to hear the recusal motion. Golden Corral Corporation ("Golden Corral") objected to Judge Stephens under section 74.053(b), but Judge Stephens overruled that objection by written order.

Following Judge Stephens' ruling, the Perritts sought mandamus from the court of appeals based on Golden Corral's objection. Apparently neither Golden Corral nor Golden Corral Franchising Systems, Inc. participated in this proceeding, and the court of appeals denied all relief. The Perritts then filed the present original proceeding in this Court, and Golden Corral moved to join as Relators.

Although Judge Stephens clearly refused to recuse himself, the record does not reflect that the Perritts either joined Golden Corral's objection or independently asked Judge Stephens to step aside. Thus, we must first decide whether the Perritts may seek mandamus relief based on another party's objection in the trial court.

A party's right to mandamus relief generally requires a predicate request for some action and a refusal of that request. *Axelson, Inc. v. McIlhany*, 798 S.W.2d 550, 556 (Tex. 1990). Thus, real parties in interest argue that the Perritts' failure to object in the trial court defeats their right to mandamus relief here. On rare occasions we have relaxed this predicate when the circumstances confirmed that "the request would have been futile and the refusal little more than a formality." *Terrazas v. Ramirez*, 829 S.W.2d 712, 723 (Tex. 1991). This is one of those occasions.

Golden Corral's objection clearly advised the trial court of its basis under section 74.053(b). Because the objection was timely, the assigned judge's disqualification was automatic if his assignment was under section 74.053. *In re Houston Lighting & Power Co.*, 976 S.W.2d 671, 672 (Tex. 1998). Golden Corral did not have to provide a reason for the judge's removal. *Houston Lighting & Power*, 976 S.W.2d at 672. The Perritts likewise could have objected to Judge Stephens under section 74.053(b). Had the Perritts filed their own formal objection to Judge Stephens, it would have added nothing for the court's consideration. Their objection would have been the same as Golden Corral's. In these unusual circumstances, the Perritts' joinder in Golden Corral's objection in the trial court was not necessary. We conclude that the Perritts have standing.

Chapter 74 of the Government Code, the Court Administration Act, divides the state into nine administrative judicial regions, provides for the appointment of regional presiding judges, and authorizes these presiding judges to assign visiting judges to the courts in their region, among other things. Section 74.053(b) grants each party to a civil case one unqualified objection to any judge assigned by the presiding judge under the chapter. TEX. GOV'T CODE § 74.053(b). When a party timely objects to the assignment, the assigned judge's removal is mandatory and may be enforced by mandamus. *Mitchell Energy Corp. v. Ashworth*, 943 S.W.2d 436, 437 (Tex. 1997).

This right to an unqualified objection, however, only applies to judges assigned under Chapter 74. *Houston Lighting & Power*, 976 S.W.2d at 672. Real parties argue that Judge Stephens' assignment was not under Chapter 74, but rather was authorized by Rule 18a. Real parties further argue that this rule empowers the presiding judge to assign judges to hear recusal motions and that such power is independent of that conferred under Chapter 74. Real parties conclude that because the presiding judge's authority to assign Judge Stephens to hear the recusal motion did not derive from Chapter 74, Golden Corral's objection was improper.

We have never specifically considered the argument that Rule 18a independently authorizes the presiding judge to assign judges to hear recusal motions. We have, however, previously granted mandamus to enforce a Chapter 74 objection to a judge assigned to hear a recusal motion under Rule 18a. *See Flores v. Banner*, 932 S.W.2d 500, 501 (Tex. 1996). While Rule 18a sets out the procedure for a trial judge's recusal or disqualification, it does not provide an independent basis apart from Chapter 74 for presiding judges to assign judges to hear such motions.

Rule 18a requires a trial judge who does not agree to recusal to refer the matter to the presiding judge of the administrative judicial district, who in turn may hear the motion or designate another judge to do so. TEX.R. CIV. P. 18a(d). When the presiding judge assigns the matter to another judge, he or she does so under authority as presiding judge of the administrative judicial district. Chapter 74 of the Government Code furnishes that authority in this instance, not our rules of civil procedure. Although this Court has the power to authorize the assignment of judges through a self- executing rule, we did not choose to do this when adopting Rule 18a.

We therefore hold that Judge Stephens abused his discretion when he overruled the timely objection to his assignment to hear the recusal motion. Because disqualification is mandatory, mandamus is the appropriate remedy to compel the performance of this ministerial act. *Mitchell Energy*, 943 S.W.2d at 437; *Flores*, 932 S.W.2d at 501. Without hearing oral argument, we conditionally grant the writ of mandamus and direct Judge Stephens to disqualify himself from any further proceedings in this matter. TEX.R.APP. P. 52.8(c). The writ will issue only if Judge Stephens fails to comply.

In re CANALES
v.
In re THE COUNTY OF JIM WELLS

52 S.W.3d 698
(Tex. 2001)

Facts: The judge of the administrative district assigned to Judge Densen to preside, as a visiting judge, over the 79th District Court. Judge Densen heard and ruled on two motions in the underlying case. Subsequently, Judge Densen was assigned to hear the case in question. Then, Barrera, for the first time, filed an objection to Judge Densen's assignment, which was overruled. The court of appeals instructed Judge Densen to disqualify himself. 9 S.W.3d 386.

Issue: When do you have to object to the assignment of a judge? Before the first hearing. Was the objection timely here? NO.

Writ of mandamus will issue. Barrera waived her objection to Judge Densen by waiting to file it until after he had conducted two pretrial hearings. Under TEX. GOV'T CODE section 74.053, the parties to a civil case may object to an assigned judge, if the objection is filed before the first hearing or trial in the case, including pretrial hearings, over which the assigned judge is to preside—without regard to the terms of the particular order under which the judge is assigned. The statute does not confer a new opportunity to object when a visiting judge, who has already heard matters in the case is reassigned by a new assignment order.

From the court of appeal opinion (9 S.W.3d 386, 388)**:**

> In the present case, Judge Densen's status as either a former or retired judge is in dispute. The only evidence of Judge Densen's status in the record before us is Judge Densen's own statement, made during the hearing on Barrera's objection to his assignment. Judge Densen noted that he "was a former judge when [he] left the bench . . . however . . . at that time, I was a vested judge." This statement is ambiguous, at best, and provides little evidence of Judge Densen's true status. Fortunately, however, Judge Densen's status is irrelevant to the issue before us as only one objection to his assignment has been lodged. More to the point, regardless of Judge Densen's status, any objection made to his assignment under chapter 74.053 was required to be timely. *See* TEX. GOV'T CODE ANN. § 74.053(c) (Vernon 1998).

In re O'CONNOR

92 S.W.3d 446
(Tex. 2002)

Facts: In this mandamus proceeding, O'Connor seeks to disqualify the trial judge from presiding over her suit for modification of the parent-child relationship. O'Connor filed her motion to disqualify under Texas Rule of Civil Procedure 18b(1)(a) after discovering that the trial judge had been her former attorney's law partner during the time that her former attorney represented her in the initial divorce action. The judge declined to disqualify himself.

Issue: Is a judge is vicariously disqualified under the Constitution as having "been counsel in the case" if a lawyer with whom the judge previously practiced law represented one of the parties concerning the matter before the court? Yes.

Writ of mandamus will issue. The judge is disqualified from presiding over the modification proceeding.

Issue: Are the orders of a constitutionally disqualified judge void, if the judge sits in a case? Yes.

Any orders or judgments the disqualified judge rendered in the modification proceeding are void and without effect. Rule 18b(1)(a) recognizes that a judge is vicariously disqualified under the Constitution as having "been counsel in the case" if a lawyer with whom the judge previously practiced law served as counsel to a party concerning the matter during their association. The temporary orders resolved matters concerning custody, visitation, and the right to determine the child's residence. O'Connor's modification proceeding raised these matters again, because O'Connor sought to increase her possession periods and to have the exclusive right to determine the child's residence. Thus, the divorce action and the modification proceeding involved the same matter in controversy - custody, visitation, and the right to determine the child's residence.

TESCO AMERICAN, INC.
v.
STRONG INDUSTRIES, INC.
221 S.W.3d 550
(Tex. 2006)

An appellate judge is disqualified because, unbeknownst to her, before she took the bench, another attorney at her very large firm played a very small role in the early stages of this appeal. TEX. CONST. ART. V, § 11, and TEX. R. CIV. P. 18b(1)(a), requires vicarious disqualification. The constitutional protection against "counsel in the case" becoming a judge in the case, makes no distinction between trial and appellate judges.

Any orders or judgments rendered by a trial judge who is constitutionally disqualified are void and without effect. However the questions or issues before an appellate court the appellate courts, judgments and the opinions of the court are generally rendered by a multi-member court, not a single judge; unless *every* judge who participates is constitutionally disqualified, the single-judge rule does not easily fit the multi-judge situation. Thus, when an opinion is issued by a court of appeals, with one disqualified judge sitting, the judgment is not void. Here, the First Court of Appeals certainly had jurisdiction of the parties and the subject matter, jurisdiction to enter judgment, and capacity to act as a court. But the judgment must be reversed, because the opinion on which it was based was authored by a justice who was constitutionally disqualified. The two remaining justices may decide this case, but they must do so without the participation of a disqualified justice.

Notes

1. *Dow Chemical Company v. Francis*, 46 S.W.3d 237 (Tex. 2001): The discretion vested in the trial court over the conduct of a trial is great. A trial court has the authority to express itself in exercising this broad discretion. Further, a trial court may properly intervene to maintain control in the courtroom, to expedite the trial, and to prevent what it considers to be a waste of time. Judicial rulings alone almost never constitute a valid basis for a bias or partiality motion, and opinions the judge forms during a trial do not necessitate recusal, unless they display a deep-seated favoritism or antagonism that would make fair judgment impossible. Thus, judicial remarks during the course of a trial that are critical or disapproving of, or even hostile to, counsel, the parties, or their cases, ordinarily do not support a bias or partiality challenge. Further, expressions of impatience, dissatisfaction, annoyance, and even anger do not establish bias or partiality. A judge's ordinary efforts at courtroom administration—even a stern and short-tempered judge's efforts—remain immune. Objection to a trial court's alleged improper conduct or comment must be made when it occurs, if a party is to preserve error for appellate review, unless the conduct or comment cannot be rendered harmless by proper instruction.

2. *Commission For Lawyer Discipline v. Schaefer*, 364 S.W.3d 831 (Tex. 2012): The Office of the Chief Disciplinary Counsel (CDC) of the State Bar of Texas investigated three grievances against attorney Heather Schaefer and found just cause to have the grievances adjudicated. When Schaefer did not elect to have the grievances adjudicated in the district court, the CDC assigned them to an evidentiary panel appointed by a District Grievance Committees for attorney disciplinary actions. A quorum of that panel heard the grievances against Schaefer and unanimously recommended that she be disbarred. The panel's "Evidentiary Hearing Report" listed the second public-member position on the six-person panel as "vacant." Although the quorum of panelists present for the hearing met the required ratio of lawyers to non-lawyers, Schaefer appealed to the Board of Disciplinary Appeals on the ground that the evidentiary panel was not composed of the required ratio of one-third public to two-thirds attorney members. BODA ruled the error was void as the panel had no capacity to act and vacated the panel's judgment and remanded for a new hearing because the evidentiary panel was improperly composed. ***Held***: A properly constituted quorum of an improperly constituted evidentiary panel has the authority to act in an attorney disciplinary matter. "In the appellate context, where multiple judges are empaneled, a judgment is merely voidable unless every judge on the panel is disqualified." As such a violation of a

procedural rule, statute, or even a constitutional requirement will not rendered an appellate judgment "void." Instead, such violations generally only result in a "voidable" or erroneous judgment. Describing the "rare circumstances" that would void a judgment, as only when it is apparent that the court rendering the judgment had no jurisdiction of the parties, no jurisdiction of the subject matter, no jurisdiction to enter the judgment, or no capacity to act as a court." Although "[t]he Grievance Committee should timely advise respondent attorneys of the composition of the evidentiary panel from which the quorum was drawn to hear the case," here "the [evidentiary panel] chair introduced only the members present on the record and did not name the absent members of the panel," thus creating uncertainty as to whether the evidentiary panel lacked a necessary public member." Nonetheless, "reasonable diligence by the attorney requires more than occurred here. Faced with an incomplete evidentiary panel, the respondent attorney must inquire as to panel composition and object if the composition requirements are not satisfied. Should an attorney fail to appear at an evidentiary hearing, she makes her task more difficult and should obtain the hearing report and preserve error through a timely post-judgment motion." Schaefer waived error by failing to appear and object at the hearing and by failing to file a timely post-judgment motion after receiving the panel's report.

3. *In re Blevins*, --- S.W.3d ----, 2013 WL 5878910 (Tex.), 57 Tex. Sup. Ct. J. 38 (November 1, 2013): "This original proceeding arises from an order in a Suit Affecting the Parent–Child Relationship (SAPCR). The order transferred possession of two children who had been living with foster parents to the children's father. The foster parents assert that the trial court abused its discretion by transferring possession and seek a writ of mandamus directing the trial judge to set aside the order. However, because the trial judge who signed the order has recused from the case, we abate the proceedings in this Court. We direct the trial judge now presiding over the case to consider the matters underlying the challenged order and determine whether the challenged order should remain in effect, be modified, or be set aside, and to render its own order accordingly. The trial judge is not limited to considering only evidence on which the order was based."

4. TEX. R. APP. PROC. 16.1. Grounds for Disqualification

The grounds for disqualification of an appellate court justice or judge are determined by the Constitution and laws of Texas.

5. TEX. R. APP. PROC. 16.2. Grounds for Recusal

The grounds for recusal of an appellate court justice or judge are the same as those provided in the Rules of Civil Procedure. In addition, a justice or judge must recuse in a proceeding if it presents a material issue which the justice or judge participated in deciding while serving on another court in which the proceeding was pending.

6. TEX. R. APP. PROC. 16.3. Procedure for Recusal

(a) Motion. A party may file a motion to recuse a justice or judge before whom the case is pending. The motion must be filed promptly after the party has reason to believe that the justice or judge should not participate in deciding the case.

(b) Decision. Before any further proceeding in the case, the challenged justice or judge must either remove himself or herself from all participation in the case or certify the matter to the entire court, which will decide the motion by a majority of the remaining judges sitting en banc. The challenged justice or judge must not sit with the remainder of the court to consider the motion as to him or her.

(c) Appeal. An order of recusal is not reviewable, but the denial of a recusal motion is reviewable.

ROCHA
v.
AHMAD
662 S.W.2d 77
(Tex. App.—San Antonio 1983, no writ)

A judge is not required to disqualify himself/herself because of the receipt of campaign contributions from an attorney appearing before that judge.

Kilgarlin & Bruch, *Disqualification and Recusal of Judges,* 17 ST. MARY'S L.J. 599, 638 (1986); Calvert, *Disqualification of Judges,* 47 TEX.B.J. 1330, 1337-38 (1984).

WILLIAMS
v.
VISWANATHAN
65 S.W.3d 685
(Tex. App.—Amarillo 2001, no pet.)

A judge is not required (under TEX. R. CIV. P. 18b(2(c) concerning impartiality) to disqualify herself/himself because one of the attorney's for a party supported the judge's opponent in a recent election.

A judge's employment as an attorney for a client, before assuming office, does not disqualify the judge from hearing a case that arose thereafter.

A judge serving as an adjunct professor at a University involved in a case before the court is not disqualified from sitting on the case. The type of interest required for disqualification must be of pecuniary nature so that he judge would gain or lose by the judgment rendered in the case.

7. *Transfer of Cases Among Courts*

Note

In re U.S. Silica Co., 157 S.W.3d 434 (Tex. 2005): This is an original mandamus proceeding. Ten silicosis cases, involving hundreds of plaintiffs, were filed in Cameron County, and randomly assigned to six different courts. At the behest of different parties, three judges issued conflicting orders asserting jurisdiction over cases in their own courts or others. **Held:** Because the Cameron County local rules permit a unilateral transfer only by the court where the first case was filed, the Supreme Court conditionally grants a writ of mandamus directing the others to vacate orders forbidding that transfer.

TEX. GOV'T CODE § 74.092(1) assigns to local administrative judges the statutory duty (among others) to "implement and execute the local rules of administration, including the assignment, docketing, transfer, and hearing of cases." This statute, however, does not give local administrative judges authority to review and reverse conflicting rulings of coordinate courts. While the local administrative judge may transfer cases pursuant to local rules, enforcing or overruling competing orders is the duty of a higher court.

As the relators challenge only the conflicting transfer orders, the propriety of consolidating such a large number of claims is not before the Court. While the Supreme Court has encouraged consolidation for pretrial purposes (most recently pursuant to legislative mandate), it has avoided placing such decisions in the hands of one of the players. Local consolidation rules have made similar arrangements to avoid the awkward problem of one court taking a case from another. But the only issue before the Court is which court, if any, could unilaterally transfer to itself related Cameron County cases. Accordingly, the Court does not address whether the transfers here would (as the local rules also require) "facilitate orderly and efficient disposition of the litigation."

8. *The Trial*

Read Rules 265, 266, 267, 269 and 270 Texas Rules of Civil Procedure and Rule 614 Texas Rules of Civil Evidence.

Note

In the following pages a brief presentation will be given of the significant procedural rules concerning the conduct of a trial. Although it is beyond the scope of this book to given any detailed presentation of the methods for admission and exclusion of evidence [this is the subject of courses in Evidence and Trial Advocacy], many of the cases presented in this book address various problems associated with the preservation of error based upon alleged erroneous evidentiary rulings made by the trial court. However, the focus of this section is to point out several specific procedural rules which address the conduct of the trial.

GUERRERO
v.
SMITH

864 S.W.2d 797
(Tex. App.—Houston [14th Dist.] 1993, no writ)

David L. Elmers, Houston, for appellants.
Edwin McAninch, Houston, for appellees.

ELLIS, JUSTICE.

Appellees, Joy Lee Smith and Kevin Lee Smith, sued appellant, Dr. Guerrero, for injuries sustained by Joy as a result of appellant's medical malpractice. The jury ruled in favor of Joy and found that appellant was negligent, grossly negligent, and committed fraud while acting in a fiduciary capacity. The jury also found that appellant's actions constituted reckless disregard for the safety of Joy and were the intentional infliction of emotional distress. The jury awarded Joy (hereinafter "appellee") $2,000,000 in actual damages and $1,250,000 in exemplary damages. Kevin Lee Smith, since divorced from appellee, did not participate in the trial and received no award. We affirm.

Appellant is a licensed medical doctor practicing homeopathic medicine. The record indicates that appellee consulted appellant for several different ailments, including migraine headaches and a sprained wrist. As treatment for appellee's ailments, appellant would inject appellee with a "concoction" made up of vitamins, minerals, and dimethyl sulfoxide (DMSO) which has not been approved for human use by the Food and Drug Administration. Appellee entered into evidence the Medical Practices Act which states that a physician must provide a written statement informing the patient that DMSO is not approved by the FDA. Appellant admitted that he did not provide such a written statement to appellee.

Before injecting appellee, appellant would not prepare the skin to sterilize it for the injection. He would inject appellant several different times and use the same needle without sterilizing either the needle or appellee's skin. He injected her in her head, between her eyes, in her throat, neck, arms, wrists, hands, elbows, stomach, abdomen, and the outside and inside of her vagina.

Appellee became infected in the exact spots where appellant administered the injections. When appellee asked for antibiotics, appellant refused to give them to her and told her to drink her morning urine instead. Appellee refused to do so and became massively infected. She was taken to an emergency room where she was found to be near death from septic shock. She was forced to undergo fasciotomies which involve cutting the skin, subcutaneous tissue, and the layer over the muscle so that swelling due to deep infection does not constrict the blood vessels and press on the nerves causing the limb to die. One of her fingers, parts of her labia, buttocks, and groin were removed. She bears permanent scars and disfigurement and incurred over $300,000 in medical bills.

At trial, Dr. Winston, a licensed medical doctor, testified as an expert witness. It was his opinion that appellant was practicing medicine beneath the standard of care in Harris County or of any physician he had seen. He stated that appellant was practicing medicine outside the law and unsafely. He further testified that in his opinion appellant's conduct constituted gross negligence, intentional infliction of emotional stress, and fraud. He estimated that appellee's future medical bills would be $1,000,000.

Appellant asserts three points of error. First, that the trial court erred in denying his motion for mistrial after appellee's counsel, during his opening statement, had displayed to the jury an inflammatory photograph which had not been introduced into evidence. Second, that the trial court erred in overruling his objection to the testimony of a witness for appellee who had been seated in the courtroom for several hours prior to her testimony, even though the Rule had been invoked. Third, that the trial court erred in overruling his objection to the testimony of a physician as an expert witness for appellee who did not possess the pertinent qualifications required by statute.

In his first point of error, appellant asserts that the trial court should have granted a mistrial after counsel for appellee surreptitiously displayed a photograph of appellee to the jury during his opening statement. Counsel for appellant did not object at the time the photograph was displayed, claiming that he did not see opposing counsel display the photograph because opposing counsel's back was to him. However, the court reporter saw the display, made record of it, and told counsel for appellant at the break. Immediately after the break, counsel for appellant moved for a mistrial, which was denied, and he made a bill of exception. The trial court instructed the jury not to consider any evidence they may have seen prior to appellee's case-in-chief. The same photograph was later admitted into evidence without objection by counsel for appellant.

Rule 265 of the Texas Rules of Civil Procedure governs the order of proceedings in a trial by jury. Rule 265(a) speaks specifically about opening statements and provides in pertinent part: (a) The party upon whom rests the burden of proof on the whole case shall state to the jury briefly the nature of his claim or defense and what said party expects to prove and the relief sought. TEX. R. CIV. P. 265(a).

This rule does not afford counsel the right to detail to the jury the evidence which he intends to offer, nor to read or display the documents and photographs he proposes to offer. Where counsel is allowed to detail expectations in the opening statement, he places matters before the jury without the determination of their admissibility. *See Ranger Ins. Co. v. Rogers*, 530 S.W.2d 162, 170 (Tex. Civ. App.—Austin 1975, writ ref'd n.r.e). This practice misleads and confuses the jurors as between counsel's mere expectations and evidence that is actually admitted. *Id.*

Although this conduct should not have been tolerated by the trial court, we are bound by the abuse of discretion standard which gives trial courts wide latitude in limiting opening statements. *Id.* We must be convinced that the court's failure to grant the motion for mistrial was such error so as to cause the rendition of an improper judgment. *Id.* at 171. We are not convinced that a different judgment would have resulted in this case had counsel for appellee not displayed the photograph.

First, the record reflects that the same photograph was later entered into evidence with no objection from appellant. The general rule is that error in the admission of evidence is deemed harmless if the objecting party subsequently permits the same or similar evidence to be introduced without objection. *Richardson v. Green*, 677 S.W.2d 497, 501 (Tex. 1984). Since the photograph was later introduced without objection by appellant, the display of it by counsel for appellee during his opening statement is deemed harmless.

Second, to obtain reversal of a judgment based on error in the admission or exclusion of evidence, appellant must show error that was calculated to cause and probably did cause the rendition of an improper judgment. *Texaco, Inc. v. Pennzoil, Co.*, 729 S.W.2d 768, 837 (Tex. App.—Houston [1st Dist.] 1987, writ ref'd n.r.e), *cert. dism'd*, 485 U.S. 994, 108 S.Ct. 1305, 99 L.Ed.2d 686 (1988). In our review of the record, we see that other pictures of appellee during her stages of the infection were admitted into evidence. In addition, there is an abundance of testimony regarding appellant's unorthodox practices. In light of all of the other evidence supporting the jury's verdict, we cannot say that the display of the photograph during opening statement by counsel for appellee caused the rendition of an improper verdict. Although we do not approve of counsel's unprofessionalism, we hold that the trial court did not abuse its discretion in denying the motion for mistrial and, therefore, overrule appellant's first point of error.

In his second point of error, appellant contends that the trial court erred in overruling his objection to the testimony of a witness for appellee who had been seated in the courtroom several hours prior to her testimony even though the Rule had been invoked. *See* TEX. R. CIV. EVID. 614. The witness, Deborah Lessard, was a spectator at the trial and had heard appellant's testimony. During the break, she approached counsel for appellee and told him that she had worked as a nurse at Twelve Oaks Hospital where some of appellant's patients had allegedly been taken. She said that she had personal knowledge to refute appellant's testimony and to impeach him. Her testimony did not concern appellee's injuries, causation, or damages, but was for impeachment purposes only.

Specifically, Ms. Lessard testified that while working as a nurse in the emergency room at Twelve Oaks Hospital, she recalled providing health care to people who claimed to be patients of appellant. She could only remember the name of one of the patients and stated that the patient reeked of urine. She testified that the patient had been drinking her own urine.

An explanation of the Rule was best given in *Triton Oil & Gas Corp. v. E.W. Moran Drilling Co.*: The Rule permits the trial court, at the request of either party in a civil case, to swear and remove the witnesses from the courtroom so they cannot hear the testimony given by any other witness in the case. It has been held that the Rule is directory, not mandatory. When the Rule has been properly invoked, as it was in the case at bar, and a party tenders a witness who has not been placed thereunder or there is some other violation of the rule [sic], the trial court, in the exercise of judicial discretion, must determine whether the witness' testimony will be received. Taking into consideration all of the circumstances, the trial judge may bar the witness from the stand, and his ruling will be upset only on a showing of abuse of discretion. Conversely, upon a similar consideration, the trial judge may, in his discretion, permit the witness to testify, and again the ruling may be upset only upon a showing of manifest abuse of discretion. *Triton Oil & Gas Corp. v. E.W. Moran Drilling Co.*, 509 S.W.2d 678, 685 (Tex. Civ. App.—Fort Worth 1974, writ ref'd n.r.e.) (citations omitted); *see also Southwestern Bell Telephone Co. v. Johnson*, 389 S.W.2d 645, 647-48 (Tex. 1965); *Parham v. Wilborn*, 746 S.W.2d 347, 349 (Tex. App.—Fort Worth 1988, no writ); *Holmes v. Holmes*, 588 S.W.2d 674, 676 (Tex. Civ. App.—Beaumont 1979, no writ). Thus, we must review all of the circumstances to see if the trial court abused its discretion. In our review, we may not substitute our own judgment for that of the trial court even if we would have decided the matter differently. *Gaines v. Frawley*, 739 S.W.2d 950, 955 (Tex. App.—Fort Worth 1987, no writ).

Normally, rulings on questions of excluding or admitting evidence will not be reversed unless the whole case turns on the evidence admitted or excluded. *Nichols v. Howard Trucking Co.*, 839 S.W.2d 155, 158 (Tex. App.—Beaumont 1992, no writ) (*citing Atlantic Mutual Insurance Co. v. Middleman*, 661 S.W.2d 182, 185 (Tex. App.—San Antonio 1983, writ ref'd n.r.e.)). Since the witness' testimony did not concern the appellee's injuries, but was used only for impeachment, we cannot say that the whole case turned upon it. Furthermore, appellant was impeached only as to a matter that did not concern appellee. The trial court did not abuse its discretion in allowing this witness to testify, thus, appellant's second point of error is overruled.

In his third point of error, appellant argues that the trial court erred in overruling his objection to the testimony of a physician as an expert who did not possess the qualifications as an expert witness required by statute. TEX. REV. CIV. STAT. ANN. art. 4590i s 14.01 (Vernon Supp. 1993) states:

> (a) In a suit involving a health care liability claim against a physician for injury to or death of a patient, a person may qualify as an expert witness on the issue of whether the physician departed from accepted standards of medical care only if: (1) the person is practicing at the time such testimony is given or was practicing at the time the claim arose and has knowledge of accepted standards of medical care for the diagnosis, care, or treatment of the illness, injury, or condition involved in the claim; or (2) the court, after a hearing conducted outside the presence of the jury, determines that the person is otherwise qualified to give expert testimony on said issue. (b) For the purpose of this section, "practicing" includes, but is not limited to, training residents or students at an accredited school of medicine or osteopathy or serving as a consulting physician to other physicians who provide direct patient care, upon the request of such other physicians.

Appellant specifically complains that Dr. Winston, who testified as an expert witness for appellee, is not qualified to do so because he claimed to be a surgeon but has not performed surgery since 1983. However, at the beginning of Dr. Winston's testimony, counsel for appellant stipulated that Dr. Winston was a qualified expert. Shortly thereafter, counsel for appellant took Dr. Winston on voir dire and objected to him testifying as an expert witness. The trial judge overruled the objection on the grounds that counsel for appellant had already stipulated to Dr. Winston's qualification as an expert witness and that the court had made an independent finding that Dr. Winston was qualified.

Stipulations comprising the record will be observed and the reviewing court is bound by the stipulation. *Amoco Prod. Co. v. Texas Elec. Serv. Co.*, 614 S.W.2d 194, 196 (Tex. Civ. App.—Houston [14th Dist.] 1981, no writ) (*citing, New v. First Nat'l Bank of Midland*, 476 S.W.2d 121 (Tex. Civ. App.—El Paso 1971, writ ref'd n.r.e.)). Although the trial court has the power to modify or set aside a stipulation, if it is not set aside, it is conclusive as to the facts stipulated and all matters necessarily included therein. *Sadler v. Duvall*, 815 S.W.2d 285, 289 (Tex. App.—Texarkana 1991, writ denied). In the present case, the trial court did not set aside the stipulation and since we, as a reviewing court, are bound by the stipulation, we are in no position to disturb it.

Furthermore, the trial court made an independent finding, after a hearing outside the presence of the jury, that Dr. Winston was a qualified expert. TEX. REV. CIV. STAT. ANN. art. 4590i s 14.01(b) (Vernon Supp. 1993) specifically grants the trial court the power to make an independent determination that the witness is "otherwise qualified" as an expert. The determination of whether a particular witness is qualified to testify as an expert is a matter of judicial discretion and the trial court's decision will not be overturned unless it clearly abused its discretion. *Warner v. Hurt*, 834 S.W.2d 404, 406 (Tex. App.—Houston [14th Dist.] 1992, no writ). After a review of the record, we cannot say that the trial court abuse its discretion in allowing Dr. Winston to testify as an expert witness. Appellant's third point of error is overruled.

Accordingly, the judgment of the trial court is affirmed.

4M LINEN & UNIFORM SUPPLY CO.
v.
W.P. BALLARD & CO., INC.

793 S.W.2d 320
(Tex. App.—Houston [1st Dist.] 1990, writ denied)

Andrew J. Mytelka, John A. Buckley, Jr., Galveston, for appellant.
Robert E. Lapin, Galveston, for appellee.

O'CONNOR, JUSTICE.

This is an appeal from a suit on a sworn account. We grant appellant's motion for rehearing, withdraw our original opinion issued November 16, 1989, and substitute the following opinion.

W.P. Ballard & Co., Inc. (Ballard & Co.) filed suit on a sworn account against 4M Linen & Uniform Supply Co., Inc. (4M Linen). In response, 4M Linen filed a counterclaim alleging breach of implied warranty, breach of contract, and violation of the Deceptive Trade Practices Act (DTPA). Before trial, on stipulated facts, the court entered an instructed verdict for Ballard & Co. for $51,996.11 on its sworn account claim and on 4M Linen's counterclaim. After the evidence, the trial court submitted Ballard & Co.'s issue on attorney's fees, and 4M Linen's defensive issues on misrepresentations and breach of warranties. The jury answered all the issues in favor of Ballard & Co. The trial court disregarded the finding on attorney's fees, and signed a judgment awarding Ballard & Co. $51,996.11, plus interest. Both parties appealed. We modify and affirm the judgment.

This suit arises out of a contract between Ballard & Co. and 4M Linen, under which Ballard & Co. supplied laundry products, produced and recommended by Diamond Shamrock, to 4M Linen. A sales representative for Ballard & Co. visited the 4M Linen plant each week to inventory 4M Linen's supplies. Based on that inventory, Ballard & Co. delivered chemicals. 4M Linen paid Ballard & Co. for the chemicals until July 1985. Beginning in June, 4M Linen started having problems with mildew. 4M Linen refused to pay Ballard & Co. for the supplies that it delivered from July 1985 through October 1985. The main issue at trial was whether Ballard & Co. had a duty to tell 4M Linen that Tex-Stat, one of the chemicals recommended by Diamond Shamrock and supplied by Ballard & Co., was not a mildewcide.

* * *

In its third point of error, 4M Linen argues the trial court erred in denying it the opportunity to open and close on final argument, in violation of TEX. R. CIV. P. 266 and 269. Before trial, the court granted a motion for directed verdict on 4M Linen's stipulation of liability on the sworn account. Ballard & Co.'s only remaining issue to go to the jury was attorney's fees. 4M Linen contends the trial court should have permitted it to open and close the argument because the central issue was its DTPA claim.

There are two rules that control the order of final argument: TEX. R. CIV. P. 266, which governs both the order of presenting evidence and final argument; and TEX. R. CIV. P. 269, which governs the argument.

Rule 266, which is subject to rule 269, provides that the plaintiff has the right to open and close argument. There are two exceptions in rule 266. First, a defendant has the right to open and close if the burden of proof for the entire case under the pleadings is on defendant. TEX. R. CIV. P. 266. Second, a defendant has the right to open and close if, before trial begins, defendant admits that plaintiff is entitled to recover, subject to proof of defensive allegations in the answer. *Id.*

Rule 269 provides that the party who has the burden of proof on the whole case, or the party who has the burden on all matters in the charge, has the right to open and close the argument. TEX. R. CIV. P. 269(a). There is an exception in rule 269: When there are several parties who have separate claims or defenses, the court "shall" determine the order of argument.

4M Linen claims that it had the right to open and close the argument because it had the burden of proof on the whole case and cites three cases in support of its point of error. In *Community Public Serv. Co. v. Andrews*, 590 S.W.2d 563, 566 (Tex. Civ. App.—Houston [1st Dist.] 1979, writ ref'd n.r.e.), this Court found the trial court properly permitted defendant to open and close because defendant had the burden of proof on all issues submitted to the jury. We agree with the holding in Andrews: when a defendant has the burden on all issues submitted to the jury, and the trial court permits defendant to open and close, we will affirm the ruling on appeal. Those are not the facts in this case.

In *Dreeben v. Sidor*, 254 S.W.2d 908, 912 (Tex. Civ. App.—Amarillo 1952, writ ref'd n.r.e.), another case cited by 4M Linen, the defendant in a suit on a note admitted executing the note, but claimed he signed it relying on plaintiff's misrepresentations. The Amarillo Court of Appeals held the trial court properly permitted defendant to open and close arguments because he had the burden of proof on issues raised by the pleadings. *Id.* The court did not address whether plaintiff had the burden of proof on any of the special issues submitted to the jury, or the effect that burden had on the right to open and close.

4M Linen also cites *Meece v. Wade*, 512 S.W.2d 372 (Tex. Civ. App.—Austin 1974, writ ref'd n.r.e.), where defendants made a similar argument to that made by 4M Linen. In *Meece*, plaintiff, an architect sued defendants to recover for breach of contract. Defendants counterclaimed, asserting malpractice. By the end of the trial, plaintiff had proved most of his case as a matter of law, and the trial court only submitted one damage issue for him. The court submitted defendants' counterclaims in six issues. Defendants had the burden on all liability issues and one damage issue, while plaintiff had the burden on only one issue. *Id.* at 373. On appeal, the *Meece* defendants argued that they should have been permitted to open and close final arguments because they had the "burden of proof on the whole case." The Austin Court of Appeals rejected defendants' argument because plaintiff had the burden of proof under the pleadings and defendants did not have the burden of proof on all issues submitted to the jury. *Id.* at 374.

The same is true here. As in *Meece*, plaintiff proved its case as a matter of law, and defendant's counterclaims were submitted to the jury, along with one issue for plaintiff. *Meece* supports the trial court's ruling.

Ballard & Co. cites us to *Horton v. Dental Capital Leasing Corp.*, 649 S.W.2d 655 (Tex. App.—Texarkana 1983, no writ) in defense of the trial court's ruling. The Texarkana Court of Appeals said a defendant "must have the burden of proof on the whole case under the pleadings or have the burden of proof on all issues submitted" to have the right to open and close. *Horton*, 649 S.W.2d at 657. The court held defendant did not have that right when plaintiff still had the burden on the issue of attorney's fees.

In this case, the trial court submitted six issues to the jury, one of which was Ballard & Co.'s issue on attorney's fees. 4M Linen had the burden of proof on the remainder of the issues submitted. After looking to the pleadings of the case, we determine that Ballard & Co. carried the burden of proof on the whole case. The trial court properly denied 4M Linen's request to open and close final arguments.

We overrule 4M Linen's third point of error.

* * *

We modify the judgment to reinstate the jury's award of attorney's fees for Ballard & Co., and, as modified, affirm the judgment.

Note

In *Pace Corp. v. Jackson*, 155 Tex. 179, 284 S.W.2d 340 (1955), the Court interpreting the phrase "the burden of proof on the whole case" stated:

> The question here, then, is who had 'the burden of proof on the whole case'? * * * Ordinarily one who first requests the intervention of a court in his behalf—who asserts a right or a duty and demands a remedy—is properly required to carry the burden of proving his right to the remedy and is entitled to such tactical advantages as inhere in his obligations. As our procedure is expanded to include new techniques and remedies, such as declaratory judgment, we must look to the reason behind 'ordinary rules' lest we apply them blindly and unjustly. In the usual and ordinary case the burden of proof is not imposed on the plaintiff merely because he files his petition first but because he asks for action on his behalf from the court, either preventive or in the nature of redress. The other party is usually content with the status quo. Both logic and fairness demand that the plaintiff shoulder the responsibility of convincing the court that action should be taken. When, by statute, a litigant is allowed to initiate judicial action merely to determine his legal relationships, the logic of the above situation is unchanged. Although, as petitioners point out, declaratory judgment actions may be brought either before or after breach of a contract, nevertheless, if one party is asserting a right to damages or some other active relief in his own behalf, the burden of proving his right to that relief still rests upon him. The time sequence in the filing of pleadings can neither relieve him of his responsibilities nor deprive him of his advantages.

CHAPTER 3.
PREPARATION OF THE JURY CHARGE AND RECEIPT OF THE VERDICT

1. *Charge of the Court*

SAHR
v.
BIERD
354 Mich. 353
92 N.W.2d 467 (1958)

Van Benschoten & Van Benschoten, Saginaw, for plaintiff, appellant and cross-appellee.
Heilman & Purcell, Saginaw, for defendant, appellee and cross-appellant.

SMITH, JUSTICE.

Here we have an automobile accident at the intersection of two country roads. It happened in broad daylight. The roads were clear and dry. A jury verdict was returned for defendant. Plaintiff asserts error, pointing to the court's refusal to submit two special questions to the jury, to the court's refusal of the charge that if upon the facts shown the defendant drove out into the intersection he was guilty of negligence as a matter of law, and to the court's inclusions of instructions upon intervening negligence when nothing had intervened. The case will be reversed. If defendant in truth drove out into the intersection under the conditions presented he was guilty of negligence as a matter of law and the jury should have been so instructed.

The inclusion of the special questions, and the controversy over their use, compels us, as well, to examine in detail this cumbersome procedural device which came into the law to lessen the peril of the jury's attaint. It was made statutory at an early time in this jurisdiction and has since been embodied in our court rules. It is prolific of disagreement, dissent (*see* our recent division in *Richards v. Birmingham School District*, 348 Mich. 490, 83 N.W.2d 643), and distinctions so dubious that Mr. JUSTICE HART of the Supreme Court of Ohio (*McNees v. Cincinnati Street Ry. Co.*, 152 Ohio St. 269, 284, 89 N.E.2d 138, 146, dissent) referred to them as metaphysical. Viewing the procedure in operation we are not impressed with its utility.

The plaintiff was a 10-year-old boy. He was riding in a Chrysler automobile being driven by his father in a westerly direction on Hess Road a two-lane, hard-surfaced, east and west, through highway. There is testimony that the father had had some beer prior to the accident. He had a restrictive driver's license only, since he had but one arm, and was required to have a knob on his steering wheel. Defendant Jack Bierd was driving his Ford south on Towerline road. This also was a hard-surfaced, two-lane road, running generally north and south. A stop sign at the Hess-Towerline intersection required traffic on Towerline to stop before entering Hess.

It is undisputed that the two cars collided. As to how and why they collided the parties differ. Plaintiff asserts that the defendant turned left through the intersection in the path of plaintiff's oncoming car and that the collision actually occurred in the northeast corner of the intersection 'where defendant had no right to be.' Defendant, however, testified that he came to a full stop 'about even with the culvert, which was two or three feet off Hess,' and that he was standing still when hit and had not entered the intersection.

Appellant first asserts error in the refusal of the trial court to submit to the jury two special questions:

> '1. Did the collision occur on the northeast corner of the intersection of Hess and Towerline road as claimed by the plaintiff?
>
> '2. Did the collision occur on Towerline road north of Hess road as claimed by the defendant?'

In support of his claimed right to the submission of such questions, appellant cites to us C.L.1948, § 618.39 (Stat.Ann. § 27.1019), providing as follows:

> 'In all cases where an issue of facts is tried before any court of record, the court shall at the request in writing, of the counsel of either party, instruct the jury if they return a general verdict, also to find upon particular questions of facts, respecting which the issue is joined, to be stated in writing, and shall direct a written finding thereon: *Provided*, Such special questions shall not exceed 5 in number, and shall be each in single, short sentences, readily answered by yes or no. The special verdict, or finding,

> shall be filed with the clerk, and entered upon the minutes, and when any special finding of facts shall be inconsistent with a general verdict, the former shall control the latter, and the court give judgment accordingly.'

Thus appellant relies upon the 'special questions' statute, also a part of Rule No. 37, § 6, rather than the 'special verdict' section of the court rules, § 7 of Rule 37. As JUSTICE BLACK has pointed out in *Richards v. Birmingham School District*, 348 Mich. 490, 512, 514, 83 N.W.2d 643, these sections are not to be confused. Section 6 (special questions, or special interrogatories) is an outgrowth of an ancient practice. Section 7 (the rule-authorized special verdict) is a modern device, urged by the leading students of our generation, espoused by distinguished judges, made a part not only of our State practice but of the Federal practice as well, commended by those who have employed it, yet permitted by us of the profession to gather dust in the back room. Meanwhile the jury function, guaranteed us by the Constitution, is permitted slowly to break down under the weight of burdens far beyond its capabilities, as the numbers of the jury-waived cases now so eloquently attest. We have too much faith in the jury function to acquiesce tacitly in its gradual elimination.

The problems confronting us in this case cannot be answered upon authority and principle without an examination of the origins and purposes of the special practice which it is here sought to employ. Behind the rule under examination we have one of the darkest of the common-law doctrines, that of the attaint of the jury. This, as Thayer tells us, was for centuries the great check upon the jury. If, upon appeal to a grand jury, the verdict of the first jury was found to be erroneous (even if 'based upon a misconception of a nice point of law,' *Morgan*, *supra*, p. 576) the first judgment was reversed and (3 Blackstone, Commentaries) 'the judgment by the common law was, that the jurors should lose their liberam legem (free law) and become forever infamous; should forfeit their goods and the profits of their lands; should themselves be imprisoned, and their wives and children thrown out of doors; should have their houses razed, their trees extirpated, and their meadows ploughed; and that the plaintiff should be restored to all that he lost by reason of the unjust verdict.'

The obvious unfairness to the jury of such procedures resulted in their being permitted to bring in a special verdict at a very early period in the common law. Scott, FUNDAMENTALS OF PROCEDURE, 95. They merely found the facts in issue, the court deciding on the legal effect of such facts. A primary difficulty with the common-law special verdict, however, was the rigid rule that if the judge failed to require the jury to find on every material issue of ultimate fact the verdict could not stand. As Dean Leon Green described it (*A New Development in Jury Trial*, 13 A.B.A.J. 715):

> 'When employed, it must be complete; the jury must find all the material facts, disputed and undisputed, and not merely the evidence from which the facts can be inferred, nor mere conclusions. Nothing must be left for the judge to do except pronounce judgment upon the facts found. The changes which have been rung on these requisites are numberless, likewise unintelligent and futile. At bottom the special verdict represents a valuable idea, but as put into operation it has no vitality. To require such excessive exactness of a lay body, or even of lawyers, in the heat of trial, is to demand the impossible. Such requirements cramped the life out of the special verdict. While provision for it is found in most states, it is practically just so much dead weight. Had its development been normal it should have superseded the general verdict centuries ago.'

As distinguished from the common-law special verdict the early law also saw the use of special interrogatories. (This is generally the procedure authorized by statute and court Rule 37, § 6, quoted, *supra*.) The answers to the special questions are not (as was the common-law special verdict) used in lieu of a general verdict but rather to explain and to test it. The general charge, with all its length and complexity, and the general verdict, remain in use, the special questions merely revealing how the jury dealt with specific issues. If (it is provided by statute) the special findings are 'inconsistent' with the general verdict the former shall control. Here lies the first great difficulty. When, in truth, do we have an inconsistency? Modern courts, in effecting reconciliation between the general verdict and the answers to the special questions, have resort to niceties of reasoning and subtleties of thought that would cause even a medieval logician to blanch. In *McNees v. Cincinnati Street Ry. Co.*, 152 Ohio St. 269, 89 N.W.2d 138, the plaintiff's decedent had suffered a coronary thrombosis while operating one of defendant's buses under adverse conditions, due to equipment casualty, during a heavy fog, and while being pushed by another bus. The special question (as to whether 'the cause of Taylor McNees' death' was 'the mental strain and excitement of the driving conditions' then prevailing) was answered affirmatively. The general verdict, however, was for the defendant. These were held to be reconcilable by the court on the ground that the special question related only to cause, and that it said nothing of proximate cause. *See also La Pointe v. Chevrette*, 264 Mich. 482, 250 N.W. 272. It will not profit us to explore their murky techniques of such reconciliations. The point to be made is that any legal doctrine requiring the final result of a controversy to turn upon what in effect are two simultaneous verdicts invites disagreement and discord. We need only to go to the digests for further illustrations. Dean Green's observations, made many years ago in 13 A.B.A.J. 715, 716, are equally applicable today: 'Innumerable refinements have been developed in their [the special questions'] use and especially in determining when the general verdict is controlled by the special finding and, all in all, the practice rather tends to retard than to expedite the disposition of cases, and has not met any wide approval.'

In addition to the difficulties encountered by reason of the reconciliation doctrine, the form of the questions themselves has given rise to much litigation. (This difficulty, it is noted, will also be encountered in the modern special verdict procedure authorized in Rule 37, § 7.) In the case before us appellee, correctly discussing both special questions as governed by the same principles, objects to the first question (relating to the corner of the intersection where the accident occurred) on the ground that answer thereto 'would in no manner settle the question as to whether or not such entry was negligent, or whether such negligence, if any, was a proximate cause of the accident.' Appellee misconstrues the nature of the answer demanded by the rule. The requirements are that it must be an ultimate fact as distinguished from an evidentiary fact (although this is, obviously, a matter of degree only) and it must have a controlling, rather than a collateral, bearing upon the verdict and issues. *Bennett v. Hill*, 342 Mich. 754, 71 N.W.2d 220. As to the factual aspect, it is impossible, we know, to frame a comprehensive definition of an ultimate fact, or to draw a precise boundary line between evidentiary facts and ultimate facts, since an ultimate fact in one case will not be so in another. Different issues may be involved. The Hon. Merrill E. Otis, one of our most distinguished Federal judges, in speaking before the Judicial Conference of the Eighth Circuit (Improvements in Statement of Findings of Fact and Conclusions of Law, 1 F.R.D. 83) expressed the pertinent factors in these words:

> 'Requirements 3 and 4 have been stated hundreds of times by appellate courts, scores of times by the supreme court of the United States. In its wording the principle is simple. The difficulty in its application is in determining what are the ultimate facts in a given case. It seems to be conceded by all who have given serious thought to the matter that it is not possible to form a definition which will be a sure guide at all times. We know that an ultimate fact is to be distinguished from mere evidence. The Supreme Court has said that. Old Equity Rule 25, 28 U.S.C.A. following section 723, which concerns the framing of a complaint in equity, makes that distinction. The distinction is presented in the very word 'ultimate' in the phrase 'ultimate fact.' Perhaps, in any given case, we may say that a fact which is offered in evidence for the purpose of proving some other fact is not itself an 'ultimate fact.' Perhaps we may say as to any fact, whether it has been directly proved in evidence or is an inference from facts proved, if it serves the sole function of supporting (not some other inference of fact) but the final legal conclusion that either plaintiff or defendant shall prevail, perhaps we may say as to such a fact, it is an 'ultimate fact.' It occurs to me that there are two tests with which every federal judge is familiar which the judge may use to determine whether facts he is considering for his findings are ultimate facts. The tests are these. 1. If he were drawing a complaint for the plaintiff in the case before him what allegations of fact would he make to support the prayer of his complaint? 2. If the case were a jury case, what facts would he in his charge require the jury to find as a basis for a verdict for the plaintiff? These are the 'ultimate facts' required to support a judgment for the plaintiff. I consider that often a finding of one ultimate fact (or two or three ultimate facts at the most) may be sufficient to support a judgment for the defendant.'

As to the requirement that the answer to a special question be 'controlling' of the main issue, we examined this aspect of the problem with care in the opinion on rehearing in *Tyler v. Wright*, 188 Mich. 561, 155 N.W. 353, 158 N.W. 1025, wherein we held:

> 'Upon the rehearing in this case, counsel for defendants questioned the rule laid down by this court for the submission of special questions to the jury. In holding that the trial court was not in error in refusing to submit the proffered questions, it was said in the opinion:
>
> "Neither question, standing by itself, calls for an answer which would have been controlling. Under the statute which allows the submission of special questions they must be so framed as to call for an answer which may be controlling of the main issue.'

> 'We were persuaded by the discussion had upon the rehearing that this construction given the statute (C.L.1897, § 10237) was rather too restricted. While no express construction of this phase of the statute appears to have been made by this court, we are of the opinion that if the questions proposed, taken singly or as a whole, call for findings which might be controlling of the main issue, they should be submitted by the trial court. The questions in controversy, which are set out in the opinion, taken together, come within this rule, and therefore should have been submitted.'

In the case before us the primary issue was whether defendant had pulled into the intersection in the path of the oncoming car and had been there struck, or whether he was struck as he sat helpless on Towerline road without having entered the intersection to any substantial extent. The answers to the special questions proposed dealt directly with this issue and the answers thereto, under the principles above set forth, would be both relevant and controlling. Thus they were unobjectionable as to content. So much, however, cannot be said for their form. The function of the special question is to determine facts without regard to their effect upon their general verdict, and hence upon the results to the litigants. To inform the jury of the correlation of their answers with the claims of the parties litigant is to frustrate the entire purpose of the quizzing. We ruled upon this issue in the case of *Taylor v. Davarn*, 191 Mich. 243, 251, 157 N.W. 572, 575, wherein we said, quoting an earlier case, that:

> "The object of the statute (Comp.Laws 1871, § 6026; How.Ann.St.1882, § 7606) requiring the jury to answer specifically questions giving their conclusions on the facts necessary to be found to entitle a party to recover, was to ascertain whether or not they had found sufficient facts from the evidence to support their general verdict under the law as given them by the court. It is the province of the jury to find these facts from the evidence, without aid or suggestion from the court, and this can never be done if the jury are told in advance what facts are necessary to be found to support the verdict, or what answers to the questions propounded will be consistent therewith, or what they must find in order to answer a question propounded in the negative or affirmative. This practice will make the general verdict control the findings, instead of the findings control the general verdict; and thereby the object of the framers of the statute will be defeated. This was the result of the practice indulged in this case. The effect is to make the court, and not the jury, decide the main issues in the case. *Cole v. Boyd*, 47 Mich. 98 (10 N.W. 124). The special findings of the jury were sufficient to support the general verdict, had the proceedings upon which they were based not been erroneous."

See, also, Anderson v. Seelow, 224 Wis. 230, 271 N.W. 844. The case of *Hormel's Estate v. Harris*, 348 Mich. 201, 82 N.W.2d 450, relied upon by appellant, did not purport to rule upon this issue. The questions were, therefore, properly denied.

The confusion existing between section 6 and section 7 procedures (compare, e. g., concurring opinion in *Skidmore v. Baltimore & O. R. Co.*, 2 Cir., 167 F.2d 54, 70, referring to comparable paragraphs (a) and (b) of Rule 49, Federal Rules of Civil Procedure) may warrant a discussion of the latter in order that its vastly different procedures be thoroughly recognized and appreciated. Both involve the use of special questions. But here the similarity stops. Under section 7 there is no general verdict by the jury and there is no general charge to the jury. The jury merely answers written questions concerning material issues of fact. The court then applies the law and renders judgment. This procedure was framed for reasons well stated by Professor Sunderland in his leading article in 29 YALE L.J. 253, 258 (*Verdicts, General and Special*), reading in part as follows:

> 'The peculiarity of the general verdict is the merger into a single indivisible residuum of all matters, however numerous, whether of law or fact. It is a compound made by the jury which is incapable of being broken up into its constituent parts. No judicial reagents exist for either a qualitative or a quantitative analysis. The law supplies the means for determining neither what facts were found, nor what principles of law were applied, nor how the application was made. There are therefore three unknown elements which enter into the general verdict: (a) the facts; (b) the law; (c) the application of the law to the facts. And it is clear that the verdict is liable to three sources of error, corresponding to these three elements. It is also clear that if error does occur in any of these matters it cannot be discovered, for the constituents of the compound cannot be ascertained. No one but the jurors can tell what was put into it and the jurors will not be heard to say. The general verdict is as inscrutable and essentially mysterious as the judgment which issued from the ancient oracle of Delphi. Both stand on the same foundation—a presumption of wisdom. The court protects the jury from all investigation and in-

quiry as fully as the temple authorities protected the priestess who spoke to the suppliant votary at the shrine. It is quite probable that the law is wise in not permitting jurors to testify as to how they compounded their verdict, for all stability would disappear if such inquiries were open. But it does not follow that there is not some better way of deciding controversies than by means of this mysterious agency. If the compound cannot be subjected to analysis perhaps it can be dispensed with.

'As to the first element in the general verdict, the finding of facts, it is much better done by means of the special verdict. Every advantage which the jury is popularly supposed to have over the court as a trier of facts, is retained, with the very great additional advantage that the analysis and separation of the facts in the case which the court and the attorneys must necessarily effect in employing the special verdict, materially reduces the chance of error. It is easy to make mistakes in dealing at large with aggregates of facts. The special verdict compels detailed consideration. But above all it enables the public, the parties and the court to see what the jury really has done. The general verdict is either all wrong or all right, because it is an inseparable and inscrutable unit. A single error completely destroys it. But the special verdict enables errors to be localized so that the sound portions of the verdict may be saved and only the unsound portions be subject to redetermination through a new trial. The morale of the jury also is aided by throwing off the cloak of secrecy, for only through publicity is there developed the proper feeling of responsibility in public servants. So far, then, as the facts go, they can be much more effectively, conveniently and usefully tried by abandoning the general verdict and substituting the special verdict.

'As to the second element in the general verdict, the law, it is a matter upon which the jury is necessarily ignorant. The jurors are taken from the body of the county, and it is safe to say that the last man who would be called or allowed to sit would be a lawyer. They are second-hand dealers in law, and must get it from the judge. They can supply nothing themselves; they are a mere conduit pipe through which the court supplies the law that goes into the general verdict. But while the jury can contribute nothing of value so far as the law is concerned, it has infinite capacity for mischief, for twelve men can easily misunderstand more law in a minute than the judge can explain in an hour. Indeed, can anything be more fatuous than the expectation that the law which the judge so carefully, learnedly and laboriously expounds to the laymen in the jury box will become operative in their minds in its true form? One who has never studied a science cannot understand or appreciate its intricacies, and the law is no exception to this rule. The very theory of the jury and its general verdict is thus predicated upon a premise which makes practically certain an imperfect or erroneous view of the principles of law which are to be compounded into the verdict. The instructions upon the law given by the court to the jury are an effort to give, in the space of a few minutes, a legal education to twelve laymen upon a branch of the law involved in the case. Law cannot be taught in any such way. As to this element, accordingly, the general verdict is almost necessarily a failure.

'As to the third element in the general verdict—the application of the law to the facts, we find the same difficulty as in the case of the first element,—a merging of the law into the verdict in such a way that it is impossible to tell how or whether the jury applied the law. They may have applied it in a wholly wrong way, or they may have failed to apply it at all. No analysis of the verdict can be made which will throw any light on the process. Since the case can ordinarily go to the jury only if a verdict either way is legally possible, whatever the jury does is presumed to be right, and this presumption excludes any inquiry from the jurors themselves. Cases may arise where the verdict shows on its face a failure to properly apply the law, usually as relating to the measure of damages, but in the vast majority of cases the verdict is a complete mystery, throwing a mantle of impenetrable darkness over the operations of the jury. Whether the jurors deliberately and openly threw the law into the discard, and rendered a verdict out of their own heads, or whether they applied the law correctly as instructed by the court, or whether they tried to apply it properly but failed for lack of understanding,—these are questions respecting which the verdict discloses nothing. So far, therefore, as the third element goes, the general verdict is an unknown and unknowable mystery, with the balance of probability against it.'

It was to avoid these serious defects in the general verdict procedure that our court rules have embodied section 7 of Rule 37, providing:

> 'Sec. 7. In any civil case, the court in its discretion may at any time, on its own motion or on request of either party, direct the jury to find a special verdict, and in such case no general verdict shall be returned. Such verdict shall be prepared by the court in the form of questions in writing, relating only to material issues of fact and admitting a direct answer, to which the jury shall make answer in writing. Instructions to the jury shall be limited to such matters as are material to the question submitted. Whenever any special verdict shall be submitted to a jury and there is omitted therefrom some controverted matter of fact not brought to the attention of the trial court by request for submission, but essential to sustain the judgment, such matter of fact shall be deemed determined by the court in conformity with its judgment, and the neglect or omission to request a finding by the jury on such a matter shall be deemed a waiver of a jury trial pro tanto and a consent that such omitted fact be determined by the court. The finding or determination of such omitted fact by the court may be reviewed on appeal without any exception thereto.'

Under this procedure the jury is not expected to assimilate that mass of abstract law known as the instructions or the general charge. The difficulties with the charge have been known to the profession for years. Dean Green's well-known study, the Judge and Jury, examines the problem on page 351 thereof:

> 'The instructions of a judge to a jury normally relate to the law applicable to the possible findings of facts, stated hypothetically, which are supported by the evidence. In any but the simplest cases, they are long and involved, phrased in terms of the nicest distinctions, capable of being understood only by lawyers, and, more frequently than not, inaccurate. No one seriously claims that they are understood by juries or that they assist a jury in reaching a verdict. For most part they are ritual. Nevertheless, these instructions are the greatest single source of reversible error and both trial and appellate courts would be relieved of their greatest source of annoyance if the general **charge** could be eliminated from trial procedure.'

Thoughtful jurists have been no less outspoken. It was Judge Driver of the Federal bench who put the problem in these terms:

> 'Appellate courts must assume that the jury has dutifully considered, has understood and has correctly applied the instructions and, therefore, that if the court's statement of the law is in any substantial particular incorrect, incomplete, or inaccurate, the general verdict has thereby been affected. The assumption, of course, is absurd. It is impossible in a few minutes to educate twelve laymen on the law of a case, embracing, as it often does, complex and technical rules of law, involved exceptions, and finely drawn legal instructions. Many times in my experience the foreman of a jury has sent me a note by the bailiff asking some question which indicated that the jurors did not have even a vague conception of the meaning of the court's instructions.' *The Special Verdict-Theory and Practice*, 26 WASH.L.REV. 21, 22.

Much the same criticism is often voiced by members of the bar. Mr. Leonard O. Thomas, of the Kansas Bar, addresses himself to the subject in his article in 23 U. OF KANSAS CITY L.REV. 194, 195:

> 'It is interesting to note that, if all juries followed the Court's instructions, there would, in the ordinary case, be no purpose whatever in requiring them to answer any special questions. Every question would be answered in accordance with the Court's instructions, and there would be no inconsistency between the answers and the general verdict. However, ninety years' experience with the juries' answers to special questions has demonstrated that juries do frequently render verdicts based on passion or prejudice and not in accordance with the instructions. One of the reasons is not the venality of the members of the jury, or their lack of sympathy with the law given by the court, but their inability to understand the instructions. Thus in an ordinary negligence action in Kansas the instructions may number twenty pages or more of complicated rules of exceedingly technical abstract law. It is no wonder that a jury that wishes to render an unbiased verdict is frequently unable to understand what verdict it must render on the facts found. This ninety years of experience in Kansas has led our appellate court to recognize the imperfection in the jury system and to base its affirmance or reversal of a case primarily on the answers to the special questions and not the instruction. Thus, judgments are very seldom reversed in Kansas on the instructions, which state general rules of law only, but are reversed very frequently on the answers to the special questions.'

The section 7 procedure is designed to eliminate this criticism. Under the procedure of this section no general charge is given, although, as noted hereafter, some instruction to the jury as to the law cannot be avoided. The jury, under the procedure, undertakes merely a fact-finding function, and it has been suggested that under the constraint of answering particular fact questions they will adhere more closely to the evidence adduced. As was said by Judge Driver: 'I have reason to believe also that while many jurors will complacently acquiesce in a general verdict they are much more hesitant about subscribing to a special verdict fact finding which they think is not supported by the evidence.' Moreover, since the questions presented are not identified with either party, or related to his winning or losing (the court, in fact, not the jury, decides the case) the danger that a verdict will be controlled by bias or prejudice is lessened. The intricacies and chances of error inherent in general instructions (which remain even under the special interrogatories procedure) are avoided. In fact, if the court misapplies the law to the facts in may correct its own error and without the need for a special trial. Moreover, the greatest single source of difficulty with the common-law special verdict has been eliminated. Under the old practice it was required that the jury find all of the material facts in issue. The omission of any would necessitate a new trial. Under the modern practice, however, and that embodied in section 7 of our rules, controverted matters of fact essential to sustain judgment but not brought to the attention of the trial court by requests for submission are deemed determined by the court in conformity with its judgment, and the omission to request such finding deemed a waiver of jury trial pro tanto. Thus has been eliminated the danger of necessity for new trial because of inadvertent omission of findings of some material fact. So far as the appellate tribunal is concerned, the specific findings upon the material issues should simplify and expedite its work.

The special verdict procedure is not, of course, to be thought of as a panacea. The distinction between an ultimate fact and a mere evidentiary fact must still be made. Moreover, the whole process may be defeated simply by an ultraliteral interpretation of the word 'fact' since (once we go beyond such basic facts as those of birth and death) most material facts seem to involve the application to human-conduct of legal standards, thus arriving at a material and ultimate 'fact' (e. g., of negligence). It may happen, of course, that a case will be so complicated, the application of the law to the facts so involved, that little or nothing would be gained in simplicity by attempting the special verdict procedure. Even in such case, however, the utilization of another modern device, the pre-trial procedure, should enable the factual issues to be narrowed to the point where a special verdict might be employed. If this seems impracticable the procedure need not be used, for the rule wisely leaves its application to the discretion of the trial court. It should be noted again, also, that the special verdict procedure of section 7 does not completely eliminate instructions to the jury. To some degree they must have guidance and explanation as to legal terms sometimes necessary to be employed in the questions.

Thus difficulties will remain. The problem of the litigated issue has no easy solution. But in the final analysis, whether the special verdict works to simplify the administration of justice and lower its cost will depend upon whether we of the profession want it to work. We would do well, in the light of today's prolific multiplication of boards, bureaus, and commissions, all deciding controverted issues of law (a function nonetheless judicial in fact because sugar-coated with a 'quasi') to ponder Professor Sunderland's words of over a quarter-century ago, spoken in Detroit at a joint meeting of the American Bar Association and the Michigan State Bar Association, with reference to our professional attitude towards procedural problems:

> 'The profession is inclined to take a rather fatalistic attitude, as though rules of practice, especially if hallowed by long observance, were immutable, like the law of gravity, and the public must make the best of them, just as it makes the best of the various forces of nature. But the profession is suffering from the complaisance which affects every monopolistic institution. Instead of expecting commercial, industrial and social relations to adjust themselves to the obsolete equipment with which the judicial establishment does business, the profession should, as it has done in England, scrap a large part of the machinery and provide new devices to correct the defects which have become an intolerable burden upon society.'

The special verdict procedure of section 7 may, indeed, for reasons not anticipated by those responsible for its formulation and adoption (some of whom have heretofore been quoted), prove unworkable in practice in this State. If so it may well be that lessons learned from its attempted employment will point up the need for wiser measures looking towards a better solution of the public's (and our) problem. The provisions of section 7, on their face, and in the light of the experience therewith where tried, both in Federal and State courts, would seem to warrant at least a tentative utilization. This Court, in the exercise of its constitutional duties of rule-making and supervision, may be persuaded by the appropriate committees of the bar and of the judicial council to eliminate section 6 and its statutory base (Comp.Laws 1948, § 618.39, Stat.Ann. § 27.1019) and hence the requirement of general instructions and a general verdict in favor of the discretionarily employable section 7. But let no one delude himself that a mere change in rules will effectuate a change in practice. Unless and until the bench and bar are convinced that only a modernization of ancient practices will halt the flight to lay boards and commissions which has already taken place in great areas of the law the mere adoption of a rule will do nothing. Harris put the matter in The Rule-Making Power, 2 F.R.D. 67, 72-73, in these words:

> 'It is obvious that the court-rule method does not of itself guarantee a flexible and changeable procedure. In fact that method may be one of the best devices to solidify the existing practice. Observe the procedure in Michigan since 1950 and in Colorado for over twenty-five years after 1913. Procedural changes depend more on the 'will to change' which is held by large numbers of the bench and bar rather than on any particular method of change. In fact experience teaches that formal changes will be of little effect unless accepted with a spirit of change. This requires a clear recognition of the real basis of legal procedure. Primarily it is not found in rules or statutes but in the habits and attitudes of the legal group. Legal procedure is merely the way lawyers and judges do their work. Written rules are an attempt to make those practices articulate. Recognizing this, it is pure fantasy to assume that a rule of court or statute will by some magical process develop a new system. Any change, whether by court rule or by statute, must come through the willingness of the legal group to adopt new ways of doing things and new attitudes toward those practices.'

So much for the procedure sought to be utilized in this case. Appellant's allegations of error, however, do not stop here. His proposed instruction No. 2, which the trial court refused to give to the jury, read in part as follows:

> 'I charge you in this case that if you find that the defendant, Jack Bierd, drove out into the intersection in the path of the vehicle occupied by Kenneth Sahr, then and in that case and under the facts of this case you will find the defendant, Jack Bierd, guilty of negligence as a matter of law, since such conduct would mean as a matter of law that the defendant's conduct was at least one of the causes of this accident and the plaintiff's injuries. I further charge you that the defendant, in pulling out into such an intersection, has the duty to maintain a look-out and to see and detect any vehicle entering the intersection from the east on Hess Road. Under such circumstances, the defendant would be guilty of negligence as a matter of law if you find that he drove into the intersection in the path of the vehicle occupied by plaintiff, and you would then turn to the question of damages since I instruct you as a matter of law that a driving into the intersection by the defendant under the facts of this case, in the path of the vehicle occupied by the plaintiff, would be at least one of the causes of the plaintiff's injuries.'

An analysis of the factual situation before the court amply justifies the instruction prayed. Defendant admitted that when he had brought his car to a final stop at the intersection, he saw the plaintiff's Chrysler approaching at a distance of from 250 to 300 feet. ' I had been driving about twenty-three years, and I would estimate its speed at about 80 miles an hour,' he testified. It was zigzagging, 'going back and forth across the road.' There can be no doubt that 'under the facts of this case' (as the requested instructions read) 'if the defendant, Jack Bierd, drove out into the intersection in the path of' the oncoming driver, who would have covered the intervening distance (if at 300 feet) in approximately 2 1/2 seconds, he would have been guilty of negligence as a matter of law. No reasonable man could conclude otherwise. It is to be doubted, in fact, if a car traveling at 80 miles per hour can be brought to a stop within 300 feet. A widely published figure for stopping at 60 miles per hour (the tables do not go as high as 80 miles per hour) is 336 feet. We do not, however, place decision on the factor of the testified speed alone. The zigzagging of the car, even at a low rate of speed, should indicate to a reasonably prudent observer that proper control of the oncoming car is for some reason lacking and that entry into its path is fraught with peril. Plaintiff was entitled to the requested instruction.

The defendant cross-appeals on the theory that the court should have granted his motion for a directed verdict made at the close of plaintiff's proofs. At the close of plaintiff's proofs the jury had before it testimony that the car in which plaintiff was riding was traveling from 70 to 80 miles per hour on a bumpy tarvia road, on the wrong side thereof, that he 'passed over to the north side of the road,' that subsequent thereto 'he put on his brakes,' witness Arnst stating that 'I could hear the noise of the wheels on the pavement. . . . I heard the squeal all the way until the crash.' The same witness testified that the Chrysler slewed sideways as it approached the intersection, with the back wheels on the (north) edge of the pavement, the front of the car 'slightly over the crown of the road or the middle of the road,' and that the Ford, at the moment of collision 'would be in the same position that the Chrysler was.' We need not get into the testimony respecting skid marks, damage to the cars, and other evidence. All of this, viewed as it must be on the motion, in the light most favorable to plaintiff, warrants submission of plaintiff's case to the jury. There was no error in the denial of the motion.

No other error of reversible nature appears. Reversed and remanded for new trial. Costs to appellant.

BLACK, VOELKER and KAVANAGH, JJ., concurred with SMITH, J.

DETHMERS, CARR, and KELLY, JJ., concurred in result.

EDWARDS, JUSTICE.

I concur in reversal for new trial on the last ground stated by Mr. JUSTICE SMITH referring to the Court's failure to submit appellant's requested Instruction No. 2.

a. ***Questions***

Read Rules 272, 277 & 278 Texas Rules of Civil Procedure.

Note

The following is a sample charge that may be given to the jury in a negligence action.

CAUSE NO. 01-001-01

PAUL PAYNE	**IN THE 555th DISTRICT COURT**
VS.	
DON DAVIS	**ALORE COUNTY, TEXAS**

COURT'S CHARGE

Members of the Jury:

After the closing arguments, you will go to the jury room to decide the case, answer the questions that are attached, and reach a verdict. You may discuss the case with other jurors only when you are all together in the jury room.

Remember my previous instructions: Do not discuss the case with anyone else, either in person or by any other means. Do not do any independent investigation about the case or conduct any research. Do not look up any words in dictionaries or on the Internet. Do not post information about the case on the Internet. Do not share any special knowledge or experiences with the other jurors. Do not use your phone or any other electronic device during your deliberations for any reason. I will give you a number where others may contact you in case of an emergency.

Any notes you have taken are for your own personal use. You may take your notes back into the jury room and consult them during deliberations, but do not show or read your notes to your fellow jurors during your deliberations. Your notes are not evidence. Each of you should rely on your independent recollection of the evidence and not be influenced by the fact that another juror has or has not taken notes.

You must leave your notes with the bailiff when you are not deliberating. The bailiff will give your notes to me promptly after collecting them from you. I will make sure your notes are kept in a safe, secure location and not disclosed to anyone. After you complete your deliberations, the bailiff will collect your notes. When you are released from jury duty, the bailiff will promptly destroy your notes so that nobody can read what you wrote.

Here are the instructions for answering the questions.

1. Do not let bias, prejudice, or sympathy play any part in your decision.

2. Base your answers only on the evidence admitted in court and on the law that is in these instructions and questions. Do not consider or discuss any evidence that was not admitted in the courtroom.

3. You are to make up your own minds about the facts. You are the sole judges of the credibility of the witnesses and the weight to give their testimony. But on matters of law, you must follow all of my instructions.

4. If my instructions use a word in a way that is different from its ordinary meaning, use the meaning I give you, which will be a proper legal definition.

5. All the questions and answers are important. No one should say that any question or answer is not important.

6. Answer "yes" or "no" to all questions unless you are told otherwise. A "yes" answer must be based on a preponderance of the evidence. Whenever a question requires an answer other than "yes" or "no," your answer must be based on a preponderance of the evidence.

The term "preponderance of the evidence" means the greater weight of credible evidence presented in this case. If you do not find that a preponderance of the evidence supports a "yes" answer, then answer "no." A preponderance of the evidence is not measured by the number of witnesses or by the number of documents admitted in evidence. For a fact to be proved by a preponderance of the evidence, you must find that the fact is more likely true than not true.

7. Do not decide who you think should win before you answer the questions and then just answer the questions to match your decision. Answer each question carefully without considering who will win. Do not discuss or consider the effect your answers will have.

8. Do not answer questions by drawing straws or by any method of chance.

9. Some questions might ask you for a dollar amount. Do not agree in advance to decide on a dollar amount by adding up each juror's amount and then figuring the average.

10. Do not trade your answers. For example, do not say, "I will answer this question your way if you answer another question my way."

11. The answers to the questions must be based on the decision of at least 10 of the 12 jurors. The same 10 jurors must agree on every answer. Do not agree to be bound by a vote of anything less than 10 jurors, even if it would be a majority.

As I have said before, if you do not follow these instructions, you will be guilty of juror misconduct, and I might have to order a new trial and start this process over again. This would waste your time and the parties' money, and would require the taxpayers of this county to pay for another trial. If a juror breaks any of these rules, tell that person to stop and report it to me immediately.

"Negligence" means failure to use ordinary care, that is, failing to do that which a person of ordinary prudence would have done under the same or similar circumstances or doing that which a person of ordinary prudence would not have done under the same or similar circumstances.

"Ordinary care" means that degree of care that would be used by a person of ordinary prudence under the same or similar circumstances.

"Proximate cause" means that cause which, in a natural and continuous sequence, produces an event, and without which cause such event would not have occurred. In order to be a proximate cause, the act or omission complained of must be such that a person using ordinary care would have foreseen that the event, or some similar event, might reasonably result there from. There may be more than one proximate cause of an event.

An occurrence may be an "unavoidable accident," that is, an event not proximately caused by the negligence of any party to it.

If an occurrence is caused solely by an "act of God," it is not caused by the negligence of any person. An occurrence is caused by an act of God if it is caused directly and exclusively by the violence of nature, without human intervention or cause, and could not have been prevented by reasonable foresight or care.

QUESTION 1

Did the negligence, if any, of the persons named below proximately cause the occurrence in question? Answer "Yes" or "No" for each of the following:

a. Don Davis ________

b. Paul Payne ________

If, in answer to Question 1, you have found that the negligence of more than one of the persons named below proximately caused the occurrence, then answer the following question. Otherwise, do not answer the following question.

QUESTION 2

What percentage of the negligence that caused the occurrence do you find to be attributable to each of those found by you, in your answer to Question 1, to have been negligent?

The percentages you find must total 100 percent. The negligence attributable to a person named below is not necessarily measured by the number of acts or omissions found. The percentage attributable to a person need not be the same percentage attributed to that person in answering another question.

a. Don Davis ________

b. Paul Payne ________

Total 100%

If in answer to question 3, you have found that 50 percent or less of the negligence that caused the occurrence is attributed to Paul Payne or if, in answer to Question 1, you have found that only the negligence of Don Davis proximately caused the occurrence, then answer Questions 4. Otherwise, do not answer Questions 4.

QUESTION 3

What sum of money, if paid now in cash, would fairly and reasonably compensate Paul Payne for his injuries, if any, that resulted from the occurrence in question?

Consider the elements of damages listed below and none other. Consider each element separately. Do not include damages for one element in any other element. Do not include interest on any amount of damages you find.

Physical pain and mental anguish.

Loss of earning capacity.

Disfigurement.

Physical impairment.

Medical care.

Do not reduce the amounts, if any, in your answers because of the negligence, if any, of Paul Payne.

Answer in dollars and cents for damages, if any, that were sustained in the past and that in reasonable probability will be sustained in the future.

Answer: ___________

Presiding Juror:

1. When you go into the jury room to answer the questions, the first thing you will need to do is choose a presiding juror.

2. The presiding juror has these duties:

a. have the complete charge read aloud if it will be helpful to your deliberations;
b. preside over your deliberations, meaning manage the discussions, and see that you follow these instructions;
c. give written questions or comments to the bailiff who will give them to the judge;
d. write down the answers you agree on;
e. get the signatures for the verdict certificate; and
f. notify the bailiff that you have reached a verdict.

Do you understand the duties of the presiding juror? If you do not, please tell me now.

Instructions for Signing the Verdict Certificate:

1. Unless otherwise instructed you may answer the questions on a vote of 10 jurors. The same 10 jurors must agree on every answer in the charge. This means you may not have one group of 10 jurors agree on one answer and a different group of 10 jurors agree on another answer.

2. If 10 jurors agree on every answer, those 10 jurors sign the verdict. If 11 jurors agree on every answer, those 11 jurors sign the verdict. If all 12 of you agree on every answer, you are unanimous and only the presiding juror signs the verdict.

3. All jurors should deliberate on every question. You may end up with all 12 of you agreeing on some answers, while only 10 or 11 of you agree on other answers. But when you sign the verdict, only those 10 who agree on every answer will sign the verdict.

Do you understand these instructions? If you do not, please tell me now.

____
Judge Presiding

Verdict Certificate

Check one:

___ Our verdict is unanimous. All 12 of us have agreed to each and every answer. The presiding juror has signed the certificate for all 12 of us.

___________________________	___________________________
Signature of Presiding Juror	Printed Name of Presiding Juror

___ Our verdict is not unanimous. Eleven of us have agreed to each and every answer and have signed the certificate below.

___ Our verdict is not unanimous. Ten of us have agreed to each and every answer and have signed the certificate below.

	SIGNATURE	NAME PRINTED
1.	____________________	____________________
2.	____________________	____________________
3.	____________________	____________________
4.	____________________	____________________
5.	____________________	____________________
6.	____________________	____________________
7.	____________________	____________________

8. ______________________________ ____
9. ______________________________ ____
10. ______________________________ ____
11. ______________________________ ____

BURK ROYALTY COMPANY
v.
WALLS

616 S.W.2d 911
(Tex. 1981)

Groce, Locke & Hebdon, Thomas H. Crofts, Jr., San Antonio, Stan Carter, Wichita Falls, for petitioners.
J. Michael Smith, Gilmer, Clifton L. Holmes, Kilgore, for respondent.

SPEARS, JUSTICE.

This suit for exemplary damages was brought by respondent Sally Walls, individually and as next friend and guardian of Jeffery Paul Walls, Jr., her minor son, against the employer of her deceased husband, Jeffery Paul Walls. Mrs. Walls alleged that both the employer, Burk Royalty Company, through its district superintendent, Kenneth Swetnam, and Swetnam, individually, were grossly negligent. Having already received workers' compensation benefits, this suit for exemplary damages was brought by Mrs. Walls pursuant to article XVI § 26 of the Texas Constitution and a statute, article 8306, § 5. Judgment was rendered for the Walls based on the jury's verdict. The court of civil appeals reformed the amount of the judgment but remanded the cause to the trial court to allocate the award between Mrs. Walls and her son. 596 S.W.2d 932. We affirm the judgment of the court of civil appeals.

The principal question presented is whether there is some evidence to support the jury's finding that Kenneth Swetnam was grossly negligent on the occasion in question. Since Burk Royalty concedes that Swetnam was a vice-principal, if the jury finding is supported by some evidence, Burk Royalty is also liable for exemplary damages. Underlying issues concern the definition of gross negligence and the standard of review of gross negligence jury findings. A third point concerns broad submission of negligence issues.

The deceased, Jeff Walls, was an employee of Burk Royalty on November 8, 1974, when he was burned to death at an oil well site in Rusk County. The fatal fire occurred while he was working as a member of a four-man crew pulling wet tubing from an oil well so that the pump at the bottom could be replaced and production restored. Walls was working on the tubing board or derrick board about twenty-five feet up in the derrick above the floor of the well. Before work had begun that day, Billy Lay, Burk's operator in charge of the well, had intended to get in his truck and look for Boyd Ehl, the toolpusher in charge of the crew, to find out how they should remove the fluid that would be trapped in the tubing (wet tubing) held in by the standing valve at the bottom of the tubing. In the meantime, Swetnam drove up to deliver the crew's paychecks, and Lay asked him instead.

Swetnam was Burk Royalty's District Superintendent in charge of all the company's operations in the East Texas area including safety for that district. Lay suggested that an explosive charge be dropped in the well to blow a hole in the tubing and let the fluid drain out at the bottom, a process called "shooting the tube." However, Swetnam told Lay not to use that method, but rather to pull the tubing until they reached fluid, then "swab" the remainder of the tubing in the hole into the "cellar" from which it was to be hauled off by truck. During the conversation, Swetnam said nothing about safety. He remained in his car and did not check for fire extinguishers or any other safety equipment.

After Swetnam left, the crew began pulling tubing. Walls' job up on the tubing board was to take the 30-foot sections ("joints") of pipe as they were pulled up and place them in a rack. He had a safety belt strapped around his shoulders and waist and attached to the derrick to prevent his falling. David Barnes and Stephen Van Meter, two other crew members, were working on the floor directly below the tubing board. Billy Lay was working from the "goat stand" on the rig where he operated the winch (drum) and cable that pulled the tubing up.

The tubing closest to the surface contained no fluid. Shortly before noon after pulling approximately twenty dry joints, the crew reached wet tubing, i. e., full of fluid. Before the next joint could be pulled, some pressurized gas escaped, causing oil to spew out of the tubing up into the derrick, covering Walls' body with oil. Somehow the gas ignited and shot flames like a torch to the top of the derrick, igniting the oil on Walls' body. The fire lasted for about a minute. Walls struggled to get out of his safety belt but couldn't. One witness described Walls "kind of jumping around . . . he jumped over to the side, you know, and his clothes and stuff was falling off him. It burned all of his clothes off and he was kicking around a bit." Some of the crew tried unsuccessfully to extinguish the fire on Walls by throwing buckets of water at him. There were no fire extinguishers on the rig. After the fire, Walls' body hung in mid-air, suspended by his safety belt, until taken down two hours later.

Special issue No. 1 submitted to the jury asked: "Do you find from a preponderance of the evidence that on the occasion in question Kenneth Swetnam failed to follow approved safety practices for pulling wet tubing?" The jury answered "Yes." The jury next found that such failure was negligence and a proximate cause of the occurrence in question. After finding substantial actual damages for the widow and son, the jury found in special issue No. 8 that on the occasion in question, "the failure of Kenneth Swetnam" was gross negligence. In the instruction accompanying this issue the jury was instructed:

> You are instructed in connection with the foregoing Special Issue that "gross negligence" is the exercise of so little care as to justify the belief that such action was a heedless and reckless disregard to the safety of Jeffrey Paul Walls and others.
>
> "Heedless and reckless disregard" means more than momentary thoughtlessness, inadvertence, or error of judgment. It means such an entire want of care as to indicate that the act or omission in question was the result of conscious indifference to the rights, welfare, or safety of the persons affected by it.

This instruction is not attacked here by the defendants although the court's general submission of the negligence issue is attacked. In special issue No. 9, the jury found exemplary damages of $150,000, which the court of civil appeals reformed to $100,000 to conform to plaintiffs' pleading. The court of civil appeals held that there was some evidence to support the jury's finding of gross negligence. The court further held that there was some evidence that defendant's negligence was a proximate cause of Walls' death in that Swetnam failed "to have available at prescribed positions the two (2) fire extinguishers prescribed by paragraph No. 14 of the company safety rules."

* * *

BROAD SUBMISSION OF NEGLIGENCE ISSUE

Burk Royalty also attacks the trial court's broad submission of the negligence issue. We hold that the court of civil appeals correctly approved the trial court's broad submission of an issue which asked about negligence in the following words:

> Do you find from a preponderance of the evidence that on the occasion in question, Kenneth Swetnam failed to follow approved safety practices for pulling wet tubing?

Burk Royalty argues that there was a variance between the pleadings and proof. This is a pleading problem, one that is handled by objections to the evidence and one which requires distinct objections to the charge which specifically advise the court of each variance. TEX. R. CIV. P. 274. The objections leveled at the charge by Burk Royalty do not distinctly point to any specific variance; thus the point was waived. *Davis v. Campbell*, 572 S.W.2d 660, 663 (Tex. 1978).

In *Brown v. American Transfer and Storage Co.*, 601 S.W.2d 931 (Tex.1980), we restated the purpose of Rule 277.[1] We further pointed out that *Scott v. Atchison, Topeka, and Santa Fe Ry.*, 572 S.W.2d 273 (Tex.

---

[1] [For purposes of this book, only selected footnotes appear n the various court's opinions will be used. Instead of using specific court's numbering system all footnotes will be numbered consecutively in each Chapter.] Rule 277 provides in part:

> It shall be discretionary with the court whether to submit separate questions with respect to each element of a case or to submit issues broadly. It shall not be objectionable that a question is general or includes a combination of elements or issues. Inferential rebuttal issues shall not be submitted. The plac-

1978) concerned a situation where the facts plaintiff alleged were left unproved and the facts that were proved were unpleaded. Variance between pleadings and proof entitled one to complain only when the "wide" variance is substantial, unwaived, and the opposite party has been mislead, surprised, and prejudiced. *Brown v. American Transfer & Storage Co., supra* at 937-938; *Stone v. Lawyers Title Ins. Corp.*, 554 S.W.2d 183, 187 (Tex. 1977).

The negligence issue in this case was whether the defendant failed to follow approved safety practices for pulling wet tubing. There was no need to ask separate questions about each reason that defendant may have failed to do so. This court has repeatedly written that Rule 277 will be applied as written. In *Mobil Chemical Co. v. Bell*, 517 S.W.2d 245 (Tex. 1974), we declared that in a negligence case, the issue may be broadly asked in terms of negligence without breaking into specific inquiries. We restate that rule and state further that this rule applies to ordinary negligence cases, not just cases which concern res ipsa loquitur. We approved this form of submission again in *Siebenlist v. Harville*, 596 S.W.2d 113 (Tex. 1980), when we upheld the single issue submission of gross negligence. It is understandable that a rule requiring issues to be submitted "distinctly and separately" which prevailed from 1913 until 1973 would slowly relinquish its hold upon trial practice, but after 1973, Rule 277, as amended, permits the submission of issues broadly even though they include a combination of elements or issues. This court, in addition to the times it has written in the opinions already cited, has on a number of other occasions, approved broad submissions. [Citations omitted.]

The practice in non-negligence cases has never required the same rule of specificity that was required by *Fox v. Dallas Hotel Co.*, 111 Tex. 461, 240 S.W. 517 (1922). Prior to 1973, there was one practice for the submission of issues in non-negligence cases and a different one for negligence cases. This was expressly articulated in *Roosth & Genecov Production Co. v. White*, 152 Tex. 619, 262 S.W.2d 99 (1953). The court in *Roosth & Genecov* cited as examples of this unequal treatment *City of Houston v. Lurie*, 148 Tex. 391, 224 S.W.2d 871 (1949), and *Howell v. Howell*, 147 Tex. 14, 210 S.W.2d 978 (1948).

There may be some continuing question about our holdings concerning issue submission because we have not previously overruled those cases which have required a specific issue for each specific element of negligence. We now expressly overrule those cases that arose before the 1973 revision of Rule 277 and which followed the mandate of *Fox v. Dallas Hotel Co.* requiring a submission of "each issue distinctly and separately, avoiding all intermingling" and stating "issues should be restricted to specific acts of negligence alleged and proven." * * *

The judgment of the court of civil appeals is affirmed.

Dissenting opinion by MCGEE, J., in which DENTON and BARROW, JJ., join [opinion omitted].

Concurring opinion by GREENHILL, C. J [opinion omitted].

---

ing of the burden of proof may be accomplished by instructions rather than by inclusion in the question. In submitting the case, the court shall submit such explanatory instructions and definitions as shall be proper to enable the jury to render a verdict and in such instances the charge shall not be subject to the objection that it is a general charge.

TEXAS DEP'T OF HUMAN SERVS.
v.
E.B.
802 S.W.2d 647
(Tex. 1990)

Jim Mattox, Delmar L. Cain, Sue Berkel, Suzanne Covington, John J. Sampson, Austin, for petitioners. Leonard F. Green, Austin, for respondent.

COOK, JUSTICE.

The Respondent's motion for rehearing is overruled. Our opinion of June 20, 1990, however, is withdrawn, and the following is substituted in its place.

The issue before this court is whether Rule 277 of the Texas Rules of Civil Procedure means exactly what it says, that is, "In all jury cases the court shall, whenever feasible, submit the cause upon broad-form questions." TEX. R. CIV. P. 277. This issue arises in the context of a suit affecting the parent-child relationship in which the Texas Department of Human Services filed suit for termination of the parent-child relationship between the parents and their two female children. After a jury trial, using broad-form questions, the trial court rendered a decree of termination based upon the jury's verdict. The court of appeals reversed and remanded the cause, holding that multiple alternative submissions were proper. 766 S.W.2d 387. We reverse the judgment of the court of appeals and affirm the judgment of the trial court.

The Texas Department of Human Services sued for termination of the parent-child relationship between the mother, Respondent E.B., and her two minor daughters. The suit was based on alleged violations of the Texas Family Code § 15.02(1)(D), (E) and on the ground that the termination would be in the best interest of the children, § 15.02(2). The district court signed a Final Decree of Termination based upon the jury's verdict. There is no complaint with respect to the sufficiency of the evidence supporting the verdict of the jury.

The judge submitted a single question for each child at trial, under the Texas Family Code § 15.02(1)(D), (E), as a broad-form submission required by this court in Rule 277. We approve of this question, which was taken from volume 5, section 218.01B of Texas Pattern Jury Charges:

Question No. 1

Should the parent-child relationship between [Respondent E.B.] and the child [E.B.] be terminated?" Answer: "Yes" or "No" Answer: ______

Question No. 2

Should the parent-child relationship between [Respondent E.B.] and the child [B.B.] be terminated? Answer: "Yes" or "No" Answer: ______

Accompanying these questions were instructions, substantially in accordance with volume 5, section 218.01A of Texas Pattern Jury Charges, including a description of the rights, privileges, duties, and powers of a parent and definitions of the terms "termination," "clear and convincing evidence," and "endanger." The crucial instructions basically track the statutory grounds for termination as set forth in the Texas Family Code § 15.02(1)(D), (E). Additionally, the jury was given a list of "some of the factors to consider in determining the best interest of the child" taken directly from *Holley v. Adams*, 544 S.W.2d 367, 371-72 (Tex. 1976).

In *Fox v. Dallas Hotel Co.*, 111 Tex. 461, 475, 240 S.W. 517, 522 (1922), this court mandated the submission of "each issue distinctly and separately." Texas thus developed a very complicated system for issue submission. In 1973, Rule 277 was amended and provided in part: It shall be discretionary with the court whether to submit separate questions with respect to each element of a case or to submit issues broadly. It shall not be objectionable that a question is general or includes a combination of elements or issues.

By this amendment, the court replaced the previous language that required issues to be submitted "distinctly and separately." In *Mobil Chemical Co. v. Bell*, 517 S.W.2d 245, 255 (Tex. 1974), this court said the new rule meant what it said: simply ask whether the party was negligent. This court explained in a later decision that

Rule 277 was designed to abolish the "distinctly and separately" requirement. *Brown v. American Transfer & Storage Co.*, 601 S.W.2d 931, 937 (Tex. 1980).

Acknowledging that there "may be some continuing question" about broad-form submissions, this court in *Burk Royalty Co. v. Walls*, 616 S.W.2d 911, 925 (Tex. 1981), expressly overruled all of the cases that arose before the 1973 revisions and which followed the decisions in *Fox*. *See generally* Pope & Lowerre, *The State of the Special Verdict*, 11 ST. MARY'S L.J. 1 (1979). In the 1988 amendments to Rule 277 this court said broad-form submission "shall" be used "whenever feasible" and eliminated trial court discretion to submit separate questions with respect to each element of a case.

Rule 277 mandates broad form submissions "whenever feasible," that is, in any or every instance in which it is capable of being accomplished.

The history and struggle to recognize broad-form submission is a long one. The rule unequivocally requires broad-form submission whenever feasible. Unless extraordinary circumstances exist, a court must submit such broad-form questions. The court of appeals held that a single broad form question incorporating two independent grounds for termination of a parent-child relationship permits the state to obtain an affirmative answer without discharging the burden that the jury conclude that a parent violated one or more of the grounds for termination under the statute. TEX. FAM. CODE § 15.02 (Vernon Supp. 1990); TEX. R. CIV. P. 292.

The charge in parental rights cases should be the same as in other civil cases. The controlling question in this case was whether the parent-child relationship between the mother and each of her two children should be terminated, not what specific ground or grounds under § 15.02 the jury relied on to answer affirmatively the questions posed. All ten jurors agree that the mother had endangered the child by doing one or the other of the things listed in § 15.02. Petitioner argues that the charge, as presented to the jury, violates her due process right by depriving a natural mother of her fundamental right to the care, custody and management of her children. Recognizing her rights does not change the form of submission. The standard for review of the charge is abuse of discretion, and abuse of discretion occurs only when the trial court acts without reference to any guiding principle. Here the trial court tracked the statutory language in the instruction and then asked the controlling question. This simply does not amount to abuse of discretion.

Broad-form questions reduce conflicting jury answers, thus reducing appeals and avoiding retrials. Rule 277 expedites trials by simplifying the charge conference and making questions easier for the jury to comprehend and answer.

Accordingly, we reverse the judgment of the court of appeals and affirm the judgment of the trial court.

Notes

1. As you can tell from the last two cases the procedural rules relating to the submission of the charge to the court have undergone substantial revisions over the years. In the *Fox* case, the Supreme Court had mandated the submission of the issues raised by the pleadings and the evidence to be separate and distinct. For example, in the case one of the several issues that inquired about Mr. Fox's contributory negligence was submitted as follows:

> "Do you find from a preponderance of the evidence that Alexander Fox was guilty of contributory negligence in his conduct in, around, or about the elevator or the shaft thereof, prior to or about the time he was injured?"

Assuming the jury answered this question "We do", it would have then been asked a separate and distinct question concerning whether such contributory negligence was a proximate cause of his injuries. In 1973 the Supreme Court amended Rule 277 to give the trial court the discretion to submit the charge broadly or to submit separate questions with respect to each element of a case. The first two cases in this Chapter contain broad issues. In accordance with the amendment to Rule 277 in 1988, trial courts are now mandated to use broad form submission whenever feasible.

2. In *Hyundai Motor Company v. Rodriguez*, 955 S.W.2d 661 (Tex. 1999) the Supreme Court held that a trial court must submit in its charge to the jury all questions, instructions, and definitions raised by the pleadings and evidence. When feasible, jury questions should be in broad form, accompanied by appropriate instructions

and definitions. A single question may relate to multiple legal theories. Indeed, submission of a single question relating to multiple theories may be necessary to avoid the risk that the jury will become confused and answer questions inconsistently. The goal of the charge is to submit to the jury the issues for decision logically, simply, clearly, fairly, correctly, and completely. Toward that end, the trial judge is accorded broad discretion so long as the charge is legally correct.

3. In *Dilliard v. Texas Electric Cooperative*, 157 S.W.3d 429 (Tex. 2005) the Court noted that under broad-form submission rules, jurors need not agree on every detail of what occurred so long as they agree on the legally relevant result. Thus, jurors may agree that a defendant failed to follow approved safety practices, without deciding each reason that the defendant may have failed to do so. Similarly, the jurors here could have unanimously found the defendant's employee negligent, even if half believed the negligent act was overloading his truck and half believed it was failing to warn oncoming traffic—acts that preceded two different collisions. With respect to inferential rebuttal issues, jurors need not agree on what person or thing caused an occurrence, so long as they agree it was not the defendant.

4. In the following case the trial court submitted the charge separately and distinctly. In that case the court's charge submitted the negligence issue in five separate questions that did not include Mrs. Warner's second theory of negligence. The jury was instructed not to answer each of the second through fifth questions unless they answered the preceding question in the affirmative. In response to Question 1, the jury found that the liquid substance on the floor of the store posed an unreasonable risk of harm to Mrs. Warner. Question 2 asked the jury the following question:

> Did the defendant know or should defendant reasonably have known that there was liquid substance on the floor of its store on the occasion in question?

The jury answered this question, "No". Pursuant to the trial court's instruction, the jury did not answer questions 3, 4 or 5 which asked whether H.E.B. failed to reduce or eliminate the risk in question, whether such failure constituted negligence, and whether such negligence was a proximate cause of Mrs. Warner's injuries. Mrs. Warner had requested the court to submit a broad form question similar to the following:

> Did the negligence, if any, of those named below proximately cause the injuries to Mrs. Warner?
> With respect to the condition of the premises, HEB was negligent if—
>
> a. the condition posed an unreasonable risk of harm, and
> b. HEB knew or reasonably should have known of the danger, and
> c. HEB failed to exercise ordinary care to protect Mrs. Warner from the danger, by both failing to adequately warn her of the condition and failing to make that condition reasonable safe.
>
> "Ordinary care" when used with respect to the conduct of HEB as an owner or occupier of a premises, means that degree of care that would be used by an owner or occupier of ordinary prudence under the same or similar circumstances.
>
> Answer "Yes" or "No" for each of the following:
>
> a. HEB ________
> b. Mrs. Warner ________

5. As will be demonstrated by subsequent cases the holding in *E.B.* has been eroded, insofar as the Court discusses broad form submission. In the context of the termination of parental rights (which involves issues of constitutional dimension), the court seems to be ready to revisit the issue of whether the same ten jurors must agree on the answers to each question. In *In the Interest of J. F.*, 96 S.W.3d 256, 275 (Tex. 2002), the court mentioned, but failed to reach (because error was not preserved) the question of whether the trial court erred in failing to instruct the jury that the same ten jurors must agree that at least one statutorily described course of parental conduct occurred, and that termination is in the best interest of the children.

H.E. BUTT GROCERY CO.
v.
WARNER
845 S.W.2d 258
(Tex. 1993)

Beverly Willis Bracken, Steve L. Moody, Waco, for petitioner.
Scott Rothenberg, Kevin O'Malley, Houston, Louis S. Muldrow, Waco, for respondents.

CORNYN, JUSTICE.

This slip and fall case concerns the pleading and requested submission requirements for independent, alternative theories of recovery. The trial court submitted only the plaintiff's (Warner's) premises liability theory, which the jury answered favorably to H.E.B. Based upon its holding that Warner was erroneously denied submission of an additional theory of recovery, the court of appeals reversed the trial court's take-nothing judgment and remanded the cause for a new trial. 820 S.W.2d 819. Because we hold that Warner pleaded and requested submission of only a premises liability theory of recovery, which was submitted by the trial court, and failed to submit a requested jury question supporting any other basis for recovery, we reverse the judgment of the court of appeals and remand the cause to that court for consideration of the points it has not addressed.

In July 1987 Tami Warner slipped in an eight-inch puddle of water, chicken blood, and other fluids that had accumulated on the floor of an H.E.B. store in Corsicana during a "bag your own chicken" promotion. Soon thereafter Warner and her husband sued H.E.B. to recover the damages occasioned by Warner's fall. At trial the court submitted a five-part premises liability question to the jury regarding H.E.B.'s liability. Based upon the jury's finding that H.E.B. neither knew nor should have known that there was a liquid substance on the floor on the occasion in question, the trial court rendered a take-nothing judgment against Warner and her husband.

The court of appeals held that Warner's pleadings alleged two theories of negligence: one based on a standard premises liability theory and the other based on the failure to "pre-bag" chicken to eliminate the hazardous condition presented. Holding that "[t]he court's charge erroneously submitted the negligence issue in five separate questions which did not include Warner's second theory of negligence," the court of appeals reversed the judgment of the trial court and remanded the cause for a new trial. 820 S.W.2d at 819.

Warner's First Amended Original Petition specifically alleged: Defendant, and its agents, servants, and employees, at the time and on the occasion in question, engaged in certain omissions, among others, are as follows: (a) In failing to provide the Plaintiff and the general public with a safe place in which to shop; (b) In failing to abate a dangerous condition on such premises; (c) In failing to warn the Plaintiff and the general public of the dangerous condition on such premises.

While Warner's petition alleged specific acts of negligence "among others," we hold that her First Amended Original Petition, fairly read, alleged only a claim based upon premises liability. *See Corbin v. Safeway Stores, Inc.*, 648 S.W.2d 292, 295 (Tex. 1983). Although Warner maintains that she has been denied her alternative, negligent failure to pre-bag chicken theory of liability, it is undisputed that she was injured by a condition of the premises—a puddle of water, chicken blood, and other fluids that had accumulated on the floor—rather than a negligently conducted activity. *See Keetch v. Kroger*, 845 S.W.2d 262 (Tex. 1992) (distinguishing premise liability and negligent activity causes of action). Thus, Warner's only potential cause of action is limited to a premises liability theory, which was submitted by the trial court.

Warner also claims that the trial court erred in failing to submit her requested broad-form question, which was based on her premises liability theory. Texas Rule of Civil Procedure 277 mandates broad-form submissions whenever they are "feasible." *See Texas Dept. of Human Serv. v. E.B.*, 802 S.W.2d 647, 649 (Tex. 1990). Because Warner tendered a proper broad-form question with appropriate instructions, the trial court should have granted her request. However, its failure to do so was not harmful error. TEX. R. APP. P. 81(b)(1). Although submitted in granulated form, the jury questions contained the proper elements of a premises liability action. Because the charge fairly submitted to the jury the disputed issues of fact and because the charge incorporated a correct legal standard for the jury to apply, we hold that the trial court's refusal to submit Warner's tendered question and instructions did not amount to harmful error.

Therefore, without hearing oral argument and pursuant to Texas Rule of Civil Procedure 170, the court reverses the judgment of the court of appeals and remands this cause to that court for consideration of those points of error it did not address.

GAMMAGE, J., concurring.

MAUZY, J., joined by DOGGETT, J., dissenting [opinion omitted].

CROWN LIFE INSURANCE COMPANY
v.
CASTEEL
22 S.W.3d 378
(Tex. 2000)

G. Alan Waldrop, Austin, John L. Hill, Jr., Houston, Edwin R. DeYoung, Austin, Roger B. Cowie, Dallas, Barbara M. Ellis, Austin, for Petitioner.

Kent Hance, Gary F. DeShazo, Jerome J. Schiefelbein, Terry Scarborough, Cyndy Olson Bourland, Austin, for Respondent.

JUSTICE ABBOTT delivered the opinion for a unanimous Court.

We overrule Casteel's Motion for Rehearing and grant in part Crown Life's Motion for Rehearing. We withdraw our opinion dated July 1, 1999, and substitute the following.

William E. Casteel sold insurance policies as an independent agent of Crown Life Insurance Company. One of the policies sold by Casteel led to a lawsuit by policyholders against Casteel and Crown. In that lawsuit, Casteel filed a cross-claim against Crown. In this appeal from that lawsuit, we consider several issues: (1) whether Casteel, who alleges that he has been injured by the unfair and deceptive practices of Crown, has standing to sue Crown under Article 21.21 of the Texas Insurance Code; (2) whether that standing extends to Article 21.21 claims that allow recovery for Deceptive Trade Practices Act violations; and (3) whether the inclusion of invalid theories of liability submitted to the jury in a single broad-form question constitutes harmful error. We hold that Casteel does have standing to sue Crown under Article 21.21; but Casteel does not have standing under Article 21.21 to allege DTPA-based claims that require consumer status by their terms. We also hold that submitting invalid theories of liability in a single broad-form jury question is harmful error when it cannot be determined whether the jury based its verdict on one or more of the invalid theories. We affirm in part, reverse and render judgment in part, vacate in part, and reverse and remand in part the judgment of the court of appeals.

I

Between 1986 and 1989, Casteel sold Modified Vanishing Premium ("MVP") policies as an agent for Crown. The MVP policies provided that substantial premiums be paid over a short period of time, after which the premiums would "vanish" and the policy would carry itself through fruition by the reinvestment of policy dividends. Crown provided Casteel with information about how the policies worked, and Casteel provided biographical information on prospective clients to Crown. Crown then produced illustrations tailored to the proposed insureds, which Casteel presented as part of his sales packages. Many of Casteel's clients who purchased MVP policies were friends from his church.

Casteel's clients began complaining about the MVP policies in 1990. The premiums had not vanished as Casteel had represented and, in some cases, never would. In the case of Randall and Sandra Ferguson, Casteel sold an MVP policy that would pay $5,000,000 to the survivor in the event that one of them died. Based on Crown's projections, Casteel had initially informed them that the premiums would total approximately $91,520 before vanishing, but the Fergusons later discovered that the premiums would never vanish and could total as much as $800,000. The Fergusons sued Casteel and Crown alleging DTPA, Article 21.21, and common-law causes of action.

Casteel filed a cross-claim against Crown alleging violations of Article 21.21, which included claims based on DTPA provisions incorporated in Article 21.21. Casteel also brought common-law claims for negligence, gross negligence, breach of fiduciary duty, breach of a duty of good faith and fair dealing, fraud, and constructive fraud. Crown moved for summary judgment on Casteel's claims, and the trial court granted partial summary judgment in Crown's favor on the common-law causes of action. Casteel's Article 21.21 claims, including those based on the DTPA, proceeded to trial with the Fergusons' claims.

With regard to the Fergusons' claims, the jury found that both Crown and Casteel had engaged in unfair or deceptive acts or practices that were a producing cause of damages to the Fergusons. The jury found that Crown had committed the alleged wrongful acts knowingly and was ninety-nine percent responsible for the Fergusons' damages, while Casteel, who was found not to have acted knowingly, bore only one percent of the responsibility. On Casteel's claims against Crown, the jury found that Crown had knowingly engaged in false, misleading, unfair, or deceptive acts or practices that were a producing cause of damages to Casteel. The jury awarded Casteel $400,000 for past lost income, $1,000,000 for future lost income, $6,000,000 for past mental anguish, and $100,000 for future mental anguish. Additionally, the jury awarded Casteel attorney's fees in the amount of forty percent of his recovery.

Following trial, Crown and the Fergusons settled. Under the settlement terms, the Fergusons assigned their rights against Casteel to Crown, so that Crown now stands in place of the Fergusons for purposes of this appeal. Crown moved for judgment notwithstanding the verdict on Casteel's claims. The trial court rendered judgment that Casteel take nothing against Crown, holding that Casteel was neither a "person" as defined under Article 21.21, nor a "consumer" under the DTPA, and therefore lacked standing to bring suit under those statutes. The court dismissed the Fergusons' claims against Crown with prejudice due to their settlement. The court rendered judgment on the verdict with respect to the Fergusons' claims against Casteel, holding Casteel individually liable for the Fergusons' actual damages, attorney's fees, and prejudgment interest in the amount of $1,366,983. The court of appeals held that Casteel was a "person" with standing to sue Crown under Article 21.21, but that Casteel did not have standing to sue under the incorporated DTPA provisions because he was not a "consumer." 3 S.W.3d 582, 593.

The court of appeals reversed and rendered judgment in favor of Casteel in the amount of $1,400,000 for lost past and future income. *Id.* at 597. The court held, however, that Casteel was not entitled to the $6,100,000 in mental anguish damages awarded by the jury because there was legally insufficient evidence to support the award. *Id.* at 597. In addition, the court remanded the case to the trial court for further proceedings on the issues of settlement credit application, calculation of prejudgment interest, and attorney's fees. *Id.* at 597. The rest of the judgment, including partial summary judgment in favor of Crown on Casteel's common-law claims, was affirmed. *Id.* at 597.

II

* * *

III

Crown next challenges the court of appeals' conclusion that the erroneous submission of Casteel's DTPA-based Article 21.21 claims was harmless. The trial court submitted a single broad-form question on the issue of Crown's liability to Casteel. The question instructed the jury on thirteen independent grounds for liability, the first five of which were taken from the DTPA section 17.46(b) laundry list.[2] The question requested a single answer on Crown's liability, which the jury answered affirmatively.

---

[2] The question instructed the jury on DTPA-based Article 21.21 liability theories as follows:

Question 16(a), "Representing that the insurance policies had characteristics, uses, benefits and quantities which they did not have," tracks DTPA § 17.46(b)(5). Question 16(b), "Representing that the insurance policies were of a particular standard, quality or grade if they were of another," tracks DTPA § 17.46(b)(7).

Question 16(c), "Advertising insurance policies with intent not to sell them as advertised," tracks DTPA § 17.46(b)(9).

Casteel contends that Crown waived any defect in the liability question by failing to preserve error at the trial court. In particular, Casteel argues that Crown's objection was not specific enough because Crown objected to the question generally, instead of to each subsection. We disagree. Crown preserved error by obtaining a ruling on its timely objection to the question on the ground that Casteel did not have standing to pursue any DTPA-based Article 21.21 claims because he was not a consumer. *See Religious of the Sacred Heart v. City of Houston*, 836 S.W.2d 606, 613-14 (Tex. 1992).

The court of appeals concluded that the trial court erred by submitting the DTPA-based theories of liability because Casteel did not have standing to bring them. Nevertheless, the court held that this error was harmless because Crown did not "affirmatively demonstrate that the error probably caused rendition of an improper judgment." 3 S.W.3d at 594. We hold that it was error to submit four of the five DTPA-based theories of liability because Casteel was required to have consumer status to maintain an Article 21.21 cause of action under them. We now decide whether that error was harmful.

The court of appeals based its holding on the harmless error rule in former Texas Rule of Appellate Procedure 81(b)(1), which stated:

> No judgment shall be reversed on appeal and a new trial ordered [because of error] . . . unless the appellate court shall be of the opinion that the error complained of amounted to such a denial of the rights of the appellant as was reasonably calculated to cause and probably did cause rendition of an improper judgment . . . .

TEX.R.APP. P. 81(b)(1) (repealed 1997). In addition, the court cited four decisions from three other courts of appeals holding that the submission of an invalid theory of liability in a single broad-form question is harmless if any evidence supports a finding of liability on a valid theory. *See Provident Am. Ins. Co. v. Castaneda*, 914 S.W.2d 273, 277-78 (Tex. App.—El Paso 1996), rev'd on other grounds, 988 S.W.2d 189 (Tex. 1998); *Hart v. Berko, Inc.*, 881 S.W.2d 502, 510-11 (Tex. App.—El Paso 1994, writ denied); *Bernstein v. Portland Sav. & Loan Ass'n*, 850 S.W.2d 694, 702 (Tex. App.—Corpus Christi 1993, writ denied); *Ford Motor Co. v. Pool*, 688 S.W.2d 879, 882 (Tex. App.—Texarkana 1985), aff'd in part and rev'd in part on other grounds, 715 S.W.2d 629 (Tex. 1986).

Notwithstanding that authority, the court of appeals erred by holding this error harmless. It is fundamental to our system of justice that parties have the right to be judged by a jury properly instructed in the law. Yet, when a jury bases a finding of liability on a single broad-form question that commingles invalid theories of liability with valid theories, the appellate court is often unable to determine the effect of this error. The best the court can do is determine that some evidence could have supported the jury's conclusion on a legally valid theory. To hold this error harmless would allow a defendant to be held liable without a judicial determination that a factfinder actually found that the defendant should be held liable on proper, legal grounds. *See* Muldrow & Underwood, *Application of the Harmless Error Standard to Errors in the Charge*, 48 BAYLOR L. REV. 815, 838-40 (1996); Dorsaneo, *Broad-Form Submission of Jury Questions and the Standard of Review*, 46 S.M.U. L. REV. 601, 634-36 (1992). Accordingly, we hold that when a trial court submits a single broad-form liability question incorporating multiple theories of liability, the error is harmful and a new trial is required when the appellate court cannot determine whether the jury based its verdict on an improperly submitted invalid theory. *See* TEX.R.APP. P. 61.1 ("No judgment may be reversed on appeal . . . unless the Supreme Court concludes that the error complained of . . . probably prevented the petitioner from properly presenting the case to the appellate courts."); *see also* TEX.R. APP. P. 44.1(a).

It is essential that the theories submitted be authorized and supported by the law governing the case. If they are not, the appellate court must, at a minimum, be able to determine whether properly submitted theories constituted the basis of the jury's verdict. Here, four of the thirteen theories in the single liability question were improperly submitted because they required that Casteel be a consumer. Yet the language of these theories was

---

Question 16(d), "Representing that agreements conferred or involved rights, remedies or obligations which they did not have or involve," tracks DTPA § 17.46(b)(12).

Question 16(e), "Failing to disclose information concerning an insurance policy which was known at the time of the transaction with the intention to induce another into a transaction," tracks DTPA § 17.46(b)(23).

altered to remove any reference to their consumer-status requirements. Thus, the jury was confronted with four liability theories available only to consumers, but was given no indication that Casteel was required to be a consumer to succeed under any of them. Given these facts, it is possible that the jury based Crown's liability solely on one or more of these erroneously submitted theories. At any rate, it is impossible for us to conclude that the jury's answer was not based on one of the improperly submitted theories.

Although we have not considered this issue since we adopted the harmless error doctrine, we have previously held that submitting multiple independent liability theories in a single jury question is harmful when one of the theories is invalid and it cannot be determined whether liability was based on the invalid theory. *See Lancaster v. Fitch*, 112 Tex. 293, 246 S.W. 1015, 1016 (1923). In *Lancaster*, the trial court submitted a single general negligence issue with instructions regarding three distinct theories of negligence liability. *Id.* at 1015-16. The jury returned a verdict for the plaintiff. On appeal, the defendant established that the trial court should not have submitted one of the theories. The court of appeals nevertheless concluded that the error was harmless because the jury could have based its verdict on either of the properly submitted theories. We disagreed, reasoning:

> The jury may have found for [plaintiff] on each of the two issues properly submitted. On the other hand, as authorized by the pleading and the charge of the court, they may have found for [plaintiff] only on the issue that was improperly submitted. In order for courts to be able to administer the law in such cases with reasonable certainty and to lay down and maintain just and practical rules for determining the rights of parties, it is necessary that the issues made and submitted to juries, and upon which they are required to pass, be authorized and supported by the law governing the case.

Id. at 1016.

Today, we reaffirm this reasoning. When a single broad-form liability question erroneously commingles valid and invalid liability theories and the appellant's objection is timely and specific, the error is harmful when it cannot be determined whether the improperly submitted theories formed the sole basis for the jury's finding. We disapprove of those courts of appeals' decisions holding that this error is harmless if any evidence supports a properly submitted liability theory. *See Provident*, 914 S.W.2d at 277-78; *Hart*, 881 S.W.2d at 511; *Bernstein*, 850 S.W.2d at 702; *Pool*, 688 S.W.2d at 882.

However, when questions are submitted in a manner that allows the appellate court to determine that the jury's verdict was actually based on a valid liability theory, the error may be harmless. *See City of Brownsville v. Alvarado*, 897 S.W.2d 750, 752 (Tex. 1995) ("Submission of an improper jury question can be harmless error if the jury's answers to other questions render the improper question immaterial."); *Boatland of Houston, Inc. v. Bailey*, 609 S.W.2d 743, 749-50 (Tex. 1980) (holding that the potentially improper submission of defensive issues was harmless error when the jury also found for the defendant on independent grounds).

Casteel argues that Texas Rule of Civil Procedure 277 required the trial court to submit all liability theories in a single broad-form question, and that the verdict should not be overturned because the trial court simply followed that rule. *See* TEX.R. CIV. P. 277. Rule 277 states, "In all jury cases the court shall, whenever feasible, submit the cause upon broad-form questions. The court shall submit such instructions and definitions as shall be proper to enable the jury to render a verdict." *Id.*

Rule 277 is not absolute; rather, it mandates broad-form submission "whenever feasible." *See Westgate, Ltd. v. State*, 843 S.W.2d 448, 455 n. 6 (Tex. 1992). In *Westgate*, we noted that "[s]ubmitting alternative liability standards when the governing law is unsettled might very well be a situation where broad-form submission is not feasible." *Id.* Similarly, when the trial court is unsure whether it should submit a particular theory of liability, separating liability theories best serves the policy of judicial economy underlying Rule 277 by avoiding the need for a new trial when the basis for liability cannot be determined. Furthermore, Rule 277 mandates that "[t]he court shall submit such instructions and definitions as shall be proper to enable the jury to render a verdict." TEX.R. CIV. P. 277. It is implicit in this mandate that the jury be able to base its verdict on legally valid questions and instructions. Thus, it may not be feasible to submit a single broad-form liability question that incorporates wholly separate theories of liability.

Because the error in the charge was harmful and Crown properly objected, we reverse the judgment of the court of appeals, and remand the case to the trial court for a new trial on the issue of whether Crown is liable to Casteel under Article 21.21 for unfair or deceptive practices that do not require Casteel to be a consumer.

* * *

In conclusion, we hold that Casteel is a "person" with standing to sue Crown for violations of Article 21.21 of the Insurance Code, but Casteel does not have standing to sue Crown for violations of those DTPA provisions incorporated within Article 21.21 that, by their terms, require Casteel to be a consumer, including DTPA sections 17.46(b)(5), (7), (9), and (23). We further hold that the inclusion of four invalid theories in a single broad-form liability question was harmful error, requiring a new trial. In addition, we hold that Crown is entitled to summary judgment on Casteel's common-law claims.

Accordingly, we affirm in part the court of appeals' judgment that Casteel take nothing on his common-law claims. Because Crown has released the judgment against Casteel, we vacate that portion of the court of appeals' judgment remanding to the trial court for application of the settlement credit. We reverse in part the court of appeals' judgment in favor of Casteel on his Article 21.21 claims for the violation of DTPA sections 17.46(b)(5), (7), (9), and (23) and render judgment that Casteel take nothing on these claims. We further reverse in part the court of appeals' judgment in favor of Casteel on his other Article 21.21 claims and remand to the trial court for proceedings consistent with this opinion.

Notes

1. *Harris County, Texas v. Smith*, 96 S.W. 3d 230 (Tex. 2002): The rules of appellate procedure set out two conditions upon which a judgment may be reversed for an error of law. The first [TEX. R. APP. P. 61.1(a).] is an error which "probably caused the rendition of an improper judgment." The second [TEX. R. APP. P. 61.1(b)] is an error which "probably prevented the petitioner from properly presenting the case to the appellate courts." Here, the trial court's charge error in this case caused actual harm because it prevented Harris County from properly presenting its case to the appellate courts.

When properly utilized, broad-form submission can simplify charge conferences and provide more comprehensible questions for the jury. But it is not always practicable to submit every issue in a case broadly. Broader is not always better. For example, that broad-form submission may not be feasible when the governing law is unsettled. Then, submitting alternative liability standards permits the appellate court to settle the law and render the correct judgment. Similarly, it would be contrary to judicial economy to insist on broad-form submission when a specific objection raises substantial concern that a particular theory of liability will infect the proposed broad-form question with error. And in a case such as this one, asking the jury to record its verdict as to each element of damages when there is doubt as to the legal sufficiency of the evidence will permit the losing party to preserve error without complicating the charge or the jury's deliberations.

Whether a granulated or broad-form charge is submitted, the trial court's duty is to submit only those questions, instructions, and definitions raised by the pleadings and the evidence. But using the harmless error rule to permit the indiscriminate mixture of valid and invalid liability theories or damage elements, without recourse, undermines a party's incentive to request legally correct definitions, instructions, and questions. A timely objection, plainly informing the court that a specific element of damages should not be included in a broad-form question because there is no evidence to support its submission, preserves the error for appellate review.

2. *Traxler v. Entergy Gulf States, Inc.*, 376 S.W.3d 742 (Tex. 2012): Traxler was riding atop a house that was being moved. He suffered injuries when he was struck by a power line belonging to Entergy Gulf States, Inc. The line was about 20 feet from the ground, while the peak of the house's roof was about 17 feet from the ground. Traxler fell from the house and suffered injuries from the fall and from electrical shock. Traxler sued Entergy and his employer Burkhart, alleging several theories of negligence including negligence per se. Question No. 1 of the jury charge asked whether the negligence of Entergy, Traxler, or Burkhart proximately caused injury to Traxler. General instructions on negligence, ordinary care, proximate cause, and new and independent cause were included with this question. With regard to the alleged negligence per se of Entergy, the jury was instructed that "negligence" also meant the failure to comply with a statutory requirement "that at any place where a transmission line crosses a highway or road it shall be at least twenty-two (22) feet above the surface of the traffic lane." Entergy contends that a *Casteel* problem is presented because both the negligence per se claim against Entergy (concerning the 22–foot requirement), and the common-law negligence claim against Entergy (concerning Entergy's alleged "do not call" policy) were invalid theories of liability. Entergy reasons that if either theory presented in the broad-form liability question is invalid, a *Casteel* problem is presented. "When a

single broad-form liability question erroneously commingles valid and invalid liability theories and the appellant's objection is timely and specific, the error is harmful when it cannot be determined whether the improperly submitted theories formed the sole basis for the jury's finding." No "Casteel" problem is presented, since the negligence per se and common law negligence theories were both valid.

3. *Thota v. Young,* 366 S.W.3d 678 (Tex. 2012): Reversible error is presumed when a broad-form question submitted to the jury incorporates multiple theories of liability and one or more of those theories is invalid, or when the broad-form question commingles damage elements that are unsupported by legally sufficient evidence. ***Held:*** Presumed harm analysis applies to a broad-form submission in a single-theory-of-liability case when the negligence charge includes both an improper defensive theory of contributory negligence and an improper inferential rebuttal instruction. For the reasons explained below, we hold that it does not, and that meaningful appellate review is provided through a traditional harm analysis. Inasmuch as the court of appeals ruled otherwise, we reverse its judgment and remand the case to that court for further consideration consistent with this opinion.

Nearly three years after Dr. Thota performed a catheterization procedure on Ronnie Young at North Texas Cardiology Center, Ronnie died of leukemia, which had developed as a complication of his prolonged struggle with a rare blood disorder. After his death, his widow Margaret, individually and on behalf of Ronnie's estate, sued Dr. Thota, alleging multiple negligent acts and omissions, and NTCC on the basis of respondeat superior. At Dr. Thota's request, and over Young's objection, the trial court submitted a jury question inquiring as to Ronnie's contributory negligence, as well as instructions on new and independent cause and unavoidable accident. In accordance with the jury's findings that Ronnie's negligence was a proximate cause of his death and Dr. Thota's was not, the trial court rendered a take-nothing judgment. The court of appeals reversed, holding the trial court committed reversible error by including in the charge the question on Ronnie's contributory negligence and the new and independent cause instruction. In so doing, the court held that the presumed harm analysis applied in *Crown Life Ins. Co. v. Casteel,* 22 S.W.3d 378, 388 (Tex. 2000), applied to a broad-form question that incorporates multiple theories of liability, one or more of which is invalid and distinguished *Bed, Bath & Beyond, Inc. v. Urista,* 211 S.W.3d 753, 756-57 (2006). ***Held:*** In a single-theory-of-liability case, if the negligence charge includes both an improper defensive theory of contributory negligence and an improper inferential rebuttal instruction on new and independent cause, meaningful appellate review is provided through a traditional harm analysis; therefore, *Casteel*'s presumed harm analysis does not apply. As the Court held in *State Dep't of Highways v. Payne,* 838 S.W.2d 235, 241 (Tex. 1992), "the procedural requirements for determining whether a party has preserved error in the jury charge are explained by one basic test: 'whether the party made the trial court aware of the complaint, timely and plainly, and obtained a ruling.'" Young met the *Payne* test; she not only made a specific and timely no-evidence objection to the contributory negligence question and specifically objected to the new and independent cause instruction but she also submitted a proposed charge that omitted both. "Young did not have to cite or reference *Casteel* specifically to preserve the right for the appellate court to apply the presumed harm analysis, if applicable, to the disputed charge issues." However, unlike the *Casteel* charge, which involved one answer blank for thirteen independent grounds of liability, the charge here provided separate answer blanks for Dr. Thota's and Ronnie's negligence. Consequently, the contributory negligence charge does not raise the issue raised in *Casteel* – the inability to determine the basis for the jury's verdict. On the new and independent cause instruction, the Court states:

> [E]ven assuming the new and independent cause instruction in this charge constituted error, it does not raise a *Casteel* issue. Like *Urista,* this case involves a single liability theory—negligence—so *Casteel's* multiple-liability-theory analysis does not apply. *See* [*Bed, Bath & Beyond, Inc. v. Urista,* 211 S.W.3d 753, 756-57 (2006)]. Moreover, as we noted in *Urista,* "when a defensive theory is submitted through an inferential rebuttal instruction, *Casteel's* solution of departing from broad-form submission and instead employing granulated submission cannot apply." *Id.* at 757. Inferential rebuttal issues are distinct from theories of liability and damage elements because they "cannot be submitted in the jury charge as separate questions and instead must be presented through jury instructions." *Id.* Like the inferential rebuttal instruction on unavoidable accident in *Urista,* the new and independent cause instruction "was given in reference to the causation element of the plaintiff's negligence claim." *Id.* at 756–57. While appellate courts may presume harm when meaningful appellate review is precluded because the submitted charge mixes valid and invalid theories of liability or commingles improper damage elements, the courts do not presume harm because of improper inferential rebuttal instructions on defensive theories.

> *See id.* at 757. Therefore, assuming without deciding that the submission of the new and independent cause instruction was an abuse of discretion, we hold that this charge error does not present a *Casteel* problem.

Applying traditional harm analysis, the Court holds no harm is shown for four reasons: (1) The jury failed to find that Dr. Thota was negligent in causing the tear in Ronnie's artery; and that finding is entirely separate from the jury's finding that Ronnie was contributorily negligent; (2) considering the entire charge, as the Court must, it is clear that "the clarifying instructions at the end of Question 1 made it clear that the jury could answer" "Yes" to both Dr. Thota and Ronnie, "No" to both, or "Yes" to one and "No" to the other; (3) the definition of proximate cause clearly informed the jury that "[t]here may be more than one proximate cause of an event"; and (4) in light of the jury's failure to find that Dr. Thota was negligent, the jury's answer in response to the question on Ronnie's contributory negligence was immaterial, *i.e.*, it could not alter the effect of the verdict. The Court further holds no harm is shown from inclusion of the new and independent cause instruction because, based on the conflicting evidence, the jury could have reasonably concluded that Dr. Thota did not breach the standard of care without reaching the issue of proximate cause and therefore without regard to the new and independent cause instruction, which pertains only to the proximate cause element.

4. *Texas Com'n on Human Rights v. Morrison*, -----S.W.3d ----, ----Tex. Sup. Ct. J.----, 2012 WL 3800884 (Tex. 2012): In this employer retaliation case, the jury was asked: Did the Texas Commission on Human Rights (TCHR) take adverse personnel actions against Marilou Morrison because of her opposition to an unlawful discriminatory practice? This was a broad-form jury question allowed the jury to find liability based on a legal theory that was jurisdictionally barred and thus could not support liability. ***Held:*** Reversed and remanded. As held in In *Crown Life Ins. Co. v. Casteel*, 22 S.W.3d 378, 389 (Tex. 2000)., when a single broad-form liability question erroneously commingles valid and invalid liability theories and the appellant's objection is timely and specific, the error is harmful when it cannot be determined whether the improperly submitted theories formed the sole basis for the jury's finding." As in *Casteel*, it cannot be determined in this case whether the jury relied on the invalid theory.

The jury was asked: Did the Texas Commission on Human Rights (TCHR) take adverse personnel actions against Marilou Morrison because of her opposition to an unlawful discriminatory practice? The charge did not define "adverse personnel actions." TCHR objected, arguing the broad-form submission improperly commingled adverse personnel actions. Specifically, TCHR objected that the term adverse personnel actions would allow the jury to find liability without unanimity because there were multiple occurrences the jury could view as adverse personnel actions. TCHR tendered a liability question that focused solely on the termination. The trial court denied the objection. The jury found TCHR liable for retaliation and awarded $300,000 in compensatory damages. ***Held:*** Reversed and remanded. Error was preserved by TDCHR. *Casteel* error may be preserved without specifically mentioning *Casteel.* During the charge conference, TCHR argued that the charge lumped TCHR's different actions together, that the case was "really, about retaliation and termination," and that it would not be possible to determine what adverse acts would form the basis of the jury's verdict. This is the problem identified in *Casteel*–commingling valid and invalid theories of liability in a broad-form question. This is especially true given that, from the outset of the underlying proceeding, the scope of what adverse personnel actions could form the basis of the suit was a contentious issue.

TCHR timely objected to the question at issue, which allowed the jury to find liability based on an invalid legal theory. Therefore, harm is presumed.

BENGE
v.
WILLIAMS
548 S.W.3d 466
(Tex. 2018)

William David George, Amy L. Nilsen, Earnest W. Wotring, Baker Wotring LLP, Houston, TX, for Petitioners Jim P. Benge, Kelsey-Seybold Medical Group PLLC.

Lucy H. Forbes, The Forbes Firm, PLLC, Chelsie King Garza, Randall O. Sorrels, Abraham Watkins Nichols Sorrels Agosto & Friend, Houston, TX, for Respondent Lauren Williams.

Jeffrey B. McClure, Andrews & Kurth LLP, Houston, TX, for Amicus Curiae Baylor College of Medicine.

Diana L. Faust, Kyle M. Burke, R. Brent Cooper, Cooper & Scully, P.C. Founders Square for Amicus Curiaes Texas Alliance for Patient Access, Texas Medical Association, Texas Osteopathic Medical Association, Dallas, TX.

Ann Seymore, Houston TX, for Amicus Curiae Memorial Hermann Health System.

CHIEF JUSTICE HECHT delivered the opinion of the Court.

At the trial of this healthcare-liability case, the patient argued and offered evidence that her physician was negligent both in using an inexperienced resident to assist with performing her surgery and in not disclosing the resident's level of involvement, although she does not claim a right to recover for the nondisclosure. The jury was asked simply whether the physician was negligent without being instructed not to consider the nondisclosure. A divided court of appeals concluded that the trial court's refusal to instruct the jury as requested was harmful error, and we agree. * * * We affirm the judgment of the court of appeals remanding the case to the trial court for a new trial.

During a laparoscopic-assisted vaginal hysterectomy ("LAVH") to remove her uterus, ovaries, and fallopian tubes, Lauren Williams, 39, suffered a bowel perforation that was not immediately diagnosed, resulting in catastrophic post-surgical consequences. She sued the surgeon, Dr. Jim Benge, a board-certified obstetrician and gynecologist, and his practice group, Kelsey-Seybold Medical Group, PLLC (together referred to as "Dr. Benge"). The jury found that Dr. Benge's negligence caused Williams' injuries. We summarize the evidence in the light most favorable to the verdict.

A week before the surgery, Dr. Benge and Williams discussed the LAVH procedure and reviewed written consent forms setting out all required disclosures of risks, including damage to the bowel. By filling out the forms and signing them, Williams stated:

> I *Lauren R. Williams* voluntarily request Dr. *Benge* as my physician, and such associates, technical assistants and other health care providers as they may deem necessary, to treat my condition . . . .
>
> * * *
>
> I . . . understand that the physician may require other physicians including residents to perform important tasks based on their skill set and, in the case of residents, under the supervision of the responsible physician. (Residents are doctors who have finished medical school but are getting more training.)

Dr. Benge testified that in explaining the consent forms, he told Williams that he "would be doing the surgery with an assistant." Williams testified that Dr. Benge did not tell her the resident would actually be performing part of the surgery.

Dr. Benge was assisted by Dr. Lauren Giacobbe, a resident in the third year of a 4-year program. Dr. Giacobbe had significant experience with hysterectomies and laparoscopic surgeries, but she had not previously assisted with an LAVH surgery, a fact Dr. Benge did not disclose to Williams. Dr. Giacobbe testified that she explained to Dr. Benge her experience level before the surgery began and that he determined the tasks she would perform. She also testified that she introduced herself to Williams on the morning of the surgery and told Williams that she was a resident and was going to be assisting Dr. Benge with the surgery. Dr. Giacobbe admitted she did not identify the surgical tasks she would perform but explained that she did not know those details until after the surgery began. Williams testified that she did not speak with Dr. Giacobbe on the morning of her surgery and would not have undergone the surgery if she had known it was Dr. Giacobbe's first time assisting an LAVH procedure.

* * *

When they finished, Dr. Benge examined the surgical area, saw no sign that Williams' bowel had been perforated, and noted no complications in the post-operative report. But within hours, Williams began to complain of severe pain, abdominal tenderness, and nausea. By the time Dr. Benge saw Williams the next morning, she had a fever and was anemic, tachycardic, and in constant pain. Dr. Benge started her on intravenous antibiotics and ordered an x-ray of her chest to ensure that she did not have pneumonia. He did not suspect that she had a perforated bowel. Dr. Benge did not see Williams again that day because he went home ill.

Williams' condition continued to deteriorate. She began experiencing rectal bleeding. Her hemoglobin and hematocrit levels fell significantly. She required a multi-unit blood transfusion and continued experiencing constant pain. Three days post-surgery, a gastroenterologist diagnosed her with a bowel perforation that was leaking feces from her intestines into her abdomen. The doctors repaired the perforation, which was on Williams' left side where Dr. Giacobbe had operated, but a colostomy was required. Williams developed sepsis, underwent a tracheotomy, was put on a mechanical ventilator, and remained in a chemically induced coma for 3 weeks. Once discharged, she required home health assistance for an extended recovery period and was unable to work.

Williams had a second surgery to reverse the colostomy, but it could not be completed successfully, and the colostomy was replaced with an ileostomy. A third surgery to replace the ileostomy with another colostomy was successful, but the colostomy became permanent. Williams has had 2 subsequent surgeries to address complications related to the colostomy.

* * *

Williams offered evidence that Dr. Benge failed to disclose Dr. Giacobbe's experience level and degree of involvement in the surgery. Williams argued throughout the trial that Dr. Benge's nondisclosure was deceitful and betrayed her trust in him. Dr. Patsner further testified that the lack of disclosure violated the standard of care and was negligent. But Williams has never claimed that the nondisclosure precluded her informed consent or otherwise provides a basis for liability. The jury was asked a single question on liability: Did Dr. Benge's negligence proximately cause Williams' injuries? Dr. Benge objected to the question because it "allow[ed] the jury to base its finding on a violation of informed consent" that Williams did not claim. Dr. Benge requested that the jury be "instructed that in deciding whether [Dr. Benge] was negligent, you cannot consider what [Dr. Benge] told, or did not tell, [Williams] about [Dr. Giacobbe's] being involved with the surgery." The trial court overruled Dr. Benge's objection and refused to give the jury the requested instruction.

The trial court rendered judgment on the verdict for Williams for almost $2 million. On appeal, * * * Dr. Benge also argued that the jury was allowed to find Dr. Benge negligent for failing to disclose Dr. Giacobbe's experience and involvement in the surgery, a basis for liability Williams had disclaimed, thus requiring a new trial. A deeply divided court of appeals agreed only with the second argument and reversed and remanded the case for a new trial. We granted Williams' and Dr. Benge's petitions for review.

* * *

We turn now to Dr. Benge's argument that the trial court's refusal to instruct the jury not to consider "what [he] told, or did not tell, [Williams] about [Dr. Giacobbe's] being involved with the surgery" was error requiring a new trial.

At trial and on appeal, Williams has steadfastly disclaimed any assertion that Dr. Benge is liable for failing to obtain her informed consent to surgery. She acknowledges that she consented in writing to the possible involvement of a resident in her LAVH procedure. She does not contend that she misunderstood the consent forms she signed. She does contend that Dr. Benge is nonetheless liable for his negligence in allowing Dr. Giacobbe in particular—with no experience in performing the surgery—to assist in the LAVH procedure, in assigning her the surgical tasks he did, and in supervising her work. Her disclaimer of an informed-consent claim does not, of course, foreclose that negligence claim.

But Williams also contends that Dr. Benge not only allowed Dr. Giacobbe to assist in surgery, he failed to disclose that Dr. Giacobbe had never performed an LAVH procedure and that she would be significantly involved in the surgery. Indeed, Williams' nondisclosure contention was front and center beginning to end. The first words out of Williams' counsel's mouth in his opening statement to the jury were that a surgeon "cannot pass off part of [a] surgery to a resident without the express permission of the patient." "[T]he reasons . . . we're bringing suit", he told the jury, were: "First, [Dr. Benge] betrayed [Williams]. He told her he was going to do the surgery. She trusted him to do the surgery. He did not, and he will admit to you he did not live up to his end of the deal." Dr. Benge betrayed Williams, counsel continued, by having "a secret surgeon, a first-time resident do a significant part of this procedure." "The first thing you must do" as a surgeon being assisted by a resident, counsel said, "is you must inform the patient." Dr. Benge "didn't tell [Williams] that [r]esident Lauren Giacobbe was going to do the procedure. He didn't tell her that the resident had never done the procedure before." "We're suing", Williams' counsel repeated, because Dr. Benge brought in "a surgeon who had no permission, who had no consent to put her hands on [Williams]." That, he reiterated, was the "[f]irst reason". The other reasons were Dr. Benge's conduct of the surgery and his post-surgical failure to promptly diagnose and treat Williams' bowel perforation.

Williams' counsel repeatedly asked Dr. Benge on the stand whether he had told Williams that Dr. Giacobbe would be involved in the surgery or her level of experience. * * * In all, Dr. Benge was asked about his nondisclosure of Dr. Giacobbe's involvement and Williams' lack of consent some 20 times. Williams' testimony likewise centered on Dr. Benge's failure to disclose, and her failure to consent to, Dr. Giacobbe's involvement.

In summation, Williams' counsel again told the jury that the "[n]umber one" reason Williams had sued was because Dr. Benge had not disclosed to her Dr. Giacobbe's lack of experience and involvement in the surgery.

Williams argues that her evidence of Dr. Benge's nondisclosure was not a claim of lack of informed consent for which he could be liable. As already noted, she disclaims any such basis for liability. But Williams' argument is contradicted by the record. Dr. Patsner, Williams' expert, testified repeatedly that Dr. Benge's nondisclosure violated the standard of care—that it was negligent. * * *

Williams argues that her claim of nondisclosure, which she clearly makes, is not the same as a claim of lack of informed consent, which she disclaims. We fail to see the difference. Williams concedes that in her written consent, she acknowledged the possible involvement of a resident in surgery. But she contends that she was not told enough about that involvement: who the resident would be, what the resident would do, and the resident's experience. Though she acknowledges informed consent to the risks of surgery and the involvement of a resident, she has repeatedly denied informed consent to the involvement of Dr. Giacobbe, calling it a betrayal and deceitful. Her nondisclosure claim cannot be viewed as anything other than a claim of lack of informed consent.

* * * The issues of whether Dr. Benge was negligent in involving Dr. Giacobbe and supervising her in the surgery, and whether Dr. Benge was negligent in failing to disclose to Williams what was required to obtain her informed consent, are completely different. Williams' evidence and argument at trial confused them.

Based on Dr. Patsner's testimony, the jury could have found that Dr. Benge was negligent in failing to disclose Dr. Giacobbe's involvement in the surgery and her lack of experience. But Williams does not assert that claim. Therefore, Dr. Benge argues, the jury should have been instructed not to consider the lack of disclosure in determining negligence, and the trial court erred in refusing the requested instruction. He contends that the error must be presumed harmful under our decision in *Crown Life Insurance Co. v. Casteel* and its progeny.

In *Casteel*, the jury was asked to find whether the defendant was liable for engaging in any of 13 practices listed in a single question. For 4 of the listed practices, the plaintiff could not recover because he was not a consumer. Hence, the question included both valid and invalid liability theories. The court of appeals held that the mixing of valid and invalid theories was error but that the error was harmless because there was some evidence to support a finding of liability under at least one of the valid theories. We disagreed, holding that "when a trial court submits a single broad-form liability question incorporating multiple theories of liability, the error is harmful and a new trial is required when the appellate court cannot determine whether the jury based its verdict on an improperly submitted invalid theory."

The jury question in the present case, unlike the one in *Casteel*, did not include multiple theories, some valid and some invalid. It inquired about a single theory: negligence. But we have twice held that when the question allows a finding of liability based on evidence that cannot support recovery, the same presumption-of-harm rule must be applied.

In *Columbia Rio Grande Healthcare, L.P. v. Hawley*, the liability question to the jury was stated the same as in the present case: Was the hospital's negligence a proximate cause of the plaintiff's injuries? The jury was instructed that the hospital could "act only through its employees, agents, nurses, and servants." The charge did not define "agent". There was evidence in the case of a physician's negligence, and the hospital requested that the jury be instructed that the physician was not its agent. The trial court refused. We held that while the case presented "a different jury charge problem" than *Casteel* did, the trial court's error "effectively preclude[d] reviewing courts from determining whether the jury found liability on an invalid basis, preclude[d] determination of whether the error probably caused the rendition of an improper judgment, and [was] harmful because it prevent[ed] proper presentation of the case on appeal."

Likewise, in *Texas Commission on Human Rights v. Morrison*, the liability question to the jury asked about a single theory: employer retaliation. The plaintiff complained of several adverse actions taken by her employer, including the denial of a promotion, but liability could not be based on the denied promotion because the plaintiff had not included that particular action in her EEOC complaint. Over the employer's objection, the trial court submitted a single question asking whether the employer took "adverse personnel actions" against the plaintiff. The plaintiff argued on appeal, as Williams does here, that there was no charge error because "no invalid theory was directly submitted to the jury". We rejected that argument, and even though the employer had not requested a limiting instruction, held that the error in overruling the objection was presumed harmful.

Here, as in *Hawley* and *Morrison*, while the jury was asked about a single liability theory, the plaintiff advanced multiple claims in the evidence. Dr. Benge was negligent, Williams claimed, in allowing Dr. Giacobbe to assist, failing to disclose her involvement, improperly supervising her, and failing to promptly detect the bowel perforation. Dr. Patsner testified that Dr. Benge's nondisclosure fell below the standard of care. The jury could have based its finding of negligence only on that nondisclosure or any 1 or more of Williams' other claims. Williams has disclaimed recovery for Dr. Benge's nondisclosure. Dr. Benge requested that the jury be instructed, correctly, that it could not consider the nondisclosure in deciding whether he was negligent. Because the trial court refused the instruction, we cannot determine whether it was the basis for the jury's finding. As in *Hawley* and *Morrison*, as well as *Casteel*, because an appellate court cannot determine whether the jury found liability on an improper basis, we must presume that the error in denying Dr. Benge's limiting instruction was harmful. The rule "both encourage[s] and require[s] parties not to submit issues that have no basis in law and fact in such a way that the error cannot be corrected without retrial."

* * *

We need not decide whether the trial court erred by admitting evidence of Dr. Benge's failure to disclose Dr. Giacobbe's involvement to Williams, or whether Dr. Benge preserved his objection. Whether Dr. Benge has an evidentiary complaint or not, the complaint he makes is that the charge allowed the jury to consider what he did or did not tell Williams about Dr. Giacobbe's involvement in the surgery in deciding negligence, even though Williams does not seek recovery on that basis. He objected to the charge and requested a limiting instruction.

In *Morrison*, we held that an objection to the charge even without a requested question or instruction preserved the complaint that the evidence would allow the jury to find liability in answer to a single broad-form question, on a theory on which the plaintiff could not recover. Dr. Benge's objection and requested instruction went as far as that case requires.

The court of appeals was correct in concluding that the charge error requires a new trial.

* * *

Accordingly, the judgment of the court of appeals is *Affirmed.*

WILLIAMS
v.
OLIVO
952 S.W.2d 523
Tex.,1997

Scott Patrick Stolley, Dallas, Andrew L. Kerr, K. Blake Coffee, San Antonio, Thomas J. Mitchell, III, Austin, John Alex Huddleston, San Antonio, for Petitioners.

Carlos Villarreal, Corpus Christi, Sam C. Fugate, Kingsville, for Respondents.

BAKER, JUSTICE, delivered the opinion of the Court, in which PHILLIPS, CHIEF JUSTICE, GONZALEZ, HECHT, CORNYN, ENOCH, OWEN and ABBOTT, JUSTICES, join.

In this case, we consider the liability of a general contractor and its on-site representative for injuries to an independent contractor's employee. The trial court rendered judgment on a jury verdict for the employee, and the court of appeals affirmed in part. 912 S.W.2d 319. Because the employee obtained no findings on the general contractor's or the representative's liability for a premises defects, we reverse the court of appeals' judgment and render judgment that the Olivos take nothing.

I. BACKGROUND

Clayton Williams, Jr., Inc. (Williams) operated an oil and gas lease in LaSalle County. Odis Graham served as Williams' on-site representative. Williams contracted with Diamond M Onshore, Incorporated to drill a well on the lease. Diamond M in turn hired David Olivo to work on a drilling crew as a floor hand. One of Olivo's duties was to roll joints of drill pipe off a pipe rack onto a catwalk, where the pipe was then hoisted up a ramp to the rig floor for connection to drill pipe already in the well. Early one morning, while moving several pipes onto the catwalk, Olivo suddenly slipped as he stepped down off the pipe rack. As he fell to the ground a few feet below, Olivo landed on his back on one of several drill pipe thread protectors that had been left on the ground during the previous shift. As a result of this injury, Olivo was partially paralyzed.

Olivo and his wife, Rosielinda, sued Williams and Graham for negligence and gross negligence. The Olivos sought both actual and exemplary damages. The trial court rendered judgment on a jury verdict for the Olivos for $2,028,354 in actual damages, plus $21,800 in exemplary damages from Graham and $500,000 in exemplary damages from Williams. Liberty Mutual Insurance Company, Diamond M's workers' compensation carrier that intervened in the case, was awarded its subrogation claim for the compensation payments it previously made to Olivo.

The court of appeals, en banc, reversed the exemplary damages awards because the evidence of gross negligence was insufficient. It affirmed in all other respects and rendered judgment.

II. DUTY

At the outset, we must determine what duty, if any, Williams owed to Olivo, the employee of an independent contractor. Williams occupied the leased land and was Diamond M's general contractor. Therefore, the hybrid body of law that lies at the intersection of premises liability and agency law governs this case. *See Exxon Corp. v. Tidwell,* 867 S.W.2d 19, 21 (Tex. 1993). An owner or occupier of land generally has a duty to use reasonable care to make and keep the premises safe for business invitees. *Redinger v. Living, Inc.,* 689 S.W.2d 415, 417 (Tex. 1985); *Smith v. Henger,* 148 Tex. 456, 226 S.W.2d 425, 431 (1950). A general contractor in control of the premises is charged with the same duty as an owner or occupier. *Redinger,* 689 S.W.2d at 417. Williams thus has overlapping duties as both the occupier of the land and the general contractor who hired an independent contractor. We must now determine the scope of those duties.

III. SCOPE OF DUTIES

A general contractor in control of the premises may be liable for two types of negligence in failing to keep the premises safe: that arising from an activity on the premises, and that arising from a premises defect. *Redinger,* 689 S.W.2d at 417. This is not a negligent-activity case because Olivo alleges that he was injured by thread protectors previously left on the ground, not as a contemporaneous result of someone's negligence. *See Keetch v. Kroger Co.,* 845 S.W.2d 262, 264 (Tex. 1992)(holding that recovery on a negligent activity theory requires that the plaintiff be harmed by or as a contemporaneous result of the activity itself); *H.E. Butt Grocery Co. v. Warner,* 845 S.W.2d 258, 259 (Tex. 1992)(same). Instead, this is a premises defect case.

There are two types of premises defects for which an independent contractor's employee may seek to hold the general contractor liable. The first category are those defects that exist on the premises when the business invitee entered for business purposes or that are created through some means unrelated to the activity of the injured employee or his employer. *Shell Chem. Co. v. Lamb,* 493 S.W.2d 742, 746 (Tex. 1973). In this situation, the general contractor has a duty to inspect the premises and warn the invitee of those dangerous conditions of which the general contractor knows or should know. *Lamb,* 493 S.W.2d at 746.

The second category of premises defects are those defects the independent contractor (or its injured employee) created by its work activity. *Lamb,* 493 S.W.2d at 746-47. When the independent contractor creates the dangerous condition, the general contractor ordinarily has no duty to warn the independent contractor's employees of the premises defect. *Pence Constr. Corp. v. Watson,* 470 S.W.2d 637, 639 (Tex. 1971). The rationale for this rule is that a general contractor normally has no duty to ensure that an independent contractor performs its work in a safe manner. *See Exxon Corp. v. Quinn,* 726 S.W.2d 17, 19-20 (Tex. 1987); *Abalos v. Oil Dev. Co. of Texas,* 544 S.W.2d 627, 631-32 (Tex. 1976).

However, this Court has long recognized that under some circumstances the general contractor does have a duty to warn an independent contractor's employees of any dangerous conditions arising out of the independent contractor's work. *See Lamb,* 493 S.W.2d at 747-48. In *Redinger,* we defined the scope of that duty by adopting section 414 of the *Restatement (Second) of Torts:*

> One who entrusts work to an independent contractor, but who retains the control of any part of the work, is subject to liability for physical harm to others for whose safety the employer owes a duty to exercise reasonable care, which is caused by his failure to exercise his control with reasonable care.

RESTATEMENT (SECOND) OF TORTS § 414 (1965), *quoted in Redinger,* 689 S.W.2d at 418. This duty requires a general contractor to exercise any retained supervisory control "with reasonable care so as to prevent the work which he has ordered to be done from causing injury to others." RESTATEMENT (SECOND) OF TORTS § 414 cmt. a, *quoted in Redinger,* 689 S.W.2d at 418. For the general contractor to be liable for negligence, its supervisory control must relate to the condition or activity that caused the injury. *Tidwell,* 867 S.W.2d at 23; *see also Welch v. McDougal,* 876 S.W.2d 218, 223-24 (Tex. App.—Amarillo 1994, writ denied); *Tirres v. El Paso Sand Prods., Inc.,* 808 S.W.2d 672, 676 (Tex. App.—El Paso 1991, writ denied).

It is typically the general contractor's right of control over the injury-causing activity or condition that gives rise to a duty to ensure that the independent contractor performs its work safely. *Pollard v. Missouri Pac. R.R.,* 759 S.W.2d 670, 671 (Tex. 1988); *Tovar v. Amarillo Oil Co.,* 692 S.W.2d 469, 470 (Tex. 1985). If there is no contractual right to control, however, the general contractor can be liable if it actually exercised control, contrary to the contract's terms. *Tidwell,* 867 S.W.2d at 21 n. 3.

In *Redinger,* the "right to control" rule subjected the general contractor to liability for the independent contractor's negligent activities on the premises. *Redinger,* 689 S.W.2d at 418. The "right to control" rule also applies to premises defect cases. *Tidwell,* 867 S.W.2d at 21-23. As the *Restatement* explains:

> The rule stated in this Section is usually, though not exclusively, applicable when a principal contractor entrusts a part of the work to subcontractors, but himself or through a foreman superintends the entire job. In such a situation, the principal contractor is subject to liability if he fails to prevent the subcontractors from doing even the details of the work in a way unreasonably dangerous to others, if he knows or by the exercise of reasonable care should know that the subcontractors' work is being so done, and has the opportunity to prevent it by exercising the power of control which he has retained in himself. *So too, he is subject to liability if he knows or should know that the subcontractors have carelessly done their work in such a way as to create a dangerous condition, and fails to exercise reasonable care either to remedy it himself or by the exercise of his control cause the subcontractor to do so.*

RESTATEMENT (SECOND) OF TORTS § 414 cmt. b (emphasis added). When a premises defect arises from the independent contractor's work, then, the general contractor who retains a right to control or exercises control can be liable for negligence in exercising or failing to exercise control over the part of the independent contractor's work that created the dangerous condition. *See Tidwell,* 867 S.W.2d at 23; *Barham v. Turner Constr. Co.,* 803 S.W.2d 731, 735-36 (Tex. App.—Dallas 1990, writ denied).

IV. PREMISES DEFECT-THE JURY CHARGE

The court of appeals correctly recognized that this case fits in the second category we have discussed and involves a premises defect that the independent contractor allegedly created rather than a negligent activity. However, the court of appeals erred in holding that the Olivos could recover from Williams for negligent control without establishing the premises defect elements. To recover against a general contractor for a premises defect, the injured plaintiff must establish both the general contractor's right to control the defect-producing work and a breach of that duty according to the traditional premises defect elements. *See Corbin v. Safeway Stores, Inc.*, 648 S.W.2d 292, 296 (Tex. 1983) (setting forth traditional elements of premises liability claim); RESTATEMENT (SECOND) OF TORTS § 414 cmt. b (incorporating premises liability elements into right-to-control liability). The plaintiff may submit this cause of action to the jury through a question about the general contractor's right to control the defect-producing work, to establish a duty, and a broad-form negligence question. However, instructions that incorporate the *Corbin* premises defect elements must accompany the questions. *See Tidwell,* 867 S.W.2d at 23; *Keetch,* 845 S.W.2d at 266-67; *Barham,* 803 S.W.2d at 736-37. Because premises defect cases and negligent activity cases are based on independent theories of recovery, a simple negligence question, unaccompanied by the *Corbin* elements as instructions or definitions, cannot support a recovery in a premises defect case. *See Keetch*, 845 S.W.2d at 266-67; *Warner*, 845 S.W.2d at 259-60.

Here, the Olivos did not request that the trial court submit a control question, the premises defect elements, or a negligence question against Williams. Therefore, there are no jury findings against Williams on any of these issues. Instead, the trial court submitted a single simple negligence question about Graham's alleged negligence. Under the trial court's charge, the jury found that Graham was Williams' employee and that Graham was negligent and proximately caused Olivo's injuries.

Initially, the Olivos requested a question asking whether Graham was negligent in failing to provide Olivo a safe place to work. Their proposed question defined negligence according to the *Corbin* factors. However, the trial court did not rule on the Olivos' request nor did it submit their proposed question. Thus, the trial court's charge omitted essential elements of a premises defects claim. On appeal, the Olivos do not complain, even conditionally, that the trial court should have submitted their proposed question that included the *Corbin* elements. Instead, they assert that *Corbin* and *Keetch* do not apply here. We disagree. We have explicitly required that the trial court submit the *Corbin* elements in a premises defect case. *Keetch,* 845 S.W.2d at 266-67; *Warner,* 845 S.W.2d at 259-60; *Hernandez v. Kroger Co.,* 711 S.W.2d 3, 4-5 (Tex. 1986).

Alternatively, the Olivos contend that the *Corbin* elements should be deemed found to support the trial court's judgment. The premises defect elements cannot be deemed found against Graham. The simple negligence question submitted to the jury relates only to the theory that Graham was liable for control over any negligent activities. *Keetch,* 845 S.W.2d at 264. However, as we have explained, this is not a negligent activity case. It is a premises defect case. The missing *Corbin* premises defect elements about knowledge and risk of harm are not necessarily referable to the negligent activity question submitted to the jury. *See Stanley Stores, Inc. v. Veazey,* 838 S.W.2d 884, 886 (Tex. App.—Beaumont 1992, writ denied); *Physicians & Surgeons Gen. Hosp. v. Koblizek,* 752 S.W.2d 657, 659-60 (Tex. App.—Corpus Christi 1988, writ denied); TEX.R. CIV. P. 279. Because the Olivos did not obtain a jury finding that included essential elements of their premises defect claim, they cannot recover against Graham. TEX.R. CIV. P. 279.

Because the Olivos did not secure a jury finding about Williams' negligence but did obtain a finding that Graham was Williams' employee, their only liability theory against Williams was respondeat superior for Graham's negligence. We need not decide whether, under these facts, Graham could incur individual liability. *See Leitch v. Hornsby,* 935 S.W.2d 114, 117 (Tex. 1996) (corporate agent can assume individual liability for breach of duty to provide safe workplace if agent owes independent duty of care); *Werner v. Colwell,* 909 S.W.2d 866, 868 (Tex. 1995)(same). Because the Olivos did not obtain findings to support premises defect liability against Graham, however, they have not established respondeat superior liability against Williams through Graham.

V. CONCLUSION

The court of appeals erred in holding that Clayton Williams, Inc., and Odis Graham could be liable for David Olivo's injuries without regard to whether the injuries arose from a negligent activity or a premises defect. Because the Olivos did not secure proper jury findings on their only viable cause of action, premises defect, they waived that claim and are not entitled to any relief from Williams or Graham. Accordingly, we reverse that part of the court of appeals' judgment affirming actual damages and render judgment that the Olivos take nothing.

SPECTOR, JUSTICE, concurring and dissenting (omitted).

TORRINGTON COMPANY v. STUTZMAN

46 S.W. 3d 829
(Tex. 2000)

William Powers, Jr., University of Texas School of Law, Austin, Roger Townsend, Richard P. Hogan, Jr., Hogan Dubose & Townsend, Jennifer Bruch Hogan, Hogan Dubose & Townsend, L.L.P., Kevin H. Dubose, David M. Gunn, Hogan Dubose & Townsend, Houston, William M. Tolin, III, Benckenstein & Oxford, Beaumont, David H. Brown, D. Ferguson McNiel, Vinson & Elkins, Houston, for petitioners.

King Waters, Waters & Waters, JoAnn Storey, Storey, Moore & McCally, Tracy J. Willi, Womble & Cotellesse, Houston, Justin Williams, Williams Kasperitis & Gowan, David J. Fisher, Orgain Bell & Tucker, Silsbee, Claudia Wilson Frost, Matthew P. Eastus, Slusser & Frost, L.L.P., Houston, Gilbert I. "Buddy" Low, Orgain, Bell & Tucker, Beaumont, Ernest H. Cannon, Ernest H. Cannon & Associates, Houston, Finis E. Cowan, Jr., Dickinson, Joe E. Broussard, Mehaffy & Weber, Beaumont, for respondents.

JUSTICE O'NEILL delivered the opinion of the court joined by CHIEF JUSTICE PHILLIPS, JUSTICE ENOCH, JUSTICE BAKER, JUSTICE ABBOTT, JUSTICE HANKINSON, and JUSTICE GONZALES.

This case arises out of a Navy helicopter crash that killed two Marines. A jury found that a defective bearing in the helicopter's tail rotor assembly caused the crash. The trial court rendered judgment for the plaintiffs against the bearing's manufacturer and the manufacturer's successor. We consider a number of issues, including (1) whether the plaintiffs' negligent undertaking claim against the successor corporation was properly submitted to the jury, (2) whether the successor is contractually obligated to indemnify the manufacturer, (3) whether legally sufficient evidence supports the judgment against the bearing's manufacturer, (4) whether the trial court erred in refusing to submit a jury question on the government-contractor defense, (5) whether the trial court applied the appropriate state's law governing damages, (6) whether the jury verdict may be vitiated based upon excessiveness, and (7) whether the successor waived its objection to the trial court's determining attorney ad litem fees without an evidentiary hearing.

We conclude that the broad-form negligence question the trial court submitted to the jury omitted elements necessary to impose liability upon the successor under a negligent undertaking theory. Accordingly, we reverse the judgment against the successor and remand the plaintiffs' claims against the successor to the trial court in the interest of justice. We further hold that the trial court did not err in enforcing the successor's contractual indemnity obligation, and that the successor has standing to challenge the judgment against the manufacturer. Additionally, we hold that legally sufficient evidence supports the judgment against the manufacturer. We also hold that the trial court did not err in refusing to submit the government-contractor defense to the jury, and that the trial court properly applied choice-of-law principles. Further, we hold that, on this record, we may not vitiate the jury verdict based upon excessiveness. Finally, we hold that the successor waived its claim that the trial court erred by determining ad litem fees without an evidentiary hearing. Accordingly, we affirm the judgment against the manufacturer. We also affirm that portion of the judgment against the successor based upon its contractual indemnity.

I
Background

On July 31, 1992, a Navy helicopter crashed, killing two Marines, Phillip D. Stutzman and James Pulaski. It is undisputed that the crash was caused by the failure of a bearing, although the parties dispute what caused the bearing to fail. The bearing was manufactured in 1984 by Fafnir Bearings, a division of Textron, Inc. Textron is also the parent company of Bell Helicopter Textron, Inc. (Bell), the company that manufactured the helicopter. Fafnir was purchased in 1985 by Torrington's parent corporation, Ingersoll-Rand Co., and became a division of Torrington. The purchase agreement requires Ingersoll-Rand to indemnify Textron for products liability claims based upon the bearing.

Textron (and later Torrington) manufactured two types of bearings: (1) a nonregreasable—05 bearing used primarily in military helicopters designed and sold by Bell, and (2) a regreasable—03 bearing used in civilian helicopters. At the time the bearing involved in the crash was sold, both—03 and—05 bearings were manufactured at Textron's New Britain, Connecticut, plant. The bearing that failed was a—05 bearing. It was acquired by the Navy sometime in or before 1984, but was not placed in a helicopter until 1990. That helicopter flew for 444 hours. In 1992, the defective bearing was placed into the helicopter involved in this crash.

The—05 bearing is a sealed bearing; grease is injected into it when it is assembled, and the bearing is not designed to be greased again after that. Like other—05 bearings made by Textron at the time, the bearing that failed had no serial number.

The—05 bearing is part of the helicopter's hangar assembly, which is part of the drivetrain that turns the tail rotor. The bearing is composed of two rings, called the inner and outer races. Sealed in between the races are steel balls lubricated with grease. The bearings support the shaft that drives the tail rotor; the shaft rests on the inner race, which turns with it.

After acquiring Textron's bearing manufacturing operation in 1985, Torrington sold—05 bearings directly to the military and to Bell. Bell installed some of the bearings in the helicopters it manufactured, and also resold some to the military. In 1988, Torrington moved its production of—03 and—05 bearings to a plant in Newington, Connecticut. Seeking Bell's approval for the move, Torrington represented that the Newington equipment, personnel, and processes were the same as or superior to those at its New Britain operation.

In 1991, a Bell civilian helicopter crashed. This incident is referred to in the record as "the Rood crash." An investigation of the Rood crash concluded that a—03 bearing in the helicopter's tail rotor had failed. After this accident, Bell, Torrington, and the FAA inspected the Newington plant. The inspection revealed a number of problems with the manufacturing process at the plant affecting both—03 and—05 bearings, including the lack of a shelf-life control policy for bearing grease and metal contamination of bearing components.

After the inspection, Bell pulled all of its—03 and—05 bearings from the shelves, and recalled those—03 and—05 bearings it had sold the military. Bell asked Torrington for the serial numbers of all—03 and—05 bearings to include in a warning bulletin to be issued to owners and operators of Bell helicopters. Torrington gave Bell the numbers for—03 and—05 bearings made at Newington and New Britain, but did not mention the unserialized bearings that Textron had made at New Britain. The Bell bulletin, referred to as an "Alert Service Bulletin," listed the serial numbers of some—03 and—05 bearings, but stated that bearings without serial numbers were not affected. The bulletin directed mechanics to inspect the listed bearings for signs of overheating, grease leakage, or roughness. After Bell issued its bulletin, Torrington's president wrote Bell, taking issue with the bulletin's reference to bearing contamination and advising that Torrington was "most anxious to participate in any evaluation you are currently performing." The letter also stated that Torrington intended to "continue to actively participate with the [National Transportation Safety Board] in their investigation [of the Rood crash and that] [w]e feel it is important to investigate all possible causes of the incident to assure the continued air worthiness of the Bell Helicopter."

The Navy issued its own bulletin in response to Bell's. This bulletin, known as a DCB-80, directed mechanics to "remove and replace" all bearings with the serial numbers listed in Bell's bulletin "not later than the next phase inspection." The DCB-80 also directed mechanics to "maintain vigilant normal required daily inspection" of bearings.

On March 12, 1992, some four months before this crash, a Navy mechanic inspected the helicopter involved in this suit. After the inspection, the mechanic filled out a maintenance service card. On the card, under the heading "discrepancy," the mechanic wrote, "Remove and Replace . . . hangar bearing for compliance with DCB-80." Because the hangar bearing did not have a serial number, it was not listed on the DCB-80. Under the heading "corrective action," the mechanic wrote, "R and R'd . . . hangar bearing for compliance with DCB-80 (not complied with)." The mechanic left the bearing in the helicopter.

The crash occurred on July 31, 1992. Upon initial inspection, the Navy thought the bearing had failed because its grease was too old. Later, after more testing, the Navy concluded that "the most likely cause of the failure was misalignment." The Navy JAG report concluded that the crash was caused by "misalignment and lubrication breakdown." The Navy's metallurgy lab wrote that the bearing failed because of overheating. The Navy lab concluded that "the cause of the overheating cannot be positively identified . . . however, the spalling on the # 1 outer race indicated a misalignment." There is evidence in the record, however, indicating that contaminants in the grease caused the spalling.

After the crash, Stutzman's and Pulaski's survivors filed this wrongful death and survival suit against more than thirty corporate entities. Except for Torrington, Textron, Mobil, and Bell, all of the remaining defendants were either nonsuited or received directed verdicts. The plaintiffs asserted various products liability and negligence claims. Although the plaintiffs sued Bell and several related entities alleging that the helicopter was defective, at trial they focused on Textron's bearing as the cause of the crash. The plaintiffs presented evidence that grease in a Textron tail rotor bearing degraded over time. They contended that the bearing was defectively designed and marketed because it had no serial number to facilitate an appropriate tracking system, and because Textron gave the Navy erroneous information about the grease's shelf-life. They also presented evidence that Textron's manufacturing processes allowed contaminants in the bearings. Torrington, as a third-party petitioner against Bell, presented evidence suggesting that the tail rotor assembly that housed the bearing was misaligned, which damaged the bearing and caused its failure.

The jury found that the bearing was defectively designed, manufactured, and marketed, that Textron and Torrington were negligent, and that Bell was not. They apportioned one percent of the liability to Textron and ninety-nine percent to Torrington. The jury awarded actual damages totaling $35,765,000, which the trial court remitted to $29 million. They also found that Torrington was grossly negligent and awarded $50 million in exemplary damages, which the trial court remitted to $5 million. In a separate bench trial, the trial court found that Ingersoll-Rand, Torrington's parent, was required to indemnify Textron under the terms of its purchase agreement.

Torrington appealed; Textron did not. The court of appeals, with JUSTICE BURGESS dissenting, found no evidence to support the gross negligence finding and reversed the exemplary damages award. *See* 46 S.W.3d at 852. The court affirmed the trial court's judgment in all other respects. *See id.* We affirm the court of appeals' judgment in part, and reverse and remand in part.

II

Torrington's Liability

A. Propriety of Jury Submission

Torrington argues that the judgment against it cannot stand because Texas does not recognize a post-sale duty to warn of product defects not discovered until after manufacture and sale. Torrington further argues that the court of appeals erred in holding that it owed the plaintiffs a duty under *Bell Helicopter Co. v. Bradshaw*, 594 S.W.2d 519 (Tex. Civ. App.—Corpus Christi 1979, writ ref'd n.r.e.).

In *Bradshaw*, the court of appeals held that a manufacturer who regained control of a product but failed to remedy a defect before it was resold could be liable in both strict liability and negligence. *Id.* at 531-32. In this case, the plaintiffs do not base Torrington's liability upon its status as the bearing's manufacturer or upon any control that it may have regained over the bearing. Instead, the plaintiffs contend that Torrington assumed a duty toward them by undertaking to investigate and identify defective bearings. Thus, we are not called upon to recognize any post-sale duty to warn, or to determine whether the control-based duty the *Bradshaw* court recognized applies. And although the plaintiffs cite several other sections of the RESTATEMENT OF TORTS: *Products Liability*, including sections 10, 11, 12, and 13, they expressly disavow an intent to have this Court recognize any new duties, and merely argue that their undertaking theory comports with mainstream case law. Thus, we express no opinion whether those Restatement sections are consistent with established Texas law. Instead, we will analyze Torrington's liability under the plaintiffs' undertaking theory.

In response to a broad-form negligence question, the jury found that Torrington's negligence proximately caused the crash. The court's charge defined the terms "negligence," "ordinary care," and "proximate cause," but provided no further instructions or definitions applicable to the negligence question.[1] Torrington contends that the jury's negligence finding cannot support the judgment against it because the charge omitted elements necessary to impose liability under the plaintiffs' undertaking theory. We agree.

To sustain their negligence claim, the plaintiffs were required to establish that Torrington violated a legal duty owed to them. *See Abalos v. Oil Dev. Co. of Texas*, 544 S.W.2d 627, 631 (Tex. 1976). Texas law generally imposes no duty to take action to prevent harm to others absent certain special relationships or circumstances. *See SmithKline Beecham Corp. v. Doe*, 903 S.W.2d 347, 353 (Tex. 1995); *see also* RESTATEMENT (SECOND) OF TORTS § 314 (1965) ("The fact that [an] actor realizes or should realize that action on his part is necessary for another's aid or protection does not of itself impose upon him a duty to take such action."). As we recently explained:

> There are many instances in which it may be said, as a matter of law, that there is a duty to do something, and in others it may be said, as a matter of law, that there is no such duty. Using familiar illustrations, it may be said generally, on the one hand, that if a party negligently creates a dangerous situation it then becomes his duty to do something about it to prevent injury to others if it reasonably appears or should appear to him that others in the exercise of their lawful rights may be injured thereby. On the other hand, it may be said generally, as a matter of law, that a mere bystander who did not create the dangerous situation is not required to become the good Samaritan and prevent injury to others. *SmithKline Beecham*, 903 S.W.2d at 353 (quoting *Buchanan v. Rose*, 138 Tex. 390, 159 S.W.2d 109, 110 (1942)).

In this case, the plaintiffs contend that Torrington assumed a duty toward them to investigate and identify potentially defective bearings. While Texas law imposes no general duty to "become [a] good Samaritan," we have recognized that a duty to use reasonable care may arise when a person undertakes to provide services to another, either gratuitously or for compensation. *Fort Bend County Drainage Dist. v. Sbrusch*, 818 S.W.2d 392, 396 (Tex. 1991); *Colonial Sav. Ass'n v. Taylor*, 544 S.W.2d 116, 120 (Tex. 1976); RESTATEMENT (SECOND) OF TORTS §§ 323, 324A (1965). In *Colonial Savings*, 544 S.W.2d at 119-20, we relied upon section 323 of the RESTATEMENT, which provides:

> One who undertakes, gratuitously or for consideration, to render services to another which he should recognize as necessary for the protection of the other's person or things, is subject to liability to the other for physical harm resulting from his failure to exercise reasonable care to perform his undertaking, if
>
> (a) his failure to exercise such care increases the risk of such harm, or
>
> (b) the harm is suffered because of the other's reliance upon the undertaking.

RESTATEMENT (SECOND) OF TORTS § 323 (1965).

The plaintiffs contend that Torrington assumed a duty toward them under the RESTATEMENT and *Colonial Savings*. They further contend that the broad-form negligence question they submitted was sufficient to support the judgment against Torrington.

---

[1] The negligence question asked: "Did the negligence, if any, of the parties named below proximately cause the occurrence in question?"

"Negligence" means failure to use ordinary care, that is, failing to do that which a person of ordinary prudence would have done under the same or similar circumstances or doing that which a person of ordinary prudence would not have done under the same or similar circumstances.

"Ordinary care" means that degree of care that would be used by a person of ordinary prudence under the same or similar circumstances.

"Proximate cause" means that cause which, in a natural and continuous sequence, produces an event, and without which cause such event would not have occurred. In order to be a proximate cause, the act or omission complained of must be such that a person using ordinary care would have foreseen that the event, or some similar event, might reasonably result therefrom. There may be more than one proximate cause of an event.

In an analogous context, we have rejected the argument that a broad-form negligence question, without more, can support a judgment against a possessor of land. *See Clayton W. Williams, Jr., Inc. v. Olivo*, 952 S.W.2d 523, 529 (Tex. 1997). In *Olivo*, we held that a broad-form negligence question that omitted instructions about the knowledge and risk-of-harm elements of a premises liability claim was insufficient. *Id.* Premises liability cases are similar to undertaking cases in that the plaintiff seeks to impose a duty on another to take protective action based upon special circumstances or the relationship between the parties. *See* RESTATEMENT (SECOND) OF TORTS *Scope Note*, Topic 7 (1965) (comparing duties of affirmative action described in Topic 7 with duties imposed upon possessors of land). In premises liability cases, like undertaking cases, a possessor of land may be held liable only if certain conditions are met. *See* RESTATEMENT (SECOND) OF TORTS §§ 342, 343 (1965) (describing, respectively, conditions upon which land possessors may be held liable to licensees and invitees).

Here, the broad-form negligence question allowed the jury to hold Torrington liable regardless of whether Torrington knew or should have known that its services were necessary to protect others. *Cf. Spencer v. Eagle Star Ins. Co. of Am.*, 876 S.W.2d 154, 157 (Tex. 1994). The question also allowed an affirmative answer regardless of whether anyone relied upon Torrington's undertaking, or whether Torrington's performance of its undertaking increased the plaintiffs' risk of harm. Because the question allowed the jury to find Torrington liable even if the plaintiffs did not establish the necessary factual predicates for a negligent undertaking duty, it was erroneous. *See id.* These essential elements of an undertaking claim should be included in the instructions accompanying a broad-form negligence question. *Cf. Ketch v. Kroger Co.*, 845 S.W.2d 262, 267 (Tex. 1992). Thus, the jury should have been instructed that Torrington was negligent only if (1) Torrington undertook to perform services that it knew or should have known were necessary for the plaintiffs' protection, (2) Torrington failed to exercise reasonable care in performing those services, and either (3) the Navy relied upon Torrington's performance, or (4) Torrington's performance increased the plaintiffs' risk of harm. *See Colonial Savings*, 544 S.W.2d at 119-20; RESTATEMENT (SECOND) OF TORTS § 323 (1965).[2]

Furthermore, while the record contains some evidence that Torrington engaged in an undertaking, the scope of the undertaking is unclear. In a letter to Bell Helicopter's president, Torrington represented that it was investigating the cause of the Rood crash "to assure the continued air worthiness of the Bell Helicopters." Because the helicopter involved in the Rood crash was a civilian helicopter that used a—03 bearing, Torrington interprets this letter to establish, at most, an undertaking to identify defective—03 bearings manufactured after Torrington acquired Fafnir. On the other hand, the plaintiffs contend that Torrington assumed a broader undertaking to investigate and identify all potentially defective bearings, an interpretation supported to some extent by the fact that Torrington ultimately gave Textron a list of serial numbers for both—03 and—05 bearings, some of which were manufactured at the New Britain plant. In *Sbrusch*, we observed that "[a] person's duty to exercise reasonable care in performing a voluntarily assumed undertaking is limited to that undertaking." *Sbrusch*, 818 S.W.2d at 397. When, as here, the facts about the scope of the assumed duty are in dispute, the jury should be instructed to that effect.

B. Effect of Erroneous Submission

Because the broad-form negligence question omitted elements necessary to establish an undertaking claim, it was erroneous. We must now decide whether that error requires us to render judgment or remand the case to the trial court for a new trial.

Our disposition of charge-error cases in recent years has been less than clear. *See, e.g., State v. San Miguel*, 981 S.W.2d 342, 352-53 (Tex. App.—Houston [14th Dist.] 1998) (EDELMAN, J., dissenting), *rev'd on other grounds*, 2 S.W.3d 249 (Tex. 1999); Edwin J. Terry et al., *Trends in Preservation of Error (at Trial, Charge, and Post Verdict)*, in STATE BAR OF TEX. PROF. DEV. PROGRAM, ADVANCED CIVIL APPELLATE PRACTICE COURSE E, E-41 (1999). In *Olivo*, we rendered judgment when a broad-form negligence question was submitted without appropriate instructions on the premises liability factors we identified in *Corbin v. Safeway Stores, Inc.*,

---

[2] We note that Torrington objected to the negligence question on the basis that it owed the plaintiffs no duty. Until our opinion today, it was not clear whether or how the factual predicates for an undertaking duty should be submitted. Under these circumstances, Torrington's no-duty objection was sufficient to preserve error and to prevent deemed findings against it. *See* State Dep't of Highways & Pub. Transp. v. Payne, 838 S.W.2d 235, 241 (Tex. 1992).

648 S.W.2d 292, 296 (Tex. 1983). *Olivo*, 952 S.W.2d at 530. But in *Spencer*, we remanded for a new trial when the trial court submitted a liability question to the jury without necessary instructions. 876 S.W.2d at 158. There, we explained that rendition is appropriate only when the question submitted is immaterial. *Id.* at 157. We concluded that the question in *Spencer* was not immaterial because it "plainly attempted to request a finding on a statutory cause of action." *Id.* Our rendition in *Olivo* did not discuss whether the omitted instructions made the question immaterial or merely defective. Nevertheless, by our disposition of the case we implicitly concluded that the defectively submitted question was immaterial. In a number of cases since *Spencer*, we have remanded for a new trial after concluding that the charge error did not make the question submitted immaterial. *See, e.g.*, *Borneman v. Steak & Ale of Texas, Inc.*, 22 S.W.3d 411, 413 (Tex. 2000) (holding that remand was proper when plaintiff plainly attempted to request a finding on a statutory cause of action); *Southeastern Pipe Line Co. v. Tichacek*, 997 S.W.2d 166, 172 (Tex. 1999) (remanding when question failed to confine jury to drainage that occurred before units in an oilfield were pooled); *but see Dallas Mkt. Ctr. Dev. Co. v. Liedeker*, 958 S.W.2d 382 (Tex. 1997) (per curiam) (remanding defectively submitted premises-liability case without discussing question's materiality).

In the cases in which we have concluded that a question was merely defective, as opposed to immaterial, the question at issue attempted to submit a theory to the jury that did not require the determination of predicate facts to establish a legal duty, and thus attempted to submit a controlling issue, albeit defectively. *See, e.g.*, *Borneman*, 22 S.W.3d at 413; *Tichacek*, 997 S.W.2d at 171-72. But in *Olivo*, the defendant owed no duty toward the plaintiff unless specific factual predicates were established. Without any determination that the specific factual predicates were met, the question did not submit a controlling issue. In other words, absent any determination that the factual predicates giving rise to a legal duty were satisfied, the defendants' failure to use reasonable care was of no legal consequence. *See Triplex Communications, Inc. v. Riley*, 900 S.W.2d 716, 720 (Tex. 1995).

In this case, Torrington owed no legal duty toward the plaintiffs absent the factual predicates we have discussed. Without a determination of these predicate duty elements, Torrington's failure to use ordinary care is immaterial and rendition would normally be proper. Nevertheless, our rules allow us to remand in the interest of justice when appropriate, even if rendition would ordinarily be warranted. *See* TEX. R. APP. P. 60.3. We did not do so in *Olivo*, because the distinction between premises liability claims and negligent activity cases, and the requirement that the *Corbin* elements be submitted in premises liability cases, were well established by the time the case was decided. *See Olivo*, 952 S.W.2d at 530 (SPECTOR, J., dissenting); *Keetch v. Kroger Co.*, 845 S.W.2d 262 (Tex. 1992). But we have remanded in the interest of justice when our decisions have altered or clarified the way in which a claim should be submitted to the jury. *See, e.g.*, *L.M.B. Corp. v. Gurecky*, 501 S.W.2d 300, 303 (Tex. 1973); *Scott v.. Liebman*, 404 S.W.2d 288, 294 (Tex. 1966).

We have never considered how an undertaking claim should be submitted to the jury, nor had the courts of appeals directly addressed the issue at the time this case was tried. *Cf. Transportation Ins. Co. v. Moriel*, 879 S.W.2d 10, 26 (Tex. 1994) (remanding in the interest of justice when trial had been conducted before any opinion of the Court had specifically addressed the standards governing the imposition of punitive damages in bad faith cases). Until our opinion today, no appellate decision has discussed whether the factual predicates giving rise to an undertaking claim should be submitted to a jury or decided by the court as a question of law. *Colonial Savings* was decided under this state's former special issues practice, and thus did not address whether a broad-form negligence question would support recovery on a negligent undertaking theory. *See* 544 S.W.2d at 118. And since *Colonial Savings* was decided, only one appellate decision has discussed the submission of an undertaking case. In that case, the parents of a boy injured while driving a four-wheeler sued the vehicle's owners alleging, among other things, that they were negligent in allowing the boy to ride without providing him a helmet or adequate safety instruction. *See Park v. Larison*, 28 S.W.3d 106, 113 (Tex. App.—Texarkana 2000, no pet.). The court of appeals held that the trial court did not abuse its discretion in refusing to instruct the jury on the factual predicates necessary to an undertaking claim. *Id.* The court reasoned:

> The instruction requested by the Parks is a correct statement of Texas law, in accordance with the Texas Supreme Court's holding in *Colonial Savings Association v. Taylor* . . . . The instruction requested by the Parks discusses the extent of one's legal duty to render services to protect another's person or property. Duty is an issue of law for the court; not the jury. As such, the requested instruction was not necessary to enable the jury to render a verdict. *Id.* (citations omitted). To the extent that Park suggests that the factual predicates for an undertaking duty are to be decided by the court, we disap-

prove it. In any event, Park demonstrates that the law regarding the submission of these types of claims has remained unclear.

Because neither this Court nor any other appellate court had written about the proper submission of an undertaking claim at the time this case was tried, it is appropriate to remand this case in the interest of justice. Accordingly, we reverse the court of appeals' judgment and remand the plaintiffs' negligent undertaking claim against Torrington to the trial court. *Cf. Wilson v. Texas Parks & Wildlife Dep't.*, 8 S.W.3d 634, 635-36 (Tex. 1999) (denying petition for review when court of appeals remanded in the interest of justice claim that would properly be presented as undertaking claim). We next consider Torrington's liability as Textron's indemnitor.

* * *

Conclusion

In summary, we hold that the broad-form negligence question against Torrington was immaterial, but we remand the plaintiffs' undertaking claim against Torrington to the trial court in the interest of justice. . . .

JUSTICE HECHT, joined by JUSTICE OWEN, dissenting.

I respectfully dissent. A new trial in this case is not justified. The record before us contains no evidence to support a judgment against Torrington on plaintiffs' voluntary-undertaking theory or against Textron for product liability. I would render judgment that the plaintiffs take nothing.

* * *

MUSTANG PIPELINE COMPANY, INC.
v.
DRIVER PIPELINE COMPANY, INC.

134 S.W.3d 195
(Tex. 2004)

PER CURIAM.

In this breach of contract case, both parties, Mustang Pipeline Co. (Mustang), and Driver Pipeline Co. (Driver), obtained favorable jury findings as to the other's breach of a pipeline construction contract. Mustang initially brought suit against Driver for Driver's failure to complete work in a timely manner. Driver counterclaimed for Mustang's wrongful termination of the contract. It is a fundamental principle of contract law that when one party to a contract commits a material breach of that contract, the other party is discharged or excused from further performance. *Hernandez v. Gulf Group Lloyds,* 875 S.W.2d 691, 692 (Tex. 1994). Furthermore, if it is clear the parties intend that time is of the essence to a contract, timely performance is essential to a party's right to require performance by the other party. *D.E.W., Inc. v. Depco Forms, Inc.*, 827 S.W.2d 379, 382 (Tex.App.—San Antonio 1992, no writ). The court of appeals, in affirming the trial court, held that Mustang could not recover damages because Mustang failed to get a jury finding that Driver's breach was material. We hold that an express jury finding on the issue of materiality is not required when "time is of the essence." Because time was of the essence under the contract and Driver failed to timely perform, Mustang was thereafter excused from performance. We reverse in part and render judgment that Driver take nothing.

In January 1997, Mustang entered into a contract under which Driver was to construct the northern 100 miles of a 200 mile pipeline from Mont Belvieu to Longview, Texas. During the bidding process, Mustang stressed that time was of the essence and that the pipeline construction had to be completed no later than April 30, 1997. In response to this time demand, Driver increased its original bid by approximately ten percent, but was still awarded the contract. The parties agreed on a fourteen-week schedule, working eleven hours per day, seven days a week. Driver contends that extensive rains delayed the project soon after work began. On March 3, 1997, Driver proposed shutting down pipeline construction until the weather improved. On March 5, Driver officially requested a thirty-day extension to the agreed completion date, citing adverse weather and safety concerns as the reason for the delay. At a meeting on March 6, Driver reiterated its intent to shut-down operations and wait for drier weather, and it proposed a new 161-day construction schedule.

Fifty-eight days into the ninety-eight day construction schedule, Driver had completed only fifteen miles of pipeline and suspended operations. The parties dispute whether Driver could have accomplished more during this time by using different equipment or reassigning crews to work on drier areas. The contract includes provisions explaining how the crews and pipeline welds could be protected while working in the rain, suggesting that the parties anticipated working despite at least some inclement weather. By March 17, Driver stated that it was still not ready to resume work on the pipeline, so Mustang's project engineer certified Driver to be in default under the contract. Mustang then contracted with Sunland Corporation to finish Driver's portion of the pipeline, which it completed in September 1997. Mustang sued Driver for breach of contract to recover the cost of completion, lost profits, and attorney's fees. Driver countersued for breach of contract, alleging that Mustang wrongfully terminated the contract, and sought damages, lost profits and attorney's fees. In their respective answers, both parties raised the other's material breach as an affirmative defense. The case was tried to a jury. At the close of trial, the following questions were included in the charge:

> 1) Did Driver Pipeline Company fail to comply with the contract it had with Mustang Pipeline Company?
>
> 2) Was Mustang Pipeline Company justified or not justified in terminating Driver Pipeline Company?
>
> 3) What sum of money, if any, if now paid in cash would fairly and reasonably compensate Mustang Pipeline Company for its damages, if any, that resulted from such failure to comply?
>
> 4) What sum of money would fairly and reasonably compensate Driver for its damages, if any, that resulted from Mustang's failure to comply with the Contract?

The jury found that Driver failed to comply with the terms of the contract but also found that Mustang was not justified in terminating the contract. It awarded Mustang $2,104,601 in damages for Driver's breach of contract and awarded Driver $2,515,958 in damages for Mustang's wrongful termination.

Both parties moved for judgment notwithstanding the verdict. Mustang asked the trial court to disregard the jury's finding that Mustang wrongfully terminated the contract and the damages awarded to Driver. Mustang contended that once the jury found that Driver breached the contract, it could not also find that Mustang wrongfully terminated the contract because a breaching party cannot subsequently enforce the contract. The trial court denied Mustang's motion. Driver's motion for judgment notwithstanding the verdict asked the trial court to disregard the jury's finding that Driver breached the contract and the damages awarded to Mustang. Driver argued there was no evidence of probative force to sustain the jury's answers on either the breach of contract or damages questions. The trial court refused to disregard the jury's finding that Driver breached the contract but granted Driver's motion to disregard Mustang's damage award. Thus, the trial court rendered judgment for Driver and awarded Driver actual damages, plus attorney's fees and interest. Both parties appealed. * * * Mustang raised several issues on appeal, arguing that: (1) the trial court erred by refusing to disregard the jury's answer to the wrongful termination question as immaterial; (2) there was legally and factually insufficient evidence to support the jury's wrongful termination finding and the claim was precluded by the contract's termination for convenience provision; * * *

The court of appeals affirmed the trial court's judgment. The court of appeals reasoned that the jury's finding of Driver's breach was relevant to Mustang's liability only if the breach was material. 69 S.W.3d at 789. The court of appeals concluded that whether a party's breach is material is a fact question, and, absent an express jury finding, the trial court was not required to treat the breach as material as a matter of law. *Id.* at 790. The court of appeals also concluded there was factually and legally sufficient evidence to support the jury's wrongful termination finding, and the contract's "termination for convenience" clause did not preclude Driver's claim because Mustang did not raise this issue in the trial court. *Id.* * * * Accordingly, the court of appeals affirmed the trial court's judgment. *Id.* at 791.

Mustang petitioned this court for review, asking us to reverse the court of appeals' judgment and render judgment for Mustang, or in the alternative, grant a new trial. First we must consider whether the trial court erred in denying Mustang's motion for judgment notwithstanding the verdict. Mustang argues that the jury's answer regarding Driver's breach rendered the jury's answer regarding Mustang's wrongful termination immaterial, because once a party has breached it cannot later sue on the contract. *See Dobbins v. Redden,* 785 S.W.2d 377, 378 (Tex.1990). Accordingly, Mustang contends that the trial court should have disregarded the jury's answer to the second question and granted its motion for judgment notwithstanding the verdict. The court of appeals rejected Mustang's argument. It reasoned that because the jury question did not ask whether the breach was material, the trial court was not required to hold the breach material as a matter of law. 69 S.W.3d at 790. Thus, according to the court of appeals, the trial court did not err in overruling Mustang's motion for judgment notwithstanding the verdict. The court of appeals was correct in holding that a party is released from further obligation under the contract only if the other party materially breached. However, we disagree with the court's requirement that Mustang obtain an express jury finding that Driver's breach was material. Texas Rule of Civil Procedure 277 mandates that a trial court "shall, whenever feasible, submit the cause upon broad-form questions." TEX.R. CIV. P. 277. The jury question regarding Driver's breach tracks the Texas Pattern Jury Charge language for the recommended breach of contract question, asking "Did Driver Pipeline Company fail to comply with the contract it had with Mustang Pipeline Company?" COMM. ON PATTERN JURY CHARGES, STATE BAR OF TEX., TEXAS PATTERN JURY CHARGES-BUSINESS, CONSUMER, EMPLOYMENT PJC 101.2 (2000) ("Did [defendant] fail to comply with the agreement?"). The jury answered yes.

The evidence presented at trial established that Driver's failure to comply was a material breach. The Restatement lists five circumstances significant in determining whether a failure to perform is material:

> (a) the extent to which the injured party will be deprived of the benefit which he reasonably expected;
>
> (b) the extent to which the injured party can be adequately compensated for the part of that benefit of which he will be deprived;
>
> (c) the extent to which the party failing to perform or to offer to perform will suffer forfeiture;
>
> (d) the likelihood that the party failing to perform or to offer to perform will cure his failure, taking account of the circumstances including any reasonable assurances;
>
> (e) the extent to which the behavior of the party failing to perform or to offer to perform comports with standards of good faith and fair dealing.

See RESTATEMENT (SECOND) OF CONTRACTS § 241 (1981). The Restatement also articulates circumstances that are significant in determining when a party's duties are discharged under a contract due to the other party's material breach. The relevant factors, in addition to those listed above, are:

> (1) the extent to which it reasonably appears to the injured party that delay may prevent or hinder him in making reasonable substitute arrangements.
>
> (2) the extent to which the agreement provides for performance without delay, but a material failure to perform or to offer to perform on a stated day does not of itself discharge the other party's remaining duties unless the circumstances, including the language of the agreement, indicate that performance or an offer to perform by that day is important.

See RESTATEMENT (SECOND) OF CONTRACTS § 242 (1981). The evidence presented established both that Driver's breach was material and that Mustang was discharged from its duties under the contract based on that breach. Evidence exists to prove, as a matter of law, that time was a material element of the contract. Driver placed an initial bid with Mustang in October 1996, but it increased its bid significantly in January 1997 after learning of the April 30 deadline. The contract specifically stated that "all time limits stated in the Contract are of the essence to the Contract," and the contract called for "100 percent completion of the pipeline system no later than April 30, 1997." In addition to the contract's emphasis on timely completion, it also required that "sufficient forces and equipment . . . be furnished at all times to adequately perform work with ample margin for emergencies and unexpected events, to carry on the work at a sufficient rate of progress to ensure completion within the time specified in the Contract." In late February 1997, when Mustang realized Driver was behind on the construction schedule, it asked for assurances from Driver that the work would be completed by the deadline. Although Driver had workers, equipment and supervision on the job site, it accomplished only minimal pipeline construction. Mustang also requested a plan from Driver on how it would finish the project by the end of April. It recognized the unseasonably wet conditions, but offered suggestions to Driver about how it might expedite construction. The evidence indicates that Driver never provided a revised plan on how it would attempt to meet the construction schedule. When Mustang terminated the contract, it had approximately forty days before the April 30, 1997 deadline to complete construction on eighty-five miles of pipeline. Even the most ambitious of construction schedules would have great difficulty successfully meeting that deadline. At the point at which Mustang terminated the contract, there was virtually no chance that Driver would be able to cure its breach and complete the construction on time.

Based on this evidence, we hold that as a matter of law Driver committed a material breach. Mustang was thereafter discharged from its duties under the contract. Therefore, the trial court should have disregarded the jury's answer to the wrongful termination question and granted Mustang judgment notwithstanding the verdict.

These problems could have been avoided had the trial court submitted the breach of contract question disjunctively ("Did Driver Pipeline Company or Mustang Pipeline Company fail to comply with the parties' contract?") accompanied by an appropriate instruction directing the jury to decide who committed the first material breach. *See* TEX.R. CIV. P. 277 ("The court may submit a question disjunctively when it is apparent from the evidence that one or the other of the conditions or facts inquired about necessarily exists."); COMM. ON PATTERN JURY CHARGES, STATE BAR OF TEX., TEXAS PATTERN JURY CHARGES—BUSINESS, CONSUMER, EMPLOYMENT PJC 101.22 (2002). In the standard contract dispute, one party cancels the contract or refuses to pay due to alleged breaches by the other; in such circumstances, jurors will often find *both* parties failed to comply with the contract (as the jury did here) unless instructed that they must decide who committed the first material breach. *See Mead v. Johnson Group, Inc.*, 615 S.W.2d 685, 689 (Tex.1981) (default by one contracting party excuses performance by the other); *see also Lake LBJ Mun. Util. Dist. v. Coulson,* 692 S.W.2d 897, 908 (Tex.App.—Austin 1985), *rev'd on other grounds,* 734 S.W.2d 649 (Tex.1987) (suggesting disjunctive submission in such cases).

* * *

Accordingly, we grant Mustang's petition for review and, without hearing oral argument, affirm the court of appeals' judgment in part, reverse in part, and render judgment that Driver take nothing.

b. *Instructions or Definitions*

i. *General*

H.E. BUTT GROCERY COMPANY
v.
BILOTTO

985 S.W.2d 22
(Tex. 1998)

Wade B. Shelton, Wallace B. Jefferson, Sunny J. Jansma, San Antonio, for Petitioner.
Les Mendelsohn, Ricky J. Poole, San Antonio, for Respondent.

SPECTOR, JUSTICE, delivered the opinion of the Court, in which PHILLIPS, CHIEF JUSTICE, GONZALEZ AND ABBOTT, JUSTICES, and LINDA THOMAS, JUSTICE (Assigned).[3]

The issue in this cause is whether a jury charge instruction predicating a damages question on a finding of fifty percent or less comparative negligence violates Rule 277 of the Texas Rules of Civil Procedure. The trial court submitted the jury instruction over HEB's objection and the jury found HEB and Bilotto each were fifty percent negligent. The court of appeals affirmed. 928 S.W.2d 197. We now affirm the judgment of the court of appeals. Vinnie Bilotto suffered back injuries when he slipped and fell in an H.E. Butt Grocery Company (HEB) store. He sued HEB for negligence and gross negligence. The case was tried to a jury. Before the trial court charged the jury, HEB objected to a proposed instruction given after jury question number two. Question one read as follows:

[3] JUSTICE LINDA THOMAS, Chief Justice of the Court of Appeals for the Fifth District of Texas at Dallas, sitting by special appointment under TEX. GOV'T CODE § 22.005.

Did the negligence, if any, of the persons named below proximately cause the occurrence in question?

Answer "YES" or "NO" for each of the following:

(a) H.E. BUTT GROCERY COMPANY ----
(b) VINNIE BILOTTO ----

The jury answered "YES" for both HEB and Bilotto. Question two then asked the jury:

What percentage of the negligence that caused the occurrence in question do you find to be attributable to each of those found by you, in your answer to Question No. 1, to have been negligent?

(a) H.E. BUTT GROCERY COMPANY ----
(b) VINNIE BILOTTO ----

The jury found both HEB and Bilotto fifty percent negligent. The instruction that followed question two, which is nearly identical to Texas Pattern Jury Charge 80.1, read:

> If, in answer to Question No. 1, you have answered "NO" for VINNIE BILOTTO, or if, in answer to Question No. 2 you have found that 50 percent or less of the negligence that caused the occurrence is attributable to VINNIE BILOTTO, then answer Question No. 3. Otherwise, do not answer Question No. 3. Question three then asked the jury to assess the damages, if any, that would reasonably compensate Bilotto.

HEB objected that the instruction after question two impermissibly informed the jury of the legal effect of its answer. The trial court overruled the objection and then instructed the jury. The jury found that HEB and Bilotto were each fifty percent negligent and awarded Bilotto damages. The issue we must resolve is whether the trial court erred in submitting the jury instruction.

The trial court is given wide latitude to determine the propriety of explanatory instructions and definitions. *See Mobil Chem. Co. v. Bell*, 517 S.W.2d 245, 256 (Tex.1974). We hold that the trial court did not err in giving this instruction.

We adopted Rule 277 in 1941. TEX. R. CIV. P. 277 (3 TEX. B..J. 566 (1940)). At the time, Texas courts were required by statute to submit the jury charge using special issues. *See* William V. Dorsaneo, III, *Broad-Form Submission of Jury Questions and the Standard of Review*, 46 S.M.U. L. REV. 601, 606-07 (1992). Over the years, however, it became apparent that this special- issue approach had overloaded the charge with "granulated issues" and had led to more and more reversals on appeal. *Id.* at 607-08. As a result of these problems, in 1973 we amended Rule 277 to permit the broad-form submission of jury questions. TEX. R. CIV. P. 277 (493-494 S.W.2d (Tex. Cases) xxxi, xxxii- xxxiii).

In 1987, we again amended Rule 277 and made the broad-form submission of the jury charge mandatory. More importantly for this case, we also added language indicating that "[t]he court may predicate the damage question or questions upon affirmative findings of liability." TEX. R. CIV. P. 277. This language determines the outcome of this dispute.

In response to question one, the jury determined that both HEB and Bilotto proximately caused Bilotto's injuries. In question two, the jury found that each party was fifty percent negligent. Because the jury found Bilotto only fifty percent negligent, in light of our comparative negligence law, the effect of the jury's answer to question two was to establish HEB's liability. The instruction that followed question two predicated the damages question on the affirmative finding of HEB's liability found in question two. The 1987 amendment to Rule 277 expressly authorizes such a conditional submission. Therefore, because this instruction is expressly authorized by Rule 277, the court did not err in giving the instruction. *See Borden, Inc. v. Price*, 939 S.W.2d 247, 254 (Tex. App.—Amarillo 1997, writ denied).

HEB nevertheless contends that the instruction was improper because it informed the jury of the legal effect of its answers. However, Rule 277 states that "[t]he court's charge shall not be objectionable on the ground that it incidentally constitutes a comment on the weight of the evidence or advises the jury of the effect of their answers when it is properly a part of an instruction or definition." *Id.* (emphasis added). Thus, following the Rule, the court's charge was not objectionable on the grounds HEB asserts if it only incidentally informed the jury of the legal effect of its answers.

Initially, we note that the clear trend among states that have considered the issue is to permit the jury to know the ultimate effect of its answers. *See Wheeler v. Bagley*, 254 Neb. 232, 575 N.W.2d 616, 619 (1998) (discussing and collecting cases on the "strong, if not overwhelming, recent trend" toward informing the jury). Nevertheless, when an instruction merely directs the jury to answer a damages question only if some condition or conditions have been met, it does not directly instruct the jury about the legal effect of its answers. *See Borden*, 939 S.W.2d at 254.

To be a direct comment on the weight of the evidence, the issue submitted must suggest to the jury the trial court's opinion on the matter. *See Southmark Management Corp. v. Vick*, 692 S.W.2d 157, 160 (Tex. App.—Houston [1st Dist.] 1985, writ ref'd n.r.e.). Similarly, to directly advise the jury of the legal effect of its answers, the issue submitted must instruct the jury how to answer each question in order for the plaintiff or defendant to prevail. *See* Pope & Lowerre, *The State of the Special Verdict—1979*, 11 ST. MARY'S L.J. 1, 43 (1979). PJC 80.1 does not directly inform the jury of the legal effect of its answers, but merely directs the jury to answer the damages question only if certain conditions are satisfied. Therefore, PJC 80.1 merely incidentally informs the jury of the legal effect of its answers.

HEB argues that our decision in *Grasso v. Cannon Ball Motor Freight Lines*, 125 Tex. 154, 81 S.W.2d 482 (Tex. Com. App. 1935), controls the outcome of this case. In *Grasso*, the trial court instructed the jury:

> If, in response to the foregoing question, you have answered that the defendant's truck was operated in a negligent manner, and that such negligence, if any, caused the injury to the plaintiff, and if you have also answered that the plaintiff was not guilty of negligence, contributing to the accident, then you will answer the following question; otherwise, you need not answer the following question.

Id. at 487. We held that this instruction impermissibly told the jury "that they must find the defendant guilty of negligence, and the plaintiff not guilty of contributory negligence, in order for the plaintiff to recover." *Id.* We held that "[s]uch a charge is undoubtedly in violation of our special issue statutes." *Id.*

PJC 80.1, albeit logically indistinguishable from the instruction we found impermissible in *Grasso*, does not violate Rule 277. The reason PJC 80.1 is permissible where the *Grasso* instruction was not is that *Grasso* predated the amendments to Rule 277. *See Borden*, 939 S.W.2d at 254.

The effect of our amendments to Rule 277 is that the rule now allows instructions such as the one at issue in *Grasso* and in this case. First, the Rule specifically authorizes courts to condition a damage question on an affirmative finding of liability. Next, this instruction only incidentally informs the jury of the legal effect of its answers. Therefore, it is in line with current Rule 277.

We do not overrule today the decades of Texas case law that holds that Texas juries cannot be directly informed of the legal effect of their answers. We do hold, however, that because conditional damages jury instructions such as PJC 80.1 are expressly permitted by Rule 277, the trial court did not err in giving the instruction. As a result, this charge is permissible under Rule 277 of the Texas Rules of Civil Procedure. Accordingly, we affirm the judgment of the court of appeals.

HANKINSON, JUSTICE, did not participate in the decision.

GONZALEZ, JUSTICE, concurring.

I agree with the Court that the charge in this case is permissible because it only incidentally informed the jury of the effect of its answers. However, I think it is time to reconsider whether it makes sense to try to keep juries in the dark about the effect of their answers in these cases. When we moved from special issue practice to broad-form submissions, we dramatically reduced the number of cases in which the jury might not know for sure the effect of its answers. In the few remaining cases in which the jury might not know the legal effect of its answers, I question whether it serves the cause of justice to continue blindfolding the jury. I would join the growing number of states that allow the jury to know the legal effect of its answers.

* * *

HECHT, JUSTICE, joined by OWEN, JUSTICE, dissenting [opinion omitted].

BAKER, JUSTICE, joined by ENOCH and OWEN, JUSTICES, dissenting.

A trial court must submit charge instructions in compliance with Rule 277. *See* TEX. R. CIV. P. 278; *see also Gulf Coast State Bank v. Emenhiser*, 562 S.W.2d 449, 452-53 (Tex. 1978). "The trial court may predicate the damage question or questions upon affirmative findings of liability." TEX. R. CIV. P. 277. Today the Court asserts that this language from Rule 277 determines the outcome of this case. Having said that, the Court rushes headlong to its preordained conclusion that Rule 277 expressly authorizes the instruction the trial court gave in this case. Accordingly, the Court holds the trial court did not err in giving the instruction. 985 S.W.2d 22.

I believe the Court focuses on the wrong part of Rule 277. The rule also states: The Court shall not in its charge comment directly on the weight of the evidence or advise the jury of the effect of their answers, but the Court's charge shall not be objectionable on the ground that it incidently constitutes a comment on the weight of the evidence or advises the jury of the effect of their answers when it is properly a part of an instruction or definition. TEX.R. CIV. P. 277. By ignoring the prohibition against advising the jury of the effect of its answers, the Court erroneously concludes that the charge in this case does not violate Rule 277. Accordingly, I dissent.

I. JURY INSTRUCTIONS

The jury's concern is to find disputed facts, rather than to achieve a particular result. *See Emenhiser*, 562 S.W.2d at 453. The trial court's charge need not and should not burden the jury with surplus instructions. *See Acord v. General Motors Corp.*, 669 S.W.2d 111, 116 (Tex. 1984). This is so even though an instruction may be a correct statement of law. *See Acord*, 669 S.W.2d at 116. This Court has treated surplus instructions to the charge as impermissible comments that tilt or nudge the jury one way or the other. *See Lemos v. Montez*, 680 S.W.2d 798, 801 (Tex. 1984); *Acord*, 669 S.W.2d at 116; *Emenhiser*, 562 S.W.2d at 453.

We first approved instructions conditioning damages findings on an affirmative liability finding in *Grieger v. Vega*, 153 Tex. 498, 271 S.W.2d 85 (1954). In *Grieger*, the charge instructed the jury to answer the damages question only if it found the defendant's conduct wrongful. *See Grieger*, 271 S.W.2d at 86. The Court held that this instruction did not violate the longstanding rule against informing the jury of the legal effect of their answers. The Court observed that any juror of ordinary intelligence would know that a defendant does not owe a plaintiff damages unless the defendant is liable for the plaintiff's injuries. *See Grieger*, 271 S.W.2d at 87. In 1988 the Court amended Rule 277 to expressly permit instructions conditioning damages on a liability finding. *See* TEX.R. CIV. P. 277.

However, Rule 277 does not permit conditioning damages on a finding of a certain percentage of comparative negligence. A jury's answer to the comparative negligence question is not a "finding of liability" under Rule 277. Instead, a finding of comparative negligence greater than 50% is a finding of an affirmative defense to liability. *See* TEX. R. CIV. P. 94; *Lawson v. Estate of McDonald*, 524 S.W.2d 351, 355 (Tex. Civ. App.—Waco 1975, writ ref'd n.r.e.). We held in *Grasso* that conditioning damages on a negative finding of contributory negligence impermissibly tells the jury the legal effect of their answers. *See Grasso v. Cannon Ball Motor Freight Lines*, 125 Tex. 154, 81 S.W.2d 482, 487 (Tex. Com. App. 1935). Although *Grasso* involved contributory negligence as an absolute bar to a plaintiff's recovery instead of the current 51% bar, *Grasso's* reasoning applies here. The law of contributory negligence is not within the realm of an ordinary juror's knowledge. *See Grieger*, 271 S.W.2d at 87 (approving conditioning damages on a finding of liability and distinguishing *Grasso*); *Finck Cigar Co. v. Campbell*, 134 Tex. 250, 133 S.W.2d 759, 760 (Tex. Com. App. 1939)(approving conditioning damages on a finding of liability and distinguishing *Grasso*). This is true whether the bar to recovery is at 1% or 51% and whether it is called "contributory negligence," "comparative negligence," "comparative responsibility," or "proportionate responsibility." Instructing the jury on the legal effect of a plaintiff's percentage of responsibility is more than "incidental"—it impermissibly allows the jury to determine the plaintiff's ultimate recovery in the trial court's judgment.

II. ANALYSIS

Here, the instruction informed the jury that for Bilotto to recover damages, they had to find him 50% or less responsible for his injuries. T his instruction essentially told the jury what it needed to do to ensure Bilotto's recovery.

The Court concedes that PJC 80.1 is logically indistinguishable from the instruction the Court found impermissible in *Grasso*. However, the Court asserts the instruction does not violate Rule 277. The Court attempts to discount *Grasso* because it was decided before the 1988 amendments. However, the additions to Rule 277 do not affect *Grasso's* primary reasoning. The 1988 amendments did not remove the language prohibiting jury instructions from informing jurors about the legal effect of their answers. The Court does not argue that the average juror knows the 50% rule, and rightfully so because that argument cannot seriously be made. In my view, it is clear that the instruction in this case told the jury something they did not know about the findings they were making. *Grasso* clearly prohibits such an instruction. Therefore, *Grasso* is still good law and supports the proposition that the jury instruction in this case did more than incidentally inform the jury about the legal effect of their answers.

There are also policy reasons why the trial court should not condition damage findings on a finding that a plaintiff is no more than 50% negligent. That bar to recovery is only one part of a comprehensive legislative comparative negligence scheme. Without question, such an instruction provides the jury with information they can use to thwart legislative policy. Clearly, if the trial court instructs the jury on how the comparative fault system operates, then the jury can adjust its answers accordingly. This instruction to the jury is a surplus instruction that is an impermissible comment that tilts or nudges the jury one way. *See Lemos*, 680 S.W.2d at 801; *Acord*, 669 S.W.2d at 116.

For these reasons, I would hold that the trial court abused its discretion by overruling H.E.B.'s objection to the 51% bar instruction. *See Walker v. Packer*, 827 S.W.2d 833, 840 (Tex. 1992) (stating that the trial court's clear failure to analyze or apply the law correctly is an abuse of discretion). The trial court's reliance on PJC 80.01 in submitting the 51% bar instruction does not make the instruction proper. Texas Pattern Jury Charges are not law. *See Keetch v. Kroger Co.*, 845 S.W.2d 276, 281 (Tex. App.—Dallas 1990), aff'd, 845 S.W.2d 262 (Tex. 1992).

I would also hold that the trial court's abuse of discretion was harmful, and therefore, reversible. *See* TEX. R. APP. P. 61.1(a). The record shows that the parties hotly contested their comparative responsibility. During deliberations, the jury asked the trial court to "please clarify the if/or situation at the end of Question 2." The trial court then asked the jury to be more specific in its inquiry. The jury did not reply to the trial court's response. The jury's request for an explanation of the 51% bar instruction and their subsequent 10-2 verdict finding Bilotto and H.E.B. each 50% negligent suggest that the instruction heavily influenced the jury's deliberations. *See Reinhart v. Young*, 906 S.W.2d 471, 473 (Tex. 1995) (recognizing that a superfluous instruction would be more likely to influence the jury improperly in a close case).

III. CONCLUSION

The 51% bar instruction allowed the jury to decide whether Bilotto or H.E.B. should "win" the case and by how much. The instruction was reasonably calculated to cause and probably did cause the rendition of an improper judgment. *See* TEX. R. APP. P. 61.1(a); *Reinhart*, 906 S.W.2d at 473. I respectfully dissent.

Notes

1. Explanatory instructions combine the special issue and the general charge methods of submission so as to preserve the advantages of both. The purpose of the explanatory instruction is to simplify issues, avoid confusion and eliminate double negatives. From 1941-1973, they could only be used when ". . . necessary to enable the jury to render a verdict. In 1973, "necessary" was changed to "proper," thereby enlarging their role. One danger is that instructions tend to comment on the weight of the evidence or to advise the jury of the effect of their answers, neither of which is permissible. Rule 277 expressly prohibits *direct* comments, but allows *incidental* comments.

2. *Quantum Chemical Corporation v. Toennies*, 47 S.W.3d 473 (Tex. 2001): An incorrect jury instruction is only grounds for reversal if it probably caused the rendition of an improper judgment. To determine whether the instruction probably caused an improper judgment, the Court examines the entire record. An improper instruction is especially likely to cause an unfair trial when the trial is contested and the evidence sharply conflicting, as it was in the present case. In this case, the trial court's instruction to the jury, to consider Quantum's discharge of Toennies "because of his age," was ambiguous and could be reasonably be interpreted to require

that the improper motivation be either the sole factor or one of several factors that led to Toennies's firing. That this ambiguity confused the jurors is readily apparent from their initial deadlock and note to the trial judge, inquiring whether Toennies had to show that age was a determining factor or the sole determining factor.

LONE STAR GAS CO.
v.
LEMOND
897 S.W.2d 755
(Tex. 1995)

PER CURIAM.

The court of appeals held in this case that it was reversible error for the trial court to add the following sentence to the standard jury charge for marketing defects: "A seller's duty to warn arises only where the dangers to be warned of are reasonably foreseeable and are such that a consumer cannot reasonably be expected to be aware of them." ____ S.W.2d ____. We disagree because, under the record before us, any error was harmless.

Phares Lemond was injured and his wife killed in an explosion that resulted when natural gas which had accumulated in the crawl space under their home was ignited by the water heater's pilot light. Lemond sued the gas distributor, Lone Star Gas Co., claiming that it was negligent and that the gas was unreasonably dangerous as designed, manufactured, and marketed. Lemond alleged that Lone Star failed to maintain its distribution lines properly, allowing gas to leak out and up through the soil below Lemond's house, and that the odorant which should have allowed the gas to be detected was defective for a number of reasons. The trial court charged the jury on all of Lemond's theories except manufacturing defect. After a three-week trial, the jury failed to find that any negligence of Lone Star or any defect in the design and marketing of the gas caused Lemond's injuries. The trial court rendered judgment on the verdict for Lone Star.

The jury charge on marketing defect tracked the standard question and instruction prescribed by the Texas Pattern Jury Charge, 3 STATE BAR OF TEXAS, TEXAS PATTERN JURY CHARGES, PJC 71.06 (1990), except for the addition of the one sentence quoted above. Lemond does not contend, and the court of appeals did not conclude, that the additional sentence misstates the law. Rather, Lemond argues, and the court of appeals agreed, that it was error to include the sentence in the charge because it is the kind of surplus instruction discouraged by *Acord v. General Motors Corp.*, 669 S.W.2d 111 (Tex. 1984), and *Lemos v. Montez*, 680 S.W.2d 798 (Tex. 1984). The appeals court concluded that the error was not harmless because the sentence (1) conflicted with and diverted the jury's attention from other language in the charge, thereby confusing them, and (2) probably tilted or nudged the jury "one way or the other", thereby prejudicing the verdict.

Assuming, without deciding, that it was error to include the sentence in the charge, we do not agree that the error requires reversal. Besides the sentence quoted above, the trial court instructed the jury as follows: A "marketing defect" with respect to the product means the failure to give adequate warnings of the product's dangers that were known, or by the application of reasonably developed human skill or foresight should have been known, or failure to give adequate instructions to avoid such dangers, which failure rendered the product unreasonably dangerous as marketed.

* * *

An "unreasonably dangerous" product is one that is dangerous to an extent beyond that which would be contemplated by the ordinary user of the product with the ordinary knowledge common to the community as to the product's characteristics. The court of appeals did not identify the conflict between this language and the sentence complained of, and a comparison readily demonstrates there is none. It is not clear why the appeals court thought that the sentence diverted the jury's attention from the rest of the charge, but assuming it did, we do not see how the sentence could have misled or confused the jury. Also, because the sentence was entirely consistent with the charge as a whole, we do not see how it could have nudged the jury improperly. Unlike *Acord*, this case was not closely contended. After a three-week trial, the jury did not make a liability finding in Lemond's favor. The record does not reflect that Lemond's marketing defect claim was any stronger than his other claims, and we cannot see how the jury would have made a different finding. The court of appeals erred in reversing the trial court's judgment. TEX. R. APP. P. 81(b).

Lemond complains that he was entitled to an instruction on manufacturing defect, and that distributors of natural gas should be held to a higher standard of care because of the dangers that inhere in the product. The court of appeals addressed these complaints fully and, we believe, rejected them correctly.

Accordingly, a majority of the Court, without hearing oral argument, reverses the judgment of the court of appeals to the extent that it reverses the judgment of the trial court, affirms it in all other respects, and renders judgment that Lemond take nothing. TEX. R. APP. P. 170.

ENOCH, J., took no part in the consideration or decision of this case.

Note

Ford Motor Co. v. Ledesma, 242 S.W.3d 32 (Tex. 2007): In this products liability case, involving a Ford truck, in defining defect, the trial court followed Texas Pattern Jury Charge (PJC) 71.3. As specified in the comment to PJC 71.3, the trial court included in the question the definition of producing cause found in PJC 70.1. Defendant-Ford objected that both PJC 71.3 and PJC 70.1 were "not accurate under the law", and failed to track the Supreme Court's precedent. The jury sided with Ledesma, finding that a manufacturing defect caused the accident, and that Plaintiff-Ledesma was not contributorily negligent, and awarding economic damages of $215,380. The court of appeals affirmed. ***Held:*** Reversed and remanded. The jury here received a legally incorrect charge. The trial court submitted the pattern jury charge's definition on manufacturing defect. However, the model charge is erroneous, as it does not include the requirement that a manufacturing defect must deviate from its specifications, or planned output, in a manner that renders the product unreasonably dangerous. The requirement of a deviation from the manufacturer's specifications or planned output serves the essential purpose of distinguishing a manufacturing defect from a design defect. The distinction is material. The danger of allowing a jury to conclude that the defect was, or might have been, a design defect is that a design defect claim requires proof and a jury finding of a safer alternative design. The charge did not make such an inquiry.

The trial court, following PJC 70.1, instructed the jury: " 'Producing cause' means an efficient, exciting, or contributing cause that, in a natural sequence, produces the incident in question. There may be more than one producing cause." The second part of the court's definition, recognizing that there may be more than one producing cause of an event, is correct. However, while the Court has seemed to sanction the first part, it has also described a producing cause as one "that is a substantial factor that brings about injury and without which the injury would not have occurred." To say that a producing cause is "an efficient, exciting, or contributing cause that, in a natural sequence, produces the incident in question" is incomplete and, more importantly, provides little concrete guidance to the jury. Juries must ponder the meaning of "efficient" and "exciting" in this context. These adjectives are foreign to modern English language as a means to describe a cause, and offer little practical help to a jury striving to make the often difficult causation determination in a products case. *Defining producing cause as being a substantial factor in bringing about an injury, and without which the injury would not have occurred,* is easily understood and conveys the essential components of producing cause that (1) the cause must be a substantial cause of the event in issue and (2) it must be a but-for cause, namely one without which the event would not have occurred. This is the definition that should be given in the jury charge.

SPENCER
v.
EAGLE STAR INS. CO. OF AMERICA

876 S.W.2d 154
(Tex. 1994)

Mark Kincaid, Austin, for Nat. Furniture Store.

Joe Longley and Tim Labadie, Austin, for Charles Spencer.

Randy Nelson, Roger D. Higgins, Belinda Vrielink, and Patrick Stolley, Dallas, for Eagle Star Ins. Co.

HECHT, JUSTICE.

We withdraw our opinion of June 30, 1993, substitute the following in its stead, and overrule respondent's motion for rehearing.

The issue we address in this case is whether error in the instruction accompanying a jury question on liability for an "unfair practice in the business of insurance" made the question immaterial or merely defective. If the question is immaterial, the trial court properly disregarded the jury's affirmative answer and rendered judgment notwithstanding the verdict for the defendant. But if the question and instruction are merely defective, defendant is entitled only to a new trial. The court of appeals held that the jury question was immaterial and affirmed the trial court's judgment. 780 S.W.2d 837. We disagree and therefore reverse the judgment of the court of appeals and remand the case for a new trial.

As proprietors of the Natural Furniture Store, the Spencers were insured by Eagle Star Insurance Company against loss of the store's contents and interruption of its business. After the store was destroyed by fire, an investigator hired by Eagle Star reported that the fire had been intentionally set inside the store, and that the fire department's chief suspect was Charles Spencer. Spencer was never charged with any offense in connection with the fire.

While the investigation was pending, Eagle Star made no payments to the Spencers, and as a result, the Spencers claim, they were unable to reopen their business, service their bank loan, or resume their rent payments for the store after the fire-damaged areas were repaired. The Spencers hired an attorney and complained to the State Board of Insurance that Eagle Star had not responded to their agent's requests for information on the status of their claim and had not paid them anything under their policy. The Board forwarded their complaint to Eagle Star. Two days later, and more than five months after the fire, Eagle Star agreed to pay the full policy limits for coverage of the store's contents. The Spencers also demanded the policy limits for business interruption coverage. After Eagle Star decided that the Spencers were entitled to only a lesser amount, which it offered to pay, the Spencers sued Eagle Star for breach of contract, breach of the common law duty of good faith and fair dealing, and violations of the Texas Deceptive Trade Practices—Consumer Protection Act, TEX. BUS. & COM. CODE §§ 17.41-.63, Texas Insurance Code art. 21.21, and Board of Insurance Orders 41060 and 41454. After the Spencers filed suit, Eagle Star paid them the amount it had determined was due.

The trial court submitted two questions to the jury regarding Eagle Star's liability. Question 1A asked whether Eagle Star's handling of the Spencers' claim for loss of earnings was an "unfair practice in the business of insurance" defined by an accompanying instruction as "any act or series of acts which is arbitrary, without justification, or takes advantage of a person to the extent that an unjust or inequitable result is obtained." Question 1B asked whether Eagle Star had engaged in unconscionable conduct as defined in section 17.45(5)(A) of the DTPA. Eagle Star objected to the questions and instructions on the grounds that neither question "is based upon a cause of action recognized under Texas law," and "more specifically . . . that [Question 1A] permits the jury to determine what duty, if any, is owed to the Spencers, which is a question of law for the Court, and not one of fact for the jury." The jury answered Question 1A "yes" and Question 1B "no". The trial court granted Eagle Star judgment notwithstanding the verdict on the ground that Question 1A was insufficient to support recovery by the Spencers. The court of appeals affirmed.

A trial court may disregard a jury finding only if it is unsupported by evidence, a condition not met in this case, or if the issue is immaterial. *C. & R. Transport, Inc. v. Campbell*, 406 S.W.2d 191, 194 (Tex. 1966). A question is immaterial when it should not have been submitted, or when it was properly submitted but has been rendered immaterial by other findings. *Id.* A question which calls for a finding beyond the province of the jury, such as a question of law, may be deemed immaterial. 4 ROY W. MCDONALD, TEXAS CIVIL PRACTICE IN DISTRICT & COUNTY COURTS § 17.31 (1984 & Supp. 1988).

Both lower courts correctly held that Question 1A was defective. When liability is asserted based upon a provision of a statute or regulation, a jury charge should track the language of the provision as closely as possible. *Brown v. American Transfer & Storage Co.*, 601 S.W.2d 931, 937 (Tex. 1980), *cert. denied*, 449 U.S. 1015, 101 S.Ct. 575, 66 L.Ed.2d 474 (1980). The charge here fails this test. Although the language of Question 1A—"unfair practice in the business of insurance"—appears to have been taken from TEX. INS. CODE art. 21.21, § 16(a), that statute by its express terms does not refer to every such practice imaginable but only to those specified by certain other statutes and regulations. *Supra* note 2. Without an instruction specifying the actions for which Eagle Star could be liable, Question 1A was improper. The instruction which accompanied Question 1A did not meet this requirement. It allowed the jury to find an unfair insurance practice based upon any action by Eagle Star that took advantage of the Spencers and resulted in an inequitable result. Liability cannot be imposed on any of the claims asserted by the Spencers on so broad and ill-defined a finding.

However, Question 1A plainly attempted to request a finding on a statutory cause of action, and while it was defective, it was not immaterial. To the contrary, it was the heart of the Spencers' case. Since Question 1A was material, the trial court could not disregard the jury's answer and render judgment notwithstanding the verdict. But because the charge was defective, and Eagle Star properly objected, it is entitled to a new trial. *See generally State Dept. of Highways v. Payne*, 838 S.W.2d 235 (Tex. 1992).

As we held in *Moulton v. Alamo Ambulance Serv., Inc.*, 414 S.W.2d 444, 449-50 (Tex. 1967), an objection is sufficient to preserve error in a defective instruction. A request of substantially correct language is not required. The applicable rule is Rule 274, TEX. R. CIV. P., which states in part: A party objecting to a charge must point out distinctly the objectionable matter and the grounds of the objection. Any complaint as to a question, definition, or instruction, on account of any defect, omission, or fault in pleading, is waived unless specifically included in the objections. Eagle Star's objection fully complied with this rule.

The trial court was authorized only to grant a new trial, not to render judgment notwithstanding the verdict. Eagle Star and two amici curiae argue that in these circumstances judgment should be rendered against the Spencers, just as judgment was rendered against the plaintiffs in *Payne*. *Payne* is distinguishable. There, plaintiffs refused to submit a theory of recovery; here, plaintiffs submitted their theory defectively. In *Payne*, plaintiffs abandoned one basis of liability by refusing to submit it over defendant's objection; here, plaintiffs never abandoned their statutory claim but requested an improper submission of it to the jury. Inasmuch as the trial court should have granted a new trial, the same relief should be granted on appeal. *See* TEX. R. APP. P. 81(c), 184.

In other cases cited by Eagle Star and the amici, the party suffering rendition failed to submit any jury question on a controlling issue. *See Cosgrove v. Grimes*, 774 S.W.2d 662, 666 (Tex. 1989) (rejecting plaintiff's argument that jury findings on attorney's failure to exercise "reasonable and ordinary care" supported recovery for DTPA claim based on breach of implied warranty), reversing and affirming in part 757 S.W.2d 508 (Tex. App.—Houston [1st Dist.] 1988) (noting that plaintiff failed to submit any issues supporting his DTPA claim). *See also Woods v. Mercer*, 769 S.W.2d 515, 518 (Tex. 1988) (plaintiff neither pleaded nor requested jury findings on discovery rule). Another cited case, *W.O. Bankston Nissan, Inc. v. Walters*, 754 S.W.2d 127 (Tex. 1988), is also distinguishable. Plaintiff, who bought a truck represented to be a year newer than it was, obtained as his only findings pertinent to actual damages, an amount for the fair market value of the car traded in. He failed, as the Court noted, to submit a proper measure of damages, for either the loss of the benefit of the bargain—the truck as represented and as received—or his out-of-pocket losses. The Court concluded first, however, that plaintiff had failed to meet his burden of proof, by showing his losses under either measure of damages.

Eagle Star and the amici argue that to remand this case for a new trial punishes Eagle Star, even though it objected to the improper charge, and gives the Spencers "a second bite at the apple". They argue that a remand only encourages plaintiffs to request submission of erroneous charges in hopes of a favorable verdict, knowing that their only risk is a new trial. The first answer to this argument is that submission of the charge is the trial court's responsibility, and the consequences of the trial court's error should not fall unduly upon plaintiffs. Further, even if plaintiffs controlled submission of the charge, the prospect of a new trial is ordinarily sufficient disincentive to request submission of an improper charge. Finally, we do not foreclose the possibility that a plaintiff's request would be so defective that a new trial would not be warranted. Such circumstances are not present in this case.

We believe the correct remedy in this case is a new trial. Accordingly, we reverse the judgment of the court of appeals and remand the case to the trial court for further proceedings.

DOGGETT, JUSTICE, concurring and dissenting.

Here the majority consents to a new trial for small business owners, Charles and Sharon Spencer, who operate the Natural Furniture Store in Austin. This means that after waiting three and one-half years for this court to act, the Spencers finally get the privilege of retrying the case on which they received a favorable jury finding in 1987. Because of errors in both the trial court and court of appeals, I agree that this cause must be reversed and remanded. I disagree completely with both the majority's method of handling this matter and its ultimate disposition. A new trial is not mandated here because Eagle Star has waived the error of which it now complains.

The sole issue considered today is whether the jury charge properly submitted a violation of the Texas Insurance Code, which imposes liability for "unfair or deceptive acts or practices in the business of insurance." TEX. INS. CODE, art. 21.21, § 16(a). Question 1A asked the jury to determine whether Eagle Star's handling of the Spencers' claim for loss of earnings was: "A. An unfair practice in the business of insurance?"

A jury charge should track the statutory language upon which it is based as closely as possible. *Brown v. American Transfer & Storage Co.*, 601 S.W.2d 931, 937 (Tex.), *cert. denied*, 449 U.S. 1015, 101 S.Ct. 575, 66 L.Ed.2d 474 (1980). Utilizing the term "unfair practice in the business of insurance," the text of Question 1A does just that with a near verbatim quote of the statutory language. Despite the rather obvious similarity between the question submitted and the statutory language, the majority summarily dismisses the Spencers' submission as failing "this test" of "track[ing] the language of the provision as closely as possible," even while conceding that the question "plainly attempted to request a finding or statutory cause of action."

The majority's determination that the question was defective is not premised on the question at all, but is instead directed to disapproval of the accompanying definition, which provided: "Unfair practice" means any act or series of acts which is arbitrary, without justification, or takes advantage of a person to the extent that an unjust or inequitable result is obtained. This definition is paraphrased in the court's conclusion that the "question" was defective by "allow[ing] the jury to find an unfair insurance practice based on any action by Eagle Star that took advantage of the Spencers and resulted in an inequitable result." Eagle Star never properly objected to the definition submitted. Rather, following its objections to the question, the insurer contended only that "we object to the instructions submitted for these [same] reasons." Rule 274 does not permit the use of such cross-references in objections.

Today's blurring of the line between questions and definitions perpetuates the refusal to adhere to the rules governing objections to the charge so recently announced in *State Dep't of Highways v. Payne*, 838 S.W.2d 235, 237 (Tex. 1992), upon which the majority relies. The effect of these decisions is to absolve objecting parties from any obligation to assist the trial judge in clarifying the charge. *See id.* at 243 (MAUZY, J., dissenting); *id.* at 246 (GONZALEZ, J., dissenting opinion on second motion for rehearing). Because general objections now suffice, the trial court submits "broad form" jury questions at its peril. Today's approval of "broad form" objections has rendered Rule 278, TEX. R. CIV. P., setting forth explicit procedures for complaint concerning instructions and definitions in the charge, meaningless. If the rules are to change, it should not be by opinion, *Alvarado v. Farah Mfg. Co.*, 830 S.W.2d 911, 915 (Tex. 1992), but by ordered consideration and public comment.

Because Eagle Star has waived error, a new trial is not required. I would reverse the court of appeals' judgment and remand to the trial court for rendition of judgment.

SPECTOR, J., joins in this concurring and dissenting opinion.

Notes

1. *Drafting.* When liability is asserted based upon a provision of a statute or regulation, a jury charge should track the language of the provision as closely as possible. The charge here fails this test. When a defective issue is submitted, and error is preserved, the case must be remanded for a new trial.

2. *Disregarding.* While a material defective issue cannot be disregarded, a trial court may disregard an immaterial issue or a material issue, when it has been rendered immaterial by other findings. The court can also disregard the answer to a material issue when the jury finding is not supported by, a condition not met in this case.

3. *Materiality.* Stated another way, a question is immaterial when it should not have been submitted, or when it was properly submitted but has been rendered immaterial by other findings. A question which calls for a finding beyond the province of the jury, such as a question of law, may be deemed immaterial.

4. *Preservation of Error.* An objection is sufficient to preserve error in a defective instruction. A request for an instruction in substantially correct language is not required.

5. *Texas Workers' Compensation Insurance Fund v. Mandlbauer*, 988 S. W. 2d 750 (Tex. 2000): In this workers' compensation claim, the worker, Mandlbauer, was not entitled to jury instructions on "producing cause" because the jury charge did not mention producing cause. When a trial court refuses to submit a requested instruction, the question on appeal is whether the request was reasonably necessary to enable the jury to render a proper verdict. Further, for an instruction to be proper, it must (1) assist the jury; (2) accurately state the law; and (3) find support in the pleadings and the evidence.

REDWINE
v.
AAA LIFE INS. CO.
852 S.W.2d 10
(Tex. App.—Dallas 1993, no writ)

David R. Weiner, Law Offices of Windle Turley, P.C., Dallas and Frank Herrera, Jr., Herrera & Vega, Inc., San Antonio, for appellant.
John Zavitsanos, Baker & Botts, Houston, for appellee.

BARBER, JUSTICE.

This suit arises out of an insurance policy. Deanne Redwine filed suit against AAA Life Insurance Company when she was denied benefits under a travel accident insurance policy. Redwine alleged various causes of action, including breach of contract and breach of the duty of good faith and fair dealing. The lawsuit was tried before a jury. At the close of Redwine's case, the trial court granted AAA Life's counterclaim for declaratory judgment that Redwine's injuries were not covered by the insurance policy. The trial court also granted AAA Life's motion for directed verdict on Redwine's claim for breach of the duty of good faith and fair dealing. At the close of all the evidence, the trial court submitted instructions that advised the jury that these two issues had been resolved in AAA Life's favor. In her sole point of error, Redwine contends that these instructions constituted impermissible comments on the weight of the evidence. In a cross-point, AAA Life contends that the trial court erred in failing to award it attorney's fees in accordance with the Texas Uniform Declaratory Judgment Act. We sustain Redwine's point of error, overrule AAA Life's cross-point, and reverse and remand this cause to the trial court for proceedings consistent with this opinion.

FACTUAL AND PROCEDURAL BACKGROUND

Redwine's mother received a direct-mail advertisement from AAA Life promoting the sale of "365 Travel Accident Insurance." Knowing that her daughter would be travelling abroad, Mrs. Redwine called an employee of AAA, a legal entity separate and distinct from AAA Life, to discuss the policy. Mrs. Redwine maintains that she discussed the policy with the AAA employee. The AAA employee denies that he discussed the terms of the policy with Mrs. Redwine. Nonetheless, Mrs. Redwine testified that, based on the advertisement and the information provided by the AAA employee, she believed that the policy would cover any injuries sustained in a serious travel accident. Mrs. Redwine returned the application form that accompanied the advertisement and paid the $36 annual premium. AAA Life issued a policy in Deanne Redwine's name.

Several months later, Deanne Redwine was injured in an automobile accident. She suffered a spinal cord injury and incomplete paralysis of her lower limbs. Redwine filed a claim with AAA Life to collect under the 365 policy. Rather than cover any injuries sustained in a serious travel accident as Mrs. Redwine believed, the 365 policy provided coverage only in the event of death, loss of limb, or loss of sight. Redwine tried to recover under the "loss of limb" provision because the advertisement material did not define "loss of limb" and Redwine thought the provision broad enough to encompass "loss of use." "Loss of limb" was defined in the certificate of insurance mailed to Mrs. Redwine after she sent in the enrollment card with her premium, however, as "severance at or above the wrist or ankle joint." AAA Life denied the claim, contending that the injuries were not covered under the policy.

Deanne Redwine filed suit against AAA Life, alleging breach of contract, violations under the Deceptive Trade Practices—Consumer Protection Act (DTPA), violations under article 21.21 of the Texas Insurance Code, common-law fraud, fraudulent inducement, and breach of the duty of good faith and fair dealing. At the jury trial, Redwine offered expert testimony that AAA Life's advertisement was misleading because the contents of the advertisement differed from the contents of the policy. The advertisement failed to delineate the specific conditions under which benefits were recoverable. Specifically, the advertisement failed to define "loss of limb." Mrs. Redwine testified that she would not have bought the policy had she known the limitations on the coverage.

At the close of Redwine's case, the trial court granted AAA Life's request for affirmative relief declaring that Redwine's injuries were not covered by the insurance policy and granted AAA Life's motion for directed verdict on Redwine's claim for breach of the duty of good faith and fair dealing. At the close of all the evidence, the trial court submitted instructions which advised the jury that these two issues had been resolved in AAA Life's favor. The jury found in favor of AAA Life on the remaining causes of action and awarded AAA Life $145,000 for attorney's fees. Redwine filed a motion to disregard the jury's findings on the question of attorney's fees. The trial court granted her motion and entered a final judgment for AAA Life but denied recovery of attorney's fees to AAA Life. This appeal follows.

COMMENTS ON WEIGHT OF EVIDENCE

In her sole point of error, Redwine contends that the trial court erred in submitting instructions that Redwine's injuries were not covered by the insurance policy and that AAA Life was not liable for breach of the duty of good faith and fair dealing. The court instructed the jury as follows: You are hereby instructed that AAA Life Insurance Company did not breach its fiduciary duty of good faith and fair dealing, or otherwise act in bad faith, by denying Deanne Redwine's claim under the 365 Travel Accident Policy. You are hereby instructed that Deanne Redwine's claim pursuant to the injuries received were not covered by the 365 Travel Accident Policy. Redwine contends that these instructions constituted impermissible comments on the weight of the evidence that were calculated to cause and probably did cause the rendition of an improper judgment. We agree and sustain this point of error.

Preservation of Error

AAA Life contends that Redwine failed to properly preserve error for appellate review, alleging that her objections to the jury instructions were too general. To preserve a complaint for appellate review, a party must present to the trial court a timely objection, stating the specific grounds for the ruling he desires the court to make if the specific grounds are not apparent from the context. TEX. R. APP. P. 52(a). It is insufficient to object to a jury charge by stating that the instruction constitutes a comment on the weight of the evidence. *Baker Material Handling Corp. v. Cummings*, 692 S.W.2d 142, 145 (Tex. App.—Dallas 1985, writ dism'd by agr.). Moreover, it is insufficient to state that the objectionable elements of a charge may confuse the jury. *Castleberry v. Branscum*, 721 S.W.2d 270, 276-77 (Tex. 1986).

Redwine, however, made the following more specific objections: "such instruction[s] [are] unlawful comment[s] on the weight of the evidence, and . . . the Jury could reasonably conclude, therefore, from th[ese] comment[s], that the rest of the allegations contained therein would also be a part of th[ese]—would be included in th[ese] instruction[s]." "Because [they are] unlawful comment[s] on the weight of the evidence, [they] could lead to a confusion of the Jury in answering the liability issues" presented by the remaining causes of action. We conclude that this objection was specific enough to preserve Redwine's complaint for appellate review.

Applicable Law

The trial court has considerable discretion in framing a jury charge. *Barham v. Turner Constr. Co.*, 803 S.W.2d 731, 735 (Tex. App.—Dallas 1990, writ denied). In determining whether there has been an abuse of discretion, this Court may not substitute its judgment for that of the trial court but must determine only whether the trial court's action was arbitrary or unreasonable. *Id.*

In framing a jury charge, the trial court must submit such explanatory instructions and definitions as will aid and assist the jury in answering the jury questions submitted. TEX. R. CIV. P. 277; *First Nat'l Bank v. Jarnigan*, 794 S.W.2d 54, 61 (Tex. App.—Amarillo 1990, writ denied). Anything that does not aid the jury in answering the jury questions submitted, regardless of how interesting or otherwise relevant to the case, must be excluded from the charge. *Jarnigan*, 794 S.W.2d at 61.

In its charge, the trial court may not comment on the evidence or the weight thereof in any manner. TEX. R. CIV. P. 277. An impermissible comment on the weight of the evidence occurs when, after examining the entire charge, it is determined that the judge assumed the truth of a material controverted fact or exaggerated, minimized, or withdrew some pertinent evidence from the jury's consideration. *Jarnigan*, 794 S.W.2d at 61; *American Bankers Ins. Co. v. Caruth*, 786 S.W.2d 427, 434 (Tex. App.—Dallas 1990, no writ); *Lively Exploration Co. v. Valero Transmission Co.*, 751 S.W.2d 649, 653 (Tex. App.—San Antonio 1988, writ denied), appeal dismissed, 493 U.S. 1065, 110 S.Ct. 1104, 107 L.Ed.2d 1013 (1990). An instruction also will be held to be an improper comment on the weight of the evidence if it suggests to the jury the trial judge's opinion concerning the matter about which the jury is asked. *Ferguson v. DRG/Colony N., Ltd.*, 764 S.W.2d 874, 886 (Tex. App.—Austin 1989, writ denied). Reversal is required if an improper comment on the weight of the evidence is one that was calculated to cause and probably did cause the rendition of an improper judgment. *Id.* A court may incidentally comment on the weight of the evidence, however, where the comment is properly a part of an instruction or definition. TEX. R. CIV. P. 277.

In several instances the courts have found that charging the jury on issues decided as a matter of law constituted an unlawful comment on the weight of the evidence. The leading decision is *Board of Regents v. Denton Construction Co.*, 652 S.W.2d 588 (Tex. App.—Fort Worth 1983, writ ref'd n.r.e.). *Board of Regents* arose out of two construction contracts for the renovation and construction of several buildings at North Texas State University. At the conclusion of all of the evidence, the trial court rendered judgment as a matter of law on two elements of damages sued for by both parties. *Id.* at 594. In the court's charge, the court instructed the jury on the partial instructed verdict entered in favor of the appellee contractor. *Id.* The court of appeals concluded that such instructions constituted impermissible comments on the weight of the evidence calculated to prejudice the rights of the appellants in the eyes of the jury. *Id.* The court of appeals explained as follows: We are at a loss to determine why this instruction was included in the charge. It was not an instruction, so far as we can see, designed to be helpful or instructive to the jury in answering any of the special issues in the court's charge . . . . [T]his instruction was not explanatory of anything, except that the court had ruled as a matter of law that appellee was entitled to prevail on the questions of the air conditioning screens and liquidated damages . . . . We think this tended to imply to the jury that the court thought the law and the facts were with the appellee, and as such, the instruction was erroneously prejudicial. *Id.* at 594-95.

In *Mader v. Aetna Casualty and Surety Co.*, 683 S.W.2d 731 (Tex. App.—Corpus Christi 1984, no writ), the trial court submitted an instruction that informed the jury that, as a matter of law, one of the plaintiffs was not a consumer within the meaning of DTPA. *Id.* at 733. This instruction was given in connection with the bad faith and harassment issue that was submitted as to this plaintiff. *Id.* The court of appeals agreed that the instruction was an improper comment on the weight of the evidence: The trial court, in effect, informed the jury on a finding which it had made as a matter of law. This was error. [Citing Board of Regents]. This instruction informed the jury to the effect that the trial court looked with favor on the appellees' case, at least in part. By informing the jury that it found that Robert Mader was not a consumer, we believe that the instruction strongly suggested to the jury that they should answer the accompanying issue accordingly . . . . We can see no useful purpose for the instruction other than to steer the jury toward an affirmative finding on those issues [of bad faith and harassment]. As such, we find that the instruction was an impermissible comment on the evidence; it announced an opinion on behalf of the trial court as to the ultimate facts that were to be inquired about. *Id.* at 733.

American Bankers Insurance Co. v. Caruth, 786 S.W.2d 427 (Tex. App.—Dallas 1990, no writ), arose out of an equine mortality insurance policy. When the insured horse died of a covered peril, the owners made demand for payment on the insurance company. *Id.* at 429. The insurance company filed suit, seeking a declaratory judgment to determine the actual value of the horse. *Id.* The owners counterclaimed, asserting various causes of action. *Id.* The insurance company repeatedly failed to comply with discovery requests. *Id.* at 429-30. The trial court, as a sanction, struck the insurance company's pleadings. *Id.* at 430. The trial court then entered a default judgment on liability and liquidated damages. *Id.* At the jury trial to determine unliquidated damages, the court charged the jury on thirty-six "findings of fact" which included the facts leading up to the lawsuit; the court's conclusion that the insurance company breach its implied warranty of fitness, breached its duty of good faith and fair dealing, and engaged in unfair insurance practices; and the court's conclusion that the owner suffered actual damages in the amount of $150,000 as a direct result of the insurance company's "misrepresentations, deceptive trade practices, acts, omissions, and conduct." *Id.* at 431-34. This Court concluded that these "findings of fact" constituted impermissible comments on the weight of the evidence: We hold that the findings of fact were unnecessary and impermissible comments on the weight of the evidence which were calculated to prejudice the rights of American Bankers in the eyes of the jury. The findings of fact were not designed to be helpful to the jury in answering any of the questions in the court's charge, and . . . the findings of fact were not instructive to the jury in answering any of the questions in the charge. Consequently, we conclude that the trial court's comments tended to imply to the jury that the trial judge thought the law and the facts were in favor of Caruth and MJC and that they should be compensated commensurately. *Id.* at 435; *see also Jarnigan*, 794 S.W.2d at 61-63; *American Petrofina, Inc. v. PPG Indus., Inc.*, 679 S.W.2d 740, 756-57 (Tex. App.—Fort Worth 1984, writ dism'd by agr.).

Application of Law to Facts

Redwine contends that the instructions submitted to the jury concerning the issues decided as matters of law—that Redwine's injuries were not covered by the insurance policy and that AAA Life was not liable for breach of the duty of good faith and fair dealing—were improper comments on the weight of the evidence, citing Board of Regents, Mader, Caruth, and the other cases. She argues that the instructions were in no way designed to be helpful or instructive to the jury in answering any of the questions submitted concerning the remaining issues. She contends that the instructions tended only to imply to the jury that the court thought that the law and the facts favored AAA Life.

AAA Life initially contends that the jury instructions were not "comments on the weight of the evidence," as that term has been defined by the courts, because they did not refer to controverted issues. AAA Life cites those cases which stand for the proposition that an impermissible comment on the weight of the evidence occurs when the judge assumes the truth of a material controverted fact or exaggerates, minimizes, or withdraws some pertinent evidence from the jury's consideration. *Jarnigan*, 794 S.W.2d at 61; *Caruth*, 786 S.W.2d at 434; *Lively Exploration Co.*, 751 S.W.2d at 653. As a corollary, the courts generally hold that if the trial court assumes an uncontroverted fact in charging the jury, such is not held to be a comment on the weight of the evidence. *McDaniel v. Tucker*, 520 S.W.2d 543, 548 (Tex. Civ. App.—Corpus Christi 1975, no writ).

Although the assumption of an uncontroverted fact in the jury charge is generally not held to be a comment on the weight of the evidence, we cannot conclude that the instructions given in the instant case concerning issues decided as a matter of law—and therefore inherently uncontroverted—were not comments on the weight of the evidence. In each of the cases cited above, *Board of Regents*, 652 S.W.2d 588; *Mader*, 683 S.W.2d 731; *Jarnigan*, 794 S.W.2d 54; *Caruth*, 786 S.W.2d 427; and *American Petrofina*, 679 S.W.2d 740, the courts held that jury instructions concerning issues decided as a matter of law were improper comments on the weight of the evidence because they suggested to the jury how the remaining issues should be resolved. Moreover, we note that the courts have also more broadly defined "comments on the weight of the evidence" to include instructions that suggest to the jury the trial judge's opinion concerning the matter about which the jury was asked. *See Ferguson*, 764 S.W.2d at 886. Jury instructions concerning issues decided as a matter of law, and therefore inherently uncontroverted, can be improper comments on the weight of the evidence.

In the alternative, AAA Life asserts that the trial court did not err in instructing the jury on the issues decided as a matter of law because the instructions were incidental comments required to clarify issues for the jury. AAA Life points out that the jury heard evidence regarding the scope of the policy coverage both before and after the directed verdict. AAA Life contends that the complained-of instructions indicated to the jury that, notwithstanding this evidence, there was no issue for the jury to decide regarding coverage under the policy.

After reviewing the record, we cannot conclude that the complained-of jury instructions were necessary to clarify issues for the jury. Although testimony was admitted throughout the trial as to the scope of coverage under the policy, such testimony was always in the context of the misleading nature of the advertisement, an issue that was still before the jury. The instructions were not helpful to the jury in answering any of the questions in the charge.

We hold that the complained-of jury instructions constituted comments on the weight of the evidence. Redwine's original petition and four amended petitions were introduced into evidence and given to the jury during deliberations. In several of these petitions, Redwine alleged causes of action for breach of contract and breach of the duty of good faith and fair dealing. The trial court's instructions to the jury that Redwine's injuries were not covered by the 365 policy and that AAA Life did not breach its fiduciary duty of good faith and fair dealing by denying Redwine's claim under the 365 policy were necessarily comments on the weight of the evidence. The instructions suggested to the jurors that the trial court viewed AAA Life's case favorably and that they should resolve the remaining causes of action in AAA Life's favor as well.

To warrant reversal, the comments must be ones that were reasonably calculated to cause, and probably did cause, the rendition of an improper judgment. *See* TEX. R. APP. P. 81(b)(1). We conclude that the judgment itself reflects that the instructions were erroneously prejudicial. *Caruth*, 786 S.W.2d at 435. We sustain appellant's point of error.

* * *

CONCLUSION

The judgment of the trial court is affirmed in part and reversed in part. The portion of the judgment in favor of AAA Life Insurance Company with respect to Redwine's claims for breach of contract and breach of the duty of good faith and fair dealing is affirmed, and the judgment denying AAA Life Insurance Company's request for attorney fees is affirmed. In all other respects, the judgment of the trial court is reversed, and this cause is remanded to the trial court for a new trial.

Notes

1. *Framing.* In framing a jury charge, the trial court must submit such explanatory instructions and definitions as will aid and assist the jury in answering the jury questions submitted. Anything that does not aid the jury in answering the jury questions submitted, regardless of how interesting or otherwise relevant to the case, must be excluded from the charge.

2. *Preserving.* To preserve a complaint for appellate review of an improper jury instruction, a party must present to the trial court *a timely objection*, stating the specific grounds. It is insufficient to object that the instruction constitutes a comment on the weight of the evidence, or that the objectionable elements of a charge may confuse the jury. However, an objecting that a comment on the weight of evidence will confuse the jury may be sufficient.

3. *Commenting.* In its charge, the trial court may not comment on the evidence or the weight thereof in any manner. It is an impermissible comment on the weight of the evidence when the judge assumes the truth of a material controverted fact or exaggerates, minimizes, withdraws some pertinent evidence from the jury's consideration, or if it suggests to the jury the trial judge's opinion concerning the matter about which the jury is asked.

4. *Union Pacific Railroad Co. v. Williams*, 45 S.W.3d 262 (Tex. 2002): In this FELA case, the evidence on foreseeability was conflicting. The trial court submitted an instruction defining negligence based on the Fifth Circuit Court of Appeals' Pattern Jury Charge, which the Texas approved in *Mitchell v. Missouri-Kansas-Texas R.R. Co.*, 786 S.W.2d 659, 662-63 (Tex. 1990). The charge did not instruct the jury to consider whether Union

Pacific could foresee the dangerous condition for purposes of imposing a duty in this case. *Held:* The trial court erred in refusing to submit Union Pacific's proposed foreseeability instruction in the jury charge. *Mitchell* is overruled to the extent that it rejected a foreseeability instruction when the evidence about that element of the railroad's duty was disputed. It also overrules *Mitchell* to the extent that it approved the Fifth Circuit's pattern instruction, even though the railroad's knowledge was disputed on the erroneous basis that it does not place the issue of duty before the jury. When the evidence about foreseeability, as it relates to the railroad's duty, is disputed, the trial court should instruct the jury about this element so it can resolve the factual issue. Union Pacific's submitted a written proposed instruction advising the jury that "you must be satisfied" that Union Pacific had knowledge about the dangerous condition. was substantially correct. State courts trying FELA claims must apply federal law about burdens of proof. Contrary to Texas law, federal law provides that "you must be satisfied" expresses the same burden of proof standard as "preponderance of the evidence." Accordingly, Union Pacific's request preserved error on its jury charge complaint, because the request was substantially correct.

COLUMBIA RIO GRANDE HEALTHCARE, L.P.
v.
HAWLEY
284 S.W.3d 851
(Tex. 2009)

R. Brent Cooper, Diana L. Faust, Devon J. Singh, Heather Jean Reynolds Johnson, Cooper & Scully, P.C., Dallas, TX, Raul Javier Guerra, Green, DuBois & Guerra, San Antonio, TX, Mike A. Hatchell and Charles R. Watson Jr., Locke Lord Bissell & Liddell LLP, Austin, TX, for Petitioner.

Darrin M. Walker, Law Office of Darrin Walker, Kingwood, TX, Laura R. Pazin Porter, Clarence V. Lyons, Loan Kim Vo, Lyons & Rhodes, P.C., San Antonio, TX, Roberto J. Yzaguirre, and Jose E. Chapa, Yzaguirre & Chapa, McAllen, TX, for Respondents.

Linda C. Breck, Corpus Christi, TX, for Amicus Curiae.

JUSTICE JOHNSON delivered the opinion of the Court, in which CHIEF JUSTICE JEFFERSON, JUSTICE HECHT, JUSTICE WAINWRIGHT, JUSTICE BRISTER, JUSTICE GREEN and JUSTICE WILLETT joined, and in all but Part II-D 2 of which JUSTICE O'NEILL and JUSTICE MEDINA joined.

In this health care liability case against a hospital we consider whether the trial court erred by refusing to give jury instructions as to new and independent cause, a physician's status as an independent contractor, and lost chance of survival. Concluding the trial court erred by refusing instructions on the physician's independent contractor status and lost chance of survival, we reverse and remand for a new trial.

On November 22, 2000, Alice Hawley visited Dr. Armando Arechiga, complaining of cramps, nausea, and vomiting. Dr. Arechiga admitted her to Columbia Rio Grande Regional Hospital ("Columbia" or "the hospital"). The next day Dr. Jesus Rodriguez operated on Alice, performed a colon resection, and sent a tissue specimen to the hospital's pathology laboratory. There, Dr. Jose Valencia, an independent pathologist whose office was located inside the hospital, discovered Alice had cancer. He diagnosed its severity as Stage 3, or what is known as Duke's C cancer.

Because some doctors had complained of not receiving pathology reports, the hospital had adopted a written policy (the policy) in regard to notifying patients' doctors of cancer diagnoses. The policy was in place at the time of Alice's surgery and called for a copy of the pathology report to be placed in the patient's hospital record. It also specified the following:

A. PATHOLOGIST WILL VERBALLY NOTIFY PHYSICIAN(S) OF RECORD.
B. PATHOLOGY SECRETARY WILL FAX REPORT TO PHYSICIAN(S) OF RECORD.
C. REPORTS WILL BE DELIVERED TO PHYSICIAN(S) OF RECORD VIA CERTIFIED MAIL.

The policy identified the "physician(s) of record" as the admitting physician and the surgeon, if the surgeon was not the admitting physician. In this case, the physicians of record were Drs. Arechiga and Rodriguez.

Alice's medical records and the pathology lab records showed the pathology report was placed in her hospital chart one day before she was discharged, although Dr. Arechiga did not see it when he completed his discharge summary. The hospital disputes whether all parts of its written notification policy must be complied with as to each cancer diagnosis, and the parties disagreed as to whether all parts were actually complied with in Alice's particular case. However, there is no dispute that Alice was not told she had cancer and did not receive treatment for cancer until long after the initial diagnosis by Dr. Valencia.

During a routine checkup in the summer of 2001, Dr. Arechiga found Alice's liver enzymes to be elevated. The enzymes were much higher when she returned for another appointment in September, so Dr. Arechiga ordered tests that revealed she had liver cancer. Even though treatment began immediately, the disease was terminal.

Alice and her husband, James Hawley, sued the hospital, Dr. Rodriguez, and Dr. Valencia. They alleged the hospital was negligent in failing to timely and properly convey the cancer diagnosis to Alice and Drs. Rodriguez and Arechiga and in failing to follow its policies and procedures for reporting the pathology results. The Hawleys nonsuited the doctors before trial.

The case was tried to a jury. The jury found that Columbia's negligence was a proximate cause of Alice's injuries. The trial court entered judgment against Columbia based on the jury verdict. The court of appeals affirmed. 188 S.W.3d 838.

Columbia argues that the trial court erred in charging the jury, * * * It asserts charge error based on the trial court's refusal to give jury instructions as to: * * * (2) the independent contractor status of Dr. Valencia, and (3) lost chance of survival.

A trial court must, when feasible, submit a cause to the jury by broad-form questions. TEX. R. CIV. P. 277. It is also required to give "such instructions and definitions as shall be proper to enable the jury to render a verdict." *Id.* An instruction is proper if it (1) assists the jury, (2) accurately states the law, and (3) finds support in the pleadings and evidence. *Tex. Workers' Comp. Ins. Fund v. Mandlbauer,* 34 S.W.3d 909, 912 (Tex. 2000). Determining necessary and proper jury instructions is a matter within the trial court's discretion, and appellate review is for abuse of that discretion. *Shupe v. Lingafelter,* 192 S.W.3d 577, 579 (Tex. 2006). One way in which a trial court abuses its discretion is by failing to follow guiding rules and principles. *Bocquet v. Herring,* 972 S.W.2d 19, 21 (Tex. 1998).

A judgment will not be reversed for charge error unless the error was harmful because it probably caused the rendition of an improper verdict or probably prevented the petitioner from properly presenting the case to the appellate courts. TEX.R.APP. P. 61.1. Charge error is generally considered harmful if it relates to a contested, critical issue. *See Bel-Ton Elec. Serv., Inc. v. Pickle,* 915 S.W.2d 480, 481 (Tex. 1996) (per curiam); *Sw. Bell Tel. Co. v. John Carlo Tex., Inc.,* 843 S.W.2d 470, 472 (Tex. 1992).

* * *

The court's charge in this case defined "proximate cause" as follows:

> "Proximate cause," when used with respect to the conduct of [the hospital], means that cause which, in a natural and continuous sequence, produces an event, and without which cause such event would not have occurred. In order to be a proximate cause, the act or omission complained of must be such that a hospital using ordinary care would have foreseen that the event, or some similar event, might reasonably result therefrom. There may be more than one proximate cause of any event.

Columbia argues that because the evidence of Alice's chance of survival at the time of Dr. Valencia's cancer diagnosis was conflicting, the court erred in refusing to give the following additional instruction:

> You are instructed that Alice H. Hawley must have had greater than a fifty percent (50%) chance of survival on November 28, 2000 for the negligence of Rio Grande Regional Hospital to be a proximate cause of injury to Alice H. Hawley.

The Hawleys do not assert that Columbia's requested instruction was an incorrect statement of the law or that the issue was not raised by the evidence. Rather, they argue (1) because the court's proximate cause definition specified that Columbia's negligence could not be a proximate cause of Alice's injuries unless her injuries would not have occurred absent the negligence, the definition adequately instructed the jury on the issue of causation and the requested instruction would have been redundant and would not have further assisted the jury; and (2) the lawyers argued to the jury that under the law, the Hawleys had the burden to prove Alice probably would have survived the cancer if the defendant's negligence had not resulted in delayed treatment. Citing *Lemos v. Montez,* 680 S.W.2d 798, 801 (Tex. 1984), the Hawleys urge the charge was sufficient and should not have been embellished because it tracked the language of the pattern jury charge. *See id.* ("Judicial history teaches that broad issues and accepted definitions suffice and that a workable jury system demands strict adherence to simplicity in jury charges."). We disagree with the Hawleys' contentions.

Recovery in a medical malpractice case requires proof to a reasonable medical probability that the injuries complained of were proximately caused by the negligence of a defendant. *Park Place Hosp. v. Estate of Milo,* 909 S.W.2d 508, 511 (Tex. 1995). Proximate cause includes two components: cause-in-fact and foreseeability. *LMB, Ltd. v. Moreno,* 201 S.W.3d 686, 688 (Tex. 2006) (per curiam). Proof that negligence was a cause-in-fact of injury requires proof that (1) the negligence was a substantial factor in causing the injury, and (2) without the act or omission, the harm would not have occurred. *Id.* These standards bar recovery by a patient if a condition preexists the negligence of a health care provider and at the time of the negligence, the condition resulted in the patient having a 50% or less chance of cure or survival. *Kramer v. Lewisville Mem'l Hosp.,* 858 S.W.2d 397, 400 (Tex. 1993).

The parties address the loss of chance question as a lost chance of survival even though Alice was alive at the time of trial. We will address the issue as the parties have briefed and presented it for two reasons. First, no one disputed that at the time of trial Alice's disease was terminal. Second, whatever injuries she suffered from the alleged negligence of the hospital, the Hawleys' burden of proof was the same-they had to prove that the hospital's actions were a cause-in-fact of injuries above and beyond those Alice would have suffered even if she had received treatment promptly after Dr. Valencia's diagnosis in November 2000. * * *

In *Kramer,* the Court was faced with the issue of whether to adopt the loss of chance doctrine as part of Texas common law * * * The Court held that recovery for a loss of chance required proof that at the time of the defendant's alleged negligence, there was less than a 50% chance the claimed injuries would have occurred without that defendant's negligence. *Id.* at 406-07 * * * Thus, proof that a patient lost *some* chance of avoiding a medical condition or of surviving the cancer because of a defendant's negligence is not enough for recovery of damages.

The testimony as to Alice's loss of chance was inconsistent and the Hawleys do not dispute that the parties hotly contested her probability of a cure or survival had she immediately begun treatment following Dr. Valencia's diagnosis in November 2000. * * *

The Hawleys contend the trial court did not need to instruct the jury that in order for Columbia's negligence to be a proximate cause of injury to Alice, she must have had a greater than 50% chance of surviving the cancer because the lawyers explained that was the law. But the jurors took oaths to render their verdict according to "the law as it may be given to you in the Charge of the Court" and evidence submitted under rulings of the court. *See* TEX.R. CIV. P. 236. The judge instructed the jurors that at the conclusion of the evidence, they would receive a written charge from him on the law. The charge itself instructed the jury that "in matters of law, you must be governed by the instructions in this charge" and if the jury "disregarded any of these instructions it will be jury misconduct." *See* TEX.R. CIV. P. 226a. The jury is presumed to have followed the court's instructions. *See Golden Eagle Archery, Inc. v. Jackson,* 116 S.W.3d 757, 771 (Tex. 2003) (noting that unless the record demonstrates otherwise, appellate courts must presume the jury followed instructions given in the jury charge). Statements from lawyers as to the law do not take the place of instructions from the judge as to the law. It is the trial court's prerogative and duty to instruct the jury on the applicable law.

Columbia's requested instruction would not have been redundant, as the Hawleys assert. The instruction would have provided to the jury the standard it was required by law to apply in making its finding on a hotly-contested issue. The opinion in *Kramer* highlights the subtleties among various approaches to valuing a loss of chance, the difficulty in properly framing the loss of chance issue as a legal matter, and the reason juries need to be instructed as to the law on loss of chance. As this Court stated over a century ago when considering alleged charge error, "[w]e must look at the court's charge as practical experience teaches that a jury, untrained in the law, would view it." *Galveston, H. & S.A. Ry. Co. v. Washington,* 94 Tex. 510, 63 S.W. 534, 538 (1901). It asks too much of lay jurors, untrained in the law, to distill the correct Texas legal standard for loss of chance from the general proximate cause instruction given by the trial court. Columbia's requested loss of chance instruction would have assisted the jury, was an accurate statement of applicable law, and was supported by the pleadings and evidence. *See Mandlbauer,* 34 S.W.3d at 912. The trial court abused its discretion by refusing to give it.

One way in which a trial court's error in refusing an instruction can be reversible is if the error probably caused the rendition of an improper judgment. TEX.R.APP. P. 61.1(a); *Union Pac. R.R. Co. v. Williams,* 85 S.W.3d 162, 170 (Tex. 2002). The instruction Columbia requested related to a contested, critical issue. *See Bel-Ton Elec. Serv.,* 915 S.W.2d at 481; *Sw. Bell Tel. Co.,* 843 S.W.2d at 472. Under the evidence, there was little question that because of the negligence as found by the jury, Alice lost some chance of cure and survival. Unless the jury applied the law as expressed in Columbia's proposed instruction, it could have found that because she lost at least some chance of reduced medical treatment and survival, even if that chance was much less than 50%, the hospital's negligence proximately caused injury to her. Such a result was specifically rejected in *Kramer.* 858 S.W.2d at 407. Considering the pleadings of the parties and the nature of the case, the evidence presented at trial, and the charge in its entirety, the refusal to give the requested instruction on loss of chance was reasonably calculated to and probably did cause the rendition of an improper judgment. *See Sterling Trust Co. v. Adderley,* 168 S.W.3d 835, 843 (Tex. 2005); *Island Recreational Dev. Corp. v. Republic of Tex. Sav. Ass'n,* 710 S.W.2d 551, 555 (Tex. 1986).

A hospital ordinarily is not liable for the negligence of an independent contractor physician. *Baptist Mem'l Hosp. Sys. v. Sampson,* 969 S.W.2d 945, 948 (Tex. 1998). Columbia asserts the trial court erred by refusing to instruct the jury, in accordance with the foregoing principle, that the jury should not consider the actions or omissions of Dr. Valencia when determining the hospital's negligence.

The Hawleys urge that the refusal to give such an instruction was not erroneous, even though they do not contend the hospital was liable for the actions or omissions of Dr. Valencia. They note (1) "[n]o one suggested that Valencia was an agent of the Hospital for whose conduct the Hospital could be held liable," (2) it was undisputed and repeatedly emphasized that Dr. Valencia was not a hospital employee, and (3) their lawyers did not dispute Columbia's jury argument that Dr. Valencia did not work for the hospital. The Hawleys also say the jury was instructed to consider only the acts of the hospital's employees. One problem with this assertion is that the jury instructions and liability question did not limit the jury's considerations as the Hawleys claim. The jury charge stated:

> You are hereby instructed that RIO GRANDE REGIONAL HOSPITAL acts or fails to act only through its employees, agents, nurses, and servants.

The one liability question then asked:

> Was the negligence, if any, of RIO GRANDE REGIONAL HOSPITAL, a proximate cause of injuries to Alice H. Hawley?

Columbia does not contend the trial court's instructing the jury that a hospital acts through its employees, agents, nurses, and servants was improper or a misstatement of the law. Rather, Columbia contends the jury should have also been given the following instruction to prevent the hospital from being found liable because the jury improperly considered Dr. Valencia as its agent:

> In considering the negligence of Rio Grande Regional Hospital, do not consider the acts or omissions of the pathologist, Dr. Valencia.

The evidence showed Dr. Valencia was an employee of Useda and Associates, pathologists with offices in the hospital. Dr. Useda, a member of the group, testified he was the medical director of Columbia's pathology laboratory. Drs. Useda and Valencia each testified they had input into the hospital's policy that specified the pathologist was to verbally notify doctors of record when cancer was diagnosed. Dr. Valencia testified he expected the laboratory secretaries to follow the protocol and when he came to work in the laboratory he usually reviewed the certified mail receipts from reports the secretaries had sent the day before. He also testified that only around one-fifth of physicians called about a cancer report would call the laboratory back, so many times he would not personally tell physicians of record about cancer diagnoses. Dr. Valencia could not recall specifically telling either Dr. Arechiga or Dr. Rodriguez that Alice had cancer. Both Drs. Arechiga and Rodriguez denied having been told of the diagnosis.

When considered in light of the evidence and the instruction given, the liability question allowed the jury to consider actions or omissions of any hospital "agent" when determining the hospital's negligence. The court instructed the jury that:

> When words are used in this charge in a sense which varies from the meaning commonly understood, you are given a proper legal definition, which you are bound to accept in place of any other meaning.

There was no definition given for "agent." Thus, the jury could have considered Dr. Valencia as the hospital's agent. *See* WEBSTER'S NEW UNIVERSAL UNABRIDGED DICTIONARY 38 (1996) (defining an agent, in part, as "a person or business authorized to act on another's behalf"). The hospital's request was designed to prevent that from happening. The instruction was effectively a limiting and proper definition of the term under the evidence. The requested instruction would have assisted the jury, was an accurate statement of applicable law, and was supported by the pleadings and the evidence. *See Mandlbauer,* 34 S.W.3d at 912. The Hawleys do not complain that the instruction would have "tilted" the jury against them in some manner; indeed, one reason they say the failure to give the instruction was not error is because it was undisputed that Dr. Valencia was not an employee of the hospital through whose actions the hospital acted.

In refusing to give the instruction, the trial court failed to follow guiding principles and therefore abused its discretion. We next consider whether the error was harmful.

Columbia asserts that failing to submit the instruction was harmful because the error prevents it from properly presenting the case on appeal. *See* TEX.R.APP. P. 61.1(b) ("No judgment may be reversed on appeal on the ground that the trial court made an error of law unless the Supreme Court concludes that the error complained of . . . (b) probably prevented the petitioner from properly presenting the case to the appellate courts."); *see also* TEX.R.APP. P. 44.1(a)(2). Columbia's position is that under the charge and record there is no way to tell if the jury found it liable because of acts of employees, agents, and servants-for whom it could properly be held liable-or because of acts and omissions of Dr. Valencia-for whom it could not. * * *

And although in most cases where a trial court errs by refusing to give a proposed instruction the harm analysis will be based on whether the refusal probably caused the rendition of an improper judgment, *see Union Pacific Railroad Co. v. Williams,* 85 S.W.3d 162, 170 (Tex. 2002), the harm analysis of Rule 61.1(b) applies here because the jury could have found Columbia liable based on Dr. Valencia's acts or omissions under the charge as given, and there is no way for Columbia or an appellate court to tell if it did so. *See Harris County,* 96 S.W.3d at 234-35. Such an error effectively precludes reviewing courts from determining whether the jury found liability on an invalid basis, precludes determination of whether the error probably caused the rendition of an improper judgment, and is harmful because it prevents proper presentation of the case on appeal. TEX.R.APP. P. 61.1(b). We sustain Columbia's issue.

* * *

The trial court erred in refusing to submit Columbia's proposed jury instructions as to Dr. Valencia's actions as an independent contractor and as to Alice's loss of chance. The judgment of the court of appeals is reversed and the case is remanded to the trial court for a new trial.

ii. *Inferential Rebuttals*

Notes

1. Under TEX. R. CIV. P. 277, an "Inferential rebuttal question shall not be submitted in the charge. * * *"

2. An inferential rebuttal issue is one which seeks to disprove the existence of an essential element submitted in another issue. *Wirtz v. Orr*, 533 S.W.2d 468 (Tex. Civ. App.—Eastland 1976, writ ref'd n.r.e.). Inferential rebuttal issues have been variously referred to as denial issues or argumentative denials rather than direct negatives. *Scott v. The Atchison, Topeka and Santa Fe Railway Company*, 572 S.W.2d 273 (Tex. 1978). The reasoning behind such labels is that "they disprove by establishing the truth of a positive factual theory which is inconsistent with the existence of some factual element of the ground of recovery or defense relied upon by the opponent, and are therefore to be distinguished from a flat denial . . . ." Hodges, Special Issue Submission in

Texas, Section 15, at 40. The basic characteristic of an inferential rebuttal is that it presents a contrary or inconsistent theory from the claim relied upon for recovery.

REINHART
v.
YOUNG
906 S.W.2d 471
(Tex. 1995)

Rex Easley, Victoria, for petitioners.
Clifford J. Vacek and Jeffrey Lee Hoffman, Houston, for respondent.

PHILLIPS, CHIEF JUSTICE.

The issue we address is whether the trial court committed reversible error by including an instruction regarding the doctrine of unavoidable accident in its charge to the jury. Because we hold that the trial court's error, if any, was harmless, we affirm the judgment of the court of appeals. 874 S.W.2d 773.

I.

Sallye Treme was driving her car on Highway 59 near Houston at about fifty miles per hour during the morning of March 17, 1989. The weather was good, and traffic was generally light. After Treme drove over an overpass, she came to an abrupt stop when a car cutting across the highway caused the traffic in front of her to halt. About four seconds later, a pickup truck driven by William Carl Young crashed into the rear end of Treme's car, allegedly injuring her and a passenger, Thelma Reinhart.

Alleging common-law negligence, Treme and Reinhart sued Young. In his First Amended Original Answer, Young asserted, inter alia, that the collision "was an unavoidable accident," and that "he was confronted by an emergency arising suddenly and unexpectedly which was not proximately caused by any negligence on his part and . . . required immediate action without time for deliberation and that he used ordinary care after such emergency arose."

The parties disagreed about the exact location of the accident. Treme claimed that the collision occurred away from the overpass, close to a bridge that crosses Highway 59. Young testified that he was traveling about one-eighth to one-fourth of a mile behind Treme and contended that the collision took place on the crest of the overpass.

Based solely on its conclusion that the incline or elevation of the overpass constituted a non-human event which proximately caused the accident, the trial court submitted an instruction to the jury in the charge of the court concerning the doctrine of unavoidable accident. The instruction stated: "An occurrence may be an 'unavoidable accident,' that is, an event not proximately caused by the negligence of any party to it." After the jury unanimously found that he was not negligent in rear-ending the automobile carrying Treme and Reinhart, the trial court rendered judgment in Young's favor. A divided court of appeals affirmed, holding that the instruction was proper because the overpass constituted an obstruction of view. 874 S.W.2d at 774.

II.

An unavoidable accident is "an event not proximately caused by the negligence of any party to it." *Dallas Ry. & Terminal Co. v. Bailey*, 151 Tex. 359, 250 S.W.2d 379, 385 (1952). The only purpose of the instruction is to ensure that the jury will understand that "they do not necessarily have to find that one or the other parties to the suit was to blame for the occurrence complained of." *Yarborough v. Berner*, 467 S.W.2d 188, 192 (Tex. 1971). The instruction is most often used to inquire about the causal effect of some physical condition or circumstance such as fog, snow, sleet, wet or slick pavement, or obstruction of view, or to resolve a case involving a very young child who is legally incapable of negligence. *Hill v. Winn Dixie Texas, Inc.*, 849 S.W.2d 802 (Tex. 1992). Here, for example, Young argues that an obstruction of view caused the accident.

Just two terms ago, we noted that, except in certain types of cases, "courts should refrain from submitting an unavoidable accident instruction . . . due to the risk that the jury will be misled or confused by the perception that the instruction represents a separate issue distinct from general principles of negligence." *Id.* at 803 (*citing* KEETON ET AL., PROSSER AND KEETON ON THE LAW OF TORTS § 29 at 163-64 (5th ed. 1984)). We are not alone in this concern. At least eighteen of our sister states, agreeing that the instruction confuses and misleads the jury, have prohibited its use in negligence cases. Ten other jurisdictions have severely limited the circumstances under which trial courts may instruct juries regarding unavoidable accident. And among the states that still retain the instruction, many courts have expressed concerns about its applicability in routine negligence cases. We share these reservations.

III.

Nevertheless, we did not in *Hill* reverse the judgment of the court of appeals since we concluded, based on the record as a whole, that the error was harmless. 849 S.W.2d at 803-04. We find nothing in the record before us today to suggest a different result.

Error in the jury charge is reversible only if, in the light of the entire record, it was reasonably calculated to and probably did cause the rendition of an improper judgment. *See* TEX. R. APP. P. 81(b)(1). No evidence in this case even remotely suggests that the unavoidable accident instruction in any way caused the case to be decided differently than it would have been without it.

First, Young introduced ample evidence at trial to support the jury's failure to find him negligent. Tony Pullings, Jr., the Texas Department of Public Safety officer who investigated the accident, agreed with Young's attorney that "by looking at the length of the skid marks [from Young's car], it was pretty obvious . . . that . . . Young was not exceeding the speed limit when he applied his brakes." Furthermore, Treme herself testified that she did not notice Young following her too closely, nor did she hear his tires squeal prior to the collision. This was not a close case, where a superfluous instruction would be more likely to influence the jury improperly. *See Hukill v. H.E.B. Food Stores, Inc.*, 756 S.W.2d 840, 844 (Tex. App.—Corpus Christi 1988, no writ). To the contrary, it was a case in which the defendant produced strong evidence and secured a unanimous jury verdict of no liability. *See Acord v. General Motors Corp.*, 669 S.W.2d 111, 116 (Tex. 1984).

Second, and even more important, the charge contained an instruction concerning the doctrine of sudden emergency. That instruction stated:

> When a person is confronted by an "emergency" arising suddenly and unexpectedly, which was not proximately caused by negligence on his part and which, to a reasonable person, requires immediate action without time for deliberation, his conduct in such an emergency is not negligence or failure to use ordinary care if, after such emergency arises, he acts as a person of ordinary prudence would have acted under the same or similar circumstances.

Plaintiffs made no objection whatsoever to this instruction, even though it reiterates much of the unavoidable accident instruction. *See* KEETON ET AL., *supra*, § 29 at 162 n. 1 ("The unavoidable accident doctrine logically subsumes the narrower . . . [doctrine] of . . . sudden emergency."). It is difficult to attribute an improper verdict, if any, to the unavoidable accident instruction when the charge also included without objection this instruction regarding sudden emergency.

Finally, nothing suggests that the jury in any way based its verdict on the unavoidable accident instruction. None of the witnesses referred to this term in their testimony. Furthermore, Young's attorney made little mention of it in his closing argument. In thirty minutes and fifty-three transcribed pages of argument, his only comment to the jury regarding the instruction was that Young "couldn't see . . . [Treme's car] until he got . . . on top of the hill, and there she was. And that makes it an unavoidable accident." By contrast, he spoke at much greater length about the doctrine of sudden emergency. After reading to the jurors the entire definition of a sudden emergency as stated in the charge, Young's attorney urged them to think about that particular definition when you are in there during your deliberations. If you will recall Mrs. Treme's testimony that she was stopped in the fast lane of the freeway in response to something that had happened ahead of her. And, folks, in light traffic on the freeway that is [a] . . . sudden [and] unexpected event that Mr. Young came upon. And we're going to talk more about that, but I want you to keep that definition in mind.

Returning from briefly addressing other issues, he again implored the jury that Young had faced a sudden emergency, stating: "Folks, I think that this case meets the definition that the court gave you of a sudden emergency. Mrs. Treme either stopped or going real slow in the fast lane of traffic created a sudden emergency for Mr. Young."

In light of the statement of facts and the instruction regarding sudden emergency, we fail to see how the unavoidable accident instruction could have confused or misled the jury. Moreover, this case was tried months before Hill on a charge whose elements had, at the time, never been questioned by this Court. The trial court committed no error which would justify a reversal under our well-settled principles of harmful error. Accordingly, we affirm the judgment of the court of appeals.

JUSTICE HECHT, joined by JUSTICE OWEN, concurring.

I agree, for the reasons expressed by CHIEF JUSTICE PHILLIPS in his plurality opinion, that it was not reasonably calculated to and probably did not cause the rendition of an improper judgment in this case for the trial court to instruct the jury that "[a]n occurrence may be an 'unavoidable accident,' that is, an event not proximately caused by the negligence of any party to it". I do not, however, share his reservations about the propriety of the instruction in cases in which it has long been used.

An unavoidable accident is defined as "an event not proximately caused by the negligence of any party to it." *Dallas Ry. & Terminal Co. v. Bailey*, 151 Tex. 359, 250 S.W.2d 379, 385 (1952); *see* 1 STATE BAR OF TEXAS, TEXAS PATTERN JURY CHARGES PJC 3.04 (1987). "The issue of unavoidable accident is raised when there is evidence tending to prove that the injury resulted from some cause other than the negligence of the parties." *Orange & N.W. R.R. v. Harris*, 127 Tex. 13, 89 S.W.2d 973, 975 (1936). When Texas courts permitted submission of separate jury questions to which an affirmative answer would negate liability—called "inferential rebuttal issues"—it was reversible error to refuse to inquire of the jury whether an accident was unavoidable if there was evidence that it was. *Id.*; *Galveston, H. & S.A. Ry. v. Washington*, 94 Tex. 510, 63 S.W. 534, 537-538 (1901).

Fifty years ago the unavoidable accident instruction was already entrenched in Texas jurisprudence. In *Hicks v. Brown*, 151 S.W.2d 790, 793 (Tex. 1941), we wrote:

> The rule is now too well settled in this court to be longer regarded as open to question that, where the evidence raises an issue that a plaintiff's injuries were the result of an unavoidable accident, the defendant has the right under his pleading of a general denial to have such issue separately submitted to the jury in such manner as to cast upon the plaintiff the burden of proving that his injuries were not the result of such accident.

The purpose of the instruction, we have explained, "is to call the matter to the attention of the jury, so that it will not be overlooked, and so that the jury will understand that they do not necessarily have to find that one or the other parties to the suit was to blame for the occurrence complained of." *Wheeler v. Glazer*, 137 Tex. 341, 153 S.W.2d 449, 452 (1941).

When Texas departed from its special issue practice of submitting granulated issues to the jury and adopted a broader form of jury submission, we continued to hold that a party is entitled to have the jury told about unavoidable accident when the evidence raises the issue, although the method was by instruction rather than by issue. Compare *Yarborough v. Berner*, 467 S.W.2d 188, 191 (Tex. 1971) (instruction) with *Dixie Motor Coach Corp. v. Galvan*, 126 Tex. 109, 86 S.W.2d 633, 634 (1935) (issue). The instruction, like its predecessor issue, is often referred to as being in the nature of an "inferential rebuttal". *Select Ins. Co. v. Boucher*, 561 S.W.2d 474, 477 (Tex. 1978). In *Lemos v. Montez*, 680 S.W.2d 798, 800-801 (Tex. 1984), we criticized the embellishment of jury charges with unnecessary instructions that tended to nudge the jury one way or another. Even in that context, however, we reaffirmed the use of an unavoidable accident instruction.

As recently as two terms ago this Court reaffirmed the propriety of the unavoidable accident instruction in certain cases. *Hill v. Winn Dixie Texas, Inc.*, 849 S.W.2d 802, 803 (Tex. 1992). We explained:

> An unavoidable accident instruction is proper only when there is evidence that the event was proximately caused by a nonhuman condition and not by the negligence of any party to the event . . . . The instruction is ordinarily given in cases involving environmental conditions such as fog, snow, sleet, wet or slick pavement, or obstruction of view . . . . The instruction may also be proper when there is evi-

> dence indicating that a very young child, legally incapable of negligence, was the only human cause of the accident . . . . When there is no evidence that the accident was caused by some such peculiar circumstance, submission of the instruction is generally improper . . . . Courts should refrain from submitting an unavoidable accident instruction in other circumstances due to the risk that the jury will be misled or confused by the perception that the instruction represents a separate issue distinct from general principles of negligence . . . .

(Citations omitted.) The present case, involving an alleged obstruction of view, is one situation in which *Hill* specifically approved the use of the instruction.

Some courts have criticized the instruction, as CHIEF JUSTICE PHILLIPS cites. But it is still used in a majority of states, at least in car wreck cases like this one. George L. Blum, *Annotation, Instructions on "Unavoidable Accident," "Mere Accident," or the Like, in Motor Vehicle Cases—Modern Cases*, 21 A.L.R.5TH 82, 105 (1994) ("The majority of courts still recognize that it is permissible for a trial judge to instruct juries in motor vehicle collision cases on the doctrine of unavoidable accident, mere accident or the like . . . ."). Continued use of the instruction is justified. One universally regarded commentary, not itself entirely enamored with the instruction, has acknowledged:

> Probably a majority of jurisdictions still permit the instruction in appropriate cases, however, and the instruction is still stoutly defended as helpful in focusing the issues in proper cases. Neither the unavoidable accident doctrine nor instructions thereon should be expected to wither away completely any time soon because of the notion's underlying logical simplicity and because such instructions, properly applied, may usefully serve to translate the arcane words and concepts of the law into a common sense perspective of everyday life and experience that jurors can readily understand. W. Page KEETON ET AL., PROSSER & KEETON ON THE LAW OF TORTS § 29, at 164 (5th ed. 1984) (footnotes omitted).

Concern that the instruction may mislead and confuse the jury is completely unfounded. The absolute truth, of course, is that some accidents are unavoidable. How the jury may become confused from being told the truth is not clear. There is no concrete evidence to suggest that such confusion actually occurs, and if there were, I would share JUSTICE PEEPLES' observation in *Perez v. Weingarten Realty Investors*, 881 S.W.2d 490, 498 (Tex. App.—San Antonio 1994, writ denied) (PEEPLES, J., concurring):

> If juries are not intellectually capable of understanding an inferential rebuttal instruction, we need to ask whether we have overestimated their capacity for exercising the vast power we have given them in deciding the controlling issues.
>
> Witnesses and lawyers can tell the jury all they like about an accident being unavoidable and no one fears that the jury will be confused or misled. It is not clear why the idea is confusing or misleading only when the court mentions it.
>
> Nor is the instruction redundant merely because it negatives plaintiff's case. This Court met and refuted this argument ninety-four years ago in Washington:
>
> It is claimed by counsel for appellee [the plaintiff] that the defense [of unavoidable accident] was covered by the general charge of the court in which the jury were instructed: "The burden of proof is upon the plaintiff to prove by a preponderance of the evidence each material allegation in his petition upon which he relies for recovery; and if the jury believe, from the evidence, that the plaintiff has failed to prove by a preponderance any one or more of the allegations of his petition, upon all such issues they will find for the defendant." In its general charge the court stated to the jury that the issues presented on the part of the plaintiff were that his injury was occasioned by the negligence of the defendant, specifying particularly the acts of negligence which produced the injury, and that the defendant pleaded a general denial and contributory negligence on the part of the injured boy. We must look at the court's charge as practical experience teaches that a jury, untrained in the law, would view it; and, so regarding it, we are of opinion that a jury might not have understood that the general denial made the issue of unavoidable accident, or that the injury had occurred in a manner not alleged and claimed by the plaintiff, neither of which issues was expressed in the charge of the court. While it is true that the general terms in which the court's charge is expressed would, as matter of law, include [unavoidable accident], . . . it is not to be supposed that the jury considered an issue not developed by the charge of the court.

63 S.W. at 538 (emphasis added). What we said ninety-four years ago is no less true today. While it is possible to deduce from standard instructions on ordinary care, negligence and proximate cause that some accidents are no one's fault, a party is entitled to have that fact pointed out to a jury, untrained in the law. It bears repeating: "it is not to be supposed that the jury considered an issue not developed by the charge of the court." *Id.*

This Court has approved of other inferential rebuttal instructions in numerous cases. *E.g., Dresser Indus., Inc. v. Lee*, 880 S.W.2d 750, 754-755 (Tex. 1993) (sole proximate cause); *Scott v. Atchison, T. & S.F. Ry.*, 572 S.W.2d 273, 279 (Tex. 1978) (act of God); *McDonald Transit, Inc. v. Moore*, 565 S.W.2d 43, 45 (Tex. 1978) (sudden emergency); *Davila v. Sanders*, 557 S.W.2d 770, 771 (Tex. 1977) (per curiam) (sudden emergency); *Jackson v. Fontaine's Clinics, Inc.*, 499 S.W.2d 87, 90-91 (Tex. 1973) (sole proximate cause); *Del Bosque v. Heitmann Bering-Cortes Co.*, 474 S.W.2d 450, 452-453 (Tex. 1971) (sudden emergency); *Yarborough v. Berner*, 467 S.W.2d 188, 190-191 (Tex. 1971) (sudden emergency; unavoidable accident); *Texas Motor Coaches, Inc. v. Palmer*, 132 Tex. 77, 121 S.W.2d 323, 323-324 (1938) (new and independent cause); *Tarry Warehouse & Storage Co. v. Duvall*, 131 Tex. 466, 115 S.W.2d 401, 405 (1938) (new and independent cause); *Young v. Massey*, 128 Tex. 638, 101 S.W.2d 809, 810 (1937) (new and independent cause); *Southland Greyhound Lines, Inc. v. Cotten*, 126 Tex. 596, 91 S.W.2d 326, 327-328 (1936) (new and independent cause); *Orange & N.W. R.R. v. Harris*, 127 Tex. 13, 89 S.W.2d 973, 975 (1936) (new and independent cause; unavoidable accident); *Dixie Motor Coach Corp. v. Galvan*, 126 Tex. 109, 86 S.W.2d 633, 634 (1935) (new and independent cause; sole proximate cause; unavoidable accident); *Phoenix Ref. Co. v. Tips*, 125 Tex. 69, 81 S.W.2d 60, 61-62 (1935) (new and independent cause). Just as we have continued to approve these instructions, an unavoidable accident instruction is equally proper in appropriate cases, like the present one.

The district court did not err in giving the jury an unavoidable accident instruction. Accordingly, I concur in the judgment of the Court.

JUSTICE ENOCH, concurring.

I agree with Chief Justice Phillips' opinion and the judgment of the Court. While I concur that the submission of the unavoidable accident instruction was not harmful error in this case, I write separately to express my view that the instruction should be discarded entirely.

The standard negligence and ordinary care instructions are predicated upon conduct occurring under the "same or similar circumstances." The unavoidable accident instruction, like the sudden emergency instruction, is subsumed in the standard negligence inquiry. *Thomas v. Oldham*, 895 S.W.2d 352 (Tex. 1995) (ENOCH, J., concurring). At best, these instructions are superfluous distractions that lead the jury away from determining negligence, and at worst, the reiteration of the negligence standard may be perceived by the jury as a subtle hint to find no negligence.

For over twenty years this Court has attempted to simplify jury instructions in the interest of justice. *See Lemos v. Montez*, 680 S.W.2d 798, 801 (Tex. 1984) (tracing history of jury charge reform to 1973). It is my hope that in the appropriate case the Court will completely discard this instruction that serves no useful purpose.

JUSTICE HIGHTOWER, joined by JUSTICE CORNYN and JUSTICE GAMMAGE, dissenting.

Because I would abolish the unavoidable accident instruction, which I view as misleading, confusing and unnecessary, I respectfully dissent.

The Court observes that at least eighteen states have determined that the unavoidable accident instruction is never appropriate in a negligence case and that fifteen other states have severely criticized or limited the instruction's use. The Court notes that "it shares [the] reservations" of these jurisdictions yet fails to give litigants any additional guidance regarding the proper application of an instruction which the Court admits may mislead the jury. 906 S.W.2d at 472.

I.

An examination of the unavoidable accident instruction reveals three weaknesses: there are no readily available criteria for determining whether the instruction is appropriate, the instruction may mislead and confuse the jury, and the instruction is redundant.

This Court has given only the most general directions about what conditions make the unavoidable accident instruction appropriate. For example, this Court recently observed that an unavoidable accident instruction is indicated only when there is "affirmative evidence of an extrinsic, unavoidable event" which caused the accident. *Hill v. Winn Dixie Texas, Inc.*, 849 S.W.2d 802, 803 (Tex. 1992). It has been said that the instruction is only considered proper when the event was proximately caused by a non-human condition and not by the negligence of any party to the event. *Yarborough v. Berner*, 467 S.W.2d 188, 190-91 (Tex. 1971). Another cause of an unavoidable accident might be an "unexpected catastrophe." *Hicks v. Brown*, 136 Tex. 399, 151 S.W.2d 790, 792 (1941). These ambiguous criteria make it difficult to determine the circumstances which make the instruction appropriate. Indeed, recent cases applying the instruction are in complete disarray and it appears that courts tend to determine the propriety of the instruction more on whim than on principle.

Today's majority opinion fails to clarify for litigants the circumstances under which the instruction is appropriate. I contend that this failure has occurred because no clear criteria can be enunciated. Those courts which have attempted to develop guidelines have been reduced to enumerating laundry lists of potential fact scenarios, as this Court does today, or to promulgating vague definitions. For example, in *Cooper v. Pay-N-Save Drugs, Inc.*, 59 Wash.2d 829, 371 P.2d 43, 47 (1962), the Supreme Court of Washington tried to articulate a rule for the proper application of the instruction with the following results:

> An instruction on unavoidable accident is only authorized when the evidence shows or justifies an inference that an unavoidable accident has occurred as that term has been defined. In other words, facts must be present in the case on the issue of unavoidable accident, and unless they are so present it is reversible error to give an instruction on that question.

See also Galbraith v. Fleming, 245 Va. 173, 427 S.E.2d 187, 188 (1968) (allowing instruction if "there is a reasonable theory of the evidence under which the parties involved may be held to have exercised due care notwithstanding that the accident occurred"); *Athey v. Bingham*, 823 P.2d 347, 350 (Okla. 1991) (disapproving of instruction "in the absence of a showing of some factor over which the parties had no control or could not have predicted"); *Howard v. Sanborn*, 483 N.W.2d 796, 799 (S.D. 1992) (holding that instruction may be used when element of "surprise" is present, such as sudden and unexpected presence of ice) and *Houston v. Adams*, 239 Ark. 346, 389 S.W.2d 872, 875 (1965) (noting that instruction may be appropriate when driver with no prior history of coronary disease suffers a sudden heart attack). Clearly, these cases do little to clarify when the instruction may be properly given.

The confused application of the unavoidable accident instruction results in needless appeals which waste judicial resources. The appellate courts must spend precious hours attempting to divine, for example, whether a hill constituted an "obstruction of view" or whether a cookie's placement on a grocery floor was an "extrinsic unavoidable event." *See e.g. Hill*, 849 S.W.2d at 802-3. Retaining this superfluous instruction does little to guide juries towards the correct analysis of the core concepts of negligence and proximate cause, and, as the Court concedes, may actually confuse and mislead jurors. This Court and the courts of appeal are left with the task, in effect, of micro-managing the charge on a case-by-case basis in an effort to determine whether the precise facts justify the unavoidable accident instruction.

* * *

Notes

1. *Yarborough v Brenner,* 467 S.W.2d 188 (Tex. 1971). Child of 4-5 years struck by car of D. Unavoidable accident plead and proven, as was sudden emergency. These, however, are inferential rebuttal defenses which, like new and independent cause, should not be submitted to jury as issues, but should be submitted as instructions or definitions. This holding became part of TEX.R.CIV.P. 277 in 1973 ("Inferential rebuttal question shall not be submitted in the charge.")

2. *Thomas v. Oldham*, 895 S.W.2d 352 (Tex. 1995). When the pleadings and evidence raise an issue of sudden emergency, a party is entitled to a jury instruction on the subject. This is an inferential rebuttal issue which cannot be submitted to the jury as a question, but must be submitted to the jury as an instruction, when it is raised by the evidence. Here, however, the trial court's failure was not an abuse of discretion. The court does not accept Justice Enoch's invitation to eliminate even jury instructions on inferential rebuttal matters.

3. In *Dresser Indus. v. Lee*, 880 S.W.2d 750 (Tex. 1993), the Supreme Court held that "[a] defendant in a products liability case [involving comparative causation, ed.] is entitled to have the jury instructed regarding sole cause if that issue is raised by the evidence."

4. *Louisiana-Pacific Corporation v. Knight*, 976 S.W.2d 674 (Tex. 1998). This is a personal injury case arising from a three-party rear-end collision involving Rachel Knighten, a truck owned by Louisiana-Pacific Corporation (LPC), and a truck (Cable Texas). When the collision occurred it was raining and the streets were wet. Knighten had to stop suddenly, because the car in front of her stopped without warning. Next, the LPC truck ran into the back of Knighten. Then, the Cable Texas truck hit the LPC truck from behind, and caused it to hit Knighten a second time. Knighten then sued LPC and Cable Texas for negligence. The trial court instructed the jury on sudden emergency. The court of appeals reversed, holding that it was error to submit the instruction on sudden emergency. *Held:* Reversed and rendered. The trial court did not abuse its discretion in submitting the sudden emergency instruction. The evidence supported a sudden emergency instruction for both LPC and Cable Texas. The trial court has great latitude and considerable discretion to determine necessary and proper jury instructions. If an instruction might aid the jury in answering the issues presented to them, or if there is any support in the evidence for an instruction, the instruction is proper.

5. *Dew v. Crown Derrick Errectors, Inc.*, --- S.W.3d ----, 2006 WL 1792216 (Tex.): The issue, in this wrongful death and survival action, is whether the trial court erred in refusing to submit an inferential rebuttal instruction on "new and independent cause." The court of appeals reversed and remanded for new trial. 117 S.W.3d 526, 537. ***Held:*** Reversed and remanded to the court of appeals to consider the other issues raised in the appeal. The evidence [detailed in the opinion] in this case did not require the submission of this additional instruction. Where the intervening act's risk is the very same risk that renders the original actor negligent, the intervening act cannot serve as a superseding cause.

A new and independent cause is one that intervenes between the original wrong and the final injury, such that the injury is attributed to the new cause, rather than the first and more remote cause. An intervening cause thus supersedes the defendant's negligence by destroying the causal connection between that negligence and the plaintiff's injury thereby relieving that defendant of liability. The purpose of an instruction, on new and independent cause, is to advise the jurors, in the appropriate case, that they do not have to place blame on a particular defendant to the suit if the true cause for the accident lies elsewhere. The instruction is necessary when the evidence in the case raises a fact issue on new and independent cause.

If the intervening force was foreseeable at the time of the defendant's negligence, the force is considered to be a concurring cause of the plaintiff's injuries, and the defendant remains liable for the original negligence. If, on the other hand, the intervening act is extraordinary under the circumstances, not foreseeable in the normal course of events, or independent of, or far removed from, the defendant's conduct, it may well be a superseding act. What generally distinguishes a superseding cause from one that merely concurs in the injury is that the intervening force was not only unforeseeable, but its consequences also unexpected: A superseding cause is one that alters the natural sequence of events and produces results that would not otherwise have occurred. Or one that is of such an extraordinary nature or so attenuates defendant's negligence from the ultimate injury that responsibility for the injury may not be reasonably attributed to the defendant.

DILLARD
v.
TEXAS ELECTRIC COOPERATIVE

157 S.W.3d 429
(Tex. 2005)

R. Matt Dawson, Dawson & Sodd, P.C., Corsicana, Roland G. Brown, Law Offices of Roland G. Brown, Jacksonville, Glenn Sodd, Richard Neal Green, Dawson & Sodd, P.C., Corsicana, Anatole Robert Barnstone, Law Office of Anatole Barnstone, Austin, for petitioners.

Michael V. Winchester, Winchester & Associates, P.C., Plano, Stephen Paul Bumstead., D. Bradley Dickinson, Dickinson & Associates, P.C., Dallas, for respondents.

JUSTICE O'NEILL delivered the opinion of the Court.

In this personal injury and wrongful death case, we must decide whether the trial court abused its discretion in refusing to submit one of two different instructions on the defendants' inferential rebuttal defenses. An inferential rebuttal defense operates to rebut an essential element of the plaintiff's case by proof of other facts. For example, the defendants in this case contended at trial that the fatal auto accident in issue was not caused by their negligence, but rather by the presence of cattle on the roadway or by the conduct of the cattle's owner who allowed them to be there. The jury rejected these defenses and returned a verdict for the plaintiffs, upon which the trial court rendered judgment. The court of appeals, however, reversed and remanded the case for a new trial, concluding that the jury needed more than one inferential rebuttal instruction for a full consideration of the case. ___ S.W.3d ____, 2003 WL 1884296. Because we conclude that the trial court's instruction sufficiently informed the jury about the defendants' inferential rebuttal defenses, we reverse the court of appeals' judgment and remand the case for that court to consider other issues that the defendants raised but the court did not address.

I

Texas Electric Cooperative (TEC) of Jasper, Texas, manufactures and sells utility poles. On the evening of May 27, 1996, TEC dispatched Stephen Bumstead to deliver a load of poles to Muenster, Texas, 304 miles away. About 120 miles out, traveling west on U.S. Highway 175 at about ten o'clock at night, Bumstead crested a hill and saw several dark cows on the road. Unable to stop his loaded tractor-trailer rig quickly enough without jeopardizing control, Bumstead collided with one or more of the cows, leaving one dead in the eastbound lane about 250 feet from a bridge crossing the Neches River. Maintaining control, Bumstead proceeded over the bridge and parked his truck on the shoulder about 1,500 feet beyond the dead cow. Bumstead immediately radioed an approaching trucker to warn him of the hazard ahead. Learning that the trucker had a cell phone, Bumstead requested that he call 911 to report the accident. Bumstead turned off his headlights and waited in his truck for help to arrive.

A few minutes later, Mae Joyce Brown drove past Bumstead's rig on to the bridge heading east on Highway 175. At the same time, the Dillards were approaching the bridge from the east in the unobstructed westbound lane. Crossing the bridge, Brown saw the approaching headlights of the Dillards' vehicle but did not see the dead cow in her lane of traffic. When she hit the cow, her car was thrown into the westbound lane and into the Dillards' vehicle, killing Kenneth Dillard and injuring his wife and daughter. Brown, too, was injured in the accident.

The Dillards sued TEC and Bumstead for negligence, seeking damages for their personal injuries and for Kenneth's death. Brown intervened in the suit. The Dillards and Brown subsequently joined a number of surrounding landowners as defendants, but these claims were dismissed or abandoned before trial because the cattle involved in the accident could not be traced to any of these defendants. Also before trial, Brown settled her claims against TEC and Bumstead, leaving only the Dillards' claims for the jury.

At trial, the Dillards contended that TEC and Bumstead were negligent in operating an overloaded and top-heavy truck that could not be safely stopped when it encountered obstacles in the road, and in failing to warn approaching motorists, like Brown, of the hazard that the first accident created. TEC responded that its driver had insufficient time to take evasive action and thus could not have avoided hitting the cows despite the exercise of ordinary care. TEC also claimed that its driver was not responsible for the second accident that killed Kenneth Dillard and injured his wife and daughter because that accident was solely caused by the conduct of whatever unknown person allowed the cows to be on the roadway in the first instance.

At the charge conference, TEC requested that its defensive theories be presented to the jury in two inferential rebuttal instructions, one on unavoidable accident and the other on sole proximate cause. On sole proximate cause, TEC asked that the definition of proximate cause include the following sentence:

> There may be more than one proximate cause of an event, but if an act or omission of any person not a party to the suit was the 'sole proximate cause' of an occurrence, then no act or omission of any other persons could have been a proximate cause.

See Comm. on Pattern Jury Charges, State Bar of Tex., Texas Pattern Jury Charges—General Negligence & Intentional Personal Torts PJC 3.2 (2003) (Sole Proximate Cause). The trial court refused to include this instruction, but agreed to instruct the jury on unavoidable accident, which it did in the following definition of proximate cause:

> PROXIMATE CAUSE means that cause which, in a natural and continuous sequence, produces an event, and without which cause such event would not have occurred. In order to be a proximate cause, the act or omission complained of must be such that a person using ordinary care would have foreseen that the event, or some similar event, might reasonably result therefrom. There may be more than one proximate cause of an event. An occurrence may be an "unavoidable accident," that is, an event not proximately caused by the negligence of any party to it.

See id. PJC 2.4 (Proximate Cause) & PJC 3.4 (Unavoidable Accident). The charge also included an instruction on spoliation based upon TEC's failure to produce Bumstead's trip logbook and any evidence of time and speed that it might contain. Guided by the court's charge, the jury returned a verdict upon which the trial court rendered judgment in the Dillards' favor.

In the court of appeals, TEC complained of four errors: (1) the trial court's refusal to submit a sole cause instruction, (2) the trial court's submission of a spoliation instruction, (3) the trial court's refusal to admit certain opinion testimony concerning causation, and (4) the factual insufficiency of the evidence to support the jury's finding of negligence and causation. Examining only the first issue, the court of appeals concluded that the trial court erred in refusing TEC's sole-cause instruction because a jury could have reasonably inferred from the cows' presence on the roadway that whoever owned them was the sole cause of both accidents. ___ S.W.3d at ____ & n. 2, 2003 WL 1884296, at *3-4 & n. 2. The court of appeals reversed the trial court's judgment and remanded the case for a new trial. *Id.* at ----, 2003 WL 1884296. We granted the Dillards' petition for review to consider the propriety of the trial court's charge in light of the instructions that were given.

II

When defendants blame an occurrence on someone or something other than themselves, the Texas Pattern Jury Charges provide multiple alternatives. There is a sole-proximate-cause instruction if the occurrence is caused by a "person not a party to the suit." There is an unavoidable-accident instruction if the occurrence is not caused by "the negligence of any party to it." There is a new-and-independent-cause instruction if the occurrence is caused by someone else later. There is a sudden-emergency instruction if the occurrence is caused by something other than the defendant's negligence and arises suddenly. And finally, there is an act-of-God instruction if the occurrence is caused by "the violence of nature." The purpose of these instructions is to advise the jurors, in the appropriate case, that they do not have to place blame on a party to the suit if the evidence shows that conditions beyond the party's control caused the accident in question or that the conduct of some person not a party to the litigation caused it. *Reinhart v. Young*, 906 S.W.2d 471, 472 (Tex. 1995).

TEC urges that it was entitled to two separate inferential rebuttal instructions here because there is evidence that the accidents may have been caused by a condition beyond its control-the cattle on the roadway—or by someone not a party to the litigation—either the unknown cattle owner or Brown. The Dillards contend, however, that there is no evidence that an unknown cattle owner did or failed to do anything to cause these accidents. They further maintain that TEC abandoned its claim that Brown caused the second accident by arguing at trial that no one involved in the accident was to blame—they were just "all in the wrong place at the wrong time." But rather than focus on whether or not there was evidence to support each of TEC's proposed inferential rebuttal defenses, we think it more appropriate to examine the adequacy of the charge that was given.

The trial court's charge included the following instruction: "An occurrence may be an 'unavoidable accident,' that is, an event not proximately caused by the negligence of any party to it." That instruction is a verbatim recitation from the Texas Pattern Jury Charges. Comm. on Pattern Jury Charges, State Bar of Tex., Texas Pattern Jury Charges—General Negligence & Intentional Personal Torts PJC 3.4 (2003); *see also Dallas Ry. & Terminal Co. v. Bailey*, 151 Tex. 359, 250 S.W.2d 379, 385 (1952) (approving this language). Although we have previously said that this instruction ordinarily applies to causes such as "fog, snow, sleet, wet or slick pavement, or obstruction of view," or to resolve a case involving "a very young child [who is] legally incapable of negligence," *Hill v. Winn Dixie Tex., Inc.*, 849 S.W.2d 802, 803 (Tex. 1992) (*citing Yarborough v. Berner*, 467 S.W.2d 188, 191 (Tex. 1971)), the instruction's language is not so limiting. The instruction merely informs the jury that it may consider causes of the occurrence other than the negligence of the parties. *See Galveston, H. & S.A. Ry. v. Washington*, 94 Tex. 510, 63 S.W. 534, 538 (1901) ("We must look at the court's charge as practical experience teaches that a jury, untrained in the law, would view it[.]").

Under the unavoidable-accident instruction that the trial court submitted, TEC was free to argue to the jury that no one's conduct—including Brown's—caused the accident, a far easier burden than showing that others were negligent. And that's what TEC chose to do. Although TEC pled in the alternative that Brown's negligence was the sole proximate cause of the second accident, TEC did not contend during trial that Brown was to blame for the accident. This perhaps explains why the court of appeals' opinion does not mention her conduct. The defense that TEC presented at trial focused solely on the cattle obstructing the road, implicating only the conduct of their unknown owner. Accordingly, the court of appeals relied solely on this conduct as the basis for its holding that a separate sole-proximate-cause instruction should have been submitted. Whatever the conduct of an unknown cattle owner might have been, it did not justify two separate inferential rebuttal instructions on what essentially was one defense. Because the instruction the trial court gave was sufficiently broad to include all shades of TEC's inferential rebuttal theories concerning the cattle, the trial court did not err in rejecting TEC's additional request on this same issue.

Although, as we have said, the traditional instructions do not always further the jury's understanding of the defense or conform to current broad-form practices, we believe that they do serve a legitimate purpose. *But see Reinhart*, 906 S.W.2d at 477 (ENOCH, J., concurring) (opining that the unavoidable-accident instruction should be discarded); (HIGHTOWER, J., dissenting) (same). The standard broad-form question is structured such that the jury is not asked whether any particular person was negligent, but whether "the negligence, if any," of particular persons proximately caused an occurrence. There is at least a potential implication in this phraseology that the occurrence was caused by someone's negligence. *See Hill*, 849 S.W.2d at 805 (HECHT, J., dissenting) (noting the unavoidable-accident instruction simply tells the jury "what the law recognizes—that some accidents occur without anyone's negligence"). We see no harm in explaining to the jury through an inferential rebuttal instruction that no such implication is intended. But giving multiple instructions on every possible rebuttal inference has the potential to skew the jury's analysis in the other direction.

As we have noted, the Texas Pattern Jury Charges presently parse inferential rebuttal defenses into five separate instructions. Comm. On Pattern Jury Charges, State Bar of Tex., Texas Pattern Jury Charges—General Negligence & Intentional Personal Torts PJC 3.1-3.5 (2003). Many of these instructions overlap to create redundancies that encourage parties to request several so that the point can be repeatedly emphasized. *See Schuhmacher Co. v. Holcomb*, 142 Tex. 332, 177 S.W.2d 951, 953 (1944) (holding defendant was entitled to both unavoidable-accident and sole-proximate-cause instructions, despite objection that this allowed defendant to "slice two defenses from precisely the same facts"). For example, an occurrence caused by severe weather could justify either an unavoidable-accident or an act-of-God instruction. *See Reinhart*, 906 S.W.2d at 474 (noting that the sudden-emergency instruction "reiterates much of the unavoidable accident instruction"). Similarly, the instructions on new and independent cause and sole proximate cause can cover much of the same territory. Such redundancy is contrary to the spirit of broad-form submission. *See Lemos v. Montez*, 680 S.W.2d 798, 801 (Tex. 1984).

More important, these instructions often draw distinctions among outside causes that are irrelevant to what jurors must decide. Under broad-form submission rules, jurors need not agree on every detail of what occurred so long as they agree on the legally relevant result. Thus, jurors may agree that a defendant failed to follow approved safety practices without deciding each reason that the defendant may have failed to do so. *Burk Royalty Co. v. Walls*, 616 S.W.2d 911, 924 (Tex. 1981). Similarly, the jurors here could have unanimously found Bumstead negligent, even if half believed the negligent act was overloading his truck and half believed it was failing to warn oncoming traffic—acts that preceded two different collisions.

With respect to inferential rebuttal issues, jurors need not agree on what person or thing caused an occurrence, so long as they agree it was not the defendant. If some jurors here blamed the cattle (unavoidable accident or sudden emergency) and the rest blamed the unknown cow owner (sole proximate cause), their differences would be irrelevant—they would properly return a unanimous defense verdict. Just as jurors may find against a defendant without agreeing on which precise acts were negligent, they should be able to find the opposite without agreeing on the precise reason. The trial court's instruction presented that alternative to the jury, and TEC was entitled to nothing more.

III

Because the trial court's charge adequately informed the jury about TEC's inferential rebuttal defenses, the court of appeals erred in holding that the case should be retried under a more elaborate and granulated charge. Accordingly, we reverse the judgment of the court of appeals and remand the case to that court for consideration of the other issues that TEC raised.

Note

A specific order in maritime law is one where a seaman is ordered to do a specific task in a specific manner or is ordered to do a task that can only be accomplished in one way. If a seaman is injured when carrying out a specific order his recovery of damages is not reduced by his own contributory negligence.

KING FISHER MARINE SERVICE, L.P.
v.
TAMEZ

443 S.W.3d 838
(Tex. 2014)

Daniel D. Pipitone, Steven Jon Knight, Chamberlain Hrdlicka White Williams & Aughtry, Houston, TX, for Petitioner King Fisher Marine Service, L.P.

John C. Schwambach Jr., Stevenson & Murray, P.C., Houston, TX, Respondent Jose H. Tamez.

JUSTICE BROWN delivered the opinion of the Court, in which JUSTICE JOHNSON, JUSTICE WILLETT, JUSTICE LEHRMANN, and JUSTICE BOYD joined.

In this case we consider whether a trial court must entertain charge objections up to the time it charges the jury or whether it acts within its discretion in setting an earlier deadline. . . . The court of appeals concluded the trial court acted within its discretion in refusing to hear a last-minute charge objection . . . . For the reasons below, we affirm.

We first address whether the trial court erred in refusing to consider for inclusion in the jury charge King Fisher's proposed definition of a specific order. King Fisher's request came the morning after the formal charge conference and minutes before the trial court would read the charge to the jury. Upon receiving King Fisher's objection to the charge and proposed definition, the trial court asked Tamez's counsel whether he had seen the offer. Counsel acknowledged seeing it but maintained he had not had enough time to verify that it was "the proper instruction in substantially correct form." The trial court then refused the instruction "mainly because it's not timely," adding that "we needed to have all this stuff done and in by yesterday."

When King Fisher's counsel protested that he was entitled under the Rules of Civil Procedure to lodge his objection, the trial court responded: "And that may be the rules, but my ruling to you was, everything needed to be in beforehand, and yesterday was the charge conference, and therefore, it needed to be done before the charge conference, not, you know, two minutes before I'm bringing in the jury." Indeed, as King Fisher's counsel finished making his objections to the charge at the formal charge conference the previous afternoon, the trial court warned the parties: "[T]omorrow when we come in, 'I'm not going to mess with this any further . . . . [W]hen you leave, you better be very happy with it, or unhappy, but satisfied that we got everything in that reflects my ruling." The parties apparently understood the seriousness of this warning; when King Fisher's counsel offered the specific-order definition the next morning, he conceded his understanding "from the discussions yesterday that all [King Fisher's new] objections will be overruled." He added: "I apologize for not making [the objections] yesterday, and I appreciate the Court's ruling on them before the charge is read."

Nevertheless, King Fisher argues the trial court abused its discretion in refusing its proposed definition as untimely. According to King Fisher, both Rule 272 of the Rules of Civil Procedure and our precedent in *State Department of Highways & Public Transportation v. Payne*, 838 S.W.2d 235 (Tex. 1992), provide that King Fisher's objection was timely and preserved error on appeal. The court of appeals disagreed, concluding that the trial court afforded King Fisher ample opportunity to present its proposed instruction and that refusing the instruction on the morning the charge was to be read was not an abuse of discretion. *King Fisher Marine Serv., L.P. v. Tamez*, No. 13-10-00425-CV, 2012 WL 1964567, at *6 (Tex. App.—Corpus Christi May 31, 2012, pet. granted) (mem.op.).

We review de novo any question regarding the proper interpretation of Rule 272. See *Long v. Castle Tex. Prod. Ltd. P'ship*, 426 S.W.3d 73, 78 (Tex. 2014). A trial court's rejection of a proposed definition is reviewed for abuse of discretion. *In re V.L.K.*, 24 S.W.3d 338, 341 (Tex. 2000).

King Fisher argues that Rule 272 of the Rules of Civil Procedure mandates that a trial court accept objections to the charge up to the moment it is read to the jury and that trial courts have no discretion to alter this deadline. The trial court's only discretion in the matter, King Fisher maintains, is its latitude in determining when it will charge the jury, which in turn sets a concomitant deadline for objections to the charge.

Tamez, on the other hand, argues the trial court's discretion allowed it to set an earlier deadline for charge objections and that Rule 272 demands only that the trial court afford the parties a "reasonable time" to "examine and present objections" to the charge. The trial court gave King Fisher sufficient time to review the charge and make objections, Tamez argues, and the trial court acted within its discretion in refusing to consider King Fisher's objection, made just minutes before the trial court was to read the charge.

Trial courts have "inherent power to control the disposition of cases 'with economy of time and effort for itself, for counsel, and for litigants.' " *Dow Chem. Co. v. Francis*, 46 S.W.3d 237, 240 (Tex. 2001) (per curiam) (quoting *Landis v. N. Am. Co.*, 299 U.S. 248, 254, 57 S.Ct. 163, 81 L.Ed. 153 (1936)). Accordingly, the " 'discretion vested in the trial court over the conduct of a trial is great.' " *Id.* (quoting *Schroeder v. Brandon*, 141 Tex. 319, 172 S.W.2d 488, 491 (1943)). This discretion empowers a trial court to fulfill "a duty to schedule its cases in such a manner as to expeditiously dispose of them." *Clanton v. Clark*, 639 S.W.2d 929, 930 (Tex. 1982).

Nevertheless, King Fisher argues Rule 272 prohibits trial courts from establishing a deadline for charge objections earlier than the reading of the charge to the jury. Rule 272 provides in pertinent part:

> The charge shall be in writing, signed by the court, and filed with the clerk, and shall be a part of the record of the cause. It shall be submitted to the respective parties or their attorneys for their inspection, and a reasonable time given them in which to examine and present objections thereto outside the presence of the jury, which objections shall in every instance be presented to the court in writing, or be dictated to the court reporter in the presence of the court and opposing counsel, before the charge is read to the jury. All objections not so presented shall be considered as waived.

TEX.R. CIV. P. 272.

The rule provides that a trial court may not consider any objections made after the charge is read to the jury. But it does not follow that a trial court is obligated to consider every objection made before the charge is read to the jury. Instead, the plain language of the rule sets an outside limit for charge objections. Tamez correctly argues that objecting before the charge is read to the jury is a necessary, but not always sufficient, step toward having the trial court review the merits of the objection.

Rule 272 mandates trial courts to afford the parties a "reasonable time" to inspect the charge and present objections outside the presence of the jury. Nothing in the rule prohibits a trial court from setting a deadline for charge objections that may expire before it charges the jury as long as the deadline affords the parties a "reasonable time" to inspect and object to the charge. Rule 272's reliance on reasonableness invites, rather than restricts, trial-court discretion. Accordingly, while the rule strictly prohibits objections after the charge is read, it affords trial courts latitude in addressing objections made before. And it is not surprising that many trial courts would prefer to avoid the confusion and scheduling difficulties that would arise if objections were allowed up to the moment the court plans to charge the jury.

Those courts of appeals which have encountered charge-objection deadlines all have one thing in common—none has questioned trial courts' authority to set such a deadline. Rather, in each case the inquiry focused on the reasonableness of the time allowed to review and object to the charge, which is exactly what the plain language of Rule 272 contemplates.

* * *

Although none of these cases is on all fours with this case or binding upon this Court, they demonstrate that while several courts of appeals have encountered charge-objection deadlines, none has balked at the trial court's authority to impose them. Instead, each has simply reviewed whether the trial court gave the parties what Rule 272 requires—a "reasonable time" to review and object to the charge. Rule 272's plain language has led to the courts of appeals' consistent analysis in this regard. We likewise conclude Rule 272 plainly grants trial courts authority to set a deadline for charge objections that falls before the reading of the charge to the jury. When such a deadline is set, we ask only whether a reasonable time was allowed to review and object to the charge.

Although King Fisher did not meet the trial court's charge-objection deadline, it did preserve error under Rule 272's requirement to object before the jury was charged and under the standard we set forward in *Payne*. 838 S.W.2d at 241. There is no question the trial court was aware of King Fisher's complaint before the jury was charged and ruled on it. Error was preserved, and the only remaining issue is whether the trial court's charge-objection deadline resulted in an unreasonable amount of time for the parties to review and object to the charge.

We find the time afforded was reasonable. King Fisher knew well in advance of trial that the specific-orders exception would be an issue in the jury charge. Tamez filed with the trial court eighteen days before trial a proposed jury charge including a specific-order question, putting King Fisher on notice that Tamez would push to have the question included. King Fisher responded with a "trial memorandum" six days later, arguing that the specific-orders exception did not apply.

Four days into trial the trial court held what the parties describe in their briefing as an informal charge conference. At that time, Tamez's counsel told the court the specific-order question was a significant point of disagreement between the parties. The trial court urged the parties to work together that evening to resolve charge issues in anticipation of a formal charge conference the next day.

At 9:05 the next morning, Tamez filed an amended proposed jury charge. After evidence closed shortly after noon, Tamez's counsel informed the trial court his new proposed charge contained modifications the parties agreed to the previous evening. The trial court apparently had not yet seen the new proposed charge and instructed the parties to return that afternoon for the formal charge conference. The record suggests the parties likely spent some of the intervening time working on the charge with the trial court off the record. At any rate, it is clear the trial court added the specific-order question to the charge before the formal charge conference began.

At the formal charge conference, King Fisher lodged three objections to the specific-order question, but never proposed a definition. The formal charge conference lasted nearly an hour, and near its conclusion the trial court admonished the parties that all objections should be made before the conference ended and that the trial court would not revisit the charge the next morning. Importantly, the trial court never set a deadline for the formal charge conference to end, nor did it limit the time the parties had to review its charge. It simply required the parties to make all their objections at the formal charge conference, and it did not end the formal charge conference until the parties had exhausted their objections. The parties were not under pressure to lodge objections by a time certain, nor was the formal charge conference adjourned under protest from either party.

Because the specific-orders exception was an issue between the parties in this case well before trial, the trial court's inclusion of a specific-order question in its charge could not have taken King Fisher by surprise. Even if the parties received the court's charge immediately before the formal charge conference, King Fisher does not argue anything in the charge departed from the trial court's prior rulings or that the trial court did anything more than capture what the parties had already discussed and knew was coming. The parties knew the first order of business when the trial court reconvened the next morning was to charge the jury. Yet King Fisher did not offer its proposed definition until just before the trial court was to bring in the jury. Under these facts, the trial court provided the parties a "reasonable time" to review and object to the charge, and acted within its discretion in refusing as untimely King Fisher's proposed definition.

Though we hold the trial court did not abuse its discretion, we do not necessarily endorse its decision. Trial courts can and should encourage adherence to their deadlines. Keeping a trial on schedule benefits everyone involved—trial courts benefit from the ability to manage the demands presented by their overall docket, jurors benefit from a managed, efficient trial that minimizes what already is an imposition on their daily lives, and parties and their counsel benefit from the equity that follows clear expectations. Nevertheless, these interests should be balanced with a trial judge's ultimate duty to provide the jury with a legally correct charge.

This Court has previously observed that "[o]ne of the main purposes of Rule 272 is to enable the trial court to submit a proper charge to the jury and to have the prior benefit of counsel's objections so as to correct any errors that might otherwise occur." *Mo. Pac. R.R. Co. v. Cross*, 501 S.W.2d 868, 873 (Tex. 1973). We also have recognized that the preparation of the charge comes "at that very difficult point of the trial between the close of the evidence and summation" and often forces counsel to navigate "complex, intricate, sometimes contradictory, unpredictable rules, just when counsel is contemplating the last words he or she will say to the jury." *Payne*, 838 S.W.2d at 240. Even the most skilled and experienced counsel will sometimes miss valid charge objections during informal and formal charge conferences. An objection that may seem obvious to an appellate court perusing a cold record may occur to battle-weary trial counsel only when the fog of war has lifted after a long day in the courtroom, or simply after a decent night's sleep. Trial courts should therefore make every effort to entertain on the merits a charge objection brought in good faith after conclusion of the formal charge conference but before the charge is read to the jury.

In this case, there is no evidence King Fisher raised its last-minute objection in bad faith or that its objection was groundless or intended only to delay the proceedings. The trial court presumably could have entertained the objection at issue with minimal delay to the day's proceedings. In refusing to do so, the trial court potentially risked placing its own schedule above the integrity of the charge.

But we decline to fashion a rule constraining all trial courts based on the facts of this case. A mandate for trial courts to entertain objections lodged at any time up until the charge is read to the jury is at odds with the discretion built into the plain language of Rule 272. Moreover, it is not sound policy. The rule King Fisher proposes essentially would put attorneys in charge of the trial in the time between the formal charge conference and the reading of the charge to the jury. Under such a paradigm, counsel may not take the formal charge conference seriously or prepare studiously knowing the court is powerless to refuse objections made after the charge conference is over. Moreover, such a rule would cripple the trial court's ability to prevent intentional or unnecessary delay caused by objections brought after the formal charge conference.

* * *

To summarize, we hold that Rule 272 affords trial courts the discretion to set a deadline for charge objections that precedes the reading of the charge to the jury as long as a reasonable amount of time is afforded for counsel to examine and object to the charge. We agree with the court of appeals that the trial court provided a reasonable amount of time in this case. Accordingly, we affirm the court of appeals' determination that the trial court did not abuse its discretion in refusing King Fisher's last-minute objection and proposed definition for the specific-order question.

* * *

Having concluded the trial court did not abuse its discretion in refusing to consider King Fisher's requested specific-order definition and that there was sufficient evidence to support the jury's specific-order finding, we reject both of King Fisher's arguments and affirm the judgment of the court of appeals.

JUSTICE GUZMAN, joined by CHIEF JUSTICE HECHT, JUSTICE GREEN and JUSTICE DEVINE, dissents.

For almost 100 years, our rules have expressly allowed a party to lodge objections to the charge before the trial court reads the charge to the jury. Unsurprisingly, we previously observed that Texas Rule of Civil Procedure 272 "requires a party to object to the charge . . . before the court reads the charge to the jury." Equally unsurprising is the fact that before this case, no party had asked this Court if Rule 272 means what it says or if we stand by our prior observation. Yet today, the Court reverses course and discards the Rule's brightline approach in favor of a system riddled with uncertainty and potential for abuse. In addition to conflicting with the plain language of the Rule and our prior interpretation, the Court's interpretation is at odds with our principle of liberally interpreting rules of procedure in order to resolve cases on the merits instead of relying on procedural technicalities.

The petitioner here complied with the Rule and our prior interpretation of it by objecting shortly before the trial court read the charge—only to have the trial court reject the objection as untimely. In affirming this ruling, the Court today elevates adjudication on procedural technicalities above adjudication on the merits, despite both our longstanding preference to the contrary and the plain language of the Rule. I respectfully dissent.

* * *

Jury trials are by their very nature multi-faceted, complex and fast-moving endeavors. There, perhaps more so than at any other phase in a lawsuit, it is critical to have consistent and brightline rules that ensure the parties fully understand how to preserve error. Undeniably, brightline rules necessarily implicate a balancing between efficiently managing dockets and juror resources and protecting the parties' right to have their cases adjudicated on the merits. Rule 272 already provides litigants with a brightline rule for timely submitting objections to a proposed jury charge: object before the court reads the charge. This unambiguous deadline appropriately provides all parties—plaintiffs and defendants alike—with clarity at a point in the trial in which the stakes are high and the pressure is acute, and it rewards the effort invested in the trial with a disposition on the merits. Promoting the adjudication of cases on the merits rather than on technicalities has long been a goal of this Court. Because the Court today departs from this overriding principle in straying from the plain language of Rule 272, I respectfully dissent.

2. *Requests for Submission and Objections to the Court's Charge: Preservation of Error*

Read Rules 274 & 279 Texas Rules of Civil Procedure.

PLACENCIO
v.
ALLIED INDUSTRIAL INT'L

724 S.W.2d 20
(Tex. 1987)

Russell H. McMains, William R. Edwards, Edwards, McMains, Constant & Terry, Corpus Christi, Guy Allison, Law Offices of Guy Allison, Corpus Christi, for petitioner.

Richard C. Keene, Gray & Keene, San Antonio and G. Thomas Coghlan, Lang, Cross, Ladon, Boldrick & Green, San Antonio, for respondents.

RAY, JUSTICE.

This is a products liability case. Jose Placencio was injured while operating a grinding wheel. The wheel flew apart and fragmented the right guard of the bench grinder to which the wheel was attached. The guard fragments struck Placencio in the head and face, causing severe injuries. Placencio sued Allied International, Inc. and Coast Industrial Exchange, Inc., distributors of the bench grinder. Based upon jury findings that the bench grinder was defectively marketed and designed, the trial court rendered a joint and several judgment against Allied and Coast. The court of appeals reversed the trial court's judgment and remanded the cause for a new trial, holding that the misuse issues requested by Allied should have been submitted to the jury.[1] 685 S.W.2d 364. We reverse the judgment of the court of appeals and affirm that of the trial court.

The misuse issues and definition, as requested by Allied, were as follows: "Misuse" means a use of the bench grinder that Defendant could not have reasonably foreseen. Special Issue No. 2 Do you find from a preponderance of the evidence that Jose Placencio misused the bench grinder in question? We the Jury answer ____

[1] This trial began before our decision in Duncan v. Cessna Aircraft Co., 665 S.W.2d 414 (Tex. 1984), which prospectively replaced the defense of misuse with the doctrine of comparative causation.

If you have answered the foregoing question "yes" and only in that event, answer the following question. Special Issue No. 3 Was such misuse a proximate cause of the occurrence in question? Answer "yes" or "no." We the Jury answer ____ Special Issue No. 4 Find from a preponderance of the evidence the respective percentage by which each cause contributed to the occurrence in question. Answer by stating the percentage, if any, opposite each name. The percentage you find must total 100%.

Plaintiff's misuse	_____%
Product defect	_____%
Total	100%

Placencio contends that Allied's misuse issues were not submitted to the trial court in substantially correct form and therefore that the court of appeals erred in reversing the trial court's judgment.

This situation is controlled by TEX. R. CIV. P. 279 which provides that the trial court's failure to submit an issue shall not be a ground for reversal of the judgment unless the issue was tendered in substantially correct wording. [S]ubstantially correct . . . does not mean that it must be absolutely correct, nor does it mean one that is merely sufficient to call the matter to the attention of the court will suffice. It means one that in substance and in the main is correct, and that is not affirmatively incorrect. *Modica v. Howard*, 161 S.W.2d 1093, 1094 (Tex. Civ. App.—Beaumont 1942, no writ) (emphasis added), *citing* CHIEF JUSTICE ALEXANDER'S lecture before the judicial section of the State Bar of Texas, July 3, 1941. Issue No. 4, as tendered by Allied, is affirmatively incorrect because it assumes material controverted facts. *See Johnson v. Zurich General Accident & Liability Ins. Co.*, 146 Tex. 232, 205 S.W.2d 353 (1947). The words "each cause" assume an affirmative finding of more than one cause; and it is clear that the causes referred to are the plaintiff's misuse and the product's defect. The multiple assumptions are that the product was defective, that it was misused by the plaintiff, and that both of these causes contributed to the occurrence. Because the issue as submitted by Allied assumed the truth of material controverted facts, it would have constituted a comment on the weight of the evidence. *See Shihab v. Express-News Corp.*, 604 S.W.2d 204 (Tex. Civ. App.—San Antonio 1980, writ ref'd n.r.e.).

Allied contends that this Court confronted the same question in *Alvarez v. Missouri-Kansas-Texas Railroad Co.*, 683 S.W.2d 375 (Tex. 1984) and there held that an implied comment within an issue would not require reversal. However, *Alvarez* involved a situation in which the trial court had submitted the disputed issue; therefore, we were faced with determining whether an implied comment in a submitted issue was cause for reversal of the trial court's judgment. In this case we are faced with determining whether an implied comment in a tendered issue was cause for the trial court to refuse the issue. We concluded in *Alvarez* that if there were error in the submission of the disputed issue, it was at most a harmless error and not a proper ground for reversal of the trial court. Thus, we merely applied the general rule that not every trial court error will warrant reversal of its judgment; a trial court's error must be harmful error in order to warrant reversal by an appellate court. TEX. R. APP. P. 81(b), 184.

If in spite of an implied comment, Allied's Issue No. 4 could be deemed "substantially correct," the trial court would have been forced to choose between (1) submitting it and possibly being reversed in the event of appeal by Placencio, or (2) refusing it and being reversed in the event of appeal by Allied. We will not impose such a dilemma upon a trial judge. It was Allied's duty to present the judge with an issue that was not affirmatively incorrect. We hold that the trial court's refusal to submit an affirmatively incorrect issue does not justify reversal; therefore the court of appeals erred in reversing the trial court's judgment.

Allied could have submitted Issue No. 4 in proper form by conditioning it on affirmative answers to prior issues establishing the assumed facts. We approve the State Bar's suggested form of misuse submission in the Texas Pattern Jury Charges. Unlike Allied's issue, the form suggested by the Texas Pattern Jury Charges is preceded by conditioning language that reads: If you have found that the product in question was defective in some manner that was a producing cause of the occurrence in question and you have also found that (the plaintiff) misused the product in some manner that was a proximate cause of the occurrence in question, and only in that event, then answer Question 3. 3 STATE BAR OF TEXAS, TEXAS PATTERN JURY CHARGES PJC § 72.02A (1982).

Allied also tendered a series of ten other more specific misuse issues. Each of these issues also assumed a disputed fact issue. Therefore, the trial court was justified in refusing to submit them. TEX. R. CIV. P. 279.

* * *

We reverse the judgment of the court of appeals and affirm the judgment of the trial court.

SPEARS, J., concurs with opinion.
HILL, CHIEF JUSTICE, dissenting.

I dissent. The trial court's refusal to submit a requested special issue constitutes reversible error if (1) there is evidence supporting submission of the issue, TEX. R. CIV. P. 277, and (2) the party requesting the issue tendered it to the court in substantially correct form, TEX. R. CIV. P. 279. Having searched the record, I find that there is some evidence that Placencio improperly installed the grinding wheel as an integral part of the working unit, that he applied excessive pressure to the side of the grinding wheel, and that he jammed the drill bit between the grinding wheel and the bench grinder's guard. Thus, there is evidence to support a finding that Placencio's misuse proximately caused this injury and this evidence supports the submission of Allied's misuse issues to the jury. Allied's misuse issues therefore should have been submitted unless they were not tendered in substantially correct form.

Allied's misuse instruction and special issues numbers 2 and 3 were contained in the Texas Pattern Jury Charges. 3 STATE BAR OF TEXAS, TEXAS PATTERN JURY CHARGES PJC 72.02B (1982). Special issue number 4 was also contained in the Texas Pattern Jury Charges; however, the pattern jury charge is preceded by the following conditioning language: If you have found that the product in question was defective in some manner that was a producing cause of the occurrence in question and you have also found that [the plaintiff] misused the product in some manner that was a proximate cause of the occurrence in question, and only in that event, then answer [the following question]. *Id.* Because Allied did not similarly condition its requested special issue number 4, the majority has concluded that the issue was a comment on the weight of the evidence. According to the majority, the words "each cause" suggested that both Allied and Placencio must have contributed to the accident. Thus, the majority reasons that the trial court properly refused to submit the issue to the jury because Allied did not submit the issue in substantially correct form.

I disagree. Allied positioned special issue number 4 after two other requested issues which asked whether the plaintiff misused the product, and if so, whether such misuse was a proximate cause of the occurrence. In addition, special issue number 4 specifically stated that the jury should not assign a percentage of the fault to Placencio unless his misuse of the bench grinder, "if any," contributed to the accident. Because Allied's special issue number 4 was positioned after those two other issues and because it contained the "if any" language, I believe that any impermissible comment on the weight of the evidence was eliminated, and that Allied's tendered misuse issues were in substantially correct form. "Substantially correct form" does not mean perfect. *Fawcett v. Bellah*, 556 S.W.2d 598, 602 (Tex. Civ. App.—Corpus Christi 1977, no writ); *Call of Houston, Inc. v. Mulvey*, 343 S.W.2d 522 (Tex. Civ. App.—Houston 1961, no writ); *Modica v. Howard*, 161 S.W.2d 1093 (Tex. Civ. App.—Beaumont 1942, no writ).

The majority does not, of course, deny that this Court would have upheld the submission of Allied's special issues if the trial court had actually submitted them. To the contrary, this Court would have upheld the submission of those issues on the ground that any implied comment on the weight of the evidence was harmless error. *See Alvarez v. Missouri-Kansas-Texas Railroad Co.*, 683 S.W.2d 375 (Tex. 1984). Yet, despite this fact, the majority has taken the anomalous position that Allied's requested issues are affirmatively incorrect.

As its reliance on nearly forty-year-old precedent demonstrates, the majority opinion signals a retreat back to the hypertechnical special issues practices previously disavowed by this Court. "[I]n an already complicated field like that of special issues, we cannot strain too hard for perfection without ultimate damage to the whole jury system in civil cases." *Id.* at 378; *Mason v. Yellow Cab & Baggage Co.*, 153 Tex. 344, 349, 269 S.W.2d 329, 331 (1954). Accordingly, I would affirm the judgment of the court of appeals and remand the cause for new trial.

CAMPBELL and GONZALEZ, JJ., join in this dissent.

LYLES
v.
TEXAS EMPLOYERS' INSURANCE ASSOCIATION

405 S.W.2d 725
(Tex. Civ. App.—Waco 1966, writ ref'd, n.r.e.)

Phelps, Kilgarlin & Snell, Houston, for appellant.
Fulbright, Crooker, Freeman, Bates & Jaworski, Jerry V. Walker, Houston, for appellee.

WILSON, JUSTICE.

The points in this workmen's compensation death case relate to the court's charge to the jury on 'producing cause' of death, a comment by the trial judge concerning whether medical text books had been 'accepted in evidence', and refusal to place witnesses 'under the rule' as authorized by Rule 267, Texas Rules of Civil Procedure. Judgment was rendered against the carrier for temporary total incapacity benefits and medical and hospital expenses prior to the employee's death.

The cause of death was controverted. Other facts were not in issue, and the court submitted one special issue: 'Do you find from a preponderance of the evidence that the accidental injury of Monroe Lyles on July 13, 1959 was a producing cause of the death of Monroe Lyles?' The jury answered, 'We do not.'

The court defined 'injury' as damage or harm to the physical structure of the body and such diseases or infection as naturally result therefrom, or the indictment, acceleration or aggravation of any disease previously or subsequently existing by reason of such damage or harm to the physical structure of the body.' The term 'producing cause' was defined as:

> 'That cause which in a natural and continuous sequence produces the death and without which the death would not have occurred.'

There are no objections to the charge.

Plaintiff's requested definition: 'By the term 'producing cause' is meant a cause which in a natural and continuous sequence, by itself, or in connection with other cause or causes, produces disability or death of a person, and without which such disability or death would not have occurred. There may be more than one producing cause', was refused.

Failure to object to a charge before submission waives the objection, under Rule 274, Texas Rules of Civil Procedure. *Texas Emp. Ins. Ass'n v. Neuman*, Tex.Sup., 379 S.W.2d 295; *Allen v. American Nat. Ins. Co.*, Tex. Sup., 380 S.W.2d 604.

Although it is now well established, we repeat that under Rules 273, 274, 276, and the first paragraph of Rule 279, a Request for submission is the method of preserving the right to complain of Omission of, or failure to submit an Issue which is relied on by the Complaining party. Objection, however, is the proper method of preserving complaint as to (1) an issue actually Submitted, but claimed to be defective; or (2) Failure to submit, where the ground of recovery or defense is Relied on by the opposing party.

In the case of explanatory instructions and Definitions: if they are Omitted, under Rule 279 a Request is prerequisite to complaint of the omission by any party, irrespective of reliance on an issue. *Great American Indemnity Co. v. Sams*, 142 Tex. 121, 176 S.W.2d 312, syl. 4; *Yellow Cab and Baggage Company v. Green*, 154 Tex. 330, 277 S.W.2d 92, 93. If the Definition is Given, but is claimed to be Defective, under Rule 274 Objection is the means of preserving the complaint. *Angelina Casualty Company v. Holt*, Tex. Sup., 362 S.W.2d 99, 101. *Texas Employers' Ins. Ass'n v. Mallard*, 143 Tex. 77, 182 S.W.2d 1000, 1002.

A request for submission is not an available alternative to an objection as a means of pointing out a defect in, or preserving a complaint to a submitted definition or instruction. The request embodying an element omitted will not be given effect as an objection under Rule 274; *City of Dallas v. Priolo*, 150 Tex. 423, 242 S.W.2d 176, 179, syl. 4; *Texas Employers' Insurance Ass'n v. Neuman*, Tex. Sup., 379 S.W.2d 295, 296; *Stuckey v. Union Mortgage & Investment Company*, Tex. Civ. App., 383 S.W.2d 429, 439, writ ref. n.r.e.; *Foley, v. Foley*, Tex. Civ. App., 350 S.W.2d 890, 892; *Southwestern Settlement & Develop. Corp. v. State*, Tex. Civ. App., 282 S.W.2d 78, 85, writ ref. n.r.e.; *White v. Southwest Coaches*, Tex. Civ. App., 292 S.W.2d 823; Hodges, Special

Issue Submission, 154, 162. Appellants' complaint as to the element asserted to be omitted is not preserved by objection, and the points are overruled.

* * *

Affirmed.

Notes

1. *Lyles* represents the "traditional" reading of the rules related to preservation of error to jury charges. As will be seen, the modern judges chaff under this "traditional" reading, and, while the rules have not changed, the interpretation has.

2. *Dallas Market Center Development Co. v. Liedeker,* 958 S.W.2d 382 (Tex. 1997). An objection is sufficient to preserve error in a defective instruction. A request of substantially correct language is not required. The trial court's statements on the record preserved DMC's complaint that the case should have been submitted to the jury on a premises liability theory, rather than a negligent activity theory. Thus, an endorsement by the trial court is not the exclusive means of preserving error for refusing a charge request. In this case, the trial court admitted that he had considered the requested question, had refused it, and had meant to endorse it, but simply filed to do so, for which he was sorry. The error was preserved.

3. *St. Joseph Hospital v. Wolff,* 94 S.W.3d 513 (Tex. 2002): Whether a definition used in the charge misstated the law is a legal question, which is reviewed de novo. The sufficiency of the evidence is measured against the jury charge that was actually submitted, which the appellants claimed was defective, and not against the charge that the trial court should have submitted, when the opposing party fails to object to the charge. Here, however, St. Joseph properly preserved error by objecting to the joint enterprise definition used in the charge. Because the trial court submitted an erroneous definition of joint enterprise over a proper objection, the legal sufficiency of the evidence is supporting the jury's finding of joint enterprise is measured against the Restatement's definition of joint enterprise.

4. *Holubec v. Brandenberger*, 111 S.W.3d 32 (Tex. 2003): In this nuisance case, the defendants, the Holubecs, specifically objected to the date submission in Question 8 of the charge, which read: "Have the conditions or circumstances complained of as constituting the basis for the nuisance action . . . remained substantially unchanged since December 31, 1986?". Held: Although the Holubecs' requested submission was not specifically tied to "the conditions or circumstances complained of as constituting the basis for the nuisance action", they plainly sought the submission of their statutory defense that the operation in question had existed substantially unchanged since on or before July 30, 1997. Because the question actually submitted was defective (because it submitted the wrong date), however, the Holubecs did not have to submit their own substantially correct question. The Holubecs' objection was sufficient to preserve error. TEX. R. CIV. P. 274.

MORRIS
v.
HOLT

714 S.W.2d 311
(Tex. 1986)

Patrick A. Pirtle, Amarillo, for petitioner.
Rick Keffler, Amarillo, for respondent.

RAY, JUSTICE.

This is a suit to recover an equity interest in two restaurants. We are asked whether Defendant's issue tendered in substantially correct form, but refused, is sufficient under TEX. R. CIV. P. 279 to preserve error concerning an omitted issue relied upon by the opponent. We are additionally faced with the situation that the jury answers do not support a judgment for the Plaintiff, Jim Holt. After a jury trial, the trial court rendered judgment favorable to Holt. The court of appeals affirmed in an unpublished opinion. We reverse the judgments of the trial court and the court of appeals and render a judgment that Holt take nothing.

In May, 1979, Holt and Morris agreed in writing that Holt was to manage two restaurants owned by Morris. For his performance of services, Holt would receive a salary plus twenty percent (20%) of the net profits from the two restaurants. The agreement also provided that Morris was to retain the net profits from the two restaurants until they equaled twenty percent (20%) of the total $400,000 estimated value of the restaurants or until five (5) years had passed, whichever occurred first. Upon the happening of these events, Holt would own twenty percent (20%) of both restaurants. In November, 1980, the parties orally agreed to change the twenty percent (20%) figures in their agreement to fifty percent (50%).

In November, 1981, Holt terminated his employment with Morris and later sued Morris for "breach of an agreement to form a partnership" because Morris refused to sign a partnership agreement contract. Morris responded by denying the parties had ever agreed to form a partnership. He also pleaded the statute of frauds as an affirmative defense. Morris additionally argued that Holt breached the employment contract by failing to remain as manager of the restaurants for a period of five (5) years.

Morris tendered issues inquiring whether the parties had agreed to form a partnership and whether the parties had agreed that if Holt terminated his employment prior to five years that Morris was to purchase Holt's accumulated equity interest. These issues were refused, although they were supported by Holt's pleadings. Morris then objected that the submitted Issue No. 1 improperly placed the burden on him as defendant. Holt, however, requested no issue which could support a favorable judgment for him. Nor did he move for a summary judgment or instructed verdict.

The trial court submitted two issues to the jury. The first issue is set out as follows:

Issue No. 1

Do you find from a preponderance of the evidence that the parties agreed that Jim Holt was required to work five years for Abe Morris before he would own any equity interest in the two Sirloin Stockades? Answer: "They did agree" or "They did not agree." The jury answered "they did not agree." The second issue dealt with the statute of frauds and whether the oral agreement between Morris and Holt could have been performed within one year. The jury found the agreement was performable within one year. Upon the two jury findings, the trial court rendered judgment for Holt.

In his appeal, Morris argued the trial court erred in refusing to submit his requested issues. Morris explains that in response to the trial court's inquiry as to what objections he had to the proposed charge, Morris orally requested the court to submit the issues. When this was denied, he tendered a written request for the same issues. These were refused by the trial court. The court of appeals held that for Morris to preserve error on these omitted issues, he was required to object to the charge for failure to submit an issue relied upon by Holt.

> The court of appeals, relying upon the opinion in *Jon-T Farms Inc. v. Goodpasture, Inc.*, 554 S.W.2d 743, 751 (Tex. Civ. App.—Amarillo 1977, writ ref'd n.r.e.), concluded that Morris' written request for submission of the issues was insufficient to preserve his complaint on appeal as to the trial court's failure to submit the issues. We disagree with this interpretation of Rule 279, TEX. R. CIV. P. which provides in pertinent part as follows: Failure to submit an issue shall not be deemed a ground for reversal of the judgment, unless its submission, in substantially correct wording, has been requested in writing and tendered by the party complaining of the judgment; provided, however, that objection to such failure shall suffice in such respect if the issue is one relied upon by the opposing party. Rule 279 permits a party in Morris' position to preserve error as to the trial court's failure to submit an issue by making a timely, specific objection or by requesting submission of the issue in substantially correct form.

We believe *Clarostat Mfg., Inc. v. Alcor Aviation, Inc.*, 544 S.W.2d 788 (Tex. Civ. App.—San Antonio 1976, writ ref'd n.r.e.) correctly analyzes this issue: [T]here is nothing in the Rule to support the conclusion that an objection is the only way of calling such omission to the attention of the trial court. Rule 279 requires tender of an issue in substantially correct form, but then goes on to provide that where the omitted issue is one relied upon by the opposing party, an objection shall be sufficient. A statement to the effect that an objection is "sufficient" cannot be construed reasonably as a statement to the effect that an objection is "the sole method by which the error can be preserved." All the Rule says is that when the omitted issue is an issue relied on by the opponent, it shall not be necessary to tender an issue in substantially correct form. It does not say that in case of such an omission the tender of an issue in substantially correct form is insufficient. The purpose of the Rule is to place a more onerous burden on the party relying on the omitted issue than on the opponent. There is nothing in the language to indicate that a party who notes the omission of an issue relied on by his opponent cannot call the omission to the court's attention by tendering the omitted issue for submission. 544 S.W.2d at 794.

The issues tendered by Defendant Morris were sufficient to preserve error under Rule 279.

In his pleadings, Holt requested relief based upon a theory that Morris had breached an agreement to form a partnership. At trial, the case was apparently tried by consent under a theory that Morris had breached an oral agreement which, although not constituting an agreement to form a partnership, did call for Holt to request submission of any issues relating to either of these theories of recovery. Finally, Holt may not rely upon the jury's negative answers to the two submitted defensive issues. The trial court cannot use a negative finding of a defensive issue to support a plaintiff's claim for affirmative relief. *Grenwelge v. Shamrock Reconstructors, Inc.*, 705 S.W.2d 693 (Tex. 1986).

Since no jury answers were obtained as to any issue supporting Holt's recovery and the only jury answers examined were negative findings to Morris' defensive issues, we reverse the judgment of the court of appeals and render judgment that Holt take nothing.

STATE DEP'T OF HIGHWAYS & PUBLIC TRANSP.
v.
PAYNE
838 S.W.2d 235
(Tex. 1992)

Dan Morales, Randy Hill, Austin, for petitioner.
John L. Pierce, II, Navasota, Samuel J. Lee, II, Angleton, for respondents.

HECHT, JUSTICE.

On motion for rehearing, our opinion of September 11, 1991, is withdrawn, and the following is now the opinion of the Court.

Kenneth Payne and his wife sued the State Department of Highways and Public Transportation to recover damages for injuries which he sustained when he walked off the end of a culvert built and maintained by the State. A jury found that Payne's injuries were caused 60% by the negligence of the State and 40% by his own negligence, and the trial court rendered judgment in Payne's favor for $148,800 plus interest. The court of appeals affirmed. 781 S.W.2d 318 (Tex. App. 1989). The two principal issues now before us are first, whether the trial court held the State to a higher standard of care than that imposed by section 101.022 of the Texas Tort Claims Act, TEX. CIV. PRAC. & REM. CODE § 101.022, and thus failed to submit the controlling question of fact to the jury, and second, whether the State has preserved this complaint for appeal. We answer both issues in the affirmative, and consequently reverse the judgment of the court of appeals and render judgment that Payne take nothing.

I

Payne's injury occurred before sunrise one morning as he walked from his home in the country across a two-lane paved road toward a deer blind he had constructed in a field. A culvert ran perpendicular to and beneath the road, ending about 22 feet from the roadbed on the deer blind side. In the dark, Payne stepped off the culvert and fell about 12 feet into a drainage ditch, sustaining injuries. Although Payne knew there was a culvert near where he was walking, he claimed that he did not see where it ended that morning because vegetation obscured it and a reflective marker was missing.

Payne alleged in his pleadings that the culvert was both a special defect and a premise defect; the State denied that the culvert was a defect of any kind. If the culvert was a premise defect, the State owed Payne the same duty a private landowner owes a licensee. TEX. CIV. PRAC. & REM. CODE § 101.022(a); *State v. Tennison*, 509 S.W.2d 560, 562 (Tex. 1974). That duty requires that a landowner not injure a licensee by willful, wanton or grossly negligent conduct, and that the owner use ordinary care either to warn a licensee of, or to make reasonably safe, a dangerous condition of which the owner is aware and the licensee is not. *Id.*; *see* RESTATEMENT (SECOND) OF TORTS § 342 (1965). If the culvert was a special defect, the State owed Payne the same duty to warn that a private landowner owes an invitee. TEX. CIV. PRAC. & REM. CODE § 101.022(b); *Harris County v. Eaton*, 573 S.W.2d 177, 180 (Tex. 1978). That duty requires an owner to use ordinary care to reduce or eliminate an unreasonable risk of harm created by a premises condition of which the owner is or reasonably should be aware.

* * *

There are two differences between these theories. The first is that a licensee must prove that the premises owner actually knew of the dangerous condition, while an invitee need only prove that the owner knew or reasonably should have known. The second difference is that a licensee must prove that he did not know of the dangerous condition, while an invitee need not do so.

In this case, the State built the culvert and thus knew of its existence. That element under either theory of liability is not in dispute. Nor do the parties dispute that Payne knew of the existence of the culvert. The point of contention is whether Payne knew the culvert was in his path as he walked through the undergrowth in the dark. After all, Payne argues, he would hardly have stepped off the edge and fallen twelve feet to serious injury had he known, or had he been adequately warned, that the culvert was in front of him. But, the State responds, he nevertheless knew that the culvert was there somewhere, and his knowledge precludes imposition of liability on the State unless the culvert was a special defect. Both parties introduced evidence regarding Payne's knowledge of the location of the culvert.

At the close of the evidence the trial court gave the jury a charge which asked two liability questions. The first question inquired whether Payne's or the State's negligence was a proximate cause of the occurrence. The second question asked what percentage of such negligence was attributable to each. In addition to the standard definitions of negligence, proximate cause and ordinary care, the trial court gave the jury the following instructions: "GOVERNMENTAL LIABILITY": A governmental unit in the state is liable for personal injury and death so caused by a condition or use of tangible personal or real property if the governmental unit would, were it a private person, be liable to the claimant according to Texas law. "DUTY OWED: SPECIAL DEFECT": Where there is a special defect such as an excavation or obstruction on or adjacent to a highway, road, or street or where there is the absence or malfunction of a traffic sign, signal or warning device that is required by law, the governmental unit owes to the plaintiff a duty to warn of such special defect. The duty owed is a duty to use ordinary care to either warn of a dangerous condition or to make such dangerous condition reasonable safe, provided the governmental unit had knowledge of the dangerous condition, or through the exercise of ordinary care, should have had knowledge of the dangerous condition. "DANGEROUS CONDITION" means a condition other than normally connected with the use of the roadway, excavation or obstruction, and a person using ordinary care could not encounter such condition with safety. The State's complaint is that the jury charge erroneously assumed that the culvert was a special defect and did not submit Payne's premise defect liability theory to the jury. Specifically, the State complains that the charge does not request the jury to find whether Payne knew of the location of the culvert at the time of his accident.

In effect, the trial court determined that the culvert was a special defect as a matter of law. The court of appeals agreed. 781 S.W.2d at 322. To the extent they treated the issue as a question of law rather than of fact, both courts were correct. Whether a condition is a premise defect or a special defect is a question of duty involving statutory interpretation and thus an issue of law for the court to decide. *Eaton*, 573 S.W.2d at 179-80; *see also Blankenship v. County of Galveston*, 775 S.W.2d 439, 441-42 (Tex. App.—Houston [1st Dist.] 1989, no writ). However, both courts incorrectly determined the status of the culvert.

Special defects are excavations or obstructions on highways, roads, or streets. TEX. CIV. PRAC. & REM. CODE § 101.022(b); *see Eaton*, 573 S.W.2d at 179. These examples set forth in the statute itself all present an unexpected and unusual danger to ordinary users of roadways. The culvert in this case was not a special defect. The end of the culvert was located far enough from the paved surface that vehicular passengers and other normal users of the roadway were unlikely to encounter it. Payne, unlike an ordinary user of the road, was walking perpendicular to the paved surface into the adjacent field. Only such a pedestrian, whose destination required him to leave the proximity of the road, was ever likely to fall off the end of the culvert. If there was a defect, it was in the field where Payne was walking. The State's duty of care with respect to such a defect is covered by the ordinary rule for premise defects under section 101.022(a).

II

Payne nevertheless argues that the State has not preserved its complaint that the trial court erred in refusing to inquire of the jury concerning his knowledge of the culvert. The State's sole objection to the charge was that the "Duty Owed" paragraph quoted above "constitutes a comment upon the weight of the evidence and amounts to an instruction to the jury that there is, in fact, a special defect, removes that issue from the province of the jury and keeps from it being a fact issue as it should be." Payne argues that this objection was not sufficiently clear to call to the trial court's attention the State's complaint that the culvert should not have been assumed to be a special defect. This argument is rather dubious in the circumstances of this case. The trial court's failure to submit Payne's premise liability theory could hardly have been an oversight. The very fact that it included instructions concerning special defects in the charge indicates that the trial court decided that the culvert was a special defect and not a premise defect. Furthermore, the trial court had allowed the parties to present evidence and argument concerning Payne's knowledge, which would have been irrelevant if the culvert was a special defect. The trial court was certainly aware that the issue was disputed.

Even if the State's objection was insufficient, the State preserved error by requesting the trial court to inquire of the jury concerning Payne's knowledge of the culvert. *Morris v. Holt*, 714 S.W.2d 311 (Tex. 1986). Specifically, the State requested the trial court to include the following question in the charge: Do you find from a preponderance of the evidence that Kenneth Herschel Payne had actual knowledge that the culvert was at the location in question on F.M. 1301? Although this question places the burden of proof on the State rather than on Payne where it belongs, Payne can hardly complain. The trial court's refusal to ask the question requested by the State constituted a clear refusal to submit a premise defect theory to the jury.[2]

We do not suggest, of course, that the trial court should have submitted the case to the jury on specific questions rather than broad-form questions, as required by Rule 277, TEX. R. CIV. P. The issue is not whether the trial court should have asked the jury the specific question requested by the State; rather, the issue is whether the State's request called the trial court's attention to the State's complaint that no premise liability theory was submitted to the jury sufficiently to preserve that complaint for appeal. The State's requested question clearly called the trial court's attention to the State's complaint because it was the sole element of premise defect liability missing from the charge. Payne appears to argue that the State would have preserved error if it had plainly objected: "The charge submits only a special defect theory and not a premise defect theory." The State's request is clearer than such an objection because it calls attention to the very element of the premise defect theory omitted from the charge. The request not only objects to the omission of the theory, it suggests the missing language necessary to correct the omission. The trial court should have included the missing element in its broad-form submission in an appropriate manner.

We have received two amicus briefs concerning the proper method for preserving a complaint about the jury charge, like the State's complaint in this case. In our State's procedural jurisprudence, there are no rules more recondite than those pertaining to the preparation of the jury charge. As Professor McDonald observed forty years ago: "No aspect of procedure has developed a greater tangle of perplexities than that which embraces the rules as to the charge of the court to the jury." 3 ROY W. MCDONALD, TEXAS CIVIL PRACTICE IN DISTRICT AND COUNTY COURTS § 12.01, at 222 (Frank W. Elliott ed., 1983). The passage of time has not improved things. Dozens of cases decided since Professor McDonald wrote, many of them flatly contradictory, attest to myriad uncertainties in preserving complaints of error in the jury charge. The rules governing charge procedures are difficult enough; the caselaw applying them has made compliance a labyrinth daunting to the most experienced trial lawyer. Today, it is fair to say that the process of telling the jury the applicable law and inquiring of them their verdict is a risky gambit in which counsel has less reason to know that he or she has protected a client's rights than at any other time in the trial.

---

2 The issue of Payne's knowledge of the location of the culvert is not merely a "phase or shade" of the broad question of the State's liability, as the dissent argues. Rather, it is a key issue in dispute in the case. Nor would a finding that Payne knew of the culvert's location have conflicted with a finding that the State was negligent, as the dissent argues. Rather, such a finding would simply have precluded liability.

The preparation of the jury charge, coming as it ordinarily does at that very difficult point of the trial between the close of the evidence and summation, ought to be simpler. To complicate this process with complex, intricate, sometimes contradictory, unpredictable rules, just when counsel is contemplating the last words he or she will say to the jury, hardly subserves the fair and just presentation of the case. Yet that is our procedure. To preserve a complaint about the charge a party must sometimes request the inclusion of specific, substantially correct language in writing, which frequently requires that even well prepared counsel scribble it out in longhand sitting in the courtroom. The rules of procedure require that the judge endorse each request with specific language, although sometimes this requirement is ignored. Sometimes a request is not sufficient and may not even be appropriate; instead, counsel must object. The objection must be specific enough to call the court's attention to the asserted error in the charge. It is not clear whether a request will serve as an objection or an objection as a request. Rather than attempt to decide under the pressure of the courtroom and in peril of losing appellate rights, whether an objection or a request is called for, cautious counsel might choose to do both in all cases—request and object. But if they are not kept separate, or if an appellate court later decides that the duplication obscured the real complaint, counsel's precaution may still result in a decision that the complaint was waived.

The procedure has been further complicated by our adoption of broad issue submission, a change intended to have the opposite effect. When special issue practice flourished in Texas, it was easier to determine which party had responsibility for submission of a particular matter to the jury, and which party had the obligation to object to misstatements in order to preserve error. That practice, however, had a host of troubles of its own, causing this Court to reject it in the last decade in favor of broad form submission. Now, however, it is impossible to determine which party has responsibility for each part of a charge. Because many instructions in a broad form charge bear upon elements of proof not easily divisible among the parties, it is hard to know who should complain. Recently it was argued before this Court that a party who objected to any submission at all of an issue proposed by his opponent, waived that objection if, alternatively, he proposed different language more favorable to his position. The process is becoming worse, not better.

The flaws in our charge procedures stem partly from the rules governing those procedures and partly from caselaw applying those rules. Last year we asked a special task force to recommend changes in the rules to simplify charge procedures, and amendments are under consideration. Rules changes must await the completion of that process; we do not revise our rules by opinion. *Alvarado v. Farah Mfg. Co.*, 830 S.W.2d 911, 915 (Tex. 1992). We can, however, begin to reduce the complexity that caselaw has contributed to charge procedures. The procedure for preparing and objecting to the jury charge has lost its philosophical moorings. There should be but one test for determining if a party has preserved error in the jury charge, and that is whether the party made the trial court aware of the complaint, timely and plainly, and obtained a ruling. The more specific requirements of the rules should be applied, while they remain, to serve rather than defeat this principle. In this case, the State clearly met this test.

* * *

Payne was not entitled to recover on his special defect theory as a matter of law. To prevail on his premise defect theory, Payne was required to obtain a finding that he lacked knowledge of the culvert. This element of his claim was not included in the broad-form charge which the trial court submitted to the jury.[3] A finding on this one element cannot be deemed in Payne's favor because the State objected to the omission by requesting a jury question on that issue. TEX. R. CIV. P. 279; *Morris*, 714 S.W.2d 311, 312-13. Thus, the verdict does not support a judgment in Payne's favor.

Accordingly, the judgment of the court of appeals is reversed, and judgment is rendered that Payne take nothing.

---

[3] The transcript does not reveal whether Payne requested that these elements of his claim be submitted to the jury. If he had requested them in substantially correct form, it would have been error for the trial court to refuse to submit them. TEX.R.CIV.P. 278. If any such error occurred, however, Payne has waived it because he can not demonstrate from the record that he requested submission of these elements.

MAUZY, JUSTICE, dissenting.

The dissenting opinion of September 11, 1991 is withdrawn, and the following is substituted in its place.

Today the court reaches an issue improperly, decides it wrongly, and disposes of the case unfairly. I dissent.

I.

In its eagerness to reach the issue of the State's duty, the court takes pains to excuse the State's failure to make a proper objection to the jury charge. Because any complaint regarding a defective instruction is waived unless specifically included in a proper objection, TEX. R. CIV. P. 274, I would hold that the State has waived the error it now asserts.

The trial court submitted a broad-form jury charge along with instructions regarding the State's duty. The instructions explained the duty associated with a special defect, but did not discuss the duty applicable in the absence of a special defect. Guided by those instructions, the jury found the State negligent. The trial court rendered judgment on the verdict, reducing the jury's award in accordance with separate findings on comparative negligence.

The State now argues that the obscured culvert should have been treated as an ordinary premise defect, rather than a special defect, as a matter of law. We do not know how the trial court would have responded to this argument, because there is no indication in the record that the State ever urged this view at trial. In fact, the State's only objection to the charge took a very different position: the State argued, wrongly, that the characterization of the culvert should be left to the jury. The objection did not assert that the property's condition was an ordinary premise defect; nor did it point out any inadequacy concerning the duty applicable to an ordinary premise defect.

To preserve any contention that the trial court erroneously charged the jury on the State's duty to Payne, the State was required to object to the trial court's instructions. TEX. R. CIV. P. 274; *see Yellow Cab and Baggage Co. v. Green*, 154 Tex. 330, 277 S.W.2d 92, 93 (1955) (holding that when trial court gives erroneous instruction, objection is required to preserve error). A vague or incorrect objection, however, does not suffice to preserve error. An objection to the charge must distinctly point out the objectionable matters and the grounds of the objection. TEX. R. CIV. P. 274; *Wilgus v. Bond*, 730 S.W.2d 670, 677 (Tex. 1987). An objection is insufficient to preserve error if it fails to adequately explain why an instruction is legally incorrect. *Castleberry v. Branscum*, 721 S.W.2d 270, 277 (Tex. 1987). On several occasions, we have held that an objection based upon one ground did not preserve error on another ground. *See Aero Energy, Inc. v. Circle C Drilling Co.*, 699 S.W.2d 821, 822 (Tex. 1985); *Davis v. Campbell*, 572 S.W.2d 660 (Tex. 1978).

Although the State objected to the charge, it did so on the basis that the instruction was a comment on the weight of the evidence, not on the ground that it misstated the State's legal duty to Payne. I would hold that this objection did not adequately state the "specific grounds for the ruling [the State] desired the court to make." TEX. R. APP. P. 52(a); *see Davis v. Campbell*, 572 S.W.2d at 663 (holding that a "no evidence" objection did not amount to a complaint that a special issue was immaterial). A litigant cannot base an objection at trial on one ground and then complain on appeal that the trial court erred on another ground.

If the State's current assertion is correct—that is, if, as a matter of law, the defect in this case was not a special defect—then the instructions submitted were fatally flawed. The instructions permitted the jury to impose the duty applicable to special defects, and provided no guidance regarding the State's duty in the absence of a special defect. The instructions did not give the jury the opportunity to apply the standard which the State now urges.

Disregarding the defects in the charge, the majority holds that the State preserved error regarding the characterization of the defect by requesting a jury question concerning Payne's knowledge of the culvert. This view is not only inconsistent with our rules; it is also unsound as a matter of practice. Only by proper objection does a litigant afford the trial court sufficient opportunity to correct defects in the charge. *See Wilgus v. Bond*, 730 S.W.2d 670, 672 (Tex. 1987). Thus, when the charge contains a defective instruction, the mere tender of a correct issue does not preserve error. *See* TEX. R. CIV. P. 274.

What was the trial court to do when the State requested a question regarding Payne's knowledge of the defect? The majority holds that the trial court reversibly erred by refusing the question; but under settled law, the trial court would have erred by submitting it. As explained by University of Texas Law Professor Patrick Hazel, an amicus on rehearing, the requested question was unacceptable. First, the question represented a "phase or shade" of the broad question; and separately submitting one element of a broad question is inconsistent with the concepts underlying broad-form submission. Second, submitting the question could have led to a conflict in the jury's answers, since a "yes" answer to both questions would have meant both that the State was negligent and that the State had no duty. Finally, the request was not in substantially correct wording, as required by Rule 278: it placed the burden of proving Payne's knowledge on the State, while the majority places it on Payne.

Professors J.H. Edgar of the Texas Tech University School of Law and John J. Sampson of the University of Texas School of Law, as amici curiae, agree that the State failed to preserve the error it now asserts. Yet, the majority persists in rewriting established Texas procedure to permit preservation of error by making an incorrect objection and requesting an improper question.

In rejecting the views of legal scholars, the majority continues its abandonment of the principles underlying broad-form submission. *See Keetch v. Kroger* (Tex. 1992) (MAUZY, J., dissenting); *Westgate v. State*, 35 Tex.S.Ct.J. 1042, 1052-53, 1992 WL 148114 (July 1, 1992) (DOGGETT, J., dissenting). Broad-form submission reduces conflicting jury answers, thus reducing appeals and avoiding retrials. *Texas Dept. of Human Serv. v. E.B.*, 802 S.W.2d 647 (Tex. 1990). The proper remedy for a defective instruction, then, is to correct the instruction. If the instruction stands uncorrected, additional issues will muddle the charge and foster conflicting jury answers, increasing the likelihood of appeal and retrial. Today's opinion effectively endorses that approach. I would not. In the interest of comprehensible jury submissions, I would affirm the judgment of the court of appeals without reaching the issue of the State's duty.

* * *

DOGGETT, AND GAMMAGE, JJ., join in this dissenting opinion.

GONZALEZ, J., dissenting.

On further reflection and study, I believe that the Court's writing on preservation of error is incorrect. For the reasons expressed in the dissenting opinion, 838 S.W.2d 235, 241 (MAUZY, J., dissenting on motion for rehearing), I would grant the motion for rehearing and affirm the judgment of the court of appeals.

BURBAGE
v.
BURBAGE AND BURBAGE FUNERAL HOME

447 S.W.3d 249
(Tex. 2014)

David Greene, Electronic Frontier Foundation, San Francisco, CA, Marc A. Fuller, Vinson & Elkins LLP, Dallas, TX, for Amicus Curiae, Electronic Frontier Foundation.

James J. Scheske, James J. Scheske, PLLC, Peter D. Kennedy, William Gerow Christian, Graves Dougherty Hearon & Moody PC, Austin, TX, Jason P. Steed, Bell Nunnally & Martin LLP, Dallas, TX, for Petitioner, Allen Chadwick Burbage.

Gregory Scott Cagle, Savrick, Schumann, Johnson, McGarr Kaminski & Shirley, LLP, Austin, TX, for Respondent, W. Kirk Burbage and Burbage Funeral Home.

JUSTICE GREEN delivered the opinion of the Court.

In this defamation case, a jury assessed compensatory and exemplary damages against Allen Chadwick Burbage (Chad) for ten statements defaming his brother, W. Kirk Burbage (Kirk). The trial court also permanently enjoined Chad from making similar statements. We are presented with three issues: (1) whether any defamatory statements fell within a qualified privilege; (2) whether evidence supports the jury's damage awards; and (3) whether the trial court abused its discretion by issuing the permanent injunction. Because we hold that Chad failed to preserve error in the charge, we do not reach the issue of qualified privilege. We also hold that the permanent injunction operates as an impermissible prior restraint on freedom of speech. Accordingly, we affirm those parts of the court of appeals' judgment. But, on damages, we hold that no evidence supports the compensatory damage award. We reverse that part of the court of appeals' judgment.

* * *

[In this definition case] [t]he trial court submitted the ten statements—four unprivileged and six potentially privileged—for the jury to determine if each statement was substantially true at the time it was made. On damages, the trial court submitted broad-form questions that incorporated the jury's answers for all ten statements. If the qualified privilege applied to any statements, then, the broad-form damages questions incorporated both valid and invalid bases for liability. Such commingling may result in harmful error. *Cf. Crown Life Ins. Co. v. Casteel*, 22 S.W.3d 378, 388 (Tex. 2000) (reversing for new trial due to erroneous commingling of valid and invalid liability theories in a single broad-form liability question). To obtain reversal due to such a charge error, Chad must have preserved the error at trial. *In re B.L.D.*, 113 S.W.3d 340, 349 (Tex. 2003) ("[A]ny complaint to a jury charge is waived unless specifically included in an objection."). We now turn to this preservation question.

B. Preservation of Charge Error

The court of appeals held that Chad waived any claim of error in the submission of potentially privileged statements because he "did not object in the trial court to the submission of broad-form damages questions." —— S.W.3d at —— (*citing In re B.L.D.*, 113 S.W.3d at 349). In *In re B.L.D.*, we held that the court of appeals erred by reviewing a jury charge complaint when the parties did not object at trial to the form of submission. 113 S.W.3d at 349, 355. Chad suggests that this case differs because he raised an objection on qualified privilege, which preserved error in any derivative damages question. Kirk responds that Chad must specifically object to the damages question's form, not merely to the underlying liability issue. Kirk further argues that even Chad's qualified privilege objection failed to preserve error.

1. Charge Error Based on Valid and Invalid Liability Theories

"It is fundamental to our system of justice that parties have the right to be judged by a jury properly instructed in the law." *Casteel*, 22 S.W.3d at 388. Thus, in *Casteel*, we required a new trial when a timely and specific objection preserved the issue of erroneous commingling of valid and invalid theories of liability in a broad-form liability question, such that the appellate court could not determine whether the jury based its verdict on an improperly submitted theory. *Id.* (*citing* TEX. R. APP. P. 61.1). Extending this principle in *Harris County v. Smith*, 96 S.W.3d 230, 234 (Tex. 2002), we determined that a broad-form damages submission mixing valid and invalid elements of damages created the same type of harmful error. And in *Romero v. KPH Consolidation, Inc.*, 166 S.W.3d 212, 225 (Tex. 2005), where evidence supported the jury's negligence finding but not its malicious credentialing finding, we held that the trial court committed harmful error by submitting an apportionment question which allowed the jury to consider malicious credentialing. We explained that "[e]ven if the jury could still have made the same apportionment of fault [without considering malicious credentialing], the error in the question is nevertheless reversible because it effectively prevents [the appellant] from complaining on appeal that they would not have done so." *Id.* at 226.

We continue to adhere to these principles. Yet in addition to the common animating principle of properly instructing the jury in the law, these cases share another link: some timely and specific objection. *Romero*, 166 S.W.3d at 229; *Harris Cnty.*, 96 S.W.3d at 232; *Casteel*, 22 S.W.3d at 387. In other words, in situations where a party does not raise a Casteel-type objection, that party surely cannot raise a Casteel issue when it failed to preserve a claim of an invalid theory of liability that forms the basis of a *Casteel*-type error. If we allowed litigants to raise a *Casteel* issue with no valid objection, either to liability or submission form, those litigants could use a post-trial motion to raise a lack of evidence on the liability question, thus bypassing the crucial step of allowing the trial judge to correct any errors in the charge.

In Romero, we declined to address whether the appellant must object both to the lack of evidence to support submission of a jury question and the form of the submission, because in that case the appellant did both. 166 S.W.3d at 229 & n. 55 (acknowledging the difficult question of whether an additional broad-form objection is required) (*citing Pan E. Exploration Co. v. Hufo Oils*, 855 F.2d 1106, 1124 (5th Cir.1988)). But whether or not an objection to both is required, some timely and specific objection must raise the issue in the trial court. *See Thota v. Young*, 366 S.W.3d 678, 691 (Tex. 2012) (requiring "some objection to the charge," whether to evidentiary support or to form, to preserve error for appellate review). Here, Chad objected based on qualified privilege, but he made no objection to the form of submission. If Chad's initial objection on qualified privilege did not preserve error, we need not address whether a further Casteel-type objection is required.

2. Specific Objections

Our rules of procedure establish the preservation requirements to raise a jury-charge complaint on appeal. *Id.* at 689. The complaining party must object before the trial court and "must point out distinctly the objectionable matter and the grounds of the objection." TEX. R. CIV. P. 274; *see also* TEX. R. APP. P. 33.1. Under Rule of Civil Procedure 274, "[a]ny complaint as to a question, definition, or instruction, on account of any defect, omission, or fault in pleading, is waived unless specifically included in the objections." TEX. R. CIV. P. 274. As a general rule, preservation requires (1) a timely objection "stating the grounds for the ruling that the complaining party sought from the trial court with sufficient specificity to make the trial court aware of the complaint, unless the specific grounds were apparent from the context," and (2) a ruling. *See* TEX. R. APP. P. 33.1. Stated differently, the test ultimately asks "whether the party made the trial court aware of the complaint, timely and plainly, and obtained a ruling." *State Dep't of Highways & Pub. Transp. v. Payne*, 838 S.W.2d 235, 241 (Tex. 1992).

Importantly, the "purpose of Rule 274 is to afford trial courts an opportunity to correct errors in the charge by requiring objections both to clearly designate the error and to explain the grounds for complaint." *Wilgus v. Bond*, 730 S.W.2d 670, 672 (Tex. 1987); *see Payne*, 838 S.W.2d at 243 (MAUZY, J., dissenting) ("Only by proper objection does a litigant afford the trial court sufficient opportunity to correct defects in the charge."). We apply these rules to Chad's objection.

3. Chad's Objection

The following dialogue occurred at the formal charge conference:

> Mr. Cagle: I'm not sure if this is an objection. I apologize, Your Honor. But the matter of in the amended—defendant's amended—first amendment to the original response, defendant has requested that there be a qualified privilege relative to the letter, and the reason for the qualified privilege is it represents common interests, a continuation of a prior judicial proceeding in Maryland and a continuation of trying to resolve matters of mutual concern between the parties of the cemetery.
>
> The Court: All right. Do you have a requested instruction that you're asking the Court to consider and to include in the charge?
>
> Mr. A. Burbage: I have—it seems as though it would—it would require the—a question in the line after—after you find that the statement inflammatory, then there would be a question do you find the statement blah-blah-blah was false at the time it was made as it related to—
>
> The Court: All right. Anything further on that? On that particular issue is there anything further?
>
> Mr. A. Burbage: No. It was—it's been mentioned in the testimony.
>
> The Court: All right. The objection is overruled. The requested instruction is denied.

Chad claims that the trial court erred in submitting liability questions on the potentially privileged statements. Therefore, Chad's objection needed to communicate to the trial court that it was improper to submit Questions 5 through 10 (on statements in the Phillips letters) to the jury. The objection does raise the subject of the qualified privilege. But, crucially, the objection must apprise the trial court of the error alleged such that the court has the opportunity to correct the problem. *See Wilgus*, 730 S.W.2d at 672. When the trial court asked Chad whether he had a requested instruction, Chad responded only with a request for a question that appears to address the falsity of the statements themselves. As Chad has argued, a qualified privilege may still apply even when the statements are false. *See O'Neil*, 456 S.W.2d at 898. It is unclear what Chad hoped to accomplish by requesting an additional question if he wanted the court to withhold Question 5 through 10 from the jury. And it is uncertain even to which questions Chad referred (presumably Questions 5 through 10, but the word "inflammatory," which Chad uses to describe the placement of his proposed question, appears nowhere in the charge). Quite simply, Chad has not provided a specific objection indicating the alleged error in the charge and allowing the trial court the opportunity to correct the error.

We note that when Chad wanted to object to a specific question at the charge conference, he did so. Before the objection on qualified privilege at issue here, Chad objected to Question 10 because it duplicated elements of

Questions 7 and 8. The trial court initially sustained this objection (although it reversed that ruling at the end of the charge conference). Chad's objection to qualified privilege, in order to preserve error, needed to distinctly raise the issue of withdrawing Questions 5 through 10 from the jury. By its language, it does not do this. And it would make little sense for Chad to raise an objection to qualified privilege to eliminate Questions 5 through 10 when, only moments before, he eliminated Question 10 only because it was duplicative of Questions 7 and 8, not because the Questions 7 and 8 were improper to submit to the jury. With this in mind, we cannot conclude that Chad's intent to remove Questions 5 through 10 was "apparent from the context." TEX. R. APP. P. 31.1(a)(1)(A). We hold that Chad's objection was insufficiently specific and did not preserve his claim of error in the submission of Questions 5 through 10.

Our procedural rules are technical, but not trivial. We construe such rules liberally so that the right to appeal is not lost unnecessarily. *Arkoma Basin Exploration Co. v. FMF Assocs. 1990-A, Ltd.*, 249 S.W.3d 380, 388 (Tex. 2008). But when an objection fails to explain the nature of the error, we cannot make assumptions. Preservation of error reflects important prudential considerations recognizing that the judicial process benefits greatly when trial courts have the opportunity to first consider and rule on error. *In re B.L.D.*, 113 S.W.3d at 350 (*citing In re C.O.S.*, 988 S.W.2d 760, 765 (Tex. 1999)). Affording courts this opportunity conserves judicial resources and promotes fairness by ensuring that a party does not neglect a complaint at trial and raise it for the first time on appeal. *Id.* (*citing Pirtle v. Gregory*, 629 S.W.2d 919, 920 (Tex. 1982) (per curiam)). Nor may we stray from these rules because Chad represented himself at trial. *See Mansfield State Bank v. Cohn*, 573 S.W.2d 181, 184-85 (Tex. 1978).

4. Application

Chad argues that the court impermissibly combined valid and invalid theories of liability when the broad-form damages question incorporated privileged statements. Chad did not make a Casteel-type objection to form; thus, to preserve error, Chad must have raised some specific objection to the submission of Questions 5 through 10. *See In re B.L.D.*, 113 S.W.3d at 349-50 (holding that a complaint to a jury charge was waived because it was not specifically included in an objection). He did not. Thus, we hold that Chad's failure to object waives his right to complain of the charge on appeal.

Notes

1. *In the Interest of A.V.*, 113 S.W.3d 355 (Tex. 2003): To preserve error to a broad form issue in a jury charge, on the ground that it was based on a theory without evidentiary support, a party must make a timely objection, plainly informing the court that a specific element should not be included in a broad-form question, because there is no evidence to support its submission. In other words, a specific objection to the charge is required to put a trial court on notice to submit a granulated question to the jury. If such an objection is not made, and the complaint is waived, the courts then look only to see if one of the grounds submitted to the jury is a valid ground upon which, in this case, the father's parental rights could be terminated.

2. *In the Interest of B.L.D.*, 113 S.W.3d 340 (Tex. 2003): In this action to terminate the parental rights of the Dosseys, the trial court submitted a jury charge with the two statutory grounds alleged against the parents in the disjunctive, and with broad-form jury questions regarding whether the parent-child relationships should be terminated. The Dosseys did not object that the disjunctive instruction and broad-form submission of the jury questions violated the Dosseys' alleged constitutional rights to have ten jurors agree on the specific statutory findings underlying the verdict. The jury found against them, and the Dosseys' parental rights were terminated. The court of appeals held that the charge violated the Dosseys' due process right to have at least ten jurors agree on either or both statutory grounds supporting termination. They concluded that "core" jury charge issues in termination cases should be reviewed, even when not preserved. **Held**: Reversed and rendered. The fundamental-error doctrine does not permit appellate review of the complaint of unpreserved charge error in this case. Because termination cases do not apply criminal procedural or evidentiary rules (that are only applicable to criminal cases), they do not necessarily incorporate the concomitant criminal fundamental-error doctrine. The fundamental error doctrine cannot be used to review unpreserved complaints about a jury charge in a case to terminate the rights of parents.

While the parents' and State's interests in obtaining review of unpreserved error, in cases brought to terminate parental rights, may be high, the State's additional competing interest in protecting the best interests of the children through judicial economy, certainty, and finality is at least equally compelling. Because heightened procedural protections have been provided in termination cases, there is a low risk that consistently applying the preservation of error rules will result in erroneous deprivation. Thus, the *Matthews v. Eldridge*, 424 U.S. 319, 335 (1976) factors do not rebut the presumption that Texas preservation rules comport with due process. As a general rule, due process does not mandate that appellate courts review unpreserved complaints of charge error in parental rights termination cases.

3. In *Equistar Chemicals, L.P. v. Dresser-Rand Co.*, --- S.W.3d ----, 50 Tex. Sup. Ct. J. 727, 2007 WL 1299161 (Tex. 2007) involved an action arising out of the failure of a product supplied by Dresser, Equistar alleged causes of action for negligence; strict liability for manufacturing, marketing and design defects; and breach of implied warranty of merchantability. The jury was asked to find only one damages amount. The jury was not instructed to distinguish damages, resulting from its findings that Dresser committed torts, from its finding that Dresser breached an implied warranty. The jury was instructed to consider only the cost of repairs "to restore the Equistar Chemicals' ethylene plant to the condition it was in immediately prior to the occurrence(s) in question." Dresser did not object to the damages question or instruction except for objections to the legal and factual sufficiency of the evidence. Dresser did file a motion for judgment n. o. v. ***Held:*** Dresser's no-evidence objections and motions for judgment n.o.v., without more, did not preserve error, as to the economic loss rule. Dresser failed to preserve error to challenge the measure of damages the jury was instructed to use. Thus, damages are measured by the question and instruction given.

4. *Ulico Casualty Co. v. Allied Pilots Assn.*, 262 S.W.3d 773 (Tex. 2008): Ulico preserved error, as to jury questions three and four, which submitted waiver and estoppel. Ulico did not waive or invite error as to waiver and estoppel by submitting proposed questions, which the trial court included in the charge, since Ulico consistently maintained that the issues would not support recovery, and were not supported by evidence. They stated they submitted the issues only because APA's requested questions were objectionable.

5. *Cruz v. Andrews Restoration, Inc.*, 364 S.W.3d 817 (Tex. 2012): The court held that a party waives the error in failing to submit a jury question regarding its attorney's fees for trial and trial preparation. Under the standard announced in *Payne*, "[f]iling a pretrial charge that includes a question containing that subpart, when no other part of the record reflects a discussion of the issue or objection to the question ultimately submitted, does not sufficiently alert the trial court to the issue." A party may rely on a charge requested before trial only if "the record shows that the trial court knew of the written request and refused to submit it." That was not shown in this case.

ALANIZ
v.
JONES & NEUSE, INC.

907 S.W.2d 450
(Tex. 1995)

Jerry Guerra and William J. Tinning, Corpus Christi, for petitioner.
Frank E. Weathered and John A. Smith, III, Corpus Christi, for respondent.

PER CURIAM.

Servando Alaniz sued Jones & Neuse, Inc. for damages to his Exxon service station caused by one of its trucks. The trial court rendered judgment on a jury verdict awarding Alaniz his repair costs, past lost profits and mental anguish. Alaniz nevertheless appealed, complaining that the trial court erred in refusing to submit his requested jury question on future lost profits. The court of appeals affirmed, holding that Alaniz failed to preserve his complaint. 878 S.W.2d 244.

As trial began, Alaniz submitted to the trial court a complete requested charge which contained on one page a question concerning various elements of damages, including future lost profits. The trial court included that very page in the jury charge, with the references to future lost profits simply redacted. Alaniz objected on the record to the omission, and this was the only objection he made to the charge. The trial court overruled the objection.

The court of appeals acknowledged that Alaniz may have preserved his objection for complaint on appeal under our decision in *State Department of Highways v. Payne*, 838 S.W.2d 235 (Tex. 1992), since it is obvious that the trial court was fully aware of Alaniz' request and refused it. The court of appeals declined to follow Payne, however, holding instead that Alaniz did not meet the requirements of Rule 273, TEX. R. CIV. P., which states:

> Either party may present to the court and request written questions, definitions, and instructions to be given to the jury; and the court may give them or a part thereof, or may refuse to give them, as may be proper. Such requests shall be prepared and presented to the court and submitted to opposing counsel for examination and objection within a reasonable time after the charge is given to the parties or their attorneys for examination. A request by either party for any questions, definitions, or instructions shall be made separate and apart from such party's objections to the court's charge.

Specifically, the appeals court faulted Alaniz in three respects: for including his request in a complete charge; for submitting his request before trial and not "after the charge [was] given to the parties"; and for not making his request "separate and apart from [his] objections". 878 S.W.2d at 245.

In each respect the court of appeals erred. First, Alaniz' request was "written" as Rule 273 requires. The rule does not prohibit including the request in a complete charge as long as it is not obscured. Second, to say that a party does not present a request after the charge is given to the parties simply because he first submitted it earlier, when the trial court was clearly aware of the request, is too strained a reading of Rule 273. Alaniz raised the issue after the charge was prepared and should not be penalized for also raising it earlier. Third, Alaniz' written request was plainly separate from his oral objection, and the appeals court's view that the two were "improperly entwined", 878 S.W.2d at 245, was incorrect.

The court of appeals also erred in concluding that *Payne* conflicts with Rule 273. In *Payne* we held that a party has preserved error in the jury charge when he has made the trial court reasonably aware of the complaint, timely and plainly, and obtained a ruling. 838 S.W.2d at 241. While Payne does not revise the requirements of the rules of procedure regarding the jury charge, it does mandate that those requirements be applied in a common sense manner to serve the purposes of the rules, rather than in a technical manner which defeats them. Under the reading of Rule 273 *Payne* requires, Alaniz preserved his jury charge complaint.

We therefore disapprove the court of appeals' opinion. We conclude, however, that Alaniz' complaint is without merit. He neither pleaded nor offered legally sufficient evidence of lost future profits to support submission of a jury question on these damages. Accordingly, Alaniz' application for writ of error is denied.

KEETCH
v.
KROGER CO.
845 S.W.2d 262
(Tex. 1992)

Michael A. Robertson, Grand Prairie, for petitioner.
Brian J. Brandstetter and Scott W. MacLaren, Dallas, for respondent.

COOK, JUSTICE.

The opinion of June 3, 1992, is withdrawn and the motion for rehearing is overruled.

This case presents questions of the appropriate jury submission of a case involving a slip and fall in a Kroger store. For the reasons set out below, we affirm the judgment of the court of appeals.

Linda Keetch was in a Kroger store to buy a loaf of bread. Having selected a loaf of bread, Keetch was walking towards the checkout counter by way of the floral department. Kroger displays and sells plants in its floral department. As part of the process of preparing the plants for sale, many of the plants are lightly sprayed with a product called Green Glo to shine the leaves. On the day Keetch was in the Kroger store, a number of plants had been sprayed on a desk in the floral department. Keetch slipped and fell when she was near the desk. Keetch argues that Green Glo overspray collected on the floor by the desk and created a slick spot.

A witness who heard Keetch fall and saw her on the floor testified that there was a waxy type substance on the floor near the floral desk. However, the Kroger employees working in the floral department on the day of the accident testified that they did not notice any slippery spots on the floor. Additionally, both Kroger employees who are assigned to work in the floral department testified that they had never noticed a slippery spot on the floor after spraying plant leaves. One of the employees had worked in the floral department for six years and the other had worked in the floral department for approximately three years.

Keetch sought to hold Kroger liable under both a premises condition and a negligent activity theory. The trial court submitted the case to the jury on only a premises condition theory. The jury found that there was a slippery spot on the floor which presented an unreasonable risk of harm to Keetch. However, the jury refused to find that Kroger knew or should have known of the slippery spot, so the trial court rendered a take nothing judgment. The court of appeals affirmed the judgment of the trial court. 845 S.W.2d 276. We affirm the judgment of the court of appeals.

Keetch argues the trial court erred: (1) when the court refused to submit Keetch's negligent activity claim; (2) when the court submitted a question asking whether Kroger knew or should have known of the slippery spot on the floor rather than a question asking whether Kroger created the slippery spot; and (3) when the court refused to submit a broad form negligence question.

I.

Keetch argues that the trial judge erred by not submitting her negligent activity theory of liability to the jury. Recovery on a negligent activity theory requires that the person have been injured by or as a contemporaneous result of the activity itself rather than by a condition created by the activity. *See, e.g., Redinger v. Living, Inc.*, 689 S.W.2d 415 (Tex. 1985); *Abalos v. Oil Development Co. of Texas*, 544 S.W.2d 627 (Tex. 1976); *Hernandez v. Heldenfels*, 374 S.W.2d 196 (Tex. 1964). Keetch's theory is that Kroger exposed its customers to the unreasonable risk of a fall by negligently conducting its plant spraying activity in an area of its store that was open to its customers.

A Kroger employee sprayed the plants sometime prior to her 7:00 p.m. quitting time. Keetch slipped on the floor and fell at approximately 7:30 p.m. There was no ongoing activity when Keetch was injured. Keetch may have been injured by a condition created by the spraying but she was not injured by the activity of spraying. At some point, almost every artificial condition can be said to have been created by an activity. We decline to eliminate all distinction between premises conditions and negligent activities. The trial court properly did not submit a negligent activity theory of liability on these facts.

II.

We stated the elements of a premises liability cause of action in *Corbin v. Safeway Stores, Inc.*, 648 S.W.2d 292 (Tex. 1983). The elements are: (1) Actual or constructive knowledge of some condition on the premises by the owner/operator; (2) That the condition posed an unreasonable risk of harm; (3) That the owner/operator did not exercise reasonable care to reduce or eliminate the risk; and (4) That the owner/operator's failure to use such care proximately caused the plaintiff's injuries. *Corbin*, 648 S.W.2d at 296; *Hernandez v. Kroger Co.*, 711 S.W.2d 3, 4 (Tex. 1986). In this case, the trial court submitted a question based on Texas Pattern Jury Charge 61.02 that incorporated the *Corbin* elements.[4]

The first element, actual or constructive knowledge of some condition on the premises by the owner or operator, is the key point for this case. Keetch argues that if Kroger created the condition then Kroger is charged with knowledge of the condition as a matter of law. Keetch's argument is incorrect. Keetch's theory is supported by a series of court of appeals opinions. The approach of these courts of appeals is that an owner or occupier

---

[4] The relevant questions submitted by the court were: Question 1: On the occasion in question, was there a slippery spot in the Floral Department on Kroger's floor that presented an unreasonable risk of harm to Linda Keetch? If you have answered Question 1 "Yes," and only in that event, then answer Question 2. Question 2: Did Kroger know, or in the exercise of ordinary care should it have known, that the slippery spot, if any, was on the floor? If you have answered Question 2 "Yes," and only in that event, then answer Question 3. Question 3: Was Kroger's failure to remove the slippery spot, if any, negligence? If you have answered Question 3 "Yes," and only in that event, then answer Question 4. Question 4: Was that negligence a proximate cause of the occurrence in question?

has sufficient knowledge of a condition to be liable for the injuries caused by the condition if the plaintiff proves the defendant:

> (1) put the foreign substance on the floor; or (2) knew that it was on the floor and negligently failed to remove it; or (3) that the foreign substance was on the floor so long that it should have been discovered and removed in the exercise of ordinary care.

Robledo v. Kroger Co., 597 S.W.2d 560, 560 (Tex. App.—Eastland 1980, writ ref'd n.r.e.) (numbers added); *see also* cases cited in note 3, *supra*. Keetch relies on the first of the three alternatives. However, none of the court of appeals opinions we have been directed to or have located rely on the first alternative to establish liability. The fact that the owner or occupier of a premises created a condition that posed an unreasonable risk of harm may support an inference of knowledge. However, the jury still must find that the owner or occupier knew or should have known of the condition. *Corbin*, 648 S.W.2d at 296. Making the inference as a matter of law is improper unless knowledge is uncontroverted. Kroger denied knowledge of the condition so the inference of knowledge could not be made as a matter of law.

Three of our cases are particularly instructive on the determination when knowledge may be inferred from the creation of a condition. First, in *Corbin*, Corbin was injured when he slipped on a grape that had fallen from a self-service grape display. Safeway admitted that at the time Corbin fell it had actual knowledge of the unusually high risk of harm associated with its grape display. *Corbin*, 648 S.W.2d at 296. The court rejected Safeway's argument that Safeway was held to a lower standard if a customer, rather than a Safeway employee, actually knocked a grape off of the display. The *Corbin* court held that Safeway's knowledge of the unusually high risk of harm associated with the self-serve display satisfied the knowledge requirement. Safeway did not have to know that a particular grape was on the floor at a particular time because it knew that the grapes would be on the floor due to the nature of the display.

Second, in *Coffee v. F.W. Woolworth Co.*, we addressed a premises liability case where there was no direct evidence that Woolworth knew of the dangerous condition. 536 S.W.2d 539 (Tex. 1976). After the court of appeals affirmed a judgment non obstante verdicto for Woolworth, we reversed both courts, holding that the jury could have inferred knowledge on two grounds. First, knowledge could have been inferred because of the length of time that the condition existed. Second, we held that the jury could reasonably infer that Woolworth had actual knowledge of the dangerous condition because store employees were working on the display stand which caused the injury. The hazard was obvious to the store employees working on the display. The fact that Woolworth created the condition was circumstantial evidence of knowledge. This is very different from establishing knowledge as a matter of law when the store owner or operator creates a condition.

Third, *Seideneck v. Cal Bayreuther Associates*, was a premises liability case where Cal Bayreuther Associates created the condition that caused Seideneck's injury. 451 S.W.2d 752 (Tex. 1970). Cal Bayreuther operated a showroom in the Trade Mart in Dallas. Seideneck was in the showroom and tripped on a throw-rug that was under a display table. Cal Bayreuther had placed the rug under the table. However, we held that there was no evidence that Cal Bayreuther knew the rug presented an unreasonable risk of harm. Proof that the premises owner or occupier created a condition which poses an unreasonable risk of harm may constitute circumstantial evidence that the owner or occupier knew of the condition. However, creating the condition does not establish knowledge as a matter of law for purposes of premises liability. The trial court properly submitted the question asking whether Kroger knew or should have known of the condition.

III.

The trial court submitted a jury question based on Texas Pattern Jury Charge 61.02. This question properly sets out the Corbin elements for a premises liability case. Keetch argues that the submission is improper because it is not in broad form.

Texas Rule of Civil Procedure 277 mandates broad form submission "whenever feasible." Accompanied by appropriate instructions, a general negligence question such as Pattern Jury Charge 66.04 is a correct broad form premises liability question. *See Parker v. Highland Park*, 565 S.W.2d 512, 519 (Tex. 1978) (abolishing doctrine that the occupier has no duty to warn or protect invitees when dangerous condition is open and obvious; replaced no-duty rule with ordinary negligence principles). In *Corbin*, we held that general negligence principles in a premises liability case are stated in Section 343 of the RESTATEMENT SECOND OF TORTS (1965). 648 S.W.2d at 295. *Corbin* stated the principles of Section 343 as four elements. Therefore, appropriate instructions in a premises liability case must incorporate the four *Corbin* elements. *Hernandez*, 711 S.W.2d at 4; *Corbin*, 648 S.W.2d at 295-96.

One formulation of a negligence definition incorporating the *Corbin* standard was affirmed by the Eleventh Court of Appeals in *Prudential Insurance Company of America v. Henson*, 753 S.W.2d 415 (Tex. App.—Eastland 1988, no writ). The trial court in *Prudential* submitted the following: NEGLIGENCE by an owner or occupier of a premises is the failure to use ordinary care to reduce or eliminate an unreasonable risk of harm created by a premises condition which the occupier knows about or in the exercise of ordinary care should know about. An owner or occupier's negligence depends on whether he acted reasonably in light of what he knew or should have known about the risks accompanying a premises condition. 753 S.W.2d at 416. *Prudential* demonstrates the feasibility of submitting premises liability questions in broad form. However, this Court recommends the following instructions accompany Texas Pattern Jury Charge 66.04 in the submission of a premises liability case involving an invitee. "Negligence," when used with respect to an owner or occupier of a premises, means failure to use ordinary care to reduce or eliminate an unreasonable risk of harm created by a premises condition which the owner or occupier knows about or in the exercise of ordinary care should know about. "Ordinary care," when used with respect to an owner or occupier of a premises, means that degree of care which would be used by an owner or occupier of ordinary prudence under the same or similar circumstances.

In this case, we need not decide whether failure to submit in broad form was reversible error because Keetch did not provide the trial judge with any indication that her complaint was with the trial court's failure to submit in broad form. Error in the charge must be preserved by distinctly designating the error and the grounds for the objection. TEX. R. CIV. P. 274; *Wilgus v. Bond*, 730 S.W.2d 670, 672 (Tex. 1987). Keetch first complained of the trial court's failure to submit in broad form in her application for writ of error to this court. Because there was not a timely objection, Keetch did not preserve error, if any, in the failure to submit in broad form.

IV.

We affirm the judgment of the court of appeals.

HECHT, JUSTICE, concurring.

I concur in the Court's opinion and write separately only to respond to the dissent.

* * *

The dissent also argues that to submit jury questions in broad form in premises liability cases, an element of liability—in this case, whether the owner had actual or constructive knowledge of the unreasonable risk—must be omitted from the charge. It should hardly need be said that broad form submission does not entail omitting elements of proof from the charge. Broad form involves inclusion of multiple elements within a single question, usually by adding accompanying instructions, when it is feasible to do so. It alters only the form of the charge, not the substance. One element which must be proved to establish liability in the circumstances of this case is that the premises owner or occupier knew or reasonably should have known of the dangerous condition before the accident occurred. Keetch was obliged to obtain a jury finding on this issue. The trial court might have submitted the matter to the jury in the manner the Court suggests, by including the element as part of the definition of negligence, instead of submitting a separate question to the jury. But it could not omit the finding altogether, as the dissent contends.

Finally, the dissent charges that the Court holds Keetch specifically, and plaintiffs generally, to a higher standard for preserving error in the charge than it set in *State Dept. of Public Highways v. Payne*, 838 S.W.2d 235 (Tex. 1992). The dissent claims "that Keetch objected to the trial court's granulated jury charge". *Ante*, at 272. But the objection the dissent refers to did not so much as hint that the trial court's granulated submission was improper or that the charge should have been in broad form. Keetch did request the same question the Court suggests today, but she requested no accompanying instructions. A party does not object to a failure to submit a jury charge in broad form by requesting questions without the necessary instructions. This case is quite different from *Payne*, where the State specifically requested a question on the one element of proof missing from the charge under the proper theory of liability. Keetch did not complain to the trial court that the charge was not submitted in broad form. Even if she had, I would not hold that the trial court's refusal to submit a broad form charge in this case was reversible error. *See H.E. Butt Grocery Co. v. Warner*, 845 S.W.2d 258, 259-60 (Tex. 1992).

PHILLIPS, C.J., and CORNYN, J., join in this concurring opinion.

Mauzy, J., dissenting on motion for rehearing [opinion omitted].

DOGGETT and GAMMAGE, JJ., join in this dissenting opinion.

3. *Effect of Failure to Preserve Error to Charge*

a. *Deemed Findings*

Read Rule 279 Texas Rules of Civil Procedure.

RAMOS
v.
FRITO-LAY
784 S.W.2d 667
(Tex. 1990)

Clinton F. Cross, El Paso, for petitioner.
Jack L. Brewster, El Paso, for respondent.

DOGGETT, JUSTICE.

The central issue in this appeal is whether an employer may be held liable in exemplary damages for the actions of its management-level employee in performing a non-managerial task. The court of appeals reversed the trial court's award of exemplary damages in this cause because Frito-Lay's sales manager was not performing a managerial task. 770 S.W.2d 887. We reverse the judgment of the court of appeals and remand the cause to that court for consideration of points it did not reach.

Liability in the trial court was premised on the intentional tort of Jose Padilla, a Frito-Lay employee, resulting in injury to Petitioner Salvador Ramos. Padilla held the title of district sales manager and had supervisory authority over twelve sales employees. On the day of the incident in question, Padilla was substituting for one of these salesmen who was on vacation, as he was unable to secure a replacement. Padilla made a route stop at Sal's Beverage Shop, a convenience store owned and operated by Ramos. A dispute arose between Padilla and Ramos concerning the ownership of a display rack, and a shoving incident ensued in which Ramos was injured.

The jury found that Padilla had committed an assault and battery proximately causing damage to Ramos and that Padilla was not deviating from the service of Frito-Lay in the furtherance of its business. The trial court entered judgment on the verdict, including an award for physical pain, medical expenses and exemplary damages. The court of appeals reversed as to medical expenses and exemplary damages but affirmed the trial court's award of damages for physical pain.

We must first consider whether error has been properly preserved. Ramos contends that Frito-Lay has waived its right to complain of the exemplary damage award because it failed to make specific objection in the trial court as to premising such award on Padilla's managerial capacity as required by Rule 52(a), Texas Rules of Appellate Procedure. Frito-Lay responds, not by pointing to a specific objection preserving error, but by contending that it was Ramos' burden to obtain affirmative jury findings on all elements necessary to predicate liability for exemplary damages. Since Ramos failed to submit issues as to managerial capacity, Frito-Lay asserts it had no obligation to object.

There can be no question that it was Ramos' burden to obtain affirmative answers to jury questions as to the necessary elements of his cause of action. If an entire theory were omitted from the charge it would be waived; and Frito-Lay would indeed have no duty to object. TEX. R. CIV. P 279; *see Strauss v. LaMark*, 366 S.W.2d 555, 557 (Tex. 1963). Where, however, issues are omitted which constitute only a part of a complete and independent ground and other issues necessarily referable to that ground are submitted and answered, the omitted elements are deemed found in support of the judgment if no objection is made and they are supported by some evidence. TEX. R. CIV. P 279; *see Strauss*, 366 S.W.2d at 557.

Here, the jury found that Padilla committed an intentional tort while in the scope of his employment and awarded exemplary damages against Frito-Lay. The trial court's judgment included an award for exemplary damages. Although the question of whether Padilla was employed in a managerial capacity and acting in the scope of his employment constituted an element of Ramos' cause of action, it did not encompass an independent ground of recovery. *See Treasure City v. Strange*, 620 S.W.2d 811, 813 (Tex. Civ. App.—Dallas 1981, no writ). Objection by Frito-Lay to the omission of the element of managerial capacity was thus necessary to prevent a deemed finding against it. *See Accent Builders Co. v. Southwest Concrete Systems, Inc.*, 679 S.W.2d 106, 110-11 (Tex. App.—Dallas 1984, writ ref'd n.r.e.). Frito-Lay did not object, nor did it request specific findings by the trial court. If the omitted element of managerial capacity is supported by some evidence, we must deem it found against Frito-Lay under Rule 279. *See Payne v. Snyder*, 661 S.W.2d 134, 142 (Tex. App.—Amarillo 1983, writ ref'd n.r.e.); *Freedom Homes of Texas, Inc. v. Dickinson*, 598 S.W.2d 714, 717 (Tex. Civ. App.—Corpus Christi 1980, writ ref'd n.r.e.).

We then turn to the question of whether the omitted element is supported by some evidence. The rule is well settled in Texas that an employer may be held liable in exemplary damages for the acts of an employee who is "employed in a managerial capacity and was acting in the scope of employment." *King v. McGuff*, 149 Tex. 432, 435, 234 S.W.2d 403, 405 (1950); *see also Purvis v. Prattco, Inc.*, 595 S.W.2d 103, 104 (Tex. 1980); *Fisher v. Carrousel Motor Hotel, Inc.*, 424 S.W.2d 627, 630 (Tex. 1967). In applying this rule to the facts of this case, the court of appeals found there was no evidence to support the exemplary damage award, stating that "the controlling factor is that at the time of the incident in question, Mr. Padilla was not performing the tasks of a sales manager, he was driving a delivery van and performing the usual task of a route salesman." 770 S.W.2d 889-90. Under the court of appeals' formulation, it is the character of the employee's act, managerial or non-managerial, and not simply whether the employee was acting in the scope of employment that determines whether exemplary damages are recoverable.

We disagree and hold that an employer may be held liable in exemplary damages for the actions of its management-level employee in performing a non-managerial task. The Texas rule set forth in *King v. McGuff* quotes the language now contained in Section 909(c) of the RESTATEMENT (SECOND) OF TORTS. The purpose of the rule permitting exemplary damages to be imposed upon an employer for the acts of its employee is to serve "as a deterrent to the employment of unfit persons for important positions." RESTATEMENT (SECOND) OF TORTS § 909, comment b (1979). To permit an employer to escape liability for the outrageous acts of its management-level employee because the employee was performing a non-managerial task would severely undercut this purpose. Moreover, we are unwilling to draw a distinction, unsupported by the RESTATEMENT or by case law, between managerial and non-managerial tasks. This line is a very grey one indeed. In this case, Padilla testified that it was his responsibility to find someone to cover for the vacationing route salesman or to cover for the salesman himself. Padilla can be described as performing the ordinary duties of a non-managerial employee in driving the delivery van and making sales, yet he can also be described as performing the often necessary managerial duty of stepping into the breach when required. He retained his title of district sales manager and his supervisory authority over twelve employees at the time he was performing these tasks. The record contains evidence to support the deemed finding that Padilla was employed in a managerial capacity and was acting in the scope of his employment.

We reverse the judgment of the court of appeals and remand the cause to that court for consideration of points it did not reach.

In re J.F.C.
96 S.W.3d 256
(Tex. 2002)

JUSTICE OWEN delivered the opinion of the Court in which CHIEF JUSTICE PHILLIPS, JUSTICE HECHT, JUSTICE JEFFERSON, and JUSTICE SMITH joined.

After a jury trial, the trial court in this case rendered a judgment terminating the rights of both the mother and father to three of their children. A divided court of appeals reversed and remanded, holding that omission of an instruction that termination must be in the children's best interest from material parts of the jury charge was fundamental error that could be raised for the first time on appeal, and that the error probably caused rendition of an improper judgment. We hold that:

1) although the trial court's charge was erroneous because it omitted the children's best interest as a prerequisite for termination in material parts of the charge, Texas Rule of Civil Procedure 279 requires us to supply the omitted finding in support of the judgment because there is either an express or deemed finding by the trial court that termination is in the children's best interest;

2) the concept of "fundamental error" cannot be used to circumvent the application of Rule 279 of our rules of procedure;

3) applying Rule 279 does not violate the due process clause of the United States Constitution or due course of law provision of the Texas Constitution;

4) because parental conduct on which termination could be based was conclusively established, we do not reach whether the trial court erred in failing to instruct the jury that the same ten jurors must agree that at least one statutorily described course of parental conduct occurred and that termination is in the best interest of the children; and

5) assuming, without deciding, that a judgment could be set aside in a parental termination case based on ineffective assistance of a parent's counsel, assistance of counsel in this case was not ineffective.

The factual sufficiency issues raised by the parents in the court of appeals pertain to a ground of termination that is unnecessary to the trial court's judgment. The remaining issues raised by the parents do not require reversal of the trial court's judgment terminating the parents' rights. Accordingly, we reverse the court of appeals' judgment and render judgment that the parent- child relationships are terminated.

I

Because we consider the record in this case in some detail later in this opinion, we include here only minimal facts and the procedural history. The three children who are the subject of this proceeding were removed from their parents' home by the Texas Department of Protective and Regulatory Services (DPRS) in October 1997. At that time, the children's respective ages were four years, two years, and seven months.

The children were initially removed without a court order. The next day, the trial court held an emergency removal hearing and appointed the DPRS temporary managing conservator of the children. Five days later, the court held an adversary hearing, continued the removal, and issued temporary orders appointing the DPRS temporary managing conservator.

The trial court thereafter entered various orders directing the parents to perform specific acts to avoid restriction or termination of their parental rights. After working with the family for six months following the children's removal, the DPRS amended its petition in the trial court to seek termination of both parents' rights. A jury trial was held in February 1999, and the trial court rendered judgment in March 1999 terminating the parent-child relationship between each parent and the three children who had been removed from the home seventeen months earlier, in October 1997. A fourth child had been born in January 1999 shortly before trial. That child was removed from the parents at birth but was not the subject of any of the proceedings in this case. The parents appealed, and the court of appeals, with one justice dissenting, reversed the trial court's judgment and remanded the case for a new trial. The court of appeals concluded that the charge permitted the jury to find that the parents' respective rights should be terminated without finding that termination would be in the children's best interest. Although the parents had not objected to the charge on this basis, the court of appeals held that the omission went to a "core issue" in a termination case, and that failing to review the unpreserved error on appeal would violate "Fourteenth Amendment procedural due process" requirements under the United States Constitution. The parents had also complained for the first time on appeal that it was error in a parental termination case to use broad-form submission because less than ten jurors could rely on one basis for termination while other jurors could rely on another basis. The parents contended that there must be a separate finding with regard to each element necessary for termination. The court of appeals rejected these arguments, concluding that broad-form submission was permissible. The dissent would have affirmed the trial court's judgment on the basis that there was either an express or implied finding that termination of parental rights was in the children's best interest.

II

We first consider the jury charge's submission of the best interest of the children. There is no indication in the record that the trial court or any counsel in the case was under any misapprehension that there are two prerequisites for termination of parental rights under section 161.001 of the Texas Family Code. Section 161.001 sets forth nineteen different courses of parental conduct, any one of which may satisfy the first prerequisite for termination. The second prerequisite under section 161.001 is that termination must be in the child's best interest. However, the written charge to the jury in this case omitted the children's best interest as an element in three material parts of the charge, perhaps because of a typographical error. The submission of the termination issues was as follows:

> With regards to [**THE MOTHER**], for the parent-child relationship to be terminated in this case, it must be proved by clear and convincing evidence that she has done at least one of the following:
>
> 1) Engaged in conduct or knowingly placed the child with persons who engaged in conduct which endangers the physical or emotional well-being of the child;
>
> OR
>
> 2) Failed to comply with the provisions of a court order that specifically established the actions necessary for the parent to obtain the return of the child who has been in the permanent or temporary managing conservatorship of the Department of Protective and Regulatory Services for not less than nine months as a result of the child's removal from the parent under Chapter 262 for abuse or neglect of the child.
>
> With regards to [**THE FATHER**], for the parent-child relationship to be terminated in this case, it must be proved by clear and convincing evidence that he has done at least one of the following:
>
> • Knowingly placed or knowingly allowed the children to remain in conditions or surroundings which endanger the physical or emotional well-being of the children;
>
> OR
>
> • Failed to comply with the provisions of a court order that specifically established the actions necessary for the parent to obtain the return of the child who has been in the permanent or temporary managing conservatorship of the Department of Protective and Regulatory Services for not less than nine months as a result of the child's removal from the parent under Chapter 262 for abuse or neglect of the child. For the parent-child relationship to be terminated in this case, it must also be proved by clear and convincing evidence that termination of the parent-child relationship would be in the best interest of the children.
>
> Some factors to consider in determining the best interest of the child are:
>
> 1. the desires of the child,
> 2. the emotional and physical needs of the child now and in the future,
> 3. any emotional and physical danger to the child now and in the future,
> 4. the parenting ability of the individuals seeking custody,
> 5. the programs available to assist those individuals to promote the best interest of the child,
> 6. the plans for the child by those individuals or by the agency seeking custody,
> 7. the stability of the home or proposed placement,

8. the acts or omissions of the parent that may indicate that the existing parent-child relationship is not a proper one, and

9. any excuse for the acts or omissions of the parent.

QUESTION 1:

Should the parent-child relationship between [**THE MOTHER**] and [**J.F.C.**] be terminated?

Answer "Yes" or "No."

Answer:

[similar questions as to the other two children]

QUESTION 4:

Should the parent-child relationship between [**THE FATHER**] and [**J.F.C.**] be terminated?

Answer "Yes" or "No."

Answer:

[similar questions as to the other two children]

The charge would have accurately instructed the jury regarding the children's best interest if a hard return had been inserted in the instruction regarding the father just before the words "For the parent-child relationship to be terminated . . . ." But as can be seen, the written instruction regarding the father's parental rights mentioned the best interest of the children only in connection with one of the two alternative descriptions of parental conduct. The jury was free to conclude that if the father had endangered the children, his rights could be terminated without any consideration of the children's best interest. Because of the way the written charge was structured, the factors the jury was to consider in determining the best interest of the children were referable only to whether the father had failed to comply with a court order establishing the actions necessary for return of the children.

The written instruction to the jury regarding the mother's parental rights omitted any reference to the best interest of the children. The jury was instructed that her rights could be terminated if there was clear and convincing evidence that she either engaged in conduct that endangered the children or failed to comply with a court order establishing the actions necessary for the return of her children. Accordingly, the charge in this case omitted a statutorily prescribed element for parental termination. There was no objection to this omission.

A

Rule 279 of the Texas Rules of Civil Procedure prescribes the consequences for failing to object to the omission of an element of a ground of recovery. The current version of Rule 279, like its predecessor, embodies long-standing case law that when some but not all elements of a claim or cause of action are submitted to and found by a jury, and there is no request or objection with regard to the missing element, a trial court may expressly make a finding on the omitted element or, if it does not, the omitted element is deemed found by the court in a manner supporting the judgment if the deemed finding is supported by some evidence. Rule 279 thus directs courts how to proceed when an element of a "ground of recovery or defense" is omitted from a jury charge.

In this case, the trial court's judgment contains an express finding that termination is in the best interest of the children. It recites that

> the Court having reviewed the said verdict of the Jury and the pleadings and the evidence herein is of the opinion that the Petitioners are entitled to the judgment of termination with regard to the children in whose interest this suit is brought, and that such judgment is in the best interest of the children in whose interest this suit is brought.

There is no indication in the record that this finding was made at the request of either party, or after notice and hearing before rendition of judgment, as Rule 279 contemplates. However, there was no objection to the inclusion of this finding in the judgment. But irrespective of whether that written finding satisfies Rule 279 regarding an express finding, the "omitted element or elements shall be deemed found by the court in such manner as to support the judgment" if there is evidence to support such a finding. Because the judgment terminated parental rights, we must determine whether there is evidence to support a deemed finding that termination is in the children's best interest.

* * *

The parents have an additional complaint about the jury charge. There are two predicates to parental termination under section 161.001 of the Texas Family Code. The first is that one or more courses of parental conduct must be established. The second is that termination must be in the best interest of the children. The gravamen of the parents' complaint is that the charge does not require the same ten jurors to agree that a parent engaged in at least one particular course of conduct described by section 161.001(1) and that termination is in the children's best interest. The charge only requires that ten jurors agree that the parent-child relationships should be terminated. They thus contend that this broad-form submission did not satisfy federal due process requirements.

This constitutional challenge was not raised in the trial court. However, even assuming, without deciding, that 1) this argument could be raised for the first time on appeal, and 2) the charge erred in this regard, we do not reach the constitutional challenge because the evidence conclusively establishes that each parent engaged in a course of conduct described by subsection 161.001(1) of the Family Code. Therefore, the alleged error did not cause the rendition of an improper judgment or prevent the parents "from properly presenting the case to the court of appeals."

In sum, any errors committed by the trial court did not require reversal.

* * *

For the foregoing reasons, we reverse the judgment of the court of appeals and render judgment terminating the parent-child relationships between each of the children, J.F.C., A.B.C., and M.B.C., and their mother and father.

JUSTICE O'NEILL concurred in the judgment only.

JUSTICE HANKINSON filed a dissenting opinion, in which JUSTICE ENOCH joined.

JUSTICE SCHNEIDER filed a dissenting opinion.

JUSTICE HANKINSON dissenting, joined by JUSTICE ENOCH.

The Court states the issue in this case as "whether there is legally sufficient evidence to support the trial court's express or deemed finding that termination is in the best interest of the children." This statement of the issue will come as a surprise to the parties and the court of appeals, as no one has raised, briefed, or addressed this issue at any stage of these proceedings. In this parental-rights-termination case the State asked us to decide whether due process requires a court of appeals to review alleged errors in the charge when the parents did not object to those errors at trial. Instead of answering that question, the Court explains the consequences of the parents' failure to object to the first alleged charge error (omission of a statutory element required for termination) under Texas Rule of Civil Procedure 279. But those consequences are not at issue, and rule 279 does not answer the actual question presented of whether, in light of the constitutional interests at stake, our law requires an appellate court to consider the parents' complaints as if they did object to the charge, even though they admit they did not. The Court does not even attempt to explain how it can review the parents' second unpreserved claim of charge error (concerning broad-form submission), instead simply concluding that the error, if any, was harmless. Refusing to answer the question presented does a disservice to our courts of appeals by failing to resolve the conflict among them as to whether they may review unpreserved error in termination cases; a disservice to our established jurisprudence, which permits us to review only preserved complaints unless a recognized exception exists; and most importantly, a disservice to the parents and children who are entitled to consistent and efficient appellate review that fairly adjudicates their complaints in these time-sensitive and compelling cases. I therefore dissent and write separately to explain how I would resolve the actual issue presented in this case. Because I conclude that Texas' common-law doctrine of fundamental error permits us to review the alleged charge errors, I would hold that Texas procedures for reviewing unpreserved charge error in parental-rights-termination cases do not violate due process. Having considered the alleged errors, however, I disagree with the court of appeals that the omission in the jury charge was harmful, and I would therefore remand this cause to the court of appeals for it to consider the remaining issues it did not yet address.

* * *

As a general rule, no error may be reviewed on appeal that was not raised before the trial court. TEX.R.APP. P. 33.1. Nevertheless, like most other jurisdictions, our civil jurisprudence is well settled that appellate courts may consider unpreserved error that is "fundamental." *See McCauley v. Consol. Underwriters*, 157 Tex. 475, 304 S.W.2d 265, 266 (1957); *Ramsey v. Dunlop*, 146 Tex. 196, 205 S.W.2d 979, 982 (1947); *see also* 6 McDonald & Carlson, TEXAS CIVIL PRACTICE § 47:4, at 1201-02 (2d ed.1998) (recognizing fundamental error as an exception to the general rule of preservation); W. James Kronzer, *Laying the Foundation for Appellate Review, in Appellate Procedure in Texas* (STATE BAR OF TEXAS, 2d ed.1979), § 9.2, at 204-06 (same); Allen Wood, *The Bill of Exceptions as Basis for Review*, in *id.* § 11.5, at 248-49 (same). While most jurisdictions recognize some type of fundamental error, they do not define it uniformly. BLACK'S LAW DICTIONARY defines the essence of fundamental error as that which is "so obvious and prejudicial that an appellate court should address it despite the parties' failure to raise a proper objection." BLACK'S LAW DICTIONARY 563 (7th ed.1999) (defining also "plain error" and "error apparent of record"). Our own application of fundamental error review has changed throughout the years. Consequently, an analysis of its evolution in our jurisprudence is useful to understanding how and when we should apply it.

We first recognized fundamental error as a principle firmly rooted in the common law. In *Jones v. Black*, 1 Tex. 527 (1846), this Court observed that as a general rule, "the record being silent as to any judicial action either sought or had upon the issues of law, they will be considered as waived, and will not be made the subject of revision here." *Id.* at 529. Nevertheless, this Court held that " 'if the foundation of the action has manifestly failed, we can not, without shocking the common sense of justice, allow a recovery to stand.' " *Id.* at 530 (quoting *Palmer v. Lorillard*, 16 *Johnson* 343, [348], 1819 WL 1790 (N.Y. 1819)); *see also Siese v. Malsch*, 54 Tex. 355, 357 (1881) (objections that go to merits and foundation of action will be considered though unassigned as error); *Rankert v. Clow*, 16 Tex. 9, 13 (1856) (same); *Salinas v. Wright*, 11 Tex. 572, 577 (1854) (same); *Wetmore v. Woodhouse*, 10 Tex. 33, 34 (1853) (same).

Although these early cases considered fundamental error to be a principle of common law, our Legislature had already codified its own version of fundamental-error review. In 1846, the Legislature enacted a statute that provided for supreme court review of "error in law either assigned or apparent on the face of the record." Act approved May 12, 1846, 1st Leg., § 24, 1846 Tex. Gen. Laws 249, 256-57, reprinted in 2 H.P.N. GAMMEL, THE LAWS OF TEXAS 1838-1846, at 1555, 1562-63 (Austin, Gammel Book Co. 1898). But in 1850, the Legislature enacted a statute providing that "[t]he appellant or plaintiff in error, shall in all cases file with the clerk of the court below, an assignment of errors, distinctly specifying the grounds on which he relies . . . and all errors not so distinctly specified, shall be considered by the Supreme Court as waived." Act approved Feb. 11, 1850, 3rd Leg., R.S., ch. 139, § 9, 1850 Tex. Gen. Laws 171, 173-74, reprinted in 3 GAMMEL, LAWS OF TEXAS 1847-1854, at 609, 611-12 (1898). Both statutes were made applicable to the courts of civil appeals when those courts were organized. *See* Act approved Apr. 13, 1892, 22nd Leg., 1st C.S., ch. 15, §§ 24, 25, 1892 Tex. Gen. Laws 25, 29, reprinted in 10 GAMMEL, LAWS OF TEXAS 1891-1897, at 389, 393 (1898). Although by its terms, the 1850 statute appeared to repeal the 1846 statute, our courts continued to consider fundamental error without acknowledging any effect of the 1850 statute. *See Ramsey*, 205 S.W.2d at 982. *But see Oar v. Davis*, 105 Tex. 479, 151 S.W. 794, 796 (1912) (holding that the statutes could be harmonized). In one of the first cases to construe the 1846 statute, *Wilson v. Johnson*, 94 Tex. 272, 60 S.W. 242 (1900), this Court stated that "it is difficult to tell what is meant by this language; but we incline to think it intended to signify a prominent error, either fundamental in character, or one determining a question upon which the very right of the case depends." *Id.* at 243; *see also Houston Oil Co. of Tex. v. Kimball*, 103 Tex. 94, 122 S.W. 533, 537 (1909) ("Perhaps the best expression is that it must be a fundamental error, such error as being readily seen lies at the base and foundation of the proceeding and affects the judgment necessarily."). Thus, " 'fundamental error' is not a statutory term, but is one coined by the courts in interpreting our [statutes]." *Texas & Pac. Ry. Co. v. Lilly*, 118 Tex. 644, 23 S.W.2d 697, 698 (1930).

Our decisions from the pre-rules era disclose two policies that informed the application of fundamental-error review. First, as a matter of efficiency and economy, appellate courts were not required to examine the record in order to ascertain whether there was a basis for claiming error. *See Wilson*, 60 S.W. at 243 ("The purpose of assignments of error is to point out the errors complained of, and not to leave the appellate court to grope through the record to ascertain whether error has been committed or not."); *see also Ford & Damon v. Flewellen*, 276 S.W. 903, 903-04 (Tex.Com.App.1925, judgm't adopted) ("Any other rule . . . would place an almost unbearable burden upon our appellate courts."). Thus, appellate courts considered unpreserved error only when the complaint could be seen on the face of the "record"—defined as "those proceedings which lie at the foundation of the court's power to render the judgment," such as the pleadings, the charge, the verdict, and the judgment itself. *Texas & Pac. Ry. Co.*, 23 S.W.2d at 699; *see Yardley v. Houston Oil Co. of Tex.*, 288 S.W. 861, 868 (Tex. Civ. App.—Beaumont 1926, writ dism'd) ("[I]n considering fundamental error, the Court of Civil Appeals can only read the pleadings of the parties, the charge of the court, the verdict of the jury, and the judgment of the court . . . ."). If determining whether there was error required examining the statement of facts, the courts would not consider it "fundamental." *See, e.g., Yardley*, 288 S.W. at 868 (trial court's allegedly erroneous construction of deed was not "fundamental" because it would require reviewing the evidence). Second, appellate courts only reviewed unpreserved error when there was "a good and sufficient ground for the court to interfere to prevent injustice being done to one of the parties." *Houston Oil Co.*, 122 S.W. at 537; *see also Hollingsworth v. Holshousen*, 17 Tex. 41, 47-48 (1856) (citing the court's practice to review an erroneous jury charge when there is reason to believe it influenced the verdict to the prejudice of a party); *Jones*, 1 Tex. at 530 (rejecting a challenge to improper venue as merely a "dilatory" challenge and not a foundational objection).

In 1941, both statutes were repealed by the act vesting the Supreme Court with rulemaking authority. Tex.Rev.Civ. Stat. Ann. art. 1731a, §§ 1, 2 (Vernon 1948); *see City of Santa Anna v. Leach*, 173 S.W.2d 193, 197-98 (Tex. Civ. App.—Eastland 1943, writ ref'd w.o.m.). We effectively "re-enacted" the 1850 statute in the form of Texas Rule of Civil Procedure 374, which required that any errors had to be presented in the court below or would be waived. For the few years immediately following the promulgation of the 1941 rules, a few courts of civil appeals held that they could no longer review fundamental error. *See Brown v. O'Meara*, 193 S.W.2d 715, 721 (Tex. Civ. App.—Galveston 1946, writ ref'd n.r.e.); *Leach*, 173 S.W.2d at 198.

* * *

Ramsey and *McCauley* were watershed decisions, establishing that fundamental-error review is not barred by our procedural rules. In the forty years since those decisions, Texas courts have consistently recognized and reaffirmed the existence of the fundamental-error doctrine. Because there is no statute defining the principle, we tend to agree with the commentator who noted that "[t]here is no single satisfactory definition of the phrase, nor can one easily analyze the cases for prognostic purposes." *Kronzer, supra*, § 9.2, at 205. In reviewing our caselaw, however, we are able to distill two types of error that our courts have consistently recognized are subject to fundamental-error review.

First, and most commonly, we apply fundamental-error review when a jurisdictional defect exists in the case. *See, e.g., Texas Ass'n of Bus. v. Texas Air Control Bd.*, 852 S.W.2d 440, 445-46 (Tex. 1993) (holding that standing is a jurisdictional issue that can be raised for the first time on appeal); *New York Underwriters Ins. Co. v. Sanchez*, 799 S.W.2d 677, 678 (Tex. 1990) (holding that lack of appellate jurisdiction is fundamental error); *McCauley*, 304 S.W.2d at 265-66 (applying fundamental-error review because intermediate court lacked jurisdiction). With "jurisdictional-based" fundamental-error review, an appellate court may reverse the judgment of the court below for error—without conducting a review for harm—even if the error is not preserved. *See Baker v. Hansen*, 679 S.W.2d 480, 481 (Tex. 1984).

Second, we apply fundamental-error review when an important public interest or public policy is at stake. *See, e.g., Ramsey*, 205 S.W.2d at 983. "Public- interest-based" fundamental error differs from jurisdiction-based fundamental error in both a procedural and substantive way: As a procedural matter, public-interest-based fundamental-error review does not mandate automatic reversal. Instead, after an appellate court determines that it will consider the unpreserved error, the court conducts the next two steps of appellate review and determines whether an error in fact occurred, and whether the error is harmful. *See* W. Wendell Hall, *Standards of Review in Civil Appeals*, 24 ST. MARY'S L.J. 1045, 1056 (1993); *see, e.g., In re C.O.S.*, 988 S.W.2d 760, 767 (Tex. 1999) (concluding that failure to give statutory admonishments, while fundamental error, was not harmful error requiring reversal); *State v. Santana*, 444 S.W.2d 614, 615 (Tex. 1969) (holding that jury charge in juvenile case warranted fundamental-error review and analyzing whether charge violated due process), vacated on other grounds, 397 U.S. 596, 90 S.Ct. 1350, 25 L.Ed.2d 594, on remand, 457 S.W.2d 275 (Tex. 1970).

Substantively, public-interest-based fundamental error is rare, implicated only when our most significant state public interests are at stake. The meaning of the "public interest" that is adversely affected must be extremely circumscribed, or the exception would swallow the rule. Thus, it cannot be enough to allege that an error violates a party's constitutional rights. *See Texas Dep't of Protective & Regulatory Servs. v. Sherry*, 46

S.W.3d 857, 861 (Tex. 2001) (holding that constitutional claim that paternity suit should not be barred by statute of limitations is waived by failing to raise the issue before the trial court) (citing *Dreyer v. Greene*, 871 S.W.2d 697, 698 (Tex.1993)). In *Ramsey*, we characterized the type of public interest that must be at stake as one "declared in the statutes or Constitution of this state." *Ramsey*, 205 S.W.2d at 983. However, we carefully declined to create an "all-inclusive" definition of a public interest that requires fundamental-error review. *Id.* Subsequent cases have identified statements of public interest based on our constitution and reflected in our caselaw. *See, e.g., Santana*, 444 S.W.2d at 615 (citing "the constitutional importance of this case to the public generally"); *Woodard v. Texas Dep't of Human Res.*, 573 S.W.2d 596, 597 (Tex. Civ. App.—Amarillo 1978, writ rev'd n.r.e.) (citing Texas Supreme Court precedent for the proposition "that the interest of the public is affected when the custody of a child is at issue").

Since *Ramsey*, our courts have categorically recognized only one other type of public interest so significant that fundamental-error review applies—the state's interest in the rights and welfare of minors. In particular, our courts have recognized fundamental-error review in the following cases: the failure to give statutory admonishments in a juvenile delinquency proceeding, *see In re C.O.S.*, 988 S.W.2d at 767; a jury charge submitting "preponderance of the evidence" as the burden of proof in a juvenile delinquency case, *see Santana*, 444 S.W.2d at 615; a jury charge based on an invalid theory of liability in a juvenile delinquency case, *see R.A.M. v. State*, 599 S.W.2d 841, 846 (Tex. Civ. App.—San Antonio 1980, no writ); the submission of "preponderance of the evidence" as the burden of proof in a parental-rights-termination case, *see Woodard*, 573 S.W.2d at 597; and an omission in a jury charge in a divorce case that deprived a minor child of the right to support, *see Rey v. Rey*, 487 S.W.2d 245, 248 (Tex. Civ. App.—El Paso 1972, no writ).

But not all cases involving children trigger fundamental-error review. In one case involving a minor, we rejected fundamental-error review because the error affected only the immediate private litigants and did not impact a matter of more general public concern. *See Newman v. King*, 433 S.W.2d 420, 422 (Tex. 1968) (failure to appoint a guardian ad litem for a minor plaintiff in a change-of-name proceeding action does not warrant fundamental-error review because only the rights of the particular minor and litigants are affected). Our courts of appeals have reached the same result in other cases. *See Wristen v. Kosel*, 742 S.W.2d 868, 870-71 (Tex. App.—Eastland 1987, writ denied) (no fundamental-error review in a custody case between two fit parents in which "[n]either parent's parental rights have been terminated"); *Ingram v. Ingram*, 249 S.W.2d 86, 88 (Tex. Civ. App.—Galveston 1952, no writ) (no fundamental-error review in a divorce case in which "the result of the suit can be of consequence to the litigants involved alone and . . . no broad question of public interest is involved").

Having reviewed our case law in this area, we are left with two guiding principles for determining whether fundamental-error review should apply to a matter of public interest: (1) the error complained of must implicate a significant public interest or policy of the state, articulated by our statutes, constitution, or caselaw; and (2) the nature of the error must be such that it impacts a truly general public interest, and not solely that of private litigants. To guide our determination in difficult cases, we should apply fundamental-error review to further its underlying policy of promoting judicial economy while avoiding manifest injustice.

With these principles in mind, I would turn to the errors alleged in this case to determine whether the fundamental-error doctrine applies. First, the Coxes allege that the trial court erroneously failed to instruct the jury that it must find termination of the Coxes' rights to be in the best interest of the child. The Coxes admit that they did not object at trial to the errors that they raised on appeal. Because charge error does not implicate the essential jurisdiction of the trial court to act, we should not review the error unless we determine that the public-interest basis for fundamental-error review applies. Applying the principles identified above, I would conclude that this charge error warrants fundamental-error review.

Our first inquiry should be whether the error affects a significant public interest, articulated in our statutes, constitution, or caselaw. *See Ramsey*, 205 S.W.2d at 983. In the statute governing suits affecting the parent-child relationship, our Legislature has declared that "[t]he public policy of this state is to . . . assure that children will have frequent and continuing contact with parents who have shown the ability to act in the best interest of the child." TEX. FAM.CODE § 153.001(a). The statute further provides that "[t]he best interest of the child shall always be the primary consideration of the court in determining the issues of conservatorship and possession of and access to the child." *Id.* § 153.002. And in the Family Code subchapter governing the termination of parent-child relationships, the Legislature has emphasized repeatedly that the "best interest of the child" is the state's foremost priority in determining the welfare of children. *See* TEX. FAM.CODE §§ 161.001(2) (court must find by clear and convincing evidence that termination is in the best interest of the child), .003(a)(5) (court may order termination based on inability to care for a child if it is in the child's best interest), .004(a)(4) (court may order termination based on a subsequent petition if it is in the child's best interest), . 005(a) (court may order termination when parent is petitioner if in the best interest of the child), .007(3) (court may order termination if pregnancy results from parent's criminal act and if in the best interest of the child), .204 (court may order termination based on affidavit of waiver of interest if it is in the best interest of the child); *see also* §§ 107.001(b) (court must appoint guardian ad litem to represent best interest of the child in a termination suit brought by the government); 153.433 (court shall order access to a grandchild by a grandparent if in the best interest of the child). Here, the charge omits the instruction that the jury must consider the "best interest of the children." Thus, the charge directly affects a statutorily defined public interest.

Further, the charge error directly affects the public policies stated in our caselaw. We presume as a matter of public policy that the best interest of a child is usually served by maintaining the parent-child relationship. *See In re G.M.*, 596 S.W.2d 846, 847 (Tex. 1980); *Wiley v. Spratlan*, 543 S.W.2d 349, 352 (Tex. 1976). Here, the State's effort to involuntarily terminate the Coxes' rights affects the public interest in maintaining the parent-child relationship. In addition, we employ a higher standard of proof in parental-termination cases than we do in ordinary civil cases, reflecting the particular importance of ensuring a correct judgment in these cases. *In re G.M.*, 596 S.W.2d at 847 (citing *Addington v. State*, 441 U.S. 418, 99 S.Ct. 1804, 60 L.Ed.2d 323 (1979)); *see also* TEX. FAM.CODE § 161.001 (codifying *In re G.M.* by establishing "clear and convincing evidence" as the burden of proof). In this case, the charge omits a required finding for termination and therefore directly and adversely impacts the public interest in reaching a correct judgment.

Having determined that the error alleged here affects a significant public interest, we should look to see whether the error impacts the public generally, and not just the immediate litigants. *See Newman*, 433 S.W.2d at 422. I would hold that an involuntary termination suit impacts the public generally. Parents have primary responsibility for the " 'custody, care and nurture' " of their children. *In re G.M.*, 596 S.W.2d at 846 (quoting *Stanley v. Illinois*, 405 U.S. 645, 92 S.Ct. 1208, 31 L.Ed.2d 551 (1972)). The State has a right and duty to look after the welfare of the children within its borders. *See Wicks v. Cox*, 146 Tex. 489, 208 S.W.2d 876, 878 (1948). Consequently, when the State acts to terminate a parent's rights, the State assumes the responsibility for the children's welfare. The State's responsibility for the support of children is "obviously a matter of public interest" that "transcends the interest of the parties" to the immediate action. *Rey*, 487 S.W.2d at 248; *cf. Wristen*, 742 S.W.2d at 870-71 (public interest not affected by the issue of which parent is appointed as managing conservator when both parents are able to take care of the child). The charge in this case allowed the trial court to terminate Tawnya Cox's and Paige Cox's parental rights without specifically instructing the jury that it must first find termination to be in the best interest of each child. Accordingly, the jury charge in this case had a potentially adverse impact on the Cox children's best interest, which is a matter of public interest in a case that affects the public generally.

Concluding that the jury charge error alleged here is subject to fundamental- error review does not undermine the general policy of judicial economy that underlies our rule for preservation of trial error. In *Pirtle v. Gregory*, 629 S.W.2d 919 (Tex. 1982), we explained that one rationale for requiring preservation is to avoid surprise to the opponent on appeal. *Id.* at 920. Here, the State had the burden of proving all the statutory elements of termination. TEX. FAM.CODE § 161.001. The State can hardly say that it was "surprised" to find that the jury charge did not contain the elements that the statute clearly requires it to prove. Moreover, if the error likely caused an improper verdict, the State's interest would be furthered by appellate review, because the State's overriding concern is the children's best interest, not the termination of parental rights.

Accordingly, I would hold that our courts may review unpreserved jury-charge error relating to the required statutory findings in a parental-rights-termination case under our common-law doctrine of fundamental-error review. As a result of this holding, I would conclude that Texas procedures for reviewing unpreserved charge error in parental-rights-termination cases do not violate due process.

* * *

For the reasons expressed above, I respectfully dissent to the Court's opinion and judgment in this cause. The Court belabors the consequences of failing to preserve error, instead of deciding whether we can review that unpreserved error. The Court then inexplicably reviews an unpreserved complaint that it decides is harmless. Not only does the Court reach issues not presented by the parties and that are unnecessary to the resolution of the case, it retreats from our error-preservation standards, thereby adding further uncertainty to the already conflicting decisions from the courts of appeals. The only general proposition I can draw from the Court's opinion is that courts of appeals should review error when they can determine from the record that the error is ultimately harmless. But my greatest concern is that the Court abandons its responsibility to ensure that parents and children receive fair, consistent, and expeditious appellate review in these most difficult cases. Accordingly, I respectfully dissent.

JUSTICE SCHNEIDER, dissenting (opinion omitted).

Note

Texas Department of Transportation v. York, 284 S.W.3d 844 (Tex. 2009): In this Tort Claims action, York also cannot recover under an ordinary premise-defect claim. The trial court submitted to the jury only a special-defect charge, with an invitee standard of care that York had prepared. The court overruled TxDOT's objection that a premise-defect charge with a licensee standard was the proper charge under the evidence, and refused TxDOT's proffered premise-defect charge that correctly set forth the elements of liability under that theory. To establish TxDOT's liability for an ordinary premise defect, York was required to obtain findings that TxDOT had actual knowledge of the dangerous condition and that she did not. Because TxDOT objected to the omission of these elements in the jury charge (elements on which York had the burden of proof), findings cannot be deemed on the elements York's favor. The verdict thus does not support a judgment in York's favor.

b. *Trial by Implied Consent*

Read Rules 67, 90, & 274 TRCP.

HARKEY
v.
TEXAS EMPLOYERS' INS. ASS'N.

146 Tex. 504, 208 S.W.2d 919
(1948)

Richard Critz, of Austin, John J. Watts, and Mike R. Mason, both of Odessa, and Critz, Kuykendall, Bauknight, Mann & Stevenson, of Austin, for petitioner.
Whitaker, Turpin, Kerr, Smith & Brooks and Robert Turpin, all Midland, for respondent.

BREWSTER, JUSTICE.

This is a suit for workman's compensation filed by H. L. Harkey, petitioner, against Texas Employers' Insurance Association, respondent. A trial court judgment for petitioner was reversed by the Court of Civil Appeals and the cause was remanded to the trial court. 208 S.W.2d 915.

The questions for decision relate to the matter of good cause for the failure of petitioner to file with the Industrial Accident Board his claim for compensation within six months after he received his injuries; and they involve the construction and application of Rules 67, 90, and 279 Texas Rules of Civil Procedure.

As good cause for failure to file his claim within the time required by law, petitioner alleged that 'he was advised by the doctors for the defendant insurance carrier that his injuries were not serious and that he had recovered from same and was in perfect shape to return to work, and . . . that he did return to work and was able to work for a period of several months until on or about January 17, 1946, at which time he began having severe headaches and dizziness and discovered that his injuries were serious and thereupon he immediately filed claim for compensation . . . .'

Petitioner testified that he did not file his claim within the six months' period because 'Dr. Clayton told me I would be all right and could go back to work in about 30 days, or in 30 days, anyhow, and that I couldn't go back to work before that on account of my hand would be too sore'; that he believed Dr. Clayton and relied upon what he said; that he went back to work approximately four weeks from the time he got hurt and worked about a month, when he 'began to feel worse and have headaches all the time, every day'; that his headaches grew worse but that he continued to work until some time in January 1946, with a loss of only three or four days.

Respondent offered no objection that this testimony was not supported by petitioner's pleadings.

The issues submitting good cause were in substantial conformity with petitioner's testimony and were as follows: 'Do you find from a preponderance of the evidence that Dr. Clayton advised plaintiff that he was not seriously injured and could return to work in thirty days?' 'Do you find from a preponderance of the evidence that plaintiff relied upon such doctor's representations, if any, to such an extent that plaintiff refrained from filing claim for compensation sooner than same was actually filed?' 'Do you find from a preponderance of the evidence that plaintiff relying on said doctor's representations (if you have found that he did) constitutes 'good cause', as that term is defined herein, for not filing his claim for compensation sooner than same was actually filed?' 'By the term 'good cause' as used in this charge is meant whether or not the claimant has used in the prosecution of his claim that degree of diligence which a man of ordinary prudence, situated as plaintiff was, would have used under the same or similar circumstances.'

Respondent timely objected to each of these issues 'because there is no pleading authorizing the submission of such issue.'

In support of his contention that the judgment of the court of civil appeals should be reversed and that of the trial court affirmed, petitioner presents two points of error. The first is that since his testimony as to good cause was admitted without objection and since no exception was taken to his petition for failure affirmatively to allege reliance upon the advice of Dr. Clayton, the issues were tried by implied consent of the parties and must be treated as if they had been alleged in his petition, under Rules 67 and 90, *supra*.

There are several distinct factual bases for good cause under Art. 8307, sec. 4a, R. S. 1925, Vernon's Ann. Civ. St. art. 8307, s 4a. Claimant's belief in good faith that his injuries are not serious is one, provided a reasonably prudent person in the same or similar circumstances would have delayed filing his claim. *Texas Employer's Insurance Association v. Clark*, Tex. Civ. App., 23 S.W.2d 405, error dismissed. And while such belief continues, the fact that almost constant pain exists does not affect the issue; since pain and suffering are not compensable. *Texas Employers' Ins. Ass'n v. Roberts*, 135 Tex. 123, 139 S.W.2d 80. Advice from a physician that his injuries are not serious constitutes good cause for failure to file a claim within the prescribed time, provided the claimant, in the exercise of ordinary care, believes and relies upon that advice. *Consolidated Underwriters v. Pruitt*, Tex. Civ. App., 180 S.W.2d 461, er. ref., want of merit.

His allegations showed clearly that petitioner was basing his excuse for the tardy filing of his claim on his own belief that his injuries were not serious, under the factual situation dealt with in the *Clark* and *Roberts* cases, *supra*. Although he did allege that respondent's doctor advised that his injuries were not serious and that he was in perfect shape to return to work, the remainder of his allegations are inconsistent with any idea that he returned to work because he believed and relied on what the doctor told him. On that point he says: 'Plaintiff alleges that he did return to work and was able to work for a period of several months, until on or about January 17, 1946, at which time he began having severe headaches and dizziness and discovered that his injuries were serious . . . and plaintiff pleads the foregoing facts as constituting good cause for failing to file claim for compensation sooner than same was actually filed.' (Italics ours.)

Yet his testimony presented a clear case of good cause under the *Pruitt* case, *supra*, that is, that the doctor told him he would be all right and could go back to work in about 30 days but not earlier; that he believed the doctor and relied upon what the doctor said; that he went back to work in about four weeks after he got hurt and worked until some time in January, 1946, with the loss of only three or four days; but that about a month after he returned to work he began to have headaches every day and that the headaches grew worse until he quit.

Thus it is clear that petitioner alleged one group of facts recognized as constituting good cause and proved another. But he seeks to avoid the consequences of that situation on the theory that the issue proved was tried by the implied consent of respondent under Rules 67 and 90, *supra*, because the latter neither objected to the testimony as to reliance upon the advice of Dr. Clayton nor excepted to petitioner's pleading for its failure to allege such reliance. We do not believe that the rules sustain that contention.

Rule 67 says that when issues not raised by the pleadings are tried by the express or implied consent of the parties, they shall be treated as if they had been raised in the pleadings; that when unpleaded issues are so tried by consent of the parties the court may permit the pleadings to be amended so as to conform them to the evidence and to raise the issues, upon motion of any party at any time before submission of the case to the court or jury; but that failure so to amend shall not affect the result of the trial of such issues not pleaded but tried by consent.

We see nothing in that language to support the contention that respondent consented to the trial of the unpleaded issue of good cause based on reliance on the advice of Dr. Clayton. While it is true that it made no objection to the testimony to that effect, nevertheless it did object to the submission of the three issues covering that question, on the plainly stated ground that 'there is no pleading authorizing' that submission. Certainly issues are not tried merely by the hearing of the testimony thereon; submission to the jury undoubtedly is part of the process. So, although the complaining party does not object to the testimony on the issues but does object to their submission on some tenable ground, he cannot be regarded as impliedly consenting that they be tried when not raised by the pleadings, as contemplated by Rule 67.

Moreover, as respondent forcefully suggests, all the testimony by petitioner as to reliance on the advice of Dr. Clayton amounted to a failure to prove his alleged ground of his own belief that his injuries were not serious. Under those circumstances, we do not think respondent was called on to object; but when, after no proof on the alleged ground had been offered, the court tendered the parties a charge submitting the proved but unpleaded ground, respondent made the obvious objection that it was not supported by any pleading. No consent by implication could arise from that situation.

It is suggested that the objection was not specific enough to call the court's attention to the variance. If the pleading in question had been long and involved or of difficult and doubtful meaning, or if the testimony had been of like character so that the court's time would have been unduly consumed in weighing the force of the objection, the suggestion would have merit. But the allegation of good cause was pointed, brief, concise; the testimony briefly, clearly and unequivocally presented a wholly different state of facts. Under those circumstances we think the vice in the charge was sufficiently called to the court's attention.

Rule 90 has no application to the questions before us. It deals with defective pleadings. There was nothing wrong with petitioner's pleadings; the trouble arose from the failure of the proof to correspond thereto.

We have considered all the cases cited by petitioner on his contention of trial by implied consent and have decided that they have no application to the fact situation of this case. In *Connor v. Boyd*, Tex. Civ. App., 176 S.W.2d 212, 214, er. ref., want of merit, no objection was made 'to any part of the court's charge as submitted to the jury.' In *Tew et al. v. Griffith*, Tex. Civ. App., 187 S.W.2d 408, er ref., want of merit, not only was there no objection before the issues were submitted to the jury but there was none prior to rendition of judgment. In *Texas Osage Co-op Royalty Pool v. Kemper*, Tex. Civ. App., 170 S.W.2d 849, er. ref., and *Litterst v. Edmonds*, Tex. Civ. App., 176 S.W.2d 342, er. ref., want of merit, no objection was interposed before judgment. In *Thompson et al. v. Haney*, Tex. Civ. App., 191 S.W.2d 491, and *Consolidated Underwriters v. Christal et al.* Tex. Civ. App., 135 S.W.2d 127, er. ref., no objection was made in the trial court. Those facts furnished a solid basis for the theory of trial by implied consent.

* * *

The judgment of the court of civil appeals is affirmed.

Notes

1. The problems presented by "laying behind the log" and making an objection at the time of the preparation of the charge has in large part been cured by the liberal rules relating to trial amendments. As shown in an earlier Chapter, under the present case law in Texas a trial court has no discretion to refuse an amendment to the pleading at the time of the preparation of the charge after the evidence has been admitted without objection, unless the complaining party presents evidence of surprise or prejudice, or the amendment contains the assertion of a new cause of action or defense. *See, e.g., Greenhalgh v. Service Lloyds Ins. Co.*, 787 S.W.2d 938 (Tex. 1990). Thus, if the party objecting to the submission of the question, fails to satisfy his burden of proof, the amendment the pleadings will be permitted. In such a case the question will be supported by evidence and pleadings.

Therefore, as a practical matter in most cases, a party needs to object to any attempt to introduce evidence unsupported by the pleadings, in order to prevent the later amendment of the pleadings and a submission of a question.

2. *Ingram v. Deere*, 288 S.W.3d 886 (Tex.2009): "As an initial matter, we must address Deere's contention that Ingram failed to preserve his no evidence argument regarding the existence of a partnership. First, Deere argues Ingram failed to preserve his no evidence argument because he did not file a verified denial in response to Deere's claim that they were partners, which Texas Rule of Civil Procedure 93(5) requires. It is undisputed that Ingram did not file the requisite verified denial. However, this issue was tried by consent of the parties. When both parties present evidence on an issue and the issue is developed during trial without objection, any defects in the pleadings are cured at trial, and the defects are waived. TEX.R. CIV. P. 67; *Sage St. Assocs. v. Northdale Constr. Co.,* 863 S.W.2d 438, 445-46 (Tex. 1993)."

"We addressed a similar issue in *Sage Street.* In that case, we discussed whether the trial court should have submitted a contract's ambiguity to the jury, although neither party pleaded it. *Sage St.,* 863 S.W.2d at 444-46. We reiterated the long-standing rule that an issue is "not tried merely by the hearing of testimony thereon." *Id.* at 446 (citing *Harkey v. Tex. Employers' Ins. Ass'n,* 146 Tex. 504, 208 S.W.2d 919, 922 (1948)). However, because *both* parties presented conflicting testimony on the subject and allowed the issue to be raised in the jury charge, the contract's ambiguity was tried by consent. *Id.* Here, not only did both parties present evidence at trial to affirm or controvert the existence of a partnership, but Deere, the party arguing that a partnership existed, also submitted the issue in the jury charge. The issue was developed at trial, and both parties understood that it was contested. Accordingly, the failure to file a verified denial did not preclude Ingram from raising the issue on appeal."

4. *Jury Deliberations and Additional Instructions*

Read Rules 226, 280-289 Texas Rules of Civil Procedure.

MISSOURI PACIFIC R.R. CO.
v.
CROSS
501 S.W.2d 868
(Tex. 1973)

Atchley, Russell, Hutchison & Waldrop, Howard Waldrop, Texarkana, for petitioner.

Brown, Kronzer, Abraham, Watkins & Steely, W. James Kronzer, Houston, Cahill Hitt, Texarkana, for respondent.

DANIEL, JUSTICE.

This appeal involves a judgment in favor of the plaintiff, David L. Cross, against the Missouri Pacific Railroad Company, defendant, in a personal injury suit brought under the Federal Employers' Liability Act, 45 U.S.C.A. Sec. 51 et seq. Upon a jury finding of total damages to Cross in the sum of $30,000, and findings that the negligence of Missouri Pacific was the proximate cause 'in whole or in part, of the injuries,' the trial court rendered judgment for Cross in the entire amount, although there were jury findings that Cross was contributorily negligent and that his negligence amounted to thirty percent of the entire negligent which caused his injuries.

For reasons hereinafter explained, the Court of Civil Appeals held that the trial court did not err in disregarding the jury's findings relating to the negligence of Cross (Special Issues 10, 11 and 12), and affirmed. 487 S.W.2d 206. We reverse and remand.

On the night of February 8, 1969, Cross, while in the course of his employment by Missouri Pacific, tripped over a protruding nail while unloading mail from an unlighted 'piggy-back' trailer. Cross fell from the trailer, across a conveyor belt, and onto the railroad's dock, suffering extensive injuries. He alleged that Missouri Pacific failed to furnish a safe place in which to perform his work and that the trailer was not properly lighted.

The jury found in answer to Special Issue No. 1 that the defendant railroad failed to furnish David Cross a safe place to work, and in answer to Special Issue No. 2 that such failure was a cause, 'in whole or in part,' of the injuries sustained by Cross on the occasion in question. In answer to Special Issue No. 3, the jury found that the defendant railroad failed to provide adequate lighting in the trailer at the time and on the occasion in question, and in answer to Special Issue No. 4 found that such failure was a cause, 'in whole or in part,' of the injuries sustained by Cross.

The above quoted words of the causation issues were taken verbatim from Sec. 52 of the Federal Employers' Liability Act, Sec. 53 of which eliminates contributory negligence as a bar to recovery by an employee but permits contributory negligence to diminish damages under the doctrine of proportional or comparative negligence. The Federal Act prescribes the substantive rights of the parties in F.E.L.A. cases, but when filed in our State courts, they are generally to be tried in accordance with our own Rules of Civil Procedure. *Thompson v. Robbins*, 157 Tex. 463, 304 S.W.2d 111 (1957).

Special Issues 5 through 9 inquired whether Cross failed to keep a proper lookout and whether he failed to inspect the trailer, each being followed by conditional inquiries as to whether such acts were proximate causes of his injuries. In this series, only the issue on failure to inspect was answered against him; the negligence and proximate cause issues being answered in his favor or left unanswered. Then followed the three issues and answers which give rise to this appeal: SPECIAL ISSUE NO. 10. Do you find from a preponderance of the evidence that the failure of David L. Cross to obtain a drop cord at the time and on the occasion in question was negligence? Answer 'Yes' or 'No'. Answer: Yes In the event you have answered the foregoing Special Issue 'Yes' and in that event only you will answer the following Special Issue. SPECIAL ISSUE NO. 11. Do you find from a preponderance of the evidence that the negligence, if any you have so found of David L. Cross in failing to obtain a drop cord at the time and on the occasion in question was Negligence? (emphasis added) Answer 'Yes' or 'No'. Answer: Yes If by your answer to any of the already submitted Special Issues you have found (1) that Plaintiff, David L. Cross, was negligent in his acts or conduct and further that such negligence was a proximate cause of his injuries, and (2) that Defendant, Missouri Pacific Railroad Company, was negligent in any of the respects charged by Plaintiff and that such negligence resulted in whole or in part in Plaintiff's injuries, then, and in that event only, will you answer the following Special Issue. SPECIAL ISSUE NO. 12. What per cent, if any, do you find from a preponderance of the evidence does the negligence, if any, of the Plaintiff bear to the entire negligence, if any, of both the Plaintiff and the Defendant? Answer by giving the percentage. Answer: 30%

As heretofore indicated, the final Special Issue (No. 13) inquired 'what sum of money . . . would fairly and reasonably compensate David Cross for his injuries, if any, which . . . resulted from the occurrence in question?', and the jury answered $30,000.

It will be noted that Special Issue No. 11 is not worded as a proximate cause issue. It merely asks if 'the negligence, if any' of Cross in failing to obtain a drop cord (light) 'was negligence'. About twenty minutes after the jury retired, and while counsel for plaintiff was dictating his objections to the charge, counsel for defendant discovered this typographical error in Issue No. 11 and filed a motion with the Court to have it corrected so that the last phrase would read, 'was a proximate cause of the injuries for which he sues here?' The trial court refused, citing an agreement made by the court and the attorneys 'that Objections and Exceptions to the charge could be made while the jury was deliberating provided there would be no new issues or definitions requested by either party,' all of which was clearly in violation of Rule 272, Texas Rules of Civil Procedure.

After the jury had deliberated for approximately an hour and thirty minutes, the foreman sent the following written message to the trial court: 'We would like to have issue #10 and #11 explained to us.' Whereupon, again by agreement of court and counsel and contrary to Rules 272 and 286, the court and counsel proceeded from the courtroom to another floor on which the jury room was located, and met with the jury in the hallway. The foreman repeated the request orally and the trial court orally stated that Special Issue No. 10 inquired whether or not failure to obtain a drop cord was negligence and that Special Issue No. 11 inquired whether or not it was a proximate cause of the injuries for which plaintiff sued. Upon returning to his chambers with counsel for both parties, the court drafted a different written response to the jury, as follows: 'In answer to your question, please resume your deliberations and answer the issues from a preponderance of the evidence.' Whereupon, counsel for the defendant railroad moved for a mistrial because of the facts related above and because the additional written charge did not conform to the oral charge as given by the court. This and another Motion for

Correction of the typographical error in Special Issue No. 11 were denied by the trial court. The jury returned its verdict on September 1, 1971; on September 13, 1971, Cross filed a motion for judgment in his favor 'in response to the answers of the jury to the charge of the Court;' and on October 7, 1971, the trial court rendered judgment for Cross in the full amount of $30,000. Obviously, the trial court disregarded the jury's answers to Special Issues 10, 11 and 12, although such action was not requested in plaintiff's motion for judgment or referred to in the trial court's judgment.

Having found Cross contributorily negligent by its answer to Special Issue No. 10, it seems abundantly clear from its 'thirty percent' answer to Special Issue No. 12 (which was conditioned on a finding of both plaintiff and defendant being guilty of negligence which caused plaintiff's injuries) that the jury intended its answer to Special Issue No. 11 as a finding that the negligence of Cross was a proximate cause of this injuries. Otherwise there would have been no reason to have answered that his negligence was thirty percent of the total negligence found by them to have occurred.

The Court of Civil Appeals affirmed on the grounds that, in spite of any alleged errors which might have been made in the violation of Rule 272 and the trial court's handling of Special Issue No. 11, it properly disregarded Special Issues 10, 11 and 12, because Missouri Pacific had failed to discharge the burden of obtaining a proper series of issues concerning the alleged contributory negligence of Cross. The Court's reasoning is that 'the evidence was far from conclusive that drop-cords were available on the evening in question, thus making it necessary for appellant (Missouri Pacific) to submit an issue to the jury for them to decide' on that question. The thrust of this reasoning is, as now argued by Cross, that Special Issue No. 10 was objectionable because it assumed an ultimate disputed fact issue. There may be some merit to this reasoning if the issue and the court's charge had been properly and timely objected to by Cross in the trial court, but this was not done. In accordance with the aforementioned agreement between the trial court and counsel, neither of the parties made any objections to the charge until after it was read to the jury. In fact, the transcript reveals that Cross's objections to the charge were not reduced to writing before January 14, 1972, and were not filed until March 27, 1972.

Rule 272 reads in part: The charge shall be in writing, signed by the judge, and filed with the clerk, and shall be a part of the record of the cause. It shall be prepared after the evidence has been concluded and shall be submitted to the respective parties or their attorneys for inspection, and a reasonable time given them in which to examine and present objections thereto, which objections shall in every instance be presented to the court in writing before the charge is read to the jury, and all objections not so made and presented shall be considered as waived. . . . The requirement that the objections to the court's charge shall be in writing will be sufficiently complied with if such objections are dictated to the court reporter in the presence of and with the consent of the court and opposing counsel, Before the reading of the court's charge to the jury, and are subsequently transcribed and the court's ruling and official signature endorsed thereon and filed with the clerk in time to be included in the transcript. (Emphasis added).

The Texas Rules of Civil Procedure have the same force and effect as statutes. *Freeman v. Freeman*, 160 Tex. 148, 327 S.W.2d 428, 433 (1959). They are to be given a liberal construction to the end of accomplishing their objective 'to obtain a just, fair, equitable and impartial adjudication of the rights of litigants under established principles of substantive law . . . .' (Rule 1), but they are not to be ignored by agreements of courts and counsel to operate contrary thereto and in violation thereof. Especially is this true when such agreements lead to unfair and harmful results to either or both litigants as in this case. Here, the agreement contrary to Rule 272 led to a series of other Rule violations and errors of the trial court. Had Rule 272 been followed, even to the extent of dictating the objections to the charge 'to the court reporter in the presence of and with the consent of the court and opposing counsel, Before the reading of the court's charge to the jury . . . .' (emphasis added), the typographical error in Issue No. 11 would have been discovered before the charge was given to the jury. This is evident from the fact that the error was discovered during the dictation of plaintiff's objections to this issue, but such dictation was after the reading of the court's charge to the jury; after counsel had completed their arguments; and about twenty minutes after the jury had retired twenty minutes after the jury had retired for its deliberations. One of the main purposes of Rule 272 is to enable the trial court to submit a proper charge to the jury and to have the prior benefit of counsel's objections so as to correct any errors that might otherwise occur. This beneficial purpose of the Rule was defeated by the agreement between the court and counsel in this case. Having been parties to the agreement, neither plaintiff nor defendant is in a position to complain, and neither has complained, of its direct effect on procedural rights to which either was justly entitled. However, we consider the question necessarily before us in connection with points and counterpoints presented on this appeal, and we hold that it was clearly error for the trial court to approve the agreement in violation of Rule 272. *See State v. Davis*, 228 S.W.2d 359 (Tex. Civ. App. 1950, no writ) and cases therein cited. Since all objections of both parties to the court's charge were dictated after the charge was read to the jury, we consider them as waived. Rule 272.

The subsequently discovered error in the wording of Special Issue No. 11 could have been corrected by written instructions of the trial court under Rule 286 after the jury retired. It was an obvious error pointed out and objected to by plaintiff after the jury retired, and a correction was thereafter immediately requested by the defendant, but denied by the trial court. As heretofore indicated, the error became obvious even to the jury, which submitted a written request to the court stating, 'We would like to have issue #10 and #11 explained to us.' The court erred in its attempted oral explanation in the hallway and abused its discretion in failing to correct the issue by a written instruction to the jury in accordance with Rule 286.

It is obvious that these procedural errors were prejudicial. They resulted in either an intended proximate cause finding court's oral explanation of the meaning of Special Issue No. 11, or a conflict between its answers to Special Issues 10 and 11 and its answer to Special Issue No. 12, the latter being predicated upon a finding of negligence and proximate cause against the plaintiff. Further, the trial court's disregard of Special Issue No. 12 left plaintiff with two findings of negligent acts by defendant which were causes 'in whole or in part,' of plaintiff's injuries, but without the jury having been permitted to speak with certainty the truth of its findings on which it based diminishment of damages 'in proportion to the amount of negligence attributable to such employee,' as provided by Sec. 53, 45 U.S.C.A.

Accordingly, the judgments of the courts below are reversed and the cause is remanded to the trial court for a new trial.

Notes

1. *In re Health Care Unlimited, Inc.*, 429 S.W.3d 600 (Tex. 2014) (per curiam): Abuse of discretion to grant new trial because no showing that communications between juror and employee of Defendant met standards for a new trial. Conversation was not material and there was no showing that it probably resulted in injury.

2. *In re Whataburger*, 429 S.W.3d 597 (Tex. 2014) (per curiam): Abuse of discretion to grant new trial in *In Re Health Care* because no showing that communications between juror and employee of Defendant met standards for a new trial. Trial court used an "appearance of impropriety" standard. But conversation was (1) not material and (2) there was no showing that it probably resulted in injury. Abuse of discretion to grant new trial in *In re Whataburger* because juror failed to disclose she had been involved in other lawsuits. Failed to meet above standards for new trial.

3. *King Fisher Marine Service, L.P. v. Tamez*, 443 S.W.3d 838 (Tex. 2014): A trial court does not have to entertain charge objections up to the time it charges the jury. The trial court acts within its discretion in setting an earlier deadline for the end of the charge conference. Thus, the trial court acted within its discretion in refusing to hear a last-minute charge objection.

4. Rule 286 of the Texas Rules of Civil Procedures provides: **Jury May Receive Further Instructions**: After having retired, the jury may receive further instructions from the court touching any matter of law, either at their request or upon the court's own motion. For this purpose they shall appear before the judge in open court in a body, and if the instruction is being given at their request, they shall through their presiding juror state to the court, in writing, the particular question of law upon which they desire further instruction. The court shall give such instruction in writing, but no instruction shall be given except in conformity with the rules relating to the charge. Additional argument may be allowed in the discretion of the court.

FIRST EMPLOYEES INS. CO.
v.
SKINNER

646 S.W.2d 170
(Tex. 1983)

Facts: This is a worker's compensation case. This is an appeal from a judgment rendered on the jury verdict awarding Jessie Skinner workers' compensation benefits for total and permanent incapacity. The court of appeals affirmed.

Issue: After the parties have rested and the charge read to the jury, is the trial court to send to the jury room the exhibits admitted at trial?

Held: Yes: We hold that Rule 281 requires that the exhibits be sent to the jury room and, therefore, the trial court erred in refusing to do so when requested by First Employees.

Issue: If exhibits are to be sent to the jury room, is the failure to do so harmful?

Held: Not here. We conclude, however, that the error was harmless under the record in this case and affirm the judgment of the court of appeals. This is a judgment call entrusted to the sound discretion and good sense of the reviewing court from an evaluation of the whole case.

Rule 281 provides: The jury may take with them in their retirement the charges and instructions, general or special, which were given and read to them, and any written evidence, except the depositions of witnesses, but shall not take with them any special charges which have been refused. Where part only of a paper has been read in evidence, the jury shall not take the same with them, unless the part so read to them is detached from that which was excluded.

We conclude that Rule 281 is mandatory and that the trial court is required to send all exhibits admitted into evidence to the jury room during the deliberations of the jury. Furthermore, this rule is self-operative and requires no request from the jurors or counsel. We recognize that an exhibit may be so large and cumbersome that it would not be feasible to send such exhibit to the jury room. This problem, however, is not presented here.

Note

Rule 281 of the Texas Rules of Civil Procedures provides as follows: **Papers Taken to the Jury Room.** With the court's permission, the jury may take with them to the jury room any notes they took during the trial. In addition, the jury may, and on request shall, take with them in their retirement the charges and instructions, general or special, which were given and read to them, and any written evidence, except the depositions of witnesses, but shall not take with them any special charges which have been refused. Where only part of a paper has been read in evidence, the jury shall not take the same with them, unless the part so read to them is detached from that which was excluded.

GOLDEN
v.
FIRST CITY NAT'L BANK

751 S.W.2d 639
(Tex. App.—Dallas 1988, no writ)

Tim Tyner, Susan Leigh Sanders, Arlington, for appellant.
James F. Boyle, Grand Prairie, for appellee.

ENOCH, CHIEF JUSTICE.

Appellant James Golden (Golden) appeals the trial court's judgment in a conversion action brought against him by appellee First City National Bank in Grand Prairie (First City). In six points of error, Golden contends that the district court erred in delivering to the jury a supplemental, verdict-urging instruction commonly known as an Allen-type charge. *See Allen v. United States*, 164 U.S. 492, 17 S.Ct. 154, 41 L.Ed. 528 (1896). Golden further urges that the court erred in denying his motion for new trial based upon jury misconduct. For the reasons discussed below, we affirm the judgment of the district court.

First City sued Golden to recover $11,700.00. First City contended that Golden came to the bank to cash checks worth approximately $1,300.00, but that First City's teller mistakenly gave him $13,000.00. Golden denied these allegations.

The case was tried to a jury. The court submitted one special issue to the jury inquiring whether Golden had received $11,700.00 belonging to First City. After deliberating approximately three hours, the jury sent a note to the trial judge stating that the jurors could not agree on an answer to the special issue. After consulting with counsel, the judge sent a supplemental, verdict-urging instruction to the jury. Approximately thirty minutes later, the jury returned a ten-to-two verdict in favor of First City.

In its brief, First City correctly points out that Golden has failed to provide an appellate record which demonstrates either the exact contents of the jury's note to the judge or the length of the jury's deliberations before and after receiving the supplemental charge. For purposes of this opinion, however, we will accept the description in Golden's brief.

After trial, First City filed a motion for judgment on the verdict. Golden filed a response and motion for new trial. The motion for new trial alleged jury misconduct and was supported with an affidavit from one of the jurors. In the affidavit, the juror stated that he did not believe that First City had proven its case against Golden. However, he felt pressured into changing his vote in favor of First City because, after receiving the supplemental charge, he was led to believe that a hung jury was not allowed.

The judge granted First City's motion for judgment on the verdict and overruled Golden's motion for new trial. Twenty-nine days after the trial court's ruling on his first motion for new trial, Golden submitted a second motion for new trial. Despite some changes in wording, the grounds for this motion were essentially the same as in the first motion. The trial court's docket sheet shows that this motion was also denied.

THE SUPPLEMENTAL INSTRUCTION

All of Golden's points of error, in one manner or another, concern whether the supplemental instruction was coercive. Therefore, we will review the instruction before discussing Golden's points of error. The court submitted the following charge to the jury. Members of the Jury: I have your note that you are unable to reach a decision on the charge submitted to you by the Court. I am going to ask you to return to the jury room to continue your deliberations. This case has been ably tried by competent attorneys and you are a representative jury of the citizens of Dallas County. In the interest of justice, if you could end this litigation by your verdict, you should do so. I do not mean to say that any individual person on the jury should yield his or her own conscience and positive conviction, but I do mean that when you are in the jury room, you should discuss this matter among yourselves carefully and listen to each other, and try, if you can, to reach a conclusion on the issues. It is the duty of jurors to keep their minds open and free to every reasonable argument that may be presented by fellow jurors that they may arrive at a decision which justly answers the consciences of the individuals making up the jury. A juror should not surrender any conscientious views founded upon the evidence unless convinced of his or her error by fellow jurors. It has cost the citizens of Dallas County considerable expense to have this case tried before a jury over the past few days. I am satisfied, ladies and gentlemen, that you have not deliberated sufficiently so that, in good conscience, I can accept a report that you cannot reach a decision. Accordingly, please return to the jury room to continue your deliberations.

In *Stevens v. Travelers Insurance Company*, 563 S.W.2d 223 (Tex. 1978), the supreme court sets forth the procedure for evaluating whether a verdict-urging instruction is coercive. First, the court must examine the charge for possibly coercive statements. If a possibly coercive statement is found, the court then must consider the charge as a whole and the circumstances surrounding it. *Id.* at 229-32.

In this case, the charge presented by the district court is substantially similar to the charge considered in *Stevens*, except that the trial court in this case eliminated a statement identified in *Stevens* as potentially coercive. Nevertheless, Golden asserts that the instruction contains two statements which render it coercive.

First, Golden points to the statement: "It has cost the citizens of Dallas County considerable expense to have this case tried before a jury over the past few days." Golden argues that this statement is coercive. He contends that its placement in a separate paragraph near the bottom of the charge lends it undue emphasis. Despite Golden's arguments, we cannot agree that this statement is coercive. The charge in *Stevens* contained a substantially identical statement in a substantially identical position in the charge. Although the court in Stevens did not approve this statement, it stated that, "if it is given, it is not, without more, coercive." *Stevens*, 563 S.W.2d at 231-32. Golden has pointed to no factors which differentiate the cost statement in this charge from the cost statement in *Stevens*. Therefore, following *Stevens*, we conclude that this statement is not coercive.

The second statement which Golden considers improper is "I am satisfied, ladies and gentlemen, that you have not deliberated sufficiently so that, in good conscience, I can accept a report that you cannot reach a decision. Accordingly, please return to the jury room to continue your deliberations." Again, this statement is substantially similar to one which the *Stevens* court found non-coercive. Golden points out that this statement differs from the statement in *Stevens* in that the trial court in this case used the words "reach a decision" while the charge in *Stevens* used the words "arrive at an agreement." This difference is without significance, and we hold that the statement in this case is not coercive.

Golden further argues, though, that the court's charge was unduly coercive because it was not tailored to take into account the circumstances of the case and the susceptibility of this particular jury to the effects of the charge. Golden did not suggest, however, either to the trial court or in his brief, any particular way in which the trial court should have tailored its charge. Nor did he identify any characteristics of the case or the jury which would have indicated, at the time that the charge was submitted, that such tailoring was required. Golden urges, however, that the juror's affidavit supporting his motion for new trial demonstrates that the charge had the effect of being coercive.

The procedure prescribed by *Stevens* requires a court to consider the surrounding circumstances in evaluating a supplemental, verdict-urging instruction only if the court determines that the instruction contains potentially coercive statements. *Anzaldua v. American Guarantee Liability & Insurance Co.*, 596 S.W.2d 222 (Tex. Civ. App.—Houston [14th Dist.] 1980, writ ref'd n.r.e.). In this case, the supplemental instruction contains no such statements. Therefore, we need not consider the surrounding circumstances. Regardless, if we were to consider the surrounding circumstances, Texas Rule of Civil Procedure 327(b) and Texas Rule of Civil Evidence 606(b), discussed below, preclude consideration of the juror's affidavit. Without the affidavit, the only factor stated by Golden as demonstrating a coercive effect is the jury's returning its verdict thirty minutes after receiving the charge. Given that the total deliberations lasted only three and one-half hours, this does not demonstrate that the charge was coercive. Nothing in our review suggests that the instruction in this case was coercive.

We now consider Golden's points of error.

Points of Error Two and Three

In points of error two and three, Golden contends that the trial court erred in submitting the supplemental instruction to the jury and failing to accept its deadlocked verdict. First City argues that Golden has waived any error regarding the supplemental charge because he failed to object at the time the charge was submitted. We agree.

Under Texas Rule of Civil Procedure 272, litigants must present their objections to the charge before it is presented to the jury. Objections not so presented are waived. TEX. R. CIV. P. 272; *see also Missouri Pacific Railroad Company v. Cross*, 501 S.W.2d 868, 873 (Tex. 1973). Rule 272 is most clearly applicable to objections to the court's initial charge to the jury. The rule that objections must be presented before the charge has been given to the jury, however, has also been applied to supplemental instructions, including instructions which a litigant later contends were coercive. *Texas Pacific Indemnity Company v. Building Material Distributors, Inc.*, 508 S.W.2d 488 (Tex. Civ. App.—Waco 1974, writ ref'd n.r.e.). At oral argument, Golden asserted that a litigant should not be required to object at the time that a verdict-urging instruction is presented to the jury because the instruction's coercive effect may not be apparent until later. We disagree.

Although the parties may not be able to predict the effect of a verdict-urging instruction with complete accuracy, this does not relieve them of their obligation to review the text of the court's charge and point out to the trial court any statements which they find potentially coercive. A primary purpose of Rule 272 is to allow the trial court the benefit of counsel's objections so that it might correct any errors before the charge is given to the jury. *Cross*, 501 S.W.2d at 873. Given this purpose, the requirement of a prior objection seems particularly appropriate in a delicate area such as a verdict-urging instruction. A party may not speculate on the effect of the charge on the jury's verdict and then complain for the first time when that verdict goes against him. *See Colls v. Price's Creameries*, 244 S.W.2d 900, 906 (Tex. Civ. App.—El Paso 1951, writ ref'd n.r.e.). Furthermore, even if Golden had preserved error as to points two and three, our analysis shows that the charge was not coercive. Golden's second and third points of error are overruled.

* * *

We AFFIRM the judgment of the trial court.

5. *Receipt of the Verdict*

Read Rules 292 and 294 Texas Rules of Civil Procedure.

Note

A verdict is without force or effect until it has been received and accepted by the court. *See, e.g., Guest v. American Petrofina Company*, 485 S.W .2d 926 (Tex. Civ. App.—Texarkana 1972, no writ). A losing party has the opportunity to poll the jury before the verdict is received. *See* Rule 294 Texas Rules of Civil Procedure. Any juror may effectively dissent until the trial judge has received the verdict. *See, e.g., State v. Finch*, 349 S.W.2d 780 (Tex. Civ. App.—San Antonio 1961, no writ). Once received and accepted by the court, the verdict may not be impeached by a showing that the verdict was less than unanimous [or less than 10-2] at some point during the deliberations. *See, e.g., Jones v. Square Deal Cab Co.*, 506 S.W.2d 855 (Tex. 1974).

a. *Incomplete Verdict*

FLEET
v.
FLEET
711 S.W.2d 1
(Tex. 1986)

Philip Durst, Austin, for petitioner.
Garrett Morris, Morris & Schieffer, Fort Worth, for respondent.

PER CURIAM.

This is a suit against an executor for breach of fiduciary duties. The trial court rendered a take nothing judgment against Peggy Fleet based on an incomplete verdict. In an unpublished opinion, the court of appeals affirmed the judgment.

The issue on appeal is whether the trial judge properly rendered judgment based on an incomplete verdict, and whether the court of appeals properly affirmed. We grant the application for writ of error and, pursuant to Rule 483 without hearing oral argument, reverse the judgment of the court of appeals and remand the cause for a new trial.

Claud Fleet's former mother-in-law, Irene Lewis, died on September 17, 1970, leaving a will which named Claud Fleet independent executor. In 1982, Peggy Fleet, Claud Fleet's former wife and Irene Lewis' surviving daughter, sued Claud Fleet for various breaches of fiduciary duties. The trial judge presented the acts alleged as breaches in one issue, lettered "A" through "K." Each lettered question contained a different act. The jury found "We Do Not" to questions "D" and "H," and "We Do" to questions "I," "J," and "K." The jury left the remaining questions unanswered.

Issue number seven, lettered to correspond to issue number one, asked the jury to find when "Peggy Fleet discovered or by reasonable diligence should have discovered Respondent Claud Fleet's acts . . . ." The jury left blank questions "A" through "H," and found dates for "I" through "K" of April 15, 1977, February 4, 1975, and September 14, 1973 respectively.

The trial judge rendered a take nothing judgment against Peggy Fleet, concluding, based on the jury's answers to issue seven, that Peggy Fleet was barred by the applicable statute of limitations. The court of appeals affirmed the judgment. Peggy Fleet brings two complaints to this court: (1) that the court of appeals erred in holding that the statute of limitations barred her claim; and, (2) that the trial court erred in rendering judgment and not declaring a mistrial when the jury could not agree to answers to material issues in issue number one.

Peggy Fleet's second complaint is correct and dispositive of the case because the trial court's and court of appeal's judgments conflict directly with our prior opinion in *Powers v. Standard Acc. Ins. Co.*, 144 Tex. 415, 191 S.W.2d 7 (1945). We held in *Powers* that a judgment cannot be based on a verdict containing unanswered issues, supported by some evidence, unless the issues are immaterial. Issues are only immaterial if their answers can be found elsewhere in the charge or if they cannot alter the effect of the verdict. 191 S.W.2d at 9. The issues this jury left unanswered are material, for each issue inquires about a different act; none duplicate. Further, while the jury found that Peggy Fleet discovered the acts in the answered issues outside of the applicable statute of limitations period, it may have found that she discovered the unanswered acts within the applicable statute of limitations period.

Faced with a verdict which leaves material issues supported by some evidence unanswered, the trial court must instruct the jury to deliberate further on the issues. If upon further deliberation the jury cannot agree on answers to the issues, the trial court may declare a mistrial, but the trial court may not render judgment based on the incomplete verdict. *Powers*, 191 S.W.2d at 9. The trial court will not be reversed for rendering judgment, however, unless the party who would benefit from answers to the issues objects to the incomplete verdict before the jury is discharged, making it clear that he desires that the jury redeliberate on the issues or that the trial court grant a mistrial. *Continental Casualty Co. v. Street*, 379 S.W.2d 648 (Tex. 1964); *Lewis v. Texas Employers Ins. Ass'n*, 151 Tex. 95, 246 S.W.2d 599 (1952).

Peggy Fleet properly objected to the incomplete verdict before the court discharged the jury by asking that the jury be instructed to further deliberate or that the trial judge grant a mistrial. Rather than instructing the jury to deliberate further, the trial court asked each juror if further deliberations would help them agree to answers. When the jurors said "no," the judge discharged the jury. The trial court later denied Peggy Fleet's motion for mistrial and rendered the take nothing judgment against her.

We hold that the trial court erred by rendering judgment on the incomplete verdict and not ordering a mistrial when it realized that the jury could not agree to answers to material, evidenced issues. *Powers*, 191 S.W.2d at 9. Because the resolution of this point of error fully disposes of this case, we do not reach Peggy Fleet's point on the statute of limitations. Accordingly, we reverse the judgment of the court of appeals and remand the cause to the probate court for a new trial.

Notes

1. *Powers v. Standard Acc. Ins. Co.*, 144 Tex. 415, 191 S.W.2d 7 (1945). Where the verdict is partial, the right to judgment depends on whether the unanswered issues could have affected the results of a judgment. Where the evidence is sufficient to support the submission of an issue to the jury, the party with the burden of proof must secure a favorable jury finding to any issue submitted. Negative answers to those issues will entitle the opponent to a judgment on that issue, but the failure to answer the issues will not authorize a judgment for the opponent, unless other answers to other issues render the unanswered issues immaterial. When material issues are not answered, the verdict is incomplete, and a mistrial should be granted.

2. In *Osterberg v. Peca*, 12 S.W.3d 31 (Tex. 2000) the Court made the following comments on the basis for reversing a judgment on an incomplete verdict:

> Finally, Peca complains that the court of appeals erred in holding that he waived recovery of attorney's fees. Section 253.131 entitles an opposing candidate who proves a violation of Chapter 253 to recover, in addition to damages based on the value of the unlawful contribution or expenditure, "reasonable attorney's fees incurred in the suit." TEX. ELEC. CODE § 253.131(d)(2). The trial court submitted a question asking the jury to "[f]ind, in dollars and cents, the total amount that would be a reasonable attorney's fee for the services by 'Plaintiff's attorney' incurred in this case." The jury informed the trial court that it was deadlocked on that question. After that disclosure, Peca failed to object or request an answer to his attorney's fees question. Instead, Peca asked the trial court to accept the incomplete verdict, and then asked the court to enter judgment as a matter of law for his attorney's fees. The trial court refused, and the court of appeals affirmed, holding that Peca had waived the issue for appeal. 952 S.W.2d at 132. Peca argues that his failure to request a jury answer did not waive his right to attorney's fees because his uncontroverted evidence entitled him to attorney's fees as a matter of law. In finding that Peca waived his right to attorney's fees, the court of appeals relied on this Court's decision in *Fleet v. Fleet*, 711 S.W.2d 1 (Tex.1986). In *Fleet*, we held that a trial court will not be reversed for rendering judgment on an incomplete verdict unless the party who would benefit from answers to the unanswered issues objects to the incomplete verdict before the jury is discharged. . . . Peca, by failing to object when the jury did not return an answer, waived any benefit from the jury question, waived any right to have the trial judge supply his own factfinding or grant a new trial on the issue, and waived his right to appeal a judgment on the issue of attorney's fees. We affirm the court of appeals' judgment regarding attorney's fees.

b. *Conflict in Jury's Answers*

Read Rule 295 Texas Rules of Civil Procedure.

USAA TEXAS LLOYDS CO.
v.
MENCHACA
545 S.W.3d 479
(Tex. 2018)

Wallace B. Jefferson, Rachel A. Ekery, Alexander Dubose, Jefferson & Townsend LLP, Mary Margaret Roark, Thomas R. Phillips, Baker Botts LLP, Austin TX, Charles T. Frazier Jr., Alexander Dubose, Jefferson & Townsend LLP, Dallas TX, Bruce E. Ramage, Martin Disiere Jefferson & Wisdom LLP, Christopher W. Martin, Levon G. Hovnatanian, Paul Wayne Pickering, Robert T. Owen, Martin Disiere Jefferson & Wisdom LLP, Tanya Dugas, Raley & Bowick, LLP, Houston TX, for Petitioner USAA Texas Lloyds Company.

Jennifer Bruch Hogan, James C. Marrow, Richard P. Hogan Jr., Hogan & Hogan, Pennzoil Place, John Steven Mostyn, The Mostyn Law Firm, Houston TX, Gilberto Hinojosa, Law Offices of Gilberto, Hinojosa & Associates, P.C., Brownsville TX, Randal G. Cashiola, Cashiola & Bean, Beaumont TX, for Respondent Menchaca, Gail.

Michael A. Choyke, Thomas C. Wright, Lisa Wright, Wright, Close & Barger, LLP, Houston TX, for Amicus Curiae, Lexington Insurance Company.

Brendan K. McBride, The McBride Law Firm, Marc E. Gravely, Matthew R. Pearson, Gravely & Pearson, LLP, San Antonio TX, for Amicus Curiae, Brass Real Estate Funds, Texas Automobile Dealers Association, Texas Independent Automobile Dealers Association, Texas Organization of Rural & Community, Hospitals.

Russell S. Post, Beck Redden LLP, Houston TX, for Amicus Curiae, Cameron, a Schlumberger Company.

Dale Wainwright, Kendyl Taylor Hanks, Greenberg Traurig, LLP, Austin TX, Lindsay E. Hagans, Houston TX, for Amicus Curiae, Chamber of Commerce of the United States of America.

Catherine L. Hanna, Hanna & Plaut LLP, Austin TX 7870, for Amicus Curiae, Insurance Council of Texas.

Hugh Rice Kelly, Texans for Lawsuit Reform, Houston TX, for Amicus Curiae, Texans for Lawsuit Reform.

Marc S. Tabolsky, Penelope E. Nicholson, Schiffer Odom Hicks & Johnson PLLC, Houston TX, for Amicus Curiae, United Policyholders.

JUSTICE BOYD announced the Court's judgment and delivered the Court's opinion as to Parts I, II, and III.A, in which CHIEF JUSTICE HECHT, JUSTICE GREEN, JUSTICE GUZMAN, JUSTICE LEHRMANN, JUSTICE DEVINE, and JUSTICE BROWN joined, a plurality opinion as to Parts III.B and III.C, in which CHIEF JUSTICE HECHT, JUSTICE LEHRMANN, and JUSTICE DEVINE joined, and an opinion as to Parts III.D, III.E, III.F, and III.G, in which JUSTICE LEHRMANN and JUSTICE DEVINE joined.

After Hurricane Ike struck Galveston Island in September 2008, Gail Menchaca contacted her homeowner's insurance company, USAA Texas Lloyds, and reported that the storm had damaged her home. The adjuster USAA sent to investigate Menchaca's claim found only minimal damage. Based on the adjuster's findings, USAA determined that its policy covered some of the damage but declined to pay Menchaca any benefits because the total estimated repair costs did not exceed the policy's deductible. About five months later, at Menchaca's request, USAA sent another adjuster to re-inspect the property. This adjuster generally confirmed the first adjuster's findings, and USAA again refused to pay any policy benefits. Menchaca sued USAA for breach of the insurance policy and for unfair settlement practices in violation of the Texas Insurance Code.

* * *

* * * the jury in this case (1) failed to find in answer to Question 1 that USAA failed to comply with its obligations under the insurance policy; (2) found in answer to Question 2 that USAA violated the Insurance Code by failing to pay Menchaca's claim for policy benefits "without conducting a reasonable investigation with respect to" that claim; and (3) found in answer to Question 3 that USAA's statutory violation resulted in Mencha-

ca incurring damages of $11,350, representing the amount of policy benefits USAA "should have paid" Menchaca.

* * *

* * * Here, the jury's answer to Question 3 (USAA "should have paid" $11,350 in policy benefits to Menchaca) necessarily addresses the same material fact as its answer to Question 1 (USAA "fail[ed] to comply with the terms of the insurance policy"), because both requested findings on whether USAA failed to pay benefits Menchaca was entitled to under the policy. The answers conflict because if USAA "should have paid" Menchaca benefits under the policy and did not, then USAA necessarily failed to comply with the policy's terms.

* * *

When an irreconcilable conflict involves one jury answer that would require a judgment in favor of the plaintiff and another that would require a judgment in favor of the defendant, the conflict is fatal. *Little Rock Furniture Mfg. Co. v. Dunn*, 148 Tex. 197, 222 S.W.2d 985, 991 (1949). Here, both questions address the decisive issue—whether USAA failed to pay benefits Menchaca was entitled to under the policy. Without Questions 2 and 3, the jury's answer to Question 1 would require a judgment in USAA's favor. But without Question 1, the jury's answers to Questions 2 and 3 would require a judgment in Menchaca's favor. We thus conclude that the answers created a fatal conflict.

Our determination that the verdict contained a fatal conflict does not end the inquiry. Of course, a trial court should not enter judgment based on a verdict containing a fatal conflict until "the disputed question of fact . . . has been resolved." *Meyer*, 502 S.W.2d at 679. But we must decide whether we can consider a trial court's error in entering such a judgment when neither party has objected to the conflict.

Generally, as "a prerequisite to presenting a complaint for appellate review, the record must show that . . . the complaint was made to the trial court by a timely request, objection, or motion." TEX. R. APP. P. 33.1(a)(1)(A). This rule "conserves judicial resources by giving trial courts an opportunity to correct an error before an appeal proceeds," promotes "fairness among litigants" by prohibiting them from surprising their opponents on appeal, and furthers "the goal of accuracy in judicial decision-making" by allowing the parties to "develop and refine their arguments" and allowing the trial court to "analyze the questions at issue." *In re B.L.D.*, 113 S.W.3d 340, 350 (Tex. 2003). Under, this rule, we will not consider an error that was not properly raised in the trial court "unless a recognized exception exists." *Id.*

An exception to the preservation-of-error requirement applies when the alleged error is "fundamental." * * *

* * *

* * * we conclude that the fatal conflict in the jury's verdict in this case does not constitute fundamental error, and as a result, we cannot consider that conflict unless the error was properly preserved. *Mack Trucks*, 206 S.W.3d at 577.

We next consider how and when a party must properly preserve error based on a fatal conflict in a jury verdict. rule 295, entitled "Correction of Verdict," provides that if a jury's answers "are in conflict," the trial court must give the jury written instructions regarding the nature of the conflict "and retire the jury for further deliberations." TEX. R. CIV. P. 295. * * *

* * *

We agree with the courts of appeals that to preserve error based on fatally conflicting jury answers, parties must raise that objection before the trial court discharges the jury. As we have explained, our "procedural rules are technical, but not trivial." *Burbage v. Burbage,* 447 S.W.3d 249, 258 (Tex. 2014). They require timely error preservation because affording trial courts an opportunity to consider and rule on alleged error "conserves judicial resources and promotes fairness by ensuring that a party does not neglect a complaint at trial and raise it for the first time on appeal." *Id.* When the alleged error is an incomplete, nonresponsive, or conflicting jury verdict, rule 295 requires the trial court to correct that error by providing additional instructions and retiring the jury "for further deliberations." TEX. R. CIV. P. 295. Once the court has discharged the jury, it cannot reform the conflicting answers as rule 295 requires. *See Roling*, 840 S.W.2d at 109 ("Once the jury is discharged, a conflict in the jury's answers cannot be reformed."). As the Austin Court of Appeals has explained, "What the jury intended by findings that potentially conflict is best determined by the jury itself," and that is the solution rule 295 requires. *Springs Window Fashions*, 184 S.W.3d at 867.

The Dissent claims that rule 295 allows for other preservation mechanisms because the rule states that a trial court "may direct [the verdict] to be reformed." Post at —— (GREEN, J., dissenting) (*quoting* TEX. R. CIV. P. 295). The rule does not mandate reformation because reformation is not always needed. The trial court's first resort is to reconcile the jury's findings. *Bender*, 600 S.W.2d at 260 (stating that the trial court "must" reconcile findings "when possible"). Should reconciliation fail, only then need the court recall the jury. We do not ignore the "may" in rule 295; we have applied the manners of recourse in the appropriate order.

As mentioned, rule 295 provides the procedure for resolving incomplete and nonresponsive jury verdicts as well as those containing conflicting answers. TEX. R. CIV. P. 295. Addressing incomplete verdicts, we have long held that a judgment will not be reversed "unless the party who would benefit from answers to the issues objects to the incomplete verdict before the jury is discharged, making it clear that he desires that the jury redeliberate on the issues or that the trial court grant a mistrial." *Fleet v. Fleet*, 711 S.W.2d 1, 3 (Tex. 1986); *see also Continental Cas. Co. v. Street*, 379 S.W.2d 648, 650 (Tex. 1964) (holding party failed to preserve error because he "did not object to the acceptance of the jury verdict as incomplete, and thus by timely objection afford the trial court the opportunity, before the jury was discharged, of correcting the error (if such it was) of accepting the verdict with the issues unanswered"). We conclude that the same error-preservation requirement applies when a party complains of a judgment based on conflicting jury answers.

Having concluded that the entry of a judgment based on fatally conflicting jury answers does not constitute fundamental error and that the error must be preserved by an objection asserted before the court discharges the jury, we must now address who bore the burden of preservation and the proper disposition of this case in light of the fact that neither USAA nor Menchaca timely objected. Amicus for USAA argues that the fatal conflict "should preclude any recovery" by Menchaca. Although USAA does not agree that the jury's answers fatally conflict, it argues that if they do conflict, it was Menchaca's burden to object and she waived the error by failing to do so before the trial court dismissed the jury. We disagree. In the jury's answers to Questions 2 and 3, Menchaca obtained all of the findings necessary to recover on her statutory-violation claim, and USAA is the party who must rely on the conflicting answer to Question 1 to prevent Menchaca from recovering based on the answers to Questions 2 and 3. As the party who must rely on the conflicting answer to avoid the effect of answers that establish liability, USAA bore the burden to object. *See, e.g., Burbage*, 447 S.W.3d at 256 ("The complaining party must object before the trial court and 'must point out distinctly the objectionable matter and the grounds of the objection.' ") (emphasis added) (*quoting* TEX. R. CIV. P. 274; TEX. R. APP. P. 33.1); *cf. Fleet*, 711 S.W.2d at 3 ("The trial court will not be reversed for rendering judgment, however, unless the party who would benefit from answers to the issues objects to the incomplete verdict before the jury is discharged.").

When we held in our early decisions that fatally conflicting jury answers constitute fundamental error, we reasoned that the error is fundamental in part because appellate courts lack the power to render a judgment based on conflicting answers. *See Radford*, 299 S.W. at 853 (stating that the law deprives the courts of "the power to render judgment . . . which is given by law and not by consent of the parties") (internal citations omitted). We explained that when it is "impossible to determine from these irreconcilable statements, with any degree of certainty, what the jury really meant by these findings, . . . no judgment can be rendered upon it." *Van Valkenberg*, 3 S.W. at 748. Because fatally conflicting answers result in "no sufficient verdict to support the judgment of the court below, or any other judgment which might be rendered," we concluded that the judgment "must be set aside, and the case remanded for a new trial." *Moore,* 3 S.W. at 286.

Under our modern, rules-based, restricted fundamental-error doctrine, however, we have discarded these concerns in favor of the efficiency and fairness our error-preservation requirement provides. Now, as before, courts "must 'reconcile apparent conflicts in the jury's findings' if reasonably possible in light of the pleadings and evidence, the manner of submission, and the other findings considered as a whole." *Bender*, 600 S.W.2d at 260 (*quoting Ford*, 216 S.W.2d at 562). And if a trial court concludes it cannot reconcile the conflict, it must provide additional instructions and retire the jury for further deliberations. TEX. R. CIV. P. 295. But if the court does not identify a conflict and no party raises it before the court discharges the jury, the conflict provides no basis for reversal on appeal, even if it is "fatal." The failure to preserve the error does not merely prevent the parties from raising the conflict on appeal, it prevents the appellate courts from considering the conflict or treating it as a basis for reversing the trial court's judgment. *Columbia Med. Ctr.*, 290 S.W.3d at 211 ("Appellate judges have much less discretion [than trial courts] because they are limited to the issues urged and record presented by the parties."); *Mack Trucks*, 206 S.W.3d at 577 ("Except for fundamental error, appellate courts are not authorized to consider issues not properly raised by the parties."); *C.O.S.*, 988 S.W.2d at 765 ("Generally, our civil rules of procedure and our decisions thereunder require a party to apprise a trial court of its error before that error can become the basis for reversal of a judgment.").

Here, USAA raised numerous objections, both to the proposed charge before its submission and to the jury's answers after the jury returned its verdict. But USAA failed to properly preserve any error based on conflicting jury answers before the trial court discharged the jury. As a result, the trial court discharged the jury without giving it the opportunity to resolve its conflicting answers. The trial court then attempted to resolve the conflict by disregarding the jury's failure to find a breach of contract. USAA properly preserved its argument that the court erred in disregarding that answer, and we have agreed with USAA that the trial court erred. We have disagreed, however, with USAA's argument that Menchaca's failure to prevail on her contract claim automatically negates the findings she obtained on her statutory claim. We are thus left with a judgment based on fatally conflicting jury answers, but since neither party preserved that error, we cannot consider the conflict as a basis for reversing the trial court's judgment.

* * *

Having concluded that the trial court and court of appeals erred in disregarding the jury's answer to Question 1, we are left with findings that support the judgment in Menchaca's favor based on statutory violations but that also contain a fatal conflict. We could render judgment for Menchaca based on the jury's verdict because USAA failed to preserve that conflict. In the interest of justice, however, we could also "remand the case to the trial court even if a rendition of judgment is otherwise appropriate." TEX. R. APP. P. 60.3. Such a remand is particularly appropriate when it appears that one or more parties "proceeded under the wrong legal theory," *Boyles v. Kerr*, 855 S.W.2d 593, 603 (Tex. 1993), especially when "the applicable law has . . . evolved between the time of trial and the disposition of the appeal." *Nat. Gas Pipeline Co. of Am. v. Justiss*, 397 S.W.3d 150, 162 (Tex. 2012); *see Hamrick v. Ward*, 446 S.W.3d 377, 385 (Tex. 2014) (remanding in the interest of justice "in light of our clarification of the law"); *Moriel*, 879 S.W.2d at 26 (same, in light of our "substantial clarification"). In light of the parties' obvious and understandable confusion over our relevant precedent and the effect of that confusion on their arguments in this case, as well as our clarification of the requirements to preserve error based on conflicting jury answers, we conclude that a remand is necessary here in the interest of justice.

* * *

For the reasons explained, we reverse the court of appeals' judgment and remand the case to the trial court for a new trial in the interest of justice.

CHIEF JUSTICE HECHT filed a concurring opinion (omitted).

JUSTICE BLACKLOCK concurs in the judgment without opinion.

JUSTICE GREEN filed a dissenting opinion in which JUSTICE GUZMAN and JUSTICE BROWN joined as to Parts I, II, and IV, and a plurality opinion as to Part III, in which CHIEF JUSTICE HECHT, JUSTICE GUZMAN, and JUSTICE BROWN joined (omitted).

JUSTICE JOHNSON did not participate in the decision.

ARVIZU
v.
ESTATE OF PUCKETT
364 S.W.3d 273
(Tex. 2012)

Toni M. Triplett, Triplett Law Firm, Houston, for Juana Lorena Arvizu.

Levon G. Hovnatanian, Martin Disiere Jefferson & Wisdom LLP, Philip Werner, Michele Anne Le, Scott Eugene Raynes, Werner & Ayers, L.L.P., Houston, for The Estate of George Puckett d/b/a Puckett Auto Sales.

Thomas E. Quirk, Aaron & Quirk, Marie Alice Haspil, ACCG General Agency, San Antonio, for Allstate Insurance Company.

John Michael "Jack" McKineley, Robert L. Ramey, John F. Elwood, Ramey Chandler McKinley & Zito, P.C., Houston, for Montgomery County Auto Auction.

PER CURIAM.

Juana Lorena Arvizu and her son were injured when her car was struck by a pickup truck driven by Edward Cantu. Montgomery County Auto Auction employed Cantu. Puckett Auto Sales owned the truck. Cantu's negligence was stipulated. A jury found that, although MCAA was his employer, Cantu drove the vehicle for Puckett's benefit. The jury found that MCAA, as Cantu's employer, had the right to direct the details of his work. It also found that Cantu was subject to Puckett's control "as to the details of the mission" when the accident occurred. The trial court rendered judgment for Arvizu. The court of appeals remanded for a new trial, holding that a jury could not logically find MCAA and Puckett to have simultaneously controlled Cantu's conduct, as the trial court had instructed the jury that Cantu could not have been an employee of both. But the jury also found that MCAA was subject to Puckett's control and was on a mission for Puckett's benefit—which comprise the elements of a principal—agent relationship. MCAA is vicariously liable for its employee's negligence; Puckett as principal is responsible for its agent's conduct. Because we are able to reconcile the jury's answers on that agency theory, we reverse the court of appeals' judgment.

Puckett Auto Sales buys used cars and sells them at public auctions. Puckett had a longstanding commercial relationship with Montgomery County Auto Auction in which MCAA would not only auction Puckett's vehicles, but would also transport unsold vehicles to other auction houses or back to Puckett's car lot. When Puckett's pickup truck did not sell, Puckett instructed MCAA to deliver it to another auction house. MCAA assigned its employee Edward Cantu to accomplish that directive, and the accident with Arvizu occurred in transit.

Arvizu sued Cantu, MCAA, and Puckett for her and her son's personal injuries. MCAA and Puckett both filed cross-claims—MCAA against Puckett for contribution and Puckett against MCAA for property damage. All parties stipulated that Cantu's negligence proximately caused the injuries. The question was who—MCAA, Puckett, or both—was vicariously liable for Cantu's negligence.

The jury found (1) that Cantu was MCAA's employee, not Puckett's, (2) that Cantu was transporting the pickup for Puckett's benefit and was subject to Puckett's control as to the details of the mission, and (3) that MCAA was transporting the vehicle for Puckett's benefit and was subject to Puckett's control as to the details of the mission. The jury awarded Arvizu $1.2 million for her and her son's injuries. Based on these findings, the trial court, over Puckett's objection, rendered judgment on the verdict against Cantu, MCAA, and Puckett, jointly and severally.

The questions submitted to the jury were as follows:

Question No. 1: "On the occasion in question, was Edward Cantu acting as an employee of Montgomery County Auto Auction or George Puckett d/b/a Puckett Auto Sales?"

Question No. 2: "On the occasion in question, was Edward Cantu transporting the vehicle in the furtherance of a mission for the benefit of George Pucket[t] D/B/A Puckett Auto Sales and subject to control by George Pucket[t] D/B/A Puckett Auto Sales as to the details of the mission?"

> Question No. 3: "On the occasion in question, was Montgomery County Auto Auction transporting the vehicle in the furtherance of a mission for the benefit of George Pucket[t] D/B/A Puckett Auto Sales and subject to control by George Pucket[t] D/B/A Puckett Auto Sales as to the details of the mission?"

Questions 2 and 3 track the Texas Pattern Jury Charge's language for nonemployee mission liability. *See* COMM. ON PATTERN JURY CHARGES, STATE BAR OF TEX., TEXAS PATTERN JURY CHARGES: GENERAL NEGLIGENCE & INTENTIONAL PERSONAL TORTS PJC 10.10 (2010 ed.). Nonemployee mission liability is a form of "respondeat superior liability outside the employment context." *St. Joseph Hosp. v. Wolff,* 94 S.W.3d 513, 537 (Tex. 2002); *see also* COMM. ON PATTERN JURY CHARGES, at PJC 10.10 cmt. ("PJC 10.10 should be given if the respondeat superior doctrine is raised in a case not involving an ordinary employee."). "The key elements of such a theory are (1) benefit to the defendant and (2) right of control." *Wolff,* 94 S.W.3d at 537.

Puckett's sole argument on appeal was that the jury findings fatally conflicted, and the court of appeals agreed. 364 S.W.3d 309, 311. The court determined that Questions 1 and 2 concerned the same material fact because both questions turned "upon the issue of whether MCAA or [Puckett] had the right to control Cantu's work." *Id.* at 316. Because Puckett and MCAA could not both have had the right to control Cantu's work, the court analyzed whether the conflicting findings would compel the rendition of different judgments. *Id.* at 315.

When taking the finding in Question 1 as true and disregarding the finding in Question 2, the court concluded that MCAA would be vicariously liable because it had the right to control Cantu's work. *Id.* at 316-17. But when taking Question 2's finding as true and disregarding Question 1's, Puckett would be vicariously liable because it had the right to control Cantu's work. *Id.* The court said both cannot be true at the same time, and therefore held that the answers fatally conflicted. *Id.* The court reversed and remanded the trial court's judgment as to Puckett. *Id.* Arvizu, Cantu, and MCAA petitioned this Court for review, each contending that Puckett cannot escape liability for its role in the Arvizus' injuries.

We think the court of appeals' analysis, so far as it goes, is correct. The threshold question in reviewing jury findings for fatal conflict is "whether the findings are about the same material fact." *Bender v. S. Pac. Transp. Co.,* 600 S.W.2d 257, 260 (Tex. 1980). In making this determination, courts have a "duty to harmonize jury findings when possible." *Producers Chem. Co. v. McKay,* 366 S.W.2d 220, 224 (Tex. 1963). Courts must uphold jury findings if "there is any reasonably possible basis upon which they may be reconciled." *Bender,* 600 S.W.2d at 260. The inquiry does not end, however, if the court determines that the findings create a conflict about the same material fact. The court must determine whether the conflict is fatal to the entry of judgment. *Bay Petroleum Corp. v. Crumpler,* 372 S.W.2d 318, 319 (Tex. 1963).

To determine whether a conflict is fatal, the court must consider each of the answers claimed to be in conflict, disregarding the alleged conflicting answer but taking into consideration all of the rest of the verdict, and if, so considered, one of the answers would require a judgment in favor of the plaintiff and the other would require a judgment in favor of the defendant, then the answers are fatally in conflict. *Little Rock Furniture Mfg. Co. v. Dunn,* 148 Tex. 197, 222 S.W.2d 985, 991 (1949). Thus, to satisfy this test, the party claiming conflict must show that one of the conflicting findings "necessarily requires the entry of a judgment different from that which the court has entered." *Id.*

We need not question whether the "control" findings are inconsistent if the verdict nevertheless supports the trial court's judgment. Findings can be "inconsistent or in conflict, or even in irreconcilable conflict," and still not be fatal to the entry of judgment. *Bay Petroleum Corp.,* 372 S.W.2d at 319.

Puckett cannot show that one of the findings necessarily requires a judgment different from the trial court's. Applying the *Little Rock* test, when the finding in Question 1 is disregarded, judgment would be rendered against Puckett because Question 2's finding establishes nonemployee mission liability against it. The result does not change when Question 2's finding is disregarded. Although the court of appeals correctly noted that Question 1 establishes vicarious liability against MCAA, 364 S.W.3d at 316-17, that finding must be considered with "all of the rest of the verdict," *Little Rock,* 222 S.W.2d at 991, which, importantly, includes the finding for Question 3.

Question 3 establishes a principal-agent relationship between Puckett and MCAA. The jury found that MCAA, a nonemployee, was on a mission for the benefit of Puckett and subject to Puckett's control. *See Wolff,* 94 S.W.3d at 537 (noting that nonemployee mission liability is a form of "respondeat superior liability outside the employment context" under which the key elements are "(1) benefit to the defendant and (2) right of control"); COMM. ON PATTERN JURY CHARGES, at PJC 10. 10 (explaining that the nonemployee mission liability question "should be given if the respondeat superior doctrine is raised in a case not involving an ordinary employee"). Puckett does not dispute that it had the right to control MCAA's truck-transporting mission or that the mission was for Puckett's benefit. *Cf. Duff v. Spearman,* 322 S.W.3d 869, 879-80 (Tex. App.—Beaumont 2010, pet. denied) (refusing to impose nonemployee mission liability because the evidence supported the jury's finding that the principal did not "exercise[ ] control over the means and details of [the agent's] mission"); *Omega Contracting, Inc. v. Torres,* 191 S.W.3d 828, 848 (Tex. App.—Fort Worth 2006, no pet.) (en banc) (noting that the threshold issue for nonemployee mission liability is control and holding that the alleged principal "conclusively negated the essential element of its alleged right to control" the agent).

MCAA worked for Puckett; Puckett controlled the details of the mission; and the accident occurred during this transaction. Combined with the finding in Question 1 that Cantu was MCAA's employee, there existed a subagency relationship between Cantu and Puckett for which Puckett is vicariously liable. *See* RESTATEMENT (THIRD) OF AGENCY § 3.15 (2006) ("A subagent is a person appointed by an agent to perform functions that the agent has consented to perform on behalf of the agent's principal and for whose conduct the appointing agent is responsible to the principal."); *id.* § 3.15 cmt. d ("As to third parties, an action taken by a subagent carries the legal consequences for the principal that would follow were the action instead taken by the appointing agent."); *see also Royal Mortg. Corp. v. Montague,* 41 S.W.3d 721, 735 (Tex. App.—Fort Worth 2001) ("[W]e note that a subagent is a person appointed by an agent to perform some duty or the whole of the business relating to his agency. He may be the agent of the agent or an agent of the principal depending upon the agreement creating the primary agency or upon the circumstances."), *abrogated on other grounds by Michiana Easy Livin' Country, Inc. v. Holten,* 168 S.W.3d 777, 788-89 (Tex. 2005). Based on the combined findings in Questions 1 and 3, the judgment is valid against Puckett even if Question 2 had not been submitted. Thus, Puckett would lose under both steps of the *Little Rock* analysis, rendering any conflict between the jury findings immaterial to the judgment.

Because Puckett cannot show that one of the purportedly conflicting findings necessarily requires the entry of a judgment different from that which the trial court rendered, the court of appeals erred in reversing the trial court's judgment. Accordingly, without hearing oral argument, we grant the petitions for review, reverse the court of appeals' judgment, and reinstate the trial court's judgment. TEX.R.APP. P. 59.1, 60.2(c).

Notes

1. In determining whether jury findings are in conflict, the following general observations can be made:

(1) The threshold question is whether the findings pertain to the same material fact.
(2) If the findings pertain to the same material facts, then the court must then determine whether they can be reconciled.
(3) Apparent conflicts must be reconciled if it is possible to do so, taking into consideration the pleadings, evidence, manner of submission and other findings. Thus, if the issues can be given more than one reasonable construction, that which avoids a conflict in the answer is usually adopted.

2. In resolving apparent conflicts, the following test, taken from *Little Rock Furniture Company v. Dunn,* 222 S.W.2d 985 (Tex. 1949), is used: The court is to determine whether, taking the finding alone in the one instance, a judgment should be entered in favor of the plaintiff; and taking it alone in the other, judgment should be entered in favor of the defendant. The court considers each of the answers claimed to be in conflict, disregarding the alleged conflicting answer but looking at the rest of the verdict. If so considered, on of the answers would require judgment in favor of the defendant, then the answers are fatally in conflict. One of the conflicting answers of the jury, in connection with the rest of the verdict, except the issue with which it conflicts, must necessarily require the entry of a judgment different from that which the court has entered.

3. *Luck v. Buffalo Lakes*, 144 S.W.2d 672, (Tex. Civ. App.—Amarillo 1940, writ dism' w,o.j.): "In determining conflicts in the findings of a jury in *Casualty Underwriters v. Rhone et al.*, 134 Tex. 50, 132 S.W.2d 97, 99, the court said: " 'It will never be presumed that jurors intend to return conflicting answers, but the presumption is always to the contrary. Courts properly refuse to strike down answers on the ground of conflict, if there is any reasonable basis upon which they may be reconciled. This is elementary.' "

4. In *Roling v. Alamo Group*, 840 S.W.2d 107 (Tex. App.—Eastland 1992, writ denied), the court held that an objection to conflicting jury findings must be made before the jury is discharged in order to preserve error. In *Roling* the appellant raised the issue of irreconcilable conflicting jury answers for the first time in her motion for new trial. The appellate court held that she had waived her complaint relying upon the underlying purpose of former Rule 52(a) of the Texas Rules of Appellate Procedure [Rule 33 of the present Rules of Appellate Procedure]—the trial court must be made aware of an alleged error so that it can prevent or correct the error. The court noted that under Rule 295 of the Texas Rules of Civil Procedure a trial court can attempt to cure such a defective verdict by instructing the jury on the nature of the conflict and retiring the jury for further deliberations; however, once the jury is discharged, a conflict in the jury's answers cannot be cured.

5. *Kish v. Van Note,* 692 S.W.2d 463, 466-467 (Tex. 1985): "If the jury verdict contains more than one acceptable measure of damages, a plaintiff may be forced to elect prior to judgment the recovery he wants by waiving the surplus findings with respect to the damages. TEX. R. CIV. P. 440; *Butler v. Joseph's Wine Shop, Inc.*, 633 S.W.2d 926, 933 (Tex. Civ. App.—Houston [14th Dist.] 1982, writ ref'd n.r.e.). The Kishes attempted to make such an election when they filed their Motions to Disregard Jury Finding and Motions for Judgment. The trial court erred in denying these motions.

6. *Birchfield v. Texarkana Memorial Hosp.*, 747 S.W.2d 361, 367 (Tex. 1987): "The judgment of the court should be "so framed as to give the party all the relief to which he may be entitled." TEX. R. CIV. P. 301, (emphasis added). While a formal waiver by the Birchfields would have been in order, it was not a prerequisite to the recovery of all of the damages to which they were lawfully entitled. *Hargrove v. Trinity Universal Insurance Co.*, 152 Tex. 243, 256 S.W.2d 73, 75 (1953). We hold that where the prevailing party fails to elect between alternative measures of damages, the court should utilize the findings affording the greater recovery and render judgment accordingly."

CHAPTER 4.
NO EVIDENCE REVIEW AND TAKING THE CASE AWAY FROM THE JURY

1. *Instructed Verdict: Taking the Case Away From the Jury Before the Verdict*

Read Rule 268 Texas Rules of Civil Procedure.

Notes

1. It is the admitted function of a jury to pass upon and determine the facts of a case when the evidence is conflicting. The jury also has the sole responsibility to determine the credibility of the witnesses and the weight to be given to their testimony. On the other hand, it is the function of a trial judge to determine issues of law. The purpose of the instructed verdict [also referred to as directed verdict] is to take the case away from the jury prior to its deliberations and to permit the trial judge to enter a judgment in a case. Given the function of juries, the entry of an instructed verdict is proper only in situations where there are no fact questions which would effect the outcome of the case. As a general rule, "[a]n instructed verdict is proper if (1) a specifically indicated defect in the nonmovant's pleading makes the pleading insufficient to support a judgment; (2) the evidence proves conclusively the truth of fact propositions that, under the substantive law, establish the right of the movant or negate the right of the nonmovant to judgment; or (3) the evidence is insufficient to raise a fact issue as to one or more fact propositions that must be established for the nonmovant to be entitled to judgment." *Gonzales v. Hearst Corporation*, 930 S.W.2d 275 (Tex. App.—Houston [14th Dist.] 1996, no writ). As a practical matter, it is fairly easy for courts to determine when a pleading will not support the entry of judgment, but it is not an easy task for courts to determine when a fact has either been "conclusively established" or where there is "no evidence" [also referred to as less than a scintilla] to support a fact. However, in both of these cases, the trial court as well as an appellate court reviewing the granting or denial of the motion for instructed verdict is concerned with the *legal sufficiency* of the evidence—not its factual sufficiency.

2. A plaintiff is entitled to an instructed verdict if the evidence conclusively establishes each element of his cause of action as a "matter of law". *See Collora v. Navarro*, 574 S.W.2d 65 (Tex. 1978). It is proper for a trial court to grant an instructed verdict for a defendant if a court finds that there is "no evidence" presented which raises a fact issue concerning a fact proposition essential to the plaintiff's recovery. *See Duff v. Yelin*, 751 S.W.2d 175 (Tex. 1988). It is also proper for a trial court to grant an instructed verdict for a defendant on the basis of an affirmative defense, if each element of that affirmative defense is conclusively established. *See, e.g,, Kassen v. Hatley*, 887 S.W. 4 (Tex. 1994); *Watts v. St. Mary's Hall*, 662 S.W.2d 55 (Tex. App.—San Antonio 1983, writ ref'd n.r.e.). To say that a fact has been established conclusively is to say that the evidence is such that reasonable minds could not differ as to the conclusion to be drawn from it. *See Triton Oil & Gas Corp. v. Marine Contractors*, 644 S.W.2d 443 (1982). A fact conclusively established can be contrasted to its legal opposite—"no evidence". For example, in a "no evidence" situation, the party with the burden of proof on a particular fact has failed to produce enough evidence to raise a fact question for the jury; on the other hand when a fact as been conclusively established, the party, who has the burden of proof on that fact, has introduced sufficient evidence to conclusively establish the fact, thus, eliminating any need for the jury to determine that fact. Both of these tests involved an evaluation of what is referred to in Texas as the legal sufficiency of the evidence. The Court in *Transportation Ins. Co. v. Moriel*, 879 S.W.2d 10 (Tex. 1994), discussed the concept of legal sufficiency as follows:

> In evaluating legal sufficiency, we are required to determine whether the proffered evidence as a whole rises to a level that would enable reasonable and fair-minded people to differ in their conclusions. William Powers, Jr. & Jack Ratliff, *Another Look at "No Evidence" and "Insufficient Evidence,"* 69 TEX. L. REV. 515, 522, 523 (1991) ("[T]he court must be persuaded that reasonable minds could not differ on the matter . . . . Ultimately, the test for "conclusive evidence" . . . is similar to the test for "no evidence" . . . the court asks whether reasonable minds could differ about the fact determination to be made by the jury."); [Robert W.] Calvert, [*"No Evidence" and "Insufficient Points of Error"*, 38 TEX. L. REV. 361 (1960)], *supra*, at 363-65 ("The rule as generally stated is that if reasonable minds cannot differ from the conclusion that the evidence lacks probative force it will be held to the legal equivalent of no evidence."); . . . .

Simply put, an instructed verdict should be granted when the evidence is such that no other verdict could be rendered on the evidence and the movant is entitled to judgment as a matter of law; however, if the evidence is such that reasonable minds may differ as to the truth of the material facts, an instructed verdict is not warranted, and it would be error for a trial court to enter an instructed verdict.

3. As the cases below will show, the legal concept of "no evidence" does not mean that a proponent has literally failed to introduce any evidence on that fact; however, it does mean that the evidence which has been introduced has no legally probative value, and therefore, there is no fact question for the jury. In discussing the concept of "no evidence" the Supreme Court in *Cecil v. Smith*, 804 S.W.2d 509 (1991) stated that "no evidence" refers to the following situations:

(1) a complete absence of evidence of a vital fact,

(2) the court is barred by rules of law or of evidence from giving weight to the only evidence offered to prove a vital fact,

(3) the evidence offered to prove a vital fact is no more than a mere scintilla, and

(4) the evidence established conclusively the opposite of the vital fact.

4. The problems facing Texas courts dealing with the concepts of "no evidence" and "conclusive evidence" is exacerbated under Texas law by the requirement that if the evidence is merely factual insufficient the court may not grant a directed verdict, but must submit the case to the jury for its determination. Thus, a real problem constantly plaguing Texas courts is how to determine when the evidence is legally insufficient, or merely factually insufficient. In discussing these issues in *Kindred v. Con/Chem, Inc.*, 650 S.W.2d 61 (Tex. 1983) the Court stated:

> "The factual insufficiency of the evidence to support an affirmative answer to an opponent's issue furnishes no basis for refusal to submit the issue." *Clarostat Manufacturing Inc. v. Alcor*, 544 S.W.2d 788, 791 (Tex. Civ. App.—San Antonio 1976, writ ref'd n.r.e.). The trial court may decline to submit a relevant issue, only if there is no evidence to support it. *Garza v. Alviar*, 395 S.W.2d 821, 824 (Tex. 1965). When the evidence offered to prove a vital fact is so weak as to do no more than create a mere surmise or suspicion of its existence, the evidence is no more than a scintilla and, in legal effect, is no evidence. *Seideneck v. Cal Bayreuther Associates*, 451 S.W.2d 752, 755 (Tex. 1970); *Joske v. Irvin*, 91 Tex. 574, 581-82, 44 S.W. 1059, 1062 (1898). *See* Calvert, *"No Evidence" and "Insufficient Evidence" Points of Error*, 38 TEX. L. REV. 361 (1960) and 5 W. DORSANEO, TEXAS LITIGATION GUIDE, s 122.03(2)(a) (1983). The test for the application of this no evidence/scintilla rule is that if reasonable minds cannot differ from the conclusion that the evidence offered to support the existence of a vital fact lacks probative force, it will be held to be the legal equivalent of no evidence. However, there is some evidence, more than a scintilla, if the evidence furnishes some reasonable basis for differing conclusions by reasonable minds as to the existence of the vital fact. *Martinez v. Delta Brands, Inc.*, 515 S.W.2d 263, 265 (Tex. 1974).

5. The following note case is provided to assist the student in reading *Joske v. Irvine* which follows. *Wal-Mart Stores, Inc. v. Rodriguez*, 92 S.W.3d 502 (Tex. 2002): The essential elements of false imprisonment are: (1) willful detention; (2) without consent; and (3) without authority of law. A defendant may be liable for instigating an unlawful arrest if he knowingly provides false information to law enforcement authorities resulting in the arrest. Applying that principle here, Rodriguez has alleged that Wal-Mart failed to disclose that its check identification system was unreliable, but not that it knowingly provided false information to law enforcement authorities resulting in the arrest. Failing to make a full and fair disclosure is not the equivalent of knowingly providing false information. Although a private citizen may be liable for directing an arrest that results in false imprisonment, the law will not generally permit inferring such direction simply from a report of crime made to the authorities. Such an inference is justified when a party provides information in its report that it knows is false. Merely providing inaccurate or incomplete information, however will not make a party liable for instigating a subsequent false imprisonment. False imprisonment is an intentional tort, requiring willful detention by the defendant.

JOSKE
v.
IRVINE
91 Tex. 574, 44 S.W. 1059
(1898)

Franklin & Cobbs, for plaintiff in error.
C. K. Breneman, for defendant in error.

DENMAN, J.

Joe Shely, an officer of the city of San Antonio, arrested James Irvine without a warrant, and confined him nearly 24 hours in the city prison. Irvine sued Alexander Joske to recover damages, claiming that such arrest was unlawful and directed by him. The arrest was not sought to be justified under any statute or charter provision, but under a city ordinance authorizing the arrest of suspicious characters without warrant. The trial court having instructed the jury that the arrest was unlawful, verdict and judgment were for plaintiff for $250, which having been affirmed by the court of civil appeals, Joske has brought the case to this court upon writ of error.

Said charge is assigned as error. The court of civil appeals overruled the assignment on the ground that the city charter did not authorize the council to pass such an ordinance. We were inclined to hold otherwise at the time of granting the application for writ of error, but do not feel called upon to determine the question, for the reason that we do not consider there is any evidence in the record of the existence of such an ordinance. . . .

From a careful examination of the cases, it appears (1) that it is the duty of the court to instruct a verdict, though there be slight testimony, if its probative force be so weak that it only raises a mere surmise or suspicion of the existence of the fact sought to be established, such testimony, in legal contemplation, falling short of being 'any evidence'; and (2) that it is the duty of the court to determine whether the testimony has more than that degree of probative force. If it so determines, the law presumes that the jury could not 'reasonably infer the existence of the alleged fact,' and 'that there is no room for ordinary minds to differ as to the conclusion to be drawn from it.' The broad and wise policy of the law, formed in and descending to us through the crucibles of time, does not permit the citizen to be deprived of his property, his liberty, or his life upon mere surmise or suspicion, and places upon a trained judiciary the grave responsibility of determining as a question of law whether the testimony establishes more. 'There is, no doubt, a possibility, in all cases where the judges have to determine whether there is evidence on which the jury may reasonably find a fact, that the judges may differ in opinion, and it is possible that the majority may be wrong. Indeed, whenever a decision of the court below on such a point is reversed, the majority must have been so either in the court above or the court below. This is an infirmity which must affect all tribunals.' *Ryder v. Wombwell, supra.*

We are, then, called upon to determine whether the testimony in this case does more than to create a mere surmise or suspicion that Joske 'requested or directed' Irvine's arrest. We think it does not, if it can be said to go that far. It shows clearly that Joske was urging the officers to ferret out and recover, if possible, his goods, which Irvine had received and had not returned, and that both he and the officers were endeavoring to ascertain from Irvine the circumstances attending their loss, so that they might be traced. This Joske had a clear legal right to do, and we are of opinion that from the mere exercise of this right the law will not permit the inference to be drawn that he 'requested or directed' the arrest, though it be conceded that but for its exercise the arrest would never have been made. It would be against reason to hold that the mere fact that a citizen has called upon the officer of the law to search for and recover his lost or stolen property will authorize the inference that he 'requested or directed' the arrest subsequently made. NEWELL, MAL. PROS. p. 108, § 7, and authorities cited; TAYL. EV. § 118, and authorities cited. The evidence would probably justify a finding that the arrest was made in Joske's presence, though it would be difficult to conclude therefrom that Shely did not fully determine upon and in legal contemplation make the arrest at the time Irvine refused to go to his room, or give any explanation as to the circumstances under which the goods were lost. It would be a grave question whether any statement made by Irvine after that time would be admissible against him if on trial for a criminal offense. But if it be conceded that the evidence warrants the inference that the arrest was not made until they returned to the store, and Shely had the conversation with Joske, still we are of opinion that nothing is shown to have occurred there that would warrant the inference that Joske 'requested or directed' Shely to make the arrest. The conversation, as detailed by Shely, Joske, and Hilgers, shows the contrary, and that Shely made the arrest on his own responsibility, against Joske's request; and it is difficult to perceive just how Joske could have prevented the arrest at that time if he had seen fit to go beyond the exercise of his clear legal right to remain passive. But, if it be conceded that the jury had the right to lay out of the case the testimony of all these witnesses, then we are left without information as to the conversation, except that Irvine says that Joske said, 'I will make an affidavit against him anyhow.' We are of the opinion that this remark does not tend to show that Joske 'requested or directed' Shely to then make the arrest, but, on the contrary, if taken as true, it indicates a purpose on Joske's part to proceed in the mode prescribed by law, by making an affidavit, and thus placing the matter before the courts. If this purpose had been carried out, this suit for an illegal arrest could not have been maintained, though one for malicious prosecution may have been, under certain circumstances not necessary to mention here. *Mullen v. Brown*, 138 Mass. 114. Would the mere fact that Shely made the arrest immediately after leaving Joske warrant the conclusion that the latter 'requested or directed' him to make it? We think not. The whole case shows that Joske was pressing both the officers and Irvine to aid him in the recovery of his goods. This he had the legal right to do. There are no circumstances tending to show any collusion between Joske and the officers, or that he had or attempted to exercise any authority or control over them in the performance of what they supposed to be their duties, or that he, while ostensibly trying to recover his goods, was covertly seeking to procure Irvine's arrest. There is no direct testimony that Joske 'requested or directed' the arrest, and we are of the opinion that such fact cannot be reasonably inferred from the circumstances. 'An inference is a deduction which the reason of the jury makes from the facts proved.' 1 RICE, EV. § 36. If the jury cannot reasonably make the deduction, the law does not authorize it. Upon the whole case, we are of opinion that the probative force of the testimony does not go beyond the point of creating a mere surmise or suspicion that Joske 'requested or directed' the arrest, and that, therefore, under the principles above discussed, there is not, in legal contemplation, 'any evidence' of that fact. It results that it was error for the court to give the charge complained of, for which the judgments of the court of civil appeals and the trial court will be reversed, and the cause remanded.

Notes

1. The holding in *Joske* is frequently referred to the "scintilla of the evidence rule," meaning that there must be more than a scintilla of the evidence to raise a fact issue for the jury.

2. Recently, the Texas Supreme Court has begun to use new terminology, referring to *"meager circumstantial evidence,"* to express the same, or possibly an even more restrictive rule. An example occurs in the case of *Hammerly Oaks, Inc. v. Edwards,* 958 S.W.2d 387 (Tex. 1997):

> The fact that Montgomery was alone in the leasing office, when Roman Gonzales threatened Edwards, was no evidence that Montgomery was in charge at that moment in time. The trier of fact may draw inferences, but only reasonable and logical ones. The evidence on which Edwards relies is 'meager circumstantial evidence,' which could give rise to any number of inferences, none more probable than another. A jury may not infer an ultimate fact from such evidence. Under the theory advanced by Edwards, a jury could conclude that a receptionist or secretary was a vice principal simply because at times, such persons were the only employees of the corporation in the office authorized to converse with the public and to relay information to and from the corporation.

See also: Wal-Mart Stores, Inc. v. Gonzalez, 968 S.W.2d 934 (Tex. 1998). When reviewing a legal sufficiency point, this court must consider only the evidence and inferences tending to support the trial court's finding, disregarding all contrary evidence and inferences. However, meager circumstantial evidence from which equally plausible but opposite inferences may be drawn is speculative and thus legally insufficient to support a finding.

3. *Jackson v. Axelrad*, 221 S.W.3d 650 (Tex. 2007) was a medical malpractice case. Both physician (Jackson, an internist) and patient (Axelrad, a psychiatrist) were doctors. At trial, Axelrad insisted he told Dr. Jackson his pain started in the left lower quadrant. It was up to the jurors to resolve this conflict in the testimony. Each claimed the other was negligent, and a jury agreed that both were. As the jury assessed slightly more fault to the plaintiff (51 percent) than the defendant (49 percent), the trial court entered a take-nothing judgment. The court of appeals reversed and remanded for a new trial, disregarding the finding of the plaintiff's negligence, because laymen generally have no duty to volunteer information during medical treatment. 142 S.W.3d 418. ***Held:*** Reversed and the jury's verdict is reinstated, because there was some evidence the plaintiff doctor

failed to report a critical symptom when he should have. The plaintiff here was not a layman, and jurors judging his actions could consider his expertise, especially as he emphasized it throughout the trial. When there are conflicts in testimony the courts must presume jurors decided all of them in favor of the verdict if reasonable human beings could do so. But evidence may support one part of a verdict but not another. Here, one version (that Axelrad reported where his pain began) supports the verdict against Dr. Jackson, while the other version (that he did not) supports the verdict against Axelrad. Reasonable jurors could not have believed both—Axelrad either *did* or *did not* report where his pain began. But because either answer would support part of the verdict, which one must the Court presume jurors believed? The presumption serves to protect jury verdicts from second-guessing on appeal. As a result, *it operates in favor of any jury finding a litigant asks an appellate court to set aside.* Here, the court of appeals set aside only one jury finding—that Axelrad was negligent. To ensure that the appellate court did not substitute its own judgment for that of the jury, the courts must presume the jury decided all conflicts in favor of this finding. There are some cases in which this general rule will not apply. Courts cannot presume findings in favor of one part of a verdict if doing so creates an irreconcilable conflict with another. But that is not the case here, as there was evidence Dr. Jackson was negligent even if Axelrad failed to report all his symptoms. Accordingly, the Court must presume jurors found Axelrad did not report where his abdominal pain began.

4. In *Central Ready Mix Concrete Co. v. Islas*, 228 S.W.3d 649 (Tex. 2007) the Court stated that in reviewing a take-nothing judgment, the appellate court is to examine the record for evidence supporting the jury finding, and ignore all evidence to the contrary, so long as a reviewing court keeps in mind that some contrary evidence cannot be ignored. The standard for reviewing a judgment notwithstanding the verdict, like all other motions rendering judgment, as a matter of law, requires a reviewing court to credit evidence favoring the jury verdict, if reasonable jurors could, and disregard contrary evidence unless reasonable jurors could not.

CITY OF KELLER v. WILSON

168 S.W.3d 802
(Tex. 2005)

Dabney D. Bassel, Larry Bracken, Law Snakard & Gambill, P.C., Fort Worth, Douglas H. Conner III, L. Stanton Lowry, Boyle & Lowry, L.L.P., Irving, for petitioner.

James B. Barlow, Barlow & Garsek, Fort Worth, Robert L. Russell Bush, Bush & Morrison, Arlington, David R. Casey, Hurst, for respondents.

Jay Doegey, Assistant City Attorney for the City of Corpus Christi, Texas, Corpus Christi, Theodore P. Gorski Jr., Office of the City Attorney for City of Fort Worth, Mark G. Daniel, Evans Gandy Daniel & Moore, Fritz Quast, Taylor Olson Adkins Sralla & Elam, LLP, Fort Worth, Monte Akers, Texas Municipal League, Austin, Michael A. Bucek, Senior Assistant City Attorney, Irving, Robert F. Brown, Brown & Hofmeister, L.L.P., Richardson, Bruce S. Powers, Assistant County Attorney, Michael A. Stafford, Harris County Attorney, Houston, for Amicus Curiae.

JUSTICE BRISTER delivered the opinion of the Court, in which CHIEF JUSTICE JEFFERSON, JUSTICE HECHT, JUSTICE WAINWRIGHT, and JUSTICE GREEN joined, and in which JUSTICE O'NEILL and JUSTICE MEDINA joined as to Parts I through IV.

Must an appellate court reviewing a verdict for legal sufficiency start by considering all the evidence or only part? Over the years, we have stated both as the proper scope of review. While some see the standards as opposing, we disagree; like a glass that is half-full or half-empty, both arrive at the same point regardless of where they start.

But both standards must be properly applied. Rules and reason sometimes compel that evidence must be credited or discarded whether it supports a verdict or contradicts it. Under either scope of review, appellate courts must view the evidence in the light favorable to the verdict, crediting favorable evidence if reasonable jurors could, and disregarding contrary evidence unless reasonable jurors could not. As we find the evidence here meets neither standard, we reverse.

I. Factual and Procedural History

The City of Keller is one of several fast-growing communities on the outskirts of Fort Worth. As part of that growth, the City approved plans for two new subdivisions, Estates of Oak Run and Rancho Serena, including plans for storm water drainage. The Wilsons own property southeast of the new subdivisions, with a tract owned by Z.T. Sebastian lying between. Before development, surface water flowed generally north to south from the land where the subdivisions were built, across the Sebastian and Wilson properties, and into the Little Bear Creek Watershed.

In 1991, the City adopted a Master Drainage Plan providing for drainage easements across both the Sebastian and Wilson properties, and thence into Little Bear Creek. The City's codes require developers to comply with the Master Plan, to provide drainage for a 100-year rain event, and to avoid increasing the volume or velocity of water discharged upon downhill properties.

The developers of Oak Run and Rancho Serena submitted plans to the City indicating they would buy a drainage easement and build a ditch forty-five feet wide and more than two hundred yards long across the Sebastian property, and deed both to the City upon completion. The plans also included detention basins on the subdivision properties, but omitted any drainage easement or ditch across the Wilsons' property. The City's director of public works approved the developers' plans, and the City accepted the works on completion and maintained after the developers' departure.

In accordance with the Master Plan, the City built a box culvert south of the Wilsons' property. But as the developers' drainage ditch ended at the Wilsons' north property line, there was no link between the two. The Wilsons alleged and the jury found this omission increased flooding on the Wilsons' property, ruining eight acres of farmland the jury valued at almost $300,000.

To recover damages for inverse condemnation, the Wilsons had to prove the City intentionally took or damaged their property for public use, or was substantially certain that would be the result. They do not allege the City intentionally flooded their land, but do allege it approved revised plans that it knew were substantially certain to have that effect.

The City contends no evidence supports the jury's finding of an intentional taking. It presented evidence that engineers for the developers, for the City, and for an outside firm the City retained all certified that the revised drainage plan complied with the City's codes and regulations—including the ban against increasing downstream runoff. Thus, the City asserts it had no reason to be substantially certain the opposite would occur, until it did.

A divided court of appeals rejected this contention. In its legal sufficiency review, the court refused to consider the various engineers' certifications because "we are to consider only the evidence and inferences that tend to support the finding and disregard all evidence and inferences to the contrary." The City challenges this omission as applying the wrong scope of review.

We have on many occasions stated the scope of review precisely as the court of appeals says (the "exclusive" standard). But we have also stated that a reviewing court must consider "all of the evidence" in the light favorable to the verdict (the "inclusive" standard). Sometimes we have mentioned neither reviewing all evidence nor disregarding some part of it. Finally, we have sometimes expressly mentioned both.

Although this Court has used both the exclusive and the inclusive standards interchangeably over the years, commentators say the two are different. Because this important issue is dispositive here, we address it in some detail, and reserve for another day the City's arguments that a governmental entity cannot be liable for approving a developer's plans, or accepting rather than constructing the works at issue.

II. Contrary Evidence That Cannot Be Disregarded

The question presented here is not a new one. More than 40 years ago, then JUSTICE CALVERT addressed the standards for reviewing legal and factual sufficiency in the most-cited law review article in Texas legal history. Frustrated that despite this Court's efforts to explain those standards "a growing number of recent decisions indicate a continuing misunderstanding," the author summarized and attempted to clarify Texas law up to 1960. The article's impact remains substantial today, having been cited more than 100 times by Texas courts in the last five years.

According to the article:

> "No evidence" points must, and may only, be sustained when the record discloses one of the following situations: (a) a complete absence of evidence of a vital fact; (b) the court is barred by rules of law or of evidence from giving weight to the only evidence offered to prove a vital fact; (c) the evidence offered to prove a vital fact is no more than a mere scintilla; (d) the evidence establishes conclusively the opposite of the vital fact.

We have quoted a similar formulation on many occasions.

Notably, JUSTICE CALVERT then proceeded to put the question before us in the proper context:

> It is in deciding "no evidence" points in situation (c) that the courts follow the further rule of viewing the evidence in its most favorable light in support of the finding of the vital fact, considering only the evidence and the inferences which support the finding and rejecting the evidence and the inferences which are contrary to the finding.

Clearly, the traditional rule in Texas has never been that appellate courts must reject contrary evidence in every no-evidence review. Instead, the traditional scope of review does not disregard contrary evidence if there is no favorable evidence (situation (a) above), or if contrary evidence renders supporting evidence incompetent (situation (b) above) or conclusively establishes the opposite (situation (d) above).

As the following examples show, this has remained the rule since. We do not presume to categorize all circumstances in which contrary evidence must be considered in a legal sufficiency review. Evidence can be disregarded whenever reasonable jurors could do so, an inquiry that is necessarily fact-specific. But it is important that when courts use the exclusive standard and disregard contrary evidence, they must recognize certain exceptions to it.

A. Contextual Evidence

In JUSTICE CALVERT's first situation—a complete absence of evidence of a vital fact—it is generally irrelevant whether a reviewing court considers contrary evidence. If supporting evidence is absent, opposing evidence cannot change that result. But in a number of cases, the lack of supporting evidence may not appear until all the evidence is reviewed in context.

For example, publications alleged to be defamatory must be viewed as a whole—including accompanying statements, headlines, pictures, and the general tenor and reputation of the source itself. A court reviewing legal sufficiency cannot disregard parts of a publication, considering only false statements to support a plaintiff's verdict or only true ones to support a defense verdict.

Similarly, reviewing courts must construe contracts as a whole; we do not consider only the parts favoring one party and disregard the remainder, as that would render the latter meaningless. Even writings executed at different times must be considered together if they pertain to the same transaction.

It is not just writings that reviewing courts must consider in context. For example, in reviewing intentional infliction of emotional distress claims for legal sufficiency, "we consider the context and the relationship between the parties." Acts that might constitute outrageous conduct when dealing with a hearing-impaired consumer may be legally insufficient between business parties. In our no-evidence reviews of successful claims, we have invariably reviewed not just evidence showing the conduct was outrageous, but also evidence showing that, in context, it was not.

More generally, evidence cannot be taken out of context in a way that makes it seem to support a verdict when in fact it never did. If a witness's statement "I did not do that" is contrary to the jury's verdict, a reviewing court may need to disregard the whole statement, but cannot rewrite it by disregarding the middle word alone.

Thus, if evidence may be legally sufficient in one context but insufficient in another, the context cannot be disregarded even if that means rendering judgment contrary to the jury's verdict. Either "evidence contrary to the verdict" must be defined to exclude material contextual evidence, or it must be an exception to the general rule.

B. Competency Evidence

It has long been the rule in Texas that incompetent evidence is legally insufficient to support a judgment, even if admitted without objection. Thus, evidence showing it to be incompetent cannot be disregarded, even if the result is contrary to the verdict. If the rule were otherwise, incompetent evidence would always be legally sufficient, because the evidence showing it to be incompetent could never be considered.

Thus, for example, if an eyewitness's location renders a clear view of an accident "physically impossible," it is no evidence of what occurred, even if the eyewitness thinks otherwise. Similarly, an employee's testimony that he was in the course and scope of his employment is legally insufficient to support a verdict against his employer if the evidence shows that legal conclusion to be incompetent.

This exception frequently applies to expert testimony. When expert testimony is required, lay evidence supporting liability is legally insufficient. In such cases, a no-evidence review cannot disregard contrary evidence showing the witness was unqualified to give an opinion. And if an expert's opinion is based on certain assumptions about the facts, we cannot disregard evidence showing those assumptions were unfounded.

After we adopted gate-keeping standards for expert testimony, evidence that failed to meet reliability standards was rendered not only inadmissible but incompetent as well. Thus, an appellate court conducting a no-evidence review cannot consider only an expert's bare opinion, but must also consider contrary evidence showing it has no scientific basis. Similarly, review of an expert's damage estimates cannot disregard the expert's admission on cross-examination that none can be verified.

Thus, evidence that might be "some evidence" when considered in isolation is nevertheless rendered "no evidence" when contrary evidence shows it to be incompetent. Again, such evidence cannot be disregarded; it must be an exception either to the exclusive standard of review or to the definition of contrary evidence.

C. Circumstantial Equal Evidence

As noted above, JUSTICE CALVERT believed the exclusive standard applied only when a no-evidence challenge asserted the evidence was no more than a scintilla. But he went on to note a "variation" that required contrary inferences to be considered when the equal-inference rule applied.

In claims or defenses supported only by meager circumstantial evidence, the evidence does not rise above a scintilla (and thus is legally insufficient) if jurors would have to guess whether a vital fact exists. "When the circumstances are equally consistent with either of two facts, neither fact may be inferred." In such cases, we must "view each piece of circumstantial evidence, not in isolation, but in light of all the known circumstances."

JUSTICE CALVERT argued there was "no necessity for the variation" because drawing an inference based on meager evidence was unreasonable whether or not the reviewing court considered the opposing inferences. Nevertheless, he recognized that "[t]he opposing inference is present and it does no harm to note its presence."

In subsequent cases this Court has continued to note rather than disregard the presence of equal but opposite inferences, often because lower courts have overlooked them. Thus, for example, one might infer from cart tracks in spilled macaroni salad that it had been on the floor a long time, but one might also infer the opposite—that a sloppy shopper recently did both. Similarly, when injury or death occurs without eyewitnesses and only meager circumstantial evidence suggests what happened, we cannot disregard other meager evidence of equally likely causes.

Thus, when the circumstantial evidence of a vital fact is meager, a reviewing court must consider not just favorable but all the circumstantial evidence, and competing inferences as well.

D. Conclusive Evidence

Next, JUSTICE CALVERT noted that Texas courts conducting a no-evidence review traditionally do not disregard contrary evidence that conclusively establishes the opposite of a vital fact. He argued that this is to some extent not a "true" no-evidence claim, as proponents may have to show not only that no evidence supports the verdict but that the opposite was proved as a matter of law. There are several types of conclusive evidence. First, an appellate court conducting a legal sufficiency review cannot "disregard undisputed evidence that allows of only one logical inference." By definition, such evidence can be viewed in only one light, and reasonable jurors can reach only one conclusion from it. Jurors are not free to reach a verdict contrary to such evidence; indeed, uncontroverted issues need not be submitted to a jury at all.

Reviewing legal sufficiency in such cases encompasses a general no-evidence review, because if some evidence supports the verdict then the contrary evidence was not "undisputed." But the review does not stop there; the evidence must also have only one logical inference. Undisputed evidence that reasonable jurors could disbelieve has two: (1) it is true, or (2) it is not.

Most often, undisputed contrary evidence becomes conclusive (and thus cannot be disregarded) when it concerns physical facts that cannot be denied. Thus, no evidence supports an impaired-access claim if it is undisputed that access remains along 90 percent of a tract's frontage. Evidence that a buyer believed a product had been repaired is conclusively negated by an accompanying letter to the contrary. And an insured's liability has not been determined by an "actual trial" if the insured did not appear, present evidence, or challenge anything presented by his opponent.

* * *

Proper legal-sufficiency review prevents reviewing courts from substituting their opinions on credibility for those of the jurors, but proper review also prevents jurors from substituting their opinions for undisputed truth. When evidence contrary to a verdict is conclusive, it cannot be disregarded.

E. Clear-and-Convincing Evidence

Since the time of JUSTICE CALVERT's article, new claims and burdens of proof have arisen that require additions to the four types of no-evidence review JUSTICE CALVERT considered exhaustive. Beginning with the United States Supreme Court's opinion in *Jackson v. Virginia*, appellate courts have recognized that, while "one slender bit of evidence" may be all a reviewing court needs to affirm a verdict based on the preponderance of the evidence, a higher burden of proof requires a higher standard of review. As we recently stated, the standard for legal sufficiency works in tandem with the standard of review—"whenever the standard of proof at trial is elevated, the standard of appellate review must likewise be elevated." If the rule were otherwise, legally sufficient evidence to support a preponderance-of-the-evidence verdict would satisfy the higher burdens as well, thus rendering their differences meaningless. Accordingly, we have held that a legal sufficiency review must consider all the evidence (not just that favoring the verdict) in reviewing cases of parental termination, defamation, and punitive damages. In such cases, again, evidence contrary to a verdict cannot be disregarded.

F. Consciousness Evidence

Further, we have had to particularize legal-sufficiency review in cases involving what a party knew or why it took a certain course, as they are not amenable to review under the exclusive standard. Long before gross negligence had to meet a clear-and-convincing burden, we recognized in *Burk Royalty Co. v. Walls* that no-evidence review of such findings had to include "all of the surrounding facts, circumstances, and conditions, not just individual elements or facts." As then CHIEF JUSTICE GREENHILL noted in concurring, speeding and running a red light may not be legally sufficient evidence of gross negligence if one's wife and daughter are bleeding to death in the back seat. Reviewing courts assessing evidence of conscious indifference cannot disregard part of what a party was conscious of.

For the same reasons, the exclusive standard of review has proven problematic in insurance bad-faith cases. Liability in such cases requires proof that the insurer denied coverage after it became reasonably clear. But that standard will always be met if reviewing courts must disregard any evidence that coverage was unclear. Subsequent cases show that reviewing courts are in fact looking at all the evidence to determine whether coverage was reasonably clear.

This problem arises in other contexts as well. In discrimination cases, discharged employees will never have to prove that the reason given for termination was a pretext if no-evidence review must disregard that reason. Government officials will never be entitled to immunity if we consider only evidence suggesting they should have acted differently. And limitations will never run under the discovery rule if reviewing courts must disregard all evidence that claimants knew of their claims.

This is not to say a reviewing court may credit a losing party's explanations or excuses if jurors could disregard them. For example, while an insurer's reliance on an expert report may foreclose bad faith recovery, it will not do so if the insurer had some reason to doubt the report. But a reviewing court cannot review whether jurors could reasonably disregard a losing party's explanations or excuses without considering what they were.

III. Contrary Evidence That Must Be Disregarded

As trials normally focus on issues that jurors could decide either way, reviewing courts must disregard evidence contrary to the verdict far more often than they must consider it. Just as no-evidence review that starts by disregarding contrary evidence often must end up considering considerably more, no-evidence review that begins by considering all the evidence must usually end up considering considerably less. Again, we do not presume to categorize all circumstances in which contrary evidence must be disregarded; a few examples serve to demonstrate that even under the inclusive standard, viewing all the evidence in a light favorable to the verdict often requires that much of it be disregarded.

A. Credibility Evidence

Jurors are the sole judges of the credibility of the witnesses and the weight to give their testimony. They may choose to believe one witness and disbelieve another. Reviewing courts cannot impose their own opinions to the contrary.

Most credibility questions are implicit rather than explicit in a jury's verdict. Thus, reviewing courts must assume jurors decided all of them in favor of the verdict if reasonable human beings could do so. Courts reviewing all the evidence in a light favorable to the verdict thus assume that jurors credited testimony favorable to the verdict and disbelieved testimony contrary to it. For example, viewing the evidence in the light favorable to the verdict means that if both parties in a traffic accident testify they had the green light, an appellate court must presume the prevailing party did and the losing party did not. If the parties to an oral contract testify to conflicting terms, a reviewing court must presume the terms were those asserted by the winner. When all the evidence is viewed in the light most favorable to the jury verdict, some of it must be completely discounted. Though not disregarded at the outset, the end result is the same. This has always been our practice in cases using the inclusive scope of review. Thus, we have concluded that a bailee sold cotton without the bailor's consent, despite the former's denials, because the jury verdict favored the latter. And we have affirmed a gross negligence verdict based on testimony that the defendant's speed was 80 miles per hour, without mentioning his own testimony to a speed half that.

Nor is it necessary to have testimony from both parties before jurors may disbelieve either. Jurors may disregard even uncontradicted and unimpeached testimony from disinterested witnesses. Thus, an architect's uncontradicted testimony that he relied on a 20-year warranty was not binding on jurors when the bid specifications he prepared included only much shorter warranties. Nor was an insured's uncontradicted testimony about lost furnishings binding on jurors when the fire scene contained several indications of arson but few of burnt furniture. Even uncontroverted expert testimony does not bind jurors unless the subject matter is one for experts alone.

Of course, "[t]he jury's decisions regarding credibility must be reasonable." Jurors cannot ignore undisputed testimony that is clear, positive, direct, otherwise credible, free from contradictions and inconsistencies, and could have been readily controverted. And as noted above, they are not free to believe testimony that is conclusively negated by undisputed facts. But whenever reasonable jurors could decide what testimony to discard, a reviewing court must assume they did so in favor of their verdict, and disregard it in the course of legal sufficiency review.

B. Conflicting Evidence

It is the province of the jury to resolve conflicts in the evidence. Accordingly, courts reviewing all the evidence in a light favorable to the verdict must assume that jurors resolved all conflicts in accordance with that verdict.

Again, this has always been the case even in those cases using the inclusive scope of review. For example, in such cases we have sometimes detailed only the evidence that supported a jury's fraud finding. We have affirmed a bad-faith verdict for legal sufficiency despite "significant evidence" that the insurer acted in good faith. We have found some evidence of lost profits, even though income tax returns showed the contrary. And we have affirmed a jury's negligence finding despite a defendant's evidence asserting it could not have prevented the accident.

In none of these cases did we state that the scope of review required us to disregard evidence contrary to the verdict; instead, we started by considering the entire record in each. But in each case we either discounted or never mentioned conflicting evidence contrary to the verdict because viewing the evidence in the light favorable to the verdict required us to do so.

Of course, it is not always clear whether evidence is conflicting. Evidence is not conflicting just because the parties cannot agree to it. For example, evidence that a hospital controlled a doctor's rotation and patient assignments raises no material conflict with evidence that a different entity controlled the details of medical treatment, as only the latter is material in a malpractice case. Similarly, evidence showing the terms of one loan does not conflict with undisputed evidence that the parties never reached an agreement regarding the terms of another.

But in every circumstance in which reasonable jurors could resolve conflicting evidence either way, reviewing courts must presume they did so in favor of the prevailing party, and disregard the conflicting evidence in their legal sufficiency review.

C. Conflicting Inferences

Even if evidence is undisputed, it is the province of the jury to draw from it whatever inferences they wish, so long as more than one is possible and the jury must not simply guess. Thus, in product liability cases jurors may find evidence of a defect from subsequent modifications, even if there were plenty of other reasons for the changes. Even if a defendant admits approaching an intersection from the wrong way on a one-way street, jurors may infer the plaintiff failed to keep a proper lookout, as that is one possible inference from the accident itself. Similarly, jurors may infer that relatives tore down posters of a missing child to assist the child's father, even though another inference was that the signs simply embarrassed them.

Accordingly, courts reviewing all the evidence in a light favorable to the verdict must assume jurors made all inferences in favor of their verdict if reasonable minds could, and disregard all other inferences in their legal sufficiency review.

IV. Reconciling the Standards

Having noted the dual lines of authority stating the scope of no-evidence review, and the proper application and exceptions to each, we turn to the question of which one is correct.

* * *

As both the inclusive and exclusive standards for the scope of legal-sufficiency review have a long history in Texas, as both have been used in other contexts to review matter-of-law motions, as the federal courts have decided the differences between the two are more semantic than real, and as both—properly applied—must arrive at the same result, we see no compelling reason to choose among them.

The key qualifier, of course, is "properly applied." The final test for legal sufficiency must always be whether the evidence at trial would enable reasonable and fair-minded people to reach the verdict under review. Whether a reviewing court begins by considering all the evidence or only the evidence supporting the verdict, legal-sufficiency review in the proper light must credit favorable evidence if reasonable jurors could, and disregard contrary evidence unless reasonable jurors could not.

While judges and lawyers often disagree about legal sufficiency in particular cases, the disagreements are almost always about what evidence jurors can or must credit and what inferences they can or must make. It is inevitable in human affairs that reasonable people sometimes disagree; thus, it is also inevitable that they will sometimes disagree about what reasonable people can disagree about. This is not a new problem; . . .

V. Application to the Facts

It remains to apply the scope of review to the facts presented.

A majority of the court of appeals affirmed the verdict for the Wilsons, finding legally sufficient evidence that the City knew increased flooding on the Wilsons' property was substantially certain to occur. The majority pointed to the following proof. First, the Wilsons' expert testified that the revised plan was certain to create flooding. Second, as the City admittedly knew that development would increase runoff and the Sebastian ditch would channel it toward the Wilsons, so it knew "with absolute certainty" that flooding would be the result.

Third, the City "did not explain" why the Master Plan required a drainage ditch across the Wilsons' property but the revised plan did not, thus allowing jurors to infer that the City knew this omission would cause flooding.

Of course, the City did explain why it approved the new plan—because three sets of engineers said the omitted ditch was unnecessary—but the court felt compelled by the scope of review to disregard that evidence. For several of the reasons stated earlier, we believe the court of appeals did not properly apply the scope of review. The critical question in this case was the City's state of mind—the Wilsons had to prove the City knew (not should have known) that flooding was substantially certain. A reviewing court cannot evaluate what the City knew by disregarding most of what it was told.

Moreover, when a case involves scientific or technical issues requiring expert advice (as this one does), jurors cannot disregard a party's reliance on experts hired for that very purpose without some evidence supplying a reasonable basis for doing so. Here, it was uncontroverted that three sets of engineers certified that the revised plans met the City's codes and regulations—and thus would not increase downstream flooding. The same firm that drew up the original Master Plan certified the revised one; unless the City had some reason to know the first certification was true and the second one was false (of which there was no evidence), there was only one logical inference jurors could draw.

None of the evidence cited by the court of appeals showed the City knew more than it was told by the engineers. The Wilsons' expert testified that flooding was (in his opinion) inevitable, but not that the City knew it was inevitable. The Wilsons' expert gave no opinion on the latter point.

Second, ending a ditch at a neighbor's property line may be evidence that a defendant was substantially certain of the result in some cases, but not in the context of this one. City witnesses admitted knowing development would increase runoff at the head of this drainage system, but not flooding at its foot. Calculating the effect of detention ponds and absorption in a grassy drainage ditch forty-five feet wide and over two hundred yards long required hydrological formulas, computer models, and mathematical calculations. The omission of the ditch across the Wilsons' property obviously raised concerns that the City investigated, but was no evidence that the City knew the advice it received in response was wrong.

The Wilsons also point to a letter Sebastian's attorney wrote the City demanding indemnity in case the new ditch flooded the Wilsons. But attorneys must protect a client from potential liability whether it is real or imagined—and justly so. In the letter, the attorney never purports to be an expert in hydrology, or cite the opinions of anyone who was. This letter may have required the City to investigate, but again is no evidence it knew the advice it received was wrong.

Our concurring colleagues believe reasonable jurors could nevertheless disregard what all the engineers certified because the City had a financial incentive to believe them rather than pay the Wilsons. Of course, defendants have a financial incentive to avoid paying damages in every case; if that incentive alone is some evidence of liability, then plaintiffs create enough evidence to go to the jury every time they file suit.

But more important, this ignores what the Wilsons had to prove—not that the City might have disbelieved the engineers' reports, but that it did. This requires evidence of "objective indicia of intent" showing the City knew identifiable harm was occurring or substantially certain to result. Jurors' doubts about the engineers' reports or the City's motives could not supply them with objective indicia that the City knew flooding would occur.

Constitutional concerns about the roles of judge and jury do not allow either to make such evidence up.

We agree with the court of appeals that the Wilsons presented some evidence that the City damaged their property, and that in drawing up and approving drainage plans it was acting for a public purpose. The missing piece in the evidence here is proof that the City knew the plans it approved were substantially certain to increase flooding on the Wilsons' properties. While the City certainly knew that fact after the flooding started, the Wilsons never pleaded or submitted to the jury any takings theory other than the City's initial approval.

Crediting all favorable evidence that reasonable jurors could believe and disregarding all contrary evidence except that which they could not ignore, we hold there was no evidence the City's approval of the revised drainage plan was an intentional taking.

Accordingly, we reverse the court of appeals' judgment against the City under article I, section 17 of the Texas Constitution. Because the court of appeals declined to address the jury's alternate verdict for the Wilsons on a claim under the Texas Water Code, we remand the case to that court to determine that issue.

JUSTICE JOHNSON did not participate in the decision.

JUSTICE O'NEILL, joined by JUSTICE MEDINA, concurring (omitted).

Note

King Ranch, Inc. v. Chapman, 118 S.W.3d 742 (Tex. 2003): In this dispute over part of the land (the Rincon) making up the King Ranch, the Chapman heirs have cobbled together a series of interesting historical tidbits and Texas folklore in an effort to regain title to one-half of the Rincon—an interest they claim is worth a substantial sum. Viewed separately, each of these tidbits fails to provide evidence of King's extrinsic fraud, and aggregated, they fare no better. While anything more than a scintilla of evidence is legally sufficient to survive a no-evidence summary judgment motion, some suspicion linked to other suspicion produces only more suspicion, which is not the same as some evidence. We cannot conclude that conspiracy theories—fascinating but unsupported by evidence—may be used to upend a one hundred twenty year old judgment quieting title to the property. Because the Chapman heirs failed to produce even a scintilla of evidence of Richard King's alleged extrinsic fraud, their bill of review fails.

WHITE
v.
SOUTHWESTERN BELL TELEPHONE COMPANY, INC.

651 S.W.2d 260
(Tex. 1983)

Atlas & Hall, David H. Hockema and Lisa Powell, McAllen, for petitioner.

Ewers, Toothaker, Ewers, Abbott, Talbot, Hamilton & Jarvis, Neil Norquest, McAllen, Jerry R. Tucker, Jr., San Antonio, for respondent.

RAY, JUSTICE.

Richard White, doing business as Hewlett-White, instituted this suit against Southwestern Bell Telephone Company, Inc., for lost profits resulting from Southwestern Bell's incorrect listing of his telephone number in the yellow pages. The trial court granted Southwestern Bell's motion for an instructed verdict. The court of appeals affirmed. We reverse the judgments of the courts below and remand the cause to the trial court.

In 1977, Richard White, the owner of Hewlett-White florist shop, sought to expand his business and entered into an agreement with Southwestern Bell for advertising in the yellow pages of the telephone book to be released in February, 1978. When the new issue came out, the phone number for Hewlett-White was listed correctly in the white pages and in one small yellow-page listing. The number, however, was listed incorrectly in the large pictorial yellow-page advertisement purchased by White. The testimony indicated that the number listed for Hewlett-White was that of an insurance company. After White complained, the telephone company assured him that an "intercept" service would be instituted, enabling incoming calls to that number to be screened and then routed to the correct party, either to the flower shop or to the insurance company. Whether this was done or not is disputed by the parties. White testified that some times, when he called the number, he would receive a message that it was not a working number.

Southwestern Bell filed a motion for instructed verdict on several grounds. The trial court granted the motion, but failed to specify the basis for its instructed verdict. The court of appeals affirmed the judgment on the basis that White did not establish a loss in net profits with a reasonable degree of certainty.

In reviewing the trial court's granting of an instructed verdict, the evidence must be considered in the light most favorable to the party against whom the verdict is instructed. *Texas Employers Insurance Association v. Page*, 553 S.W.2d 98 (Tex. 1977). If there is any conflicting evidence of probative nature in the record, a determination of the issue is for the jury. *Air Conditioning, Inc. v. Harrison-Wilson-Pearson*, 151 Tex. 635, 253

S.W.2d 422 (1952). After considering all of the evidence in the light most favorable to White, we have determined that the case should have been submitted to the jury.

To recover for a loss of profits, it is not necessary that the loss be susceptible to exact calculation. *Southwest Battery Corporation v. Owen*, 131 Tex. 423, 115 S.W.2d 1097, 1098 (1938). It is sufficient that the amount of loss is shown by competent evidence with reasonable certainty. *Id.* Where there is an established business, pre-existing profits may be used to evidence the amount of loss with reasonable certainty. *Atomic Fuel Extraction Corporation v. Estate of Tom Slick*, 386 S.W.2d 180, 188 (Tex. Civ. App.—San Antonio 1964, writ ref'd n.r.e. per curiam, 403 S.W.2d 784 (Tex. 1965); *Richker v. Georgandis*, 323 S.W.2d 90, 98 (Tex. Civ. App.—Houston 1959, writ ref'd n.r.e.). Furthermore, in calculating the loss in profits, the normal increase in the business which might have been expected in the light of past developments and existing conditions may be considered. *Southwest Battery Corporation v. Owen*, 115 S.W.2d at 1099.

The evidence showed that Hewlett-White has been an established business for thirty-three years and has consistently shown profits. Additionally, there was evidence that the sale of flowers is not an uncertain or speculative business. A representative for Southwestern Bell testified that directory advertising is a very effective method of attracting business for florists. The representative further added that a business would be hurt if its telephone number was incorrectly listed in the yellow pages.

Hewlett-White's business records were introduced to show the gross sales in the years 1974 through 1980, and 1978 was the only year with a decline in gross receipts. White's certified public accountant, using "linear regression" analysis, testified what White's sales should have been in 1978. According to her figures, there was a projected loss of gross receipts in the amount of $40,000. There was testimony that Hewlett-White's sales through wire services, which are unrelated to yellow-page advertising, increased in 1978. White's income tax returns and other testimony conflicted with these figures; however, the determination of which figure is correct is for the jury. *Air Conditioning, Inc. v. Harrison-Wilson-Pearson*, 253 S.W.2d at 425.

White testified that twenty-five to thirty percent of his gross receipts is profit. Additionally, he testified that his overhead expenses remain static, and once these expenses are met, the only additional expense is the cost of the flowers themselves which are marked up five hundred percent. His estimate as to what percentage of his receipts is profit was reasonably certain because of his experience in the field.

Under the facts of this case, it cannot be said, as a matter of law, that White is not entitled to recovery for his lost profits. We hold White's evidence presented a fact question for jury determination.

The telephone company, as an additional basis for its motion for instructed verdict, asserted that White has no standing as a "consumer" under the Deceptive Trade Practices Act. TEX. BUS. & COM. CODE ANN. § 17.45(4). This contention is without merit as White sought and paid for additional telephone lines and yellow-page advertising, and therefore is a consumer under the Act. Further, Southwestern Bell alleged that its affirmative defense of accord and satisfaction was conclusively proved because White agreed to an eighty percent reduction in his monthly advertising rates. We hold that a fact question exists as to whether the elements of this defense are established. *See Jenkins v. Henry C. Beck Co.*, 449 S.W.2d 454 (Tex. 1969). Consequently, the instructed verdict cannot be upheld on this point.

Southwestern Bell contends that its liability, if any, is limited by its tariff and advertising contract. These points are not fully briefed and may be further developed on remand.

The judgments of the courts below are reversed and the cause is remanded to the trial court.

Notes

1. *Phillips v. Carlton Energy Group*, 475 S.W.3d 265 (Tex. 2015) in discussing what evidence was necessary to recovery for lost profits the court stated:

> "With respect to the recovery of lost profits as consequential damages, the law is well-settled: lost profits can be recovered only when the amount is proved with reasonable certainty. Proof need not be exact, but neither can it be speculative. The reasonable certainty requirement "is intended to be flexible enough to accommodate the myriad circumstances in which claims for lost profits arise." But [p]rofits which are largely speculative, as from an activity dependent on uncertain or changing market condi-

tions, or on chancy business opportunities, or on promotion of untested products or entry into unknown or unviable markets, or on the success of a new and unproven enterprise, cannot be recovered. Factors like these and others which make a business venture risky in prospect preclude recovery of lost profits in retrospect.

"It is impossible to announce with exact certainty any rule measuring the profits the loss for which recovery may be had." "What constitutes reasonably certain evidence of lost profits is a fact intensive determination." We have denied recovery of lost profits that the claimant contended would have been realized from the bid that would have been offered on a construction project had the claimant known the truth about site conditions; from retirement accounts taken by a competitor; from a lost opportunity to develop and market a new, unique, voice-prompted, programmable thermostat; from the lost use of a bulldozer; and from the sale of oil and gas leases, had defendant drilled a second well as agreed, even though the first well was a dry hole. We have upheld recoveries of lost profits from an established account of an asbestos abatement business; from farmers' crop loss; from an established florist shop; from an established cigarette vending business; and from selling car batteries (in the 1930s). The only common thread running through these cases is the necessity that the claim of lost profits not be hypothetical or hopeful but substantial in the circumstances.

But while whether to allow a recovery of lost profits is a fact-dependent inquiry, "[t]his does not mean . . . that the 'reasonable certainty' test lacks clear parameters." "As a minimum, opinions or estimates of lost profits must be based on objective facts, figures, or data from which the amount of lost profits can be ascertained." Though the breach or tort may be clear, profits "not susceptible of being established by proof to that degree of certainty which the law demands" cannot be recovered as damages. Still, courts draw a distinction between uncertainty merely as to the amount and uncertainty as to the fact of legal damages. Cases may be cited which hold that uncertainty as to the fact of legal damages is fatal to recovery, but uncertainty as to the amount will not defeat recovery. A party who breaks his contract cannot escape liability because it is impossible to state or prove a perfect measure of damages."

2. *St. Joseph Hospital v. Wolff*, 94 S.W.3d 513 (Tex. 2002): In evaluating the legal sufficiency of the evidence to support a finding, the court determines whether the proffered evidence as a whole rises to a level that would enable reasonable and fair-minded people to differ in their conclusions. Thus, the court considers all the evidence in the light most favorable to the prevailing party, indulging every reasonable inference in that party's favor. Although it is often stated that a reviewing court performing a no-evidence review must disregard all evidence contrary to the finding in question, a court need not disregard undisputed evidence that allows of only one logical inference. Nevertheless, a no-evidence point is sustained only if there is no more than a scintilla of evidence proving each element of the cause of action (here joint enterprise).

SZCZEPANIK
v.
FIRST SOUTHERN TRUST CO.

883 S.W.2d 648
(Tex. 1994)

Harvey G. Joseph, John A. Koepke, and A. David Gross, Dallas, for petitioners.

Thomas K. Boone, Monte M. Bond, Dallas, and June E. Higgins, Spring, for respondents.

PER CURIAM.

This case involves alleged lost profits sustained by First Southern Trust Company (FST), a wholly owned subsidiary of First Southern Holding Company (FSH), when certain officers and employees left FST and formed a competing business.

FST manages retirement assets primarily for retired airline pilots. In 1991, after serving for a brief period of time as president of FST and FSH, Richard Szczepanik resigned and formed a new corporation, Retirement Advisors of America, Inc. (RAAI), with other former officers and employees of FST and FSH. RAAI also manages retirement assets for retired airline pilots. Some of FST's clients transferred their retirement assets totaling

$36 million from FST to RAAI. Szczepanik sued FSH for payment of his salary during the time he had served as president of FST and FSH. FST counterclaimed under numerous theories for damages resulting from the loss of customers to RAAI. After several days of testimony offered in FST's case in chief, the trial court excluded evidence of damages by FST under TEX. R. CIV. P. 215(5) for failing to supplement discovery that sought information as to the amount of damages, the method of calculating damages, and expert witnesses who would testify as to damages. The trial court granted Petitioners' motion for instructed verdict on the grounds that there was no evidence of damages. The court of appeals reversed and remanded the case holding that the evidence raised a fact issue concerning lost profits damages that precluded an instructed verdict on FST's claims, but affirmed the trial court's judgment awarding Szczepanik $97,803 on his salary claim. 880 S.W.2d 10. Because we hold there is no evidence of lost profits damages, we reverse the judgment of the court of appeals concerning the instructed verdict and remand to the court of appeals for consideration of FST's other points of error.

In reviewing the granting of an instructed verdict, we must determine whether there is any evidence of probative force to raise a fact issue on the material questions presented. *Collora v. Navarro*, 574 S.W.2d 65, 68 (Tex. 1978). We consider all of the evidence in a light most favorable to the party against whom the verdict was instructed and disregard all contrary evidence and inferences; we give the losing party the benefit of all reasonable inferences created by the evidence. *White v. Southwestern Bell Tel. Co.*, 651 S.W.2d 260, 262 (Tex. 1983). If there is any conflicting evidence of probative value on any theory of recovery, an instructed verdict is improper and the case must be reversed and remanded for jury determination of that issue. *White*, 651 S.W.2d at 262.

At trial, FST attempted to offer evidence of the lost profits it sustained and would sustain as a result of the transfer of assets to RAAI. FST offered evidence that $36 million in account assets were transferred to RAAI and that FST collected annual fees of .75% to 1% on account assets. FST also offered testimony that absent the interference of RAAI, FST would have expected to retain its customers' accounts for the lifetime of the individual account holders. FST also offered evidence that in 1991 it managed assets of $350 million and expected to make a profit of $250,000 to $500,000 per year beginning in 1991.

Recovery of lost profits does not require that the loss be susceptible to exact calculation. *Texas Instruments v. Teletron Energy Management, Inc.*, 877 S.W.2d 276, 279 (Tex. 1994). However, the injured party must do more than show that they suffered some lost profits. *Id.* The amount of the loss must be shown by competent evidence with reasonable certainty. *Id.* What constitutes reasonably certain evidence of lost profits is a fact intensive determination. *Holt Atherton Ind., Inc. v. Heine*, 835 S.W.2d 80, 84 (Tex. 1992). At a minimum, opinions or estimates of lost profits must be based on objective facts, figures, or data from which the amount of lost profits may be ascertained. *Id.* Recovery of lost profits must be predicated on one complete calculation. *Id.* at 85.

The evidence that FST expected to make a profit beginning in 1991 of $250,000 to $500,000 per year is legally insufficient to show lost profits. First, this evidence, elicited from the testimony of FST's secretary and treasurer, is pure speculation. There is nothing in the record to show how FST determined the amount of lost profits. *See Holt Atherton*, 835 S.W.2d at 84. Second, there is nothing in the record that relates the total amount of profits FST expected to make beginning in 1991 to the profits FST lost as a result of the transfer of retirement accounts to RAAI.

The evidence that FST lost $36 million in assets to RAAI and earned .75% to 1% in annual fees on such assets also is legally insufficient to show lost profits. While this evidence suggests that FST lost $270,000 to $360,000 in annual fees on the accounts transferred to RAAI, this evidence is legally insufficient to show lost profits because there is no evidence that FST could have expected to retain all of those accounts for any period of time. Rather, the uncontradicted evidence shows that the individual account holders could transfer their accounts to another trustee or retirement fund manager at any time. Without evidence that FST could have expected to retain the $36 million in retirement accounts for any length of time, there is no evidence that FST could have expected to earn profits on those accounts for any period of time.

The court of appeals' reliance on the testimony that FST could have expected to retain the accounts for the lifetime of the individual account holders does not support reversal of the trial court's judgment. First, this evidence is without any evidentiary foundation and therefore, is purely speculative and conclusory. Second, even considering this evidence, there is no evidence of the life expectancy of the individual account holders. Thus, again, there is no basis to determine the length of time FST could have expected to retain the $36 million in retirement assets. Third, there is no evidence that the individual account holders representing the $36 million in retirement assets were still alive at the time of trial. In short, there is no evidence that FST would have kept the $36 million or any portion thereof for any period of time.

We hold that on this record, there is no evidence of lost profits damages and Petitioners were entitled to an instructed verdict on damages. We reverse the judgment of the court of appeals and remand this matter to the court of appeals for consideration of FST's additional points of error.

Notes

1. The evidence given only by the plaintiff to conclusively establish one or more of the elements of his cause of action is sufficient, if that evidence is clear, direct, and positive, and was uncontradicted by the defendant who had the means and opportunity of disproving the testimony or the credibility of the plaintiff and failed to do so. *See Collora v. Navarro*, 574 S.W.2d 65 (Tex. 1978). This is the same rule which is used in summary judgment practice. *See* Rule 166a(c) of the Texas Rules of Civil Procedure.

2. It is a well-settled rule that a defendant whose motion for instructed verdict is denied following the introduction of all of a plaintiff's evidence, and who then proceeds with the introduction of his own evidence, waives his motion for instructed verdict, unless the motion is reurged at the close of his case. *See Texas Steel Co. v. Douglas*, 533 S.W.2d 111 (Tex. Civ. App.—Fort Worth 1976, writ ref'd n.r.e.).

3. Since the judge in a nonjury case is the arbiter of both facts and law, a motion for judgment can be based either on the legal insufficiency or the factual insufficiency of the evidence. *See Qantel Business Sys., Inc. v. Custom Controls Co.*, 761 S.W.2d 302 (Tex. 1988).

4. *Coastal Transport Company, Inc. v. Crown Central Petroleum Corp.*, 136 S.W.3d 227 (Tex. 2004): In this case, Crown Central Petroleum sued Coastal Transport for negligence and gross negligence, after a Coastal gasoline truck caused a fire that destroyed a Crown Central gasoline-loading facility. *Held*: Coastal did not waive its right to complain that there is legally insufficient evidence of gross negligence, by failing to object to the admission of expert testimony on gross negligence. An objection is not needed to preserve a no-evidence challenge to conclusory expert testimony. Such an objection is required, only when a challenge to expert testimony questions the underlying methodology, technique, or foundational data used by the witness. A Daubert/Robinson challenge to the reliability of a scientific process or technique, for example, must be timely made, in order to allow the court to exercise its gatekeeper function.

2. *Motion for Judgment Notwithstanding the Verdict and Motion to Disregard a Jury Finding: Taking the Case Away From the Jury After the Verdict*

Read Rule 301 Texas Rules of Civil Procedure.

SHERMAN
v.
FIRST NATIONAL BANK IN CENTER, TEXAS

760 S.W.2d 240
(Tex. 1988)

Thomas R. McLeroy, Jr., Center, for petitioner.
Bill Warren, Center, for respondent.

PER CURIAM.

R.L. Sherman sued First National Bank of Center, Texas for wrongful foreclosure on certain real estate. The Bank had advanced Sherman funds to purchase the real estate and secured the funds by a deed of trust upon the property. Eventually, the substitute trustee of the deed of trust gave notice of sale and sold the property. The jury returned a verdict which was favorable to Sherman on the wrongful foreclosure suit. Accordingly, the judge rendered judgment for Sherman. In an unpublished, per curiam opinion, the court of appeals reversed the judgment of the trial court and rendered judgment for the Bank, holding there was "absolutely no evidence" to support the jury's answers to the issues. We reverse the judgment of the court of appeals and affirm that of the trial court.

Sherman and his deceased wife, Annie Sherman, executed a deed of trust and note payable to the Bank to secure a $75,000 loan advanced for the purchase of real estate. The loan was renewed and due for payment on October 20, 1982. In December of 1981, Sherman received a letter from the Bank demanding the payment of several notes, including the $75,000 real estate note which was not due and owing at that time. In an unsuccessful attempt to settle the matter, Sherman offered to pay the notes with cash and certificates of deposit and brought to the Bank's attention the fact that the real estate note was not due at that time.

In July of 1982, the Bank filed suit in Cause No. 20,914 in Shelby County against Sherman, seeking to recover the balance on the notes, including the $75,000 real estate note, or to foreclose on the property securing the notes. The Bank alleged in its pleading in that cause that all notes, except the real estate note, were due. The Bank, through various employees, admitted throughout litigation that the Bank knew the $75,000 real estate note was not due; however, because the Bank was feeling insecure, the Bank included the real estate note in its petition to "run a bluff" against Sherman.

At the time Cause No. 20,914 was filed, Sherman had remarried Jimmie Boles Sherman. He was incarcerated in a federal penitentiary in Fort Worth. Sherman was never served with citation in Cause No. 20,914 and never appeared of record. He only learned of the cause through his wife, Jimmie Boles Sherman, who had learned of the suit through a newspaper article.

After notifying Sherman of the pending suit, Jimmie Boles Sherman visited with bank officials in an attempt to resolve the matter. She put up collateral for several of the notes, and certificates of deposit were liquidated to extinguish the remainder of the indebtedness. Thereafter, the Bank moved the court to dismiss Cause No. 20,914 with prejudice to refile the matter. The court granted the motion and dismissed the entire case with prejudice. However, the Bank urges now that the $75,000 real estate note was excluded from the settlement.

In October of 1982, only two months after Cause No. 20,914 was dismissed with prejudice, the Bank gave Sherman notice of its intent to foreclose on the property securing the $75,000 real estate note. Sherman filed this action seeking to enjoin the foreclosure. The substitute trustee sold the property under the deed of trust in December of 1982. Thereafter, Sherman amended his petition to include a cause of action for wrongful foreclosure.

At trial of the wrongful foreclosure cause of action the jury returned a verdict for Sherman, finding that Cause No. 20,914, including the $75,000 real estate note, was compromised and settled between the Bank and Sherman. Therefore, the Bank wrongfully foreclosed on the real estate. The Bank moved for a judgment notwithstanding the verdict, but the trial court denied the motion on December 31, 1986.

Thereafter, the Bank appealed to the court of appeals. In the court of appeals, the Bank urged that the trial court erred in failing to grant judgment notwithstanding the verdict. For appellate purposes, a complaint that the trial court erred in refusing to grant a judgment notwithstanding the verdict, raises only a no evidence point for appellate review. The court of appeals held there was "absolutely no evidence" that Sherman had settled the real estate note with the Bank.

Sherman urges here that the court of appeals erred in holding there was no evidence to support the jury verdict. "In deciding a no evidence point, an appellate court must consider only the evidence and inferences tending to support the finding and disregard all evidence and inferences to the contrary." *See Alm v. Aluminum Co. of America*, 717 S.W.2d 588, 593 (Tex. 1986), *citing Garza v. Alviar*, 395 S.W.2d 821, 823 (Tex. 1965). When there is more than a scintilla of evidence, the appellate court may not overturn the jury's finding on a "no evidence" point of error.

At trial, Sherman introduced as Plaintiff's Exhibit One the record of Cause No. 20,914. The record of Cause No. 20,914 reflects that the Bank filed a petition seeking to foreclose the security interest on all notes including the $75,000 real estate note. The record in Cause No. 20,914 also reflects that according to the Bank's "Motion to Dismiss" and "Order of Dismissal" with prejudice "all matters [including the real estate note] in dispute between the parties have been fully and finally compromised and settled." (emphasis added).

This evidence constitutes more than a scintilla of evidence that Cause No. 20,914 as compromised and settled included the real estate note. Admittedly, the record in this cause reveals contradictory evidence which is set forth by the court of appeals in its unpublished per curiam opinion. However, the court of appeals should not have considered this contradictory evidence under a no evidence review.

Again, we reiterate, an appellate court is limited to reviewing only the evidence tending to support the jury findings in a "no evidence" point of error. The opinion and judgment of the court of appeals is in conflict with this court's repeated holdings. *See e.g. Garcia v. Insurance Co. of the State of Pennsylvania*, 751 S.W.2d 857 (Tex. 1988); *Alm v. Aluminum Co. of America*, 717 S.W.2d at 593; *International Armament Corp. v. King*, 686 S.W.2d 595 (Tex. 1985); *Garza v. Alviar*, 395 S.W.2d at 823. Therefore, pursuant to TEX. R. APP. P. 133(b), we grant Sherman's application for writ of error, and without hearing oral argument, a majority of the court reverses the judgment of the court of appeals and reinstates the judgment of the trial court.

Note

"*In City of Keller v. Wilson*, the Texas Supreme Court recognized the different scopes of review applicable to no evidence cases, referring to them as exclusive (considering only the evidence favorable to the finding) and inclusive (considering all of the evidence), but the court held that whether the legal sufficiency scope of review was all of the evidence or only the evidence favorable to the jury's verdict made no real difference. Following the United States Supreme Court, the Texas Supreme Court held that any difference between the inclusive and exclusive standards was 'more semantic than real.' The court held that whether a reviewing court reviews all of the evidence or only part of the evidence in a legal-sufficiency review, 'there can be no disagreement about where that review should end': 'Under either scope of review, appellate courts must view the evidence in the light most favorable to the verdict, crediting favorable evidence if reasonable jurors could, and disregarding contrary evidence unless reasonable jurors could not.' The court further explained:

> If the evidence at trial would enable reasonable and fair-minded people to differ in their conclusions, then jurors must be allowed to do so. A reviewing court cannot substitute its judgment for that of the trier-of-fact, so long as the evidence falls within this zone of reasonable disagreement.

Similarly, there is no disagreement about how a reviewing court should view evidence in the process of that review. Whether a reviewing court starts with all or only part of the record, the court must consider evidence in the light most favorable to the verdict, and indulge every reasonable inference that would support it. But if the evidence allows of only one inference, neither jurors nor the reviewing court may disregard it." W. Wendell Hall, *Standards of Review in Texas*, 38 ST. MARY'S L. J. 47, 247-248 (2006) (permission granted).

MANCORP
v.
CULPEPPER

802 S.W.2d 226
(Tex. 1990)

R. Scott Hogarty, James W. Paulsen, and Bill Jones, Houston, for petitioner.
James L. Wright, and Eva C. Ramos, Austin, for respondents.

SPEARS, JUSTICE.

Mancorp, Inc. sued John C. Culpepper, Jr. and Culpepper Properties, Inc. for breach of a construction contract. Mancorp alleged that it had performed the contract by completing work on the First Bank Galleria building in Bryan, Texas, and that it was owed $510,650, the unpaid balance under the contract. Culpepper and Culpepper Properties, Inc. counterclaimed for breach of contract, breach of warranty, and deceptive trade practices, alleging material defects in the building. The jury found (1) that Mancorp substantially performed its contract with Culpepper Properties, Inc., (2) that Culpepper Properties, Inc. was entitled to an offset for necessary repairs to the building totaling $289,376.90, (3) that Culpepper Properties, Inc. was the alter ego of John C. Culpepper, Jr., (4) that Mancorp was not in breach of its contract with Culpepper Properties, Inc., and (5) that Mancorp was entitled to reasonable and necessary attorneys' fees. Culpepper and Culpepper Properties, Inc. moved for judgment non obstante veredicto on the jury's alter ego finding. The trial court rendered judgment for Mancorp in the amount of $221,273.10 (contract price less the offset) but rendered judgment n.o.v. for Culpepper on the alter ego finding. The court of appeals reformed the trial court's judgment by reducing Mancorp's recovery by $2000, and affirmed the judgment as reformed. 781 S.W.2d 618. We reverse the judgment of the court of appeals and remand this cause to that court for consideration of the factual insufficiency point that Culpepper raised in the appeal below.

ALTER EGO

In order to uphold a trial court's judgment notwithstanding the verdict, an appellate court must determine that no evidence supports the jury's findings. *Williams v. Bennett*, 610 S.W.2d 144, 145 (Tex. 1980). When reviewing a no evidence point, an appellate court is limited to reviewing only the evidence tending to support the jury's verdict and must disregard all evidence to the contrary. *Sherman v. First Nat'l Bank*, 760 S.W.2d 240, 242 (Tex. 1988) (per curiam); *Garcia v. Insurance Co. of Pa.*, 751 S.W.2d 857, 858 (Tex. 1988) (per curiam). If more than a scintilla of evidence supports the jury finding, it must be upheld. *Garcia*, 751 S.W.2d at 858. Thus, appellate courts must consider the evidence and inferences as they tend to support the verdict and not with a view toward supporting the judgment. *See, id.* ("If there is more than a scintilla of evidence to support the jury finding, it must be upheld.") (emphasis added). With this standard in mind, we now examine the evidence to determine whether the jury's alter ego finding is supported by more than a scintilla of evidence.

Under the alter ego theory, courts disregard the corporate entity when there exists such unity between corporation and individual that the corporation ceases to be separate and when holding only the corporation liable would promote injustice. *Castleberry v. Branscum*, 721 S.W.2d 270, 272 (Tex. 1986). An alter ego relationship may be shown from the total dealings of the corporation and the individual. *Id.* This showing may include evidence of "the degree to which corporate formalities have been followed and corporate and individual property have been kept separately, the amount of financial interest, ownership and control the individual maintains over the corporation, and whether the corporation has been used for personal purposes." *Id.*

In the instant case, the court of appeals found that the only testimony concerning alter ego was that of Culpepper. His testimony showed noncompliance with corporate formalities and payment of alleged corporate debts with his personal checks. The court of appeals viewed this testimony standing alone, and the reasonable inferences drawn from it, as constituting no evidence that Culpepper Properties, Inc. is Culpepper's alter ego. The court also considered evidence of checks drawn on the account of "John C. Culpepper, Jr., Bank Tower Project," which Culpepper wrote without a designation that he was the agent of Culpepper Properties, Inc., to be no evidence of alter ego and further stated that Culpepper's business card—"Culpepper Properties, Inc., John C. Culpepper, Jr., his self"—amounted to less than a scintilla of evidence. Finally, the court could find no evidence of gross fraud that would result in injustice.

Instead of considering this evidence and the reasonable inferences supporting the jury's finding of alter ego, the court of appeals drew inferences from the evidence which tended to support the trial court's judgment n.o.v. that Culpepper Properties, Inc. was not the alter ego of Culpepper. Certainly, reasonable minds could differ about whether Culpepper's testimony established that Culpepper failed to observe corporate formalities. However, it was not unreasonable for the jury to infer from Culpepper's testimony that he and the corporation were alter egos. The evidence of the checks could support an inference that the account was used solely for Culpepper's personal business investments. Similarly, evidence of Culpepper's business card may have led the jury to infer that Culpepper considered Culpepper Properties, Inc. indistinguishable from himself.

These pieces of evidence, however, do not stand alone; we consider them along with other pieces of evidence. There was testimony that throughout their dealings Culpepper led Mancorp to believe it was dealing with Culpepper as an individual. During negotiations, Culpepper told Mancorp's vice president that he personally backed the First Bank Galleria project. All of these pieces of evidence, taken together and in light of other evidence in the record showing Culpepper's and Culpepper Properties, Inc.'s total dealings, constitute more than a scintilla of evidence to support a finding that there is such unity between the corporation and the individual that the separateness of the corporation has ceased. *See Castleberry*, 721 S.W.2d at 276.

Likewise, there is more than a scintilla of evidence that failure to pierce the corporate veil will result in injustice. *See Matthews Constr. Co. v. Houston Pipe & Supply Co.*, 796 S.W.2d 692, 693 (Tex. 1990) (when corporate form is used as essentially unfair device courts may act in equity and disregard corporate form to avoid inequitable result). "Where a corporate entity is owned or controlled by an individual who operates the company in a manner indistinguishable from his personal affairs and in a manner calculated to mislead those dealing with him to their detriment," the corporate fiction may be disregarded in order to prevent injustice. *See Loomis Land & Cattle Co. v. Wood*, 699 S.W.2d 594, 597 (Tex. App.—Texarkana 1985, writ ref'd n.r.e.); *see also Sagebrush Sales Co. v. Strauss*, 605 S.W.2d 857 (Tex. 1980). In contract cases, inequity frequently results from reasonable reliance on the financial backing of the corporation's owners should the corporation become insolvent. *Pan Eastern Exploration Co. v. Hufo Oils*, 855 F.2d 1106, 1133 (5th Cir. 1988). Without this reliance on an owner's representations of financial backing, a contract claimant would otherwise assume the risk of insolvency as part of its bargain with the corporate entity. *Id.* (*citing Bell Oil & Gas Co. v. Allied Chem. Corp.*, 431 S.W.2d 336 (Tex. 1968); *Edwards Co. v. Monogram Indus., Inc.*, 730 F.2d 977 (5th Cir. 1984) (en banc)).

Viewing the evidence in the light most favorable to the jury's verdict, the evidence in this case tends to show the following: (1) Ryan Mortgage Company made the construction loan for the First Bank Galleria project to Culpepper Properties, Inc. and Culpepper individually; (2) Culpepper personally guaranteed the loan; (3) Culpepper told Richard Darrah, Mancorp's vice president, that he was personally behind the project; (4) Ryan Mortgage confirmed to Darrah that Culpepper was personally behind the project; (5) Culpepper did business under the corporate name of Culpepper Properties, Inc. and personally under the name Culpepper Properties; (6) Mancorp submitted the proposal for the bank project to "Culpepper Properties," not Culpepper Properties, Inc.; (7) Culpepper signed an order for changes in the construction documents personally under the name of Culpepper Properties; and (8) Mancorp thought it was doing business with Culpepper, the individual, and that he was paying for the job. The record also shows that Ryan Mortgage foreclosed on the project and that two of the project's creditors went unpaid. Based on this evidence, a jury could reasonably infer that injustice would result if Culpepper was not held personally liable because Mancorp relied on Culpepper's misleading representations to the effect that he was backing the project. Moreover, the evidence of the mortgage company's foreclosure of the project and the fact that two of the project's creditors were unpaid could have led the jury to reasonably infer that Mancorp might go unpaid by Culpepper Properties, Inc., and this would result in injustice. Therefore, based upon the evidence concerning the total dealings between Culpepper and Culpepper Properties, Inc., we hold that more than a scintilla of evidence supports the jury's alter ego finding and the court of appeals erred in concluding otherwise.

* * *

We reverse the judgment of the court of appeals and remand this cause to that court for consideration of the factual insufficiency point that Culpepper raised by cross-point in the appeal below.

HECHT, JUSTICE, dissenting.

I dissent. There is no evidence in this record from which the jury could have found that John C. Culpepper, Jr. was the alter ego of Culpepper Properties, Inc. The trial court reached this conclusion and rendered judgment notwithstanding the verdict for John Culpepper. The court of appeals reached the same conclusion and affirmed this portion of the trial court's judgment. Now this Court concludes that there is evidence of alter ego. The Court cannot point to a shred of evidence which, by itself, implies that John Culpepper was the alter ego of Culpepper Properties. Instead, it takes various bits and pieces of evidence, each of which is no evidence of alter ego, adds them together, notes that Mancorp thought John Culpepper might be Culpepper Properties' alter ego, and comes up with evidence of alter ego. Nothing plus nothing plus nothing is still nothing, no matter how hard you believe, or hope, that it may be something.

The Court states that to prove that a corporation is merely the alter ego of a person, one must show two things: first, that "there exists such unity between corporation and individual that the corporation ceases to be separate," and second, that "holding only the corporation liable would promote injustice." *Supra* at 228. Alter ego, the Court acknowledges, "is shown from the total dealings of the corporation and the individual." *Castleberry v. Branscum*, 721 S.W.2d 270, 272 (Tex. 1986) (emphasis added). The Court, however, does not review the total dealings between John Culpepper and Culpepper Properties; rather, it looks only to those dealings which support a finding of alter ego. This restricted review of the evidence is justified, the Court says, because legal sufficiency of the evidence must be determined by considering only the evidence and inferences favorable to the jury finding. Even under this restricted view, there is no evidence to support a finding of alter ego in this case.

* * *

I agree with the Court that the dealings between John Culpepper and Culpepper Properties must be viewed in their totality, although the Court takes a much narrower perspective of the record here. Nevertheless, even if the evidence cited by the Court were all there was in this record on the issue of alter ego, it would not allow alter ego to be inferred. I agree that weak inferences, no one of which is alone enough to support a finding of alter ego, may together do so. But pieces of evidence from which nothing can be inferred cannot be combined somehow to produce an implication. That is the situation here. The jury could reasonably have suspected that John Culpepper treated Culpepper Properties as his alter ego, as I believe the Court does, but it could not have inferred alter ego from this record. Several smoldering sticks, no one of them flaming, may together build a fire. But all the sticks there are, piled up without spark or heat, make neither smoke nor fire; they are nothing but a big pile of sticks, and one cannot infer from the pile that they must be afire. If the shield from personal liability which the corporate form affords shareholders can be overcome by sheer volume of evidence bereft of substance, that shield is very little protection.

On remand, the court of appeals is left to determine whether the evidence of alter ego, of which it found none at all before, is factually insufficient to support the verdict. If that court is consistent with its prior opinion, it will remand this case for a new trial on the issue of alter ego. Because I would affirm the judgment of the court of appeals, I dissent.

PHILLIPS, C.J., joins in this dissenting opinion.

HARRIS COUNTY, Texas
v.
McFERREN

788 S.W.2d 76
(Tex. App.—Houston [1st Dist.] 1990, writ denied)

Mike Driscoll, County Atty., Frank Sanders, Asst. County Atty., Houston, for appellant.
Merry Miller, Houston, for appellee.

DUGGAN, JUSTICE.

This is an appeal from a plaintiff's judgment entered in a premises liability action after the court disregarded a jury answer favorable to the defendant. We reverse and render a take-nothing judgment.

Appellee, William McFerren, individually, and as next friend of his minor daughter, Shannon McFerren, sued appellant, Harris County, Texas, under the Texas Tort Claims Act, TEX. CIV. PRAC. & REM. CODE ANN. § 101.022 (Vernon 1986), as a result of injuries Shannon received at a county-owned park.

Shannon McFerren had attended a high school pep rally and bonfire on November 17, 1983, at Sylvan Beach Park, and was standing in front of a picnic table shelter afterward, waiting for her grandmother to pick her up. A boy had climbed on top of the shelter while his brother stood next to it, shaking one of its pillars back and forth. The shelter collapsed and struck Shannon's leg, breaking her right ankle. It is undisputed that Sylvan Beach Park is owned, operated, and maintained by Harris County.

In answers to questions submitted, the jury found that the picnic table shelter that fell on Shannon's leg constituted a dangerous condition (Question 1); that the County did not have actual knowledge of the dangerous condition (Question 2); that the County failed to make the dangerous condition reasonably safe (Question 7); and, based on Question 7, that the County was 100 percent liable (Question 12). The trial court disregarded the jury's answer to Question 2 and entered judgment for the jury's monetary award to the McFerrens based on: (1) the jury's findings of a dangerous condition, the County's negligence in failing to make the dangerous condition reasonably safe, the County's 100 percent liability, and proximate cause; and (2) the trial court's holding, as a matter of law, that the County knew of the dangerous condition. The plaintiffs did not plead gross negligence on the part of the County, and no jury question on the issue was requested or submitted. Because the jury found in answer to Question 2 that the County did not have actual knowledge of the dangerous condition, the jury did not answer the predicated question that followed as to whether the County failed to warn of the condition.

Harris County's second point of error is dispositive of the appeal, and we therefore consider it first. In its second point of error, Harris County asserts that the trial court erred in disregarding the jury's answer to Question 2.

A trial court may not properly disregard a jury's negative finding and substitute its own affirmative finding unless the evidence conclusively establishes such an affirmative finding. *New Process Steel Corp. v. Steel Corp.*, 703 S.W.2d 209, 216 (Tex. App.—Houston [1st Dist.] 1985, writ ref'd n.r.e.). Neither may the trial court disregard a jury's answer that has some support in the evidence, even though the great weight and preponderance of the evidence may be to the contrary. *Gulf, C. & Santa Fe Ry. v. Deen*, 158 Tex. 466, 470, 312 S.W.2d 933, 937, cert. denied, 358 U.S. 874, 79 S.Ct. 111, 3 L.Ed.2d 105 (1958).

A contention on appeal that an answer to a jury question should not have been disregarded presents a "no evidence" point. *Harper Bldg. Sys. v. Upjohn Co.*, 564 S.W.2d 123, 125 (Tex. Civ. App.—Beaumont 1978, writ ref'd n.r.e.) (where some evidence of probative force existed to support a jury's finding of lost profits, an award of damages for lost profits should not have been disregarded); *see also Harbin v. Seale*, 461 S.W.2d 591, 592 (Tex. 1970) (before a judgment n.o.v. is proper, there must be no evidence of probative force upon which the jury could have made the finding relied upon). To sustain the trial court's action in granting a motion to disregard the jury's answer to a specific question, an appeals court must determine that there is no evidence upon which the jury could have made the finding. *Alm v. Aluminum Co. of Am.*, 717 S.W.2d 588, 593 (Tex. 1986).

In acting on a motion to disregard a jury answer, all evidence must be considered in the light most favorable to the party against whom the motion is sought, and every reasonable inference deducible from the evidence is to be indulged in that party's favor. *Alm*, 717 S.W.2d at 593; *New Process Steel Corp.*, 703 S.W.2d at 216 (where evidence was sufficient to support the jury's finding on damages, granting of a motion to disregard was improper); *Berlow v. Sheraton Dallas Corp.*, 629 S.W.2d 818, 821 (Tex. App.—Dallas 1982, writ ref'd n.r.e.) (when there was some evidence to support jury's finding that the hotel's negligence was the proximate cause of the loss, judgment n.o.v. was improper).

A trial court may disregard a jury finding on a question only if it has no support in the evidence, TEX. R. CIV. P. 301, or if it is rendered immaterial by other findings. *Eubanks v. Winn*, 420 S.W.2d 698, 701 (Tex. 1967); *New Process Steel Corp.*, 703 S.W.2d at 213.

The Texas Tort Claims Act establishes that the question of the County's lack of knowledge of the defect is material. Section 101.022 provides that if a claim arises from a premises defect, the governmental unit owes the claimant "only the duty that a private person owes to a licensee on private property unless the claimant pays for the use of the premises." TEX. CIV. PRAC. & REM. CODE ANN. § 101.022 (Vernon 1986); *see also Vela v. Cameron County*, 703 S.W.2d 721, 724 (Tex. App.—Corpus Christi 1985, writ ref'd n.r.e.) (swimmer was a licensee rather than a business invitee where he did not pay for use of county beach). In our case, Shannon did not pay for the use of the premises.

A private person owes licensees on private property the duty not to injure them by willful or wanton conduct, or by gross negligence. *State v. Tennison*, 509 S.W.2d 560, 562 (Tex. 1974). As stated earlier, gross negligence was not pleaded or submitted to the jury. However, apart from willful or wanton conduct, or gross negligence, when the licensor has actual knowledge of the dangerous condition and the licensee does not, the licensor has the duty either to warn the licensee or to make the condition reasonably safe. *Lower Neches Valley Auth. v. Murphy*, 536 S.W.2d 561, 562-63 (Tex. 1976). The duty to warn licensees of dangerous conditions arises only in those instances where the licensor knows of the condition likely to cause injury. *Tennison*, 509 S.W.2d at 562. Thus, a jury finding of no actual knowledge of the dangerous condition becomes material when, as here, there is no duty other than to avoid injuring the claimant willfully, wantonly, or through gross negligence.

Having determined that the County's knowledge, or lack of knowledge, of the dangerous condition is a material issue, we next consider whether there is evidence of probative force in the record to support the jury's finding that the County did not have actual knowledge. In making this determination, we consider only the evidence favorable to appellant, and disregard all contrary evidence. *Alm*, 717 S.W.2d at 593. If there is any evidence of probative force to support the jury's answer, then the trial court erred in disregarding the answer, even though the evidence may not have been clear, convincing, and unambiguous. *Mitchell v. Porter*, 349 S.W.2d 785, 786 (Tex. Civ. App.—Houston 1961, writ ref'd n.r.e.).

From our examination of the record, we find, as summarized below, that there is evidence favorable to the jury's answer that appellant did not have actual knowledge of the dangerous condition of the park shelter.

Two County employees testified that when the shelter legs were installed, the legs were placed in holes three to four feet deep, which were then filled with concrete. John Parker, the assistant park superintendent, testified that the legs on this shelter were set in concrete below the ground and were installed properly. He testified that he personally checked all the equipment in the park after Hurricane Alicia, and within two months before Shannon's accident. There was no water standing around the picnic shelters after the hurricane. As far as Parker could tell, the equipment was perfectly safe, and the picnic shelter in question was still in good condition. He knew of no other injuries involving such shelters, and had received no complaints about the condition of the park equipment after Hurricane Alicia.

Parker also testified that the picnic shelter tables had been used many times, that they had been checked along with all the other playground equipment in the time period between Hurricane Alicia and Shannon McFerren's accident, and that he had never seen any holes, gaps, or "wallowed-out places" (such as plaintiffs' witnesses testified about) on the sides of the posts of any of the picnic shelters. After the hurricane, everything in the park was cleaned and inspected; the park was completely clean when it was opened prior to Shannon's accident. As of the day of the occurrence in question, Parker was not aware of anything wrong with the picnic shelters; if there had been a problem, the shelters would have been removed.

Park employee Marshall Ojeda testified that the picnic shelter in question was inspected after Hurricane Alicia, and "everything seemed to be okay." Ojeda checked the shelters before the hurricane, and found them to be sturdy and firm. He further testified that no one had ever complained about the shelters at Sylvan Beach.

Park superintendent Michael Parrott testified that the tables were solid in the ground; that if anyone had reported to him that a shelter had moved or shifted, it would have been replaced or its roof removed; and that the county had neither experienced problems with, nor received complaints about, shelters at any other county park.

We find that this testimony constitutes some evidence of probative force to support the jury's negative answer to Question 2, namely, that the County had no actual knowledge of the picnic shelter's dangerous condition. The trial court therefore erred in disregarding the jury's answer.

* * *

We next consider whether the trial court's error in disregarding the answer was reasonably calculated to cause, and probably did cause, rendition of an improper judgment. TEX. R. APP. P. 81(b)(1). The jury answered that the County failed to make the dangerous condition reasonably safe (Question 7), and that such failure was negligence (Question 8). Based on these answers, the jury found the County 100 percent liable for the damages (Question 12).

As previously stated, liability to a licensee for a premises defect must be predicated on a finding, on the one hand, of willful, wanton, or grossly negligent conduct, or, on the other hand, that the licensor had actual knowledge of the dangerous condition and failed to warn or make the condition reasonably safe. *Lower Neches Valley Auth.*, 536 S.W.2d at 562-63. In light of the jury's finding that there was no actual knowledge of the dangerous condition on the part of the County, we turn to consider whether the alternate basis for recovery exists, that is, whether the County's conduct was willful, wanton, or grossly negligent.

However, the McFerrens did not plead willful, wanton, or grossly negligent conduct, and did not request a question regarding these issues. Ordinary negligence was the only standard submitted for the jury's consideration.

Question 8 asked if the failure to make the condition reasonably safe constituted negligence, not gross negligence. Ordinary negligence was the only standard submitted for the jury's consideration. Accordingly, Question 8 does not inquire about a proper standard of care; neither does it provide a basis of recovery to impose liability upon a licensor for a premises defect. *Tennison*, 509 S.W.2d at 562.

Because the jury did not find that the County had actual knowledge of the picnic shelter's dangerous condition, and was not asked to find gross negligence, no basis exists for the County's liability. The error in disregarding the jury's answer therefore did cause rendition of an improper judgment. TEX. R. APP. P. 81(b)(1).

The County's second point of error is sustained.

* * *

The trial court's judgment is reversed, and judgment is hereby rendered that the McFerrens take nothing.

Note

Procedure in Moving for and Granting Judgment Notwithstanding the Verdict:

a. Timing. The motion for judgment n.o.v. is filed and argued before judgment is rendered, but may be filed and considered after the rendition of judgment, before the court loses plenary power over its judgment.

b. Failure to Move for Instructed Verdict Not Waiver. Unlike federal procedure, Texas does not condition a motion for judgment n.o.v. upon a prior motion for instructed verdict.

c. Filing of Motion for Judgment on the Verdict Can be a Wavier. By moving for judgment on the verdict, a party is considered to have affirmed the verdict and may have waived the right to judgment n.o.v.. It is not a waiver if the motion for judgment is based on grounds unrelated to the m for judgment n.o.v..

d. Motion. The motion for judgment notwithstanding the verdict should be as specific as a motion for directed verdict.

3. *Motion for New Trial*

Read Rules 320 & 324 Texas Rules of Civil Procedure.

a. *Introduction*

CECIL
v.
SMITH
804 S.W.2d 509
(Tex. 1991)

M. Keith Dollahite, Tyler, Michael G. George, Athens, for petitioner.
James A. Attaway, Jr., Quitman, for respondent.

HIGHTOWER, JUSTICE.

The issue before this court is whether a timely filed motion for new trial which is overruled by operation of law preserves appellate complaints of no evidence and factual insufficiency of the evidence to support a jury finding. The trial court, after a jury trial, rendered judgment concerning ownership of a certificate of deposit and the validity and delivery of a deed. Mildred Cecil (Cecil) timely filed a motion for new trial and an amended motion for new trial asserting, among other things, that there was no evidence and factually insufficient evidence to support the jury findings. The amended motion for new trial was overruled by operation of law. The court of appeals affirmed. 790 S.W.2d 709. The court of appeals held that Cecil failed to preserve her points of error because she failed "to call the trial court's attention to her timely filed motion for new trial . . . ." 790 S.W.2d at 716 (emphasis in original). We reverse and remand this cause to the court of appeals.

Martha L. Wisdom (Decedent) died testate in 1985. Her will was admitted to probate and named Charles Madison Smith (Smith) independent executor and left the entire estate to Smith and Cecil. In 1988, Smith filed an application to recover possession of the proceeds of a certificate of deposit allegedly belonging to Decedent's estate. Subsequently, Cecil and others filed suit against Smith seeking to remove him as independent executor and to set aside a deed executed by Decedent in favor of Smith. Both proceedings were transferred to the Henderson County Court At Law.

After a jury trial, judgment was rendered on the jury's verdict in favor of Smith that the deed in question was valid, that Decedent delivered the deed to Smith prior to her death and that Decedent's estate owned the certificate of deposit. Cecil timely filed a motion for new trial. Cecil's motion for new trial asserted, among other things, the following: (1) the evidence was factually insufficient to support each finding; (2) the jury's failure to find that Decedent did not deliver the deed to Smith was contrary to the overwhelming weight and preponderance of the evidence; (3) there was no evidence to support the findings; and (4) the contrary of each finding was established as a matter of law. The trial court did not hear or otherwise consider the amended motion for new trial and the motion was overruled by operation of law. The court of appeals concluded sua sponte that Cecil failed to preserve her points of error asserting that there was no evidence or factually insufficient evidence to support the jury's findings. The court of appeals stated: "Our legal conclusion that Cecil's points of error . . . were not preserved for review rests upon Cecil's failure to call the trial court's attention to her timely filed motion for new trial that alleges those claimed errors." 790 S.W.2d at 716 (emphasis in original).

Cecil argues that her motion for new trial which was overruled by operation of law preserves appellate complaints of no evidence and factual insufficiency of the evidence to support the jury's findings. We agree.

A point in a motion for new trial is a prerequisite to complain on appeal that the evidence is factually insufficient to support a jury finding and that a jury finding is against the overwhelming weight of the evidence. TEX. R. CIV. P. 324(b)(2) and (3). *See* TEX. R. APP. P. 52(d). "No evidence"[1] points may be raised by either (1) a motion for instructed verdict, (2) a motion for judgment notwithstanding the verdict, (3) an objection to the submission of the issue to the jury, (4) a motion to disregard the jury's answer to a vital fact issue or (5) a motion for new trial. *Aero Energy, Inc. v. Circle C Drilling Co.*, 699 S.W.2d 821, 822 (Tex. 1985). Cecil's no evidence points of error were raised only in her motion for new trial.

A motion for new trial must be filed prior to or within thirty days after the judgment is signed. TEX. R. CIV. P 329b(a). One or more amended motions for new trial may be filed without leave of court before any preceding motion for new trial filed by the movant is overruled and within thirty days after the judgment is signed. TEX. R. CIV. P 329b(b). If an original or amended motion for new trial is not determined by written order signed within seventy-five days after the judgment was signed, it is overruled by operation of law. TEX. R. CIV. P. 329b(c).

In requiring Cecil to call the trial court's attention to her motion for new trial, the court of appeals relied upon the "presentment requirement" in Rule 52(a) of the Texas Rules of Appellate Procedure and *Moore v. Mauldin*, 428 S.W.2d 808 (Tex. 1968). Rule 52(a) states the general rule for preserving appellate complaints and provides in relevant part:

> In order to preserve a complaint for appellate review, a party must have presented to the trial court a timely request, objection or motion, stating the specific grounds for the ruling he desired the court to make if the specific grounds were not apparent from the context. It is also necessary for the complaining party to obtain a ruling upon the party's request, objection or motion. TEX. R. APP. P. 52(a)

While Rule 52(a) provides the general rule for preserving appellate complaints, Rule 52(d) specifically applies to preserving complaints in motions for new trial. Rule 52(d) provides that "[a] point in a motion for new trial is a prerequisite to appellate complaint in those instances provided in paragraph (b) of Rule 324 of the Texas Rules of Civil Procedure." Rule 52(d) expressly applies when Rule 324(b) requires error to be preserved in a motion for new trial. When Rule 324(b) requires a motion for new trial to preserve error, the complaining party is required only to comply with the filing requirements in Rule 329b to preserve the points of error. *See general-*

[1] No evidence points of error may only be sustained when the record discloses (1) a complete absence of evidence of a vital fact, (2) the court is barred by rules of law or of evidence from giving weight to the only evidence offered to prove a vital fact, (3) the evidence offered to prove a vital fact is no more than a mere scintilla, and (4) the evidence established conclusively the opposite of the vital fact. *See* Calvert, *"No Evidence" and "Insufficient Evidence" Points of Error*, 38 TEX. L. REV. 361, 362-63 (1960). Cecil's points that (1) there was no evidence to support the findings and (2) the contrary of each finding was established as a matter of law will hereinafter collectively be referred to as her "no evidence" points.

ly Riley v. Meriwether, 780 S.W.2d 919, 922 (Tex. App.—El Paso 1989, no writ); *Metot v. Danielson*, 780 S.W.2d 283, 286 (Tex. App.—Tyler 1989, writ denied); *Texaco, Inc. v. Pennzoil, Co.*, 729 S.W.2d 768, 852 (Tex. App.—Houston [1st Dist] 1987, writ ref'd n.r.e.), *cert dismissed*, 485 U.S. 994, 108 S.Ct. 1305, 99 L.Ed.2d 686 (1988).

Factual insufficiency points of error are expressly required by Rule 324(b) to be raised in a motion for new trial. Therefore, we hold that Cecil's motion for new trial points complaining that the evidence was factually insufficient are preserved for appellate review by her compliance with the filing requirements of Rule 329b and the subsequent overruling of the motion for new trial by operation of law. *See Riley v. Meriwether*, 780 S.W.2d at 922; *Metot v. Danielson*, 780 S.W.2d at 286.

Concerning Cecil's no evidence points of error, Rule 324 does not require no evidence points of error to be raised in a motion for new trial to preserve the complaint for appeal. However, no evidence complaints may be raised in a motion for new trial. *Aero Energy, Inc. v. Circle C Drilling Co.*, 699 S.W.2d at 822. In this case, Cecil's no evidence points of error were raised only in her motion for new trial. Although Rule 52(d) only specifically refers to Rule 324(b) error preservable by motion for new trial, we see no reason to distinguish between error specifically preservable by motion for new trial in Rule 324(b) and other error preservable by motion for new trial. Requiring compliance with Rule 52(a) in addition to Rule 329b's filing requirement would unnecessarily resurrect the "presentment" requirement which this court eliminated in 1981 to motions for new trial. TEX. R. CIV. P 329b comment (Vernon Supp. 1990). Furthermore, requiring the additional compliance with Rule 52(a) would undermine our goal of judicial economy by creating needless expense and delay. *See Cherne Industries, Inc. v. Magallanes*, 763 S.W.2d 768, 772 (Tex. 1989). Consequently, we hold that no evidence complaints are preserved for appellate review if Rule 329b's filing requirements for motions for new trial are met. *See Riley v. Meriwether*, 780 S.W.2d at 922; *Metot v. Danielson*, 780 S.W.2d at 286.

The court of appeals did not consider Cecil's points of error asserting that the evidence was legally and factually insufficient to support the jury findings. Because the unaddressed points of error include attacks on the sufficiency of the evidence, we remand the cause to the court of appeals for consideration of the previously unaddressed points. *See Coulson & CAE, Inc. v. Lake LBJ Municipal Utility District*, 734 S.W.2d 649, 652 (Tex. 1987).

Accordingly, we reverse and remand the cause to the court of appeals.

CORNYN, J., dissenting [opinion omitted].

Note

Rule 33 of the new Rules of Appellate Procedure incorporates the essence of former Rule 52(a) of the Texas Rules of Appellate Procedure, but omits former rule 52(d) as unnecessary given Rules 324(a) and (b) of the Texas Rules of Civil Procedure. Thus, *Cecil v. Smith* is still a valid legal precedent.

In re BENT
487 S.W.3d 170
(2016)

Ana Ene, Richard D. Daly, Daly & Black, P.C., Eric Michael Adams, Mehaffy & Weber PC, Ernest W. Boyd, Butch Boyd Law Firm, Jonathan Daniel Simon, Simon Law Firm, Marilyn Vilandos, The Vilandos Firm, P.C., Houston, Melissa Waden Wray, Daly & Black, P.C., Waco, for Relators.

Russell S. Post, Beck Redden LLP, Houston, for Amicus Curiae.

Christopher Avery, Thompson, Coe, Cousins & Irons, LLP, Christopher W. Martin, Levon G. Hovnatanian, Robert T. Owen, Martin Disiere Jefferson & Wisdom, L.L.P., Tanya Dugas, Raley & Bowick, LLP, Houston, for Real Party in Interest.

JUSTICE BROWN delivered the opinion of the Court.

In recent years this Court has sought to protect the constitutional right to a trial by jury by requiring trial courts to provide litigants with "an understandable, reasonably specific explanation" for setting aside a jury verdict and ordering a new trial. *In re Columbia Med. Ctr. of Las Colinas, Subsidiary, L.P.*, 290 S.W.3d 204, 213 (Tex. 2009). Generally, this requirement is satisfied when a trial court's stated reason is "a reason for which a new trial is legally appropriate" and "is specific enough to indicate that the trial court did not simply parrot a pro forma template, but rather derived the articulated reasons from the particular facts and circumstances of the case at hand." *In re United Scaffolding, Inc.*, 377 S.W.3d 685, 688-89 (Tex. 2012). When a new-trial order satisfies these facial requirements, we have further empowered appellate courts to "conduct a merits review of the bases for a new trial order" and grant mandamus relief "[i]f the record does not support the trial court's rationale for ordering a new trial." *In re Toyota Motor Sales, U.S.A., Inc.*, 407 S.W.3d 746, 749 (Tex. 2013).

In this case, the court of appeals concluded the trial court abused its discretion in ordering a new trial because each basis for doing so was either facially insufficient or could not withstand a *Toyota* merits review. Relators Stacey and Mark Bent now ask us to uphold the trial court's new-trial order and both parties seek this Court's guidance on the scope of the merits review we established in *Toyota*. Specifically, the parties have inquired as to the court of appeals' authority, within the context of an abuse-of-discretion standard of review, to re-weigh evidence considered by the trial court in determining whether there is insufficient evidence to support a jury's finding or that a finding is against the great weight and preponderance of the evidence. We ultimately do not reach that issue because we conclude the bases for the trial court's order implicating factual-sufficiency analysis did not comply with the facial requirements we established in *Columbia* and *United Scaffolding*. Therefore, we need not determine whether the court of appeals properly conducted its merits review of those bases. Though we would not have been as generous in applying our facial-requirements precedents, we nonetheless agree with the court of appeals' ultimate disposition of the trial court's bases for a new trial. Accordingly, we deny the Bents' mandamus petition.

I.

Stacey and Mark Bent owned a home in Piney Point Village, a small municipality surrounded by Houston's sprawling city limits. The Bents' home, purchased in 2005 and insured by USAA, suffered a hurricane, a flood, and eventually foreclosure. Their dispute with USAA spans each of these unfortunate events.

This case began as a routine claim on a homeowner's policy for damage sustained in September 2008 from Hurricane Ike. A USAA adjuster inspected the Bents' home and assessed damages at $14,302.33. Not included in this amount was the cost of removing fallen trees on the Bents' lot, which the adjuster told the Bents their policy did not cover. USAA sent the Bents two letters on October 23, 2008: one informing them that USAA had approved their claim, and another including a $1,162.33 check to cover the Bents' claim minus their one-percent deductible.

The Bents' home later sustained flood damage in April 2009. The homeowner's policy at issue in this case did not cover flood damage; however, the Bents held a separate flood-insurance policy with an affiliated carrier. While repairing the flood damage, workers discovered mold within the walls of the Bents' home. At trial, the Bents argued that Ike-related roof damage, undiscovered by USAA, caused water to leak into the home, which eventually developed into mold.

USAA re-inspected the house in May 2009. Based on that inspection, USAA approved an additional payment. Furthermore, and contrary to the previous adjuster's representation, the adjuster told the Bents their homeowner's policy did in fact cover at least some of the tree-removal costs. Once again, USAA issued two letters—one notifying the Bents of claim approval and another with a $49,471.67 check—on June 6, 2009.

The following month USAA received notice from Stacey claiming additional Ike-related damage had been discovered. USAA performed a third inspection of the house on July 21, 2009. And as before, USAA revised its estimate and again separately issued, on July 25, 2009, a claim-approval letter and apparently issued a $11,072.78 check the day before.

On October 1, 2009, the Bents again contacted USAA regarding additional and previously unclaimed Ike-related damage. This time, however, USAA took the position that it could not consider the new claim without more specific itemization of the alleged damage. After a series of letters and phone calls, the Bents requested yet another inspection, and USAA obliged. At this November 11, 2009 re-inspection, the adjuster explained what additional information was needed for USAA to consider the Bents' claim. After receiving nothing further from the Bents, USAA invoked the policy's appraisal provision. USAA finally heard from the Bents in December 2009 when their attorney sent a letter contesting USAA's right to an appraisal.

Negotiations wore on between USAA and the Bents' first attorney, and then with the Bents themselves, and then with a second attorney retained in July 2010. Following yet another re-inspection, USAA sent a letter to the Bents' counsel in August 2010 presenting a "revised dwelling estimate," detailing $136,539.41 in damages attributable to Hurricane Ike, which USAA asked counsel to "review . . . with Mr. and Mrs. Bent." After accounting for depreciation and the Bents' deductible, USAA stated it was "prepared to send an additional actual cash value payment" of $27,416.86, an amount that would bring total payments made by USAA to $89,123.64. In the letter, USAA described that amount as an "actual cash value settlement" and stated: "The Loss Settlement Provision stipulates that the loss to your covered property be settled at actual cash value." Unlike with USAA's previous letters, no concurrent payment accompanied this one. USAA argued at trial that the August 2010 letter was a settlement offer not payable without the Bents' acceptance. But the Bents did not accept the offer and instead sued USAA for breach of their homeowner's policy and various violations of the Texas Insurance Code. In March 2012, with litigation ongoing, USAA nonetheless mailed the Bents a check for $27,416.86 plus interest. USAA characterizes this payment as "an unsuccessful attempt to resolve the claim . . . even though the Bents never indicated any agreement with USAA's proposed compromise."

As this saga between the Bents and USAA unfolded, the Bents were also dealing with the City of Piney Point Village's restrictions on their efforts to repair their home. After Ike, Stacey met several times with Annette Arriaga, Piney Point Village's director of planning, development, and permits and secretary of both the city's Planning and Zoning Commission and Board of Adjustments. These meetings culminated in a June 2010 letter from Arriaga to the Bents informing them that the city estimated the extent of the damage triggered an ordinance requiring the home to be rebuilt one foot above the floodplain in which it sat. Arriaga further wrote that she was "apprehensive about the [overall] health and welfare of the structure" and recommended the home be "replaced" or "re-built." The Bents therefore argued their home was, in effect, a total loss.

In late 2010 the Bents stopped making mortgage payments and their lender foreclosed on their home. The Bents' case against USAA, however, proceeded to trial. At its conclusion, the jury found that USAA had not breached the homeowner's policy but that it did make a "statement in such a manner as to mislead a reasonably prudent person to a false conclusion of a material fact" in violation of chapter 541 of the Insurance Code. This finding was apparently based on the initial adjuster's misrepresentation that the Bents' policy did not cover tree removal. Based on this finding, the jury awarded damages of $150,000 for the diminished value of the home and $250,000 for mental anguish. The jury further awarded the Bents $185,000 in attorney's fees through trial but awarded no appellate attorney's fees.

The trial court initially entered judgment on the jury's verdict but later granted the Bents' motion for new trial. The trial court gave five bases in its order: (1) the jury's finding that USAA did not breach the homeowner's policy was contrary to the great weight and preponderance of the evidence; (2) USAA violated the trial court's order in limine regarding the Bents' failure to seek a variance from the relevant Piney Point Village city ordinance; (3) the evidence did not support the jury's award for the diminished value of the Bents' home; * * *.

USAA sought relief from the court of appeals. Concluding the trial court abused its discretion on each of its bases for ordering a new trial, the court of appeals conditionally granted a writ of mandamus directing the trial court to vacate its order and render judgment on the jury's verdict. The Bents then sought relief from this Court, arguing that the trial court acted within its discretion on every basis except for the mental-anguish-damages predicate, which the Bents do not present for our review.

II.

Trial courts have traditionally been afforded broad discretion in granting new trials. *See Columbia,* 290 S.W.3d at 210 (citing *Johnson v. Fourth Court of Appeals,* 700 S.W.2d 916, 917 (Tex.1985)). Our rules of civil procedure vest trial courts with broad authority to order new trials "for good cause" and "when the damages are manifestly too small or too large." TEX. R. CIV. P. 320. Historically, trial courts sometimes granted new trials with little or no explanation, and "[o]ur decisions approved the practice of trial courts failing to specify reasons for setting aside jury verdicts." *Columbia,* 290 S.W.3d at 208.

The Texas Constitution, however, guarantees that the right to trial by jury "shall remain inviolate." TEX. CONST. art. I, § 15. It follows that trial judges cannot enjoy unfettered authority to order new trials. Within the past decade, this Court's jurisprudence has evolved to more firmly secure Texans' constitutional right to a jury trial in the new-trial context. In *Columbia,* we acknowledged trial judges' authority to order new trials is "not limitless." 290 S.W.3d at 210. We also held that, at the very least, parties to a jury trial "are entitled to an understandable, reasonably specific explanation why their expectations are frustrated by a jury verdict being disregarded or set aside, the trial process being nullified, and the case having to be retried." *Id.* at 213.

Our holding in *Columbia* arose from an order premised on the bare assertion that a new trial was "in the interests of justice and fairness." *Id.* at 206. We concluded that "such a vague explanation in setting aside a jury verdict does not enhance respect for the judiciary or the rule of law, detracts from transparency we strive to achieve in our legal system, and does not sufficiently respect the reasonable expectations of parties and the public when a lawsuit is tried to a jury." *Id.* at 213. We further held that "the significance of the issue—protection of the right to jury trial"—justified mandamus review under the circumstances. *Id.* at 209.

We expanded on the trial court's obligation in *In re United Scaffolding.* In that case we held a trial court does not abuse its discretion in ordering a new trial "so long as its stated reason for granting a new trial (1) is a reason for which a new trial is legally appropriate (such as a well-defined legal standard or a defect that probably resulted in an improper verdict); and (2) is specific enough to indicate that the trial court did not simply parrot a pro forma template, but rather derived the articulated reasons from the particular facts and circumstances of the case at hand." 377 S.W.3d at 688-89.

We went on in *United Scaffolding* to identify examples in which a new-trial order would amount to an abuse of discretion, such as when: (1) "the given reason, specific or not, is not one for which a new trial is legally valid"; (2) "the articulated reasons plainly state that the trial court merely substituted its own judgment for the jury's"; or (3) "the order, though rubber-stamped with a valid new-trial rationale, provides little or no insight into the judge's reasoning." *Id.* at 689. We also made several observations about what a facially valid new-trial order looks like. We rejected a *Pool*-like standard of review, which would require trial courts to " 'detail the evidence relevant to the issue in consideration.' " *Id.* at 687 (quoting *Pool v. Ford Motor Co.,* 715 S.W.2d 629, 635 (Tex. 1986)). Rather, we took the view that a trial court "need not provide a detailed catalog of the evidence" as long as it provides a "cogent and reasonably specific explanation" of its reasoning. *Id.* at 688. Accordingly, we counseled reviewing courts to focus "not on the length or detail of the reasons a trial court gives, but on how well those reasons serve the general purpose of assuring the parties that the jury's decision was set aside only after careful thought and for valid reasons." *Id.* (citing *Columbia,* 290 S.W.3d at 213).

In urging quality over quantity, however, we did not relieve any trial court of its responsibility to point to evidence that played a pivotal role in its decision. We noted that "mere recitation of a legal standard, such as a statement that a finding is against the great weight and preponderance of the evidence, will not suffice." *Id.* at 689. To be facially valid, a new-trial order based on a factual-sufficiency review "must indicate that the trial judge considered the specific facts and circumstances of the case at hand and explain how the evidence (or lack of evidence) undermines the jury's findings." *Id.*

In *In re Toyota* we took the next logical step: deciding "whether, on mandamus review, an appellate court may evaluate the merits of a new[-]trial order that states a clear, legally appropriate, and reasonably specific reason for granting a new trial." 407 S.W.3d at 757. In other words, "if a trial court's order facially comports with *Columbia* and *United Scaffolding,* may an appellate court review the correctness of the stated reasons for granting a new trial?" *Id.* We concluded that "[h]aving already decided that new[-]trial orders must meet these requirements and that noncompliant orders will be subject to mandamus review, it would make little sense to conclude now that the correctness or validity of the orders' articulated reasons cannot also be evaluated." *Id.* at 758. To do otherwise "would mean that a trial court could set aside a verdict for reasons that are unsupported by the law or the evidence, as long as those reasons are facially valid." *Id.* Accordingly, we held "[a]ppellate courts must be able to conduct merits-based review of new[-]trial orders" and if "a trial court's articulated reasons are not supported by the underlying record, the new[-]trial order cannot stand." *Id.*

We acknowledged that while the new-trial order in *Toyota* satisfied the facial requirements elucidated by *Columbia* and *United Scaffolding,* "the record squarely conflict[ed] with the trial judge's expressed reasons for granting [a] new trial." *Id.* at 759. That expressed reason was that Toyota's counsel "willfully disregarded" and "brazenly and intentionally violated" a limine order that precluded introduction of a police officer's deposition testimony regarding the plaintiff's seat-belt usage. *Id.* at 761. However, the record revealed it was the plaintiff's attorney—not Toyota's—who introduced the deposition testimony by reading it into the record when making an offer of proof under the rule of optional completeness, and afterward failed to object or ask for a curative or limiting instruction. *Id.* at 760-61. Toyota's counsel then referred to the deposition testimony in subsequent witness examinations and closing arguments. When plaintiff's counsel protested, the trial court ruled the evidence was part of the record and Toyota was no longer prohibited from referencing it. *Id.* We agreed with Toyota that the record clearly established Toyota never violated the trial court's limine order. Accordingly, the expressed basis for the new-trial order was unsupported and thus the order itself was invalid. *Id.*

The Bents correctly point out a distinction between *Toyota* and this case. In *Toyota,* the record "directly contravene[d]" the basis for the new-trial order. *See id.* at 761. But here, several of the trial court's rulings are based on a conclusion that the jury's findings were against the great weight and preponderance of the evidence—a conclusion implicating the shades of gray inherent in weighing evidence and the appropriate level of deference afforded a trial court's estimation of that evidence. Accordingly, the Bents ask "[h]ow exacting can or should an appellate court's review be when there is no direct conflict" between the record and the stated bases for a new trial. We do not directly engage that question because in this case we do not proceed beyond holding that the trial court's order was facially insufficient. However, we observe that merits review is not uncharted territory; on the contrary, we recognized in *Toyota* that "it is old hat to our colleagues on the federal bench." *Id.* at 758. And those courts do not hesitate to review new-trial orders based on factual-sufficiency analyses. *See id.* at 759 (discussing *Cruthirds v. RCI, Inc.,* 624 F.2d 632, 635, 636 (5th Cir.1980)). We have not adopted the Fifth Circuit's approach to merits review and do not suggest that more cannot be said on the subject, but appellate courts are hardly without precedent to guide them.

Importantly, this Court has never suggested merits review of new-trial orders should be conducted under anything other than the abuse-of-discretion standard that is familiar and inherent to mandamus proceedings. *See Walker v. Packer,* 827 S.W.2d 833, 839-42 (Tex. 1992). *Columbia, United Scaffolding,* and *Toyota* all broke new ground, but they did so within an abuse-of-discretion framework. In *Toyota* we opened the gates to reviewing the merits of a new-trial order, but we did not create a new standard of review. Indeed, we concluded in *Toyota* that the trial court "abused its discretion" because its "stated reasons, though complying in form with the requirements of *Columbia* and *United Scaffolding,* lacked substantive merit." *Toyota,* 407 S.W.3d at 762. Accordingly, it is inaccurate to say, as one court of appeals has suggested, that we have "enunciated a new standard of review for intermediate appellate courts to use in implementing [our] directive: the 'merits-based review.' " *In re Wyatt Field Serv. Co.,* 454 S.W.3d 145, 150 (Tex. App.—Houston [14th Dist.] 2014, mand. filed) (orig. proceeding). "Merits review" was simply a reference to the new authority granted to courts of appeals to consider, in mandamus proceedings, whether the record supports the trial court's rationale for ordering a new trial. *See Toyota,* 407 S.W.3d at 749. It is not a new standard of review; the abuse-of-discretion standard applies to merits review just as it does in all mandamus proceedings.

III

A

We now turn to the trial court's bases for granting a new trial. The first was the jury's finding that USAA did not breach the Bents' homeowner's policy—a conclusion the trial court deemed "so contrary to the great weight and preponderance of the evidence in this case as to be clearly wrong and manifestly unjust." The trial court's determination on this point apparently turned on its reading of the policy's prompt-payment provision, which the trial court quoted as follows:

> If we notify you that we will pay your claim, or part of your claim, we must pay within business days after we notify you. If payment of your claim or part of your claim requires the performance of an act by you, we must pay within 5 business days after the date you perform the act.

From that provision and the evidence presented at trial, the trial court drew the following conclusions concerning the jury's finding that USAA did not breach the policy:

> Hurricane Ike hit the Texas coast on September 13, 2008. The testimony of Stacey Bent established that Plaintiffs made an insurance claim within days of that event and that Defendant notified Plaintiffs it would pay Plaintiffs' claim. Further, the testimony of Stacey Bent and the individual adjusters on the claim established that six different, and increasing, estimates were made by Defendant between the initial estimate on October 6, 2008, and the final estimate on August 28, 2010, and none of Defendant's payments to Plaintiffs were made within the required 5 business days.

Defendant did not offer any testimony to controvert Plaintiffs' evidence that Defendant failed to make the required payment within 5 business days.

The court of appeals decided this explanation satisfied *Columbia* and *United Scaffolding*'s facial requirements but, after conducting a merits review, ultimately determined the trial court's rationale was unsupported by the record. *In re United Servs. Auto Ass'n,* 446 S.W.3d 162, 171-72 (Tex. App.—Houston [1st Dist.] 2014). We think the court of appeals was too generous—the trial court's explanation is insufficient on its face.

First, the trial court's explanation suggests a muddled legal- and factual-sufficiency evaluation of the evidence. A reference to the "great weight and preponderance of the evidence" signals a factual-sufficiency analysis, but the remainder of the explanation gives the impression USAA breached the policy as a matter of law. The trial court concluded Stacey's testimony "established" the Bents made a claim and USAA notified them it would pay, but that "none of Defendant's payments to Plaintiffs were made within the required 5 business days." The trial court further asserted that USAA "did not offer any testimony to controvert Plaintiffs' evidence that Defendant failed to make the required payments within 5 business days." If true, it appears judgment notwithstanding the verdict, not a new trial, was appropriate. If the Bents conclusively established their claim, and USAA presented no contrary evidence, the trial court has not articulated "a reason for which a new trial is legally appropriate." *See United Scaffolding,* 377 S.W.3d at 688-89.

Furthermore, if the trial court believed, as it obviously did, that no payment was made within five days after USAA notified the Bents a payment was forthcoming, its duty was to "explain how the evidence (or lack of evidence) undermines the jury's findings." *See id.* at 689. The trial court failed to do so. It noted the Bents made a claim "within days" after Hurricane Ike and that USAA "notified Plaintiffs it would pay Plaintiffs' claim." But this muddy reference to USAA's notification "provides little or no insight into the judge's reasoning." *See id.* With no mention of when the notification occurred or in what capacity it was made, the parties must speculate as to which of the many contacts between USAA and the Bents triggered the five-day prompt-payment provision. We reiterate that the trial court is not obligated to provide a "detailed catalog of the evidence." *Id.* at 688. However, in a case where liability turns on a specific event occurring on a specific date and the passage of a fixed amount of time after that event, something more than simply stating that USAA "notified Plaintiffs it would pay Plaintiffs' claim" is required. As it is, the trial court's explanation does little to "assur[e] the parties that the jury's decision was set aside only after careful thought and for valid reasons." *See id.*

The trial court ostensibly provides more explanation, but only through a vague reference to "six different, and increasing, estimates . . . between the initial estimate on October 6, 2008, and the final estimate on August 28, 2010." From this, the trial court proclaims that "none of [USAA's] payments to Plaintiffs were made within the required 5 business days." Yet there is no indication that "estimates" have any bearing on *notification* under the prompt-payment provision, which turns not on an estimate but when a policyholder is actually notified that their claim was approved. At worst, the trial court's explanation is based on a misreading of the policy that results in a legally improper basis for ordering a new trial. At best, it never rises to a "cogent and reasonably specific explanation" of the trial court's reasoning and inspires no confidence that the trial court "derived the articulated reasons from the particular facts and circumstances of the case at hand." *See id.* at 688-89. Simply put, the trial court never pinpoints the events or dates it believed triggered USAA's prompt-payment obligation. On the contrary, its explanation serves only to suggest the trial court failed to properly ascertain the nature of that provision.

Because we conclude the trial court's explanation did not meet *Columbia* and *United Scaffolding*'s facial requirements, we need not determine if the trial court's rationale is supported by the record. The court of appeals, however, undertook that review and concluded that the record did not support the trial court's rationale. Specifically, the court of appeals concluded the record directly contravened the trial court's assertion that USAA "did not offer any testimony to controvert Plaintiffs' evidence that [USAA] failed to make the required payments within 5 business days." In actuality, USAA's claim records were admitted into evidence and showed USAA simultaneously issued checks on the Bents' claims each time USAA approved payments in October 2008 and June 2009, and issued a July 2009 payment the day before the Bents were notified USAA would make a payment. The court of appeals concluded "the record contains no evidence that USAA ever notified the Bents that it would pay a claimed amount and then failed to make a timely payment in that amount." *United Servs. Auto Ass'n,* 446 S.W.3d at 172. The court of appeals deemed the evidence "inconclusive" as to whether the Bents were required to take additional action before USAA was obligated to pay the amount approved in its August 2010 letter, noting testimony from USAA's corporate representative that the letter constituted a settlement attempt, not an unconditional agreement to pay the approved amount. Based on its review of the evidence, the court of appeals concluded the trial court "[did] not actually identify any evidence tending to show that USAA did not comply with the loss payment provision of the policy." *Id.* at 173. The court of appeals also held that the trial court's statement that USAA did not offer any evidence to the contrary was incorrect, as USAA "offered such evidence in the form of the claims log and [the corporate representative's] testimony regarding the log, the timing of payments, and the August 2010 letter." *Id.*

We do not pass judgment on the court of appeals' review of the record; we need not consider it to conclude that the trial court's order was facially insufficient. We acknowledge, however, the Bents' argument that trial courts should be granted deference in concluding a jury finding was against the great weight and preponderance of the evidence or insufficiently supported by the evidence. We can hardly disagree with that general proposition, but an appellate court does not necessarily re-weigh the evidence presented at trial simply by conducting a merits review of a factual-sufficiency-based new-trial order. Here, the trial court claimed USAA offered *no* evidence contradicting the Bents' evidence that USAA failed to comply with the prompt-payment provision. The court of appeals concluded this was demonstrably untrue and identified contradictory evidence in the record. It was not necessary to re-weigh the evidence concerning USAA's payments to conclude the trial court's claim is unsupported by the record. *See Toyota,* 407 S.W.3d at 749 ("If the record does not support the trial court's rationale for ordering a new trial, the appellate court may grant mandamus relief."). The amount of deference given to a trial court's evaluation of the evidence will likely be a point of contention in review of some new-trial orders, but it is not implicated in *every* review of an order ostensibly based on a factual-sufficiency analysis.

B

The second basis for a new trial given by the trial court was that USAA violated the court's limine order when it discussed a potential variance to Piney Point Village's city ordinance that effectively required the Bents' home to be rebuilt in light of the damage it sustained. The trial court's order noted that the Bents filed a motion in limine seeking to prevent USAA from making "[a]ny reference to, or insinuation regarding, [the Bents] not attempting to get a variance from the Piney Point ordinance requiring the house be brought up to code, or argument or insinuation that they could have, or should have, attempted to get one, or would have received one if they had tried." The trial court stated it granted the motion in part, "specifically requiring USAA to approach the bench before raising such issues." Nevertheless, the trial court stated that "counsel raised the variance subject with [Arriaga] in an attempt to suggest [the Bents] could have, or would have, gotten a variance if they had applied for one," and "spent a considerable amount of time discussing the variance issue in closing." The trial court further provided examples by way of quoting USAA's counsel's argument from the record, including statements such as:

- "It's interesting that they want consequential damages when they never gave us these documents, when they never sought a variance, when [Arriaga] tells us the City of Piney Point gives variances for flood damage and other natural disasters."
- "[T]he last question asked of Ms. Arriaga was, 'Does the City of Piney Point ever grant a variance?' And she said—remember?—'Oh, yes, for natural disasters, like floods.' They give them a variance. That means they don't have to demolish the house just because it's one foot below the level."
- "[W]e asked [Arriaga] on cross-examination, 'Isn't it true that not a single contractor has come into Piney Point and asked you to pull a permit on this house, asked to do any work on this house or asked you for a variance of this house?' And Ms. [Arriaga] said, 'No. No. No.' "

The trial court declared USAA's questioning of Arriaga invited "pure speculation" and that there is no evidence in the record to support counsel's closing argument. Accordingly, the trial court concluded that "USAA's jury argument on the issue of variance was improper" and "materially prejudiced Plaintiffs."

Because the trial court's order was "specific" and a "violation of an order in limine can serve as the basis of a new[-]trial order," the court of appeals concluded *Columbia* and *United Scaffolding* were satisfied. *United Servs. Auto Ass'n,* 446 S.W.3d at 174-75. In this instance we agree. Unlike the prompt-payment provision, we can ascertain both an appropriate legal basis for the trial court's ruling and understand why the trial court made it. Like the court of appeals, we must next turn to the record and determine if it supports the trial court's explanation.

After an examination of the record, the court of appeals determined the trial court indeed granted the Bents' motion in limine in part. But contrary to the trial court's statement that the limine order "specifically requir[ed] USAA to approach the bench before raising such issues," the trial court actually allowed USAA more latitude. The following exchange regarding the Bents' motion in limine took place at a pre-trial conference:

> USAA'S COUNSEL: I mean, I think it's absolutely relevant to ask whether or not they got a variance or requested a variance. I think that is absolutely within—
>
> THE COURT: I don't have a problem with that. I think—
>
> USAA'S COUNSEL: As far as the routine activities of the board—I think that's something that we could approach the bench with at the time, and if Ms. Arriaga is prepared or qualified to answer that, then we can proceed in that regard.
>
> THE COURT: Yeah. I'm not going to limine out the entire issue of a variance, but whether or not they would've, all that—those kind of questions, you're going to have to talk with me about—
>
> USAA'S COUNSEL: Absolutely.
>
> THE COURT: —before you come up. So sort of granted in part and denied in part.

The trial court suggests USAA first violated its limine order by raising the variance issue while questioning Arriaga "in an attempt to suggest [the Bents] could have, or would have, gotten a variance if they had applied for one." The trial court further stated it sustained the Bents' objection when USAA questioned Arriaga regarding a variance. But the court of appeals' review of the record revealed the Bents did not actually object to any part of USAA's questioning of Arriaga concerning variances, nor did they object to USAA's closing argument. Our review of the record confirms that conclusion. Furthermore, USAA asked only "whether residents of Piney Point can request variances, whether Arriaga educated the Bents regarding this fact, whether Stacey ever requested a variance, and what factors the Board of Adjustments considers when deciding whether to approve a variance." *Id.* at 175. Because the trial court's order only limited questions as to whether the Bents would have received a variance if they applied for one, we agree with the court of appeals that USAA did not violate the order by asking whether the Bents *could have* requested one.

We further agree with the court of appeals that USAA's closing argument did not violate the limine order. USAA's counsel reminded the jury that the Bents never applied for a variance, even though Arriaga testified variances are sometimes granted after natural disasters. Importantly, USAA's counsel never said the Bents would have been granted a variance had they applied for one. Moreover, once Arriaga's testimony was admitted "without objection or a request that it be stricken or that the jury be instructed to disregard—it was in [the record] for all purposes and a proper subject of closing argument." *See Toyota,* 407 S.W.3d at 760.

We agree with the court of appeals that the record clearly establishes USAA did not violate the limine order, and in fact directly controverts the trial court's stated rationale for ordering a new trial.

C

The trial court's third basis for ordering a new trial is that the evidence does not support the jury's $150,000 award to the Bents for their home's diminished value. On this the parties agreed, and the trial court acknowledged USAA argued the jury should have awarded no damages while the Bents argued the only evidence placed the diminished value in excess of $900,000. The trial court explained its ruling as follows:

> The Court agrees that the $150,000.00 damage award seems arbitrary, given the evidence that was presented. But the Court is not inclined to substitute its opinion for that of the jury. Texas Rule of Civil Procedure 320 specifically provides that "new trials may be granted when the damages are manifestly too small or too large." The Court believes that the damages awarded by the jury for diminished value of [the Bents'] home was not supported by the evidence at trial.

The court of appeals concluded this explanation passes muster under *Columbia* because it is "specific enough both to permit USAA to attack it and to enable our review of it" but fails under *United Scaffolding* because it does not " 'elaborate, with reference to the evidence adduced at trial, how the jury's answers are contrary to the great weight and preponderance of the evidence.' " *United Servs. Auto Ass'n,* 446 S.W.3d at 176 (quoting *United Scaffolding,* 377 S.W.3d at 690). That is, the court of appeals concluded that while the order "discusses the parties' arguments as to what the evidence showed," it "does not actually discuss the evidence itself." *Id.*

We agree. The trial court's explanation makes no reference to the evidence at all. It offers only the conclusory comment that the jury's award "seems arbitrary." Rule 320 does permit a trial court to grant a new trial when "damages are manifestly too small or too large," but the trial court does not specify which scenario applies here and makes no effort to point to any evidence supporting its rationale. The trial court's opinion that the jury's award "seems arbitrary" does not amount to a "cogent and reasonably specific explanation of the reasoning that led the court to conclude that a new trial was warranted." *See United Scaffolding,* 377 S.W.3d at 688. Nor does it provide the parties any assurance "that the jury's decision was set aside only after careful thought and for valid reasons." *See id.* Again, we reiterate that the trial court need not "provide a detailed catalog of evidence" to support its reasoning. *See id.* But here the court offered *none*. Accordingly, we agree with the court of appeals that the trial court abused its discretion by ordering a new trial based on the jury's diminished-value award.

D

The trial court's final basis for a new trial was the jury's failure to award the Bents appellate attorney's fees. The trial court found this oversight "erroneous and against the overwhelming weight of the evidence." It explained:

> Texas Civil Practice and Remedies Code Sections 38.001–38.003 mandates an award of attorney's fees when a Plaintiff prevails on a breach of contract claim. Sections 541 and 542 of the Texas Insurance Code have similar provisions. When a statute mandates an award of trial attorney's fees, an award of appellate attorney's fees is likewise mandatory. (citations omitted).
>
> Since [the Bents] prevailed on their Section 541 claims, they were entitled to an award of attorney's fees for trial and through appeal. Moreover, as was mentioned above, the Court finds that USAA breached the insurance agreement as a matter of law. The jury answered "no" to the breach of contract question. Thus, it is unclear how that answer affected the total attorney's fees awarded by the jury ($185,000). That number may very well have been higher had the jury properly answered the breach of contract question. In any event, the jury could not legitimately award $0.00 for Plaintiffs' attorney's fees on appeal.

We have already confirmed the trial court abused its discretion by ordering a new trial based on the jury's finding that USAA did not breach the policy. Because much of the trial court's analysis is contingent on that first basis, the references to attorney's-fees provisions in the Civil Practice and Remedies Code, as well as the prompt-payment provisions in chapter 542 of the Insurance Code, no longer apply. Reducing the trial court's reasoning to the statutory provisions and analysis thereof as consistent with the jury's answers, the order essentially becomes:

> The jury awarded $0.00 for Plaintiffs' attorney's fees. This award was erroneous and against the overwhelming weight of the evidence . . . .
>
> Sections 541 . . . of the Texas Insurance Code ha[s] [a] similar [mandatory attorney's fees] provision[ ]. When a statute mandates an award of trial attorney's fees, an award of appellate attorney's fees is likewise mandatory . . . .
>
> Since [the Bents] prevailed on their Section 541 claims, they were entitled to an award of attorney's fees for trial and through appeal.

Although the trial court again couches its conclusion in factual-sufficiency nomenclature ("against the overwhelming weight of the evidence"), its rationale for ordering a new trial turns on a legal conclusion: that chapter 541 mandates an award of attorney's fees based on, in this case, the jury's determination that USAA made "a statement in such a manner as to mislead a reasonably prudent person to a false conclusion of a material fact."

The court of appeals considered the trial court's explanation facially sufficient. We cannot agree. Chapter 541 of the Insurance Code provides that a prevailing plaintiff "may obtain . . . reasonable and necessary attorney's fees." TEX. INS. CODE § 541.152(a)(1). We assume "may obtain" renders an attorney's-fee award mandatory, *see Bocquet v. Herring,* 972 S.W.2d 19, 20-21 (Tex. 1998), but by its own terms it is not automatic—a prevailing party bears the burden to establish the fees are "reasonable and necessary," *see Arthur Andersen & Co. v. Perry Equip. Corp.,* 945 S.W.2d 812, 819 (Tex. 1997) ("[T]he plaintiff must prove that the amount of fees was both reasonably incurred and necessary to the prosecution of the case at bar, and must ask the jury to award the fees in a specific dollar amount, not as a percentage of the judgment."). And a jury does not necessarily err in awarding no attorney's fees if the party seeking them fails to establish its requested fees are "reasonable and necessary." *See Rosenblatt v. Freedom Life Ins. Co. of Am.,* 240 S.W.3d 315, 320-24 (Tex. App.—Houston [1st Dist.] 2007, no pet.); *Cain v. Pruett,* 938 S.W.2d 152, 159-60 (Tex. App.—Dallas 1996, no writ). Accordingly, absent any reference to what evidence was adduced as to reasonable and necessary attorney's fees, the failure to award attorney's fees under a mandatory-fee statute is not in itself a reason for which a new trial is legally appropriate. *See United Scaffolding,* 377 S.W.3d at 689 ("[A]n order granting a new trial may amount to a clear abuse of discretion if the given reason, specific or not, is not one for which a new trial is legally valid."). Here, the order summarily states that evidence supporting an award of reasonable and necessary attorney's fees is "overwhelming." This is insufficient; the order "must indicate that the trial judge considered the specific facts and circumstances of the case at hand and explain how the evidence (or lack of evidence) undermines the jury's findings." *Id.* at 689. The trial court made no such effort, rendering this basis for a new trial facially insufficient.

* * *

We conclude that three of the trial court's bases for ordering a new trial fail to satisfy the facial requirements set forth in *Columbia* and *United Scaffolding.* On the remaining basis, we agree with the court of appeals that the record does not support the trial court's stated rationale. The trial court abused its discretion and the court of appeals acted appropriately in conditionally granting mandamus relief directing the trial court to vacate its order and enter judgment on the jury's verdict. Accordingly, we deny the Bents' petition for writ of mandamus.

JUSTICE JOHNSON did not participate in the decision.

Notes

1. The granting of a new trial is an interlocutory order which can not be appealed under Texas law. As a result, an original proceeding by mandamus is the only relief available for a party complaining of the granting of the new trial.

2. Prior to April 1, 1984, following a trial by jury, a complaint in a motion for new trial specifically pointing out an alleged error made by the trial judge was necessary to preserve that error for appellate review, except in a few instances. The 1984 amendments to Rule 324 changed that practice dramatically. The present rule eliminates the need for a motion for new trial as the method of preservation of error for appellate review in most cases. However, lawyers still use the motion to bring to a court's attention alleged errors committed during the pretrial and trial stages which were previously pointed out by objection, motion, or otherwise pursuant to Rule 33 of the Texas Rules of Appellate Procedure. The purpose of such a motion is to give the trial court one last chance to change its mind and grant a new trial prior to commencing the appellate process. More importantly, as well be discussed in Chapter 16 of this casebook, the filing of a motion for new trial in a jury case extends the appellate timetables. *See* Rules 26, 32 & 35 of the Texas Rules of Appellate Procedure. The remaining section of this chapter will focus on some of the complaints which must be contained in a motion for new trial in order to preserve an error for appellate review.

3. *In re United Scaffolding, Inc.*, 301 S.W.3d 661 (Tex. 2010): This case involved the granting of a new trial in the interest of justice and fairness before *In re Columbia Medical Center of Las Colinas*, 290 S.W.3d 204 (Tex. 2009). In *Columbia Medical* the Court held that the trial court abused its discretion by disregarding a jury verdict and granting a new trial when the reason it gave for doing so was "in the interest of justice and fairness." While the trial judge followed the applicable law in effect at the time the order granting a new trial was issued, an erroneous legal conclusion is an abuse of discretion, even if it may not have been clearly erroneous when made.

b. *Misconduct of Jury or Court Official*

Read Rule 327 Texas Rules of Civil Procedure and Rule 606 Texas Rules of Civil Evidence.

DANIELS
v.
MELTON TRUCK LINES, INC.

704 S.W.2d 142
(Tex. App.—Eastland 1986, writ ref'd n.r.e.)

J. Gene Bailey, Rex A. Nichols, Nichols, Bailey & Watson, Longview, for appellant.
Crawford Parker, Jr., Rick McPherson, Parker & McPherson, Carthage, James W. Sharp, Sharp, Ward, Price & Hightower, Longview, for appellee.

DICKENSON, JUSTICE.

This motor vehicle collision case was tried by a jury which refused to find that either driver's actions were a proximate cause of the collision. Both sides appeal the judgment that all plaintiffs and counter-plaintiffs take nothing. We affirm.

The plaintiffs were riding in a 1978 Ford Van which collided with a 1979 Freightliner Tractor Trailer. Plaintiffs sued the owner, the Lessee, and the driver of the truck. Each of those defendants filed a counterclaim against the estate of the van's driver.

Each side used expert witnesses to "reconstruct the accident" which occurred on State Highway 149 between Carthage and Longview on November 5, 1980, at 1:30 a.m. The people in the van were on their way home to Carthage after attending a Ronnie Millsap concert in Longview. The truck was on its way to Oklahoma with a load of plywood. The experts agreed that the vehicles had a left-front to left-front collision and that the impact was on the van's side of the center stripe. They reached different conclusions as to which driver caused the collision to occur.

The driver of the van was killed, and all four of his passengers testified that they were sleeping and, consequently, did not know what caused the collision. The truck driver testified that the van was on the truck driver's side of the highway, that he pulled the truck to his left to avoid the collision, and that the van then came back across the center stripe. The highway patrolman testified that two of the young men who were riding in the van told him at the scene of the accident that their driver went to sleep and drifted onto the wrong side of the road, that one of the passengers saw the truck lights and yelled, and that their driver pulled back to his right. Two witnesses who arrived at the scene before the highway patrolman said the two young men told them that they did not know what caused the collision and did not say anything about their driver going to sleep and getting on the wrong side of the road.

The jury's verdict can be summarized as shown:

1. Joseph D. Stephens (the truck driver) did not fail to apply his brakes; did not fail to keep a proper lookout; did not fail to turn to the right; did not go to sleep at the wheel; did not fail to yield; and was not operating his vehicle at an excessive speed.

2. Joseph D. Stephens (the truck driver) failed to keep his vehicle completely within the right half of the roadway.

3. Such failure was not a proximate cause of the collision.

4. Jimmy Dial Craig (driver of the van) was negligent: as to lookout; failure to drive on the right half of the roadway; failure to give the truck driver at least one-half of the highway; failure to yield the right-of-way; and falling asleep. The jury refused to find proximate cause as to any of the negligent acts and omissions.

Under the instructions of the court, the jury was not required to answer any of the other special issues. Those issues related to the apportionment of fault and the amount of damages to each plaintiff and counter-plaintiff.

Plaintiffs urge a single point of error. They argue that the trial court erred in overruling their motion for new trial because statements made by one of the jurors during the jury's deliberations constituted jury misconduct and was an "outside influence" improperly brought to bear on the jury's deliberations.

This point is overruled because of TEX. R. EVID. 606(b) which was adopted before the trial of this case and which now states:

> Upon an inquiry into the validity of a verdict or indictment, a juror may not testify as to any matter or statement occurring during the course of the jury's deliberations or to the effect of anything upon his or any other juror's mind or emotions as influencing him to assent to or dissent from the verdict or indictment or concerning his mental processes in connection therewith, except that a juror may testify whether any outside influence was improperly brought to bear upon any juror. Nor may his affidavit or evidence of any statement by him concerning a matter about which he would be precluded from testifying be received for these purposes.

The trial court properly refused to consider the jurors' affidavits and bills of exception testimony of six of the jurors that during their lengthy deliberations one of the jurors, Shirley Hamilton:

> [K]ept repeating that she was a police officer for the City of Carthage and her duties included patrolling, investigating accidents and issuing tickets . . . . Juror Hamilton did not directly threaten to use her outside influence and police power on those who disagreed with her, but all jurors had become tired and exhausted and they very easily probably felt both consciously and subconsciously that the power Juror Hamilton had outside the jury room as a police officer would be used against them if they did not agree with her.
>
> * * *
>
> She left the distinct impression that if we did not answer the questions as she thought they should be answered, that we would see her later and could suffer the consequences . . . . It is my sincere belief

> that Juror Hamilton used her outside position as a peace officer to influence and intimidate other members of the jury.
>
> * * *
>
> It is my opinion the emphasis of her right to make arrests outside the jury room had an influence on some of the jurors changing and siding with her.
>
> * * *
>
> I really believed that both sides were negligent and the injured persons should have been granted damages but I did not want to have any future problems with Officer Hamilton. She never directly threatened anyone but indirectly she indicated those disagreeing with her could see her later in the patrol car.
>
> * * *
>
> Juror Hamilton did not directly threaten anyone but she was angry and shouted down those who disagreed with her. I can see how the jurors that changed their votes could have felt they would see Juror Hamilton later if they did not vote the way she did.
>
> * * *
>
> It is probable that one or more of them were influenced by the repeated and forceful assertions of Juror Hamilton concerning her outside position as a police officer.

Rule 606(b) is clear. None of the jurors may testify as to "any matter or statement occurring during the course of the jury's deliberations." Those statements concerning Juror Hamilton, accepted as true, do not show "outside influence" within the meaning of the exception stated in this rule. *See* Black, *Article VI: Witnesses*, 20 HOUSTON LAW REVIEW 409 at 421 (1983 TEXAS RULES OF EVIDENCE HANDBOOK):

> The Texas rule, though similar to federal rule 606(b), is more restrictive than its federal counterpart. Both versions allow a juror to testify about whether outside influence was improperly brought to bear. However, the federal rule also permits testimony "on the question whether extraneous prejudicial information was improperly brought to the jury's attention." The Texas Supreme Court deleted this phrase from the rule proposed by the Liaison Committee.
>
> * * *
>
> The term "extraneous prejudicial information" refers to information that is external to the jury, rather than that which is outside the record. Thus, information that is injected into the jury's deliberations by sources other than the jurors themselves constitutes extraneous prejudicial information.
>
> * * *
>
> [T]he drafters of the federal rule clearly did not intend for the "extraneous prejudicial information" exception to be used to reach any matters and statements occurring during jury deliberations. To this extent, there is no difference in the effects of the Texas and federal versions of the rule.

All of the cases cited by appellant were decided prior to September 1, 1983, the effective date of TEX. R. EVID. 606(b). Appellant argues that to construe this rule as barring proof of all statements made by the jurors during the course of their deliberations would bar the proof of serious jury misconduct, such as: (1) threats by one juror to do physical violence to another after they leave the courthouse if he does not change his vote; (2) offers of a bribe by one juror to change his vote, to be paid after the jury is discharged; (3) unsworn testimony by a juror about material facts; (4) discussions in violations of the court's instructions to not discuss insurance, attorney's fees, or the effect of their answers to the special issues. As now written, Rule 606(b) bars testimony by any juror as to all matters or statements occurring during the course of their deliberations, except for testimony that "any outside influence was improperly brought to bear upon any juror." As we read this rule, the statements by Juror Hamilton do not come within the exception and, consequently, proof of her statements and their effect is barred by the rule. *See United States v. Greer*, 620 F.2d 1383 (10th Cir. 1980), for a discussion of federal Rule 606(b).

* * *

The judgment of the trial court is affirmed.

GOLDEN EAGLE ARCHERY, INC.
v.
JACKSON
24 S.W.3d 362
(Tex. 2000)

Lipscomb Norvell, Jr., Benckenstein Norvell & Nathan, Beaumont, for Petitioner.

David B. Gaultney, John Cash Smith, Mehaffy & Weber, Beaumont, George Barron, Orange, for Respondent.

JUSTICE GONZALES delivered the opinion of the Court, in which CHIEF JUSTICE PHILLIPS, JUSTICE HECHT, JUSTICE ENOCH, JUSTICE OWEN, JUSTICE BAKER, JUSTICE HANKINSON and JUSTICE O'NEILL joined.

The main issue in this case is whether procedural and evidentiary rules may constitutionally prohibit jurors from testifying post-verdict about statements made during deliberations, unless such statements concern outside influences. *See* TEX. R. CIV. P. 327(b); TEX. R. CIV. EVID. 606(b). Ronald Jackson obtained a verdict in a products liability case, but moved for a new trial on several grounds, including juror misconduct, juror bias, and the adequacy of the verdict. After a hearing, the trial court denied the motion. The court of appeals reversed and remanded for a new trial, holding that Texas Rule of Civil Procedure 327(b) denied Jackson his constitutional right to a fair and impartial jury trial because it prohibited him from proving jury misconduct during deliberations. 974 S.W.2d 952, 954. Because we conclude that the rule is constitutional, we reverse the court of appeal's judgment and remand to that court to consider Jackson's other points of error that the court of appeals did not reach.

I

Jackson's wife bought him a Golden Eagle compound bow from a Wal-Mart store. When Jackson drew back the string the bow slipped out of his hand and a cable guard struck his eye, causing severe injuries. He sued Golden Eagle Archery, Inc., Coleman Company, Inc., and Wal-Mart, Inc. for negligence and products liability. The trial court dismissed the claims against Coleman and Wal-Mart, leaving Golden Eagle as the sole defendant. The jury found that Golden Eagle defectively marketed the bow but failed to find that the bow was defectively designed. The jury also found that Jackson was negligent, and attributed to him 45% of the responsibility for his injury. The jury found Jackson's damages to be approximately $25,000 for medical care, $2,500 for physical pain and mental anguish, $2,500 for vision loss, $0 for physical impairment other than vision loss, $1,500 for disfigurement, and $4,600 for past lost earnings. Ten of the twelve jurors signed the verdict. The trial court asked the ten if they agreed to the entire verdict, but neither party asked to poll the individual jurors. The trial court then rendered a judgment for approximately $20,000 damages and $6,700 prejudgment interest.

Jackson moved for a new trial. He challenged the legal and factual sufficiency of the evidence to support several of the jury's answers, contested the trial court's exclusion of certain evidence, and alleged that juror Barbara Maxwell concealed a bias during voir dire and that she and other jurors committed misconduct before and during formal deliberations. The motion attached affidavits from one of Jackson's attorneys and three jurors. Two of the affidavits were from the jurors who did not vote for the verdict, Donald Frederick and Janet Cline. A third was from the presiding juror, Shawn Lynch. The motion asserted that even though Texas Rule of Civil Procedure 327(b) prohibits consideration of juror affidavits to impeach the verdict, to ignore the evidence of misconduct during deliberations would unconstitutionally deny Jackson his right to a fair trial. Golden Eagle responded that both Rule 327(b) and Texas Rule of Civil Evidence 606(b) prohibit the court from considering the juror's affidavits, that Jackson's attorney's affidavit primarily recounted hearsay statements about what some jurors told him, and that Jackson waived any juror-bias complaint because he did not conduct a sufficient voir dire.

At the hearing on his motion for new trial, Jackson offered the four affidavits as well as juror Frederick's testimony. The trial court admitted the testimony and affidavits without limitation "to the extent they contain appropriate evidentiary matters for consideration under Rule 327," and otherwise for the purposes of Jackson's bill of exceptions. At the hearing, Jackson's attorney read passages from the voir dire questioning of the jurors to demonstrate that Maxwell had hidden her bias against lawsuits of this kind. Jackson's attorney began voir dire with a lengthy question about whether any jurors were opposed to lawsuits, or could not be fair, or simply did not want to be on a jury. A panel member raised his hand. Jackson's attorney told the juror he would ask him more questions later, then asked the panel, "Anyone else?" No one responded. Jackson's attorney continued:

> Is there anybody here, by the same token, who would just say, "Look, I just can't do that. I can't—I don't believe in it. I just can't give a verdict that means that somebody is going to have to pay a lot of money"? Anybody here that—again, if you do, now is the time. You owe it to yourself and you owe it to these people and to the Court to be honest about it because we—all we can do is ask you about it, but you have to tell us. Anybody here that could not do that?

Again, no one responded. Finally, Jackson's attorney asked the panel if any of them had served on a jury. Maxwell answered that she had served on both a civil and a criminal case. She said the civil case involved a man's death in an accident. Jackson's attorney asked:

Q Did you—did you reach a verdict in that case?
A No.
Q Anything about that case that would keep you from being fair here?
A No, sir.

Frederick testified in his affidavit and at the hearing about a conversation he had with Maxwell during a trial recess. According to Frederick, Maxwell told him that previously she had served on a jury that awarded nothing for a wrongful death claim, which Frederick thought contradicted her voir dire statements, and further told him she did not believe in "awarding money in stuff like that," and that "we are the ones who end up paying for it."

The remaining juror testimony concerned events occurring after the jury retired to begin deliberating the evidence. Frederick, Cline, and Lynch all recalled that the jury bartered on the amounts to award for disfigurement and loss of vision, although their accounts contradict each other in the specifics. Frederick said that initially ten jurors had agreed to award $2,500 for disfigurement and nine had agreed to award $2,500 for loss of vision, but traded votes to award $1,500 for disfigurement and $2,500 for loss of vision. Lynch, however, claimed that initially ten jurors had agreed on $1,500 for loss of vision, and eight agreed on $2,500 for disfigurement, but ultimately decided to switch these amounts. Cline merely remembered that the jurors "traded off" on these answers.

Frederick also stated that during the jury's discussion of damages, Maxwell told other jurors that "there is too much of this going on," which he took to mean the filing of lawsuits. He said that she "held up a document which showed the name of Wal-Mart and said something to the effect that the plaintiff had probably already gotten a big settlement from Wal-Mart and did not need any more money out of this case."

Frederick and Lynch additionally testified that during jury room deliberations Maxwell speculated whether Jackson had been drinking alcoholic beverages when the accident occurred. Finally, all three juror affidavits claim that Maxwell strongly argued against Jackson's position throughout the jury room deliberations.

The trial court overruled Jackson's motion for a new trial explaining its ruling in a letter to the parties. The court advised it would not sustain Jackson's jury misconduct arguments because the jurors' affidavits and testimony all pertained to jury deliberations and were therefore incompetent. The court also rejected Jackson's complaints about undisclosed juror bias. Acknowledging that the same evidence offered to show jury misconduct "would certainly support a conclusion that the juror in question was biased against product liability suits" the court did not resolve whether Maxwell was in fact biased. Instead, the court concluded that Jackson's attorney's voir dire questioning of Maxwell was not specific enough to show she purposefully concealed any bias. Jackson did not request the trial court to make any fact findings about any of these issues.

On appeal, Jackson asserted eight points of error, any one of which, if sustained, would result in a new trial. His first six points challenged the sufficiency of the amount of the damages awarded, the weight of the evidence supporting the jury's verdict, and the exclusion of certain evidence. The court of appeals addressed only Jackson's last two points about jury misconduct and juror bias. A divided court of appeals reversed the trial court's judgment and remanded the case for a new trial. The court expressed its concern about "the ever increasing lack of veracity of jurors on voir dire . . . ." 974 S.W.2d at 957. The court held that because Rule 327(b) denied Jackson the only evidence available to prove misconduct, it denied him his right to a fair and impartial trial. It concluded that the evidence established Maxwell's misconduct, and that the misconduct was material and caused harm. Golden Eagle petitioned this Court for review, and we granted the petition.

II

This case turns on whether, and to what extent, the jurors' affidavits and testimony are admissible to show juror misconduct such as undisclosed bias. The problem of jury misconduct or bias presents difficult choices about how best to promote the jury system's "purity and efficiency" under Article I, Section 15 of the Texas Constitution. On the one hand, it may be desirable in a particular case to rectify a verdict improperly decided because of juror bias or misconduct. A fair trial before an impartial tribunal is a basic requirement of due process. *See In re Murchison*, 349 U.S. 133, 136, 75 S.Ct. 623, 99 L.Ed. 942 (1955). However, the goal of a trial by a jury free from bias or misconduct must be balanced against other legitimate interests. *See Maldonado v. Missouri Pac. Ry. Co.*, 798 F.2d 764, 770 (5th Cir.1986). Courts and commentators have noted several policy reasons why losing parties should not be allowed to conduct unfettered investigations into the jury's deliberations to try to prove such allegations, in essence putting the jury on trial.

First, jury deliberations must be kept private to encourage jurors to candidly discuss the case. A verdict is a collaborative effort requiring individuals from different backgrounds to reach a consensus. A juror should feel free to raise and consider an unpopular viewpoint. To discharge their duties effectively, jurors must be able to discuss the evidence and issues without fear that their deliberations will later be held up to public scrutiny. Second, there is a recognized need to protect jurors from post-trial harassment or tampering. The losing party has every incentive to try to get jurors to testify to defects in their deliberations. The winning party would likewise want to investigate in order to protect the judgment.

Jury service will be less attractive if the litigants can harass a juror after trial, call a juror to testify about jury deliberations, and make juror deliberations public. Third, a disgruntled juror whose view did not prevail in the jury room would have an avenue for vindication by overturning the verdict. This is a significant concern in Texas civil trials, in which the verdict may be less than unanimous. Fourth is the need for finality. Litigation must end at some point if the public is to have any confidence in judgments . . . .

* * *

In 1983, our Court adopted Texas Rule of Civil Evidence 606(b). *See* TEX. R. CIV. EVID. 606(b), 641-642 S.W.2d (Texas Cases) LII (1983); 1 MCCORMICK & RAY, TEXAS LAW OF EVIDENCE § 1612 (Texas Practice 1980). The State Bar Liaison Committee on the Rules of Evidence had recommended that we adopt Federal Rule of Evidence 606(b) verbatim. *See* Black, *Article VI: Witnesses*, 20 HOUS. L. REV. 409, 422-23 (1983). The rule as adopted provided:

> Rule 606. Competency of Juror as Witness
>
> (b) Inquiry into validity of verdict or indictment
>
> Upon an inquiry into the validity of a verdict or indictment, a juror may not testify as to any matter or statement occurring during the course of the jury's deliberations or to the effect of anything upon his or any other juror's mind or emotions as influencing him to assent or dissent from the verdict or indictment or concerning his mental process in connection therewith, except that a juror may testify on the question whether any outside influence was improperly brought to bear upon any juror. Nor may his affidavit or evidence of any statement by him concerning a matter about which he would be precluded from testifying be received for these purposes.

TEX. R. CIV. EVID. 606(b). The rule differs from Federal Rule 606(b) only in that it deletes the federal exception that allows a juror to testify "whether extraneous prejudicial information was improperly brought to the jury's attention." *Compare* TEX. R. CIV. EVID. 606(b) with FED R. EVID. 606(b). The same year the Court amended Rule 327(b) to incorporate the provisions of Rule 606(b) into the procedures for seeking a new trial:

> b. A juror may not testify as to any matter or statement occurring during the course of the jury's deliberations or to the effect of anything upon his or any other juror's mind or emotions as influencing him to assent to or dissent from the verdict concerning his mental processes in connection therewith, except that a juror may testify whether any outside influence was improperly brought to bear upon any juror. Nor may his affidavit or evidence of any statement by him concerning a matter about which he would be precluded from testifying be received for these purposes.

TEX. R. CIV. P. 327(b). Our Court did not explain the significance of its decision to reject an exception for extraneous prejudicial information, leaving scholars to speculate whether the Texas rules are more restrictive than the federal rule. *Compare* Addison, *Conduct Unbecoming a Jury: Rule 606(b)*, 50 TEX. BAR J. 872, 872 (1987) (stating that the Texas rule is more restrictive), *with* Black, *supra*, 20 HOUS. L. REV. at 423 (concluding that the federal exceptions for "extraneous prejudicial information" and "outside influences" are largely redundant).

III

Before we consider the constitutional questions, we first determine if, and to what extent, the rules bar the evidence Jackson offered in this case. Golden Eagle argues that Rule 327(b) precludes proof of all jury misconduct except misconduct resulting from outside influences. Both Rule 327(b) and Rule 606(b) state that jurors may not testify about statements or matters occurring during deliberations, but they may testify about outside influences. *See* TEX. R. CIV. P. 327(b); TEX. R. CIV. EVID. 606(b). A number of cases and commentators have concluded that the Texas rules forbid all proof of jury misconduct unless it involves outside influences. Many of these cases rely on a statement in *Weaver v. Westchester Fire Insurance Company*:

> [A] motion for new trial based on jury misconduct must be supported by a juror's affidavit alleging "outside influences" were brought to bear upon the jury.

739 S.W.2d 23, 24 (Tex. 1987). However, our statement in *Weaver* was overly broad, because the rules' limitations on affidavits and testimony as grounds for a new trial expressly do not apply to non-jurors. A court may, of course, admit competent evidence of juror misconduct from any other source. *See, e.g., Mayo v. State*, 708 S.W.2d 854, 856 (Tex. Crim. App. 1986) (considering testimony of witness contacted by juror); *Fillinger v.. Fuller*, 746 S.W.2d 506, 508 (Tex. App.—Texarkana 1988, no writ) (holding that rules do not require that affidavits be from jurors only); *Goode, supra*, § 606.2 & n. 42. There is no competent non-juror evidence of misconduct here, however. Jackson's attorney's affidavit relates in part to statements made in open court during voir dire; the remainder of the attorney's testimony is objected-to hearsay concerning what the jurors told him another juror said. *See Mitchell v. Southern Pac. Trans. Co.*, 955 S.W.2d 300, 322 (Tex. App.—San Antonio 1997, no writ) (holding non-juror's affidavit about what occurred in jury deliberations was hearsay); *Clancy v. Zale Corp.*, 705 S.W.2d 820, 828 (Tex. App.—Dallas 1986, writ ref'd n.r.e.); *Tenngasco Gas Gathering Co. v. Fischer*, 624 S.W.2d 301, 305 (Tex. App.—Corpus Christi 1981, writ ref'd n.r.e.). While we may consider the record of the voir dire, it alone contains no suggestion of jury misconduct.

We now turn to the juror testimony. Here three jurors testified as to (1) matters alleged to have occurred after the jury retired to begin deliberating the evidence and (2) a conversation alleged to have occurred during a trial break. We consider first the jurors' testimony about events occurring after retiring to begin deliberations. In support of a motion for new trial, Rule 327(a) provides:

> When the ground of a motion for new trial, supported by affidavit, is misconduct of the jury or of the officer in charge of them, or because of any communication made to the jury or that a juror gave an erroneous or incorrect answer on voir dire examination, the court shall hear evidence thereof from the jury or others in open court.

TEX.R. CIV. P. 327(a). Jackson argues that when we harmonize Rules 327(a) and 327(b), the latter does not apply when the purpose of the juror's affidavit is to show that another juror lied on voir dire and concealed bias and prejudice. Thus, Jackson argues that Rule 327(a) permits juror testimony about statements made during deliberations if offered to show that a juror gave an erroneous or incorrect answer on voir dire examination. But, if Jackson's interpretation is correct, and Rule 327(a) is an exception to Rule 327(b), then the scope of inquiry into jury deliberations may legitimately include not just incorrect answers on voir dire but any "misconduct of the jury", including misconduct occurring during formal deliberations. If so, the 1983 amendments to Rule 327 greatly expanded the scope of inquiry into the jury's deliberations rather than restricting them.

Certainly, there is no basis for concluding that the Court intended to expand the scope of inquiry into the jury's deliberations by adopting Rule 327(a) as an exception to Rule 327(b). Rule 327(b) operates to prohibit jurors from testifying about matters and statements occurring during deliberations. Harmonizing both sections, subsection (b) applies regardless of the grounds alleged for a new trial. Jackson suggests that Rule 327(a)'s provision for juror testimony would be meaningless if Rule 327(b) precludes a juror from testifying about statements made during deliberations. We disagree. Rule 327(b) does not preclude juror testimony about improper contacts with individuals outside the jury, nor juror testimony about matters or statements not "occurring during the course of the jury's deliberations." A juror may testify about jury misconduct provided it does not require delving into deliberations. For example, a juror could testify that another juror improperly viewed the scene of the events giving rise to the litigation. Likewise, a juror could testify about reasons for disqualifying another juror provided the testifying juror's knowledge was gained independent of deliberations. Juror Maxwell, had she been called to testify, could have been questioned about the facts of her prior jury service without violating Rule 327(b).

Despite the rules' prohibition against juror testimony about deliberations, both Rule 327(b) and Rule 606(b) allow jurors to testify about outside influences. Jackson argues that we should broadly interpret the exception for outside influences and consider the jurors' testimony because it falls within the exception in the rules for "outside influences." We have not defined what kind of "outside influence" a juror may testify about. In *Weaver*, our only case on the subject, we gave examples of what is not an outside influence. *Weaver v. Westchester Fire Ins. Co.*, 739 S.W.2d 23, 24 (Tex. 1987). In that case, a worker's compensation claimant obtained a juror's affidavit claiming that the jury had discussed the failure of certain witnesses to appear and testify and the probability that the claimant lacked hospitalization insurance. *See id.* We concluded that the affidavit was not evidence of an outside influence. *See id.*

Most Texas courts considering the question have held that the rules prevent a juror from testifying that the jury discussed improper matters during deliberation. *See, e.g., Soliz v. Saenz*, 779 S.W.2d 929, 933 (Tex. App.—Corpus Christi 1989, writ denied); *King v. Bauer*, 767 S.W.2d 197, 198 (Tex. App.-Corpus Christi 1989, writ denied); *Baley v. W/W Interests, Inc.*, 754 S.W.2d 313, 316 (Tex. App.—Houston [14th Dist.] 1988, writ denied); *Robinson Elec. Supply Co. v. Cadillac Cable Corp.*, 706 S.W.2d 130, 132 (Tex. App.—Houston [14th Dist.] 1986, writ ref'd n.r.e.); *Clancy v. Zale Corp.*, 705 S.W.2d 820, 828-29 (Tex. App.—Dallas 1986, writ ref'd n.r.e.). We agree. The rules contemplate that an "outside influence" originates from sources other than the jurors themselves. Accordingly, here the accounts that some jurors speculated whether alcohol was involved in the accident and that Jackson may have received a settlement, or that the jurors traded answers on two issues, are all juror statements about matters occurring during their deliberations. They are not evidence of outside influences.

Jackson also argues that we should consider Maxwell herself an "outside influence" because she brought prejudices into the jury room. A number of cases have also rejected this argument, holding that the rules preclude evidence from a juror that another juror exhibited bias during jury deliberations. *See, e.g., United States v. Duzac*, 622 F.2d 911, 913 (5th Cir.1980) (holding that the "proper time to discover such prejudices is when the jury is being selected and peremptory challenges are available to the attorneys"); *Soliz*, 779 S.W.2d at 933 (holding that evidence emanating from inside jury deliberations not admissible to show bias); *Baker Marine Corp. v. Weatherby Eng'g Co.*, 710 S.W.2d 690, 692-93 (Tex. App.—Corpus Christi 1986, no writ) (holding that juror testimony that fellow juror seemed biased during deliberation was inadmissable). Moreover, while failure to disclose bias is a form of juror misconduct that justifies a new trial under the appropriate circumstances, proof of a juror's failure to disclose bias must come from some source other than a fellow juror's testimony about deliberations. *See Durbin v. Dal-Briar Corp.*, 871 S.W.2d 263, 272 (Tex. App.—El Paso 1994, writ denied).

In the same vein, Jackson contends that Maxwell was an outside influence because her bias statutorily disqualified her from serving on the jury. *See* TEX. GOV'T CODE § 62.105(4). However, Jackson did not timely raise statutory disqualification as a basis for new trial. *See* TEX. R. CIV. P. 329(b). But even if Jackson had timely raised it, Jackson must depend on proof other than matters prohibited by Rule 327(b) to establish statutory disqualification.

Finally, we consider the alleged conversation between Frederick and Maxwell during a trial break. Jackson argues that the conversation should not be considered "deliberations" and therefore barred by Rule 606(b) and Rule 327(b). We agree. The Texas Rules of Civil Procedure use the term "deliberations" as meaning formal jury deliberations—when the jury weighs the evidence to arrive at a verdict. In at least one rule the term is used to refer to the stage of trial after the court has charged the jury but before it has returned a verdict. Rule 287 provides:

> The court, during the deliberations of the jury, may proceed with other business or recess from time to time, but shall be deemed open for all purposes connected with the case before the jury.

TEX. R. CIV. P. 287. Clearly, here the rule refers to formal deliberations and not incidental discussions that might occur between jurors during trial.

Other rules use the term "deliberation" to refer to the formal process beginning after the close of evidence and the jury charge, when the jury retires to weigh the evidence to arrive at a verdict. For example, Rule 282 provides that a "jury may either decide a case in court or retire for deliberation." Rule 283 constrains the officer in charge of the jury from revealing "the state of [the jury's] deliberations." If polling the jury reveals a problem with the verdict, or it is otherwise defective or incomplete, Rules 294 and 295 provide for "further deliberations." None of the rules contemplate that the jury may begin deliberating during a trial break. On the contrary, the approved jury instructions direct courts to admonish the jury against informal discussions of the case:

> Do not even discuss this case among yourselves until after you have heard all of the evidence, the court's charge, the attorneys' arguments and until I have sent you to the jury room to consider your verdict.

TEX. R. CIV. P. 226a (approved instructions) pt II.

A court of appeals adopted an opposing view interpreting the term "deliberations" in Rules 606 and 327(b) to include discussions before the charge was read and formal deliberations had begun:

> Any conversation regarding the case occurring between or among jurors is a part of jury deliberations regardless of the time and place where it occurs.

To hold otherwise would reinstate the post-trial questioning of jurors under prior law. *Baley v. W/W Interests, Inc.*, 754 S.W.2d 313, 316 (Tex. App.—Houston [14th Dist.] 1988, writ denied). A number of courts have followed this holding from *Baley* without discussion. This expansive reading, however, is not required by the language of the rules. Thus, we disapprove of the definition of the term "deliberations" in these cases. And contrary to the court of appeal's suggestion in *Baley*, Rule 606(b) and Rule 327(b) were not intended to eliminate post-trial questioning altogether. Juror testimony is still permitted on the issues of juror misconduct, communications to the jury, and erroneous answers on voir dire, provided such testimony does not require delving into deliberations. TEX. R. CIV. P. 327(a), (b).

Consequently, we conclude that Rules 327(b) and 606(b) do not bar Frederick's testimony about his conversation with Maxwell during a trial break. However, because this evidence does not conclusively establish that Maxwell prevaricated or concealed bias during voir dire, we do not agree that the trial court abused its discretion in failing to grant a new trial.

To warrant a new trial for jury misconduct, the movant must establish (1) that the misconduct occurred, (2) it was material, and (3) probably caused injury. Rule 327 provides that a trial court: may grant a new trial if . . . the erroneous or incorrect answer on voir dire examination, be material, and if it reasonably appears from the evidence both on the hearing of the motion and the trial of the case and from the record as a whole that injury probably resulted to the complaining party. TEX. R. CIV. P. 327(a). Whether misconduct occurred and caused injury is a question of fact for the trial court. *See Pharo v. Chambers County*, 922 S.W.2d 945, 948 (Tex. 1996). Absent findings to the contrary, we must assume that the trial court made all findings in support of its decision to deny the motion for new trial. *See id.* Consequently, Jackson had the burden to conclusively establish that Maxwell committed jury misconduct, a burden he did not discharge.

* * *

Jackson contends that Frederick's testimony established that Maxwell prevaricated on voir dire. When Jackson's attorney asked the panel about prior jury service, Maxwell volunteered she had served on juries in a criminal matter and a civil matter involving a death. The attorney asked if the jury had reached a verdict in the civil case, and Maxwell answered "no". The attorney did not ask Maxwell any further questions.

We conclude that Frederick's affidavit and testimony do not conclusively establish that Maxwell failed to answer Jackson's voir dire questions truthfully. The other party to the conversation, Maxwell, did not testify at the new trial hearing nor does the record indicate that anyone called her to testify. It is at least possible that Maxwell misunderstood the voir dire question about whether the jury had reached a verdict in the wrongful death case and thought it meant whether the jury had awarded any damages in the case. There is no other evidence in the record about this conversation or the facts of Maxwell's prior jury service. This evidence does not conclusively establish that Maxwell intentionally answered incorrectly.

Jackson also contends that Frederick's testimony demonstrates that Maxwell concealed bias during voir dire. If, as Frederick testified, Maxwell said that she did not believe in "things like that" or "lawsuits like that" or in awarding money in "stuff like that" or "things like that", all referring to the wrongful death action, or that she did not believe in "lawsuits like this", referring to the present case, did she mean lawsuits that she considered to be lacking in merit or all personal injury actions? The latter is a reasonable inference, but so is the former. Frederick's testimony, if credible, was inconclusive.

But the trial court may not have considered Frederick's testimony to have been credible. It was certainly hearsay, and while no objection was made to its admission to preclude the trial court from considering it, the trial court was nevertheless free on its own to disregard the testimony.

We conclude that the evidence about discussions prior to formal deliberations does not establish jury misconduct here, and Rules 606(b) and 327(b) prohibit considering the testimony about matters and statements occurring in the course of the jury's formal deliberations. We turn now to Jackson's constitutional arguments.

IV

Jackson argues that Rule 327(b) conflicts with the guarantees of the right to a fair and impartial jury trial in Article I, Section 15 and Article V, Section 10 of the Texas Constitution. He also suggests that Rule 327(b) violates federal due process. We disagree with both contentions. The United States Constitution does not guarantee a jury trial in state courts. The Sixth Amendment guarantee of a jury trial applies to the states, but by its terms applies only to criminal prosecutions. The right to a jury trial in civil cases in federal courts is found in the Seventh Amendment, but it has never been extended to the states . . . .

* * *

The United States Supreme Court has extensively discussed the constitutionality of Federal Rule of Evidence 606(b) in only one case, *Tanner v. United States*, 483 U.S. 107, 107 S.Ct. 2739, 97 L.Ed.2d 90 (1987). The two defendants in that case sought a hearing on jury misconduct based on juror affidavits that jurors were severely impaired during trial by alcohol and drug abuse. The defendants claimed that Federal Rule 606(b) deprived them of their Sixth Amendment right to a fair jury trial. The Court rejected the claim, noting the substantial policy considerations that support common-law rules against juror impeachment of verdicts in general, and Federal Rule 606(b) in particular. The Court went so far as to suggest that the jury system could not survive if courts permitted extensive post-verdict investigations into juries' internal deliberative processes. *Id.* at 120.

Important to the Supreme Court's analysis in *Tanner* is its emphasis on the protection provided by other aspects of federal trial procedure. The Court noted that the suitability of a potential juror can be tested during voir dire, "jurors may report inappropriate behavior to the court before they render a verdict," and verdicts may be impeached post-trial by non-juror evidence. *Id.* at 127, 107 S.Ct. 2739. Although a federal Sixth Amendment case, we believe that the approach taken in *Tanner* is appropriate to our analysis under the Texas Constitution. Rules 606(b) and 327(b) cannot be viewed in isolation from other trial procedures designed to further the Constitution's goal of a fair and impartial jury. Our system provides other procedures to protect against undesirable jurors. Litigants may question potential jurors on voir dire to detect potential bias and either challenge for cause or exercise peremptory challenges. *See Babcock v. Northwest Mem'l Hosp.*, 767 S.W.2d 705, 708-09 (Tex. 1989).

Rules 327(b) and 606(b) expressly apply only to post-verdict juror testimony. If a problem develops during trial, the court may question the jury by voir dire and take corrective measures such as instructing the jury, dismissing particular jurors, or declaring a mistrial. *See, e.g., Doucet v. Owens-Corning Fiberglas Corp.*, 966 S.W.2d 161, 165 (Tex. App.—Beaumont 1998, pet. denied). When the jury returns the verdict, the court may also poll the individual jurors. *See Branham v. Brown*, 925 S.W.2d 365, 368 (Tex. App.—Houston [1st Dist.] 1996, no writ). Finally, Texas rules concerning attorneys' post-trial juror contact are more permissive than federal court rules. *See Commission For Lawyer Discipline v. Benton*, 980 S.W.2d 425, 433 (Tex. 1998) (noting that Texas law permit attorneys to respectfully contact jurors post trial).

We conclude that Rules 327(b) and 606(b) do not deprive the litigants of a fair trial under the Texas Constitution, nor do they fail to afford litigants due process. The rules are designed to balance concerns about the threat of jury misconduct with the threat from post-verdict juror investigation and impeachment of verdicts.

V

The trial court did not abuse its discretion by denying a new trial on grounds of jury misconduct because Jackson did not present competent evidence. Accordingly, we reverse the judgment of the court of appeals and remand the case to that court to consider Jackson's other issues that it did not reach.

JUSTICE HECHT filed a concurring opinion, in which JUSTICE OWEN joined [omitted].

JUSTICE ABBOTT filed a concurring opinion [omitted].

Notes

1. *Mitchell v. Southern Pacific Transp. Co.*, 955 S.W.2d 300, 322 (Tex. App.—San Antonio 1997, no history): "To preserve error regarding jury misconduct, the complaining party must present evidence proving the misconduct at a hearing on a motion for new trial. TEX. R. CIV. P. 324(b)(1); TEX. R. CIV. P. 327. Although this evidence may generally include testimony from any person with knowledge of the misconduct, jurors may not testify about their deliberations or their mental processes during deliberations, but only about any outside influence that was improperly brought to bear on any juror. *Wooten v. Southern Pacific Transp. Co.*, 928 S.W.2d 76, 78 (Tex. App.—Houston [14th Dist.] 1995, no writ). Rule 327(a) mandates that the court hear evidence of juror misconduct if it is properly presented. *Texaco, Inc.*, 729 S.W.2d at 851." *See also Wooten v. Southern Pacific Transp. Co.,* 928 S.W.2d 76 (Tex. App.—Houston [14th Dist.] 1995, no writ) [Note: While *b*oth *Mitchell* and *Wooten* were disapproved by the Supreme Court in the *Jackson* case, it is obvious that the disapproval concerned the court of appeals holding on what constituted an outside influence, and not the procedure for establishing jury misconduct.

2. *Pharo v. Chambers County, Texas,* 922 S.W.2d 945 (1966): Determining whether jury misconduct occurred is a question of fact for the trial court, and if there is conflicting evidence on this issue the trial court's finding must be upheld on appeal. The trial court's determination as to whether jury misconduct occurred "is ordinarily binding on the reviewing courts and will be reversed only where a clear abuse of discretion is shown." In the context of this damage suit against the County, the bailiff's reference to "raising taxes," overheard by jurors considering an action against the county, was improper. This misconduct, however, justifies a new trial only if it reasonably appears from the record that "injury probably resulted to the complaining party." TEX. R. CIV. P. 327(a). "To show probable injury, there must be some indication in the record that the alleged misconduct most likely caused a juror to vote differently than he 'would otherwise have done on one or more issues vital to the judgment'." Determining the existence of probable injury is a question of law.

3. *Ford Motor Co. v. Castillo*, 279 S.W.3d 656 (Tex. 2009): TEX. R. CIV. P. 327(b); TEX. R. EVID. 606(b) provide jurors may not testify about matters or statements made during jury deliberations. This does not protect the jury's deliberations from all discovery. But, by their plain language, the rules apply to motions for new trials, reasons jurors voted for or against verdicts, and inquiries into the validity of verdicts or indictments. Even when those types of issues are involved, the rules specifically allow jurors to testify about outside influence brought to bear on any of them. In this case, there was no verdict. Discovery involving jurors will not be appropriate in most cases, but in this case there was more than just a suspicion that something suspect occurred—there was some circumstantial evidence that it did. Discovery involving jurors should, ordinarily, be limited to facts and evidence relevant to (1) whether any outside influence was improperly brought to bear upon any juror, and (2) rebuttal of a claim that a juror was not qualified to serve. And although the trial court abused its discretion by entirely depriving Ford of discovery on the breach of contract claim, it remains within the trial court's discretion to reasonably control the limits of discovery and the manner in which the discovery may be obtained. "We express no opinion about discovery or matters involving the breach of contract claim other than discovery involving jurors."

4. *Pena-Rodriguez v. Colorado*, 137 S.Ct. 855 (2017): "Where a juror makes a clear statement indicating that he or she relied on racial stereotypes or animus to convict a criminal defendant, the Sixth Amendment requires that the no-impeachment rule give way in order to permit the trial court to consider the evidence of the juror's statement and any resulting denial of the jury trial guarantee."

c. *Insufficient Evidence and Great Weight and Preponderance of the Evidence*

GUERRA
v.
WAL-MART STORES, INC.
943 S.W.2d 56
(Tex. App.—San Antonio 1997, no writ)

Hugo Xavier De Los Santos, San Antonio, for Appellant.

Harold R. Loftin, Jr., Small, Craig & Werkenthin, P.C., Austin, Stephen R. Fogle, Small, Craig & Werkenthin, P.C., San Antonio, for Appellee.

HARDBERGER, CHIEF JUSTICE.

This is a negligence case. San Juana Guerra claimed that a Sam's Wholesale Club employee negligently threw a cart, which struck her and injured her back. The case was tried to a jury, which unanimously found in favor of the defendant, Wal-Mart Stores, Inc., d/b/a Sam's Wholesale Club (Sam's). The trial court entered judgment in favor of Sam's. We affirm.

FACTS

The actual occurrence made the basis of Guerra's suit against Sam's is disputed by the parties. Guerra claimed that when she visited a Sam's store on April 30, 1990 accompanied by her daughter, she was struck from behind by a shopping cart thrown by a Sam's employee who was not watching what he was doing. Guerra contended that she suffered injury to her back as a result of this incident. Guerra said that she reported the accident immediately to store personnel. Sam's maintained at trial that the accident never occurred, and claimed that the accident was never reported to store personnel. The jury found that Sam's did not cause a shopping cart to come into contact with Guerra, that the negligence of Sam's did not proximately cause the occurrence in question, and that Guerra should be awarded no damages.

* * * Guerra contends that the trial court erred in . . . not overruling the jury's verdict in favor of the defendant because the same was contrary to the great weight and preponderance of the evidence . . . .

* * *

In her second point of error, Guerra claims that the jury's verdict was against the great weight and preponderance of the evidence. The jury was asked three questions. Questions one and two and the jury's answers were as follows:

Question No. 1

On the occasion in question, did Wal-Mart Stores, Inc. d/b/a Sam's Wholesale Club cause a shopping cart to come into contact with the body of San Juana Guerra?

Answer "Yes" or "No."

Answer: No

Question No. 2

Did the negligence, if any, of Wal-Mart Stores, Inc. d/b/a Sam's Wholesale Club proximately cause the occurrence in question?

Answer "Yes" or "No."

Answer: No

The third question inquired about damages, to which the jury returned an answer of zero.

Guerra had the burden of proof on all three questions submitted to the jury. In reviewing a factual sufficiency point on which the complaining party had the burden of proof, we assess all the evidence and reverse for a new trial only if the challenged findings are so against the great weight and preponderance of the evidence as to be clearly wrong and manifestly unjust. *Pool v. Ford Motor Co.*, 715 S.W.2d 629, 635 (Tex. 1986); *Cain v. Bain*, 709 S.W.2d 175, 176 (Tex. 1986). The same standard applies and a reversal is proper if the jury's failure to find a fact is against the great weight and preponderance of the evidence. *Cropper v. Caterpillar Tractor Co.*, 754 S.W.2d 646, 651 (Tex. 1988). However, in evaluating great-weight points complaining of a jury's failure to find a fact, we must be mindful that the jury was not convinced by a preponderance of the evidence. *Herbert v. Herbert*, 754 S.W.2d 141, 144 (Tex. 1988). We can reverse only if a detailing of the evidence shows that the great weight of the evidence clearly supports an affirmative answer. *Id.*

A review of the evidence in this case indicates that the jury's failure to answer questions one and two in the affirmative was not against the great weight and preponderance of the evidence. Guerra's evidence at trial consisted almost entirely of her own testimony and that of her children and experts. Guerra testified that she and her daughter visited a Sam's store on April 30, 1990. She stated that a Sam's employee threw a steel shopping cart, hitting her in the back and injuring her. Guerra's daughter, Eulalia, then testified that a male Sam's employee who had been greeting incoming customers and arranging shopping carts threw a cart backwards without looking. Eulalia stated that the shopping cart hit her mother in the back. Guerra and her daughter both testified that they spoke to a Sam's representative who made a report of the incident. Finally, Guerra's experts testified that Guerra suffered serious bodily injury as a result of the April 30, 1990 incident, and that she had incurred medical bills for treatment of the injury.

In addition to the above evidence, the jury was also entitled to consider the evidence presented by Sam's, which could have suggested to the jury that the accident never occurred. Representatives of Sam's testified at length regarding the policies and procedures employed by Sam's with respect to in-store accidents. The evidence established that Sam's had specific policies requiring that records be maintained regarding such accidents and that medical assistance be offered to injured patrons. Yet, no records of Guerra's accident were located. The jury could infer from the absence of such records that no accident occurred. *See Sudduth v. Commonwealth County Mut. Ins. Co.*, 454 S.W.2d 196, 197 (Tex. 1970).

Although evidence was presented at trial tending to support the positions of both parties in this case, we are not convinced that the overwhelming weight of the evidence supported only an affirmative answer to questions one and two. Nearly all of the witnesses called by Guerra were interested witnesses, and the jury was the sole judge of the credibility of these witnesses. *E.g., Gray v. Floyd*, 783 S.W.2d 214, 216 (Tex. App.—Houston [1st Dist.] 1990, no writ); *Tatum v. Huddleston*, 711 S.W.2d 367, 369 (Tex. App.—Texarkana 1986, no writ). The jury simply chose to disbelieve these witnesses. The jury's refusal to answer questions one and two in the affirmative is not so contrary to the great weight and preponderance of the evidence as to be clearly wrong and unjust. Having found that the jury's determinations in questions one and two were not against the great weight and preponderance of the evidence, the issue of compensation addressed in question three becomes irrelevant. "It has long been the law in Texas that a finding of zero damages, even if contrary to the uncontroverted evidence, is rendered immaterial by a finding of no liability." *Ramsey v. Lucky Stores*, 853 S.W.2d 623, 635 (Tex. App.—Houston [1st Dist.] 1993, writ denied). A jury's answer is immaterial if it will not change the effect of the verdict. *Fleet v. Fleet*, 711 S.W.2d 1, 2 (Tex. 1986). Regardless of the jury's answer in question three in this case, the trial court would have been compelled to enter a take-nothing judgment against plaintiffs as a result of the jury's findings of no liability. Consequently, the issue of compensation was immaterial.

Guerra's second point of error is overruled.

* * *

The judgment of the trial court is affirmed.

Notes

1. As discussed above, the phrases "no evidence" and "conclusive evidence" are terms used to describe situations where there are no fact questions to be decided by the jury, and therefore, a judgment can be entered by a court. These phrases are used by courts to describe the *legal sufficiency* of the evidence. On the other hand the phrases "insufficient evidence" and "against the great weight and preponderance of the evidence" are used by courts to describe the overall state of the *factual sufficiency* of the evidence. Under Texas law, a trial court should submit a question to the jury for its determination when more than a scintilla of evidence, but less that enough to conclusively establish the fact, supports an affirmative answer to the fact question; but the same trial court should grant a new trial to a party who successfully establishes that jury's affirmative answer to a submitted question is either supported by "insufficient evidence" or that the jury's negative answer is "against the great weight and preponderance of the evidence". To say that there is insufficient evidence to support a particular affirmative finding of the jury, one is asserting that there is more than "no evidence" to support the jury's finding; but the jury's answer is greatly outweighed by contrary evidence. To say that the jury's negative answer is against the great weight and preponderance, one is asserting that there is not enough evidence to conclusively establish the opposite of the jury's answer, but that there is substantial more evidence of probative force for the existence of a particular fact than there is for its nonexistence. In either event—when the jury's affirmative answer to a question is supported by insufficient evidence; or when the jury's negative answer is against the great weight and preponderance of the evidence—the trial court should grant a new trial. In neither of these situations of *factual sufficiency* should a trial court take a case away from the jury and enter a judgment as he can in the case where the evidence is *legally sufficient or insufficient* evidence. These troublesome issues will be revisited in Chapters 16 and 17 of this casebook.

2. "The 'great weight and preponderance' standard is used to review a jury's negative finding in a question of fact for which the appellant carried the burden of proof at trial. * * * The proper standard of review for an appellant challenging the factual sufficiency of the evidence supporting the jury's affirmative findings on fact questions for which the appellant did not have the burden of proof is the 'insufficiency evidence' standard." *Sanchez v. Guerrero*, 885 S.W.2d 487 (Tex. App.—El Paso 1994, no writ) (citations omitted).

3. "[N]o court is free to substitute its judgment for that of the jury." *Larson v. Cactus Utility Co.*, 730 S.W.2d 640 (Tex. 1987). Neither the trial court nor appellate courts have the power to "second guess the fact finder." *State v. $11,014.00*, 820 S.W.2d 783 (Tex. 1991).

4. Assume a personal injury/products liability case. P sues D. Jury finds that (1) D was guilty of negligence which proximately caused the accident, but (2) the D's product was not defectively designed, (3) P was not guilty of contributory negligence, and [4] P sustained damages totaling 10,000,000,000.

a. The D would attack the first finding with a no evidence point or an insufficient evidence point. [P had the burden of proof and secured a favorable finding].

b. The plaintiff would attack the second finding with a matter of law point /great weight and preponderance of the evidence point. [P had the burden of proof and failed to secure a favorable finding].

c. The D would attack the third finding with matter of law/great weight points. [D had the burden of proof and failed to secure a favorable finding].

d. The D would attack the damages finding with a no evidence or [more likely] an insufficient evidence point.

5. *Dow Chemical Company v. Francis*, 46 S.W.3d 237, 241-42 (Tex. 2001): "When a party attacks the legal sufficiency of an adverse finding on an issue on which she has the burden of proof, she must demonstrate on appeal that the evidence establishes, as a matter of law, all vital facts in support of the issue. *Sterner v. Marathon Oil Co.*, 767 S.W.2d 686, 690 (Tex. 1989); Hall, *Standards of Review in Texas*, 29 ST. MARY'S L.J. 351, 481-82 (1998)." In reviewing a "matter of law" challenge, the reviewing court must first examine the record for evidence that supports the finding, while ignoring all evidence to the contrary. *Sterner*, 767 S.W.2d at 690; *Hall*, *supra*, at 482. If there is no evidence to support the finding, the reviewing court will then examine the entire record to determine if the contrary proposition is established as a matter of law. *Sterner*, 767 S.W.2d at 690; *Hall*, *supra*, at 482. The point of error should be sustained only if the contrary proposition is conclusively established. *Coucher v. Coucher*, 660 S.W.2d 55, 58 (Tex. 1983); *Hall*, *supra*, at 482. Here, Francis had the

burden of proof on her retaliation claim. *See* TEX. LAB. CODE § 451.002(c). Thus, in considering only the evidence favorable to Francis, the court of appeals did not conduct a proper "matter of law" review.

When a party attacks the factual sufficiency of an adverse finding on an issue on which she has the burden of proof, she must demonstrate on appeal that the adverse finding is against the great weight and preponderance of the evidence. *Coucher*, 660 S.W.2d at 58; *Hall, supra*, at 485. The court of appeals must consider and weigh all of the evidence, and can set aside a verdict only if the evidence is so weak or if the finding is so against the great weight and preponderance of the evidence that it is clearly wrong and unjust. *See Pool v. Ford Motor Co.*, 715 S.W.2d 629, 635 (Tex. 1986); *Hall, supra*, at 484. In doing so, the court of appeals must "detail the evidence relevant to the issue" and "state in what regard the contrary evidence greatly outweighs the evidence in support of the verdict." *Pool*, 715 S.W.2d at 635. Here, the court of appeals improperly considered only the evidence favorable to Francis' retaliation claim and did not review the evidence supporting the jury verdict. Thus, we conclude that the court of appeals did not conduct a proper factual-sufficiency review."

6. *In the Interest of M.S.*, 115 S.W.3d 534 (Tex. 2003): In this action to terminate parental rights, Strickland's trial counsel failed to file a motion for new trial, and thus failed to preserve the factual sufficiency point for review. As a result, the court of appeals refused to consider her factual sufficiency complaint. Held: Reversed and remanded to the court of appeals to determine whether counsel's failure to preserve the factual sufficiency issue was not objectively reasonable, and whether this error deprived Strickland of a fair trial. That a motion for new trial is required for appellate review of a factual sufficiency issue is something that competent trial counsel in Texas should know. And filing such a motion is not a difficult task. Counsel's failure to preserve the factual sufficiency issue may constitute ineffective assistance of counsel.

d. *Erroneous Answers During Voir Dire*

Reread *Palmer Well Services, Inc. v. Mack Trucks, infra* Chapter 10.

Notes

1. TEX. GOV'T CODE section 62.102 disqualifies a person to serve as a petit juror if he is under indictment or other legal accusation of misdemeanor or felony theft, or any other felony.

2. TEX. R. CIV. P. 230. Certain Questions Not To Be Asked. "In examining a juror, he shall not be asked a question the answer to which may show that he has been convicted of an offense which disqualifies him or that he stands charged by some legal accusation with theft or any felony." Under Rule 230, it is up to the trial court to ask the jury panel whether any of them have been convicted or are under indictment, and it is up to the attorney to use due diligence to see that this is done. The attorney, however, cannot ask the question.

3. In *Texaco v. Pennzoil Co.*, 729 S.W.2d 768 (Tex. App.—Houston [1st Dist.] 1987, writ ref'd n.r.e), *cert. denied*, 485 U.S. 994 (1988), the court addressed the question of erroneous or false answers given on voir dire as follows:

> For erroneous or false answers given on voir dire to entitle a party to a new trial, there must be a concealment by the juror. *Dunn v. Sears Roebuck & Co.*, 371 S.W.2d 731, 735 (Tex. Civ. App.—Houston 1963, writ ref'd n.r.e.). Before there can be concealment, the questions asked must call for disclosure; the questions asked must be direct and specific. *Id.*; *Roy L. Jones Truck Line v. Johnson*, 225 S.W.2d 888, 896 (Tex. Civ. App.—Galveston 1949, writ ref'd n.r.e.). A catch-all question asking "was there anything in" the juror's experience "that would cause [them] to lean one way or the other in this type of case" does not meet the requirement of specificity. 4 R. MCDONALD, TEXAS CIVIL PRACTICE IN DISTRICT & COUNTY COURTS § 11.10.3 (1983); *see also Roy L. Jones Truck Line*, 225 S.W.2d at 896.
>
> In the instant case, the question asked was not so direct or specific as to require juror Shannon to reveal the fact that his wife had lost her job in a corporate takeover. Although harm is suggested, no harm has been shown. In addition, as a matter of law, the question was insufficient to elicit the information Texaco complains it should have received. *Id.*

Texaco next alleges juror misconduct in juror Lawler's failure to answer the following questions: "Is anybody here on the panel that's left or any member of your family that's ever had any business dealings with Texaco? . . . Any business relationship with Texaco? You or your employers or members of your family?" Texaco asserts that juror misconduct occurred because juror Lawler failed to inform the court that his father-in-law was a Texaco employee.

The affidavit in support of Texaco's new trial motion states: 6. After the jury's verdict was returned, Texaco learned for the first time that the jury's presiding juror, Richard Lawler, was related by marriage to a long-time Texaco employee, Jimmie R. Paull. I interviewed Mr. Paull on December 9, 1985, and learned for the first time that he is the father of Cheryl Paull, Mr. Lawler's wife, that he and his daughter are estranged, and that he has not seen his daughter since 1977, when Mr. Lawler and his daughter were married. He has neither seen nor spoken to his son-in-law during this period and he has never seen or spoken to his two grandchildren. Attached hereto in support of these points is the affidavit of Jimmie R. Paull. 7. Juror Lawler should have divulged this information in the voir dire examination of the jury panel in response to the following question from Mr. Jamail: Is anybody here on the panel that's left or any member of your family that's ever had any business dealings with Texaco? . . . any business relationship with Texaco? You or your employers or members of your family? 8. Lawler responded but only that his employer had a "lot of business with Texaco." He did not mention his father-in-law's long-time employment. When I interviewed Mr. Lawler after the verdict and asked him about his father-in-law, he told me he did not learn his father-in-law was a Texaco employee until two months into the trial or later, and that this was the reason he did not disclose his relationship with Texaco. This relationship between Lawler and his father-in-law was relevant to Texaco's consideration of whether Juror Lawler was qualified to serve on the jury. Had Texaco been aware of this information, which would have a tendency to bias Lawler against Texaco, it would have moved to excuse Lawler for cause. Had that motion not been granted, Texaco would have used one of its peremptory [sic] challenges to excuse Lawler.

The affidavit fails as a matter of law to establish concealment. By its own wording, the affidavit establishes that juror Lawler did not know the work relationship between his father-in-law and Texaco until the trial was two months old. Failure to disclose information about which a juror had no knowledge or had forgotten at the time of voir dire does not constitute concealment. *McDonough Brothers v. Lewis*, 464 S.W.2d 457, 466 (Tex. Civ. App.—San Antonio 1971, writ ref'd n.r.e.).; *see also Childers v. Texas Employers Insurance Association*, 154 Tex. 88, 273 S.W.2d 587, 588 (1954).

e. *Jury Argument*

Read Rule 269 Texas Rules of Civil Procedure.

SOUTHWESTERN GREYHOUND LINES, INC.
v.
DICKSON
236 S.W.2d 115, 149 Tex. 599
(Tex. 1951)

Types of jury arguments, which may involve error, include:

Criticism, censure or abuse of parties or witnesses.
Abusive language and criticism in general.
Opprobrious terms and expressions.
Appeal to passion and prejudice generally.
Appeal to sympathy, generally.

Invited arguments (arguments made in reply to a prior argument of an opponent, which would otherwise be excessive or improper) are justified by similar argument or other type of "invitation" coming from the opposing side. This is so only when the relation between the argument under attack, and the alleged provocation is one of reason and fairness. Otherwise counsel might well hesitate to use even the politest criticism for fear of justifying an unrestrained reply or, on the other hand, both sides may properly elect to abandon all restraint.

The aggregate (cumulative) effect of multiple "borderline" statements, which, while not each in itself improper argument, may yet be taken to enhance the effect of those which are definitely improper, and thus show harm.

LIVING CENTERS OF TEXAS, INC.
v.
PEÑALVER
256 S.W.3d 678
(Tex. 2008)

Diana L. Faust, R. Brent Cooper, Devon J. Singh, Cooper & Scully, P.C., Dallas TX, Thomas A. Countryman, Fulbright & Jaworski L.L.P., San Antonio TX, Lori Campione Ferguson, Hanson Bridgett Marcus Vlahos & Rudy LLP, Sacramento CA, for Petitioners.
George W. Mauze II, Mauze Law Firm, San Antonio TX, for Respondents.

PER CURIAM.

Living Centers of Texas, Inc., defendant in a wrongful death suit, stipulated liability. During final argument of the trial on damages, plaintiff's counsel compared Living Centers' lawyer's attempts to minimize damages to a World War II German program in which elderly and infirm persons were used for medical experimentation and killed. Concluding that the jury argument was improper and incurable, we reverse and remand for a new trial.

Belia Peñalver moved into a nursing home in 1997. In September 2000, a nursing home employee dropped Belia, who was then 90 years old, while transferring her from a wheelchair to a bed. She died the next day from injuries suffered in the incident. Belia's sons sued Living Centers of Texas, Inc., its administrator, and its director of nursing (collectively, "Living Centers") seeking wrongful death and survivor damages.

A first jury trial resulted in judgment in favor of the Peñalvers for $356,000 actual and $362,000 punitive damages, reduced from $500,000 when the trial court applied the statutory cap on punitive damages. The court of appeals reversed and remanded for a new trial because of improperly admitted evidence of previous falls at the nursing home. Before the second trial, Living Centers stipulated that its negligence proximately caused Belia's injuries and death, so the only issue at trial was the amount of damages.

During closing argument at the second trial, the Peñalvers' counsel referred to Germany's World War II T-4 Project and defense counsel's trial conduct:

> In World War II the Germans had a project called T-Four. You probably read about it in history books.
>
> But what they did is they took all the people who they thought were inferior in society, primarily older people, impaired people, and they used them for experiments. They killed them. Over 400,000. That culture 60 years ago didn't consider the impaired and elderly valuable.
>
> Our culture has never looked at that. We went to war to stop that, the biggest war in the history of the world to stop those atrocities that were going on. And we're not at the point where we're tolerant today, as the defense would like you to be, of this wrongful death.
>
> * * *
>
> But [the defense lawyers'] job here is to convince you that the damages are insignificant to minimize the damages. How have they done that? At the very beginning in opening statement [they] said they only have two defenses, if you want to call it defense. She is old and she is impaired.

* * *

> So it really goes back to that, the initial issue, where are we as a society? Have we regressed to 1944, 1945 Germany? Have we regressed or gone ahead so far now, 60 years later now, we have a different attitude, that a wrongful death of an elderly or impaired person is not every bit as significant and has every bit as significant damages as the wrongful death of anyone else?

Living Center's counsel did not object to the argument, but attempted to counter it by arguing that "there are no Nazis in this courtroom" and "I've never been accused of being a Nazi before."

The jury awarded almost three times the actual damages awarded in the first trial. The second jury awarded actual damages of $510,000 to Belia's estate and $300,000 to each of her two sons-a total of $1,110,000. Living Centers filed a motion for new trial based, in part, on allegations that the Peñalvers' jury argument as to the T-4 Project was improper, incurable, and harmful. The trial court denied the motion for new trial.

Living Centers appealed. The court of appeals affirmed, with one justice dissenting. 217 S.W.3d 44. In its petition for review, Living Centers continues to complain of the final jury argument which criticized Living Centers' counsel and referenced Germany's World War II T-4 Project.

Error as to improper jury argument must ordinarily be preserved by a timely objection which is overruled. *Tex. Employers' Ins. Ass'n v. Haywood*, 153 Tex. 242, 266 S.W.2d 856, 858 (1954). The complaining party must not have invited or provoked the improper argument. *Standard Fire Ins. Co. v. Reese*, 584 S.W.2d 835, 839 (1979). Typically, retraction of the argument or instruction from the court can cure any probable harm, but in rare instances the probable harm or prejudice cannot be cured. In such instances the argument is incurable and complaint about the argument may be made even though objection was not timely made. *See* TEX. R. CIV. P. 324(b)(5); *Haywood*, 266 S.W.2d at 858. To prevail on a claim that improper argument was incurable, the complaining party generally must show that the argument by its nature, degree, and extent constituted such error that an instruction from the court or retraction of the argument could not remove its effects. *See Haywood*, 266 S.W.2d at 858. The test is the amount of harm from the argument:

> whether the argument, considered in its proper setting, was reasonably calculated to cause such prejudice to the opposing litigant that a withdrawal by counsel or an instruction by the court, or both, could not eliminate the probability that it resulted in an improper verdict.

Id. But jury argument that strikes at the appearance of and the actual impartiality, equality, and fairness of justice rendered by courts is incurably harmful not only because of its harm to the litigants involved, but also because of its capacity to damage the judicial system. Such argument is not subject to the general harmless error analysis.

In *Reese*, this Court discussed different types of jury argument that constitute incurable error. For example, appeals to racial prejudice adversely affect the fairness and equality of justice rendered by courts because they improperly induce consideration of a party's race to be used as a factor in the jury's decision. *See Reese*, 584 S.W.2d at 840 (*citing Haywood*, 266 S.W.2d at 858); *see also Moss v. Sanger*, 75 Tex. 321, 12 S.W. 619, 620 (1889). Unsupported, extreme, and personal attacks on opposing parties and witnesses can similarly compromise the basic premise that a trial provides impartial, equal justice. *See Reese*, 584 S.W.2d at 840 (*citing Howsley & Jacobs v. Kendall*, 376 S.W.2d 562 (Tex. 1964) and *Sw. Greyhound Lines, Inc. v. Dickson*, 149 Tex. 599, 236 S.W.2d 115 (1951)). Further, accusing the opposing party of manipulating a witness, without evidence of witness tampering, can be incurable, harmful argument. *See Howsley & Jacobs*, 376 S.W.2d at 565-66.

The serious effects of arguments not based on evidence or invited by opposing counsel, such as the one under consideration here, are recognized in our Rules of Civil Procedure. Rule 269 provides that during final arguments, "[m]ere personal criticism by counsel upon each other shall be avoided, and when indulged in shall be promptly corrected as a contempt of court." TEX. R. CIV. P. 269(e). Trial courts are not required to wait for objections before correcting improper argument, but should guard against such conduct and correct it sua sponte. TEX. R. CIV. P. 269(g).

Incurable argument is, however, rare. Not all personally critical comments concerning opposing counsel are incurable. But arguments that strike at the courts' impartiality, equality, and fairness inflict damage beyond the parties and the individual case under consideration if not corrected. Such arguments damage the judicial system itself by impairing the confidence which our citizens have in the system, and courts countenance very little tolerance of such arguments. *See Reese*, 584 S.W.2d at 840 ("The injection of new and inflammatory matters into the case through argument has in exceptional instances been regarded as incurable by an instruction . . . . [A]n affront to the court and the equality which it must portray will be dealt with harshly.").

The argument which Living Centers complains of struck at Living Centers and its trial counsel by comparing trial counsel to perpetrators of the T-4 Project atrocities. The T-4 Project was brought up only once during trial when, upon inquiry by the Peñalvers' counsel, a witness testified that he was not familiar with the program. There was no evidence that Living Centers either intended to injure or kill Belia or that Living Centers performed medical experiments on her. The extreme final argument cannot be said to have been invited by the actions of Living Centers' counsel in pointing out what the evidence clearly showed: Belia was elderly and had certain impairments that accompanied the aging process. The Peñalvers' improper comments were not inadvertent, and the jury argument was designed to incite passions of the jury and turn the jurors against defense counsel for doing what lawyers are ethically bound to do: advocate clients' interests within the bounds of law. Counsel for Living Centers was entitled to urge a smaller damages amount than the plaintiffs sought without being painted as modern-day equivalents of T-4 Project operators who experimented on and purposefully killed humans.

The argument struck at the integrity of the courts by utilizing an argument that was improper, unsupported, and uninvited. Failure to deal harshly with this type of argument can only lead to its emulation and the entire judicial system will suffer as a result.

Our analysis and conclusion is not altered because it was Living Centers' counsel who first used the term "Nazi." The right to complain of improper, incurable jury argument is not lost by counsel's attempting to respond to and reduce the effect of such argument. *See* TEX. R. CIV. P. 269(e); *Panhandle & S.F. Ry. Co. v. Huckabee*, 216 S.W. 666, 668 (Tex. Civ. App.1919).

We agree with the dissenting justice in the court of appeals: the argument complained of struck at the heart of the jury trial system, was designed to turn the jury against opposing counsel and his clients, and was incurable. The judgment of the court of appeals is reversed, and the case is remanded for a new trial.

STANDARD FIRE INSURANCE COMPANY
v.
REESE, Jr.
584 S.W.2d 835
(Tex. 1979)

Thurlow & Hennessey, Edward J. Hennessey and Randall D. Wilkins, Houston, for petitioner.
Stevens F. Mafrige and George A. Sellnau, Houston, for respondent.

POPE, JUSTICE.

The question presented by this appeal is whether plaintiff, Arthur Reese, Jr., sustained his burden to prove that a jury argument made by counsel for Standard Fire Insurance Company constituted reversible error in the absence of an objection or motion that the court instruct the jury to disregard the argument. The Industrial Accident Board had awarded Reese $1,120.00 for temporary total incapacity, $2,528.10 for permanent partial incapacity and $1,329.00 for medical expenses, a total of $4,977.10. Standard appealed, and the trial court rendered judgment for Reese on a jury verdict for the sum of $870.00 for total incapacity for the period from March 14, 1975, to June 10, 1975; medical benefits in the sum of $1,239.00, and interest in the amount of $179.91, for a total of $2,278.91. The judgment should have been for $2,288.91. Mr. Reese, the worker, appealed from that judgment, and the court of civil appeals reversed the judgment by reason of a jury argument. 567 S.W.2d 861. From our review of the whole record, we conclude that the argument by Standard's attorney was neither improper nor reversibly harmful. We reverse the judgment of the court of civil appeals and affirm the judgment of the trial court.

Counsel for Standard Fire Insurance Company made this jury argument which is the basis for the reversal by the court of civil appeals:

> But that won't make this claim valuable enough. So, we have to run in Dr. Buning. Enter Dr. Buning, April 8, 1975, approximately three and a half weeks after this incident. Dr. Buning in Spring Branch, Mr. Reese, Astrodome. He drove by a thousand doctors between the Astrodome and Spring Branch. Aren't you curious as to why he went to Dr. Buning? Aren't you curious as to why Mr. Mafrige sent him to Dr. Buning? Does not a sham or a plot evolve out of all of this? What does Buning do then? Let's send him over to old Mort, give him the old 1-6-8-9-11-15 treatment. That's good. That looks good on paper. We can pump on him for about six or eight weeks, build those medical bills up real high. The higher the medical bills, obviously he has got to be hurt if he has got all of those medical bills. It will look good in front of a jury. Does that not make itself abundantly clear to you? Does that not eat away at the credibility of this entire situation? Reese's counsel neither objected to the argument nor asked the court to give any instruction to the jury about it. Standard's trial theory and its argument was that Reese had incurred unnecessary charges for physical therapy in the amount of $1,458.00 even though the treatments were doing him no good.

Standard attacked the credibility of the worker's claim in light of the evidence that Reese resumed regular employment a short time after his initial treatment, worked full time and earned more money than he had ever earned before. Standard's counsel also argued that two doctors had examined Reese and released him as able to return to work, and those two doctors had not testified. He then argued that the evidence showed that Reese received therapy from April to June of 1975, was released from further treatments, but resumed those unnecessary treatments seven months later for the purpose of building up the amount of the medical expenses. He questioned whether Reese had any disability at all, and he argued that the decision in the case would turn upon Reese's credibility. He then continued,

> Maybe you all feel like I am rationalizing. Maybe I am. But Mr. Reese, when he tells you he is hurt and can't do this and can't do that and will never ever be the same again, maybe Mr. Reese really believes that. And if he does, then he is telling the truth. But it is not credible, folks. It is not credible when you put all of these facts together, when you put in the Mafrige-Bachynsky-Buning combination.
>
> MR. MAFRIGE: Your Honor, I object. There is no evidence of any combination and he keeps making inferences and slanderous remarks and I strenuously object. He is outside the record.
>
> THE COURT: You may reply to that on closing argument.

The argument was not improper because there was direct evidence, as well as inferences from the evidence, which supported the argument. Mr. Reese testified that he was on his job on March 14, 1975, performing his work as a cement worker. He was standing in about six inches of cement when he sustained a "pop" in his back. Another employee helped him step from the cement, and Reese's employer immediately had him taken to the Torno Medical Center that was located in Pasadena near the job site. Dr. Torno examined and treated Reese for about a month. He prescribed physical therapy treatments which Reese received for an estimated five or ten times. Dr. Torno, in turn, referred Reese to a Dr. Podniac, an orthopedic surgeon. Both of those doctors, after about six weeks, dismissed Reese as able to return to work. At that point, Reese went to see Dr. Eric Buning, whom he not previously known.

Dr. Buning's office was at that time located in Spring Branch. Reese testified that he went to see Dr. Buning because his lawyer sent him. Mr. Mafrige was his lawyer. Reese also testified that he lived in South Park near the Astrodome. When Mr. Mafrige was questioning Reese, his client, there was this exchange:

> "Q. How was it you got to Dr. Buning's office?
> "A. You sent me to Dr. Buning.
> "Q. Your lawyer did?
> "A. Yes."

Reese was hurt on Friday, March 14, 1975; he went to see his lawyer four days later. There are three pharmacy bills in evidence. They are in the name of Arthur Reese but have typed on each of them the notation, "bill Steven F. Mafrige," who was Reese's attorney.

Dr. Buning, after examining Reese, prescribed physical therapy which he detailed on a printed prescription form. The prescription that Dr. Buning signed was not on Dr. Buning's prescription form; it was on the prescription bearing the name of Mort Moriarty, L.P.T. (licensed physical therapist). Mr. Moriarty had his offices in the same building in which Dr. Buning was located. Mr. Moriarty testified that he and Dr. Buning were personal friends. Dr. Buning "would just come by and visit the office. He had time to kill," he said.

Dr. Buning wrote two different prescriptions for physical therapy. The first one was for the treatments from April 8, 1975, until June 9, when they were terminated on orders from Dr. Buning. Dr. Buning wrote a second prescription about seven months later on January 5, 1976, calling for daily treatments for two to four weeks. On that same date Reese resumed his treatments, and they continued until March 5, 1976. By that time the bill for physical therapy had grown to the amount of $1,458.00.

Dr. Buning died sometime about February, 1976, and Dr. Nicholas Bachynsky took over his office and patients. He saw Reese on March 2 and March 10, made an examination but prescribed no treatment. Dr. Bachynsky testified that he did not prescribe therapy treatments, because "I don't think it would have any benefit to him." Reese did not return to Dr. Bachynsky until November 2, 1976, and then, according to the evidence, because "The lawyer wanted him to come by for re-evaluation." Dr. Bachynsky's total charges amounted only to $50.00. He expressed the opinion that Reese suffered from pain caused by a nerve root impingement and also degenerative arthritis, that Reese did not have any symptom that could be called an objective one, that every symptom of the injury required his reliance upon the credibility of the patient, and that in his opinion, Reese had a sixty percent permanent disability. That opinion statement is the only evidence in the record of the extent of Reese's incapacity.

The jury argument about Mr. Moriarty's therapy treatments cannot be understood except in the context of this additional evidence. Mr. Moriarty testified that his billings listed twenty-one different kinds of therapy which he was capable of providing. They were numerically coded at the bottom of each statement. For example, the treatments he gave Mr. Reese were coded in this fashion, as he explained:

> "Q. Like No. 1 is hot packs. No. 6 is ultrasound. No. 8 is massage. No. 9 is electrical stimulation. No. 11 is therapeutic exercise. And No. 15
> "A. Pelvic traction.
>
> "Q. Intermittent pelvic traction, right. Now it looks to me like you gave him the 1-6-8-9-11-15 treatment every time he was there.
> "A. Because that's what was prescribed."

Standard's defense was that Reese's claim was a weak one and had almost no medical basis. Two physicians released him as able to do work, and the evidence showed that he returned to work in 1976, worked continuously as a cement worker and earned more than he had ever earned before. Standard urged that the only evidence of any incapacity rested upon Reese's own subjective statements, as Dr. Bachynsky acknowledged.

From this record, we conclude that there was direct evidence of a close relationship between Reese's attorney, Mr. Mafrige, and Dr. Buning, Morton Moriarty, and Dr. Bachynsky. Whether by cross-examination or advocacy, the relationship between witnesses and a party is properly weighed, evaluated, and tested. It is the jury's function to evaluate the evidence in that context.

Standard's argument that Reese "drove by a thousand doctors between the Astrodome and Spring Branch" to see Dr. Buning was not improper. Hyperbole has long been one of the figurative techniques of oral advocacy. Such arguments are a part of our legal heritage and language. Shakespeare wrote about "a thousand blushing apparitions" and "a thousand innocent shames," in Much Ado About Nothing. In the Tempest he wrote, "Now would I give a thousand furlongs of sea for an acre of barren ground"; in King Richard III, "My conscience hath a thousand several tongues, and every tongue brings in a several tale . . . "; in Hamlet, "And by a sleep to say we end the heartache and the thousand natural shocks that flesh is heir to"; in Hamlet again, "To be honest, as this world goes, is to be one man picked out of ten thousand," and in Romeo and Juliet, he has Juliet saying, "A thousand times good-night!" The method has often been employed to make a point.[1]

[1] "Those thousand decencies that daily flow from all her words and actions." John Milton, Paradise Lost.

"Thousands at his bidding speed, And post o'er land and ocean without rest;
They also serve who only stand and wait." Milton, On the Late Massacre in Piedmont.

The Harmless Error Rule

The harmless error rule is one that ebbs and flows. Its very existence contemplates that an error has been committed, but judicial expectations for perfect trials find presumed harm continually contending for a revival. In 1941, after an inconsistent history which saw appellate courts alternately range between a burden on the winner to prove no-harm to that of a burden on the loser to prove harm, Texas adopted Rules 434 and 503 and harmless error. Its intended effect was uncertain at first. *See Airline Motor Coaches, Inc. v. Bennett*, 144 Tex. 36, 187 S.W.2d 982 (1945); *Myers v. Thomas*, 143 Tex. 502, 186 S.W.2d 811 (1945); *Rojas v. Vuocolo*, 142 Tex. 152, 177 S.W.2d 962 (1944); *Dallas Ry. & Term. Co. v. Hendricks*, 140 Tex. 93, 166 S.W.2d 116 (1942).

Harmless error creeps back into the practice when subjective evaluations replace a more objective and structured testing of error. For that reason, decisions since 1941 have resisted the tide of presumed harm by surrounding the decision about reversibility with several tests. In the case of improper jury argument, the complainant must prove a number of things. He has the burden to prove (1) an error (2) that was not invited or provoked, (3) that was preserved by the proper trial predicate, such as an objection, a motion to instruct, or a motion

---

"But thousands die without or this or that
Die, and endow a college or a cat." Alexander Pope, Moral Essays, Epistle III.

"Man's inhumanity to man
Makes countless thousands mourn." Robert Burns, Man Was Made to Mourn.

"And homeless near a thousand homes I stood,
And near a thousand tables pined and wanted food." William Wordsworth, Guilt and Sorrow.

"Strange that a harp of thousand strings
Should keep in tune so long!" Isaac Watts, Hymns and Spiritual Songs.

"The lamps shown o'er fair women and brave men.
A thousand hearts beat happily." Lord Byron, Childe Harold's Pilgrimage.

"He left a corsair's name to other times,
Link'd with one virtue, and a thousand crimes." Lord Byron, The Corsair.

"But in vayne shee did conjure him
To depart her presence soe;
Having a thousand tongues to allure him,
And but one to bid him goe." Thomas Percy, King John and The Abbot of Canterbury.

"If winged thoughts that flit to thee a thousand in an hour." John Moultrie, Forget Thee.

"Earth with her thousand voices, praises God." Samuel Taylor Coleridge, Hymn in the Vale of Chamouni.

"Ring out old shapes of foul disease,
Ring out the narrowing lust of gold;
Ring out the thousand wars of old,
Ring in the thousand years of peace." Alfred Lord Tennyson, In Memoriam.
"There are a thousand hacking at the branches of evil to one who is striking at the root." Henry David Thoreau, Walden.

"Hundreds of people can talk for one who can think, but thousands can think for one who can see." John Ruskin, Modern Painters.

"The lowliest men would sooner face
A thousand dreadful deaths, than come
Before their loved ones in disgrace." John Davidson, A Ballad of a Coward.

"One man in a thousand, Solomon says,
Will stick more close than a brother." Rudyard Kipling, The Thousandth Man.

"For every beast of the forest is mine, and the cattle upon a thousand hills." Psalms 50:10.

Ed McMahon to Karnack, the Mystic from the East, April 4, 1979, "A thousand welcomes to you." Tonight Show, NBC.

Sadat on April 5, 1979, "Any act of terrorism against Egypt will be repaid one thousand fold."

for mistrial, and (4) was not curable by an instruction, a prompt withdrawal of the statement, or a reprimand by the judge. 3 MCDONALD, TEXAS CIVIL PRACTICE § 13.17.2 (1970). There are only rare instances of incurable harm from improper argument. The complainant has the further burden to prove (5) that the argument by its nature, degree and extent constituted reversibly harmful error. How long the argument continued, whether it was repeated or abandoned and whether there was cumulative error are proper inquiries. All of the evidence must be closely examined to determine (6) the argument's probable effect on a material finding. (7) Importantly, a reversal must come from an evaluation of the whole case, which begins with the voir dire and ends with the closing argument. The record may show that the cause is weak, strong, or very close. From all of these factors, the complainant must show that the probability that the improper argument caused harm is greater than the probability that the verdict was grounded on the proper proceedings and evidence. *Aultman v. Dallas Ry. & Term. Co.*, 152 Tex. 509, 260 S.W.2d 596 (1953). Rules 434, 503, TEX. R. CIV. P.

There was evidence in this record, partly supplied by counsel for Reese, himself, which showed the close connection between the lawyers and those treating Reese. There was no objection to the first argument about which he now complains; there was no motion to instruct as to either of the two arguments. Reese's counsel had the opportunity to reply and did so in his closing argument, and the argument was not so severe or prolonged as to amount to reversible error.

Precedents that arose prior to 1941 and hold that argument was prejudicial are unreliable, but even under the discarded rule of presumed harm, one who sat by while hearing an improper argument without objection or motion was not later heard to complain about it. *Gulf, C. & S.F. Ry. Co. v. Greenlee*, 70 Tex. 553, 8 S.W. 129, 131 (1888). A pre-1941 instance of the requirement that one promptly object and request a jury instruction to disregard the argument is *Ramirez v. Acker*, 134 Tex. 647, 138 S.W.2d 1054 (1940). In *Ramirez*, counsel argued that plaintiff's suit was one that "stinks," that plaintiff was a victim of a "scheme or design by somebody to use him," that someone ought to be indicted for filing and prosecuting the suit, that defendants were not going to pay "blood-money" in the form of a settlement as had been exacted from others. The petitioner urged that the argument left the inference that plaintiff's counsel conspired with plaintiff to bring the suit for some malicious or fraudulent purpose. *Ramirez v. Acker*, 124 S.W.2d 905, 909 (Tex. Civ. App.—Beaumont 1939), Aff'd, 134 Tex. 647, 138 S.W.2d 1054 (1940). Since that argument was held curable even under the old rule of presumed harm, the brief argument in this case, to which there was no objection, A fortiori, was curable under the rule of harmless error. In *Wade v. Texas Employers' Ins. Ass'n*, 150 Tex. 557, 244 S.W.2d 197, 199 (1951), this court noted the strength of the rule requiring timely objection to improper argument even prior to 1941 and wrote that the supreme court had gone to some length in holding that even strong appeals to prejudice become harmless when a jury is instructed to disregard them, "for which reason it is logical to require an objection and instruction."

The injection of new and inflammatory matters into the case through argument has in exceptional instances been regarded as incurable by an instruction. An appeal to racial prejudice falls into the category. *Texas Employers Ins. Ass'n v. Haywood*, 153 Tex. 242, 266 S.W.2d 856 (1954). The use in argument of the epithets, "liar," "fraud," "faker," "cheat," and "imposter" in disregard of objections that were made was harmful. *Southwestern Greyhound Lines, Inc. v. Dickson*, 149 Tex. 599, 236 S.W.2d 115 (1951). The unsupported charge of perjury was incurable. *Howsley & Jacobs v. Kendall*, 376 S.W.2d 562 (Tex. 1964). Those cases, similar to *Texas Employers' Ins. Ass'n v. McCaslin*, 159 Tex. 273, 317 S.W.2d 916 (1958), show that an affront to the court and the equality which it must portray will be dealt with harshly. However, an argument in a condemnation case that charged the condemnor with fraud was considered harmless and curable when there was no objection even when there was no support in the evidence for the argument. *City of Dallas v. Andrews*, 149 Tex. 609, 236 S.W.2d 609 (1951).

It is our opinion that Reese, by failing to object and press for an instruction at the time of the argument, waived his complaint. *Turner v. Turner*, 385 S.W.2d 230 (Tex. 1964); *Maston v. Texas Employer's Ins. Ass'n*, 160 Tex. 439, 331 S.W.2d 907, 910 (1960); *Texas & N.O.R. Co. v. Sturgeon*, 142 Tex. 222, 177 S.W.2d 264, 267 (1944).

In looking at the whole record, the state of the evidence, the strength and weakness of the case, and the verdict, we conclude that the jury carefully considered its verdict and the evidence. It made favorable findings for Reese on several issues. It found that Reese was injured, he suffered total incapacity for the period from March 14, 1975, to June 10, 1975, and the jury awarded him $1,239.00 for his medical, therapy and drug expenses covering that period. It denied all claims thereafter. During that period Dr. Buning charged $185.00 for his services, Morton Moriarty charged $972.00 for his therapy treatments, and drug bills amounted to $72.00 for a total of $1,229.00. The jury verdict drew a sharp line between the period during which, from the evidence, Reese did not and could not work and the time that he was able to work and did so.

The probabilities are that the jury would have reached its same conclusion from the evidence without regard to Standard's argument. This is the evidence from the whole record. Two physicians released Reese to return to work. There was a long gap between the time Reese stopped seeing any doctor and when he returned. He did not see Dr. Buning from May 29 to January 5. He did not see Dr. Bachynsky from June, 1976, to November. Mr. Moriarty's therapy treatments ceased during the period from June 9, 1975, to January 5, 1976. Reese went to see Dr. Bachynsky in March, 1976. It was Dr. Bachynsky, Reese's doctor, who testified that all of Reese's symptoms were only subjectively supported. It was Dr. Bachynsky who said that the therapy treatments that Dr. Buning prescribed were not beneficial and also that he never prescribed them. The jury accepted that judgment of Mr. Reese's doctor by denying the claimed medical and therapy expenses incurred after June 9, 1976, the end of the total incapacity period. Reese testified that he went back to full-time work in four or five months after his injury. He said that he worked until each job was finished, returned to his union for the next assignment, was never discharged, and earned wages as a cement worker in excess of any prior time during his life. The probabilities are that the jury believed this testimony of Reese and his own doctor and that the jury rendered a careful verdict upon the basis of the evidence.

The judgment of the court of civil appeals is reversed and that of the trial court is affirmed.

STEAKLEY, JUSTICE, dissenting.

I am dismayed by the action of the Court in reversing the judgment of the Court of Civil Appeals by means of the holding that the jury argument here in question "was neither improper nor reversibly harmful." We ought to confront more positively the particular seriousness in jury argument of attacks upon the professional ethics and integrity of opposing counsel. In my view, and as held by the unanimous Court of Civil Appeals, 567 S.W.2d 861, the jury arguments were improper, without support in the evidence and by their very nature incurable.

* * *

Notes

1. In *Otis Elevator Co. v. Wood*, 436 S.W.2d 324 (Tex. 1968) the Supreme Court succinctly stated the Texas law concerning improper jury argument in the following language:

> Otis has points calling for a remand of the cause because of the jury argument of plaintiffs' counsel. In most instances, the objections of defendant's counsel were sustained and would not require a remand, and it would require an undue lengthening of this opinion to set them out. The substance of one of the points, however, is as follows: During the argument, counsel referred several times to the fact that Mrs. Wood had been required to have her breast removed in order to combat the effect of cancer. He strongly intimated that the cancer was caused by the escalator accident. There was no evidence to this effect in the record. The first two times counsel referred to the breast surgery, no objection was made. The third reference to the surgery was objected to by opposing counsel and a jury instruction to disregard was requested. The following occurred: 'THE COURT: Well, I'll instruct Mr. Dunham to stay in the evidence and argue the evidence. 'MR. DUNHAM, JR.: We're trying to do exactly that, Your Honor. 'THE COURT: Well, you do it.' Counsel resumed his argument with another point.
>
> Improper jury arguments are usually referred to as one of two types: 'curable' or 'incurable.' A jury argument is 'curable' when the harmful effect of the argument can be eliminated by a trial judge's instruction to the jury to disregard what they have just heard. The error is 'cured' and rendered harmless by the instruction. On the other hand, an argument may be so inflammatory that its harmfulness could not be eliminated by an instruction to the jury to disregard it. The prejudicial nature of the argument is so acute that it is 'incurable.'
>
> If the argument is of a 'curable' nature, an objection to it must be promptly made and an instruction requested or the error is waived. But if the argument is 'incurable,' the failure to object does not

result in a waiver. The reasoning is that 'counsel making the argument is the offender so the law will not require opposing counsel to take a chance on prejudicing his cause with the jury by making the objection.' *Smerke v. Office Equipment Co.*, 138 Tex. 236, 158 S.W.2d 302 (Tex. Com. App. 1941).

We have concluded that the argument complained of was improper, but that its prejudicial effect was curable by an instruction to disregard. Otis failed to object in the first two instances in which the argument was made; and as to those instances, the error was waived. The third time the same argument was made Otis objected. It is at least doubtful that the instructions given were clearly understood by the jury. The trial court should have been less equivocal in instructing Mrs. Wood's counsel to confine his argument to injuries that had support in the record. The question arises whether the instruction, by possibly leaving the jury with the impression that the trial judge himself did not think counsel was arguing outside the record, was 'calculated to cause and probably did cause the rendition of an improper judgment . . . .' *See* Rules 434 and 503, Texas Rules of Civil Procedure.

We have concluded that the inference that the trial judge regarded the argument as proper was not strong enough to constitute harmful error. The trial judge did not overrule Otis' objection, and his admonition to counsel to argue the evidence is susceptible to the interpretation that he thought counsel had not been doing so. We do not regard the court's ruling or instructions as reversible error.

2. The concurring opinion of then JUSTICE GONZALEZ [now on the Supreme Court] of the Thirteenth Court of Appeals in the case of *Ford Motor Co. v. Nowak*, 638 S.W.2d 582 (Tex. App.—Corpus Christi 1982, writ ref'd n.r.e.) is instructive on the scope of permissible jury argument.

The majority recognizes that there are rare instances of incurable harm from improper jury argument. This Court, in *Hartford Accident and Indemnity Co. v. Thurmond*, 527 S.W.2d 180, 193 (Tex. Civ. App.—Corpus Christi 1975, writ ref'd n.r.e.), explained the distinction between curable and incurable jury arguments as follows: "Improper jury arguments are usually referred to as one of two types 'curable' or 'incurable.' A jury argument is curable when the harmful effect of the argument can be eliminated by a trial judge's instruction to the jury to disregard what they have just heard. The error is cured and rendered harmless by the instruction. On the other hand, an argument may be so inflammatory that its harmfulness could not be eliminated by an objection or an instruction to the jury to disregard it. The prejudicial nature of the argument is so acute that it is incurable."

Therefore, if an improper jury argument is so prejudicial that its harmful effect on the jury cannot be cured by an instruction to disregard it, the argument is incurable and no objection is necessary to preserve the error.

The jury argument made by the District Attorney, who was employed as local counsel for appellees, is as follows: ". . . You see the Frank Nowaks of this world and I live with these people and I know them and if I use terms that may offend some of you it is because I use them with love and they, I hope, love me back. Czechs, Bohemians, I can do it, oil field trash, oil field people, but since I am with them I use those terms they know that I do not mean anything offensive towards them, but Frank is a little man sitting out there on Allenhurst Road. You heard his deposition. He certainly is not any college professor and he certainly is not able to take on the people of Ford. You talk about David and Goliath, Frank Nowak has no chance against Ford Motor Company. His resources, mental ability and everything else is just like a midget or a flea climbing up an elephant . . . ."

In discussing the difference between burden of proof in a civil case and in a criminal case, the appellees' attorney went on to state: ". . . He didn't tell you that they [Ford] had hired a million dollar Watergate lawyer to represent them against a country prosecutor like me and he didn't tell you that they had to prove that beyond a reasonable doubt. In this case, and in the Court's charge Frank Nowak has to prove his case to you by a preponderance of the evidence, 51% or the greater weight of the believable evidence that you have heard. They tried to mislead you there and then they attacked the first little guy on the stand, Bob Taylor. They attacked Nubbins Chambless, the guy that went out and made the movie. They attacked, of course, Dr. Reed, then yesterday I thought was the crowning blow was Scott King. That was reprehensible and shows the arrogance, the complete condescending attitude that Ford has towards you, towards this Court, towards us and towards Frank Nowak. They start being condescending to you in saying, you may not be able to understand, we're going to try to make it as simple so you poor people can understand, and it has been that way throughout this trial. We are the great Ford Motor Company. We're going to send these lawyers down here from Houston and fool those folks down there in the country . . . ." Regarding Ford's engineers, he said: "The work that Cannon did as opposes to this little engineer over here, with his tailor made suit and his Italian shoes, ...

* * *

* * * Then they jump on little Scott King [plaintiff's witness], well, I have known him as long as I have known some of you people, they jump on him, and they come out with some ridiculous story, if that doesn't destroy him and if you believe anything that Carr [Ford's expert witness] says after those two instances, then you believe in the tooth fairy, . . . If you pull musical strings, Carr will dance to any tune that Ford sings, he is completely their man . . . ."

In discussing punitive damages with the jury, the attorney said: ". . . Ladies and Gentlemen, in this area it is hard because we are dealing with such a large sum of money to you and I, it is peanuts to Ford."

As correctly noted by the majority, the function of the jury was to impartially balance the product's utility against the likelihood of and the gravity of injury from its use. With the district attorney of a small county fanning the fires of regional prejudice and passion against "big bad" corporation with Watergate lawyers and engineers wearing tailor made suits and Italian shoes, the jury was incapable, as a matter of law, to properly carry its function.

The masterful jury argument also contained continuous references to matters outside the record and vouched for the credibility of the appellees' witnesses, and, therefore, in my opinion, was improper. Since I believe that the issue of Ford's liability was close, I find it ludicrous to say that this argument did not have an effect on the jury's verdict.

I do not expect perfect trials. This is why we have the harmless error rule. I also believe that some appeals to a juror's bias and prejudice are inevitable and a necessary part of our adversary system of justice. I am also aware that cases have rarely been reversed because of unobjected to jury arguments. However, in the context of this case, the argument as a whole was improper and could not have been cured by an instruction. It was so prejudicial that it was reasonably calculated to cause and probably did cause the rendition of an improper judgment. Rule 434, TEX. R. CIV. P. (1976).

3. Jury argument are to be confined to the evidence and reasonable inferences which may be drawn from the evidence. What constitutes a reasonable inference is, of course, a question of law. For example, in *Standard Fire Ins. Co. v. Reese*, 584 S.W.2d 835 (Tex. 1979), the Court found no error in an argument that the plaintiff had driven "by a thousand doctors between the Astrodome and Spring Branch" when the evidence was silent on the number of doctors between the plaintiff's treating physician and the plaintiff's residence. The Court viewed this as mere hyperbole, rather than argument outside the scope of the evidence. More recently, in *Gorman v. Life Ins. Co. of North America*, 859 S.W.2d 383 (Tex. App.—Houston [1st Dist.] 1993, no writ) the court discussed in some detail a point of error complaining that a jury argument had gone beyond a reasonable inference from the evidence. The court stated:

> In cross-point two, LINA asserts that the jury answered the travel and sojourn question in favor of the plaintiffs because the argument of appellants included incurable jury argument. To obtain reversal of a judgment on the basis of improper jury argument, an appellant must prove (1) an error, (2) that was not invited or provoked, (3) that was preserved by the proper trial predicate, such as an objection, a motion to instruct, or a motion for mistrial, (4) that was not curable by an instruction, by a prompt withdrawal of the statement, or by a reprimand by the judge, and (5) the argument by its nature, degree, and extent, constituted reversibly harmful error. *Standard Fire Ins. Co. v. Reese*, 584 S.W.2d 835, 839-40 (Tex. 1979). The reviewing court must determine if the probability that the improper argument caused harm is greater than the probability that the verdict was based upon proper proceedings and evidence. *Id.* at 839-40. The improper jury argument must be evaluated in light of the whole case, beginning with voir dire and ending with closing argument. *Luna v. North Star Dodge Sales, Inc.*, 667 S.W.2d 115, 120 (Tex. 1984).
>
> LINA notes that the argument of appellants included accusations of "bold-faced lies," "misrepresentation and concealment, lies and deceit," "efforts to tailor . . . testimony," and efforts "to block the

evidence from coming in" by agents of LINA. LINA also points to appellants' argument that an affirmative finding in regard to their claims was necessary for the "widows" of this state, and that it was further necessary for the jury to leave a "legacy" for and send a "message" to Amanda Gorman that would demonstrate that her father was not guilty of cheating on his employer.

LINA's objections to this argument were sustained, but its motions for mistrial were denied. LINA did not request an instruction to the jury to disregard the argument. LINA claims that the jury's affirmative finding to special issue number one was motivated by sympathy, passion, and prejudice brought about by the impermissible jury argument and that the argument was incurable by instruction.

Our review of the record shows that, shortly after the accident, Thornton, a Tenneco supervisor, conducted an investigation. Thornton talked with many of the people who were at the seminar with Gorman on the day of his death, and with people who had been with Gorman at the afternoon meeting at the Tenneco building. Most of these witnesses stated that Gorman expressed an intention to return to the seminar. The results of Thornton's investigation were turned over to Nitsch, corporate counsel for Tenneco. Nitsch also conducted his own investigation and talked to most of the same people as Thornton.

The record shows that Tenneco directed a letter to Mrs. Gorman's counsel that stated, contrary to what the witnesses had told Thornton: "There was no indication that Mr. Gorman was traveling on company business at the time of his accident . . . . Further, it appears that Mr. Gorman left work early for personal reasons during the afternoon of August 4, 1982."

A few weeks later, Tenneco forwarded the appellants' claim form to LINA. Tenneco did not furnish LINA with the results of its investigation or with the names of the witnesses who had stated that Dale Gorman told them he was returning to the seminar.

The jury also heard evidence that Tenneco responded to appellant's interrogatories over a year after the investigations by stating that "no information or evidence has been discovered or produced to Tenneco, Inc. indicating that Mr. Gorman was in the course and scope of his employment at the time of his automobile accident" and that "there is no indication that Mr. Gorman was returning to the training class in the U.S. Homes Building at the time of his accident," and that "there was conversation indicating that he may have been on his way home at the time of the accident and his secretaries were not advised of his intention to return to the training class."

Based on the foregoing, counsel for appellants accused Tenneco of "bald-faced lies," "misrepresentation and concealment, lies and deceit," and efforts "to block the evidence." Counsel may properly argue reasonable inferences from the evidence. *See Reese*, 584 S.W.2d at 837. Whether by cross-examination or advocacy, the jury may be encouraged to weigh, evaluate, and test the evidence before it. *Id.* at 838. Our review of the entire record reveals ample evidence from which the jury could conclude that the corporate representative for Tenneco engaged in misrepresentation of the facts or concealment of the evidence. The jury argument was not improper.

4. *Phillips v. Bramlett*, 288 S.W.3d 876 (Tex. 2009): During final argument, in this medical malpractice case, plaintiffs' counsel stated: "For years, in this very conservative community, juries have been very liberal with the doctors, very liberal. What I mean is: Their verdicts didn't send much of a message at all." The doctor's counsel immediately objected with the following: "Judge, I object to any testimony about the propriety of other trials and the verdicts reached by other juries in Lubbock." The trial court responded: "This is his argument, and it is not testimony." The doctor's counsel did not offer any further explanation of his objection, and plaintiffs' counsel thereafter continued to argue that the jury needed to send a message to the doctors of Lubbock, without further objection. ***Held***: Any error in the jury argument was not preserved, because the trial court's response indicated that it did not understand the objection, and counsel made no further attempt to clarify the court's understanding, or obtain a ruling on his objection. The argument was not fundamental error. Incurable argument is that which strikes at the very core of the judicial process. The party claiming incurable harm must persuade the court that, based on the record as a whole, the offensive argument was so extreme that a juror of ordinary intelligence could have been persuaded by that argument to agree to a verdict contrary to that to which he would have agreed but for such argument. A finding of incurable harm typically involved unsubstantiated attacks on the integrity or veracity of a party or counsel, appeals to racial prejudice, or the like. Counsel's

plea to send a message to the doctors was not of this same class of impropriety, and, considering the record as a whole, not so extreme as to be incapable of cure.

TEXAS EMPLOYERS' INS. ASS'N
v.
GUERRERO
800 S.W.2d 859
(Tex. App.—San Antonio 1990, writ denied)

W. Wendell Hall, Xavier Rodriguez, Fulbright & Jaworski, San Antonio, for appellant.
Catherine M. Stone, Watkins & Brock, Timothy Patton, Pasqual & Pozza, San Antonio, for appellee.

PEEPLES, JUSTICE.

Appellee's motion for rehearing is denied. Our previous opinion is withdrawn and replaced by the following.

Texas Employers' Insurance Association (TEIA) appeals from a judgment rendered on a jury verdict awarding plaintiff Roman Guerrero worker's compensation benefits for total and permanent disability. TEIA's complaints fall into three categories: . . . (3) jury argument. We reverse and remand for a new trial.

The evidence, considered favorably to the verdict, shows that on January 16, 1982, while working for TEIA's insured, H.G. Farms, Guerrero fell from his tractor, landing on his rear and injuring his tailbone. The employer sent him to Dr. Kimmel, who diagnosed a chipped coccyx. For three months Dr. Kimmel treated Guerrero and TEIA paid workers' compensation benefits and medical expenses. On April 15, 1982, Guerrero returned to work, and he continued to work for H.G. Farms until the company closed in October 1984. On January 19, 1985—three years after the January 1982 injury—Guerrero saw Dr. Rios, who diagnosed a herniated lumbar disc and operated four months later.

* * *

JURY ARGUMENT

TEIA complains that Guerrero's counsel made an appeal for ethnic unity in his closing jury argument. The record shows that eleven of the twelve jurors had Spanish surnames, as did Guerrero, his trial attorney, and his treating doctor, Dr. Rios. The challenged argument reads as follows (emphasis added):

MR. BARRIENTOS (Guerrero's counsel): I am tickled to death to be here and I will represent him and any man like him in Zavala, Maverick, Dimmit, Cameron, any county in the State of Texas any time. Octavio Paz, a well-known author said one time, and I will quote him and I already translated it. He said, "Things that unite us far exceed those things that divide us." You apply that to evidence. The things, the preponderance of the evidence, that unite in favor of Mr. Guerrero, far exceed those inconsistencies, the legal problems. He is not a perfect man, neither is his medical. But heck, he went back to work after he got cut, things of this nature. The things that unite us, exceed those that divide us. There is a time to be united. Right now is a time to be united. An example is politics. We don't have to agree with all the candidates, with the same ones. But by golly there comes a time when we have got to stick together as a community. We have to stick together as a jury of peers of a man to pass judgment and help that person if he is entitled to [sic] under the evidence. MR. KURTH (TEIA's counsel): Your Honor, this is getting a little inflammatory in asking the jury to take that position—MR. BARRIENTOS: No, No. I didn't ask them, sir, I said, We. I think that is proper. THE COURT: Well, you have got two minutes. MR. BARRIENTOS: Thank you, your Honor. Because if one is united, one has hope. And with hope, one can live. He still has a lot of years to live. And it is all going to depend on you.

TEIA contends that this argument was a subtle but nonetheless real request for the jury to be united and on Guerrero's side for ethnic reasons. Guerrero's appellate counsel defends the argument by characterizing it as a request that the jury view Guerrero's case as more united by consistencies than divided by legal technicalities. Counsel's brief then concludes that there is nothing inflammatory or incurable about the argument. The quoted remarks were made three minutes before counsel finished his closing argument and the jury retired to deliberate.

Appeals to racial prejudice are of course prohibited. *Standard Fire Ins. Co. v. Reese*, 584 S.W.2d 835, 840 (Tex. 1979); *Texas Employers' Ins. Ass'n v. Haywood*, 153 Tex. 242, 266 S.W.2d 856 (1954). They are "universally condemned." *See* Annotation, Statement by Counsel Relating to Race, Nationality, or Religion in Civil Action as Prejudicial, 99 A.L.R. 2D 1249, 1254 (1965). No one suggests that appeals to ethnic prejudice should be treated differently from racial ones.

We think the argument was a request for ethnic solidarity that cannot be plausibly explained away as a suggestion that the jury simply remember the things that "unite" Guerrero's case. Counsel said that the things that unite "us" exceed the things that divide "us," and then said, "There is a time to be united. Right now is a time to be united." The argument did more than simply say, "In this case the evidence for Mr. Guerrero is united," which counsel now urges was his true meaning. Words such as "By golly, there comes a time when we have got to stick together as a community" cannot be excused as simply a declaration that Guerrero's case was more unified than divided. A realistic assessment of the argument in context leads to the inescapable conclusion that an appeal for ethnic unity was made. We cannot accept any suggestion that such ethnic pleas are permissible when they are dressed up and mingled with advice that the jury should follow the evidence. The argument was a forbidden ethnic plea. We must therefore decide whether it constitutes reversible error.

While most improper jury arguments can be cured by objection and instruction to disregard, appeals to racial prejudice are one of the exceptional kinds of argument that are considered incurable. *See Standard Fire Ins. Co. v. Reese*, 584 S.W.2d at 840. As we read *Reese*, an appeal to racial prejudice—as opposed to the mere incidental mention of race—constitutes reversible error even if no objection was made. While the court in 1954 in *Haywood* had evaluated a racial argument's harmful impact after a review of the entire record, *Reese* held in 1979 that such arguments are "exceptional," and unlike other arguments that require an objection and are curable by an instruction to disregard, they are incurable and reversibly harmful. In most situations, said the court, an instruction to disregard will cure the prejudice and make it harmless:

In [an earlier case], this court noted the strength of the rule requiring timely objection to improper argument even prior to 1941 and wrote that the supreme court had gone to some length in holding that even strong appeals to prejudice become harmless when a jury is instructed to disregard them, "for which reason it is logical to require an objection and instruction." *Id.* at 840 (emphasis added). But in rare instances—such as the injection of racial prejudice into the case—an instruction will not cure the harm: The injection of new and inflammatory matters into the case through argument has in exceptional instances been regarded as incurable by an instruction. An appeal to racial prejudice falls into the category. [Citation omitted]. The use in argument of the epithets, "liar," "fraud," "faker," "cheat," and "imposter" in disregard of objections that were made was harmful. [Citation omitted]. The unsupported charge of perjury was incurable. [Citation omitted]. Those cases . . . show that an affront to the court and the equality which it must portray will be dealt with harshly. *Id.* (emphasis added).

According to the dissent, "incurable" simply means "no objection necessary," and incurable arguments will not require reversal if the appellate court considers them harmless. Clearly an incurable argument does not require an objection, but to go further and hold that an argument can be incurable and yet harmless is a contradiction in terms. The dissent's view cannot be squared with the passage quoted above, in which the *Reese* court used the terms "incurable" and "harmful" almost interchangeably. Other language in *Reese* makes clear that "cure" refers to harm and not only to preservation of error, as the dissent urges. The *Reese* court said there are "rare instances of incurable harm from improper argument," *id.* at 839 (emphasis added), and a later passage refers to an argument that was considered "harmless and curable." *Id.* at 840. The portion of the *Reese* opinion that discusses how a court should assess harmfulness applies to the "unexceptional" mass of cases in which harm must be shown based on the entire record.

Reese's equation of "incurable" with "harmful" is consistent with the supreme court's earlier statements that the notion of "cure" refers to removing the argument's harmful effect. The court said so at great length in *Otis Elevator Co. v. Wood*, 436 S.W.2d 324, 333 (Tex. 1968) (emphasis added): Improper jury arguments are usually referred to as one of two types: "curable" or "incurable." A jury argument is "curable " when the harmful effect of the argument can be eliminated by a trial judge's instruction to the jury to disregard what they have just heard. The error is "cured" and rendered harmless by the instruction. On the other hand, an argument may be so inflammatory that its harmfulness could not be eliminated by an instruction to the jury to disregard it. The prejudicial nature of the argument is so acute that it is "incurable." If the argument is of a "curable" nature, an objection to it must be promptly made and an instruction requested or the error is waived. But if the argument is "incurable," the failure to object does not result in a waiver . . . . We have concluded that the argument complained of was improper, but that its prejudicial effect was curable by an instruction to disregard. Later cases have continued to equate the terms "incurable" and "harmful," holding that the evil that cannot be "cured" is the harmful, prejudicial nature of the argument. *See, e.g., Gannett Outdoor Co. v. Kubeczka*, 710 S.W.2d 79, 86 (Tex. App.—Houston [14th Dist.] 1986, no writ); *American Home Assur. Co. v. Coronado*, 628 S.W.2d 818, 823-24 (Tex. App.—Amarillo 1981, writ ref'd n.r.e.); *Houston Lighting & Power Co. v. Fisher*, 559 S.W.2d 682, 685 (Tex. Civ. App.—Houston [14th Dist.] 1977, writ ref'd n.r.e.). We hold that incurable does not mean simply that no objection need be made; it also means that the argument's harmfulness, its reversible impact, cannot be cured or corrected by an instruction.

It is true that the veiled and subtle ethnic references in this case are not nearly so explicit and brazen as those in *Texas Employers' Ins. Ass'n v. Haywood*, 153 Tex. 242, 266 S.W.2d 856 (1954), but we cannot affirm the judgment on that basis. "The statement, to be objectionable, may be indirect or implied, as well as direct or express . . . ." Annotation, Statement by Counsel Relating to Race, Nationality, or Religion in Civil Action as Prejudicial, 99 A.L.R.2D 1249, 1254-55 (1965). The law should not stoop to evaluating subtle distinctions such as whether an argument was too crude and revolting, or on the other hand sufficiently slick and artful to pass muster. To permit the sophisticated ethnic plea while condemning those that are open and unabashed would simply reward counsel for ingenuity in packaging. Inevitably, lawyers representing their clients zealously within the bounds of the law would test the limits and fine-tune their arguments to avoid being too explicit. Courts would be asked to label some arguments permissible and uphold them with a wink when everyone knew that an ethnic appeal had been made. That course would demean the law and perhaps deepen the divisions from which society already suffers.

The *Reese* court condemned such appeals to prejudice as "exceptional" and as "an affront to the court and the equality which it must portray." Such arguments, the court said, "will be dealt with harshly." 584 S.W.2d at 840. We think there are compelling reasons for *Reese's* harsh, incurable-error approach. When a racial or ethnic appeal is made, the dispute is no longer confined to the litigants; there has been an attack on the social glue that helps bind society together. *Reese* characterized it as an affront to the court. The offense is against society, and it makes no difference whether the victimized-litigant has shown harm. Lawyers have no right to undermine the ethnic harmony of society simply to win a lawsuit.

The dissent's reversible-error approach would do nothing to discourage the well-packaged ethnic argument. It would unwittingly permit lawyers to craft subtle ethnic arguments, thereby putting the burden on the opposing attorney to object and seek an instruction to disregard. Because an instruction could cure the harm—and failure to seek an instruction would waive any error—the offending lawyer would have almost nothing to lose. Ethnic arguments would not cause reversal unless the victimized attorney made an objection, sought an instruction to disregard, and obtained an appellate ruling that the argument was reasonably calculated to cause and probably did cause rendition of an improper judgment. Presumably, under the dissent's view, the victimized attorney would also have to make a post-verdict record to establish the actual ethnic makeup of the jury in order to establish harm.

If we were to affirm the judgment before us, we would establish a precedent permitting calculated, subtle racial or ethnic arguments by all litigants in all types of cases—personal injury, family law, commercial—provided the arguments were properly dressed up and disguised. Such a decision would insulate appeals for "unity" when minority litigants found themselves in court before juries in other parts of this state. That is a real and frightening prospect in this nation of immigrants. All litigants—anglo, black, hispanic, native American, oriental, and all others, including governmental and business entities—should feel free to litigate their cases before juries in all 254 counties without facing state-of-the-art ethnic pleas in closing argument. Such arguments are forbidden, and it matters not whether counsel suggests—depending upon the venue—that the jury reward or penalize a litigant for belonging or not belonging to a racial or ethnic group. *Angelina Casualty Co. v. Ryan*, 282 S.W.2d 310, 313 (Tex. Civ. App.—Galveston 1955, writ ref'd n.r.e.); *Cooke-Teague Motor Co. v. Johnson*, 50 S.W.2d 399, 401 (Tex. Civ. App.—Fort Worth 1932, no writ); Annotation, *supra*, 99 A.L.R.2d at 1255 ("a statement calculated to create bias in favor of a litigant may be as prejudicial as one calculated to create prejudice against him") (emphasis added).

The Texas courts have consistently condemned jury arguments based on grounds of race, ethnicity, religion, and national origin. In the last twenty-five years such tactics have almost vanished, at least in the reported decisions. We think the scarcity of such arguments in recent years, and the consistent condemnation of them by our appellate courts, indicates that society considers them utterly beyond the pale. Recently adopted Canon 3A(9) of the Code of Judicial Conduct further demonstrates our legal system's commitment to prejudice-free trials:

A judge shall perform judicial duties without bias or prejudice. A judge shall not, in the performance of judicial duties, manifest bias or prejudice by words or conduct and shall not knowingly permit staff, court officials and others subject to the judge's direction and control to do so. A judge shall require lawyers in proceedings before the court to refrain from manifesting, by words or conduct, bias or prejudice based on race, sex, religion or national origin against parties, counsel or others.

We hold that incurable reversible error occurs whenever any attorney suggests, either openly or with subtlety and finesse, that a jury feel solidarity with or animus toward a litigant or a witness because of race or ethnicity. Because such a jury argument was made in the court below, we reverse the judgment and remand the cause for a new trial. We stress that our holding does not encompass incidental references to the race of parties and witnesses; instead, we deal here with an intentional appeal for a verdict on the basis of ethnicity.

TEIA also complains that plaintiff's counsel argued that defense counsel had "lied" to the jury. Such an argument is clearly improper; Reese arguably placed the epithets "liar," "fraud," "faker," "cheat," and "imposter" in the same category of rare incurable arguments as appeals to racial prejudice. *See* 584 S.W.2d at 840. Because this case must be retried for other reasons, we simply call attention to the supreme court's strong and express disapproval of such terminology.

IV. TRIAL COURT'S DUTY TO SUPPRESS IMPROPER JURY ARGUMENT.

We also take this opportunity to emphasize the responsibilities of trial judges when improper jury argument occurs. Under *Reese* many arguments are considered curable and harmless. But that does not mean that they are proper or that the trial court should permit them. *Reese* did not suggest in the slightest that trial courts should adopt a passive "anything goes" attitude toward improper jury argument. *Reese* simply outlined the reversible error burden that appellants face in the appellate court when they complain of jury argument.

Rule 269 commands courts to correct improper argument sua sponte: Rule 269. Argument

* * *

(e) Arguments on the facts should be addressed to the jury, when one is impaneled in a case that is being tried, under the supervision of the court. Counsel shall be required to confine the argument strictly to the evidence and to the arguments of opposing counsel. Mere personal criticism by counsel upon each other shall be avoided, and when indulged in shall be promptly corrected as a contempt of court. (f) Side-bar remarks, and remarks by counsel of one side, not addressed to the court, while the counsel on the other side is examining a witness or arguing any question to the court, or addressing the jury, will be rigidly repressed by the court. (g) The court will not be required to wait for objections to be made when the rules as to arguments are violated; but should they not be noticed and corrected by the court, opposing counsel may ask leave of the court to rise and present his point of objection. But the court shall protect counsel from any unnecessary interruption made on frivolous and unimportant grounds. TEX. R. CIV. P. 269 (emphasis added). These portions of rule 269 have been the law in Texas since 1892 with no change in wording.

Three years before the above-quoted rules were adopted, the supreme court underscored the duty of trial judges to police jury argument. In an 1889 case, in which counsel flagrantly criticized the adverse parties for being Jewish, the supreme court condemned the argument and reminded trial judges of their responsibilities in the strongest language: Cases ought to be tried in a court of justice upon the facts proved; and whether a party be Jew or gentile, white or black, is a matter of indifference. The course pursued in this case was one that no court of justice ought for a moment to tolerate; and it certainly must be true that the judge who tried this cause did not fully understand the language of counsel, or he would not have permitted it,—would have rebuked it, and ought to have punished its author. *Moss v. Sanger*, 75 Tex. 321, 12 S.W. 619, 620 (1889) (emphasis added).

In keeping with these rules, court decisions have consistently urged trial judges not to take a laissez-faire approach. We note the following words of a unanimous supreme court in 1954: We realize that in the course of a hotly contested trial lawyers are apt, even prone, to "pull off the gloves"; but lawyers are officers of the court and proper and ethical conduct requires that there be limitations on the extent to which counsel may go in the injection of prejudicial and inadmissible matters, whether by way of cross-examination of witnesses or by way of jury argument. When these limits are transgressed a trial ceases to be a test of right and wrong by standards of law in a court of justice and becomes a "catch-as-catch-can, no-holds-barred" spectacle not unlike a modern wrestling match. It is not only the province but the duty of the trial judge, acting on his own volition if necessary, to prevent any such deterioration of judicial dignity. *Texas Employers' Ins. Ass'n v. Haywood*, 266 S.W.2d at 859-60 (emphasis added). In view of these authorities, it cannot be said that this decision imposes a new responsibility on trial judges. The trial court's duty to police jury argument sua sponte has existed in Texas for 100 years.

We wholeheartedly reaffirm the words of our own court in *Motley v. Lawrence*, 283 S.W. 699, 702-703 (Tex. Civ. App.—San Antonio 1926, writ dism'd): We copy these rules [the predecessors to present rule 269] for the purpose, too, of emphasizing to the trial courts their duty to protect litigants and witnesses and parties who are forced against their will in court trials from unnecessary abuse at the hands of enthusiastic and too energetic counsel. There are many, yes, the great majority of trial judges, who control their courts and rebuke counsel who indulge in such practices, as the rules of court require, without waiting for opposite counsel to arise and stop the proceedings to present his objections. So it is the duty of a watchful trial judge to quickly act in such cases.

* * *

District courts are charged with a high duty in respect to trials before them. It is their duty to protect their courts from the contempt of counsel who flagrantly violate the rules of court, and, if necessary, to do so they have the full power to punish for contempt. The time is ripe for the enforcement of law and order and due respect for constituted authority. Trials in courts must proceed in an orderly way and command respect, so that they shall mean something, not only to those litigating in the courts, but to mankind.

The judgment is reversed and the cause is remanded for a new trial.

BIERY, J., dissenting [opinion omitted].

STATE OF TEXAS
v.
BROOKS

432 S.W.2d 188
(Tex. Civ. App.—Waco 1968, writ ref'd n.r.e.)

Crawford C. Martin, Atty. Gen., Austin, Woodrow Curtis, Asst. Atty. Gen., for appellant.
Hugh D. Reed, Jr., Fairfield, W. A. Keils, Jr., Teague, for appellees.

MCDONALD, CHIEF JUSTICE.

This is a condemnation case wherein the State of Texas condemned an approximately 17-acre strip through the middle of a 160 acre tract belonging to the Brooks'. After the taking, a remainder of approximately 143 acres was left consisting of two tracts: one approximately 38 acres, and the other, approximately 105 acres. Trial to a jury resulted in a verdict of $3,770.10 for the land taken; a value of $32,229.90 of the remainder before the taking; and a value of $22,017.10 of the remainder, after the taking. The trial court rendered judgment on the verdict for defendants for $11,603.90 ($13,982.90 less $2379.00 deposited by the State after award by the Commissioners).

Plaintiff appeals on five points, contending:

1) Numerous prejudicial, harmful, abusive, inflammatory remarks and misstatements, made by counsel for defendants, prejudiced the rights of the State.

2) There is no evidence to support the jury answers of $22,017, as the value of the remainder after the taking.

Plaintiff lists some 37 statements made by counsel for defendants, either during the trial, on voir dire examination of the jury panel, or from oral argument, which it contends were improper. Plaintiff contends these remarks, either individually or cumulatively, prejudiced the State's rights so that a new trial should be required . While it is not feasible to detail all of the complained of statements, we have considered the record as a whole and have concluded that none present reversible error under Rule 434 Texas Rules of Civil Procedure. Some of the complained of statements were not objected to; some were objected to, and the trial court sustained objections; and some of the complained of jury argument was invited.

One matter complained of by plaintiff is the argument of one of defendants' counsel to the jury, wherein he told the jury: 'Mr. Hemphill, I believe you bought testimony.' The record reflects that one of the State's expert appraiser witnesses testified he was making a charge for his work and time in court. Mr. Hemphill, counsel for the State, in his prior argument, told the jury how much work the witness had done, and how he had qualified himself as an appraiser; and that his 'fees sound high'. He then argued to the jury: '* * * are we buying testimony or are we paying fair prices for work?' Counsel for defendants thereafter argued to the jury: 'Mr. Hemphill, I know you asked the jury one question there. 'Do you think when Mr. Watson was testifying we were buying testimony or if we were paying for service.' Mr. Hemphill, I believe you bought testimony.'

The argument was invited, and cannot be attacked as improper and calculated to wring from the jury an improper verdict in such circumstances. *Transport Ins. Co. v. Reid*, Tex. Civ. App., (n.w.h.) 384 S.W.2d 204.

The jury found the remainder valued at $22,017.10 after the taking . Plaintiff contends the answer without support in the evidence, and that the evidence supports only a value of $20,530.00 after the taking.

We think the jury authorized to value the land after the taking as they did, but in any event the plaintiff is not in a position to complain of a smaller amount of damages found to the remainder than the jury could have found under the evidence. *See Corpus Christi v. Nemec*, Tex. Civ. App., n.w.h., 404 S.W.2d 834.

All of plaintiff's points and contentions are overruled. The judgment is correct.

Affirmed.

f. *Newly Discovered Evidence*

NEW AMSTERDAM CASUALTY CO.
v.
JORDAN

359 S.W.2d 864
(Tex. 1962)

Fulbright, Crooker, Freeman, Bates & Jaworski, Jerry V. Walker and Larry W. Starr, Houston, for petitioner.

John H. Holloway, Houston, for respondent.

STEAKLEY, JUSTICE.

This is a compensation case in which respondent (plaintiff below) had judgment based on jury findings of total incapacity for fifty-five weeks and partial incapacity for seventy-five additional weeks. Respondent appealed and urged nine points of error. The Court of Civil Appeals classified the 'principal contentions' of respondent as six, overruled five, and sustained the sixth described by the Court of Civil Appeals as 'The Trial Court abused its discretion in denying a new trial on the ground of material 'newly discovered evidence' of additional surgery performed on plaintiff after the trial of the case but before Motion for New Trial was acted on.' One Justice dissented on motion for rehearing in the latter respect. 353 S.W.2d 256.

We granted writ of error on petitioner's single point of error which urged that 'The Court of Civil Appeals erred in holding that the trial court abused its discretion in refusing to grant respondent a new trial upon grounds of newly discovered evidence.'

Respondent was injured on September 12, 1957, and underwent back surgery on November 4, 1957. The case was tried during the week of October 15, 1959, but the judgment of the trial court was not entered until July 25, 1960. On August 22, 1960, respondent filed his amended motion for new trial based in part, on the proposition that on August 18, 1960, he had undergone a second back operation necessitated by the injury of September 12, 1957, which resulted in his temporary incapacity extending longer than the seventy-five weeks found by the jury in the trial of the case.

We mention at this point that the procedure for determining liability of the association for medical services furnished to or received by an injured employee after the date of judgment, provided by the amendment to Section 5 of Article 8307, Vernon's Ann. Civ. St. (Acts 1957, 55th Leg., p. 1186, Ch. 397) is not involved here. It is to be noted in this connection that no such procedure is provided in contemplation of post-trial developments bearing on the question of liability for a greater or lesser period of incapacity than found upon trial of the case, and as embodied in the judgment of the court.

The principles governing post-trial evidence developments were long ago established by this Court. In *Mitchell v. Bass*, 26 Tex. 372 (1862), CHIEF JUSTICE WHEELER wrote: * * * In deciding upon motions for new trials on the ground of newly discovered evidence, courts have found it necessary to lay down stringent rules, and to scrutinize such applications with much strictness, to prevent the mischiefs which would otherwise be produced. * * * Such motions are received with careful scrutiny, and are held to address themselves very much to the discretion of the court; and where the court has refused an application made upon this ground, the appellate court will not reverse, unless it shall appear that the court below has not exercised its discretion according to the established rules of law. * * * Where there can be any doubt of the justice of the verdict, to refuse a new trial, when the party has really discovered new evidence of a conclusive tendency, would be against justice and precedent; and by new evidence is meant proof of some new and material fact in the case which has come to light since the trial.'

In holding that the newly discovered evidence under review in the above case was not cumulative and afforded a proper basis for new trial, the court continued: '* * * It is not proposed to multiply witnesses to any distinct fact or circumstance testified to by witnesses upon the trial; but it brings to light a new and independent truth, which the testimony upon the trial sought, but in vain, to prove. '* * * The new evidence relates to the proof of a fact by means so dissimilar from that used upon the trial, as to afford no ground for treating it as cumulative merely of the evidence upon the trial. It is of so decisive a nature, so material to the just decision of the matter in controversy, ...'

CHIEF JUSTICE GOULD in *Wolf v. Mahan*, 57 Tex. 171, 172 (1882), said: 'The reason of the rule forbidding a new trial for the purpose of admitting cumulative testimony does not apply where the party has had no fair opportunity to procure and adduce evidence on an issue raised by his adversary for the first time, during the trial, by the introduction of evidence which could not be anticipated. The reason of the rule is that public policy, looking to the finality of trials, requires that parties be held to diligence in preparing their cases, and that they shall not be allowed a second trial because they mistook the amount of testimony requisite. *Powell v. Jones*, 42 Barb. 30 (42 N.Y. 30). But the policy which seeks to limit continued litigation does not apply where a party has had no fair opportunity to present his side of the case-no real day in court. In discussing this subject, CHIEF JUSTICE WHEELER said: 'It is desirable that there should be an end of litigation with as little delay and expense as possible, consistently with the great end of litigation—a correct decision of causes according to their real merits; but it should always be sought in subordination to the great end to be attained.' *Mitchell v. Bass*, 26 Tex. (372) 377.'

In *Houston & Texas Central Railway Co. v. Forsyth*, 49 Tex. 171, 180 (1878), the Court discussed the problem of cumulative evidence as follows: '* * * Cumulative evidence, as has been often said, is additional evidence of the same kind to the same point. Although evidence tends to prove the same proposition as that previously introduced, yet it is not cumulative when it is of a different character, and merely tends to prove the former proposition by proof of a new and distinct fact. 'The meaning of the rule, says Judge Woodbury, in *Aiken v. Bemis*, 3 Wood. & Min., (348) 358, 'cannot be to exclude, as cumulative, newly-discovered evidence of subordinate points or facts bearing on the general question; for in such a view, no new trial for new evidence could ever be obtained, all new evidence relating, as it must if it be pertinent to the general ground or general fact put in issue before. But it must mean that new evidence to a subordinate point or fact, is not competent where the subordinate point or particular fact was before gone into; because it is then cumulative or additional as to that fact.'

'A new trial will not be granted on the ground of newly-discovered evidence, unless it is made to appear that it has come to the knowledge of the applicant since the trial; that it could not have been sooner discovered by the exercise of diligence; that it is not merely cumulative; that it is not for the purpose of impeachment.' *Conwill v. Gulf, C. & S. F. Ry. Co.*, 85 Tex. 96, 19 S.W. 1017 (1892).

See also MCDONALD, TEXAS CIVIL PRACTICE, Vol. 4, Sec. 18.16; 31 TEX. JUR., Sec. 81, p. 90 et seq.; *Texas Employers' Insurance Ass'n v. Moser* (Tex. Civ. App.), 152 S.W.2d 390.

The principles thus announced have been applied to the problem of granting new trials upon the ground that subsequent events show a more serious personal injury than indicated at the time of the trial. *See* 39 AMER. JUR., Sec. 176, p. 180, and annotations in 31 L.R.A.2d 1236, and 45 L.R.A.,N.S., 87. Respondent relies on the Kentucky case of *Anshutz v. Louisville R. Co.*, 152 Ky. 741, 154 S.W. 13, 45 L.R.A.,N.S., 87, which was the subject of the foregoing annotations. The analysis of this case by the Supreme Court of Missouri in *Curry v. Thompson*, 247 S.W.2d 792, 31 A.L.R. 2D 1225, is particularly relevant: 'The *Anshutz* case facts are readily distinguishable from our case here. In the *Anshutz* case the medical opinions there given by the doctors (and upon which the verdict was there based) were bottomed upon an assumption of certain physical facts (prior removal of both fallopian tubes) which assumption the after-trial facts demonstrably proved to be erroneous. In the instant case the questions made an issue by the evidence (and now pertinent) are as to the extent and severity of plaintiff's injuries, i.e., whether such injuries are so permanent as to prevent plaintiff ever returning to his former railroad switching employment. Those issues were here litigated and there was expert opinion evidence upon every side of those issues. In the *Anshutz* case the verdict was based on evidence that the operation had rendered plaintiff barren but the after-trial facts showed that a child was developing at the time of the trial. In *Woods v. Kentucky Traction & Term. Co., supra*, in discussing the *Anshutz* case, the court said (252 Ky. 78, 65 S.W.2d (961) 966): 'If this operation had been performed, as testified to by the doctors—that is, if the fallopian tubes had been removed—Mrs. Anshutz could not have had a baby, but she did have one, and the tumor turned out to be a boy.' Mrs. Anshutz' barrenness was not there an issue of the evidence for in that case there was no testimony to contradict that of the surgeons who operated her that they had actually removed her fallopian tubes and that naturally, surgically and physiologically, she had been thereby rendered barren. But in our case here the permanency of plaintiff's injuries, their extent and severity, and whether he could ever return to his former railroad switching employment were all issues of the evidence.'

Missouri-Kansas-Texas R. Co. v. Evans, 151 Tex. 340, 250 S.W.2d 385, considered by the majority of the Court of Civil Appeals to be controlling in the instant case, is likewise distinguishable; cancer as the cause of incapacity was not 'of the evidence' in the trial of the case. As said in the dissenting opinion below, *Evans* involved 'an entirely new, unknown, different and unknowable cause of incapacity,' which was discovered by a post-trial operation. The operation did not cause or result in additional or extended incapacity; it revealed cancer as the possible cause of the whole incapacity and, as this Court pointed out in its opinion, cancer as a possible cause was not mentioned in the trial of the case and was not before the jury in any respect in passing upon the merits of the case. In the words of this Court in *Mitchell v. Bass, supra*, the evidence of cancer in *Evans* was 'new evidence of a conclusive tendency'; it brought to light 'a new and independent truth,' and was 'decisive' in nature and 'so material to the just decision of the matter in controversy.'

On the other hand, the after-trial evidence in the case at bar, consisting of a second back operation over three years after the injury, two years and nine months after the previous back operation, and ten months after the trial of the case, was not 'dissimilar to that used upon the trial' and was 'additional evidence of the same kind to the same point' as that introduced at the trial touching the question of respondent's incapacity. It is true that the second back operation was a new fact but it did not 'bring to light a new and independent truth,' and we do not think it can be said that respondent has not had his day in court or that the requirements for overriding the public policy requiring finality of trials have been met. Moreover, the evidence does not, in our opinion, partake of a conclusiveness and decisiveness upon the merits of the case to the extent of showing that justice has not been attained and that, as a matter of law, the trial court abused its discretion in denying the motion.

Apart, then, from the question of whether or not the post-trial facts alleged in the motion for a new trial were sufficiently established at the hearing (which we do not decide), we hold that the Court of Civil Appeals erred in reversing and remanding the case for another trial upon the ground of newly discovered evidence.

* * *

The judgment of the Court of Civil Appeals is reversed, and that of the trial court is affirmed.

g. *Equitable Motion for New Trial*

See earlier discussion in Chapter 2 of this Casebook.

CHAPTER 5.
NON-JURY TRIALS

1. *Request for Findings of Fact and Conclusions of Law*

Read Rules 296-297 Texas Rules of Civil Procedure.

Notes

1. *Wagner v. Riske,* 142 Tex. 337, 178 S.W.2d 117 (1944): ". . . [T]he general rule [is] that the failure of the trial court to file conclusions of law and fact constituted reversible error, where the party complaining complied with statutory requirements in an effort to secure such filing. * * *

"In spite of the above rules, a failure of a trial court to prepare and file findings of fact or conclusions of law under Rule 296, or additional or amended findings of fact or conclusions of law under Rule 298, will not call for a reversal of the trial court's judgment, if the record before the appellate court affirmatively shows that the complaining party has suffered no injury in the premises."

2. *Ad Villarai LLC v. Chan Il,* 519 S.W.3d 132 (Tex. 2017): Neither a newly elected district-court judge or the former judge she replaced may file findings of fact following a bench trial over which the former judge presided before his term expired.

CHERNE INDUS.
v.
MAGALLANES
763 S.W.2d 768
(Tex. 1989)

Summary: The Court dispenses with the requirement that the initial request for findings of fact and conclusions of law be presented to the trial judge. The court holds that timely filing a copy of the initial request for findings and conclusions with the clerk of the court is sufficient under TEX.R.CIV.P. 296. The failure to file findings of fact and conclusions of law when they were timely and properly requested is presumed harmful unless the record affirmatively shows a lack of injury. When the trial court has the ability to correct the error, remand to the trial court is not required to correct the error; a stay will be ordered.

Notes

1. Following the *Cherne Industries* case, the Supreme Court amended both Rules 296 and 297 of the Texas Rules of Civil Procedure to require that a party only has the obligation to file timely with the clerk of the court the Request for Findings of Fact and Conclusions of Law and the Notice of Past Due Findings of Fact and Conclusions of Law. Notice of these filings must be served on other parties. The Rules impose the duty upon the clerk of calling the filings to the attention of the court. Following the logic of the *Cherne Industries* case, the failure of a clerk to notify a judge, should not negate the duty of the court to file the findings and conclusions. In such a case, if the findings and conclusions are not filed and an appellate court determines that the court's error in failing to file them was harmful, the appellate court should direct the trial judge to supplement the record with appropriate findings of fact and conclusions of law. *See* Rule 44.4 Texas Rules of Appellate Procedure.

2. If a court does not file findings of fact or conclusions of law following the initial request, a party must file the Notice of Past Due Findings of Fact and Conclusions of Law in a timely fashion. The failure to file this reminder waives the right to complain on appeal of the trial court's failure to file the findings or conclusions. Thus, the case will be treated in the same manner as one where no initial request was made. In such a case, as will be shown in the next section of this Chapter, the appellate court will imply all necessary findings in support of the trial court's judgment. *See, e.g., Las Vegas Pecan & Cattle Co., Inc. v. Zavala County*, 682 S.W.2d 254 (Tex. 1984). *See also Pharo v. Chambers County, Texas*, 922 S.W.2d 945 (Tex. 1996) (in the absence of findings of fact the appellate court must assume that the trial court made all findings in support of its judgment).

2. *Failure to Request Findings of Fact and Conclusions of Law*

BURNETT
v.
MOTYKA
610 S.W.2d 735
(Tex. 1980)

Summary: In a nonjury trial, where no findings of fact or conclusions of law are filed or requested, it will be implied that the trial court made all the necessary findings to support its judgment. These implied findings may be attacked on appeal by "no evidence" or "insufficient evidence" points of error. In determining a "no evidence" to support an implied finding, the appellate court can only consider that evidence that is favorable to the judgment and must disregard entirely that which is opposed to it. In determining an insufficient evidence point, the court must consider and weigh all the evidence, including any evidence contrary to the trial court's judgment.

3. *Request for Additional Findings of Fact and Conclusions of Law*

Read Rule 298 Texas Rules of Civil Procedure

Note

After the court files original findings of fact and conclusions of law, any party may file "a request for specified additional or amended findings or conclusions." TEX. R. CIV. P. 298. The Supreme Court held long ago that "Rule 298 contemplates that the request for further additional or amended findings . . . shall specify the further additional or amended findings that the party making the request desires the trial court to make and file." *Wagner v. Riske*, 142 Tex. 337, 178 S.W.2d 117, 119-20 (1944). "A bare request is not sufficient; proposed findings must be submitted." *Alvarez v. Espinosa*, 844 S.W.2d 238 (Tex. Civ. App.—San Antonio, 1992, writ dism'd w.o.j.).

ASAI
v.
VANCO INSULATION ABATEMENT, INC.
932 S.W.2d 118
(Tex. App.—El Paso 1996, no writ)

Facts: This is an appeal from a trial court judgment in favor of Appellee. Appellee sued Appellant for breach of contract in payment of the sales price of a vacuum used for picking up asbestos. Appellant agreed to purchase the vacuum from Appellee for $11,000 plus $600 for delivery to Albuquerque, New Mexico. Appellant paid $2,600 down, with $4,500 due in August and $4,500 due in September 1993. After delivery to Albuquerque, a litany of difficulties arose.

On December 1, 1993, Appellee brought suit against Appellant for breach of contract in payment of the sales price. In its answer, Appellant asserted that Appellee was not entitled to recover the purchase price because it had breached the sales agreement and had breached express and implied warranties. Appellant counterclaimed for damages, or alternatively, that it be allowed an offset due to the defective equipment. The case was tried to the court, and judgment was entered granting recovery to Appellee for the sum of $9,000, plus attorney's fees.

Issue: Did the trial court err in failing to find additional findings of fact (that there was an implied warranty of fitness)?

Held: No. The trial court's failure to comply with TEX.R.CIV.P. 298 concerning additional findings is not reversible if the requested finding is covered by and directly contrary to the original findings filed by the trial court. The trial court found that Appellee did not breach any implied warranties. Such a finding is in direct opposition to Appellant's requested finding. The trial court's failure to comply with Appellant's request is not reversible error if the finding made is supported by the evidence. To determine the necessary evidentiary support, we must consider the concomitant arguments under point of error two.

TEX.R.CIV.P. 298 provides, in pertinent part:

> The court shall file any additional or amended findings and conclusions that are appropriate within ten days after such request is filed, and cause a copy to be mailed to each party to the suit. No findings or conclusions shall be deemed or presumed by any failure of the court to make any additional findings or conclusions.

Issue: Was there factually sufficient evidence to support the trial's court's finding of an implied warranty? Yes. We find the evidence sufficient to support the determination.

Findings of fact are reviewable for legal and factual sufficiency of the evidence by the same standards that are applied in reviewing the evidence supporting a jury's answer. Conclusions of law are reviewable de novo.

Immaterial Issue: Did the trial court's implied finding, that an implied warranty of fitness for a particular purpose, does not apply to used equipment. We disagree, finding that the trial court impliedly found that the implied warranty of fitness applies to used goods.

Issue: When is the trial court required to make additional findings of fact? Were they necessary here? No.

Held: No. The trial court is only required to make additional findings of fact and conclusions of law that are appropriate. If the refusal does not prevent the adequate presentation on appeal, there is no reversible error. TEX.R.CIV.P. 298 requires additional findings of fact and conclusions of law only if they relate to "ultimate or controlling issues." The trial court is not required to make findings that are unsupported in the record, that relate merely to evidentiary matters, or that are contrary to other previous findings.

4. *Omitted Findings of Fact*

Read Rule 299 Texas Rules of Civil Procedure

HERNANDEZ CONSTR. & SUPPLY CO.
v.
NATIONAL BANK OF COMMERCE
578 S.W.2d 675
(Tex. 1979)

Summary: Where one or more elements of an action or defense have been found by the trial court, omitted unrequested elements, where supported by evidence, will be supplied by presumption in support of the judgment. While an express finding of fact cannot extend by implication to cover independent grounds of defense, it can cover an omitted element of the action or defense if another element is expressly found. Thus, there reasonableness and unreasonableness of attorney's fees are not further independent issuable facts. The challenge to the reasonableness of attorney's fees is one ground of defense comprised of two elements: (1) the contractual fee is unreasonable, and (2) a lesser fee is reasonable under the circumstances.

Facts: This is a suit to collect principal, interest and attorney's fees on a promissory note. The sole issue here concerns an award of attorney's fees based upon a fixed percentage of the principal and interest due on the note. Specifically, the issue is whether an omitted, unrequested finding that the contractual fee is unreasonable will be supplied by presumption in support of the trial court judgment, if the trial court expressly finds that a lesser fee is reasonable and the omitted finding of unreasonableness is supported by the evidence.

The National Bank of Commerce of Brownsville, respondent here, brought suit as holder of a promissory note executed by Hernandez Construction Company, Inc., et al., petitioners here. The note provided that "in the event that this note is placed into the hands of an attorney for collection . . . an additional fifteen percent (15%) on the amount of principal and interest then owing shall be added to the same as attorney's fees." The trial court rendered judgment in favor of the Bank for principal and interest of $105,916.74 and attorney's fees of $10,000. In response to the Bank's request for findings of fact and conclusions of law, the trial court found that the Bank agreed to pay its attorney 15% of the outstanding principal and interest due on the note as an attorney's fee, and that $10,000 is a reasonable sum for the services rendered by the Bank's attorney.

The Bank appealed, contending that it is entitled to the contractual percentage of fees provided for in the note. The court of civil appeals reversed that part of the trial court's judgment awarding attorney's fees, and rendered judgment for the Bank in the amount of $15,887.51, an amount equal to 15% of the principal and interest due on the note. 564 S.W.2d 499. We reverse the judgment of the court of civil appeals and affirm the judgment of the trial court.

Issue: Is an agreement to pay a percentage of an unpaid balance as attorney's fees an absolute promise to pay the contractual amount? No. Texas courts do not regard agreements to pay attorney's fees based on a percentage of the unpaid balance and interest on a promissory note as absolute promises to pay the contractual amount, but as contracts to indemnify the holder of the note for attorney's expenses actually incurred in collecting the principal and interest on the note. Consequently, the obligor of the note can challenge the reasonableness of contractual attorney's fees.

Issue: How is the reasonableness of the percentage attorney fees challenged?

Held: Upon a proper showing the holder will be limited to an amount which is reasonable under the circumstances, and may be denied any recovery where it appears that no expense has been incurred as a result of the maker's default.

Issue: What is required to establish the affirmative defense of unreasonableness of attorney's fees?

Held: (1) In order to make a "proper showing" that the fee should be reduced, the obligor must first plead and prove that the contractual fee is unreasonable. (2) To complete the showing, however, the obligor must also prove a lesser amount that is reasonable under the circumstances. These two elements comprise the affirmative defense of unreasonableness of attorney's fees.

In their answer, Hernandez pled that "the payment of fifteen (15%) additional as attorney's fees . . . would be an unreasonable amount and not representative of the work involved in the collection of said note." At the nonjury trial, the parties did not dispute that principal and interest in the amount of $105,914.74 was due on the note. The sole disputed issue at trial concerned the reasonableness of the attorney's fees provided for in the note. An officer of the Bank testified that the Bank agreed to pay its attorney the contractual fee for collecting the note. Another witness testified that the $15,000 was an unreasonable amount and that $5,000 would be reasonable under the circumstances. The trial court, after hearing this testimony, initially announced judgment for the Bank "in the amount of $15,916.74 as agreed to by the parties at the time of entering into the agreement;" however, the court stated that it would accept briefs on the issue of attorney's fees. After studying the briefs submitted by the parties, the trial court set aside its previous judgment and set an evidentiary hearing on the reasonableness of the contractual attorney's fees.

At the hearing, both parties presented evidence. One attorney testified that 15% of the principal and interest due was unreasonable because of the large principal due under the note and the time required for an attorney to collect a note in circumstances similar to those before us. Both parties presented evidence on the amount of time required for an attorney to collect a note and the hourly wage of attorneys employed to collect notes. The Bank's attorney testified on what he did to collect this particular note.

Issue: What findings were made here? The trial court expressly found one of the elements of the defense relied on by Hernandez: the lesser fee of $10,000 is a reasonable fee. The other element of the defense is supported by evidence that the contractual fee is unreasonable.

Issue: When can an omitted finding be presumed from an express finding? Rule 299 states the situation in which omitted findings will be presumed from express findings:

> Where findings of fact are filed by the trial court they shall form the basis of the judgment upon all grounds of recovery and of defense embraced therein. The judgment may not be supported upon appeal by a presumption of finding upon any ground of recovery or defense, no element of which has been found by the trial court; but where one or more elements thereof have been found by the trial court, omitted unrequested elements, where supported by evidence, will be supplied by presumption in support of the judgment. Refusal of the court to make a finding requested shall be reviewable on appeal.

The trial court expressly found one of the elements of the defense relied on by Hernandez: the lesser fee of $10,000 is a reasonable fee. The other element of the defense are supported by evidence that the contractual fee is unreasonable. A finding of unreasonableness is an "omitted unrequested element" of a defense, "supported by the evidence" and "will be supplied by presumption in support of the judgment." By the express terms of Rule 299, we hold that unreasonableness of a contractual attorney's fee will be presumed from the express trial court finding that a lesser sum is a reasonable fee.

Issue: Did the express finding that $10,000 was a reasonable attorney fee include the implied finding that a $15,000 fee was unreasonable?

Held: Yes. An express finding of fact cannot extend by implication to cover independent grounds of defense. However, this rule is not applicable in this cause. Reasonableness and unreasonableness of attorney's fees are not further independent issuable facts. The challenge to the reasonableness of attorney's fees is one ground of defense comprised of two elements: (1) the contractual fee is unreasonable, and (2) a lesser fee is reasonable under the circumstances Hernandez pled that the contractual fee was unreasonable. At a trial in which the only disputed issue was the reasonableness of the contractual fee, Hernandez presented evidence that the fee was unreasonable and that a lesser fee would be reasonable. At an evidentiary hearing set solely to determine the reasonableness of attorney's fees, evidence was presented showing unreasonableness and a lesser reasonable amount. The question of reasonableness of attorney's fees was squarely before the trial court. In this context, the issue of reasonableness and unreasonableness is so intertwined that a specific finding of a reasonable attorney fee does not then require the obligor of the note to request a specific finding that the contractual fee is unreasonable. *See*, 4 R. McDonald, TEXAS CIVIL PRACTICE s 16.09 (rev. 1971).

Notes

1. *Texas Eastern Transmission Corp. v. Sealy Ind. Sch. Dist.*, 572 S.W.2d 49 (Tex. Civ. App.—Houston [1st Dist.] 1978, no writ): The trial court need not make findings about:

> Facts that are admitted;
> Facts that are immaterial to the resolution of any controlling issue;
> Facts that are evidentiary only; and
> Facts that do not relate to the ultimate or controlling issue(s) in the case.

In making the findings, the trial court is not limited to the requests made.

2. *Davis v. Moreno*, 579 S.W.2d 309 (Tex. Civ. App.—Corpus Christi 1979, no writ): The trial court, in this personal injury case, did not err in refusing to find whether the plaintiff had an enlarged spleen before the collision. As a general rule, the trial judge, upon proper request, is only required to make findings on ultimate, controlling and material issues. The judge is not required to make findings:

> upon matters which are adequately covered by findings already made,
> upon evidentiary matters, or
> upon every other controverted issues of fact.

The existence of a pre-existing condition is not an ultimate issue in a personal injury case based upon negligence.

3. In interlocutory appeals, the trial court may file findings if they do not delay the filing of the record in the appellate court.

But, the judge can refuse to make findings in interlocutory appeals.
There is no authority to make findings in appeals from summary judgments.
There is no authority to make findings in appeals from judgments by default.

4. *Mayhew v. Town of Sunnyvale*, 964 S.W.2d 922 (Tex. 1998). Although determining whether a property regulation is unconstitutional requires the consideration of a number of factual issues, the ultimate question of whether a zoning ordinance constitutes a compensable taking, or violates due process or equal protection is a question of law, not a question of fact. In resolving this legal issue, the Court considers all surrounding circumstances. While the Supreme Court depends on the district court to resolve disputed facts, regarding the extent of government intrusion on the property, the ultimate determination, of whether the facts are sufficient to constitute a taking, is a question of law.

5. *Preservation of Error in Non-Jury Cases*

Notes

1. The following excerpt from *Regan v. Lee*, 879 S.W.2d 133 (Tex. App.—Houston [14th Dist.] 1994, no writ) discusses the major differences between preservation of error in non-jury trials as opposed to jury trials.

> In the history of Texas law, to raise a "no evidence" point before an appellate court after a jury trial, the appellant must have filed one or more predicate motions designed to bring the error to the trial judge's attention, enabling the judge to correct the error and render judgment for the movant before jurisdiction was lost. *Bluebonnet Exp. v. Employers Ins. of Wausau*, 651 S.W.2d 345, 351-52 (Tex. App.—Houston [14th Dist.] 1983, writ ref'd n.r.e.). These predicate motions include: (1) a motion for instructed verdict; (2) a motion for judgment notwithstanding the verdict; (3) an objection to the submission of the issue to the jury; (4) a motion to disregard the jury's answer to a vital fact issue; or (5) a motion for new trial specifically raising the complaint. *Aero Energy, Inc. v. Circle C Drilling Co.*, 699 S.W.2d 821, 822 (Tex. 1985). However, no such predicate motion requirements have been imposed on appeals from nonjury trials and it has been possible to raise both legal and factual sufficiency of the evidence points for the first time on appeal as long as the complaint has somehow been brought to the trial judge's attention. *Bluebonnet Exp.*, 651 S.W.2d at 352 (*citing, Kissman v. Bendix Home Systems*, 587 S.W.2d 675, 677-78 (Tex. 1979)).
>
> Furthermore, TEX. R. APP. P. 52(a) requires a party to present to the trial court a timely request, objection or motion in order to preserve appellate review. The rule was amended in 1990 to clarify appellate requisites from nonjury trials. The amended portion of Rule 52(d) reads as follows: A party desiring to complain on appeal in a nonjury case that the evidence was legally or factually insufficient to support a finding of fact, that a finding of fact was established as a matter of law or was against the overwhelming weight of the evidence, or of the inadequacy or excessiveness of the damages found by the court shall not be required to comply with paragraph (a) of this rule.
>
> In other words, challenges to a finding of fact's legal and factual sufficiency can be made for the first time on appeal from nonjury trials. *Westech Eng. v. Clearwater Constructors*, 835 S.W.2d 190, 196-97 (Tex. App.—Austin 1992, no writ). Therefore, no predicate was required for appellant to challenge the legal and factual insufficiency of findings of fact on appeal.

2. TEX. R. APP. P. 52(a) became TEX. R. APP Rule 33, effective in 1999. Old Rule 52(d) has been eliminated as unnecessary in light of TEX. R. CIV. P. 324(a) and (b). Effective January 1, 2003, old Rule 52(d) is reinstated as Rule 33.1(d), which reads:

> (d) Sufficiency of Evidence Complaints in Non jury Cases. In a nonjury case, a complaint regarding the legal or factual insufficiency of the evidence e—including a complaint that the damages found by the court are excessive or inadequate, as distinguished from a complaint that the trial court erred in refusing to amend a fact finding or to make an additional finding of fact—may be made for the first time on appeal in the complaining party's brief.

Thus, all that is necessary to challenge findings of fact on the basis of factual or legal sufficiency of the evidence is to raise a proper point of error in a brief filed in the appellate court and to include a statement of facts in the record.

3. *Office of the Atty. Gen. of Texas v. Burton,* 369 S.W.3d 173 (Tex. 2012): Although the Attorney General argued that Burton's child support arrearage was $57,000, the trial court ruled after a bench trial that it was $0. The court of appeals affirmed, holding that the Attorney General waived its no-evidence complaint by not first presenting it to the trial court. ***Held***: The Attorney General was not required to present the no-evidence complaint to the trial court. Texas Rule of Appellate Procedure 33.1(d) provides that "[i]n a nonjury case, a complaint regarding the legal or factual insufficiency of the evidence … may be made for the first time on appeal in the complaining party's brief."

4. Prior to the new Rules of Appellate Procedure, there was a disagreement among the various courts of appeal on the necessity of preserving error to conclusions of law filed by a trial court. Several courts asserted that preservation of error was not required. *See, e.g., Sammons v. Elder*, 940 S.W.2d 276 (Tex. App.—Waco 1997, no writ) (holding that conclusions of law in a nonjury trial are reviewable by this Court without preservation under Rule 52(a)). *See also Spiller v. Spiller*, 901 S.W.2d 553, 556 (Tex. App.—San Antonio 1995, writ denied); *Westech Eng. v. Clearwater Constructors*, 835 S.W.2d 190, 196 (Tex. App.—Austin 1992, no writ). Other courts, however, required a post-judgment request, objection, or motion in compliance with Rule 52(a). *Regan v. Lee*, 879 S.W.2d 133, 136 (Tex. App.—Houston [14th Dist.] 1994, no writ); *Winters v. Arm Refining Co., Inc*., 830 S.W.2d 737, 738-39 (Tex. App.—Corpus Christi 1992, writ denied). The new Rules do not directly address the point. However, in order to avoid a possible waiver, the wise practitioner should preserve his complaint by making an appropriate objection or motion.

6. *Perfection of Appeal in Nonjury Cases*

Read Rules 25 and 26.1(a) Texas Rules of Appellate Procedure

IKB INDUSTRIES (Nigeria) Limited
v.
PRO-LINE CORPORATION
938 S.W.2d 440
(Tex. 1997)

Robert H. Westerburg, Dallas, for petitioner.
Robert R. Gibbons, Dallas, for respondent.

HECHT, JUSTICE.

Here, the sole question is whether requesting findings of fact and conclusions of law following dismissal of a case as a sanction for discovery abuse extends the time for perfecting appeal under Rule 41(a)(1) [Now Rule 26.1(a)(1)] of the Texas Rules of Appellate Procedure. The court of appeals answered no. 901 S.W.2d 568. Under the circumstances of this case, as we explain, we disagree.

IKB Industries (Nigeria) Limited sued Pro-Line Corporation. Pro-Line moved to dismiss IKB's action as a sanction for discovery abuse. *See* TEX. R. CIV. P. 215. After a hearing, for which there is no statement of facts, the district court granted the motion, struck IKB's pleadings, and dismissed the action with prejudice. The court's judgment recites that the court considered "the Court's file—including all pleadings, affidavits, and deposition excerpts filed with the Court (and of which the Court takes judicial notice) and . . . the testimony and argument of counsel." (Emphasis added.) The judgment contains seven pages of findings that the court made, as the judgment recites, "from the evidence before it".

Notwithstanding these findings, IKB filed a request for findings of fact and conclusions of law, referencing Rule 296 of the Texas Rules of Civil Procedure. Rule 296 states in part: In any case tried in the district or county court without a jury, any party may request the court to state in writing its findings of fact and conclusions of law. Such request . . . shall be filed within twenty days after judgment is signed . . . . IKB's request was filed eight days after the dismissal order was signed. The district court did not respond to IKB's request.

A timely filed request for findings of fact and conclusions of law extends the deadline for perfecting appeal from 30 to 90 days after the judgment is signed "in a case tried without a jury." TEX. R. APP. P. 41(a)(1). Since IKB filed a cost bond 49 days after the dismissal order was signed, IKB perfected appeal only if its request for findings and conclusions extended the deadline for doing so from 30 to 90 days—that is, only if the case was "tried without a jury" within the meaning of Rule 41(a)(1).

Not every case finally adjudicated without a jury trial is "a case tried without a jury" within the meaning of Rule 41(a)(1). For instance, we held in *Linwood v. NCNB Texas*, 885 S.W.2d 102, 103 (Tex. 1994), that a request for findings in a case concluded by summary judgment does not extend appellate deadlines. The reason is not that a summary judgment proceeding is in no sense a trial. On the contrary, we have held that "[a] summary judgment proceeding is a trial within the meaning of Rule 63" of the Texas Rules of Civil Procedure, which governs amendment of pleadings. *Goswami v. Metropolitan Sav. & Loan Ass'n*, 751 S.W.2d 487, 490 (Tex. 1988). True, a "summary judgment proceeding is not a conventional trial but rather an exception to the usual and traditional form of procedure wherein witnesses are heard in open court and documentary evidence is offered and received in evidence." *Richards v. Allen*, 402 S.W.2d 158, 160 (Tex. 1966). But this distinction was not the basis for our decision in *Linwood.*

Instead, *Linwood* takes a functional approach to Rule 41(a)(1). It holds, not that a summary judgment is not a trial within the meaning of the rule, but that "findings of fact and conclusions of law have no place in a summary judgment proceeding". *Linwood*, 885 S.W.2d at 103. The reason findings and conclusions "have no place" in a summary judgment proceeding is that for summary judgment to be rendered, there cannot be a "genuine issue as to any material fact", TEX. R. CIV. P. 166a(c), and the legal grounds are limited to those stated in the motion and response, *Stiles v. Resolution Trust Corp.*, 867 S.W.2d 24, 26 (Tex. 1993). In other words, if summary judgment is proper, there are no facts to find, and the legal conclusions have already been stated in the motion and response. The trial court should not make, and an appellate court cannot consider, findings of fact in connection with a summary judgment. Because a request for findings and conclusions following summary judgment can have no purpose, should not be filed, and if filed, should be ignored by the trial court, such a request should not extend appellate deadlines. *Linwood* rejects a broad construction of Rule 41(a)(1) that would cause the filing of a request for findings and conclusions to extend the time for perfecting appeal in every case adjudicated without a jury.

The most restrictive construction of Rule 41(a)(1) would not allow a request for findings and conclusions to extend the time for perfecting appeal unless the request was proper under Rule 296—that is, "[i]n any case tried in the district or county court without a jury". Our approach to applying this language, similar to the language of Rule 41(a)(1), has also been functional. A party is not entitled to findings of fact and conclusions of law following summary judgment, *Linwood*, 885 S.W.2d at 103, judgment non obstante veredicto, *Fancher v. Cadwell*, 159 Tex. 8, 314 S.W.2d 820, 822 (1958), or judgment after directed verdict, *Ditto v. Ditto Investment Co.*, 158 Tex. 104, 309 S.W.2d 219, 220 (1958), again, not because these adjudications are in no sense trials. Indeed, judgment non obstante veredicto is rendered after a full trial and verdict. Rather, a party is not entitled to findings and conclusions in such instances because judgment must be rendered as a matter of law. Were there facts to find the three judgments we have listed are the only ones to which Rule 296 does not apply. The point is simply that Rule 296, like Rule 41(a)(1), is not governed by a definition of the word, "trial", common to both, but by their respective purposes.

The problem with a restrictive construction of Rule 41(a)(1)—not allowing a party's request for findings and conclusions to extend the time for perfecting appeal unless the party is entitled to findings and conclusions under Rule 296—is that it conflicts with the purpose of Rule 41(a)(1). This is because the purposes of Rule 296 and Rule 41(a)(1) are not identical.

The purpose of Rule 296 is to give a party a right to findings of fact and conclusions of law finally adjudicated after a conventional trial on the merits before the court. In other cases findings and conclusions are proper, but a party is not entitled to them. For example, in a case like this one in which judgment is rendered as a sanction for discovery abuse, findings for imposing sanctions may be helpful, and we have encouraged their use. *TransAmerican Nat. Gas Corp. v. Powell*, 811 S.W.2d 913, 919 n. 9 (Tex. 1991); *Chrysler Corp. v. Blackmon*, 841 S.W.2d 844, 852 (Tex. 1992). But we do not require them for two reasons. One is practical: they are often unnecessary, and requiring them in every case would unduly burden trial courts. As we explained in *Blackmon*:

> [W]e do not wish to unnecessarily burden our trial courts by requiring them to make written findings in all cases in which death penalty sanctions are imposed. First, the benefit of the trial court's explanation in the record of why it believes death penalty sanctions are justified may be sufficient to guide the appellate court. Second, written findings are not needed in the vast majority of relatively uncomplicated cases or even more complex cases involving only a few issues pertinent to the propriety of death penalty sanctions. We doubt that findings in such cases would meaningfully assist appellate review.

841 S.W.2d at 852. The other reason findings are not required whenever they may be useful is that appellate courts are not obliged to give them the same level of deference. A legally correct judgment based on findings of fact made after a trial on the merits cannot be set aside on appeal if the findings are supported by sufficient evidence. *Harris County Flood Control Dist. v. Shell Pipe Line Corp.*, 591 S.W.2d 798, 799 (Tex. 1979). An order imposing discovery sanctions, on the other hand, may be reversed for an abuse of discretion even if findings and evidence support it. *Blackmon*, 841 S.W.2d at 852-853. There is less reason to require findings when they are not as binding on appeal.

The purpose of Rule 41, on the other hand, is to prescribe the time for perfecting appeal. The deadline is 30 days after the judgment is signed, unless extended by the filing of a motion for new trial or of a request for findings and conclusions in a case tried without a jury. The first exception affords the trial court time to consider and decide the motion. The second exception allows the trial court time to state the basis for its judgment so that a party may determine whether to appeal. Often, perhaps usually, the decision to appeal is not controlled by the court's findings and conclusions; nevertheless, the purpose of Rule 41(a)(1) is to allow time for the court to make them and the parties to consider them. The purpose of the second exception is served not only when findings are required by Rule 296, but whenever they may be useful for appellate review—as when a case has been dismissed for discovery abuse.

Allowing a request for findings and conclusions to extend the deadline for perfecting appeal when a party is not entitled to findings and conclusions under Rule 296 does not impair the purpose of Rule 296. However, not to allow such a request to extend appellate deadlines does impair the purpose of Rule 41(a)(1) by depriving a party of a statement of the basis of the trial court's ruling to allow the party to determine whether to appeal. A restrictive construction of Rule 41(a)(1) thus conflicts with the core rationale of *Linwood*—that the rule should be construed to accomplish its purpose.

To summarize: A request for findings of fact and conclusions of law does not extend the time for perfecting appeal of a judgment rendered as a matter of law, where findings and conclusions can have no purpose and should not be requested, made, or considered on appeal. Examples are summary judgment, judgment after directed verdict, judgment non obstante veredicto, default judgment awarding liquidated damages, dismissal for want of prosecution without an evidentiary hearing, dismissal for want of jurisdiction without an evidentiary hearing, dismissal based on the pleadings or special exceptions, and any judgment rendered without an evidentiary hearing. A timely filed request for findings of fact and conclusions of law extends the time for perfecting appeal when findings and conclusions are required by Rule 296, or when they are not required by Rule 296 but are not without purpose—that is, they could properly be considered by the appellate court. Examples are judgment after a conventional trial before the court, default judgment on a claim for unliquidated damages, judgment rendered as sanctions, and any judgment based in any part on an evidentiary hearing.

In the present case, although sanctions were imposed largely on the basis of discovery requests and responses that are a matter of record and indisputable, there appears to be a factual dispute over IKB's explanations for its alleged discovery abuse. The trial court's extensive findings themselves indicate a resolution of disputed factual matters apart from the filings included in the transcript. Applying the rule we have adopted, we hold that IKB's request for findings and conclusions extended the deadline for perfecting appeal. Thus, the court of appeals erred in dismissing the appeal.

The dissent argues that whether a request for findings extends the time for perfecting appeal should depend upon the standard of review. By this standard, a request for findings following dismissal for discovery abuse, as in this case, would not extend the time for appeal even though we have encouraged trial courts to make these findings, and they can be considered on appeal. Moreover, it sometimes happens that the standard of review has not been finally determined. *Ruiz v. Conoco, Inc.*, 868 S.W.2d 752, 757-758 (Tex. 1993). Thus the standard the dissent would apply is less certain than the one we adopt.

Accordingly, the Court grants IKB's application for writ of error and without hearing oral argument reverses the judgment of the court of appeals and remands the case to that court for a consideration of other issues raised. TEX. R. APP. P. 170.

BAKER, JUSTICE, dissenting.

Today the Court holds that a timely request for findings of fact and conclusions of law extends the time for perfecting appeal when findings and conclusions are required by Rule 296, or when they are not required by Rule 296 but are not without purpose—that is, they could properly be considered by the appellate court. The Court opines that its new rule does not conflict with the core rationale of *Linwood*—which is a functional approach that rejects a broad construction of Rule 41(a)(1) that would allow the filing of a request for findings and conclusions to extend the time for perfecting appeal in every case adjudicated without a jury. *See Linwood v. NCNB of Texas*, 876 S.W.2d 393 (Tex. App.—Dallas), *rev'd on other grounds*, 885 S.W.2d 102 (Tex. 1994).

I respectfully disagree. The rule the Court adopts continues to unduly complicate, rather than simplify, the issue raised in this case. In my view, the rule the Court adopts: Is in fact contrary to *Linwood's* functional approach to construing Rule 41(a)(1); Requires the appellate court to review the entire record to accurately determine if the evidentiary hearing did in fact involve the trial court's resolution of discrete fact issues outside the scope of the pleadings, motions, documents, and arguments of counsel; Ignores appellate standards of review that establish whether the trial court must resolve discrete fact questions, and the impact these standards of review have upon a particular appeal; and Adds delay to many appeals—an additional sixty days—when the judicial system is under fire from the legal community and the general public for the inordinate time—and concomitant costs—it takes to process a controversy through the system.

I believe a more appropriate and more workable rule is that whether a request for findings of fact and conclusions of law extends the time to appeal depends upon the standard of review that applies to the particular appeal. In my view, this rule would: Support *Linwood's* functional approach to construing Rule 41(a)(1); . Permit the parties to determine immediately whether findings and conclusions are necessary to the appeal and therefore necessary to request and extend the time to perfect the appeal; Permit the appellate court to determine immediately—without the necessity of reviewing the entire record—whether the request for findings and conclusions extends the time to perfect the appeal; and Avoid additional delays in processing and disposing of many appeals.

I. REQUESTS FOR FINDINGS OF FACT

Rule 41(a)(1) clearly relates to Rule 296. *See* TEX. R. APP. P. 41(a)(1) and TEX. R. CIV. P. 296. Rule 296 only entitles a party to findings of fact and conclusions of law in cases tried in district or county court without a jury. *Chavez v. Housing Auth. of El Paso*, 897 S.W.2d 523, 525 (Tex. App.—El Paso 1995, writ denied). A court tries a case when there is an evidentiary hearing upon conflicting evidence. *Linwood*, 876 S.W.2d at 395; *Chavez*, 897 S.W.2d at 525. Accordingly, findings of fact are appropriate only when the court is deciding fact issues. *Chavez*, 897 S.W.2d at 525. Where the court rules without determining discrete fact questions, requests for finding of fact and conclusions of law are neither appropriate nor effective for extending appellate deadlines. *WISD Taxpayers Ass'n v. Waco Indep. Sch. Dist.*, 912 S.W.2d 392, 394 (Tex. App.—Waco 1996, no writ); *Chavez*, 897 S.W.2d at 525-26. Findings specifically tied to an appropriate legal standard are the only type of findings that can be truly beneficial to appellate review. *Chrysler Corp. v. Blackmon*, 841 S.W.2d 844, 853 (Tex. 1992).

II. PRINCIPAL APPELLATE STANDARDS OF REVIEW

A. ABUSE OF DISCRETION

Under an abuse of discretion standard, the appellate court reviews the entire record to determine if the trial court acted arbitrarily and unreasonably, and thus abused its discretion. *Morrow v. H.E.B., Inc.*, 714 S.W.2d 297, 298 (Tex. 1986). The reviewing court may not reverse the trial court for an abuse of discretion because it disagrees with the trial court's decision so long as that decision is within the trial court's discretionary authority. *Beaumont Bank v. Buller*, 806 S.W.2d 223, 226 (Tex. 1991); *Downer v. Aquamarine Operators, Inc.*, 701 S.W.2d 238, 242 (Tex. 1985).

Under an abuse of discretion standard of review, the appellate court does not review factual issues decided by the trial court under legal or factual sufficiency standards. *Crouch v. Tenneco, Inc.*, 853 S.W.2d 643, 649 (Tex. App.—Waco 1993, writ denied). Under an abuse of discretion standard of review, legal and factual sufficiency claims are not independent, reversible grounds of error, but rather merely factors to consider in assessing whether the trial court abused its discretion. *Buller*, 806 S.W.2d at 226. Under an abuse of discretion standard of review, findings of fact and conclusions of law are neither appropriate nor required. *Crouch*, 853 S.W.2d at 649.

An abuse of discretion does not exist if the trial court bases its decision on conflicting evidence and some evidence supports the trial court's decision. *See Ruiz v. Conoco, Inc.*, 868 S.W.2d 752, 758 (Tex. 1993). An abuse of discretion does not exist if some evidence in the record shows the trial court followed guiding rules and statutes. *Crouch*, 853 S.W.2d at 649.

B. EVIDENTIARY STANDARD OF REVIEW

Legal and factual sufficiency of the evidence standards of review govern appeals of nonjury trials on the merits. *Blackmon*, 841 S.W.2d at 852; Hall, *Standards of Appellate Review in Civil Appeals*, 21 ST. MARY'S L.J. 865, 919-20 (1990). When a party appeals from a nonjury trial, it must complain of specific findings and conclusions of the trial court, because a general complaint against the trial court's judgment does not present a justiciable question. *Fiduciary Mortgage Co. v. City Nat'l Bank*, 762 S.W.2d 196, 204 (Tex. App.—Dallas 1988, writ denied). Accordingly, findings of fact and conclusions of law are mandatory for a party to file to avoid the onerous presumptions that apply in an appeal from a nonjury trial. When an appellant does not request or file findings and conclusions by the trial court, the appellate court presumes the trial court found all fact questions in support of its judgment, and the reviewing court must affirm that judgment on any legal theory finding support in the pleadings and evidence. *Point Lookout West, Inc. v. Whorton*, 742 S.W.2d 277, 278 (Tex. 1987).

If the appellant does not challenge the trial court's findings of fact, when filed, these facts are binding upon both the party and the appellate court. *Wade v. Anderson*, 602 S.W.2d 347, 349 (Tex. Civ. App.—Beaumont 1980, writ ref'd n.r.e.). Accordingly, it is incumbent for the appellant to attack the findings by appropriate legal and factual sufficiency points of error. *Lovejoy v. Lillie*, 569 S.W.2d 501, 504 (Tex. Civ. App.—Tyler 1978, writ ref'd n.r.e.).

In an appeal of a nonjury trial, findings are specifically and meaningfully tied to appropriate standards of appellate review and are therefore truly beneficial to appellate review. *See Blackmon*, 841 S.W.2d at 853.

III. DISMISSAL AS A DISCOVERY SANCTION

The appellate standard of review of a trial court order dismissing a case as a discovery sanction is abuse of discretion. *Blackmon*, 841 S.W.2d at 852; *TransAmerican Nat. Gas Corp. v. Powell*, 811 S.W.2d 913, 919 n. 9 (Tex. 1991). Findings are neither appropriate nor required under an abuse of discretion standard. *Crouch*, 853 S.W.2d at 649. Findings are not tied to the appellate standard of review and are not necessarily beneficial to appellate review. Accordingly, under the rule I propose, I would hold that findings and conclusions did not extend the appellate timetable in this case. I would affirm the court of appeals' judgment dismissing the appeal and deny the writ.

IV. CONCLUSION

The Court asserts that the rule it adopts is better than the one I propose because it sometimes happens that the appellate standard of review has not been finally determined. Thus, the Court concludes that the standard I would apply is less certain than the one it adopts. I beg to differ again.

There is a substantial body of statutory and case law that establishes appellate standards of review. Moreover, the bench and bar are fortunate to have available two excellent law review articles that put this body of law together for ready reference. *See generally* Hall, *Standards of Appellate Review in Civil Appeals*, 21 ST. MARY'S L.J. 865 (1990) *and* Hall, *Revisiting Standards of Review in Civil Appeals*, 24 ST. MARY'S L.J. 1045 (1993). "The law prescribing the standard of review to a particular ruling is complex but relatively well settled." Hecht, *Forward: Revisiting Standards of Review in Civil Appeals*, 24 ST. MARY'S L.J. 1041, 1041 (1993).

Today the Court needlessly establishes a new standard when existing standards will better solve the problem. I respectfully dissent.

Note

Rule 26.1(a)(4) of the Rules of Appellate Procedure incorporates the holding in the *IKB Industries* case.

PHILLIPS
v.
BEAVERS
938 S.W.2d 446
(Tex. 1997)

Carl David Adams, C. Sellers Aycock, Dallas, for petitioners.
Mitchell Madden, Thomas V. Murto, III, Dallas, for respondents.

PER CURIAM.

The sole question in this case is whether a request for findings of fact and conclusions of law extends the time for filing the appellate record under Rule 54(a) of the Texas Rules of Appellate Procedure if the case is dismissed for want of prosecution. The court of appeals dismissed the appeal. 906 S.W.2d 254. We hold that the time for filing the record was extended because the dismissal was based on an evidentiary hearing.

On January 10, 1983, R. Lowell Phillips, George T. Worley, Jr. and Worley Geological Services, Inc. filed this suit against Carl D. Beavers and others seeking more than $6 million actual damages and $18 million exemplary damages relating to interests in certain oil and gas properties. Twelve years later, on February 1, 1995, after an evidentiary hearing, the district court dismissed the suit for want of prosecution. The order recites that the court considered the testimony at the evidentiary hearing in finding that plaintiffs had failed to exercise due diligence in prosecuting the case. Nine days later Phillips and Worley Geological requested the court's factual findings and legal conclusions. Phillips and Worley Geological each filed a cost bond to perfect appeal twenty-six days after the order of dismissal was signed. George Worley did not appeal. The transcript and statement of facts were filed ninety-two days after the dismissal order was signed.

Rule 54(a) provides in part: The transcript and statement of facts, if any, shall be filed in the appellate court within sixty days after the judgment is signed, or, if a timely motion for new trial or to modify the judgment has been filed by any party, or if any party has timely filed a request for findings of fact and conclusions of law in a case tried without a jury, within one hundred twenty days after the judgment is signed. If Phillips and Worley Geological's request for findings extended the deadline for filing the record, it was timely filed; if the request did not extend the filing deadline, the record was late.

In *IKB Industries (Nigeria) Ltd. v. Pro-Line Corp.*, 938 S.W.2d 440, 443 (Tex. 1997) (per curiam), also decided today, we held that "[a] timely filed request for findings of fact and conclusions of law extends the time for perfecting appeal when findings and conclusions are required by Rule 296, or when they are not required by Rule 296 but are not without purpose—that is, they could properly be considered by the appellate court." We determined that this rule was consistent with the purpose of Rule 41 by allowing time for findings to be made when they may be useful for appellate review. *Id.* at 442. An example included "any judgment based in any part on an evidentiary hearing." *Id.* at 443. The same rule should apply in determining the deadlines for filing the appellate record under Rule 54(a). Consistently, we hold that a timely filed request for findings of fact and conclusions of law extends the deadline for filing the appellate record under Rule 54(a) when findings and conclusions are required by Rule 296, or when they are not required by Rule 296 but are not without purpose—that is, they could properly be considered by the appellate court.

Although the district court appears to have based its decision largely on the filings in the transcript and the argument of counsel, it also expressly considered live testimony. Applying the rule we have adopted, we hold that Phillips and Worley Geological's request for findings and conclusions extended the deadline for filing the appellate record under Rule 54. The court of appeals therefore erred in dismissing the appeal.

Accordingly, the Court grants petitioners' application for writ of error and, without hearing argument, reverses the judgment of the court of appeals and remands the case to that court for a consideration of other issues raised. TEX. R. APP. P. 170.

BAKER, J., dissents for reasons stated in his dissenting opinion issued this date in *IKB Industries (Nigeria) Ltd. v. Pro-Line Corp.*, 938 S.W.2d 440, 443.

Note

Gene Duke Builders, Inc. v. Abilene Housing Authority, 138 S.W.3d 907 (Tex. 2004): Duke and Abilene were involved in a construction contract dispute, and Duke, pursuant to provisions in the contract, demanded arbitration. Abilene refused, and Duke brought this suit to compel arbitration. The trial court, after a hearing, granted Abilene's motion to dismiss for lack of subject matter jurisdiction, based on the conclusion that Duke was first required to bring a claim under the administrative procedure outlined in chapter 2260 of the Government Code. *Held:* Duke extended its time for filing a notice of appeal under TEX. R. APP. P. 26.1 by making a request for findings of fact and conclusions of law after the trial court granted Abilene's plea to the jurisdiction. Duke's time was extended because the findings of fact and conclusions of law filed by the trial court were based on an evidentiary hearing. Although Duke made no formal offer of evidence at the hearing on the plea to the jurisdiction, it submitted a deposition, affidavits, and exhibits attached to its pleadings showing that Abilene identified itself as part of the City of Abilene. Duke then used this evidence to argue that Abilene was a municipality and, therefore, not subject to TEX. GOV'T CODE § 2260.001(4). Because the trial court took evidence and because the trial court's findings could properly be considered by the appellate court, the time for filing notice of appeal was extended. The purposes of extending the deadline to file a notice of appeal are to give the trial court time to state the basis for its judgment so that a party may determine whether to appeal and to provide the court of appeals with a useful tool for appellate review.

7. *Appellate Review of Nonjury Cases*

ROBERSON
v.
ROBINSON
768 S.W.2d 280
(Tex. 1989)

Parker Ellzey, Alice, for petitioners.

Bernice Y. Shapiro, San Antonio, for respondent.

PER CURIAM.

Raymond Robinson, individually and as Executor of the Estate of Etta Moyer, filed this suit for rents against Charles E. Roberson and Roberson's Funeral Home, Inc. ("Roberson"). After a nonjury trial, the trial court rendered judgment against Roberson. The court of appeals reformed the trial court's judgment in part and affirmed. 761 S.W.2d 51. We reverse the judgment of the court of appeals.

Roberson brought forth a statement of facts on appeal, but did not request the trial court to make any findings of fact or conclusions of law. In the court of appeals, Roberson challenged the legal and factual sufficiency of the evidence to support the trial court's judgment. In purporting to resolve these points, the court of appeals stated:

> In determining if there is any evidence to support the judgment and implied findings of fact, we can consider only the evidence favorable to the implied findings and disregard any contrary evidence. 761 S.W.2d at 53. The court then proceeded to consider only that evidence favorable to the trial court's judgment.

In a nonjury trial, where no findings of fact or conclusions of law are filed or requested, it is implied that the trial court made all the necessary findings to support its judgment. *Goodyear Tire and Rubber Co. v. Jefferson Constr. Co.*, 565 S.W.2d 916, 918 (Tex. 1978); *Buchanan v. Byrd*, 519 S.W.2d 841, 842 (Tex. 1975). When a statement of facts is brought forward, these implied findings may be challenged by factual sufficiency and legal sufficiency points the same as jury findings or a trial court's findings of fact. *Burnett v. Motyka*, 610 S.W.2d 735, 736 (Tex. 1980); see also *Seaman v. Seaman*, 425 S.W.2d 339, 341 (Tex. 1968); *Bishop v. Bishop*, 359 S.W.2d 869, 872 (Tex. 1962).

In this case, it is clear that the court of appeals, in applying only a no evidence standard of review, failed to consider and weigh all of the evidence, thereby failing to properly rule on Roberson's factual sufficiency points. We conclude that this cause therefore must be remanded to that court for consideration of these points. *Burnett v. Motyka*, 610 S.W.2d at 736.

Pursuant to Rule 133(b), Texas Rules of Appellate Procedure, we grant Roberson's motion for rehearing, grant the application for writ of error and, without hearing oral argument, a majority of the court reverses the judgment of the court of appeals and remands the cause to that court for consideration of Roberson's factual sufficiency points.

TENERY
v.
TENERY

932 S.W.2d 29
(Tex. 1996)

Roger D. Bellows, Three Rivers, for Petitioner.
Sharon Trigo, Laredo, for Respondent.

PER CURIAM.

In this divorce case, the trial court refused three requests to make findings of fact and conclusions of law about the division of a marital estate and the amount of child support. The court of appeals held that the trial court's refusal was not harmful error. _____ S.W.2d _____, _____, 1995 WL 714203. We affirm in part and reverse in part.

The trial court awarded Gloria Tenery a disproportionate amount of the marital estate. It also ordered her husband, Wilbur, to pay $550 per month in child support for the care of one minor child. At the time of trial, Wilbur was collecting $980 per month in unemployment benefits. After the trial, Wilbur filed a timely request for findings of fact and conclusions of law under Texas Rule of Civil Procedure 296. Wilbur later submitted a notice of past due findings and conclusions and requested additional or amended findings and conclusions. *See* TEX. R. CIV. P. 297-98.

The court of appeals correctly held that Wilbur was not harmed by the trial court's failure to make findings of fact and conclusions of law about the division of the marital estate because there was ample evidence in the record to support the judgment. _____ S.W.2d at _____. The trial court has wide latitude to divide the marital estate "in a manner that the court deems just and right." TEX. FAM. CODE § 3.63; *see also Murff v. Murff*, 615 S.W.2d 696, 699 (Tex. 1981). Here, the record contains evidence that Wilbur had more earning capacity than Gloria, that he was at fault for the breakup of the marriage, and that Gloria would have been the one to benefit financially if the marriage continued. This evidence supports the trial court's decision to award Gloria a disproportionate amount of the marital estate. A trial court's failure to make findings is not harmful error if "the record before the appellate court affirmatively shows that the complaining party suffered no injury." *Cherne Indus. v. Magallanes*, 763 S.W.2d 768, 772 (Tex. 1989).

The court of appeals erred, however, when it held that Wilbur was not harmed by the trial court's failure to make findings of fact and conclusions of law about the amount of child support payments. _____ S.W.2d at _____. The Family Code guides the calculation of child support and bases that calculation on a percentage of monthly resources. *See* TEX. FAM. CODE § 154.125. Under the Family Code, resources include wage and salary income, interest income, self-employment income, net rental income, and all other income actually being received. *Id.* § 154.062(b). If the trial court uses factors other than net resources in determining the amount of child support, the Family Code specifies the findings the trial court must make. *Id.* § 154.130.

The record reveals that at the time of trial Wilbur's net resources were limited to $980 per month. Section 154.125 would require Wilbur, who was supporting one minor child, to pay $196 per month. The trial court ordered Wilbur to pay Gloria $550 per month. In his request for additional or amended findings, Wilbur asked for findings explaining why the amount of child support per month ordered by the court varied from the amount computed under section 154.125 guidelines. The trial court has the discretion to deviate from the guidelines and consider other factors. *Id.* § 154.123. But if a trial court deviates, as it did here, it must, upon request, make written findings of fact and conclusions of law. *Id.* § 154.130(a)(3); *see also Chamberlain v. Chamberlain*, 788 S.W.2d 455, 455 (Tex. App.—Houston 1990, writ denied) (holding that the language in the Family Code is mandatory and that the trial court's failure to make written findings upon request was reversible error).

Under Texas Rule of Civil Procedure 296, harm to the complaining party is presumed unless the contrary appears on the face of the record when the party makes a proper and timely request for findings and the trial court fails to comply. *Cherne*, 763 S.W.2d at 772 (*citing Wagner v. Riske*, 142 Tex. 337, 178 S.W.2d 117, 120 (1944)). Error is harmful if it prevents an appellant from properly presenting a case to the appellate court. TEX. R. APP. P. 81(b). In this case, the trial court's refusal to abide by the Family Code's child support provisions prevented Wilbur from effectively contesting the trial court's deviation from the guidelines in section 154.125.

Accordingly, under Texas Rule of Appellate Procedure 170 and without hearing oral argument, the Court grants the application for writ of error, reverses the portion of the judgment of the court of appeals that concerns child support, and remands this cause to the court of appeals with instructions for it to direct the trial court to correct its error under Texas Rule of Appellate Procedure 81(a).

Notes

1. In the case of *In re Jane Doe,* 19 S.W. 3d 249 (Tex. 2000), in discussing the standard of review for findings of fact the Supreme Court expounded:

> The standard of review to be applied in reviewing a trial court rulings on a minor's application to consent to an abortion without notifying her parents, pursuant to TEX. FAM. CODE section 33.004 is a legal or factual standard of review. The "mature and sufficiently well informed" requirement of section 33.003 is a question of fact. Section 33.003 provides that the trial judge should determine these questions by "a preponderance of the evidence." This requirement implies that the trial judge is to weigh the evidence and determine the credibility of the minor or any other witnesses. The trial court's factual findings on these issues are subject to a legal and factual sufficiency review standard. The abuse of discretion standard applies when a trial court has discretion either to grant or deny relief based on its factual determinations. This standard is especially appropriate when the trial court must weigh competing policy considerations and balance interests in determining whether to grant relief. Thus, the abuse of discretion standard is typically applied to procedural or other trial management determinations. By contrast, in this case the trial court has no discretion over the order. The statute provides that if the court finds that the minor is "mature and sufficiently well informed," it "shall enter an order authorizing the minor to consent to the performance of the abortion without notification to either of her parents . . . ." Furthermore, in determining whether a minor is "mature and sufficiently well informed," the trial court is not to weigh policy considerations; it simply makes a factual determination. When the trial court acts primarily as a factfinder, appellate courts normally review its determinations under the legal and factual sufficiency standards. Therefore, that standard of review is applied to this appeal. Unlike

the courts of appeals, the Supreme Court may only engage in legal sufficiency review. In reviewing legal sufficiency, however, the Supreme Court may set forth factors and principles for lower courts to follow in determining and reviewing whether a minor is "mature and sufficiently well informed" to make this decision without parental notification.

2. *Hone v. Hanafin*, 104 S.W.3d 884 (Tex. 2003): Courts and scholars disagree about whether filing a request for findings of fact and conclusions of law extends the deadline for perfecting an appeal when the appeal is accelerated. TEX. R. APP. P. 26.1(a)(4) does not clearly state that such a request does not extend the time period within which to file a notice of appeal. Under these circumstances, Petitioners could have plausibly assumed that their request for findings of fact would extend the time for filing a notice of appeal under Rule 26.1(a)(4). "Because we do not reach Petitioners' second issue, we do not consider whether a request for findings of fact and conclusions of law extends the appellate timetable in an interlocutory appeal under Rule 26.1(b)."

3. *Quiroz v. Gray*, 441 S.W.3d 588, 591 (Tex. App.—El Paso 2014, no pet.): "In each of their complaints, Appellants assert the trial court "erred in all findings and conclusions to the contrary." However, Appellants fail to identify any particular finding that they claim is palpably contrary to the evidence. Nor do they specifically identify any conclusion that they allege is erroneous. Generally, an attack on the sufficiency of the evidence must be directed at specific findings of fact rather than at the judgment as a whole. *In re M.S.F.*, 383 S.W.3d 712, 716 (Tex. App.—Amarillo 2012, no pet.). Unchallenged findings are binding upon the appellate court. *Id.* However, unidentified findings of fact may be reviewed on appeal if the appellate court can fairly determine from the argument the specific finding of fact that is being challenged. *In re M.S.F.*, 383 S.W.3d at 716. Because we can fairly determine from Appellants' argument the specific findings being challenged, we will address each of their complaints."

WESTECH ENG'G
v.
CLEARWATER CONSTRUCTORS

835 S.W.2d 190
(Tex. App.—Austin 1992, no writ)

William Knolle, Hearne, Knolle, LeWallen, Livingston & Holcomb, Austin, for appellant.
Brian S. Greig, Mary S. Canfield, Fulbright & Jaworski, Austin, for appellee.

B.A. SMITH, JUSTICE.

This case involves a construction contract. In twenty-three points of error, the sub-contractor, WesTech Engineering, Inc. (WesTech), has challenged the trial court's determination that it entered into and subsequently breached an agreement with the general contractor, Clearwater Constructors, Inc. (Clearwater) to provide wastewater-treatment equipment. In sixteen points of error, WesTech attacks the legal or factual sufficiency of the evidence supporting the trial court's judgment that WesTech pay damages to Clearwater for breach of contract; in the remaining seven points of error, WesTech attacks particular conclusions of law underlying the judgment. Clearwater, in turn, has brought two cross-points complaining of the trial court's denial of consequential damages and certain expenses. We will affirm the judgment of the trial court as modified.

THE CONTROVERSY

This appeal arises from WesTech and Clearwater's business dealings during 1987 and 1988. In the summer of 1987, the City of Austin undertook to expand and improve its Walnut Creek Wastewater Treatment Facility. Early in the process, the City retained the engineering firm of Camp, Dressar & McKee (CDM) to prepare the plans and specifications for the project. The City then solicited bids from general contractors, one of which was Clearwater Constructors.

WesTech was aware of the Walnut Creek Facility expansion and made bids to prospective general contractors, including Clearwater, in an attempt to secure a portion of the project. In these bids, WesTech offered to supply particular water-treatment equipment called for in the plant expansion. Specifically, WesTech sought to supply (1) two final clarifier mechanisms ("clarifiers"), and (2) a dissolved air flotation sludge thickening system ("DAF"). On June 30, 1987, Clearwater received a bid from WesTech on these two items and used WesTech's figures when formulating its own bid to the City.

In August 1987, the City chose Clearwater as the general contractor for the plant expansion project. In a letter of intent dated September 15th, notifying WesTech that it had been selected to supply the clarifiers and the DAF, Clearwater indicated that it would forward to WesTech a purchase agreement "in the very near future." WesTech received an unsigned agreement from Clearwater in mid-December.

A WesTech representative signed the purchase agreement but attached a letter to Clearwater indicating that the agreement contained terms that differed from WesTech's initial proposal. In its letter dated December 16, 1987, WesTech expressed its intent that the terms of its original proposal be "made a part of the [purchase] order." In its findings of fact, the trial court found that Clearwater subsequently signed the purchase agreement and dated it December 18, 1987. In separate findings, the trial court referred to this purchase agreement as "the contract" between the parties.

Initially, relations between WesTech and Clearwater proceeded normally. WesTech submitted to Clearwater specific data concerning both the clarifiers and the DAF. Problems arose, however, when the project engineering firm, CDM, determined that WesTech's clarifier equipment would not meet the particular specifications set out in the City's contract. The parties conducted a number of meetings to resolve these problems. For its part, WesTech supplied additional data on its proposed equipment, which Clearwater and CDM re-evaluated. Nevertheless, CDM decided that the WesTech equipment would not comply with the City's contract requirements.

Ultimately CDM concluded that the central-drive gears to be used in WesTech's clarifiers did not meet the durability requirements set out in the City's plans and specifications. Clearwater notified WesTech of its decision to seek an alternate source for the clarifiers and informed WesTech that it would be liable for Clearwater's increased procurement costs, if any.

In March 1988, WesTech supplied Clearwater with its DAF equipment submittal. Later that month, CDM engineers rejected WesTech's DAF submittal on the grounds that WesTech lacked the DAF installation experience called for in the City contract. Clearwater again notified WesTech of the rejection and informed WesTech it would be accountable for any increased costs in procuring DAF equipment from an alternate source. Eventually Clearwater obtained the clarifiers and the DAF from other companies, but at a cost greater than that contracted for with WesTech.

In March 1990, Clearwater filed suit against WesTech for breach of contract, hoping to recover its increased costs for the equipment. After a trial before the court, Clearwater was awarded $123,495 in "cover" costs resulting from WesTech's breach, plus prejudgment interest and attorney's fees. WesTech now appeals the trial court's judgment.

STANDARDS OF REVIEW

At WesTech's request, the trial court filed findings of fact and conclusions of law in support of its judgment; some eighty-nine findings of fact and twenty-seven conclusions of law are contained in the record. In addition, the record contains a statement of facts from the proceedings.

Findings of Fact

We attach to findings of fact the same weight that we attach to a jury's verdict upon jury questions. *City of Clute v. City of Lake Jackson*, 559 S.W.2d 391, 395 (Tex. Civ. App. 1977, writ ref'd n.r.e.). Findings of fact are reviewable for legal and factual sufficiency of the evidence by the same standards used to review jury findings. *Okon v. Levy*, 612 S.W.2d 938, 941 (Tex. Civ. App. 1981, writ ref'd n.r.e.) (*citing Hall v. Villarreal Dev. Corp*., 522 S.W.2d 195 (Tex. 1975)).

An appellant who challenges the legal sufficiency of the evidence supporting an issue upon which it did not have the burden of proof must demonstrate that there is no evidence to support the adverse finding. *Raw Hide Oil & Gas, Inc. v. Maxus Exploration Co.*, 766 S.W.2d 264, 275 (Tex. App. 1988, writ denied). In reviewing a no-evidence point, we consider only the evidence supporting the finding and we disregard all evidence to the contrary. *Best v. Ryan Auto Group, Inc.*, 786 S.W.2d 670, 671 (Tex. 1990). If there is any evidence supporting the finding, we must overrule the point and uphold the finding.

When challenging the factual sufficiency of the evidence supporting an adverse finding upon which it did not carry the burden of proof, an appellant must demonstrate that there is insufficient evidence to support the adverse finding. *Maxus Exploration Co.*, 766 S.W.2d at 275-76. We will consider and weigh all the evidence in support of and contrary to the finding. *Plas-Tex, Inc. v. U.S. Steel Corp.*, 772 S.W.2d 442, 445 (Tex. 1989). The contested finding will be upheld unless we find that (1) the evidence is too weak to support the finding, or (2) the finding is so against the overwhelming weight of the evidence as to be manifestly unjust. *Garza v. Alviar*, 395 S.W.2d 821, 823 (Tex. 1965). We will not substitute our judgment for that of the trier of fact merely because we reach a different fact conclusion. *Otis Elevator Co. v. Joseph*, 749 S.W.2d 920, 923 (Tex. App. 1988, no writ).

On those issues on which an appellant has the burden of proof, it must prevail on a no-evidence challenge and then must demonstrate on appeal that the evidence conclusively establishes the issue in its favor as a matter of law. *Holley v. Watts*, 629 S.W.2d 694, 696 (Tex. 1982). Only when the contrary proposition is established conclusively by the evidence will we sustain the point of error. *Meyerland Community Improvement Ass'n v. Temple*, 700 S.W.2d 263, 267 (Tex. App. 1985, writ ref'd n.r.e.).

Conclusions of Law

The trial court's conclusions of law are always reviewable. *Middleton v. Kawasaki Steel Corp.*, 687 S.W.2d 42, 44 (Tex. App. 1985, writ ref'd n.r.e.). Conclusions of law will be upheld on appeal if the judgment can be sustained on any legal theory supported by the evidence. *Simpson v. Simpson*, 727 S.W.2d 662, 664 (Tex. App. 1987, no writ). Incorrect conclusions of law will not require reversal, however, if the controlling findings of facts will support a correct legal theory. *Valencia v. Garza*, 765 S.W.2d 893, 898 (Tex. App. 1989, no writ). Moreover, conclusions of law may not be reversed unless they are erroneous as a matter of law. *Mercer*, 715 S.W.2d at 697.

* * *

CONCLUSION

We sustain appellant's twenty-third point complaining of the trial court's unconditional award of attorney's fees and modify the judgment to reflect an award of such fees only upon success on appeal. As modified, we affirm the judgment of the district court.

POWERS, J., did not participate.

HOFLAND
v.
FIREMAN'S FUND INSURANCE COMPANY

907 S.W.2d 597
(Tex. App.—Corpus Christi 1995, no writ)

Kathryn Snapka, Corpus Christi, J. Robert McKissick, John D. Charbonnet, Jr., Spagnoletti & Associates, Houston, Ricardo Gonzalez, Oxford, Oxford & Gonzalez, Edinburg, for appellants.
Richard E. Griffin, Fred A. Simpson, Annelie Menke, Griffin & Laser, Houston, for appellee.
Kathleen Walsh Beirne, Houston, for real party in interest.

YANEZ, JUSTICE.

This case arises out of a dispute over insurance coverage. The trial court held that La Joya Gin, Inc. (La Joya) was not covered by the insurance policy; therefore, the insurance company had no duty to defend or indemnify La Joya. By three points of error, La Joya and Larry Hofland appeal from this declaratory judgment. We affirm.

Appellants, Hofland and La Joya, initiated this lawsuit against Fireman's Fund Insurance Company (FFIC) as a result of FFIC's refusal to defend and indemnify La Joya for a judgment entered against it in a separate lawsuit filed by Filiberto and Maria Garza. In that lawsuit, the Garzas alleged that Robert Clyde Smith, acting as an agent of La Joya, was driving a pickup truck in the course and scope of his employment with La Joya when a flatbed trailer he was towing became disengaged and collided with Mr. Garza's vehicle. The Garzas sued, among others, La Joya and its owner, Larry Hofland. The trial judge concluded that Smith acted as an agent of La Joya and negligently attached the trailer to his vehicle. Thereupon, the trial judge entered a judgment against La Joya in the amount of $1,000,000.00.

In the present lawsuit, the breach of contract claim was severed from the other claims and tried by the court without a jury. The parties stipulated to limit the issues to the proper interpretation of the policy provisions, specifically Exclusion 2(b) of the policy, and its applicability to the Garza lawsuit. The parties further stipulated that the court's interpretation shall control the issue of FFIC's duty to defend or indemnify La Joya. La Joya is the only named insured of the insurance policy. Exclusion 2(b) provides that the insurance does not apply to bodily injury or property damage arising out of the ownership, maintenance, operation, use, loading or unloading of (1) any automobile or aircraft owned or operated by or rented or loaned to any insured, or (2) any other automobile or aircraft operated by any person in the course of his employment by any insured.

At the conclusion of the bench trial, the court entered a take-nothing declaratory judgment against appellants. The court made the following findings:

(1) FFIC had no duty to defend La Joya in the Garza lawsuit;

(2) FFIC had no duty to indemnify La Joya for the $1,000,000.00 judgment;

(3) the provisions of the insurance policy are unambiguous; and

(4) the relationship between Robert Clyde Smith and La Joya was adequately adjudicated by the court in the Garza lawsuit.

Hofland and La Joya appeal from this judgment.

By three points of error, appellants complain that there is no evidence to support the court's findings that FFIC had no duty to defend or indemnify and assert that, as a matter of law, the policy provisions were ambiguous. We address these three points together.

Conclusions of law will be upheld on appeal if the judgment can be sustained on any legal theory supported by the evidence. *Westech Eng'g, Inc. v. Clearwater Constructors, Inc.*, 835 S.W.2d 190, 196 (Tex. App.—Austin 1992, no writ); *Kotis v. Nowlin Jewelry, Inc.*, 844 S.W.2d 920, 922 (Tex. App.—Houston [14th Dist.] 1992, no writ). Conclusions of law will not be reversed unless they are erroneous as a matter of law. *Westech Eng'g, Inc.*, 835 S.W.2d at 196; *Mercer v. Bludworth*, 715 S.W.2d 693, 697 (Tex. App.—Houston [1st Dist.] 1986), rev'd on other grounds, 801 S.W.2d 890 (Tex. 1991).

The dispositive issue is whether Exclusion 2(b) applies, and thus, results in La Joya not being covered by its insurance policy. Appellants urge that the plain meaning of Exclusion 2(b) precludes its applicability, or alternatively, the provision is ambiguous and should be construed against the insurer. Appellants contend that as worded, the exclusion is susceptible to more than one reasonable interpretation. The interpretation appellants advocate in claiming the exclusion does not apply is twofold: 1) although the trailer was "used," it was not being "operated" at the time it was hitched and 2) although Smith may have been acting "in the course of his employment," he was not an "employee" of La Joya. A second reasonable interpretation, according to appellants and the one urged by FFIC, is that Smith "used" and "operated" the trailer and that the term "employment" applies not only to "employees" but to other persons as well.

Whether a contract is ambiguous is a question of law for the court to decide by looking at the contract as a whole in light of the circumstances present when the contract was entered. *Coker v. Coker*, 650 S.W.2d 391, 394 (Tex. 1983); *R & P Enters. v. LaGuarta, Gavrel & Kirk, Inc.*, 596 S.W.2d 517, 518 (Tex. 1980). If the contract can be given a certain or definite legal meaning or interpretation, then it is not ambiguous and the court will construe the contract as a matter of law. *Coker*, 650 S.W.2d at 393; *Corriveau v. 3005 Investment Corp.*, 697 S.W.2d 766, 767 (Tex. App.—Corpus Christi 1985, writ ref'd n.r.e.). The contractual provision, however, is ambiguous if its meaning is uncertain and doubtful and it is reasonably susceptible to more than one interpretation. *Coker*, 650 S.W.2d at 393; *RGS, Cardox Recovery, Inc. v. Dorchester Enhanced Recovery Co.*, 700 S.W.2d 635, 638 (Tex. App.—Corpus Christi 1985, writ ref'd n.r.e.).

Nevertheless, not every difference in the interpretation of a contract or an insurance policy amounts to an ambiguity. *Forbau v. Aetna Life Ins. Co.*, 876 S.W.2d 132, 134 (Tex. 1994). Both the insured and the insurer are likely to take conflicting views of coverage, but disagreement over the interpretation of an instrument does not automatically make it ambiguous. *Id.* Likewise, uncertainty or lack of clarity in the language chosen by the parties is insufficient to render a contract ambiguous. *Preston Ridge Fin. Servs. Corp. v. Tyler*, 796 S.W.2d 772, 777 (Tex. App.—Dallas 1990, writ denied); *Medical Towers v. St. Luke's Episcopal Hosp.*, 750 S.W.2d 820, 822 (Tex. App.—Houston [14th Dist.] 1988, writ denied).

In construing contracts, the primary concern of the court is to ascertain the true intention of the parties as expressed in the instrument. *Coker*, 650 S.W.2d at 393; *R & P Enters.*, 596 S.W.2d at 518. In ascertaining the true intention of the parties, the courts will examine and consider the entire writing, seeking as best they can, to harmonize and to give effect to all the provisions of the contract so that none will be rendered meaningless. *Universal CIT Credit Corp. v. Daniel*, 150 Tex. 513, 243 S.W.2d 154, 158 (1951); *Corriveau*, 697 S.W.2d at 767. Language used by parties in a contract should be accorded its plain, grammatical meaning unless it definitely appears that the intention of the parties would thereby be defeated. *Lyons v. Montgomery*, 701 S.W.2d 641, 643 (Tex. 1985).

We agree with the trial court that the exclusion provision is unambiguous. Appellants' main contention is that the negligent act of hitching the trailer to the truck constitutes a use and not an operation of the trailer; therefore, the requirements of the exclusion are not satisfied. Appellants focus only on one specific act. However, the exclusion is more expansive. The exclusion provides that insurance does not apply to bodily injury arising out of the use or loading of an automobile operated by a person in the course of his employment by the insured. The parties agree that the definition of "automobile" includes a trailer. Attaching the trailer to the truck is a use or even a loading of the automobile.

Our analysis does not stop here, as argued by appellants. The Garza court not only found that Smith was negligent in attaching the trailer to his truck, but also that the trailer came loose from the truck, struck Garza, and caused him severe injuries. Thus, we also look to the facts leading up to the detachment of the trailer which caused Garza's injuries. Smith operated the trailer when he drove his truck and towed the trailer. FFIC's expert, John McKinley, testified that one operates a trailer by hitching it to another vehicle and pulling it. Thus, the operation of a trailer includes hitching the trailer so that it can be towed. Consequently, Garza's injuries arose out of the use and operation of the trailer.

We now address whether Smith was acting in the course of La Joya's employment. Appellants assert that because the Garza court only found that Smith was acting as an agent for La Joya and did not find that he was an employee, Exclusion 2(b) does not apply. The exclusion provides that the automobile had to be operated by any person in the course of the insured's employment; the exclusion does not refer to an "employee." The term "agent" refers to a form of employment. *Ackley v. State*, 592 S.W.2d 606, 608 (Tex. Crim. App. [Panel Op.] 1980). An agent is the employee of his principal. *Id.* The term "employee" includes "servant" and "agent." *Id.* "Employment" is commonly defined as use, purpose, or the act of employing. WEBSTER'S NINTH NEW COLLEGIATE DICTIONARY 408 (1987). "Employ" means "to make use of" or "to use or engage the services of." *Id.* Thus, the Garza court's finding that Smith acted as La Joya's agent satisfies the language of the exclusion since he is a person acting in the course of his employment by La Joya.

Having found that the provision is unambiguous and that Exclusion 2(b) applies, we hold that FFIC had no duty to defend or indemnify La Joya. We overrule appellants' three points of error.

Accordingly, we affirm the judgment of the trial court.

FEDERAL DEPOSIT INS. CORP.
v.
MORRIS

782 S.W.2d 521
(Tex. App.—Dallas 1990, no writ)

T. Ray Guy, William C. Scott, Jenkens & Gilchrist, Dallas, for appellant.
J. Kent Newsom, Newsom, Terry & Newsom, Dallas, for appellees.

ENOCH, CHIEF JUSTICE.

Federal Deposit Insurance Corp. (FDIC), in its capacity as receiver of First National Bank of Irving (FNB-I), appeals the trial court's judgment against it in a suit brought by Robert Morris, Jr., and William O. Shields. In a single point of error, FDIC claims that the trial court erred in failing to make findings of fact and conclusions of law, thus depriving FDIC of the opportunity to urge other points of error concerning the factual and legal foundations of the judgment. We agree. The judgment of the trial court is reversed and the cause is remanded for a new trial.

PROCEDURAL BACKGROUND

Trial was held before the court without a jury in the early fall of 1988, an election year. At trial, Morris and Shields sought recovery for damages they incurred by FNB-I's failure to convey an apartment building. FDIC asserted various legal and factual defenses. The trial judge lost his election to a full term on the court and did not sign a final judgment before leaving office. However, a final judgment was entered in favor of Morris and Shields on January 23, 1989, by the successor judge.

On January 31, 1989, FDIC, pursuant to rule 296 of the Texas Rules of Civil Procedure, requested the new presiding judge to make findings of fact and conclusions of law. The trial court judge acknowledged receipt of the request for findings of fact and conclusions of law on February 6, 1989. On February 24, 1989, FDIC, pursuant to rule 297 of the Texas Rules of Civil Procedure, filed a motion with the judge reminding him that findings of fact and conclusions of law had been requested and as of that date had not yet been filed with the clerk of the court. No findings of fact or conclusions of law were ever filed with the clerk.

FINDINGS OF FACT AND CONCLUSIONS OF LAW REQUIRED

Texas Rule of Civil Procedure 296 reads as follows: In any case tried in the district or county court without a jury, the judge shall, at the request of either party, state in writing his findings of fact and conclusions of law. Such request shall be filed within ten days after the final judgment is signed. Notice of the filing of the request shall be served on the opposite party as provided in Rule 21a. TEX. R. CIV. P. 296 (emphasis added).

Texas Rule of Civil Procedure 297 reads: When demand is made therefor, the court shall prepare its findings of fact and conclusions of law and file same within thirty days after the judgment is signed. Such findings of fact and conclusions of law shall be filed with the clerk and shall be part of the record. If the trial judge shall fail so to file them, the party so demanding, in order to complain of the failure, shall, in writing, within five days after such date, call the omission to the attention of the judge, whereupon the period for preparation and filing shall be automatically extended for five days after such notification. TEX. R. CIV. P. 297 (emphasis added).

Morris and Shields respond that the record does contain findings of fact and conclusions of law and that such findings and conclusions are located in the judgment itself. They point to case law for the proposition that when findings of fact and conclusions of law are set forth as recitations in the judgment appealed from, they shall be treated as findings of fact and conclusions of law filed in accordance with rule 296 of the Texas Rules of Civil Procedure. *Cottle v. Knapper*, 571 S.W.2d 59, 64 (Tex. Civ. App.—Tyler 1978, no writ). Indeed, a plethora of Texas cases so holds. *See Lee v. Uvalde County*, 616 S.W.2d 367, 369 (Tex. Civ. App.—Tyler 1981, no writ); *Bradley v. Jones*, 604 S.W.2d 450, 453 (Tex. Civ. App.—Tyler 1980, no writ); *Peterson v. Peterson*, 595 S.W.2d 889, 891 (Tex. Civ. App.—Austin 1980, writ dism'd); *Hemphill v. S & Q Clothiers*, 579 S.W.2d 564, 567 (Tex. Civ. App.—Fort Worth 1979, no writ).

However, we note that in these cases, no request was made by any of the parties for findings of fact or conclusions of law pursuant to rule 296. The court in *Hemphill* simply concludes that, "the findings of fact recited in this judgment are to be given the same consideration as if they had been separately filed." *Hemphill*, 579 S.W.2d at 567. In *Cottle*, however, the court pointed out that the preferable practice is to file findings of fact and conclusions of law in a separate instrument from that of the judgment. *Cottle*, 571 S.W.2d at 64. In the case before us, a timely request for findings of fact and conclusions of law was made. Once the request was properly and timely made, the judge had thirty days in which to file findings of fact and conclusions of law. TEX. R. CIV. P. 297. Morris and Shields fail to point out in the record where findings and conclusions by the trial court have been filed. Rules 296 and 297 clearly contemplate a separate instrument is to be filed.

When a party makes a proper and timely request for findings of fact and conclusions of law pursuant to rule 296, the trial court may not rely upon a reference back to recitals in the judgment itself to satisfy that request. Such recitals tend to mislead a party into failing to request specific findings, or as in this case, to request findings believing that none have been made and then bringing forth a point of error on appeal asserting failure of the trial court to respond to the request. *See generally Gonzalez v. Cavazos*, 601 S.W.2d 202, 203 (Tex. Civ. App.—Corpus Christi 1980, no writ) (holding that recitals in the judgment are not tantamount to findings of fact or conclusions of law); *Texas Hauling Contractors v. Rose Sales Co.*, 565 S.W.2d 240, 244 (Tex. Civ. App.—Corpus Christi 1977, no writ) ("Such recitations [of findings of fact and legal conclusions] in the judgment are not proper. It tends to mislead the parties, sometimes resulting in failure by them to request and receive specific findings"); *Cottle*, 571 S.W.2d at 64 (The preferable practice is to file findings of fact and conclusions of law in a separate instrument).

FDIC made a request for findings of fact and conclusions of law within ten days after the judgment was entered. No such findings having been filed, FDIC gave its reminder notice under rule 297. We hold that the trial court was in error in failing to make findings of fact and conclusions of law. *Anzaldua v. Anzaldua*, 742 S.W.2d 782, 783 (Tex. App.—Corpus Christi 1987, writ denied); *Fine v. Scott*, 592 S.W.2d 56, 58 (Tex. Civ. App.—Eastland 1979, writ ref'd n.r.e.).

Having concluded that the trial court erred in failing to file findings of fact and conclusions of law, the only issue remaining is whether we are required to either abate the appeal and order the trial court to enter findings and conclusions or remand this cause for a new trial. *See Joseph v. Joseph*, 731 S.W.2d 597, 598-60 (Tex. App.—Houston [14th Dist.] 1987, no writ).

HARM

The general rule in Texas is that the failure of the trial court to file findings of fact and conclusions of law constitutes error, where the complaining party has complied with the appropriate rules of procedure in an effort to secure such findings. *Wagner v. Riske*, 142 Tex. 337, 342, 178 S.W.2d 117, 119 (1944); *Joseph*, 731 S.W.2d at 598. However, failure of the trial court to prepare and file findings of fact or conclusions of law under rule 296 does not require reversal of the trial court's judgment if the record before the appellate court affirmatively shows the complaining party suffered no harm. *Las Vegas Pecan & Cattle Co. v. Zavala County*, 682 S.W.2d 254, 256 (Tex. 1984); *Wagner*, 178 S.W.2d at 120; *Sheldon Pollack Corp. v. Pioneer Concrete*, 765 S.W.2d 843, 845 (Tex. App.—Dallas 1989, writ denied).

In *Sheldon Pollack Corp.*, this Court stated that the test for determining whether the complaining party has suffered harm by the trial court's failure to file findings is: [W]hether the circumstances of the particular case would require an appellant to have to guess the reason or reasons that the judge has ruled against it. *See Fraser v. Goldberg*, 552 S.W.2d 592, 594 (Tex. Civ. App.—Beaumont 1977, writ ref'd n.r.e.). The issue is whether there are disputed facts to be resolved. *See Barnes v. Coffman*, 753 S.W.2d 823 (Tex. App.—Houston [14th Dist.] 1988, writ denied). *Sheldon*, 765 S.W.2d at 845. In *Fraser v. Goldberg*, the court stated: In factually complicated situations in which there are two or more possible grounds for recovery or defense, an undue burden would be placed upon an appellant. Having to try to guess the reason or reasons the trial judge rules against him should not be required. *Fraser*, 552 S.W.2d at 597. The test used in *Fraser* applies to the facts of this case. Here, several grounds for recovery were alleged and several defenses to liability were urged. We have already held that the recitations in the judgment do not satisfy the rule 296 request. A party is not required to guess first where findings are located and then guess what they are.

As to whether abatement of the appeal or remand of the cause is necessitated, we conclude that remand is mandated by the peculiar facts of this case. The remedy of abatement is not available. The original trial judge is no longer on the court and, consequently, no longer available to respond to our order to enter findings of fact and conclusions of law. *See Anzaldua v. Anzaldua*, 742 S.W.2d 782, 783 (Tex. App.—Corpus Christi 1987, writ denied); *see also Cherne Industries, Inc. v. Juan Magallanes*, 763 S.W.2d 768, 773 (Tex. 1989) (here the court held that "[b]ecause the trial judge continues to serve on the district court, . . . the error in this case is remediable").

The judgment of the trial court is reversed and this cause is remanded to that court for a new trial.

Note

Texas Eastern Transmission Corp. v. Sealy Ind. Sch. Dist., 572 S.W.2d 49 (Tex. Civ. App.—Houston [1st Dist.] 1978, no writ): The trial court need not make findings about:

Facts that are admitted;
Facts that are immaterial to the resolution of any controlling issue;
Facts that are evidentiary only;
Facts that do not relate to the ultimate or controlling issue(s) in the case.
In making the findings, the trial court is not limited to the requests made.

Chapter 6.
Preclusion: Res Judicata and Collateral Estoppel

1. *Res Judicata*

CORMIER
v.
HIGHWAY TRUCKING COMPANY
312 S.W.2d 406
(Tex. Civ. App.—San Antonio 1958, no writ)

Jack Fields, Port Lavaca, for appellant.
Lewright, Dyer & Redford, James W. Wray, Jr., Corpus Christi, for appellees.

W. O. Murray, Chief Justice.

This suit was instituted in the County Court of Calhoun County by Matthew Cormier against Highway Trucking Company and Solomon Gonzales, seeking to recover damages to the automobile of plaintiff resulting from a collision between plaintiff's automobile and a truck driven by Solomon Gonzales and owned by Highway Trucking Company. There had been a previous suit between these parties, based on the same collision, in which plaintiff recovered judgment against the defendants for personal injuries sustained by him in that collision. The defendants plead the judgment in the District Court as a bar to the cause of action in the County Court. The trial court sustained the plea of bar and granted a summary judgment that plaintiff take nothing as against the defendants. Matthew Cormier has prosecuted this appeal.

Appellant clearly states that the question here presented is: 'May a Plaintiff who receives injuries to his person and damages to his property in a single occurrence bring two separate actions for damages against the same Defendant or Defendants, one for the injuries to his person and one for the injuries to his property without a recovery in one barring a recovery in the other?' This is a question of first impression in this State. There are two early cases which have a bearing on the matter: *Watson v. Texas & P. Railway Co.*, 8 Tex. Civ. App. 144, 27 S.W. 924, and *Texas & P. R. Co. v. Nelson*, 9 Tex. Civ. App. 156, 29 S.W. 78. The facts in those cases distinguish them from the case we have before us and, therefore, do not settle the question here raised.

The authorities of other jurisdictions are not in accord on this question. There is clearly a majority rule and a minority rule. In 127 A.L.R. at page 1081, the majority rule is stated as follows: '* * * a single wrongful or negligent act or omission causing an injury to both the person and the property of the same individual constitutes but one cause of action with separate items of damage, and * * * hence, the cause of action cannot be split, and a recovery of a judgment for either item of damage may be pleaded in bar of an action to recover for the other item of damage, * * *.' In 127 A.L.R. at page 1083, the minority rule is stated as follows: '* * * damage to goods and injury to the person, although the result of the same wrongful act, are infringements of different rights, and give rise to distinct causes of action, and hence a recovery under one cause of action cannot be pleaded in bar of a recovery on the other cause of action, * * *.'

We are of the opinion that the majority rule is the better rule, because it prevents a multiplicity of suits and at the same time does justice between litigants. Here a party, while driving his car, has a collision with a motor vehicle driven by another party, and as a result of such collision he sustains personal injury and damages to his automobile. He should seek to recover both of these items of damage in one lawsuit. There is no good reason why the parties should be put through the expense and trouble of two lawsuits when the grounds of recovery of the two items of damages must be based on exactly the same facts. We realize that there are exceptions to this rule, but none of these exceptions are involved here and need not be discussed.

The provisions of Rule 97, Texas Rules of Civil Procedure, relating to compulsory counterclaims, and the provisions of Article 5539b, Vernon's Ann Civ. Stats., relating to limitation as affecting amended and supplemental pleadings, indicate that the public policy of this State favors the bringing of but one suit to collect these two items of damages.

The judgment of the trial court is affirmed.

Notes

1. *Pustejovsky v. Rapid-American Corporation*, 35 S.W.3d 643 (Tex. 2000): Generally, the single action rule, also known as the rule against splitting claims, provides a plaintiff one indivisible cause of action for all damages arising from a defendant's single breach of a legal duty. A corollary rule concerns the accrual of a cause of action: A cause of action accrues when the plaintiff knows or reasonably should know that he had been legally injured by the alleged wrong, however slightly. The fact that the plaintiff's actual damages may not be fully known until much later does not affect the determination of the accrual date.

2. Two other terms are useful in the discussion of res judicata. These terms are "merger" and "bar."

   a. If P recovered in the first action that cause of action is merged into the judgment and cannot be reasserted. Even unadjudicated claims are barred when they constitute a part of the same cause of action.

   b. If the P lost in the first action, the cause of action and all claims comprising it are barred by the judgment.

3. Res judicata includes the concepts of merger & bar (claim preclusion) and the doctrines of collateral estoppel or estoppel by judgment (issue preclusion). The part of the chapter titled "Res Judicata" refers to the doctrine of merger and bar (claim preclusion). The second part of the chapter refers to issue preclusion, otherwise referred to as Collateral Estoppel.

BARR
v.
RESOLUTION TRUST CORP.
837 S.W.2d 627
(Tex. 1992)

Albert B. Greco, Jr., Barbara L. Wohlrabe, Dallas, for petitioner.
Jack N. Ross, II, Dallas, for respondent.

GONZALEZ, JUSTICE.

The issue in this case is whether a claim by Sunbelt Federal Savings against George Barr based on a partnership promissory note and guarantee agreement is barred by the doctrine of res judicata. The trial court granted Barr's motion for summary judgment based on res judicata. The court of appeals, with one Justice dissenting, reversed the trial court's judgment, holding that the doctrine did not apply. 824 S.W.2d 600. We reverse the judgment of the court of appeals and affirm the trial court's judgment.

In 1985, Barr and Ron Knott were partners in the Bar III Venture. On March 14, 1985, Bar III executed a promissory note for $369,750 in favor of Sunbelt's predecessor in interest. The same day, Barr and Knott executed a personal guarantee of the note. In March 1987, Bar III defaulted on the note.

On May 24, 1988, Sunbelt filed two separate lawsuits on the note. In one suit, Sunbelt alleged liability against the partnership as maker of the note and against Knott as guarantor of the note. In the other, Sunbelt alleged that Barr was personally liable because of his unconditional guarantee of the note.

Barr moved for summary judgment in the latter lawsuit on the grounds that the terms of the guaranty agreement were too uncertain to be enforceable. Barr argued that the agreement, a standard form containing a number of options to choose and blanks to complete, was not sufficiently completed to ascertain his liability. The trial court granted the motion, and rendered a final take-nothing judgment. Sunbelt did not appeal the judgment.

Thereafter, Sunbelt amended its pleadings in the suit against the partnership and Knott by adding Barr as a defendant, alleging that his status as a partner created liability for the note. Barr's answer asserted res judicata, among other defenses.

Barr moved for summary judgment on the grounds that the take-nothing judgment in the first lawsuit barred litigation of the claims against him in the second lawsuit. Sunbelt also moved for summary judgment, requesting a judgment on the note. The trial court granted Barr's motion and denied Sunbelt's. This interlocutory judgment became final when the court rendered judgment for Sunbelt on its claims against the partnership and Knott for the full amount of the note.

Sunbelt appealed, arguing that the trial court should have granted its summary judgment instead of Barr's. The court of appeals, with one justice dissenting, determined that the first suit did not bar the second. However, the court concluded that questions of fact prevented rendition in Sunbelt's favor, and thus remanded the case to the trial court. Both Barr and Sunbelt sought review in our court.

Much of the difficulty associated with the doctrine of res judicata is due to the confusion of several related theories. Broadly speaking, res judicata is the generic term for a group of related concepts concerning the conclusive effects given final judgments. *Puga v. Donna Fruit Co.*, 634 S.W.2d 677, 679 (Tex. 1982). Within this general doctrine, there are two principal categories: (1) claim preclusion (also known as res judicata); and (2) issue preclusion (also known as collateral estoppel).[1] Res judicata, or claims preclusion, prevents the relitigation of a claim or cause of action that has been finally adjudicated, as well as related matters that, with the use of diligence, should have been litigated in the prior suit. *Gracia v. RC Cola-7-Up Bottling Co.*, 667 S.W.2d 517, 519 (Tex. 1984); *Bonniwell v. Beech Aircraft Corp.*, 663 S.W.2d 816, 818 (Tex. 1984). Issue preclusion, or collateral estoppel, prevents relitigation of particular issues already resolved in a prior suit.[2] *Bonniwell*, 663 S.W.2d at 818. Barr's argument, that Sunbelt should have brought all theories of liability in one suit, is the defense of claim preclusion.

Claim preclusion prevents splitting a cause of action. *Jeanes v. Henderson*, 688 S.W.2d 100, 103 (Tex. 1985). The policies behind the doctrine reflect the need to bring all litigation to an end, prevent vexatious litigation, maintain stability of court decisions, promote judicial economy, and prevent double recovery. Zollie Steakley & Weldon U. Howell, Jr., *Ruminations on Res Judicata*, 28 Sw. L.J. 355, 358-59 (1974).

The question that has given courts the most difficulty is determining what claims should have been litigated in the prior suit. Early on, this Court held that res judicata "is not only final as to the matter actually determined, but as to every other matter which the parties might litigate in the cause, and which they might have decided." *Foster v. Wells*, 4 Tex. 101, 104 (1849). We have never repudiated this definition of claim preclusion, and it appears in some form in most definitions of res judicata. *See, e.g., Jeanes v. Henderson*, 688 S.W.2d 100, 103 (Tex. 1985) (res judicata bars not only what was actually litigated but also claims that could have been litigated in the original cause of action). If taken literally, this definition of the rule would require that all disputes existing between parties be joined, regardless of whether the disputes have anything in common. This court has re-

---

1 Res judicata may be further categorized into merger and bar, because the doctrine has different applications depending on which party is successful in the prior suit. If the party asserting a claim prevails, the cause of action is merged into the judgment, and the cause of action as such ceases to exist. Jeanes v. Henderson, 688 S.W.2d 100, 103 (Tex. 1985). If the party defending a claim prevails in the prior suit, the judgment acts as a bar to matters which could have been litigated in the original suit. *Id.*

2 An example of the confusion concerning collateral estoppel is the court of appeals' holding that "res judicata does not preclude relitigation of issues that the first court did not actually try and determine, unless a determination of those issues was essential to the judgment in the first suit." 824 S.W.2d at 602. The court relied on RESTATEMENT (SECOND) OF JUDGMENTS § 27 (1982), which is entitled "Issue Preclusion—General Rule", i.e., collateral estoppel. *See id.* § 17(3), and comment (c). We disapprove similar language in the case cited by the court, Faour v. Faour, 762 S.W.2d 361 (Tex. App.—Houston [1st Dist.] 1988, writ denied). Our own recent holdings have contributed to the confusion by holding without elaboration that res judicata requires an "identity of issues" between the prior and subsequent suits. *See, e.g.*, Coalition of Cities for Affordable Utility Rates v. Public Utilities Commission, 798 S.W.2d 560, 563 (Tex. 1990); Byrom v. Pendley, 717 S.W.2d 602, 606 (Tex. 1986); Bonniwell v. Beech Aircraft Corp., 663 S.W.2d 816, 818 (Tex. 1984). If an identity of issues is strictly required, then there is no basis for precluding issues that should have been raised in the prior suit but were not, and there is no distinction between claim preclusion and issue preclusion. *See* Flores v. Edinburg Consolidated Indep. School Dist., 741 F.2d 773, 776 (5th Cir. 1984).

sorted to a wide variety of theories and tests to give res judicata a more restrictive application. *See generally* 5 WILLIAM V. DORSANEO III, TEXAS LITIGATION GUIDE § 131.06[4][b][ii] (1991); *Steakley*, 28 SW.L.J. 355.

Even if only cases from more recent times are considered, our holdings with respect to res judicata are difficult to reconcile. In *Griffin v. Holiday Inns of America*, 496 S.W.2d 535 (Tex. 1973) the court determined that a take-nothing judgment in a suit to recover in contract for services and materials did not preclude a subsequent suit to be compensated in quantum meruit. The court rejected the view that a judgment as to one claim is res judicata of all claims or causes of action arising out of the same transaction, and stated that, "[a]s a general rule a judgment on the merits in a suit on one cause of action is not conclusive of a subsequent suit on a different cause of action except as to issues of fact actually litigated and determined in the first suit." *Id.* at 538. The court acknowledged, however, that alternative theories of recovery for the same "claim" may not be brought in different lawsuits.

Thus, in *Griffin*, the court determined that a "cause of action" for res judicata purposes is something more than the set of facts necessary to establish a single theory of recovery but not necessarily the entire transaction between the parties. *Id.* at 537-38. The court gave no guidance on the question of how to make this fine distinction between a mere alternative theory of recovery and a different cause of action. Every theory of recovery has its unique elements of proof. As the *Griffin* case illustrates, only slight variations of the facts to support different theories of the same incident can result in a court finding different causes of action, thus thwarting the purposes of res judicata. *See Steakley*, 28 SW. L.J. at 361-62.

The court took an entirely different approach in *Westinghouse Credit Corp. v. Kownslar*, 496 S.W.2d 531 (Tex. 1973). In that case Kownslar had guaranteed all promissory notes by the maker. The issue was whether res judicata required that Westinghouse bring in one suit its claims for all notes guaranteed by Kownslar that were then in default. Rather than decide whether there was more than one cause of action involved, the court decided the case solely on whether it appeared that the policies of res judicata required such a result.

This pure policy approach as exemplified by *Westinghouse* makes it virtually impossible to determine in advance what policy will win out in any given case. Without any objective standards, each case is decided ad hoc, and therefore the doctrine is "inherently unpredictable" and "affords little basis for consistency and formulation of precedent." *Steakley*, 28 SW. L.J. at 362-63. *Westinghouse* is the only case we have decided solely on policy grounds.

Then, in *Texas Water Rights Comm. v. Crow Iron Works*, 582 S.W.2d 768 (Tex. 1979), the court shifted the focus from the cause of action to the subject matter of the litigation. The question was whether a major lawsuit instigated to sort out water rights to the lower Rio Grande river precluded a subsequent suit based on the claim that during the pendency of that suit the plaintiff had purchased additional rights. The court concluded that the subsequent claim was barred, noting that: The scope of res judicata is not limited to matters actually litigated; the judgment in the first suit precludes a second action by the parties and their privies not only on matters actually litigated, but also on causes of action or defenses which arise out of the same subject matter and which might have been litigated in the first suit. *Id.* at 771-72 (emphasis added). *Accord, Gracia*, 667 S.W.2d at 519. Thus this definition is not consistent with earlier formulations of the rule, such as in *Griffin*, that only issues related to a single cause of action are barred in a subsequent suit. While we did not expressly overrule the *Griffin* test in either *Crow Iron Works* or *Gracia* we do so now.

A determination of what constitutes the subject matter of a suit necessarily requires an examination of the factual basis of the claim or claims in the prior litigation. It requires an analysis of the factual matters that make up the gist of the complaint, without regard to the form of action. Any cause of action which arises out of those same facts should, if practicable, be litigated in the same lawsuit. *Gracia*, 667 S.W.2d at 519; *Crow Iron Works*, 582 S.W.2d at 772.

The definition of res judicata in *Gracia* and *Crow Iron Works* is substantially similar to the rule of compulsory counterclaims embodied in the rules of civil procedure. A party defending a claim must bring as a counterclaim any claim that "arises out of the transaction or occurrence that is the subject matter of the opposing party's claim . . . ." TEX. R. CIV. P. 97.

The RESTATEMENT OF JUDGMENTS also takes the transactional approach to claims preclusion. It provides that a final judgment on an action extinguishes the right to bring suit on the transaction, or series of connected transactions, out of which the action arose. RESTATEMENT OF JUDGMENTS § 24(1). A "transaction" under the RESTATEMENT is not equivalent to a sequence of events, however; the determination is to be made pragmatically, "giving weight to such considerations as whether the facts are related in time, space, origin, or motivation, whether they form a convenient trial unit, and whether their treatment as a trial unit conforms to the parties' expectations or business understanding or usage." *Id.* s 24(2).

We conclude that the transactional approach to claims preclusion of the RESTATEMENT effectuates the policy of res judicata with no more hardship than encountered under rule 97(a) of the rules of civil procedure. Modern rules of procedure obviate the need to give parties two bites at the apple, as was done in *Griffin*, to ensure that a claim receives full adjudication. Discovery should put a claimant on notice of any need for alternative pleading. Moreover, if success on one theory becomes doubtful because of developments during trial, a party is free to seek a trial amendment.

In the case now before us, there is no valid reason to subject Barr to two different lawsuits. In the suit brought previously against Barr, the bank alleged that he executed the guarantee on the same day and as part of the "same transaction" as the promissory note. In both suits Sunbelt seeks to hold Barr primarily liable for payment of the note and seeks the same amount of damages. Both suits require proof establishing the notes of the partnership, that the notes are due, and that the partnership has defaulted. The only factual allegation that Sunbelt pleaded in the second suit that was not in the first is that Barr is a general partner of Bar III Venture.

It is clear that in this case the execution of the partnership note and Barr's guarantee of it were related in time and space and motivation, and the parties considered it as a single transaction. The issues of both claims form a convenient trial unit, whereas separate lawsuits would require significant duplication of effort of the court and the parties involved. With due diligence, the claim that Barr was liable because he is a partner could have been joined in the suit on his guarantee of the partnership note.

We reaffirm the "transactional" approach to res judicata. A subsequent suit will be barred if it arises out of the same subject matter of a previous suit and which through the exercise of diligence, could have been litigated in a prior suit. For these reasons, the judgment of the court of appeals is reversed and that of the trial court is affirmed.

GETTY OIL COMPANY
v.
INSURANCE COMPANY OF NORTH AMERICA, NL.

845 S.W.2d 794
(Tex. 1992)

Joe G. Roady, Mel Smith, Patrick L. Hughes, Mary Ann A. Bellatti, and Karen S. Cook, Houston, for petitioners.

Tom Lorance, Jr., Byron Lee, Tom Bayko, John C. Allen, Jack G. Carnegie, Linda C. Schoonmaker, Houston, Michael W. Jahnke, New York City, David W. Prasifka, Houston, Thomas Engelhardt, Chicago, Ill., and William K. Luyties, Houston, for respondents.

PHILLIPS, CHIEF JUSTICE.

The purchaser of certain chemicals brought suit against the seller and its insurers, claiming that they were contractually obligated to provide insurance to cover a judgment against the purchaser in a wrongful death action precipitated by the explosion of the chemicals. The trial court granted summary judgment for the defendants on four grounds: (1) a contract provision requiring the seller to purchase liability insurance for the buyer violated the Texas Oilfield Anti-Indemnity Statute, TEX.REV.CIV.STAT.ANN. art. 2212b (now codified and amended at TEX.CIV.PRAC. & REM.CODE §§ 127.001-.007 (Vernon 1986 & Supp.1992)); (2) the same contractual provision violated the common law express negligence rule; (3) the prior litigation of a related indemnity provision precluded the present suit under the doctrine of res judicata; and (4) specific issues were precluded by collateral estoppel. The court of appeals affirmed on the theory of res judicata. 819 S.W.2d 908 (Tex. App.—

Houston 1991). We affirm the judgment of the court of appeals in part, reverse in part, and remand the cause to the trial court for further proceedings.

I. Facts and Procedural Background

Getty Oil Company ("Getty") purchased various chemicals from NL Industries, Inc. ("NL") for Getty's oil production and exploration operations in the Midland, Texas, area. A purchase order numbered "HB-5357" was in effect from August 1, 1983, to July 31, 1984. It included the following provisions:

> 4. INSURANCE AND INDEMNITY: Seller agrees to maintain at Seller's sole cost and expense, from the time operations are commenced hereunder until Order is fully performed and discharged insurance of all types and with minimum limits as follows, and furnish certificates to Purchaser's Purchasing Department evidencing such insurance with insurers acceptable to Purchaser * * *
>
> All insurance coverages carried by Seller, whether or nor required hereby, shall extend to and protect Purchaser . . . to the full amount of such coverages and shall be sufficiently endorsed to waive any and all claims by the underwriters or insurers against Purchaser . . .
>
> Seller shall indemnify, defend and hold harmless Purchaser . . . from any and all losses, claims, actions, costs, expenses, judgments, subrogations, or other damages resulting from injury to any person (including injury resulting in death), or damage (including loss or destruction to property of whatsoever nature of any person[ )] arising out of or incident to the performance of the terms of this Order by Seller (including, but not limited to, Seller's employees, agents, subcontractors, and others designated by Seller to perform work or services in, about, or attendant to, the work and services under the terms of this Order.) Seller shall not be held responsible for any losses, expenses, claims, subrogations, actions, costs, judgments, or other damages, directly, solely, and proximately caused by the negligence of Purchaser. Insurance covering this indemnity agreement shall be provided by Seller.
>
> The liability of Seller, as herein above provided, shall not be limited by the insurance coverage required of Seller.

On November 22, 1983, a barrel of chemical demulsifier delivered by NL under Order No. HB-5357 exploded in the vicinity of a Getty well, killing Carl Duncan, an independent contractor working for Getty.

Duncan's estate and survivors brought wrongful death and survival actions in the 130th Judicial Court of Matagorda County against Getty, NL and its subsidiaries, and others. Getty filed a cross-claim against NL, alleging that NL's negligence proximately caused the injury to Duncan, that the chemicals manufactured by NL were defective, and that NL breached warranties in connection with the sale of the chemicals. Getty also asserted a contractual right of indemnity against NL under the terms of HB-5357 (quoted above), and a contribution claim because of NL's negligence. The jury found Getty 100% negligent and grossly negligent in causing the accident. The trial court rendered judgment on the jury verdict for $3,757,000 actual damages and $25,000,000 punitive damages. The trial court also rendered judgment that "all Cross-Actions for contributions and/or indemnity based upon the contracts are denied." Getty appealed the portion of the judgment denying it contribution and indemnity, and the court of appeals affirmed the judgment of the trial court. *Getty Oil Corp. v. Duncan,* 721 S.W.2d 475 (Tex. App.—Corpus Christi 1986, writ ref'd n.r.e.). Getty's insurers, Travellers Insurance Company, Travellers Indemnity Company, and English & American Insurance Company, settled the claim for $14 million.

Getty then filed an insurance claim with NL's insurers. After they refused to honor the claim, Getty sued NL and its primary and excess insurance carriers, Insurance Company of North America ("INA") and Youell and Companies ("Youell"), respectively. Getty alleged that, pursuant to the terms of the HB-5357 "Insurance and Indemnity" provision, NL's insurance should cover Getty for its liability in the *Duncan* case. Getty brought claims against NL for breach of the contract to purchase insurance in its behalf, violation of TEX.BUS. & COM.CODE § 1.203 (Tex. UCC) (Vernon 1968) (obligation of good faith), breach of the duty of good faith and fair dealing, negligence, violation of the Texas Deceptive Trade Practices Act (DTPA), TEX.BUS. & COM.CODE §§ 17.41-.63 (Vernon 1987 & Supp.1992), and common law fraud. Against INA and Youell, Getty asserted claims for breach of the contract to extend it insurance coverage, violation of TEX.INS.CODE art. 3.62 (Vernon 1981) (repealed) (failure to pay claim), breach of the duty of good faith and fair dealing, negligence, violation of the DTPA, and common law fraud.

NL, INA and Youell jointly moved for summary judgment, arguing that (1) the terms of HB-5357 did not make Getty an additional insured under NL's policies; (2) the Insurance and Indemnity scheme of HB-5357 was prohibited by the Texas Oilfield Anti-Indemnity Statute, TEX.REV.CIV.STAT.ANN. art. 2212b (now codified and amended at TEX.CIV.PRAC. & REM.CODE §§ 127.001-.007); and (3) Getty's claims were barred by res judicata and collateral estoppel. The defendants also joined Getty's insurers as third party defendants, claiming that Getty's policies with them at least partially relieved the defendants of covering Getty's liability.

On May 3, 1990, the trial court granted the defendants' motions for summary judgment. The trial court also granted the defendants' motion to sever the third party claims against Getty's insurers, and ordered that the severed actions not go forward until resolution of the action between Getty and the defendants. Getty appealed the summary judgment for defendants, and the court of appeals affirmed on res judicata grounds, holding that Getty's claims were barred because it was seeking the same relief under a different theory that it unsuccessfully sought in the first suit. 819 S.W.2d at 915. Getty now seeks a reversal of the court of appeals' judgment and the trial court's summary judgment.

II. Res Judicata

A. Getty v. NL

We recently clarified that Texas follows the "transactional" approach to res judicata. *See Barr v. Resolution Trust Corp.,* 837 S.W.2d 627 (Tex. 1992). Under this approach, a judgment in an earlier suit "precludes a second action by the parties and their privies not only on matters actually litigated, but also on causes of action or defenses which arise out of the same subject matter and which might have been litigated in the first suit." *Id.* at 630; *Texas Water Rights Comm. v. Crow Iron Works,* 582 S.W.2d 768, 771-72 (Tex. 1979).

We conclude that Getty's present suit arises out of the same subject matter as its earlier cross-claim against NL asserted in the *Duncan* suit. The Restatement (Second) of Judgments, which recognizes the transactional test, suggests that factors to consider in determining whether facts constitute a single "transaction" are "their relatedness in time, space, origin, or motivation, and whether, taken together, they form a convenient unit for trial purposes." Restatement (Second) of Judgments § 24 cmt. b (1980). Getty's present action against NL arose from the same accident that was adjudicated in the *Duncan* suit. The present suit also concerns the same contract, HB-5357, and the same section of that contract, the "Insurance and Indemnity" section. Finally, Getty seeks the same relief against NL here as in its earlier cross-claim: reimbursement for Getty's liability to Duncan's estate and beneficiaries. Thus, both Getty's actions against NL derived from the same transaction.

Getty argues that res judicata cannot bar its present claims against NL because these claims did not accrue until judgment was rendered in the *Duncan* suit. That is, Getty had no liability and hence no need for insurance coverage until liability was assigned. The contingent nature of these claims, however, does not preclude the operation of res judicata. We held in *Barr* that "[a] subsequent suit will be barred if it arises out of the same subject matter of a previous suit and which, through the exercise of diligence, could have been litigated in a prior suit." 837 S.W.2d at 631. Getty could have asserted its present claims in the *Duncan* suit, with their resolution being contingent on the plaintiffs' claims. Texas Rule of Civil Procedure 51(b) provides:

> **Joinder of Remedies.** Whenever a claim is one heretofore cognizable only after another claim has been prosecuted to a conclusion, the two claims may be joined in a single action; but the court shall grant relief in that action only in accordance with the relative substantive rights of the parties.

See Parkhill Produce Co. v. Pecos Valley Southern Ry. Co., 348 S.W.2d 208 (Tex. Civ. App.—San Antonio 1961, writ ref'd n.r.e.). For example, we have held that an indemnitee may bring a claim against an indemnitor before judgment is assigned against the indemnitee. *See Gulf, Colorado & Santa Fe Ry. Co. v. McBride,* 159 Tex. 442, 446, 322 S.W.2d 492, 495 (Tex. 1958); *Mitchell's, Inc. v. Friedman,* 157 Tex. 424, 431, 303 S.W.2d 775, 779 (Tex. 1957); *K & S Oil Well Service, Inc. v. Cabot Corp.,* 491 S.W.2d 733, 739 (Tex. Civ. App.—Corpus Christi 1973, writ ref'd n.r.e.). Forcing the indemnity suit to wait for judgment in the liability suit "would contravene the policy of the courts to encourage settlements and to minimize litigation." *Id.*

Getty itself took advantage of this rule in its initial cross-action against NL, in which Getty asserted its claim under the indemnity provision of HB-5357. The fact that Getty had no claim for indemnity against NL until the trial court rendered judgment did not preclude this cross-claim. Likewise, Getty could have brought its other contingent cross-claims against NL in the *Duncan* action. The fact that Getty's claims against NL were contingent on Getty incurring liability in the *Duncan* suit does not in and of itself preclude operation of res judicata.

We do not hold that a defendant must assert a cross-claim against a co-defendant simply because it arises from the same subject matter as plaintiff's claim. TEX.R.CIV.P. 97(e) clearly makes such a cross-claim permissive; the defendant may assert it, but is not required to. Rule 97(e) comports with the principle that res judicata applies only to *adverse* parties. Where two parties are aligned in the first action and no issues are drawn between them, the judgment in that action does not preclude later claims between those parties. *See Smith v. Baker,* 380 S.W.2d 725, 726 (Tex. Civ. App.—Waco 1964, writ ref'd n.r.e.); *Green v. City of San Antonio,* 282 S.W.2d 769, 776 (Tex. Civ. App.—San Antonio 1955, writ ref'd n.r.e.); *Second Nat'l Bank of Houston v. Fuqua,* 262 S.W.2d 834, 835 (Tex. Civ. App.—Waco 1953, writ ref'd n.r.e.). However, where a defendant *does* assert a cross-claim against a co-party, they become adverse, and the principles of res judicata apply. The cross-claimant becomes a plaintiff for res judicata purposes, and is required to assert all claims against the cross-defendant arising from the subject matter of the original cross-claim. *Cf.* Restatement (Second) Judgments § 23 (1980) ("Where a defendant interposes a claim as a counterclaim and a valid and final judgment is rendered against him on the counterclaim, the rules of bar are applicable to the judgment.").

Getty relies on *Chandler v. Cashaway Building Materials, Inc.,* 584 S.W.2d 950, 954 (Tex. App.—El Paso 1979, no writ), where the court held that res judicata "applies to the cause of action which was actually filed by the plaintiff and not cross-actions which might have been filed by a defendant, unless, of course, the compulsory counterclaim rule is applicable." *See also Swiss Avenue Bank v. Slivka,* 724 S.W.2d 394, 396-97 (Tex. App.—Dallas 1986, no writ). These cases merely reiterate the principle of Rule 97(e) that a party is not required to assert a cross-claim against an otherwise non-adverse party. Neither *Chandler* nor *Slivka* involved a situation where a party asserted some but not all of its cross-claims.

Getty was not required to bring any of its cross-claims against NL in the *Duncan* suit. Once it chose to bring some of those claims, however, it was required under res judicata to bring them all in the same action. Accordingly, we agree with the court of appeals' holding as to this issue.

B. Getty v. INA and Youell

The court of appeals also held that Getty's claims against INA and Youell, NL's primary and excess insurance carriers, were barred by res judicata. Although INA and Youell were not parties to the *Duncan* suit, the court reasoned that res judicata bars a second suit "against the same parties *or their privies.*" 819 S.W.2d at 910 (emphasis added).

Under Texas law, a former judgment bars a second suit against all who were in "privity" with the parties to the first suit. *Benson v. Wanda Petroleum Co.,* 468 S.W.2d 361, 363 (Tex. 1971). There is no general definition of privity that can be automatically applied in all res judicata cases; the circumstances of each case must be examined. *See Dairyland County Mutual Ins. Co. of Texas v. Childress,* 650 S.W.2d 770, 773-74 (Tex. 1983); *Benson,* 468 S.W.2d at 363. Those in privity with a party may include persons who exert control over the action, persons whose interests are represented by the party, or successors in interest to the party. *See Dairyland,* 650 S.W.2d at 774.

Getty replies that even if INA and Youell were in privity with NL, res judicata would not bar Getty's present claims against them because Getty could not have asserted those claims in the *Duncan* suit. The insurance policies themselves specifically prohibited any claim from being brought against INA or Youell before the insured's liability was reduced to judgment or compromised. We have held that when such "no action" policy provisions exist, "a third party's right of action against the insurer does not arise until he has secured such an agreement or a judgment against the insured." *Great American Ins. Co. v. Murray,* 437 S.W.2d 264, 265-66 (Tex. 1969); *see also State Farm County Mut. Ins. Co. of Texas v. Ollis,* 768 S.W.2d 722, 723 (Tex. 1989).

Moreover, TEX.R.CIV.P. 38(c) prohibited Getty from joining INA and Youell in the *Duncan* suit. This rule provides, with respect to the joinder of third parties:

> (c) This rule shall not be applied, in tort cases, so as to permit the joinder of a liability or indemnity insurance company, unless such company is by statute or contract liable to the person injured or damaged.

Rule 38(c) has been held to prohibit the joinder of insurers in situations resembling this case. *See Langdeau v. Pittman,* 337 S.W.2d 343, 355 (Tex. Civ. App.—Austin 1960, writ ref'd n.r.e.).

Since Getty could not have asserted its present claims against INA or Youell in the *Duncan* suit, it is not now precluded by res judicata from bringing these claims. We accordingly reverse the judgment of the court of appeals affirming the trial court's summary judgment against INA and Youell on the ground of res judicata, and we remand this portion of the cause to the trial court for further proceedings.

III. Collateral Estoppel

The trial court also granted summary judgment for respondents on the basis of collateral estoppel. The court of appeals did not reach this question.

The doctrine of collateral estoppel precludes relitigation of ultimate issues of fact actually litigated and essential to the judgment in a prior suit. *Tarter v. Metropolitan Savings & Loan Ass'n,* 744 S.W.2d 926, 927 (Tex. 1988), *Bonniwell v. Beech Aircraft Corp.,* 663 S.W.2d 816, 818 (Tex. 1984); Restatement (Second) of Judgments § 27 (1980). NL first argues that Getty seeks to relitigate the issue of whether Duncan's accident arose in connection with NL's performance of the purchase order. This issue is important because HB-5357 requires NL to provide insurance for Getty only for losses "arising out of or incident to the performance of the terms of this Order by [NL] . . . ." NL contends that the jury decided this issue adversely to Getty in the *Duncan* case.

Collateral estoppel requires that the issue decided in the first action be identical to the issue in the pending action. *See Price v. Texas Employers' Ins. Ass'n,* 782 S.W.2d 938, 940 (Tex. App.—Tyler 1989, writ ref'd n.r.e.). The jury in the *Duncan* suit found that NL was not negligent and that it placed adequate warnings on the chemicals, but neither the jury nor the trial court expressly found that the accident did not arise out of or incident to NL's performance of the purchase order. NL contends, however, that the phrase "incident to [NL's] performance" in HB-5357 refers only to losses caused by NL's negligence, and thus the jury's answers necessarily equate to a finding that Duncan's accident was not incident to the performance of HB-5357. The court in the *Duncan* case, however, apparently made no finding regarding this question. Also, we do not consider the language necessarily to be as narrow as NL contends. Getty's construction-that an injury is "incident to performance" as long as it results from chemicals delivered by NL under the contract-is also arguable under the literal language of the agreement. The parties have not focused on the proper interpretation of this language in their briefing and argument to this Court, and thus we are unable under the present record to conclude that NL's obligation to provide insurance applied only for accidents caused by NL's negligence. Without such a finding, we cannot conclude that Getty is attempting to relitigate a factual issue decided by the jury in the *Duncan* case, and NL's collateral estoppel argument must therefore fail.

NL further argues that Getty is attempting to relitigate a legal issue previously decided in the *Duncan* suit: whether Getty has a right of indemnity from NL. Collateral estoppel also precludes the relitigation of essential issues of law that were litigated and determined in a prior action. *Price,* 782 S.W.2d at 940-41; *Withers v. Republic Nat'l Bank of Dallas,* 248 S.W.2d 271, 282 (Tex. Civ. App.—Beaumont 1952, writ ref'd n.r.e.); Restatement (Second) of Judgments § 27 (1980). It was determined in the *Duncan* suit that Getty had no right of indemnity from NL, but Getty is not attempting to relitigate that issue here. Rather, it is seeking damages for NL's failure to extend insurance coverage to Getty. Although the latter action arose from the same transaction as the former and, with respect to Getty's claim against NL, is barred by res judicata, it is based on a different provision of HB-5357 and does not present the same legal issue. As indicated, collateral estoppel only applies where the *identical* issue was litigated in the prior suit. *Price,* 782 S.W.2d at 940.

For the foregoing reasons, the court of appeals' judgment cannot be affirmed on the basis of collateral estoppel.

* * *

VI. Conclusion

We affirm the judgment of the court of appeals as to Getty's claims against NL. We reverse the judgment of the court of appeals as to Getty's claims against INA and Youell, and remand those claims to the trial court for further proceedings consistent with this opinion. We express no opinion regarding whether Getty is an additional insured under NL's insurance policies with INA or Youell, or the extent of such coverage, if it exists.

Concurring and dissenting opinion by GONZALEZ, J., joined by MAUZY and DOGGETT, JJ.GONZALEZ, JUSTICE concurring and dissenting (omitted).

Notes

1. Res judicata requires proof of three elements. Those elements are: (1) a prior final judgment on the merits by a court of competent jurisdiction; (2) identity of parties or those in privity with them; and (3) a second action based on the same claims as were raised or could have been raised in the first action. *See Texas Water Rights Comm'n v. Crow Iron Works*, 582 S.W. 768 (Tex. 1979). The issue of privity in the context of res judicata was addressed by the Court recently in *Amstadt v. United States Brass Corp.*, 919 S.W.2d 644 (Tex. 1996). In that case a homeowner brought a suit to recover damages allegedly caused by a defective plumbing system. The prior owner of the house had brought the same lawsuit against the identical parties and a final judgment had been rendered in that case. The defendant's asserted that the second case was barred by the doctrine of res judicata arguing that the second homeowner was in privity with the former homeowner from who he purchased his house. The Court said:

> Generally people are not bound by a judgment in a suit to which they were not parties. *See* TEX. CIV. PRAC. & REM. CODE § 37.006(a). The doctrine of res judicata creates an exception to this rule by forbidding a second suit arising out of the same subject matter of an earlier suit by those in privity with the parties to the original suit. *See Crow Iron Works*, 582 S.W.2d at 771-72. The purposes of the exception are to ensure that a defendant is not twice vexed for the same acts, and to achieve judicial economy by precluding those who have had a fair trial from relitigating claims. *Benson v. Wanda Petroleum Co.*, 468 S.W.2d 361, 363 (Tex. 1971).
>
> People can be in privity in at least three ways: (1) they can control an action even if they are not parties to it; (2) their interests can be represented by a party to the action; or (3) they can be successors in interest, deriving their claims through a party to the prior action. *Getty Oil Co. v. Insurance Co. of N. Am.*, 845 S.W.2d 794, 800 (Tex. 1992); *Benson*, 468 S.W.2d at 363.
>
> To determine whether subsequent plaintiffs are in privity with prior plaintiffs, we examine the interests the parties shared. *See Texas Real Estate Comm'n v. Nagle*, 767 S.W.2d 691, 694 (Tex. 1989). Privity exists if the parties share an identity of interests in the basic legal right that is the subject of litigation. *Id.* To determine whether a prior and later lawsuit involve the same basic subject matter, we focus on the factual basis of the complaint. *Barr*, 837 S.W.2d at 630. If the second plaintiffs seek to relitigate the matter which was the subject of the earlier litigation, res judicata bars the suit even if the second plaintiffs do not allege causes of action identical to those asserted by the first. *See id.* at 630; *Crow Iron Works*, 582 S.W.2d at 771-72. Res judicata also precludes a second action on claims that arise out of the same subject matter and which might have been litigated in the first suit. *Crow Iron Works*, 582 S.W.2d at 772; *Cain v. Balcom*, 130 Tex. 497, 109 S.W.2d 1044, 1045-46 (1937). Under the foregoing standards, we consider whether the Knowlton plaintiffs were in privity with the Diehl plaintiffs, so that res judicata bars the Knowltons' suit.
>
> U.S. Brass and Celanese argue that the Knowlton plaintiffs were in privity with the Diehl plaintiffs because the Knowlton plaintiffs were successors in interest who derived their rights in property from the Diehl plaintiffs. We agree. " '[A]ll persons are privy to a judgment whose succession to the rights of property therein adjudicated are derived through or under one or the other of the parties to the action, and which accrued subsequent to the commencement of the action.' " *Kirby Lumber Corp. v. Southern Lumber Co.*, 145 Tex. 151, 196 S.W.2d 387, 388 (1946) (*quoting Cain*, 109 S.W.2d at 1046). As a matter of law, the Knowlton plaintiffs were in privity with the Diehl plaintiffs because they succeeded to the rights of property in the homes. *See id.* ("Privity, in this connection, means the mutual or successive relationship to the same rights of property."). Although the rule that res judicata bars the claims of successors in title arose in the context of land and property rights disputes, *see, e.g., Freeman v. McAninch*, 87 Tex. 132, 27 S.W. 97, 98-100 (1894), it applies here as well. As we stated in a water rights dispute, "one acquiring an interest in the property involved in a lawsuit takes the interest subject to the parties' rights as finally determined by the court." *Crow Iron Works*, 582 S.W.2d at 771.

For both the Diehl and Knowlton plaintiffs, the right at issue was the right to be compensated for injuries caused by the defective plumbing systems. The two lawsuits involved the same subject matter, the same houses, and the same plumbing systems. The negligence, gross negligence, products liability, and DTPA claims were virtually identical. Because the Knowlton plaintiffs are the Diehl plaintiffs' successors in interest and because they brought virtually identical claims concerning the same subject matter, we hold that res judicata bars the Knowlton plaintiffs' suit.

2. Sec. 31.004, TEX. CIV. PRAC. & REM CODE. Effect of Adjudication in Lower Trial Court.

(a) A judgment or a determination of factor law in a proceeding in a lower trial court is not res judicata and is not a basis for estoppel by judgment in a proceeding in a district court, except that a judgment rendered in a lower trial court is binding on the parties thereto as to recovery or denial of recovery.

(b) This section does not apply to a judgment in probate, guardianship, mental health, or other matter in which a lower trial court has exclusive subject matter jurisdiction on a basis other than the amount in controversy.

(c) For purposes of this section, a "lower trial court" is a small claims court, a justice of the peace court, a county court, or a statutory county court.

3. Sec. 31.005, TEX.CIV.PRAC. & REM CODE. Effect of Adjudication in Small Claims or Justice of the Peace Court.

A judgment or a determination of fact or law in a proceeding in small claims court or justice of the peace court is not res judicata and does not constitute a basis for estoppel by judgment in a proceeding in a county court or statutory county court, except that the judgment rendered in binding on the parties thereto as to recovery or denial of recovery.

4. *John G. and Marie Stella Kenedy Memorial Foundation v. Dewhurst*, 90 S.W.3d 268 (Tex. 2002): Determinations of law are not generally given preclusive effect.

The Court's interpretation of the civil law in *Luttes* is reasonable and workable, and it has provided a rule for determining boundaries for more than forty years. While the Court recognizes that the subject is not beyond reconsideration, *stare decisis* is never stronger than in protecting land titles, as to which there is great virtue in certainty. Accordingly, the Court reaffirms that shoreline boundaries in civil law land grants must be determined with reference to measured mean daily high water levels.

5. In *Igal v. Brighstar Information Technology Group, Inc.*, ---S.W.3d ----, Tex. Sup. Ct. J. 184, 2007 WL 4276545 (Tex. 2007) the Court addressed the doctrine of res judicata in the area of administrative orders. The Court noted that to further the public policy discouraging prolonged and piecemeal litigation, the administrative orders of certain administrative agencies bar the same claims being relitigated in the court system. When an administrative agency is acting in a judicial capacity and resolves disputed issues of fact properly before it, which the parties have had an adequate opportunity to litigate, the courts apply res judicata to enforce repose. In deciding wage claims under Section 61, Texas Workers' Commission (TWC) acts in a judicial capacity. Res judicata, therefore, will generally apply to final TWC orders. Igal had the option of seeking relief for alleged unpaid wages in an administrative proceeding under the Payday Day Law or pursuing a common law debt action in state court. He chose the former. Only after TWC entered a final judgment on the merits, which Igal elected not to appeal, did Igal seek redress in the courts. The doctrine of res judicata bars Igal from pursuing relief in a court of law after obtaining a final decision in TWC for the same transaction. The parties had an adequate opportunity to litigate their claims through an adversarial process in which TWC finally decided disputed issues of fact.

6. In *Citizens Insurance Co. of America v. Daaach,* 217 S.W. 3d 430 (Tex. 2007) the court addressed the effect of res judicata in class action law suits. The court noted that class certification under Rule 42 was never meant to be an exception to res judicata, or to exist in some sort of alternative universe outside the normal jurisprudence of Texas. Basic principles of res judicata apply to class actions just as they do to any other form of litigation. Accordingly, claims not pursued, or abandoned, in a class suit seeking damages that proceeds to final judgment on other claims arising from the same subject matter are subject to preclusion from relitigation by the principles of res judicata. Having given putative class members the opportunity to choose, however, the courts will ordinarily hold class actions to the same res judicata standards as other forms of litigation, including enforc-

ing the preclusion on abandoned claims which could have been litigated in the suit. Class members may be precluded from asserting those claims in subsequent individual litigation if they arose from the same transaction or subject matter and could have been litigated in the prior suit. Aggregation of claims in an appropriate class action is a more efficient way to resolve numerous disputes at once. However, efficiency is defeated if the tactfully structured dispute that is finally resolved in class suits may be relitigated in the same or other forums. To have preclusive effect a prior judgment cannot be "constitutionally infirm." Due process requires that the named plaintiff at all times adequately represent the interests of the absent class members, as well as notice plus an opportunity to be heard and participate in the litigation. Due process may require that class members be given notice of the class action and an opportunity to opt out and preserve claims that a class representative has abandoned. Thus, TEX. R. CIV. P. 42 requires the trial court, as part of its rigorous analysis, to consider the risk that a judgment in the class action may preclude subsequent litigation of claims not alleged, abandoned, or split from the class action. The trial court abuses its discretion if it fails to consider the preclusive effect of a judgment on abandoned claims, as res judicata could undermine the adequacy of representation requirement.

LEONARD
v.
TEXACO, INC.
422 S.W.2d 160
(Tex. 1967)

R. E. Swift, Palestine, Garrett & Stahala, Robert Stahala, Fort Worth, for petitioner.

Bob Reeves, Palestine, William S. Clarke, Houston, for respondent.

NORVELL, JUSTICE.

This case involves a limitation problem. The action is one for damages by a surface owner against the mineral lessee allegedly growing out of seismic operations on the lease. Texaco, Inc., defendant in the trial court and respondent here, contends that the action was barred by the two year statute of limitations. Article 5526 [now 16.003 TEX. CIV. PRAC. & REM. CODE] reads in part as follows:

> 'There shall be commenced and prosecuted within two years after the cause of action shall have accrued, and not afterward, all actions or suits in court of the following description:
>
> '1. Actions of trespass for injury done to the estate or the property of another. * * *'

O. P. Leonard, the plaintiff in the trial court and petitioner here, takes the position that the statute was tolled for a few days by agreement of the parties so that his petition was filed within the prescribed statutory period and that a subsequent amendment of the petition was embraced by Article 5539b (now TEX. CIV. PRAC. & REM. CODE 16. 065) which provides:

> 'Whenever any pleading is filed by any party to a suit embracing any cause of action, cross-action, counterclaim, or defense, and at the time of filing such pleading such cause of action, cross-action, counterclaim, or defense is not subject to a plea of limitation, no subsequent amendment or supplement changing any of the facts or grounds of liability or of defense shall be subject to a plea of limitation, provided such amendment or supplement is not wholly based upon and grows out of a new, distinct or different transaction and occurrence. Provided, however, when any such amendment or supplement is filed, if any new or different facts are alleged, upon application of the opposite party, the court may postpone or continue the case as Justice may require.'

The trial court gave judgment for plaintiff but the Court of Civil Appeals reversed upon a holding that the amendment to Leonard's petition did not come within the provisions of said Article 5539b. 409 S.W.2d 901. We reverse the judgment of the Court of Civil Appeals and affirm that of the trial court.

Leonard, the surface owner of approximately 12,000 acres of land in Anderson County, Texas, sued Texaco, the holder of an oil, gas and mineral lease covering the tract, claiming that his cattle, fences, roads and road crossing had been injured or damaged by Texaco's seismic operations. Such damages were alleged to have been suffered in the year 1959, and Leonard filed suit on July 6, 1961. The Court of Civil Appeals held that the cause of action alleged in his original petition was not barred by the two year statute of limitations. We agree with this holding. (Texaco asserts that this holding is erroneous and such contention will be discussed by us in reviewing the points of error contained in Texaco's brief in the Court of Civil Appeals.) That court, however, held that as the original petition set up a claim in tort and the subsequent amendments thereto filed in 1964 and 1965 asserted a claim in contract, Article 5539b did not operate to save the cause of action based upon contract from the bar of the two year statute.

Leonard's original petition asserted that Texaco had made an excessive and unreasonable use of the surface estate in conducting its seismic operations. By a 1964 amendment and a trial amendment thereto filed on March 8, 1965, Leonard retained the charge that Texaco had made an unreasonable and excessive use of the surface but also alleged that Texaco had contracted and agreed to pay all damages resulting to the surface as a result of its exploratory operations. The case was submitted upon the contract theory of liability and the jury found that prior to the time Texaco began its seismic operations, it agreed with Leonard to pay all damages to his property that might be caused by such operations and that Leonard had been damaged in a number of particulars aggregating the sum of $3,998.00.

The holding of the Court of Civil Appeals that the contract action asserted by Leonard in his trial pleadings was barred by limitation is based upon the circumstance that while the original petition sounded in tort, unreasonable and unnecessary use, the amended petition was based upon an agreement to pay damages. In other words, the Court of Civil Appeals followed the 'cause of action' concept in applying Article 5539b to this case and concluded that although a cause of action in tort had been declared upon within the statutory limitation period, this would not save from the bar of limitations a cause of action based on contract which was first pleaded long after two years had expired from the date the damages were allegedly sustained.

The Court of Civil Appeals relied primarily upon *Hopper v. Hargrove*, 154 S.W.2d 978 (Tex. Civ. App. 1941, writ ref'd), which followed *Phoenix Lumber Company v. Houston Water Company*, 94 Tex. 456, 61 S.W. 707 (1901), a case decided before 1931 when Article 5539b was adopted. *See*, Acts 1931, 42nd Leg., p. 194, ch. 115. In *Hopper*, it appeared that the plaintiff by an amended petition sought recovery of a tract of land not mentioned in her previous petitions. The Court of Civil Appeals held that Article 5539b did not operate to avoid the bar of limitation. While the holding might be justified upon other grounds, the opinion cited the Phoenix Lumber Company case and stated that it was 'clear that the third amended original petition declares upon a New cause of action in so far as the land in controversy is concerned.' (Emphasis added.)

In *Global Corporation v. Vincent*, 156 Tex. 398, 295 S.W.2d 640 (1956), this Court quoted with approval the following from *Texas Pacific Coal & Oil Co. v. Smith*, 130 S.W.2d 425 (Tex. Civ. App. 1939, writ dis'm judgm. cor.):

> 'Unless the cause of action alleged in an amended pleading involves a different transaction from that in the original pleading, the latter having declared upon a cause of action not then barred, it is immaterial that the cause of action alleged in the amended pleading be different from the cause of action originally alleged. The test which Vernon's Ann.Civ.St. art. 5539b makes proper is whether or not the cause of action alleged in the amended pleading be 'wholly based upon and grows out of a new, distinct or different transaction and occurrence.' *Farmers & Merchants Nat. Bank v. Arrington*, Tex. Civ. App., 98 S.W.2d 378, 379; *Universal Life & Accident Ins. Co. v. Johnson*, Tex. Civ. App., 120 S.W.2d 314.'

The emergency clause of the 1931 act referred to 'the importance of simplifying Court procedure' and evinced an intention to effect some change in the law as it theretofore existed.

In *Hallaway v. Thompson*, 148 Tex. 471, 226 S.W.2d 816 (1950), we said:

> 'The obvious purpose of Article 5539b was to limit the application of the statutes of limitations to amended pleadings. It was evidently intended to modify the previously existing rule for determining whether limitation should apply to an amended pleading, as first announced in *Phoenix Lumber Co. v. Houston Water Co.*, 94 Tex. 456, 61 S.W. 707. * * * Article 5539b expressly provides that an amendment to a pleading shall not be subject to a plea of limitation where the amendment is not wholly based on or grows out of a new, distinct or different transaction or occurrence.'

See also, First State Bank & Trust Co. of Rio Grande City v. Ramirez, 133 Tex. 178, 126 S.W.2d 16 (1939); *City of Houston v. Magness*, 364 S.W.2d 702 (Tex. Civ. App. 1963, writ ref'd).

The test under Article 5539b as amended in 1931 is no longer based upon a difference in causes of action declared upon in the original and amended petitions and the expressions contained in *Hopper v. Hargrove, supra*, indicating the contrary must be disapproved. The test is whether the cause of action alleged in the amended petition is 'wholly based upon and grows out of a new, distinct or different transaction and occurrence.'

In this particular case, while the original petition sounded in tort and alleged an excessive use of the land, and the amended petition set up a promise to pay such damages as Texaco might cause to the surface estate through its seismic operations, it cannot be said that a petition setting up the agreement to pay stated a cause of action wholly based upon and growing out of a different transaction or occurrence. In fact, the difference in the tort and contract actions in the present case would have little practical effect so far as trial preparation is concerned.

When Texaco notified Leonard that it intended to conduct exploratory operations, Leonard protested that the land was wet—'just as wet as a frog,' due to recent rains. He wanted Texaco to stay all the premises until they dried up. 'I didn't want them in there tearing up the country with that heavy equipment they use for seismographing.' Discussions were had in regard to paying Leonard $1,000.00 for surface damage, which he refused, and One Dollar per acre, which Texaco refused. Finally, according to Leonard, a Texaco representative stated that they were going ahead with their seismic operations but would pay Leonard for damages to the surface. This agreement was later partially confirmed by letter. The seismic operations undertaken by Texaco over the protests of Leonard based upon the wetness of the ground and consequent greater damage to the premises was the transaction or occurrence out of which grew both the claim in tort and the claim in contract.

We hold that as the original cause of action declared upon in the original petition filed on July 6, 1961 was not barred by the two year statute, the cause of action alleged in the amended petition filed in 1964 and the trial amendment thereto, was not barred by the two year statute because of the provisions of Article 5539b.

* * *

Note

Lexington Ins. Co. v. Daybreak Exp., Inc., ----S.W.3d -----, 55 Tex. Sup. Ct. J. 1416, 2012 WL 3800881 (Tex. 2012): The principal question in this case is whether, for purposes of Section 16.068 of the Texas Civil Practice and Remedies Code, an action for cargo damage against a common carrier, brought under the Carmack Amendment to the Interstate Commerce Act, 49 U.S.C. § 14706, relates back to an action for breach of an agreement to settle the cargo-damage claim. The answer depends on whether the cargo-damage claim is, in the words of Section 16.068, "wholly based on a new, distinct, or different transaction or occurrence" than the breach-of-settlement claim. A divided court of appeals held that a cargo-damage claim does not relate back and is therefore barred by limitations. 342 S.W.3d 795 (Tex.App.-Houston [14th Dist.] 2011). We disagree and accordingly reverse the judgment of the court of appeals and render judgment for the plaintiff.

"Transaction or occurrence" is a concept fundamental to modern civil procedure. *See, e.g.,* TEX. R. CIV. P. (third-party practice), 40 (joinder), 50 (pleading), 97 (counterclaims and cross-claims); TEX. CIV. PRAC. & REM. CODE (limitations); *Barr v. Resolution Trust Corp.,* 837 S.W.2d 627 (Tex.1992) (res judicata). The United States Supreme Court has observed that " '[t]ransaction' is a word of flexible meaning. It may comprehend a series of many occurrences, depending not so much upon the immediateness of their connection as upon their logical relationship." *Moore v. N.Y. Cotton Exch.,* 270 U.S. 593, 610, 46 S.Ct. 367, 70 L.Ed. 750 (1926). Rule 15(c)(1)(B) of the Federal Rules of Civil Procedure employs a standard similar to Section 16.068, allowing relation back of a claim, pleaded by amendment, "that arose out of the conduct, transaction, or occurrence set out—or attempted to be set out—in the original pleading." FED.R.CIV.P. 15(c)(1)(B). "[T]he search ... is for a common core of operative facts in the two pleadings." 6 CHARLES ALAN WRIGHT, ARTHUR R. MILLER, & MARY K. KANE, FEDERAL PRACTICE & PROCEDURE § 1497 (3rd ed.2010). "Although not expressly mentioned in the rule, the courts also inquire into whether the opposing party has been put on notice regarding the claim or defense raised by the amended pleading." *Id.; see also* 2 ROY W. MCDONALD & ELAINE A. GRAFTON CARLSON, TEXAS CIVIL PRACTICE § 10.18 (2d ed.2002) ("The inquiry applied should be the pragmatic one of notice . . . .").

In the present case, the cargo-damage claim and the breach-of-settlement claim both arose out of the same occurrence: Daybreak's shipment of Burr's computer equipment. The settlement was an effort to reach agreement on the damages recoverable under the Carmack Amendment. Although Lexington might recover on the breach-of-settlement claim without proving the amount of damage to the equipment, that damage was the basis for the settlement agreement. Daybreak might well argue that it is unreasonable to believe that it agreed to pay thirty times more than it actually paid. Daybreak had fair notice that the amount of damage might be in issue, as well as whether an agreement had been reached.

The court of appeals' conclusion that the two claims are based on two separate transactions is contradicted by our decision in *Leonard v. Texaco, Inc.,* 422 S.W.2d 160 (Tex.1967). There, a surface owner sued the mineral lessee for property damages caused by the lessee's seismic operations. Later, after limitations had run, the surface owner amended his petition to add a claim that the lessee had breached an agreement to pay for the damages, possibly to avoid having to prove negligence. *Id.* at 161, 162; see *Humble Oil & Ref. Co. v. Williams,* 420 S.W.2d 133, 134 (Tex.1967) ("A person who seeks to recover from the lessee for damages to the surface has the burden of alleging and proving either specific acts of negligence or that more of the land was used by the lessee than was reasonably necessary."). In *Leonard,* the surface owner prevailed on the contract claim at trial, but the court of civil appeals reversed, holding under Section 16.068's predecessor, which contained the same relation-back standard, that the contract claim did not relate back to the property damage claim and was therefore barred by limitations. We disagreed. *Id.* at 162. Though the initial claim "sounded in tort and alleged an excessive use of land" and the later claim "set up a promise to pay ... damages" that sounded in contract, we concluded: "it cannot be said" that the latter was "wholly based upon and growing out of a different transaction or occurrence." *Id.* at 163.

In *Leonard,* as in the present case, one claim centered on damage to property and the other on an alleged agreement to pay for the damage. And in each case, the requirements for proof of the two claims were somewhat different. But the claims in each cases arose out of the same occurrence and involved the same injury to property. *Leonard's* holding that the two claims were not based on wholly different transactions forecloses the court of appeals' contrary conclusion in this case.

In re UNITED SERVICES AUTO. ASS'N

307 S.W.3d 299
(Tex. 2010)

Lacey L. Gourley, Bracewell & Giuliani, L.L.P., Pamela Stanton Baron, Thomas R. Phillips, Baker Botts L.L.P., Austin, TX, Mario A. Barrera, Bracewell & Giuliani LLP, San Antonio, TX, William H. Ford, Ford & Massey, P.C., San Antonio, TX, for Relator.

Jeffrey D. Small, Law Office of Jeff Small, Jeffrey Alan Goldberg, Cynthia A. Cano, Law Offices of Jeffrey A. Goldberg, San Antonio, TX, for Real Party in Interest.

Charles C. High Jr., Kemp Smith P.C., El Paso, TX, for Amicus Curiae Texas Association of Business.

Vanetta Loraine Christ, Vinson & Elkins LLP, Houston, TX, for Amicus Curiae Texas Employment Law Council.

Daniel L. Geyser, Asst. Solicitor General, James C. Ho, Solicitor General of Texas, David S. Morales, Office of the Attorney General of Texas, Clarence Andrew Weber, First Assistant Attorney General, Greg W. Abbott, Attorney General of Texas, Austin, TX, for Amicus Curiae State of Texas.

CHIEF JUSTICE JEFFERSON delivered the opinion of the Court.

* * *

James Steven Brite sued USAA, his former employer, alleging that it had illegally discriminated against him based on his age, violating the Texas Commission on Human Rights Act (TCHRA). See generally *United Servs. Auto. Ass'n v. Brite*, 215 S.W.3d 400 (Tex.2007) (" *Brite I* "). He filed suit in the Bexar County Court at Law No. 7, which has jurisdiction concurrent with that of the district court in "civil cases in which the matter in controversy exceeds $500 but does not exceed $100,000, excluding interest, statutory or punitive damages and penalties, and attorney's fees and costs, as alleged on the face of the petition . . . ." TEX. GOV'T CODE § 25.0003(c)(1). Brite asserted in his original petition that his damages exceeded the $500 statutory minimum, but he did not plead that his damages were below the $100,000 maximum. *Brite I*, 215 S.W.3d at 401. He pleaded that "[i]n all reasonable probability, [his] loss of income and benefits will continue into the future, if not for the balance of [his] natural life" and sought "compensation due Plaintiff that accrued at the time of filing this Petition" (back pay), "the present value of unaccrued wage payments" (front pay), punitive damages, and attorney's fees. *Id.*

Before limitations expired, USAA filed a plea to the jurisdiction, contending that Brite's damage claims exceeded the $100,000 jurisdictional limit of the statutory county court, excluding interest, statutory or punitive damages, and attorney's fees and costs. USAA argued that because Brite's annual salary was almost $74,000 when he was terminated, his front pay and back pay allegations alone exceeded the county court's jurisdictional maximum. Brite opposed, and the trial court twice denied, USAA's jurisdictional plea. Shortly thereafter, Brite amended his petition to seek damages of $1.6 million, and subsequently claimed in discovery responses that " 'his lost wages and benefits in the future, until age 65, total approximately $1,000,000.00.' " *Brite I*, 215 S.W.3d at 401 (quoting discovery responses). After a jury trial, the trial court awarded Brite $188,406 in back pay, $350,000 in front pay, $300,000 in punitive damages, $129,387 in attorney's fees, and prejudgment interest. *Id.*

A divided court of appeals affirmed the trial court's judgment. *See United Servs. Auto. Ass'n v. Brite*, 161 S.W.3d 566, 579 (Tex. App.—San Antonio 2005, pet. granted). We reversed, concluding that the amount in controversy at the time Brite filed suit exceeded $100,000, depriving the county court at law of jurisdiction over the matter. *Brite I*, 215 S.W.3d at 402. We dismissed the underlying suit for want of jurisdiction. *Id.* at 403.

Within sixty days of our judgment dismissing the county court case, Brite refiled his claim in Bexar County district court. USAA filed a plea to the jurisdiction and moved for summary judgment asserting, among other things, that the trial court lacked subject matter jurisdiction because Brite failed to file suit within TCHRA's two-year time limit; that the tolling provision in section 16.064 of the Civil Practice and Remedies Code did not apply to TCHRA claims; and that even if it did, Brite's original suit was filed with "intentional disregard of proper jurisdiction," depriving him of that provision's protection. The trial court denied the plea and motion. The court of appeals denied relief, concluding that USAA had not established that its appellate remedy was inadequate. 2007 WL 3003131, at *1, 2007 Tex.App. LEXIS 8206, at *1-*2. USAA now petitions this Court for mandamus relief.

II. Is TCHRA's two-year period for filing suit jurisdictional?

USAA argues that TCHRA's two year deadline for filing suit is jurisdictional, precluding application of the tolling statute. * * *

In *Dubai Petroleum Co. v. Kazi*, 12 S.W.3d 71, 76 (Tex.2000) (quoting Restatement (Second) of Judgments § 12 cmt. b. at 118 (1982)), we observed that " '[t]he classification of a matter as one of jurisdiction . . . opens the way to making judgments vulnerable to delayed attack for a variety of irregularities that perhaps better ought to be sealed in a judgment.' " Thus, "[a]lthough Mingus represented the dominant approach when it was decided, 'the modern direction of policy is to reduce the vulnerability of final judgments to attack on the ground that the tribunal lacked subject matter jurisdiction.' " *Dubai*, 12 S.W.3d at 76 (quoting Restatement (Second) of Judgments § 11 cmt. e. at 113). We overruled Mingus "to the extent that it characterized the plaintiff's failure to establish a statutory prerequisite as jurisdictional." *Id.* Instead, we held that " '[t]he right of a plaintiff to maintain a suit, while frequently treated as going to the question of jurisdiction, has been said to go in reality to the right of the plaintiff to relief rather than to the jurisdiction of the court to afford it.' " *Id.* at 76-77 (quoting 21 C.J.S. Courts § 16, at 23 (1990)).

Since *Dubai*, we have been "reluctant to conclude that a provision is jurisdictional, absent clear legislative intent to that effect." *City of DeSoto v. White*, 288 S.W.3d 389, 393 (Tex.2009). * * *

In keeping with the statute's language, *Dubai* and subsequent cases, as well as the purposes behind TCHRA and federal interpretations of Title VII, we conclude that the two-year period for filing suit is mandatory but not jurisdictional, and we overrule *Schroeder* to the extent it held otherwise.

II. Does the tolling statute, TEX. CIV. PRAC. & REM. CODE § 16.064, apply to a TCHRA claim?

In pertinent part, section 16.064 provides:

> The period between the date of filing an action in a trial court and the date of a second filing of the same action in a different court suspends the running of the applicable statute of limitations for the period if:
>
> (1) because of lack of jurisdiction in the trial court where the action was first filed, the action is dismissed or the judgment is set aside or annulled in a direct proceeding; and
> (2) not later than the 60th day after the date the dismissal or other disposition becomes final, the action is commenced in a court of proper jurisdiction.

TEX. CIV. PRAC. & REM. CODE § 16.064(a).

USAA contends that, even if the limitations period is not jurisdictional, the tolling statute does not apply, citing a string of cases holding generally that section 16.064 does not apply to special statutory proceedings. *See, e.g., Heart Hosp. IV, L.P. v. King*, 116 S.W.3d 831, 836 (Tex. App.—Austin 2003, pet. denied); *Argonaut Sw. Ins. Co. v. Walker*, 64 S.W.3d 654, 657 (Tex. App.—Texarkana 2001, pet. denied); *Gutierrez v. Lee*, 812 S.W.2d 388, 392 (Tex. App.—Austin 1991, writ denied); *Castillo v. Allied Ins. Co.*, 537 S.W.2d 486, 487 (Tex. Civ. App.—Amarillo 1976, writ ref'd n.r.e.); *Pan Am. Fire & Cas. Co. v. Rowlett*, 479 S.W.2d 782, 783 (Tex. Civ. App.—Eastland 1972, writ ref'd n.r.e.); *Braden v. Transp. Ins. Co.*, 307 S.W.2d 655, 656 (Tex. Civ. App.—Dallas 1957, no writ); *Leadon v. Truck Ins. Exch.*, 253 S.W.2d 903, 905 (Tex. Civ. App.—Galveston 1952, no writ); *Bear v. Donna Indep. School Dist.*, 85 S.W.2d 797, 799 (Tex. Civ. App.—San Antonio 1935, writ dism'd w.o.j.).

But there are at least three problems with this approach. First, we have never endorsed the theory that section 16.064 is inapplicable to causes of action created by statute. All of those decisions were from our courts of appeals, and most predate *Dubai*. Second, those cases are based on the *Mingus* rationale, overruled in *Dubai*, that a "dichotomy [exists] between common-law and statutory actions," with mandatory statutory provisions also being jurisdictional. *Dubai*, 12 S.W.3d at 76. Post-*Dubai*, we have rejected such a distinction, adopting instead "an approach to jurisdictional questions designed to strengthen finality and reduce the possibility of delayed attacks on judgments, regardless of whether the claim was anchored in common law or was a specially-created statutory action." *City of DeSoto*, 288 S.W.3d at 394 (emphasis added).

Third, the argument conflates equitable tolling with statutory tolling. The former is a court-created doctrine, *see e.g., Taliani v. Chrans*, 189 F.3d 597, 597 (7th Cir.1999) (noting that "equitable tolling [is] the judge-made doctrine . . . that excuses a timely filing when the plaintiff could not, despite the exercise of reasonable diligence, have discovered all the information he needed in order to be able to file his claim on time"), that may not apply if a statutory requirement is deemed jurisdictional, *see Zipes*, 455 U.S. at 393, 102 S.Ct. 1127 (holding that "filing a timely charge of discrimination with the EEOC is not a jurisdictional prerequisite to suit, . . . but a requirement that, like a statute of limitations, is subject to waiver, estoppel, and equitable tolling"). The latter is a legislative dictate that limitations be tolled for " any action" filed in the wrong court. See Act approved Apr. 27, 1931, 42d Leg., R.S., ch. 81, 1931 Tex. Gen. Laws 124, 124, current version at TEX. CIV. PRAC. & REM. CODE § 16.064 (emphasis added).

Here we must construe two statutes—one that creates a limitations period and a second that tolls it. There is no reason, absent clear legislative intent, that we should not harmonize the two. *See La Sara Grain Co. v. First Nat'l Bank*, 673 S.W.2d 558, 565 (Tex. 1984) ("Generally, courts are to construe statutes so as to harmonize with other relevant laws, if possible."). Had the Legislature wanted to prohibit statutory tolling, it could have done so, but TCHRA is devoid of any such indication. *Cf.* TEX. CIV. PRAC. & REM. CODE § 74.251(a) (creating limitations period that applies "[n]otwithstanding any other law"); *Liggett v. Blocher*, 849 S.W.2d 846, 850 (Tex. App.—Houston [1st Dist.] 1993, no writ) (holding that "notwithstanding any other law" meant that statutory tolling provision did not apply to health care liability claims). Thus, absent language indicating that section 16.064 was not intended to apply to TCHRA claims, the statute of limitations is tolled for those cases falling within section 16.064's savings provision.

IV. Was Brite's first suit filed with "intentional disregard of proper jurisdiction"?

Section 16.064 will not save a later-filed claim if the first action was filed "with intentional disregard of proper jurisdiction." TEX. CIV. PRAC. & REM. CODE § 16.064(b). USAA contends that is what happened here, while Brite asserts that a jury must decide whether he intended to evade jurisdiction, given that he vigorously denies doing so. We agree with USAA.

Noting "[t]he importance of simplifying Court procedure," the Texas Judicial Council in 1930 drafted the tolling statute. *See* Second Annual Report of the Texas Civil Judicial Council to the Governor and Supreme Court, Bill No. 6, at 10-12 (1930). The Legislature made a single change-extending the refiling period from thirty to sixty days-and passed the bill. *See* Act approved Apr. 27, 1931, 42d Leg., R.S., ch. 81, 1931 Tex. Gen. Laws 124, 124, current version at TEX. CIV. PRAC. & REM. CODE § 16.064; *see also Burford v. Sun Oil Co.*, 186 S.W.2d 306, 310 (Tex. Civ. App.—Austin 1944, writ ref'd w.o.m.). In its recommendation accompanying the bill, the Council noted

> [t]hat the wrong court is frequently and in good faith chosen by capable lawyers, [as] evidenced by the hundreds of cases cited in the annotations upon the subject given in Vernon's Annotated Texas Statutes, 9 pages upon Justice Court, 17 pages upon county court and 29 pages upon district court jurisdiction.

Second Annual Report, at 11. The Council explained that the Texas bill was based on a Kentucky statute that tolled limitations for actions "commenced in due time and in good faith" in a court that lacked jurisdiction. *Id.* (*citing* CARROLL'S KY. STAT. § 2545 (1922)). The Council stated that its bill was "like that of Kentucky in substance, but . . . a definition of 'good faith' [is] supplied." *Id.* at 11-12. It is that definition that is at issue here.

As we noted in *Brite I*, "[t]he jurisdictional statute for county courts at law values the matter in controversy on the amount of damages 'alleged' by the plaintiff . . . ." *Brite I*, 215 S.W.3d at 402-03 (*quoting* TEX. GOV'T CODE § 25.0003(c)(1)). Here, Brite's petition omitted the statement required by our rules-that the "damages sought are within the jurisdictional limits of the court," TEX.R. CIV. P. 47(b)—and instead pleaded only that his damages exceeded $500. Brite has never contended that he was unaware of or confused about the county court's jurisdictional limitation. *See, e.g., Clary Corp. v. Smith*, 949 S.W.2d 452, 461 (Tex. App.—Fort Worth 1997, pet. denied) (noting that 16.064 did not apply because "there [was] no evidence of mistake here," as plaintiffs "have neither alleged nor presented evidence that they were unaware of the trial court's amount in controversy limits"). While such confusion would be understandable, as other statutory county courts (even those in one county adjacent to Bexar County) have no such restriction, he instead argued that "the amount in controversy should not be calculated by the damages originally sued for, but instead by the amount of damages that, more likely than not, the plaintiff would recover." *Brite I*, 215 S.W.3d at 402. We rejected that argument, concluding that "[t]he amount in controversy in this case exceeded $100,000 at the time Brite filed suit." *Id.* at 403.

The parties disagree about the proper standard for intentional disregard under the tolling statute, which requires that USAA "show in abatement that the first filing was made with intentional disregard of proper jurisdiction." TEX. CIV. PRAC. & REM. CODE § 16.064(b). Brite contends that intent is always a fact issue, inappropriate for resolution on summary judgment, while USAA asserts it has met its burden through circumstantial evidence of Brite's intent and that Brite is charged with knowledge of the law. We have never before addressed this issue.

We agree, in part, with USAA. Once an adverse party has moved for relief under the "intentional disregard" provision, the nonmovant must show that he did not intentionally disregard proper jurisdiction when filing the case. As it is the nonmovant who has this information, he should bear the burden of producing it. *Cf. Brown v. Shores*, 77 S.W.3d 884, 889 (Tex. App.—Houston [14th Dist.] 2002, no pet.) (BRISTER, J., concurring) (noting that, because "diligent-service question focuses almost entirely on the efforts and thoughts of plaintiff's counsel, so the initial burden of presenting evidence should rest there, too"; "[o]therwise, every one of these numerous cases will begin with the defendant sending a notice to depose plaintiff's counsel and a subpoena for all files").

We disagree, however, that a plaintiff's mistake about the court's jurisdiction would never satisfy the requirement. Section 16.064's intent standard is similar to that required for setting aside a default judgment, *see Craddock v. Sunshine Bus Lines, Inc.*, 134 Tex. 388, 133 S.W.2d 124, 126 (1939) (requiring new trial if defendant proves three elements, the first of which is that default was neither intentional nor due to conscious indifference), and we have held that a mistake of law may be a sufficient excuse, *Bank One, Tex., N.A. v. Moody*, 830 S.W.2d 81, 84 (Tex. 1992). Moreover, section 16.064 was drafted precisely because "capable lawyers" often make "good faith" mistakes about the jurisdiction of Texas courts. *See* Second Annual Report, at 11; *see also* Citizens' Commission on the Texas Judicial System, Report and Recommendations—Into the Twenty-First Century, at 17 (1993) ("No one person understands or can hope to understand all the nuances and intricacies of Texas' thousands of trial courts.").

But while the tolling statute protects plaintiffs who mistakenly file suit in a forum that lacks jurisdiction, it does not apply to a strategic decision to seek relief from such a court-which is what happened here. *Hotvedt v. Schlumberger, Ltd. (N.V.)*, 942 F.2d 294, 297 (5th Cir.1991) (refusing to apply section 16.064 because "[i]t is clear . . . that errors in [an attorney's] tactical decisions were not meant to be remedied by the savings statute"); *Clary*, 949 S.W.2d at 461 (holding that "[s]ection 16.064 was not intended to remedy . . . tactical decisions"); *see also Brite I*, 161 S.W.3d at 586 (DUNCAN, J., dissenting) (noting that "the record, taken as a whole, establishes that Brite's trial attorney filed the Original Petition with full knowledge that Brite sought far more than $100,000 in actual damages and purposefully drafted the Original Petition to conceal that fact by omitting the statement required by Rule 47(b)"). Because Brite unquestionably sought damages in excess of the county court at law's jurisdiction, it matters not that he subjectively anticipated a verdict within the jurisdictional limits. For that reason, limitations was not tolled. His second suit, filed long after the expiration of the two year statute, is therefore barred.

V. Is USAA entitled to mandamus relief?

Finally, we must decide whether mandamus relief is appropriate. Deciding whether the benefits of mandamus outweigh the detriments requires us to weigh public and private interests, recognizing that-rather than categorical determinations—"the adequacy of an appeal depends on the facts involved in each case." *In re McAllen Med. Ctr., Inc.*, 275 S.W.3d 458, 469 (Tex. 2008); *In re The Prudential Ins. Co. of Am.*, 148 S.W.3d 124, 136-37 (Tex. 2004).

In *CSR Ltd. v. Link*, 925 S.W.2d 591, 596-97 (Tex. 1996), we conditionally granted mandamus relief ordering the trial court to grant CSR's special appearance in a toxic tort case. We held that "extraordinary circumstances" (namely the enormous number of potential claimants and the most efficient use of the state's judicial resources) warranted extraordinary relief, even though it was typically unavailable for the denial of a special appearance. *CSR*, 925 S.W.2d at 596; *see also Canadian Helicopters Ltd. v. Wittig*, 876 S.W.2d 304, 308-09 (Tex. 1994).

And although "mandamus is generally unavailable when a trial court denies summary judgment, no matter how meritorious the motion," that rule is based in part on the fact that "trying a case in which summary judgment would have been appropriate does not mean the case will have to be tried twice"—a justification not applicable here. *In re McAllen Med. Ctr.*, 275 S.W.3d at 465-66. USAA has already endured one trial in a forum that lacked jurisdiction (and then a subsequent appeal to the court of appeals and this Court) and is facing a second trial on a claim that we have just held to be barred by limitations. Two wasted trials are not "[t]he most efficient use of the state's judicial resources." *CSR*, 925 S.W.2d at 596; *cf. In re McAllen Med. Ctr.*, 275 S.W.3d at 466. Denying mandamus relief here would thwart the legislative intent that non-tolled TCHRA claims be brought within two years (as well as the tolling provision's inapplicability to suits filed with intentional disregard of proper jurisdiction), and we should not "frustrate th[at] purpose by a too-strict application of our own procedural devices." *In re McAllen Med. Ctr.*, 275 S.W.3d at 467.

Because the extraordinary circumstances presented here merit extraordinary relief, we conditionally grant the writ and direct the trial court to grant USAA's motion for summary judgment. We are confident the trial court will comply, and our writ will issue only if it does not.

JUSTICE JOHNSON did not participate in the decision.

2. *Collateral Estoppel*

EAGLE PROPERTIES
v.
SCHARBAUER
807 S.W.2d 714
(Tex. 1990)

James E. Ingram, San Antonio, and Clinard J. Hanby and W. James Kronzer, Houston, for petitioners.

James W. Paulsen, Houston, John H. McElhaney, Morris Harrell, Donald Colleluori and Bruce A. Budner, Dallas, John E. O'Neill and David T. Hedges, Houston, W.B. Browder, Jr., Midland, David C. Holmes, Houston, and Michael V. Powell, Dallas, for respondents.

COOK, JUSTICE.

This court's opinion of December 19, 1990, is withdrawn and the following is substituted in its place. Petitioners' and Respondents' motions for rehearing are overruled.

This is a single cause which originated from two related cases. The first case presents us with the question of whether the doctrines of res judicata and collateral estoppel preclude a state action following the settlement of a federal court case that involved different parties but the same subject matter. The second case presents similar questions of res judicata and collateral estoppel but also addresses whether the statute of limitations for causes of action in fraud is two years or four years. We hold that the statute of limitations does not bar the claims for fraud in the second case, that res judicata does not bar the claims in either case, and that collateral estoppel bars only some of the claims presented in both cases. Therefore, we reverse the judgment of the court of appeals in part and affirm in part, 758 S.W.2d 911, and remand this cause to the court of appeals for further consideration of whether Branum's claims other than fraud against TCB, First Republic, and Peat Marwick are barred by the relevant statutes of limitations.

In 1982, First National Bank of Midland (First Midland) was experiencing financial problems due to a large portfolio of energy-related loans. To improve the financial position of First Midland, Eagle Properties, Ltd., was formed to purchase First Midland's twenty-four story office building, ten-story parking garage, and drive-in banking facilities for $75 million. M.W. Branum and Thomas C. Brown were the general partners of Eagle. Charles Fraser, the president and chairman of the board of First Midland, hand-picked the Eagle partners and solicited their participation. The consideration consisted of $25 million in unsecured promissory notes from Eagle and two unfunded letters of credit, each for $25 million, provided by Texas Commerce Bank (TCB) and InterFirst Bank Dallas. Eagle agreed to lease the premises back to First Midland for three years and to allow First Midland to manage the properties.

The financial condition of First Midland continued to deteriorate, and in June 1983 Eagle agreed to the funding of the letters of credit six months before they were scheduled to be funded. On October 14, 1983, First Midland was declared insolvent, and the Federal Deposit Insurance Corporation (FDIC) was appointed receiver. The FDIC accelerated payment on the notes and filed suit in federal court in February 1984 to collect on them. Eagle counterclaimed for declaratory judgment on grounds of common law fraud, violations of the Securities Exchange Act, failure of consideration, violations of the Bank Holding Company Act, and the operation of two subordination agreements. In a non-jury trial, the federal court held for the FDIC. In particular, the federal court held that First Midland did not fraudulently induce Eagle to enter into the transaction, execute the promissory notes, or agree to the early funding of the letters of credit. *FDIC v. Eagle Properties, Ltd.*, 664 F.Supp. 1027 (W.D.Tex. 1985).

Eagle filed an appeal to the United States Court of Appeals for the Fifth Circuit. While the case was on appeal, the parties entered into a settlement agreement which explicitly preserved Eagle's right to file claims against the officers and directors of First Midland. The settlement did not call for the judgment of the trial court to be vacated. At one point during the negotiations, however, Eagle offered the FDIC an additional one million dollars in settlement if it would move the Fifth Circuit to reverse or vacate and remand the judgment of the district court for a take-nothing judgment, and if these events in fact occurred. The FDIC declined this offer.

Subsequent to the settlement agreement, two suits were filed in state court. In the first suit, *Eagle Properties, Ltd. v. Mays*, Eagle and the individual partners sued certain officers and directors of First Midland (the Directors), alleging common law and statutory fraud, violations of the Deceptive Trade Practices Act, and negligence/breach of fiduciary duties. The second suit, *Branum v. Scharbauer*, was originally filed by M.W. Branum alone, but Eagle and the remaining partners, except Thomas C. Brown, subsequently intervened as additional plaintiffs. This suit was brought against the Directors, TCB, InterFirst Bank Dallas (now First Republic Dallas), and Main Hurdman (now Peat Marwick). The suit alleged common law and statutory fraud and violations of the Deceptive Trade Practices Act against all defendants, breach of contract/promissory estoppel against TCB and InterFirst, and negligence by TCB, InterFirst (hereinafter "First Republic"), and Main Hurdman (hereinafter "Peat Marwick").

Each of the defendants moved for summary judgment in the trial court, with the exception of two of the Directors, Joel T. Mays and John P. Butler. The trial court consolidated the two causes, and severed plaintiffs' claims against Joel T. Mays and John P. Butler, the claims between Thomas C. Brown and the other plaintiffs, and the counterclaims filed by some of the Directors, TCB, and First Republic. These claims were made the subject of a separate action, *Eagle Properties, Ltd. v. Fraser*. The trial court then entered final judgment with respect to the remaining claims in favor of the Directors, TCB, First Republic, and Peat Marwick. The summary judgment in *Mays* was based upon res judicata, collateral estoppel, and plaintiffs' lack of standing to bring the negligent mismanagement claims. The summary judgment in *Branum* was based on res judicata, collateral estoppel, and the relevant statute of limitations.

Eagle Properties and its two general partners, Branum and Brown, appealed from the judgment of the trial court. The court of appeals affirmed the judgment of the trial court.

Petitioners challenge the judgment of the court of appeals and the trial court's granting of both summary judgments. We agree in part with petitioners' contentions, and we reverse the judgment of the court of appeals in part, affirm in part, and remand to the court of appeals for further consideration of whether Branum's claims other than fraud against TCB, First Republic, and Peat Marwick are barred by the relevant statutes of limitations.

Res Judicata

* * * [The Court noted that since first suit was decided by a federal court that the federal law of res judicata applied. After an extensive review of the federal law of res judicata the Court noted that res judicata does not preclude Eagle and Branum from bringing their state law claims in this case.]

Collateral Estoppel

Next, we address the issue of collateral estoppel. The threshold question is what law governs collateral estoppel. In this case, the same result will be reached whether federal or state law is applied to the issue of collateral estoppel. Therefore, we do not decide the choice of law question.

In order to invoke the doctrine of collateral estoppel, a party must establish "(1) the facts sought to be litigated in the first action were fully and fairly litigated in the prior action; (2) those facts were essential to the judgment in the first action; and (3) the parties were cast as adversaries in the first action." *Bonniwell v. Beech Aircraft Corp*., 663 S.W.2d 816, 818 (Tex. 1984). *See Allen v. McCurry*, 449 U.S. 90, 94-95, 101 S.Ct. 411, 414-15, 66 L.Ed.2d 308 (1980); *Hicks v. Quaker Oats Co*., 662 F.2d 1158, 1166 (5th Cir. 1981).

A. No Requirement of Mutuality

In *Benson v. Wanda Petroleum Co*., 468 S.W.2d 361 (Tex. 1971), this Court stated, The rule [of collateral estoppel] is generally stated as binding a party and those in privity with him . . . . Due process requires that the rule of collateral estoppel operate only against persons who have had their day in court either as a party to the prior suit or as a privy, and, where not so, that, at the least, the presently asserted interest was actually and adequately represented in the prior trial. *Id.* at 363. This definition does not require mutuality for the invocation of collateral estoppel; rather, it is only necessary that the party against whom the plea of collateral estoppel is being asserted be a party or in privity with a party in the prior litigation. *Myrick v. Moody Nat'l Bank*, 590 S.W.2d 766, 769 (Tex. Civ. App.—Houston [14th Dist.] 1979, writ ref'd n.r.e.); *Hardy v. Fleming*, 553 S.W.2d 790, 792-93 (Tex. Civ. App.—El Paso 1977, writ ref'd n.r.e.). As this Court stated in *Tarter v. Metropolitan Sav. &*

Loan Ass'n, "The doctrine applies when the party against whom collateral estoppel is asserted had a full and fair opportunity to litigate the issue in the prior suit" (emphasis added). 744 S.W.2d 926, 927 (Tex. 1988) (*citing Bonniwell*). Although Eagle cites several cases for the proposition that a party cannot avail himself of the doctrine of collateral estoppel unless he was a party or in privity with a party in the prior litigation, in each of those cases we held only that collateral estoppel cannot be asserted against a party who was not a party or in privity with a party in the prior litigation. *See Employers Casualty Co. v. Block*, 744 S.W.2d 940 (Tex. 1988); *Bonniwell*, 663 S.W.2d 816; *Wilhite v. Adams*, 640 S.W.2d 875 (Tex. 1982); *Benson*, 468 S.W.2d 361. Similarly, the U.S. Supreme Court abandoned the requirement of mutuality in applying collateral estoppel in *Blonder-Tongue v. Univ. of Illinois Foundation*, 402 U.S. 313, 91 S.Ct. 1434, 28 L.Ed.2d 788 (1971). Therefore, the Directors, TCB, First Republic and Peat Marwick are not barred from asserting collateral estoppel by a requirement of mutuality; it is sufficient that Eagle and Branum were both parties in *FDIC v. Eagle*.

B. Issues Essential to the Federal Judgment

Next, we must address the question of whether the federal court's findings regarding fraud in the transaction were essential to its judgment. Under state law, collateral estoppel only precludes the relitigation of identical issues of fact or law which were actually litigated and essential to the prior judgment. *Tarter*, 744 S.W.2d at 927; *Van Dyke v. Boswell, O'Toole, Davis & Pickering*, 697 S.W.2d 381, 384 (Tex. 1985). THE RESTATEMENT (SECOND) OF JUDGMENTS § 27, comment (i) (1982) provides in part, "If a judgment of a court of first instance is based on determinations of two issues, either of which standing independently would be sufficient to support the result, the judgment is not conclusive with respect to either issue standing alone." The rationale for this rule is that a determination in the alternative may not have been as rigorously considered as it would have been if necessary to the result, and the losing party may be dissuaded from appealing one determination because of the likelihood that the other will be upheld. *Id.*

In *FDIC v. Eagle*, the court found that neither First Midland nor its president, Charles Fraser, fraudulently induced Eagle and its partners to enter into the sale-leaseback transaction or execute the promissory notes in issue. 664 F.Supp. at 1045. The court also indicated, however, that the FDIC had a defense to these fraud claims because the FDIC did not have actual knowledge of the fraud at the time it entered into the purchase and assumption agreement. *Id.* at 1037. The court stated, "[I]f the Court had to, the Court would find that the FDIC did not have actual knowledge of conduct or communications that would give rise to a finding of fraud." *Id.* at 1045-46.

The statement of the federal court regarding FDIC's knowledge of any fraud, viewed in the context of the entire opinion, does not constitute an alternative holding so as to prevent its holding on the fraud claims from having preclusive effect. While this alternative reasoning may have had some adverse effect on defendants' desire to appeal the judgment, it is clear that the federal court "rigorously considered" defendants' claims of fraudulent inducement, carefully reviewing each contention. *Id.* at 1037-45. Therefore, applying state law to the circumstances of this case, we hold that the defendants' claims of fraudulent inducement were "actually tried" in the federal court and that the court's findings on fraudulent inducement were "essential" to its judgment for the purposes of preclusion by collateral estoppel.

The same result would be reached under federal law. For collateral estoppel to bar relitigation of an issue, that issue must have been "necessarily determined" in the prior litigation. *United States v. Garza*, 754 F.2d 1202, 1209 (5th Cir. 1985); *Hicks*, 662 F.2d at 1168. Nevertheless, except in very unusual cases, the abandonment of estoppel for the reason that a prior judgment rests on multiple grounds is inconsistent with the general rule in federal courts that a party is only entitled to one full and fair opportunity to litigate an issue. 1B MOORE'S FEDERAL PRACTICE P 0.443[5.-2] (1988). While the Fifth Circuit has adopted the reasoning of the RESTATEMENT (SECOND) OF JUDGMENTS § 27 comment (i), it did so only in the context of offensive collateral estoppel. *Hicks*, 662 F.2d at 1169-70. Because this case only involves the defensive use of collateral estoppel, and because we have found the findings of the federal court in *FDIC v. Eagle* to be "essential" to that judgment and rigorously considered by that court, we hold that under federal law the alternative "findings" of the federal court do not preclude the application of collateral estoppel in the present litigation.

C. Preclusion of Eagle's Claims

We now turn to the question of whether any of the issues in Eagle's case, Mays, were litigated in the prior action, thereby estopping Eagle from asserting the claims in this action.

1. Common Law and Statutory Fraud

Eagle's first cause of action against the Directors is for common law fraud. The elements of actionable fraud are that: (1) a material representation was made; (2) the representation was false; (3) when the representation was made the speaker knew it was false or made it recklessly without any knowledge of its truth and as a positive assertion; (4) the speaker made the representation with the intent that it should be acted upon by the party; (5) the party acted in reliance upon the representation; and (6) the party thereby suffered injury. *Trenholm v. Ratcliff*, 646 S.W.2d 927, 930 (Tex. 1983); *Stone v. Lawyers Title Ins. Corp.*, 554 S.W.2d 183, 185 (Tex. 1977).

Eagle bases its actions for common law and statutory fraud on the grounds that the Directors made false representations or material omissions with the intent of inducing Eagle to enter into the sales-leaseback transaction and agree to early funding of the letters of credit. First, Eagle alleges that the Directors misrepresented the bank's financial condition. The court in *FDIC v. Eagle* found that a fiduciary relationship did not exist between Charles Fraser and the individual defendants, that Fraser's disclosures and representations were adequate to inform Eagle and its partners of the bank's financial position and the reasons for selling the building, that Fraser had represented to each Eagle partner that an unfavorable financial report had been received from bank examiners, and that each defendant knew the bank had definite financial problems. *FDIC v. Eagle*, 664 F.Supp. at 1043-44.

Second, Eagle alleges that the Directors misrepresented that Eagle could depreciate the property and that the completed sale would occur in 1982. The federal court found that these representations were only expressions of opinion with legal implications. Generally, misrepresentations as to matters of law are not actionable fraud. *Sawyer v. Pierce*, 580 S.W.2d 117, 125 (Tex. Civ. App.—Corpus Christi 1979, writ ref'd n.r.e.). Such misrepresentations may be actionable between fiduciaries or where the representor has superior knowledge or information and uses it unfairly. The court found, however, that there was no fiduciary relationship between Fraser and First Midland and the individual defendants and that Fraser did not have a decided advantage over them. *FDIC v. Eagle*, 664 F.Supp. at 1042.

Eagle also alleges that the Directors misrepresented the fair market value of the property and the existence of an appraisal in the amount of $75 million. The federal court found that the representation of such an appraisal was false and material, but that none of the defendants who heard the representation relied upon it, in that they did not request to view the appraisal and did not condition their participation on reviewing the appraisal. Furthermore, the court found that the defendants should have taken the precaution of reviewing an appraisal and informing themselves of the value of the properties. *FDIC v. Eagle*, 664 F.Supp. at 1042-43.

Finally, Eagle alleges that the Directors failed to inform them that the SEC and the Office of the Comptroller of the Currency had concerns about the validity of the original transaction. The federal court found, however, that Fraser accurately represented that the OCC viewed the sale as a positive step for the bank. *FDIC v. Eagle*, 664 F.Supp. at 1044.

The court in *FDIC v. Eagle* held, following its extensive review of the facts surrounding the transaction, that neither Fraser nor First Midland fraudulently induced the defendants to enter into the sale-leaseback transaction, execute the promissory notes, or agree to early funding of the letters of credit. *FDIC v. Eagle*, 664 F.Supp. at 1045, 1048. We hold that the findings of the federal court collaterally estop Eagle's actions for common law and statutory fraud in Mays.

2. Deceptive Trade Practices Act

Eagle also brings claims under the Deceptive Trade Practices Act (DTPA). Based on the same allegations underlying its fraud claims, Eagle alleges that the foregoing representations and omissions violate TEX. BUS. & COM. CODE § 17.46(b) because they constitute representations or omissions that (1) the real property has characteristics, uses or benefits which it does not have, § 17.46(b)(5); (2) the real property is of a particular standard, quality or grade when it is another, § 17.46(b)(7); and (3) an agreement confers or involves rights, remedies or obligations which it does not have or involve, or which are prohibited by law, § 17.46(b)(12).

A defendant may be held liable for the deceptive trade practices described in § 17.46(b)(5), (7) and (12) even if the defendant did not know that the representations made were false or did not intend to deceive anyone. *Pennington v. Singleton*, 606 S.W.2d 682, 690 (Tex. 1980). Subdivisions (5) and (7) are designed to ensure the accuracy of descriptions of goods and services, and covers both general and specific descriptions. *Id.* Thus, misrepresentations which do not necessarily constitute common law fraud may be actionable under the DTPA. *See Smith v. Baldwin*, 611 S.W.2d 611, 616 (Tex. 1980) (noting that a primary purpose of the DTPA was "to provide consumers a cause of action for deceptive trade practices without the burden of proof and numerous defenses encountered in a common law fraud or breach of warranty suit"). To the extent that the federal court found that Charles Fraser and First Midland did not misrepresent the bank's financial condition and the position of the OCC regarding the transaction, DTPA claims may not be brought on this basis. However, Eagle is not collaterally estopped from bringing causes of action under § 17.46(b)(5) or (7) based on other allegations, including representations that there was an appraisal justifying the asking price of $75 million, which the federal court found to be false.

Eagle also alleges that the failure to disclose certain information about the real estate was intended to induce it into a transaction into which it would not have otherwise entered, § 17.46(b)(23). This subdivision includes an element of intent, and the court in *FDIC v. Eagle* held that neither Fraser nor the Bank fraudulently induced the defendants to enter into the sale-leaseback transaction, execute the promissory notes, or agree to early funding of the letters of credit. *FDIC v. Eagle*, 664 F.Supp. at 1045, 1048. Eagle is therefore estopped from bringing a claim under § 17.46(b)(23) of the DTPA. Therefore, summary judgment was proper on the basis of collateral estoppel on the DTPA claims brought under § 17.46(b)(23).

3. Negligent Mismanagement

Eagle's final cause of action against the Directors is for negligent conduct in the performance of their duties, thereby breaching a fiduciary duty owed to Eagle. In *FDIC v. Eagle*, the federal court held that a fiduciary relationship did not exist between Charles Fraser and First Midland and Eagle's partners. *FDIC v. Eagle*, 664 F.Supp. at 1043-44. Since the Directors did not owe a fiduciary duty to Eagle's partners, and Eagle suing on its own behalf as a creditor cannot maintain a personal action against the Directors of the corporation for breaching their duty to the corporation, *see Sutton v. Reagan & Gee*, 405 S.W.2d 828, 834-35 (Tex. Civ. App.—San Antonio 1966, writ ref'd n.r.e.), summary judgment was properly granted for the Directors on Eagle's negligent management cause of action.

D. Preclusion of Branum's claims

Finally, we turn to the question of whether Branum is collaterally estopped from bringing his claims in Branum. Branum is collaterally estopped to the same extent as Eagle from bringing claims of fraud against the Directors and DTPA claims against the Directors under TEX. BUS. & COM. CODE § 17.46(b)(5), (7), (12) & (23).

In addition to the DTPA claims that parallel Eagle's DTPA claims, Branum has brought a claim under TEX. BUS. & COM. CODE § 17.50(a)(3), alleging that the Directors' actions constitute an unconscionable course of conduct. An act or practice that "results in a gross disparity between the value received and consideration paid, in a transaction involving transfer of consideration," is considered unconscionable conduct under the DTPA. TEX. BUS. & COM. CODE § 17.45(5) (Vernon 1987). In this case, the consideration received by First Midland in the sale-leaseback transaction was $75 million. The transaction was entered into on December 31, 1982. The record shows that the bank property was appraised at $35 million as of November 23, 1982. Collateral estoppel does not bar Branum from bringing a DTPA claim on this basis.

As part of his suit, Branum also alleges that TCB and First Republic owed him a fiduciary duty, and has brought claims of fraud, negligence, and breach of contract/promissory estoppel against TCB and First Republic with respect to their participation in the sale of the First Midland property, a rehabilitation funding program following the sale, and the funding of the $50 million letters of credit. These claims include allegations that Branum would not have agreed to the early funding of the $50 million letters of credit if he had known that TCB and First Republic were not going to fund First Midland with $200 million under the rehabilitation program. Branum has also presented claims against Peat Marwick for fraud, negligence, gross negligence, and accounting malpractice with respect to the sale-leaseback transaction. Branum's suit also includes DTPA claims against these parties.

In *FDIC v. Eagle*, the federal court only held that Charles Fraser and First Midland did not fraudulently induce Eagle into the sale-leaseback transaction, the execution of the promissory notes, and the early funding of the letters of credit. The issues which were actually litigated and essential to that judgment are different from the issues presented in Branum's suit against TCB, First Republic, and Peat Marwick. Therefore, Branum is not collaterally estopped from bringing his claims against these parties.

Statute of Limitations

With respect to the suit filed by Branum, the summary judgment in favor of TCB, First Republic, and Peat Marwick was based in part on the grounds that Branum's claims were barred by the relevant statute of limitations. Branum's claims which are based on fraud are governed by a four-year statute of limitations, *Williams v. Khalaf*, 802 S.W.2d 651 (1990), not a two-year statute of limitations as held by the court of appeals. Branum's original petition was filed on October 11, 1985. Therefore, the summary judgment on Branum's fraud claims cannot be upheld on the statute of limitations grounds. Branum's other claims against TCB, First Republic, and Peat Marwick may be barred by the relevant statutes of limitations. We therefore remand this cause to the court of appeals to determine which, if any, of Branum's claims other than fraud against TCB, First Republic, and Peat Marwick are barred by the relevant statutes of limitations, and whether fact questions existed, sufficient to withstand summary judgment, regarding the date Branum knew or should have known of the actionable conduct, where necessary for determination of the statute of limitations questions. TEX. R. APP. P. 90(a).

Conclusion

We hold that res judicata does not preclude Eagle and Branum from bringing their state law claims in this case. Collateral estoppel bars Eagle and Branum from bringing claims of common law and statutory fraud against the Directors, some of the DTPA claims against the Directors, and Eagle's negligent mismanagement claim against the Directors. The remaining DTPA claims brought against the Directors and the claims brought by Branum against TCB, First Republic, and Peat Marwick are not collaterally estopped by the federal judgment. Finally, Branum's fraud claims are not barred by the relevant statute of limitations. Accordingly, we reverse the judgment of the court of appeals in part, affirm in part, and remand this cause to the court of appeals for further consideration of whether Branum's claims other than fraud against TCB, First Republic, and Peat Marwick are barred by the relevant statutes of limitations.

MOWER v. BOYER

811 S.W.2d 560
(Tex. 1991)

Kathleen W. Osman, Andy Taylor, Laura Gibson, Houston, for petitioner.
Dale F. Carrington, David P. Willis, Houston, for respondent.

COOK, JUSTICE.

This case involves two inconsistent final judgments in two actions brought by the same creditor on the same promissory note. The first final judgment was rendered by the probate court, the second by the district court. We hold that the finding of the probate court that the note had been fully satisfied precluded the district court from rendering judgment for the creditor, Boyer.

Jack Boyer sued Lowell Kendall Mower, Jr., L. Kendall Mower, Sr., and Patricia Mower for allegedly failing to make any payments on a $15,000 note signed by Mower Jr. and Mower Sr. The district court rendered an interlocutory partial summary judgment against Mower Jr. and Mower Sr., stating in its written order that "Summary Judgment should be granted on all issues, except recei[pt] of consideration and the amount of the attorney's fees." The Mowers' pleadings, as amended before the trial court signed its written order, generally denied Boyer's allegations and raised lack of consideration as an affirmative defense.

Mower Sr. died while the district court action was still pending, and Boyer brought an action on the same note in probate court against the decedent's estate. After trial on the merits, the probate court rendered judgment that Boyer take nothing, on the ground that the note had been fully satisfied. Boyer did not appeal this judgment.

In the district court action, Mower Jr. moved to set aside the partial summary judgment, amended his answer to plead satisfaction and the preclusive effect of the probate court's judgment, and moved for summary judgment on these grounds. The district court denied his motion for summary judgment, tried the issues of consideration and attorney's fees, and rendered judgment for Boyer against Mower Jr. only. The court of appeals affirmed, holding that res judicata precluded Mower Jr. from raising satisfaction as an affirmative defense in the probate court because he failed to raise it in the prior summary judgment proceeding in the district court. 795 S.W.2d 292, 293. The court of appeals also held that the district court's partial summary judgment was "final" for collateral estoppel purposes and precluded the probate court from determining the issue of liability against Boyer. 795 S.W.2d at 293. We reverse the judgment of the court of appeals and render judgment for Mower Jr.

At the outset, we note that the district court's interlocutory partial summary judgment was not entitled to either res judicata or collateral estoppel effect. A partial summary judgment that is interlocutory and non-appealable is not final and cannot support a plea of res judicata. *See Homeright Co. v. Exchange Warehouses, Inc.*, 526 S.W.2d 241, 244-45 (Tex. Civ. App.—Tyler 1975, writ ref'd n.r.e.); RESTATEMENT (SECOND) OF JUDGMENTS § 13 (1982). In this case, the interlocutory partial summary judgment was not final because it expressly left open the issue of consideration, and thus it was not entitled to res judicata effect.

Nor was the partial summary judgment entitled to collateral estoppel effect on the issue of satisfaction of the note. A prior adjudication of an issue will be given estoppel effect only if it was adequately deliberated and firm. The factors to be considered in making this determination are (1) whether the parties were fully heard, (2) that the court supported its decision with a reasoned opinion, and (3) that the decision was subject to appeal or was in fact reviewed on appeal. *See Scurlock Oil Co. v. Smithwick*, 724 S.W.2d 1, 6 (Tex. 1986); *Van Dyke v. Boswell, O'Toole, Davis & Pickering*, 697 S.W.2d 381, 385 (Tex. 1985); RESTATEMENT (SECOND) OF JUDGMENTS § 13, comment g (1982). The interlocutory partial summary judgment of the district court does not meet any of these criteria, as the issue of satisfaction was not expressly raised or decided, the decision was not supported by a reasoned opinion, and the judgment was not reviewable by appeal.

Although the partial summary judgment in the district court was not entitled to preclusive effect, the final judgment of the probate court on Boyer's claim against Mower Sr.'s estate was entitled to preclusive effect in the district court. When a probate court exercises jurisdiction over a decedent's estate, its judgment, regular on its face, is immune from collateral attack. *Graham v. Graham*, 733 S.W.2d 374, 377-78 (Tex. App.—Amarillo 1987, writ ref'd n.r.e.); *Wybrants v. Lehman*, 307 S.W.2d 339, 341-42 (Tex. Civ. App.—Eastland 1957, writ ref'd n.r.e.); *see also Dallas Joint Stock Land Bank of Dallas v. Forsyth*, 130 Tex. 563, 109 S.W.2d 1046, 1050 (1937), reh'g granted in part and overruled in part, 130 Tex. 563, 112 S.W.2d 173 (1938) (probate court acting within its statutory powers is a court of general jurisdiction and its judgments are immune from collateral attack).[1] Neither party contends that the probate court's judgment is void. If Boyer wished to challenge the judgment of the probate court on the ground that it should have been precluded by the partial summary judgment in the district court, he could have appealed the judgment of the probate court and asserted this argument on appeal. He chose not to do so, and instead proceeded to try his case in the district court. In the district court, however, he was not entitled to challenge the probate court's judgment by collateral attack. Given that the probate court proceeded to judgment first, its judgment was not void, and the partial summary judgment of the district court was not entitled to preclusive effect, the only remaining question is whether the probate court's judgment precluded the district court from rendering judgment for Boyer.

Relitigation of an issue will be barred by collateral estoppel if "(1) the facts sought to be litigated in the first action were fully and fairly litigated in the prior action; (2) those facts were essential to the judgment in the first action; and (3) the parties were cast as adversaries in the first action." *Eagle Properties v. Scharbauer*, 807 S.W.2d 714, 721 (Tex. 1991); *Bonniwell v. Beech Aircraft Corp.*, 663 S.W.2d 816, 818 (Tex. 1984). For collateral estoppel to be invoked, it is only necessary that the party against whom the plea of collateral estoppel is

---

[1] As a general rule, the court in which suit is first filed acquires dominant jurisdiction to the exclusion of other coordinate courts, and any subsequent suit involving the same parties and the same controversy must be dismissed if a party to the subsequent suit calls the second court's attention to the pendency of the prior suit by a plea in abatement. Wyatt v. Shaw Plumbing Co., 760 S.W.2d 245, 247-48 (Tex. 1988); Curtis v. Gibbs, 511 S.W.2d 263, 267 (Tex. 1974). However, if the second court has jurisdiction over the subject matter and the proper party does not file a dilatory plea in abatement in the second court at the proper stage, the second court can determine the issues before it and if it proceeds to judgment first, its judgment may have preclusive effect on the pending proceeding in the other court. *See* Estate of Maxey, 559 S.W.2d 458, 460-61 (Tex. Civ. App.—Texarkana 1977, writ ref'd n.r.e.). On the record before us, it appears that an order of abatement was neither sought nor obtained in the probate court.

being asserted be a party or in privity with a party in the prior litigation. *Eagle Properties*, at 720-22; *Tarter v. Metropolitan Sav. & Loan Ass'n*, 744 S.W.2d 926, 927 (Tex. 1988).

Each of the requirements for collateral estoppel is met in the present case. First, the issue of satisfaction was fully and fairly litigated in the probate court, which decided the issue against Boyer. Second, the satisfaction of the note was the basis for the probate court's decision, so it was clearly essential to its judgment. Third, Boyer was both plaintiff in district court and claimant in probate court, seeking to recover on the same note in both actions. Therefore, we conclude that the district court erred in failing to give collateral estoppel effect to the probate court's determination that Boyer could not recover on the note because it had been fully satisfied.

For the reasons stated, we reverse the judgment of the court of appeals and render judgment that Jack Boyer take nothing on his claim against Lowell Kendall Mower, Jr.

TARTER
v.
METROPOLITAN SAVINGS & LOAN ASSOCIATION

744 S.W.2d 926
(Tex. 1987)

Kenneth L. King, Bruce Claycombe, Richard E. McGary, Jones, Claycombe & King, Dallas, for petitioners.
Thomas L. Case and Cynthia J. MaHowald, St. Claire & Case, Dallas, for respondent.

SPEARS, JUSTICE.

This cause concerns the extent to which the doctrine of collateral estoppel bars claims arising from an alleged wrongful foreclosure. Respondent Metropolitan Savings and Loan Association (Metropolitan) was the holder of a note and first lien deed of trust on the home of Petitioners Jack and Margaret Tarter. The Tarters fell into arrears on the note, and Metropolitan notified them of its intent to foreclose. Before the Tarters could reinstate the loan, Metropolitan sold the note and first lien deed of trust to the holders of a second lien deed of trust on the Tarter home. The trustee then sold the Tarter property. In a suit brought prior to the instant case, the Tarters sued the second lien holders for wrongful foreclosure. The trial court found that the foreclosure was valid and rendered judgment awarding the second lien holders title and possession of the property. The Tarters then brought suit against Metropolitan for breach of contract and deceptive trade practices. The trial court rendered judgment in favor of the Tarters. The court of appeals reversed the judgment of the trial court, holding that the doctrine of collateral estoppel barred all of the Tarters' claims against Metropolitan. 730 S.W.2d 1. We reverse the judgment of the court of appeals and remand the cause to that court for a consideration of the points of error not previously reached.

In 1979, the Tarters failed to make four scheduled payments on the note that Metropolitan held on the Tarter property. Metropolitan consequently accelerated the note, notified the Tarters of its intent to foreclose, and directed the trustee to post notices of sale. The Tarters assert that after receiving the acceleration notice, they contacted Metropolitan and were told that their loan would be reinstated if they paid the arrearages and other reinstatement charges before the foreclosure sale. Jack Tarter testified that he brought a cashier's check for the agreed amount to Metropolitan's office on the morning of the sale. He testified that he was told that Metropolitan had just sold the note and deed of trust to Ronald Albers and Joseph Brownsted, the holders of a second deed of trust on the Tarters' property. Before the Tarters could contact Albers and Brownsted, the trustee sold the Tarter property.

The Tarters sued Albers and the trustee to recover title to the property and for damages. Brownsted intervened in the action. The trial court denied the Tarters' claim for damages and found that the foreclosure was valid. The court awarded title and possession of the property to Albers and Brownsted. That judgment is now final.

The Tarters then filed this suit against Metropolitan, alleging that (1) the foreclosure was wrongful because Metropolitan failed to give notice of its intent to accelerate the note; (2) Metropolitan breached its own contract with the Tarters by selling the note before the Tarters could reinstate the loan; and (3) Metropolitan engaged in deceptive trade practices by falsely representing that it would reinstate the loan if the Tarters paid the agreed amount before the foreclosure sale.

The trial court granted summary judgment in favor of Metropolitan on the wrongful foreclosure claim, holding that the claim was barred under the doctrine of collateral estoppel. The trial court, however, permitted the remaining claims to be presented to the jury. The jury found that Metropolitan had breached its oral contract with the Tarters and had knowingly violated the Texas Deceptive Trade Practices Act, TEX. BUS. & COMM. CODE Ann. §§ 17.46(b)(12), 17.50(a)(3) (Vernon 1987). The trial court rendered judgment for the Tarters.

The court of appeals reversed the judgment of the trial court and rendered judgment that the Tarters take nothing. The court of appeals held that the doctrine of collateral estoppel barred the Tarters' claims against Metropolitan because the Tarters' prior suit against Albers and Brownsted and this suit against Metropolitan presented the same ultimate issue—the validity of the foreclosure. The court of appeals concluded that the determination of the wrongful foreclosure issue in the first suit "precludes relitigation of that issue on alternative evidentiary grounds, such as breach of contract or deceptive trade practices, that could result in an inconsistent determination of that ultimate issue." 730 S.W.2d at 3.

The doctrine of collateral estoppel precludes relitigation of any ultimate issue of fact actually litigated and essential to the judgment in a prior suit. *Bonniwell v. Beech Aircraft Corp.*, 663 S.W.2d 816, 818 (Tex. 1984). The doctrine applies when the party against whom collateral estoppel is asserted had a full and fair opportunity to litigate the issue in the prior suit. *Id.* The question in this case, therefore, is whether the same ultimate issue litigated by the Tarters in the wrongful foreclosure suit against Albers and Brownsted is presented in the Tarters' suit against Metropolitan. Because we conclude that the ultimate issue in this case is whether Metropolitan breached the contract or committed a deceptive trade practice without regard to the validity of the foreclosure, we hold that the doctrine of collateral estoppel does not bar the Tarters' claims against Metropolitan.

Metropolitan contends that the issue of wrongfulness of the foreclosure, determined against the Tarters in their suit against Albers and Brownsted, is the same ultimate issue presented in this suit. Metropolitan maintains that the prior determination that the foreclosure was valid necessarily presupposed that Metropolitan had not engaged in any conduct that would invalidate the foreclosure. Metropolitan argues that if the Tarters established their claims of breach of contract and deceptive trade practices, they would also establish the wrongfulness of the foreclosure. Metropolitan thus asserts that any finding of a breach of contract or deceptive trade practice would be contrary to the prior determination that the foreclosure was valid.

Ultimate issues are those factual determinations submitted to a jury that are necessary to form the basis of a judgment. *Van Dyke v. Boswell, O'Toole, Davis & Pickering*, 697 S.W.2d 381, 384-85 (Tex. 1985); *Dreeben v. Sidor*, 254 S.W.2d 908, 910 (Tex. Civ. App.—Amarillo 1953, writ ref'd n.r.e.). The term "ultimate issue" does not refer to a cause of action or claim. *Wilhite v. Adams*, 640 S.W.2d 875, 876 (Tex. 1982); *Northern Texas Traction Co. v. Bruce*, 77 S.W.2d 889, 890 (Tex. Civ. App.—Dallas 1934, writ dism'd). The ultimate issues in the Tarters' suit against Metropolitan were neither expressly nor necessarily adjudicated in the suit against Albers and Brownsted.

In their suit against Albers and Brownsted, the Tarters' cause of action was wrongful foreclosure. *See Owens v. Grimes*, 539 S.W.2d 387, 389 (Tex. Civ. App.—Tyler 1976, writ ref'd n.r.e.). The Tarters alleged that there were procedural irregularities in the foreclosure sale. The validity of the foreclosure, therefore, was the legal conclusion that was drawn from the jury's finding on the ultimate issue—whether certain procedural irregularities occurred in the sale of the property.

In the Tarters' suit against Metropolitan, the causes of action on which the Tarters prevailed were breach of contract and violation of the Texas Deceptive Trade Practices Act. The ultimate issues submitted to the jury inquired into the component elements of each cause of action. *See* 3 MCDONALD, TEXAS CIVIL PRACTICE § 12.06.1, at 239 (1983). These issues were clearly different from the issue submitted to the jury in the Tarters' suit against Albers and Brownsted. Affirmative answers to these issues established Metropolitan's liability without reference to the validity of the foreclosure sale. Breach of contract and deceptive trade practices were not merely alternative evidentiary grounds for the claim of wrongful foreclosure but were, instead, separate and independent causes of action.

Metropolitan contends that the doctrine of collateral estoppel nevertheless applies because of the implied negative finding in the suit against Albers and Brownsted that Metropolitan did not breach its contract or commit a deceptive trade practice. Metropolitan, however, was not a party to the prior action nor was its conduct an issue in the trial. There is nothing in the record to show that a question of fact regarding Metropolitan's conduct was necessarily determined as a prerequisite to the rendition of the first judgment. *Van Dyke*, 697 S.W.2d at 385; RESTATEMENT (SECOND) OF JUDGMENTS § 27 comment h (1982). Thus, an affirmative jury finding that Metropolitan breached the contract or committed a deceptive trade practice is not fundamentally inconsistent with the prior determination of a valid foreclosure. The doctrine of collateral estoppel applies when relitigation could result in an inconsistent determination of the same ultimate issue; it does not bar litigation merely because the outcomes of two suits may appear to be inconsistent. *See* 2 A. FREEMAN, FREEMAN ON JUDGMENTS § 677, at 1429-32 (5th ed. 1925).

The judgment of the court of appeals is reversed and the cause remanded to that court for a consideration of points of error not previously reached.

CULVER, J., not sitting.

Notes

1. *Johnson & Higgins of Texas, Inc. v. Kenneco Energy, Inc.*, 962 S.W.2d 507 *(Tex.* 1998). Collateral estoppel may preclude relitigation of issues previously litigated even though the subsequent suit is based upon a different cause of action. If a cause of action in the second lawsuit involves an element already decided in the first lawsuit, that cause of action is barred. For this to be true, however, the issue decided in the first action must be actually litigated, essential to that lawsuit's judgment, and identical to the issue in the pending action.

Generally, there cannot be estoppel by alternative findings. If a judgment of a court of first instance is based on determinations of two issues, either of which standing independently would be sufficient to support the result, the judgment is not conclusive with respect to either issue standing alone. An exception exists to the general rule of no preclusion when alternative holdings are appealed and affirmed. If the judgment of the court of first instance was based on a determination of two issues, either of which standing independently would be sufficient to support the result, and the appellate court upholds both of these determinations as sufficient, and accordingly affirms the judgment, the judgment is conclusive as to both determinations.

2. *Quinney Electric, Inc. v.. Kondos Entertainment, Inc*, 988 S W.2d 212 (Tex. 1999). Kondos Entertainment retained Quinney Electric to do electrical work. Snyder represented Kondos in its dealings with Quinney. In partial payment of its work for Kondos, Quinney received checks Snyder signed and issued from an account in V-Ball, Inc.'s name. When Quinney stopped receiving checks for its work, it sued Kondos, V-Ball, and Snyder in state court for the unpaid contract balance, interest and attorneys' fees. Four months later, V-Ball filed for bankruptcy and Quinney filed a proof of an unsecured claim for the $83,991.21 contract balance in the bankruptcy court. V-Ball contested Quinney's claim. The bankruptcy court entered an order allowing Quinney's claim as a general unsecured claim for $83,724.76 and ordered V-Ball to pay the claim. Quinney pursued its state court claim against Kondos and Snyder. The trial court rendered judgment for Quinney for actual damages, prejudgment interest, attorney's fees, court costs, and post-judgment interest. The trial court then credited the judgment with the $83,724.76 bankruptcy judgment that V-Ball paid. The court of appeals reversed the trial court's judgment and rendered judgment for Kondos and Snyder. 948 S.W.2d 820, 825. The court of appeals held that the bankruptcy judgment collaterally estopped Quinney from relitigating the contract claim in state court. The Supreme Court reversed and remanded to the court of appeals to consider Kondos and Snyder's additional points of error. The doctrine of collateral estoppel generally applies when the issue was fully and fairly litigated in the previous action and was essential to the judgment in the previous action. The basic function of collateral estoppel is to prevent a party from relitigating an issue that the party previously litigated and lost. It could not estop Quinney, who prevailed on the contract issues in bankruptcy court, from relitigating the issues in its state court suit against Kondos and Snyder. Quinney prevailed on the issues it sought to relitigate and therefore, was not collaterally estopped from relitigating them. Instead, the trial court properly foreclosed Quinney's double recovery of contract damages by crediting Quinney's judgment against Kondos and Snyder with the amount Quinney received from the bankruptcy court judgment. Further, the parties agree that they did not litigate attorney's fees, interest, and costs issues in the bankruptcy proceeding. Thus, these issues are not subject to collateral estoppel in state court.

3. There is an ultimate limit on a plaintiff's potential recovery. *See Bradshaw v. Baylor*, 84 S.W.2d 703, 705 (Tex. 1935) ("[A]n injured party is entitled but one satisfaction for the injuries sustained by him.").

4. *Sky View at Las Palmas LLC v. Mendez*, 555 S.W.3d 101 (Tex. 2018): Martinez, who loaned Sky View money to start a development project, sued Sky View and Israely, for failing to repay the loan and for fraud for Israely's net worth misrepresentation when applying for the loan. Martinez also sued a title company and two law firms that settled. In his suit Martinez won $2.6 million. Sky View argued that the award should be reduced by the $2.3 million that Martinez had received in settling with the title company and the law firms. The trial court denied the motion and the court of appeals affirmed. The Supreme Court reversed and remanded holding that the one satisfaction rule applies and the trial court erred by denying the non-settling defendants settlement credits. The cause of action pleaded are not the proper inquiry in applying the one satisfaction rule. The proper question is whether the plaintiff suffered a single indivisible injury. Although Martinez had asserted various cause of action against the defendants all of his allegation were based on the same injury—the nonpayment of the loan. He sought to recover his economic loss of the loan's principal and accumulated interest plus attorney's fees.

5. *HECI Exploration Company v. Neel*, 982 S.W.2d 881 (Tex. 1998). A lessee cannot collaterally estop royalty owners in a suit against an adjoining operator for damages to the reservoir, absent an assignment by the royalty owner to the lessee or an agreement that the lessee will represent the royalty owner. The elements of collateral estoppel are that: (1) the facts sought to be litigated in the first action were fully and fairly litigated in the prior action; (2) those facts were essential to the judgment in the first action; and (3) the parties were cast as adversaries in the first action. Collateral estoppel binds only the party against whom estoppel is sought or those in privity. A lessee and royalty owners are not in privity for purposes of collateral estoppel. Although the circumstances of each case must be examined, generally, parties are in privity for purposes of collateral estoppel when: (1) they control an action, even if they are not parties to it; (2) their interests are represented by a party to the action; or (3) they are successors in interest, deriving their claims through a party to the prior action.

6. On the issue of election of remedies, *see Bocanegra v Aetna Life Insurance Co,* 605 S.W.2d 848 (Tex. 1980).

7. Steven C. Malin, *Collateral Estoppel: The Fairness Exception,* 53 J. AIR L. COM. 959, 959 (1988). "The doctrine of collateral estoppel, or issue preclusion, prevents a party from contesting an issue that he as previously litigated and lost. The related doctrine of res judicata, or claim preclusion, on the other hand precludes a party from asserting or contesting a claim that he has previously litigated and lost. To illustrate, assume A, a patent holder, sues B, a competitor, claiming that one of B's products is an infringement of A's patent. Upon trial, the court finds the patent invalid and holds for B, the competitor. If A against sues B claiming that B's same product is an infringement, A would be barred by res judicata, because the suit is upon the same claim. If, instead, A sues B claiming that a different product of B is an infringement of A's patent, B would plead collateral estoppel since A's patent had been conclusively determined invalid in the first action.

The two doctrines differ in other ways. As a rule, res judicata applies regardless of whether there has been an adversarial contest on the matter; conversely, collateral estoppel operates only when the parties actually have litigated the issue. Further, res judicata precludes only subsequent suits on the same cause of action; collateral estoppel, on the other hand, may preclude relitigation of issues in later suits on any cause of action. Finally, while res judicata is mandatory in nature, collateral estoppel is within the trial court's discretion."

8. *Texas Department of Public Safety v. Petta,* 44 S.W 3d 575 (Tex.2001): A fact found in a criminal proceeding may collaterally estop the retrial of that issue in a subsequent civil case. In *Petta,* , a jury found Petta guilty of fleeing or attempting to elude a police officer. Despite her conviction, Petta, in this case, sued the police officer individually for assault. Held: The jury's determination in the criminal case, that Petta did not reasonably believe that she was in danger of imminent harm when she fled, collaterally estops Petta from maintaining an action for assault against Rivera. Collateral estoppel applies when, as here, the party against whom it is asserted had a full and fair opportunity to litigate the issue in the prior suit.

9. *Sysco Food Servs. v. Trapnell*, 890 S.W.2d 796 (Tex. 1994): The doctrine of collateral estoppel or issue preclusion is designed to (1) promote judicial efficiency, (2) protect parties from multiple lawsuits, and (3) prevent inconsistent judgments by precluding relitigation of issues. When the application of the doctrine would not accomplish these purposes, and the result would be unfair, the courts should not apply the doctrine, even

though the issue in question (here, were there potato whiteners in the fruit salad) was fully and fairly litigated in the first suit.

Here, applying collateral estoppel would not conserve judicial resources because the parties not joined in the first action could still relitigate the issue.

Collateral estoppel would not protect the defendants from multiple lawsuits, since the defendants in the first action will not have to defend two suits.

Application of collateral estoppel also will not necessarily prevent the possibility of inconsistent findings. The defendants not joined in the first action, were free to litigate the issue litigated in the first action. "Due process requires that the rule of collateral estoppel operate only against persons who have had their day in court either as a party to the prior suit or as a privy . . . ."

Application of collateral estoppel also involves considerations of fairness not encompassed by the "full and fair opportunity" inquiry. The Trapnells were prevented from filing all of their claims in one suit by case law that has subsequently been overruled by statute. If collateral estoppel were applied, the Trapnells would foreclosed from litigating the potato whitener issue as to one set of defendants, yet the issue would remain in the case as a defense to the Trapnells' claims against the remaining defendants.

This holding is a narrow one, given the unusual procedural posture of this case and the fact that statutory changes make it unlikely that this situation will recur in the future.

3. *Election of Remedies*

BOCANEGRA
v.
AETNA LIFE INSURANCE COMPANY
605 S.W.2d 848
(Tex. 1980)

Branton & Mendelsohn, Les Mendelsohn, Chrys A. Lambros and L. Wayne Scott, San Antonio, for petitioner.
Joe Meador, San Antonio, for respondent.

POPE, JUSTICE.

Plaintiff, Janie Bocanegra, sued Aetna Life Insurance Company on a group medical and hospital policy and recovered judgment upon a jury finding that certain medical and hospital services she needed resulted from a non-occupational disease. Previously Mrs. Bocanegra had filed with the Industrial Accident Board a claim, which she settled, for an occupational injury. The court of civil appeals held the settlement was an election, which barred her later suit. That court reversed the judgment of the trial court and rendered judgment for Aetna. 572 S.W.2d 355. We hold that Mrs. Bocanegra did not make an informed election that barred her in this action. We reverse the judgment of the court of civil appeals and affirm the judgment of the trial court.

Mrs. Bocanegra began working for Clegg Company in 1965 as a book binder. Her work required her to lift and handle books. As she got out of bed one morning in April of 1975, she experienced a sharp pain in her lower back. She reported for work but did not tell her employer about her pain. On June 3, 1975, again on arising from bed, she had another severe pain, but still did not report any job-related injury. On June 29 the pain became so severe that she went to the emergency room of the Baptist Hospital. Her physician, Dr. Larry Miller, prescribed conservative treatment including two weeks in traction. He told Mrs. Bocanegra that she might have hurt her back at work. Failing to get any relief and after extensive tests, on August 11, she underwent surgery for a slipped disc. Dr. William Dossman performed the surgery. Mrs. Bocanegra never gave notice to her employer that she had sustained an occupational injury, but on August 18, after her operation, she filed with the Texas Industrial Accident Board her Notice of Injury or Occupational Disease and Claim for Compensation. In that notice she wrote, "I was lifting telephone books in the course and scope of my employment and injured my back and body generally." In her accompanying hardship affidavit, she swore, "I was hurt on the job on the above date while working for the above employer." On July 21, she filed a claim under the Aetna group policy on which she checked the box which asked if the claim was based on an accident. She also wrote on that claim form that the accident occurred "At work by lifting and bending." On July 29, she filed a second claim with Aetna on which she checked "No" to the question whether her claim was based on an accident. She also filed a claim with American Security Life Insurance Company on September 13 in which she stated that the accident occurred at work while lifting and bending. On September 17, she filed a similar claim with Presidential Life Insurance Company, which gave the same information.

On October 27, Mrs. Bocanegra settled her worker's compensation claim for a general injury for $12,000, which the compensation carrier paid. The settlement agreement was "solely for lost wages and future impaired earning capacity," and it expressly excluded any payment for past or future medical or hospital expenses, the items that are here in question. Mrs. Bocanegra, after her surgery and the settlement of her claim for an occupational injury, commenced these proceedings against Aetna to recover the amount of her medical and hospital bills. She asserted, and the jury found, that the medical and hospital services resulted from a non-occupational injury. She supported this claim by her own testimony that she was not injured on the job but that she did not know that fact until after her operation. At that time Dr. Dossman, her surgeon, told her that her back problem was the result of a degenerative disc disease that pre-dated but lingered after the onset of the initial back pain. She denied that she at any time ever told her doctors that she had sustained an injury on the job. Dr. Dossman confirmed Mrs. Bocanegra's testimony and testified that, in his opinion, her disc trouble was not related to her occupation. He testified: "About half of the time in this problem there is no known injury or cause of the problem, it just happens. About half of the time there is a history of some specific injury producing the problem." The court of civil appeals concluded that Mrs. Bocanegra's claim for an occupational injury was, as a matter of law, inconsistent with the state of facts upon which she later relied to obtain a judgment in her suit on the health policy that she had a non-occupational injury. The court rendered judgment that she take nothing.

The doctrine of election, although widely criticized, survives in wide-ranging branches of the law that stretch from the widow's election in probate law to the choice in contract law between a suit for damages and one for rescission. *See* 5 WILLISTON ON CONTRACTS §§ 683-688 (3d ed. Jaeger 1961). Election, an affirmative defense, has been held to bar remedies, rights, and inconsistent positions arising out of the same state of facts. 25 AM. JUR. 2D *Election of Remedies* § 7 (1966); Annot., 116 A.L.R. 601, 602 (1938). The situations in which an election might arise are so variable that an all-inclusive definition has been elusive, and discussions of the doctrine often borrow terms that may also appropriately relate to other affirmative defenses. For that reason, election is often confused with or likened to judicial estoppel, equitable estoppel, ratification, waiver or satisfaction. Those doctrines sometimes do not reach a situation that equity and good conscience need to reach through the doctrine of election.

A judicial estoppel may arise when a question necessary for the determination of a prior adjudication is decided. It constitutes a bar to a redetermination of that issue in a different cause. *Benson v. Wanda Petroleum Co.*, 468 S.W.2d 361 (Tex. 1971); *Long v. Knox*, 155 Tex. 581, 291 S.W.2d 292 (1956); *Houston Terminal Land Co. v. Westergreen*, 119 Tex. 204, 27 S.W.2d 526 (1930). Equitable estoppel differs from each of the above defenses, because it requires some deception that is practiced upon a party who relies upon it to his prejudice. *Barfield v. Howard M. Smith Co. of Amarillo*, 426 S.W.2d 834 (Tex. 1968); *Concord Oil Co. v. Alco Oil and Gas Corp.*, 387 S.W.2d 635 (Tex. 1965); *Gulbenkian v. Penn*, 151 Tex. 412, 252 S.W.2d 929 (1952). A ratification rests upon a manifestation of assent to confirm one's prior act or that of another. It may occur without any prior litigation and in the absence of any change of position by or prejudice to the other party. *Texas & Pac. Coal & Oil Co. v. Kirtley*, 288 S.W. 619 (Tex. Civ. App.—Eastland 1926, writ ref'd). Waiver, the voluntary relinquishment of a known right, is sometimes spoken of as intentional conduct inconsistent with the assertion of a known right. *Ford v. State Farm Mut. Auto. Ins. Co.*, 550 S.W.2d 663, 667 (Tex. 1977). Full satisfaction will bar a claim because the law will not permit double redress. *James and Company, Inc. v. Statham*, 558 S.W.2d 865 (Tex. 1977); *McMillen v. Klingensmith*, 467 S.W.2d 193 (Tex. 1971); *Bradshaw v. Baylor University*, 126 Tex. 99, 84 S.W.2d 703 (1935).

The single underlying principle of the election doctrine has not been found. Estoppel in some form, ratification and unjust enrichment have been suggested as the basic reasons for an election, and in many instances they suffice. *Schenck v. State Line Telephone Co.*, 238 N.Y. 308, 144 N.E. 592 (1924); *Metroflight, Inc. v. Shaffer*, 581 S.W.2d 704 (Tex. Civ. App.—Dallas 1979, writ ref'd n. r. e.). The court of civil appeals in this case has, perhaps more soundly, held that inconsistency will bar an action in instances of manifest injustice. Even though the inconsistent position may not fit the mold of a better defined principle, an election will bar recovery when the inconsistency in the assertion of a remedy, right, or state of facts is so unconscionable, dishonest, contrary to fair dealing, or so stultifies the legal process or trifles with justice or the courts as to be manifestly unjust.

A similar loosely defined but useful equitable doctrine is the constructive trust. It is unlike other trusts, but equity raised it up in the name of good conscience, fair dealing, honesty, and good morals. *Omohundro v. Matthews*, 161 Tex. 367, 341 S.W.2d 401, 405 (1960). "A constructive trust is the formula through which the conscience of equity finds expression." *Beatty v. Guggenheim Exploration Co.*, 225 N.Y. 380, 386, 122 N.E. 378, 380 (1919). Equity provides the idea of constructive trusts as a tool to "frustrate skullduggery," 4 R. POWELL, REAL PROPERTY § 593 (1949), even though that kind of a trust is also grounded upon elusive principles. Such a trust is purely a creature of equity. Its form is practically without limit, and its existence depends upon the circumstances. *Simmons v. Wilson*, 216 S.W.2d 847, 849 (Tex. Civ. App.—Waco 1949, no writ).

The election doctrine, therefore, may constitute a bar to relief when (1) one successfully exercises an informed choice (2) between two or more remedies, rights, or states of facts (3) which are so inconsistent as to (4) constitute manifest injustice. *See Custom Leasing, Inc. v. Texas Bank & Trust Co. of Dallas*, 491 S.W.2d 869 (Tex. 1973).

A number of seemingly inconsistent positions do not rise to the level of an election which will bar recovery. One may, for example, plead alternative and inconsistent facts without being barred. Rules 48 and 51, Texas Rules of Civil Procedure, authorize such procedures. One who pleads alternative or inconsistent facts or remedies against two or more parties may settle with one of them on the basis of one remedy or state of facts and still recover a judgment against the others based on the pleaded alternative or inconsistent remedies or facts. By analogy, an insurer's voluntary payment to a worker of weekly compensation benefits will not bar the defense that there was no accidental injury. *Lopez v. Associated Employers Ins. Co.*, 330 S.W.2d 522 (Tex. Civ. App.—San Antonio 1959, writ ref'd). *See also Southern Underwriters v. Schoolcraft*, 138 Tex. 323, 158 S.W.2d 991 (1942). The basis for the holding was to encourage prompt payments of compensation following injury. A holding that the payments were inconsistent with a denial of an accidental injury or that they constituted an admission of an injury would discourage prompt payment of weekly benefits. *Hartford Accident and Indemnity Co. v. Hale*, 400 S.W.2d 310, 312-13 (Tex. 1966).

There is no election, that is, no inconsistency in choices, when one first unsuccessfully pursues a right or remedy which proves unfounded and then pursues the one that is allowed. *Poe v. Continental Oil & Cotton Co.*, 231 S.W. 717 (Tex. Com. App. 1921, holding approved); *Schwartz v. National Loan & Investment Co.*, 133 S.W.2d 133 (Tex. Civ. App.—Dallas 1939, writ ref'd); *Breland v. Guaranty Building & Loan Co.*, 119 S.W.2d 690 (Tex. Civ. App.—Fort Worth 1938, writ ref'd); 25 AM. JUR. 2D, *Election of Remedies* § 9. One may assert concurrent but inconsistent remedies or distinct causes of action against different persons arising out of independent transactions. *Shriro Corp. v. Ward*, 570 S.W.2d 395 (Tex. 1978); *American Savings & Loan Ass'n of Houston v. Musick*, 531 S.W.2d 581, 588-89 (Tex. 1975); *Custom Leasing, Inc. v. Texas Bank & Trust Co. of Dallas*, 491 S.W.2d 869, 871 (Tex. 1973); *Liberty Mutual Ins. Co. v. First National Bank in Dallas*, 151 Tex. 12, 245 S.W.2d 237 (1951).

One's choice between inconsistent remedies, rights or states of facts does not amount to an election which will bar further action unless the choice is made with a full and clear understanding of the problem, facts, and remedies essential to the exercise of an intelligent choice. *Leonard v. Hare*, 161 Tex. 28, 336 S.W.2d 619 (1960); *Slay v. Burnett Trust*, 143 Tex. 621, 187 S.W.2d 377, 379 (1945); *Loveless v. Texas Employers Ins. Ass'n*, 269 S.W.2d 454 (Tex. Civ. App.—Austin 1954, writ ref'd); 5 WILLISTON ON CONTRACTS § 685 (3d ed. Jaeger 1961); MERREM, ELECTION OF REMEDIES IN TEXAS, 8 Sw.L.J. 109, 110 (1954); 25 AM. JUR. 2D, *Election of Remedies* § 21 (1966). An exception to that rule exists when the choice of a course of action, though made in ignorance of the facts, will cause harm to an innocent party. *Slay v. Burnett Trust*, *supra* at 394; *Employers' Indemnity Corp. v. Felter*, 277 S.W. 376 (Tex. Com. App. 1925).

This present case aptly illustrates the reason that election should not bar a suit when a previous course of action or a settlement for less than the claim was grounded upon uncertain and undetermined facts. The definition of an occupational disease contained in section 20 of article 8306 is itself complex and difficult:

> Whenever the term "Occupational Disease" is used in the Workmen's Compensation Laws of this State, such term shall be construed to mean any disease arising out of and in the course of employment which causes damage or harm to the physical structure of the body and such other diseases or infections as naturally result therefrom. An "Occupational Disease" shall also include damage or harm to the physical structure of the body occurring as the result of repetitious physical traumatic activities extending over a period of time and arising in the course of employment; provided, that the date of the cumulative injury shall be the date disability was caused thereby. Ordinary diseases of life to which the general public is exposed outside of the employment shall not be compensable, except where such diseases follow as an incident to an "Occupational Disease" or "Injury" as defined in this section.

Under that definition, Mrs. Bocanegra's injury may have been an occupational one which was compensable, it may have been an "ordinary disease of life" which was not, or it may have been both. TEX. REV. CIV. STAT. ANN. art. 8306, § 22. Many diseases, do not fit neatly within an either/or distribution, and the dispute whether such a condition is compensable or not is an ongoing one. Uncertainty in many complex areas of medicine and law is more the rule than the exception. It would be a harsh rule that charges a layman with knowledge of medical causes when, as in this case, physicians and lawyers do not know them. Mrs. Bocanegra's first physician, Dr. Miller, was of the opinion that the lifting and bending at the work bench was the cause of an occupational injury. Dr. Dossman advised her to the contrary after the surgery. The settlement agreement that Mrs. Bocanegra made with her compensation carrier showed that the carrier disputed liability, the period of time lost for the claimed occupational disease, and past and future medical expenses for which the carrier paid nothing. Mrs. Bocanegra lacked the requisite knowledge to bind her to an informed election.

Some of the Texas decisions cannot be harmonized, and they need discussion. *Seamans Oil Co. v. Guy*, 115 Tex. 93, 276 S.W. 424 (1925), while reaching a correct result, intermingles the doctrines of election, estoppel, and satisfaction. J. H. Guy and wife, lessors of an oil and mineral lease instituted suit against Seamans Oil Company and Empire Gas & Fuel Company for the cancellation of the lease. During the pendency of the suit against them, Seamans and Empire Gas could exercise none of the rights accorded by the lease, but they kept the lease alive by tendering timely delay rental payments which the Guys refused to accept. Just before the lease expired by its own terms, the Guys adopted an inconsistent posture, dismissed their suit for cancellation and drew a check on the bank for the delay rentals that they had previously rejected. By that time, the Guys' suit had fully accomplished its purpose to defeat any drilling or other operations. The court held that "(i)t would be shocking to a sense of justice to hold that the Guys could destroy the value of the leasehold by the claim that it did not exist and at the same time collect delay rentals upon the basis that it was a valid lease." The opinion, though primarily grounded upon an election, is an instance of full satisfaction which the Guys had already achieved through their lawsuit. Even though it was dismissed, the suit had fully accomplished the same purpose that a favorable judgment would have achieved. *Seamans* quotes from 10 RULING CASE LAW 703, 704:

> If one having a right to pursue one of several inconsistent remedies makes his election, institutes suit, and prosecutes it to final judgment or receives anything of value under the claim thus asserted, or if the other party has been affected adversely, such election constitutes an estoppel thereafter to pursue another and inconsistent remedy. And where the right in the subsequent suit is inconsistent with that set up in the former suit, as distinguished from a merely inconsistent remedy, the party is estopped though the former suit may not have proceeded to judgment. But where the inconsistency is in the remedies it is generally considered that there is no estoppel where the former suit was dismissed without trial or before judgment.

The quotation is an early statement of the election doctrine and contains errors. An election may arise short of one's prosecution of a claim to final judgment. One may also receive something by way of settlement, even of substantial value, under an uncertain claim without making an election which bars recovery against another person. The quotation may be illustrative of some situations which might rise to the level of an election, but it is an unreliable statement of a general rule, and we reject it. *Lomas and Nettleton Co. v. Huckabee*, 558 S.W.2d 863 (Tex. 1977) relied upon *Seamans, supra*, in holding there was an election. The Huckabees first asserted in their lawsuit that two insurance companies had insured the Huckabees' real and personal property that was destroyed in a fire. The Huckabees, upon the strength of that state of facts, recovered in a settlement one hundred percent of their claim for the destroyed realty and eighty percent of their claim for the destroyed personality. Their lawsuit was then dismissed with prejudice. After succeeding with their claim that their property was insured, they adopted the inconsistent position that it was not insured and sued their agent for his neglect. We held that the Huckabees, after successfully asserting their claim on one state of facts and receiving almost the whole of their claim, would not be permitted a second recovery against another party by denying the truth of that state of facts. The case was correctly decided, but the quotation from *Seamans*, as discussed above, includes errors concerning the election doctrine. *Cf. Shriro Corp. v. Ward*, 570 S.W.2d 395 (Tex. 1978).

The court of civil appeals in *Metroflight, Inc. v. Shaffer*, 581 S.W.2d 704 (Tex. Civ. App.—Dallas 1979, writ ref'd n. r. e.), followed but criticized Huckabee. As is characteristic of this whole area of law, the opinion mixes equitable estoppel, ratification, satisfaction, judicial estoppel, unjust enrichment and other matters. Perhaps the underlying flaw in the analysis of the court of civil appeals in Metroflight is its basic assumption. Metroflight had sued in federal court claiming that it had insurance coverage for losses arising out of a plane crash. The defendant insurer denied coverage but later paid Metroflight eighty percent of the total claim. Metroflight, after dismissing its action in which it asserted insurance coverage, proceeded with a suit against its agent for damages on the basis of the inconsistent fact that the plane was not insured. The trial court held that Metroflight was barred by election. The court of civil appeals affirmed but criticized the Huckabee case, which it felt bound to follow. The Metroflight court assumed that Metroflight had dismissed its federal court claim asserting insurance coverage because pre-trial discovery had shown that claim to be groundless and certain to fail. This assumption, twice stated, is wrong. The insurer's settlement for eighty percent of the very large coverage-based claim shows the validity and strength of the claim that insurance actually existed.

In *Seamans*, *Huckabee*, and *Metroflight*, the respective plaintiffs realized most or all of what they claimed by asserting facts about which they were certain. By contrast, however, the fact upon which Mrs. Bocanegra relied in settling with her compensation carrier, the nature of her complex disease, was highly uncertain which was evidenced by the small settlement which included none of her hospital and medical bills. The judgment of the court of civil appeals is reversed and the judgment of the trial court is affirmed.

GARWOOD, J., not sitting.

CAMPBELL, JUSTICE, concurring.

We should not attempt to draw an artificial distinction between this case and the decisions in *Huckabee* and *Metroflight* merely to avoid an admission that those decisions were erroneous. * * *

Proper regard for these principles compels a conclusion that a mere compromise and settlement of a claim asserting facts inconsistent to those asserted in a claim against a different defendant should not bar the latter claim. The contrary conclusion, in effect, compels a party to proceed to final judgment against two or more defendants instead of settling with a defendant who is desirous of settlement. This would not diminish assertion of inconsistent claims but would merely diminish settlements.

We should concede our error and expressly overrule *Huckabee* and hold there is no election until final judgment on the merits.

Notes

1. In *Medina v. Herrera,* 927 S.W.2d 597 (Tex. 1996), the Court applied the election of remedies doctrine in a personal injury case, that arose out of and on-the-job injury. Plaintiff-Medina was working at Interstate, riding a forklift, when he was struck by his supervisor, Herrera. Medina lost his balance, fell, and injured his back. He filed for, and received, workers' compensation benefits. On the claim form prepared by his attorney, Medina described the circumstances of his injury consistently with his present allegations. The trial court granted summary judgment for both defendants, Herrera and Interstate. The court of appeals affirmed. 905 S.W.2d 624. The Supreme Court affirmed as to Interstate; reversed and remanded as against Herrera, holding that the Workers' Compensation Act does not apply to a worker's intentional tort claim against the employer. Thus, Medina's intentional tort claim against Interstate has not been barred by the Legislature, but rather by his own voluntary election of an inconsistent remedy, under the Workers' Compensation Act. The receipt of workers compensation benefits is inconsistent with his present intentional tort claim against his employer, but not Medina. While the remedies would not be factually inconsistent, they would still be mutually exclusive for purposes of the election of remedies doctrine.

The Court in *Medina* reasoned that because Medina's present claim against Interstate is fundamentally inconsistent with his earlier pursuit of compensation benefits, and because Medina is charged with knowledge of the ramifications of his actions, he made an informed choice of remedy as to Interstate. Medina was represented by an attorney both in submitting his formal claim for compensation benefits, and in securing continued temporary income benefits at the contested hearing. By the time Medina filed this suit for common-law tort damages, he had been receiving benefits for almost two years, the entire time represented by counsel. Under these circumstances, Medina must, as a matter of law, be charged with knowledge of his remedies. Further, while he may not have appreciated the extent of his back injury when he applied for benefits, it is not the extent of injury, but rather the circumstances surrounding the accident which dictate whether it should be pursued as a workers' compensation claim, or a common-law intentional tort claim.

2. *Texas Adjutant General's Office v. Ngakoue*, 408 S.W.3d 350 (Tex. 2013): Election of remedies does not preclude a plaintiff, who sues a government employee acting within the scope of his employment from asserting a claim against the proper defendant—the government employer. The statutory procedure for the dismissal of the suit against such employee is immaterial to whether the suit may now be maintained against the proper defendant.

CHAPTER 7.
THE COURT OF APPEALS

1. *Jurisdiction*

Notes

1. Section 22.220(a) of the Texas Government Code states in part:

Each court of appeals has appellate jurisdiction of all civil cases within its district of which the district courts or county courts have jurisdiction when the amount in controversy or the judgment rendered exceeds $250, exclusive or interest and costs.

2. Section 22.225 of the Texas Government Code states in part:

A judgment of a court of appeals is conclusive on the facts of the case in all civil cases.

TEXAS DEPARTMENT OF PUBLIC SAFETY
v.
BARLOW

48 S.W.3d 174
(Tex. 2001)

S. Kyle Duncan, Kevin Michael Givens, Gregory S. Coleman, Austin, Stephen Edward Dennis, Conroe, John Cornyn, Attorney General of Texas, Andy Taylor, Linda Eads, Jeffrey S. Boyd, Austin, for Petitioner.

Travis B. Bryan, III, Youngkin, Catlin, Bryan & Stacy, David S. Barron, Law Office of David S. Barron, Bryan, for Respondent.

JUSTICE O'NEILL delivered the opinion of the Court, joined by CHIEF JUSTICE PHILLIPS, JUSTICE ENOCH, JUSTICE BAKER, JUSTICE ABBOTT, JUSTICE HANKINSON and JUSTICE JEFFERSON.

This case presents a dispute between the Texas Department of Public Safety and a driver over the driver's license suspension. We must decide whether Texas courts of appeals have jurisdiction over appeals from county courts at law in license suspension cases arising from a driver's refusal to submit to a blood alcohol concentration test. We hold that the courts of appeals do have jurisdiction over such appeals. Accordingly, we reverse the court of appeals' judgment dismissing this case for lack of jurisdiction and remand the case to the court of appeals for further proceedings.

I

Benjamin Barlow was arrested on suspicion of drunk driving and was asked to submit a breath specimen for a blood alcohol concentration ("BAC") test. He refused, and the Department of Public Safety suspended his driver's license. *See* TEX. TRANSP. CODE § 724.035 (authorizing the Department to suspend a driver's license if the driver refuses a BAC test). Barlow timely requested an administrative hearing, and the administrative law judge sustained the suspension. *See id.* § 724.041. Barlow appealed to the county court at law, which reversed the suspension. *See id.* §§ 724.047, 524.041. The Department sought to appeal the county court at law's decision, but the court of appeals dismissed the appeal, holding that (1) it did not have general jurisdiction because the record contained no evidence that the case met the minimum amount in controversy requirement the Legislature established under the Texas Constitution, *see* TEX. GOV'T CODE § 22.220(a); TEX. CIV. PRAC. & REM. CODE § 51.012; and (2) there was no specific statutory grant of jurisdiction over license suspension appeals from county courts at law, *see* TEX. TRANSP. CODE § 524.002; TEX. GOV'T CODE § 2001.901. 992 S.W.2d 732, 740-41. We granted the Department's petition for review to consider whether the court of appeals correctly decided its jurisdiction. *See Del Valle Indep. Sch. Dist. v. Lopez*, 845 S.W.2d 808, 809 (Tex. 1992).

II

The court of appeals' jurisdiction over this appeal must be based on either the constitution's general jurisdictional grant, *see* TEX. CONST. art. V, § 6, or a specific statutory jurisdictional grant. The Department claims that both jurisdictional bases exist in this case. We begin by considering whether the court of appeals had general jurisdiction over this appeal.

Our constitution vests jurisdiction over appeals from final judgments of district and county courts in the courts of appeals, subject to any restrictions and regulations prescribed by law. TEX. CONST. art. V, § 6. The Legislature has limited courts of appeals' jurisdiction to cases in which the amount in controversy or the judgment exceeds $100. *See* TEX. GOV'T CODE § 22.220(a); TEX. CIV. PRAC. & REM. CODE § 51.012. Thus, the court of appeals erred in dismissing the Department's appeal if the amount in controversy in a driver's license suspension case exceeds $100.

The "amount in controversy," in the jurisdictional sense, is not limited to the money damages sought. Rather, "[t]he subjective value of a privilege, if asserted in good faith, establishes jurisdiction if that value meets the requisite amount in controversy." *Tune v. Texas Dep't of Pub. Safety*, 23 S.W.3d 358, 361 (Tex. 2000). In *Tune*, we held that the amount of money that a citizen is willing to pay for a privilege is some evidence of its value. *Id.* at 362. Thus, statutes that require payment for a person to be afforded a particular privilege, such as a licensing fee, may establish a minimum value. *Id.* That is not because the fee is somehow in controversy, but because "the standard fee offers the minimum measure of 'the [privilege's] value.' " *Id.* We concluded in *Tune* that the $140 statutory fee for a handgun license established its minimum value for jurisdictional purposes. *Id.*

We apply *Tune's* reasoning to the situation presented here. The Department charges a $24 fee for issuing or renewing a driver's license. TEX. TRANSP. CODE § 521.421. That a driver is willing to pay this amount to obtain a license in the first instance is some indication of its minimum value. *See Tune*, 23 S.W.3d at 362. In addition, a driver whose license has been suspended must pay "a fee of $100 in addition to any other fee required by law" to be reinstated or to obtain another driver's license. TEX. TRANSP. CODE § 724.046(a). These amounts indicate a minimum value that a driver such as Barlow is willing to pay for the privilege of driving and together meet the minimum jurisdictional threshold. *See Tune*, 23 S.W.3d at 362.

Barlow contends that the Department failed to meet its burden to establish jurisdiction because it did not plead and prove a specific amount in controversy. But as we have said, by seeking to retain his driver's license, Barlow put the value of his driving privileges at issue. And neither party needed to introduce evidence about what Barlow subjectively thinks his driving privileges are worth because the Transportation Code itself establishes an objective minimum value. *See id.*

III

Because the amount in controversy in this case exceeds the $100 jurisdictional minimum, the court of appeals had jurisdiction over the Department's appeal from the county court's decision reversing Barlow's driver's license suspension. And because the court of appeals had general jurisdiction, we do not reach the Department's alternative argument that Chapter 524 of the Texas Transportation Code contains a specific jurisdictional grant. We reverse the court of appeals' judgment dismissing this case for lack of jurisdiction, and remand the case to that court to consider the merits.

JUSTICE HECHT, joined by JUSTICE OWEN, concurring in the judgment.

The amount of the fee that the government charges for a particular license rarely has anything at all to do with the value of the license to the licensee or the amount the licensee would be willing to pay for the privilege conveyed. This is certainly true for a driver's license, which costs $24 and is good for at least six years. Surely the right to drive a car—and beyond doubt the right to drive a pickup—in Texas is worth much more than eight cents a week. (It is worth noting that a Department employee was recently charged with selling driver's licenses illegally for $300-$775 apiece, which is perhaps some indication of what a "market price" would be.) A license to operate a motorcycle or moped costs $32. Is that because the right to drive a motorcycle or moped is worth a third more than the right to drive a car or pickup? Of course not! Does a driver's license worth only $24 before it is suspended suddenly become worth $124 after the driver pays $100 to reinstate it? No. If any explanation for the amount of a driver's license fee exists, and it may well be that the charge is more or less arbitrary, it certainly relates more to the administrative costs of processing applications, giving examinations, and issuing licenses than it does to the value of the license to a driver. The Court in its search for a dollar figure written down somewhere to satisfy the court of appeals' $100 jurisdictional minimum ignores the plain fact that the value of a driver's license and the value of the State's interest in curbing drunk driving—both of which are involved in this appeal—are worth considerably more than $100. I agree that the court of appeals should not have dismissed the appeal for want of jurisdiction.

Notes

1. There are some limitations upon the right to appeal. For example, as stated in *Texas State Bank v. Amaro*, 87 S.W.3d 538 (Tex. 2002): A litigant cannot treat a judgment as both right and wrong, and if he has voluntarily accepted the benefits of a judgment, he cannot afterward prosecute an appeal therefrom. There is a narrow exception to this rule that as long as an appellant accepts only that which appellee concedes, or is bound to concede, to be due him under the judgment he is not estopped to prosecute an appeal which involves only his right to a further recovery.

2. In *Sultan v. Mathew*, 178 S.W.3d 747 (Tex. 2005) the court noted a limitation on the appellate jurisdiction of the courts of appeals: A party dissatisfied with a small claims court judgment may appeal to the county court or county court at law for a de novo trial if the amount in controversy exceeds $20. TEX. GOV'T CODE §§ 28.052(a), 28.053(b). The Texas Government Code provides that a "[j]udgment of the county court or county court at law on the appeal [from the small claims court] is **final**." *Id.* § 28.053(d) (emphasis added). The question here is whether the word "final" in section 28.053(d) means final and appealable or final and not appealable. The Court concluded that the word "final" in section 28.053(d) meant "that there is no further appeal beyond the county court or county court at law."

2. *The Process of Appeal*

a. *Preservation of Complaint at the Trial Court*

Read Rule 33 Texas Rules of Appellate Procedure and Rule 103 of the Texas Rules of Civil Evidence.

BUSHELL
v.
DEAN
803 S.W.2d 711
(Tex. 1991)

PER CURIAM.

Syndex's motion for rehearing is granted in part and overruled in part. This court's opinion and judgment of November 21, 1990, are withdrawn, and the following is substituted in their place.

Mary Dean brought this action against Bill Bushell and the Syndex Corporation, her former manager and employer, claiming assault, intentional infliction of emotional distress, and sexual harassment pursuant to TEX. REV. CIV. STAT. ANN. art. 5221k, § 5.01 (1985). Dean obtained a favorable jury determination on each cause and the trial court rendered judgment awarding Dean $195,600 in actual and punitive damages and $123,000 in attorney's fees. The court of appeals reversed that part of the judgment awarding damages and attorney's fees for the sexual harassment claim and remanded that part of the cause for new trial. 781 S.W.2d 652. Because the court of appeals based this part of its judgment on unpreserved error, we reverse the judgment of the court of appeals and remand the cause to that court for further proceedings.

By three points of error to the court of appeals, Syndex attacked the trial court's admission of testimony by one of Dean's experts, Dr. Lucia Gilbert. Syndex asserted that the testimony was irrelevant, TEX. R. CIV. EVID. 402; that the probative value of the testimony was substantially outweighed by unfair prejudice, TEX. R. CIV.

EVID. 403; and that the testimony was inadmissible character evidence. TEX. R. CIV. EVID. 404. The court of appeals sustained all three points of error.

Syndex did not preserve its objection to Dr. Gilbert's testimony at trial. On direct examination, Dr. Gilbert indicated that he was going to give a "working definition" of sexual harassment, including "general things that are true about a person who harasses." Syndex's counsel objected, stating, I am objecting to the testimony of this expert witness as a whole to the extent that it goes to questions of profile of someone who harasses . . . . I think it is likely to create a great deal of prejudice and to confuse the jury and issues that they actually have to decide in this case, and that involves a mixture of law and fact. The trial judge responded, I [have] expressed a concern that at some point I did not think that the questions to the witness had crossed the point yet, but at some point it might cross the line into character evidence prohibitions, at which time if you believe that it does you will need to reurge your—any objection. Some time later, Dr. Gilbert testified about the "profile" of a sexual harasser, but Syndex did not make any further objection.

In order to preserve a complaint for appellate review, a party must present to the trial court a timely request, objection or motion, state the specific grounds therefor, and obtain a ruling. TEX. R. APP. P. 52(a). Therefore, Syndex's points of error relating to this testimony were not before the appellate court for review, and the court of appeals erred in holding that the testimony was inadmissible. *See Lemons v. EMW Mfg. Co.*, 747 S.W.2d 372 (Tex. 1988).

The court of appeals did not consider several of Syndex's points of error. These points include arguments which, if sustained, would require a modification of the trial court's judgment or a remand for new trial. Therefore, we remand the cause to the court of appeals for consideration of these points of error. *See McKelvy v. Barber*, 381 S.W.2d 59, 64 (Tex. 1964).

The applications for writ of error brought by Bill Bushell and Syndex Corporation are denied.

Pursuant to TEX. R. APP. P. 170, a majority of the court, without hearing oral argument, reverses the judgment of the court of appeals and remands the cause to that court for further consideration in accordance with this opinion.

Note

Maritime Overseas Corporation v. Ellis 971 S.W.2d 402 (Tex. 1998): Maritime did not object before trial, or when the evidence was offered, that the scientific evidence offered by Ellis's experts was scientifically unreliable. On appeal, Maritime argues that the federal standard articulated in *Daubert v. Merrell Dow Pharm., Inc.*, 509 U.S. 579 (1993); 1997), and the state standard articulated in *E.I. duPont de Nemours v. Robinson,* 923 S.W.2d 549 (Tex. 1995) and *Merrell Dow Pharm., Inc. v. Havner*, 953 S.W.2d 706 (Tex. 1997) are the proper standards for reviewing the sufficiency of Ellis's damages evidence. * * * . . . Maritime's position is that, if the court of appeals applied a proper scientific methodology test to Ellis's experts' testimony, the testimony would be legally insufficient to show that the long-term conditions, which Ellis claims he suffers, were caused by delayed neurotoxicity. Thus, Maritime concludes, by way of its complaints about the court of appeals" factual sufficiency review, that there is no evidence of some of Ellis's actual damages. Held: Affirmed. Maritime's argument is flawed. To preserve a complaint that scientific evidence is unreliable and thus, no evidence, a party must object to the evidence before trial or when the evidence is offered.

McCRAW
v.
MARIS

837 S.W.2d 646
(Tex. App.—Dallas 1990, no writ)

Facts: Dispute over proceedings of an insurance policy.

Issue: Did the trial court err in refusing to allow McCraw & Wiggins to pay a jury fee prior to trial when the case was set on the jury docket. Not reached.

Issue: Was the error preserved? No?

Held: The formal bill did not bear the signature of the trial judge, and was not approved by the opposing counsel, and so did not preserve error. It was not a bystander's bill. It is not in compliance with TEX. R. APP. P. Rule 52(c). It therefore presents nothing for review, and is not considered.

MCLAUGHLIN
v.
FIRST NATIONAL BANK OF JEFFERSON, TEXAS

858 S.W.2d 511
(Tex. App.—Texarkana 1993, writ denied)

Facts: Formal bill shows that the trial judge told the attorneys for McLaughlin that they had been dismissed from the suit by all parties, and that the attorney did not need to participate in preparing the jury charge. As a result, McLauglin's counsel did not preserve error to the charge. Judgement was entered against McLauglin and others. The Bank's attorneys approved the bill and the judge found it to be correct.

Issue: Does the approved formal bill control over the record of the proceedings? Yes.

Held: If the trial court and the opposing party find the bill of exceptions to be correct, it is to be signed by the judge and filed as part of the record. The bill of exceptions then controls on the issue in question. The agreement to the bill of exceptions, by the judge and the opposing party, conclusively establishes the proposition stated in the bill of exceptions, as a matter of law (here that McLaughlin was dismissed prior to the submission of the charge to the jury).

Notes

1. Former Rule 52(c) has been rewritten so that the procedure for making a formal bill of exception is more clearly and definitely stated. *See* Rule 33.2 of the Texas Rules of Appellate Procedure. Under the old rule, when a party was dissatisfied with the formal bill filed by the judge, he could prepare what was referred to as a bystanders bill of exception. Rule 33.2 dispenses with the language "three respectable bystanders" and merely state "three people". It is unlikely that the case law concerning who may qualify to sign the "bystanders bill of exception" has been affected by this change. In *Smith v. United Gas Pipe Line Co.*, 149 Tex. 69, 228 S.W.2d 139 (1950), the Court held that bystander's bills are defective if supported only by affidavits of the attorneys participating in the case. In *Harris County Flood Control Dist. v. Cohen*, 282 S.W.2d 917 (Tex. Civ. App.—Galveston 1955, writ ref'd n.r.e.), the court held that the term "bystander" "relates to one who has no concern in the outcome of the case on trial." *Id.* at 919.

2. *Goodpasture v. Coastal Industrial Water Authority*. 490 S.W.2d 883(Tex. App.—Houston [1st Dist] 1973, no writ). A bill of exceptions that is not approved by either the trial judge or opposing counsel, and that is not a bystanders' bill, presents nothing for appellate review.

3. Richard Orsinger: *The New Texas Rules of Appellate Procedure* (STATE BAR OF TEXAS INSTITUTE ON PRACTICING UNDER THE NEW TEXAS RULES OF APPELLATE PROCEDURE, 1997, at page B-9):

> *Informal Bills of Exception and Offer of Proof.* Old (pre-9/1/97) TRAP Rule 52(b), specifically discussed making an offer of proof when evidence is excluded at trial. That provision has been deleted from the new TEX. R. APP. P. The requirement to make an offer of proof when evidence has been excluded is now set out in TEX.R.CIV.EVID. 103(b).
>
> *Deadline for Formal Bills of Exception.* Under old TRAP 52(c)(11), formal bills of exception were due sixty (60) days after the judgment is signed, or ninety (90) days if a motion for new trial was timely filed. Under new TRAP 33.2(c)(1), the time for filing formal bills of exception in civil cases is always 30 days after the filing party perfects appeal. The deadline does *not* vary depending on timely filing of a motion for new trial, etc. The deadline can be extended upon a proper motion to extend the deadline, filed within 15 days after the deadline. New TRAP 33.2(e)(3).
>
> *Sanctions for Frivolous Original Proceedings.* The old TEX. R. APP. P. 84 (court of appeals) and old TRAP 182 (Supreme Court), regarding damages for delay on appeal, did not authorize sanctions in original proceedings. That has been changed. Under new TRAP 52.10 the appellate court can award 'just sanctions' after notice and a reasonable opportunity to respond, on a party or attorney who is not "acting in good faith." Lack of good faith is demonstrated by: (i) filing a petition that is groundless; (ii) bringing a petition solely for delay of the underlying proceeding; (iii) grossly misstating or omitting an obviously important and material fact in the petition or response; or (iv) filing an appendix that is clearly misleading because of the omission of obviously important and material evidence or documents.

b. *The Jurisdictional Prerequisite: The Notice of Appeal*

Read Rules 25 and 26 Texas Rules of Appellate Procedure.

Notes

1. Prior to September 1, 1997, an appeal bond, or its equivalent, was a jurisdictional prerequisite to perfect an appeal from a trial court to a court of appeals. This requirement has been repealed under the new appellate rules, and replaced with the requirement that an appeal is perfected when a written notice of appeal is filed. *See* Rule 25.1 Texas Rules of Appellate Procedure. Rule 25.1(c), unlike the former rules, requires that anyone (including an appellee) who seeks to alter a trial court's appealable order must file a notice of appeal. As well be shown below, the former rules did not always require that an appellee perfect an appeal in order to obtain a more favorable judgment in the court of appeals than he had received in the trial court.

Rule 25.1(d) dictates the information which must be contained in the notice of appeal. Rule 25.1(e) specifies that the notice be filed with the trial court clerk, with copies served on all parties to the trial courts appealable order and the clerk of the appellate court. Rule 26 specifies the time within which the notice of appeal must be filed. Like the former rules, Rule 26.3 permits an extension of time for late filing of the notice of appeal. Nothing in the new rules indicates that the Supreme Court intended to modify previous case law concerning an appellate court's jurisdiction over an appeal when a "bona fide" attempt has been made to invoke its jurisdiction. In fact, Rule 25.1(f) states that defects in a notice of appeal may be corrected at any time prior to the filing of the appellant's brief. Furthermore, Rule 44.3 requires that before a court of appeals affirms, dismisses, or reverse a judgment for a "formal defect or irregularities in appellate procedure", it must give a party a reasonable time to correct the problem.

2. The appeal is perfected by filing a notice of appeal 30 days after the judgment is signed, or if a post-judgment motion, or request for findings of fact and conclusions of law are made, 90 days after the judgment is signed. TEX.R.APP.P. 26.1(a). The longer time period will apply if any party timely files a (i) motion for new trial; (ii) motion to modify the judgment; (iii) motion to reinstate after dismissal for want of prosecution (DWOP); or (iv) a request for findings and conclusions where they are required or can be properly considered by the appellate court. Under TEX.R.APP.P. 4.3(a), the modification of a judgment during the trial court's period of plenary power restarts the appellate timetable.

3. The deadline for perfecting the appeal may be extended if, within 15-days after the deadline, and within that same period, a motion is filed in the appellate court reasonably explaining the need for the extension, as required by TEX.R.APP.P. 10.5(b).

4. A prematurely filed notice of appeal is effective. TEX. R. APP. P. 27.1.

5. The notice of appeal is filed with the trial clerk, but the appellant must file a copy of the notice with the appellate court clerk. TEX. R. CIV. P. 25.1(c).

6. TEX. R. APP. P. 9.2 provides that "A document received within ten days after the filing deadline is considered timely filed if: (A) it was sent to the proper clerk by United States Postal Service first-class, express, registered, or certified mail; (B) it was placed in an envelope or wrapper properly addressed and stamped; and (C) it was deposited in the mail on or before the last day for filing."

7. *Williams v. Flores*, 80 S.W.3d 631 (Tex. 2002): Since William's filed a motion for new trial within 30 days of the date the trial court signed the final judgment confirming an arbitration award, he had 90 days in which to file a notice of appeal. Even though the notice of appeal was filed 12 after the 90 day deadline expired, Williams had, under TEX. R. APP. P. 26.3, he had 15 days in which to file a motion to extend the time for filing the notice of appeal. Since the motion to extend time was placed in the mail on the 15th day after the notice of appeal was due, and, since it was received by the court of appeals within 10 days of the deadline for filing the motion to extend time, under TEX. R. APP. P. 9.2, the motion to extend time was timely filed, and the appeal was timely perfected.

MAXFIELD
v.
TERRY

888 S.W.2d 809
(Tex. 1994)

Donald P. Wiley and Mark Mueller, Dallas, for petitioner.
Scott Pelley and Rayburn M. (Rim) Nall, Sherman, for respondent.

PER CURIAM.

This appeal from a will contest between family members presents the issue of whether the failure to perfect separate appeals from separate orders rendered in the same probate proceeding required the court of appeals to dismiss the appeal of one of the orders for want of jurisdiction. We hold that J.R. Maxfield invoked the jurisdiction of the court of appeals by filing a cash deposit for one of the probate orders, and that the court of appeals erred by sua sponte dismissing the appeal of the second probate order for want of jurisdiction. We reverse the judgment of the court of appeals and remand the cause to that court for further proceedings.

On September 7, 1991, Marie Maxfield died in a nursing home in Florida. Her will, executed two weeks prior to her death, appointed John Robert Terry as her personal representative and bequeathed her estate to the children of her brother, William Maxfield. The original death certificate stated her Texas address. It was later amended and replaced the Texas address with a Florida address. Thereafter, probate proceedings were commenced in Florida. J.R. Maxfield, brother of Marie Maxfield, contested the Florida proceedings, alleging that Marie Maxfield was a domiciliary of Texas and thus the will should be probated in Texas. J.R. Maxfield voluntarily dismissed the will contest in Florida and three days later filed a suit in Texas for a declaratory judgment on the domicile issue. This case was assigned cause number 91-04482-P(A). Prior to the declaratory judgment suit, J.R. Maxfield had filed an Application for Letters of Administration in Texas, cause number 91-04482-P. Terry sought a summary judgment in the declaratory judgment action on the basis of res judicata asserting that the issue of Marie Maxfield's domicile had been fully litigated in the Florida court. The probate court granted summary judgment in the declaratory judgment action and in a separate order denied J.R. Maxfield his application for letters of administration. Each probate order received its own cause number. On appeal, J.R. Maxfield filed the cash deposit in lieu of bond under cause number 91-04482-P. No cash deposit or bond was filed for the declaratory judgment action, cause number 91-04482-P(A). No cash deposit or bond was filed for the declaratory judgment action, cause number 91-04482-P(A). J.R. Maxfield brought points of error in his brief, however, complaining of the court's decisions with respect to both the letters of administration and the declaratory judgment actions. Terry filed a motion to sever and dismiss a portion of the appeal for want of jurisdiction because J.R. Maxfield failed to perfect an appeal. The court of appeals overruled the motion and made no mention of any "defect" in the appeal. After oral argument, however, the court of appeals dismissed the case for want of jurisdiction on the declaratory judgment action and overruled J.R. Maxfield's point of error on the letters of administration.

To invoke the jurisdiction of the court of appeals, an instrument must be filed pursuant to Texas Rules of Appellate Procedure 40(a) and 41(a). Recently, in *Jamar v. Patterson*, 868 S.W.2d 318, 319 (Tex. 1993), we stated that, "[i]t is our policy to construe rules reasonably but liberally, when possible, so that the right to appeal is not lost by creating a requirement not absolutely necessary from the literal words of the rule." *See e.g. City of San Antonio v. Rodriguez*, 828 S.W.2d 417 (Tex. 1992) (failing to put the correct cause number on the cost bond will not preclude appellant's attempt to invoke appellate jurisdiction); *Grand Prairie Indep. Sch. Dist. v. Southern Parts Imports*, 813 S.W.2d 499, 500 (Tex. 1991) (dismissing appeal is improper "[i]f the appellant timely files a document in a bona fide attempt to invoke the appellate court's jurisdiction, [unless] the court of appeals, . . . allow[s] the appellant an opportunity to amend or refile the instrument . . . to perfect the appeal") (emphasis added).

Although each probate order was final and appealable, the court of appeals dismissed the declaratory judgment order, holding that "a party must file a separate cost bond, cash deposit, or affidavit of inability to pay for each of the probate court's final orders." 870 S.W.2d 614. Under this Court's policy of liberally construing the Rules of Appellate Procedure, J.R. Maxfield made a bona fide attempt to invoke the jurisdiction of the court of appeals by filing one "instrument" for both probate orders. *See e.g. Ashmore v. North Dallas Bank & Trust*, 804 S.W.2d 156, 157-58 (Tex. App.—Dallas 1990, no writ) (invoking appellate jurisdiction over three separate probate orders by filing one notice of appeal). The court of appeals should have given J.R. Maxfield the opportunity to correct any defect in the appeal before dismissing. *Grand Prairie Indep. Sch. Dist.*, 813 S.W.2d at 500.

A majority of the court grants the application of J.R. Maxfield and, without hearing argument, reverses the judgment of the court of appeals and remands to that court for further proceedings in accordance with this opinion. TEX. R. APP. P. 170.

VERBURGT
v.
DORNER
959 S.W.2d 615
(Tex. 1997)

Jaay D. Neal, San Antonio, for Petitioners.

Edward C. Mainz, Jr., San Antonio, Laurence E. Best, Steven D. Naumann, Houston, for Respondents.

SPECTOR, J., JUSTICE, delivered the opinion of the Court, in which PHILLIPS, CHIEF JUSTICE, GONZALEZ, HECHT, and OWEN, JUSTICES, join.

In this case, we decide whether the court of appeals erred in dismissing an appeal for want of jurisdiction. The appellant, John Verburgt, filed a cost bond on the thirty-fourth day after the trial court rendered judgment against him. Verburgt mistakenly believed that he had timely complied with Rule 41(a)(1) of the Rules of Appellate Procedure in filing the bond and did not concurrently move to extend the time to file under Rule 41(a)(2). We hold that a motion for extension of time is implied when a party, acting good faith, files a cost bond within the fifteen-day period in which Rule 41(a)(2) permits parties to file a motion to extend. We therefore reverse the judgment of the court of appeals and remand to that court.

Verburgt, in his individual capacity and as his children's next friend, sued Constance Clear, Patricia Dorner, and the Methodist Mission Home for intentional infliction of emotional distress and negligent interference with familial relationships. After Verburgt nonsuited Clear, the trial court granted summary judgment for the remaining defendants. The judgment was signed on October 10, 1995. Because no motion for new trial was filed, Verburgt's cost bond was due within thirty days, by November 9th. *See* TEX. R. APP. P. 41(a)(1). Verburgt did not file the bond until November 13th, nor did he file a motion to extend the time to file the bond within fifteen days of the bond's due date. *See* TEX.R.APP. P. 41(a)(2).

Several weeks later, the court of appeals ordered Verburgt to show cause why it should not dismiss his appeal for lack of jurisdiction. Verburgt's response demonstrated that his counsel had simply miscalculated the date the bond was due. *See* 928 S.W.2d 654, 655. Initially, the court of appeals decided to retain jurisdiction of Verburgt's appeal. But on rehearing en banc, the court reversed itself.

The court of appeals in this case recognized the "patent unfairness" of the result it reached:

> We are, therefore, confronted with the question of whether the appellate rules condone a result that allows a litigant who knows he is late with his bond to save his appeal, but rejects the appeal of the litigant who erroneously, but in good faith, believes he has timely filed his bond and, thus satisfied, also believes he has no need to file for an extension of time.

Id. Although it acknowledged the arbitrariness of dismissal under these circumstances, the court of appeals nevertheless believed that the interest in finality of judgments outweighed the policy of disposing of appeals on their merits. *Id.* at 656.

In dismissing Verburgt's appeal, the appellate court also relied largely upon a decision by the Court of Criminal Appeals, *Olivo v. State*, 918 S.W.2d 519 (Tex. Crim. App. 1996). But the Court of Criminal Appeals itself recognized in *Olivo* that its approach to the perfection of appeals in criminal cases has differed significantly from our more liberal approach. *See id.* at 524-25; *compare Jones v. State*, 796 S.W.2d 183, 186-87 (Tex. Crim. App. 1990) (holding that Rule 83 of the Texas Rules of Appellate Procedure did not entitle appellant who filed defective notice of appeal to amend notice beyond the time allowed by Rule 41(a)(2) when the appellant had not requested an extension of time under Rule 41(b)(2)) with *Grand Prairie Indep. Sch. Dist. v. Southern Parts Imports, Inc.*, 813 S.W.2d 499, 500 (Tex. 1991) (holding that an appellate court may not dismiss an appeal when the appellant filed the wrong instrument required to perfect the appeal without giving the appellant an opportunity to correct the error).

This Court has never wavered from the principle that appellate courts should not dismiss an appeal for a procedural defect whenever any arguable interpretation of the Rules of Appellate Procedure would preserve the appeal. We have repeatedly held that a court of appeals has jurisdiction over any appeal in which the appellant files an instrument in a bona fide attempt to invoke the appellate court's jurisdiction. *Linwood v. NCNB Texas*, 885 S.W.2d 102, 103 (Tex.1994); *Grand Prairie Indep. Sch. Dist.*, 813 S.W.2d at 500. Our decisions reflect the policy embodied in our appellate rules that disfavors disposing of appeals based upon harmless procedural defects. *See Grand Prairie Indep. Sch. Dist.*, 813 S.W.2d at 500. Thus, we have instructed the courts of appeals to construe the Rules of Appellate Procedure reasonably, yet liberally, so that the right to appeal is not lost by imposing requirements not absolutely necessary to effect the purpose of a rule. *See Jamar v. Patterson*, 868 S.W.2d 318, 319 (Tex. 1993); *see also Crown Life Ins. Co. v. Estate of Gonzalez*, 820 S.W.2d 121, 121-22 (Tex. 1991); *Gay v. City of Hillsboro*, 545 S.W.2d 765, 766 (Tex. 1977).

As the dissenting justice in the court of appeals pointed out, the result the court of appeals reached was not "absolutely necessary" under these facts. 928 S.W.2d at 657 (DUNCAN, J., dissenting) ("[T]he issue is not whether the rules condone a patently unfair result but whether they require it.") (emphasis in original). Here, the court of appeals acknowledged that Verburgt demonstrated that he had made a bona fide attempt to timely perfect an appeal. *See id.* at 655.

We hold that a motion for extension of time is necessarily implied when an appellant acting in good faith files a bond beyond the time allowed by Rule 41(a)(1), but within the fifteen-day period in which the appellant would be entitled to move to extend the filing deadline under Rule 41(a)(2). Our holding does not indefinitely extend the time in which parties may perfect an appeal, as Justice Enoch implies. Instead, once the period for granting a motion for extension of time under Rule 41(a)(2) has passed, a party can no longer invoke the appellate court's jurisdiction. It also does not alter the time for perfecting an appeal beyond the period authorized by Rule 41(a). Nor does our holding undermine finality of judgments, as the court of appeals believed. *See* 928 S.W.2d at 656. Parties who prevail in the trial court will still know within the time specified in Rule 41(a)(2) whether their opponents will seek to perfect an appeal. We decline to elevate form over substance, as the dissenters would.

Accordingly, we reverse the judgment of the court of appeals and remand to that court to allow it to determine whether Verburgt offered a reasonable explanation for his failure to timely file his bond. *See* TEX. R. APP. 41(a)(2).

ENOCH, JUSTICE, joined by ABBOTT and HANKINSON, JUSTICES, dissenting.

From today forward, one need no longer timely appeal to invoke an appellate court's jurisdiction. But just two months ago, this Court retained the longstanding rule that only a timely filed appeal invokes appellate jurisdiction. We insisted that to perfect appeal in a civil case, the notice of appeal must be filed within the time prescribed in the rules. *See* TEX.R.APP. P. 26.1. Further, we insisted that to extend the time in which to file the notice of appeal, one must file not only the notice of appeal, but in addition " a motion" that "must state: . . . [among other things] the facts relied on to reasonably explain the need for an extension." TEX. R. APP. P. 26.3, 10.5(b)(1)(C). Like our new rules, the plain language of the rule that applies to this case, Rule 41(a)(2), mandates that the appeal be timely; consequently, it compels the result the court of appeals reached in this case. Is this a bad result? For the hopeful appellant, perhaps (assuming that the appeal is, in fact, meritorious). But denuding the Court's rules to achieve the Court's chosen result is bad law. I dissent.

Rule 41(a)(2) permits a party who fails to timely appeal to seek an extension of time. But to do so, the party has to file, within fifteen days of the original due date, both the cost bond and a motion for extension of time reasonably explaining the need for the extension. The majority's holding, that an "implicit motion" is filed if a would-be appellant files late and files only a cost bond, 959 S.W.2d at 615, simply ignores the rule's requirement that both instruments must be filed. Moreover, Rule 41(a)(2) gives the court of appeals discretion whether to allow an extension of time, but this discretion is triggered only by the filing of a motion reasonably explaining the need for the extension. In the absence of a motion, the court of appeals' discretion is never invoked and the late-filed cost bond has no effect. Here, Verburgt did not file a motion to extend time, and he did not file the cost bond timely. He simply did not do what Rule 41(a)(2) clearly requires.

The Court does not cite a single case holding that the untimely filing of an appeal can still be a bona fide attempt to invoke the court of appeals' jurisdiction. To the contrary, we have consistently and routinely held that the appeal must be filed timely. *See Davies v. Massey*, 561 S.W.2d 799, 801 (Tex. 1978) ("Filing a cost bond . . . is a necessary and jurisdictional step in perfecting an appeal."); *Glidden Co. v. Aetna Cas. & Sur. Co.*, 155 Tex. 591, 291 S.W.2d 315, 318 (1956) ("It is well settled . . . that the requirement that the bond be filed within thirty days is mandatory and jurisdictional."). Indeed, the court of appeals' decision in this case is predicated on this crucial point:

> [W]hile the supreme court has liberally construed the rules regarding the instruments necessary to confer jurisdiction, we do not discern a retreat in that court from the fundamental requirement that in order to invoke the jurisdiction of the court of appeals, some instrument, whether or not it is the correct instrument, must be timely filed.

928 S.W.2d at 656 (explaining two decisions on which the Court relies today: *Linwood v. NCNB Texas*, 885 S.W.2d 102, 103 (Tex. 1994) and *Grand Prairie Indep. Sch. Dist. v. Southern Parts Imports, Inc.*, 813 S.W.2d 499, 500 (Tex. 1991); *see also Olivo v. State*, 918 S.W.2d 519, 524 (Tex. Crim. App. 1996) (correctly noting that the "liberal policy" espoused by this Court in Linwood and Grand Prairie "concerns the substitution of a correct instrument for an incorrect instrument, which has been timely filed ").

I agree with the majority that "appellate courts should not dismiss an appeal for a procedural defect whenever any arguable interpretation of the Rules of Appellate Procedure would preserve the appeal." 959 S.W.2d at 616 (emphasis added)(*citing Linwood* and *Grand Prairie*). But surely that interpretation must be arguable. Interpreting Rule 41(a)(2) in contradiction to its plain language is not arguable; indeed, it is remarkably harmful to the concept of justice.

Under any number of circumstances, time plays a critical role in justice. For example, statutes of limitation and repose exist to ensure that claims are made in a timely fashion. *See, e.g., Trinity River Auth. v. URS Consultants, Inc.*, 889 S.W.2d 259, 263 (Tex. 1994) ("We start with the unassailable premise that statutes of limitation, in general, serve a public function. They 'compel the exercise of a right of action within a reasonable time so that the opposing party has a fair opportunity to defend while witnesses are available and the evidence is fresh in their minds.' ") (*quoting Robinson v. Weaver*, 550 S.W.2d 18, 20 (Tex. 1977)). Timely exercise of one's appellate rights is no less significant to predictability, and consequently, to justice. Failure to timely file an appeal has always been a jurisdictional error that precludes an appellate court from reaching the merits. *See Davies*, 561 S.W.2d at 801; *Glidden*, 291 S.W.2d at 318. It rightfully should remain so.

The majority's flawed reasoning is also apparent from the cases it cites. In *Linwood* and *Grand Prairie*, we held that a party's bona fide attempt to invoke the appellate court's jurisdiction will preserve its appeal. What is clearly apparent in these opinions is that the procedural defect, which rendered the party's effort at appeal only a bona fide attempt, was correctable. Concomitantly, the hopeful appellant had the obligation to correct this defect. But how would one correct untimeliness? One can't. Neither of these cases remotely signals a retreat from the principle that a party must timely appeal to invoke the court's jurisdiction.

The majority responds to my criticism by claiming that its decision "does not indefinitely extend the time in which parties may perfect an appeal" because parties supposedly "will still know within the time specified in Rule 41(a)(2) whether their opponents will seek to perfect an appeal." 659 S.W.2d at 617. My colleagues demonstrate that they do not understand what they do. The "indefiniteness" has nothing to do with not knowing whether an appeal will be filed within thirty days or forty-five days. It has everything to do with not knowing when the Court will simply "imply" a condition that never occurred to reach the result it prefers. When next will the Court "imply" filings that were never made? If the clear language of its own rules does not constrain the Court, then what will? If this is not "indefinite," then perhaps I do not understand the meaning of the word.

Finally, the majority mistakenly believes that ignoring its own rules somehow enhances "fairness." Playing by the rules is fair. Changing the rules to produce a particular result is not.

The judgment of the court of appeals should be affirmed. I dissent.

BAKER, JUSTICE, dissenting.

The court of appeals reached the decision required by applying the plain and unambiguous language of Rule 41(a)(2). *See* TEX. R. APP. P. 41(a)(1) and (2); *Davies v. Massey*, 561 S.W.2d 799, 801 (Tex. 1978); *Glidden Co. v. Aetna Cas. & Sur. Co.*, 155 Tex. 591, 291 S.W.2d 315, 318 (1956); *see also Miller v. Miller*, 848 S.W.2d 344, 345 (Tex. App.—Texarkana 1993, no writ); *El Paso Sharky's Billiard Parlor, Inc. v. Amparan*, 831 S.W.2d 3, 5 (Tex. App.—El Paso 1992, writ denied).

The Court's opinion dispenses with Rule 41(a)(2)'s requirements, and amends the rule by judicial fiat. The Court's opinion is contrary to its own precedent. *See State Dept. of Highways & Public Transportation v. Payne*, 838 S.W.2d 235, 241 (Tex. 1992) ("[W]e do not revise our rules by opinion."); *Alvarado v. Farah Mfg. Co.*, 830 S.W.2d 911, 915 (Tex. 1992) (same). I would deny the writ because the Court decides otherwise, I dissent.

Notes

1. *Hone v. Hanafin*, 104 S.W.3d 884 (Tex. 2003): The Supreme Court has established a liberal standard for considering untimely appeals. Thus, under TEX. R. CIV. P. 26.3, a court of appeals cannot require appellants to admit that their filings were untimely, if they offer a plausible good faith justification for filing their notice of appeal when they did. Absent a finding that an appellant's conduct was deliberate or intentional, the court of appeals should ordinarily accept the appellant's explanations as reasonable.

Pursuant to Texas Rule of Appellate Procedure 26.3, an appellate court may extend the time to file a notice of appeal if, within fifteen days after the deadline for filing the appeal notice, the party files a notice of appeal in the trial court and a motion for extension of time in the court of appeals. Under *Verburgt v. Dorner*, 959 S.W.2d 615 (Tex. 1997), a motion for extension of time is implied when an appellant, acting in good faith, files an appeal notice within Rule 26.3's fifteen-day period permitting an appellant to move to extend the filing deadline. The motion for extension must, however, still be filed with, and accepted by the court of appeals.

Here, Petitioners contended that the filing of a request for findings of fact, in an interlocutory appeal, extended their time for filing their notice of appeal. The court of appeals could have, but refused to consider Petitioners' notice of appeal as an implied motion for extension of time to file a notice of appeal. The Court reversed and remanded to the court of appeals. Petitioners' contention regarding their request for findings of fact and conclusions of law constituted a reasonable explanation for filing their notice of appeal beyond the twenty-day deadline. A reasonable explanation is any plausible statement of circumstances indicating that failure to file within the specified period was not deliberate or intentional, but was the result of inadvertence, mistake or mischance. This standard is applied to all cases in which an appellant fails to file a notice of appeal timely. Any conduct short of deliberate or intentional noncompliance qualifies as inadvertence, mistake or mischance.

2. *City of San Benito v. Rio Grande Valley Gas Company*, 109 S.W.3d 750 (Tex. 2003): An appeal can, generally, only be brought by a named party to the suit. However, the doctrine of virtual representation is an exception to the general rule. An appellant is a deemed party under virtual representation when: (1) it is bound by the judgment; (2) its privity of estate, title, or interest appears from the record; and (3) there is an identity of interest between the appellant and a party to the judgment. Unnamed class members have been deemed to be parties under this doctrine. Because the unnamed class members here would be bound to the judgment approving the settlement, they should be considered "parties" for purposes of appeal.

There is no interlocutory appeal from an order denying a party the right to opt out of a class.

While it is true that the cities seeking to opt out of a class settlement could have attempted to seek mandamus relief in the Supreme Court, after the court of appeals denied mandamus relief, filing a request for an extraordinary writ is not a prerequisite to an appeal.

An attorney has implied authority to nonsuit a client's claim when the nonsuit does not affect a substantial right or bar the bringing of another suit based on the same cause of action.

3. *See* L. Wayne Scott, *The Dilemma of Interpreting Rules of Civil Procedure: A Proposal for Elastic Formalism*, 47 ST. MARY'S L. J. 569 (2016).

HOUSER
v.
McELVEEN

243 S.W.3d 646.
(Tex. 2008)

Bruce Wayne Houser, Beaumont, TX, pro se.
Kenneth W. McElveen, Edna, TX, pro se.
Barbara Vanecek, Edna, TX, pro se.

PER CURIAM.

Petitioner Bruce Wayne Houser, a pro se inmate, sued for mandamus compelling respondent Kenneth McElveen, the county clerk of Jackson County, to probate Houser's father's will. The trial court dismissed the petition, and Houser asserts, without challenge, that he deposited his notice of appeal in the prison mail 35 days later. The court of appeals received it on the 46th day after the judgment was signed and dismissed the appeal as not having been timely perfected. 2006 WL 328134 (Tex. App.—Corpus Christi 2006) (per curiam).

The notice of appeal was required to be filed within 30 days of the judgment, TEX.R.APP. P. 26.1, but the court of appeals should have extended that time if, within the next 15 days, Houser filed his notice of appeal and a motion for extension with a reasonable explanation, TEX.R.APP. P. 10.5(b), 25.1(a), 26.3. The notice of appeal was deemed filed on the day he mailed it, since it was received one day after the 15-day deadline, TEX.R.APP. P. 9.2(b), *Ramos v. Richardson,* 228 S.W.3d 671, 673 (Tex. 2007) (per curiam), and a motion for extension was thereby implied, *Verburgt v. Dorner,* 959 S.W.2d 615, 617 (Tex. 1997). The question, then, is whether there is "any plausible statement of circumstances indicating that failure to file within the [specified] period was not deliberate or intentional, but was the result of inadvertence, mistake, or mischance." *Meshwert v. Meshwert,* 549 S.W.2d 383, 384 (Tex. 1977).

In his notice of appeal, and in his petition here without challenge, Houser states that he mailed a motion for new trial nine days after the judgment, and a copy of a transmittal letter bearing that date is attached. There is no motion for new trial in the trial court's record, but Houser could reasonably have believed that the clerk would receive it within three weeks of when he says he mailed it. An inmate who does everything in his power to satisfy timeliness requirements may not be penalized for the error or tardiness of prison officials. *See Williams v. T.D.C.J.-I.D.,* 142 S.W.3d 308, 309-310 (Tex. 2004) (per curiam). If a motion for new trial had been received within 30 days of the judgment, Houser's notice of appeal would have been timely filed. TEX.R.APP. P. 26.1(a)(1). This plausible statement of circumstances indicates that Houser's failure to timely file his notice of appeal was not intentional but inadvertent. *See Hone v. Hanafin,* 104 S.W.3d 884, 886 (Tex. 2003) (per curiam).

Houser was entitled to an extension of time in which to file his notice of appeal, and thus the court of appeals should not have dismissed the appeal. Accordingly, we grant the petition for review, and without hearing oral argument, we reverse the court of appeals' judgment and remand the case for further proceedings. TEX.R.APP. P. 59.1.

SAN ANTONIO
v.
RODRIGUEZ

828 S.W.2d 417
(Tex. 1992)

Lowell F. Denton, Sarah B. Duncan, San Antonio, Thomas F. Nye, Corpus Christi, David W. Ross, Allan K. DuBois, Laura Cavaretta, San Antonio, for petitioner.
Randall C. Jackson, Jr., Les Mendelsohn, San Antonio, for respondents.

PER CURIAM.

We consider whether a notice of appeal, timely filed in the proper court and carrying the correct style but displaying the wrong cause number, is sufficient to perfect appeal and avoid dismissal.

On October 1, 1990, the deadline for perfection of appeal in the present case, the City of San Antonio (the City) filed notice of appeal along with a post-judgment motion to modify or correct judgment. The City placed the proper style, *Abraham Rodriguez and Alicia Rodriguez v. City of San Antonio*, but the wrong cause number, No. 88-CI-14572 instead of No. 87-CI-23305, on both its notice of appeal and its post-judgment motion.

The district clerk of Bexar County maintains the files and records pertaining to pending cases according to the cause number rather than the style of the case. On October 18, 1990, a deputy district clerk received a telephone inquiry concerning cause No. 87-CI-23305. Upon review of the record for that case, the deputy district clerk initially found that no notice of appeal or post-judgment motion had been filed. Upon further investigation, however, she discovered that the instruments had been filed, but had been docketed under the wrong cause number, 88-CI-14572. After finding this error and discussing the problem with a supervisor, the deputy district clerk drew a line through the erroneous cause number, 88-CI-14572, and substituted the correct cause number, 87-CI-23305, on both instruments. She then called the City's attorneys to notify them of the mistake and to inform them that the correction had been made and that refiling was unnecessary.

Subsequently, the court of appeals granted the Rodriguezes' motion to dismiss the City's appeal, reasoning that, because its notice of appeal was defective, the City failed to perfect its appeal in a timely manner. In taking this action, the court of appeals relied upon *Philbrook v. Berry*, 683 S.W.2d 378 (Tex. 1985), a default judgment case in which the motion for new trial was filed under the original cause number rather than the severed cause number. *Id.* at 379. Assuming that *Philbrook* was correctly decided, it is not controlling in this case. In *Philbrook*, the party names associated with the original and severed cause numbers were identical. Consequently, the different cause numbers were crucial to the proper management of the two cases. In the instant case, the cause number incorrectly transcribed on the City's notice of appeal has no association with or similarity to the style of the case now before us, and, there is no suggestion of confusion regarding the judgment from which the City sought appeal. *See El Paso Cent. Appraisal Dist. v. Montrose Partners*, 754 S.W.2d 797, 799 (Tex. App.—El Paso 1988, writ denied) (because misnomer in notice of appeal did not disadvantage or mislead appellee, dismissal inappropriate).

We have held that a court of appeals has jurisdiction over an appeal when the appellant files an instrument that is "a bona fide attempt to invoke appellate court jurisdiction." *Grand Prairie Indep. Sch. Dist. v. Southern Parts Imports, Inc.*, 813 S.W.2d 499, 500 (Tex. 1991) (per curiam) (emphasis added) (citations omitted). More recently, we reaffirmed the policy that "the decisions of the courts of appeals [should] turn on substance rather than procedural technicality." *Crown Life Ins. Co. v. Estate of Gonzales*, 820 S.W.2d 121 (Tex. 1991) (per curiam) (citations omitted). Here, there can be no doubt that the City's attempt to perfect an appeal was "bona fide" because, but for the erroneous cause number, the City's notice of appeal complied with the provisions of TEX. R. APP. P. 40(a)(2). We hold that the City's notation of the incorrect cause number on its notice of appeal does not defeat the jurisdiction of the court of appeals.

Accordingly, pursuant to TEX. R. APP. P. 170, without hearing oral argument, a majority of this court grants the City's application for writ of error, reverses the judgment of the court of appeals, and remands this case to that court for further proceedings consistent with this opinion.

Notes

1. In the case of an appeal by way of a restricted appeal from the trial court to the Court of Appeals [as opposed to the ordinary appeal] the appellant has six months to perfect his appeal by filing notice of appeal. *See* Rule 26.1(c) Texas Rules of Appellate Procedure.

2. In *Biffle v. Morton Rubber Indus.* 785 S.W.2d 143 (Tex. 1990), the Supreme Court reiterated its long held position that "[a]n instrument is deemed in law filed at the time it is delivered to the clerk, regardless of whether the instrument is filemarked."

3. TEX. R. APP. P. 32.1, while not jurisdictional, states that a "docketing statement" must be filed following the perfecting of an appeal. It is for administrative purposes, and is to contain information on the parties and their attorneys. The docketing statement is to provide essential information about the case, including [paraphrased]:

> (a)(1) The name of the appellant, and the name, address, telephone number, fax number, if any, and State Bar of Texas identification number of the appellant's lead counsel; or
> (a)(2) if the party is unrepresented, the party's name, address, telephone number, and fax number, if any;
> (b) the date the notice of appeal was filed or mailed;
> (c) the trial court's name and county, the name of the judge who tried the case, and the date the judgment or order appealed from was signed;
> (d) the date of filing of any motion for new trial, motion to modify the judgment, request for findings of fact, motion to reinstate, or other filing that affects the time for perfecting the appeal;
> (e) the names of all parties to the trial court's judgment or the order appealed from, and the vital information of the other attorney or party.
> (f) the general nature of the case—for example, personal injury, breach of contract, or temporary injunction;
> (g) whether the appeal's submission should be given priority or whether the appeal is an accelerated one under Rule 28 or another rule or statute;
> (h) whether the appellant has requested, or will request, a reporter's record, and whether the trial was electronically recorded;
> (i) the name of the court reporter;
> (j) whether the appellant intends to seek temporary or ancillary relief while the appeal is pending;
> (k) specific information if an affidavit of indigence is filed;
> (l) whether the appellant has filed or will file a supersedeas bond; and
> (m) any other information the appellate court requires.

4. *Williams v. Flores,* 46 Tex. Sup. Ct. J. 26, 2002 WL 31259895 (Oct. 10, 2002): Since William's filed a motion for new trial within 30 days of the date the trial court signed the final judgment confirming an arbitration award, he had 90 days in which to file a notice of appeal. Even though the notice of appeal was filed 12 days after the 90 day deadline expired, Williams had, under TEX. R. APP. P. 26.3, 15 days in which to file a motion to extend the time for filing the notice of appeal. Since the motion to extend time was placed in the mail on the 15th day after the notice of appeal was due, and, since it was received by the court of appeals within 10 days of the deadline for filing the motion to extend time, under TEX. R. APP. P. 9.2, the motion to extend time was timely filed, and the appeal was timely perfected.

5. *Warwick Towers Council of Co-Owners v. Park Warwick, L.P.*, 244 S.W.3d 838 (Tex: 2008): An insurer, asserting rights to subrogation, did not waive its right to appeal by filing the notice of appeal in its insured's name. The notice of appeal in the insured's name was a bona fide attempt to invoke the appellate court's jurisdiction. If the appellant timely files a document in a bona fide attempt to invoke the appellate court's jurisdiction, the court of appeals, on appellant's motion, must allow the appellant an opportunity to amend or refile the instrument required by law or Rules to perfect the appeal. The Supreme Court's policy is to apply rules of procedure liberally to reach the merits of the appeal whenever possible.

c. *Supersedeas Bond*

Read Rule 24 Texas Rules of Appellate Procedure.

In re RON SMITH

192 S.W.3d 564
(Tex. 2006)

R. Brent Cooper, Diana L. Faust, Heather Jean Reynolds Johnson, Cooper & Scully, P.C., Dallas, for Relator.

Mark S. McQuality, Cheryl C. Turner, Bragg, Chumlea, McQuality & Smithers, Dallas, Gregory Stuart Love, Timothy G. Chovanec, Law Offices of Timothy G. Chovanec, P.C., Fort Worth, for Real Party In Interest.

PER CURIAM.

Judgment debtors Ron Smith and Main Place Custom Homes, Inc. filed motions seeking review of the trial court's order setting aside their cash deposits in lieu of supersedeas bond to suspend enforcement of the trial court's judgment and sustaining the judgment creditors' challenge to their net worth affidavits. We treat the motions as petitions for writ of mandamus and conditionally grant in part and deny in part the relief sought.

Texas law provides that when a judgment is for money, the amount of security required to suspend enforcement of the judgment pending appeal may not exceed the lesser of: (1) fifty percent of the judgment debtor's net worth; or (2) twenty-five million dollars. TEX. CIV. PRAC. & REM. CODE § 52.006(b); TEX. R. APP. P. 24.2(a)(1). Under Texas Rule of Appellate Procedure 24.2(c)(1), a judgment debtor who provides a bond, deposit, or security based upon its net worth "must simultaneously file an affidavit that states complete, detailed information concerning the debtor's assets and liabilities from which net worth can be ascertained." A judgment creditor may challenge the debtor's affidavits, and the trial court must hear the judgment creditor's challenge promptly after reasonable discovery concerning the judgment debtor's net worth is complete. TEX. R. APP. P. 24.2(c)(2)-3). Following the hearing, "[t]he trial court must issue an order that states the debtor's net worth and states with particularity the factual basis for that determination." TEX. R. APP. P. 24.2(c)(3).

Richard and Ginger Honaker obtained a judgment against Smith and Main Place in the total amount of $800,820.44, plus post-judgment interest. Smith and Main Place filed notices of appeal in September of 2004 with the Second Court of Appeals. In March of 2005, the Honakers began conducting post-judgment discovery in an effort to enforce the judgment. The parties then entered into protracted negotiations over the date for Smith's deposition. On June 14, 2005, two days before the agreed upon date for Smith's deposition, Smith and Main Place filed cash deposits in lieu of bond in the amount of $10.00 each and net worth affidavits to supersede enforcement of the trial court's judgment and to stay post-judgment discovery. In the affidavits, Smith averred that his net worth was negative $167,206.00 and that Main Place's net worth was $0.00.

The Honakers immediately filed a contest to the affidavits of net worth and moved the trial court to set aside the cash deposits in lieu of bond. They also filed a motion for sanctions and to compel discovery responses in aid of the judgment. The Honakers contended that the net worth affidavits were "manipulative and false" and that Smith's affidavit testimony that Main Place had no assets was not verifiable without discovery. Nevertheless, the Honakers claimed that they had obtained sufficient information through discovery to establish that Smith's closely held corporation, R.A. Smith & Company, Inc. (an entity not named in the Honakers' lawsuit), was Smith's alter ego. Therefore, the Honakers argued, all of that company's assets should be included in the calculation of Smith's net worth.

The trial court held hearings on the Honakers' motions in August of 2005. On October 14, 2005, the trial court issued two separate orders which Smith and Main Place challenge here. In the first order, the trial court sustained the Honakers' contest. The trial court found that the net worth affidavits were insufficient to adequately describe Smith's and Main Place's net worth. The trial court also found that the affidavits were designed to mislead the court and work an injustice on the Honakers by inappropriately staying execution and post-judgment discovery efforts. Without stating the basis for its calculation, the trial court found that Smith's net worth as of June 14, 2005 was $1,142,951; however, the court did not determine Main Place's net worth. The trial court further ordered that any future attempts by Smith and Main Place to stay enforcement of the judgment or post-judgment discovery must be approved in advance and must comply with the finding that R.A. Smith & Company, Inc. is Smith's alter ego. In the second order, the trial court reiterated its alter ego finding, granted the Honakers' motion to compel, ordered Smith and Main Place to respond to the Honakers' discovery requests, and sanctioned Smith $11,275 for expenses, plus attorney's fees.

As Texas Rule of Appellate Procedure 24.4 permits, Smith and Main Place filed a motion with the court of appeals seeking review of the trial court's order setting aside their cash deposits in lieu of bond and determining Smith's net worth. They subsequently filed a separate appeal of the discovery order.

Smith and Main Place also filed a motion for additional findings of fact and conclusions of law with the trial court. In that motion, Main Place requested that the trial court state Main Place's net worth and the factual basis for that determination. Smith requested that the trial court state with particularity the factual basis for the determination that he had a net worth of $1,142,951. Smith also requested additional findings to support the trial court's determination that R.A. Smith & Company, Inc. was his alter ego.

On January 5, 2006, the court of appeals issued an order denying Smith and Main Place's Rule 24.4 motion. One justice dissented, arguing that the trial court improperly based its determination of Smith's net worth on its finding that R.A. Smith & Company, Inc. was Smith's alter ego. *Main Place Custom Homes, Inc., v. Honaker*, 192 S.W.3d 604, No. 02-04-275-CV (Tex. App.—Fort Worth March 23, 2006, dissent to corrected order denying appellants' "Texas Appellate Rule 24.4 Motion") (GARDNER, J., dissenting).

The trial court subsequently denied Smith and Main Place's request for additional findings of fact and conclusions of law on the grounds that the request was moot because the court of appeals denied their Rule 24.4 motion.

Smith and Main Place then sought review from this Court by filing motions pursuant to Rule 24.4. The Honakers challenge this Court's jurisdiction to hear the motions. In response, Smith and Main Place argue that Rule 24.4 provides a basis for this Court to assert jurisdiction over the motions, but request in the alternative that we treat the motions as petitions for writ of mandamus. We treat the motions as petitions for writ of mandamus and conditionally grant in part and deny in part the petitions. *See Isern v. Ninth Court of Appeals*, 925 S.W.2d 604 (Tex. 1996) (orig. proceeding) (reviewing by mandamus a trial court's order permitting the judgment debtor to post alternate security to supersede execution of the judgment).

When a judgment creditor files a contest to the judgment debtor's affidavit of net worth, the trial court must hold a hearing and "issue an order that states the debtor's net worth and states with particularity the factual basis for that determination." TEX. R. APP. P. 24.2(c)(3). The trial court abused its discretion here because it failed to state with particularity the factual basis for its determination that Smith's net worth was $1,142,951. The trial court did not make any findings that would permit a reviewing court to ascertain the basis for that determination. Further, the trial court found that R.A. Smith & Company, Inc. was Smith's alter ego without stating the factual or legal basis for that conclusion.

Smith argues that the trial court abused its discretion by basing the determination that he had a net worth of $1,142,951 on the alter ego finding. He argues that the Honakers were foreclosed from raising that theory post-judgment and presented legally and factually insufficient evidence to support it. Because we conclude that the trial court must enter additional findings to support its alter ego determination, and because post-judgment discovery is still ongoing, we reserve judgment on whether the trial court abused its discretion in determining that R.A. Smith & Company, Inc. is Smith's alter ego for purposes of Rule 24.2(c).

However, as to Smith's argument that the trial court abused its discretion by considering the alter ego theory in the post-judgment net worth proceeding, we disagree. Because "[a]lter ego applies when there is such unity between corporation and individual that the separateness of the corporation has ceased," *Castleberry v. Branscum*, 721 S.W.2d 270, 272 (Tex. 1986), an alter ego finding is relevant to the determination of the judgment debtor's net worth. Therefore, the trial court did not abuse its discretion by considering the alter ego theory in determining Smith's net worth pursuant to Rule 24.

Although the trial court did not abuse its discretion by considering the alter ego theory, that does not mean that the trial court's alter ego finding may be used to hold R.A. Smith & Company, Inc. or any other nonparty liable for the judgment. A judgment may not be amended to include an alter ego that was not named in the suit. *Matthews Const. Co., Inc. v. Rosen*, 796 S.W.2d 692, 693 (Tex. 1990). Therefore, an alter ego finding in a post-judgment net worth proceeding may not be used to enforce the judgment against the unnamed alter ego or any other nonjudgment debtor, but only to determine the judgment debtor's net worth for the purposes of Rule 24.

In addition to the failure to make adequate fact findings supporting its determination of Smith's net worth, the trial court failed to determine Main Place's net worth as required by Rule 24.2(c)(3). Even though the Honakers did not complete discovery concerning Smith's and Main Place's net worth before the hearing, under Rule 24.2(c)(3) "[t]he trial court must hear a judgment creditor's contest promptly after any discovery has been completed." Rule 24.2(c)(3) clearly provides that after the hearing the trial court must issue an order that states the judgment debtor's net worth. To the extent that a judgment debtor is uncooperative with reasonable discovery concerning the judgment debtor's net worth, the trial court may take appropriate steps (e.g. compel responses, issue sanctions, etc.) to ensure that discovery is completed before the hearing on the judgment creditor's contest. *See Arndt v. Farris*, 633 S.W.2d 497 (Tex. 1982) (trial court had jurisdiction to enter sanctions order for failure to comply with post-judgment discovery requests).

Smith and Main Place also argue that the trial court abused its discretion by compelling responses to the Honakers' post-judgment enforcement discovery requests because the Honakers were foreclosed by Texas Rule of Civil Procedure 621a from seeking responses to the requests after Smith and Main Place superseded the judgment by filing affidavits of net worth and cash deposits in lieu of bond. We disagree. Smith and Main Place refused to answer much of the written post-judgment enforcement discovery even though it was relevant to determining what assets were available to satisfy the judgment. Further, the parties had been engaged in post-judgment enforcement discovery for several months, and it was not until the eve of Smith's deposition that Smith and Main Place filed their cash deposits in lieu of bond and affidavits of net worth to supersede enforcement of the judgment. The trial court's conclusion that Smith and Main Place were attempting to avoid answering post-judgment enforcement discovery by filing the cash deposits in lieu of bond and affidavits of net worth was reasonable. In addition, Rule 24.2(c)(2) allows the judgment creditor to conduct reasonable discovery concerning the judgment debtor's net worth. The discovery in question sought information regarding assets owned by Smith and Main Place; therefore, the discovery was reasonably calculated to lead to information relevant to the net worth proceeding. In these circumstances, the trial court did not abuse its discretion by ordering Smith and Main Place to respond to the discovery requests.

We decline Smith's and Main Place's requests to review the discovery sanctions order in this proceeding. A sanctions order is appealable when the judgment is signed. *Arndt*, 633 S.W.2d at 500. Smith and Main Place filed a separate appeal of the trial court's sanctions order; accordingly, they have an adequate remedy by appeal. *Walker v. Packer*, 827 S.W.2d 833, 840 (Tex. 1992) (orig. proceeding). In addition, Rule 24.4 does not provide a basis for reviewing a discovery sanctions order.

Finally, Smith and Main Place argue that the court of appeals erred in not conducting a legal and factual sufficiency analysis of the trial court's net worth determination. We agree that the court of appeals should have conducted a legal and factual sufficiency analysis of the trial court's net worth determination, but the trial court's failure to make the required findings prevented the court of appeals from conducting the necessary sufficiency review. We trust that if it is called upon to do so again, the court of appeals will review the trial court's net worth determinations for legal and factual sufficiency. *See City of Keller v. Wilson*, 168 S.W.3d 802, 822 (Tex. 2005) (discussing standards for legal sufficiency review); *Pool v. Ford Motor Co.*, 715 S.W.2d 629, 635 (Tex. 1986) (discussing standards for factual sufficiency review); *cf. Beaumont Bank v. Buller*, 806 S.W.2d 223, 226 (Tex. 1991) (noting court of appeals should have reviewed turnover order under an abuse of discretion standard instead of reversing on the ground that there was "no evidence" to support issuance of the order).

We hold that the trial court abused its discretion by issuing an order that did not state with particularity the factual basis for its determination of Smith's net worth and that did not state Main Place's net worth as required by Rule 24. Accordingly, without hearing oral argument, we conditionally grant the writ and direct the trial court to enter additional findings as to Smith's net worth and the determination that R.A. Smith & Company, Inc. is Smith's alter ego. TEX. R. APP. P. 52.8(c). We further direct the trial court to determine Main Place's net worth and to issue an order that states with particularity the factual basis for that determination. All other relief is denied. We are confident that the trial court will comply, and our writ will issue only if the trial court fails to do so.

In re CROW-BILLINGSLEY AIR PARK, LTD.
98 S.W.3d 178
(Tex. 2003)

Stephanie Michelle Dooley, Tod B. Edel, Christopher John Akin, Carrington Coleman Sloman & Blunenthal, Dallas, for Relator.

David W Elrod, Elizabeth L. Reding, Rochelle Elrod Hutcheson, LLP, Dallas, for Respondent.

PER CURIAM.

The relators in this original proceeding, Crow-Billingsley Air Park, Ltd., Crow-Billingsley Berkeley, Ltd., Henry Billingsley, and Lucy Crow-Billingsley (collectively "Billingsley"), seek a writ of mandamus directing the trial court to enforce its final judgment in the underlying case involving a disputed zoning committee election. Because the trial court abused its discretion by failing to enforce its unsuperseded final judgment, we conditionally grant the writ.

Air Parks Estates is a residential and commercial subdivision subject to certain restrictive covenants. These covenants established the Air Park-Dallas Zoning Committee ("Zoning Committee"), an unincorporated association, and gave it certain powers. The Zoning Committee's membership includes three members who are elected biennially by a majority vote of the lot owners on a one vote per lot basis.

Billingsley, who owns a large number of lots in Air Parks Estates, sued the Zoning Committee, in part, to enjoin the June 2000 Zoning Committee election, alleging that Billingsley was wrongly being denied the right to participate in the upcoming election. After a bench trial, the district court rendered judgment on July 23, 2001, ordering a Zoning Committee election to be held on September 21, 2001, and making various rulings as to Billingsley's eligibility to vote and run for a place on the Zoning Committee. On September 5, 2001, the Zoning Committee, attempting to stay the election, filed a motion asking the court to set security. Billingsley responded with a motion to require the Committee's attorney to show authority. TEX.R. CIV. P. 12. Following an evidentiary hearing, the court granted the motion and struck the Committee's motion to set security. The Zoning Committee never refiled its motion. On September 19, the court ordered the election to proceed as previously ordered, but the results of the election were suspended until further order of the court and a determination by the court that the election procedure complied with the terms of the July 23rd final judgment.

On the day of the September 21st election, Billingsley filed a motion to enforce the judgment, seeking a declaration of the election winners under the terms of the July 23rd final judgment. But both the Zoning Committee and Billingsley had taken actions before the election that may have affected the eligibility of certain Billingsley lots to cast votes. Thus, in order to declare the winners of the election, the trial court needed to conduct an evidentiary hearing to determine what lots were eligible to vote according to the terms of the July 23rd judgment. Before the trial court ruled on the motion to enforce, both the Zoning Committee and Billingsley appealed the July 23rd judgment. The Zoning Committee then filed a motion in the trial court to dismiss the enforcement motion, arguing that the court had no continuing jurisdiction to hear it. The court granted the motion to dismiss for lack of jurisdiction. This left the result of the court-ordered election unresolved even though the judgment had not been superseded.

A trial court has an affirmative duty to enforce its judgment. TEX.R. CIV. P. 308. And the Declaratory Judgments Act expressly empowers a trial court to make supplemental rulings to aid enforcement of a declaratory judgment. TEX. CIV. PRAC. & REM.CODE § 37.011. Our procedural rules allow a judgment debtor to supersede a judgment, thereby suspending enforcement, by posting security set by the trial court, not by merely filing an appeal. TEX.R.APP. P. 24.1, 24.2(a)(3). Accordingly, we hold that the trial court had jurisdiction to hear the motion to enforce its final judgment, despite the fact that the judgment had been appealed.

Mandamus is an extraordinary remedy available only in limited circumstances to correct a clear abuse of discretion or the violation of a duty imposed by law when the relator has no adequate remedy by appeal. *Republican Party of Texas v. Dietz,* 940 S.W.2d 86, 88 (Tex. 1997); *Walker v. Packer,* 827 S.W.2d 833, 839-44 (Tex. 1992). A party is entitled to mandamus relief to vacate an order that wrongly denies a prevailing party's attempt to enforce an unsuperseded judgment. *See In re Dryden,* 52 S.W.3d 257, 261-65 (Tex. App.—Corpus Christi 2001, orig. proceeding); *Gonzales v. Daniel,* 854 S.W.2d 253, 256 (Tex. App.—Corpus Christi 1993, orig. proceeding); *Anderson v. Lykes,* 761 S.W.2d 831, 834 (Tex. App.—Dallas 1988, orig. proceeding), *overruled on other grounds, Walker v. Packer,* 827 S.W.2d at 842.

We hold that the trial court abused its discretion when it refused to hear the motion to enforce the unsuperseded final judgment and dismissed Billingsley's enforcement motion for want of jurisdiction. A writ of mandamus will issue only if the trial court fails to comply with this opinion.

JUSTICE WAINWRIGHT did not participate in the decision.

Notes

1. Once the judgment of a trial court becomes final, in the sense that the trial court's plenary power over the judgment has expired, the successful party (the judgment creditor) has the right to execute on the judgment. Contrary to the common law, the perfection of an appeal by the losing party (the judgment debtor) does not preclude execution on the assets of the losing party pending appeal. For many years, a supersedeas bond was the only way to prevent execution pending appeal. It remains the primary means of suspending execution pending appeal. However, after the trial and appeal of the *Pennzoil Co. v. Texaco* case, provision was made to "soften" the rule. *See: Pennzoil v. Texaco, Inc.,* 481 U.S. 1, 95 L. Ed. 2d 1, 107 S. Ct. 1519 (1987).

2. Texas Civil Practice and Remedies Code § 52.006. Amount of Security for Money Judgment

(a) Subject to Subsection (b), when a judgment is for money, the amount of security must equal the sum of:
(1) the amount of compensatory damages awarded in the judgment;
(2) interest for the estimated duration of the appeal; and
(3) costs awarded in the judgment.

(b) Notwithstanding any other law or rule of court, when a judgment is for money, the amount of security must not exceed the lesser of:
(1) 50 percent of the judgment debtor's net worth; or
(2) $25 million.

(c) On a showing by the judgment debtor that the judgment debtor is likely to suffer substantial economic harm if required to post security in an amount required under Subsection (a) or (b), the trial court shall lower the amount of the security to an amount that will not cause the judgment debtor substantial economic harm.

(d) An appellate court may review the amount of security as allowed under Rule 24, Texas Rules of Appellate Procedure, except that when a judgment is for money, the appellate court may not modify the amount of security to exceed the amount allowed under this section.

(e) Nothing in this section prevents a trial court from enjoining the judgment debtor from dissipating or transferring assets to avoid satisfaction of the judgment, but the trial court may not make any order that interferes with the judgment debtor's use, transfer, conveyance, or dissipation of assets in the normal course of business.

3. The perfection of an appeal will *not* ordinarily suspend the execution of a judgment.

4. *Mudd v. Mudd,* 665 S.W.2d 128 (Tex. App.—San Antonio 1983, mandamus overruled). The supersedes bond must be in an amount, and with sufficient sureties, to enable the appellee to collect the judgment. The amount should include estimated interest, but the trial court cannot set the amount at an excessive rate so as to be inequitable. The court of appeals can review to determine whether the bond is excessive.

5. *In Re Dallas Area Rapid Transit,* 967 S.W.2d 358(Tex. 1998). The district court abused its discretion in denying supersedeas of the judgment ordering production of information, under the "Open Records Act,"

Texas Public Information Act, TEX. GOV'T CODE sections 552.001-.353. TEX. R. APP. P. 47(f) [now Rule 24.2(a)(3)] affords the trial court a measure of discretion. But that discretion does not extend to denying a party any appeal whatsoever. To allow a trial court discretion to refuse to supersede a judgment requiring production of information under the Act is to give that court the power to deny the governmental body any effective appeal, for once the requested information is produced, an appeal is moot.

6. *See* TEX. R. APP. P. 24.3(a)(5) for the general provision for supersedeas in cases involving government entities.

7. *Isern v. Ninth Court of Appeals*, 925 S.W.2d 604 (Tex. 1996): The trial court can allow alternate security in personal injury cases. There is no conflict between TEX. CIV. PRAC. & REM. CODE section 52.002 and TEX. R. APP. P. 47(b)(1) [now 24.2]. Section 52.002 does not apply to appeals from personal injury judgments. Under Rule 47(b)(1), the trial court has discretion to set the supersedeas bond at a lesser amount than that awarded in a personal injury judgment.

8. Certain parties are exempt from the need to file a supersedeas bond:

The State, any county, any department of State, any department head acting in an official capacity, and certain Federal agencies. TEX. CIV. P. REM. CODE section 6.001(b).

Incorporated cities and towns. TEX. CIV. P. REM. CODE section 6.002.

Water districts, water control districts, levee districts, and drainage districts. TEX. CIV. P. REM. CODE section 6.003.

Executors, administrators, guardians, and other personal representatives in their fiduciary capacity. TEX. PROB. CODE, section 29.

Persons who are exempt under several other special statutes. *See* TEX. CIV. PRAC. & REM. CODE Sec. 43.001; TEX. CIV. PRAC. & REM. CODE, Sec. 104.006, TEX. TRANS. CODE, Sec. 452.054(b).

9. *In re State Bd. for Educator Certification*, 411 S.W.3d 576 (Tex. App.—Austin 2013 orig. proceeding), *remand. denied,* 452 S.W.3d 802 (Tex. 2014). **Supersedeas May Be Denied To Any Party – Including the State In Non-Monetary, Non-Profit Case:** Mandamus proceeding. A governmental entity's notice of appeal does not deprive a trial court of discretion to refuse suspension of its judgment if the appellee posts security in accordance with TEX. R. APP. P. 24(a)(3). Put in practical terms, a trial court has discretion to prevent the Board from re-revoking a teacher's professional license while the Board appeals, for however long, the court's rejection of the Board's initial revocation. The Government's right to supersede a judgment may be automatic, but it is not absolute.

d. *The Appellate Record*

Read Rules 34, 35 and 37 Texas Rules of Appellate Procedure.

Note

The appellate record consists of the clerk's record [formerly known as the transcript] and the reporter's record [formerly known as the statement of facts]. Unlike the former rules, the duty to file the record in the appellate court in a timely fashion rests upon the clerk of the trial court and the court reporter. *See* Rule 35.3 of the Texas Rules of Appellate Procedure. However, the obligation to file the record does not arise unless a notice of appeal has been filed, payment for the entire record has been made or arranged to be paid, and the appellant has timely requested the court reporter to prepare the reporter's record. *Id.* The record is to be filed in the normal case thirty days after the first notice of appeal is filed. The appellate courts are required to permit the filing of late records, if the delay is not the appellant's fault and may permit late filing even if the delay is the appellant's fault. *Id.* However, like the former rules, if no clerk's record is filed as a result of the fault of the appellant [that is, the appellant did not pay or make arrangements to pay for the clerk's record], the court may dismiss the appeal; and if no reporter's record is filed as a result of the fault of the appellant [that is, the appellant did not request one be prepared or did not pay or make arrangements to pay for the record], the court can consider and decide those issues which do not need that record. *See* Rule 37.3 of the Texas Rules of Appellate Procedure.

The rules also provide a method for one incapable of paying the fees to have a record prepared. *See* Rule 20 of the Texas Rules of Appellate Procedure.

VERNCO CONSTRUCTION, INC.,
v.
DAVID NELSON
460 S.W.3d 145
(Tex. 2015)

Dana Livingston, Alexander Dubose Jefferson & Townsend LLP, Austin, David M. Evans, Sara Murray, Langley & Banack, Inc., San Antonio, Peter L. Kilpatrick, Langley & Banack, Inc., San Antonio, Rachel Anne Ekery, Wallace B. Jefferson, Alexander Dubose Jefferson & Townsend LLP, Austin, for Petitioner Vernco Construction, Inc.

Darrell F. Smith, Darrell Frank Smith, P.C., San Antonio, Jerry T. Steed, Baucum, Steed & Barker, San Antonio, Ruth G. Malinas, Plunkett & Griesenbeck, Inc., San Antonio, for Respondent E.E. Hood & Sons, Inc.

Eric Scott, Kortney M. Kloppe-Orton, William H. Oliver, Pipkin & Oliver, L.L.P., San Antonio, for Respondent David Nelson.

In this complex commercial dispute, Vernco Construction, Inc., obtained a multi-million dollar breach-of-contract and tort judgment against E.E. Hood & Sons, Inc., and David Nelson, individually and d/b/a Collective Contracting (collectively, the Respondents). The Respondents appealed the judgment on various grounds, but the only issue before this Court is whether Vernco lacked standing to maintain the lawsuit because it assigned the claims to its commercial lender either before or after filing the lawsuit. The trial court found that Vernco had standing, but the court of appeals reversed, vacated the judgment, and dismissed for want of jurisdiction. 406 S.W.3d 374, 380 (Tex. App.—El Paso 2013). The court of appeals based its analysis on the terms of a forbearance agreement between Vernco and its lender but declined to consider an addendum to that agreement, erroneously stating that the document is "not a part of the record on appeal" and "was not before the trial court." *Id.* at 380. Because the court of appeals failed to consider pertinent evidence before the trial court, we reverse and remand the cause to that court for reconsideration.

* * *

After the trial court rendered judgment of more than $6 million in Vernco's favor on favorable jury findings, the Respondents appealed, raising numerous complaints and challenging the trial court's denial of their motion to dismiss for lack of standing. The court of appeals, relying solely on the four corners of the forbearance agreement, concluded that Vernco assigned all of its interest in the claims to the Bank and therefore had no standing to maintain an action for damages on those claims. 406 S.W.3d at 380. The court therefore vacated the trial-court judgment and dismissed the case for want of jurisdiction. *Id.*

The court refused to consider the addendum as part of the standing analysis because it had not been included in an offer of proof during the trial on the merits. *Id.* The court further intimated that the addendum was not in the appellate record at all and had merely been appended to Vernco's appellate brief. *Id.* (declaring that the addendum "was not before the trial court and is not before this Court" because "Vernco did not make an offer of proof of the [addendum] to the trial court and the [addendum] was not admitted into evidence but is merely appended to Vernco's brief"). The court further rejected Vernco's claim to possess standing in a representative capacity, noting the absence of evidence that the Bank had authorized Vernco to pursue the claims against the Respondents on its behalf. *Id.* The court never mentioned the hearing on the motion to dismiss or the existence of the addendum as an exhibit to Vernco's response to the motion to dismiss.

In declining to consider the addendum, the court of appeals appears to have overlooked the addendum in the record and misunderstood when the substantive jurisdictional ruling occurred. According to the court, "[t]he trial court 'denied the bill,' and thereafter, in its written order, denied the motion to dismiss and found Vernco had standing and the trial court had subject[-]matter jurisdiction." 406 S.W.3d at 377. In fact, the trial court ruled on the motion to dismiss following a pretrial hearing, and the ruling judge's November 9, 2010 order denying the Respondents' motion to dismiss.

The standing inquiry "focuses on the question of who may bring an action." *Patterson v. Planned Parenthood,* 971 S.W.2d 439, 442 (Tex. 1998). Courts lack subject-matter jurisdiction to adjudicate disputes initiated by parties lacking standing. *The M.D. Anderson Cancer Center v. Novak,* 52 S.W.3d 704, 708 (Tex. 2001); *Tex. Ass'n of Business v. Tex. Air Control Bd.*, 852 S.W.2d 440, 443-44 (Tex. 1993). Whether a court has subject-matter jurisdiction is a question of law. *Tex. Dep't of Parks & Wildlife v. Miranda*, 133 S.W.3d 217, 226 (Tex. 2004).

Because standing is a component of subject[-]matter jurisdiction, we consider [standing issues] as we would a plea to the jurisdiction." *Brown v. Todd,* 53 S.W.3d 297, 305 n.3 (Tex. 2001). The trial court can rule on a jurisdictional plea by submission or after an evidentiary hearing: "[A] court deciding a plea to the jurisdiction is not required to look solely to the pleadings but may consider evidence and must do so when necessary to resolve the jurisdictional issues." *Bland Indep. School Dist. v. Blue*, 34 S.W.3d 547, 555 (Tex. 2000) (trial court determined jurisdictional issue after an evidentiary hearing at which witnesses testified); see *State v. Lueck,* 290 S.W.3d 876, 884 (Tex. 2009) (jurisdictional challenge may be asserted in a motion for summary judgment). When a jurisdictional issue is not intertwined with the merits of the claims, which is the case here, disputed fact issues are resolved by the court, not the jury. *E.g., Bland*, 34 S.W.3d at 554-55; *Univ. of Tex. v. Poindexter*, 306 S.W.3d 798, 806-07 (Tex. App.—Austin 2009, no pet.); see *Miranda*, 133 S.W.3d at 226 (quoting *Cameron v. Children's Hosp. Med. Ctr.*, 131 F.3d 1167, 1170 (6th Cir. 1997), for the proposition that "whether a district court has subject[-]matter jurisdiction is a question for the court, not a jury, to decide, even if the determination requires making factual findings, unless the jurisdictional issue is inextricably bound to the merits of the case"). The jurisdictional determination should be made as soon as practicable because a court should not proceed with a case over which it has no jurisdiction; however, the court has discretion to defer the decision until the case has been more fully developed. *Miranda*, 133 S.W.3d at 227.

The Respondents filed a pretrial motion to dismiss for want of jurisdiction, alleging the absence of standing agreement and the addendum, among other items. The Respondents requested an evidentiary hearing and gave notice that the hearing had been set. The order denying the motion states that, as requested, "All Parties appeared by and through counsel, and the Court heard evidence and argument." After hearing the evidence and argument, the trial court expressly found that Vernco had standing and concluded that the court had subject-matter jurisdiction.

The judge presiding over the trial-court proceedings had discretion to consider the jurisdictional matter in a pretrial hearing rather than awaiting further development of the case. *Id.* Furthermore, when the successor judge was assigned to preside over the jury trial, she had discretion to reconsider the pretrial judge's interlocutory ruling but was not required to do so. *Cf. Velez v. DeLara*, 905 S.W.2d 43, 45 (Tex. App.—San Antonio 1995, no writ) (under Bexar County's central docket system "the jurisdiction to reconsider an interlocutory ruling is vested in the court rather than the individual judge, and since one district judge may hold court for another district judge," the successor judge has the right to reconsider a previously entered interlocutory order). After reviewing the pertinent pleadings, the trial judge declined to reconsider the ruling. Accordingly, we must review the evidence before the trial court at the motion-to-dismiss hearing in considering the trial court's determination that, as a legal and factual matter, Vernco has standing. Contrary to the court of appeals' suggestion otherwise, we are not limited to reviewing evidence provided in an offer of proof at the trial on the merits.

This matter presents two issues concerning the contents of the appellate record. First, the court of appeals erroneously concluded that the addendum was not before the trial court and not part of the appellate record. Both the forbearance agreement and the addendum are included with the pleadings germane to the motion to dismiss, which were before the pretrial judge when he determined the standing issue. The court of appeals should have considered all the evidence presented for the pretrial judge's consideration.

The second issue is that there is no record of the plea to the jurisdiction hearing, which may or may not have been evidentiary. "If all the evidence is filed with the clerk and only arguments by counsel are presented in open court, the appeal should be decided on the clerk's record alone." *Michiana Easy Livin' Country, Inc. v. Holten*, 168 S.W.3d 777, 782 (Tex. 2005). A reporter's record is required, however, to preserve evidentiary complaints for appellate review when evidence is introduced in open court. *Id.* at 782, 783. Absent a specific indication or assertion to the contrary, we generally presume that pretrial hearings are nonevidentiary. *Id.* at 782-83. But, "[i]f the proceeding's nature, the trial court's order, the party's briefs, or other indications show that an evidentiary hearing took place in open court, then a complaining party must present a record of that hearing to establish harmful error." *Id.*

The record here suggests that the pretrial hearing regarding Vernco's standing was evidentiary. In the motion to dismiss, the Respondents requested an evidentiary hearing and asserted that lack of jurisdiction would be established by "the evidence submitted with [the] motion, and the testimony that will be offered at the hearing." Although the forbearance agreement and addendum might be construed as a matter of law, Vernco's response asserted both legal and factual matters in opposition to the motion to dismiss, including whether a foreclosure occurred and whether Vernco was authorized to act as the Bank's representative. The pretrial judge's order further states that he "heard evidence and argument" at the dismissal. Elsewhere in the record, there are statements to the effect that the pretrial judge devoted the better a part of a day to the hearing, which implies that the hearing encompassed more than counsel's argument regarding evidence already on file. On the other hand, the parties have not mentioned any void in the record or discussed how its absence might impact the standing inquiry. *Cf. Schafer v. Conner*, 813 S.W.2d 154, 155 (Tex. 1991) (an appellant challenging sufficiency of the evidence to support the trial court's judgment cannot meet that burden without presenting a sufficient record on appeal because it is presumed that the omitted portions of the record support the trial court's judgment); *Guthrie v. Nat'l Homes Corp.*, 394 S.W.2d 494, 495 (Tex. 1965) (absent a reporter's record, the court must presume the evidence at trial supported the jury's finding). At this point, we could only speculate as to the nature of the hearing.

Clearly, however, the addendum is part of the clerk's record before the trial court and certainly must be considered if the matter was determined on the pleadings. If evidence was introduced at the motion-to-dismiss hearing, no reporter's record of that hearing has been included with the appellate record. Because the court of appeals did not consider evidence in the relevant portion of the appellate record, we reverse the court's judgment and remand this case to that court for further proceedings, including reconsideration of the standing issue. *See* TEX. R. APP. P. 59.1.

i. *The Reporter's Record*

Notes

1. TEX. R. APP. P. 34.6(b)(3) provides that "[a]n appellate court must not refuse to file a reporter's record or a supplemental reporter's record because of a failure to timely request it."

2. Once the record is requested by the party, it becomes the duty of the clerk of the court of appeals to see that the record is filed with the court of appeals. TEX. R. APP. P. 37.3.

3. *Caveat.* Beware of TEX. R. APP. P. 37.3(b) and (c). If the clerk's record or the reporter's records are not filed due to the fault of the appellant, dire consequences may ensue. If the clerk's record is not timely filed because of the failure to make arrangements to pay the clerk's fee, the court of appeals may dismiss for want of prosecution (after giving the appellant a reasonable opportunity to cure). If the reporter's record is not filed because the appellant did not request it, after a reasonable opportunity to cure, the court may consider and decide the issues.

PUBLIC UTIL. COUNSEL
v.
PUBLIC UTIL. COMM'N
878 S.W.2d 598
(Tex. 1994)

Stephen Fogel and Walter Washington, Austin, for petitioner.

Richard P. Noland and Paula Mueller, Austin, for respondents in No. D-4400.

Philip F. Ricketts, Austin, Debra Champagne, Houston, Fernando Rodriguez, Austin, John Dewey, Lake Jackson, Paul W. Phillips, Washington, DC, Mark Witcher and Allen H. King, Austin, Hugh Rice Kelly and George W. Schalles, Houston, Robert J. Hearon, Jr., Robin A. Melvin, Roy Q. Minton, John L. Foster and Selden Anne Wallace, Austin, Peggy Wells Dobbins, Coral Gables, FL, Marianne Carroll, Norma K. Scogin, Elizabeth R.B. Sterling and Dan Morales, Austin, Jonathan Day and Frederick D. Junkin, Houston, Raupaco T. Gonzalez, W. Scott McCoullough and Michael G. Shirley, Austin, Ana Guerrero Cummings, Houston, for respondents.

PER CURIAM.

We decide if a court of appeals may affirm a trial court judgment upholding a contested Public Utility Commission of Texas ("PUC") ratemaking order on the sole ground that the appellant has not timely filed a statement of facts. *See* TEX. R. APP. P. 54. We hold that the court of appeals erred by failing to identify and address issues that may be resolved without a statement of facts. *See* TEX. R. APP. P. 50(a), 90(a). We also hold the court of appeals erred by refusing to take judicial notice of the published order of the PUC, which forms the basis for this appeal.

In an order dated October 23, 1991, the PUC granted the Houston Lighting and Power Company ("HL & P") a $313 million rate increase based upon a non-unanimous stipulation between HL & P and several ratepayer organizations. The Office of Public Utility Counsel ("OPUC"), which had not joined the stipulation, appealed the order to a Travis County district court. The district court affirmed. OPUC appealed again, but the court of appeals affirmed the judgment of the district court without considering the merits of OPUC's appeal because OPUC had not timely filed the statement of facts. 859 S.W.2d 71; TEX. R. APP. P. 54(a).

On September 18, 1992, OPUC timely requested preparation and transmission of the statement of facts "which should include . . . the complete record of the proceeding conducted by the Public Utility Commission of Texas and entered into the District Court record as Plaintiff['s] Exhibit No. 1." OPUC timely filed the transcript with the court of appeals, including "all original exhibits with [the trial court]," pursuant to a sua sponte trial court order of August 31, 1992. The clerk of the court of appeals filed the administrative record on November 5, 1992. *Office of Public Util. Counsel v. Public Util. Comm'n*, 859 S.W.2d 71, 72 (Tex. App.—Austin 1993) (same case). When OPUC realized, in February, 1993, that the statement of facts had not been filed, it moved for an extension of time to file the statement of facts. Because OPUC did not timely file its motion, however, the court of appeals overruled it. TEX. R. APP. P. 54(a); *B.D. Click Co. v. Safari Drilling Corp.*, 638 S.W.2d 860, 862 (Tex. 1982). Moreover, without a statement of facts, the court of appeals held that it could not verify that the trial court had admitted the administrative record into evidence. *See* TEX. GOV'T CODE ANN. s 2001.175(d) (Vernon Supp. 1994) (formerly Administrative Procedure and Texas Record Act, TEX. REV. CIV. STAT. art. 6252-13a, s 19(d)(3)).

Although TEX. R. APP. P. 54(a) precludes a court of appeals from considering a late-filed statement of facts, *see id.* ("[the court] shall have no authority to consider a late filed transcript or statement of facts"), it does not require the court to affirm the judgment appealed from as a matter of course. For example, the court of appeals may exercise other remedies, such as "disregarding materials filed, or applying presumptions against the appellant." TEX. R. APP. P. 54(a); *see Day v. State Bar*, 821 S.W.2d 172, 174 (Tex. App.—Eastland 1991, writ denied).

The record on appeal consists of "a transcript and, where necessary to the appeal, a statement of facts." TEX. R. APP. P. 50(a) (emphasis added). The court of appeals is obligated to "address every issue raised and necessary to final disposition of the appeal," TEX. R. APP. P. 90(a), and resolution of some issues will not necessarily require a statement of facts. While a court of appeals generally cannot determine whether an agency finding is supported by "substantial evidence" without reviewing the administrative record, *see* TEX. GOV'T CODE ANN. § 2001.174(2)(E) (Vernon Supp. 1994), this does not preclude the court from addressing issues, such as those involving legal error, the determination of which would not require a statement of facts. *Segrest v. Segrest*, 649 S.W.2d 610, 611 (Tex. 1983), *cert. denied*, 464 U.S. 894, 104 S.Ct. 242, 78 L.Ed.2d 232 (1983) ("[The requirement of a statement of facts] applies to issues which require reference to the evidence and not to matters which are strictly questions of law."); *Day*, 821 S.W.2d at 174.

The court of appeals also erred by refusing to take judicial notice of the published order of the PUC. To be the proper subject of judicial notice, a fact must be "capable of accurate and ready determination by resort to sources whose accuracy cannot reasonably be questioned." TEX. R. CIV. EVID. 201(b)(2). Judicial notice is mandatory if "requested by a party and [the court is] supplied with the necessary information." TEX. R. CIV. EVID. 201(d). A court of appeals has the power to take judicial notice for the first time on appeal. *See Langdale v. Villamil*, 813 S.W.2d 187, 189-90 (Tex. App.—Houston [14th Dist.] 1991, no writ); *City of Dallas v. Moreau*, 718 S.W.2d 776, 781 (Tex. App.—Corpus Christi 1986, writ ref'd n.r.e.). In its motion to take judicial notice, OPUC directed the court's attention to the PUC's order, published at 17 TEX. P.U.C. BULL. 3063-3423, which the trial court affirmed in its entirety. The authenticity and contents of the PUC ratemaking order are capable of accurate and ready determination by resort to a published record whose accuracy cannot reasonably be questioned.

Among other legal issues OPUC argues it has raised on appeal are the PUC's treatment of deferred charges under section 41(a) of the Public Utility Regulatory Act ("PURA"), TEX. REV. CIV. STAT. ANN. art. 1446c, § 41(a) (Vernon Supp. 1994), and the PUC's calculation of HL & P's federal income tax expense using methods that violate PURA §§ 41(c)(2), (3), and *Public Util. Comm'n v. Houston Lighting & Power Co.*, 748 S.W.2d 439 (Tex. 1987). Even if issues such as these could not have been resolved without the statement of facts, the court of appeals should have explained why this was so. We hold the court of appeals erred by affirming the trial court judgment without determining which issues it could resolve absent a statement of facts and resolving every such issue OPUC raised. Pursuant to Rule 170, TEX. R. APP. P., a majority of the court, without hearing oral argument, reverses the judgment of the court of appeals and remands this cause to that court for further proceedings consistent with this opinion.

ii. *The Effect of a Partial Reporter's Record*

Read Rule 34.6(c) Texas Rules of Appellate Procedure.

Notes

1. JUSTICE GONZALEZ, concurring in the case of *Beaumont Bank v. Buller*, 806 S.W.2d 223 (Tex. 1991), in discussing those points of error which may be reviewed by appellate courts in the absence of a complete reporter's record [statement of facts] noted:

> Generally, points dependent on the state of the evidence cannot be reviewed in the absence of a complete statement of facts. *Lane v. Fair Stores*, 150 Tex. 566, 243 S.W.2d 683, 684 (1952). As we said in *The Englander Co. v. Kennedy*, 428 S.W.2d 806 (Tex. 1968): The burden is on a party appealing from a trial court judgment to show that the judgment is erroneous in order to obtain a reversal. When the complaint is that the evidence is factually or legally insufficient to support vital findings of fact, or that the evidence conclusively refutes vital findings, this burden cannot be discharged in the absence of a complete or an agreed statement of facts. *Id.* at 807. . . .
>
> The absence of a complete record is not always fatal to appellate review or review by original proceeding. Since the time of *The Englander Co.*, we have amended the rules to allow for limited appeals. TEX. R. APP. P. 53(d). By following this rule the presumption is the reverse of that in the usual appeal, in that the appellate court will assume that nothing in the record that was not brought forward is relevant to the determination of the appeal. *Producer's Const. Co. v. Muegge*, 669 S.W.2d 717, 718 (Tex. 1984). Also, a court may consider matters that are fundamentally erroneous even in the absence of a statement of facts. *Lane*, 243 S.W.2d at 684-85. Pure questions of law, not dependent on the evidence,

may be reviewed without a statement of facts. *Segrest v. Segrest*, 649 S.W.2d 610 (Tex. 1983). In a mandamus proceeding, we held that since it was undisputed that no evidence was presented at a discovery hearing, no statement of facts was necessary to determine the discovery questions. *Barnes v. Whittington*, 751 S.W.2d 493, 495 (Tex. 1988) (orig. proceeding). The common thread in these exceptions is that the presence or absence of a statement of facts has no bearing on the resolution of the controlling issues. Since there was no attempt in the case at bar to limit the appeal under rule 53(d), the court of appeals should have presumed that the omitted portion of the statement of facts supported the trial court's judgment. *Christiansen v. Prezelski*, 782 S.W.2d 842, 843 (Tex. 1990).

2. TEX. R. APP. PROC. 34.6 (c) now sets out the procedure for the use of a partial reporter's record.

a. *Effect on appellate points or issues.* If the appellant requests a partial reporter's record, the appellant must include in the request a statement of the points or issues to be presented on appeal and will then be limited to those points or issues.

b. *Other parties may designate additions.* Any other party may designate additional exhibits and portions of the testimony to be included in the reporter's record.

c. *Costs; requesting unnecessary matter.* Additions requested by another party must be included in the reporter's record at the appellant's cost. But if the trial court finds that all or part of the designed additions are unnecessary to the appeal, the trial may order the other party to pay the costs for the preparation of the unnecessary additions. This paragraph does not affect the appellate court's power to tax costs differently.

CHRISTIANSEN
v.
PEZELSKI
782 S.W.2d 842
(Tex. 1990)

Thomas H. Crofts, Jr., R. Jo Reser, San Antonio, for petitioner.
Arnold A. Vickery, Elizabeth Kilbride, Houston, for respondents.

PER CURIAM.

The issue in this case is whether a court of appeals may properly find reversible error when it does not have a complete record of the case before it and the appellant has not complied with TEX. R. APP. P. 53(d). We hold that it cannot. Accordingly, we grant the application for writ of error and, without hearing oral argument, we reverse the judgment of the court of appeals and render judgment for the Petitioner. *See* TEX. R. APP. P. 133(b).

Robert L. Christiansen, D.D.S., performed oral surgery on Gloria Prezelski. She subsequently sued him for malpractice. Following a jury trial, judgment was rendered in Christiansen's favor. At trial, Prezelski called and examined Christiansen as an adverse witness. During his cross-examination of Christiansen, Christiansen's counsel advised the court that he would like to call his two expert witnesses, proceed with eliciting their testimony, and then complete his examination of Christiansen. The attorney explained that he had previously discussed this proposal with Prezelski, and that it was his understanding that he would be able to call his experts out of turn. This action was necessitated by a continuance sought and obtained by Prezelski; Christiansen's experts were from out of town and securing their attendance on another day would have been inconvenient.

Prezelski acceded to this request on the condition that the experts not be placed on the stand until after Christiansen's counsel had finished the cross-examination and she had been afforded an opportunity to redirect. The trial court rejected the condition proposed by Prezelski and allowed Christiansen's attorney to call the expert witnesses.

After the experts were excused, the cross-examination of Christiansen was completed by his attorney. Prezelski's counsel then elicited, on re-direct, that Christiansen had not taken a cephalometric x-ray; Christiansen had previously testified that he had taken such x-rays. Additionally, the expert witnesses previously called by Christiansen indicated by their testimony that they believed that he had taken cephalometric x-rays. Despite this revelation, Prezelski did not request that Christiansen's experts be recalled to the stand for impeachment purposes.

The court of appeals concluded that the trial court's refusal to allow Prezelski time to examine Dr. Christiansen before the experts were allowed to testify, and its failure to grant Prezelski's motion for new trial constituted harmful error. The court made this finding based upon an examination of a partial statement of facts. With one justice dissenting, the court of appeals reversed the judgment of the trial court and remanded the cause for a new trial. 775 S.W.2d 764.

Prezelski requested that only part of the record be sent to the court of appeals, but she failed to comply with Texas Rule of Appellate Procedure 53(d), which states: If appellant requests or prepares a partial statement of facts, he shall include in his request or proposal a statement of the points to be relied on and shall thereafter be limited to such points. If such statement is filed, there shall be a presumption on appeal that nothing omitted from the record is relevant to any of the points specified or to the disposition of the appeal. Any other party may designate additional portions of the evidence to be included in the statement of facts. TEX. R. APP. P. 53(d). The burden is on the appellant to see that a sufficient record is presented to show error requiring reversal. TEX. R. APP. P. 50(d); *Escontriadas v. Apodaca*, 629 S.W.2d 697, 699 (Tex. 1982). It is undisputed that a complete statement of facts was not brought up for review.

An appellant must either comply with rule 53(d) or file a complete statement of facts; otherwise, it will be presumed that the omitted portions are relevant to the disposition of the appeal. A reviewing court must examine the entire record in a case in order to determine whether an error was reasonably calculated to cause and probably did cause the rendition of an improper judgment. *Gomez Leon v. State*, 426 S.W.2d 562, 565 (Tex. 1968). When an appellant has neither complied with rule 53(d) nor filed a complete statement of facts, the reviewing court is unable to ascertain whether a particular ruling by the trial court is harmful in the context of the entire case.

Unaided by the presumption resulting from compliance with rule 53(d), and unable to review the entire record in the case, the court of appeals in the instant case could not properly determine that the trial court ruling in question was harmful error. Accordingly, a majority of the court reverses the judgment of the court of appeals and renders judgment for Christiansen.

SCHAFER
v.
CONNER

813 S.W.2d 154
(Tex. 1991)

Vincent A. Gamal, Houston and Myrta Kaye Applewhite, Magnolia, for petitioners.
Ernest Coker, Jr., Conroe, for respondents.

PER CURIAM.

C.L. Conner and others (Conner) developed a mobile home subdivision and sold certain lots to Ralph Schafer and others (Schafer). Schafer sued Conner for breach of contract and for violations of the Texas Deceptive Trade Practices—Consumer Protection Act (DTPA) for Conner's failure to satisfactorily develop the subdivision. At a bifurcated trial, the jury found that Conner breached the contract and violated the DTPA and the trial court assessed damages and entered judgment for some plaintiffs while rendering take nothing judgments against other plaintiffs. The prevailing plaintiffs who recovered damages appealed and challenged the adequacy of the damage award. They brought forth only a partial statement of facts and selectively included witness testimony. The court of appeals affirmed in part and reversed and rendered in part. 805 S.W.2d 554. The court of appeals overruled Schafer's factual insufficiency complaints because Schafer failed (1) to bring forth an entire statement of facts and (2) to comply with TEX. R. APP. P. 53(d) by including "a statement of the points to be relied on in his request to the court reporter."

This court has held that when an appellant complains of the factual or legal sufficiency of the evidence, the appellant's burden to show that the judgment is erroneous cannot be discharged in the absence of a complete or an agreed statement of facts. *Englander Co. v. Kennedy*, 428 S.W.2d 806, 807 (Tex. 1968). It is undisputed that Schafer failed to bring forth an entire statement of facts or an agreed statement of facts. Therefore, the court of appeals correctly overruled Schafer's complaints concerning the adequacy of the damages because in the absence of a complete statement of facts, it is presumed that the omitted evidence supports the trial court's judgment. *See Englander Co. v. Kennedy*, 428 S.W.2d at 806; *Woodward v. Higdon*, 643 S.W.2d 470, 471 (Tex. App.—Waco 1982, writ ref'd n.r.e.); *Ruffin v. Ruffin*, 753 S.W.2d 824, 828 (Tex. App.—Houston [14th Dist.] 1988, no writ).

Although the court of appeals correctly overruled Schafer's complaints concerning the adequacy of the damages, a majority of the court disapproves the court of appeals' "hypertechnical" interpretation of TEX. R. APP. P. 53(d) which would require a statement of points to be relied upon on appeal to be filed in rather than with appellant's request for a partial statement of facts. *See Alford v. Whaley*, 794 S.W.2d 920, 923 (Tex. App.—Houston [1st Dist.] 1990, no writ).

Accordingly, Schafer's application for writ of error is denied.

Note

Is *Schafer v. Conner* good law in light of TEX. R. APP. P. 34.6 (c)(4)? Yes, because points were not designated. That provisions provides:

> *Presumptions.* The appellate court must presume that the partial reporter's record designed by the parties constitutes the entire record for purposes of reviewing the stated points or issues. This presumption applies even if the statement includes a point or issue complaining of the legal or factual insufficiency of the evidence to support a specific factual finding identified in that point or issue.

GARDNER
v.
BAKER & BOTTS, L.L.P.

6 S.W.3d 295
(Tex. App.—Houston [1st] 1999, pet. denied.]

George M. Bishop, Chappell Hill, for Appellant.
Eric J.R. Nichols, David J. Beck, Houston, for Appellee.

Panel consists of CHIEF JUSTICE SCHNEIDER and JUSTICES WILSON and ANDELL.

MICHAEL H. SCHNEIDER, CHIEF JUSTICE.

Appellants appeal a jury's verdict finding no liability on their legal malpractice, breach of fiduciary duty, and deceptive trade practices claims against appellees, Baker & Botts, L.L.P. We affirm.

The Partial Record

As a preliminary matter, Baker & Botts argues the judgment of the trial court should be affirmed because appellants failed to comply with former Rule of Appellate Procedure 53(d)[1] in requesting a partial statement of facts.

Following trial, counsel for appellants asked the court reporter to prepare the statement of facts, excluding voir dire, opening and closing statements, and the testimony of Harold Metts, Ken Studdard, and Clifford Fry. By requesting only a partial record, appellants had to comply with Rule 53(d), which provides:

> If appellant requests or prepares a partial statement of facts, he shall include in his request or proposal a statement of the points to be relied on and shall thereafter be limited to such points. If such a statement

[1] This appeal is governed by former Texas Rules of Appellate Procedure because it was perfected before September 1, 1997. Rule 34.6(c)(1), which applies to all appeals perfected after September 1, 1997, contains the identical language as former Rule 53(d). TEX. R. APP. P. 34.6(c)(1).

> is filed, there shall be a presumption on appeal that nothing omitted from the record is relevant to any of the points specified or to the disposition of the appeal. Any other party may designate additional portions of the evidence to be included in the statement of facts.

TEX. R. APP. P. 53(d) (emphasis added). Appellants request for a partial statement of facts did not include a statement of the points to be relied on, as required by Rule 53(d).

Appellants did file a Notice of Limitation of Appeal pursuant to former Rule 40(a)(4)[2] They argue that this is sufficient to satisfy the requirements of Rule 53(d). We disagree. While Rule 40(a)(4) is satisfied by a general statement identifying the severable portion of the judgment appealed from, Rule 53(d) has a more specific requirement: to designate with reasonable particularity the complaints to be pursued on appeal. *See Dresser Indus., Inc. v. Forscan Corp.*, 641 S.W.2d 311, 315 (Tex. App.—Houston [14th Dist.] 1982, no writ).

Here, the only portion of appellants' Notice of Limitation of Appeal relevant to their claims on appeal was a general notice of their intent to attack certain jury answers "based on either their factual insufficiency, legal insufficiency, or that certain issues had been proven as a matter of law." However, Appellants did not state with any particularity the specific jury answers that they intended to challenge on appeal. *See Kwik Wash Laundries, Inc. v. McIntyre*, 840 S.W.2d 739, 741 (Tex. App.—Austin 1992, no writ); *see also CMM Grain Co., Inc. v. Ozgunduz*, 991 S.W.2d 437, 439-40 (Tex. App.—Fort Worth 1999, no writ) (finding a general statement identifying the portion of the judgment the party intended to appeal insufficient to satisfy Rule 34.6(c)). Absent such a specific statement, the Appellee is left to guess which additional portions of the evidence should be included in the statement of facts. *See Superior Packing, Inc. v. Worldwide Leasing & Financing, Inc.*, 880 S.W.2d 67, 70 (Tex. App.—Houston [14th Dist.]1994, writ denied) (noting that the purpose of the predecessor to Rule 53(d) is to afford the appellee an opportunity to designate additional material to be included in the statement of facts which it deems relevant to the issues raised on appeal). This is the exact situation that Rule 53(d) is designed to prevent.

Additionally, Appellants' Notice of Limitation of Appeal did not mention the other points appellants have raised on appeal. These discrepancies prevent a finding that Appellants have complied with Rule 53(d). *See Dresser Indus., Inc.*, 641 S.W.2d at 315 (holding appellant failed to comply with predecessor to Rule 53(d) because points designated differed from the points of error argued on appeal). On appeal, appellants contend: (1) the trial court erred in refusing to admit a prior judgment and a decision of the State Comptroller into evidence; (2) the trial court erred in failing to find the advice given by Baker & Botts incorrect as a matter of law; (3) there was no evidence to support the jury's finding that appellants were negligent; (4) the trial court erred in allowing the testimony of a Baker & Botts' expert because he had not been properly designated; (5) certain jury answers were against the great weight and preponderance of the evidence; and (6) the trial court erred in failing to find Baker & Botts breached its fiduciary duty owed to appellant as a matter of law.

For the reasons stated above, we find the general notice provided in Appellants' Notice of Limitation of Appeal is insufficient to satisfy the narrow purpose of Rule 53(d). Because appellants did not comply Rule 53(d), they must suffer the presumption that the omitted portions of the record support the trial court's judgment. *Christiansen v. Prezelski*, 782 S.W.2d at 843; *Schafer v. Conner*, 813 S.W.2d 154, 155 (Tex. 1991); *Tapiador v. North Am. Lloyds of Texas*, 772 S.W.2d 954, 955 (Tex. App.—Houston [1st Dist.] 1989, no writ).

Review Absent a Complete Record

First, appellants contend the trial court committed reversible error in failing to admit certain evidence, and by allowing the testimony of a Baker & Botts' expert who had not been properly designated. To determine whether the trial court's allegedly erroneous evidentiary rulings constituted harmful error, we must examine the entire record. *Christiansen*, 782 S.W.2d at 843. Because appellants failed to comply with Rule 53(d), we must presume the evidence omitted from the record would have shown that error, if any, was harmless. *Id.*

---

[2] Appellants' Notice of Limitation of Appeal stated they intended to limit their appeal to issues regarding:

> [T]he admission of evidence concerning the financial status of either the estate of Herman L. Gardner, M.D. or Lenan Briggs Gardner Bass, the ruling by the Trial Court that the Plaintiffs' claim for damages regarding the proposed oil and gas lease with Union Pacific was barred, the submission of issues to the Jury over objection of counsel for Plaintiffs and the Jury's answers to the issues based on either their factual insufficiency, legal insufficiency, or that certain issues had been proven as a matter of law.

We overrule appellants' first and fourth points of error.

Appellants also raise numerous legal and factual sufficiency points of error. However, an appellant's burden to show that the evidence is legally or factually insufficient cannot be met absent a complete record. *Schafer*, 813 S.W.2d at 155 (Tex. 1991); *Englander Co. v. Kennedy*, 428 S.W.2d 806, 807 (Tex. 1968). Because appellants failed to bring forth a complete record, we must presume the omitted portions of the record would have shown the evidence to be legally and factually sufficient. *Schafer*, 813 S.W.2d at 155; *Richards v. Schion*, 969 S.W.2d 131, 133 (Tex. App.—Houston [1st Dist.] 1998, no writ).

We overrule appellants' second, third, fifth, and sixth points of error.

The judgment of the trial court is affirmed.

DAVIE L. WILSON, JUSTICE dissenting.

Because I believe the majority is not heeding the Supreme Court's warning regarding "hypertechnical" interpretations of former appellate rule 53(d), *Schafer v. Conner*, 813 S.W.2d 154, 155 (Tex. 1991), I respectfully dissent.

Today's decision effectively denies appellants a ruling on the merits of the case and in a macro sense, makes the practice of pursuing appeals on partial records far more exacting than necessary to faithfully serve the language and purpose of the rule.

The majority seems to base its opinion on the alleged general nature of appellants' points of appeal contained in a document entitled, Notice of Limitation of Appeal, although appellant is also criticized for filing it outside of, and before, the request for partial record. Specifically, I interpret the majority's narrow holding to be that appellants' Notice of Limitation of Appeal is "insufficient to satisfy the strict requirements of Rule 53(d)" and; therefore, the appeal must be dismissed without reaching the merits.

Although the majority's language never directly states that filing a purported statement of points in a Notice of Limitation of Appeal is sufficient compliance with Rule 53(d), the majority could not decide the case as it does without first determining that the language of the points was properly before the appellee. The appellee urges in its brief that the appeal should be thrown out merely because the request for partial record did not contain the statement of points, even though the points were in another differently styled document. The majority necessarily rejects appellee's "strict" interpretation in reaching the issue it does, but then adopts "strict" guidelines in determining whether the language of the points is sufficient under the rule.

The majority cites *CMM Grain Co., Inc. v. Ozgunduz*, 991 S.W.2d 437, 439-40 (Tex. App.—Fort Worth 1999, no pet.) in support of its position. In *CMM*, the court stated that "appellants announced in their notice of appeal the desire to limit their appeal to the trial court's denial of their offset claim." *Id.* The court further noticed the absence of any attempt to provide the appellee with the statement of points or issues to be presented on appeal. *Id.* In making its decision, the court observed that "while the terminology of the statement of points need not be exact, the statement should describe the nature of the complained of error with reasonable particularity." *Id.*

The statements contained in appellants' Notice of Limitation of Appeal are far more detailed than the simple short-handed statement the court rejects in CMM and, given the points of error ultimately briefed, I would hold them as descriptive of the complained of error with reasonable particularity.

The points of error briefed were fully argued before the panel with the appellee suffering from no apparent disability from the limitation of the trial record. I would proceed to determine the merits of the appeal.

Accordingly, I dissent.

BENNETT
v.
COCHRAN
96 S.W.3d 227
(Tex. 2002)

PER CURIAM

JUSTICE SMITH did not participate in the decision.

The issue before this Court is whether, by requesting only a partial reporter's record, Bennett waived his right to challenge the legal and factual sufficiency of the evidence on appeal. The court of appeals answered this question affirmatively. __ S.W.3d __. However, Rule 34.6(c)(4)'s plain language provides that an appellant need not file a complete reporter's record to preserve legal or factual sufficiency issues. TEX. R. APP. P. 34.6(c)(4). Therefore, we reverse the court of appeals' judgment and remand the cause for further proceedings consistent with this opinion.

Robert Bennett and Les Cochran are former partners of Bennett & Cochran, L.L.P., a law partnership. After Bennett withdrew from the partnership, Cochran sued Bennett, alleging negligent misrepresentation, fraud, and breach of contract. Bennett counter-sued, asserting, *inter alia*, claims for breach of contract and battery. The jury awarded Bennett $29,000 in damages ($24,000 for Cochran's breach of contract and $5,000 resulting from Cochran's battery) and $50,000 in attorney's fees. The jury also awarded Cochran $50,000 in damages based on Bennett's negligent misrepresentations. The trial court granted Cochran's motion for judgment notwithstanding the verdict and ordered that Bennett take nothing.

Bennett appealed, challenging the legal and factual sufficiency of the evidence. The court of appeals affirmed the trial court's judgment, holding that, because Bennett requested only a partial reporter's record, he waived any complaint challenging the sufficiency of the evidence. __ S.W.3d __. Pursuant to Texas Rule of Appellate Procedure 34.6, when an appellant requests only a partial reporter's record, the appellate court must presume that the partial reporter's record . . . constitutes the entire record for purposes of reviewing the [appellant's] stated points or issues. This presumption applies even if the statement includes a point or issue complaining of the legal or factual insufficiency of the evidence to support a specific factual finding identified in that point or issue.

TEX. R. APP. P. 34.6 (c)(1), (4). The rule expressly states that an appellant need not file a complete reporter's record to preserve legal or factual sufficiency points. Accordingly, the court of appeals erred in holding that Bennett waived his legal and factual sufficiency points of error by filing an incomplete reporter's record.

Although the court of appeals did not address the issue, Cochran alleges alternatively that Bennett waived his legal and factual sufficiency challenges by failing to comply with Rule 34.6(c)(1)'s requirement to "include in the request [for a partial reporter's record] a statement of the points or issues to be presented on appeal." TEX. R. APP. P. 34.6(c)(1). Cochran does not allege that Bennett's delay prejudiced Cochran on appeal. Instead, he contends that, because Bennett failed to timely file a statement of his points or issues, he is not entitled to the presumption that the partial reporter's record constitutes the entire record for purposes of reviewing his legal and factual sufficiency challenges.

Although Bennett's statement of issues was due "[a]t or before the time for perfecting the appeal," he filed it almost two months late. TEX. R. APP. P. 34.6(b)(1). However, nothing in the record indicates that Bennett's tardiness impaired Cochran's appellate posture. Cochran had more than two months after he first received notice of Bennett's statement of issues to file his appellee's brief. Cochran does not contend that Bennett's delay prevented him from identifying the relevant issues or supplementing the reporter's record. Nor does Cochran assert that he had insufficient time to adequately prepare his appellate arguments.

There is no question that, had Bennett completely failed to submit his statement of points or issues, Rule 34.6 would require the appellate court to affirm the trial court's judgment. *See Richards v. Schion*, 969 S.W.2d 131, 133 (Tex. App.—Houston [1st Dist.] 1998, no pet.) ("When an appellant appeals with a partial reporter's record but does not provide the list of points as required by rule 34.6(c)(1), it creates the presumption that the omitted portions support the trial court's findings."). Many of our courts of appeals require "strict compliance" with all of Rule 34.6's provisions to preserve appellate review. *See, e.g., Brown v. McGuyer Homebuilders, Inc.*, 58 S.W.3d 172, 175 (Tex. App.—Houston [14th. Dist.] 2001, pet. denied) (appellant's failure to file statement of points in compliance with Rule 34.6 required appellate court to presume record's omitted portions supported trial court's judgment); *In re R.C.*, 45 S.W.3d 146, 149 (Tex. App.—Fort Worth 2000, no pet.) (appellate court permitted to review only those issues properly designated in appellant's statement of points); *Hilton v. Hillman Distrib. Co.*, 12 S.W.3d 846, 847 (Tex. App.—Texarkana 2000, no pet.) (requiring both request for partial record and statement of points to be timely filed). However, we have adopted a more flexible approach in certain cases—like this one—when a rigid application of Rule 34.6 would result in denying review on the merits, even though the appellee has not established any prejudice from a slight relaxation of the rule. *See, e.g., Schafer v. Conner*, 813 S.W.2d 154, 155 (Tex. 1991).

In *Schafer*, we rejected an interpretation of Rule 53(d)—Rule 34.6(c)'s predecessor—that would require an appellant to actually file its statement of points or issues "in" its request for the reporter's record. *Id.* at 155; *see also Furr's Supermarkets, Inc. v. Bethune*, 53 S.W.3d 375, 377 (Tex. 2001) (stating appellee's issue statement in its notice of appeal was sufficient to invoke the presumption that the partial reporter's record constituted the entire record for purposes of reviewing the stated issue). Then, in *Gallagher v. Fire Insurance Exchange*, 950 S.W.2d 370, 370-71 (Tex. 1997), we reiterated our commitment to ensuring that courts do not unfairly apply the rules of appellate procedure to avoid addressing a party's meritorious claim. There, we reversed a court of appeals' holding that the appellant waived review by failing to file a complete statement of facts in strict compliance with Rule 53(d). *Id.* at 371. We reasoned:

> The court of appeals was correct in holding that, absent a complete record on appeal, it must presume the omitted items supported the trial court's judgment. For the courts of appeals to affirm the trial court's judgment on the basis of omitted items after having denied pre-submission supplementation of those items without having determined that such would unreasonably delay disposition of the appeal, however, offends the spirit of [our appellate rules].

Id. (quoting *Crown Life Ins. Co. v. Estate of Gonzalez*, 820 S.W.2d 121, 122 (Tex. 1991)). We find this argument no less compelling today than we did in *Gallagher* or *Crown Life*. Here, Bennett did file his statement of issues or points, albeit some time after he filed his request for a partial reporter's record.

Our appellate rules are designed to further the resolution of appeals on the merits. *See Gallagher*, 950 S.W.2d at 370-71. We will interpret these rules, when possible, to achieve that aim. However, litigants should not view our relaxation of rules in a particular case as endorsing noncompliance. While we seek to resolve appeals on their merits, litigants who ignore our rules do so at the risk of forfeiting appellate relief.

Here, the objective behind Rule 34.6(c)(1) was fully served. Cochran does not allege that he was deprived of an opportunity to designate additional portions of the reporter's record, nor does he assert that Bennett's delay otherwise prejudiced the preparation or presentation of his case. Under these circumstances, we hold that Rule 34.6 does not preclude appellate review of Bennett's legal and factual sufficiency issues.

Accordingly, without hearing oral argument, we grant Bennett's petition for review, reverse the court of appeals' judgment, and remand the cause to the court of appeals for further proceedings consistent with this opinion. TEX. R. APP. P. 59.1.

Notes

1. Limited appeals, as they were formerly known, have been eliminated under the "new" Rules of Appellate Procedure. Anyone desiring to alter a lower court's appealable order must perfect his/her/its own appeal to either the court of appeals or the Supreme Court.

2. If a party wants the appellate court to affirm the trial court, that party will state reply points in the appellee's brief. This is the same as the old practice. But, if a party seeks to alter the trial court's judgment, the party must perfect his/her/its own appeal—even in a two party case. This is a major change in procedure. Under the former rules, a party could raise points seeking to alter the trial court's judgment in the appellee's brief. Now, the party must perfect his/her/its own appeal.

3. In a multiple party case, just as under the old rules, a party is, required to perfect appeal to raise any ground for relief that does not affect the interest of the appellant or bear on matters presented in the appeal brought by the appellant. For example, to invoke the appellate court's jurisdiction over a third party, the appellee must perfect his/her/its own appeal. Under TEX. R. APP. P. 26.1(d), if one party timely perfects an appeal, any other party may perfect an appeal within 14 days of the date the appeal is perfected, or 14 days of the last day to perfect the first appeal, whichever is later.

4. TEX. R. APP. P. 34.6(b)(1): A party must request preparation of the reporter's record "at or before the time for perfecting the appeal." The request must "designate the portions of the testimony to be included." TEX. R. APP. P. 34.6(c)(1): The party requesting a limited record must include a "statement of the points or issues to be presented on appeal." The party is then limited to the points or issue stated. TEX. R. APP. P. 34.6(c)(4).

iii. *Clerk's Record*

Notes

1. Under the old rules, it was the appellant's duty to see that the transcript was timely filed. The transcript is now called the clerk's record, and under the new TEX. R. APP. P. 35.3, the trial clerk is to prepare and file the clerk's record if (1) the notice of appeal is timely filed; and (2) the party responsible for paying for the preparation of the clerk's record has paid the clerk's fee, has made satisfactory arrangements with the clerk to pay the fee, or is entitled to appeal without paying the fee.

2. The new rules omit the requirement found in the old rules, that failure to make timely designation of items to be included in the transcript waived the right to complain of omissions.

3. TEX. R. APP. PROC. 37.3 requires the appellate clerk to give the trial clerk notice that the record is late within 30 days of its due date, in the case of an ordinary appeal, or 10 days, in the case of an accelerated appeal.

4. Rule 37.3(b) provides that: "If the trial clerk failed to file the clerk's record because the appellant failed to pay or make arrangements to pay the clerk's fee for preparing the clerk's record, the appellate court may—on a party's motion or its own initiative—dismiss the appeal for want of prosecution unless the appellant was entitled to proceed without paying of costs. The court must give the appellant a reasonable opportunity to cure before dismissal."

5. Under TEX. R. APP. PROC. 35.3 the clerk and the court reporter are responsible for filing the clerk's record and reporter's record if the party responsible for paying for the preparation of the clerk's or reporter's record has made satisfactory arrangements with the clerk to pay the fee, or is entitled to appeal without paying the fee. No bond is required for the perfection of an appeal. TEX. R. APP. PROC. 25.1.

iv. *Affidavit of Indigence*

Read Rule 145 of the Texas Rules of Civil Procedure and Rule 20 of the Texas Rules of Appellate Procedure.

In re ARROYO
988 S.W.2d 737
(Tex. 1998)

Edgar Santos Arroyo, Rosharon, for Relator in No. 98-0152.
Kenneth W. Lindsey, Paul J. Smith, Houston, for Respondent in No. 98- 0152.
Michael James Holloway, Abilene, for Relator in No. 98-0161.
Alan L. Busch, Joyce Horner, Dallas, for Respondent in No. 98-0161.

PER CURIAM.

The common issue presented in these two original mandamus proceedings is whether, after the 1997 amendments to the Texas Rules of Appellate Procedure, appeal affords adequate relief from an order sustaining a contest to an affidavit of indigence and thus requiring advance payment of appellate costs, so that review by mandamus is no longer available. We hold that the amended rules make appeal an adequate remedy, and accordingly we deny both petitions.

Relator Michael T. Holloway's appeal from an adverse judgment in the trial court is pending in the court of appeals. The record has not been filed because Holloway has not paid the cost for it in advance, and the trial court sustained a contest to his affidavit of indigence that, under Rule 20 of the Texas Rules of Appellate Procedure, would have relieved him of the obligation of advance payment of appellate costs. Holloway unsuccessfully petitioned the court of appeals for mandamus directing the trial court to vacate its order, and then petitioned this Court for the same relief. Relator Edgar Santos Arroyo is in the same situation in a separate appeal, except that the trial court in his case sustained a contest to his affidavit of indigence only to the extent that he be required to pay $10 costs in advance.

Before the 1997 amendments to the Rules of Appellate Procedure, a party who could not pay appellate costs in advance as required by law could perfect an appeal only by filing an affidavit of indigence. If the trial court sustained a contest to the affidavit, the party had no means of invoking the jurisdiction of the appellate court, and thus the only avenue for review was mandamus. Now, however, Rule 25.1(a) provides that a party may perfect an appeal merely by filing a notice of appeal. Providing security for costs is no longer a prerequisite to invoking the court of appeals' jurisdiction. Thus, an indigent party is no longer precluded from perfecting appeal and challenging the trial court's order sustaining a contest to the party's affidavit of indigence. If a party is required to pay for preparation of the appellate record and does not do so or make arrangements to do so, Rule 35.3 excuses the clerk and court reporter from filing the record, and Rule 37.3(b) provides that the appeal may be dismissed for want of prosecution.

This avenue of appeal is not adequate, however, unless the indigent party can obtain the record pertaining to the trial court's ruling sustaining the contest to the affidavit of indigence. The court of appeals can and should, on motion or its own initiative, require the clerk and court reporter under Rules 34.5(c)(1) and 34.6(d), respectively, to prepare and file the portions of the record necessary to review an order sustaining a contest to an affidavit of indigence. This has been the practice for obtaining the relevant record for mandamus review of such orders. The burden of obtaining the relevant portions of the record in this manner should be minimal. If the court of appeals determines that the order sustaining a contest to an affidavit of indigence should be reversed, the appellant can then obtain a full record under Rules 34.5(c)(1) and 34.6(d), and can supplement his or her briefing under Rule 38.7.

Pending resolution of an appellant's challenge to an order sustaining a contest to an affidavit of indigence, Rule 35.3(c) precludes the court of appeals from dismissing the appeal for appellant's failure to file the complete record, since the failure in such circumstances would not be appellant's fault. The court of appeals should also defer the payment of fees under Rule 5 until it determines whether payment is due. Once the trial court's ruling is affirmed, however, the appeals court may dismiss the appeal under Rule 37.3(b) if appellant fails to file the clerk's record, and may require payment of all fees due.

Thus, the amended Rules of Appellate Procedure provide not only an adequate appellate mechanism for review of an order sustaining a contest to an affidavit of indigence, but one which is functionally identical to mandamus review used previously. This adequate appellate remedy precludes mandamus relief, and therefore Holloway's and Arroyo's petitions are denied.

Notes

1. One seeking to appeal no longer files a cost bond. Rather a notice of appeal is filed. The issue of indigence, now, comes up in the context of payment for the clerk and reporters records, and the payment of filing fees in the appellate courts.

2 *In the Interest of J. W. and D. S. G*, 52 S.W.3d 730 (Tex. 2001): An affidavit of indigence should contain the information required by TEX. R. APP. P. 20.1(a). However, the court of appeals must allow the amendment of an incomplete affidavit of indigency, and must direct reconsideration of the contests, based upon any additional information provided by the appellants. Although an affidavit of indigence is no longer used to invoke appellate jurisdiction, it is no less essential to an appeal.

3. *Baughman v Baughman*, 65 S.W.3d 309 (Tex. App—Waco 2001, pet. denied): This is an appeal of an indigency contest. H filed 2 affidavits of inability to pay cost attempting to pursue an appeal without having to pay court cost. Primarily he sought to be excused from having to pay for the reporter's record and the clerk's record. His former wife, W, and the court reporter for the underlying suit each filed contest to the 2nd affidavit. The trial court sustained the contest. Held: Affirmed. H testified he had nothing of value, was unemployed, owed $70,000 in debts, was unable to borrow any money, had an inherited degenerative spinal disk condition that prevented him from working, and had incurred an on-the-job injury for which he received maximum benefits but was pursuing a claim for additional compensation. W and the court reporter testified that H was capable of holding down a job, and this same evidence had also been brought out during cross examination of H. The Court of Appeals could not say that the trial court's decision to sustain the contest to H's affidavit was not supported by any evidence; the court could have determined that H's unemployment was voluntary and that he would be able to pay the costs, or some part thereof, if he really wanted to and made a good faith effort to do so.

4. In *Hood v. Wal-Mart Stores, Inc.*, 216 S.W.3d 829 (Tex. 2007). Hood, appearing pro se, filed an assault and battery action against Wal-Mart. The trial court entered summary judgment for the defendants. When Hood filed his timely notice of appeal in the court of appeals, he failed to pay the filing fee, and had not yet filed an affidavit of indigence. The court of appeals granted an additional ten days to pay. Hood did not pay the fee, but he filed his affidavit of indigence with the court of appeals within the ten day window. Ultimately, the court of appeals denied Hood's motion to proceed in forma pauperis under Texas Rule of Appellate Procedure 20.1(c)(1), which requires the petitioner to file an affidavit of indigence with or before his notice of appeal. The court of appeals dismissed Hood's action. ***Held:*** Reversed and remanded. Under Texas Rule of Appellate Procedure 44.3, a court of appeals may not dismiss an action due to a formal defect or irregularity without first allowing the petitioner reasonable time to cure the error. Hood's affidavit discharged the filing fee requirement unless a contest to it is sustained.

5. *Higgins v. Randall County Sheriff Office*, 257 S.W.3d 684 (Tex. 2008): Higgins, a pro se inmate, timely appealed the trial court's dismissal of his civil suit for want of prosecution, but failed, either to pay the filing fee, or to file an affidavit of indigence. When the court of appeals requested payment of the filing fee within ten days, Higgins filed an affidavit of indigence, in which he did clearly attest that he had no current or expected income of any kind, and that he had no prospects for receiving any money in the future. Because Higgins failed to file the affidavit with his appeal as TEX. R. APP P. 20.1(c)(1) provides, and because the affidavit failed to fully comply with Rule 20.1(b), the court dismissed Higgins's appeal. Held: Reversed and remanded to the court of appeals. The appeal of a party asserting indigence may proceed when the affidavit lacks complete information on all of the items enumerated in TEX. R. APP. P. 20.1(b), but no contest to the affidavit is filed. This decision reflects the policy embodied in the appellate rules that disfavors disposing of appeals based upon harmless procedural defects.

GRIFFIN INDUSTRIES, INC.
v.
THE HONORABLE THIRTEENTH COURT OF APPEALS

934 S.W.2d 349
(Tex. 1996)

William Dibrell, Diane M. Henson, Austin, Lev Hunt, Corpus Christi, for Relators.
Willard G. Holgate, Corpus Christi, for Respondent.

OWEN, JUSTICE.

In this mandamus proceeding, the trial court sustained a contest to an affidavit of inability to pay costs on appeal under Rule 40(a)(3) of the Texas Rules of Appellate Procedure. The court of appeals conditionally issued a writ of mandamus concluding that the trial court had abused its discretion. 913 S.W.2d 752. Griffin Industries sought mandamus relief in this Court, and we granted leave to file. Because we agree with the holdings of the court of appeals, we deny the petition for writ of mandamus.

I

Griffin Industries recycles used cooking grease. Griffin Industries accused Villegas and her husband of stealing grease, and they were both arrested. Mr. Villegas died about three months after the incident. Ultimately, the prosecutor dropped the charges against Maria Villegas. She then sued Griffin Industries and others for malicious prosecution, false arrest, and wrongful death. After Villegas presented her case, the trial court granted a motion for a directed verdict in favor of Griffin Industries. Villegas sought to appeal and filed an affidavit of inability to pay costs. Both the court reporter and Griffin Industries contested the affidavit.

Maria Villegas has been unemployed since 1991. She has an eighth-grade education and a GED. In the past, she has worked as a secretary and has owned a cleaning business, but she testified that arthritis in her fingers and problems with her hands, for which she has undergone surgery, now foreclose her from occupation in either of those fields. Villegas's entire income, less than $500 per month, comes from Social Security Disability and Supplemental Security Income benefits. At the time of the hearing on the contest to the affidavit of inability to pay costs, she was no longer eligible for food stamps because she had moved across county lines, although she had reapplied for this assistance.

As a condition of receiving Social Security benefits, Villegas testified that the Texas Rehabilitation Commission directed her to obtain retraining in a new line of work. Accordingly, she had attended Texas State Technology College as a full-time student from 1993 to 1995 and, at the time of the hearing, was attending Bee County College on a part-time basis to complete remedial course work necessary to obtain an associates degree in building construction.

Villegas rents a one-bedroom apartment for $360 a month and pays an additional $60 to $90 in utilities. She lives with her daughter Elizabeth and her daughter's infant son Joshua. Elizabeth supplies groceries for the family from the food stamps she receives. Villegas testified that she has no savings account, stocks, bonds, real property, jewelry, or other assets, except a poorly running 1985 Buick worth at most $500. She borrows clothes from her children. Moreover, Villegas owes $6,986.17 in federal income taxes, $2500 to her attorney for the defense of the criminal action, and $689.25 for expenses already incurred in this suit.

The court of appeals held that the trial court abused its discretion in sustaining the contest to the affidavit because Villegas proved that she was indigent and unable to pay the costs of appeal. 913 S.W.2d at 756. Further, the court of appeals held that the ability of an attorney to pay for an appeal should not defeat the client's status as an indigent. *Id.*

II

Rule 40 of the Texas Rules of Appellate Procedure governs appeals by indigent parties. Under that rule, the burden of proof at the hearing on the contest to the affidavit of inability to pay costs rests on the appellant to sustain the allegations in the affidavit. TEX. R. APP. P. 40(a)(3)(D). The appellant must prove that she could not pay the costs of appeal " 'if [she] really wanted to and made a good-faith effort to do so.' " *Allred v. Lowry*, 597 S.W.2d 353, 355 (Tex. 1980) (*quoting Pinchback v. Hockless*, 139 Tex. 536, 164 S.W.2d 19, 20 (1942)). This standard is met, however, by proof that the appellant depends on public assistance. As we said in *Goffney v. Lowry*, 554 S.W.2d 157, 159-60 (Tex. 1977):

> The fact that any individual is dependent upon the charity of the public afforded through the various welfare programs is, by itself, prima facie evidence that the person is financially unable to pay the court costs or give security therefor.

This standard is consistent with the standard for an affidavit of inability to secure costs in the trial court. *See* TEX. R. CIV. P. 145. Rule 145 defines a "party who is unable to afford costs" as "a person who is presently receiving a governmental entitlement based on indigency or any other person who has no ability to pay costs." Villegas's testimony established that such programs were her only source of income.

The evidence offered by Griffin Industries does not negate this prima facie case. First, Griffin Industries pointed out that Villegas had not attempted to obtain a loan for the appellate costs by borrowing against her claim. However, Villegas's evidence established that she had no collateral and no income stream to secure a loan from any reasonable commercial lender. Requiring her to obtain formal loan rejections would exalt form over substance, as such rejections would "merely buttress th[e] conclusion that she is financially unable to meet any of the court costs or give security therefor." *Goffney*, 554 S.W.2d at 160.

Next, Griffin Industries offered evidence that in the past Villegas may have misrepresented her marital status to obtain AFDC benefits for her children. However, she no longer receives those benefits, as her children have reached majority, and such expired benefits form no part of her prima facie case. Therefore, whether she once misrepresented her marital status to obtain these benefits is irrelevant.

In addition, Griffin Industries offered Villegas's testimony from the underlying trial indicating that she may also have been untruthful about her marital status or whether her husband lived with her to doctors who treated her for the illnesses forming the basis of her compensable disability. Griffin Industries argues that Villegas's untruthfulness about her marital status is evidence that Villegas was not entitled to the government benefits that she now receives and which established her prima facie case.

Griffin Industries offered no evidence, however, that any misrepresentation by Villegas to her doctor about her marital status was financially motivated or otherwise material to the Social Security Administration's ruling that Villegas is disabled or in need of SSI. Villegas testified that she went to her doctor because she was sick, not to qualify for disability benefits, and that it was her doctor who suggested that she seek benefits. In fact, the evidence conclusively establishes that her marital status was irrelevant to her qualification for government benefits, as the Administration's hearing on whether to award Villegas benefits occurred after Mr. Villegas's death.

Griffin Industries counters that Villegas's alleged fraud in obtaining benefits is at least relevant to her credibility. However, even assuming, as we must, that Villegas misrepresented her marital status in the past to obtain now-expired AFDC benefits for her children and that she was untruthful about her marital status in discussions with doctors who treated her, such misrepresentations do not amount to evidence that Villegas obtained the government benefits she now receives by fraud. The evidence is uncontroverted that Villegas actually receives government assistance, and Griffin Industries offered no medical or other evidence suggesting that Villegas was not legally entitled to this assistance.

The dissent argues that evidence of misrepresentations by Villegas is at least relevant to her credibility. 934 S.W.2d at 356. Apparently, the dissent is of the view that even after a witness testifies that he or she is dependent on public assistance and thereby establishes a prima facie case of indigence, the trial court simply may refuse to believe that the witness is credible and may conclude that the witness is not in fact indigent. The dissent misapprehends the effect of establishing a prima facie case. To overcome a prima facie showing, an opposing party must offer evidence to rebut what has been established. The trial court is not free simply to disbelieve the direct, positive evidence that establishes the prima facie case. *See, e.g., Sansom v. Sprinkle*, 799 S.W.2d 776, 778 (Tex. App.—Fort Worth 1990, orig. proceeding).

The issues raised in *Sansom* were similar to those in the case before us. At a hearing on a contest to an affidavit of inability to pay costs on appeal, Sansom testified that he had no job, no funds to pursue an appeal, and subsisted on food stamps. *Id.* at 777. The trial court nevertheless sustained the challenge. *Id.* On appeal, the court of appeals recognized that generally a trial court is permitted, even required, to judge the credibility of testimony. *Id.* at 778. However, as the court of appeals in *Sansom* correctly held, when a prima facie case of dependence on public assistance has been established, opposing parties bear the burden of introducing some evidence that the witness is not dependent on food stamps or that other funds are available. *Id.* The trier of fact is not permitted to disregard entirely the word of the witness that he was indigent. *Id.*

Finally, Griffin Industries points out that counsel for Villegas judicially admitted at the hearing on the indigency affidavit contest that Villegas has not sought or obtained employment during the time she has been receiving disability benefits because Social Security rules prohibit recipients of disability benefits from working. From this admission and from the fact that Villegas has attended school full time and done well there, Griffin Industries contends that the trial court could have inferred that Villegas was really able to work. No "inference" can be drawn from these facts. Villegas's counsel accurately informed the trial court of the Administration's rule. Further, Villegas testified that attending school was a condition of receiving the disability benefits. To use the conditions that the government has placed on Villegas's receipt of assistance as proof that she is not really entitled to that assistance should be too ironic a Catch-22 for this Court to countenance. For these reasons, we hold that Griffin Industries has offered no evidence negating Villegas's prima facie case that she is unable to pay costs without assistance from her lawyer.

III

The only remaining issue is what effect Villegas's fee arrangement with her attorney has on the contest to her affidavit of inability to pay costs on appeal. Griffin Industries argues that because Villegas's fee agreement with her attorney provided that he would pay or advance costs, Villegas does not meet the test for indigency and that, therefore, the trial court did not abuse its discretion in sustaining the indigency contest. It is undisputed that counsel for Villegas has not paid the costs of appeal. We are thus faced with the question of how courts are to treat the truly indigent who are able to find a lawyer willing to represent them for a contingent interest in any recovery, but unwilling to pay the costs of an appeal.

The courts of appeals are divided on the question whether the existence of a contingency fee agreement is grounds for sustaining a contest to a litigant's claim that he or she is unable to pay costs. *Compare Modern Living, Inc. v. Alworth*, 730 S.W.2d 444, 446 (Tex. App.—Beaumont 1987, orig. proceeding) (holding that an attorney is not obligated to pay costs of appeal by virtue of a contingency fee agreement and that the trial court erred in sustaining contest) *with Culpepper v. Coker*, 769 S.W.2d 373, 375 (Tex. App.—Houston [14th Dist.] 1989, orig. proceeding) (holding that the trial court did not abuse its discretion in sustaining indigency contest because the appellant did not prove that his attorney could not bear the costs of appeal).

Our state Constitution and our rules of procedure recognize that our courts must be open to all with legitimate disputes, not just those who can afford to pay the fees to get in. TEX. CONST. art. 1, § 13; TEX. R. CIV. P. 145; TEX. R. APP. P. 53(j). Under the facts of this case, the contingency fee agreement should not nullify the indigency status of Villegas.

The contingent fee contract between Villegas and her attorney William Holgate is ambiguous at best regarding the payment or advancement of costs on appeal. The fee agreement provides in pertinent part:

> It is agreed that all necessary disbursements, witness fees and court costs will be separately paid by [Villegas], including traveling expenses and incidental disbursements necessary to conduct hearings or trials or to interview witnesses, etc., [Villegas] to advance sufficient sums to cover said disbursements and costs from time to time when requested by said Attorney. In the event that [Villegas] does not advance the sums as stated above for disbursements and costs at the rate of twelve percent (12%) per annum [sic]. Said Attorney is herewith granted a lien upon said cause or causes of action and any real or personal property or thing recovered therein either by [Villegas] or said attorneys to secure payment of the fees herein provided for, and of any disbursements not independently paid by [Villegas].

Resolving all ambiguities in favor of the trial court's ruling, the most that can be said about the agreement is that it obligates Holgate to loan costs of court to Villegas.

No one disputes that Holgate paid none of the costs in this case from its inception. When Holgate agreed to pursue this suit, Villegas owed him $2,500 for his earlier representation of her in the criminal proceeding. Holgate testified that he realized Villegas would not be able to pay all the court costs in the present suit and that he could not afford to do so. Accordingly, he promptly referred the case to another attorney who paid the filing and service fees and apparently some of the deposition costs. That attorney eventually withdrew and returned the file to Holgate. Holgate thereafter concluded discovery and represented Villegas in a jury trial. The trial court directed a verdict against Villegas at the close of her evidence. Villegas sought to appeal, and at the hearing contesting Villegas's affidavit of inability to pay, the evidence established that neither Villegas nor her attorney had paid costs of discovery done by Holgate.

The evidence is uncontroverted that Villegas asked her attorney to pay the costs for a statement of facts and the transcript, but that he would not or could not do so. Both Villegas and Holgate testified to this fact. It is of little solace to Villegas that the trial court concluded that her attorney had a contractual obligation to advance costs. Whatever contractual or other rights an indigent litigant has against an attorney are not a substitute for the present means to pay the costs of an appeal. A suit against the attorney after the appeal is dismissed will not revive the appeal.

We recognize, however, that the fee agreement between an attorney and an indigent client may be considered in determining if the litigant is able to pay costs on appeal. If the agreement provides that the attorney is to pay or advance costs, and the appellant makes no further showing, the agreement would be some evidence that the appellant has a source of funds from which to pay costs. But, when the facts establish that the attorney will not or cannot pay those costs, as is the case here, we cannot erect a legal fiction that an indigent has the ability to pay " 'if [she] really wanted to.' " *Allred v. Lowry*, 597 S.W.2d 353, 355 (Tex. 1980) (*quoting Pinchback v. Hockless*, 139 Tex. 536, 164 S.W.2d 19, 20 (1942)).

The right of the indigent to pursue an appeal should not turn on whether an attorney abides by an agreement to pay or to advance costs. When the attorney is obligated to the client to pay or advance costs but will not or cannot do so, the indigent should not be stripped of his or her indigent status. Through civil suits and the disciplinary process, our legal system has a means of extracting justice from attorneys who violate obligations to their clients and of deterring such conduct. To demand that indigent clients forfeit appellate rights for their attorneys' transgressions or inability to pay would leave indigents faced with a *Hobson's* choice on appeal: of the right to a statement of facts and the transcript, or they can continue to have representation by counsel on a contingent-fee basis, only to have their case dismissed for inability to pay costs if their attorneys will not or cannot pay. Such a result would effectively say that the poor could not be represented by lawyers who are unwilling to pay court costs. If a lawyer is unable or unwilling to pay out-of-pocket costs, an indigent's right to access to the courts would be at an end. In marginal (but not frivolous) cases, indigents would be penalized if they could not find an attorney who would be willing to pay appellate costs. (There has been no contention in the trial court or the court of appeals that Villegas's appeal is frivolous, and we express no opinion on that issue.)

We realize that official reporters have many demands placed on their time and that preparing appellate statements of facts without pay comes not only at a monetary sacrifice, but also at the expense of completing court business. However, our appellate rules provide some measure of protection. Under Texas Rules of Appellate Procedure 89 and 182(a), courts of appeals and this Court have the authority to tax costs against a losing party. If an indigent is successful on appeal, nothing prevents our appellate courts from ordering the losing party to pay the cost of the statement of facts. And, while the principal complaint of court reporters stems from the cases in which indigents have obtained a free statement of facts and are not successful on appeal, our rules address such cases: an indigent is entitled to a free statement of facts. TEX. R. APP. P. 53(j)(1). Trial courts could lessen the financial burden on the court reporter by seeking authorization from this Court to record court proceedings by electronic recording, at least experimentally for some cases. *See* Rules Governing the Procedure for Making a Record of Court Proceedings by Electronic Recording, reprinted in Texas Rules of Court—State 345-46 (West 1996).

For the above reasons, we agree with the court of appeals that the trial court abused its discretion in sustaining the contest to the affidavit of inability to pay costs on appeal. Therefore, we deny Griffin Industries' petition for a writ of mandamus.

BAKER, JUSTICE, joined by ENOCH, JUSTICE, dissenting [opinion omitted].

Notes

1. Under TEX. R. APP. P. 20 an indigent party may appeal without advance payment of the cost of the record and filing fees. The party claiming indigency (an inability to pay the costs in an appellate court) must file an affidavit of indigence and a timely notice of appeal.

2. TEX. R. CIV. P. 20.1(c)(1). The affidavit of indigency must be filed in the trial court with or before the notice of appeal. For original proceedings, the affidavit must be filed in the appellate court, with or before the document seeking relief. Rule 20.1(c)(2). A respondent who requests preparation of a record must *file* the affidavit of indigence in the appellate court *within 15 days after the date the respondent requests preparation of the record.* The deadline for filing the affidavit of indigence can be extended if a motion for extension is filed within 15 days after the deadline. Rule 20.1(c)(3).

3. TEX. R. APP. P. 20.1(d)(1). The affidavit is *filed with the clerk of the trial court*, and it is the clerk who must promptly forward a copy to the appropriate court reporter. If the affidavit is filed with the appellate court clerk, and the filing party seeks a free record, the appellate court clerk must send a copy of the affidavit to the trial clerk and court reporter, together with a notice stating the deadline for filing a contest.

4. A contest of the affidavit can be filed by the clerk, the court reporter, or any party. The *contest* must be *filed* on or before the *10th day after the affidavit was filed* with the trial court clerk. If the affidavit was filed with the appellate court clerk, the contest is due by the date set by the appellate court clerk. TEX. R. APP. P. 20.1(e). If no contest is filed, the affidavit, the affidavit is taken as true, and the party is allowed to appeals without paying costs. Rule 20.1(f). If a contest is filed, the party who claims indigency must prove the affidavit's allegations. For an incarcerated party, the affidavit itself is evidence and is sufficient to meet the party's burden, without the incarcerated party attending the hearing. Rule 20.1(h).

5. If the affidavit of indigence is filed in the appellate court, and the contest occurs there, the appellate court can: (i) conduct a hearing and rule; (ii) decide the contest based on the affidavit, and other timely filed documents; (iii) request written submission of additional evidence; or (iv) refer the matter to the trial court to hear evidence and grant appropriate relief. If the affidavit of indigence is filed in the trial court, or referred by the appellate court to the trial court, then the trial court must give notice and conduct a hearing. A hearing on the contest must be conducted within 10 days after the contest is filed, or after the matter was received from the appellate court. The trial court can sign an order extending the time for hearing, but that extension cannot exceed 20 days from the date of the order. Unless, within the period set for the hearing, the trial court signs an order sustaining the contest, the affidavit's allegations will be deemed true, and the party will be allowed to proceed without advance payment of costs.

6. *Morris v. Aguilar,* 369 S.W.3d 168 (Tex. 2012): The Morrises timely filed an affidavit of indigence and a notice of appeal. The court reporter (Aguilars) filed a contest to the affidavit 24 days after the 10-day deadline. The trial court sustained the contest; and the court of appeals affirmed, holding the Morrises waived the untimeliness of the contest by failing to object. ***Held*:** Texas Rule of Appellate Procedure 20.1(f) provides that, "[u]nless a contest is timely filed, no hearing will be conducted, the affidavit's allegations will be deemed true, and the party will be allowed to proceed without advance payment of costs." As the Court has previously held, "Rule 20.1(f) is mandatory to protect the indigent appellant and uphold the principle that '[c]ourts should be open to all, including those who cannot afford the costs of admission.' " Contrary to the Aguilars' argument, Texas Rule of Civil Procedure 5 may not be used to extend the 10-day deadline in Texas Rule of Appellate Procedure 20.1(f); by its terms, Rule 5 applies to deadlines in the Rules of Civil Procedure. Nor does Texas Rule of Appellate Procedure 2 authorize an extension; that rule requires "good cause," a standard that is not met by showing lack of actual notice since, as amended in 1997, Rule 20.1(d)(1) requires that, if the notice is filed with the clerk, it is the clerk that must provide a copy of the notice to the court reporter. As the Court has previously held, the clerk's failure to do so is not grounds for denying an indigent appellant the benefit of Rules 20.1(e)-(f). The Court also states, in a footnote, that it disagrees with the court of appeals' conclusion that "the truck Morris's husband used in his work, which was the couple's only vehicle, and 'items that they find useful …, largely those related to [Morris's] husband's deafness'" are "non-necessaries."

iv(a). *Record on Appeal*

Notes

1. Under TEX. R. CIV. PROC. 35.1, the appellate record must be filed in the appellate court within 60 days after the judgment is signed, except as follows:

a. *When a post-verdict motion or request for findings is filed.* If Rule 26.1 (a) applies, within 120 days after the judgment is signed. [Rule 26.1 provides that a notice of appeal must be filed within 90 days after the judgment is signed if any party timely files:

(1) a motion for new trial;
(2) a motion to modify the judgment;
(3) a motion to reinstate under Texas Rules of Civil Procedure 165a; or
(4) a proper request for findings of fact and conclusions of law are filed.

b. *In accelerated appeals.* If Rule 26.1(b) applies, within 10 days after the notice of appeal is filed. [Rule 26.1(b) relates to accelerated appeals, and require the notice of appeal to be field within 20 days after the judgment or order is signed.

c. *In restricted appeals.* If Rule 26.1(c) applies, within 30 days after the notice of appeal is filed.

2. *What If The Record Is Late?* If the record is not filed on time, the clerk (if the fee has been paid) is responsible for filing the record. If the fault for late filing is the appellant's, or if the appellant has failed to timely request the reporter's record, then the appellant should file a motion for extension of time, otherwise not. Rule 35.3(c).

3. *What If The Record Is Lost?* If the lost reporter's record is material to the appeal, a new trial will be granted. Rule 34.6(f). If a document from the clerk's record is lost, the parties can, by written stipulation substitute a copy. If the parties can't agree, the trial court must determine what, if any, is an accurate copy and include it in the record. Rule 34.5.

v. *Briefs*

Read Rule 38 Texas Rules of Appellate Procedure.

Notes

Rule 9. Texas Rules of Appellate Procedure: Papers Documents Generally

9.1. Signing

(a) *Represented Parties.* If a party is represented by counsel, a document filed on that party's behalf must be signed by at least one of the party's attorneys. For each attorney whose name appears on a document as representing that party, the document must contain that attorney's State Bar of Texas identification number, mailing address, telephone number, fax number, if any, and email address.

(b) *Unrepresented Parties.* A party not represented by counsel must sign any document that the party files and give the party's mailing address, telephone number, fax number, if any, and email address.

(c) *Electronic Signatures.* A document that is electronically served, filed, or issued by a court or clerk is considered signed if the document includes:

(1) a "/s/" and name typed in the space where the signature would otherwise appear, unless the document is notarized or sworn; or

(2) an electronic image or scanned image of the signature.

9.2. Filing

(a) *With Whom.* A document is filed in an appellate court by delivering it to:

(1) the clerk of the court in which the document is to be filed; or

(2) a justice or judge of that court who is willing to accept delivery. A justice or judge who accepts delivery must note on the document the date and time of delivery, which will be considered the time of filing, and must promptly send it to the clerk.

(b) *Filing by Mail.*

(1) Timely Filing. A document received within ten days after the filing deadline is considered timely filed if:

(A) it was sent to the proper clerk by United States Postal Service or a commercial delivery service;

(B) it was placed in an envelope or wrapper properly addressed and stamped; and

(C) it was deposited in the mail or delivered to a commercial delivery service on or before the last day for filing.

(2) Proof of Mailing. Though it may consider other proof, the appellate court will accept the following as conclusive proof of the date of mailing:

(A) a legible postmark affixed by the United States Postal Service;

(B) a receipt for registered or certified mail if the receipt is endorsed by the United States Postal Service;

(C) a certificate of mailing by the United States Postal Service; or

(D) a receipt endorsed by the commercial delivery service.

(c) *Electronic Filing.*

(1) Requirement. Attorneys in civil cases must electronically file documents. Attorneys in criminal cases must electronically file documents except for good cause shown in a motion filed in the appellate court. Unrepresented parties in civil and criminal cases may electronically file documents, but it is not required.

(2) Mechanism. Electronic filing must be done through the electronic filing manager established by the Office of Court Administration and an electronic filing service provider certified by the Office of Court Administration.

(3) Exceptions. Documents filed under seal, subject to a pending motion to seal, or to which access is otherwise restricted by law or court order must not be electronically filed. For good cause, an appellate court may permit a party to file other documents in paper form in a particular case.

(4) Timely Filing. Unless a document must be filed by a certain time of day, a document is considered timely filed if it is electronically filed at any time before midnight (in the court's time zone) on the filing deadline. An electronically filed document is deemed filed when transmitted to the filing party's electronic filing service provider, except:

(A) if a document is transmitted on a Saturday, Sunday, or legal holiday, it is deemed filed on the next day that is not a Saturday, Sunday, or legal holiday; and

(B) if a document requires a motion and an order allowing its filing, the document is deemed filed on the date the motion is granted.

(5) Technical Failure. If a document is untimely due to a technical failure or a system outage, the filing party may seek appropriate relief from the court.

(6) Confirmation of Filing. The electronic filing manager will send a filing confirmation notice to the filing party.

(7) Electronic Notices From the Court. The clerk may send notices, orders, or other communications about the case to the party electronically. A court seal may be electronic.

9.3. Texas Rules of Appellate Procedure: Number of Copies

(a) *Courts of Appeals.*

(1) Document Filed in Paper Form. If a document is not electronically filed, a party must file: the original and one unbound copy of the document unless otherwise required by local rule. The unbound copy of an appendix must contain a separate page before each document and must not include tabs that extend beyond the edge of the page.

(2) Electronically Filed Document. Unless required by local rule, a party need not file a paper copy of an electronically filed document.

(b) *Supreme Court and Court of Criminal Appeals.*

(1) Document Filed in Paper Form. If a document is not electronically filed, a party must file the original and 11 copies of any document addressed to either the Supreme Court or the Court of Criminal Appeals, except that in the Supreme Court only an original and one copy must be filed of any motion, response to the motion, and reply in support of the motion, and in the Court of Criminal Appeals, only the original must be filed of a motion for extension of time or a response to the motion, or a pleading under Code of Criminal Procedure article 11.07.

(2) Electronically Filed Document. Paper copies of each document that is electronically filed with the Supreme Court or the Court of Criminal Appeals must be mailed or hand-delivered to the Supreme Court or the Court of Criminal Appeals, as appropriate, within three business days after the document is electronically filed. The number of paper copies required shall be determined, respectively, by order of the Supreme Court or the Court of Criminal Appeals.

(c) *Exception for Record.* Only the original record need be filed in any proceeding.

9.4. Texas Rules of Appellate Procedure: Form

Except for the record, a document filed with an appellate court, including a paper copy of an electronically filed document, must — unless the court accepts another form in the interest of justice — be in the following form:

(a) *Printing.* A document may be produced by standard typographic printing or by any duplicating process that produces a distinct black image. Printing must be on one side of the paper.

(b) *Paper Type and Size.* The paper on which a document is produced must be 8½ by 11 inches, white or nearly white, and opaque.

(c) *Margins.* Documents must have at least one-inch margins on both sides and at the top and bottom.

(d) *Spacing.* Text must be double-spaced, but footnotes, block quotations, short lists, and issues or points of error may be single-spaced.

(e) *Typeface.* A document produced on a computer must be printed in a conventional typeface no smaller than 14-point except for footnotes, which must be no smaller than 12-point. A typewritten document must be printed in standard 10-character-per-inch (cpi) monospaced typeface.

(f) *Binding and Covering.* A paper document must be bound so as to ensure that it will not lose its cover or fall apart in regular use. A paper document should be stapled once in the top left-hand corner or be bound so that it will lie flat when open. A paper petition or brief should have durable front and back covers which must not be plastic or be red, black, or dark blue.

(g) *Contents of Cover.* A document's front cover, if any, must contain the case style, the case number, the title of the document being filed, the name of the party filing the document, and the name, mailing address, telephone number, fax number, if any, email address, and State Bar of Texas identification number of the lead counsel for the filing party. If a party requests oral argument in the court of appeals, the request must appear on the front cover of that party's first brief.

(h) *Appendix and Original Proceeding Record.* A paper appendix may be bound either with the document to which it is related or separately. If separately bound, the appendix must comply with paragraph (f). A paper record in an original proceeding or a paper appendix must be tabbed and indexed. An electronically filed record in an original proceeding or an electronically filed appendix that includes more than one item must contain bookmarks to assist in locating each item.

(i) *Length.*

(1) Contents Included and Excluded. In calculating the length of a document, every word and every part of the document, including headings, footnotes, and quotations, must be counted except the following: caption, identity of parties and counsel, statement regarding oral argument, table of contents, index of authorities, statement of the case, statement of issues presented, statement of jurisdiction, statement of procedural history, signature, proof of service, certification, certificate of compliance, and appendix.

(2) Maximum Length. The documents listed below must not exceed the following limits:

(A) A brief and response in a direct appeal to the Court of Criminal Appeals in a case in which the death penalty has been assessed: 37,500 words if computer-generated, and 125 pages if not.

(B) A brief and response in an appellate court (other than a brief under subparagraph (A)) and a petition and response in an original proceeding in the court of appeals: 15,000 words if computer-generated, and

50 pages if not. In a civil case in the court of appeals, the aggregate of all briefs filed by a party must not exceed 27,000 words if computer-generated, and 90 pages if not.

(C) A reply brief in an appellate court and a reply to a response to a petition in an original proceeding in the court of appeals: 7,500 words if computer-generated, and 25 pages if not.

(D) A petition and response in an original proceeding in the Supreme Court, a petition for review and response in the Supreme Court, a petition for discretionary review and response in the Court of Criminal Appeals, and a motion for rehearing and response in an appellate court: 4,500 words if computer-generated, and 15 pages if not.

(E) A reply to a response to a petition for review in the Supreme Court, a reply to a response to a petition in an original proceeding in the Supreme Court, and a reply to a petition for discretionary review in the Court of Criminal Appeals: 2,400 words if computer-generated, and 8 pages if not.

(3) Certificate of Compliance. A computer-generated document that is subject to a word limit under this rule must include a certificate by counsel or an unrepresented party stating the number of words in the document. The person certifying may rely on the word count of the computer program used to prepare the document.

(4) Extensions. A court may, on motion, permit a document that exceeds the prescribed limit.

(j) *Electronically Filed Documents*. An electronically filed document must:

(1) be in text-searchable portable document format (PDF);

(2) be directly converted to PDF rather than scanned, if possible;

(3) not be locked;

(4) be combined with any appendix into one computer file, unless that file would exceed the size limit prescribed by the electronic filing manager; and

(5) otherwise comply with the Technology Standards set by the Judicial Committee on Information Technology and approved by the Supreme Court.

(k) *Nonconforming Documents*. If a document fails to conform with these rules, the court may strike the document or identify the error and permit the party to resubmit the document in a conforming format by a specified deadline.

9.5. Texas Rules of Appellate Procedure: Service

(a) *Service of All Documents Required.* At or before the time of a document's filing, the filing party must serve a copy on all parties to the proceeding. Service on a party represented by counsel must be made on that party's lead counsel. Except in original proceedings, a party need not serve a copy of the record.

(b) *Manner of Service.*

(1) Documents Filed Electronically. A document filed electronically under Rule 9.2 must be served electronically through the electronic filing manager if the email address of the party or attorney to be served is on file with the electronic filing manager. If the email address of the party or attorney to be served is not on file with the electronic filing manager, the document may be served on that party or attorney under subparagraph (2).

(2) Documents Not Filed Electronically. A document that is not filed electronically may be served in person, by mail, by commercial delivery service, by fax, or by email. Personal service includes delivery to any responsible person at the office of the lead counsel for the party served.

(c) *When Complete.*

(1) Service by mail is complete on mailing.

(2) Service by commercial delivery service is complete when the document is placed in the control of the delivery service.

(3) Service by fax is complete on receipt.

(4) Electronic service is complete on transmission of the document to the serving party's electronic filing service provider. The electronic filing manager will send confirmation of service to the serving party.

(d) *Proof of Service.* A document presented for filing must contain a proof of service in the form of either an acknowledgment of service by the person served or a certificate of service. Proof of service may appear on or be affixed to the filed document. The clerk may permit a document to be filed without proof of service, but will require the proof to be filed promptly.

(e) *Certificate Requirements.* A certificate of service must be signed by the person who made the service and must state:

(1) the date and manner of service;

(2) the name and address of each person served; and

(3) if the person served is a party's attorney, the name of the party represented by that attorney.

CITY OF ARLINGTON
v.
STATE FARM LLOYDS
145 S.W.3d 165
(Tex. 2004)

Frank Waite, Elizabeth Lutton, Asst. City Attys., Alan Dean Lathrom, Arlington, for Petitioner.
Michael W. Minton, Law Office of Michael W. Minton, PLLC, Dallas, for Respondent.

PER CURIAM.

State Farm Lloyds (State Farm) brought a subrogation suit against the City of Arlington to recover monies it paid to an insured homeowner whose home was damaged by a sewage backup. The trial court awarded damages to State Farm, and the court of appeals affirmed. Initially, we must determine whether the City adequately preserved its argument that there was no evidence to support essential elements of State Farm's nuisance and takings claims. Because we conclude that the City adequately supported its arguments in the court of appeals with record references and citation of authority, we hold that it preserved the argument. Based on this Court's decision in *City of Dallas v. Jennings,* 142 S.W.3d 310 (Tex. 2004), we further conclude that the City of Arlington is not liable, as a matter of law, for the damages alleged in the underlying case. We therefore reverse the court of appeals' judgment and render judgment in favor of the City of Arlington.

Raw sewage backed up into the home of Michael and Sonia Bates on two occasions in 1997 and 1998, causing significant damage to their home. The Bateses' homeowners' insurer, State Farm, paid them $12,723.61 for the first occurrence and $85,582.96 for the second. State Farm brought a subrogation suit against the City of Arlington to recover the monies paid, alleging that the City's operation of the sewer lines constituted a nuisance and an unconstitutional taking under Article 1, Section 17 of the Texas Constitution. State Farm did not allege that the City operated the sewer improperly; instead, it argued that "backups of raw, noxious sewage into private residences" are "inherent in the nature" of sewer systems. State Farm argued that the City should be liable for the damage caused by the sewer system because "the City intentionally acted to maintain the system for the benefit [o]f its citizenry, knowing all the time that backups such as the one involved here are inherent" in the operation of sewer systems.

At trial, a jury found that the sewer system "create[d] a nuisance" that proximately caused damages to the house, and that the second sewage flood (but not the first) constituted "a taking of property by the City of Arlington." The jury found that $42,916 would reasonably compensate the Bateses for the damage to their home from the second backup, and the trial court rendered judgment for that amount.

The City of Arlington appealed, arguing (1) that the City was immune from nuisance liability unless the nuisance amounted to a taking under Article I, Section 17 of the Texas Constitution; (2) that State Farm had put forward no evidence that the City acted with the requisite intent to support a takings claim under Article I, Section 17; (3) that State Farm had put forward no evidence that "the property [was] taken for, or applied to, a public use"; and (4) that the trial court erred by submitting questions of law to the jury.

Without considering the merits of the City's arguments, the court of appeals held that the City waived its issues by inadequate briefing because it failed to include specific citations to the record. 141 S.W.3d 216.

We disagree that the City waived its issues. Contrary to the court of appeals' statements, the City did include record references with page numbers in its brief's Statement of Facts section to support each fact it asserted. Although it did not repeat the references under its Argument and Authorities section, we have held that "failure to restate the facts and record references under each point of error" will not waive the issues when the brief "contains all points of error relied upon, argument and authorities under each point of error, and all facts relied upon for the appeal with references to the pages in the record where those facts can be found." *Weaver v. Southwest Nat'l Bank,* 813 S.W.2d 481, 482 (Tex. 1991). Because the City's brief met the requirements laid out in *Weaver,* we conclude that the City did not waive its issues by failing to restate the record references in its Argument and Authorities section.

Nor do we agree that the City's citations to the "entire record" waived its no-evidence issues. For example, to support its assertion that "[t]here is no allegation or evidence that the [Bateses'] home was singled out or chosen by the City to facilitate an intentional sewage discharge," the City cited the "entire record." The court of appeals concluded that the City had waived its no-evidence points because it "failed to establish, with proper record references, what the evidence adduced at trial was and how that evidence supports its contentions on appeal" and concluded that "[m]erely asserting that no evidence supports the complained-of judgment will not suffice . . . . This court is not required to search a voluminous record, with no guidance from the City, to determine whether the record supports the City's contentions on appeal." 141 S.W.3d 216, 218. We disagree.

If the City's no-evidence argument had been based on the strength of the evidence—for example, if the City argued that the evidence was "so weak as to do no more than create a mere surmise or suspicion"—then the City could, and should, detail the relevant parts of the record. *See* Robert W. Calvert, *"No Evidence" and "Insufficient Evidence" Points of Error,* 38 TEX. L.REV. 361, 363 (1960). In this case, however, the City was not arguing about the strength of the evidence, but was instead arguing that there was a complete absence of evidence on critical elements of State Farm's claims. When a complete absence of evidence is alleged, the reviewing court must include the entire record within its scope of review. *See, e.g., Ford Motor Co. v. Miles,* 967 S.W.2d 377, 380 (Tex. 1998) (noting that a no-evidence point will fail if there is "any probative evidence in the entire record.").

Furthermore, neither the facts nor the evidence were truly disputed in this case; instead, the parties essentially disagreed on the legal standards that should be applied to takings and governmental nuisance claims generally. For example, the parties in this case did not dispute whether there was evidence that the City intended to damage the Bateses' home; in fact, State Farm's attorney admitted during his closing argument that the City did not intend to damage the home. Instead, the parties disputed the appropriate legal standard by which to measure the intent required to support takings claims, with State Farm arguing that liability could be predicated on the fact that the City "intentionally operated the sewer system," and the City arguing that a heightened standard of intent should apply. Similarly, the parties did not truly dispute whether there was any evidence that the City's immunity had been waived; instead, they disputed whether, as a matter of law, the City could be held liable for a nuisance even in the absence of any waiver of immunity. Consequently, the crux of the dispute was whether State Farm's claims were barred as a matter of law, and whether the trial court should therefore have granted summary judgment in the City's favor. Both parties amply supported their legal arguments with citation to relevant authority. We conclude that these issues were not waived.

Because we determine that the issues were not waived, we turn to the merits of the City's appeal. Our recent opinion in *City of Dallas v. Jennings,* 142 S.W.3d 310 (Tex. 2004), similarly dealt with a takings claim and a nuisance claim arising from a sewage backup and laid out the applicable legal standards for those claims. In that case, we held that a heightened intent standard is indeed necessary to support a takings claim, and that the mere intentional operation of a sewer system is insufficient to support liability. Specifically, we held that takings liability may arise when the governmental entity "(1) knows that a specific act is causing identifiable harm; or (2) knows that the specific property damage is substantially certain to result from an authorized government action." *Jennings,* 142 S.W.3d at 314.

In this case, there was no evidence the City possessed such knowledge; in fact, State Farm's own witnesses agreed that, at most, after "an occurrence at a certain place" there "may be a way to collect enough information to maybe predict that it's going to happen," but State Farm never alleged that such a prediction was possible in this case. Based on this record, we hold that the City did not engage in an unconstitutional taking.

Our decision in *Jennings* similarly forecloses State Farm's nuisance claim. In *Jennings,* we noted that "[a] city is immune from liability for its governmental actions unless that immunity is waived," and that "[o]peration of a sewer system is a governmental function." *Id.* (citing TEX. CIV. PRAC. & REM.CODE § 101.0215(a)(32)). We therefore concluded that "the City will not be liable for damage resulting from its operation of the sewer system without a clear waiver of governmental immunity." *Id.* We apply the same standard here, and note that

State Farm has not pointed to any applicable waiver of immunity. We therefore hold that the City of Arlington retained immunity from the nuisance claim.

For the foregoing reasons, we hold that the court of appeals erred in affirming the trial court's judgment. Pursuant to Rule 59.1 of the Texas Rules of Appellate Procedure, we grant the City's Petition for Review, and, without oral argument, render judgment that State Farm take nothing.

Notes

1. Rule 38.9 of the Rules of Appellate Procedure continues the Court adherence to liberal construction of the briefing rules.

2. *Willis v. Donnelly*, 199 S.W.2d 262 (Tex. 2006): In this breach of contract/breach of fiduciary duty case, the jury found that the Willises, shareholders in the corporations involved, had ratified the letter agreement, between the plaintiff and the corporations in question. The court of appeals held that the Willises can be held liable for breach of contract, based on this jury finding, and further held that they had waived any argument that the evidence is insufficient to support liability on the contract, based on ratification. ***Held:*** The ratification argument was preserved. As a general rule, a petitioner's complaint about the trial court's judgment must be raised in the court of appeals to preserve error in the Supreme Court. However, a party should not lose its right to appeal based on an unduly technical application of procedural rules. The Willises' opening brief (relevant portions of the brief are set forth in the opinion) in the court of appeals preserved error on this issue.

3. The Supreme Court has approved the use of a broad point of error in an appeal from the granting of a summary judgment. The Court held that a point of error alleging that "[t]he trial court erred in granting the motion for summary judgment" was sufficient to preserve error and to allow argument as to all possible grounds upon which summary judgment should have been denied. *Plexchem Int'l, Inc. v. Harris County Appraisal Dist.*, 922 S.W.2d 930 (1996); *Malooly Bros. v. Napier*, 461 S.W.2d 119 (Tex. 1970).

4. The Supreme Court has held that a court of appeals may not enter a judgment because of briefing inadequacies without first ordering the party to rebrief. *See Inpetco v. Texas American Bank*, 729 S.W.2d 300 (Tex. 1987) (per curiam) (noting that Rule 74 should be read in conjunction with TEX. R. APP. P. 83 which provides, "A judgment shall not be affirmed or reversed or an appeal dismissed for defects or irregularities in appellate procedure, either of form or substance, without allowing a reasonable time to correct or amend such defects or irregularities . . . ."). *See also* Rules 38.9 and 44.3 of the Texas Rules of Appellate Procedure.

5. The requisites for a brief in the court of appeals is now set out in TEX. R. APP. P. 38. This rule reflects a considerable change in procedure. The Texas Courts have always liberally construed the points of error presented on appeal. Now, under Rule 38(e), "The brief must state concisely *all issues or points* presented for review. The statement of an issue or point will be treated as covering every subsidiary question that is fairly included." It is understood that the appealing parties may now either state a point of error, or may, as in the federal courts, state the issue in the form of a question. This new approach should avoid declarations by the appellate courts that complaints were waived by the failure to present a sufficiently accurate point of error.

6. A sample Appellee's brief might look, in part, look like this:

Issue Presented

Question 1: Did the trial court properly hold that Section 16.068, TEX. CIV. PRAC. & REM. CODE, allowed Heritage to amend its timely filed tortious interference claim to include claims for damages resulting from contracts, which were negotiated after the suit was filed, but which could not be completed because of the original act of tortious interference?

Summary of Argument

Question 1. Limitations. Heritage sued the respondents immediately after the tortious conduct occurred. Several business transactions (Sun, Enserch, and Enron) subsequently failed, because of that tortious conduct. After the statute of limitations had run, Heritage properly amended its petition to included claims for those later transactions (Sun, Enserch, and Enron). The trial court properly found that all claims for damage accrued at the time of the tortious acts. The amended pleadings related back to the original pleadings under section 16.068, TEX. CIV. PRAC. & REM. CODE.

7. Some General Information About Briefs.

Who?: A party seeking to alter the trial court's judgment should file a brief in the court of appeals. That party is referred to as the appellant. The party seeking to preserve the judgment is the appellee. TEX. R. APP. PROC. 3.1.

What? Contents—Appellant's Brief. See TEX. R. APP. P. 38.1.

Contents—Appellee's Brief. See TEX. R. APP. P. Rule 38.2.

Length. Briefs may not exceed 50 pages, exclusive of pages containing the identity of parties and counsel, the tale of contents, the index of authorities, the statement of the case, the issues presented, the signature, the proof of service, and the appendix. A reply brief may not be longer than 25 pages, exclusive of the items stated above. The aggregate number of pages of pages of all brief filed by a party may not exceed 90 pages, exclusive of the items stated above. TEX. R. APP. PROC. sets out specifics concerning the form of the brief.

Where? The briefs are filed with the clerk of the court of appeals.

When? In an ordinary appeal: the appellant's brief is due within 30 days after the later of the date of filing of the clerk's record, or the reporter's record. The appellee's brief is due within 30 days after the date the appellant's brief is due.

In an accelerated appeal. the appellant's brief is due within 20 days after the later of the date of filing of the clerk's record, or the reporter's record. The appellee's brief is due within 20 days after the date the appellant's brief is due.

Reply briefs must be filed within 20 days after the date the appellee's brief was filed.

Extension of time may be secured by filing a motion with the court of appeals under TEX. R. APP. PROC. 10.5(b). A motion to extend time to file the brief may be filed before or after the date the brief is due.

8. *Ditta v. Conte* , --- S.W.3d ----, 52 Tex. Sup. Ct. J. 823, 2009 WL 1566989 (Tex. 2009): When the only issue is the law question of which statute of limitations applies, the court of appeals should apply the correct limitations statute even if the appellee does not file any brief. Of course, this rule does not eliminate a litigant's initial obligation to raise the statute of limitations as an affirmative defense. Further, a question is properly before this Court if it is subsidiary to, and fairly included within, an issue raised in a litigant's petition for review. This requirement is to be applied reasonably, yet liberally, so that an appellate court can reach the merits of an appeal, whenever it is reasonably possible to do so. In order to see that a just, fair, and equitable adjudication of the rights of the litigants is obtained, the Court broadly construes Petitioner's issues to encompass the core question of whether a statute of limitations should be applied at all.

vi. *Extension of Time for Late Filing of Documents in Appellate Court*

Read Rules 10.5 Texas Rules of Appellate Procedure.

Note

The appellate rules provide for a fifteen day extension of time for the filing of the notice of appeal, if the notice of appeal and motion to extend time are filed within that time. *See* Rule 26.3 of the Texas Rules of Appellate Procedure. A motion to extend the time for filing a brief may be filed before or after the brief is due. *See* Rule 38.6(d) of the Texas Rules of Appellate Procedure. In either case, Rule 10.5 states that the motion needs to contain a statement of the facts which "reasonable explain" the need for the extension. The requirement for a reasonable explanation is identical to the former rules concerning extensions of time. Thus, it is clear that the Court will adhere to its previous caselaw interpreting similar requirements of "reasonably explaining" the need for the extension or delay in filing of the appropriate document. Thus, as well be shown below, any set of factual circumstances short of conscious indifference will suffice as reasonable.

GARCIA
v.
KASTNER FARMS, INC.
774 S.W.2d 668
(Tex. 1989)

W. Michael Murray, Austin, for petitioner.
James M. Whitten, Sinton, for respondents.

RAY, JUSTICE.

The issue presented is whether Alfredo P. Garcia has reasonably explained his failure to timely file a cost bond for appeal. TEX. R. APP. P. 41(a)(2). The court of appeals held he had not and dismissed Garcia's appeal for want of jurisdiction. 761 S.W.2d 444. We reverse the judgment of the court of appeals and remand the cause to that court for further proceedings.

Garcia sued Kastner Farms, Inc. for breach of contract, and the trial court rendered judgment that Garcia take nothing. Because Garcia did not file a motion for new trial, the cost bond was due to be filed within thirty days. TEX. R. APP. P. 41(a)(1). Garcia did not file his cost bond within the thirty-day period; however, he did file a motion to extend time to file his cost bond. Garcia was late in filing his bond because he believed the cost bond could be filed after he received the trial court's findings of fact and conclusions of law. Garcia explained that he could not adequately determine the propriety or necessity of an appeal until he had received and reviewed these findings of fact and conclusions of law.

In determining whether to grant Garcia's motion, the court of appeals considered Rule 41(a)(2):

> An extension of time may be granted by the appellate court for late filing of a cost bond or notice of appeal or making the deposit required by paragraph (a)(1) or for filing the affidavit, if such bond or notice of appeal is filed, deposit is made, or affidavit is filed not later than fifteen days after the last day allowed and, within the same period, a motion is filed in the appellate court reasonably explaining the need for such extension.

The court of appeals overruled Garcia's motion and dismissed the appeal for want of jurisdiction, concluding that a misunderstanding of the law was not a reasonable explanation. 761 S.W.2d at 446. The court of appeals purported to follow the leading case of *Meshwert v. Meshwert*, 549 S.W.2d 383 (Tex. 1977), and also relied heavily on *Home Ins. Co. v. Espinoza*, 644 S.W.2d 44 (Tex. App.—Corpus Christi 1982, writ ref'd n.r.e.).

In *Meshwert*, we defined the phrase "reasonably explaining," to mean "any plausible statement of circumstances indicating that failure to file within the [required] period was not deliberate or intentional, but was the result of inadvertence, mistake or mischance." 549 S.W.2d at 384. While the definition of reasonable explanation is settled, the courts of appeals have not applied the definition consistently. Compare *Heritage Life Ins. Co. v. Heritage Group Holding Corp.*, 751 S.W.2d 229 (Tex. App.—Dallas 1988, writ denied) (holding that any conduct short of deliberate or intentional noncompliance qualifies as inadvertence, mistake or mischance—even if that conduct can also be characterized as professional negligence) with *Home Ins. Co. v. Espinoza*, 644 S.W.2d 44 (Tex. Civ. App.—Corpus Christi 1982, writ ref'd n.r.e.) (holding that failure to adequately familiarize oneself with the basic rules of appellate procedure is not a reasonable explanation).

In *Espinoza*, the attorney impliedly admitted that she was mistaken regarding the requirements under the rule, somehow having gleaned the impression that the cost bond need not be filed if a hearing on the motion for new trial is still pending. The court of appeals in *Espinoza* said that a misunderstanding of the law was not a reasonable explanation. We believe that *Espinoza* represents an unduly restrictive view of Rule 41(a)(2).

This court in *Meshwert* recognized that the reasonable explanation standard was a relaxed requirement from the old standard of good cause. 549 S.W.2d at 384. *Meshwert* followed the reasoning of the dissent in *Sloan v. Passman*, 536 S.W.2d 575 (Tex. Civ. App.—Dallas 1976, no writ) (GUITTARD, C.J., dissenting at 538 S.W.2d 1). *Sloan v. Passman* was specifically overruled by the Dallas Court of Civil Appeals in *United States Fire Ins. Co. v. Stricklin*, 547 S.W.2d 338 (Tex. Civ. App.—Dallas 1977, no writ). *Stricklin* adopted the dissenting opinion in *Sloan v. Passman*, which said that "the requirement of a reasonable explanation implies no stricter standard than that applicable to avoidance of a default judgment." 538 S.W.2d at 1. Under this standard:

> [A]ny plausible statement of circumstances indicating that failure to file . . . was not deliberate or intentional, but was the result of inadvertance, mistake, or mischance, [would] be accepted as a reasonable explanation, even though counsel or his secretary may appear to have been lacking in that degree of diligence which careful practitioners normally exercise.

Id. This liberal standard of review encompasses the negligence of counsel as a reasonable explanation for the necessity of an extension. *See Heritage Life*, 751 S.W.2d at 231-32; *Stricklin*, 547 S.W.2d at 339-40. Thus, the proper focus under *Meshwert* is on a lack of deliberate or intentional failure to comply. *See Heritage Life*, 751 S.W.2d at 232; *Meshwert*, 549 S.W.2d at 384. Any conduct short of deliberate or intentional noncompliance qualifies as inadvertence, mistake or mischance—even if that conduct can also be characterized as professional negligence. *See Heritage Life*, 751 S.W.2d at 232.

We conclude that the view espoused in *Espinoza* is too strict and that the more lenient standard enunciated in *Heritage Life* is correct. In applying the *Heritage Life* standard, we have determined Garcia's attempted late filing was not intentional or deliberate, but was due to the attorney's misunderstanding of the law. Accordingly, we hold that the explanation offered is a reasonable one within the ambit of rule 41(a)(2).

We reverse the judgment of the court of appeals and remand the cause to that court for further proceedings.

INDUSTRIAL SERVICES U.S.A., INC.
v.
AMERICAN BANK, N.A.

17 S.W.3d 358
(Tex. App.—Corpus Christi, 2000 , no pet'n)

Jim David Bickham, Austin, for Appellant.
Scott J. Duncan, Porter, Rogers, Dahlman, Gordon & Lee, Corpus Christi, for Appellee.

PER CURIAM.

This is an attempted appeal of a summary judgment granted on January 5, 2000 by the 214th District Court of Nueces County. The notice of appeal was due on February 5, 2000, and any motion to extend time for filing the notice of appeal was due on February 20, 2000. The notice of appeal was filed on February 7, 2000; no motion for extension of time to file the notice of appeal was filed.

To perfect an appeal, a notice of appeal generally must be filed within thirty days after the date the judgment is signed. TEX. R. APP. P. 26.1. A motion to extend the time to file a notice of appeal may be filed within fifteen days after the deadline for filing the notice of appeal. TEX. R. APP. P. 26.3. The motion for extension of time must contain the facts relied on to reasonably explain the need for an extension. TEX. R. APP. P. 10.5(b).

On March 8, 2000, this Court notified appellant's counsel as follows:

> Upon inspection of the clerk's record, it appears that the appeal has not been timely perfected. Pursuant to TEX. R. APP. P. 42.3, you are hereby given notice of this defect so that steps may be taken to correct the defect, if it can be done. If, after the expiration of ten days from the date of receipt of this letter, this defect is not cured, this appeal shall be dismissed.

Appellant has not responded to this notice.

In *Verburgt v. Dorner*, 959 S.W.2d 615 (Tex. 1997), the Texas Supreme Court held that "a motion for extension of time is necessarily implied when an appellant acting in good faith files a bond beyond the time allowed by Rule 41(a)(1), but within the fifteen-day period in which the appellant would be entitled to move to extend the filing deadline under Rule 41(a)(2)." *Id.* at 617. Although *Verburgt* was decided under the former rules of appellate procedure, the exception has been held applicable to the filing of the notice of appeal under the current rules. *Smith v. Houston Lighting & Power Co.*, 7 S.W.3d 287, 288 (Tex. App.—Houston [1st Dist.] 1999, no pet. h.); *Kidd v. Paxton*, 1 S.W.3d 309, 310 (Tex. App.—Amarillo 1999, no pet. h.).

However, this judicially-created implication does not extend to the requirement that the movant provide a reasonable explanation why an extension is necessary; it is still necessary to demonstrate facts that reasonably show a need to extend the time for filing the notice of appeal. *Jones v. City of Houston*, 976 S.W.2d 676, 677 (Tex. 1998) (applying the *Verburgt* rule to late-filed pauper's affidavit in lieu of appeal bond); *Smith*, 7 S.W.3d at 288-89; *Kidd*, 1 S.W.3d at 310; *Coronado v. Farming Technology, Inc.*, 994 S.W.2d 901, 901-02 (Tex. App.—Houston [1st Dist.] 1999, no pet.); *Miller v. Greenpark Surgery Center Assoc., Ltd.*, 974 S.W.2d 805, 807-08 (Tex. App.—Houston [14th Dist.] 1998, no pet.).

Appellant has failed to provide this Court with facts that reasonably show the need to extend the time for filing the notice of appeal. We hold this appeal was not timely perfected and dismiss it for want of jurisdiction.

NATIONAL UNION FIRE INS. CO.
v.
NINTH COURT OF APPEALS

864 S.W.2d 58
(Tex. 1993)

George W. Vie, III, Galveston, for relator.
E. Casey Magan, Houston, for respondent.

CORNYN, JUSTICE.

In this original mandamus proceeding, National Union Fire Insurance Company seeks relief from a January 28, 1993, order of the Ninth Court of Appeals in which it withdrew an October 15, 1992, order that had granted National an extension of time to file an electronic statement of facts. National's appeal arises from an adverse judgment in a workers' compensation action filed in Liberty County by Floyd Smith, the real party in interest. 852 S.W.2d 1. The effect of the court's January 28, 1993, order is that National has no statement of facts timely filed with the court of appeals. National argues that the court of appeals abused its discretion in withdrawing its earlier order, which allowed National an extension of time to file the statement of facts, and that it has no adequate remedy at law. We agree, and conditionally grant the writ.

The record of proceedings in the trial court, which National seeks to file with the court of appeals, consists of an electronic tape recording. This type of record is permitted by our order adopting rules for making a record of court proceedings by electronic recording in Liberty County. *See* Misc. Docket No. 91-0058, Adoption of Rules for Liberty County for Making a Record of Court Proceedings by Electronic Recording. These rules require, however, that the court recorder "shall file the statement of facts with the court of appeals within fifteen days of the perfection of an appeal or writ of error." *Id.* at p. 4. Because National perfected its appeal on September 15, 1992, its statement of facts was due by September 30, 1992. On October 14, 1992, within the fifteen days' grace period allowed for such motions by TEX. R. APP. P. 54(c), National filed its motion to extend time to file the statement of facts, and the court of appeals granted that motion on October 15, postponing National's deadline until November 17, 1992. On November 10th, however, Smith urged the court of appeals to withdraw the order extending National's deadline and to dismiss the appeal, claiming that National's October 14 motion did not reasonably explain the reason for delay. After a response by National and a reply by Smith, on January 28, 1993, the court of appeals withdrew its order of October 15, 1992, disregarding the statement of facts already filed on November 17, 1992. As a result, National has no timely filed statement of facts upon which to base its appeal. The court of appeals did not, however, dismiss the appeal.

Abuse of Discretion

TEX. R. APP. P. 54(c) provides:

> An extension of time may be granted for late filing in a court of appeals of a transcript or statement of facts, if a motion reasonably explaining the need therefor is filed by appellant with the court of appeals not later than fifteen days after the last date for filing the record.

Such motion shall also reasonably explain any delay in the request required by Rule 53(a). (emphasis added). One thing is immediately clear from the rule: the court of appeals "may" grant such a motion, but it is not required to do so. And, although we hold that the court of appeals abused its discretion, it did so not by refusing National an extension of time, but by basing its decision on an erroneous legal standard for judging the reasonableness of the movant's explanation. It would not necessarily have been an abuse of discretion to deny the extension of time; Rule 54(c) specifically makes such a decision discretionary.[3] Even "if a motion reasonably explaining the need therefor is filed," the court is not compelled to grant the motion. While a court of appeals may not grant a motion that lacks a reasonable explanation, the mere presence of a reasonable explanation does not require that the court of appeals grant the motion. Nothing in the remainder of Rule 54(c) divests the court of appeals of the discretion granted it by the word "may" in the first line.

In its opinion withdrawing its original order, the court of appeals held that National's motion was deficient because it "failed to reasonably explain the need for an extension of time for the late filing of the statement of facts in this case." 852 S.W.2d at 2. By holding that National's explanation failed to meet the standard for reasonableness in Rule 54(c), the court of appeals misapplied legal principles, and at that level committed an abuse of discretion.[4] In *Garcia v. Kastner Farms, Inc*., 774 S.W.2d 668 (Tex. 1989), we defined "reasonably explaining" in the context of TEX. R. APP. P. 41(a) as follows:

In *Meshwert* [*Meshwert v. Meshwert*, 549 S.W.2d 383 (1977)], we defined the phrase "reasonably explaining," to mean "any plausible statement of circumstances indicating that failure to file within the [required] period was not deliberate or intentional, but was the result of inadvertence, mistake or mischance." *Id.* at 669. In fact, "[a]ny conduct short of deliberate or intentional noncompliance qualifies . . . even if that conduct can also be characterized as professional negligence." *Id.* at 670. Under this generous standard, it is clear that National's explanation of its need for an extension of time qualifies as a reasonable explanation.

National's original Motion to Extend Time filed on October 14, 1992, contained ample evidence of a reasonable explanation for its need for an extension of time. National was confused about almost every element of the proper procedures that must be followed in counties authorized to make records of court proceedings by electronic recording. First, National recited the date that the judgment was signed, and from that calculated that October 19, 1992, being 120 days from that date, was the last timely date to file the statement of facts. Second, its motion related that the clerk had advised it of the fifteen-days-from-perfection deadline, but National believed the clerk to be mistaken. Third, while professing knowledge of certain rules for Harris and Dallas County, National explained that to its knowledge this court had yet to adopt rules relating to the making of a record by electronic recording for Liberty County. Fourth, National's motion explained that it needed time "so that the court reporter may transfer to this Court the certified cassette copy of the original recording of the trial proceeding." Fifth, National's motion requested an order from the court of appeals "setting out the requirements of the parties relating to any appendix and written transcription of all portions of the recorded statement of facts relevant to the error asserted." Any one of these five aspects of its motion provides a reasonable explanation under the requirements of Rule 54(c)—National was mistaken as to its obligations under this court's Adoption of Rules for Liberty County for Making a Record of Court Proceedings by Electronic Recording.

Through nine orders of this court, courts in twelve counties operate under essentially identical rules for electronic recording. There are eleven rules, the last of which specifically provides that the overall effect on the remainder of the rules of procedure should be minimal:

Other Provisions. Except to the extent inconsistent with these rules, all other statutes and rules governing the procedures in civil actions shall continue to apply to those proceedings of which a record is made by elec-

---

[3] Because the reason the court of appeals gives for its denial is a misapplication of authority from this court as to the meaning of the phrase "reasonably explains" in Rule 54(c), this mistake amounts to an abuse of discretion. Walker v. Packer, 827 S.W.2d 833, 840 (Tex. 1992).

[4] In fact, the court of appeals would have been entitled to rest its decision on discretionary grounds, but chose not to. *See* Pat Walker & Co. v. Johnson, 623 S.W.2d 306, 309 (Tex. 1981) (interpreting predecessor Rule 21(c) with identical relevant language and noting that "[b]ecause the Court of Civil Appeals has this discretion, the denial of the motion was not a ministerial act for which original mandamus will lie"). Instead, by basing its denial of an extension of time on the "if-a-motion-reasonably-explaining" clause of Rule 54(c), the court of appeals' decision must be reviewed as any other application of legal principles.

tronic tape recording. There are, however, important differences in those counties in which electronic recording is permitted, such as the elimination of the need for a stenographic record and provision for a different deadline for filing the statement of facts, calculated from perfection of the appeal and not the signing of the judgment. While we do not approve of counsel's inattention and lack of awareness of these special rules, there is no evidence that National's mistake was deliberate or intentional. Consequently, we hold that National's mistake constitutes a reasonable explanation, and the court of appeals abused its discretion by holding otherwise.

Smith argues that National's motion was further deficient in that it was not supported by either an affidavit of the court reporter or the certificate of the trial judge explaining when the statement of facts would be available for filing as required by TEX. R. APP. P. 73(i). Rule 73(i) provides: when an extension of time is requested for filing the statement of facts, the facts relied upon to reasonably explain the need for an extension must be supported by the affidavit of the court reporter, or the certificate of the trial judge, which shall include the court reporter's estimate of the earliest date when the statement of facts will be available for filing. (emphasis added). In this case, neither the court reporter nor trial judge had personal knowledge of any of the facts upon which National's explanation turned. As we have already concluded that National's own mistake as to its obligations under the special electronic recording rules suffices as a reasonable explanation, the lack of a supporting affidavit or certificate is not relevant under these facts.

No Adequate Remedy at Law

Absent mandamus, National's relief consists of proceeding through an appeal that, without a statement of facts, amounts to a useless exercise. It is difficult for a court of appeals to engage in a meaningful appellate review without the benefit of a properly filed statement of facts. In this context, it must be said that National has no adequate remedy at law. *Cf. Walker*, 827 S.W.2d at 843.

Conclusion

The Ninth Court of Appeals abused its discretion by misapplying the legal principles for interpreting the phrase "reasonably explains" in TEX. R. APP. P. 54(c). National's mistake as to its obligations under the special rules for electronic recordings in Liberty Country is a sufficient explanation under Rule 54(c). Further, as National has no adequate remedy at law, a writ of mandamus is appropriate if the Ninth Court of Appeals does not consider National's statement of facts as timely filed.

We are confident that the Ninth Court of Appeals will reconsider its decision and permit the filing of the electronic statement of facts in accordance with the views we have expressed. The clerk is instructed to issue the writ only if it does not.

Dissenting opinion by PHILLIPS, C.J., joined by GONZALEZ and ENOCH, JJ.

PHILLIPS, CHIEF JUSTICE, dissenting.

I respectfully dissent. Regardless of whether the court of appeals erred, or whether that error constituted an abuse of discretion, I believe that National Union's rights could be adequately protected through the normal appellate process.

Since mandamus is supposed to be an extraordinary remedy, we have historically used care to ensure that litigants do not make frivolous or misguided attempts to secure the writ. In our recent writings, we have emphasized that mandamus is not available where the relator has an adequate remedy by appeal, *see Walker v. Packer*, 827 S.W.2d 833, 840-44 (Tex. 1992) (and cases cited therein), and we have explained that seeking mandamus relief is never a prerequisite for obtaining full appellate review. *Id.* at 842 n. 9; *Pope v. Stephenson*, 787 S.W.2d 953, 954 (Tex. 1990).

Today's decision departs from this tenor of restraint by granting mandamus relief despite National Union's clearly adequate remedy by appeal. Assuming it does not ultimately prevail in the court of appeals, National Union could challenge that court's refusal to extend the time for filing the statement of facts by application for writ of error. How, then, could the court of appeals' ruling inflict irreparable harm justifying expedited review by mandamus?

We addressed this precise question in *Pat Walker & Co. v. Johnson*, 623 S.W.2d 306, 309 (Tex. 1981), holding that the court of appeals' refusal to extend the time for filing a statement of facts was not reviewable by mandamus because the ruling "may be addressed by this Court when properly presented in an Application for Writ of Error." I can discern no good reason for the Court's sub silentio overruling of that holding today.

The Court purportedly rests its decision on the principles of *Walker v. Packer*, 827 S.W.2d 833 (Tex. 1992). There we held that a party does not have an adequate appellate remedy from a trial court's discovery error if that error vitiates the party's ability to present a viable claim or defense to such an extent that "the trial would be a waste of judicial resources." 827 S.W.2d at 843. While imprecise, I am convinced this is as good a standard as we can articulate. But it has no application here, for at least two reasons.

First, National Union has not demonstrated that its ability to prosecute the appeal has been so severely compromised that the proceeding would truly waste judicial resources. Since National Union has not provided us with its appellate points of error, we cannot determine to what extent its appeal has been vitiated by the absence of a statement of facts. At argument, however, National Union conceded that it intends to assert at least one point of error—concerning the trial court's charge—which may be considered without a statement of facts. If National Union were to prevail on that issue, its complaint regarding the statement of facts would be moot.

Even if the court of appeals' failure to permit the filing of the statement of facts doomed National Union's chances of intermediate appellate success, however, I would not grant the writ of mandamus. However erroneous the appellate court's ruling, the delay in obtaining review in our Court by ordinary writ of error would virtually never be sufficient to justify mandamus relief. When a trial court abuses its discretion in the discovery phase of the pre-trial process, a litigant might have to wait literally years for relief. The enormous expense and delay of a full trial, requisite post-trial procedures, preparation of a full appellate record, full appellate briefing on all points, and oral argument before obtaining vindication can be of such significance as to mandate immediate attention. Our writing in *Walker v. Packer* was directed to that type of hardship.

The same circumstances are almost always lacking when the courts of appeals abuse their discretion. Errors of those courts can be reviewed through the normal writ of error process with little if any more delay, and little if any additional expense to the parties, than the mandamus action will entail. Thus, most of the writs of mandamus we have previously granted or conditionally granted against appellate courts have involved those courts' review of interlocutory trial court orders by mandamus, not errors of first impression or of review in the ordinary appellate process. *See, e.g., Scott v. Twelfth Court of Appeals*, 843 S.W.2d 439 (Tex. 1992); *Spears v. Fourth Court of Appeals*, 797 S.W.2d 654 (Tex. 1990); *Flores v. Fourth Court of Appeals*, 777 S.W.2d 38 (Tex. 1989); *Packer v. Fifth Court of Appeals*, 764 S.W.2d 775 (Tex. 1989); *Champion Int'l Corp. v. Twelfth Court of Appeals*, 762 S.W.2d 898 (Tex. 1988); *Hoffman v. Fifth Court of Appeals*, 756 S.W.2d 723 (Tex. 1988); *Stringer v. Eleventh Court of Appeals*, 720 S.W.2d 801 (Tex. 1986); *Street v. Second Court of Appeals*, 715 S.W.2d 638 (Tex. 1986); *Johnson v. Fourth Court of Appeals*, 700 S.W.2d 916 (Tex. 1985); *Jordan v. Fourth Court of Appeals*, 701 S.W.2d 644 (Tex. 1985); *Peeples v. Fourth Court of Appeals*, 701 S.W.2d 635 (Tex. 1985); *Ginsberg v. Fifth Court of Appeals*, 686 S.W.2d 105 (Tex. 1985). The cases I have found where we granted mandamus relief based on a court of appeals' error of first impression have either not addressed the critical issue of whether relator had an adequate remedy by ordinary appeal, *see Head v. Twelfth Court of Appeals*, 811 S.W.2d 570 (Tex. 1991); *Chojnacki v. First Court of Appeals*, 699 S.W.2d 193 (Tex. 1985); *Crites v. Second Court of Appeals*, 516 S.W.2d 123 (Tex. 1974), or have involved circumstances where relator clearly did not have an adequate appellate remedy. *See O'Connor v. First Court of Appeals*, 837 S.W.2d 94 (Tex. 1992) (court of appeals' refusal to allow non-panel member justice to publish dissenting opinion on motion for en banc reconsideration); *Mapco, Inc. v. Forrest*, 795 S.W.2d 700 (Tex. 1990) (refusal of court of appeals to forward application for writ of error to Supreme Court); *Doctors Hosp. Facilities v. Fifth Court of Appeals*, 750 S.W.2d 177 (Tex. 1988) (refusal of court of appeals to rule on motion for rehearing, thereby impeding Supreme Court's jurisdiction over application for writ of error); *Cowan v. Fourth Court of Appeals*, 722 S.W.2d 140 (Tex. 1987) (same). Notably, the cases on which the Court relies in finding an abuse of discretion both reached this Court through the normal appellate process, not by mandamus. *See Garcia v. Kastner Farms, Inc.*, 774 S.W.2d 668 (Tex. 1989); *Meshwert v. Meshwert*, 549 S.W.2d 383 (Tex. 1977).

The salient principle of *Walker v. Packer* was that mandamus relief should be restricted to compelling situations. Today's decision, far from being an extension of *Walker*, stands that principle on its head.

The total number of mandamus actions we passed upon in the last five years is nearly twice as great as the number during the preceding five year period. If the standards for mandamus review are not carefully confined to truly extraordinary circumstances, we risk even greater escalation of such filings. An increased diversion of appellate resources to mandamus review would, in my opinion, serve neither the bar, the litigants, nor the public.

Perhaps there are cases, where constitutional questions are implicated or rights could be irrevocably lost, that call for issuance of a conditional writ of mandamus against a court of appeals for an error committed in the ordinary appellate process. This is not such a case. I am hard pressed to think of any preliminary ruling by any lower court in Texas which, if clearly erroneous, would fail to qualify for mandamus review under today's standard. Even if this ruling is not taken as an invitation to a mandamus firesale, I see no reason to inject such uncertainty into an already cumbersome and confusing appellate structure. Therefore, I dissent.

GONZALEZ and ENOCH, JJ., join in this dissent.

Notes

1. *Hone v. Hanafin,* 104 S.W.3d 884 (Tex. 2003): To receive an extension under Rule 26.3(b), an appellant must, among other things, file a motion complying with Rule 10.5(b). TEX. R. APP. P. 26.3(b). Rule 10.5(b) requires all motions for extension of time to file a notice of appeal to set forth "the facts relied on to reasonably explain the need for an extension." TEX. R. APP. P. 10.5(b)(1)(C), (b)(2)(A).

2. On electronic recordings see: 6 MCDONALD & CARLSON **TEX. CIV. PRAC. APP. PRAC.** § 16:25 (2d ed.)

e. *Non-Suit on Appeal*

UNIVERSITY OF TEXAS MEDICAL BRANCH AT GALVESTON
v.
BLACKMON
195 S.W.3d 98
(Tex. 2006)

Greg Abbott, Attorney General of Texas, Barry Ross McBee, Edward D. Burbach, Rafael Edward Cruz, Ryan D. Clinton, Office of the Attorney General, Nichelle A. Cobb, Tort Litigation Division, Austin, for The University of Texas Medical Branch at Galveston.
Stephen A. Khoury, Kelsoe Anderson Khoury & Clark, Dallas, for The Estate of Darla Blackmom and Sheila Shultz.

PER CURIAM.

While the petitioner's interlocutory appeal from its plea to the jurisdiction was pending in the court of appeals, the respondent filed a nonsuit. We conclude that the nonsuit deprived the court of appeals of jurisdiction, and we vacate its order and dismiss this interlocutory appeal for want of jurisdiction.

Darla Blackmon died of pneumonia while incarcerated at a Texas Department of Criminal Justice substance abuse facility operated by the University of Texas Medical Branch at Galveston (UTMB). Blackmon's daughter, Sheila Shultz, brought suit for wrongful death and survival damages, claiming that UTMB negligently failed to diagnose and treat her mother's illness. Shultz alleged a waiver of sovereign immunity under the Tort Claims Act's exception for personal injury or death caused by a condition or use of tangible personal property. *See* TEX. CIV. PRAC. & REM. CODE § 101.021(2). UTMB filed a plea to the jurisdiction, which the trial court denied, and then brought an interlocutory appeal. *See id.* § 51.014(a)(8).

The court of appeals initially reversed the trial court's order and rendered judgment for UTMB, but then withdrew its judgment upon granting Shultz's motion for rehearing. Three weeks later, Shultz filed a nonsuit and moved to dismiss the appeal for want of jurisdiction. The court of appeals denied Shultz's motion, and eventually issued a new opinion denying UTMB's plea to the jurisdiction. 169 S.W.3d 712. Responding to UTMB's appeal in this Court, Shultz contends that there is no longer a case or controversy, and that her nonsuit deprived the court of appeals of jurisdiction over UTMB's appeal. We agree.

Under the Texas Rules of Civil Procedure, "[a]t any time before the plaintiff has introduced all of his evidence other than rebuttal evidence, the plaintiff may dismiss a case, or take a non-suit, which shall be entered in the minutes." TEX. R. CIV. P. 162. Rule 162 applies in this case because Shultz filed the nonsuit while this matter was pending on interlocutory appeal from UTMB's pretrial plea to the jurisdiction. Under these circumstances, the nonsuit extinguishes a case or controversy from "the moment the motion is filed" or an oral motion is made in open court; the only requirement is "the mere filing of the motion with the clerk of the court." *Shadowbrook Apts. v. Abu-Ahmad,* 783 S.W.2d 210, 211 (Tex. 1990); *see also Greenberg v. Brookshire,* 640 S.W.2d 870, 872 (Tex. 1982). While the date on which the trial court signs an order dismissing the suit is the "starting point for determining when a trial court's plenary power expires," a nonsuit is effective when it is filed. *In re Bennett,* 960 S.W.2d 35, 38 (Tex.1997); TEX. R. CIV. P. 329b. The trial court generally has no discretion to refuse to dismiss the suit, and its order doing so is ministerial. *In re Bennett,* 960 S.W.2d at 38; *Shadowbrook,* 783 S.W.2d at 211.

Of course, the trial court need not immediately dismiss the suit when notice of nonsuit is filed. Rule 162 states that the plaintiff's right to nonsuit "shall not prejudice the right of an adverse party to be heard on a pending claim for affirmative relief or excuse the payment of all costs taxed by the clerk," and a dismissal "shall have no effect on any motion for sanctions, attorney's fees or other costs, pending at the time of dismissal." TEX. R. CIV. P. 162. A claim for affirmative relief must allege a cause of action, independent of the plaintiff's claim, on which the claimant could recover compensation or relief, even if the plaintiff abandons or is unable to establish his cause of action. *BHP Petroleum Co., Inc. v. Millard,* 800 S.W.2d 838, 841 (Tex. 1990). UTMB has not raised a claim for affirmative relief, but it did request costs in its plea to the jurisdiction. Rule 162 permits the trial court to hold hearings and enter orders affecting costs, attorney's fees, and sanctions, even after notice of nonsuit is filed, while the court retains plenary power. *In re Bennett,* 960 S.W.2d at 38. Thus, the trial court has discretion to defer signing an order of dismissal so that it can "allow a reasonable amount of time" for holding hearings on these matters which are "collateral to the merits of the underlying case." *Id.* at 38-39. Although the Rule permits motions for costs, attorney's fees, and sanctions to remain viable in the trial court, it does not forestall the nonsuit's effect of rendering the merits of the case moot.

Finally, UTMB argues that a plaintiff cannot nonsuit a claim once a court has rendered a judgment on the merits. *See Hyundai Motor Co. v. Alvarado,* 892 S.W.2d 853, 854 (Tex. 1995) (holding that a nonsuit results in a dismissal with prejudice as to claims already adjudicated on partial summary judgment). In this case, however, the court of appeals withdrew its judgment for UTMB before the nonsuit was filed. As a result, the nonsuit vitiated only the trial court's interlocutory order denying UTMB's plea to the jurisdiction. That ruling favored Shultz and, consequently, its nullification did not prejudice UTMB.

The court of appeals lacked jurisdiction to issue an order and opinion on rehearing. Accordingly, without hearing oral argument, we grant the petition for review, vacate the court of appeals' order, and dismiss the appeal for want of jurisdiction. TEX. R. APP. P. 59.1, 60.2(e).

3. *The Judgment of the Court of Appeals*

Read Rules 43 and 44 Texas Rules of Appellate Procedure.

a. *Affirmance*

SEARS, ROEBUCK & CO.
v.
MARQUEZ
628 S.W.2d 772
(Tex. 1982)

Young, Taylor, Murray & Richards, Randall B. Richards, San Antonio, for petitioner.
Michael A. Chovanec, John C. Laye, Jr., and Daniel R. Rutherford, San Antonio, for respondents.

PER CURIAM.

Irene Marquez (Marquez) brought this suit against Sears, Roebuck & Company (Sears) seeking to recover damages for breach of a "Termite Control Contract and Guarantee." The trial court rendered a judgment notwithstanding the verdict in favor of Sears, ignoring the jury's verdict awarding $25,000 damages to Marquez to repair her house.

The court of appeals reviewed the evidence and agreed with the trial court's judgment that there was no legally sufficient evidence to support the jury's findings as to the existence or amount of damages. However, the court of appeals reversed the trial court, holding it erred in granting the judgment notwithstanding the verdict, and then remanded the cause in the interest of justice because: ". . . the parties are in agreement some new . . . damage occurred . . . ." 625 S.W.2d 52.

We hold that under the record and circumstances before us the court of appeals' reversal and remand in the interest of justice was not within its discretion. Under either Rule 434 or Rule 505 TEX. R. CIV. P., it is well settled that an errorless judgment of a trial court cannot be reversed in the interest of justice. *See, General Motors Corp. v. Hopkins*, 548 S.W.2d 344 (Tex. 1977); *Uselton v. State*, 499 S.W.2d 92 (Tex. 1973); Calvert, *In the Interest of Justice*, 4 ST. MARY'S L.J. 291 (1972).

An appellate court is not authorized to reverse the judgment of a trial court on the ground that the case has not been fully developed. It may only reverse for error committed at trial. *Barnum v. Lopez*, 471 S.W.2d 567 (Tex. 1971). Once an appellate court has concluded there is no evidence to support a necessary finding, it is not within its power to reverse the judgment and remand for further development of the same or similar evidence without finding some error in the judgment.

The court of appeals' failure to affirm the judgment in favor of Sears under this record conflicts with the rule in the above cited cases and Rule 434, TEX. R. CIV. P. Pursuant to Rule 483, TEX. R. CIV. P., we grant petitioner's writ of error and, without hearing oral argument, we reverse the judgment of the court of appeals and render judgment that Irene Marquez take nothing by her suit against Sears.

Note

Continental Coffee Products Co. v. Cazarez, 937 S.W. 2d 444 (Tex. 1996). The court of appeals did not err in finding some evidence to support the trial court's award of actual damages. The Court is troubled, however, by the amount of non-probative evidence cited by the court of appeals in determining that the jury's verdict was supported by factually, as well as legally, sufficient evidence. But the Court cannot determine whether the remaining probative evidence is factually sufficient. Continental and Duff have not asked the Court to remand the cause to the court of appeals for a second factual sufficiency review of the actual damages award, and the TEX. R. APP. P. 180 does not permit the Court to remand to the court of appeals for another evidentiary review in the interest of justice. Therefore, the Court affirms the award of actual damages and reverses and renders judgment that Cazarez take nothing as punitive damages.

b. *Reversal: The Ability to Render or Remand*

Note

Natural Gas Pipeline Company of America v. Pool, 124 S.W.3d 188 (Tex. 2003): For reasons of judicial economy, the Texas Supreme Court has long required that dispositive issues must be considered and resolved and that a judgment moving the case to the greatest degree of finality must be rendered. Thus, when a party presents multiple grounds for reversal of a judgment on appeal, appellate courts should first address issues that would require rendition.

DUDLEY CONSTRUCTION, LTD
v.
ACT PIPE AND SUPPLY, INC.
545 S.W.3d 532
(Tex. 2018)

Robert A. Swearingen, Byron Thompson, The Swearingen Law Firm, College Station TX, for Petitioners.

Lisa M. Norman, Robert A. Plessala, W. Jason Walker, Andrews Myers, P.C., Houston TX, for Respondent.

JUSTICE BROWN delivered the opinion of the Court.

This case presents two questions. The first is procedural: Did ACT Pipe and Supply, Inc., in defending a favorable judgment notwithstanding the jury's verdict, successfully raise a "cross-point" in the court of appeals that preserved an alternative argument proscribing the jury's original verdict? We say yes—ACT did not formally label its argument a "cross-point," but the substance of that argument, if accepted, would nonetheless vitiate the jury's original verdict. * * *

I

This appeal stems from a billing dispute between a general contractor and a pipe supplier. Dudley Construction, Ltd., the general contractor, enlisted ACT Pipe and Supply, Inc., as a supplier for two municipal water- and sewer-improvement projects: the Reclaimed Water Project in College Station and the Tabor Project in Bryan. This dispute primarily concerns the Tabor Project.

To assist Dudley in bidding for the Tabor Project, ACT's operations manager, Mark Stroud, quoted prices for the "slip-joint" pipe Dudley anticipated using for the project at $95 per unit of 36-inch and $74.53 per unit of 30-inch pipe. Dudley won the contract, and Stroud ordered the slip-joint pipe from ACT's manufacturer to lock in the quoted prices and ensure timely delivery.

After Stroud placed the order, however, the city rejected the proposed use of slip-joint pipe, insisting the project required "restrained-joint" pipe. Stroud provided Dudley a second proposal, quoting the city's preferred pipe at a more-expensive price of $109.71 per unit of 36-inch and $82 per unit of 30-inch pipe. The city approved Dudley's revised proposal, but ACT never modified the original slip-joint purchase order with the pipe manufacturer. Consequently, Dudley received slip-joint rather than restrained-joint pipe at the job site.

Dudley's project manager, Michael Ham, informed Stroud that Dudley had received the wrong pipe. Stroud advised Ham that restrained-joint pipe was available at a higher cost, but Ham insisted ACT supply the restrained-joint pipe at the same price ACT quoted for the slip-joint pipe. Dudley's owner, Richard Dudley, began working with ACT's regional manager, Curt Murray, to resolve the dispute. After reviewing the project plans, Murray told Dudley he believed that slip-joint pipe met the project's specifications and was allowed under the contract, the city's objections notwithstanding. Dudley subsequently took the position with the city that the Tabor Project contract did not specify which pipe must be used and that slip-joint pipe was adequate. The city relented, agreeing to Dudley's use of slip-joint pipe so long as it was reinforced by external restraints. Dudley agreed. Accordingly, Dudley installed the errantly ordered slip-joint pipe it had already received along with $17,500 worth of external restraints ACT supplied at no cost.

Dudley and ACT could not, however, agree on how much Dudley owed for the pipe. Dudley signed a purchase order on September 14, 2011, for the slip-joint pipe that was ultimately used at the originally quoted price of $95 and $74.53 per 36- and 30-inch unit, respectively. But after the project's completion, ACT billed Dudley for restrained-joint pipe at the second proposal's higher cost. Murray testified at trial that the parties verbally agreed to use the higher-quoted prices to offset cost reductions for pipe used in the Reclaimed Water Project. Dudley denied any such agreement, but nonetheless submitted ACT's invoices for both projects to the cities, which paid Dudley for the full amounts ACT sought. Dudley deposited these payments in its account, but citing the ongoing dispute, paid ACT nothing for either project.

ACT sued Dudley on a sworn account for $143,714.19, the total it claims Dudley owes it for the Tabor and Reclaimed Water projects. Because Dudley did not pay ACT after the cities paid Dudley the amounts due on ACT's invoices, ACT also alleged misapplication of trust funds under the Texas Construction Trust Fund Act. As to ACT's sworn-account claims, the jury found that the prices ACT charged were "in accordance with the agreement" for the Reclaimed Water Project and awarded ACT $14,214.20. For the Tabor Project, however, the jury answered that the prices ACT charged were not "in accordance with the agreement," but nonetheless awarded ACT $110,629.70 for "reasonable compensation." The jury also found ACT perfected a bond-payment claim and awarded the same damages as ACT's sworn-account claims. Finally, the jury found that Dudley misapplied trust funds under the trust-fund act but awarded no corresponding damages to compensate ACT for either project.

ACT moved for judgment notwithstanding the verdict. It urged the trial court to change the jury's answer to the sworn-account liability question for the Tabor Project. ACT argued the $110,629.70 damages award necessitated a finding that ACT had indeed charged Dudley "in accordance with the agreement." ACT also encouraged the trial court to disregard the jury's finding that it was not entitled to damages in light of the jury's finding that Dudley misapplied trust funds. ACT asked the trial court to instead substitute the $110,629.70 in damages the jury found for its sworn-account and bond-payment claims.

The trial court granted ACT's motion and issued a final judgment. In its judgment, the court set aside the jury's liability finding on ACT's sworn-account claim for the Tabor Project, instead concluding it was "conclusively proven" that the prices charged by ACT were in accordance with the parties' agreement. The trial court further found that ACT's damages were uncontroverted and conclusively proven, and substituted the jury's $110,629.50 award for the Tabor Project and $14,214.20 for the Reclaimed Water Project under the sworn-account and bond-payment claims in place of the jury's zero-damages findings for trust-fund-act damages. The judgment awarded ACT $131,823.99 in attorney's fees.

Dudley appealed on several grounds. Relevant to the case here, Dudley argued the trial court erred in rendering judgment notwithstanding the verdict on ACT's sworn-account claim because sufficient evidence supports the jury's finding that the price ACT charged for the Tabor Project was not in accordance with the parties' agreement. Dudley also argued the evidence supports the jury's zero-damages finding on ACT's trust-fund-act claim or, alternatively, that the trial court erred in awarding damages based on the amount the jury awarded for ACT's sworn-account and bond-payment claims. Finally, Dudley argues the trial court improperly awarded attorney's fees.

The court of appeals affirmed in part and reversed in part. 531 S.W.3d 744, 748 (Tex. App.—Texarkana 2016). On the claims relevant to this appeal, it agreed with Dudley that sufficient evidence supported the jury's finding that the prices ACT charged Dudley for the Tabor Project were not in accord with the parties' agreement. *Id.* at 754-55. Accordingly, the court of appeals reversed the trial court's judgment on that issue and rendered judgment that ACT take nothing on its sworn-account claim for the Tabor Project. *Id.* at 754. But it rejected Dudley's argument that the evidence supports the jury's zero-damages finding for ACT's trust-fund-act claim. *Id.* at 755 (noting Dudley cited no authority to support its argument that "there was no loss of the construction funds" as Dudley held the funds because of "a dispute between the parties due to ACT's overcharges as found by the jury").

The court of appeals concluded, however, that the trial court did not substitute "conclusively proven" trust-fund-act damages in place of the jury's zero-damages finding when it inserted the jury's $110,629.70 damages awards for the Tabor Project under ACT's sworn-account and bond-payment claims. *Id.* at 756. "From the documentation presented at trial," the court of appeals observed, "it is unclear how the jury reached its decision on the other damage questions, although it is clear that the trial court based its actions on the jury's findings to those questions." *Id.* at 756. The court of appeals therefore held that the trial court erred in determining damages for ACT's trust-fund act claim, reasoning that "it does not appear that the obligations of Dudley under any contract yielded exactly $110,629.70." *Id.*

But the court of appeals also took issue with the jury's zero-damages finding: "While the jury found zero damages, we conclude that it was conclusively proven and not really contested that there was some sum of money, more than nothing, that constituted a trust fund under the statute." *Id.* For that reason, the court of appeals reversed the trial court's judgment as to ACT's trust-fund-act damages and remanded to that court "to determine the appropriate amount of recovery." *Id.* at 754, 762.

A dissenting opinion, however, noted that ACT did not raise a cross-point on appeal asserting that the evidence did not support the jury's zero-damages finding for ACT's trust-fund-act claim as required by Texas Rule of Civil Procedure 324(c) and Texas Rule of Appellate Procedure 38.2(b)(1). In light of ACT's omission, the dissenting insisted these rules "require us to render judgment of zero damages on ACT's trust-fund cause of action." *Id.* at 762 (BURGESS, J., dissenting).

* * *

We granted Dudley's petition for review.

II

We first consider whether ACT waived its argument that the court of appeals should not enter judgment on the jury's original verdict after concluding the trial court erroneously rendered judgment notwithstanding the verdict. Like the dissenting opinion at the court of appeals, Dudley argues that two procedural rules—civil-procedure rule 324(c) and appellate-procedure rule 38.2(b)(1)—required the court of appeals to reinstate the jury's zero-damages finding after it concluded the evidence did not support the trust-fund-act damages award the trial court substituted. The rules are similar in some respects and identical in others. Texas Rule of Civil Procedure 324(c) states:

> Judgment Notwithstanding Findings; Cross-Points
>
> When judgment is rendered non obstante verdicto or notwithstanding the findings of a jury on one or more questions, the appellee may bring forward by cross-point contained in his brief filed in the Court of Appeals any ground which would have vitiated the verdict or would have prevented an affirmance of the judgment had one been rendered by the trial court in harmony with the verdict, including although not limited to the ground that one or more of the jury's findings have insufficient support in the evidence or are against the overwhelming preponderance of the evidence as a matter of fact, and the ground that the verdict and judgment based thereon should be set aside because of improper argument of counsel.
>
> The failure to bring forward by cross-points such grounds as would vitiate the verdict shall be deemed a waiver thereof; provided, however, that if a cross-point is upon a ground which requires the taking of evidence in addition to that adduced upon the trial of the cause, it is not necessary that the evidentiary

hearing be held until after the appellate court determines that the cause be remanded to consider such a cross-point.

TEX. R. CIV. P. 324(c).

Texas Rule of Appellate Procedure 38.2(b) similarly provides:

(b) *Cross–Points*.

(1) Judgment Notwithstanding the Verdict. When the trial court renders judgment notwithstanding the verdict on one or more questions, the appellee must bring forward by cross-point any issue or point that would have vitiated the verdict or that would have prevented an affirmance of the judgment if the trial court had rendered judgment on the verdict. Failure to bring forward by cross-point an issue or point that would vitiate the verdict or prevent an affirmance of the judgment waives that complaint. Included in this requirement is a point that:

(A) the verdict or one or more jury findings have insufficient evidentiary support or are against the overwhelming preponderance of the evidence as a matter of fact; or

(B) the verdict should be set aside because of improper argument of counsel;

(2) When Evidentiary Hearing Needed. The appellate court must remand a case to the trial court to take evidence if:

(A) the appellate court has sustained a point raised by the appellant; and

(B) the appellee raised a cross-point that requires the taking of additional evidence.

TEX. R. APP. P. 38.2(b).

This Court has previously articulated the upshot of these rules: "Normally, when a trial court has entered judgment notwithstanding the verdict, and an appellate court concludes that this was error, it must reverse the judgment of the trial court and enter judgment in harmony with the verdict, unless the appellee presents by cross-points grounds sufficient to vitiate the jury's verdict or to prevent an affirmance of the judgment had one been entered on the verdict." *Jackson v. Ewton*, 411 S.W.2d 715, 717 (Tex. 1967). And we have clarified the distinction between counter-points and cross-points. Counter-points "assist the appellate court in finding the answers given to the points of the appellant. From the standpoint of the advocate, their function is to show that the point or points of the opposite party are not valid." *Id.* Cross-points, on the other hand, "are really 'points' which are used to preserve error committed by the trial court. They are the means by which an appellee may bring forward complaints of some ruling or action of the trial court which the appellee alleges constituted error as to him." *Id.*

The *Jackson* court observed that Rule 324(c) serves to "require a final disposition of the case by the appellate court, where a judgment notwithstanding the verdict is erroneously rendered by the trial court, on the basis of the record before it, and to order a remand only as to questions that require the taking of additional evidence, such as jury misconduct." *Id.* at 718. This rule, and its appellate counterpart, promote judicial economy by providing for "one appeal in the case instead of two." *See id.* at 719. If an appellate court agrees with an appellant that the trial court below erroneously set aside the jury's findings and entered its own judgment, the rules have preemptively burdened the appellee to argue any alternative ground that would prevent the appellate court from restoring the jury's answers.

"Cross-points" are the rules-prescribed method for fulfilling this requirement and preserving such alternative arguments against the jury's original verdict. But we have never required rigid technical compliance with these rules. Nor do these rules themselves mandate use of particular labels; a party need not name its arguments "cross-points" to avoid waiver. Whenever possible, we reject form-over-substance requirements that favor procedural machinations over reaching the merits of a case. *See Lane Bank Equip. Co. v. Smith S. Equip., Inc.*, 10 S.W.3d 308, 314 (Tex. 2000) (HECHT, J., concurring) ("Appellate procedure should not be tricky. It should be simple, it should be certain, it should make sense, and it should facilitate consideration of the parties' arguments on the merits."); *see also* TEX. R. CIV. P. 1 ("The proper objective of rules of civil procedure is to obtain a just, fair, equitable and impartial adjudication of the rights of litigants under established principles of substantive law.").

If an appellee makes a substantive argument that would, if accepted, vitiate the jury's original verdict or prevent an affirmance of the judgment had one been rendered in harmony with the jury's verdict, it has presented a cross-point sufficient to avoid waiver. The Fourteenth Court of Appeals has modeled the correct approach, considering arguments as cross-points "even when the appellee does not explicitly refer to them as such." *JJJJ Walker, LLC v. Yollick*, 447 S.W.3d 453, 459 (Tex. App.—Houston [14th Dist.] 2014, pet. denied). If an appellee makes an argument only in response to an appellant's point of error—technically, perhaps, a "counter-point" under the *Jackson* dichotomy—appellate courts should nonetheless consider it a cross-point if, regardless of how or where it is presented, the substance of the argument would nonetheless undermine the jury's original verdict. *See Holman Street Baptist Church v. Jefferson*, 317 S.W.3d 540, 547 (Tex. App.—Houston [14th Dist.] 2010, pet. denied) ("Although [the appellee] did not explicitly term his . . . arguments as 'cross-points,' he did make . . . arguments [that would have vitiated the verdict] in response to [the appellant's] issues. We will therefore consider these arguments as cross-points and assess the merits of [the appellee's] contentions.").

Without dispute, ACT did not formally label as cross-points any of its arguments to the court of appeals. It did, however, argue in defense of the trial court's judgment notwithstanding the verdict overriding the jury's zero-damages finding for its trust-fund-act claim. And its basis for doing so was that the trial court acted properly in disregarding a finding that was against the overwhelming weight of the evidence and contrary to the jury's finding that Dudley had misapplied trust funds. ACT insisted that the "overwhelming evidence presented at trial supported entering [judgment notwithstanding the verdict]" on ACT's trust-fund-act claims. It pointed to "records subpoenaed from each city detail[ing] the amounts [Dudley] submitted in pay applications, which included the materials supplied by [ACT]." These records "included the city's approval of the payment applications and the electronic funds transfer records identifying the dates and amounts of the funds transferred to [Dudley]." Furthermore, "Mr. Dudley admitted that [Dudley] submitted and received approval from the city for pay applications that included the materials for which [ACT] is seeking recovery" and that "he received the funds for [ACT's] materials, as reflected in the city's records." And upon cross-examination, Dudley testified that "the funds he received from the city were 'widely dispersed,' but none were dispersed to [ACT]." This evidence, ACT insists, "conclusively establishes" its entitlement to damages for its trust-fund-act claim. Accordingly, ACT asked the trial court to disregard the jury's zero-damages finding and enter "the same damage amounts the jury found in response to damages questions" for ACT's sworn-account and bond-payment claims.

Dudley concedes that ACT's failure to label its argument as a "cross-point" is not fatal but insists ACT ultimately failed to preserve its argument because it substantively presented only a counter-point to Dudley's argument that the trial court improperly granted judgment notwithstanding the verdict. But ACT defends the trial court's decision precisely because it repudiates the jury's zero-damages finding. ACT's argument that "the evidence conclusively establishes ACT's entitlement to damages" and what Dudley insists it should have argued—that the overwhelming weight of the evidence is against the jury's verdict—are two sides of the same coin: to defend the judgment notwithstanding the verdict because the evidence is overwhelmingly against the jury's verdict *is* to attack the verdict. Whether *Jackson* would classify ACT's argument a "counter-point" or a "cross-point," its substance is unmistakable: the evidence commands at least some damages.

The court of appeals permissibly considered ACT's argument a "cross-point," noting that "[w]hile ACT has not explicitly set out or named any of its appellate points as 'cross-points,' it has substantively made arguments that, if accepted, vitiate the original jury verdict of zero damages." 531 S.W.3d at 756 n.16. Accordingly, it remanded the issue to the trial court "to determine the appropriate amount of recovery." *Id.* at 754, 762. Dudley argues, however, that under *Jackson* a remand is improper because "this case does not require the taking of new evidence which the parties had no opportunity to develop in the trial court." *See Jackson*, 411 S.W.2d at 718 ("The purpose of [rule 324(c)] was to require a final disposition of the case by the appellate court, where a judgment notwithstanding the verdict is erroneously rendered by the trial court, on the basis of the record before it, and to order a remand only as to questions that require the taking of additional evidence, such as jury misconduct."). On this point, we believe *Jackson*—issued more than forty years ago—may have overstated the constraints of rule 324(c) and, by implication, appellate-procedure rule 38.2(b).

Clearly, the thrust of these rules is to require appellees to present any alternative arguments that would prevent the court of appeals from reinstating the jury's verdict should it agree with the appellant that the trial court erred in rendering judgment notwithstanding the verdict. One purpose of this requirement might be to better position courts of appeals to finally dispose of cases instead of remanding them to trial courts for further proceedings. But nothing in the text of either rule compels the conclusion that a final disposition in the court of appeals is required or that a remand is always limited to instances in which new evidence must be taken. Under the circumstances here, we cannot say the court of appeals erred in remanding the case to the trial court for reconsideration of ACT's trust-fund-act damages. *See, e.g.*, *Texarkana Mem'l. Hosp., Inc. v. Murdock*, 946

S.W.2d 836, 837 (Tex. 1997) ("Because there is no evidence to support the entire amount of damages awarded by the jury, but there is legally sufficient evidence that [the defendant's] negligence caused some of the medical expenses, we reverse the judgment of the court of appeals and remand the cause for a new trial.").

We therefore affirm the court of appeals' decision on this issue and agree the case should be remanded to the trial court for further proceedings. * * *

* * *

On the issue of whether ACT preserved its argument that judgment should not be entered on the jury's verdict, we affirm the court of appeals' judgment. On the issue of the availability of attorney's fees for ACT's trust-fund-act claim, we reverse the court of appeals' judgment and render judgment that attorney's fees are unavailable. We remand the case to the trial court for further proceedings consistent with this opinion.

JUSTICE BLACKLOCK did not participate in the decision.

Notes

1. In *USAA Texas Lloyds Co. v. Menchaca,* 545 S.W.3d 479 (Tex. 2018) the supreme court addressed the issue of a remand in the interest of justice in the following words:

> Having concluded that the trial court and court of appeals erred in disregarding the jury's answer to Question 1, we are left with findings that support the judgment in Menchaca's favor based on statutory violations but that also contain a fatal conflict. We could render judgment for Menchaca based on the jury's verdict because USAA failed to preserve that conflict. In the interest of justice, however, we could also "remand the case to the trial court even if a rendition of judgment is otherwise appropriate." TEX. R. APP. P. 60.3. Such a remand is particularly appropriate when it appears that one or more parties "proceeded under the wrong legal theory," *Boyles v. Kerr*, 855 S.W.2d 593, 603 (Tex. 1993), especially when "the applicable law has . . . evolved between the time of trial and the disposition of the appeal." *Nat. Gas Pipeline Co. of Am. v. Justiss*, 397 S.W.3d 150, 162 (Tex. 2012); *see Hamrick v. Ward*, 446 S.W.3d 377, 385 (Tex. 2014) (remanding in the interest of justice "in light of our clarification of the law"); *Moriel*, 879 S.W.2d at 26 (same, in light of our "substantial clarification"). In light of the parties' obvious and understandable confusion over our relevant precedent and the effect of that confusion on their arguments in this case, as well as our clarification of the requirements to preserve error based on conflicting jury answers, we conclude that a remand is necessary here in the interest of justice.

2. Rule 43.3 of the Texas Rules of Appellate Procedure now specifically authorizes courts of appeals to reverse cases in the interest of justice. As noted above, the caselaw had recognized the ability of a court of appeals to reverse and remand in the interest of justice, rather than reverse and render, in very limited situations. It is clear that the rule change merely incorporates current caselaw, and should not be viewed as an expansion of the powers of appellate courts to remand cases for new trials, rather than rendering the judgments which should have been entered by the trial courts. It discussing the question of "the interest of justice the Dallas Court of Appeals stated:

> Having prevailed on its "no evidence" point as to attorney's fees, Gill would ordinarily be entitled to the rendition of judgment in its favor. *National Life and Accident Ins. Co. v. Blagg*, 438 S.W.2d 905, 909 (Tex. 1969); *Garza*, 395 S.W.2d at 823. However, the rules of appellate procedure authorize this court to remand for further proceedings "when it is necessary to remand . . . for further proceedings." TEX. R. APP. P. 81(c).
>
> The precursor of rule 81 was rule 434 of the rules of civil procedure.[Rule 434 required remand "when it is necessary that some matter of fact be ascertained or the damage to be assessed or the matter to be decreed is uncertain." Rule 81(c) of the rules of appellate procedure simply states that remand is allowed "when it is necessary to remand . . . for further proceedings." We consider the language of the two rules to be sufficiently similar that cases analyzing rule 434 also apply to our rule 81(c).] Under that rule, the supreme court has held that appellate courts have broad discretion to remand in the interest of justice. *Scott v. Liebman*, 404 S.W.2d 288, 294 (Tex. 1966). As early as 1911, the supreme court laid down the rule to be followed in cases where a "no evidence" point has been sustained:

> [A]s long as there is a probability that a case has for any reason not been fully developed, this court will not render judgment on the insufficiency of the evidence. In other words, it must be apparent to the court that the case has been fully developed, and that there is no probability that any other evidence can be secured before it will render judgment.

Paris and G.N.R.R. v. Robinson, 104 Tex. 482, 492, 140 S.W. 434, 439 (1911) (emphasis added*); see also Morrow v. Shotwell*, 477 S.W.2d 538, 541-42 (Tex. 1972); *City of Lucas v. North Texas Municipal Water District*, 724 S.W.2d 811, 820 (Tex. App.—Dallas 1986, writ ref'd n.r.e.); *Zion Missionary Baptist Church v. Pearson*, 695 S.W.2d 609, 613 (Tex. App.—Dallas 1985, writ ref'd n.r.e.).

> We can conceive of no case which better exemplifies the need to remand in the interest of justice than the case at bar. In this case of first impression, we have set out a rule for proving legal assistant's fees so that they are recoverable under a statute authorizing the award of attorney's fees. Because we have just enunciated this procedure, International had no reason to believe it was required to introduce the evidence we have now held necessary. Clearly, then, the case has not been fully developed as to attorney's fees.
>
> Having found error in the judgment of the trial court on the issue of attorney's fees, we possess both the power and the obligation to remand because such recourse "will subserve better the ends of justice." *Zion Missionary Baptist Church*, 695 S.W.2d at 613, *quoting Massachusetts Mutual Life Ins. Co. v. Steves*, 472 S.W.2d 332, 333 (Tex. Civ. App.—Fort Worth 1971, no writ). Accordingly, we sever International's cause of action for attorney's fees and remand same to the trial court for a determination of the reasonable amount of attorney's fees, if any, that International should recover from Gill.

Gill Savings Ass'n v. International Supply Co., Inc., 759 S.W.2d 697 (Tex. App.—Dallas 1988, writ denied).

3. As pointed out by the late Chief Justice, Robert W. Calvert, *In the Interest of Justice,* 3 ST. MARY'S L.J. 291, 292 (1972), the right to remand in the interest of justice has been recognized in Texas since, at least, the decision in *Buzard v. First National Bank*, 67 Tex. 83, 93, 2 S.W.2d 54, 59 (1886). In *Buzard,* the plaintiff's theory was that the defendants were partners, but the plaintiff failed to prove the partnership. The Court then noted that liability was possible on the theory of agency, and thus, the trial court had not considered the theory of agency. The Supreme Court remanded the case "In order that appellee (plaintiff) may take such further action in the case, by amendment or otherwise, as may be deemed proper . . . ."

In 1892, the Legislature adopted article 1771, Revised Civil Statutes of 1925, Tex. Laws. 1892, ch. 14, section 1, at 22, 10 H. GAMMEL, LAWS OF TEXAS 386 (1898), which subsequently became TEX. R. CIV. PROC. 505, giving the Supreme Court the power to "either affirm the judgment, or reverse and render such judgment as the Court of Civil Appeals should have rendered, or reverse the judgment and remand the case to the lower court, if it shall appear that the justice of the case demands another trial . . . ."

While former TEX. R. CIV. P. 434, and its later incarnations, TEX. R. APP. PROC. 80(a-c) and 81(c) (effective September 1, 1986), did not expressly grant the power to remand in the interest of justice, those courts have had that power from their inception. After the creation of the Court of Civil Appeals in 1891, the Supreme Court recognized, in *Patrick v. Smith,* 90 Tex. 267, 274, 38 S.W. 17, 21 (1896), that:

> If there be no evidence to sustain a judgment upon an issue material to a recovery, the appellate court [referring to the Court of Civil Appeals] may, in its discretion, render judgment for the appellant, or remand the cause for a new trial.

4. *Kerr-McGee v. Helton,* 133 S.W.3d 245 (Tex. 2004): While Texas Rule of Appellate Procedure 60.3, allows the Supreme Court to remand in the interest of justice, where the Court's decision does not modify any legal precept, a remand in the interest of justice cannot be justified. The fact that the Supreme Court found that the lessee's expert opinion on damages was legally incompetent, and thus no evidence does not require a remand for new trial. It is implausible to suggest, post-*Daubert/Robinson*, that parties will initially present less than their best expert evidence, in the expectation of a second chance, should their first try fail.

5. When is a reversal in the interest of justice authorized?

a. There can be no remand in the interest of justice unless there is an error in the trial court's judgment. Clearly, an appellate court cannot reverse an errorless judgment. *Davis v. Davis*, 141 Tex. 613, 175 S.W.2d 226

(1943); *Texas Employers' Ins. Ass'n v. Brandon,* 126 Tex. 636, 89 S.W.2d 982 (1936); *City of Houston v. Blackbird,* 394 S.W.2d 159 (Tex. 1965).

b. There should be a reversal in the interest of justice when a party with a meritorious claim or defense will lose the case without another opportunity to present it in the trial court. In adopting TEX. R. APP. PROC. 43.3, the courts of appeal were expressly given the power that they had possessed from the beginning. As recognized in the commentary to Rule 43.3, the new rule merely "codify current practice." While the cases discussing the power to remand in the interest of justice are not all consistent, certain situations clearly mandate the remand, while others give the court of appeals discretion to remand. After discussing the case law, Judge Calvert concluded that:

> [T]he rule is to remand wherever and when ever it appears that a party with a meritorious claim or defense will lose his case without another opportunity to present it in the trial court. There are a few cases in which the supreme court has refused to remand and, indeed, some in which it has reversed a court of civil appeals' judgment of remand, but hose cases are the exception rather than the rule, and judgment has usually been rendered only after a searching examination of the record. 4 ST. MARY'S L.J., 296.

In the early case of *Paris & G.N.R.R. v. Robinson,* 104 Tex. 482, 140 S.W. 434 (1911), this Court indicated:

> [A]s long as there is a probability that a case has *for any reason* not been fully developed, this court will not render judgment on the insufficiency of the evidence. In other words, it must be apparent to the court that the case has been fully developed, and *that there is no probability* that any other evidence can be secured before it will render judgment. 104 Tex., 482, 140 S.W., 439 (emphasis added).

c. Remand is proper to supply additional testimony, amend pleadings, or to show jurisdiction. *Associated Oil Co. v. Hart,* 277 S.W. 1043, 1045 (Tex. Comm'n App. 1925, holding approved); *Hall v. O.C. Whitaker Co.,* 143 Tx. 397, 185 S.W.2d 720 (1945) (facts not fully developed).

d. Generally, there is no remand when the trial court overturns a favorable jury verdict by entry of a judgment n.o.v. If the trial court's judgment n.o.v. is reversed, generally, judgment should be rendered on the verdict if the judgment n.o.v. is reversed. *Scott v. Liebman*, 404 S.W.2d 288, 294 (Tex. 1986); *LeMaster v. Fort Worth Transit Co.,* 138 Tex. 512, 160 S.W.2d 224 (1942); *Jackson v. Ewton,* 411 S.W.2d 715 (Tex. 1967).

e. A conscious decision to try a case one way, does not preclude a remand to try the case on a different theory. Contrary to the argument of *Oryx*, the cases indicate that an erroneous choice of legal theory, whether because of mistake of law or trial tactic, does not preclude a remand in the interest of justice. *Colbert v. Dallas Joint Stock land Bank of Dallas,* 102 S.W.2d 1031, 1036 (Tex. Com. App. 1937, opinion adopted).

f. Remand in the interest of justice requires a statement that it is a remand in the interest of justice. In *National Life & Acc. Ins. Co. v. Blagg*, 438 S.W.2d 905, 918 (Tex. 1969), this Court indicated that to remand in the interest of justice, the court of appeals must expressly state that it is doing so. It will not be inferred that a remand, rather than a rendition, is in the interest of justice: In that case Bragg had ample opportunity to develop the evidence, and conceded that in-all-likelihood no new evidence would be developed upon retrial.

> [T]he Court of Civil Appeals in this case did not remand in the interest of justice; it assigned no reason at all for remanding the cause for another trial. It is possible that the subjective intention of the court was to remand in the interest of justice, but we have no way of determining if that is so. * * * A remand under these circumstances would merely afford an opportunity for another 'bite at the apple.' *Jackson v. Ewton*, 411 S.W.2d 715 (Tex. Sup. 1967). We do not view this as a proper case in which to exercise our discretion to remand a cause in the interest of justice.

6. In the case of *Estrada v. Dillon*, 44 S.W.3d 558 (Tex. 2001) made it clear that under the Texas Rules of Appellate Procedure a remand for damages only when liability had been contested is impermissible. The Court stated: "We next consider whether the court of appeals erred in remanding the case for a new trial solely on the damages issue when Estrada and Lear Lines initially contested liability in the trial court, but did not challenge liability post-judgment or on appeal. Texas Rule of Appellate Procedure 44.1(b) provides that "[t]he court may not order a separate trial solely on unliquidated damages if liability is contested." TEX. R. APP. P. 44.1(b). If a party files a general denial in the trial court, that pleading puts a plaintiff to his or her proof on all issues, including liability; its effect extends to contesting liability in the event of remand on appeal. *See, e.g., United Savings Ass'n of Tex. v. Villanueva*, 878 S.W.2d 619, 624 (Tex. App.—Corpus Christi 1994, no writ) (remanding the issues of liability and damages in a title-to-property dispute because the defendant contested liability in the trial

court); *Little Darling Corp. v. ALD, Inc.*, 566 S.W.2d 347, 350 (Tex. Civ. App.—Dallas 1978, no writ) (holding that so long as the defendants' answer contested liability, the issues of damages and liability must be remanded). A party's failure to present on appeal an additional discrete challenge to liability when that party challenges damages does not defeat the plain language of rule 44.1(b) proscribing a separate trial on unliquidated damages when liability is contested. Estrada and Lear Lines contested liability in this case by filing a general denial and alleging in their first and second amended answers that Dillon's injuries and damages were proximately caused by his own negligence. Therefore, the court of appeals erred in remanding only the damages part of the case." The entire case was thus remanded for a new trial.

7. Remember that the appellee will be required to perfect an appeal if the party seeks to alter the trial court's judgment (Rule 25.1(c)), and must perfect a cross-point ". . . if the trial court rendered judgment notwithstanding the verdict, and the appellee seeks to present any issue or point that would have vitiated the verdict or that would have prevented an affirmance of the judgment if the trial court had rendered judgment on the verdict." Rule 38.2(b)(1).

8. TEX. R. APP. P. 38.2(b)(2) relates to the need for cross points when an evidentiary hearing is needed:

"The appellate court must remand a case tot he trial court to take evidence if:

(A) the appellate court has sustained a point raised by the appellant; and
(B) the appellee raised a cross-point that requires the taking of additional evidence."

9. *Ingram v. Deere,* 288 S.W.3d 886 (Tex. 2009): When a trial court renders judgment n.o.v., and the losing party appeals, the prevailing party may also appeal, and present points or issues on any ground that would either vitiate the verdict or preclude affirming the judgment and reinstating the verdict, including grounds not raised in the judgment n.o.v. This is an exception to the general rule that, as a prerequisite to presenting a complaint for appellate review, the record must show that the complaint was made to the trial court, and that the trial court ruled, or refused to rule, on the request.

10. *MBM Financial Corp. v. Woodlands Operating Co.*, 292 S.W.3d 660 (Tex. 2009): While the courts normally remand for a new trial when there is some evidence to support an amount of actual damages, in this case there was no evidence about the amount of damages at all. And where the record shows as a matter of law that the plaintiff is entitled only to nominal damages, the appellate court will not reverse merely to enable him to recover such damages. Accordingly, judgment is rendered that the Woodlands take nothing as damages on its breach of contract claim.

11. *Morton v. Nguyen*, --- S.W.3d ----, 2013 WL 4493799 (Tex.), 56 Tex. Sup. Ct. J. 955 (November 22, 2013): When only claim supporting attorney's fees or mental anguish is reversed, the award of those sums is also reversed.

HORROCKS
v.
TEXAS DEP'T OF TRANSP.

852 S.W.2d 498
(Tex. 1993)

Robert C. Lyon, Rowlett, for petitioners.
Edward A. Jeffords, Dan Morales, Mark Heidenheimer, Austin, for respondent.

PER CURIAM.

We consider whether an appellate court may properly render judgment on the basis of a no evidence complaint raised solely by a motion for new trial.

Police officer Jimmy Horrocks sustained permanently disabling injuries when his motorcycle struck a truck leaf spring lying on the shoulder of Interstate 20 in Grand Prairie, Texas. Horrocks and his wife Beatriz sued, alleging the State negligently failed to remove or warn of a hazardous roadway condition. Following trial, a jury determined that the spring was a "special defect" under the Texas Tort Claims Act, that the State knew or should have known of the defect, and that the State's negligence proximately caused the accident. The trial court rendered judgment on the verdict.

Although failing to challenge the sufficiency of the evidence as to its actual knowledge of the spring by objecting to jury submissions or by moving for directed verdict, for judgment notwithstanding the verdict, or to disregard jury findings, the State complained in its motion for new trial that there was no evidence to support the verdict under a premises defect theory. This motion was overruled by the trial court. The court of appeals reversed and rendered judgment for the State, holding that the truck leaf spring was not a special defect as a matter of law and that there was no evidence to support liability on a premises defect theory. 841 S.W.2d 413.

The court of appeals erred in rendering judgment based on a no evidence point preserved solely in the State's motion for new trial. Ordinarily, an appellate court should render judgment after sustaining a complaint as to the legal sufficiency of the evidence. *See National Life & Accident Ins. Co. v. Blagg*, 438 S.W.2d 905, 909 (Tex. 1969). However, in *J. Weingarten, Inc. v. Razey*, 426 S.W.2d 538 (Tex. 1968), we sustained a no evidence point but nonetheless remanded for a new trial because "we do not have before us the appellate predicate for a rendition." *Id.* at 540. Here, the State also failed to lay such a predicate.

When reversing trial court judgments, "the [appellate] court shall proceed to render such judgment or decree as the court below should have rendered . . . ." TEX. R. APP. P. 81(c) (emphasis added). Because the State requested only a new trial on the premises defect theory, that was the only relief to which it was entitled. *See, e.g., First Am. Title Co. v. Prata*, 783 S.W.2d 697, 701 (Tex. App.—El Paso 1989, writ denied); *Hebisen v. Nassau Dev. Co.*, 754 S.W.2d 345, 348 (Tex. App.—Houston [14th Dist.] 1988, writ denied); *Garland v. Vasquez*, 734 S.W.2d 92, 97 (Tex. App.—Dallas 1987, writ ref'd n.r.e.). Accordingly, pursuant to TEX. R. APP. P. 170, without hearing oral argument, a majority of this court grants the Horrocks' application for writ of error, reverses the judgment of the court of appeals and remands this case to the trial court for further proceedings in accordance with this opinion.

ENOCH, J., not sitting.

4. *The Opinion of the Court of Appeals*

Read Rule 47 Texas Rules of Appellate Procedure.

GONZALEZ
v.
MCALLEN MEDICAL CENTER, INC.

195 S.W.3d 680
(Tex. 2006)

Levon G. Hovnatanian, Martin Disiere Jefferson & Wisdom, L.L.P., John M. O'Quinn, O'Quinn Laminack & Pirtle, Houston, Jaime A. Gonzalez, Gonzalez & Associates, McAllen, David W. Holman, Godwin Pappas Langley Ronquillo, LLP, Robert Alan York, Godwin Gruber, LLP, Benjamin L. Hall III, The Hall Law Firm, and Holly Melissa Wheeler, Houston, for Petitioners.

Richard A. Sheehy, Sheehy, Serpe & Ware, P.C., Houston, Steven M. Gonzalez, Gonzales Gaytan Garza & Castillo, LLP, McAllen, Robert B. Dubose, Robert M. Roach Jr., Sean Reed Cox, Cook & Roach, L.L.P., Houston, Christopher C. Franz, The Franz Law Firm, McAllen, Charles E. Sweetman, Sweetman & Wise, Brownsville, for Respondents.

PER CURIAM.

A jury rejected the medical negligence claims brought by the family of Enrique Gonzalez against McAllen Medical Center and Dr. Jose Igoa. The plaintiffs appealed, challenging the factual sufficiency of several jury findings. The Thirteenth Court of Appeals rejected these points in a memorandum opinion, concluding in a single sentence that the evidence was factually sufficient without stating any reason why. 2003 WL 21283132, (Tex. App.—Corpus Christi 2003) (mem.op.). We agree with the plaintiffs that they are entitled to more than this, and thus reverse.

Enrique Gonzalez was voluntarily admitted to the psychiatric ward of McAllen Medical Center suffering from Alzheimer's disease. While there, another patient hit him in the face, causing him to fall and break his hip. His family sued the hospital and his treating physician. After a five-week trial, the jury answered all six liability questions in favor of the defendants.

The Gonzalez family appealed, challenging in six points the factual sufficiency of the jury's liability findings, and in a seventh the legal sufficiency of a finding that Gonzalez did not suffer a "serious, permanent, and disabling injury." The court of appeals recited the standard of review for factual sufficiency, and then concluded summarily:

> Considering the record in its entirety, we hold that appellants' factual sufficiency challenge fails because the jury's verdict was not against the great weight of the evidence. We overrule appellants' first six issues.

When the issues in a case are settled, the Texas Rules of Appellate Procedure require courts of appeals to "write a brief memorandum opinion no longer than necessary to advise the parties of the court's decision and the basic reasons for it." TEX. R. APP. P. 47.4. The opinion here does not comply with this rule because, while it advises the plaintiffs of the court's decision, it fails to articulate any reason for it.

A court of appeals must "detail the evidence . . . and clearly state why the jury's finding is factually insufficient" when reversing a jury verdict, but need not do so when affirming a jury verdict. *Compare Pool v. Ford Motor Co.*, 715 S.W.2d 629, 635 (Tex. 1986), with *Ellis County State Bank v. Keever*, 888 S.W.2d 790, 794 (Tex. 1994); *see also Citizens Nat'l Bank in Waxahachie v. Scott*, 195 S.W.3d 94 (Tex. 2006) (per curiam) (applying same principle to legal sufficiency review). Thus, neither the appellate rules nor this Court require detailed recitations of the evidence when a factual sufficiency complaint is overruled. But merely stating that it is overruled does not count as providing the "basic reasons" for that decision.

Rule 47 does not attempt to prescribe the appropriate contents of every memorandum opinion, but a court's discretion in deciding what to include should be guided by the rule's purpose. A memorandum opinion is intended primarily for the parties, who already know the background facts and procedural history. They should also be well aware of the standard of review and applicable law, as memorandum opinions are appropriate only when these are well-settled. *See* TEX. R. APP. P. 47.4. Accordingly, a memorandum opinion generally should focus on the basic reasons why the law applied to the facts leads to the court's decision.

For example, the plaintiffs here assert in their brief that the psychiatric unit was overcrowded and understaffed; the defendants respond that as the only provider in the area, the alternative to admission was turning patients out on the streets. Explaining whether reasonable jurors could discredit one or credit the other without ignoring the great weight and preponderance of the evidence should require no more words than the court of appeals expended reciting the standard of review. *Cf. Sims v. State*, 99 S.W.3d 600, 603-04 (Tex. Crim. App. 2003) (holding unpublished opinions in criminal cases "must include a discussion of the most important and relevant evidence" asserted in factual sufficiency appeals).

The plaintiffs here are entitled to a written opinion stating why the jury's verdict can or cannot be set aside. This Court has no jurisdiction of such claims, so that opinion must come from the court of appeals. Accordingly, without hearing oral argument, we reverse the court of appeals' judgment and remand for further proceedings in accordance with this opinion. *See* TEX. R. APP. P. 59.1.

LONE STAR GAS COMPANY
v.
RAILROAD COMMISSION OF TEXAS

767 S.W.2d 709
(Tex. 1989)

David C. Duggins, Clark, Thomas, Winters & Newton, Austin, for petitioners.
Jim Mattox, Atty. Gen. and Sarah F. Miller, Asst. Atty. Gen., Austin, for respondents.

PER CURIAM.

This case presents a recurring problem: the failure of the court of appeals to "address every issue raised and necessary to final disposition of the appeal." TEX. R. APP. P. 90(a). Petitioners seek a declaration that certain provisions of amended rules 30 and 34 of the Texas Railroad Commission dealing with proration and ratable take restrictions are invalid. Petitioners also seek a declaration as to the applicability of these rules to certain situations. The trial court held the rules provisions valid, within the Railroad Commission's authority to promulgate. However, the trial court dismissed the case because it concluded that the request for a declaratory judgment was not ripe. The court of appeals reversed, holding that the applicability issue is ripe for decision. However, the court of appeals refused to address the validity issue, despite the trial court's ruling, on the grounds that the trial court's "order of dismissal renders the ruling on validity mere surplusage which we will not address."

The court of appeals is obliged to "address every issue raised and necessary to final disposition of the appeal." TEX. R. APP. P. 90(a). When the court of appeals reverses the judgment of a lower court, the appeals court "shall proceed to render such judgment or decree as the court below should have rendered, except when it is necessary to remand to the court below for further proceedings." TEX. R. APP. P. 81(c). In this case, the trial court held the Railroad Commission rules provisions in issue to be valid. Notwithstanding some inconsistency in the trial court's holdings on the validity and applicability issues, the trial court's ruling on the validity issue was not "mere surplusage" and was squarely presented to the court of appeals. A holding that the rules are invalid would finally dispose of this case. A holding that the rules are valid would finally dispose of one of the two principal issues in the case. Prior to ordering a remand, points calling for rendition of judgment should be considered. *Pruitt v. Republic Bankers Life Ins. Co.*, 491 S.W.2d 109, 112 (Tex. 1973). Thus, under rule 90(a), the court of appeals was obliged to address the validity issue. Under rule 81(c), the court of appeals' duty was clear: absent a finding that further proceedings in the trial court were necessary, the appeals court should have rendered judgment that the challenged Commission rules are either valid or invalid. No purpose for remand appears in this case. The trial court would have no reason to reconsider its decision that the rules are valid. The parties neither requested the court of appeals to remand nor suggested that the evidence was not fully developed on this issue in the trial court. Therefore, the court of appeals erred in remanding the validity issue to the trial court. *See Mobil Oil Corp. v. Frederick*, 621 S.W.2d 595, 596 (Tex. 1981).

Rules 81(c) and 90(a) are mandatory. The courts of appeals are not at liberty to disregard them. These rules serve the salutary purpose of eliminating unnecessary delay and expense in the appellate process. Although the rules do not require or contemplate advisory opinions on issues not essential to the final disposition of a case, the rules do mandate full consideration of all issues raised to move the case as far as possible toward final disposition.

The court of appeals' decision in this case conflicts with rules 81(c) and 90(a). Accordingly, a majority of the Court grants petitioners' application for writ of error, and, without hearing oral argument, reverses the judgment of the court of appeals and remands the case to that court with instructions to comply with rules 81(c) and 90(a).

Notes

1. Texas Rules of Appellate Procedure allows courts of appeal to designate whether their opinions are to be published or not. The Supreme Court in *Collins v. Ison-Newsome,* 73 S.W.3d 178, (Tex. 2001) reviewed the standards by which the court of appeals should determine to publish or not publish opinions. The Supreme Court, in holding that unpublished opinions could not be used to establish "conflicts jurisdiction," stated that if the standards for publication set out in rule TEX. R. APP. P. 47.4 are carefully followed, there will likely not be many conflicts among unpublished opinions that meet the conflicts-jurisdiction standard. Unpublished opinions should be reserved for applying established law to highly fact-specific cases. If an opinion establishes a new rule of law, modifies an existing rule, applies a rule to a novel fact situation likely to recur, involves an issue of continuing public interest, criticizes existing law, or resolves a conflict, then the opinion meets the standards for publication. The standards are open to some degree of interpretation, but the guidelines they contain do suggest that rule 47.7's prohibiting citation of unpublished opinions was not designed to defeat or circumvent the Supreme Court's jurisdiction.

2. *Texas Association of School Boards, Inc. v. Bass*, 45 Tex. Sup. Ct. J. 1044, 2002 WL 1433222 (July 3, 2002): The court of appeals final disposition of a case must conform to its analysis of the case. Here, the court of appeals' final disposition of the case reversing the trial court's summary judgment for TASB does not conform to its analysis affirming summary judgment for TASB. Therefore, the judgment of the court of appeals is reversed and remanded with instructions to resolve the conflict between the court of appeals' reasoning and its judgment reversing the trial court's summary judgment in its entirety.

3. In *VanDevender v. Woods*, 222 S.W.3d 430 (Tex. 2007) Deputy Sheriff James VanDevender sought a declaratory judgment that Jefferson County and its sheriff, G. Mitch Woods, violated article III, section 52e of the Texas Constitution by failing to pay VanDevender's full salary during his second term as a deputy sheriff after he became disabled. That constitutional provision grants county law enforcement officers their "maximum salary" while they are "hospitalized or incapacitated" until their "term of office" expires. The trial court and court of appeals held that the Constitution did not entitle VanDevender to salary continuation benefits. ***Held:*** The judgment of the court of appeals is vacated, and the case is remanded to that court to address VanDevender's evidentiary arguments on causation. The court of appeals should not have reached the ultimate constitutional question, without first reviewing whether VanDevender's incapacity resulted from a job-related injury, a precondition to receiving continued salary. Judicial restraint cautions that, when a case may be decided on a non-constitutional ground, the courts should refrain from deciding the constitutional issue.

4. *Cardwell v. Whataburger Restaurants, LLC,* 484 S.W.3d 426 (Tex. 2016): P sued for on-the-job injuries and D sought to compel arbitration based on the clause in its Employee Handbook. P argued the arbitration agreement is unconscionable and illusory. The trial court denied the motion based on only some of P's unconscionability arguments and on its own research and views about arbitration. On interlocutory appeal, the Court of Appeals revered and remanded, setting out all of the parties' arguments at length but addressed only the grounds the trial court gave for its ruling. ***Held:*** Reversed and remanded to the court of appeals. The court of appeals must hand down a written opinion that addresses every issue raised and necessary to final disposition of the appeal. TEX. R. APP. P. 47.1. The court of appeals could not order arbitration without either addressing Cardwell's arguments or remanding the case to the trial court to address them.

5. *Standard for Reviewing Factual Insufficiency Points*

Notes

1. Article 5, Section 6 of the Texas Constitution provides in part:

> The state shall be divided into courts of appeals districts, with each district having a Chief Justice, two or more other Justices, and such other officials as may be provided by law . . . . Said Court of Appeals shall have appellate jurisdiction co-extensive with the limits of their respective districts, which shall extend to all cases of which the District Courts or County Courts have original or appellate jurisdiction, under such restrictions and regulations as may be prescribed by law. Provided, that the deci-

> sion of said courts shall be conclusive on all questions of fact brought before them on appeal or error. Said courts shall have such other jurisdiction, original and appellate, as may be prescribed by law.

This Constitutional provision has been interpreted as providing a general grant of appellate jurisdiction and as a limitation of the judicial authority of the courts of appeals to disturb the fact finding of the trier of facts. *See Cropper v. Caterpillar Tractor Co.*, 754 S.W.2d 646 (Tex. 1988). More specifically, the courts of appeals do not have the power to find facts [that is, to substitute its own fact finding for that of the trier of facts], but only to "unfind facts" which a judge or jury has improperly found. *See Pool v. Ford Motor Co.*, 715 S.W.2d 629 (Tex. 1986).

2. This Constitutional provision makes it clear that courts of appeals have the final jurisdiction in Texas over factual sufficiency points of error. While courts of appeals also have jurisdiction to determine legal sufficiency points of error, the Supreme Court's jurisdiction on these types of evidentiary matters is limited to legal sufficiency points of error. In discussing the distinction between "no evidence" [legal sufficiency] and "insufficient evidence" [factual sufficiency] points of error the Supreme Court has stated:

> A statement in a point of error, or in the opinion of one of our intermediate appellate courts, that the evidence is 'insufficient' to support a finding by the trier of fact is often troublesome because of its ambiguity. It can mean that the evidence is legally insufficient, i.e., there is no evidence of probative force, to support the finding in question. When that contention is made, a question of law within our jurisdiction as well as that of the Courts of Civil Appeals is presented. In deciding that question, the appellate court must consider only the evidence and the inferences tending to support the finding and disregard all evidence and inferences to the contrary. If a 'no evidence' point is sustained and the proper procedural steps have been taken, the finding under attack may be disregarded entirely and judgment is usually rendered for the appellant unless the interests of justice require another trial.
>
> On the other hand, an assertion that the evidence is 'insufficient' to support a finding of fact can mean that the evidence is factually insufficient, i.e., the evidence supporting the finding is so weak or the evidence to the contrary is so overwhelming that the finding should be set aside and a new trial ordered. When that contention is made at the appellate level, a question within the peculiar and conclusive factual jurisdiction of the Courts of Civil Appeals is presented. The intermediate court is required to consider all of the evidence in deciding the question. If the contention is sustained, the finding under attack may be set aside and a new trial ordered. Factual insufficiency of the evidence does not, however, authorize the court to disregard the finding entirely or make a contrary finding in entering final judgment for one of the parties. *See* Calvert, *'No Evidence' and 'Insufficient Evidence' Points of Error*, 38 TEX. LAW REV. 359; Garwood, *The Question of Insufficient Evidence on Appeal*, 30 TEX. LAW REV. 803; *Gulf, C. & S. F. Ry. Co. v. Deen*, 158 Tex. 466, 312 S.W.2d 933, 159 Tex. 238, 317 S.W.2d 913; *In re King's Estate*, 150 Tex. 662, 244 S.W.2d 660.

Garza v. Alviar, 395 S.W.2d 821 (Tex. 1965).

3. As well be shown in the following cases, the Supreme Court's inability to review factual insufficiency points of error has not limited its ability to review the application of the legal standard used by the courts of appeals in their review of factual insufficiency points of error.

POOL
v.
FORD MOTOR COMPANY
715 S.W.2d 629
(Tex. 1986)

Rex Houston, Wellborn, Houston, Adkinson, Mann & Sadler, Henderson, for petitioners.
Richard Grainger, Grainger, Patterson, Howard & Colley, Tyler, for respondent.

KILGARLIN, JUSTICE.

Our opinion of February 12, 1986 is withdrawn and the following is substituted.

This is a products liability action arising out of an alleged defect that caused Ronnie Pool's Ford pick-up truck to go out of control. Pool sustained serious head injuries when his truck ran off the road and collided with a tree. Pool and his wife brought this suit against Ford Motor Company alleging design and/or manufacturing defects which caused the right rear suspension system U-bolt to fall off, which, in turn, caused the accident.

The jury found that the U-bolt assembly system was defective when it left the possession of Ford Motor Company and that such defect was a producing cause of the accident. The jury failed to find that Pool was negligent in driving his pick-up while intoxicated, driving at an excessive rate of speed, in permitting his pick-up to veer off the road, or in failing to wear his seat belt. The trial court rendered judgment for Pool based on these findings and those of the jury relating to damages. The trial court subsequently ordered a remittitur of Mrs. Pool's damages for loss of future consortium and a small amount of Pool's medical expenses.

The court of appeals reversed the judgment and remanded the cause for a new trial. 688 S.W.2d 879. * * * The court also held that the jury's failure to find no contributory negligence was against the great weight and preponderance of the evidence. We affirm in part and reverse in part the judgment of the court of appeals and remand this cause to that court.

The Pools initially complain of the court of appeals' holding that the jury's failure to find that Ronnie Pool was contributorily negligent was against the great weight and preponderance of the evidence. We hold that the court of appeals committed errors of law in their review.

The court of appeals held that:

> Because statutes prohibiting driving while intoxicated and speeding are safety statutes setting minimum standards of care, the jury was not permitted to decide that either of those acts did not constitute negligence. Thus, the jury's finding that Pool was not negligent can be sustained only if there is sufficient evidence that Pool was not, in fact, intoxicated and was not, in fact, speeding at the time his vehicle left the road.

688 S.W.2d at 883. Thus, the court of appeals apparently confused negligence per se with common law negligence. The court of appeals noted that the statute in effect at that time provided for a presumption of intoxication if a person's blood alcohol level was greater than 0.10 and then noted that evidence showed Pool had a blood alcohol level of 0.119. *Id.* The court of appeals went on to find "insufficient evidence to overcome the presumption of intoxication raised by the blood test." *Id.* (emphasis added).

Similarly, the court of appeals held that another statute made Pool's speed prima facie unreasonable. *See* TEX. REV. CIV. STAT. ANN. art. 6701d, § 166 (Vernon 1977). The court stated "[w]ithout evidence of probative value rebutting excessive speed and without any evidence of emergency, incapacity, or impossibility, the statutory violation was established as a matter of law and the jury's answer must be disregarded." 688 S.W.2d at 883.

In both instances, the court of appeals misapplied the applicable statutes. The DWI statute in effect at the time of this accident did not provide for a presumption of intoxication in civil actions. Act of June 4, 1969, ch. 434, §§ 1-3, 1969 TEX. GEN. LAWS 1468-70, amended by Act of June 16, 1983, ch. 303, § 4, 1983 TEX. GEN. LAWS 1568, 1577-85. In fact, the 1971 amendment to the statute specifically provided that the presumption of intoxication would not apply in civil actions. Act of June 7, 1971, ch. 709, § 3, 1971 TEX. GEN. LAWS 2340, 2342. Thus, the court of appeals clearly erred in giving presumptive weight to Pool's blood alcohol test.

The court of appeals also apparently overlooked the statute which provides that "the provision of this act declaring maximum or minimum speed limitations shall not be construed to relieve the plaintiff in any action from the burden of proving negligence on the part of the defendant as the proximate cause of an accident." TEX. REV. CIV. STAT. ANN. art. 6701d, § 171(b) (Vernon 1977). Thus, a finding of speed in violation of the statutory limit is incomplete in a tort action when it does not include a finding of negligence. *Davis v. Gatlin*, 462 S.W.2d 54, 57 (Tex. Civ. App.—Beaumont 1970, writ ref'd n.r.e.).

As the Pattern Jury Charges note, in a civil action the key issue is the reasonableness of the speed given the circumstances, not the violation of the statutory limit. *See* 1 STATE BAR OF TEXAS, TEXAS PATTERN JURY CHARGES P.J.C. 5.02 (1970). In fact, the drafter's comment to this section explicitly states that "this submits the common law duty of the driver of a vehicle not to drive at an excessive rate of speed . . . . No issue submitting the violation of a specific speed limit is submitted because of the provision of § 171(b) of art. 6701d . . . ." *Id.*

* * *

Thus, we hold that the court of appeals erred in treating the statutory violation of the speed limit as negligence per se. Further, the court erroneously gave presumptive weight to a violation of the DWI statute.

After having found that the court of appeals applied incorrect standards in evaluating the contributory negligence allegations of speed and intoxication, we ordinarily would remand this cause to that court so that it might view factual insufficiency consistent with our instructions as to the correct standard of law.

* * *

As a further argument as to why this cause should not be remanded for factual sufficiency determination, the Pools allege that the court of appeals exercised its fact jurisdiction in such a way as to undermine the jury verdict in contravention of the constitutional guarantee of right of trial by jury. It is true that Texas Constitution article I, section 15, provides that the right of trial by jury shall remain inviolate, but it is the same Constitution in article V, section 6, that states that decisions of courts of appeals shall be conclusive on all questions of fact. The Pools' argument is not a novel one. Indeed, shortly after the 1891 adoption of the amendment creating the then courts of civil appeals and delineating their jurisdiction, this court recognized the potential constitutional conflict and sought to strike a balance. *Choate v. San Antonio & A.P. Ry. Co.*, 91 Tex. 406, 44 S.W. 69 (1898).

In essence, CHIEF JUSTICE GAINES, speaking for the court in *Choate*, wrote that it was in the province of the jury to determine questions of fact but it was in the power of courts of civil appeals to set aside the finding and to award a new trial. He stated:

> It is contrary to the genius of our institutions, as well as to the letter and spirit of every constitution ever adopted in this State, to suppose that it was ever intended to substitute the judgment of the appellate courts upon the facts of a case in place of that of the jury, and to make the determination of these courts final.

91 Tex. at 410, 44 S.W. at 70. But, *Choate*, as did so many scholarly opinions which followed, sought to harmonize the two constitutional provisions by stating that while appellate courts could not find facts, if the jury finding was so against the great weight and preponderance of the evidence, the court of appeals could unfind facts and reverse the judgment and remand the matter for a new trial. *Id.*

A case probably as often cited as any other before this court, *In Re King's Estate*, 150 Tex. 662, 244 S.W.2d 660 (1951), alluded to the seeming conflict by saying:

> But Article 5, § 6 of the Constitution, Vernon's Ann. St., is no more to be ignored than any other part of that document, and that provision, with the decisions, statutes and rules based upon it, requires the Court of Civil Appeals, upon proper assignment, to consider the fact question of weight and preponder-

ance of all the evidence and to order or deny a new trial accordingly as to the verdict may thus appear to it clearly unjust or otherwise.

150 Tex. at 666, 244 S.W.2d at 662.

Two former members of this court have provided insight into this vexing problem. JUSTICE ST. JOHN GARWOOD posited the idea of constitutional change to eliminate the reference to "facts," saying that it "is confusing at best because a court of civil appeals has no power to find facts. It may only 'unfind' facts which a jury or trial judge has improperly found." Garwood, *The Question of Insufficient Evidence on Appeal*, 30 TEXAS L. REV. 803, 813-14 (1952). Former CHIEF JUSTICE ROBERT W. CALVERT utilized the distinction between fact finding and unfinding a vital fact. He stated "[m]oreover, action by a court in 'unfinding' a vital fact is not an unconstitutional usurpation of the right of trial by jury. The same Constitution which guarantees a right of trial by jury empowers Courts of Civil Appeals finally to decide all fact questions." Calvert, *"No Evidence" and "Insufficient Evidence" Points of Error*, 38 TEXAS L. REV. 361, 368 (1960).

More recently, a current member of this court added his analysis of *In Re King's Estate*. He asserted that the holding never intended to allow courts of appeals to consider all of the facts and decide the case according to their interpretation of the evidence. *Dyson v. Olin Corp.*, 692 S.W.2d 456, 458 (Tex. 1985) (ROBERTSON, J., concurring). He stated that the courts of appeals should only exercise their fact jurisdiction to prevent a manifestly unjust result; and that those courts "are not free to reweigh the evidence and set aside a jury verdict merely because the judges feel that a different result is more reasonable." *Id.* But, JUSTICE ROBERTSON proposed no alternative interpretations to Texas Constitution article V, section 6.

While a cogent argument may be made in support of the right to hold that insufficient evidence exists to uphold a jury's affirmative finding, it becomes more difficult to rationalize why, when a jury fails to find a fact from a preponderance of the evidence, that non-finding should be set aside on a great weight and preponderance standard. That does appear to be allowing a substitution of thought processes.

Nevertheless, we do not choose to overrule *In Re King's Estate*. If a constitutional conflict exists, it remains to the electorate of this state to eliminate the conflict. Our present Constitution empowers the courts of appeals to "unfind" facts, even if they cannot "find" them. We choose to adhere to previous interpretations that harmonize the two constitutional provisions. The right of courts of appeals to review for factual insufficiency must continue undisturbed. The Pools' constitutional attack is overruled.

However, *In Re King's Estate* established that the supreme court might take jurisdiction, notwithstanding the finality of judgments of the courts of civil appeals on fact questions, in order to determine if a correct standard had been applied by the intermediate courts. A litany of subsequently decided cases, including *Puryear v. Porter*, 153 Tex. 82, 264 S.W.2d 689 (1954), *Garza v. Alviar*, 395 S.W.2d 821 (Tex. 1965), *Harmon v. Sohio Pipeline Co.*, 623 S.W.2d 314 (Tex. 1981), and culminating with *Dyson v. Olin Corp.*, serve as examples of a variety of situations in which the supreme court has reviewed factual insufficiency points because the court of appeals had utilized an incorrect test.

And even as to factual insufficiency, it has been the supreme court that has delineated the role of the courts of appeals. *In Re King's Estate* mandated those courts to consider and weigh all of the evidence in the case in determining whether the evidence is insufficient or if the verdict is so against the great weight and preponderance of the evidence as to be manifestly unjust. This court, in that opinion, recognized that in performing this task, it was not simple to describe the intellectual process to be followed by the court of appeals; how it was that there could be probative evidence to support the verdict and at the same time not be sufficient evidence. 150 Tex. at 666, 244 S.W.2d at 662.

CHIEF JUSTICE CALVERT opined that a court of appeals "should analyze the evidence on both sides of the issue, at least in a brief and general way, and point out why the finding is regarded as being contrary to the great weight and preponderance of the evidence." CALVERT, *supra*, at 368. JUSTICE GARWOOD enumerated a few of the many instances when a verdict should be set aside and a new trial granted. He cited examples of "such as to shock the conscience," "so as to be clearly unjust," "to clearly indicate bias." He suggested that in arriving at an insufficiency holding, the court of appeals "must, up to a point, follow the same kind of mental process that a jury does." GARWOOD, *supra*, at 811. Recognizing the inexact standard set for the courts of appeals, JUSTICE GARWOOD allowed that "[m]aybe some day we will develop more rules to aid trial courts and courts of civil appeals in dealing with this troublesome question." *Id.* at 812.

Our continuing review of courts of appeals decisions in which factual insufficiency points are discussed convinces us that the overwhelming majority of those opinions represent honest efforts by their scriveners to adhere to the guidelines of *In Re King's Estate*. However, there occasionally appears an opinion in which it seems that the court of appeals has merely substituted its judgment for that of the jury. Those opinions couch their holdings with the necessary "factual insufficiency" or "against the great weight and preponderance" language without providing analyses of the evidence or stating bases for the conclusions drawn. One recent opinion is particularly noteworthy in this regard. In it the court of appeals reversed a judgment on factual insufficiency grounds, saying "[t]he jury evidently believed Appellee's argument; we do not." It may well be that the court of appeals in that case and other courts in similar cases considered and weighed all the evidence before arriving at a decision of insufficiency. But, without that mental process being reflected by the opinion, it is impossible for this court to be certain that the requirements of *In Re King's Estate* have been followed.

In order that this court may in the future determine if a correct standard of review of factual insufficiency points has been utilized, courts of appeals, when reversing on insufficiency grounds, should, in their opinions, detail the evidence relevant to the issue in consideration and clearly state why the jury's finding is factually insufficient or is so against the great weight and preponderance as to be manifestly unjust; why it shocks the conscience; or clearly demonstrates bias. Further, those courts, in their opinions, should state in what regard the contrary evidence greatly outweighs the evidence in support of the verdict. It is only in this way that we will be able to determine if the requirements of *In Re King's Estate* have been satisfied.

* * *

Accordingly, we affirm in part and reverse in part the judgment of the court of appeals. We remand to that court for it to consider Ford's factual insufficiency point as to Pool's negligence and the remaining points in that court attacking the damages award as being against the great weight and preponderance of the evidence. Ford Motor Company's motion for rehearing is granted insofar as preservation of its factual insufficiency point is concerned; otherwise it is overruled.

GONZALEZ, JUSTICE, concurring [opinion omitted].

Note

Golden Eagle Archery, Inc. v. Jackson, 116 S.W.3d 757 (Tex. 2003): Jackson sued Golden Eagle, alleging that a compound hunting bow, manufactured by Golden Eagle, was defectively designed and marketed. The jury failed to find a design defect, but found that Golden Eagle did not give adequate warnings of the product's danger. A single damage question was submitted, in which the jury was permitted to award damages in six separate categories. They awarded $25,393.10 for medical care, $2,500 for physical pain and mental anguish, $2,500 for "physical impairment of loss of vision," $0 for "physical impairment other than the loss of vision," $1,500 for disfigurement, and $4,600 for loss of earnings in the past. Because the court of appeals in this case did not properly apply the standard of review set forth in *Pool v. Ford Motor Co.*, 715 S.W.2d 629, 635 (Tex. 1986), and because this Court has never before articulated the standard for factual sufficiency review when evidence pertains to more than one category of damages, the court of appeals' judgment, 29 S.W.3d 925, is reversed and remanded to that court for another factual sufficiency review. When only one category of damages is challenged on the basis that the award in that category was zero or was too low, a court should consider only whether the evidence unique to that category is so against the great weight and preponderance of the evidence as to be manifestly unjust, shock the conscience, or clearly demonstrate bias. When, as in this case, the jury's failure to find greater damages in more than one overlapping category is challenged, the court of appeals should first determine if the evidence unique to each category is factually sufficient. If it is not, the court of appeals should then consider all the overlapping evidence, together with the evidence unique to each category, to determine if the total amount awarded in the overlapping categories is factually sufficient.

In keeping with the principles that a court may not substitute its judgment for that of the jury, and that the jury is the sole judge of the weight and credibility of testimony, courts should not conclude that a jury's failure to award any damages for physical impairment is against the great weight and preponderance of the evidence simply because there is objective evidence of an injury. This does mean, however, that a verdict awarding no damages for pain and suffering should be upheld on appeal if there is objective, undisputed evidence of a significant injury, and the jury could not have compensated the injured party in some other category of damages.

CROPPER
v.
CATERPILLAR TRACTOR COMPANY

754 S.W.2d 646
(Tex. 1988)

Russell H. McMains, McMains & Constant, Corpus Christi, Pat Maloney, Law Offices of Pat Maloney, San Antonio, for petitioner.

David S. Kidder, Eugene W. Brees, II and Debora Beck McWilliams, Thompson & Knight, William Powers, Jr., Austin, for respondent.

WALLACE, JUSTICE.

In this personal injury action, we decide whether a court of appeals has the authority to remand a cause for a new trial when it concludes that a jury's failure to find in favor of a party on a particular issue is "against the great weight and preponderance of the evidence." We hold that a court of appeals has the authority to review a "failure to find" in the same manner in which it may review a jury's findings. TEX. CONST., art. V, § 6. We further hold that this review does not violate the right of trial by jury. TEX. CONST., art. I, § 15.

Anthony Paul Cropper was severely injured while operating a Caterpillar 651B Water Wagon, and brought suit against the Caterpillar Tractor Company (Caterpillar) on theories of negligence and strict products liability. The evidence at trial showed that Cropper was spraying water on an open field in order to keep the amount of dust from his employer's nearby mine at an acceptable level, and ran over the unfolded metal tracks of a backhoe tractor being repaired by another employee. After the water wagon rolled over the tracks, the impact of the wagon's cab returning to the ground forced the operator's chair to bottom out, resulting in a compression fracture of Cropper's lower back and other injuries.

The jury answered all issues favorably to Cropper, including the following defensive issue submitted at Caterpillar's request:

> Was ANTHONY CROPPER negligent in the operation of the Water Wagon on the occasion in question?
>
> ANSWER: No.

The trial court rendered judgment on the jury's verdict, awarding Cropper over $2.5 million in actual damages and assessing $250,000 in punitive damages against Caterpillar.

On appeal Caterpillar contended, among other things, that: (1) the jury's failure to find contributory negligence was against the great weight and preponderance of the evidence; (2) the evidence supporting several of the jury's findings was factually insufficient; and (3) the damages awarded by the jury were excessive and not supported by the evidence, thus authorizing the court of appeals to order a remittitur. The court of appeals reversed and remanded for new trial, sustaining the first of these contentions without passing upon the remainder of Caterpillar's points of error. 720 S.W.2d 824.

Although Cropper contends that Caterpillar waived this first contention by failing to assign it as error in its motion for new trial, we find no merit to this argument. Caterpillar contended in its motion for new trial that the jury's negative answer to the above issue was "so against the great weight and preponderance of the evidence as to be manifestly unjust"; and thereby preserved this complaint. TEX. R. CIV. P. 324. We granted Cropper's application for writ of error to consider the following questions:

> (1) when a jury refuses to find in favor of a party on a particular fact issue, and that party had the burden of proof at trial on this particular issue, is it within the authority of the court of appeals to review the jury's action in this respect and, upon concluding that the jury's "negative finding" was against the great weight and preponderance of the evidence, remand for a new trial?
> (2) if such power exists, does it violate the right of trial by jury?
> (3) if such power exists and does not violate the right of trial by jury, was that power properly exercised in this case?

Although these questions are somewhat intertwined, our initial focus is upon the source and parameters of the courts of appeals' jurisdiction over fact questions.

I.

The constitutional origin of appellate court jurisdiction over fact questions.

The Texas Constitution confers upon the courts of appeals "appellate jurisdiction . . . under such restrictions and regulations as may be prescribed by law," and further provides that "the decision of said courts shall be conclusive upon all questions of fact brought before them by appeal or error." TEX. CONST. art. V, § 6. These two clauses have independent significance, and have quite different consequences upon the allocation of jurisdiction between this court and the intermediate appellate courts. The former operates as a general grant of "appellate jurisdiction," and is in fact the only clause in Article V which purports to vest judicial authority in the intermediate courts. The latter, which will be referred to as the "factual conclusivity clause," functions not as a grant of authority to the courts of appeals but as a limitation upon the judicial authority of this court. *Choate v. San Antonio & A.P. Ry. Co.*, 91 Tex. 406, 44 S.W. 69 (1898).

In one of the earliest reported decisions of this court, we held that a court operating under a general grant of "appellate jurisdiction" had the power to review fact questions. *Bailey v. Haddy*, Dallam 376 (1841). Then, as now, the constitution provided that the right of trial by jury should remain "inviolate." REPUB. OF TEX. CONST., Ninth Declaration of Right (1836). That same constitution vested this court with "appellate jurisdiction," just as our present constitution confers such authority upon the courts of appeals. REPUB. OF TEX. CONST., art. IV, § 8. Construing the constitution and related statutes, we explicitly recognized that the grant of "appellate jurisdiction" empowered this court to review both fact and law questions, although we recognized that such powers might not exist in a common law court reviewing a jury-tried case. *Dallam* at 378. The court concluded that in a jury-tried case, its powers of review embraced those of a common law court as well as a civil law court or court of equity, subject to the restriction that the right of trial by jury should remain inviolate. *Id.; see also Republic v. Smith*, *Dallam* 407 (1841) (recognizing that the court could review both the fact and the law questions in a criminal case).

In the fifty year interval between the *Bailey* decision and the constitutional amendments of 1891, we continued to recognize that this court had the power to review jury verdicts on factual issues. Due to the court's deference to jury verdicts in general, the cases where review actually led to reversal are far less in number than the cases where we merely acknowledged this power of review. Nonetheless, they exist. The cases where this power was apparently exercised include *Hall v. Layton*, 16 Tex. 262 (1856) appeal after remand 25 Tex. 204 (1860); *Garvin v. Stover*, 17 Tex. 292 (1856); *Chandler v. Meckling*, 22 Tex. 37 (1858); *Carlton v. Baldwin*, 22 Tex. 724 (1859) appeal after remand 27 Tex. 572 (1864); *McQueen v. Fulgham*, 27 Tex. 464 (1864); *Willis v. Lewis*, 28 Tex. 185 (1866); *Weisiger v. Chisholm*, 28 Tex. 780 (1866); *Harnage v. Berry*, 43 Tex. 567 (1875); *Houston & Tex. Cent. Ry. Co. v. Knapp*, 51 Tex. 569 (1879); *Redus v. Burnett*, 59 Tex. 576 (1883); *Houston & T.C. Ry. Co. v. Schmidt*, 61 Tex. 282 (1884); *Dimmit v. Robbins*, 12 S.W. 94 (Tex. 1889); and *Missouri Pac. Ry. Co. v. Somers*, 14 S.W. 779 (Tex. 1890). In *Somers*, the court briefly summarized the nature of its authority to reverse jury verdicts on fact issues:

> Although this court has the power to review a case upon the facts, and to set aside a verdict which has evidence to support it, that power has been reluctantly exercised. But it is the right and duty of this court to set aside a verdict, when it is against such a preponderance of the evidence that it is clearly wrong.

14 S.W. at 779.

By creating the courts of appeals and vesting them with "appellate jurisdiction," the 1891 amendment to the constitution conferred upon those courts the same power over fact questions that this court exercised prior to that amendment. *Choate*, 44 S.W.2d at 69-70. Thus, the court below, in reviewing the jury's verdict in favor of Cropper, was possessed of the same powers that this court could previously exercise prior to 1891, the same powers alluded to in *Somers*. *Id.* In the exercise of those powers, the court below concluded that "the jury's finding that Cropper was not negligent in his operation of the water wagon was so contrary to the great weight of the evidence as to be manifestly unjust." 720 S.W.2d at 826. Although the court below was technically incorrect in implying that it was reviewing a jury's finding, there can be no doubt that it had the power to reverse and remand unless there is some dispositive distinction between appellate review of "findings" and appellate review of "non-findings" or "failures to find."

II.

The authority of the courts of appeal to review a "non-finding."

In *Pool v. Ford Motor Co.*, 715 S.W.2d 629 (Tex. 1986), the court recently intimated in dicta that there might be some such distinction between review of findings and nonfindings. While recognizing that the constitution empowers courts to "unfind" a jury's findings, the court observed that it was "more difficult to rationalize" why a non-finding should be reviewable under a great weight and preponderance standard. 715 S.W.2d at 634. This difference between findings and non-findings had previously been described as "a distinction which exists in semantics and theory only but which does not exist in reality." *Dyson v. Olin Corp.*, 692 S.W.2d 456, 458 (Tex. 1985) (ROBERTSON, J., concurring). If there is any inference in *Pool* that there is a distinction between review of findings and review of non-findings, we lay that question to rest.

In the fifty years of case law preceding the adoption of the 1891 constitutional amendments, this court never once indicated that it lacked the authority to review a jury's "non-finding." However, this issue could only rarely arise in those days, since so-called "non-findings" are merely the byproducts of the system of special issue submission. When cases were submitted upon general charges, as was largely the practice in the nineteenth century, the jury was called upon to make one of only two possible "findings": it either "found" for the plaintiff or "found" for the defendant. Yet, prior to 1891, when we reviewed and set aside a general verdict because the jury failed to find a particular fact, we necessarily reviewed its "non-finding" since a general verdict for either plaintiff or defendant impliedly resolved every contested issue in favor of the verdict winner. *Hardy v. DeLeon*, 5 Tex. 211 (1849); *Hamilton v. Rice*, 15 Tex. 282 (1855). It is perfectly clear that regardless of which party had the burden of proof at trial, and regardless of which party prevailed before the jury, the verdict loser had the right to assert on appeal that the jury's verdict was either not supported by the evidence or was against the great weight and preponderance of the evidence, as appropriate.

The *Somers* case demonstrates this principle. There, the plaintiff had sued his employer for an injury he received, and we had earlier set aside a jury verdict in his favor and remanded for new trial. *See* 14 S.W. 741 (Tex. 1888). On retrial, the principal dispute was whether the plaintiff had assumed the risk of injury, and the jury refused to find that he had assumed the risk. We set aside that verdict, which was based upon the jury's "non-finding" of assumption of risk, because it was "against such a preponderance of the evidence" that it was "clearly wrong." 14 S.W. at 779.

Another illustrative case is *Dimmitt v. Robbins*, 12 S.W. 94 (Tex. 1889). In that case, Robbins brought suit against Dimmitt, after his failure to pay an alleged loan. Dimmitt generally denied the indebtedness, and also alleged that any promise he had made to Robbins was vitiated by duress or fraud. It is clear that Dimmitt had the burden of proof at trial on these latter allegations. The jury returned a verdict for Robbins, rejecting Dimmit's contentions of duress and fraud. Upon reviewing the evidence, the court set aside the jury's verdict in favor of Robbins and remanded for new trial, observing that the jury's failure to find fraud and duress was "manifestly against the great weight of the testimony." 12 S.W. at 99.

In *Houston & T.C. Ry. Co. v. Schmidt*, 61 Tex. 282 (1884), the court confronted a situation where, as in the instant case, the jury had failed to find contributory negligence on the part of the plaintiff. The defendant argued on appeal that either the evidence showed that Schmidt was not injured in the manner he had alleged, or that the injury he received was the result of his own contributory negligence. 61 Tex. at 285. The court sustained both of these contentions, holding that the verdict was "contrary to the evidence" and "against the great preponderance of evidence." *Id.* at 286.

The advent of issue submission and the decline of the general charge had no effect whatsoever upon the courts of appeals' authority to review a jury's non-findings. Our adoption of issue submission through the rules has not been and should not be construed to have limited the authority of the courts of appeals to review jury-tried cases. TEX. R. CIV. P. 816. In *Parrish v. Hunt*, 331 S.W.2d 304 (Tex. 1960), we unanimously held that Article V, § 6 of the Texas Constitution required the appellate court to properly pass upon contentions that a jury's non-findings were against the great weight and preponderance of the evidence. *Id.* at 305-6. In *Traylor v. Goulding*, 497 S.W.2d 944 (Tex. 1973), we reaffirmed our holding in *Parrish*, and reversed and remanded to the court of appeals so that it could properly pass upon the plaintiff's contention that the jury's non-findings were against the great weight and preponderance of the evidence. *Id.* at 948.

More recently, we reaffirmed the existence of such authority in the courts of appeals in *Pool v. Ford Motor Co.*, 715 S.W.2d at 634. In that case, as here, the jury had refused to find that the plaintiff was contributorily negligent, and the court of appeals held that this "failure to find" was against the great weight and preponderance of the evidence. Despite language in the opinion of the court indicating some discomfort with the holding, we recognized that the court of appeals had such authority to remand the case for new trial.

In sum, we have held that regardless of the manner in which the case was submitted to the jury, the court of appeals' jurisdiction extends to all fact questions in the case, whether the jury has expressly or impliedly answered "yes" or "no" to a particular question. Given our recent tendency to favor broad issue submission, a contrary rule would be simply unworkable. Under the current practice of issue submission, defensive issues may be submitted by instruction or be otherwise combined with non-defensive issues, provided that the burden of proof is properly placed. *Lemos v. Montez*, 680 S.W.2d 798, 800 (Tex. 1984). If we countenanced this distinction between "findings" and "non-findings," we would greatly complicate the process of appellate review, since it would frequently be impossible for a court of appeals to determine whether a jury's response to such a broad issue was motivated by its reviewable "finding" or its nonreviewable "non-finding" of one or more of the sub-issues. We decline to depart from our previous holdings, or to visit such dilemmas upon the courts of appeals. We hold that the court of appeals may reverse and remand a case for a new trial when it concludes that the jury's "failure to find" is against the great weight and preponderance of the evidence.

III.

The right of trial by jury and appellate review of a jury's non-finding.

It is well established that an appellate court cannot merely substitute its judgment for that of a jury, because the court cannot exercise its constitutional authority to the detriment of the right of trial by jury, which is of equal constitutional stature. It has been suggested that when a court of appeals engages in determining whether a jury's "non-finding" is against the great weight and preponderance of the evidence, it must necessarily substitute its thought process, if not its "judgment," for that of the jury. *Pool*, 715 S.W.2d at 634. Yet, in that same opinion, we upheld the authority of the court of appeals to review such a "non-finding." *Id.*

Today, we reaffirm the holding of *Pool*. The limitations we have imposed upon the courts of appeals are more than adequate to assure that the right of trial by jury shall remain "inviolate." TEX. CONST. art. I, § 15. The historical safeguards of that right are found in the deferential standards of review applied, *see e.g., Houston & T.C. Ry. Co. v. Schmidt*, 61 Tex. 282 (1884); *Willis v. Lewis*, 28 Tex. 185 (1866); and the prohibition against rendition of judgment upon a "great weight" or "factual insufficiency" point of error, *Choate*, 44 S.W. at 69-70. Recently, we have created an additional safeguard by requiring the courts of appeals to set forth in detail the evidence in the case along with its reasons for concluding that the jury's verdict was contrary to the evidence, if it so concludes. *Pool*, 715 S.W.2d at 634-5. However, it is clear that when a court of appeals properly reaches a conclusion that a verdict is against the great weight of the evidence, it may return the case for trial before a different jury without violating the right of trial by jury.

The fact that the court of appeals might engage in "thought processes" akin to the jury's, as noted in *Pool*, does not establish a violation of the right of trial by jury. *Texas & New Orleans Ry. Co. v. Syfan*, 44 S.W. 1064 (Tex. 1898). Moreover, in light of our rejection of the so called distinction between the review of "findings" and "non-findings," our decision in *Hopson v. Gulf Oil Corp.*, 150 Tex. 1, 237 S.W.2d 352 (1951) is dispositive. In response to a contention that the appellate courts' "factual insufficiency" review of a jury's finding was unconstitutional, we said:

> Review of the jury's verdict by the Court of Civil Appeals under its jurisdiction over the facts, with reversal for want of sufficient evidence, does not amount to denial of the right to trial by jury. The Court of Civil Appeals does not and cannot substitute fact findings of its own for the findings of the jury, but in exercising its jurisdiction over the facts the Court of Civil Appeals may reverse the trial court's judgment and remand the case for another trial when it finds that the verdict is so contrary to the great weight and preponderance of the evidence as to be clearly wrong. The power thus exercised is the same as that exercised by the trial court when it sets aside the jury's verdict on account of insufficient

> evidence and awards a new trial. And this practice is not a denial of the right of trial by jury. *Choate v. San Antonio & A.P. Ry. Co.*, 91 Tex. 406, 409-410, 44 S.W. 69.

Id., 237 S.W.2d at 358; *accord Schaff v. Verble*, 240 S.W. 597, 602 (Tex. Civ. App.—San Antonio, 1922) aff'd 251 S.W. 1023 (Tex. Comm'n App. 1923, judgmt adopted).

We long ago recognized that an occasional "corrupt, biased or silly verdict is not enough for condemnation" of the jury system. *Bailey, Dallam* at 380. No one would argue that the constitutional right of trial by jury should or could be abrogated by this court, merely because the court reached the conclusion that too many juries were reaching clearly wrong decisions. It is no different to suggest that we should or could restrict or abolish the courts of appeals' constitutional authority to review fact questions, merely because there are occasional opinions that reflect too little deference to the judgment of the jury. *See Pool*, 715 S.W.2d at 635 (discussing such "occasional" opinions). The right of trial by jury and appellate court review of fact questions have peacefully co-existed for almost one hundred and fifty years, and are thoroughly rooted in our constitution and judicial system. Aside from the inescapable fact that this court cannot amend the constitution, we are not prepared to sacrifice either for the benefit of the other.

IV.

Proper exercise of appellate court review.

The court below clearly sustained Caterpillar's contentions that the jury's failure to find contributory negligence was against the great weight and preponderance of the evidence. 720 S.W.2d at 826-7. However, it is suggested that there is language in the opinion of the court of appeals indicating that it improperly found Cropper was contributorily negligent and thereby effectively foreclosed the jury's consideration of that issue on remand. The language of the opinion indicating this purported "finding" is as follows:

> A jury will have to determine, of course, the degree to which this conduct on Cropper's part contributed to cause the accident. Such a determination has not been made because that issue was contingent upon the jury's affirmative answer to the contributory negligence issue.

720 S.W.2d at 827. Cropper argues that this language establishes that the court of appeals either conclusively determined the fact of Cropper's contributory negligence, or held that Cropper was contributorily negligent as a matter of law.

We do not agree with Cropper's interpretation of the court of appeals' disposition of the case. Viewing the opinion of the court of appeals as a whole, its language in context, and its judgment that the cause should be remanded for trial, it appears that the holding of that court is that the "non-finding" of the jury is against the great weight and preponderance of the evidence. *Tippett v. Brannon*, 493 S.W.2d 511 (Tex. 1973). To the extent that the above quoted language could be viewed as settling the issue of Cropper's contributory negligence, we disapprove that language.

Cropper also argues that we should reverse the judgment of the court of appeals and remand to that court, because it failed to comply with the dictates of *Pool v. Ford Motor Company*. In *Pool*, we held that a court of appeals should "detail the evidence relevant to the issue in consideration and clearly state why the jury's finding . . . is so against the great weight and preponderance as to be manifestly unjust." 715 S.W.2d at 629. Further, we stated that the court of appeals' opinion "should state in what regard the contrary evidence greatly outweighs the evidence in support of the verdict." *Id.*

In his motion for rehearing, Cropper brought to the attention of the court of appeals certain testimony and evidence that was not referred to by the court in its opinion and which somewhat contradicted the version of the facts recited by the court in its opinion. *Cf. Garza v. Alviar*, 395 S.W.2d 821, 823 (Tex. 1965). Further, the evidence specifically referred to in Cropper's motion lent substantial support to the jury's verdict. Cropper has thus preserved his complaint that the court of appeals' opinion does not comply with the guidelines established by this court in *Pool v. Ford Motor Company*. We sustain this point of error.

The judgment of the court of appeals is reversed and the cause is remanded to that court for further consideration in light of this opinion.

ROBERTSON, JUSTICE, dissenting joined by RAY and MAUZY, JJ. [opinion omitted].

Notes

1. *In the Interest of C. H.*, 89 S.W.3d 17 (Tex. 2002): In parental termination cases, the burden of proof at trial is by clear and convincing evidence. On appeal, termination findings must be upheld, against a factual sufficiency challenge, if the evidence is such that a reasonable jury could form a firm belief or conviction that grounds exist for termination under TEX. FAM. CODE §§ 161.001 and 161.206(a).

When reversing on insufficiency grounds, the reviewing court must detail the evidence relevant to the issue of parental termination and clearly state why the evidence is insufficient to support a termination finding by clear and convincing evidence. In the interest of uniform decision-making, the Court rejects any articulation of the standard that varies from the standard announced today

While the court of appeals recited the "highly probable" standard that the Court now disavow, the recitation of an erroneous standard as harmful error in and of itself. But, because the court of appeals disregarded much of the evidence supporting the finding that termination would be in C.H.'s best interest, and failed to clearly explain why it concluded a reasonable jury could not form a firm conviction or belief from all the evidence that termination would be in C.H.'s best interest, the court of appeals has erred.

The Supreme Court does not have jurisdiction to conduct a factual sufficiency review, but we may ensure that the courts of appeals adhere to the proper legal standard of review.

2. *In the Interest of K. M. S.,* 91 S.W.3d 331 (Tex. 2002): In this suit to establish paternity, on appeal, the court of appeals "decline[d] to follow" *Texas Department of Protective & Regulatory Services v. Sherry*, 46 S.W.3d 857 (Tex. 2001), in which this Court interpreted various provisions of the Texas Family Code. The court's refusal to follow *Sherry* does not affect the disposition of this case. Nevertheless, in reaching their conclusions, courts of appeals are not free to disregard pronouncements from this Court, as did the court of appeals here. The petitions for review are denied.

3. *In the Interest of J. F. C.*, 96 S.W.3d 256 (Tex. 2002): Due process requires the application of the clear and convincing evidence standard of proof in parental termination cases. 'Clear and convincing evidence' means the measure or degree of proof that will produce in the mind of the trier of fact a firm belief or conviction as to the truth of the allegations sought to be established.

The distinction between legal and factual sufficiency, when the burden of proof is clear and convincing evidence, may be a fine one in some cases, but there is a distinction in how the evidence is reviewed. If, after conducting its legal sufficiency review of the record evidence, a court determines that no reasonable factfinder could form a firm belief or conviction that the matter that must be proven is true, then that court must conclude that the evidence is legally insufficient. Rendition of judgment in favor of the parent would generally be required, if there is legally insufficient evidence. In a factual sufficiency review, if, in light of the entire record, the disputed evidence that a reasonable factfinder could not have credited in favor of the finding is so significant that a factfinder could not reasonably have formed a firm belief or conviction, then the evidence is factually insufficient. A court of appeals should detail in its opinion why it has concluded that a reasonable factfinder could not have credited disputed evidence in favor of the finding.

In the absence of any contention that the federal constitution requires a de novo review of the evidence, the Court leaves open whether the United States Constitution requires de novo review in parental termination of rights cases, and if so, whether the standards set forth in this opinion would comport with the de novo review required by those decisions.

Statements in the Court's decision in *Garza v. Maverick Market, Inc.* 768 S.W.2d 273 (Tex. 1989), concerning review of proof (which must be by clear and convincing evidence) of a putative child in a wrongful death case where paternity is challenged, do not control when, as here, the Court is considering a constitutionally mandated clear and convincing evidence burden of proof. In the wrongful death cases, the Court had adopted the clear and convincing evidence standard, in such cases, to maintain consistency with the Legislature's choice of the clear and convincing evidence standard in connection with other legitimacy issues under the Probate Code and the Family Code. The United States Supreme Court had not mandated a clear and convincing evidence burden of proof in those cases.

4. *Bentley v. Bunton*, 94 S.W.3d 561 (Tex. 2002): The requirement of independent appellate review is a rule of federal constitutional law. The question whether the evidence in the record in a defamation case is of the convincing clarity required to strip the utterance of First Amendment protection is not merely a question for the trier of fact.

The independent review required by the First Amendment is unlike the evidentiary review to which appellate courts are accustomed in that the deference to be given the fact finder's determinations is limited. Indeed, the question whether the evidence in the record in a defamation case is sufficient to support a finding of actual malice is a question of law. On questions of law the Supreme Court ordinarily does not defer to a lower court at all. But the sufficiency of disputed evidence to support a finding cannot be treated as a pure question of law when there are issues of credibility. Here, the Court concludes that the evidence that Bunton acted with actual malice in defaming Bentley was clear and convincing. As to Gates, the Court finds that "although the issue is a close one, we hold that the evidence of Gates's actual malice was not clear and convincing."

5. *Citizens National Bank in Waxahachie v. Scott*, 195 S.W.3d 94 (Tex. 2006): This is a suit on a note. The trial court entered judgment for the plaintiffs. The court of appeals reversed and rendered judgment for the defendants, reciting the facts, and then stating only that "the evidence conclusively establishes, as a matter of law, all vital facts to support a finding of payment." ***Held:*** Reversed and remanded to the court of appeals for more detailed consideration. While memorandum opinions are intended to be brief in scope, a memorandum opinion issued by a court of appeals, advising the parties of the court's decision but failing to articulate any reason for that decision, does not comply with Texas Rule of Appellate Procedure 47.4. Additionally, when a court of appeals disturbs the judgment of a lower tribunal, merely saying that the court has reviewed all the evidence and reached a conclusion contrary to that of the trier of fact, is not enough. Instead, the court should explain, with specificity, why it has substituted its judgment for that of the trial court.

6. *In re John Doe, a/k/a Trooper*, 444 S.W.3d 603 (Tex. 2014): Rule 202 of the Texas Rules of Civil Procedure allows "a proper court" to authorize a deposition to investigate a potential claim before suit is filed, but a proper court must have personal jurisdiction over the potential defendant. The Court does not reach a due process issue.

JAFFE AIRCRAFT CORP.
v.
CARR

867 S.W.2d 27
(Tex. 1993)

John H. Martin, Deborah G. Hankinson, Beverly Ray Burlingame, Dallas, Kenneth L. Fuller, San Antonio, for petitioners.

Charles Nicholson, Warren N. Weir, Scott Roberts, San Antonio, Risley C. Triche, Napoleonville, LA, Pat Maloney, Sr., San Antonio, for respondents.

DOGGETT, JUSTICE.

In this appeal we determine that the Court of Appeals applied an incorrect legal standard in its review of the factual sufficiency of the evidence supporting a jury finding.

This action arises from the death of Nathan Carr, a passenger in a prototype aircraft, which crashed during a demonstration flight. Mary Carr, on behalf of her family and her deceased husband's estate, brought suit against the owner, Jaffe Aircraft Corporation and Jafftech Industries (Jaffe), who had purchased the prototype with the intention of developing it into a pilot-trainer for military use.

It is undisputed that immediately prior to the crash the airplane had been traveling at less than its maximum rated speed on a straight flight path when the right wing separated as the result of metal fatigue. The only contested issue at trial was the cause of this fatigue. Carr claimed negligence by Jaffe's pilot and vice-president, Forest Molberg, who had allegedly stressed the wing beyond its designated operational limits. Both Carr and Molberg were killed in the crash. Jaffe filed a general denial. The trial court entered a take nothing judgment based on the jury's answer to the question: "Did the negligence of (Jaffe) proximately cause the occurrence in question?" The Court of Appeals reversed on grounds that the jury's failure to respond affirmatively to this query "was so against the great weight and preponderance of the evidence as to be wrong and unjust and remanded the cause for a new trial." 863 S.W.2d 71, 75 (1992).

Central to our system of justice is reliance upon the factfinder to resolve disputed issues of fact. In Texas this usually means that a jury, composed of a cross section of a local community, will be entrusted with the vital responsibility to act as "the sole judges of the credibility of the witnesses and the weight to be given their testimony." TEX. R. CIV. P. 226a(III).

While it may review the factual sufficiency of the evidence supporting a jury finding to prevent a manifestly unjust result, a court of appeals may not set aside such a finding merely because the judges believe that they would have reached a different and more reasonable result had they been jurors. *Pool v. Ford Motor Co.*, 715 S.W.2d 629, 634 (Tex. 1986). To ensure that courts of appeals do not simply substitute themselves as factfinders for properly constituted juries, we have required that these courts when reversing on insufficiency grounds, should, in their opinions, detail the evidence relevant to the issue in consideration and clearly state why the jury's finding is factually insufficient or is so against the great weight and preponderance as to be manifestly unjust; why it shocks the conscience; or clearly demonstrates bias. Further, those courts, in their opinions, should state in what regard the contrary evidence greatly outweighs the evidence in support of the verdict. *Id.* at 635 (emphasis added). *See also Lofton v. Texas Brine Corp.*, 777 S.W.2d 384 (Tex. 1989). In *Cropper v. Caterpillar Tractor Co.*, 754 S.W.2d 646, 649-53 (Tex. 1988), we held that this requirement applies as fully to a court of appeals, which is reviewing the evidence in support of a jury's answer of "no" to a finding as it does when the answer is "yes." Factual sufficiency review in our intermediate courts is not a one way street. Our law must be as fair to a defendant challenging an appellate reversal of a negative jury finding as it is to a plaintiff who challenges appellate reversal of an affirmative jury finding. The court of appeals in the instant case has not satisfied this standard as reflected in our decisions.

While properly detailing evidence that Jaffe's vice-president Molberg had routinely flown the airplane over the recommended flying speed and performed high speed aerobatics for which the plane was ill-suited, the court of appeals failed to discuss thoroughly the contrary evidence supportive of the jury's negative finding on the issues of causation and negligence. Never mentioned is some of the testimony of the manufacturer, Ed Swearingen, to whom Molberg purportedly indicated that he had not exceeded the recommended flying speed and that the only aerobatics he performed were gentle ones. Persons who had previously flown with Molberg in the prototype also testified that he was an able pilot and had not engaged in any reckless behavior. Additional witnesses attested to Molberg's piloting habits and reputation as a safe and conscientious pilot, who recognized aircraft design limitations. None of this evidence is addressed by the court of appeals in its opinion, which contains only a single reference to evidence supporting the verdict.

Swearingen further suggested that occasional performance of aerobatic maneuvers would have been neither negligent nor would they have produced sufficient metal fatigue to pose a probable cause of wing failure. There was also testimony that a test pilot of a potential military trainer has a duty to determine whether the operational limits designated by the manufacturer are realistic. Having omitted any mention of the above evidence as well as any explanation of how a jury finding that considered it "is so against the great weight and preponderance as to be manifestly unjust," the court of appeals has erred. *Id.*

While this Court has a responsibility to assure that the intermediate appellate courts properly follow applicable legal standards, we lack jurisdiction ourselves to determine the factual sufficiency of evidence supporting a jury verdict. TEX. CONST. art. V, § 6. Our holding today is therefore limited to requiring that the court of appeals apply the correct legal standard in its review of the evidence; we reverse that court's judgment and remand this cause to it for further consideration in accordance with this opinion.

GONZALEZ, JUSTICE, concurring.

I join in the Court's opinion and judgment but I write separately to once again caution about the danger of our misuse of *Pool v. Ford Motor Co.*, 715 S.W.2d 629 (Tex. 1986) to circumvent our limited authority to review a factual insufficiency holding. *See Lofton v. Texas Brine Corp.*, 777 S.W.2d 384, 387 (Tex. 1989) (GONZALEZ, J., dissenting). The standard articulated by this Court in *Pool*, although legally justified, is susceptible to abuse unless exercised with the utmost caution and restraint. This Court has no constitutional authority to review a determination by the court of appeals that a jury finding is either supported by factually insufficient evidence or is against the great weight and preponderance of the evidence. Our review of such a holding is limited to determining that it was lawfully made, not whether it was decided correctly. On rare occasions, I believe that our writings have exceeded this narrow authority. *See Lofton v. Texas Brine Corp.*, 720 S.W.2d 804 (Tex. 1986) (per curiam) (remand for second factual sufficiency review); *Lofton*, 777 S.W.2d 384 (remand for third factual sufficiency review); *See also* William Powers, Jr. & Jack Ratliff, *Another Look at "No Evidence" and Insufficient Evidence*," 69 TEX. L. REV. 515, 533 (1991).

This case, however, presents a textbook example of the appropriate exercise of our responsibility to direct the court of appeals, when reversing on insufficiency grounds, to "detail the evidence relevant to the issue in consideration and clearly state why the jury's finding is factually insufficient or is so against the great weight and preponderance as to be manifestly unjust; why it shocks the conscience; or clearly demonstrates bias." *Pool*, 715 S.W.2d at 635.

* * *

With little effort, however, this Court could, in almost any case, discover some fact in the record which is not set forth in the opinion below. By labeling that fact as "material," we could reverse the judgment of the court of appeals and remand for further proceedings. The respective jurisdictions of the courts of appeals and of this Court are best preserved when we exercise this power sparingly. With that caveat, I join in the opinion of the Court and in the judgment.

6. Clear and Convincing Evidence Review

Notes

1. *Southwestern Bell Telephone v. Garza*, 164 S.W.3d 607 (Tex. 2004): In this action for a violation of the Anti-Retaliation Law, TEX. LAB. CODE § 451.001(1), the jury found that SWBT acted with actual malice in harming the plaintiff, and awarded exemplary damages. ***Held:*** The award of exemplary damages is reversed. Under the evidence [detailed in the opinion] a reasonable trier of fact could not have formed a firm belief or conviction that SWBT acted toward Garza with ill will, spite, evil motive, or purposeful injury. While there are some indications that it might have done so, there are a great many others that it did not. An elevated standard of proof at trial—here, clear and convincing evidence—requires a correspondingly elevated standard of evidentiary review on appeal. In a legal sufficiency review, a court should look at all the evidence in the light most favorable to the finding to determine whether a reasonable trier of fact could have formed a firm belief or conviction that its finding was true. To give appropriate deference to the fact finder's conclusions, and the role of a court conducting a legal sufficiency review, looking at the evidence in the light most favorable to the judgment means that a reviewing court must assume that the factfinder resolved disputed facts in favor of its finding, if a reasonable factfinder could do so. A corollary to this requirement is that a court should disregard all evidence that a reasonable factfinder could have disbelieved or found to have been incredible. This does not mean that a court must disregard all evidence that does not support the finding. Disregarding undisputed facts that do not support the finding could skew the analysis of whether there is clear and convincing evidence. If, after conducting its legal sufficiency review of the record evidence, a court determines that no reasonable factfinder could form a firm belief or conviction that the matter that must be proven is true, then that court must conclude that the evidence is legally insufficient.

2. *In the Interest of S.M.R.*, 434 S.W.3d 576 (Tex. 2014): An appeals court, in reviewing factual-sufficiency of a parental-rights termination, must thoroughly review the entire record, but need not detail all evidence when it affirms the judgment. When the reviewing court affirms the jury verdict, the risk that the court has usurped the role of the jury disappears.

Specifically, in proceedings to terminate the parent-child relationship under Family Code section 161.001, the petitioner is required to establish one or more of the acts or omissions enumerated under subdivision (1) of the statute and must also prove that termination is in the best interest of the child. Proof under each subsection must be satisfied by clear and convincing evidence and termination may not be based solely on the best interest of the child, as determined by the trier of fact.

7. *Remittitur in the Court of Appeals*

Read Rule 46 Texas Rules of Appellate Procedure.

ROSE
v.
DOCTORS HOSP.
801 S.W.2d 841
(Tex. 1990)

Douglas D. Mulder, John H. Hagler, Ronald D. Krist, W. James Kronzer, Houston, for petitioners.

R. Brent Cooper, Robert A. Gwinn, Kenneth C. Stone, Michael W. Huddleston, Dallas, C.J. Francisco, Austin, for respondents.

COOK, JUSTICE.

The motions for rehearing are granted in part and overruled in part. This court's opinion and judgment of September 6, 1990, are withdrawn, and the following is substituted in its place.

In this case, we once again consider the constitutionality of the damages provisions of the Medical Liability and Insurance Improvement Act, TEX. REV. CIV. STAT. ANN. art. 4590i, §§ 11.02 and 11.03 (Vernon Supp. 1991) ("Medical Liability Act"), this time in the context of a wrongful death action. The court of appeals decided that the statutory damages limitations provisions are constitutional. 735 S.W.2d 244.[1] We decided subsequently to the court of appeals opinion that statutory damages limitations are unconstitutional when applied to damages in common law medical malpractice actions. *Lucas v. United States*, 757 S.W.2d 687, 692 (Tex. 1988). Our holding in *Lucas*, however, did not extend to wrongful death actions. We now hold that the legislature may, through the Medical Liability Act, constitutionally curtail damages in wrongful death actions.

The case also presents procedural issues. We are asked to decide whether a remittitur becomes fatally defective when the party filing it in the court of appeals reserves the right to complain of the standard used in arriving at the remittitur. If such a remittitur is not defective, we must consider whether, in this particular case, the court of appeals did apply the wrong standard in arriving at the remittitur. We hold that a remittitur filed in the court of appeals is unaffected by a reservation of the right to appeal the standard used in arriving at the remittitur. We further hold that the court of appeals applied the correct standard in arriving at the remittiturs in this case.

I. FACTS

The convoluted history of this case is partly explained in the original opinion of the court of appeals and in our opinion on application for writ of mandamus. 735 S.W.2d 244; 750 S.W.2d 177. For purposes of this opinion, we confine ourselves to a summary of the circumstances which brought to this court the issues we must decide today.

Rex Rose was admitted to Doctors Hospital and died there the next day. His widow, Lisa Beth, and his parents, Alton and Frances, brought a wrongful death action against the hospital, contending that Rex Rose had received a fatal dose of morphine while a patient at the hospital. The jury awarded $2,825,000 to Lisa Beth

[1] The court of appeals reversed the trial court's judgment notwithstanding the verdict and rendered judgment for the Roses subject to suggested remittiturs. The Roses filed remittiturs in the amounts suggested by the court, but they reserved the right to complain of having been erroneously required to do so. Doctors Hospital then filed a motion for rehearing complaining of the court of appeals' reversal and rendition; the hospital claimed the court of appeals should have remanded for a new trial since the remittiturs had been conditionally filed. The court of appeals agreed, and wrote an unpublished opinion which remanded the cause for a new trial. The Roses and the hospital filed applications for writ of error complaining of all opinions written by the court of appeals. Our opinion in this case addresses the issues in all court of appeals opinions.

Rose and $815,000 each to Alton and Frances Rose, but the trial court rendered judgment notwithstanding the verdict.

The court of appeals reversed, holding that there was some evidence that the hospital caused Rex Rose's death. The court did, however, suggest remittiturs to reduce the damages awarded by the jury. Lisa Beth Rose's damages were reduced in accordance with s 11.02 of the Medical Liability Act. The court suggested a remittitur reducing Alton and Frances Rose's damages to the amount supported by the evidence.

The Roses responded by filing remittiturs within the time period prescribed by the court of appeals. However, the Roses expressly reserved the right to complain of the ruling requiring the remittiturs.

The Roses argue that the court of appeals was prohibited by the Texas Constitution and our decision in Lucas from reducing the damages awarded to Lisa Beth Rose. They also contend that the court of appeals applied an erroneous standard in reviewing the evidence to arrive at the remittitur. Doctors Hospital complains that the Roses filed a "conditional" remittitur, one which was defective because it amounted to a non-acceptance of the judgment of the court of appeals. We address each issue in turn.

* * *

The Medical Liability Act delineates the interests of the state in a list of purposes found at the beginning of the statute. TEX. REV. CIV. STAT. art. 4590i, § 1.02(b) (Vernon Supp. 1991). These purposes include the reduction of excessive severity of health care liability claims, decreasing the cost of those claims, making insurance at reasonably affordable rates available to health care providers, and making affordable health care more accessible and available to the public. *Id.* The method by which the legislature chose to effect those purposes is outlined in §§ 11.02 and 11.03, the damages provisions. The damages provisions rationally relate to the interests of the state as stated in the statute's list of purposes. The statute, therefore, does not violate equal protection.

* * *

The remittitur dispute in this case highlights opposing perceptions of the nature and purpose of remittiturs. Doctors Hospital argues that a remittitur is a "take-it-or-leave-it" offer, one which allows a party no options other than straightforward acceptance or rejection. Once a party accepts the remittitur, he consents to the judgment and may not reserve a right to complain of it later. Doctors Hospital's position is that any response to a remittitur other than outright acceptance, including reservation of the right to appeal the remittitur, makes the remittitur conditional and constitutes rejection of the judgment. Under these circumstances, argues Doctors Hospital, a court of appeals has no choice but to remand for a new trial.

The Roses argue that a party may file a remittitur in the court of appeals but expressly reserve the right to complain of it on motion for rehearing and in application for writ of error to this court. The Roses not only reserved but exercised that right in this case. They argue that Doctors Hospital's rigid notion of the options available to a remitting party would deprive a litigant of his right to appeal and deprive this court of jurisdiction to decide on appeal certain issues which have traditionally come within the power of this court to address.

Critical to the Rose position is the assumption that a party complaining of a court of appeals' suggestion of remittitur has the right to appeal the imposition of the remittitur, irrespective of whether he reserves rights in the remittitur. If a party does not have that right, then a reservation of the right to appeal is meaningless. Only if the party has the right to appeal a remittitur can the question arise whether a reservation of rights contained within the remittitur filing itself destroys the right to appeal.

Rule 85(c) of the Texas Rules of Appellate Procedure addresses the function of remittiturs on appeal. The rule provides that, if a court of appeals believes that a trial court should have suggested a remittitur, the court of appeals may suggest one. Texas case law instructs that the standard of review is one of factual sufficiency. *Larson v. Cactus Util. Co.*, 730 S.W.2d 640, 641 (Tex. 1987). If the remitting party files the remittitur, then judgment is reformed and affirmed in accordance with the remittitur. If the party declines to file the remittitur, then judgment is reversed. TEX. R. APP. P. 85(c).

Rule 85(c) does not contain restrictions upon the remitting party's right to appeal. We find no Texas authorities to support the contention that the right to appeal the court of appeals' final judgment, whether a reversal or a reformation and affirmation, is in any way affected by the terms of Rule 85(c). On the contrary, this court is unquestionably empowered to review judgments resulting from the imposition of Rule 85(c) because those judgments are predicated upon the court of appeals' conclusion that the evidence is insufficient to sustain the trial court's judgment. *Larson*, 730 S.W.2d at 641. Like all legal and factual sufficiency determinations, the standards used in arriving at suggestions of remittitur are subject to examination by this court and may form the basis of a party's appeal. *See Herbert v. Herbert*, 754 S.W.2d 141, 144 (Tex. 1988), *citing Pool v. Ford Motor Co.*, 715 S.W.2d 629, 634-35 (Tex. 1986).

We now turn to the question whether the reservation of a right to appeal contained within the remittitur destroys the right to appeal. We believe that a litigant's right to appeal and the obligations of this court to review a remittitur suggestion outweigh any confusion that may be caused by the remitting party's reservation of rights. The party including such a reservation has stated nothing more than the obvious, that is, that he has a right to appeal the judgment. As long as the remitting party makes it clear to the court of appeals that he is accepting the suggestion of remittitur and the consequent reformation of the judgment, additional language reserving the right to appeal amounts to mere surplusage. Accordingly, we hold that a reservation of the right to appeal contained in an otherwise valid remittitur does not amount to a rejection of the remittitur.

Our final inquiry focuses on the standard used by the court of appeals in this case to arrive at the remittitur. As we have stated, the standard is factual sufficiency. *Larson*, 730 S.W.2d at 641. To enable this court to determine whether the standard has been properly applied, the court of appeals is obligated to detail and analyze the evidence. *See Pool*, 715 S.W.2d at 633-35 (Tex. 1986). In this case, the court of appeals has dutifully accomplished the task of analyzing the evidence. We are thus able to conclude that the court of appeals applied the proper standard in arriving at the remittitur.

In conclusion, we hold that the damages provisions of the Medical Liability Act are constitutional when applied to wrongful death actions. We hold that damages under the damages cap provisions are to be calculated on a "per defendant" basis. And finally, we hold that a reservation of rights in a remittitur filed in a court of appeals does not deprive a remitting party of the right to appeal. The judgment of the court of appeals is reversed insofar as it remands for a new trial and affirmed in all other respects. Judgment is rendered for the Roses in accordance with this opinion.

PHILLIPS, C.J., and DOGGETT, J., dissenting joined by RAY and MAUZY, JJ. [opinion omitted].

Notes

1. A remittitur may be suggested by the trial court or the court of appeals upon a determination that an excess of damages has been allowed. The plaintiff is then given the choice of remitting a part or taking a new trial.

2. *Larson v Cactus Utility Co.,* 730 S.W.2d 640 (Tex. 1987). In a suit to determine the value of a corporation, and to force the division of the assets of the corporation, the jury found that the fair market value of the corporation was $4,053,325, and awarded the plaintiff-Larson $787,053 as his share (plus attorney and accounting fees). Upon motion for new trial, the trial court ordered a remittitur of $350,000. The court of appeals affirmed stating that the order of remittitur was not manifestly unjust or an abuse of discretion. The Supreme Court reversed and remanded the case to the court of appeals for reconsideration, holding that *the standard of review for a remittitur is no longer an abuse of discretion (requiring a showing that the error was as a matter of law) standard. Rather, the Supreme Court held that the standard of review is on a factual sufficiency evidence standard.* A remittitur is proper only when the evidence is factually insufficient to support the verdict and not under an abuse of discretion standard. *The same standard applies to the trial court and to the court of appeals.*

3. The claimant at the trial court level has the option of refusing the remittitur or retrying the case. The opposing party does not have standing to appeal if the claimant does not. *City National Bank v Jacksboro Bank*, 602 S.W.2d 511 (Tex. 1980). However, reservation of the right to appeal contained in the remittitur does not amount to a rejection of the remittitur and does not destroy the right to appeal. *Rose v. Doctors Hospital,* 801 S.W.2d 841 (Tex. 1990).

4. *Formosa Plastics Corp. v. Presidio Eng's & Contractors, Inc.* 960 S.W.2d 41 (Tex. 1998): A remittitur on appeal can be effectuated only by the court of appeals suggesting a remittitur in lieu of ordering a new trial, TEX. R. APP. PROC. 46.3, or by a party voluntarily remitting if a court of appeals reverses the trial court's judgment because of a legal error that affects only part of the damages awarded by the judgment. TEX. R. APP.

PROC. 46.5. The Rules do not authorize remittitur to the Supreme Court. That Court can only consider a remittitur if the damages to the personal property have been established as a matter of law.

5. *Miga v. Jensen*, ___ Tex. Sup Ct. J. ___, 2001 WL 34038821 (Oct. 31, 2002): Shortly after the court of appeals' decision, the parties entered into an Agreed Order under which Jensen made "an unconditional tender [to Miga] . . . of the sum of $23,439,532.78 . . . toward satisfaction of the Judgment in order to terminate the accrual of post-judgment interest on that sum." Held: Jensen's appeal was not mooted. One must be able to halt the accrual of post-judgment interest, yet still preserve appellate rights. Thus, payment on a judgment will not moot an appeal of that judgment, if the judgment debtor clearly expresses an intent that he intends to exercise his right of appeal, and appellate relief is not futile. This holding does not undermine the Finance Code's post- judgment interest scheme.

8. *Motion for Rehearing in Courts of Appeals*

Read Rule 49, Texas Rules of Appellate Procedure.

9. *Accelerated Appeals*

Notes

1. *Rule 26. Time To Perfect Appeal.* An accelerated appeal must be perfected within *20 days* after the judgment or order is signed.

2. *Rule 25. Method of Perfecting Appeal and Notifying Appellate Court.* Appeals will be perfected by all parties through a notice of appeal filed in the trial court. A copy of the notice of appeal must be filed with the appellate court clerk, along with a docketing statement. *Under Rule 5, fees must be paid when a document is presented for filing.* If a party intends to proceed as an indigent, the party must also comply with Rule 20.

3. *Rule 35. Time to File Record; Responsibility For Filing Record. Time to File Record.* The appellate record in an accelerated appeal must be filed within 10 days after the notice of appeal is filed. The responsibility for filing the record has shifted from the appellant to the court reporter and the district clerk. The appellate court must allow the record to be filed late when the delay is not the appellant's fault, and may do so when the delay is the appellant's fault. The parties must still designate the clerk's record and request preparation of the court reporter's or court recorder's record and pay for the record or make satisfactory arrangements for payment.

4. *Rule 38. Requisites of Briefs.* The appellant must file a brief in an accelerated appeal within 20 days after the later of (i) the date the clerk's record is filed or (ii) the date the reporter's record is filed. The appellee must file its brief within 20 days after the date the appellant's brief is field. If the appellant has not filed a brief, then the appellee may file a brief within 20 days after the appellant's brief is due. A reply brief, if any, must be filed within 20 days after the date the appellee's brief is filed. Rule 38 specifies brief contents, form and other requirements, including the filing of an appendix. [Students should read Rule 38 in its entirety, and be familiar with its contents, including the requisites of a brief, the limits on pages, and the requirements for an appendix, including what should be, and what may be, included in an appendix.]

5. *Rule 49. Motion And Further Motion For Rehearing.* The time for filing motions for rehearing is 15 days after the court of appeals' judgment or order is rendered. The appellate court may deny the right to file a motion for rehearing in an accelerated appeal. Motions for rehearing are no longer jurisdictional prerequisites to supreme court review, but may be used.

6. *Which Appeals May Be Accelerated.* The accelerated appeal is available in appeals from the following:

a. Appealable Interlocutory Orders. Section 51.014 TEX. CIV. PRAC. & REM. CODE provides for interlocutory appeals in the following cases:

(a) "A person may appeal from an interlocutory order of a district court, county court at law, or county court that:

(1) appoints a receiver or trustee;

(2) overrules a motion to vacate an order that appoints a receiver or trustee;

(3) certifies or refuses to certify a class in a suit brought under rule 42 of the Texas Rules of Civil Procedure;

(4) grants or refuses a temporary injunction or grants or overrules a motion to dissolve a temporary injunction as provided by Chapter 65; or

(5) denies a motion for summary judgment that is based on an assertion of immunity by an individual who is an officer or employee of the sate or a political subdivision of the state." [Added in 1989].

(6) denies a motion for summary judgment that is based in whole or in part upon a claim against or defense by a member of the electronic or print media, actin in such capacity, or a person whose communication appears in or is published by the electronic or print media, arising under the free speech or free press clause of the First Amendment to the United States Constitution, or Article 1, Section 8, of the Texas constitution, or Chapter 73.

(7) grants or denies the special appearance of a defendant under Rule 120a, Texas Rules of Civil Procedure, except in a suit brought under the Family Code; or

(8) grants or denies a plea to the jurisdiction by a governmental unit as that term is defined in Section 101.001.

(b) An interlocutory appeal under Subsection (a) shall have the effect of staying the commencement of a trial in the trial court pending resolution of the appeal.

b. Quo Warranto Proceedings. ["The purpose of a quo warranto proceeding is to question the right of a person or corporation, including a municipality, to exercise a public franchise or office." *Alexander Oil Co. v. City of Seguin,* 825 S.W.2d 434, 436-437 (Tex. 1991). Section 66.001 of the Texas Civil Practice and Remedies Code specifies seven situations in which quo warranto action is available, but it is not all inclusive.'

c. Primary Election Contests.

10. *Supreme Court Review of Interlocutory Appeals*

Note

Recently revised Section 22.001(e) of the Texas Government Code changes the definition of conflict for Supreme Court jurisdiction as follows: "for purpose of Subsection (c), one court holds differently from another when there is inconsistency in their respective decisions that should be clarified to remove unnecessary uncertainty in the law and unfairness to litigants." This eliminates years of debate concerning when various decisions of the courts of appeal and or Supreme Court were in conflict.

CHAPTER 8. PROCEEDINGS TO THE SUPREME COURT

1. *Jurisdiction over Legal Sufficiency Questions*

Under Article V, Section 6, of the Texas Constitution, courts of appeals have the final jurisdiction in Texas over factual sufficiency points of error. While courts of appeals have also have jurisdiction to determine legal sufficiency points of error, the Supreme Court's jurisdiction on these types of evidentiary matters is limited to legal sufficiency points of error. The Supreme Court can determine whether the court of appeals has applied the proper legal standard in conducting their factual sufficiency review.

2. *Jurisdiction of the Texas Supreme Court*

Notes

1. I. The statutory basis for the jurisdiction to the Supreme Court is found in Section 22.001 of the Texas Government Code. That section provides:

> (a) The supreme court has appellate jurisdiction, except in criminal law matters, of an appealable order or judgment of the trial courts if the court determines that the appeal presents a question of law that is important to the jurisprudence of the state. The supreme court's jurisdiction does not include cases in which the jurisdiction of the court of appeals is made final by statute.
>
> (b) A case over which the court has jurisdiction under Subsection (a) may be carried to the supreme court by petition for review.
>
> (c) Except as provided by this subsection or other law, an appeal may be taken to the supreme court only if the appeal was first brought to the court of appeals. An appeal may be taken directly to the supreme court from an order of a trial court granting or denying an interlocutory or permanent injunction on the ground of the constitutionality of a statute of this state.
>
> (d) The supreme court has the power, on affidavit or otherwise, as the court may determine, to ascertain the matters of fact that are necessary to the proper exercise of its jurisdiction.

II. The statutory basis for the Supreme Court's acting on petitions for review is found in Section 22.007 of the Government Code. That section provides:

> (a) The supreme court may act on petitions for review when the court deems it expedient.
>
> (b) Repealed by Acts 2017, 85th Leg., ch. 150 (H.B. 1761), § 4(2).
>
> (c) Repealed by Acts 2017, 85th Leg., ch. 150 (H.B. 1761), § 4(2).
>
> (d) Repealed by Acts 2017, 85th Leg., ch. 150 (H.B. 1761), § 4(2).
>
> (e) The granting of a petition for review admits the case into the supreme court, and the supreme court shall proceed with the case as provided by law. The denial or dismissal of a petition for review has the effect of denying the admission of the case into the supreme court, except that a motion for rehearing may be made in the same manner that a motion for rehearing to the supreme court is made in a case in which the court granted review. The denial or dismissal of a petition for review may not be regarded as a precedent or authority.
>
> (f) Repealed by Acts 2017, 85th Leg., ch. 150 (H.B. 1761), § 4(2).
>
> (g) Repealed by Acts 2017, 85th Leg., ch. 150 (H.B. 1761), § 4(2).

2. Rule 53 of the Texas Rules of Appellate Procedure states that the method of Supreme Court review of a final judgment of a court of appeals is by way of petition for review [formerly, appeal was by way of writ of error]. This rule identifies what matters need to be contained in the petition, the requirements for both the response to the petition and the reply to the response, and the time and place of filing these various documents. Any party who seeks a more favorable judgment than received in the court of appeals is required to file a petition for review. Unlike the former rules, the petition does not serve the function of the brief. Briefs in cases on appeal to the Supreme Court are prepared and filed only upon request of the Court. *See* Rule 55 of the Texas Rules of Appellate Procedure. Both the petition and the petitioner's brief must contain a statement of the statutory basis of the Supreme Court's jurisdiction over the particular appeal. However, Rule 56.1 of the Texas Rules of Appellate Procedure specifically states that the decision to grant review to a case is a matter of discretion. In reaching its decision the Court may consider the factors listed in Section 22.001 of the

Government Code. However, it needs to be noted that even if the Supreme Court has potential jurisdiction pursuant to its statutory authority, the Court has the discretion not to grant a petition for review, and therefore not to hear a case. In such a case, the Court can deny or dismiss the petition, or if it agrees with the judgment and legal principles announced by the opinion of the Court of Appeals, the Court can refuse the petition. *See* Rule 56.1(b) and (c) of the Texas Rules of Appellate Procedure.

3. As noted in the last Chapter, the Supreme Court does not have jurisdiction to resolve a point of error concerning the factual sufficiency of the evidence on appeal. Section 22.225 of the Government Code limits the Court's jurisdiction over question of law. It provides:

(a) A judgment of a court of appeals is conclusive on the facts of the case in all civil cases.
(b) Repealed by Acts 2017, 85th Leg., ch. 150 (H.B. 1761), § 4(3).
(c) Repealed by Acts 2017, 85th Leg., ch. 150 (H.B. 1761), § 4(3).
(d) Repealed by Acts 2017, 85th Leg., ch. 150 (H.B. 1761), § 4(3).
(e) Repealed by Acts 2017, 85th Leg., ch. 150 (H.B. 1761), § 4(3).

4. While the courts of appeals must take the cases presented to them, the Supreme Court, generally, has discretionary review power. Under current practice and procedures, four justices of the Supreme Court must vote to grant a petition for review. This has not always been the law. The Supreme Court's present discretionary review power is substantially different from what it once was. From 1917 to 1927, the section accorded jurisdiction over "an error of law . . . of such importance to the jurisprudence of the State, as in the opinion of the Supreme Court requires correction. . . ." TEX. REV. CIV. STAT. ANN. art. 1728(6) (1925), Acts 1917, 35th Leg., ch. 75, § 1. From 1927 to 1987, the section accorded jurisdiction over "an error of substantive law" that "affects the judgment . . ." TEX. GOVT. CODE § 22.001 (Vernon 1985), Acts 1985, 69th Leg., ch. 480, § 1; *see* TEX. REV. CIV. STAT. ANN. art. 1728(6) (Vernon 1962), Acts 1927, 40th Leg., ch. 144, § 1. Since 1987, the standard has changes so that the Supreme Court's jurisdiction is no longer primarily to correct the errors of lower courts. TEX. GOVT. CODE § 22.001(a)(6) currently reads in part: "The supreme court has appellate jurisdiction . . . in . . . any other case in which it appears that an error of law has been committed by the court of appeals, and that error is of such importance to the jurisprudence of the state that, in the opinion of the supreme court, it requires correction . . . ."

The effect of the change in the law is substantial. Until the 1987 enactment, the Supreme Court was required to review erroneous judgments. That is no longer true. Now there must be an error of law by the lower court which is "of such importance to the jurisprudence of the state that . . . it requires correction." TEX. GOV'T CODE ANN. § 22.001 (Vernon 1988). It should be noted that even if the Supreme Court has potential jurisdiction pursuant to its statutory authority, the Court has the discretion not to grant a writ of error, and therefore not to hear a case. In such a case it will issue an order on the petition for review.

5. In *Dallas County v. Logan*, 407 S.W.3d 745 (Tex. 2013) that court stated that a court of appeals' judgment is ordinarily conclusive in interlocutory appeals taken pursuant to section 51.014(a), but this Court has jurisdiction to resolve conflicts. The conflict, however, must be with a prior decision. *See* TEX. GOV'T CODE § 22.001(a)(2) (granting the supreme court appellate jurisdiction in "a case in which one of the courts of appeals holds differently from a prior decision of another court of appeals or of the supreme court on a question of law material to a decision of the case"). And, although *Black* is not a "prior" decision [as it was issued after the court of appeals decision in this case], the conflict found to exist among the courts of appeals in *Black* likewise gives us jurisdiction over this appeal. *See Black,* 392 S.W.3d at 93.

3. *Exercise of Jurisdiction by the Supreme Court*

a. *In General*

In re KING'S ESTATE
150 Tex. 662, 244 S.W.2d 660
(1951)

Harry Bunnenberg, Vernon, for petitioner.

Storey, Storey & Donaghey, Vernon, Bullington, Humphrey, Humphrey & Fillmore, Wichita Falls, for respondents.

PER CURIAM.

In this will contest, a district court jury found the testatrix, Mrs. Jessie King, to lack testamentary capacity, and judgment was accordingly rendered for the contestants against petitioner, Carl King, who defended the will. Petitioner by proper points in the trial court and Court of Civil Appeals sought (unsuccessfully) a new trial on the ground that the verdict was 'so contrary to the overwhelming weight of all the evidence as to be clearly wrong and unjust.' The Court of Civil Appeals affirmed the judgment of the trial court, except in certain particulars not presently material. 242 S.W.2d 925.

In connection with petitioner's particular contention above-mentioned, the opinion of the court below correctly gives the wording of such contention. It also states that the contention is overruled. However, it further discloses beyond any doubt, that, in purporting to overrule the point, the court actually treated it as a question of law, to wit, that there was no evidence to support the verdict, rather than question of fact. The court clearly based judgment, in so far as the particular assignment is concerned, upon its application to the evidence of the legal proposition stated by it thus: 'If there is any evidence of probative force to support this finding of the jury, such finding is conclusive and binding on both the trial court and this court.' That rule, like the rule whereby the reviewing court looks only to the evidence favorable to the verdict, and the rule of whether reasonable minds could differ, applies, and applies only, to the question of whether the evidence as a matter of law requires a conclusion contrary to the verdict. *Choate v. San Antonio & A. P. Ry. Co.*, 90 Tex. 82, 84, 37 S.W. 319; *id.*, 91 Tex. 406, 44 S.W. 69; *Eastham v. Hunter*, 98 Tex. 560, 565, 86 S.W. 323, 325; *United States Gypsum Co. v. Shields*, 101 Tex. 473, 477, 108 S.W. 1165; *Wininger v. Ft. Worth & D. C. Ry. Co.*, 105 Tex. 56, 58, 143 S.W. 1150; *Cartwright v. Canode*, 106 Tex. 502, 171 S.W. 696; *Woods v. Townsend*, 144 Tex. 594, 192 S.W.2d 884; *Montgomery Ward & Co. v. Scharrenbeck*, 146 Tex. 153, 204 S.W.2d 508, 511; *Renfro Drug Co. v. Lewis*, Tex. Sup., 235 S.W.2d 609, 613, 621; *Gulf C. & S. F. Ry. Co. v. Wilson*, Tex. Civ. App., 59 S.W. 589, 591, er. dism. Such tests are not applicable to the question under consideration. The latter is one of fact. It is not infrequently described as a question of 'sufficiency' of the evidence. *See Hall Music Co. v. Robinson*, 117 Tex. 261, 1 S.W.2d 857; *Wisdom v. Smith*, 146 Tex. 420, 209 S.W.2d 164, 166. The question requires the Court of Civil Appeals, in the exercise of its peculiar powers under the constitution and Texas Rules of Civil Procedure Nos. 451, 453, and 455, to consider and weigh all of the evidence in the case and to set aside the verdict and remand the cause for a new trial, if it thus concludes that the verdict is so against the great weight and preponderance of the evidence as to be manifestly unjust—this, regardless of whether the record contains some 'evidence of probative force' in support of the verdict. *See* cases cited, *supra*. The evidence supporting the verdict is to be weighed along with the other evidence in the case, including that which is contrary to the verdict.

The holding of the court below is assigned as error here. It is in effect an erroneous ruling of law that the existence of 'any evidence of probative force' in support of the verdict determines that the verdict is not 'contrary to the overwhelming weight of all the evidence.' It is in conflict with the above cited decisions of this court. The holding also is tantamount to a refusal to pass upon the assignment in question in violation of Rules 451 et seq., *supra*.

Under these circumstances, we may properly take jurisdiction of the case, notwithstanding the finality of judgments of the Courts of Civil Appeals on the fact question of whether a verdict should be set aside and a new trial granted on the ground that the verdict is against the overwhelming weight of the evidence. *See Dallas Ry. & Terminal Co. v. Farnsworth*, 148 Tex. 584, 227 S.W.2d 1017. *See also* Rules 451 et seq., *supra*.

It is true that petitioner's assignment or point in question (No. II in his brief as appellant below) includes parenthetical references not only to the trial court's failure to grant a new trial but also to its action in failing to instruct a verdict or render judgment in petitioner's favor notwithstanding the verdict. These two latter matters can, of course, be germane only to the law question of 'no evidence' and are thus inappropriate to the fact question which the assignment or point otherwise correctly presents. Possibly the inclusion of these references was the source of the error below, but the matter of duplicitousness of the assignment is not raised, and in fact the respondents contend that the Court of Civil Appeals duly passed on the fact question as such. Whether it did or did not can only be determined from the opinion, the purport of which is that it did not. Nor may we look at the statement of facts ourselves and say what the court should or could have decided, if it had properly considered the point. The purport of the opinion we gather not only from the rule announced by the court, as above quoted, but also from the conspicuous absence of any reference to the evidence for the petitioner.

It is, indeed, not simple to describe the intellectual process to be followed by the Court of Civil Appeals in passing on the fact question—to specify just how a verdict may be supported by evidence of probative force and at the same time be on all the evidence so clearly unjust as to require a new trial. But Article 5, s 6 of the Constitution, Vernon's Ann. St., is no more to be ignored than any other part of that document, and that provision, with the decisions, statutes and rules based upon it, requires the Court of Civil Appeals, upon proper assignment, to consider the fact question of weight and preponderance of all the evidence and to order or deny a new trial accordingly as to the verdict may thus appear to it clearly unjust or otherwise. This is the meaning given the constitutional phrase 'all questions of fact brought before them on appeal or error' of Sec. 6, *supra*. But for that interpretation there would be no 'questions of fact' for the Court of Civil Appeals to determine, since it cannot, save as a matter of law on conclusive evidence or lack of evidence, determine factual issues as a basis for rendering judgment. *See Wisdom v. Smith, supra*, and similar holdings.

Since it is our view that the above matter presents the only reversible error complained of in the application for writ of error, the case is appropriate for the exercise of our powers to reverse and remand upon the application. Rule 483, Tex. Rules of Civ. Proc., *Railroad Commission v. Roberdeau*, Tex. Sup., 242 S.W.2d 881, 883, and decisions therein cited.

The judgment of the Court of Civil Appeals is reversed and the cause is remanded to that court, so that it may, in the light of this opinion, properly pass upon the assignment above-mentioned.

Read Rule 53.7(b) Texas Rules of Appellate Procedure

MAPCO
v.
FORREST
795 S.W.2d 700
(Tex. 1990)

Roger Townsend, Ben Taylor, Houston, for relators.
Thomas Lee Bartlett, Houston, for respondents.

PER CURIAM.

In this original proceeding, relators seek writ of mandamus to compel the clerk of the court of appeals to forward the application and cross-application for writ of error and case record to this court. The clerk has refused to forward the applications and record on direct orders of the justices of the court of appeals.

Relators Mapco, Inc., Mapco Underground Storage of Texas, Inc., and other aligned parties appealed the trial court judgment against them to the Ninth Court of Appeals. The case was argued June 15, 1989. At that time the three justices who heard the case were CHIEF JUSTICE MARTIN DIES and JUSTICES BURGESS and BROOKSHIRE. On August 31, 1989, CHIEF JUSTICE DIES retired, and on September 1, 1989, CHIEF JUSTICE RONALD L. WALKER assumed the bench as the appointed successor.

On November 16, 1989, the court of appeals issued its opinions and judgment JUSTICE BURGESS wrote the "majority" opinion, which reversed the trial court judgment and remanded the cause; JUSTICE BROOKSHIRE dissented. The written judgment of the court conforms to the "majority" opinion disposition. At the end of the court's opinions this notation appears: "Panel of DIES, C.J., BROOKSHIRE, J., BURGESS, J. [Next Line:] WALKER, C.J., not sitting."

On November 30, 1989, the appellees (the "Carter parties") filed their motion for rehearing. The final point of the motion for rehearing specifically alleged as error the improper court of appeals panel issue. Appellees argued that after his resignation CHIEF JUSTICE DIES was not authorized to participate in the decision, and that without his concurrence the decision was one-to-one, in violation of sections 22.216(i) and 22.222 of the Texas Government Code. On December 7, 1989, the court of appeals overruled the motion for rehearing. There is no notation concerning which justices participated in the overruling of the motion for rehearing.

On December 21, 1989, the appellees filed with the court of appeals clerk what they styled "Appellees Motion for Reconsideration, or Alternatively, for Opinion." This "motion" re-urged two points that had been in the motion for rehearing, particularly the panel issue. It urged that the opinion and judgment on their face did not show concurrence of a majority of the only "panel" that could have been sitting when the judgment was rendered, that the judgment was "void or voidable" for that reason, and that the court should at least issue a new opinion addressing the panel question.

On January 4, 1990, the court of appeals through its clerk issued a letter stating appellee's motion for reconsideration was granted, directing re-briefing and setting the case for re-argument. On January 8, 1990, appellees filed their application for writ of error with the court of appeals clerk with a cover letter stating it was to be filed . . . pursuant to Rule 130(b) of the Texas Rules of Appellate Procedure. This Application is submitted for filing subject to the Order of the Court of Appeals dated January 4, 1990 granting Appellees' Motion for Reconsideration, or Alternatively, For Opinion and ordering the subject Appeal to be reargued and rebriefed by the parties. It is our position that the decision and judgment rendered by the Court on November 16, 1989 was void or voidable based upon the lack of participation in the Judgment and Opinion rendered by a majority of the panel sitting on the Court at the time of rendition of said Judgment and, therefore, did not commence the running of the time in which Appellees may file their Application for Writ of Error. However, in an abundance of caution, Appellees submit the enclosed Application for Writ of Error in order to present their Points of Error to the Supreme Court on a timely basis in the event said void or voidable Judgment and Opinion did commence the running of the time in which Appellees may file their Application for Writ of Error. Within ten days the Mapco parties filed their conditional application for writ of error. Thereafter, the Mapco parties wrote the court of appeals clerk requesting that the applications and records be forwarded to the supreme court. The clerk responded with a letter stating that the court of appeals had "granted in full" the motion for reconsideration and that she declined to forward the applications and record to the supreme court "following direct orders and instructions from the Justices of the Ninth Court of Appeals." The Mapco parties then filed this mandamus proceeding.

Relators' argument is simply stated. The filing of the applications for writ of error deprived the court of appeals of jurisdiction to change its judgment. *Ammex Warehouse Co. v. Archer*, 381 S.W.2d 478, 482 (Tex. 1964). As this court has stated, upon the filing of the application for writ of error "the jurisdiction of the Supreme Court immediately attached," leaving the court of appeals "without authority to make any order in the case." *Johnson v. Sovereign Camp*, W.O.W., 125 Tex. 329, 336, 83 S.W.2d 605, 608 (1935).[1] Relators also argue that the court of appeals' January 4, 1990 order cannot be justified as an exercise of its plenary power over its judgments, because its period of plenary power over its judgment expired on December 31, 1989, when the term in which the judgment was rendered ended.[2] As this court has written, except for a "ministerial act" consistent with the judgment, a court of appeals "is without authority to correct or alter a judgment after the expiration of the term in which it was rendered." *Cockburn v. Hightower*, 121 Tex. 555, 557, 52 S.W.2d 365, 366 (1932).

In reply the Carter parties urge a number of innovative arguments why the court of appeals could have jurisdiction to render its order. We address two of these, to clarify holdings of this court.

The Carter parties argue that the court of appeals' plenary jurisdiction to vacate its judgment continued into the next term because the motion for reconsideration was "pending" when the term ended December 31, 1989. The appellate rules authorize a second or subsequent motion for rehearing only if the court of appeals modifies its judgment or opinion in connection with the overruling of a previous motion. TEX. R. APP. P. 100(d). A second motion for rehearing not authorized by the rules is a nullity even if the court of appeals rules on it. *Honeycutt v. Doss*, 410 S.W.2d 772 (Tex. 1966). Necessarily such a motion did not extend the court of appeals' plenary jurisdiction over the judgment in the case.

The second argument is that the court of appeals' judgment was "void" because it was contrary to section 22.222(c) of the Government Code. In fact a corresponding provision appears in the constitution: The Court of Appeals may sit in sections as authorized by law. The concurrence of a majority of the judges sitting in a section is necessary to decide a case. TEX. CONST. art. V, § 6. It is also true that in *Freeman v. Freeman*, 160 Tex. 148, 156, 327 S.W.2d 428, 433 (1959), this court stated, "Judgments are void for lack of power in courts to render them when they are rendered contrary to constitutional or valid statutory prohibition or outside limiting constitutional or statutory authority." Given only this language from *Freeman*, the Carter parties' argument is reasonably plausible that the court of appeals judgment was "void" as contrary to the "statutory prohibition" that a majority of a panel must concur to render a decision, or beyond the authority of the court because the constitution requires the concurrence of a majority of a "section" of the court of appeals.

In fact, the argument does not withstand closer scrutiny. We have spent considerable effort distinguishing and explaining the quoted language from *Freeman* in holdings that a court's action contrary to a statute or statutory equivalent means the action is erroneous or "voidable," not that the ordinary appellate or other direct procedures to correct it may be circumvented. For example, in *El Paso Pipe and Supply Co. v. Mountain States Leasing, Inc.*, 617 S.W.2d 189 (Tex. 1981), we expressly distinguished *Freeman* and held that conflict with then rule 329b, Texas Rules of Civil Procedure, although a mandatory rule dealing with the trial court's plenary power, did not make the judgment "void"; the error had to be corrected through the ordinary appellate process or other proper proceedings. Again, in *Middleton v. Murff*, 689 S.W.2d 212, 213 (Tex. 1985), we expressly

---

[1] This court recently overruled in part *Johnson v. Sovereign Camp*, but only to the extent that the court of appeals is not deprived of jurisdiction to rule on the motion for rehearing of another party that is still pending when an application for writ of error is filed. Otherwise, the rule applies with full force that appellate jurisdiction immediately attaches in this court. *See* Doctors Hospital Facilities v. Fifth Court of Appeals, 750 S.W.2d 177, 179 (Tex. 1988).

[2] TEX. GOV'T CODE ANN. § 22.218 (1988) provides: "The term of each court of appeals begins and ends with each calendar year."

disapproved the quoted statement from *Freeman* to the extent it was construed to mean that "[i]f a judgment rendered by a trial court is void it may be set aside by that court at any time." We further explained it was only a trial court judgment rendered without "jurisdictional power" in the sense of lack of subject matter jurisdiction that could be set aside by the trial court at any time.

If *Middleton v. Murff* failed to make it clear, we now expressly disapprove the quoted language from *Freeman* to the extent it is construed to apply to a court of appeals' plenary power. Absent one of those rare circumstances that makes the judgment "void," the mere fact that an action by a court of appeals is contrary to a statute, constitutional provision or rule of civil or appellate procedure makes it "voidable" or erroneous. A judgment is void only when it is apparent that the court rendering the judgment had no jurisdiction of the parties, no jurisdiction of the subject matter, no jurisdiction to enter the judgment, or no capacity to act as a court. *Cook v. Cameron*, 733 S.W.2d 137, 140 (Tex. 1987); *Browning v. Placke*, 698 S.W.2d 362, 362 (Tex. 1985). On facts substantially similar to the present case, this court in an ordinary appeal recently held the court of appeals' judgment was erroneous, and reversed and remanded the cause. *See Hayden v. Liberty Mutual Fire Ins. Co.*, 786 S.W.2d 260 (Tex. 1990). Despite its error, here the court of appeals had lost jurisdiction to correct it.

Because the orders and actions of the court of appeals and its clerk conflict with this court's decisions in *Johnson v. Sovereign Camp*, W.O.W. and *Cockburn v. Hightower*, and further with rule 132(a), TEX. R. APP. P., we grant leave to file and without oral argument a majority of the court conditionally issues the writ of mandamus. TEX. R. APP. P. 122. We direct the Ninth Court of Appeals and its clerk to forward the record and applications for writ of error to this court.

Notes

1. A motion for rehearing in the court of appeals is no longer a prerequisite to consideration by the Texas Supreme Court. TEX. R. APP. P. 49.9. It is now possible for one party to petition for review in the Supreme Court, and for the other party to file a motion for rehearing in the court of appeals. TEX. R. APP. P. 53.7. However, a party must choose one route or the other. "A party may not file a motion for rehearing in the court of appeals after the party has filed a petition for review in the Supreme Court unless the court of appeals modifies its opinion or judgment after the petition for review is filed." TEX. R. APP. P. 53.7(b).

2. TEX. R. APP. P. 53.7 (b). "* * * The filing of a petition for review does not preclude another party from filing a motion for rehearing or the court of appeals from ruling on the motion. If a motion for rehearing is timely filed after a petition for review is filed,, the petitioner must immediately notify the Supreme Court clerk of the filing of the motion, and must notify the clerk when the last timely filed motion is overruled by the court of appeals. A petition filed before the last ruling on all timely filed motions for rehearing is treated as having been filed on the date of, but after, the last ruling on any such motion."

BOSSLEY
v.
DALLAS COUNTY MENTAL HEALTH & MENTAL RETARDATION

NOT DESIGNATED FOR PUBLICATION.
UNDER TEX.R.APP.P. 47.7 UNPUBLISHED OPINIONS MAY NOT BE CITED AS AUTHORITY.
1999 WL 993901
(Tex. App.—Dallas 1999, no petition.)

OVARD, JUSTICE.

Appellants appeal the denial of their motion for new trial which appellants filed in the trial court after the Texas Supreme Court rendered judgment in this case in favor of appellees. Additionally, appellants' counsel appeals the award of sanctions against him for filing a frivolous motion for new trial. In two points of error, appellants and their counsel generally contend the trial court's order awarding sanctions is void for failing to comply with rule 13 of the Texas Rules of Civil Procedure. In three additional points of error, appellants contend the trial court erred, and violated appellants' constitutional rights, by failing to grant appellants' motion for new trial. Appellants reason that the Texas Supreme Court erroneously determined an issue of fact, thereby exceeded its jurisdiction, and as a result rendered a void judgment. Relying on the jurisdiction of the courts of appeals to review facts, appellants contend the judgment rendered by this Court prior to the appeal to the Texas Supreme Court constitutes the only valid appellate judgment in this case. We conclude we lack jurisdiction over this appeal and the trial court lacked jurisdiction to enter its order denying appellant's motion for new trial and awarding sanctions. Accordingly, we vacate the trial court's void order and dismiss this appeal.

This case was originally appealed to this Court after the trial court granted summary judgment in favor of appellees. We reversed and remanded the case to the trial court. *See Bossley v. Dallas County Mental Health*, 934 S.W.2d 689 (Tex. App.—Dallas 1995), rev'd 968 S.W.2d 339 (Tex.), *cert. denied*, 119 S.Ct. 541 (1998). The judgment of this Court, however, was appealed by writ of error to the Texas Supreme Court, which reversed our judgment and rendered judgment for appellees. *See Bossley v. Dallas County Mental Health*, 968 S.W.2d 339 (Tex.), *cert. denied*, 119 S.Ct. 541 (1998). The Texas Supreme Court subsequently overruled appellants' motion for rehearing, and the United States Supreme Court denied appellants' petition for writ of certiorari.

After the Texas Supreme Court rendered judgment in favor of appellees and against appellants, but before the Texas Supreme Court's mandate issued, counsel for appellants filed a motion for new trial with the trial court.

Generally, appellants asserted that the Texas Supreme Court lacked jurisdiction because it misstated certain facts in its opinion which, appellants contend, constitute the lynchpin of the court's decision. Appellants also asserted that the Texas Supreme Court improperly rendered judgment against Dallas County Mental Health & Mental Retardation because the court failed to account for appellants' attempt to nonsuit this defendant before the trial court rendered its judgment. Appellees responded that appellants' motion was frivolous and sought sanctions pursuant to rule 13 of the Texas Rules of Civil Procedure. On December 18, 1998, the trial court signed an order denying appellants' motion for new trial. In its order, the trial court further found that the motion for new trial was frivolous and ordered appellants' counsel to reimburse appellees' attorney's fees of $3744 incurred in responding to the motion. It is from the trial court's December 18, 1998 order that appellants bring this appeal.

On December 21, 1998, three days following the trial court's order, the Texas Supreme court issued its mandate in this case. In pertinent part, the mandate states:

IT IS THEREFORE ORDERED, in accordance with the court's opinion, that:

1) The judgment of the court of appeals is reversed;

2) Judgment is rendered that Albert Bossley, individually, Elaine Bossley, individually, and as representatives of the Estate of Roger Arthur Bossley, take nothing;

3) Dallas County Mental Health and Mental Retardation, et al., shall recover from Albert Bossley, individually, Elaine Bossley, individually, and as representatives of the estate of Roger Arthur Bossley, who shall pay the costs in this Court and in the court of appeals.

The mandate further commands the district court 'to observe the order of our said Supreme Court in this behalf, and in all things to have recognized, obeyed, and executed.'

After the Texas Supreme Court acquires exclusive jurisdiction in a case,[3] it will permit no interference from any other court. *See Dallas/Fort Worth Intern. Airport Bd. v. City of Irving*, 868 S.W.2d 750, 751 (Tex. 1993). Its jurisdiction continues until the case is fully determined by that court and its judgment is completely executed by the court below and the mandate obeyed. *See Curtis v. Nobles*, 588 S.W.2d 687, 688 (Tex. Civ. App.—Amarillo 1979, orig. proceeding); *Witherspoon v. Davis*, 163 S.W. 700, 703 (Tex. Civ. App.—Austin 1914, orig. proceeding) (quoting *Wells v. Littlefield*, 62 Tex. 28 (1884)). Rendition of a judgment by the Texas Supreme Court on the merits implies a decision by the court that it had) jurisdiction of the matter adjudged. *Cherokee Water Co. v. Ross*, 698 S.W.2d 363, 365 (Tex. 1985). A lower court has no authority to correct any alleged error in an appellate judgment. *See Martin v. Credit Protection Ass'n, Inc.*, 824 S.W.2d 254, 257 (Tex. App.—Dallas 1992, writ dism'd w.o.j.); *Jones v. Casualty Reciprocal Exch.*, 275 S.W. 279, 281 (Tex. Civ. App.—Texarkana 1925, writ ref'd). The correction, if any, must be made by the court rendering the judgment, not by one whose duty it is to obey the judgment. *See Martin*, 824 S.W.2d at 257; *Jones*, 275 S.W.2d at 281.

Accordingly, it is clear this Court has no jurisdiction to consider appellants' points of error complaining that the Texas Supreme Court lacked jurisdiction to render its judgment in this case. By rendering judgment on the merits, the Texas Supreme Court resolved any jurisdictional issue against appellants, and we lack any authority to review that decision. Appellants' attempt to rely on this Court's judgment as the last valid judgment in the case is fundamentally misdirected. This Court's judgment became a nullity upon being reversed by the Texas Supreme Court. *See Flowers v. Flowers*, 589 S.W.2d 746, 748 (Tex. Civ. App.—Dallas 1979, no writ).

It is equally clear the trial court lacked jurisdiction to consider appellants' motion for new trial. Appellants were required to file a motion for new trial within thirty days after the trial court granted summary judgment for appellees in 1991. *See* TEX.R.CIV.P. 329b(a). After the trial court's plenary jurisdiction expired, it had no jurisdiction thereafter to consider a motion for new trial. *See Clark & Co. v. Giles*, 639 S.W.2d 449, 450 (Tex. 1982); *Southern County Mut. Ins. Co. v. Powell*, 736 S.W.2d 745, 748 (Tex. App.—Hous. [14th Dist.] 1987, orig. proceeding); *see also* TEX.R.CIV.P. 329b(f). Furthermore, the Texas Supreme Court's disposition rendering judgment excluded any possibility of a new trial. Once an appellate court renders judgment, the trial court has no jurisdiction to review or interpret the appellate judgment but must observe the judgment as it was framed by the appellate court. *Martin*, 824 S.W.2d at 255 56; *see also Harris County Children's Protective Servs. v. Olvera*, 971 S.W.2d 172, 175 76 (Tex. App.—Houston [14th Dist.] 1998, pet. denied). The Texas Supreme Court's judgment in this case was a final judgment over which the trial court had no control. *See Martin*, 824 S.W.2d at 257. Because the trial court lacked jurisdiction to consider appellants' motion, its December 18, 1998 order denying the motion is void. *See Bayoud v. Bayoud*, 797 S.W.2d 304, 311(Tex. App.—Dallas 1990, writ denied) (*citing Cook v. Cameron*, 733 S.W.2d 137, 140 (Tex. 1987)).

It necessarily follows that the award of sanctions in the trial court's order is void as well. A void order has no legal effect; it is void at its inception as if it had never existed. *Ex parte Anderson*, 893 S.W.2d 195, 197 n. 4 (Tex. App.—El Paso 1995, orig. proceeding); *Watson v. Hart*, 871 S.W.2d 914, 920 (Tex. App.—Austin 1994, orig. proceeding). A court has no more power to act in sanction matters without jurisdiction than it does elsewhere. *Hjalmarson v. Langley*, 840 S.W.2d 153, 155 (Tex. App.—Waco 1992, orig. proceeding), overruled in part on other grounds by *Scott & White Mem'l Hosp. v. Schexnider*, 940 S.W.2d 594 (Tex. 1996); *see also Jobe v. Lapidus*, 874 S.W.2d 764, 768 (Tex. App.—Dallas 1994, writ denied) (holding order granting rule 13 sanctions signed after the expiration of the trial court's plenary jurisdiction was void). Accordingly, we conclude the entire December 18, 1998 order is void, including the award of attorney's fees.

---

[3] Under the appellate rules in effect during the prior appeal of this case, the jurisdiction of the Texas Supreme Court attached to a case upon the filing of an application for writ of error, and thereafter the intermediate appellate court lacked authority to make any order in the case other than to act on a pending motion for rehearing. *See Mapco, Inc. v. Forrest*, 795 S.W.2d 700, 702 (Tex. 1990).

When a party appeals from a void order and the appellate court lacks jurisdiction to consider the appeal, the proper procedure is for the appellate court to declare the order to be void and dismiss the appeal for lack of jurisdiction. *See State ex rel. Latty v. Owens*, 907 S.W.2d 484, 486 (Tex. 1995); *see also Wilson v. Kutler*, 971 S.W.2d 557, 559 (Tex. App.—Dallas 1998, no pet.). Accordingly, we vacate the trial court's December 18, 1998 order and declare it to be null and void, and we dismiss this appeal for want of jurisdiction.

Note

Texas Workers' Compensation Insurance Fund v. Mandlbauer, 34 S.W.3d 909 (Tex. 2000): In a prior per curiam decision, the Supreme Court held that Mandlbauer did not have standing to complain about the trial court's failure to submit an inferential rebuttal instruction on sole cause. Accordingly, it reversed the court of appeals' judgment and remanded the case to that court. 988 S.W.2d 750 (Tex. 1999). The Supreme Court's Mandate provided that the "Texas Workers' Compensation Insurance Fund shall recover from Mike Mandlbauer, who shall pay, the costs in this Court and in the court of appeals." The court of appeals, on remand, reversed the trial court's judgment and remanded the case for a new trial. The court of appeals also ordered that "all cost of the appeal shall be assessed against [the Fund]." Held: Reversed and rendered for the Fund. The court of appeals' mandate stating that "all costs of the appeal" be assessed against the Fund is ambiguous because it does not limit costs to the appeal on remand. The court of appeals generally has discretion to assess costs in subsequent court of appeals' proceedings. But in this instance the court's mandate could be read to include the costs in the court of appeals that this Court ordered Mandlbauer to pay. The Supreme Court judgment on this appeal, awards all costs against Mandlbauer for all appeals

b. *Specific Jurisdictional Provisions*

Read Rule 56.1 Texas Rules of Appellate Procedure.

UNIVERSITY OF THE INCARNATE WORD
v.
REDUS
518 S.W.3d 905
(Tex. 2017)

Laurence S. Kurth, Matthew F. Wymer, Akerman, LLP, San Antonio, Amy Warr, Wallace B. Jefferson, Alexander Dubose Jefferson & Townsend LLP, Austin, for Petitioner.

Brent C. Perry, Robert R. Burford, Burford Perry, LLP, Houston, Frank Herrera Jr., Jorge A. Herrera, The Herrera Law Firm, San Antonio, Mason W. Herring, Herring Law Firm, Houston, for Respondent.

JUSTICE DEVINE delivered the opinion of the Court.

The Texas Civil Practice and Remedies Code provides for an interlocutory appeal from an order that "grants or denies a plea to the jurisdiction by a governmental unit." TEX. CIV. PRAC. & REM. CODE § 51.014(a)(8). The term "governmental unit" has the same meaning here as it does in the Texas Tort Claims Act. *Id.* §§ 51.104(a)(8), 101.001 (defining the term). The issue we must decide is whether a private university that operates a state-authorized police department is such a "governmental unit." If it is, the university can pursue this interlocutory appeal from the trial court's order denying the university's plea to the jurisdiction. The court of appeals concluded, however, that the university is not a governmental unit and dismissed the appeal. 474 S.W.3d 816, 817 (Tex. App.—San Antonio 2015). Because we conclude that the university is a governmental unit for purposes of this interlocutory appeal, we reverse and remand.

Though University of the Incarnate Word (UIW) is a private university, it maintains a campus police department. The Legislature has authorized private institutions of higher education to employ and commission peace officers and operate police departments. TEX. EDUC. CODE § 51.212(a). This case arises from a UIW officer's use of deadly force following a traffic stop. The incident resulted in the death of Cameron Redus, a UIW student the officer pulled over on suspicion of driving while intoxicated.

Redus's parents sued UIW and the officer for their son's death. UIW raised governmental immunity as a defense in its answer and later asked the trial court to dismiss the suit in a plea to the jurisdiction. The trial court denied the plea, and UIW took an interlocutory appeal under section 51.014(a)(8) of the Civil Practice and Remedies Code. That provision authorizes an interlocutory appeal from an order granting or denying a governmental unit's plea to the jurisdiction. Although UIW does not claim to be a governmental unit generally, it contends it is a governmental unit when defending the actions of its police department. The court of appeals disagreed and dismissed the appeal. 474 S.W.3d at 825. We granted UIW's petition for review.

Because section 51.014(a)(8) authorizes an interlocutory appeal from the grant or denial only of a governmental unit's plea to the jurisdiction, and UIW filed the plea in this case, UIW must be a governmental unit to pursue this appeal. Section 51.014(a)(8) defines "governmental unit" by reference to the Tort Claims Act, so we must look there for its definition. TEX. CIV. PRAC. & REM. CODE § 51.014(a)(8). The Tort Claims Act defines "governmental unit" as

> (A) this state and all the several agencies of government that collectively constitute the government of this state, including other agencies bearing different designations, and all departments, bureaus, boards, commissions, offices, agencies, councils, and courts;
>
> (B) a political subdivision of this state, including any city, county, school district, junior college district, levee improvement district, drainage district, irrigation district, water improvement district, water control and improvement district, water control and preservation district, freshwater supply district, navigation district, conservation and reclamation district, soil conservation district, communication district, public health district, and river authority;
>
> (C) an emergency service organization; and
>
> (D) any other institution, agency, or organ of government the status and authority of which are derived from the Constitution of Texas or from laws passed by the legislature under the constitution.

Id. § 101.001(3)(A-D). UIW claims to be a governmental unit only under subpart D. To qualify as a governmental unit under the Tort Claims Act, then, UIW must satisfy subpart D's two conditions. First, UIW must be an "institution, agency, or organ of government," and, second, UIW must derive its "status and authority . . . from the Constitution of Texas or from laws passed by the legislature under the constitution." *Id.* § 101.001(3)(D).

UIW concedes that, as a private university, it is not generally a "governmental unit." But UIW argues that a private entity can be a governmental unit for certain purposes and that it is a governmental unit when defending lawsuits arising from its law-enforcement function. UIW contends it is a governmental unit for purposes of defending its campus police department because its "status and authority" to "create a law enforcement agency or police department" arise from laws passed by the Legislature that allow private universities to commission and deploy peace officers to enforce criminal laws. TEX. EDUC. CODE § 51.212.

The Reduses respond that UIW is a private institution and that no state law makes UIW a part of the government. Rather, the statute authorizing UIW to commission and employ peace officers "requires that [UIW] be a private or independent institution." 474 S.W.3d at 823 (citing TEX. EDUC. CODE § 51.212). The Reduses submit that previous cases recognizing ostensibly private institutions to be governmental units have relied on express statutory authority to that effect. See, e.g., *LTTS Charter Sch., Inc. v. C2 Constr., Inc.*, 342 S.W.3d 73, 77 (Tex. 2011) (citing TEX. EDUC. CODE § 12.105); *Klein v. Hernandez*, 315 S.W.3d 1, 8 (Tex. 2010) (citing TEX. HEALTH & SAFETY CODE § 312.006(b)). The Reduses argue that no comparable authority exists here.

The parties focus therefore on different aspects of subpart D's definition. TEX. CIV. PRAC. & REM. CODE § 101.001(3)(D). Relying on the latter portion of the subpart, UIW argues it is a governmental unit because state law gives it the status and authority to create a police department and enforce state and local law—a governmental function. Relying on the subpart's first requirement, the Reduses counter that no state law makes UIW an "institution, agency, or organ of government," and that the Legislature has conditioned its authorization of UIW to operate a police department on UIW's status as a private institution.

Although private institutions are not commonly understood to be a part "of government," we have held that a private institution can be a governmental unit. In *LTTS Charter School*, we determined that a private charter school was a governmental unit entitled to an interlocutory appeal under section 51.014(a)(8). 342 S.W.3d at 82. In reaching this conclusion, we pointed to specific legislative grants of authority to open-enrollment charter schools, including the grant of all powers given to traditional public schools under Title 2 of the Education Code. *Id.* at 77 (citing TEX. EDUC. CODE § 12.104(a)). We commented further that open-enrollment charter schools "have statutory entitlements to state funding" and services that "school districts receive," are generally subject to the laws and rules pertaining to public schools, and are obligated to comply with many of the requirements of educational programs that apply to traditional public schools, including accountability programs. *Id.* at 77-78 (citing TEX. EDUC. CODE §§ 12.103(a), .104, .106(a)). In addition, we noted that open-enrollment charter schools are subject "to a host of statutes that govern governmental entities outside the Education Code," including statutes imposing open-meetings requirements, public-information requirements, and record-regulation requirements. *Id.* at 78 (citing TEX. EDUC. CODE §§ 12.1051, .1052). We noted further that the Legislature expressly granted open-enrollment charter schools the same immunity from liability school districts have. *Id.* at 78 n.44. And we explained that open-enrollment charter schools are expressly considered "governmental entit[ies] for . . . [statutes] relating to property held in trust and competitive bidding," "political subdivision[s] for . . . [statutes concerning] procurement of professional services," and "local government[s] for . . . [statutes governing] authorized investments." *Id.* at 78 (internal quotes omitted) (citing TEX. EDUC. CODE § 12.1053). Finally, we expressed "confiden[ce] that the Legislature considers" open-enrollment charter schools "institution[s], agenc[ies], or organ[s] of government" under subsection 101.001(3)(D) given their statutory status as part of the public-school system, "their authority to wield" the powers given to public schools, and their right to "receive and spend state tax dollars (and in many ways to function as a governmental entity)." *Id.* (internal footnotes omitted) (citing TEX. EDUC. CODE §§ 12.104(a), .105–.107, .1053).

Relying on this discussion from LTTS Charter School, the court of appeals identified several factors as relevant to UIW's status as a governmental unit and applied those factors to hold that UIW was not a governmental unit. See 474 S.W.3d at 821-24 (listing factors). The court concluded that UIW's authority to commission and employ peace officers did not overcome several other factors indicating that UIW was not a governmental unit, such as the fact that "UIW is not 'part of the Texas public-school system'; receives no statutory entitlement to state or other government funding; is not compelled to comply with Texas's regulatory and accountability system and rules pertaining to public schools, and; is not granted authority of all powers given to traditional public schools." *Id.* at 824.

UIW complains that the court of appeals erroneously applied *LTTS Charter School*. The court missed the mark, UIW contends, because it focused on whether UIW is part of the public-education system instead of on whether UIW's police department is part of Texas's law-enforcement system. UIW maintains that the court should have limited its analysis to the university's law-enforcement function because it does not contend to be a governmental unit generally but only in cases regarding its police department.

UIW submits that it is part of the state's system of law enforcement because its campus police must have the same license and meet the same requirements as any other peace officer in the state. TEX. OCC. CODE § 1701.301. UIW's officers can enforce state law on campus and state and local law at other locations as permitted by the Texas Education Code. TEX. EDUC. CODE § 51.212(a). Moreover, UIW officers have the powers, privileges, and immunities of peace officers when on the property of the university, when performing duties assigned by the university, when in a county in which the university has land, or to the extent authorized by Section 51.2125 of the Texas Education Code. *Id.* § 51.212(b). Campus police officers take the peace officer's oath and must post bond with the Governor of Texas. *Id.* § 51.212(c). And, with respect to information relating to law-enforcement activities, campus police departments of private institutions are law-enforcement agencies and governmental bodies for the purposes of the Public Information Act. *Id.* § 51.212(f). Thus, although the university and its police department lack public funding, UIW argues it is a governmental unit as to its policing function because the Legislature created the authority by which it can commission officers, its officers have the same powers as officers commissioned by public entities, and UIW's police department is subject to the same regulations as other police departments.

UIW emphasizes that law enforcement is a quintessentially governmental function and that this weighs in favor of its status as a governmental unit. The Tort Claims Act, according to UIW, supports this argument because it lists police and fire protection first among the governmental functions "enjoined on a municipality by law and . . . given by the state as part of the state's sovereignty, to be exercised by the municipality in the interest of the general public." TEX. CIV. PRAC. & REM. CODE § 101.0215(a)(1).

UIW recognizes, however, that not all of the indicators of governmental-unit status present *in LTTS Charter School* are present here. For one thing, unlike an open-enrollment charter school, UIW receives no public funding for its police department. *LTTS Charter School*, 342 S.W.3d at 77. For another, the Education Code expressly declares open-enrollment charter schools to be "part of the public school system of this state," but no comparable declaration makes UIW's campus police department a part of any state system. *Id.* Finally, the Legislature expressly granted open-enrollment charter schools immunity from liability, implying "legislative recognition of 'governmental unit' status," but no comparable grant of general immunity exists here. *Id.* at 78 n.44.

To be a governmental unit under the Tort Claims Act, UIW must (1) be an "institution, agency, or organ of government" and (2) derive its "status and authority" as such from "laws passed by the Legislature." TEX. CIV. PRAC. & REM. CODE § 101.001(3)(D). Here, UIW clearly derives its status and authority to commission and employ peace officers and operate a police department from laws passed by the Legislature. See TEX. EDUC. CODE § 51.212 (authorizing private universities to operate police departments). The question is whether UIW is an "institution, agency, or organ of government."

Because the statute does not further define these terms, we look to the terms' common meaning. *Abutahoun v. Dow Chem. Co.*, 463 S.W.3d 42, 46 (Tex. 2015). The Oxford English Dictionary defines organ as a "body of persons or thing by which some particular purpose is carried out or some function is performed." Organ, THE COMPACT EDITION OF THE OXFORD ENGLISH DICTIONARY (1971). The New Oxford American Dictionary defines organ as "a department or organization that performs a specified function." Organ, THE NEW OXFORD AMERICAN DICTIONARY (3d ed. 2010). And Webster's Third New International Dictionary defines organ as "an instrumentality exercising some function or accomplishing some end" and "a governmental instrumentality operating as part of a larger organization." Organ, WEBSTER'S THIRD NEW INTERNATIONAL DICTIONARY (2002). These definitions indicate that an "organ of government" is an entity that operates as part of a larger governmental system.

Our case law confirms that the question here is whether UIW's campus police department is part of a larger governmental system and provides a framework for answering that question. In *LTTS Charter School*, we concluded that a private charter school was an "institution, agency or organ of government" based on a legislative scheme that made private charter schools part of the Texas public-education system. 342 S.W.3d at 76-78. Many of the same indicators of governmental-unit status present in *LTTS Charter School* are present here. For example, the Legislature granted charter schools all of the powers and privileges of public schools, *id.* at 77 (citing TEX. EDUC. CODE § 12.104(a)), and here it has given UIW the power to operate a police department like that of any city, TEX. EDUC. CODE § 51.212(b). Like the charter school, UIW must follow the same state-promulgated rules its public counterparts follow:

- To create a police department, a private university must apply for state approval and include information about its resources and capabilities in its application. 37 TEX. ADMIN. CODE § 211.16.
- Private universities can employ only state-licensed peace officers. TEX. OCC. CODE § 1701.301; 37 TEX. ADMIN. CODE § 223.2(c)(1).
- Private-university police departments must submit to the same audits as other police departments. 37 TEX. ADMIN. CODE §§ 211.26, 223.2(c).

Moreover, like state and local law-enforcement agencies, UIW must make certain records available for public review because UIW's police department is a governmental entity under the Public Information Act. TEX. EDUC. CODE § 51.212(f). And, though the Legislature has not granted private universities immunity from liability generally, as they did charter schools, the Legislature has granted limited immunity to private universities when their officers act pursuant to mutual assistance agreements with local police departments. *Id.* §§ 51.212(b)(2), .2125.

But the indicators of governmental-unit status present in *LTTS Charter School* do not precisely match those present here. Unlike the charter school, UIW lacks public funding, and the Legislature does not consider UIW a governmental entity under the Government Code and Local Government Code provisions relating to property held in trust and competitive bidding . *LTTS Charter School*, 342 S.W.3d at 78 (citing TEX. EDUC. CODE § 12.1053). Moreover, the Legislature's intended role for private universities in public law enforcement is less clear than its express inclusion of open-enrollment charter schools in the public-school system. See *id.* at 77 (citing legislation declaring open-enrollment charter schools to be "part of the public school system of this state").

Nevertheless, the Legislature has authorized UIW to enforce state and local law using the same resource municipalities and the State use to enforce law: commissioned peace officers. UIW's officers have the same powers, privileges, and immunities as other peace officers. TEX. EDUC. CODE § 51.212(b). Because law enforcement is uniquely governmental, the function the Legislature has authorized UIW to perform and the way the Legislature has authorized UIW to perform it strongly indicate that UIW is a governmental unit as to that function. We accordingly conclude that UIW is a governmental unit for purposes of law enforcement and that UIW is therefore entitled to pursue an interlocutory appeal under section 51.014(a)(8) of the Civil Practice and Remedies Code.

Our conclusion that UIW is a governmental unit is not a comment on the merits of UIW's plea to the jurisdiction. Although UIW argues that it enjoys immunity from suit and liability when sued for actions related to its law-enforcement function, that issue is not before us. The issue of immunity is instead for the court of appeals and will implicate principles of sovereign immunity that have had no bearing on our analysis here. See *Wasson Interests, Ltd. v. City of Jacksonville*, 489 S.W.3d 427, 432 (Tex. 2016) (noting that sovereign immunity is a common-law doctrine and that courts determine whether an entity is immune in the first instance); see also *Reata Constr. Corp. v. City of Dall.*, 197 S.W.3d 371, 375 (Tex. 2006) (noting that "it remains the judiciary's responsibility to define the boundaries of the common-law doctrine and to determine under what circumstances sovereign immunity exists in the first instance"). To determine whether an entity is immune, courts should rely not on the Tort Claims Act's definition of governmental unit, as we have here, but on the "nature and purposes" of sovereign immunity. *Wasson Interests*, 489 S.W.3d at 432. In short, whether an entity is entitled to an interlocutory appeal and whether an entity has sovereign immunity are separate questions with separate analytical frameworks.

As we did in *LTTS Charter School*, "[w]e leave undecided the separate issue of whether [UIW] is immune from suit." 342 S.W.3d at 78 n.44. The issue we decide is one of appellate jurisdiction only: Did the court of appeals have jurisdiction to consider UIW's interlocutory appeal? It did. Accordingly, we reverse the court of appeals' judgment and remand for it to resolve UIW's interlocutory appeal.

Note

Cases which originate in the justice courts are not usually appealable to the Texas Supreme Court. However, the Supreme Court has jurisdiction of such a case if it involves the construction of a statute. *See* TEX. GOV'T CODE § 22.225(b)(1). *Texas Department of Public Safety v. McLendon,* 35 S.W.3d 632 (Tex. 2000).

4. *Procedural Predicates in the Court of Appeals*

Notes

1. A motion for rehearing is no longer required as a predicate to an appeal to the Supreme Court. Rule 49.9.

2. If a motion for rehearing is presented to the court of appeals, it must be filed within 15 days after the court renders its judgment or order. Rule 49.1. If that deadline is missed, the party seeking the rehearing has an additional 15 days within which to request an extension of time to file the motion for rehearing.

3. If one party files a Petition for Review in the Supreme Court, this does not preclude any other party from filing a motion for rehearing in the court of appeals. Rule 53.7(b). If a timely motion for rehearing is filed after a Petition for Review, the petitioner is required to notify the Clerk of the Supreme Court of its filing and subsequent action on the motion. A prematurely filed petition is deemed filed on the date the motion for rehearing is overruled. Rule 53.7. After filing a Petition for Review, the petition in the Supreme Court cannot file a motion for rehearing in the court of appeals, unless the court of appeals subsequently modifies its opinion or judgment. TEX. R. APP. P. 53.7(b).

4. TEX. R. APP. P. 49.1. Motion for Rehearing. A motion for rehearing may be filed within 15 days after the court of appeals' judgment or order is rendered. The motion must clearly state the points relied on for the rehearing.

5. TEX. R. APP. P. 49.5. Further Motion for Rehearing. After a motion for rehearing is decided, a further motion for rehearing may be filed within 15 days of the court's action if the court:

a. modifies its judgment
b. vacates its judgment and renders a new judgment; or
c. issues an opinion in overruling a motion for rehearing.

6. TEX. R. APP. PROC. 49.10. A motion or response must be no longer than 15 pages.

5. *Supreme Court Review of Decisions of the Courts of Appeals*

a. *In General*

Read Rules 53.4 Texas Rules of Appellate Procedure.

McKELVY
v.
BARBER
381 S.W.2d 59
(Tex. 1964)

John W. Herrick, Massie Tillman, Fort Worth, for petitioner.
Cantey, Hanger, Gooch, Cravens & Scarborough, Sloan B. Blair, Fort Worth, for respondent.

WALKER, JUSTICE.

Our opinion delivered in this cause on March 4, 1964, is withdrawn and the following is substituted therefor:

Jim C. McKelvy, petitioner, brought this suit again Dr. Forrest C. Barber, respondent, to recover damages alleged to have resulted from negligent medical treatment. Respondent's motion for instructed verdict at the conclusion of all the evidence was granted by the trial court, and the Court of Civil Appeals affirmed. 368 S.W.2d 38. As the case reaches us, the appeal presents two procedural problems and two questions of substantive law. We have concluded that respondent was not entitled to a peremptory instruction on any of the grounds asserted in his motion, and the cause will be remanded for a new trial.

Petitioner injured his finger in the course of his employment by American Manufacturing Company. He was taken by the Personnel Director to the office of respondent, who treated the injury. Petitioner later developed tetanus and was totally and permanently disabled at the time of trial. He settled with Pacific Employers Insurance Company, the compensation carrier for American, prior to the institution of this suit.

While respondent's motion for instructed verdict contains twenty numbered paragraphs, it actually asserts two basic and independent grounds for granting a peremptory instruction in his favor. These are: (1) that there is no evidence to support a finding that the tetanus was proximately caused by any negligence on respondent's part; and (2) that since the undisputed evidence shows that respondent was acting as the agent, servant or employee of American and its compensation carrier in treating petitioner, he is immune from liability by virtue of the provisions of Article 8306, § 3, Vernon's Ann. Tex. Civ. Stat. The judgment of the trial court merely recites that specific grounds were set forth in the motion for instructed verdict, and that the court was of the opinion that the motion was well taken and should be granted. To reverse the judgment of the trial court under these circumstances, it was necessary for petitioner to assume the appellate burden of establishing that the peremptory instruction cannot be supported on either of the grounds set out in the motion. If he has waived the right to question either of such grounds or if either is sound, the judgment of the trial court must be affirmed.

Petitioner was not required to file a motion for new trial as a prerequisite to an appellate attack on the action of the trial court in granting a peremptory instruction. Rule 324, Texas Rules of Civil Procedure. His brief as appellant in the Court of Civil Appeals contains three points of error which assert that there is evidence to support findings that the tetanus was proximately caused by respondent's negligence. Since he did not have a point of error complaining of the action of the trial court in sustaining the motion for instructed verdict on the second ground mentioned above, respondent says that petitioner has waived any complaint he might have had with respect thereto. We do not agree.

In the introduction to his brief as appellee in the Court of Civil Appeals, respondent stated that he presumed petitioner was not contesting the motion for peremptory instruction on any grounds other than as stated in the three points of error. By his Counterpoint No. 16 and the argument thereunder, however, respondent sought to uphold the instructed verdict on the statutory immunity ground urged in the trial court. Petitioner responded with an extended discussion of the question in his reply brief, and respondent then filed an additional reply dealing only with that issue. The Court of Civil Appeals did not affirm on the theory that petitioner had waived the right to complain of any error on the part of the trial court in granting a peremptory instruction on the second ground stated in the motion for instructed verdict. On the contrary, it considered the question on the merits, concluded that the position taken by respondent was sound, and accordingly affirmed the judgment of the trial court without considering the three points of error set out in petitioner's original brief. After a point of law has thus been brief in the Court of Civil Appeals, we think it should be treated as having been properly presented for decision at the intermediate court level even though not raised by a formal point of error in the appellant's brief.

Section 3 of Article 8306 provides that the employees of a subscriber shall have no right of action against their employer or against any agent, servant or employee of said employer for damages for personal injuries. An agent, servant or employee within the meaning of this statute is ordinarily one for whose conduct the employer would, aside from the Workmen's Compensation Act, be legally responsible under the doctrine of respondent superior. The statutory immunity does not extend, for example, to an independent contractor. *See Haynes v. Taylor*, Com. App., 35 S.W.2d 104, 38 S.W.2d 1101; *Cotton v. Henger*, Tex. Civ. App., 312 S.W.2d 299 (modified and affirmed, 159 Tex. 139, 316 S.W.2d 719). The injured claimant may thus be entitled to recover in a third-party action even though the defendant would be regarded as the employer's agent for some purposes. An important consideration in such cases is whether the employer had that right to control the physical details as to manner of performance which is characteristic of the relationship of master and servant. *See American Nat. Ins. Co. v. Denke*, 128 Tex. 229, 95 S.W.2d 370, 107 A.L.R. 409.

As pointed out by the Court of Civil Appeals, it is undisputed that respondent was the doctor for American Manufacturing Company. Petitioner so testified, as did respondent and a representative of the company. Respondent says that when all parties have thus conceded that he was engaged in work for the employer, a presumption arises that the relationship of master and servant existed between them. He contends that the courts below were required to give effect to such presumption because no evidence tending to show the existence of any other relationship was introduced.

It is unnecessary to decide here whether there are circumstances under which a medical practitioner who treats a patient would be regarded as the servant of another. In the ordinary case, however, where an industrial employer or its compensation carrier arranges for and pays a particular physician or surgeon to care for employees injured in the course of their employment, the parties do not contemplate that the relation of master and servant will arise between the employer or carrier on the one hand and the physician or surgeon on the other. The doctor is generally expected to exercise and rely entirely upon his own professional knowledge and skill without interference from either the employer or the insurance carrier. There is no presumption then of a master and servant relationship where the proof merely shows that an ordinary employer or insurance company has arranged for a doctor to treat another person. *See* 41 AM. JUR. PHYSICIANS AND SURGEONS § 116; Annotation, 19 A.L.R. 1168, 1183; Annotation, 69 A.L.R. 2D 305, 320; RESTATEMENT, SECOND, AGENCY § 223, Comment a; MECHEM, OUTLINES OF THE LAW OF AGENCY, 4th ed. 1952, § 432 et seq.

It appears from the evidence in this case that respondent is engaged in the general practice of medicine. Only about fifteen or twenty per cent of his practice is of an industrial nature. He is not on a retainer with American Manufacturing Company, but is paid for his services as they are rendered. His charges for treating injured workmen are paid by Pacific Employers, while American pays his fees for making physical examinations. The details of his relationship with the company are not fully developed, but the mere fact that he is generally regarded as the 'company doctor' and is paid by Pacific Employers does not conclusively establish that he is subject to the ultimate control of either in his treatment of industrial injuries. In our opinion the evidence fails to show as a matter of law that respondent is the agent, servant or employee of American Manufacturing Company or its compensation carrier in rendering such services, and the instructed verdict cannot rest upon the second ground stated above. *See Pedigo & Pedigo v. Croom*, Tex. Civ. App., 37 S.W.2d 1074 (wr. ref.); *Hoffman v. Houston Clinic*, Tex. Civ. App., 41 S.W.2d 134 (wr. dis.). This brings us to the second procedural question raised by respondent.

As indicated above, the Court of Civil Appeals did not pass upon petitioner's three points of error which attacked the first ground set out in the motion for instructed verdict. The failure of the intermediate court to consider and sustain such points was not assigned as error in petitioner's motion for rehearing in the Court of

Civil Appeals or in his application for writ of error here. Respondent says that in this situation the judgment of the trial court must be affirmed in any event because it rests upon an independent ground which cannot now be questioned. He thus seeks to invoke the rule that applies when the intermediate court has overruled points of error attacking an independent ground upon which the judgment of the trial court rests and its action in that respect is not brought forward for review. *See City of Deer Park v. State*, 154 Tex. 174, 275 S.W.2d 77.

'(I)t seems to be the definitely settled rule that the party who prevailed in the Court of Civil Appeals is entitled to have his assignment, which were properly presented in that court, considered by the Supreme Court in so far as may be necessary to determine what judgment should have been rendered by the Court of Civil Appeals.' *Holland v. Nimitz*, 111 Tex. 419, 232 S.W. 298, 239 S.W. 185. This refers to assignments or points of error that were not passed on by the Court of Civil Appeals. We have also said on several occasions that 'when it is determined that the Court of Civil Appeals erred in basing its judgment on a particular ground, the Supreme Court is authorized to consider the briefs filed in that court, not for the purpose of reversing its judgment, but for the purpose only of determining whether, by considering other assignments therein, it could affirm such judgment.' *See Texas Employers Ins. Ass'n v. Kennedy*, 135 Tex. 486, 143 S.W.2d 583; *Driver v. Worth Construction Co.*, 154 Tex. 66, 273 S.W.2d 603; *Garcia v. Moncada*, 127 Tex. 453, 94 S.W.2d 123.

These 'ground rules' which have evolved through the years are usually applied in the ordinary case where each of several points of error in the Court of Civil Appeals, if sustained, would require that the judgment of the trial court be reversed. All complaints of that nature must be considered and overruled before the intermediate court can properly affirm. If it does affirm and the appellant brings forward only some of the points in his application for writ of error, his other points in the Court of Civil Appeals are deemed to be waived, whether passed on by that court or not. This is so because the intermediate court plainly errs when it affirms without considering contention that might lead to a reversal, and the burden is on the losing party to complain of the error if he wishes us to pass on the question.

When the Court of Civil Appeals reverses in the ordinary case mentioned above, it will either render or remand as may be required by the point or points of error which are sustained. The losing party must then bring forward for review all rulings of the intermediate court which led to a reversal. If we decide that its holdings on these questions are unsound, the brief of the prevailing party in the Court of Civil Appeals may be examined to determine whether there are other points of error which warrant an affirmance of its judgment on a ground not considered by the intermediate court. *See Meyer v. Great American Indemnity Co.*, 154 Tex. 408, 279 S.W.2d 575. We may also remand the cause to the Court of Civil Appeals to enable it to pass on points of the prevailing party there which were rendered immaterial under its initial holding, even though the sustaining of such points would lead to a judgment different from that originally entered by the intermediate court. *See Wood v. Kane Boiler Works*, 150 Tex. 191, 238 S.W.2d 172; *Ritchie v. American Surety Co.*, 145 Tex. 422, 198, S.W.2d 85; *Baker v. Baker*, 143 Tex. 191, 183 S.W.2d 724; *Block v. Aetna Casualty & Surety Co.*, 138 Tex. 420, 159 S.W.2d 470; *McKenzie Construction Co. v. City of San Antonio*, 131 Tex. 474, 115 S.W.2d 617.

This is not one of the ordinary cases, and in our opinion is not governed by the general rules, discussed above. The judgment of the trial court can rest upon two independent grounds, and both rulings of that court were brought to the Court of Civil Appeals for review. After overruling the attack on one of such grounds, the intermediate court was not required to and did not pass on the appellant's points of error which challenged the other ground. The appellant then came to us with an application for writ of error which asserts that the holding of the Court of Civil Appeals on the question decided there is erroneous but does not mention the negligence and causation points that were not considered, and we have concluded that the points of error brought forward in the application should be sustained.

There appear to be only two previous cases in which this situation has arisen. In one of them the procedural problem with which we are now concerned was not raised, and the Commission of Appeals took the position that it was under a duty to pass on the question not considered by the Court of Civil Appeals. *Elliott v. Wallace*, Tex. Com. App., 59 S.W.2d 109. In the other case, the defendants in error argued at length, as respondent does here, that the judgment of the trial court should be affirmed because it could rest on a ruling not considered by the Court of Civil Appeals and not brought forward in the application for writ of error. This practice question was not decided, because the assignment of error was treated by the Supreme Court as being sufficiently broad to embrace all rulings made by the trial court. *Independent Eastern Torpedo Co. v. Herrington*, 128 Tex. 17, 95 S.W.2d 377.

A careful and seasoned appellate practitioner would have included in his application for writ of error a point asserting that the Court of Civil Appeals erred in failing to consider and sustain the points of error dealing with negligence and causation. Respondent says, in effect, that the failure to do so here requires us to affirm the judgment of the trial court no matter how erroneous it may be. That approach might save the Supreme Court some time, but it is also calculated to entrap the inexperienced appellate advocate. The attack in this Court is upon the judgment of the Court of Civil Appeals. That judgment rests squarely upon a single holding, which has been brought forward for review. When it is determined, as we have in this instance, that the conclusion reached by the intermediate court is unsound, it would certainly be proper to remand the cause to that court for a ruling on the points of error not previously considered by it. Since these points present only law question, however, we can and do dispose of them now instead of requiring the parties to go back to the Court of Civil Appeals and then possibly return here with a second application for writ of error. In our opinion the evidence raises issues of negligence and causation that can be resolved only by the trier of fact, and the trial court erred in granting respondents' motion for instructed verdict.

In *Jecker v. Western Alliance Ins. Co.*, Tex. Sup., 369 S.W.2d 776, and *Rogers v. Winters*, 161 Tex. 451, 341 S.W.2d 417, the Court of Civil Appeals reversed and rendered judgment for the appellant. After concluding that the holding of the intermediate court on the question considered by it was unsound, we refused to pass on other points of the appellant in that court which might have entitled the appellant to a reversal and remand or modification of the trial court's judgment. It was reasoned that such complaints would, if sustained, result in an alteration of the judgment of the Court of Civil Appeals, and therefore could not be considered unless brought to this Court by cross-point. These holdings of *Jecker* and *Rogers* are not consistent with the line of cases represented by *Wood v. Kane Boiler Works, supra*, and will not be followed in the future.

The judgments of the courts below are reversed, and the cause is remanded to the district court for a new trial.

Notes

1. The new Rules of Appellate Procedure apparently change the result in the last case. A party in the position of Dr. Barber should bring forward to the Supreme Court in his response to the petition for review and in his brief the independent ground for affirmance of the court of appeal's judgment. *See* Rules 53.3(c)(2) and 55.3(c)(2) of the Texas Rules of Appellate Procedure. However, Rule 53.4 states that a party may obtain either a remand to the court of appeals or consideration by the Supreme Court of points briefed in the lower court, but not decided by that court, by filing a motion for rehearing [among other pleadings] with the Supreme Court pursuant to Rule 64; and Rule 61.3 notes that the Court will not reverse a judgment for defects or irregularities in appellate procedure without giving the party a reasonable time to correct the defect or irregularity. Until there is further direction in this area, the "seasoned lawyer" should bring forward to the Supreme Court these types of points or issues.

2. *Center for Health Care Services v. Quintanilla*, 121 S.W.3d 733 (Tex. 2003): This is an action for wrongful termination. Quintanilla is a former employee of The Center for Health Care Services, a mental health and mental retardation center. After the Center terminated him, Quintanilla sued the Center alleging, among other things, violations of section 161.134 of the Texas Health and Safety Code and the Texas Whistleblower Act. TEX. HEALTH & SAFETY CODE § 161.134; TEX. GOV'T CODE § 554.002. Then by enacting Texas Health and Safety Code section 161.134, the Legislature did not intend to waive the State's sovereign immunity from suit. In his responsive brief on the merits filed eight months after the Center's petition for review, Quintanilla, for the first time, requested reversal of that portion of the court of appeals' judgment dismissing his Whistleblower claim. He did not file a petition for review, and his response to the Center's petition does not complain of the court of appeals' dismissal of his Whistleblower Act claim. Instead, he confined his argument solely to the sovereign immunity issue. He has, therefore, waived the right to seek reversal of that portion of the court of appeals' judgment. TEX. R. APP. P. 53.1 ("A party who seeks to alter the court of appeals' judgment must file a petition for review."), 53.2 ("The petition must state concisely all issues or points presented for review.").

3. TEX. R. APP. PROC. 53.3(c)(2) now requires the respondent to state issues if "the respondent is asserting independent grounds for affirmance of the court of appeals' judgment . . . ." Likewise TEX. R. APP. PROC. 55.3(c)(2) requires the state issues if "the respondent is asserting independent grounds of affirmance of the court of appeals' judgment. . . .."

4. Before the 1997 amendments, "the Supreme Court would examine the respondent's brief to the court of appeals and affirm on any basis presented in that brief. *Roark v. Allen*, 633 S.W.2d 804 (Tex. 1982). * * * Thus, the respondent received a review of all possible grounds supporting the judgment of the court of appeals without actually presenting them to the Supreme Court. * * * If the Supreme Court overlooked a ground to affirm, the respondent was permitted to raise the matter on rehearing. Likewise, the Supreme Court inspected the respondent's brief in the court of appeals to determine if there were grounds for a judgment granting the respondent some relief, but less relief than actually granted by the court of appeals. * * * Thus, before rendering judgment against the respondent, where the court of appeals had rendered judgment for the respondent, the Supreme Court would consider any grounds presented by the respondent to the court of appeals which might require a new trial. * * * However, in *Davis v. City of San Antonio*, 752 S.W.2d 518(Tex. 1988) the Supreme Court refused to remand the respondent's factual sufficiency points to the court of appeals and refused to permit the respondent to amend its response to raise the factual sufficiency points before the Supreme Court. . . . The 1997 amendment to this rule represents a compromise between the result in Davis and the long-standing prior law. These issues must be presented to the Supreme Court in some fashion, and the Court will not notice the *sua sponte*. However, they may be raised as late as a motion for rehearing after the opinion on the merits." HANBY'S TEXAS RULES OF APPELLATE PROCEDURE ANNOTATED (1999), 171.

b. *Review of No Evidence Points of Error*

Reread Section 22.225 of the Texas Government Code.

Notes

1. In *Joske v. Irvine*, 91 Tex. 574, 44 S.W. 1059 (1898), JUSTICE DENMAN clearly articulated what has become the classic statement of the scope of review by the Supreme Court concerning no evidence points of error. He noted:

> Since the scintilla doctrine has been exploded, both in England and in this country, the preliminary question of law for the court is, not whether there is literally no evidence, or a mere scintilla, but whether there is any that ought reasonably to satisfy the jury that the fact sought to be proved is established. If there is evidence from which the jury can properly find the question for the party on whom the burden of proof rests, it should be submitted; if not, if should be withdrawn from the jury . . . . [I]t is not enough to authorize the submission of a question, as one of fact, to a jury, that there is 'some evidence.' A scintilla of evidence, or a mere surmise that there may have been negligence on the part of the defendants, would not justify the judge in leaving the case to the jury; and held that a single act of casual neglect, though admissible as evidence, as held by this court in *Cunningham v. Railway Co.*, 88 Tex. 534, 31 S. W. 629, was not sufficient to authorize a jury to find that an employee was incompetent, and that the retention of such employee in its service, after having investigated the facts connected with such act, would not authorize a finding that the company was guilty of negligence in continuing to employ him.
>
> This court in *Lee v. Railway Co.*, 89 Tex. 588, 36 S. W. 65, said: 'To authorize the court to take the question from the jury, the evidence must be of such a character that there is no room for ordinary minds to differ as to the conclusion to be drawn from it.' In *Mynning v. Railroad Co.*, 64 Mich. 93, 31 N. W. 147, the rule is stated thus: 'If the circumstances are such that reasonable minds might draw different conclusions respecting the plaintiff's fault, he is entitled to go to the jury upon the facts. The judge takes the case from the jury only when it is susceptible of but one just opinion.'

From a careful examination of the cases, it appears (1) that it is the duty of the court to instruct a verdict, though there be slight testimony, if its probative force be so weak that it only raises a mere surmise or suspicion of the existence of the fact sought to be established, such testimony, in legal contemplation, falling short of being 'any evidence'; and (2) that it is the duty of the court to determine whether the testimony has more than that degree of probative force. If it so determines, the law presumes that the jury could not 'reasonably infer the existence of the alleged fact,' and 'that there is no room for ordinary minds to differ as to the conclusion to be drawn from it.' The broad and wise policy of the law, formed in and descending to us through the crucibles of time, does not permit the citizen to be deprived of his property, his liberty, or his life upon mere surmise or suspicion, and places upon a trained judiciary the grave responsibility of determining as a question of law whether the testimony establishes more. 'There is, no doubt, a possibility, in all cases where the judges have to determine whether there is evidence on which the jury may reasonably find a fact, that the judges may differ in opinion, and it is possible that the majority may be wrong. Indeed, whenever a decision of the court below on such a point is reversed, the majority must have been so either in the court above or the court below. This is an infirmity which must affect all tribunals.' *Ryder v. Wombwell, supra.*

2. No evidence points of error may be sustained only when the record discloses (1) a complete absence of evidence of a vital fact, (2) the court is barred by rules of law or of evidence from giving weight to the only evidence offered to prove a vital fact, (3) the evidence offered to prove a vital fact is no more than a mere scintilla, and (4) the evidence established conclusively the opposite of the vital fact. *See* Calvert, *"No Evidence" and "Insufficient Evidence" Points of Error*, 38 TEX. L. REV. 361, 362-63 (1960). Thus, the standard of review for "no evidence" points entails two inquiries. The first addresses the quality of the evidence offered, inquiring whether the evidence offered has a tendency to prove the existence of a material fact. *See generally* Powers & Ratliff, *Another Look at "No Evidence" and "Insufficient Evidence" Points of Error*, 69 TEX. L. REV. 515, 521-23 (1991). The second is quantitative and inquires as to whether there is more than a mere scintilla of probative evidence. *Id.*

LEITCH
v.
HORNSBY

935 S.W.2d 114
(Tex. 1996)

Charles M. Jefferson, San Antonio, for Petitioners.
Charles A. Nicholson, San Antonio, for Respondent.

BAKER, JUSTICE.

Grady Hornsby sued his employer, Pro Com Marketing Services, Inc., for damages for back injuries Hornsby suffered when he lifted a cable reel. Hornsby also joined Russell Leitch and Hal Crews, officers, directors, and stockholders of Pro Com as defendants. The trial court rendered judgment on a jury verdict against Pro Com, Leitch, and Crews, jointly and severally for almost $700,000. The court of appeals affirmed the trial court's judgment. 885 S.W.2d 243.

This appeal raises the issue of the corporate officers' personal liability and whether there is some evidence of negligence and causation for Hornsby's injury. We conclude the court of appeals erred in affirming the trial court's judgment holding Leitch and Crews individually liable. We also conclude that Hornsby produced no probative evidence to prove causation between his back injury and Pro Com's alleged negligence. Accordingly, we reverse the court of appeals' judgment and render judgment that Grady Hornsby take nothing from Pro Com Marketing Services, Inc., Russell Leitch, and Hal Crews.

I. BACKGROUND

A. FACTS

Pro Com is a cable television servicing company. In 1989, Pro Com began installing cable wire for households to which it had sold cable services. When it began installation of cable wire, Pro Com hired Grady Hornsby to be its technical manager. As technical manager, Pro Com placed Hornsby in charge of cable installation, including the training and supervision of other Pro Com employees. While preparing to go to a job site for a Pro Com contract, Hornsby began unloading equipment from his truck including a reel of cable. Hornsby did not wear a lift belt, nor did he have a dolly available to unload the cable reel. The reel weighed about 65 pounds. When he lifted the reel he injured his back.

Before working for Pro Com, Hornsby had worked for eight to ten different cable companies. None of these companies had provided lifting belts for its employees. Hornsby testified some of his previous employers had provided their workers with safety belts but not lifting belts. Some of the companies had supplied dollies for their employees. Hornsby requested Pro Com to furnish some of this equipment. Pro Com refused to do so.

B. THE TRIAL AND APPEAL

At the time of Hornsby's injury, Pro Com did not subscribe to workers' compensation insurance. Consequently, Hornsby sued Pro Com, Leitch, and Crews for common law negligence. Hornsby asserted that all three defendants did not provide a safe work place and equipment, did not provide proper equipment, did not provide a protective lift belt, and did not give safety instructions and training. The jury found that Hornsby's injury occurred while he acted as a Pro Com employee, that the negligence of Pro Com, Leitch, and Crews proximately caused Hornsby's injuries, that Hornsby's damages were $594,000, and that Pro Com was not the alter ego of Leitch and Crews. The trial court rendered judgment on the jury verdict and held Pro Com, Leitch, and Crews jointly and severally liable for the damages the jury awarded together with prejudgment interest. The court of appeals affirmed the trial court's judgment.

* * *

III. NEGLIGENCE AND CAUSATION

Although Hornsby alleged Pro Com did not provide proper safety instructions and training, Hornsby's evidence focused on Pro Com's failure to provide proper lifting equipment. Hornsby produced no evidence of lack of proper training. Moreover, Hornsby testified that as Pro Com's technical manager, he knew how to properly lift cable wire. Pro Com, Leitch, and Crews contend that the basis of Hornsby's complaint is that he would not have injured his back if he had been furnished a lift belt or other equipment to lift the cable reel out of his truck. They argue that the evidence shows that business custom in the cable installation industry is that the industry does not provide its installers with lifting equipment such as lift belts. They assert this is evidence that they were not negligent when they declined to provide Hornsby with lifting equipment. Pro Com, Leitch, and Crews also argue that, assuming they owed a duty to furnish Hornsby with lifting equipment, their breach of such a duty was not the cause of Hornsby's injury. Finally, they assert Hornsby did not present any evidence to show his injury would not have happened if he had been provided with and had been using a lift belt or other lifting equipment.

A. APPLICABLE LAW

1. No Evidence—Standard of Review

When we review a no evidence claim, we consider only the evidence and inferences tending to support the jury's fact finding. We disregard all contrary evidence and inferences. *See Transport Ins. Co. v. Faircloth*, 898 S.W.2d 269, 275-76 (Tex. 1995); *Browning-Ferris, Inc. v. Reyna*, 865 S.W.2d 925, 928 (Tex. 1993). If there is any evidence of probative force to support the finding, we overrule the point of error and uphold the jury's finding. *Southern States Transp., Inc. v. State*, 774 S.W.2d 639, 640 (Tex. 1989); *Stafford v. Stafford*, 726 S.W.2d 14, 16 (Tex. 1987). If there is more than a scintilla of probative evidence in the record to support the finding, a no evidence challenge fails. *Stafford*, 726 S.W.2d at 16.

2. Proximate Cause

A plaintiff must plead and prove that the defendant's negligence is the proximate cause of his injury. Proximate cause consists of cause in fact and foreseeability. *See Farley v. M M Cattle Co.*, 529 S.W.2d 751, 755 (Tex. 1975). The foreseeability of a back injury in connection with regular lifting of heavy objects is judged by a reasonable person standard. *See Exxon Corp. v. Roberts*, 724 S.W.2d 863, 867 (Tex. App.—Texarkana 1986, writ ref'd n.r.e.). In a case like this one, where there is no medical testimony linking the alleged negligence to the injury, a claimant must provide probative evidence, through expert testimony, connecting the injury to the alleged negligence. *See Lenger v. Physician's Gen. Hosp., Inc.*, 455 S.W.2d 703, 706 (Tex. 1970); *Sears, Roebuck & Co. v. Hurst*, 652 S.W.2d 563, 565 (Tex. App.—Fort Worth 1983, writ ref'd n.r.e.); *Orkin Exterminating Co. v. Davis*, 620 S.W.2d 734, 736-37 (Tex. Civ. App.—Dallas 1981, writ ref'd n.r.e.); *cf. Royal Globe Ins. Co. v. Suson*, 626 S.W.2d 161, 163-64 (Tex. App.—Fort Worth 1981, writ ref'd n.r.e.)(holding that expert testimony not required to establish link between back injury and on-the-job incident). Whether proper lifting equipment would have prevented the injury is not a question that can be answered by general experience. *See Lenger*, 455 S.W.2d at 706. Incompetent opinion testimony is not evidence, and a finding supported only by such testimony cannot survive a no evidence challenge. *See Missouri Pac. R.R. Co. v. Buenrostro*, 853 S.W.2d 66, 77 (Tex. App.—San Antonio 1993, writ denied); Calvert, *"No Evidence" & "Insufficient Evidence" Points of Error*, 38 TEX. L. REV. 361, 362-63 (1960). Proof of causation cannot "turn upon speculation or conjecture." *Lenger*, 455 S.W.2d at 706.

B. APPLICATION OF LAW TO FACTS

Hornsby pleaded that Pro Com did not provide him with proper equipment to lift heavy objects and other gear related to the business. Hornsby testified that he had to carry heavy reels of cable for Pro Com. Hornsby said he frequently requested safety equipment from Pro Com such as dollies, lift belts or truck mounted reels. One of Hornsby's co-workers testified that he and Hornsby requested dollies and holders for the spools. Hornsby also testified that he had previously worked for eight to ten cable installation companies and that none of those companies had furnished lift belts. The evidence also showed that Hornsby and others requested Pro Com to provide lift belts, dollies, or truck mounted reels and Pro Com refused to do so.

We assume, without deciding, that Pro Com had a duty to provide Hornsby with proper lifting equipment. We also assume, without deciding, that Hornsby's back injury was caused by lifting the cable reel. Despite these assumptions, the record is clear, and we conclude, that no probative evidence exists that Hornsby's injury was proximately caused by the breach of any such duty.

The record shows Hornsby's treating physician testified that lifting the cable reel caused Hornsby's back injury. However, in response to a question about whether Hornsby's injury could have been prevented by the use of a lift belt, Hornsby's treating physician testified: "I would be unable to comment. I don't think there is anything that would be available to say yes or no in that respect." This testimony is no evidence of causation. *See Lenger*, 455 S.W.2d at 706-07.

Hornsby's co-worker, Larry Whidden, did not witness the incident in question. Hornsby did not offer Whidden as an expert witness. Nevertheless, Whidden expressed his opinion that the use of a lift belt would have eliminated Hornsby's injury. Pro Com argues that Whidden's testimony is no evidence, because as Pro Com objected at trial, Whidden was not qualified to testify about whether lifting equipment would have prevented Hornsby's injury. We agree. Whidden's testimony has no probative worth and is not proper evidence of causation because his testimony amounts to mere conjecture, and because he was not qualified to testify about what type of lifting devices might have prevented Hornsby's injuries. *See* TEX. R. CIV. EVID. 702; *Lenger*, 455 S.W.2d at 706; *Buenrostro*, 853 S.W.2d at 77. Therefore, this is no evidence to support the jury's verdict.

There is no other evidence in the record connecting Hornsby's injury with Pro Com's failure to provide proper lifting equipment. Thus, we conclude the court of appeals erred in holding that there was legally sufficient evidence to support the jury's finding that Pro Com's failure to furnish appropriate lifting equipment was a cause in fact of Hornsby's back injury.

IV. CONCLUSION

Because the duty to furnish a safe work place is the duty of Pro Com, Hornsby's employer, and not that of Pro Com's employees in their individual capacities, we hold that the court of appeals erred in holding Leitch and Crews individually liable for Pro Com's alleged negligence. We also hold that Hornsby did not provide legally sufficient evidence of causation between his back injury and Pro Com's alleged negligence. Accordingly, the court of appeals erred in holding that Hornsby carried his burden of proof on the causation issue.

Therefore, we reverse the court of appeals' judgment. We render judgment that Grady Hornsby take nothing from Pro Com Marketing Services, Inc., Russell Leitch, and Hal Crews.

SPECTOR, J., not sitting.

ABBOTT, JUSTICE, concurring.

I agree with the Court's judgment and with most of its opinion. I write separately only to provide a more detailed discussion of why no evidence supports the jury's verdict.

Because of constitutionally mandated limitations on our review of facts, this Court should tread very carefully whenever we are requested to determine that no evidence supports a jury's verdict. Well-established law guides our evaluation of a no evidence point of error. The Texas Constitution requires that "the decision of [the courts of appeals] shall be conclusive on all questions of fact brought before them on appeal or error." TEX. CONST. art. V, § 6. This provision "restrict[s], in express terms, the jurisdiction of the supreme court, and . . . confine[s] it to questions of law." *Choate v. San Antonio & A.P. Ry. Co.*, 91 Tex. 406, 44 S.W. 69, 69 (1898); *see Coulson v. Lake LBJ Municipal Util. Dist.*, 781 S.W.2d 594, 597 (Tex. 1989) (acknowledging that this Court has no jurisdiction to undertake factual sufficiency review); *Gulf, Colorado & Santa Fe Ry. Co. v. Deen*, 158 Tex. 466, 312 S.W.2d 933, 938 (1958) (Texas Supreme Court cannot conduct factual sufficiency review); *Wilson v. Wilson*, 145 Tex. 607, 201 S.W.2d 226, 227 (1947) ("the Supreme Court is not invested with the power to determine facts."); *see also* Hall, *Revisiting Standards of Review in Civil Appeals*, 24 ST. MARY'S L.J. 1045, 1139 (1993) (constitutional "provision . . . acts as a limitation on the judicial authority of the supreme court and confines its jurisdiction to questions of law").

When determining a no evidence point of error in accordance with these constitutional limitations, this Court "must consider only the evidence and inferences tending to support the jury's finding, viewed most favorably in support of the finding, and disregard all contrary evidence and inferences." *Havner v. E-Z Mart Stores, Inc.*, 825 S.W.2d 456, 458 (Tex. 1992); *see Garza v. Alviar*, 395 S.W.2d 821, 823 (Tex. 1965); *Cartwright v. Canode*, 106 Tex. 502, 171 S.W. 696, 698 (1914). If there is any evidence of probative force to support the finding, we overrule the point of error and uphold the jury's finding. *Southern States Transp., Inc. v. State*, 774 S.W.2d 639, 640 (Tex. 1989). If more than a scintilla of evidence exists, the claim is sufficient as a matter of law, and any challenges go merely to the weight to be accorded the evidence. *See Stafford v. Stafford*, 726 S.W.2d 14, 16 (Tex. 1987); *In re King's Estate*, 150 Tex. 662, 244 S.W.2d 660, 661 (1951).

The limitations on this Court's ability to review evidence do not mandate, however, that we abstain from reviewing a jury's verdict when a party fails to offer any evidence on an element of a cause of action. Simply because a party presents several days of testimony for the jury's consideration does not mean that this Court is exceeding its constitutional limitations by requiring that the testimony amount to a scintilla of evidence in support of the legal elements of the cause of action. While jurors are vested with the authority to evaluate the evidence and weigh the credibility of witnesses, some legally sufficient evidence must nevertheless exist to support their verdict.

Mr. Hornsby claimed that the defendants were negligent by failing to supply him a lift belt and a dolly to help him lift the cable reel and by failing to provide a safe place to work. To succeed on his negligence claims, Mr. Hornsby had to offer at least some evidence establishing that the defendants' alleged acts or omissions proximately caused his injuries.

The record shows that twelve witnesses were called to testify at trial. Only two of them, Dr. Paul Geibel and Larry Whidden, were asked a question concerning proximate cause. Dr. Geibel provided the following testimony:

> Q. And could you please tell the jury what in your opinion is the cause of his [Mr. Hornsby's] injuries?
> A. Well, he has been symptomatic from the three-level disc herniating in his back and the spondylolisthesis at the bottom level, the instability. By his history this became symptomatic at the time of his lifting injury in September of 1990.

This answer demonstrates that Mr. Hornsby's injury was caused by lifting the reel, but it offers nothing regarding whether acts or omissions of the defendants were the proximate cause of that injury.

Later, Dr. Geibel provided some testimony regarding the lift belts:

> Q. Okay. Now getting back to the belts, if they are to provide this support as you testified, how wide do they have to be to do an effective job?
> A. I don't think there is any studies proving the amount of belts or use of them or degrees of width or anything that would predict any—any decrease in amount of injuries or anything along that nature.
>
> Q. Okay. To follow-up on that just a little bit, Doctor, I get the impression that you don't think perhaps the belt is necessarily a preventative device; is that a fair statement?
> A. I don't feel that it's as totally preventative as one would feel it would be. It doesn't hurt anything.
>
> Q. Doesn't hurt but it doesn't necessarily help?
> A. Correct.
>
> Q. As far as if an accident of this nature were to occur and cause a three-level disc herniating, is that something that you think could have been prevented by the use of a belt such as we've been talking about?
> A. I would be unable to comment. I don't think there is anything that would be available to say yes or no in that respect.

The testimony quoted above is the only evidence provided by Dr. Geibel regarding proximate cause and no other questions were posed to him on that issue. Dr. Geibel's testimony demonstrates that he has no opinion on the proximate cause issue. Clearly, this evidence does not constitute any legally sufficient evidence of causation.

Mr. Hornsby's co-worker, Larry Whidden, offered only the following testimony about the proximate cause issue:

> Q. And what kind of equipment did you request from them?
> A. Dollies for the cable, lift belts, something, you know, that would make the job a little bit easier, less strain, because the equipment, most of the equipment was on the heavy side.
>
> Q. And in your opinion, would this equipment have assisted you in lifting these cable reels?
> A. Lift belt would have eliminated this injury.
>
> Mr. Walton (counsel for defense): Your Honor, I'm going to object to that. I think that calls for an expert opinion, that is well beyond any demonstrated knowledge he has.
>
> The Court: Sustained.
>
> Q. In any event, sir, do you believe this equipment you are talking about, the dollies and the safety belt, from your experience of lifting these cables, do you think that would have helped you?
> A. Yes, it would have.
>
> Q. All right.
>
> Mr. Walton: Your Honor, again, I'm going to object as far as that calls for speculation, it's not something that he has any specialized knowledge with regard to what lift belts and cable dollies did.
>
> The Witness: Well, Your Honor, I've worked with those before. The Court: Sir, I can handle it all by myself. Okay. Overruled.

The last answer demonstrates nothing more than Mr. Whidden's belief that the safety equipment would have helped Mr. Whidden and Mr. Hornsby do their jobs. It certainly does not provide even a scintilla of probative evidence connecting Mr. Hornsby's injury to the alleged negligence of the defendants.

Mr. Whidden's earlier answer, that the "lift belt would have eliminated this injury," would establish proximate cause if Whidden had been a properly qualified expert witness. However, Mr. Walton's sustained objection properly challenged Mr. Whidden's ability to provide expert testimony. Earlier testimony developed Mr. Whidden's expertise as a cable worker and as a person who has used safety equipment, but there is no testimony developing Mr. Whidden's expertise regarding the causal connection between the use of safety belts and the prevention of herniated discs. Just like an ordinary automobile driver is not qualified to testify that a seatbelt can prevent a herniated disc, Mr. Whidden was not qualified to testify that the lift belt would have prevented Mr. Hornsby's injury.

Other than the testimony detailed in this concurring opinion, there is no evidence even arguably linking Mr. Hornsby's injury to the acts or omissions of the defendants. Accordingly, I concur with the Court's judgment that "the court of appeals erred in holding that Hornsby carried his burden of proof on the causation issue."

6. *The Petition for Review*

Read Rules 53 and 55 of the Texas Rules of Appellate Procedure.

7. *Direct Appeal to the Supreme Court of Texas*

Read Rule 57 of the Texas Rules of Appellate Procedure.

STATE OF TEXAS
v.
HODGES
92 S.W.3d 489
(Tex. 2002)

Elections. Candidate Who Votes in Other Party's Election Is Ineligible to Be Nominee of Own Party.

TEX. ELEC. CODE § 162.015(a)(2), which prohibits a person from appearing on the general election ballot as a candidate for a political party "other than the party holding the primary in which the person voted or was a candidate," cannot be reasonably be construed to permit Judge David Hodges to appear as a Democratic Party candidate in the November 2002 election, since he voted in the Republican Party primary. The statute precludes Judge Hodges from running as a Democratic Party nominee in the general election, based on his participation in the Republican Party primary. Section 162.015(a)(2) is an ineligibility statute rather than an eligibility statute.

Election Code § 162.015(a)(2) Is Constitutional.

Utilizing the balancing test articulated in *Anderson v. Celebrezee*, 460 U.S. 780, 789, 103 S.Ct. 1564, 75 L.Ed.2d 547 (1983), TEX. ELEC. CODE § 162.015(a)(2) does not violate either the Texas or United States Constitutions.

Direct Appeals. Jurisdiction of Supreme Court. Extended Jurisdiction.

Under TEX. GOV'T CODE § 22.001(c) the Supreme Court has direct appeal jurisdiction from "an order of a trial court granting or denying an interlocutory or permanent injunction on the ground of the constitutionality of a statute of this state." In addition, when the Supreme Court has appellate jurisdiction over any issue, it acquires "extended jurisdiction" over all other questions of law properly preserved and presented.

Direct Appeals. Standard of Review.

The Supreme Court's review on direct appeal is confined to questions of law. Questions raising constitutional concerns are reviewed de novo.

Notes

1. In *Episcopal Diocese of Fort Worth v. Episcopal Church*, --- S.W.3d ----, 2013 WL 4608728 (Tex.), 56 Tex. Sup. Ct. J. 1034 (August 30, 2013) Justice Willett in his dissenting opinion discussed the history of the direct appeal in Texas:

> Until 1940, when Texans amended their constitution, the Supreme Court of Texas lacked any authority to decide direct appeals (i.e., appeals that leapfrog the court of appeals and pass directly to this Court). Four years later, the Legislature first exercised its new power to permit direct appeals, and in the sixty-nine years since, this Court has exercised that jurisdiction sparingly, only forty-three times. The reason is simply stated: Our direct-appeal jurisdiction is exceedingly narrow and only proper if the trial court granted or denied an injunction "on the ground of the constitutionality of a statute of this state."
>
> Today's direct appeal is directly unappealable. The trial court's order nowhere mentions any constitution or statute, much less the constitutionality of a statute. Indeed, the trial court stated verbally that it was not pivoting on the constitutionality of state law. This dispute undoubtedly has a First Amendment overlay, but for a direct appeal, constitutionality must exist not just in the ether, but in the order.
>
> As the trial court did not determine "the constitutionality of a statute of this state," its injunction could hardly be issued "on the ground of the constitutionality of a statute of this state." Accordingly, we lack jurisdiction.
>
> * * *
>
> A 1940 constitutional amendment gave the Legislature power to grant direct appeals to this Court. Not until 1944, though, did the Legislature do so. The original conferral allowed direct appeals from injunctions based on two grounds, either (1) the constitutionality or unconstitutionality of a state statute, or (2) the validity or invalidity of certain state administrative orders. Today, the statutory grant of direct-appeal jurisdiction covers just one situation: "[A]n order of a trial court granting or denying an interlocutory or permanent injunction on the ground of the constitutionality of a statute of this state."
>
> I have found only forty-three cases where we have exercised direct-appeal jurisdiction. That is, while such jurisdiction has existed for nearly seventy years, we have exercised it stintingly. In twenty-four of the forty-three cases, our opinion made clear that the trial court either made a direct holding about a statute's constitutionality or issued declaratory relief that a statute was or was not constitutional. In eleven other cases, the trial court's order clearly must have been based on constitutional grounds, either because the opinion implies that only constitutional issues were raised to the trial court or because the trial court granted an injunction enforcing a statute over constitutional objection, thus implicitly upholding the statute against constitutional attack. In two other cases, we summarily stated that the trial court granted or denied the injunction on the ground of a statute's constitutionality. But in at least six direct-appeal cases, we did not make it clear why we thought the trial court's injunction was based on constitutional grounds. These cases address jurisdiction rather cursorily, and only one of the opinions garnered a dissent on the jurisdictional issue, to which the majority opinion declined to respond.
>
> But in the vast majority of cases where we have exercised direct-appeal jurisdiction, it has been abundantly clear that the trial court issued or denied an injunction on the ground of a statute's constitutionality.
>
> We have also issued at least eleven opinions in which we *dismissed* attempted direct appeals for want of jurisdiction because the statutory test was not met. We have variously explained that our direct-appeal jurisdiction "is a limited one," that we have been "strict in applying" or have "strictly applied" direct-appeal jurisdictional requirements, and that "[w]e have strictly construed our direct appeal jurisdiction." Therefore, we have held that to meet the jurisdictional prerequisites, a trial court must actually "pass upon the constitutionality of [a] statute," "determin[e]" a statute's constitutionality, or "base its decision" on constitutional grounds. Indeed, "[i]t is not enough that a question of the constitutionality of a statute may have been raised in order for our direct appeal jurisdiction to attach in

injunction cases; in addition the trial court must have made a holding on the question based *on the grounds* of the constitutionality or unconstitutionality of the statute."

A close examination of the eleven cases where we dismissed for want of jurisdiction reveals strict adherence to the Legislature's restricted framework. For example, we held "no jurisdiction" where the trial court made the injunction decision based on res judicata or where the trial court was directed to do so by a writ of prohibition by the court of civil appeals. That is, because the trial court did not decide the merits of the constitutional issue, we lacked direct-appeal jurisdiction. Similarly, we held that we did not have such jurisdiction where the trial court denied an injunction because the plaintiffs lacked "the necessary justiciable interest" to sue. We even held that we lacked jurisdiction over a direct appeal of a temporary injunction involving a "serious question" of the constitutionality of a statute, because the real purpose of the temporary injunction was merely to preserve the status quo, and the trial court did not make any holdings finally determining the constitutional issue.

2. The judgment of an appellate court is note enforceable until the appellate court issues its mandate. Rule 18.1: Issuance of the Texas Rules of Appellate Procedure provides:

> The clerk of the appellate court that rendered the judgment must issue a mandate in accordance with the judgment and send it to the clerk of the court to which it is directed and to all parties to the proceeding when one of the following periods expires:
>
> (a) In the Court of Appeals.
>
> (1) Ten days after the time has expired for filing a motion to extend time to file a petition for review or a petition for discretionary review if:
>
> (A) no timely petition for review or petition for discretionary review has been filed;
>
> (B) no timely filed motion to extend time to file a petition for review or petition for discretionary review is pending; and
>
> (C) in a criminal case, the Court of Criminal Appeals has not granted review on its own initiative.
>
> (2) Ten days after the time has expired for filing a motion to extend time to file a motion for rehearing of a denial, refusal, or dismissal of a petition for review, or a refusal or dismissal of a petition for discretionary review, if no timely filed motion for rehearing or motion to extend time is pending.
>
> (b) In the Supreme Court and the Court of Criminal Appeals. Ten days after the time has expired for filing a motion to extend time to file a motion for rehearing if no timely filed motion for rehearing or motion to extend time is pending.
>
> (c) Agreement to Issue. The mandate may be issued earlier if the parties so agree, or for good cause on the motion of a party.

CHAPTER 9. ORIGINAL JURISDICTION OF APPELLATE COURTS

1. *Introduction*

Read Rule 52 Texas Rules of Appellate Procedure.

Notes

1. As should be obvious by now, Texas appellate courts not only have appellate jurisdiction—generally confined to a review of final orders—but also have original jurisdiction. The original jurisdiction of the Texas appellate courts extends to considering petitions for mandamus, habeas corpus, and other writs. In exercising their original jurisdiction, the Texas appellate courts are called upon to make determinations concerning the actions of trial courts and other officials of the state. The authority for these original proceedings is constitutional. In response to the constitutional grant of power the legislature has enacted statutes which define the extent of this grant of constitutional authority.

2. Article 5, Section 3 of the Texas Constitution provides in part:

> . . . The Supreme Court and the Justices thereof shall have power to issue writs of habeas corpus, as may be prescribed by law, and under such regulations as may be prescribed by law, the said courts and Justices thereof may issue the writs of mandamus, procedendo, certiorari and such other writs, as may be necessary to enforce its jurisdiction. The Legislature may confer original jurisdiction on the Supreme Court to issue writs of quo warranto and mandamus in such cases as may be specified, except as against the Governor of the State. . . .

3. Article 5, Section 6 of the Texas Constitution provides in part:

> . . . Said courts [courts of appeals] shall have such other jurisdiction, original and appellate, as may be prescribed by law. . . .

4. The Texas Government Code Section 22.002 provides:

> Writ Power
>
> (a) The supreme court or a justice of the supreme court may issue writs of procedendo and certiorari and all writs of quo warranto and mandamus agreeable to the principles of law regulating those writs, against a district judge, a court of appeals or a justice of a court of appeals, or any officer of state government except the governor, the court of criminal appeals, or a judge of the court of criminal appeals.
>
> (b) The supreme court or, in vacation, a justice of the supreme court may issue a writ of mandamus to compel a district judge to proceed to trial and judgment in a case agreeable to the principles and usages of law, returnable to the supreme court on or before the first day of the term, or during the session of the term, or before any justice of the supreme court as the nature of the case requires.
>
> (c) Only the supreme court has the authority to issue a writ of mandamus or injunction, or any other mandatory or compulsory writ or process, against any of the officers of the executive departments of the government of this state to order or compel the performance of a judicial, ministerial, or discretionary act or duty that, by state law, the officer or officers are authorized to perform.
>
> (d) Repealed by Acts 1987, 70th Leg., ch. 148, s 2.03, eff. Sept. 1, 1987.
>
> (e) The supreme court or a justice of the supreme court, either in termtime or vacation, may issue a writ of habeas corpus when a person is restrained in his liberty by virtue of an order, process, or commitment issued by a court or judge on account of the violation of an order, judgment, or decree previously made, rendered, or entered by the court or judge in a civil case. Pending the hearing of an application for a writ of habeas corpus, the supreme court or a justice of the supreme court may admit to bail a person to whom the writ of habeas corpus may be so granted.

5. The Texas Government Code section 22.221 provides:

Writ Power

(a) Each court of appeals or a justice of a court of appeals may issue a writ of mandamus and all other writs necessary to enforce the jurisdiction of the court.

(b) Each court of appeals for a court of appeals district may issue all writs of mandamus, agreeable to the principles of law regulating those writs, against a judge of a district or county court in the court of appeals district.

(c) Repealed by Acts 1987, 70th Leg., ch. 148, s 2.03, eff. Sept. 1, 1987.

(d) Concurrently with the supreme court, the court of appeals of a court of appeals district in which a person is restrained in his liberty, or a justice of the court of appeals, may issue a writ of habeas corpus when it appears that the restraint of liberty is by virtue of an order, process, or commitment issued by a court or judge because of the violation of an order, judgment, or decree previously made, rendered, or entered by the court or judge in a civil case. Pending the hearing of an application for a writ of habeas corpus, the court of appeals or a justice of the court of appeals may admit to bail a person to whom the writ of habeas corpus may be granted.

6. *Perry v. Del Rio*, 45 Tex. Sup. Ct. J. 52, ___ S.W.3d ___, 2001 WL 1285081 (Tex. 2001): The Texas Supreme Court has direct-appeal jurisdiction from "an order of a trial court granting or denying an interlocutory or permanent injunction on the ground of the constitutionality of a statute of this state." Here, the trial court's order enjoins parties from using the State's existing thirty congressional districts. Additionally, when the Supreme Court has appellate jurisdiction over any issue, it acquires "extended jurisdiction" over all other questions of law properly preserved and presented. Accordingly, the Court has direct-appeal jurisdiction to consider all the legal errors alleged in the various parties' appeals. The Supreme Court's review on direct appeal is constitutionally confined to questions of law. The Court reviews questions raising constitutional violations *de novo*.

2. *Writ of Mandamus*

BRADY
v.
FOURTEENTH COURT OF APPEALS
795 S.W.2d 712
(Tex. 1990)

Glenn A. Diddel, III, Houston, for relator.
Harold D. Hammett, Ft. Worth, W. Troy McKinney, Joe H. Reynolds, Houston, for respondent.

RAY, JUSTICE.

Our original opinion is withdrawn and the following substituted.

In this original proceeding relator seeks writ of mandamus directing the court of appeals to withdraw the writ of mandamus it issued in an original proceeding. Because the resolution of the issues presented to the court of appeals required factual determinations that could not properly be made by an appellate court in an original proceeding, we hold the court of appeals abused its discretion and conditionally grant the writ.

Relator Elaine A. Brady is the sole candidate in the Democratic primary for Place One on the First Court of Appeals. Appropriate Democratic Party officials certified her after she had submitted her application with the $2,000 filing fee and accompanying documentation to satisfy the applicable sections of the Texas Election Code. The documentation included several pages of petitions to have her placed on the ballot. The petitions bore a combined total of 302 signatures.

The incumbent justice and sole candidate in the Republican primary for Place One on the First Court of Appeals is the Honorable D. Camille Dunn. On January 24, 1990, Dunn filed an original mandamus action in the Fourteenth Court of Appeals to compel Robert Slagle in his capacity as Chairman of the Texas Democratic Executive Committee and local Democratic Party officials to remove Brady's name from the Democratic primary ballot. Dunn alleged Brady's petitions did not comply with the Election Code's sections 141.062, 141.063, and 141.065. Dunn claimed that (1) the petitions did not have at least 250 signatures by registered voters because fifty-eight signers were not on the 1990 list of registered voters; (2) other signatures were invalid for failure to include complete addresses, correct voter registration numbers, the date, a printed name, and similar defects; and (3) the person who notarized Brady's application and 35 pages of petitions did not affix her stamp or seal. Dunn's record included an affidavit from the Harris County Tax Assessor certifying that 58 signers were not on the 1990 list of registered voters.

Brady, the real party in interest, responded with an affidavit also from the Harris County Tax Assessor showing 10 of the 58 challenged signers were in fact registered. Brady also included certified copies of voter registration records from the assessor's office to show that an additional 21 of the 58 were registered. Both Slagle and Brady contended that there were factual disputes that precluded mandamus relief in an original appellate court proceeding. Slagle urged that a literal and over-strict construction of the Election Code provisions that even failed to allow for correction of clerical mistakes would, as applied to Brady's situation, violate the First and Fourteenth Amendments to the United States Constitution. For the constitutional claim, Slagle *cited Pilcher v. Rains*, 853 F.2d 334 (5th Cir. 1988), which cited *Anderson v. Celebrezze*, 460 U.S. 780, 103 S.Ct. 1564, 75 L.Ed.2d 547 (1983), and related cases.

The court of appeals issued the writ of mandamus to remove Brady's name from the primary ballot because the court concluded Brady only had 247 valid signatures, three short of the required 250. *Dunn v. Slagle*, 783 S.W.2d 953 (Tex. App.—Houston [14th Dist.] 1990, orig. proceeding). The court of appeals concluded it was "undisputed" that 27 signers were unregistered. It further concluded the number of valid signatures was reduced below 250 because of omissions and incorrect registration numbers for several of the remaining signatures. Fifteen signatures were held invalid for incorrect registration numbers. Although the briefs of Slagle and Dunn addressed the federal constitutional issue, there is no mention of it in either the court's opinion or concurring opinion.

It is well established Texas law that an appellate court may not deal with disputed areas of fact in an original mandamus proceeding. *West v. Solito*, 563 S.W.2d 240, 245 (Tex. 1978); *Dikeman v. Snell*, 490 S.W.2d 183, 186-87 (Tex. 1973). To adjudicate the controversy the court of appeals decided factual questions on inconsistent and conflicting affidavits and documents. The construction and application of the Election Code provisions Dunn asserts were violated, by the nature of the statutes involved, require a fully-developed factual record. It is impossible to construe the statutes as to factors such as the type and extent of clerical error that is permissible, without factual determinations of how many signers were in fact registered but gave incorrect voter registration numbers through clerical error. The number of registered voters who signed is a fact question that may not be determined by comparing registration names with signatures, because some signers may have used variants of their names (such as a middle name or omission of a maiden name) that would not be disclosed by simple comparison. The factual problems mentioned are not all-inclusive; the record in this case calls for factual determinations too numerous and varied to detail in this opinion.

We have a further problem with the statutory construction questions in this case that requires a fully-developed factual record. Statutes are given a construction consistent with constitutional requirements, when possible, because the legislature is presumed to have intended compliance with state and federal constitutions. *Greyhound Lines, Inc. v. Board of Equalization*, 419 S.W.2d 345, 348-49 (Tex. 1967); TEX. GOV'T CODE ANN. § 311.021(1) (Vernon 1988). Applying this principle under the issues raised in this case requires factual determinations the court of appeals could not properly make in an original mandamus proceeding.

The Supreme Court has stated that the federal constitutional rights involved in a political party's process of selecting its nominee for an elective office include the fundamental rights of freedom of association and the right to cast an effective vote. *Tashjian v. Republican Party of Connecticut*, 479 U.S. 208, 214, 107 S.Ct. 544, 548, 93 L.Ed.2d 514 (1986); *Anderson v. Celebrezze*, 460 U.S. 780, 787-88, 103 S.Ct. 1564, 1569-70, 75 L.Ed.2d 547 (1983); *Illinois State Bd. of Elections v. Socialist Workers Party*, 440 U.S. 173, 184, 99 S.Ct. 983, 990, 59 L.Ed.2d 230 (1979). In particular, the freedom of association guaranteed by the First and Fourteenth

Amendments includes the right to select a candidate who best represents the party's ideologies as decided by its members. *Eu v. San Francisco County Democratic Central Committee*, 489 U.S. 214, 109 S.Ct. 1013, 1021, 103 L.Ed.2d 271 (1989).

When a political party questions the constitutionality of state statutes regulating the party's method of selecting a candidate, as applied to a particular office or candidate, the courts must employ a balancing test. The balancing test weighs the burden on the candidate or party against the compelling state interest the state must advance to justify the regulation. *Eu v. San Francisco County Democratic Central Committee*, 109 S.Ct. at 1019; *Tashjian v. Republican Party of Connecticut*, 479 U.S. at 213-15, 107 S.Ct. at 548-49; *Anderson v. Celebrezze*, 460 U.S. at 788-90, 103 S.Ct. at 1569-71; *Illinois State Bd. v. Socialist Workers Party*, 440 U.S. at 184, 99 S.Ct. at 990; *American Party of Texas v. White*, 415 U.S. 767, 780 & n. 11, 94 S.Ct. 1296, 1305 & n. 11, 39 L.Ed.2d 744 (1974). The party challenging the statute must produce evidence to establish facts to enable a court to assess the character and magnitude of the burden imposed on the party's First and Fourteenth Amendment rights by the election law's provisions. *Anderson v. Celebrezze*, 460 U.S. at 788-90, 103 S.Ct. at 1569-71; *Socialist Labor Party v. Gilligan*, 406 U.S. 583, 588, 92 S.Ct. 1716, 1719, 32 L.Ed.2d 317 (1972). The party defending the statutory regulation must produce evidence that the burdens are necessary to further a compelling state interest. *Eu v. San Francisco County Democratic Central Committee*, 109 S.Ct. at 1021 & n. 15; *Tashjian v. Republican Party of Connecticut*, 479 U.S. at 217-18 & n. 8, 107 S.Ct. at 550-51 & n. 8; *Anderson v. Celebrezze*, 460 U.S. at 789, 103 S.Ct. at 1570. The party defending the statute must further show the statute is narrowly tailored to serve that compelling state interest. *Eu v. San Francisco County Democratic Central Committee*, 109 S.Ct. at 1019-20; *Anderson v. Celebrezze*, 460 U.S. at 806, 103 S.Ct. at 1579; *Illinois State Bd. of Elections v. Socialist Workers Party*, 440 U.S. at 185, 99 S.Ct. at 990.

In applying the balancing test, the Supreme Court has said a "court must resolve [a constitutional challenge to a state election law] by an analytic process that parallels its work in ordinary litigation." *Anderson v. Celebrezze*, 460 U.S. at 789, 103 S.Ct. at 1570 (emphasis added). Application of a constitutional balancing test is particularly dependent on a fully-developed factual record. *See, e.g., Socialist Labor Party v. Gilligan*, 406 U.S. at 588, 92 S.Ct. at 1719; *Wisconsin v. Yoder*, 406 U.S. 205, 224-27, 92 S.Ct. 1526, 1537-39, 32 L.Ed.2d 15 (1972); *see generally* Pine, *Speculation and Reality: The Role of Facts in Judicial Protection of Fundamental Rights*, 136 U. PA. L. REV. 655, 658-68, 701-702 (1988). In *Pilcher v. Rains*, 853 F.2d 334 (5th Cir. 1988), applying the balancing test to several of the Texas Election Code provisions in controversy here, the Fifth Circuit Court of Appeals concluded that as applied to the Libertarian Party's candidates on the factual record there presented, the requirement that correct voter registration numbers be listed with the signatures was unconstitutional. Our point is not that the evidence and facts as to Brady would necessarily be the same, nor that the Fifth Circuit necessarily correctly applied the constitutional balancing test, but rather that resolving the constitutional issue necessarily requires factual determinations. It is perhaps possible that the evidence to support the various balancing test factors could be stipulated or otherwise be undisputed and presented in a form that would allow meaningful constitutional analysis. We need not decide that question because it clearly is not presented in this case. Here Slagle and Brady explicitly maintained that the facts were disputed and asserted their rights to develop fully the factual record. The court of appeals abused its discretion by adjudicating constitutional issues that necessarily dealt with disputed areas of fact.

Because the court of appeals issued the writ of mandamus in an original proceeding in which it could not properly make the factual determinations raised in the case, we hold the court of appeals abused its discretion. We conditionally issue the writ of mandamus directing the court of appeals to withdraw its writ and any related orders. The actual writ will issue only if the court of appeals fails to comply with this opinion. We overrule the motion for rehearing, and no further motion for rehearing will be entertained.

MAUZY, J., concurs.

Notes

1. The question of the power of the Supreme Court to mandamus state governmental agencies is the subject of debate. *See In re TXU Electric Co.* 67 S.W.3d 130 (Tex. 2001): "In this original proceeding, relator is TXU Electric Co. and respondents are the Public Utility Commission and its three members. TXU seeks relief from portions of the Commission's orders requiring TXU to reverse efforts it has undertaken to mitigate its estimated stranded costs as part of the transition to a deregulated, competitive retail market for the sale of electricity in Texas." *Held:* Petition for writ of mandamus is denied. "Six Members of the Court vote to deny relief for different reasons. CHIEF JUSTICE PHILLIPS, joined by JUSTICES ENOCH and GODBEY, would not exercise mandamus jurisdiction because TXU has an adequate remedy at law. JUSTICE BAKER, joined by JUSTICE RODRIGUEZ, would hold that the relief TXU seeks is against the Commission, over which the Court has no original mandamus jurisdiction. JUSTICE BRISTER would hold that the portions of the Commission's orders of which TXU complains do not constitute a clear abuse of discretion. JUSTICE HECHT, joined by JUSTICE OWEN and JUSTICE JEFFERSON, would grant relief."

2. *Vondy v. Comm'rs Court of Uvalde County*, 620 S.W.2d 104, 109 (Tex. 1981): The Texas Supreme Court does not have original mandamus jurisdiction over county officials but the district court does.

3. *In re State Bar of Texas*, 113 S.W.3d 730 (Tex. 2003): The Supreme Court has concurrent jurisdiction with the Texas courts of appeals to grant mandamus relief; however, the Texas Rules of Appellate Procedure mandate that a relator first seek relief in the court of appeals. Nonetheless, a party can bypass the court of appeals if "compelling reasons" exist for this Court to grant relief. Because this case presents an issue of statewide importance - the interference by a district court in the regulation of the legal practice—the Supreme Court finds compelling reasons to exercise jurisdiction in this matter.

4. *In re Norman F. Newton*, 146 S.W.3d 648 (Tex. 2004): ART PAC's failure to petition the court of appeals for relief, ordinarily a prerequisite to a petition in the Supreme Court, was not required in this case, because the issue here was one of statewide application, and the election was imminent. Relators' interests in contributing to their opponents, as well as candidates in other races, rise to the same level, as if they were candidates for office, and as if their candidates were at stake.

5. *In re Lumbermens Mutual Casualty Co.*, 184 S.W.3d 729 (Tex. 2006): In this mandamus proceeding, Lumbermens Mutual Casualty Company seeks relief from a trial court order striking its petition in intervention in appeal. While Lumbermens I was pending, Sonat filed a motion in the trial court to increase the appellate security to $40 million. Lumbermens sought to intervene in the trial court, to contest Sonat's motion, after its insured, Cudd, conceded that an increase in security was warranted. The trial court struck Lumbermens' intervention, and granted Sonat's motion. Lumbermens then filed this petition for writ of mandamus, and a motion for temporary injunction pendente lite. ***Held:*** Writ of mandamus is denied. Lumbermens did not seek mandamus relief from the court of appeals before filing its petition in the Supreme Court, as Rule 52.3(e) of the Rules of Appellate Procedure requires, "unless there is a compelling reason not to do so." Lumbermens argues that it was justified in bypassing the court of appeals, because that court had previously denied it leave to intervene on appeal. In a separate opinion, in Lumbermens I, the Supreme Court holds that the court of appeals abused its discretion in denying Lumbermens leave to participate in Cudd's appeal, in order to raise a potentially dispositive issue that Cudd agreed to drop, in exchange for Sonat's agreement to nonsuit certain uninsured claims Sonat asserted against Cudd in a separate lawsuit. In light of this disposition, Lumbermens' petition for writ of mandamus is denied, without regard to the merits and without prejudice to Lumbermens' ability to seek relief from the trial court or the court of appeals.

In re The PRUDENTIAL INSURANCE CO. OF AMERICA
148 S.W.3d 124
(Tex. 2004)

Gino John Rossini, John A. Mackintosh Jr., G. Luke Ashley and Camille Knight, Thompson & Knight, L.L.P., Dallas, for Relators.

Luke Madole, Russell F. Nelms, Dena Jean Denooyer, Carrington Coleman Sloman & Blumenthal, Dallas, for Respondents.

JUSTICE HECHT delivered the opinion of the Court, in which JUSTICE OWEN, JUSTICE SMITH, JUSTICE WAINWRIGHT, and JUSTICE BRISTER joined.

The parties to a commercial lease agreed to waive trial by jury in any future lawsuit involving the lease, but when the tenant and its guarantors later sued for rescission and damages, they nevertheless demanded a jury trial. The trial court denied the landlord's motion to quash the demand. In this original proceeding, the landlord petitions for mandamus relief directing the trial court to enforce the parties' contractual jury waiver. We conditionally grant relief.

I

Francesco Secchi, a native of Italy, and his wife Jane, a native of England, moved to Dallas in 1981, where they have lived ever since and have become naturalized citizens. The Secchis have been in the restaurant business since 1983, and they (or entities controlled by them) own and operate two Dallas restaurants, Ferrari's and Il Grano. In October 2000, a limited partnership the Secchis controlled, Italian Cowboy Partners, Ltd., leased space in a Dallas shopping center for another restaurant. The lease agreement was the product of six months' active negotiations with the landlord, The Prudential Insurance Co. of America, and its agent, Four Partners L.L.C. doing business as Prizm Partners (collectively, "Prudential"). The Secchis had negotiated at least two other leases over the years, and they and their lawyer successfully insisted on a number of changes in Prudential's proposals. Offers went back and forth, and the agreement went through seven drafts. Francesco, whose formal education extended only to about the eighth grade, did not read the lease but left that to Jane, whose educational background was similar but whose English was better. Jane went over the agreement with their attorney but focused on the economic terms. When the Secchis and Prudential finally reached an understanding, Francesco signed the lease as manager of the partnership's general partner, Secchi, L.L.C. Prudential insisted that the Secchis personally guarantee the lease, and that agreement was also negotiated and changed by the Secchis before they signed it.

The lease contains the following paragraph:

> Counterclaim and Jury Trial. In the event that the Landlord commences any summary proceeding or action for nonpayment of rent or other charges provided for in this Lease, Tenant shall not interpose any counterclaim of any nature or description in any such proceeding or action. Tenant and Landlord both waive a trial by jury of any or all issues arising in any action or proceeding between the parties hereto or their successors, under or connected with this Lease, or any of its provisions.

Prudential did not specifically point out this provision to the Secchis, and Jane testified that she never noticed it. She also testified that notwithstanding the clear meaning of the second sentence, she never intended to waive a jury trial in any future litigation. The guaranty agreement does not contain a similar waiver but does state that the Secchis agree to guarantee the tenant's "full and timely performance and observance of all the covenants, terms, conditions, provisions, and agreements" in the lease, and in the event of the tenant's default, to "faithfully perform and fulfill all of such terms, covenants, conditions, provisions, and agreements".

Some nine months after the lease was executed, the Secchis and their limited partnership (collectively, "ICP") sued Prudential in statutory county court, claiming in part that it was impossible to do business on the premises because of a persistent odor of sewage. Prudential counterclaimed for amounts allegedly due under the lease and guaranty. When the trial court notified the parties that a date for non-jury trial had been set, ICP filed a jury demand and paid the jury fee, as required by Rule 216 of the Texas Rules of Civil Procedure. The court then notified the parties that a date for jury trial had been set. Prudential moved to quash the jury demand, based on the waiver in the lease. ICP responded that contractual jury waivers in general, and the waiver in the lease in particular, are unenforceable. . . .

After a hearing, the court denied the motion in a brief order without explanation.

Prudential petitioned the court of appeals for mandamus relief, which that court denied with a short memorandum opinion, 2002 WL 1608233, explaining only that "the relators have not shown themselves entitled to the relief requested." Prudential then petitioned for relief from this Court, and we agreed to hear argument. . . .

* * *

Having concluded that the parties' contractual jury waiver is enforceable, we turn to whether Prudential is entitled to relief by mandamus. Prudential must meet two requirements. One is to show that the trial court clearly abused its discretion. We have concluded as a matter of law that Prudential was entitled to enforcement of the jury waiver. Since "[a] trial court has no 'discretion' in determining what the law is or applying the law to the facts", even when the law is unsettled, the trial court's refusal to enforce the jury waiver was a clear abuse of discretion. Thus, Prudential has met the first requirement.

The other requirement Prudential must meet is to show that it has no adequate remedy by appeal. The operative word, "adequate", has no comprehensive definition; it is simply a proxy for the careful balance of jurisprudential considerations that determine when appellate courts will use original mandamus proceedings to review the actions of lower courts. These considerations implicate both public and private interests. Mandamus review of incidental, interlocutory rulings by the trial courts unduly interferes with trial court proceedings, distracts appellate court attention to issues that are unimportant both to the ultimate disposition of the case at hand and to the uniform development of the law, and adds unproductively to the expense and delay of civil litigation. Mandamus review of significant rulings in exceptional cases may be essential to preserve important substantive and procedural rights from impairment or loss, allow the appellate courts to give needed and helpful direction to the law that would otherwise prove elusive in appeals from final judgments, and spare private parties and the public the time and money utterly wasted enduring eventual reversal of improperly conducted proceedings. An appellate remedy is "adequate" when any benefits to mandamus review are outweighed by the detriments. When the benefits outweigh the detriments, appellate courts must consider whether the appellate remedy is adequate.

This determination is not an abstract or formulaic one; it is practical and prudential. It resists categorization, as our own decisions demonstrate. Although this Court has tried to give more concrete direction for determining the availability of mandamus review, rigid rules are necessarily inconsistent with the flexibility that is the remedy's principal virtue. Thus, we wrote in *Walker v. Packer* that "an appellate remedy is not inadequate merely because it may involve more expense or delay than obtaining an extraordinary writ." While this is certainly true, the word "merely" carries heavy freight. In *In re E.I. duPont de Nemours & Co.*, we concluded that defending the claims of more than 8,000 plaintiffs in litigation that would last for years was not mere expense and delay, and that mandamus review of the denial of duPont's special appearance was justified, even though duPont could eventually appeal and did not appear to be in any danger of succumbing to the burden of the litigation. In *Travelers Indemnity Co. v. Mayfield*, we granted mandamus review of an order requiring a carrier to pay the plaintiff's attorney fees as incurred in a compensation case, even though the carrier could have appealed from the final judgment and won recovery for the amounts paid, because the order not only cost the carrier money but "radically skew[ed] the procedural dynamics of the case" by requiring the defendant to fund the plaintiff's prosecution of her claims. In *In re Masonite Corp.*, the trial court on its own motion and without any authority whatever, split two cases into sixteen and transferred venue of fourteen of them to other counties. We held that the defendants were not required to wait until appeal to complain:

> Walker does not require us to turn a blind eye to blatant injustice nor does it mandate that we be an accomplice to sixteen trials that will amount to little more than a fiction. Appeal may be adequate for a particular party, but it is no remedy at all for the irreversible waste of judicial and public resources that would be required here if mandamus does not issue.

These cases, among a great many others that could be cited, serve to illustrate that whether an appellate remedy is "adequate" so as to preclude mandamus review depends heavily on the circumstances presented and is better guided by general principles than by simple rules.

Nor is the consideration whether to grant mandamus review confined to private concerns. No one suggested in *Masonite* that any individual party would suffer more by waiting to complain on appeal of the venue order than would any other party complaining of any other venue order in any other case. Two factors drove our decision in *Masonite*: the complete lack of authority for the trial court's order, and the impact on the legal system. We simply could not justify putting the civil justice system itself to the trouble of grinding through proceedings that were certain to be "little more than a fiction." The trial court's ruling in *Travelers* was novel but might easily have become a repeated error. Either way, the error was clear enough, and correction simple enough, that mandamus review was appropriate.

Prudent mandamus relief is also preferable to legislative enlargement of interlocutory appeals. The unavailability of mandamus relief increases the pressure for expanded interlocutory appeals. For example, when this Court refused to review venue decisions by mandamus, the Legislature responded by authorizing mandamus review of all decisions involving mandatory venue provisions. When we held that the denial of a special appearance would ordinarily not warrant mandamus review, the Legislature responded by creating an interlocutory appeal from the denial of a special appearance. When questions arose concerning the availability of mandamus to review the sufficiency of expert reports required in medical malpractice cases, the Legislature responded by creating an interlocutory appeal from the denial of dismissals of such cases for insufficient expert reports. Interlocutory appeals lie as of right and must be decided on the merits, increasing the burden on the appellate system. "Mandamus," on the other hand, "is an extraordinary remedy, not issued as a matter of right, but at the discretion of the court. Although mandamus is not an equitable remedy, its issuance is largely controlled by equitable principles." As a selective procedure, mandamus can correct clear errors in exceptional cases and afford appropriate guidance to the law without the disruption and burden of interlocutory appeal. Appellate courts must be mindful, however, that the benefits of mandamus review are easily lost by overuse.

The issue before us in the present case—whether a pre-suit waiver of trial by jury is enforceable—fits well within the types of issues for which mandamus review is not only appropriate but necessary. It is an issue of law, one of first impression for us, but likely to recur (it has already arisen in another case in the court of appeals, also on petition for mandamus. It eludes answer by appeal. In no real sense can the trial court's denial of Prudential's contractual right to have the Secchis waive a jury ever be rectified on appeal. If Prudential were to obtain judgment on a favorable jury verdict, it could not appeal, and its contractual right would be lost forever. If Prudential suffered judgment on an unfavorable verdict, Prudential could not obtain reversal for the incorrect denial of its contractual right "unless the court of appeals concludes that the error complained of . . . probably caused the rendition of an improper judgment". Even if Prudential could somehow obtain reversal based on the denial of its contractual right, it would already have lost a part of it by having been subject to the procedure it agreed to waive.

* * *

Only if a contractual waiver of trial by jury is enforced in the trial court can its propriety effectively be reviewed on appeal. The denial of trial by jury is harmless error only if there are no material fact issues to submit to a jury. But the denial of trial by jury is also reviewable by mandamus. A sentence in our opinion in *General Motors Corp. v. Gayle* suggests that this is not true, but we granted mandamus in that case to correct the trial court's denial of a jury trial, and we cited without disapproval three courts of appeals that we said "ha[d] reviewed jury trial orders by mandamus." To afford relief for the denial of a jury trial both by mandamus and by appeal, and to deny relief by either means for the refusal to enforce a jury waiver, unacceptably contorts review of the issue. Mandamus relief in a situation like this, in Professor Charles Alan Wright's words, "provides a valuable ad hoc relief valve for the pressures that are imperfectly contained by the statutes permitting appeals from final judgments and interlocutory orders."

* * *

The dissent suggests that mandamus relief should not be used to enforce contractual rights, but we used it for precisely that purpose only recently in *In re Allstate County Mutual Insurance Co.* to enforce the parties' agreement to submit to an appraisal process for determining the value of a vehicle claimed to be a total loss. The dissent states that we took "the United States Supreme Court's pronouncement that appellate delays defeated the 'core purpose' of contracts to arbitrate" as a "mandate . . . to provide an extraordinary remedy." Perhaps so, but the Supreme Court's "pronouncement" was also a statement of fact: lawsuits followed by appeals defeat the core purpose of arbitration agreements. For exactly the same reason, trial to a jury followed by appeal, if one were even allowed, defeats the reasons for agreeing to waive a jury in the first place.

The dissent argues that "authorizing mandamus relief to enforce a contractual jury waiver while relegating a party to its appellate remedy when denied its constitutional right to a jury trial" creates a procedural anomaly. If the premise were true, an anomaly would exist; but the premise is not true. We have never held that the denial of a jury trial, which can certainly be reviewed by appeal, cannot also be reviewed by mandamus. As we have already noted, we have faced the issue only once, in *General Motors Corp. v. Gayle*, and while one sentence of that opinion states that mandamus is "generally not available" to review the denial of a jury trial, we nevertheless directed the trial court to abort or mistry the nonjury trial it had commenced and to set the case on its jury docket. We also cited three court of appeals cases that had "reviewed jury trials by mandamus." *General Motors* does not preclude review of the denial of a jury trial by mandamus.

Finally, the dissent argues that "[e]ven if parties may freely waive their right to trial by jury, there is no public policy reason for encouraging them to do so." Of course, enforcing an agreement is not the same as encouraging parties to make it. By enforcing contractual jury waivers, we no more encourage them than we encourage arbitration by enforcing arbitration agreements. Parties are free to agree to such remedies as they choose, and as we have noted, they may have good reasons for agreeing to waive a jury trial. What the dissent ignores is that there is a compelling public policy reason to enforce legal agreements freely made. The dissent does not find the jury trial waiver in this case illegal or contrary to public policy, yet it would deny all viable means of enforcement.

* * *

For these reasons, we direct respondent, the Honorable Sally Montgomery, to vacate her order of June 6, 2003, and the prior order of June 19, 2002, to grant Prudential's motion to quash the jury demand and payment of jury fee, and to return the case to the nonjury docket. We are confident she will promptly comply. Our writ will issue only if she does not.

CHIEF JUSTICE PHILLIPS, joined by JUSTICE O'NEILL, JUSTICE JEFFERSON, and JUSTICE SCHNEIDER, dissenting [omitted].

3. *Habeas Corpus*

Ex parte HIGHTOWER

877 S.W.2d 17

(Tex. App.—Dallas 1994, orig. proceeding)

Aglaia D. Mauzy, Dallas, for appellant.
John B. Schorsch, Jr., Dallas and Randall Antonson, Duncanville, for ad litem.

BAKER, JUSTICE.

This is an original habeas corpus proceeding. The 302nd District Court of Dallas County held relator in contempt for not paying attorney ad litem fees and expenses as child support and costs of court. The contempt order fixed relator's punishment at confinement for ten minutes for each separate violation, or until she purged herself by payment of the ad litem fees and expenses. The order required payment of $2871 ad litem fees and expenses, $85 court costs for the contempt motion, and $1500 as attorney's fees incurred in the contempt proceeding. We conclude the trial court abused its discretion in determining the ad litem fees and expenses are child support. We hold that the failure to pay ad litem fees and expenses is the failure to pay a debt. We hold the Texas Constitution prohibits the trial court from enforcing by contempt the payment of the attorney's fees and expenses. We order relator discharged.

THE FACTUAL BACKGROUND

Relator and her husband divorced in May 1988. In June 1991, the former husband moved to change his visitation rights. In August 1993, the trial court appointed Lynn Cherry as attorney ad litem to represent the interests of the couple's child. The ad litem filed an answer for the child. The ad litem requested the court to order the parties to pay reasonable ad litem fees. She requested judgment against the parties for the fees. The ad litem also moved the court for security for costs. She requested that the relator and her former husband deposit $2500 to secure her fees and costs. In August 1993, the trial court ordered relator and her former husband to pay $2,308.84 to the ad litem as fees by September 3, 1993.

The ad litem filed another motion for security for costs. The trial court heard the motion on October 19, 1993. On November 15, 1993, the trial court ordered relator to pay $2871 to the ad litem as child support. This amount represented the unpaid balance of fees and expenses billed by the ad litem between September 1, 1993, and October 4, 1993. The trial court ordered relator to pay the $2871 by 4:00 p.m., November 19, 1993.

In early December 1993, the ad litem filed a motion for enforcement of the November order. After a hearing, the trial court found relator in contempt for failure to comply with the November order. On December 21, 1993, the trial court held relator in contempt and committed her to the county jail. The trial court's contempt order punished relator by confinement in the county jail for ten minutes per violation, and thereafter until she purged herself by payment of the ad litem fees and expenses, court costs, and attorney's fees for the ad litem's attorney. Relator immediately applied to this Court for a writ of habeas corpus. We released her on bond pending a hearing.

THE NOVEMBER ORDER

The November order that is the subject of the trial court's contempt ruling states: IT IS THEREFORE ORDERED that LAURA HIGHTOWER, Respondent (mother) shall pay the Attorney/Guardian Ad Litem Fees and Costs as child support and as costs of the representation of the minor child, JORDAN SIEGEL. IT IS FURTHER ORDERED that LAURA HIGHTOWER shall pay as child support the sum of the balance due and owing to the Attorney/Guardian Ad Litem as of the October 4, 1993 statement. Said sum being $2,871.00. IT IS THEREFORE ORDERED that LAURA HIGHTOWER shall pay as child support the sum of $2871.00, payable directly to the Attorney/Guardian Ad Litem, LYNN CHERRY, on or before 4:00 p.m., November 19, 1993 at 312 West Twelfth Street, Dallas, Texas 75208.

The record contains copies of the invoices the ad litem sent to relator and her former husband. Each invoice shows the ad litem charged an hourly rate for professional services performed and for expenses such as facsimiles, postage and copies. These invoices show the ad litem charged $6,638.34 for professional services performed and expenses incurred from August 12, 1993, through September 29, 1993. After crediting relator and her ex-husband with the amounts they paid, a $2871 balance of fees and expenses remained. The trial court ordered this balance paid by relator.

THE PARTIES' CONTENTIONS

In support of her application for writ of habeas corpus, relator asserts eleven points of error. Relator first complains that the trial court erred in holding her in contempt and confining her because the order requires imprisonment for nonpayment of a debt in violation of the Texas Constitution.

The trial court characterized the ad litem fees and expenses as child support. The ad litem responds that, because the trial court ordered the fees and expenses paid as child support, relator's imprisonment for failure to pay those sums does not violate the Constitution. The ad litem argues the trial court had the discretion to determine the fees, order them paid as child support, and thus exercise the court's contempt powers to imprison relator for failure to pay the fees.

THE ISSUE

The issue is whether the trial court can, by characterizing ad litem fees and expenses as child support, enforce by contempt payment of ad litem fees and expenses incurred in a suit affecting the parent-child relationship brought under section 11.02 of the family code.

THE APPLICABLE LAW

A. Burden of Proof

An original habeas corpus proceeding is a collateral attack on the contempt judgment. *See Ex parte Rohleder*, 424 S.W.2d 891, 892 (Tex. 1967) (orig. proceeding). In a habeas corpus proceeding, a relator bears the burden to show the contempt order is void and not merely voidable. *Ex parte Lowery*, 518 S.W.2d 897, 899 (Tex. Civ. App.—Beaumont 1975, orig. proceeding); *Ex parte Holloway*, 490 S.W.2d 624, 626 (Tex. Civ. App.—Dallas 1973, orig. proceeding). A relator must conclusively show her entitlement to a writ. *Ex parte Crawford*, 506 S.W.2d 920, 922 (Tex. Civ. App.—Tyler 1974, orig. proceeding).

B. Standard of Review

In an original habeas corpus proceeding, we do not have jurisdiction to weigh the evidence offered at the contempt hearing to determine whether it preponderates against the judgment. *Ex parte Helms*, 152 Tex. 480, 259 S.W.2d 184, 186 (1953) (orig. proceeding); *Ex parte Linder*, 783 S.W.2d 754, 760 (Tex. App.—Dallas 1990, orig. proceeding). We accord to the trial court the right to judge the witnesses' credibility and the weight given their testimony. *See Ex parte Elmore*, 161 Tex. 585, 342 S.W.2d 558, 561 (1961) (orig. proceeding); *Ex parte Karr*, 663 S.W.2d 534, 538 (Tex. App.—Amarillo 1983, orig. proceeding).

As a reviewing court, we may only determine if the trial court's contempt findings are so completely without evidentiary support that the trial court's judgment is void because it deprives a relator of liberty without due process of law. *Ex parte Helms*, 259 S.W.2d at 186; *Ex parte Karr*, 663 S.W.2d at 537. In short, we do not review the trial court's exercise of its discretion nor the sufficiency of the evidence to support the trial court's action. *Ex parte La Rocca*, 154 Tex. 618, 282 S.W.2d 700, 703 (1955) (orig. proceeding); *Ex parte Hosken*, 480 S.W.2d 18, 20 (Tex. Civ. App.—Beaumont 1972, orig. proceeding).

We have found no Texas case that expressly articulates the nature of our review of a trial court's application of the law to the facts. We conclude that the standard set by the Texas Supreme Court in original mandamus proceedings for review of a trial court's application of the law should apply in a review of a trial court's application of the law in a contempt proceeding.

In a mandamus proceeding, we review the trial court's determination of the legal principles controlling its ruling with less deference than we review factual findings. *Walker v. Packer*, 827 S.W.2d 833, 840 (Tex. 1992) (orig. proceeding). A trial court has no discretion in determining what the law is or applying the law to the facts. A trial court's clear failure to analyze or apply the law correctly is an abuse of discretion. *See Joachim v. Chambers*, 815 S.W.2d 234, 240 (Tex. 1991) (orig. proceeding); *NCNB Texas National Bank v. Coker*, 765 S.W.2d 398, 400 (Tex. 1989) (orig. proceeding).

C. Applicable Law

Under our law, a court shall not imprison a person for debt. TEX. CONST. art. I, § 18. Our law does not allow collection of attorney's fees by contempt proceedings. *Wallace v. Briggs*, 162 Tex. 485, 348 S.W.2d 523, 525-26 (1961) (orig. proceeding). However, the law does not consider attorney's fees and costs awarded in a contempt proceeding to enforce child support payments a debt. A court may enforce such fees and costs through a contempt judgment. TEX. R. CIV. P. 308a; *Ex parte Rogers*, 633 S.W.2d 666, 670-71 (Tex. App.—Amarillo 1982, orig. proceeding). A contempt order enforcing child support, including attorney's fees for enforcement, does not violate the constitutional right not to be imprisoned for debt. *Ex parte Helms*, 259 S.W.2d at 188.

However, the power to punish for contempt is one the trial court should exercise with caution. *Ex parte Rogers*, 633 S.W.2d at 671. Because of this widely accepted principle, Texas courts limit any extension of the "duty to support" to those services and costs required for enforcing child support. *See Ex parte Myrick*, 474 S.W.2d 767, 772 (Tex. Civ. App.—Houston [1st Dist.] 1971, orig. proceeding). The family code provides that after notice and hearing, the trial court may enforce by contempt any decree or court order for child support. *See* TEX. FAM. CODE ANN. § 14.40(a) (Vernon 1986).

In a suit affecting the parent-child relationship, the court may appoint an attorney to represent the child when necessary to protect the interests of the child. TEX. FAM. CODE ANN. § 11.10(c) (Vernon 1986). An attorney appointed by the court to represent a child under section 11.10(c) may receive a reasonable fee set by the court. TEX. FAM. CODE ANN. § 11.10(e) (Vernon 1986).

APPLICATION OF LAW TO FACTS

The ad litem argues the trial court's November order for payment of her fees was not for attorney's fees, but was for payment of child support. She relies on the language of the trial court's order. She argues the trial court had the discretion to determine that her fees and expenses were child support. She asserts the trial court correctly enforced payment through contempt. We disagree.

The trial court appointed the ad litem under section 11.10(c) of the family code. TEX. FAM. CODE ANN. § 11.10(c) (Vernon 1986). The unpaid ad litem fees arose from the fees the trial court awarded under section 11.10(e) of the family code. TEX. FAM. CODE ANN. § 11.10(e) (Vernon 1986). Accordingly, although the ad litem drafted the order to provide that the fees were child support, they are clearly nothing more than attorney's fees.

The fees the trial court awarded are not within the exception to the constitutional prohibition of imprisonment for debt. *See* TEX. R. CIV. P. 308a. These fees did not arise from enforcement of a child support order by a contempt order. Section 14.40 of the family code does not provide statutory support for enforcement of the ad litem's unpaid fees by contempt. TEX. FAM. CODE ANN. § 14.40 (Vernon 1986 & Supp. 1994).

The ad litem also argues that, unless we permit enforcement of ad litem fees by contempt, there is no avenue to protect ad litems from parents who refuse to pay for the ad litems' services. We disagree.

The trial court may order the parents to deposit funds into the registry of the court or into an account to defray future ad litem fees and expenses. The ad litem may secure a judgment for the unpaid fees and expenses. The ad litem then may pursue any remedy available to a judgment creditor for collection of the judgment.

Although section 11.10(e) authorizes an award of attorney's fees and costs against relator, we hold the unpaid fees and expenses is a debt and not child support. The trial court abused its discretion because it improperly applied the law to the facts. We hold the trial court did not have authority to enforce payment of the fees and expenses by contempt. TEX. CONST. art. I, § 18; *Ex parte Rogers*, 633 S.W.2d at 671. We hold the contempt order is void.

We grant the writ and discharge the relator.

Notes

1. As shown above, Section 22.221 of the Texas Government Code provides courts of appeals with limited writ power. A court of appeals' original jurisdiction to issue a writ of habeas corpus is limited to those cases in which a person's liberty is restrained because the person has violated an order, judgment, or decree entered in a civil case. Stated another way, this Court does not have original habeas corpus jurisdiction in criminal law matters. *See Ex parte Lewis*, 663 S.W.2d 153, 154 (Tex. App.—Amarillo 1983, orig. proceeding). That jurisdiction rests instead with the Court of Criminal Appeals, the District Courts, the County Courts, or any judge of said Courts. TEX. CODE CRIM. PROC. ANN. art. 11.05 (Vernon 1977); *see* TEX. CONST. art. V, §§ 5, 8, 16; TEX. GOV'T CODE ANN. §§ 25.0003, 26.047 (Vernon 1988).

2. *In Re Long,* 984 S.W.2d 623 (Tex. 1999): Contempt orders that do not involve confinement cannot be reviewed by writ of habeas corpus, and the only possible relief is a writ of mandamus.

4. *Writ of Prohibition*

HOLLOWAY
v.
FIFTH COURT OF APPEALS
767 S.W.2d 680
(Tex. 1989)

Andrew L. Smith, III, Carrollton, F. Dean Armstrong, Law Offices of F. Dean Armstrong, P.C., Flossmoor, Ill., Pat S. Holloway, Giddings, for relator.

R. Jack Ayres and Thomas V. Murto, Law Offices of R. Jack Ayres, P.C., Dallas, W. James Kronzer, Houston, John B. Kyle, Jackson, Walker, Winstead, Cantwell, & Miller, Dallas, Dennis Olson, Greenville, for respondent.

MAUZY, JUSTICE.

In this original proceeding, relator Pat S. Holloway complains that the Honorable Fifth Court of Appeals has abused its discretion by granting writs of prohibition, mandamus and injunction. *See Browning v. Ryan*, 756 S.W.2d 379 (Tex. App.—Dallas 1988, orig. proceeding). These writs were directed at the Honorable Tom Ryan, Senior Judge sitting for the 162nd Judicial District Court, who sustained a collateral attack on a previous judgment against Holloway. The judgment, which Judge Ryan declared void, had previously been appealed to the court of appeals but that appeal was dismissed. Nevertheless, the court of appeals' judgment of dismissal served as the basis for the extraordinary writs now before us.

The principal issue here then is whether an appellate court, which does not rule on the merits of an appeal but instead dismisses it, can issue a writ of prohibition to protect the judgment which was the subject of the prior appeal. We hold that it cannot. Because the court of appeals dismissed the prior appeal, it had no judgment to protect by writ of prohibition and, accordingly, abused its discretion when it granted the writ. The court of appeals also erred in issuing writs of mandamus and injunction.

The underlying litigation concerns an imperishable dispute over entitlement to the assets of Pat S. Holloway and Humble Exploration Company. The litigation dates back to 1979, but for the purposes of this proceeding we begin with the judgment rendered in 1982 by the 162nd Judicial District Court in Cause No. 79-9623-L, *Jane H. Browning, et al. v. Humble Exploration Company, Pat S. Holloway, et al.* In that suit for fraud, breach of fiduciary duties, and imposition of a constructive trust, the Brownings obtained a multi-million dollar judgment against Holloway, Humble Exploration Company and others.

Holloway and Humble appealed the 1982 judgment, but did not post a supersedeas bond. The Brownings, however, could not execute on their judgment because Holloway and Humble had previously sought protection under the federal bankruptcy laws. While Holloway's appeal was pending before the court of appeals, the Brownings filed suit in federal court to force Holloway and Humble to either post a supersedeas bond or turn over their assets to a receiver appointed in the judgment of the state court. Holloway, Humble, and their trustee in bankruptcy, Don Navarro, resisted the Brownings' efforts and filed a counterclaim asserting that the state court judgment was void because the trial in state court had not been conducted in accordance with the remand order of the bankruptcy court. The federal district court agreed and granted summary judgment for Humble, Holloway and Navarro. *Browning v. Navarro*, 37 B.R. 201 (N.D.Tex. 1983).

Following this action of the federal court, both sides filed motions in the court of appeals; the Brownings moved to dismiss the appeal, while Holloway moved to abate the state appeal until the federal decision became final on appeal. The court of appeals overruled Holloway's motion to abate and granted the Brownings' motion to dismiss. In so ruling, the court of appeals wrote that the appeal should be dismissed because Holloway had elected to pursue an inconsistent remedy in federal court. *Humble Exploration Co. v. Browning*, 677 S.W.2d 111 (Tex. App.—Dallas 1984). Although the court of appeals dismissed the appeal, it did write to express its strong disagreement with the federal district court's conclusion that the state court's judgment was void. The court of appeals' view was subsequently vindicated when the United States Fifth Circuit Court of Appeals reversed the judgment of the federal district court and remanded the cause for further proceedings. *Browning v. Navarro*, 743 F.2d 1069 (5th Cir. 1984).

Following this ruling from the Fifth Circuit, Holloway attempted to revive his state court appeal by filing a motion asking the court of appeals to reconsider its prior judgment of dismissal. The court of appeals granted this motion, vacated its prior judgment of dismissal and set the cause for hearing en banc. In the subsequent en banc opinion, a majority of the court reinstated its judgment dismissing the appeal because its plenary power over that judgment had expired prior to the filing of Holloway's motion. In other words, the court of appeals concluded that it no longer retained jurisdiction to reinstate Holloway's appeal. *Humble Exploration Co. v. Browning*, 690 S.W.2d 321 (Tex. App.—Dallas 1985, writ ref'd n.r.e.).

After this setback, Holloway initiated a new action in the 162nd Judicial District Court of Dallas County. This new action incorporated both a collateral attack on the court's prior judgment in *Browning v. Humble Exploration Company* and a direct attack by equitable bill of review. On April 13, 1988, Judge Tom Ryan, a senior district judge sitting as judge of the 162nd Judicial District Court, granted Holloway's twelfth motion for partial summary judgment and held that the final judgment previously rendered in *Browning v. Humble Exploration Company* on November 11, 1982, was void. This partial summary judgment was then made final by severing out Holloway's equitable claim for bill of review and docketing that claim as a separate cause.

This development caused the Brownings to file an original proceeding in the court of appeals seeking writs of mandamus, prohibition and injunction against Judge Ryan. The Brownings also perfected an appeal from the summary judgment rendered by Judge Ryan. The court of appeals chose to review Judge Ryan's action by means of the original proceeding, granted the Brownings' request for extraordinary relief, and held that the 1982 judgment rendered in *Browning v. Humble Exploration Company* was "a valid, existing, final judgment not subject to collateral attack or bill of review." *Browning v. Ryan*, 756 S.W.2d at 384. The court of appeals then ordered Judge Ryan to set aside his judgment and order of severance, prohibited Judge Ryan from taking any action in Holloway's bill of review other than its dismissal, and finally enjoined Holloway from using the state courts to attack the 1982 judgment of the 162nd District Court in cause No. 79-9623-L, *Browning v. Humble Exploration Company*. In issuing each of these writs, the court of appeals abused its discretion.

The threshold problem is with the court of appeals' use of the writ of prohibition. This writ operates like an injunction issued by a superior court to control, limit or prevent action in a court of inferior jurisdiction. *City of Houston v. City of Palestine*, 114 Tex. 306, 267 S.W. 663, 665 (Tex. 1924). The purpose of the writ is to enable a superior court to protect and enforce its jurisdiction and judgments. *Browne v. Rowe*, 10 Tex. 183, 184 (1853). The writ is typically used to protect the subject matter of an appeal or to prohibit an unlawful interference with the enforcement of a superior court's orders and judgments. *Texas Employers Ins. Ass'n v. Kirby*, 137 Tex. 106, 152 S.W.2d 1073 (1941).

Apparently the specific purpose for the writ of prohibition in our present case was the latter one—to prohibit the unlawful interference with the enforcement of a superior court's judgment. In voiding the prior judgment, Judge Ryan concluded that the judge who presided over the 162nd Judicial District Court when *Browning v. Humble Exploration Company* was decided never legally acquired jurisdiction over the subject matter of the case. Although the reasons for this conclusion are not important to our present decision, the court of appeals thought the reasoning to be substantially similar to that of the federal district court which had previously declared the judgment in *Browning v. Humble Exploration Company* void, only to be reversed by the Fifth Circuit. *Browning v. Navarro*, 37 B.R. 201 (N.D.Tex. 1983), *rev'd*, 743 F.2d 1069 (5th Cir. 1984).

In resolving the original proceeding below, the court of appeals looked to its original opinion in *Humble Exploration Company v. Browning*, 677 S.W.2d 111, found Judge Ryan's conclusions of law to be in conflict with it and issued the writ of prohibition to prevent Judge Ryan from interfering with its prior judgment. The error here is that Judge Ryan's judgment does not interfere with the court of appeals' judgment of dismissal in *Humble Exploration Company v. Browning*.

Apparently the court of appeals viewed its judgment in *Humble Exploration Company v. Browning* as essentially one of affirmance. When an appellate court considers the merits of an action and renders a judgment of affirmance or reversal, it has a judgment which under the appropriate circumstances can be protected by writ of prohibition. *Houston Oil Co. v. Village Mills Co.*, 123 Tex. 253, 259-60, 71 S.W.2d 1087, 1089 (1934). The court of appeals in *Humble Exploration Company v. Browning*, however, did not rule on the merits. It dismissed the appeal. Granted the court wrote on the collateral matter of the trial court's jurisdiction, but the writing was not material to, nor incorporated in, its judgment of dismissal. Even had the court of appeals chosen to rule on the merits of the appeal in its judgment of dismissal, such ruling would have been "mere surplusage" incapable of enforcement by the extraordinary writ of prohibition. *Fitch v. International Harvester Co.*, 163 Tex. 221, 221, 354 S.W.2d 372, 373 (1962).

Appellate courts have no authority to issue writs of prohibition to protect unappealed district court judgments. *Texas Employers Ins. Ass'n v. Kirby*, 137 Tex. 106, 152 S.W.2d 1073 (1941). Although the dismissal of an appeal may have the same practical affect as an affirmance of the lower court's judgment, these two appellate judgments are not in law the same. *United States v. Gomez*, 64 U.S. (23 How.) 326, 339-40, 16 L.Ed. 552, 587 (1860). A dismissal of an appeal does not merge the judgment of the trial court into the judgment of the appellate court and does not vest the appellate court with authority to issue extraordinary writs to protect the judgment of the trial court. *Oilmen's Reciprocal Ass'n v. Coe*, 29 S.W.2d 430 (Tex. Civ. App.—Eastland 1930, writ ref'd); *Cunningham v. Universal Credit Co.*, 92 S.W.2d 1097 (Tex. Civ. App.—Fort Worth 1936, no writ).

The court of appeals also issued a writ prohibiting Judge Ryan from proceeding in the bill of review which had been severed from the claim on which Holloway premised his collateral attack. Incorporated with this action was the court of appeals' writ of mandamus which directed Judge Ryan to vacate his judgment declaring the prior judgment in *Browning v. Humble Exploration Company* void, to vacate his order of severance, and to dismiss Holloway's claims for bill of review and collateral attack. Finally, the court of appeals enjoined Holloway from pursuing in the courts of this state any other claim attacking the 1982 judgment of the 162nd Judicial District Court in cause No. 79-9623-L, *Browning v. Humble Exploration Company*.

In issuing these writs, the court abused its discretion for yet another reason. At the time it ruled, the court of appeals had before it both an original proceeding seeking the issuance of the aforementioned extraordinary writs and an appeal directly attacking the judgment rendered by Judge Ryan. In choosing the original proceeding to remedy the perceived error, the court of appeals ignored a fundamental tenet of writ practice. The issuance of an extraordinary writ is not authorized when the relator has an adequate remedy by appeal. *Johnson v. Fourth Court of Appeals*, 700 S.W.2d 916, 917 (Tex. 1985). As the name implies, extraordinary writs issue "only in situations involving manifest and urgent necessity and not for grievances that may be addressed by other remedies." Sales, *Original Jurisdiction of the Supreme Court and the Courts of Civil Appeals of Texas, in Appellate Procedure in Texas*, s 1.4[1][b] at 47 (2d Ed. 1979), *citing Herring v. Houston National Exchange Bank*, 113 Tex. 337, 255 S.W. 1097 (1923). The court of appeals therefore abused its discretion when it chose the original proceeding instead of the pending appeal as the means for addressing the perceived error committed in the trial court.

Our final difficulty with the opinion of the court of appeals is its assumption that an original proceeding is the appropriate vehicle for resolving a claim of res judicata. Seventy-five years ago we expressed reservations regarding such practice in *Milam County Oil Mill Co. v. Bass*, 106 Tex. 260, 264-65, 163 S.W. 577, 578-79 (1914): The power of a court to enforce its jurisdiction does not include an authority to prevent the prosecution of any suit to which a judgment of the court may be an effectual bar, but which . . . makes no attempt to disturb it, or to interfere with its execution . . . . The assumption of such right would invest a court not merely with the control of its own judgments and authority to enforce its jurisdiction, but with a further power to govern other courts in the exercise of their lawful jurisdiction; and the result would be that the issue of the conclusiveness of a judgment upon what is urged as a distinct cause of action could never be determined except by the court that rendered it. There we advised that "the remedy provided by our system" should a trial court fail to recognize the preclusive effect of a prior judgment was appeal. *Id.* 163 S.W. at 578. Some years later, we observed that were "the rule otherwise, the defense of res judicata to suits in trial courts would soon be abandoned in all instances involving appellate court judgments in favor of original proceedings in our appellate courts." *City of Dallas v. Dixon*, 365 S.W.2d 919, 923 (Tex. 1963), rev'd on other grounds sub nom., *Donovan v. Dallas*, 377 U.S. 408, 84 S.Ct. 1579, 12 L.Ed.2d 409 (1964).

Like other courts which have considered the underlying dispute between the Brownings and Holloway, we are vexed by this hydra-headed litigation. The answer, however, is not to lock the doors of all our state courts and summarily declare the matter at an end. Litigation between these same parties has been pending in the federal courts over a similar span of time and we note that the Fifth Circuit, through normal appellate review, has succeeded in narrowing Holloways' claims to a single viable defense. *Browning v. Navarro*, 826 F.2d 335, 346 (5th Cir. 1987). The courts of this state likewise have at their disposal the means to narrow and resolve those issues in dispute. The urgency with which the court of appeals considered the original proceeding convinces us that this matter will be expeditiously resolved in that court.

We further urge the trial court to move promptly to resolve Holloway's pending bill of review, which has been on file since June 16, 1986. It is not clear why it took 22 months and 12 motions for summary judgment for the trial judge to rule on the collateral attack or why the bill of review proceeding was not then also ripe for consideration.

We conditionally grant relator's petition for writ of mandamus and direct the court of appeals to vacate its order of July 26, 1988 in *Browning v. Ryan.* We also vacate our order staying all proceedings in the appeal pending before the court of appeals to permit a review of the merits of that appeal. *See* Order of December 7, 1988, *Holloway v. Fifth Court of Appeals*, 761 S.W.2d 306 (Tex. 1988).

GONZALEZ, J., dissenting [opinion omitted].

SPEARS, J., not sitting.

CITY OF ROCKWALL
v.
HUGHES

246 S.W.3d 621
(Tex. 2008)

Terry D. Morgan, Terry Morgan & Associates, P.C., James W. Morris Jr., Goins Underkofler Crawford & Langdon, L.L.P., Dallas, F. Dayton Eckert Jr., Law Offices of F. Dayton Eckart Jr., Garland, Bob E. Shannon, Joseph R. Knight, Alice G. McAfee, Baker Botts LLP, Austin, TX, for Petitioner.

R. Matthew Molash, James A. Baker, Robert H. Mow Jr., Dwight A. Shupe, Matthew R. Miller, Garon R. Horton, Hughes & Luce, L.L.P., Dallas, TX, for Respondent.

Theodore Paul Gorski Jr., City of Fort Worth, Fort Worth, Edwin M. Snyder, City Attorney's Office, Denton, M. Scott Norman Jr., Texas Association of Builders, Scott Houston, Texas Municipal League, Austin, Darrin M. Coker, City Attorney for City of Pearland, Pearland, Brian D. Shannon, Texas Tech University School of Law, Lubbock, L. Stanton Lowry, Boyle & Lowry, LLP, Irving, TX, for Amicus Curiae.

JUSTICE JOHNSON delivered the opinion of the Court, in which CHIEF JUSTICE JEFFERSON, JUSTICE WAINWRIGHT, JUSTICE MEDINA, and JUSTICE GREEN joined.

A municipality generally must annex land pursuant to a plan giving three years' notice of its intent to annex. If an area is exempt from the three-year notice requirement, then annexation can take place by use of abbreviated procedures with less notice of a city's intent to annex.

In this case, a landowner sought inclusion in the City of Rockwall's three-year annexation plan. The City denied the request, claimed the proposed annexation was statutorily exempt from the three-year requirement, and gave notice of intent to annex the landowner's territory under abbreviated procedures. The landowner requested that the City arbitrate the dispute. When the City refused, the landowner sought a court order compelling arbitration. The trial court refused to compel arbitration and dismissed the landowner's case for lack of jurisdiction. The court of appeals held that the City must arbitrate. We reverse the judgment of the court of appeals and affirm the trial court's judgment dismissing the suit.

I. Background

A. Annexation Law

The Texas Constitution confers on cities the power to annex land. TEX. CONST. ART. XI, § 5. The Legislature prescribes procedures to be used by cities in conducting annexations. *See* TEX. LOC. GOV'T CODE ch. 43; *Alexander Oil Co. v. City of Seguin*, 825 S.W.2d 434, 439 (Tex. 1991). Statutory annexation procedures require municipalities to prepare annexation plans specifically identifying areas which may be annexed beginning on the third anniversary of the date the plan is adopted or amended (a "three-year plan"). *See* TEX. LOC. GOV'T CODE § 43.052(c). Subchapter 43C sets out annexation procedures for areas included in such three-year plans. *See id.* §§ 43.051-.057.

Section 43.052(h) lists several types of exemptions from three-year plans. One type of area exempted is a "sparsely-populated" area. *Id.* § 43.052(h)(1). If an area is exempt from inclusion in a three-year plan, annexation occurs according to procedures set out in subchapter 43C-1. *See id.* § 43.061 ("This subchapter applies to an area proposed for annexation that is not required to be included in a municipal annexation plan under Section 43.052."). Annexations of section 43.052(h)(1) sparsely-populated areas may be initiated subject to 30 days' notice of the first hearing on the proposed annexation. *Id.* § 43.062(b). Annexations under subchapter 43C-1 procedures generally must be completed within ninety days of the time proceedings are begun. *Id.* § 43.064. Cities are prohibited from using the section 43.052(h)(1) "sparsely populated" exemption to circumvent requirements that annexations be pursuant to a three-year plan. *Id.* § 43.052(i).

The controversy before us primarily involves subsections 43.052(c), (h), and (i) which in pertinent part provide as follows:

> (c) A municipality shall prepare an annexation plan that specifically identifies annexations that may occur beginning on the third anniversary of the date the annexation plan is adopted. The municipality may amend the plan to specifically identify annexations that may occur beginning on the third anniversary of the date the plan is amended.
>
> * * *
>
> (h) This section [43.052] does not apply to an area proposed for annexation if: (1) the area contains fewer than 100 separate tracts of land on which one or more residential dwellings are located on each tract . . . .
>
> (i) A municipality may not circumvent the requirements of this section by proposing to separately annex two or more areas described by Subsection (h)(1) if no reason exists under generally accepted municipal planning principles and practices for separately annexing the areas. If a municipality proposes to separately annex areas in violation of this section, a person residing or owning land in the area may petition the municipality to include the area in the municipality's annexation plan. If the municipality fails to take action on the petition, the petitioner may request arbitration of the dispute. The petitioner must request the appointment of an arbitrator in writing to the municipality. Sections 43.0564(b), (c), and (e) apply to the appointment of an arbitrator and the conduct of an arbitration proceeding under this subsection.

B. The Controversy

The estate of W.W. Caruth (the Estate) owns 405 acres of land (the Caruth property) within a part of the extraterritorial jurisdiction of the City, a home-rule city. In August 2004, the Estate applied to the City for initial approval of a residential development plan for the Caruth property. After the Estate filed its application, the City initiated annexation procedures pursuant to section 43.052(h)(l) in regard to two areas: one included the Caruth property and another included land not contiguous to the Caruth property. The City sent notices of annexation to affected persons pursuant to subchapter 43C-1 procedures for areas exempted from three-year annexation plans. The Estate objected to the City's attempt to annex using subchapter 43C-1 procedures and petitioned the City to include the Caruth property in the City's three-year annexation plan. The Rockwall City Council adopted a resolution rejecting the Estate's request. The Estate then asserted that the City was circumventing section 43.052(c)'s requirement that annexations be carried out pursuant to a three-year plan and requested arbitration pursuant to section 43.052(i). The City responded by advising the Estate that the proposed annexations were exempt from inclusion in a three-year plan and the Estate's "request for arbitration [was] not appropriate."

The Estate filed suit in district court seeking an order compelling arbitration pursuant to section 43.052(i) and a temporary restraining order and temporary injunction preventing the City from proceeding with annexation pending completion of arbitration, including related appeals, if any. The City responded, in part, by filing a plea to the jurisdiction asserting that the Estate did not have standing because the dispute concerned annexation procedures, the suit was a collateral attack on the annexation ordinances and proceedings and the only way to challenge alleged annexation procedural irregularities was through quo warranto proceedings. In support of its plea to the jurisdiction, the City argued, in part, that section 43.052(i) authorized the Estate to request arbitration if the City did not take action on the Estate's petition to be included in a three-year plan but that the City took action on the petition by denying it. The trial court denied the Estate's applications, granted the City's plea to the jurisdiction and dismissed the action.

The Estate appealed. The court of appeals agreed with the Estate's interpretation of section 43.052(i):

> [W]e read the plain language of the statute to provide that, if the City fails to take action on the petition to include the area in the [three-year] annexation plan, the landowner may request arbitration of the dispute.

153 S.W.3d 709, 713-14 (emphasis added). The court of appeals reversed and remanded with instructions that the trial court compel arbitration and enjoin the City from proceeding with annexation pending the outcome of arbitration. *Id.* at 714.

In this Court, the City, supported by amicus curiae, maintains that the court of appeals erred in concluding that section 43.052(i) grants a private right to the Estate to elect, and thereby require, arbitration of the Estate's claim even though the City took action on the Estate's petition by denying it. The Estate, also supported by amicus curiae, claims it has standing because section 43.052(i) grants it a substantive, private right to require the City to arbitrate the Estate's claim.

II. Standard of Review

Statutory construction is a legal question we review de novo. In construing statutes, we ascertain and give effect to the Legislature's intent as expressed by the language of the statute. *See State, Texas Parks and Wildlife Dept. v. Shumake*, 199 S.W.3d 279, 284 (Tex. 2006). We use definitions prescribed by the Legislature and any technical or particular meaning the words have acquired. TEX. GOV'T CODE § 311.011(b). Otherwise, we construe the statute's words according to their plain and common meaning, *Texas Department of Transportation v. City of Sunset Valley*, 146 S.W.3d 637, 642 (Tex. 2004), unless a contrary intention is apparent from the context, *Taylor v. Firemen's and Policemen's Civil Service Commission of City of Lubbock*, 616 S.W.2d 187, 189 (Tex. 1981), or unless such a construction leads to absurd results. *Univ. of Tex. S.W. Med. Ctr. v. Loutzenhiser*, 140 S.W.3d 351, 356 (Tex. 2004); *see also Tex. Dep't of Protective and Regulatory Servs. v. Mega Child Care, Inc.*, 145 S.W.3d 170, 177 (Tex. 2004) (noting that when statutory text is unambiguous, courts must adopt the interpretation supported by the statute's plain language unless that interpretation would lead to absurd results). We presume the Legislature intended a just and reasonable result by enacting the statute. TEX. GOV'T CODE § 311.021(3). When a statute's language is clear and unambiguous, it is inappropriate to resort to rules of construction or extrinsic aids to construe the language. *See St. Luke's Episcopal Hosp. v. Agbor*, 952 S.W.2d 503, 505 (Tex. 1997); *Ex parte Roloff*, 510 S.W.2d 913, 915 (Tex. 1974).

III. Analysis

The statutory language on which the issue turns provides: "If the municipality fails to take action on the petition, the petitioner may request arbitration of the dispute . . . ." TEX. LOC. GOV'T CODE § 43.052(i). The Estate urges that the statute be read differently than the plain language reads. The Estate says that the statute "expressly provides for arbitration between a landowner and a city when the city, upon the petition of a landowner, fails to act to include the landowner's property in a three year annexation plan." (Emphasis added). The Estate asks that we affirm the court of appeals' construction to that effect. We decline to do so.

We first address the City's standing argument. In challenging the Estate's standing, the City cites *Alexander Oil Co. v. City of Seguin*, 825 S.W.2d 434 (Tex. 1991), for the proposition that the Estate does not have standing because the validity of the City's annexation can only be challenged by a quo warranto proceeding unless the proposed annexation is wholly void. *See id.* at 436 ("The only proper method for attacking the validity of a city's annexation of territory is by quo warranto proceeding, unless the annexation is wholly void."). The City reasons that the trial court lacked jurisdiction to hear a suit to compel arbitration because the Estate does not allege that the City has no power to annex the areas in question or that the annexation proceedings are otherwise wholly void, but rather alleges only that the City must annex pursuant to the three-year plan procedures of subchapter 43C as opposed to using the more expedited procedures of subchapter 43C-1.

In *Alexander Oil*, the City of Seguin passed an ordinance annexing land owned by Alexander Oil Company. *Id.* at 435. Alexander Oil filed suit alleging that Seguin failed to comply with procedures required by the Municipal Annexation Act such as providing proper notice for hearings, conducting the required hearings, and providing an annexation plan. *Id.* at 436. Seguin responded that because the ordinance annexing Alexander Oil's property was not void, a quo warranto proceeding by the State was the only proper way to collaterally attack the ordinance and the case should be dismissed. *Id.* The Court agreed with Seguin that procedural irregularities render ordinances voidable, not void. *Id.* at 439. The Court also noted that the Legislature had not expressly provided a private action to set aside annexations where an annexation ordinance is merely voidable. *Id.* at 437. Thus, Alexander Oil affirmed the rule that unless an annexation is wholly void or the Legislature has expressly granted a private right to challenge the annexation in some manner, a quo warranto proceeding brought by the State is the only proper means of attacking a municipality's annexation in court. *Id.*

The Estate does not urge that the City's annexation proceeding is void or that the City lacks power to annex the area in question. Nor does the Estate challenge the authorities. The City cites various cases for its contention that the annexation process in general is procedural. *See Werthmann v. City of Fort Worth*, 121 S.W.3d 803 (Tex. App.—Fort Worth 2003, no pet.); *City of Balch Springs v. Lucas*, 101 S.W.3d 116 (Tex. App.—Dallas 2002, no pet.); *City of San Antonio v. Hardee*, 70 S.W.3d 207 (Tex. App.—San Antonio 2001, no pet.). The Estate says those authorities simply are not applicable because none of them interpret the language of section 43.052(i) which is the issue in this case. The Estate maintains that it has standing because subsequent to Alexander Oil the Legislature expressly granted landowners a substantive private right to arbitration by enacting section 43.052(i). It argues that when the Legislature enacted comprehensive changes in 1999 to impose order in annexation law, the cornerstone of the changes was section 43.052(c)'s requirement that municipalities must prepare annexation plans specifically identifying areas that may be annexed beginning on the third anniversary of the date the plan is adopted or amended. According to the Estate, the exemptions of section 43.052(h) have been used regularly by cities to circumvent the three-year planning requirement. The Estate posits that by enacting section 43.052(i), the Legislature must have intended to protect against such abuse by requiring arbitration if a municipality fails to take action on a landowner's petition to incorporate the land into the city's three-year plan and that any other interpretation of the statute would lead to absurd results. As part of its argument, the Estate references the policy of the State which favors arbitration of disputes and the short time frame necessary to complete arbitration if there are no appeals from the arbitration award. *See Jack B. Anglin Co. v. Tipps*, 842 S.W.2d 266, 268 (Tex. 1992). The Estate also argues that it would be illogical for the Legislature to have crafted a detailed statutory framework around the requirement that municipalities enact three-year annexation plans, provide for exemptions to the three-year plan requirement, allow landowners to contest whether a city is circumventing the three-year plan requirement by requesting inclusion in a three-year plan, yet require a city to arbitrate the contest only if the city ignores, or "pocket vetoes," the petition.

But we are not persuaded that the process and result called for by the plain language of the statute is illogical, much less absurd. Subchapters 43C and 43C-1 contain extensive provisions in regard to annexations. Section 43.052(i) is detailed in specifying how and when the landowner may present a complaint to the city. It incorporates by reference part, but not all, of section 43.0564's arbitration procedures. And in the midst of the detailed language, we find that the Legislature specifically addressed when arbitration may be requested: "If the municipality fails to take action on the petition . . . ." In regard to "logic," it seems to us that by crafting language specifying when arbitration of the dispute could be requested, legislators logically would have considered that there are two instances in which a dispute would need to be resolved. The first instance is if the city did not bring the landowner's petition up for consideration, or, if it was brought up for consideration, the city failed to take action on it one way or the other (what the parties refer to in this case as a "pocket veto"). The second instance is if the city denied the petition and refused to put the land into a three-year plan. It follows, logically, that because the statutory language as enacted allows arbitration to be requested only in the first instance, the Legislature's intent was not to provide for arbitration in the second instance. *See Cameron v. Terrell & Garrett, Inc.*, 618 S.W.2d 535, 540 (Tex. 1981) ("It is a rule of statutory construction that every word of a statute must be presumed to have been used for a purpose . . . [and] we believe every word excluded from a statute must also be presumed to have been excluded for a purpose.").

Contrary to the Estate's position, we see benefits from reading the statute's language literally. One significant benefit is that by not reading language into the statute when the legislature did not put it there, we do not risk crossing the line between judicial and legislative powers of government as prescribed by article II of the

Texas Constitution. Tex. Const. art. II, § 1. ("[N]o person, or collection of persons, being of one of these [three governmental] departments, shall exercise any power properly attached to either of the others, except in the instances herein expressly permitted."). Another benefit is that by interpreting statutes such as this in a straightforward manner, we build upon the principle that "ordinary citizens [should be] able 'to rely on the plain language of a statute to mean what it says.' " *Fitzgerald v. Advanced Spine Fixation Sys.*, 996 S.W.2d 864, 866 (Tex. 1999) (*quoting Addison v. Holly Hill Fruit Prods. Inc.*, 322 U.S. 607, 618, 64 S.Ct. 1215, 88 L.Ed. 1488 (1944)).

As presented in this case, construing the statute's language to mean what it says results in a landowner having the right to request arbitration only if a city refuses to include the area in question in a three-year plan, fails to deny the petition, and fails to otherwise accommodate the landowner. The statute as written, in effect, provides a structured method for landowners to seek redress from cities if landowners believe cities are annexing in violation of section 43.052(c). If a landowner petitions to be included in a three-year plan and the city acts on the petition in a way that is acceptable to the landowner, there is no dispute to be resolved. If the city denies the landowner's petition, then the landowner has notified the city of its specific complaint in writing and pursued and exhausted a legislatively-provided method for seeking redress before asking a State's attorney to disrupt the city's annexation process by filing a quo warranto action. *See* TEX. CIV. PRAC. & REM.CODE § 66.002(c) (quo warranto proceedings may be brought by the attorney general or county or district attorney on his or her own motion or at the request of an individual). And a city has the option of taking no action to either grant or deny the landowner's petition and, thereby, effectively agreeing to arbitration of the dispute if the landowner requests arbitration. Under this last scenario, the arbitration essentially is a dispute resolution process agreed to by the parties. In the event multiple landowners submit petitions, the city might delay acting on the petitions in an attempt to have all the petitioning landowners agree to join in one arbitration to resolve the issue(s). If an agreement cannot be reached to join in one arbitration, the city might choose to either grant or deny each petition. The landowners whose petitions are denied have the option of seeking institution of a quo warranto action in which the claims of all landowners will be resolved, instead of the city and each landowner being involved in individual arbitration proceedings.

* * *

V. Conclusion

We decline to read additional language into the statute as the Estate urges us to do. We go no further than the unambiguous language of the statute to interpret it. Section 43.052(i) does not create a substantive private right for a landowner to compel arbitration if a municipality takes action on the landowner's petition by denying it, as the City did. Accordingly, the Estate lacks standing to pursue the suit it filed.

We reverse the judgment of the court of appeals and render judgment dismissing the Estate's suit.

JUSTICE WILLET filed a dissenting opinion, in which JUSTICE HECHT, JUSTICE O'NEILL, and JUSTICE BRISTER joined (opinion omitted).

APPENDIX

Texas Rules of Civil Procedure

Adopted effective Sept. 1, 1941 including amendments received through January 9, 2019.

PART I.
GENERAL RULES

RULE 1. OBJECTIVE OF RULES.

The proper objective of rules of civil procedure is to obtain a just, fair, equitable and impartial adjudication of the rights of litigants under established principles of substantive law. To the end that this objective may be attained with as great expedition and dispatch and at the least expense both to the litigants and to the state as may be practicable, these rules shall be given a liberal construction.

RULE 2. SCOPE OF RULES.

These rules shall govern the procedure in the justice, county, and district courts of the State of Texas in all actions of a civil nature, with such exceptions as may be hereinafter stated. Where any statute in effect immediately prior to September 1, 1941, prescribed a rule of procedure in lunacy, guardianship, or estates of decedents, or any other probate proceedings in the county court differing from these Rules, and not included in the "List of Repealed Statutes," such statute shall apply; and where any statute in effect immediately prior to September 1, 1941, and not included in the "List of Repealed Statutes," prescribed a rule of procedure in any special statutory proceeding differing from these rules, such statute shall apply. All statutes in effect immediately prior to September 1, 1941, prescribing rules of procedure in bond or recognizance forfeitures in criminal cases are hereby continued in effect as rules of procedure governing such cases, but where such statutes prescribed no rules of procedure in such cases, these rules shall apply. All statutes in effect immediately prior to September 1, 1941, prescribing rules of procedure in tax suits are hereby continued in effect as rules of procedure governing such cases, but where such statutes prescribed no rules of procedure in such cases, these rules shall apply; provided, however, that Rule 117a shall control with respect to citation in tax suits.

(Amended by Order Sept. 20, 1941, eff. Dec. 31, 1941; June 16, 1943, eff. Dec. 31, 1943; Aug. 18, 1947, eff. Dec. 31, 1947; April 10, 1986, eff. Sept. 1, 1986.)

RULE 3. CONSTRUCTION OF RULES.

Unless otherwise expressly provided, the past, present or future tense shall each include the other; the masculine, feminine, or neuter gender shall each include the other; and the singular and plural number shall each include the other.

RULE 3a. LOCAL RULES.

Each administrative judicial region, district court, county court, county court at law, and probate court may make and amend local rules governing practice before such courts, provided:

(1) that any proposed rule or amendment shall not be inconsistent with these rules or with any rule of the administrative judicial region in which the court is located;

(2) no time period provided by these rules may be altered by local rules;

(3) any proposed local rule or amendment shall not become effective until it is submitted and approved by the Supreme Court of Texas;

(4) any proposed local rule or amendment shall not become effective until at least thirty days after its publication in a manner reasonably calculated to bring it to the attention of attorneys practicing before the court or courts for which it is made;

(5) all local rules or amendments adopted and approved in accordance herewith are made available upon request to members of the bar;

(6) no local rule, order, or practice of any court, other than local rules and amendments which fully comply with all requirements of this Rule 3a, shall ever be applied to determine the merits of any matter.

(Renumbered from former rule 817 and amended Dec. 5, 1983, eff. April 1, 1984. Amended April 10, 1986, eff. Sept. 1 1986; July 15, 1987, eff. Jan. 1, 1988; April 24, 1990, eff. Sept. 1, 1990.)

Notes and Comments

Comment to 1990 change: To make Texas Rules of Civil Procedure timetables mandatory and to preclude use of unpublished local rules or other "standing" orders to local practices to determine issues of substantive merit.

RULE 4. COMPUTATION OF TIME.

In computing any period of time prescribed or allowed by these rules, by order of court, or by any applicable statute, the day of the act, event, or default after which the designated period of time begins to run is not to be included. The last day of the period so computed is to be included, unless it is a Saturday, Sunday, or legal holiday, in which event the period runs until the end of the next day which is not a Saturday, Sunday, or legal holiday. Saturdays, Sundays, and legal holidays shall not be counted for any purpose in any time period of five days or less in these rules, except that Saturdays, Sundays, and legal holidays shall be counted for purpose of the three-day periods in Rules 21 and 21a, extending other periods by three days when service is made by mail.

(Amended by Order July 26, 1960, eff. Jan. 1, 1961; April 24, 1990, eff. Sept. 1, 1990; Aug. 16, 2013, eff. Jan. 1, 2014; Dec. 13, 2013, eff. Jan. 1, 2014.)

Notes and Comments

Comment to 1990 change: Amended to omit counting Saturdays, Sundays and legal holidays in all periods of less than five days with certain exceptions.

RULE 5. ENLARGEMENT OF TIME.

When by these rules or by a notice given thereunder or by order of court an act is required or allowed to be done at or within a specified time, the court for cause shown may, at any time in its discretion (a) with or without motion or notice, order the period enlarged if application therefor is made before the expiration of the period originally prescribed or as extended by a previous order; or (b) upon motion permit the act to be done after the expiration of the specified period where good cause is shown for the failure to act. The court may not enlarge the period for taking any action under the rules relating to new trials except as stated in these rules. If any document is sent to the proper clerk by first-class United States mail in an envelope or wrapper properly addressed and stamped and is deposited in the mail on or before the last day for filing same, the same, if received by the clerk not more than ten days tardily, shall be filed by the clerk and be deemed filed in time. A legible postmark affixed by the United States Postal Service shall be prima facie evidence of the date of mailing.

(Amended by Order Oct. 12, 1949, eff. March 1, 1950; July 21, 1970, eff. Jan. 1, 1971; Oct. 3, 1972, eff. Feb. 1, 1973; July 22, 1975, eff. Jan. 1, 1976; April 10, 1986, eff. Sept. 1, 1986; April 24, 1990, eff. Sept. 1, 1990.)

Notes and Comments

Comment to 1990 change: To make the last date for mailing under Rule 5 coincide with the last date for filing.

RULE 6. SUITS COMMENCED ON SUNDAY.

No civil suit shall be commenced nor process issued or served on Sunday, except in cases of injunction, attachment, garnishment, sequestration, or distress proceedings, provided that citation by publication published on Sunday shall be valid.

(Amended by Order Oct. 3, 1972, eff. Feb. 1, 1973.)

RULE 7. MAY APPEAR BY ATTORNEY.

Any party to a suit may appear and prosecute or defend his rights therein, either in person or by an attorney of the court.

RULE 8. ATTORNEY IN CHARGE.

On the occasion of a party's first appearance through counsel, the attorney whose signature first appears on the initial pleadings for any party shall be the attorney in charge, unless another attorney is specifically designated therein. Thereafter, until such designation is changed by written notice to the court and all other parties in accordance with Rule 21a, said attorney in charge shall be responsible for the suit as to such party. All communications from the court or other counsel with respect to a suit shall be sent to the attorney in charge.

(Amended by Order July 16, 1987, eff. Jan. 1, 1988.)

RULE 8a. [Suspended, *see* Misc. Docket No. 03-9207, Dec. 23, 2003, eff. Dec. 30, 2003.]

(Adopted by Order Oct. 9, 2003, eff. Jan. 1, 2004, only in cases filed on or after effective date. Order Dec. 23, 2003 suspends effective date pending further order of the Court.)

RULE 9. NUMBER OF COUNSEL HEARD.

Not more than two counsel on each side shall be heard on any question or on the trial, except in important cases, and upon special leave of the court.

RULE 10. WITHDRAWAL OF ATTORNEY.

An attorney may withdraw from representing a party only upon written motion for good cause shown. If another attorney is to be substituted as attorney for the party, the motion shall state: the name, address, telephone number, telecopier number, if any, and State Bar of Texas identification number of the substitute attorney; that the party approves the substitution; and that the withdrawal is not sought for delay only. If another attorney is not to be substituted as attorney for the party, the motion shall state: that a copy of the motion has been delivered to the party; that the party has been notified in writing of his right to object to the motion; whether the party consents to the motion, the party's last known address and all pending settings and deadlines. If the motion is granted, the withdrawing attorney shall immediately notify the party in writing of any additional settings or deadlines of which the attorney has knowledge at the time of the withdrawal and has not already notified the party. The Court may impose further conditions upon granting leave to withdraw. Notice or delivery to a party shall be either made to the party in person or mailed to the party's last known address by both certified and regular first class mail. If the attorney in charge withdraws and another attorney remains or becomes substituted, another attorney in charge must be designated of record with notice to all other parties in accordance with Rule 21a.

(Amended by Order July 15, 1987, eff. Jan. 1, 1988; April 24, 1990, eff. Sept. 1, 1990.)

Notes and Comments

Comment to 1990 change: The amendment repeals the present rule and clarifies the requirements for withdrawal.

RULE 11. AGREEMENTS TO BE IN WRITING.

Unless otherwise provided in these rules, no agreement between attorneys or parties touching any suit pending will be enforced unless it be in writing, signed and filed with the papers as part of the record, or unless it be made in open court and entered of record.

(Amended by Order July 15, 1987, eff. Jan. 1, 1988.)

Notes and Comments

Comment to 1988 change: The amendment makes it clear that Rule 11 is subject to modification by any other Rule of Civil Procedure.

RULE 12. ATTORNEY TO SHOW AUTHORITY.

A party in a suit or proceeding pending in a court of this state may, by sworn written motion stating that he believes the suit or proceeding is being prosecuted or defended without authority, cause the attorney to be cited to appear before the court and show his authority to act. The notice of the motion shall be served upon the challenged attorney at least ten days before the hearing on the motion. At the hearing on the motion, the burden of proof shall be upon the challenged attorney to show sufficient authority to prosecute or defend the suit on behalf of the other party. Upon his failure to show such authority, the court shall refuse to permit the attorney to appear in the cause, and shall strike the pleadings if no person who is authorized to prosecute or defend appears. The motion may be heard and determined at anytime before the parties have announced ready for trial, but the trial shall not be unnecessarily continued or delayed for the hearing.

(Amended by Order June 10, 1980, eff. Jan. 1, 1981.)

RULE 13. EFFECT OF SIGNING OF PLEADINGS, MOTIONS AND OTHER PAPERS; SANCTIONS.

The signatures of attorneys or parties constitute a certificate by them that they have read the pleading, motion, or other paper; that to the best of their knowledge, information, and belief formed after reasonable inquiry the instrument is not groundless and brought in bad faith or groundless and brought for the purpose of harassment. Attorneys or parties who shall bring a fictitious suit as an experiment to get an opinion of the court, or who shall file any fictitious pleading in a cause for such a purpose, or shall make statements in pleading which they know to be groundless and false, for the purpose of securing a delay of the trial of the cause, shall be held guilty of a contempt. If a pleading, motion or other paper is signed in violation of this rule, the court, upon motion or upon its own initiative, after notice and hearing, shall impose an appropriate sanction available under Rule 215-2b, upon the person who signed it, a represented party, or both.

Courts shall presume that pleadings, motions, and other papers are filed in good faith. No sanctions under this rule may be imposed except for good cause, the particulars of which must be stated in the sanction order. "Groundless" for purposes of this rule means no basis in law or fact and not warranted by good faith argument for the extension, modification, or reversal of existing law. A general denial does not constitute a violation of this rule. The amount requested for damages does not constitute a violation of this rule.

(Amended by Order July 15, 1987, eff. Jan. 1, 1988; April 24, 1990, eff. Sept. 1, 1990.)

Notes and Comments

Comment to 1990 change: To require notice and hearing before a court determines to impose sanctions, to specify that any sanction imposed be appropriate, and to eliminate the 90-day "grace" period provided in the former version of the rule.

RULE 14. AFFIDAVIT BY AGENT.

Whenever it may be necessary or proper for any party to a civil suit or proceeding to make an affidavit, it may be made by either the party or his agent or his attorney.

RULE 14a. [Repealed effective Sept. 1, 1986]

(Repealed by Order April 10, 1986, eff. Sept. 1, 1986.)

RULE 14b. RETURN OR OTHER DISPOSITION OF EXHIBITS.

The clerk of the court in which the exhibits are filed shall retain and dispose of the same as directed by the Supreme Court.

(Adopted by Order July 20, 1966, eff. Jan. 1, 1967. Amended by Order July 15, 1987, eff. Jan. 1, 1988.)

Supreme Court Order Relating to Retention and Disposition of Exhibits

In compliance with the provisions of Rule 14b, the Supreme Court hereby directs that exhibits offered or admitted into evidence shall be retained and disposed of by the clerk of the court in which the exhibits are filed upon the following basis.

This order shall apply only to: (1) those cases in which judgment has been rendered on service of process by publication and in which no motion for new trial was filed within two years after judgment was signed; and, (2) all other cases in which judgment has been signed for one year and in which no appeal was perfected or in which a perfected appeal was dismissed or concluded by a final judgement as to all parties and the issuance of the appellate court's mandate such that the case is no longer pending on appeal or in the trial court.

The party who offered an exhibit may withdraw it from the clerk's office within thirty days of the later of (1) a case becoming subject to this order, or (2) the effective date of this order. The clerk, unless otherwise directed by the court, may dispose of any exhibits remaining after such time period.

Misc. Docket No. 05-9026, Order Relating to Retention and Disposition of Deposition of Exhibits in Civil Case, Jan. 27, 2005, eff. June 1, 2005.

RULE 14c. DEPOSIT IN LIEU OF SURETY BOND.

Wherever these rules provide for the filing of a surety bond, the party may in lieu of filing the bond deposit cash or other negotiable obligation of the government of the United States of America or any agency thereof, or with leave of court, deposit a negotiable obligation of any bank or savings and loan association chartered by the government of the United States of America or any state thereof that is insured by the government of the United States of America or any agency thereof, in the amount fixed for the surety bond, conditioned in the same manner as would be a surety bond for the protection of other parties. Any interest thereon shall constitute a part of the deposit.

(Adopted by Order June 10, 1980, eff. Jan. 1, 1981.)

PART II.
RULES OF PRACTICE IN DISTRICT AND COUNTY COURTS

SECTION 1.
GENERAL RULES

RULE 15. WRITS AND PROCESS.

The style of all writs and process shall be "The State of Texas;" and unless otherwise specially provided by law or these rules every such writ and process shall be directed to any sheriff or any constable within the State of Texas, shall be made returnable on the Monday next after expiration of twenty days from the date of service thereof, and shall be dated and attested by the clerk with the seal of the court impressed thereon; and the date of issuance shall be noted thereon.

RULE 16. SHALL ENDORSE ALL PROCESS.

Every officer or authorized person shall endorse on all process and precepts coming to his hand the day and hour on which he received them, the manner in which he executed them, and the time and place the process was served and shall sign the returns officially.

(Amended by Order July 15, 1987, eff. Jan. 1, 1988.)

RULE 17. OFFICER TO EXECUTE PROCESS.

Except where otherwise expressly provided by law or these rules, the officer receiving any process to be executed shall not be entitled in any case to demand his fee for executing the same in advance of such execution, but his fee shall be taxed and collected as other costs in the case.

RULE 18. WHEN JUDGE DIES DURING TERM, RESIGNS OR IS DISABLED.

If the judge dies, resigns, or becomes unable to hold court during the session of court duly convened for the term, and the time provided by law for the holding of said court has not expired, such death, resignation, or inability on the part of the judge shall not operate to adjourn said court for the term, but such court shall be deemed to continue in session. If a successor to such judge shall qualify and assume office during the term, or if a judge be transferred to said district from some other judicial district, he may continue to hold said court for the term provided, and all motions undisposed of shall be heard and determined by him, and statements of facts and bills of exception shall be approved by him. If the time for holding such court expires before a successor shall qualify, and before a judge can be transferred to said district from some other judicial district, then all motions pending, including those for new trial, shall stand as continued in force until such successor has qualified and assumed office, or a judge has been transferred to said district who can hold said court, and thereupon such judge shall have power to act thereon at the succeeding term, or on an earlier day in vacation, on notice to all parties to the motion, and such orders shall have the same effect as if rendered in term time. The time for allowing statement of facts and bills of exception from such orders shall date from the time the motion was decided.

(Amended by Order June 16, 1943, eff. Dec. 31, 1943.)

RULE 18a. RECUSAL AND DISQUALIFICATION OF JUDGES.

(a) *Motion; Form and Contents.* A party in a case in any trial court other than a statutory probate court or justice court may seek to recuse or disqualify a judge who is sitting in the case by filing a motion with the clerk of the court in which the case is pending. The motion:

- (1) must be verified;
- (2) must assert one or more of the grounds listed in Rule 18.2;
- (3) must not be based solely on the judge's rulings in the case; and
- (4) must state with detail and particularity facts that:
  - (A) are within the affiant's personal knowledge, except that facts may be stated on information and belief if the basis for that belief is specifically stated;
  - (B) would be admissible in evidence; and
  - (C) if proven, would be sufficient to justify recusal or disqualification.

(b) *Time for Filing Motion.*

- (1) Motion to Recuse. A motion to recuse:
  - (A) must be filed as soon as practicable after the movant knows of the ground stated in the motion; and
  - (B) must not be filed after the tenth day before the date set for trial or other hearing unless, before that day, the movant neither knew nor reasonably should have known:
    - (i) that the judge whose recusal is sought would preside at the trial or hearing; or
    - (ii) that the ground stated in the motion existed.
- (2) Motion to Disqualify. A motion to disqualify should be filed as soon as practicable after the movant knows of the ground stated in the motion.

(c) *Response to Motion.*

- (1) By Another Party. Any other party in the case may, but need not, file a response to the motion. Any response must be filed before the motion is heard.
- (2) By the Respondent Judge. The judge whose recusal or disqualification is sought should not file a response to the motion.

(d) *Service of Motion or Response.* A party who files a motion or response must serve a copy on every other party. The method of service must be the same as the method of filing, if possible.

(e) *Duties of Clerk.*

- (1) Delivery of Motion or Response. When a motion or response is filed, the clerk of the court must immediately deliver a copy to the respondent judge and to the presiding judge of the administrative judicial region in which the court is located ("the regional presiding judge").
- (2) Delivery of Order of Recusal or Referral. When a respondent judge signs and files an order of recusal or referral, the clerk of the court must immediately deliver a copy to the regional presiding judge.

(f) *Duties of Respondent Judge; Failure to Comply.*

- (1) Responding to Motion. Regardless of whether the motion complies with this rule, the respondent judge, within three business days after the motion is filed, must either:
  - (A) sign and file with the clerk an order of recusal or disqualification; or
  - (B) sign and file with the clerk an order referring the motion to the regional presiding judge.
- (2) Restrictions on Further Action.
  - (A) Motion Filed Before Evidence Offered at Trial. If a motion is filed before evidence has been offered at trial, the respondent judge must take no further action in the case until the motion has been decided, except for good cause stated in writing or on the record.
  - (B) Motion Filed After Evidence Offered at Trial. If a motion is filed after evidence has been offered at trial, the respondent judge may proceed, subject to stay by the regional presiding judge.
  - (3) Failure to Comply. If the respondent judge fails to comply with a duty imposed by this rule, the movant may notify the regional presiding judge.

(g) Duties of Regional Presiding Judge.

(1) Motion. The regional presiding judge must rule on a referred motion or assign a judge to rule. If a party files a motion to recuse or disqualify the regional presiding judge, the regional presiding judge may still assign a judge to rule on the original, referred motion. Alternatively, the regional presiding judge may sign and file with the clerk an order referring the second motion to the Chief Justice of the Supreme Court of Texas for consideration.

(2) Order. The ruling must be by written order.

(3) Summary Denial for Noncompliance.

(A) Motion to Recuse. A motion to recuse that does not comply with this rule may be denied without an oral hearing. The order must state the nature of the noncompliance. Even if the motion is amended to correct the stated noncompliance, the motion will count for purposes of determining whether a tertiary recusal motion has been filed under the Civil Practice and Remedies Code.

(B) Motion to Disqualify. A motion to disqualify may not be denied on the ground that it was not filed or served in compliance with this rule.

(4) Interim Orders. The regional presiding judge or judge assigned to decide the motion may issue interim or ancillary orders in the pending case as justice may require.

(5) Discovery. Except by order of the regional presiding judge or the judge assigned to decide the motion, a subpoena or discovery request may not issue to the respondent judge and may be disregarded unless accompanied by the order.

(6) Hearing.

(A) Time. The motion must be heard as soon as practicable and may be heard immediately after it is referred to the regional presiding judge or an assigned judge.

(B) Notice. Notice of the hearing must be given to all parties in the case.

(C) By Telephone. The hearing may be conducted by telephone on the record. Documents submitted by facsimile or email, otherwise admissible under the rules of evidence, may be considered.

(7) Reassignment of Case if Motion Granted. If the motion is granted, the regional presiding judge must transfer the case to another court or assign another judge to the case.

(h) *Sanctions.* After notice and hearing, the judge who hears the motion may order the party or attorney who filed the motion, or both, to pay the reasonable attorney fees and expenses incurred by other parties if the judge determines that the motion was:

(1) groundless and filed in bad faith or for the purpose of harassment; or

(2) clearly brought for unnecessary delay and without sufficient cause.

(i) *Chief Justice.* The Chief Justice of the Supreme Court of Texas may assign judges and issue any orders permitted by this rule or pursuant to statute.

(j) *Appellate Review.*

(1) Order on Motion to Recuse.

(A) Denying Motion. An order denying a motion to recuse may be reviewed only for abuse of discretion on appeal from the final judgment.

(B) Granting Motion. An order granting a motion to recuse is final and cannot be reviewed by appeal, mandamus, or otherwise.

(2) Order on Motion to Disqualify. An order granting or denying a motion to disqualify may be reviewed by mandamus and may be appealed in accordance with other law.

(Added by Order June 10, 1980, eff. Jan. 1, 1981. Amended by Order Dec. 5 1983, eff. April 1, 1984; April 10, 1986, eff. Sept. 1, 1986; July 15, 1987, eff. Jan. 1, 1988; April 24, 1990, eff. Sept. 1, 1990; July 5, 2011, eff. Aug. 1, 2011; July 22, 2011, eff. Aug. 1, 2011.)

RULE 18b. GROUNDS FOR DISQUALIFICATION AND RECUSAL OF JUDGES.

(a) *Grounds for Disqualification.* A judge must disqualify in any proceeding in which:

(1) the judge has served as a lawyer in the matter in controversy, or a lawyer with whom the judge previously practiced law served during such association as a lawyer concerning the matter;

(2) the judge knows that, individually or as a fiduciary, the judge has an interest in the subject matter in controversy; or

(3) either of the parties may be related to the judge by affinity or consanguinity within the third degree.

(b) *Grounds for Recusal.* A judge must recuse in any proceeding in which:

(1) the judge's impartiality might reasonably be questioned;

(2) the judge has a personal bias or prejudice concerning the subject matter or a party;

(3) the judge has personal knowledge of disputed evidentiary facts concerning the proceeding;

(4) the judge or a lawyer with whom the judge previously practiced law has been a material witness concerning the proceeding;

(5) the judge participated as counsel, adviser, or material witness in the matter in controversy, or expressed an opinion concerning the merits of it, while acting as an attorney in government service;

(6) the judge knows that the judge, individually or as a fiduciary, or the judge's spouse or minor child residing in the judge's household, has a financial interest in the subject matter in controversy or in a party to the proceeding, or any other interest that could be substantially affected by the outcome of the proceeding;

(7) the judge or the judge's spouse, or a person within the third degree of relationship to either of them, or the spouse of such a person:

(A) is a party to the proceeding or an officer, director, or trustee of a party;

(B) is known by the judge to have an interest that could be substantially affected by the outcome of the proceeding; or

(C) is to the judge's knowledge likely to be a material witness in the proceeding; or

(8) the judge or the judge's spouse, or a person within the first degree of relationship to either of them, or the spouse of such a person, is acting as a lawyer in the proceeding.

(c) *Financial Interests.* A judge should inform himself or herself about personal and fiduciary financial interests, and make a reasonable effort to inform himself or herself about the personal financial interests of his or her spouse and minor children residing in the household.

(d) *Terminology and Standards.* In this rule:

(1) "proceeding" includes pretrial, trial, or other stages of litigation;

(2) the degree of relationship is calculated according to the civil law system;

(3) "fiduciary" includes such relationships as executor, administrator, trustee, and guardian;

(4) "financial interest" means ownership of a legal or equitable interest, however small, or a relationship as director, adviser, or other active participant in the affairs of a party, except that:

(A) ownership in a mutual or common investment fund that holds securities is not a "financial interest" in such securities unless the judge participates in the management of the fund;

(B) an office in an educational, religious, charitable, fraternal, or civic organization is not a "financial interest" in securities held by the organization;

(C) the proprietary interest of a policyholder in a mutual insurance company, of a depositor in a mutual savings association, or a similar proprietary interest, is a "financial interest" in the organization only if the outcome of the proceeding could substantially affect the value of the interest;

(D) ownership of government securities is a "financial interest" in the issuer only if the outcome of the proceeding could substantially affect the value of the securities; and

(E) an interest as a taxpayer or utility ratepayer, or any similar interest, is not a "financial interest" unless the outcome of the proceeding could substantially affect the liability of the judge or a person related to the judge within the third degree more than other judges.

(e) *Waiving Ground for Recusal.* The parties to a proceeding may waive any ground for recusal after it is fully disclosed on the record.

(f) *Discovery and Divestiture.* If a judge does not discover that the judge is recused under subparagraph (b)(6) or (b)(7)(C) until after the judge has devoted substantial time to the matter, the judge is not required to recuse himself or herself if the judge or the person related to the judge divests himself or herself of the interest that would otherwise require recusal.

(Adopted by Order July 15, 1987, eff. Jan. 1, 1988. Amended by Order April 24, 1990, eff. Sept. 1, 1990; July 5, 2011, eff. Aug. 1, 2011.)

Comment to 2011 Change: Rule 18a governs the procedure for recusing or disqualifying a judge sitting in any trial court other than a statutory probate court or justice court. Chapter 25 of the Government Code governs statutory probate courts, Rule 528 governs justice courts, and Chapter 29 of the Government Code governs municipal courts. Under Rule 18.a, a judge's rulings may not be the sole basis for a motion to recuse or disqualify the judge. But when one or more sufficient other bases are raised, the judge hearing the motion may consider evidence of rulings when considering whether to grant the motion. For purposes of this rule, the term "rulings" is not meant to encompass a judge's statements or remarks about a case.

The amendments to Rule 18b are not intended to be substantive.

RULE 18c. RECORDING AND BROADCASTING OF COURT PROCEEDINGS.

A trial court may permit broadcasting televising, recording, or photographing of proceedings in the courtroom only in the following circumstances:

(a) in accordance with guidelines promulgated by the Supreme Court for civil cases, or

(b) when broadcasting, televising, recording, or photographing will not unduly distract participants or impair the dignity of the proceedings and the parties have consented, and consent to being depicted or recorded is obtained from each witness whose testimony will be broadcast, televised, or photographed, or

(c) the broadcasting, televising, recording, or photographing of investiture, or ceremonial proceedings.

(Added by Order April 24, 1990, eff. Sept. 1, 1990.)

RULE 19. NON-ADJOURNMENT OF TERM.

Every term of court shall commence and convene by operation of law at the time fixed by statute without any act, order, or formal opening by a judge or other official thereof, and shall continue to be open at all times until and including the last day of the term unless sooner adjourned by the judge thereof.

(Amended by Order June 16, 1943, eff. Dec. 31, 1943.)

RULE 20. MINUTES READ AND SIGNED.

On the last day of the session, the minutes shall be read, corrected and signed in open court by the judge. Each special judge shall sign the minutes of such proceedings as were had by him.

RULE 21. FILING AND SERVING PLEADINGS AND MOTIONS.

(a) *Filing and Service Required.* Every pleading, plea, motion or application to the court for an order, whether in the form of a motion, plea or other form of request, unless presented during a hearing or trial, must be filed with the clerk of the court in writing, must state the grounds therefore, must set forth the relief or order sought, and at the same time a true copy must be served on all other parties, and must be noted on the docket.

(b) *Service of Notice of Hearing.* An application to the court for an order and notice of any hearing thereon, not presented during a hearing or trial, must be served upon all other parties not less than three days before the time specified for the hearing unless otherwise provided by these rules or shortened by the court.

(c) *Multiple Parties.* If there is more than one other party represented by different attorneys, one copy of each pleading must be served on each attorney in charge.

(d) *Certificate of Service.* The party or attorney of record, must certify to the court compliance with this rule in writing over signature on the filed pleading, plea, motion or application.

(e) *Additional Copies.* After one copy is served on a party that party may obtain another copy of the same pleading upon tendering reasonable payment for copying and delivering.

(f) *Electronic Filing.*

  (1) Requirement. Except in juvenile cases under Title 3 of the Family Code and truancy cases under Title 3A of the Family Code, attorneys must electronically file documents in courts where electronic filing has been mandated. Attorneys practicing in courts where electronic filing is available but not mandated and unrepresented parties may electronically file documents, but it is not required.

  (2) Email Address. The email address of an attorney or unrepresented party who electronically files a document must be included on the document.

  (3) Mechanism. Electronic filing must be done through the electronic filing manager established by the Office of Court Administration and an electronic filing service provider certified by the Office of Court Administration.

  (4) Exceptions.

    (A) Wills are not required to be filed electronically.

    (B) The following documents must not be filed electronically:

      (i) documents filed under seal or presented to the court in camera; and

      (ii) documents to which access is otherwise restricted by law or court order.

    (C) For good cause, a court may permit a party to file other documents in paper form in a particular case.

  (5) Timely Filing. Unless a document must be filed by a certain time of day, a document is considered timely filed if it is electronically filed at any time before midnight (in the court's time zone) on the filing deadline. An electronically filed document is deemed filed when transmitted to the filing party's electronic filing service provider, except:

    (A) if a document is transmitted on a Saturday, Sunday, or legal holiday, it is deemed filed on the next day that is not a Saturday, Sunday, or legal holiday; and

    (B) if a document requires a motion and an order allowing its filing, the document is deemed filed on the date that the motion is granted.

  (6) Technical Failure. If a document is untimely due to a technical failure or a system outage, the filing party may seek appropriate relief from the court. If the missed deadline is one imposed by these rules, the filing party must be given a reasonable extension of time to complete the filing.

  (7) Electronic Signatures. A document that is electronically served, filed, or issued by a court or clerk is considered signed if the document includes:

(A) a "/s/" and name typed in the space where the signature would otherwise appear, unless the document is notarized or sworn; or

(B) an electronic image or scanned image of the signature.

(8) Format. An electronically filed document must:

(A) be in text-searchable portable document format (PDF);

(B) be directly converted to PDF rather than scanned, if possible;

(C) not be locked; and

(D) otherwise comply with the Technology Standards set by the Judicial Committee on Information Technology and approved by the Supreme Court.

(9) Paper Copies. Unless required by local rule, a party need not file a paper copy of an electronically filed document.

(10) Electronic Notices From the Court. The clerk may send notices, orders, or other communications about the case to the party electronically. A court seal may be electronic.

(11) Non-Conforming Documents. The clerk may not refuse to file a document that fails to conform with this rule. But the clerk may identify the error to be corrected and state a deadline for the party to resubmit the document in a conforming format.

(12) Original Wills. When a party electronically files an application to probate a document as an original will, the original will must be filed with the clerk within three business days after the application is filed.

(13) Official Record. The clerk may designate an electronically filed document or a scanned paper document as the official court record. The clerk is not required to keep both paper and electronic versions of the same document unless otherwise required by local rule. But the clerk must retain an original will filed for probate in a numbered file folder.

(Amended by Order Sept. 20, 1941, eff. Dec. 31, 1941; Aug. 18, 1947, eff. Dec. 31, 1947; July 11, 1977, eff. Jan. 1, 1978; June 10, 1980, eff. Jan. 1, 1981; April 24, 1990, eff. Sept. 1, 1990; Aug. 16, 2013, eff. Jan. 1, 2014; Dec. 13, 2013, eff. Jan. 1, 2014; Tex. Sup. Ct. Misc. Docket No. 15-9155 Aug. 28, 2015, eff. Sept. 1, 2015.)

Comment to 2013 Change: Rule 21 is revised to incorporate rules for electronic filing, in accordance with the Supreme Court's order—Misc. Docket No. 12-9206, amended by Misc. Docket Nos. 13-9092 and 13-9164—mandating electronic filing in civil cases beginning on January 1, 2014. The mandate will be implemented according to the schedule in the order and will be completed by July 1, 2016. The revisions reflect the fact that the mandate will only apply to a subset of Texas courts until that date.

Technology Standards (These standards apply to documents filed electronically under Texas Rule of Civil Procedure 21 and Texas Rule of Appellate Procedure 9.)

RULE 21a. METHODS OF SERVICE.

(a) Methods of Service. Every notice required by these rules, and every pleading, plea, motion, or other form of request required to be served under Rule 21, other than the citation to be served upon the filing of a cause of action and except as otherwise expressly provided in these rules, may be served by delivering a copy to the party to be served, or the party's duly authorized agent or attorney of record in the manner specified below:

(1) Documents Filed Electronically. A document filed electronically under Rule 21 must be served electronically through the electronic filing manager if the email address of the party or attorney to be served is on file with the electronic filing manager. If the email address of the party or attorney to be served is not on file with the electronic filing manager, the document may be served on that party or attorney under subparagraph (2).

(2) Documents Not Filed Electronically. A document not filed electronically may be served in person, by mail, by commercial delivery service, by fax, by email, or by such other manner as the court in its discretion may direct.

(b) When Complete.

(1) Service by mail or commercial delivery service shall be complete upon deposit of the document, postpaid and properly addressed, in the mail or with a commercial delivery service.

(2) Service by fax is complete on receipt. Service completed after 5:00 p.m. local time of the recipient shall be deemed served on the following day.

(3) Electronic service is complete on transmission of the document to the serving party's electronic filing service provider. The electronic filing manager will send confirmation of service to the serving party.

(c) Time for Action After Service. Whenever a party has the right or is required to do some act within a prescribed period after the service of a notice or other paper upon him and the notice or paper is served upon him by mail, three days shall be added to the prescribed period.

(d) Who May Serve. Notice may be served by a party to the suit, an attorney of record, a sheriff or constable, or by any other person competent to testify.

(e) Proof of Service. The party or attorney of record shall certify to the court compliance with this rule in writing over signature and on the filed instrument. A certificate by a party or an attorney of record, or the return of the officer, or the affidavit of any other person showing service of a notice shall be prima facie evidence of the fact of service. Nothing herein shall preclude any party from offering proof that the document was not received, or, if service was by mail, that the document was not received within three days from the date that it was deposited in the mail, and upon so finding, the court may extend the time for taking the action required of such party or grant such other relief as it deems just.

(f) Procedures Cumulative. These provisions are cumulative of all other methods of service prescribed by these rules.

(Adopted by Order Aug. 18, 1947, eff. Dec. 31, 1947. Amended by Order July 21, 1970, eff. Jan. 1, 1971; Oct. 3, 1972, eff. Feb. 1, 1973, July 11 1977, eff. Jan. 1, 1978; June 10, 1980, eff. Jan. 1, 1981; Dec. 5, 1983, eff. April 1, 1984; April 24, 1990, eff. Sept. 1, 1990; Aug. 16, 2013, eff. Jan. 1, 2014; Dec. 13, 2013, eff. Jan. 1, 2014.)

Comment to 2013 Change: Rule 21a is revised to incorporate rules for electronic service in accordance with the Supreme Court's order—Misc. Docket No. 12-9206, amended by Misc. Docket Nos. 13-9092 and 13-9164—mandating electronic filing in civil cases beginning on January 1, 2014.

Technology Standards (These standards apply to documents filed electronically under Texas Rule of Civil Procedure 21 and Texas Rule of Appellate Procedure 9.)

RULE 21b. SANCTIONS FOR FAILURE TO SERVE OR DELIVER COPY OF PLEADINGS AND MOTIONS.

If any party fails to serve on or deliver to the other parties a copy of any pleading, plea, motion, or other application to the court for an order in accordance with Rules 21 and 21a, the court may in its discretion, after notice and hearing, impose an appropriate sanction available under Rule 215-2b.

(Adopted by Order April 24, 1990, eff. Sept. 1, 1990.)

[RULE 21c. Repealed effective September 1, 1986.]

RULE 21c. PRIVACY PROTECTION FOR FILED DOCUMENTS.

(a) Sensitive Data Defined. Sensitive data consists of:

  (1) a driver's license number, passport number, social security number, tax identification number, or similar government-issued personal identification number;

  (2) a bank account number, credit card number, or other financial account number; and

  (3) a birth date, home address, and the name of any person who was a minor when the underlying suit was filed.

(b) Filing of Documents Containing Sensitive Data Prohibited. Unless the inclusion of sensitive data is specifically required by a statute, court rule, or administrative regulation, an electronic or paper document, except for wills and documents filed under seal, containing sensitive data may not be filed with a court unless the sensitive data is redacted.

(c) Redaction of Sensitive Data; Retention Requirement. Sensitive data must be redacted by using the letter "X" in place of each omitted digit or character or by removing the sensitive data in a manner indicating that the data has been redacted. The filing party must retain an unredacted version of the filed document during the pendency of the case and any related appellate proceedings filed within six months of the date the judgment is signed.

(d) Notice to Clerk. If a document must contain sensitive data, the filing party must notify the clerk by:

  (1) designating the document as containing sensitive data when the document is electronically filed; or

  (2) if the document is not electronically filed, by including, on the upper lefthand side of the first page, the phrase: "NOTICE: THIS DOCUMENT CONTAINS SENSITIVE DATA."

(e) Non-Conforming Documents. The clerk may not refuse to file a document that contains sensitive data in violation of this rule. But the clerk may identify the error to be corrected and state a deadline for the party to resubmit a redacted, substitute document.

(f) Restriction on Remote Access. Documents that contain sensitive data in violation of this rule must not be posted on the Internet.

(Adopted by Order Aug. 16, 2013, eff. Jan. 1, 2014; Dec. 13, 2013, eff. Jan. 1, 2014.)

Comment to 2013 Change: Rule 21c is added to provide privacy protection for documents filed in civil cases.

SECTION 2.
INSTITUTION OF SUIT

RULE 22. COMMENCED BY PETITION.

A civil suit in the district or county court shall be commenced by a petition filed in the office of the clerk.

RULE 23. SUITS TO BE NUMBERED CONSECUTIVELY.

It shall be the duty of the clerk to designate the suits by regular consecutive numbers, called file numbers, and he shall mark on each paper in every case the file number of the cause.

RULE 24. DUTY OF CLERK.

When a petition is filed with the clerk he shall indorse thereon the file number, the day on which it was filed and the time of filing, and sign his name officially thereto.

RULE 25. CLERK'S FILE DOCKET.

Each clerk shall keep a file docket which shall show in convenient form the number of the suit, the names of the attorneys, the names of the parties to the suit, and the nature thereof, and, in brief form, the officer's return on the process, and all subsequent proceedings had in the case with the dates thereof.

RULE 26. CLERK'S COURT DOCKET.

Each clerk shall also keep a court docket in a permanent record that shall include the number of the case and the names of the parties, the names of the attorneys, the nature of the action, the pleas, the motions, and the ruling of the court as made.

(Amended by Order April 24, 1990, eff. Sept. 1, 1990.)

RULE 27. ORDER OF CASES.

The cases shall be placed on the docket as they are filed.

SECTION 3.
PARTIES TO SUITS

RULE 28. SUITS IN ASSUMED NAME.

Any partnership, unincorporated association, private corporation, or individual doing business under an assumed name may sue or be sued in its partnership, assumed or common name for the purpose of enforcing for or against it a substantive right, but on a motion by any party or on the court's own motion the true name may be substituted.

(Amended by Order July 21, 1970, eff. Jan. 1, 1971.)

RULE 29. SUIT ON CLAIM AGAINST DISSOLVED CORPORATION.

When no receiver has been appointed for a corporation which has dissolved, suit may be instituted on any claim against said corporation as though the same had not been dissolved, and service of process may be obtained on the president, directors, general manager, trustee, assignee, or other person in charge of the affairs of the corporation at the time it was dissolved, and judgment may be rendered as though the corporation had not been dissolved.

RULE 30. PARTIES TO SUITS.

Assignors, endorsers and other parties not primarily liable upon any instruments named in the chapter of the Business and Commerce Code, dealing with commercial paper, may be jointly sued with their principal obligors, or may be sued alone in the cases provided for by statute.

(Amended by Order July 15, 1987, eff. Jan. 1, 1988.)

RULE 31. SURETY NOT TO BE SUED ALONE.

No surety shall be sued unless his principal is joined with him, or unless a judgment has previously been rendered against his principal, except in cases otherwise provided for in the law and these rules.

RULE 32. MAY HAVE QUESTION OF SURETYSHIP TRIED.

When any suit is brought against two or more defendants upon any contract, any one or more of the defendants being surety for the other, the surety may cause the question of suretyship to be tried and determined upon the issue made for the parties defendant at the trial of the cause, or at any time before or after the trial or at a subsequent term. Such proceedings shall not delay the suit of the plaintiff.

RULE 33. SUITS OR AGAINST COUNTIES.

Suits by or against a county or incorporated city, town or village shall be in its corporate name.

RULE 34. AGAINST SHERIFF, ETC.

Whenever a sheriff, constable, or a deputy or either has been sued for damages for any act done in his official character, and has taken an indemnifying bond for the acts upon which the suit is based, he may make the principal and surety on such bond parties defendant in such suit, and the cause may be continued to obtain service on such parties.

RULE 35. ON OFFICIAL BONDS.

In suits brought by the State or any county, city, independent school district, irrigation district, or other political subdivision of the State, against any officer who has held an office for more than one term, or against any depository which has been such depository for more than one term, or has given more than one official bond the sureties on each and all such bonds may be joined as defendants in the same suit whenever it is difficult to determine when the default sued for occurred and which set of sureties on such bonds is liable therefor.

(Amended by Order June 16, 1943, eff. Dec. 13, 1943.)

RULE 36. DIFFERENT OFFICIALS AND BONDSMEN.

In suits by the State upon the official bond of a State officer, any subordinate officer who has given bond, payable either to the State or such superior officer, to cover all or part of the default sued for together with the sureties on his official bond, may be joined as defendants with such superior officer and his bondsmen whenever it is alleged in the petition that both of such officers are liable for the money sued for.

RULE 37. ADDITIONAL PARTIES.

Before a case is called for trial, additional parties, necessary or proper parties to the suit, may be brought in, either by the plaintiff or the defendant, upon such terms as the court may prescribe; but not at a time nor in a manner to unreasonably delay the trial of the case.

RULE 38. THIRD-PARTY PRACTICE.

(a) **When Defendant May Bring in Third Party.** At any time after commencement of the action a defending party, as a third-party plaintiff, may cause a citation and petition to be served upon a person not a party to the action who is or may be liable to him or to the plaintiff for all or part of the plaintiff's claim against him. The third-party plaintiff need not obtain leave to make the service if he files the third-party petition not later than thirty (30) days after he serves his original answer. Otherwise, he must obtain leave on motion upon notice to all parties to the action. The person served, hereinafter called the third-party defendant, shall make his defenses to the third-party plaintiff's claim under the rules applicable to the defendant, and his counterclaims against the third-party plaintiff and cross-claims against other third-party defendants as provided in Rule 97. The third-party defendant may assert against the plaintiff any defenses which the third-party plaintiff has to the plaintiff's claim. The third-party defendant may also assert any claim against the plaintiff arising out of the transaction or occurrence that is the subject matter of the plaintiff's claim against the third-party plaintiff The plaintiff may assert any claim against the third-party defendant arising out of the transaction or occurrence that is the subject matter of the plaintiff's claim against the third-party plaintiff, and the third-party defendant thereupon shall assert his defenses and his counterclaims and cross-claims. Any party may move to strike the third-party claim, or for its severance or separate trial. A third-party defendant may proceed under this rule against any person not a party to the action who is or who may be liable to him or to the third-party plaintiff for all or part of the claim made in the action against the third-party defendant.

(b) **When Plaintiff May Bring in Third Party.** When a counterclaim is asserted against a plaintiff, he may cause a third party to be brought in under circumstances which under this rule would entitle a defendant to do so.

(c) This rule shall not be applied, in tort cases, so as to permit the joinder of a liability or indemnity insurance company, unless such company is by statute or contract liable to the person injured or damaged.

(d) This rule shall not be applied so as to violate any venue statute, as venue would exist absent this rule.

(Amended by Order March 31, 1941, eff. Sept. 1, 1941; Dec. 5, 1983, eff. April 1, 1984.)

RULE 39. JOINDER OF PERSONS NEEDED FOR JUST ADJUDICATION.

(a) Persons to Be Joined if Feasible. A person who is subject to service of process shall be joined as a party in the action if

(1) in his absence complete relief cannot be accorded among those already parties or

(2) he claims an interest relating to the subject of the action and is so situated that the disposition of the action in his absence may

(i) as a practical matter impair or impede his ability to protect that interest or

(ii) leave any of the persons already parties subject to a substantial risk of incurring double, multiple, or otherwise inconsistent obligations by reason of his claimed interest. If he has not been so joined, the court shall order that he be made a party. If he should join as a plaintiff but refuses to do so, he may be made a defendant, or, in a proper case, an involuntary plaintiff.

(b) **Determination by Court Whenever Joinder Not Feasible.** If a person as described in subdivision (a)(1)-(2) hereof cannot be made a party, the court shall determine whether in equity and good conscience the action should proceed among the parties before it or should be dismissed, the absent person being thus regarded as indispensable. The factors to be considered by the court include: first, to what extent a judgment rendered in the person's absence might be prejudicial to him or those already parties; second, the extent to which, by protective provisions in the judgment, by the shaping of relief, or other measures the prejudice can be lessened or avoided, third whether a judgment rendered in the person's absence will be adequate; fourth, whether the plaintiff will have an adequate remedy if the action is dismissed for non-joinder.

(c) **Pleading Reasons for Nonjoinder.** A pleading asserting a claim for relief shall state the names, if known to the pleader, of any persons as described in subdivision (a)(1)-(2) hereof who are not joined, and the reasons why they are not joined.

(d) **Exception of Class Actions.** This rule is subject to the provisions of Rule 42.

(Amended by Order July 21, 1970, eff. Jan. 1, 1971.)

RULE 40. PERMISSIVE JOINDER OF PARTIES.

(a) **Permissive Joinder.** All persons may join in one action as plaintiffs if they assert any right to relief jointly, severally, or in the alternative in respect of or arising out of the same transaction, occurrence, or series of transactions or occurrences and if any question of law or fact common to all of them will arise in the action. All persons may be joined in one action as defendants if there is asserted against them jointly, severally, or in the alternative any right to relief in respect of or arising out of the same transaction, occurrence, or series of transactions or occurrences and if any question of law or fact common to all of them will arise in the action. A plaintiff or defendant need not be interested in obtaining or defending against all the relief demanded. Judgment may be given for one or more of the plaintiffs according to their respective rights to relief, and against one or more defendants according to their respective liabilities.

(b) **Separate Trials.** The court may make such orders as will prevent a party from being embarrassed, delayed, or put to expense by the inclusion of a party against whom he asserts no claim and who asserts no claim against him, and may order separate trials or make other orders to prevent delay or prejudice.

RULE 41. MISJOINDER AND NONJOINDER OF PARTIES.

Misjoinder of parties is not ground for dismissal of an action. Parties may be dropped or added, or suits filed separately may be consolidated, or actions which have been improperly joined may be severed and each ground of recovery improperly joined may be docketed as a separate suit between the same parties, by order of the court on motion of any party or on its own initiative at any stage of the action, before the time of submission to the jury or to the court if trial is without a jury, on such terms as are just. Any claim against a party may be severed and proceeded with separately.

(Amended by Order March 31, 1941, eff. Sept. 1, 1941.)

RULE 42. CLASS ACTIONS.

(a) Prerequisites to a Class Action. One or more members of a class may sue or be sued as representative parties on behalf of all only if (1) the class is so numerous that joinder of all members is impracticable, (2) there are questions of law or fact common to the class, (3) the claims or defenses of the representative parties are typical of the claims or defenses of the class, and (4) the representative parties will fairly and adequately protect the interests of the class.

(b) Class Actions Maintainable. An action may be maintained as a class action if the prerequisites of subdivision (a) are satisfied, and in addition:

(1) the prosecution of separate actions by or against individual members of the class would create a risk of

(A) inconsistent or varying adjudications with respect to individual members of the class which would establish incompatible standards of conduct for the party opposing the class, or

(B) adjudications with respect to individual members of the class which would as a practical matter be dispositive of the interests of the other members not parties to the adjudications or substantially impair or impede their ability to protect their interests; or

(2) the party opposing the class has acted or refused to act on grounds generally applicable to the class, thereby making appropriate final injunctive relief or corresponding declaratory relief with respect to the class as a whole; or

(3) the questions of law or fact common to the members of the class predominate over any questions affecting only individual members, and a class action is superior to other available methods for the fair and efficient adjudication of the controversy. The matters pertinent to these issues include:

(A) the interest of members of the class in individually controlling the prosecution or defense of separate actions;

(B) the extent and nature of any litigation concerning the controversy already commenced by or against members of the class;

(C) the desirability or undesirability of concentrating the litigation of the claims in the particular forum; and

(D) the difficulties likely to be encountered in the management of a class action.

(c) **Determination by Order Whether to Certify a Class Action; Notice and Membership in Class.**

(1) (A) When a person sues or is sued as a representative of a class, the court must—at an early practicable time—determine by order whether to certify the action as a class action.

(B) An order certifying a class action must define the class and the class claims, issues, or defenses, and must appoint class counsel under Rule 42(g).

(C) An order under Rule 42(c)(1) may be altered or amended before final judgment. The court may order the naming of additional parties in order to insure the adequacy of representation.

(D) An order granting or denying certification under Rule 42(b)(3) must state:

(i) he elements of each claim or defense asserted in the pleadings;

(ii) any issues of law or fact common to the class members;

(iii) any issues of law or fact affecting only individual class members;

(iv) the issues that will be the object of most of the efforts of the litigants and the court;

(v) other available methods of adjudication that exist for the controversy;

(vi) why the issues common to the members of the class do or do not predominate over individual issues;

(vii) why a class action is or is not superior to other available methods for the fair and efficient adjudication of the controversy; and

(viii)if a class is certified, how the class claims and any issues affecting only individual members, raised by the claims or defenses asserted in the pleadings, will be tried in a manageable, time efficient manner.

(2) (A) For any class certified under Rule 42(b)(1) or (2), the court may direct appropriate notice to the class.

(B) For any class certified under Rule 42(b)(3), the court must direct to class members the best notice practicable under the circumstances, including individual notice to all members who can be identified through reasonable effort. The notice must concisely and clearly state in plain, easily understood language:

(i) the nature of the action;

(ii) the definition of the class certified;

(iii) the class claims, issues, or defenses;

(iv) that a class member may enter an appearance through counsel if the member so desires;

(v) that the court will exclude from the class any member who requests exclusion, stating when and how members may elect to be excluded; and

(vi) the binding effect of a class judgment on class members under Rule 42(c)(3).

(3) The judgment in an action maintained as a class action under subdivision (b)(1) or (b)(2) whether or not favorable to the class, shall include and describe those whom the court finds to be members of the class. The judgment in an action maintained as a class action under subdivision (b)(3), whether or not favorable to the class, shall include and specify or describe those to whom the notice provided in subdivision (c)(2) was directed, and who have not requested exclusion, and whom the court finds to be members of the class.

(d) **Actions Conducted Partially as Class Actions; Multiple Classes and Subclasses.** When appropriate (1) an action may be brought or maintained as a class action with respect to particular issues, or (2) a class may be divided into subclasses and each subclass treated as a class, and the provisions of this rule shall then be construed and applied accordingly.

(e) **Settlement, Dismissal or, Compromise.**

(1) (A) The court must approve any settlement, dismissal, or compromise of the claims, issues, or defenses of a certified class.

(B) Notice of the material terms of the proposed settlement, dismissal or compromise, together with an explanation of when and how the members may elect to be excluded from the class, shall be given to all members in such manner as the court directs.

(C) The court may approve a settlement, dismissal, or compromise that would bind class members only after a hearing and on finding that the settlement, dismissal, or compromise is fair, reasonable, and adequate.

(2) The parties seeking approval of a settlement, dismissal, or compromise under Rule 42(e)(1) must file a statement identifying any agreement made in connection with the proposed settlement, dismissal, or compromise.

(3) In an action previously certified as a class action under Rule 42(b)(3), the court may not approve a settlement unless it affords a new opportunity to request exclusion to individual class members who had an earlier opportunity to request exclusion but did not do so.

(4)(A) Any class member may object to a proposed settlement, dismissal, or compromise that requires court approval under Rule 42(e)(1)(A).

(B) An objection made under Rule 42(e)(4)(A) may be withdrawn only with the court's approval.

(f) **Discovery.** Unnamed members of a class action are not to be considered as parties for purposes of discovery.

(g) **Class Counsel.**

(1) Appointing Class Counsel.

(A) Unless a statute provides otherwise, a court that certifies a class must appoint class counsel.

(B) An attorney appointed to serve as class counsel must fairly and adequately represent the interests of the class.

(C) In appointing class counsel, the court

(i) must consider:

- the work counsel has done in identifying or investigating potential claims in the action;
- counsel's experience in handling class actions, other complex litigation, and claims of the type asserted in the action;
- counsel's knowledge of the applicable law; and
- the resources counsel will commit to representing the class;

(ii) may consider any other matter pertinent to counsel's ability to fairly and adequately represent the interests of the class;

(iii) may direct potential class counsel to provide information on any subject pertinent to the appointment and to propose terms for attorney fees and nontaxable costs; and

(iv) may make further orders in connection with the appointment.

(2) Appointment Procedure.

(A) The court may designate interim counsel to act on behalf of the putative class before determining whether to certify the action as a class action.

(B) When there is one applicant for appointment as class counsel, the court may appoint that applicant only if the applicant is adequate under Rule 42(g)(1)(B) and (C). If more than one adequate applicant seeks appointment as class counsel, the court must appoint the applicant or applicants best able to represent the interests of the class.

(C) The order appointing class counsel may include provisions about the award of attorney fees or nontaxable costs under Rule 42(h) and (i).

(h) **Procedure for determining Attorney Fees Award.** In an action certified as a class action, the court may award attorney fees in accordance with subdivision (i) and nontaxable costs authorized by law or by agreement of the parties as follows:

(1) Motion for Award of Attorney Fees. A claim for an award of attorney fees and nontaxable costs must be made by motion, subject to the provisions of this subdivision, at a time set by the court. Notice of the motion must be served on all parties and, for motions by class counsel, directed to class members in a reasonable manner.

(2) Objections to Motion. A class member, or a party from whom payment is sought, may object to the motion.

(3) Hearing and Findings. The court must hold a hearing in open court and must find the facts and state its conclusions of law on the motion. The court must state its findings and conclusions in writing or orally on the record.

(i) **Attorney's Fees Award.**

(1) In awarding attorney fees, the court must first determine a lodestar figure by multiplying the number of hours reasonably worked times a reasonable hourly rate. The attorney fees award must be in the range of 25% to 400% of the lodestar figure. In making these determinations, the court must consider the factors specified in Rule 1.04(b), Tex. Disciplinary R. Prof. Conduct.

(2) If any portion of the benefits recovered for the class are in the form of coupons or other noncash common benefits, the attorney fees awarded in the action must be in cash and noncash amounts in the same proportion as the recovery for the class.

(j) **Effective Date.** Rule 42(i) applies only in actions filed after September 1, 2003.

(Amended by Order Sept. 20, 1941, eff. Dec. 31, 1941; May 9, 1977, eff. Sept. 1, 1977; Dec. 5, 1983, eff. April 1, 1984; Oct. 9, 2003, eff. Jan. 1, 2004, except that Rule 42(i) applies only in cases filed on or after Sept. 1, 2003.)

RULE 43. INTERPLEADER.

Persons having claims against the plaintiff may be joined as defendants and required to interplead when their claims are such that the plaintiff is or may be exposed to double or multiple liability. It is not ground for objection to the joinder that the claims of the several claimants or the titles on which their claims depend do not have a common origin or are not identical but are adverse to and independent of one another, or that the plaintiff avers that he is not liable in whole or in part to any or all of the claimants. A defendant exposed to similar liability may obtain such interpleader by way of cross-claim or counterclaim. The provisions of this rule supplement and do not in any way limit the joinder of parties permitted in any other rules.

RULE 44. MAY APPEAR BY NEXT FRIEND.

Minors, lunatics, idiots, or persons non compos mentis who have no legal guardian may sue and be represented by "next friend" under the following rules:

(1) Such next friend shall have the same rights concerning such suits as guardians have, but shall give security for costs, or affidavits in lieu thereof, when required.

(2) Such next friend or his attorney of record may with the approval of the court compromise suits and agree to judgments, and such judgments, agreements and compromises, when approved by the court, shall be forever binding and conclusive upon the party plaintiff in such suit.

SECTION 4.
PLEADING

A.
GENERAL

RULE 45. DEFINITION AND SYSTEM.

Pleadings in the district and county court shall

(a) be by petition and answer;

(b) consist of a statement in plain and concise language of the plaintiff's cause of action or the defendant's grounds of defense. That an allegation be evidentiary or be of legal conclusion shall not be grounds for an objection when fair notice to the opponent is given by the allegations as a whole; and

(c) contain any other matter which may be required by any law or rule authorizing or regulating any particular action or defense.

Pleadings that are not filed electronically must be in writing, on paper measuring approximately 8 ½ inches by 11 inches, and signed by the party or his attorney. The use of recycled paper is strongly encouraged.

All pleadings shall be construed so as to do substantial justice.

(Amended by Order July 15, 1987. eff. Jan. 1, 1988; April 24, 1990, eff. Sept. 1, 1990; Sept. 4, 1990; Dec. 13, 2013, eff. Jan. 1, 2014.)

RULE 46. PETITION AND ANSWER; EACH ONE INSTRUMENT OF WRITING.

The original petition, first supplemental petition, second supplemental petition, and every other, shall each be contained in one instrument of writing, and so with the original answer and each of the supplemental answers.

RULE 47. CLAIMS FOR RELIEF.

An original pleading which sets forth a claim for relief, whether an original petition, counterclaim, cross-claim, or third party claim, shall contain:

(a) a short statement of the cause of action sufficient to give fair notice of the claim involved;

(b) a statement that the damages sought are within the jurisdictional limits of the court;

(c) except in suits governed by the Family Code, a statement that the party seeks:

 (1) only monetary relief of $ 100,000 or less, including damages of any kind, penalties, costs, expenses, pre-judgment interest, and attorney fees; or

 (2) monetary relief of $ 100.000 or less and non-monetary relief; or

 (3) monetary relief over $ 100.000 but not more than $200.000; or

 (4) monetary relief over $200.000 but not more than $ 1.000.000; or

 (5) monetary relief over $ 1.000.000: and

(d) a demand for judgment for all the other relief to which the party deems himself entitled.

Relief in the alternative or of several different types may be demanded; provided, further, that upon special exception the court shall require the pleader to amend so as to specify the maximum amount claimed. A party that fails to comply with (c) may not conduct discovery until the party's pleading is amended to comply.

(Amended by Order July 11, 1977, eff. Jan. 1, 1978; April 24, 1990, eff. Sept. 1. 1990; Nov. 13, 2012, eff. March 1, 2013; Feb 12, 2013, eff. March 1, 2013. (Applies to cases filed on or after March 1, 2013, except those filed in justice court.))

Comment to 2013 change: Rule 47 is amended to require a more specific statement of the relief sought by a party. The amendment requires parties to plead into or out of the expedited actions process governed by Rule 169, added to implement section 22.004(h) of the Texas Government Code. Except in a in a suit governed by the Family Code, the Property Code, the Tax Code, or Chapter 74 of the Civil Practice & Remedies Code, a suit in which the original petition contains the statement in paragraph (c)(l) is governed by the expedited actions process. The further specificity in paragraphs (c)(2)-(5) is to provide information regarding the nature of cases filed and does not affect a party's substantive rights.

RULE 48. ALTERNATIVE CLAIMS FOR RELIEF.

A party may set forth two or more statements of a claim or defense alternatively or hypothetically, either in one count or defense or in separate counts or defenses. When two or more statements are made in the alternative and one of them if made independently would be sufficient, the pleading is not made insufficient by the insufficiency of one or more of the alternative statements. A party may also state as many separate claims or defenses as he has regardless of consistency and whether based upon legal or equitable grounds or both.

RULE 49. WHERE SEVERAL COUNTS.

Where there are several counts in the petition, and entire damages are given, the verdict or judgment, as the case may be, shall be good, notwithstanding one or more of such counts may be defective.

RULE 50. PARAGRAPHS, SEPARATE STATEMENTS.

All averments of claim or defense shall be made in numbered paragraphs, the contents of each of which shall be limited as far as practicable to a statement of a single set of circumstances; and a paragraph may be referred to by number in all succeeding pleadings, so long as the pleading containing such paragraph has not been superseded by an amendment as provided by Rule 65. Each claim founded upon a separate transaction or occurrence and each defense other than denials shall be stated in a separate count or defense whenever a separation facilitates the clear presentation of the matters set forth.

RULE 51. JOINDER OF CLAIMS AND REMEDIES

(a) **Joinder of Claims.** The plaintiff in his petition or in a reply setting forth a counterclaim and the defendant in an answer setting forth a counterclaim may join either as independent or as alternate claims as many claims either legal or equitable or both as he may have against an opposing party. There may be a like joinder of claims when there are multiple parties if the requirements of Rules 39, 40, and 43 are satisfied. There may be a like joinder of cross claims or third-party claims if the requirements of Rules 38 and 97, respectively, are satisfied.

(b) **Joinder of Remedies.** Whenever a claim is one heretofore cognizable only after another claim has been prosecuted to a conclusion, the two claims may be joined in a single action; but the court shall grant relief in that action only in accordance with the relative substantive rights of the parties. This rule shall not be applied in tort cases so as to permit the joinder of a liability or indemnity insurance company, unless such company is by statute or contract directly liable to the person injured or damaged.

(Amended by Order Sept. 20, 1941, eff. Dec. 31, 1941; July 26, 1960, eff. Jan. 1, 1961.)

RULE 52. ALLEGING A CORPORATION.

An allegation that a corporation is incorporated shall be taken as true, unless denied by the affidavit of the adverse party, his agent or attorney, whether such corporation is a public or private corporation and however created.

RULE 53. SPECIAL ACT OR LAW.

A pleading founded wholly or in part on any private or special act or law of this State or of the Republic of Texas need only recite the title thereof, the date of its approval, and set out in substance so much of such act or laws as may be pertinent to the cause of action or defense.

RULE 54. CONDITIONS PRECEDENT.

In pleading the performance or occurrence of conditions precedent, it shall be sufficient to aver generally that all conditions precedent have been performed or have occurred. When such performances or occurrences have been so plead, the party so pleading same shall be required to prove only such of them as are specifically denied by the opposite party.

(Amended by Order March 31, 1941, eff. Sept. 1, 1941.)

RULE 55. JUDGMENT.

In pleading a judgment or decision of a domestic or foreign court, judicial or quasi-judicial tribunal, or of a board or officer, it shall be sufficient to aver the judgment or decision without setting forth matter showing jurisdiction to render it.

RULE 56. SPECIAL DAMAGE.

When items of special damage are claimed, they shall be specifically stated.

RULE 57. SIGNING OF PLEADINGS.

Every pleading of a party represented by an attorney shall be signed by at least one attorney of record in his individual name, with his State Bar of Texas identification number, address, telephone number, email address, and if available, fax number. A party not represented by an attorney shall sign his pleadings, state his address, telephone number, email address, and, if available, fax number.

(Amended by Order June 10, 1980, eff. Jan. 1, 1981; April 24, 1990, eff. Sept. 1, 1990; Dec. 13, 2013, eff. Jan. 1, 2014.)

RULE 58. ADOPTION BY REFERENCE.

Statements in a pleading may be adopted by reference in a different part of the same pleading or in another pleading or in any motion, so long as the pleading containing such statements has not been superseded by an amendment as provided by Rule 65.

RULE 59. EXHIBITS AND PLEADING.

Notes, accounts, bonds, mortgages, records, and all other written instruments, constituting, in whole or in part, the claim sued on, or the matter set up in defense, may be made a part of the pleadings by copies thereof, or the originals, being attached or filed and referred to as such, or by copying the same in the body of the pleading in aid and explanation of the allegations in the petition or answer made in reference to said instruments and shall be deemed a part thereof for all purposes. Such pleadings shall not be deemed defective because of the lack of any allegations which can be supplied from said exhibit. No other instrument of writing shall be made an exhibit in the pleading.

RULE 60. INTERVENOR'S PLEADINGS.

Any party may intervene by filing a pleading, subject to being stricken out by the court for sufficient cause on the motion of any party.

(Amended by Order April 24, 1990, eff. Sept. 1, 1990.)

RULE 61. TRIAL: INTERVENORS: RULES APPLY TO ALL PARTIES.

These rules of pleading shall apply equally, so far as it may be practicable to intervenors and to parties, when more than one, who may plead separately.

RULE 62. AMENDMENT DEFINED.

The object of an amendment, as contra-distinguished from a supplemental petition or answer, is to add something to, or withdraw something from, that which has been previously pleaded so as to perfect that which is or may be deficient, or to correct that which has been incorrectly stated by the party making the amendment, or to plead new matter, additional to that formerly pleaded by the amending party, which constitutes an additional claim or defense permissible to the suit.

RULE 63. AMENDMENTS AND RESPONSIVE PLEADINGS.

Parties may amend their pleadings, respond to pleadings on file of other parties, file suggestions of death and make representative parties and file such other pleas as they may desire by filing such pleas with the clerk at such time as not to operate as a surprise to the opposite party; provided that any pleadings, responses or pleas offered for filing within seven days of the date of trial or thereafter, or after such time as may be ordered by the judge under Rule 166, shall be filed only after leave of the judge is obtained, which leave shall be granted by the judge unless there is a showing that such filing will operate as a surprise to the opposite party.

(Amended by Order July 26, 1960, eff. Jan. 1, 1961; April 24, 1990, eff. Sept. 1, 1990.)

RULE 64. AMENDED INSTRUMENT.

The party amending shall point out the instrument amended, as "original petition," or "plaintiff's first supplemental petition," or as "original answer," or "defendant's first supplemental answer" or other instrument filed by the party and shall amend by filing a substitute therefor, entire and complete in itself, indorsed "amended original petition," or "amended first supplemental petition," or "amended original answer," or "amended first supplemental answer," accordingly as said instruments of pleading are designated.

RULE 65. SUBSTITUTED INSTRUMENT TAKES PLACE OF ORIGINAL.

Unless the substituted instrument shall be set aside on exceptions, the instrument for which it is substituted shall no longer be regarded as a part of the pleading in the record of the cause, unless some error of the court in deciding upon the necessity of the amendment, or otherwise in superseding it, be complained of, and exception be taken to the action of the court, or unless it be necessary to look to the superseded pleading upon a question of limitation.

RULE 66. TRIAL AMENDMENT.

If evidence is objected to at the trial on the ground that it is not within the issues made by the pleading, or if during the trial any defect, fault or omission in a pleading, either of form or substance, is called to the attention of the court, the court may allow the pleadings to be amended and shall do so freely when the presentation of the merits of the action will be subserved thereby and the objecting party fails to satisfy the court that the allowance of such amendment would prejudice him in maintaining his action or defense upon the merits. The court may grant a postponement to enable the objecting party to meet such evidence.

(Amended by Order March 31, 1941, eff. Sept. 1, 1941.)

RULE 67. AMENDMENTS TO CONFORM TO ISSUES TRIED WITHOUT OBJECTION.

When issues not raised by the pleadings are tried by express or implied consent of the parties, they shall be treated in all respects as if they had been raised in the pleadings. In such case such amendment of the pleadings as may be necessary to cause them to conform to the evidence and to raise these issues may be made by leave of court upon motion of any party at any time up to the submission of the case to the Court or jury, but failure so to amend shall not affect the result of the trial of these issues; provided that written pleadings, before the time of submission, shall be necessary to the submission of questions, as is provided in Rules 277 and 279.

(Amended by Order March 31, 1941, eff. Sept. 1, 1941; April 24, 1990, eff. Sept. 1, 1990.)

RULE 68. COURT MAY ORDER REPLEADER.

The court, when deemed necessary in any case, may order a repleader on the part of one or both of the parties, in order to make their pleadings substantially conform to the rules.

RULE 69. SUPPLEMENTAL PETITION OR ANSWER.

Each supplemental petition or answer, made by either party, shall be a response to the last preceding pleading by the other party, and shall not repeat allegations formerly pleaded further than is necessary as an introduction to that which is stated in the pleading then being drawn up. These instruments, to wit, the original petition and its several supplements, and the original answer and its several supplements, shall respectively, constitute separate and distinct parts of the pleadings of each party; and the position and identity, by number and name, with the indorsement of each instrument, shall be preserved throughout the pleadings of either party.

RULE 70. PLEADING: SURPRISE: COST.

When either a supplemental or amended pleading is of such character and is presented at such time as to take the opposite party by surprise, the court may charge the continuance of the cause, if granted, to the party causing the surprise if the other party satisfactorily shows that he is not ready for trial because of the allowance of the filing of such supplemental or amended pleading, and the court may, in such event, in its discretion require the party filing such pleading to pay to the surprised party the amount of reasonable costs and expenses incurred by the other party as a result of the continuance, including attorney fees, or make such other order with respect thereto as may be just.

(Amended by Order June 10, 1980, eff. Jan. 1, 1981.)

RULE 71. MISNOMER OF PLEADING.

When a party has mistakenly designated any plea or pleading, the court, if justice so requires, shall treat the plea or pleading as if it had been properly designated. Pleadings shall be docketed as originally designated and shall remain identified as designated, unless the court orders redesignation. Upon court order filed with the clerk, the clerk shall modify the docket and all other clerk records to reflect redesignation.

(Amended by Order July 15, 1987, eff. Jan. 1, 1988.)

RULE 72. [REPEALED]

(Repealed by Order April 24, 1990, eff. Sept. 1, 1990.)

RULE 73. [REPEALED]

(Repealed by Order April 24, 1990, eff. Sept. 1, 1990.)

RULE 74. FILING WITH THE COURT DEFINED.

The filing of pleadings, other papers and exhibits as required by these rules shall be made by filing them with the clerk of the court, except that the judge may permit the papers to be filed with him, in which event he shall note thereon the filing date and time and forthwith transmit them to the office of the clerk.

(Amended by Order July 20, 1966, eff. Jan. 1, 1967.)

RULE 75. FILED PLEADINGS; WITHDRAWAL.

All filed pleadings shall remain at all times in the clerk's office or in the court or in custody of the clerk, except that the court may by order entered on the minutes allow a filed pleading to be withdrawn for a limited time whenever necessary, on leaving a certified copy on file. The party withdrawing such pleading shall pay the costs of such order and certified copy.

RULE 75a. FILING EXHIBITS: COURT REPORTER TO FILE WITH CLERK.

The court reporter or stenographer shall file with the clerk of the court all exhibits which were admitted in evidence or tendered on bill of exception during the course of any hearing, proceeding, or trial.

(Added July 20, 1966, eff. Jan. 1, 1967.)

RULE 75b. FILED EXHIBITS: WITHDRAWAL.

All filed exhibits admitted in evidence or tendered on bill of exception shall, until returned or otherwise disposed of as authorized by Rule 14b, remain at all times in the clerk's office or in the court or in the custody of the clerk except as follows:

(a) The court may by order entered on the minutes allow a filed exhibit to be withdrawn by any party only upon such party's leaving on file a certified, photo, or other reproduced copy of such exhibit. The party withdrawing such exhibit shall pay the costs of such order and copy.

(b) The court reporter or stenographer of the court conducting the hearing, proceedings, or trial in which exhibits are admitted or offered in evidence, shall have the right to withdraw filed exhibits, upon giving the clerk proper receipt therefor, whenever necessary for the court reporter or stenographer to transmit such original exhibits to an appellate court under the provisions of Rule 379 or to otherwise discharge the duties imposed by law upon said court reporter or stenographer.

(Adopted by Order July 20, 1966, eff. Jan. 1, 1967.)

RULE 76. MAY INSPECT PAPERS.

Each attorney at law practicing in any court shall be allowed at all reasonable times to inspect the papers and records relating to any suit or other matter in which he may be interested.

RULE 76a. SEALING COURT RECORDS.

1. **Standard for Sealing Court Records.** Court records may not be removed from court files except as permitted by statute or rule. No court order or opinion issued in the adjudication of a case may be sealed. Other court records, as defined in this rule, are presumed to be open to the general public and may be sealed only upon a showing of all of the following:
   (a) a specific, serious and substantial interest which clearly outweighs:
      (1) this presumption of openness;
      (2) any probable adverse effect that sealing will have upon the general public health or safety;
   (b) no less restrictive means than sealing records will adequately and effectively protect the specific interest asserted.
2. **Court Records.** For purposes of this rule, court records means:
   (a) all documents of any nature filed in connection with any matter before any civil court, except:
      (1) documents filed with a court in camera, solely for the purpose of obtaining a ruling on the discoverability of such documents;
      (2) documents in court files to which access is otherwise restricted by law;
      (3) documents filed in an action originally arising under the Family Code.
   (b) settlement agreements not filed of record, excluding all reference to any monetary consideration, that seek to restrict disclosure of information concerning matters that have a probable adverse effect upon the general public health or safety, or the administration of public office, or the operation of government.
   (c) discovery, not filed of record, concerning matters that have a probable adverse effect upon the general public health or safety, or the administration of public office, or the operation of government, except discovery in cases originally initiated to preserve bona fide trade secrets or other intangible property rights.
3. **Notice.** Court records may be sealed only upon a party's written motion, which shall be open to public inspection. The movant shall post a public notice at the place where notices for meetings of county governmental bodies are required to be posted, stating: that a hearing will be held in open court on a motion to seal court records in the specific case, that any person may intervene and be heard concerning the sealing of court records; the specific time and place of the hearing; the style and number of the case, a brief but specific description of both the nature of the case and the records which are sought to be sealed; and the identity of the movant. Immediately after posting such notice, the movant shall file a verified copy of the posted notice with the clerk of the court in which the case is pending and with the Clerk of the Supreme Court of Texas.

4. **Hearing.** A hearing, open to the public, on a motion to seal court records shall be held in open court as soon as practicable, but not less than fourteen days after the motion is filed and notice is posted. Any party may participate in the hearing. Nonparties may intervene as a matter of right for the limited purpose of participating in the proceedings, upon payment of the fee required for filing a plea in intervention. The court may inspect records in camera when necessary. The court may determine a motion relating to sealing or unsealing court records in accordance with the procedures prescribed by Rule 120a.
5. **Temporary Sealing Order.** A temporary sealing order may issue upon motion and notice to any parties who have answered in the case pursuant to Rules 21 and 21a upon a showing of compelling need for specific facts shown by affidavit or by verified petition that immediate and irreparable injury will result to a specific interest of the applicant before notice can be posted and a hearing held as otherwise provided herein. The temporary order shall set the time for the hearing required by paragraph 4 and shall direct that the movant immediately give the public notice required by paragraph 3. The court may modify or withdraw any temporary order upon motion by any party or intervenor, notice to the parties, and hearing conducted as soon as practicable. Issuance of a temporary order shall not reduce in any way the burden of proof of a party requesting sealing at the hearing required by paragraph 4.
6. **Order on Motion to Seal Court Records.** A motion relating to sealing or unsealing court records shall be decided by written order, open to the public, which shall state: the style and number of the case; the specific reasons for finding and concluding whether the showing required by paragraph 1 has been made; the specific portions of court records which are to be sealed; and the time period for which the sealed portions of the court records are to be sealed. The order shall not be included in any judgment or other order but shall be a separate document in the case; however, the failure to comply with this requirement shall not affect its appealability.
7. **Continuing Jurisdiction.** Any person may intervene as a matter of right at any time before or after judgment to seal or unseal court records. A court that issues a sealing order retains continuing jurisdiction to enforce, alter, or vacate that order. An order sealing or unsealing court records shall not be reconsidered on motion of any party or intervenor who had actual notice of the hearing preceding issuance of the order, without first showing changed circumstances materially affecting the order. Such circumstances need not be related to the case in which the order was issued. However, the burden of making the showing required by paragraph 1 shall always be on the party seeking to seal records.
8. **Appeal.** Any order (or portion of an order or judgment) relating to sealing or unsealing court records shall be deemed to be severed from the case and a final judgment which may be appealed by any party or intervenor who participated in the hearing preceding issuance of such order. The appellate court may abate the appeal and order the trial court to direct that further public notice be given, or to hold further hearings, or to make additional findings.
9. **Application.** Access to documents in court files not defined as court records by this rule remains governed by existing law. This rule does not apply to any court records sealed in an action in which a final judgment has been entered before its effective date. This rule applies to cases already pending on its effective date only with regard to:
   (a) all court records filed or exchanged after the effective date;
   (b) any motion to alter or vacate an order restricting access to court records, issued before the effective date.

(Adopted by Order April 24, 1990, eff. Sept. 1, 1990.)

RULE 77. LOST RECORDS AND PAPERS.

When any papers or records are lost or destroyed during the pendency of a suit, the parties may, with the approval of the judge, agree in writing on a brief statement of the matters contained therein; or either party may supply such lost records or papers as follows:

a. After three days' notice to the adverse party or his attorney, make written sworn motion before the court stating the loss or destruction of such record or papers, accompanied by certified copies of the originals if obtainable, or by substantial copies thereof.
b. If, upon hearing, the court be satisfied that they are substantial copies of the original, an order shall be made substituting such copies or brief statement for the originals.
c. Such substituted copies or brief statement shall be filed with the clerk, constitute a part of the cause, and have the force and effect of the originals.

(Amended by Order June 16, 1943, eff. Dec. 31, 1943.)

B.
PLEADINGS OF PLAINTIFF

RULE 78. PETITION; ORIGINAL AND SUPPLEMENTAL; INDORSEMENT.

The pleading of plaintiff shall consist of an original petition, and such supplemental petitions as may be necessary in the course of pleading by the parties to the suit. The original petition and the supplemental petitions shall be indorsed, so as to show their respective positions in the process of pleading, as "original petition," "plaintiff's first supplemental petition," "plaintiff's second supplemental petition," and so on, to be successively numbered, named, and indorsed.

RULE 78a. Repealed by order Dec. 11, 2018, eff Dec. 11, 2018.

[Civil Case Information Sheet as provided in Misc. Docket No. 13-9022, Feb. 12, 2013, eff March 1, 2013 repealed by Order Dec. 11, 2018, eff. Dec. 11, 2018.

RULE 79. THE PETITION.

The petition shall state the names of the parties and their residences, if known, together with the contents prescribed in Rule 47 above.

RULE 80. PLAINTIFF'S SUPPLEMENTAL PETITION.

The plaintiff's supplemental petitions may contain special exceptions, general denials, and the allegations of new matter not before alleged by him, in reply to those which have been alleged by the defendant.

RULE 81. DEFENSIVE MATTERS.

When the defendant sets up a counter claim, the plaintiff may plead thereto under rules prescribed for pleadings of defensive matter by the defendant, so far as applicable. Whenever the defendant is required to plead any matter of defense under oath, the plaintiff shall be required to plead such matters under oath when relied on by him.

RULE 82. SPECIAL DEFENSES.

The plaintiff need not deny any special matter of defense pleaded by the defendant, but the same shall be regarded as denied unless expressly admitted.

C.
PLEADINGS OF DEFENDANT

RULE 83. ANSWER; ORIGINAL AND SUPPLEMENTAL; INDORSEMENT.

The answer of defendant shall consist of an original answer, and such supplemental answers as may be necessary, in the course of pleading by the parties to the suit. The original answer and the supplemental answers shall be indorsed, so as to show their respective positions in the process of pleading, as "original answer," "defendant's first supplemental answer," "defendant's second supplemental answer," and so on, to be successively numbered, named and indorsed.

RULE 84. ANSWER MAY INCLUDE SEVERAL MATTERS.

The defendant in his answer may plead as many several matters, whether of law or fact, as he may think necessary for his defense, and which may be pertinent to the cause, and such matters shall be heard in such order as may be directed by the court, special appearance and motion to transfer venue, and the practice thereunder being excepted herefrom.

(Amended by Order Oct. 12, 1949, eff. March 1, 1950; April 12, 1962, eff. Sept. 1, 1962; June 15, 1983, eff. Sept. 1, 1983.)

RULE 85. ORIGINAL ANSWER; CONTENTS.

The original answer may consist of motions to transfer venue, pleas to the jurisdiction, in abatement, or any other dilatory pleas; of special exceptions, of general denial, and any defense by way of avoidance or estoppel, and it may present a cross-action, which to that extent will place defendant in the attitude of a plaintiff. Matters in avoidance and estoppel may be stated together, or in several special pleas, each presenting a distinct defense, and numbered so as to admit of separate issues to be formed on them.

(Amended by Order June 16, 1983, eff. Sept. 1, 1983.)

RULE 86. MOTION TO TRANSFER VENUE.

1. **Time to File.** An objection to improper venue is waived if not made by written motion filed prior to or concurrently with any other plea, pleading or motion except a special appearance motion provided for in Rule 120a. A written consent of the parties to transfer the case to another county may be filed with the clerk of the court at any time. A motion to transfer venue because an impartial trial cannot be had in the county where the action is pending is governed by the provisions of Rule 257.
2. **How to File.** The motion objecting to improper venue may be contained in a separate instrument filed concurrently with or prior to the filing of the movant's first responsive pleading or the motion may be combined with other objections and defenses and included in the movant's first responsive pleading.

3. **Requisites of Motion.** The motion, and any amendments to it, shall state that the action should be transferred to another specified county of proper venue because:
   (a) The county where the action is pending is not a proper county; or
   (b) Mandatory venue of the action in another county is prescribed by one or more specific statutory provisions which shall be clearly designated or indicated.

The motion shall state the legal and factual basis for the transfer of the action and request transfer of the action to a specific county of mandatory or proper venue. Verification of the motion is not required. The motion may be accompanied by supporting affidavits as provided in Rule 87.

4. **Response and Reply.** Except as provided in paragraph 3(a) of Rule 87, a response to the motion to transfer is not required. Verification of a response is not required.
5. **Service.** A copy of any instrument filed pursuant to Rule 86 shall be served in accordance with Rule 21a.

(Amended by Order March 31, 1941, eff. Sept. 1, 1941; June 16, 1943 eff. Dec. 31, 1943; July 20, 1954, eff. Jan. 1, 1955; April 12, 1962, eff. Sept. 1, 1962; June 15, 1983, eff. Sept. 1, 1983.)

RULE 87. DETERMINATION OF MOTION TO TRANSFER.

1. **Consideration of Motion.** The determination of a motion to transfer venue shall be made promptly by the court and such determination must be made in a reasonable time prior to commencement of the trial on the merits. The movant has the duty to request a setting on the motion to transfer. Except on leave of court each party is entitled to at least 45 days notice of a hearing on the motion to transfer.

Except on leave of court, any response or opposing affidavits shall be filed at least 30 days prior to the hearing of the motion to transfer. The movant is not required to file a reply to the response but any reply and any additional affidavits supporting the motion to transfer must, except on leave of court, be filed not later than 7 days prior to the hearing date.

2. **Burden of Establishing Venue.**
   (a) **In General.** A party who seeks to maintain venue of the action in a particular county in reliance upon Section 15.001 (General Rule), Sections 15.011-15.017 (Mandatory Venue), Sections 15.031-15.040 (Permissive Venue), or Sections 15.061 and 15.062 (Multiple Claims), Civil Practice and Remedies Code, has the burden to make proof, as provided in paragraph 3 of this rule, that venue is maintainable in the county of suit. A party who seeks to transfer venue of the action to another specified county under Section 15.001 (General Rule), Sections 15.011 & REM.-15.017 (Mandatory Venue), Sections 15.031-15.040 (Permissive Venue), or Sections 15.061 and 15.062 (Multiple Claims), Civil Practice and Remedies Code, has the burden to make proof, as provided in paragraph 3 of this rule, that venue is maintainable in the county to which transfer is sought. A party who seeks to transfer venue of the action to another specified county under Sections 15.011-15.017, Civil Practice and Remedies Code on the basis that a mandatory venue provision is applicable and controlling has the burden to make proof, as provided in paragraph 3 of this rule, that venue is maintainable in the county to which transfer is sought by virtue of one or more mandatory venue exceptions.
   (b) **Cause of Action.** It shall not be necessary for a claimant to prove the merits of a cause of action, but the existence of a cause of action, when pleaded properly, shall be taken as established as alleged by the pleadings. When the defendant specifically denies the venue allegations, the claimant is required, by prima facie proof as provided in paragraph 3 of this rule, to support such pleading that the cause of action taken as established by the pleadings, or a part of such cause of action, accrued in the county of suit. If a defendant seeks transfer to a county where the cause of action or a part thereof accrued, it shall be sufficient for the defendant to plead that if a cause of action exists, then the cause of action or part thereof accrued in the specific county to which transfer is sought, and such allegation shall not constitute an admission that a cause of action in fact exists. But the defendant shall be required to support his pleading by prima facie proof as provided in paragraph 3 of this rule, that, if a cause of action exists, it or a part thereof accrued in the county to which transfer is sought.
   (c) **Other Rules.** A motion to transfer venue based on the written consent of the parties shall be determined in accordance with Rule 255. A motion to transfer venue on the basis that an impartial trial cannot be had in the courts where the action is pending shall be determined in accordance with Rules 258 and 259.
3. **Proof.**
   (a) **Affidavit and Attachments.** All venue facts, when properly pleaded, shall be taken as true unless specifically denied by the adverse party. When a venue fact is specifically denied, the party pleading the venue fact must make prima facie proof of that venue fact; provided, however, that no party shall ever be required for venue purposes to support by prima facie proof the existence of a cause of action or part thereof, and at the hearing the pleadings of the parties shall be taken as conclusive on the issues of existence of a cause of action. Prima facie proof is made when the venue facts are properly pleaded and an affidavit, and any duly proved attachments to the affidavit, are filed fully and specifically setting forth the facts supporting such pleading. Affidavits shall be made on personal knowledge, shall set forth specific facts as would be admissible in evidence, and shall show affirmatively that the affiant is competent to testify.

(b) **The Hearing.** The court shall determine the motion to transfer venue on the basis of the pleadings, any stipulations made by and between the parties and such affidavits and attachments as may be filed by the parties in accordance with the preceding subdivision of this paragraph 3 or of Rule 88.

(c) If a claimant has adequately pleaded and made prima facie proof that venue is proper in the county of suit as provided in subdivision (a) of paragraph 3, then the cause shall not be transferred but shall be retained in the county of suit, unless the motion to transfer is based on the grounds that an impartial trial cannot be had in the county where the action is pending as provided in Rules 257-259 or on an established ground of mandatory venue. A ground of mandatory venue is established when the party relying upon a mandatory exception to the general rule makes prima facie proof as provided in subdivision (a) of paragraph 3 of this rule.

(d) In the event that the parties shall fail to make prima facie proof that the county of suit or the specific county to which transfer is sought is a county of proper venue, then the court may direct the parties to make further proof.

4. **No Jury.** All venue challenges shall be determined by the court without the aid of a jury.

5. **Motion for Rehearing.** If venue has been sustained as against a motion to transfer, or if an action has been transferred to a proper county in response to a motion to transfer, then no further motions to transfer shall be considered regardless of whether the movant was a party to the prior proceedings or was added as a party subsequent to the venue proceedings, unless the motion to transfer is based on the grounds that an impartial trial cannot be had under Rules 257-259 or on the ground of mandatory venue, provided that such claim was not available to the other movant or movants.

Parties who are added subsequently to an action and are precluded by this rule from having a motion to transfer considered may raise the propriety of venue on appeal, provided that the party has timely filed a motion to transfer.

6. There shall be no interlocutory appeals from such determination.

(Amended by Order Sept. 20, 1941, eff. Dec. 31, 1941; June 16, 1943, eff. Dec. 31, 1943; Aug. 18, 1947, eff. Dec. 13, 1947; June 15, 1983, eff. Sept. 1, 1983, July 15, 1987, eff. Jan. 1, 1988; April 24, 1990, eff. Sept. 1, 1990.)

RULE 88. DISCOVERY AND VENUE.

Discovery shall not be abated or otherwise affected by pendency of a motion to transfer venue. Issuing process for witnesses and taking depositions shall not constitute a waiver of a motion to transfer venue, but depositions taken in such case may be read in evidence in any subsequent suit between the same parties concerning the same subject matter in like manner as if taken in such subsequent suit. Deposition transcripts, responses to requests for admission, answers to interrogatories and other discovery products containing information relevant to a determination of proper venue may be considered by the court in making the venue determination when they are attached to, or incorporated by reference in, an affidavit of a party, a witness or an attorney who has knowledge of such discovery.

(Amended by Order June 15, 1983, eff. Sept. 1, 1983; July 15, 1987, eff. Jan. 1, 1988.)

RULE 89. TRANSFERRED IF MOTION IS SUSTAINED.

If a motion to transfer venue is sustained, the cause shall not be dismissed, but the court shall transfer said cause to the proper court; and the costs incurred prior to the time such suit is filed in the court to which said cause is transferred shall be taxed against the plaintiff. The clerk shall make up a transcript of all the orders made in said cause, certifying thereto officially under the seal of the court, and send it with the original papers in the cause to the clerk of the court to which the venue has been changed. Provided, however, if the cause be severable as to parties defendant and shall be ordered transferred as to one or more defendants but not as to all, the clerk, instead of sending the original papers, shall make certified copies of such filed papers as directed by the court and forward the same to the clerk of the court to which the venue has been changed. After the cause has been transferred, as above provided for the clerk of the court to which the cause has been transferred shall mail notification to the plaintiff or his attorney that transfer of the cause has been completed, that the filing fee in the proper court is due and payable within thirty days from the mailing of such notification, and that the case may be dismissed if the filing fee is not timely paid; and if such filing fee is timely paid, the cause will be subject to trial at the expiration of thirty days after the mailing of notification to the parties or their attorneys by the clerk that the papers have been filed in the court to which the cause has been transferred; and if the filing fee is not timely paid, any court of the transferee county to which the case might have been assigned, upon its own motion or the motion of a party, may dismiss the cause without prejudice to the refiling of same.

(Amended by Order June 16, 1943 eff. Dec. 31, 1943; June 15, 1983 eff. Sept. 1, 1983.)

RULE 90. WAIVER OF DEFECTS IN PLEADING.

General demurrers shall not be used. Every defect omission or fault in a pleading either of form or of substance, which is not specifically pointed out by exception in writing and brought to the attention of the judge in the trial court before the instruction or charge to the jury or, in a non-jury case, before the judgment is signed, shall be deemed to have been waived by the party seeking reversal on such account; provided that this rule shall not apply as to any party against whom default judgment is rendered.

(Amended by Order June 10, 1980, eff. Jan. 1, 1981.)

RULE 91. SPECIAL EXCEPTIONS.

A special exception shall not only point out the particular pleading excepted to, but it shall also point out intelligibly and with particularity the defect, omission, obscurity, duplicity, generality, or other insufficiency in the allegations in the pleading excepted to.

(Amended by Order March 31, 1941, eff. Sept. 1, 1941.)

Rule 91a. Dismissal of Baseless Causes of Action.

91a.1. Motion and Grounds.

Except in a case brought under the Family Code or a case governed by Chapter 14 of the Texas Civil Practice and Remedies Code, a party may move to dismiss a cause of action on the grounds that it has no basis in law or fact. A cause of action has no basis in law if the allegations, taken as true, together with inferences reasonably drawn from them, do not entitle the claimant to the relief sought. A cause of action has no basis in fact if no reasonable person could believe the facts pleaded.

91a.2. Contents of Motion.

A motion to dismiss must state that it is made pursuant to this rule, must identify each cause of action to which it is addressed, and must state specifically the reasons the cause of action has no basis in law, no basis in fact, or both.

91a.3. Time for Motion and Ruling.

A motion to dismiss must be:

(a) filed within 60 days after the first pleading containing the challenged cause of action is served on the movant;
(b) filed at least 21 days before the motion is heard; and
(c) granted or denied within 45 days after the motion is filed.

91a.4. Time for Response.

Any response to the motion must be filed no later than 7 days before the date of the hearing.

91a.5. Effect of Nonsuit or Amendment; Withdrawal of Motion.

(a) The court may not rule on a motion to dismiss if, at least 3 days before the date of the hearing, the respondent files a nonsuit of the challenged cause of action, or the movant files a withdrawal of the motion.
(b) If the respondent amends the challenged cause of action at least 3 days before the date of the hearing, the movant may, before the date of the hearing, file a withdrawal of the motion or an amended motion directed to the amended cause of action.
(c) Except by agreement of the parties, the court must rule on a motion unless it has been withdrawn or the cause of action has been nonsuited in accordance with (a) or (b). In ruling on the motion, the court must not consider a nonsuit or amendment not filed as permitted by paragraphs (a) or (b).
(d) An amended motion filed in accordance with (b) restarts the time periods in this rule.

91a.6. Hearing; No Evidence Considered.

Each party is entitled to at least 14 days' notice of the hearing on the motion to dismiss. The court may, but is not required to, conduct an oral hearing on the motion. Except as required by 91 a. 7, the court may not consider evidence in ruling on the motion and must decide the motion based solely on the pleading of the cause of action, together with any pleading exhibits permitted by Rule 59.

91a.7. Award of Costs and Attorney Fees Required.

Except in an action by or against a governmental entity or a public official acting in his or her official capacity or under color of law, the court must award the prevailing party on the motion all costs and reasonable and necessary attorney fees incurred with respect to the challenged cause of action in the trial court. The court must consider evidence regarding costs and fees in determining the award.

91a.8. Effect on Venue and Personal Jurisdiction.

This rule is not an exception to the pleading requirements of Rules 86 and 120a, but a party does not, by filing a motion to dismiss pursuant to this rule or obtaining a ruling on it, waive a special appearance or a motion to transfer venue. By filing a motion to dismiss, a party submits to the court's jurisdiction only in proceedings on the motion and is bound by the court's ruling, including an award of attorney fees and costs against the party.

91a.9. Dismissal Procedure Cumulative.

This rule is in addition to, and does not supersede or affect, other procedures that authorize dismissal.

(Adopted by Order Nov. 13, 2012, eff. March 1, 2013; Order Feb. 12, 2013, eff. March 1, 2013. (Applies to all cases, including those pending on March 1, 2013.))

Comment to 2013 change: Rule 91a is a new rule implementing section 22.004(g) of the Texas Government Code, which was added in 2011 and calls for rules to provide for the dismissal of causes of action that have no basis in law or fact on motion and without evidence. A motion to dismiss filed under this rule must be ruled on by the court within 45 days unless the motion, pleading, or cause of action is withdrawn, amended, or nonsuited as specified in 9 la. 5. If an amended motion is filed in response to an amended cause of action in accordance with 91a.5(b), the court must rule on the motion within 45 days of the filing of the amended motion and the respondent must be given an opportunity to respond to the amended motion. The term "hearing" in the rule includes both submission and an oral hearing. Attorney fees awarded under 91a.7 are limited to those associated with challenged cause of action, including fees for preparing or responding to the motion to dismiss.

RULE 92. GENERAL DENIAL.

A general denial of matters pleaded by the adverse party which are not required to be denied under oath, shall be sufficient to put the same in issue. When the defendant has pleaded a general denial, and the plaintiff shall afterward amend his pleading, such original denial shall be presumed to extend to all matters subsequently set up by the plaintiff.

When a counterclaim or cross-claim is served upon a party who has made an appearance in the action, the party so served, in the absence of a responsive pleading, shall be deemed to have pleaded a general denial of the counterclaim or cross-claim, but the party shall not be deemed to have waived any special appearance or motion to transfer venue. In all other respects the rules prescribed for pleadings of defensive matter are applicable to answers to counterclaims and cross-claims.

(Amended by Order Dec. 5, 1983, eff. April 1, 1984; Dec. 19, 1984, eff. April 1, 1985.)

RULE 93. CERTAIN PLEAS TO BE VERIFIED.

A pleading setting up any of the following matters, unless the truth of such matters appear of record, shall be verified by affidavit.

1. That the plaintiff has not legal capacity to sue or that the defendant has not legal capacity to be sued.
2. That the plaintiff is not entitled to recover in the capacity in which he sues, or that the defendant is not liable in the capacity in which he is sued.
3. That there is another suit pending in this State between the same parties involving the same claim.
4. That there is a defect of parties, plaintiff or defendant.
5. A denial of partnership as alleged in any pleading as to any party to the suit.
6. That any party alleged in any pleading to be a corporation is not incorporated as alleged.
7. Denial of the execution by himself or by his authority of any instrument in writing, upon which any pleading is founded, in whole or in part and charged to have been executed by him or by his authority, and not alleged to be lost or destroyed. Where such instrument in writing is charged to have been executed by a person then deceased, the affidavit shall be sufficient if it states that the affiant has reason to believe and does believe that such instrument was not executed by the decedent or by his authority. In the absence of such a sworn plea, the instrument shall be received in evidence as fully proved.
8. A denial of the genuineness of the indorsement or assignment of a written instrument upon which suit is brought by an indorsee or assignee and in the absence of such a sworn plea, the indorsement or assignment thereof shall be held as fully proved. The denial required by this subdivision of the rule may be made upon information and belief.
9. That a written instrument upon which a pleading is founded is without consideration, or that the consideration of the same has failed in whole or in part.
10. A denial of an account which is the foundation of the plaintiff's action, and supported by affidavit.
11. That a contract sued upon is usurious. Unless such plea is filed, no evidence of usurious interest as a defense shall be received.
12. That notice and proof of loss or claim for damage has not been given as alleged. Unless such plea is filed such notice and proof shall be presumed and no evidence to the contrary shall be admitted. A denial of such notice or such proof shall be made specifically and with particularity.
13. In the trial of any case appealed to the court from the Industrial Accident Board the following, if pleaded, shall be presumed to be true as pleaded and have been done and filed in legal time and manner unless denied by verified pleadings:
    (a) Notice of injury.

(b) Claim for compensation.

(c) Award of the Board.

(d) Notice of intention not to abide by the award of the Board.

(e) Filing of suit to set aside the award.

(f) That the insurance company alleged to have been the carrier of the workers' compensation insurance at the time of the alleged injury was in fact the carrier thereof.

(g) That there was good cause for not filing claim with the Industrial Accident Board within the one year period provided by statute.

(h) Wage rate. A denial of any of the matters set forth in subdivisions (a) or (g) of paragraph 13 may be made on information and belief. Any such denial may be made in original or amended pleadings; but if in amended pleadings the same must be filed not less than seven days before the case proceeds to trial. In case of such denial the things so denied shall not be presumed to be true, and if essential to the case of the party alleging them, must be proved.

14. That a party plaintiff or defendant is not doing business under an assumed name or trade name as alleged.

15. In the trial of any case brought against an automobile insurance company by an insured under the provisions of an insurance policy in force providing protection against uninsured motorists, an allegation that the insured has complied with all the terms of the policy as a condition precedent to bringing the suit shall be presumed to be true unless denied by verified pleadings which may be upon information and belief.

16. Any other matter required by statute to be pleaded under oath.

(Amended by Order March 31, 1941, eff. Sept. 1, 1941; Sept. 20, 1941 eff. Dec. 31, 1941; June 16, 1943, eff. Dec. 31, 1943; Oct. 12, 1949, eff. March 1, 1950; July 21, 1970, eff. Jan. 1, 1971; July 22, 1975, eff. Jan. 1, 1976; June 15, 1983, eff. Sept. 1, 1983; Dec. 5, 1983, eff. April 1, 1984.)

RULE 94. AFFIRMATIVE DEFENSES.

In pleading to a preceding pleading, a party shall set forth affirmatively accord and satisfaction, arbitration and award, assumption of risk, contributory negligence, discharge in bankruptcy, duress, estoppel, failure of consideration, fraud, illegality, injury by fellow servant, laches, license, payment, release, res judicata, statute of frauds, statute of limitations, waiver, and any other matter constituting an avoidance or affirmative defense. Where the suit is on an insurance contract which insures against certain general hazards, but contains other provisions limiting such general liability, the party suing on such contract shall never be required to allege that the loss was not due to a risk or cause coming within any of the exceptions specified in the contract, nor shall the insurer be allowed to raise such issue unless it shall specifically allege that the loss was due to a risk or cause coming within a particular exception to the general liability; provided that nothing herein shall be construed to change the burden of proof on such issue as it now exists.

(Amended by Order March 31, 1941, eff. Sept. 1, 1941.)

RULE 95. PLEAS OF PAYMENT.

When a defendant shall desire to prove payment, he shall file with his plea an account stating distinctly the nature of such payment, and the several items thereof; failing to do so, he shall not be allowed to prove the same, unless it be so plainly and particularly described in the plea as to give the plaintiff full notice of the character thereof.

RULE 96. NO DISCONTINUANCE.

Where the defendant has filed a counterclaim seeking affirmative relief, the plaintiff shall not be permitted by a discontinuance of his suit, to prejudice the right of the defendant to be heard on such counter-claim.

RULE 97. COUNTERCLAIM AND CROSS-CLAIM.

(a) **Compulsory Counterclaims.** A pleading shall state as a counterclaim any claim within the jurisdiction of the court, not the subject of a pending action, which at the time of filing the pleading the pleader has against any opposing party, if it arises out of the transaction or occurrence that is the subject matter of the opposing party's claim and does not require for its adjudication the presence of third parties of whom the court cannot acquire jurisdiction; provided, however, that a judgment based upon a settlement or compromise of a claim of one party to the transaction or occurrence prior to a disposition on the merits shall not operate as a bar to the continuation or assertion of the claims of any other party to the transaction or occurrence unless the latter has consented in writing that said judgment shall operate as a bar.

(b) **Permissive Counterclaims.** A pleading may state as a counterclaim any claim against an opposing party whether or not arising out of the transaction or occurrence that is the subject matter of the opposing party's claim.

(c) **Counterclaim Exceeding Opposing Claim.** A counterclaim may or may not diminish or defeat the recovery sought by the opposing party. It may claim relief exceeding in amount or different in kind from that sought in the pleading of the opposing party, so long as the subject matter is within the jurisdiction of the court.

(d) **Counterclaim Maturing or Acquired After Pleading.** A claim which either matured or was acquired by the pleader after filing his pleading may be presented as a counterclaim by amended pleading.

(e) **Cross-Claim Against Co-party.** A pleading may state as a cross-claim any claim by one party against a co-party arising out of the transaction or occurrence that is the subject matter either of the original action or of a counterclaim therein. Such cross-claim may include a claim that the party against whom it is asserted is or may be liable to the cross-claimant for all or part of a claim asserted in the action against the cross-claimant.

(f) **Additional Parties.** Persons other than those made parties to the original action may be made parties to a third party action, counterclaim or crossclaim in accordance with the provisions of Rules 38, 39 and 40.

(g) Tort shall not be the subject of set-off or counterclaim against a contractual demand nor a contractual demand against tort unless it arises out of or is incident to or is connected with same.

(h) **Separate Trials; Separate Judgments.** If the court orders separate trials as provided in Rule 174, judgment on a counterclaim or cross-claim may be rendered when the court has jurisdiction so to do, even if the claims of the opposing party have been dismissed or otherwise disposed of.

(Amended by Order March 31, 1941, eff. Sept. 1, 1941; July 21, 1970, eff. Jan. 1, 1971; Dec. 5, 1983, eff. April 1, 1984.)

RULE 98. SUPPLEMENTAL ANSWERS.

The defendant's supplemental answers may contain special exceptions, general denial, and the allegations of new matter not before alleged by him, in reply to that which has been alleged by the plaintiff.

(Amended by Order March 31, 1941, eff. Sept. 1, 1941.)

SECTION 5.
CITATION

RULE 99. ISSUANCE AND FORM OF CITATION.

a. **Issuance.** Upon the filing of the petition, the clerk, when requested, shall forthwith issue a citation and deliver the citation as directed by the requesting party. The party requesting citation shall be responsible for obtaining service of the citation and a copy of the petition. Upon request, separate or additional citations shall be issued by the clerk. The clerk must retain a copy of the citation in the court's file.

b. **Form.** The citation shall (1) be styled "The State of Texas," (2) be signed by the clerk under seal of court, (3) contain name and location of the court, (4) show date of filing of the petition, (5) show date of issuance of citation, (6) show file number, (7) show names of parties, (8) be directed to the defendant, (9) show the name and address of attorney for plaintiff, otherwise the address of plaintiff, (10) contain the time within which these rules require the defendant to file a written answer with the clerk who issued citation, (11) contain address of the clerk, and (12) shall notify the defendant that in case of failure of defendant to file an answer, judgment by default may be rendered for the relief demanded in the petition. The citation shall direct the defendant to file a written answer to the plaintiff's petition on or before 10:00 a.m. on the Monday next after the expiration of twenty days after the date of service thereof. The requirement of subsections 10 and 12 of this section shall be in the form set forth in section c of this rule.

c. **Notice.** The citation shall include the following notice to the defendant: "You have been sued. You may employ an attorney. If you or your attorney do not file a written answer with the clerk who issued this citation by 10:00 a.m. on the Monday next following the expiration of twenty days after you were served this citation and petition, a default judgment may be taken against you."

d. **Copies.** The party filing any pleading upon which citation is to be issued and served shall furnish the clerk with a sufficient number of copies thereof for use in serving the parties to be served, and when copies are so furnished the clerk shall make no charge for the copies.

(Amended by Order Oct. 10, 1945, eff. Feb. 1, 1946; July 16, 1987, eff. Jan. 1, 1988; Oct. 17, 2011, eff. Jan. 1, 2012; Order Dec. 12, 2011, eff. Jan. 1, 2012.)

RULE 100 TO 102. [REPEALED]

(Repealed by Order July 15, 1987, eff. Jan. 1, 1988.)

RULE 103. WHO MAY SERVE.

Process—including citation and other notices, writs, orders, and other papers issued by the court—may be served anywhere by (1) any sheriff or constable or other person authorized by law or, (2) any person authorized by law or by written order of the court who is not less than eighteen years of age, or (3) any person certified under order of the Supreme Court. Service by registered or certified mail and citation by publication shall, if requested, be made by the clerk of the court in which the case is pending. But no person who is a party to or interested in the outcome of a suit may serve any process. The order authorizing a person to serve process may be made without written motion and no fee may be imposed for issuance of such order.

(Amended by Order June 10, 1980, eff. Jan. 1, 1981; July 15, 1987, eff. Jan. 1, 1988; Oct. 7, 2004, eff. Feb. 1, 2005, extended by Order Jan. 27, 2005 to July. 1, 2005, in all pending cases; June 29, 2005, eff. July 1, 2005, in all pending cases.)

Comment – 2005: Subsection (a) is amended to include among the persons authorized to effect service those who meet certification requirements promulgated by the Supreme Court and to prohibit private individuals from serving certain types of process unless, in rare circumstances, a court authorizes an individual to do so.

Certification of Persons
Authorized to Serve Process Under
Rules 103 and 536(a), Texas Rules of Civil Procedure

Rules 103 and 536(a), Texas Rules of Civil Procedure, allow process to be served by any person who is not a party to or interested in the outcome of a suit and who is certified under order of the Supreme Court of Texas. To improve the standards for persons authorized to serve process and to reduce the disparity among Texas civil courts for approving persons to serve process,

IT IS ORDERED:

1. To be certified to serve process under Rules 103 and 536(a), Texas Rules of Civil Procedure, a person must file with the Clerk of the Supreme Court a sworn application in the form prescribed by the Court. The application must contain a statement that the applicant has not been convicted of a felony or of a misdemeanor involving moral turpitude. Form applications may be obtained in the Clerk's office or on the Supreme Court website. The application must include a criminal history record obtained within the preceding 90 days from the Texas Department of Public Safety in Austin, Texas, and a certificate from the director of a civil process service course approved as provided by this Order that the applicant has completed the approved course within the prior year.

2. Applications will be reviewed and approved or rejected for good cause by the Texas Process Service Review Board, appointed by the Court. The Board will notify each applicant of its action, and for each person certified, will post on a list maintained on the Supreme Court website the person's name and an assigned identification number. The Office of Court Administration will provide clerical assistance to the Board.

3. Certification is effective for three years from the last day of the month it issues.

4. Certification may be revoked for good cause, including a conviction of a felony or of a misdemeanor involving moral turpitude. A person suffering such a conviction must immediately notify the Clerk of the Supreme Court and cease to serve process.

5. A person must not represent that he or she is certified under this Order if certification has not been approved, has expired, or has been revoked.

6. The following civil process service courses are approved:

a. the course now offered by the Houston Young Lawyer's Association, for certification for every state court;

b. the course now offered by the Texas Process Server's Association, for certification except for courts in Harris County;

c. a course offered by an academy or other provider licensed or approved by the Texas Commission on Law Enforcement, for certification for every state court.

7. A civil process service course that meets the following requirements, similar to the courses approved in paragraph 6, may apply to the Board for approval by the Court:

a. a minimum of 7 hours of monitored instruction;

b. instruction on applicable laws, including the historical development of the law, with emphasis on practical training of proper service and return of service (for example, using sample returns depicting both correct and incorrect returns of service);

c. instruction on a process server's exposure to criminal liability;

d. instruction on unique issues involving family law cases; and

e. basic competence testing upon completion of the course.

8. No organization that offers an approved civil process service course may make membership in the organization a prerequisite to taking the course.

9. The effective date of this Order is July 1, 2005. A person who on that date is shown to have met the requirements for an approved private process server already in place in Dallas County, Denton County, or Harris County, having provided a criminal history record there and having completed a course listed in paragraph 6, is considered to have been certified under this Order, to the extent permitted by paragraph 6, as if the person had complied with this Order on that date.

(Adopted by Order Oct. 7, 2004, eff. Feb. 1, 2005, extended by Order Jan. 27, 2005 to July. 1, 2005; June 29, 2005, eff. July 1, 2005.)

RULE 104. [REPEALED]

(Repealed by Order July 15, 1987, eff. Jan. 1, 1988.)

RULE 105. DUTY OF OFFICER OR PERSON RECEIVING.

The officer or authorized person to whom process is delivered shall endorse thereon the day and hour on which he received it, and shall execute and return the same without delay.

(Amended by Order July 11, 1977, eff. Jan. 1, 1978; July 15, 1987, eff. Jan. 1, 1988.)

RULE 106. METHOD OF SERVICE

(a) Unless the citation or an order of the court otherwise directs, the citation shall be served by any person authorized by Rule 103 by

(1) delivering to the defendant, in person, a true copy of the citation with the date of delivery endorsed thereon with a copy of the petition attached thereto, or

(2) mailing to the defendant by registered or certified mail, return receipt requested, a true copy of the citation with a copy of the petition attached thereto.

(b) Upon motion supported by affidavit stating the location of the defendant's usual place of business or usual place of abode or other place where the defendant can probably be found and stating specifically the facts showing that service has been attempted under either (a)(1) or (a)(2) at the location named in such affidavit but has not been successful, the court may authorize service

(1) by leaving a true copy of the citation, with a copy of the petition attached, with anyone over sixteen years of age at the location specified in such affidavit, or

(2) in any other manner that the affidavit or other evidence before the court shows will be reasonably effective to give the defendant notice of the suit.

(Amended by Order Aug. 18, 1947, eff. Dec. 31, 1947; July 22, 1975, eff. Jan. 1, 1976; July 11, 1977, eff. Jan. 1, 1978; June 10, 1980, eff. Jan. 1, 1981; July 15, 1987, eff. Jan. 1, 1988; April 24, 1990, eff. Sept. 1, 1990.)

RULE 107. RETURN OF SERVICE

(a) The officer or authorized person executing the citation must complete a return of service. The return may, but need not, be endorsed on or attached to the citation.

(b) The return, together with any document to which it is attached, must include the following information:

(1) the cause number and case name;

(2) the court in which the case is filed;

(3) a description of what was served;

(4) the date and time the process was received for service;

(5) the person or entity served;

(6) the address served;

(7) the date of service or attempted service;

(8) the manner of delivery of service or attempted service;

(9) the name of the person who served or attempted to serve the process;

(10) if the person named in (9) is a process server certified under order of the Supreme Court, his or her identification number and the expiration date of his or her certification; and

(11) any other information required by rule or law.

(c) When the citation was served by registered or certified mail as authorized by Rule 106, the return by the officer or authorized person must also contain the return receipt with the addressee's signature.

(d) When the officer or authorized person has not served the citation, the return shall show the diligence used by the officer or authorized person to execute the same and the cause of failure to execute it, and where the defendant is to be found, if ascertainable.

(e) The officer or authorized person who serves or attempts to serve a citation must sign the return. If the return is signed by a person other than a sheriff, constable, or the clerk of the court, the return must either be verified or be signed under penalty of perjury. A return signed under penalty of perjury must contain the statement below in substantially the following form:

"My name is ________________________, my date of birth is
(First) (Middle) (Last)
_________, and my address is _______, ___, ____, ______, and
(Street) (City)(State)(Zip Code)
_________, I declare under penalty of perjury that the foregoing is

(Country)
true and correct.
Executed in _______ County, State of ____, on the day of _____, _____
(Month) (Year)

____
Declarant"

(f) Where citation is executed by an alternative method as authorized by Rule 106, proof of service shall be made in the manner ordered by the court.

(g) The return and any document to which it is attached must be filed with the court and may be filed electronically or by facsimile, if those methods of filing are available.

(h) No default judgment shall be granted in any cause until proof of service as provided by this rule or by Rules 108 or 108a, or as ordered by the court in the event citation is executed by alternative method under Rule 106, shall have been on file with the clerk of the court ten days, exclusive of the day of filing and the day of judgment.

(Amended by Order July 11, 1977, eff. Jan. 1, 1978; June 10, 1980, eff. Jan. 1, 1981; July 15, 1987, eff. Jan. 1, 1988; April 24, 1990, eff. Sept. 1, 1990; Oct. 17, 2011, eff. Jan. 1, 2012; Order Dec. 12, 2011, eff. Jan. 1, 2012.)

RULE 108. SERVICE IN ANOTHER STATE

Where the defendant is absent from the State, or is a nonresident of the State, the form of notice to such defendant of the institution of the suit shall be the same as prescribed for citation to a resident defendant; and such notice may be served by any disinterested person who is not less than eighteen years of age, in the same manner as provided in Rule 106 hereof The return of service in such cases shall be in accordance with Rule 107. A defendant served with such notice shall be required to appear and answer in the same manner and time and under the same penalties as if he had been personally served with a citation within this State to the full extent that he may be required to appear and answer under the Constitution of the United States in an action either in rem or in personam.

(Amended by Order July 22, 1975, eff. Jan. 1, 1976; Oct. 17, 2011, eff. Jan. 1, 2012; Order Dec. 12, 2011, eff. Jan. 1, 2012.)

RULE 108a. SERVICE OF PROCESS IN FOREIGN COUNTRIES.

(1) **Manner.** Service of process may be effected upon a party in a foreign country if service of the citation and petition is made: (a) in the manner prescribed by the law of the foreign country for service in that country in an action in any of its courts of general jurisdiction; or (b) as directed by the foreign authority in response to a letter rogatory or a letter of request; or (c) in the manner provided by Rule 106; or (d) pursuant to the terms and provisions of any applicable treaty or convention; or (e) by diplomatic or consular officials when authorized by the United States Department of State; or (f) by any other means directed by the court that is not prohibited by the law of the country where service is to be made. The method for service of process in a foreign country must be reasonably calculated, under all of the circumstances, to give actual notice of the proceedings to the defendant in time to answer and defend. A defendant served with process under this rule shall be required to appear and answer in the same manner and time and under the same penalties as if he had been personally served with citation within this state to the full extent that he may be required to appear and answer under the Constitution of the United States or under any applicable convention or treaty in an action either in rem or in personam.

(2) **Return.** Proof of service may be made as prescribed by the law of the foreign country, by order of the court, by Rule 107, or by a method provided in any applicable treaty or convention.

(Added Dec. 5, 1983, eff. April 1, 1984.)

RULE 109. CITATION BY PUBLICATION.

When a party to a suit, his agent or attorney, shall make oath that the residence of any party defendant is unknown to affiant, and to such party when the affidavit is made by his agent or attorney, or that such defendant is a transient person, and that after due diligence such party and the affiant have been unable to locate the whereabouts of such defendant, or that such defendant is absent from or is a nonresident of the State, and that the party applying for the citation has attempted to obtain personal service of nonresident notice as provided for in Rule 108, but has been unable to do so, the clerk shall issue citation for such defendant for service by publication. In such cases it shall be the duty of the court trying the case to inquire into the sufficiency of the 1 exercised in attempting to ascertain the residence or whereabouts of the defendant or to obtain service of nonresident notice, as the case may be, before granting any judgment on such service.

(Amended by Order Oct. 10, 1945, eff. Feb. 1, 1946; July 22, 1975, eff. Jan. 1, 1976; Dec. 5, 1983, eff. April 1, 1984.)

RULE 109a. OTHER SUBSTITUTED SERVICE.

Whenever citation by publication is authorized, the court may, on motion, prescribe a different method of substituted service, if the court finds, and so recites in its order, that the method so prescribed would be as likely as publication to give defendant actual notice. When such method of substituted service is authorized, the return of the officer executing the citation shall state particularly the manner in which service is accomplished, and shall attach any return receipt, returned mail, or other evidence showing the result of such service. Failure of defendant to respond to such citation shall not render the service invalid. When such substituted service has been obtained and the defendant has not appeared, the provisions of Rules 244 and 329 shall apply as if citation had been served by publication.

(Added July 22, 1975, eff. Jan. 1, 1976.)

RULE 110. EFFECT OF RULES ON OTHER STATUTES.

Where by statute or these rules citation by publication is authorized and the statute or rules do not specify the requisites of such citation or the method of service thereof, or where they direct that such citation be issued or served as in other civil actions, the provisions of these rules shall govern. Where, however, the statute authorizing citation by publication provides expressly for requisites of such citation or service thereof, or both, differing from the provisions of Rules 114, 115, and 116, these rules shall not govern, but the special statutory procedure shall continue in force; provided, however, that Rule 117a shall control with respect to citation in tax suits.

(Amended by Order Aug. 18, 1947, eff. Dec. 31, 1947.)

RULE 111. CITATION BY PUBLICATION IN ACTION AGAINST UNKNOWN HEIRS OR STOCKHOLDERS OF DEFUNCT CORPORATIONS.

If the plaintiff, his agent, or attorney, shall make oath that the names of the heirs or stockholders against whom an action is authorized by Section 17.004, Civil Practice and Remedies Code, are unknown to the affiant, the clerk shall issue a citation for service by publication. Such citation shall be addressed to the defendants by a concise description of their classification, as "the Unknown Heirs of A.B. deceased," or "Unknown Stockholders of ___________ Corporation," as the case may be, and shall contain the other requisites prescribed in Rules 114 and 115 and shall be served as provided by Rule 116.

(Amended by Order July 15, 1987, eff. Jan. 1, 1988.)

RULE 112. PARTIES TO ACTIONS AGAINST UNKNOWN OWNERS OR CLAIMANTS OF INTEREST IN LAND.

In suits authorized by Section 17.005, Civil Practice and Remedies Code, all persons claiming under such conveyance whose names are known to plaintiff shall be made parties by name and cited to appear, in the manner now provided by law as in other suits; all other persons claiming any interest in such land under such conveyance may be made parties to the suit and cited by publication under the designation "all persons claiming any title or interest in land under deed heretofore given to _______________ of ______________ as grantee" (inserting in the blanks the name and residence of grantee as given in such conveyance). It shall be permissible to join in one suit all persons claiming under two or more conveyances affecting title to the same tract of land.

(Amended by Order July 15, 1987, eff. Jan. 1, 1988.)

RULE 113. CITATION BY PUBLICATION IN ACTIONS AGAINST UNKNOWN OWNERS OR CLAIMANTS OF INTEREST IN LAND.

In suits authorized by Section 17.005, Civil Practice and Remedies Code, plaintiff, his agent or attorney shall make and file with the clerk of the court an affidavit, stating

(a) the name of the grantee as set out in the conveyance constituting source of title of defendants, and

(b) stating that affiant does not know the names of any persons claiming title or interest under such conveyance other than as stated in plaintiff's petition and

(c) if the conveyance is to a company or association name as grantee, further stating whether grantee is incorporated or unincorporated, if such fact is known and if such fact is unknown, so stating.

Said clerk shall thereupon issue a citation for service upon all persons claiming any title or interest in such land under such conveyance. The citation in such cases shall contain the requisites and be served in the manner provided by Rules 114, 115 and 116.

(Amended by Order July 20, 1954, eff. Jan. 1, 1955; July 15, 1987, eff. Jan. 1, 1988; April 24, 1990 eff. Sept. 1, 1990.)

RULE 114. CITATION BY PUBLICATION; REQUISITES.

Where citation by publication is authorized by these rules, the citation shall contain the requisites prescribed by Rules 1., and 99, in so far as they are not inconsistent herewith, provided that no copy of the plaintiff's petition shall accompany this citation, and the citation shall be styled "The State of Texas" and shall be directed to the defendant or defendants by name, if their names are known, or to the defendant or defendants as designated in the petition, if unknown or such other classification as may be fixed by any statute or by these rules. Where there are two or more defendants or classes of defendants to be served by publication, the citation may be directed to all of them by name and classification, so that service may be completed by publication of the one citation for the required number of times. The citation shall contain the names of the parties, a brief statement of the nature of the suit (which need not contain the details and particulars of the claim) a description of any property involved and of the interest of the named or unknown defendant or defendants, and, where the suit involves land, the requisites of Rule 115. If issued from the district or county court, the citation shall command such parties to appear and answer at or before 10 o'clock a.m. of the first Monday after the expiration of 42 days from the date of issuance thereof, specifying the day of the week, the day of the month, and the time of day the defendant is required to answer. If issued from the justice of the peace court, such citation shall command such parties to appear and answer on or before the first day of the first term of court which convenes after the expiration of 42 days from the date of issue thereof, specifying the day of the week, and the day of the month, that such term will meet.

(Amended by Order Sept. 20, 1941, eff. Dec. 31, 1941.)

RULE 115. FORM OF PUBLISHED CITATION IN ACTIONS INVOLVING LAND.

In citations by publication involving land, it shall be sufficient in making the brief statement of the claim in such citation to state the kind of suit, the number of acres of land involved in the suit, or the number of the lot and block, or any other plat description that may be of record if the land is situated in a city or town the survey on which and the county in which the land is situated, and any special pleas which are relied upon in such suit.

RULE 116. SERVICE OF CITATION BY PUBLICATION.

The citation, when issued, shall be served by the sheriff or any constable of any county of the State of Texas or by the clerk of the court in which the case is pending, by having the same published once each week for four (4) consecutive weeks, the first publication to be at least twenty-eight (28) days before the return day of the citation. In all suits which do not involve the title to land or the partition of real estate, such publication shall be made in the county where the suit is pending, if there be a newspaper published in said county, but if not, then in an adjoining county where a newspaper is published. In all suits which involve the title to land or partition of real estate, such publication shall be made in the county where the land, or a portion thereof, is situated, if there be a newspaper in such county, but if not, then in an adjoining county to the county where the land or a part thereof is situated, where a newspaper is published.

(Amended by Order Dec. 5, 1983, eff. April 1, 1984.)

RULE 117. RETURN OF CITATION BY PUBLICATION.

The return of the officer executing such citation shall show how and when the citation was executed, specifying the dates of such publication be signed by him officially and shall be accompanied by a printed copy of such publication.

(Amended by Order Oct. 17, 2011, eff. Jan. 1, 2012; Order Dec. 12, 2011, eff. Jan. 1, 2012.)

RULE 117a. CITATION IN SUITS FOR DELINQUENT AD VALOREM TAXES.

In all suits for collection of delinquent ad valorem taxes, the rules of civil procedure governing issuance and service of citation shall control the issuance and service of citation therein, except as herein otherwise specially provided.

1. **Personal Service: Owner and Residence Known, Within State.** Where any defendant in a tax suit is a resident of the State of Texas and is not subject to citation by publication under subdivision 3 below, the process shall conform substantially to the form hereinafter set out for personal service and shall contain the essential elements and be served and returned and otherwise regulated by the provisions of Rules 99 to 107, inclusive.
2. **Personal Service: Owner and Residence Known, Out of State.** Where any such defendant is absent from the State or is a nonresident of the State and is not subject to citation by publication under subdivision 3 below, the process shall conform substantially to the form hereinafter set out for personal service and shall contain the essential elements and be served and returned and otherwise regulated by the provisions of Rule 108.
3. **Service by Publication: Nonresident, Absent from State, Transient, Name Unknown, Residence Unknown, Owner Unknown, Heirs Unknown, Corporate Officers, Trustees, Receivers or Stockholders Unknown, Any Other Unknown Persons Owing or Claiming or Having an Interest.** Where any defendant in a tax suit is a nonresident of the State, or is absent from the State, or is a transient person, or the name or the residence of any owner of any interest in any property upon which a tax lien is sought to be foreclosed, is unknown to the attorney requesting the issuance of process or filing the suit for the taxing unit, and such attorney shall make affidavit that such defendant is a nonresident of

the State, or is absent from the State, or is a transient person, or that the name or residence of such owner is unknown and cannot be ascertained after diligent inquiry, each such person in every such class above mentioned, together with any and all other persons, including adverse claimants, owning or claiming or having any legal or equitable interest in or lien upon such property, may be cited by publication. All unknown owners of any interest in any property upon which any taxing unit seeks to foreclose a lien for taxes, including stockholders of corporations—defunct or otherwise—their successors, heirs, and assigns, may be joined in such suit under the designation of "unknown owners" and citation be had upon them as such; provided, however, that record owners of such property or of any apparent interest therein, including, without limitation, record lien holders, shall not be included in the designation of "unknown owners"; and provided further that where any record owner has rendered the property involved within five years before the tax suit is filed, citation on such record owner may not be had by publication or posting unless citation for personal service has been issued as to such record owner, with a notation thereon setting forth the same address as is contained on the rendition sheet made within such five years, and the sheriff or other person to whom citation has been delivered makes his return thereon that he is unable to locate the defendant. Where any attorney filing a tax suit for a taxing unit, or requesting the issuance of process in such suit, shall make affidavit that a corporation is the record owner of any interest in any property upon which a tax lien is sought to be foreclosed, and that he does not know, and after diligent inquiry has been unable to ascertain, the location of the place of business, if any, of such corporation, or the name or place of residence of any officer of such corporation upon whom personal service may be had, such corporation may be cited by publication as herein provided. All defendants of the classes enumerated above may be joined in the same citation by publication.

An affidavit which complies with the foregoing requirements therefor shall be sufficient basis for the citation above mentioned in connection with it but shall be held to be made upon the criminal responsibility of affiant.

Such citation by publication shall be directed to the defendants by names or by designation as hereinabove provided, and shall be issued and signed by the clerk of the court in which such tax suit is pending. It shall be sufficient if it states the file number and style of the case, the date of the filing of the petition, the names of all parties by name or by designation as hereinabove provided, and the court in which the suit is pending; shall command such parties to appear and defend such suit at or before 10 o'clock a.m. of the first Monday after the expiration of forty-two days from the date of the issuance thereof, specifying such date when such parties are required to answer; shall state the place of holding the court, the nature of the suit, and the date of the issuance of the citation; and shall be signed and sealed by the clerk.

The citation shall be published in the English language one time a week for two weeks in some newspaper published in the county in which the property is located, which newspaper must have been in general circulation for at least one year immediately prior to the first publication and shall in every respect answer the requirements of the law applicable to newspapers which are employed for such a purpose, the first publication to be not less than twenty-eight days prior to the return day fixed in the citation; and the affidavit of the editor or publisher of the newspaper giving the date of publication, together with a printed copy of the citation as published, shall constitute sufficient proof of due publication when returned and filed in court. If there is no newspaper published in the county, then the publication may be made in a newspaper in an adjoining county, which newspaper shall in every respect answer the requirements of the law applicable to newspapers which are employed for such a purpose. The maximum fee for publishing the citation shall be the lowest published word or line rate of that newspaper for classified advertising. If the publication of the citation cannot be had for this fee, chargeable as costs and payable upon sale of the property, as provided by law, and this fact is supported by the affidavit of the attorney for the plaintiff or the attorney requesting the issuance of the process, then service of the citation may be made by posting a copy at the courthouse door of the county in which the suit is pending, the citation to be posted at least twenty-eight days prior to the return day fixed in the citation. Proof of the posting of the citation shall be made by affidavit of the attorney for the plaintiff, or of the person posting it. When citation is served as here provided it shall be sufficient, and no other form of citation or notice to the named defendants therein shall be necessary.

4. **Citation in Tax Suits: General Provisions..** Any process authorized by this rule may issue jointly in behalf of all taxing units who are plaintiffs or intervenors in any tax suit. The statement of the nature of the suit, to be set out in the citation, shall be sufficient if it contains a brief general description of the property upon which the taxes are due and the amount of such taxes, exclusive of interest, penalties, and costs, and shall state, in substance, that in such suit the plaintiff and all other taxing units who may set up their claims therein seek recovery of the delinquent ad valorem taxes due on said property, and the (establishment and foreclosure) of liens, if any, securing the payment of same, as provided by law; that in addition to the taxes all interest, penalties, and costs allowed by law up to and including the day of judgment are included in the suit; and that all parties to the suit, including plaintiff, defendants, and intervenors, shall take notice that claims for any taxes on said property becoming delinquent subsequent to the filing of the suit and up to the day of judgment, together with all interest, penalties, and costs allowed by law thereon, may, upon request therefor, be recovered therein without further citation or notice to any parties thereto. Such citation need not be accompanied by a copy of plaintiff's petition and no such copy need be served. Such citation shall also show the names of all taxing units which assess and collect taxes on said property not made parties to such suit, and shall contain, in substance, a recitation that each party to such suit shall take notice of, and plead and answer to, all claims and pleadings then on file or thereafter filed in said cause by all other parties therein, or who may intervene therein and set up their respective tax claims against said property. After citation or notice has been given on behalf of any plaintiff or intervenor taxing unit, the court shall have jurisdiction to hear and determine the tax claims of all taxing units who are parties plaintiff, intervenor or defendant at the time such process is issued and of all taxing units intervening after such process is issued, not only for the tax-

es, interest, penalties, and costs which may be due on said property at the time the suit is filed, but those becoming delinquent thereon at any time thereafter up to and including the day of judgment, without the necessity of further citation or notice to any party to said suit; and any taxing unit having a tax claim against said property may, by answer or intervention, set up and have determined its tax claim without the necessity of further citation or notice to any parties to such suit.

5. **Form of Citation by Publication or Posting.** The form of citation by publication or posting shall be sufficient if it is in substantially the following form with proper changes to make the same applicable to personal property, where necessary, and if the suit includes or is for the recovery of taxes assessed on personal property, a general description of such personal property shall be sufficient:

THE STATE OF TEXAS)
COUNTY OF ________________)
In the name and by the authority of the State of Texas
Notice is hereby given as follows:
To

____

and any and all other persons, including adverse claimants, owning or having or claiming any legal or equitable interest in or lien upon the following described property delinquent to Plaintiff herein, for taxes, to-wit:

____
____
____

Which said property is delinquent to Plaintiff for taxes in the following amounts:

$ ______, exclusive of interest, penalties, and costs, and there is included in this suit in addition to the taxes all said interest, penalties, and costs thereon allowed by law up to and including the day of judgment herein.

You are hereby notified that suit has been brought by ___________ as Plaintiffs, against __________ as Defendants, by petition filed on the ______ day of ________________, 19__, in a certain suit styled ____________ v. ___________ for collection of the taxes on said property and that said suit is now pending in the District Court of ________________ County, Texas, ________________ Judicial District, and the file number of said suit is _______________, that the names of all taxing units which assess and collect taxes on the property hereinabove described not made parties to this suit, are ________________.

Plaintiff and all other taxing units who may set up their tax claims herein seek recovery of delinquent ad valorem taxes on the property hereinabove described, and in addition to the taxes all interest, penalties, and costs allowed by law thereon up to and including the day of judgment herein, and the establishment and foreclosure of liens, if any, securing the payment of same, as provided by law.

All parties to this suit, including plaintiff, defendants, and intervenors, shall take notice that claims not only for any taxes which were delinquent on said property at the time this suit was filed but all taxes becoming delinquent thereon at any time thereafter up to the day of judgment, including all interest, penalties, and costs allowed by law thereon, may, upon request therefor, be recovered herein without further citation or notice to any parties herein, and all said parties shall take notice of and plead and answer to all claims and pleadings now on file and which may hereafter be filed in said cause by all other parties herein, and all of those taxing units above named who may intervene herein and set up their respective tax claims against said property.

You are hereby commanded to appear and defend such suit on the first Monday after the expiration of forty-two (42) days from and after the date of issuance hereof, the same being the _____ day of __________ A.D., 19__ (which is the return day of such citation), before the honorable District Court of ______________ County, Texas, to be held at the courthouse thereof, then and there to show cause why judgment shall not be rendered for such taxes, penalties, interest, and costs, and condemning said property and ordering foreclosure of the constitutional and statutory tax liens thereon for taxes due the plaintiff and the taxing units parties hereto, and those who may intervene herein, together with all interest, penalties, and costs allowed by law up to and including the day of judgment herein, and all costs of this suit.

Issued and given under my hand and seal of said court in the City of __________, ____________County, Texas, this ____ day of _________, A.D., 19__.

____
Clerk of the District Court.
_____________ County, Texas,
_____________ Judicial District.

6. **Form of Citation by Personal Service In or Out of State.** The form of citation for personal service shall be sufficient if it is in substantially the following form, with proper changes to make the same applicable to personal property, where necessary, and if the suit includes or is for the recovery of taxes assessed on personal property, a general description of such personal property shall be sufficient:

THE STATE OF TEXAS

To ________________, Defendant,

GREETING:

YOU ARE HEREBY COMMANDED to appear and answer before the Honorable District Court, ________________ Judicial District, ________________ County, Texas, at the Courthouse of said county in __________, Texas, at or before 10 o'clock a.m. of the Monday next after the expiration of 20 days from the date of service of this citation, then and there to answer the petition of _____________ Plaintiff, filed in said Court on the __________ day of ___________, A.D., 19__, against ____________, Defendant, said suit being number _______ on the docket of said Court, the nature of which demand is a suit to collect delinquent ad valorem taxes on the property hereinafter described.

The amount of taxes due Plaintiff, exclusive of interest, penalties, and costs, is the sum of $ __________, said property being described as follows, to-wit: ____.

The names of all taxing units which assess and collect taxes on said property, not made parties to this suit, are: ____.

Plaintiff and all other taxing units who may set up their tax claims herein seek recovery of delinquent ad valorem taxes on the property hereinabove described, and in addition to the taxes all interest, penalties, and costs allowed by law thereon up to and including the day of judgment herein, and the establishment and foreclosure of liens securing the payment of same, as provided by law.

All parties to this suit, including plaintiff, defendants, and intervenors, shall take notice that claims not only for any taxes which were delinquent on said property at the time this suit was filed but all taxes becoming delinquent thereon at any time thereafter up to the day of judgment, including all interest, penalties, and costs allowed by law thereon, may, upon request therefor, be recovered herein without further citation or notice to any parties herein, and all said parties shall take notice of and plead and answer to all claims and pleadings now on file and which may hereafter be filed in this cause by all other parties hereto, and by all of those taxing units above named, who may intervene herein and set up their respective tax claims against said property.

If this citation is not served within 90 days after the date of its issuance, it shall be returned unserved.

The officer executing this return shall promptly serve the same according to the requirements of law and the mandates hereof and make due return as the law directs.

Issued and given under my hand and seal of said Court at ________________, Texas, this the ___________ day of _____________, A.D., 19__.

____
Clerk of the District Court of
______________ County, Texas.
By ______________________, Deputy.

(Added Aug. 18, 1947, eff. Dec. 31, 1947. Amended by Order May 4, 1948, eff. Oct. 1, 1948; July 17, 1950, eff. Dec. 1, 1950; July 15, 1987, eff. Jan. 1, 1988.)

RULE 118. AMENDMENT.

At any time in its discretion and upon such notice and on such terms as it deems just, the court may allow any process or proof of service thereof to be amended, unless it clearly appears that material prejudice would result to the substantial rights of the party against whom the process issued.

RULE 119. ACCEPTANCE OF SERVICE.

The defendant may accept service of process, or waive the issuance or service thereof by a written memorandum signed by him, or by his duly authorized agent or attorney, after suit is brought, sworn to before a proper officer other than an attorney in the case, and filed among the papers of the cause, and such waiver or acceptance shall have the same force and effect as if the citation had been issued and served as provided by law. The party signing such memorandum shall be delivered a copy of plaintiff's petition, and the receipt of the same shall be acknowledged in such memorandum. In every divorce action such memorandum shall also include the defendant's mailing address.

(Amended by Order Sept. 20, 1941, eff. Dec. 31, 1941; July 20, 1954, eff. Jan. 1, 1955; July 26, 1960, eff. Jan. 1, 1961.)

RULE 119a. COPY OF DECREE.

The district clerk shall forthwith mail a certified copy of the final divorce decree or order of dismissal to the party signing a memorandum waiving issuance or service of process. Such divorce decree or order of dismissal shall be mailed to the signer of the memorandum at the address stated in such memorandum or to the office of his attorney of record.

(Added July 20, 1954, eff. Jan. 1, 1955.)

RULE 120. ENTERING APPEARANCE.

The defendant may, in person, or by attorney, or by his duly authorized agent, enter an appearance in open court. Such appearance shall be noted by the judge upon his docket and entered in the minutes, and shall have the same force and effect as if the citation had been duly issued and served as provided by law.

RULE 120a. SPECIAL APPEARANCE.

1. Notwithstanding the provisions of Rules 121, 122 and 123, a special appearance may be made by any party either in person or by attorney for the purpose of objecting to the jurisdiction of the court over the person or property of the defendant on the ground that such party or property is not amenable to process issued by the courts of this State. A special appearance may be made as to an entire proceeding or as to any severable claim involved therein. Such special appearance shall be made by sworn motion filed prior to motion to transfer venue or any other plea, pleading or motion; provided however, that a motion to transfer venue and any other plea, pleading, or motion may be contained in the same instrument or filed subsequent thereto without waiver of such special appearance; and may be amended to cure defects. The issuance of process for witnesses, the taking of depositions, the serving of requests for admissions, and the use of discovery processes, shall not constitute a waiver of such special appearance. Every appearance, prior to judgment, not in compliance with this rule is a general appearance.
2. Any motion to challenge the jurisdiction provided for herein shall be heard and determined before a motion to transfer venue or any other plea or pleading may be heard. No determination of any issue of fact in connection with the objection to jurisdiction is a determination of the merits of the case or any aspect thereof.
3. The court shall determine the special appearance on the basis of the pleadings, any stipulations made by and between the parties, such affidavits and attachments as may be filed by the parties, the results of discovery processes, and any oral testimony. The affidavits, if any, shall be served at least seven days before the hearing, shall be made on personal knowledge, shall set forth specific facts as would be admissible in evidence, and shall show affirmatively that the affiant is competent to testify.

   Should it appear from the affidavits of a party opposing the motion that he cannot for reasons stated present by affidavit facts essential to justify his opposition, the court may order a continuance to permit affidavits to be obtained or depositions to be taken or discovery to be had or may make such other order as is just.

   Should it appear to the satisfaction of the court at any time that any of such affidavits are presented in violation of Rule 13, the court shall impose sanctions in accordance with that rule.
4. If the court sustains the objection to jurisdiction, an appropriate order shall be entered. If the objection to jurisdiction is overruled, the objecting party may thereafter appear generally for any purpose. Any such special appearance or such general appearance shall not be deemed a waiver of the objection to jurisdiction when the objecting party or subject matter is not amenable to process issued by the courts of this State.

(Added April 12, 1962, eff. Sept. 1, 1962. Amended by Order July 22, 1975, eff. Jan. 1, 1976; June 15, 1983, eff. Sept. 1, 1983; April 24, 1990, eff. Sept. 1, 1990.)

RULE 121. ANSWER IS APPEARANCE.

An answer shall constitute an appearance of the defendant so as to dispense with the necessity for the issuance or service of citation upon him.

RULE 122. CONSTRUCTIVE APPEARANCE.

If the citation or service thereof is quashed on motion of the defendant, such defendant shall be deemed to have entered his appearance at ten o'clock a.m. on the Monday next after the expiration of twenty (20) days after the day on which the citation or service is quashed, and such defendant shall be deemed to have been duly served so as to require him to appear and answer at that time, and if he fails to do so, judgment by default may be rendered against him.

RULE 123. REVERSAL OF JUDGMENT.

Where the judgment is reversed on appeal or writ of error for the want of service, or because of defective service of process, no new citation shall be issued or served, but the defendant shall be presumed to have entered his appearance to the term of the court at which the mandate shall be filed.

RULE 124. NO JUDGMENT WITHOUT SERVICE.

In no case shall judgment be rendered against any defendant unless upon service, or acceptance or waiver of process, or upon an appearance by the defendant, as prescribed in these rules, except where otherwise expressly provided by law or these rules.

When a party asserts a counterclaim or a cross-claim against another party who has entered an appearance, the claim may be served in any manner prescribed for service of citation or as provided in Rule 21(a).

(Amended by Order Dec. 5, 1983, eff. April 1, 1984.)

SECTION 6.
COSTS AND SECURITY THEREFOR

RULE 125. PARTIES RESPONSIBLE.

Each party to a suit shall be liable to the officers of the court for all costs incurred by himself.

RULE 126. FEE FOR SERVICE OF PROCESS IN A COUNTY OTHER THAN IN THE COUNTY OF SUIT.

(a) *General Rule: Fee Due Before Service.* A sheriff or constable may require payment before serving process in a case pending in a county other than the county in which the sheriff or constable is an officer.

(b) *Exception: Statement of Inability to Afford Payment of Court Costs Filed.* If a Statement of Inability to Afford Payment of Court Costs has been filed in a case in which the declarant requests service of process in a county other than in the county of suit, the clerk must indicate on the document to be served that a Statement of Inability to Afford Payment of Court Costs has been filed. The sheriff or constable must execute the service without demanding payment.

(Amended by Tex. Sup. Ct. Misc. Docket No. 16-9056, eff. Sept. 1, 2016; Tex. Sup. Ct. Misc. Docket No. 16-9122, eff. Sept. 1, 2016.)

[Statement of Inability to Afford Payment of Court Costs as provided in Tex. Sup. Ct. Misc. Docket No. 16-9122, eff. Sept. 1, 2016 and applies to any contest of, or challenge to, a claim of inability to afford payment of court costs that is pending on September 1, 2016.]

RULE 127. PARTIES LIABLE FOR OTHER COSTS.

Each party to a suit shall be liable for all costs incurred by him. If the costs cannot be collected from the party against whom they have been adjudged, execution may issue against any party in such suit for the amount of costs incurred by such party, but no more.

RULE 128. [REPEALED]

(Repealed by Order Dec. 5, 1983, eff. April 1, 1984.)

RULE 129. HOW COSTS COLLECTED.

If any party responsible for costs fails or refuses to pay the same within ten days after demand for payment, the clerk or justice of the peace may make certified copy of the bill of costs then due, and place the same in the hands of the sheriff or constable for collection. All taxes imposed on law proceedings shall be included in the bill of costs. Such certified bill of costs shall have the force and effect of an execution. The removal of a case by appeal shall not prevent the issuance of an execution for costs.

(Amended by Order Dec. 5, 1983, eff. April 1, 1984.)

RULE 130. OFFICER TO LEVY.

The sheriff or constable upon demand and failure to pay said bill of costs, may levy upon a sufficient amount of property of the person from whom said costs are due to satisfy the same, and sell such property as under execution. Where such party is not a resident of the county where such suit is pending, the payment of such costs may be demanded of his attorney of record; and neither the clerk nor justice of the peace shall be allowed to charge any fee for making out such certified bill of costs, unless he is compelled to make a levy.

RULE 131. SUCCESSFUL PARTY TO RECOVER.

The successful party to a suit shall recover of his adversary all costs incurred therein, except where otherwise provided.

RULE 132. [REPEALED]

(Repealed by Order Dec. 5, 1983, eff. April 1, 1984.)

RULE 133. COSTS OF MOTION.

The court may give or refuse costs on motions at its discretion, except where otherwise provided by law or these rules.

RULES 134 AND 135. [REPEALED]

(Repealed by Order Dec. 5, 1983, eff. April 1, 1984.)

RULE 136. DEMAND REDUCED BY PAYMENTS.

Where the plaintiff's demand is reduced by payment to an amount which would not have been within the jurisdiction of the court, the defendant shall recover his costs.

RULE 137. IN ASSAULT AND BATTERY, ETC.

In civil actions for assault and battery, slander and defamation of character, if the verdict or judgment shall be for the plaintiff, but for less than twenty dollars, the plaintiff shall not recover his costs, but each party shall be taxed with the costs incurred by him in such suit.

RULE 138. COST OF NEW TRIALS.

The costs of new trials may either abide the result of the suit or may be taxed against the party to whom the new trial is granted, as the court may adjudge when he grants such new trial.

RULE 139. ON APPEAL AND CERTIORARI.

When a case is appealed, if the judgment of the higher court be against the appellant, but for less amount than the original judgment, such party shall recover the costs of the higher court but shall be adjudged to pay the costs of the court below; if the judgment be against him for the same or a greater amount than in the court below, the adverse party shall recover the costs of both courts. If the judgment of the court above be in favor of the party appealing and for more than the original judgment, such party shall recover the costs of both courts; if the judgment be in his favor, but for the same or a less amount than in the court below, he shall recover the costs of the court below, and pay the costs of the court above.

RULE 140. NO FEE FOR COPY.

No fee for a copy of a paper not required by law or these rules to be copied shall be taxed in the bill of costs.

RULE 141. COURT MAY OTHERWISE ADJUDGE COSTS.

The court may, for good cause, to be stated on the record, adjudge the costs otherwise than as provided by law or these rules.

RULE 142. SECURITY FOR COSTS.

The clerk shall require from the plaintiff fees for services rendered before issuing any process unless filing is requested pursuant to Rule 145 of these rules.

(Amended by Order March 31, 1941, eff. Sept. 1, 1941; July 15, 1987, eff. Jan. 1, 1988.)

RULE 143. RULE FOR COSTS.

A party seeking affirmative relief may be ruled to give security for costs at any time before final judgment, upon motion of any party, or any officer of the court interested in the costs accruing in such suit, or by the court upon its own motion. If such rule be entered against any party and he failed to comply therewith on or before twenty (20) days after notice that such rule has been entered, the claim for affirmative relief of such party shall be dismissed.

(Amended by Order July 21, 1970, eff. Jan. 1, 1971.)

RULE 143a. COSTS ON APPEAL TO COUNTY COURT.

If the appellant fails to pay the costs on appeal from a judgment of a justice of the peace or small claims court within twenty (20) days after being notified to do so by the county clerk, the appeal shall be deemed not perfected and the county clerk shall return all papers in said cause to the justice of the peace having original jurisdiction and the justice of the peace shall proceed as though no appeal had been attempted.

(Added July 22, 1975, eff. Jan. 1, 1976.)

RULE 144. JUDGMENT ON COST BOND.

All bonds given as security for costs shall authorize judgment against all the obligors in such bond for the said costs, to be entered in the final judgment of the cause.

RULE 145. PAYMENT OF COSTS NOT REQUIRED.

(a) *General Rule.* A party who files a Statement of Inability to Afford Payment of Court Costs cannot be required to pay costs except by order of the court as provided by this rule. After the Statement is filed, the clerk must docket the case, issue citation, and provide any other service that is ordinarily provided to a party. The Statement must either be sworn to before a notary or made under penalty of perjury. In this rule, "declarant" means the party filing the Statement.

(b) *Supreme Court Form; Clerk to Provide.* The declarant must use the form Statement approved by the Supreme Court, or the Statement must include the information required by the Court-approved form. The clerk must make the form available to all persons without charge or request.

(c) *Costs Defined.* "Costs" mean any fee charged by the court or an officer of the court that could be taxed in a bill of costs, including, but not limited to, filing fees, fees for issuance and service of process, fees for a court-appointed professional, and fees charged by the clerk or court reporter for preparation of the appellate record.

(d) *Defects.* The clerk may refuse to file a Statement that is not sworn to before a notary or made under penalty of perjury. No other defect is a ground for refusing to file a Statement or requiring the party to pay costs. If a defect or omission in a Statement is material, the court—on its own motion or on motion of the clerk or any party—may direct the declarant to correct or clarify the Statement.

(e) *Evidence of Inability to Afford Costs Required.* The Statement must say that the declarant cannot afford to pay costs. The declarant must provide in the Statement, and, if available, in attachments to the Statement, evidence of the declarant's inability to afford costs, such as evidence that the declarant:

(1) receives benefits from a government entitlement program, eligibility for which is dependent on the recipient's means;

(2) is being represented in the case by an attorney who is providing free legal services to the declarant, without contingency, through:

(A) a provider funded by the Texas Access to Justice Foundation;

(B) a provider funded by the Legal Services Corporation; or

(C) a nonprofit that provides civil legal services to persons living at or below 200% of the federal poverty guidelines published annually by the United States Department of Health and Human Services;

(3) has applied for free legal services for the case through a provider listed in(e)(2) and was determined to be financially eligible but was declined representation; or

(4) does not have funds to afford payment of costs.

(f) *Requirement to Pay Costs Notwithstanding Statement.* The court may order the declarant to pay costs only as follows:

(1) *On Motion by the Clerk or a Party.* The clerk or any party may move to require the declarant to pay costs only if the motion contains sworn evidence, not merely on information or belief:

(A) that the Statement was materially false when it was made; or

(B) that because of changed circumstances, the Statement is no longer true in material respects.

(2) *On Motion by the Attorney Ad Litem for a Parent in Certain Cases.* An attorney ad litem appointed to represent a parent under Section 107.013,Family Code, may move to require the parent to pay costs only if the motion complies with (f)(1).

(3) *On Motion by the Court Reporter.* When the declarant requests the preparation of a reporter's record but cannot make arrangements to pay for it, the court reporter may move to require the declarant to prove the inability to afford costs.

(4) *On the Court's Own Motion.* Whenever evidence comes before the court that the declarant may be able to afford costs, or when an officer or professional must be appointed in the case, the court may require the declarant to prove the inability to afford costs.

(5) *Notice and Hearing.* The declarant may not be required to pay costs without an oral evidentiary hearing. The declarant must be given 10 days' notice of the hearing. Notice must either be in writing and served in accordance with Rule 21a or given in open court. At the hearing, the burden is on the declarant to prove the inability to afford costs.

(6) *Findings Required.* An order requiring the declarant to pay costs must be supported by detailed findings that the declarant can afford to pay costs.

(7) *Partial and Delayed Payment.* The court may order that the declarant pay the part of the costs the declarant can afford or that payment be made in installments. But the court must not delay the case if payment is made in installments.

(g) *Review of Trial Court Order.*

(1) *Only Declarant May Challenge; Motion.* Only the declarant may challenge an order issued by the trial court under this rule. The declarant may challenge the order by motion filed in the court of appeals with jurisdiction over an appeal from the judgment in the case. The declarant is not required to pay any filing fees related to the motion in the court of appeals.

(2) *Time for Filing; Extension.* The motion must be filed within 10 days after the trial court's order is signed. The court of appeals may extend the deadline by 15 days if the declarant demonstrates good cause for the extension in writing.

(3) *Record.* After a motion is filed, the court of appeals must promptly send notice to the trial court clerk and the court reporter requesting preparation of the record of all trial court proceedings on the declarant's claim of indigence. The court may set a deadline for filing the record. The record must be provided without charge.

(4) *Court of Appeals to Rule Promptly.* The court of appeals must rule on the motion at the earliest practicable time.

(h) *Judgment.* The judgment must not require the declarant to pay costs, and a provision in the judgment purporting to do so is void, unless the court has issued an order under (f), or the declarant has obtained a monetary recovery, and the court orders the recovery to be applied toward payment of costs.

Comment to 2016 Change: The rule has been rewritten. Access to the civil justice system cannot be denied because a person cannot afford to pay court costs. Whether a particular fee is a court cost is governed by this rule, Civil Practice and Remedies Code Section 31.007, and case law.

The issue is not merely whether a person can pay costs, but whether the person can afford to pay costs. A person may have sufficient cash on hand to pay filing fees, but the person cannot afford the fees if paying them would preclude the person from paying for basic essentials, like housing or food. Experience indicates that almost all filers described in (e)(1)-(3), and most filers described in (e)(4), cannot in fact afford to pay costs.

Because costs to access the system—filing fees, fees for issuance of process and notices, and fees for service and return—are kept relatively small, the expense involved in challenging a claim of inability to afford costs often exceeds the costs themselves. Thus, the rule does not allow the clerk or a party to challenge a litigant's claim of inability to afford costs without sworn evidence that the claim is false. The filing of a Statement of Inability to Afford Payment of Court Costs—which may either be sworn to before a notary or made under penalty of perjury, as permitted by Civil Practice and Remedies Code Section 132.001—is all that is needed to require the clerk to provide ordinary services without payment of fees and costs. But evidence may come to light that the claim was false when made. And the declarant's circumstances may change, so that the claim is no longer true. Importantly, costs may increase with the appointment of officers or professionals in the case, or when a reporter's record must be prepared. The reporter is always allowed to challenge a claim of inability to afford costs before incurring the substantial expense of record preparation. The trial court always retains discretion to require evidence of an inability to afford costs.

(Amended by Order Dec. 5, 1983, eff. April 1, 1984; July 15, 1987, eff. Jan. 1, 1988; Tex. Sup. Ct. Misc. Docket No. 16-9056, eff. Sept. 1, 2016; Tex. Sup. Ct. Misc. Docket No. 16-9122, eff. Sept. 1, 2016.)

[Statement of Inability to Afford Payment of Court Costs as provided in Tex. Sup. Ct. Misc. Docket No. 16-9122, eff. Sept. 1, 2016 and applies to any contest of, or challenge to, a claim of inability to afford payment of court costs that is pending on September 1, 2016.]

RULE 146. DEPOSIT FOR COSTS.

In lieu of a bond for costs, the party required to give the same may deposit with the clerk of court or the justice of the peace such sum as the court or justice from time to time may designate as sufficient to pay the accrued costs.

RULE 147. APPLIES TO ANY PARTY.

The foregoing rules as to security and rule for costs shall apply to any party who seeks a judgment against any other party.

(Amended by Order Dec. 5, 1983, eff. April 1, 1984.)

RULE 148. SECURED BY OTHER BOND.

No further security shall be required if the costs are secured by the provisions of an attachment or other bond filed by the party required to give security for costs.

RULE 149. EXECUTION FOR COSTS.

When costs have been adjudged against a party and are not paid, the clerk or justice of the court in which the suit was determined may issue execution, accompanied by an itemized bill of costs, against such party to be levied and collected as in other cases; and said officer, on demand of any party to whom any such costs are due, shall issue execution for costs at once. This rule shall not apply to executors, administrators or guardians in cases where costs are adjudged against the estate of a deceased person or of a ward. No execution shall issue in any case for costs until after judgment rendered therefor by the court.

SECTION 7.
ABATEMENT AND DISCONTINUANCE OF SUIT

RULE 150. DEATH OF PARTY.

Where the cause of action is one which survives, no suit shall abate because of the death of any party thereto before the verdict or decision of the court is rendered, but such suit may proceed to judgment as hereinafter provided.

RULE 151. DEATH OF PLAINTIFF.

If the plaintiff dies, the heirs, or the administrator or executor of such decedent may appear and upon suggestion of such death being entered of record in open court, may be made plaintiff, and the suit shall proceed in his or their name. If no such appearance and suggestion be made within a reasonable time after the death of the plaintiff, the clerk upon the application of defendant, his agent or attorney, shall issue a scire facias for the heirs or the administrator or executor of such decedent, requiring him to appear and prosecute such suit. After service of such scire facias, should such heir or administrator or executor fail to enter appearance within the time provided, the defendant may have the suit dismissed.

(Amended by Order Dec. 5, 1983, eff. April 1, 1984.)

RULE 152. DEATH OF DEFENDANT.

Where the defendant shall die, upon the suggestion of death being entered of record in open court, or upon petition of the plaintiff, the clerk shall issue a scire facias for the administrator or executor or heir requiring him to appear and defend the suit and upon the return of such service, the suit shall proceed against such administrator or executor or heir.

RULE 153. WHEN EXECUTOR, ETC., DIES.

When an executor or administrator shall be a party to any suit, whether as plaintiff or as defendant, and shall die or cease to be such executor or administrator, the suit may be continued by or against the person succeeding him in the administration, or by or against the heirs, upon like proceedings being had as provided in the two preceding rules, or the suit may be dismissed, as provided in Rule 151.

(Amended by Order Dec. 5, 1983, eff. April 1, 1984.)

RULE 154. REQUISITES OF SCIRE FACIAS.

The scire facias and returns thereon, provided for in this section, shall conform to the requisites of citations and the returns thereon, under the provisions of these rules.

RULE 155. SURVIVING PARTIES.

Where there are two or more plaintiffs or defendants, and one or more of them die, upon suggestion of such death being entered upon the record, the suit shall at the instance of either party proceed in the name of the surviving plaintiffs or against the surviving defendants, as the case may be.

RULE 156. DEATH AFTER VERDICT OR CLOSE OF EVIDENCE.

When a party in a jury case dies between verdict and judgment, or a party in a non-jury case dies after the evidence is closed and before judgment is pronounced, judgment shall be rendered and entered as if all parties were living.

(Amended by Order July 11, 1977, eff. Jan. 1, 1978.)

RULE 157. [REPEALED]

(Repealed by Order July 15, 1987, eff. Jan. 1, 1988.)

RULE 158. SUIT FOR THE USE OF ANOTHER.

When a plaintiff suing for the use of another shall die before verdict, the person for whose use such suit was brought, upon such death being suggested on the record in open court, may prosecute the suit in his own name, and shall be as responsible for costs as if he brought the suit.

RULE 159. SUIT FOR INJURIES RESULTING IN DEATH.

In cases arising under the provisions of the title relating to injuries resulting in death, the suit shall not abate by the death of either party pending the suit, but in such case, if the plaintiff dies, where there is only one plaintiff, some one or more of the parties entitled to the money recovered may be substituted and the suit prosecuted to judgment in the name of such party or parties, for the benefit of the person entitled, if the defendant dies, his executor, administrator or heir may be made a party, and the suit prosecuted to judgment.

RULE 160. DISSOLUTION OF CORPORATION.

The dissolution of a corporation shall not operate to abate any pending suit in which such corporation is a defendant, but such suit shall continue against such corporation and judgment shall be rendered as though the same were not dissolved.

RULE 161. WHERE SOME DEFENDANTS NOT SERVED.

When some of the several defendants in a suit are served with process in due time and others are not so served, the plaintiff may either dismiss as to those not so served and proceed against those who are, or he may take new process against those not served, or may obtain severance of the case as between those served and those not served, but no dismissal shall be allowed as to a principal obligor without also dismissing the parties secondarily liable except in cases provided by statute. No defendant against whom any suit may be so dismissed shall be thereby exonerated from any liability, but may at any time be proceeded against as if no such suit had been brought and no such dismissal ordered.

(Amended by Order Dec. 5, 1983, eff. April 1, 1984; April 24, 1984, eff. Oct. 1, 1984; July 15, 1987, eff. Jan. 1, 1988.)

RULE 162. DISMISSAL OR NON-SUIT.

At any time before the plaintiff has introduced all of his evidence other than rebuttal evidence, the plaintiff may dismiss a case, or take a non-suit, which shall be entered in the minutes. Notice of the dismissal or non-suit shall be served in accordance with Rule 21a on any party who has answered or has been served with process without necessity of court order.

Any dismissal pursuant to this rule shall not prejudice the right of an adverse party to be heard on a pending claim for affirmative relief or excuse the payment of all costs taxed by the clerk. A dismissal under this rule shall have no effect on any motion for sanctions, attorney's fees or other costs, pending at the time of dismissal, as determined by the court. Any dismissal pursuant to this rule which terminates the case shall authorize the clerk to tax court costs against dismissing party unless otherwise ordered by the court.

(Amended by Order Dec. 5, 1983, eff. April 1, 1984; July 15, 1987, eff. Jan. 1, 1988.)

RULE 163. DISMISSAL AS TO PARTIES SERVED, ETC.

When it will not prejudice another party, the plaintiff may dismiss his suit as to one or more of several parties who were served with process, or who have answered, but no such dismissal shall in any case, be allowed as to a principal obligor, except in the cases provided for by statute.

(Amended by Order Dec. 5, 1983, eff. April 1, 1984; July 15, 1987, eff. Jan. 1, 1988.)

RULE 164. [REPEALED]

(Repealed by Order July 15, 1987, eff. Jan. 1, 1988.)

RULE 165. ABANDONMENT.

A party who abandons any part of his claim or defense, as contained in the pleadings, may have that fact entered of record, so as to show that the matters therein were not tried.

RULE 165a. DISMISSAL FOR WANT OF PROSECUTION.

1. **Failure to Appear.** A case may be dismissed for want of prosecution on failure of any party seeking affirmative relief to appear for any hearing or trial of which the party had notice. Notice of the court's intention to dismiss and the date and place of the dismissal hearing shall be sent by the clerk to each attorney of record, and to each party not represented by an attorney and whose address is shown on the docket or in the papers on file, by posting same in the United States Postal Service. At the dismissal hearing, the court shall dismiss for want of prosecution unless there is good cause for the case to be maintained on the docket. If the court determines to maintain the case on the docket, it shall render a pretrial order assigning a trial date for the case and setting deadlines for the joining of new parties, all discovery, filing of all pleadings, the making of a response or supplemental responses to discovery and other pretrial matters. The case may be continued thereafter only for valid and compelling reasons specifically determined by court order. Notice of the signing of the order of dismissal shall be given as provided in Rule 306a. Failure to mail notices as required by this rule shall not affect any of the periods mentioned in Rule 306a except as provided in that rule.
2. **Non-compliance With Time Standards.** Any case not disposed of within time standards promulgated by the Supreme Court under its Administrative Rules may be placed on a dismissal docket.
3. **Reinstatement.** A motion to reinstate shall set forth the grounds therefor and be verified by the movant or his attorney. It shall be filed with the clerk within 30 days after the order of dismissal is signed or within the period provided by Rule 306a. A copy of the motion to reinstate shall be served on each attorney of record and each party not represented by an attorney whose address is shown on the docket or in the papers on file. The clerk shall deliver a copy of the motion to the judge, who shall set a hearing on the motion as soon as practicable. The court shall notify all parties or their attorneys of record of the date, time and place of the hearing.

   The court shall reinstate the case upon finding after a hearing that the failure of the party or his attorney was not intentional or the result of conscious indifference but was due to an accident or mistake or that the failure has been otherwise reasonably explained.

   In the event for any reason a motion for reinstatement is not decided by signed written order within seventy-five days after the judgment is signed, or, within such other time as may be allowed by Rule 306a, the motion shall be deemed overruled by operation of law. If a motion to reinstate is timely filed by any party, the trial court, regardless of whether an appeal has been perfected, has plenary power to reinstate the case until 30 days after all such timely filed motions are overruled, either by a written and signed order or by operation of law, whichever occurs first.
4. **Cumulative Remedies.** This dismissal and reinstatement procedure shall be cumulative of the rules and laws governing any other procedures available to the parties in such cases. The same reinstatement procedures and timetable are applicable to all dismissals for want of prosecution including cases which are dismissed pursuant to the court's inherent power, whether or not a motion to dismiss has been filed.

(Added Oct. 3, 1972, eff. Feb. 1, 1973. Amended July 22, 1975, eff. Jan. 1, 1976; Dec. 5, 1983; July 15, 1987, eff. Jan. 1, 1988.)

SECTION 8.
PRE-TRIAL PROCEDURE

RULE 166. PRETRIAL CONFERENCE.

In an appropriate action, to assist in the disposition of the case without undue expense or burden to the parties, the court may in its discretion direct the attorneys for the parties and the parties or their duly authorized agents to appear before it for a conference to consider:

(a) All pending dilatory pleas, motions and exceptions;

(b) The necessity or desirability of amendments to the pleadings;

(c) A discovery schedule;

(d) Requiring written statements of the parties' contentions;

(e) Contested issues of fact and simplification of the issues;

(f) The possibility of obtaining stipulations of fact;

(g) The identification of legal matters to be ruled on or decided by the court;

(h) The exchange of a list of direct fact witnesses, other than rebuttal or impeaching witnesses the necessity of whose testimony cannot reasonably be anticipated before the time of trial, who will be called to testify at trial, stating their address and telephone number, and the subject of the testimony of each such witness;

(i) The exchange of a list of expert witnesses who will be called to testify at trial, stating their address and telephone number, and the subject of the testimony and opinions that will be proffered by each expert witness;

(j) Agreed applicable propositions of law and contested issues of law;

(k) Proposed jury charge questions, instructions, and definitions for a jury case or proposed findings of fact and conclusions of law for a nonjury case;

(l) The marking and exchanging of all exhibits that any party may use at trial and stipulation to the authenticity and admissibility of exhibits to be used at trial;

(m) Written trial objections to the opposite party's exhibits, stating the basis for each objection;

(n) The advisability of a preliminary reference of issues to a master or auditor for findings to be used as evidence when the trial is to be by jury;

(o) The settlement of the case, and to aid such consideration, the court may encourage settlement;

(p) Such other matters as may aid in the disposition of the action.

The court shall make an order that recites the action taken at the pretrial conference, the amendments allowed to the pleadings, the time within which same may be filed, and the agreements made by the parties as to any of the matters considered, and which limits the issues for trial to those not disposed of by admissions, agreements of counsel, or rulings of the court; and such order when issued shall control the subsequent course of the action, unless modified at the trial to prevent manifest injustice. The court in its discretion may establish by rule a pretrial calendar on which actions may be placed for consideration as above provided and may either confine the calendar to jury actions or extend it to all actions.

Pretrial proceedings in multidistrict litigation may also be governed by Rules 11 and 13 of the Rules of Judicial Administration.

(Amended by Order July 26, 1960, eff. Jan. 1, 1961; April 24, 1990, eff. Sept. 1, 1990; Aug. 29, 2003, eff. Sept. 1, 2003.)

RULE 166a. SUMMARY JUDGMENT.

(a) **For Claimant.** A party seeking to recover upon a claim, counterclaim, or cross-claim or to obtain a declaratory judgment may, at any time after the adverse party has appeared or answered, move with or without supporting affidavits for a summary judgment in his favor upon all or any part thereof A summary judgment, interlocutory in character, may be rendered on the issue of liability alone although there is a genuine issue as to amount of damages.

(b) **For Defending Party.** A party against whom a claim, counterclaim, or cross-claim is asserted or a declaratory judgment is sought may, at any time, move with or without supporting affidavits for a summary judgment in his favor as to all or any part thereof.

(c) **Motion and Proceedings Thereon.** The motion for summary judgment shall state the specific grounds therefor. Except on leave of court, with notice to opposing counsel, the motion and any supporting affidavits shall be filed and served at least twenty-one days before the time specified for hearing. Except on leave of court, the adverse party, not later than seven days prior to the day of hearing may file and serve opposing affidavits or other written response. No oral testimony shall be received at the hearing. The judgment sought shall be rendered forthwith if (i) the deposition transcripts, interrogatory answers, and other discovery responses referenced or set forth in the motion or response, and (ii) the pleadings, admissions, affidavits, stipulations of the parties, and authenticated or certified public records, if any, on file at the time of the hearing, or filed thereafter and before judgment with permission of the court, show that, except as to the amount of damages, there is no genuine issue as to any material fact and the moving party is entitled to judgment as a matter of law on the issues expressly set out in the motion or in an answer or any other response. Issues not expressly presented to the trial court by written motion, answer or other response shall not be considered on appeal as grounds for reversal. A summary judgment may be based on uncontroverted testimonial evidence of an interested witness, or of an expert witness as to subject matter concerning which the trier of fact must be guided solely by the opinion testimony of experts, if the evidence is clear, positive and direct, otherwise credible and free from contradictions and inconsistencies, and could have been readily controverted.

(d) **Appendices, References and Other Use of Discovery Not Otherwise on File.** Discovery products not on file with the clerk may be used as summary judgment evidence if copies of the material, appendices containing the evidence, or a notice containing specific references to the discovery or specific references to other instruments, are filed and served on all parties together with a statement of intent to use the specified discovery as summary judgment proofs: (i) at least twenty-one days before the hearing if such proofs are to be used to support the summary judgment; or (ii) at least seven days before the hearing if such proofs are to be used to oppose the summary judgment.

(e) **Case Not Fully Adjudicated on Motion.** If summary judgment is not rendered upon the whole case or for all the relief asked and a trial is necessary, the judge may at the healing examine the pleadings and the evidence on file, interrogate counsel, ascertain what material fact issues exist and make an order specifying the facts that are established as a matter of law, and directing such further proceedings in the action as are just.

(f) **Form of Affidavits; Further Testimony.** Supporting and opposing affidavits shall be made on personal knowledge, shall set forth such facts as would be admissible in evidence, and shall show affirmatively that the affiant is competent to testify to the matters stated therein. Sworn or certified copies of all papers or parts thereof referred to in an affidavit shall be attached thereto or served therewith. The court may permit affidavits to be supplemented or opposed by depositions or by further affidavits. Defects in the form of affidavits or attachments will not be grounds for reversal unless specifically pointed out by objection by an opposing party with opportunity, but refusal, to amend.

(g) **When Affidavits Are Unavailable.** Should it appear from the affidavits of a party opposing the motion that he cannot for reasons stated present by affidavit facts essential to justify his opposition, the court may refuse the application for judgment or may order a continuance to permit affidavits to be obtained or depositions to be taken or discovery to be had or may make such other order as is just.

(h) **Affidavits Made in Bad Faith.** Should it appear to the satisfaction of the court at any time that any of the affidavits presented pursuant to this rule are presented in bad faith or solely for the purpose of delay, the court shall forthwith order the party employing them to pay to the other party the amount of the reasonable expenses which the filing of the affidavits caused him to incur, including reasonable attorney's fees, and any offending party or attorney may be adjudged guilty of contempt.

(i) **No-Evidence Motion.** After adequate time for discovery, a party without presenting summary judgment evidence may move for summary judgment on the ground that there is no evidence of one or more essential elements of a claim or defense on which an adverse party would have the burden of proof at trial. The motion must state the elements as to which there is no evidence. The court must grant the motion unless the respondent produces summary judgment evidence raising a genuine issue of material fact.

(Added Oct. 12, 1949. eff. March 1, 1950. Amended by Order Oct. 1, 1951, eff. March 1, 1952; July 20, 1966, eff. Jan. 1, 1967; July 21, 1970, eff. Jan. 1, 1971; July 11, 1977, eff. Jan. 1, 1978; June 10, 1980, eff. Jan. 1, 1981; Dec. 5, 1983, eff. April 1, 1984; July 15, 1987, eff. Jan. 1, 1988; April 24, 1990, eff. Sept. 1, 1990; April 16, 1997 and August 15, 1997, effective September 1, 1997.)

RULE 167. OFFER OF SETTLEMENT; AWARD OF LITIGATION COSTS.

167.1. Generally.

Certain litigation costs may be awarded against a party who rejects an offer made substantially in accordance with this rule to settle a claim for monetary damages—including a counterclaim, crossclaim, or third-party claim — except in:

(a) a class action;
(b) a shareholder's derivative action;
(c) an action by or against the State, a unit of state government, or a political subdivision of the State;
(d) an action brought under the Family Code;
(e) an action to collect workers' compensation benefits under title 5, subtitle A of the Labor Code; or
(f) an action filed in a justice of the peace court or small claims court.

167.2. Settlement Offer.

(a) *Defendant's declaration a prerequisite; deadline.* A settlement offer under this rule may not be made until a defendant — a party against whom a claim for monetary damages is made — files a declaration invoking this rule. When a defendant files such a declaration, an offer or offers may be made under this rule to settle only those claims by and against that defendant. The declaration must be filed no later than 45 days before the case is set for conventional trial on the merits.

(b) *Requirements of an offer.* A settlement offer must:

(1) be in writing;

(2) state that it is made under Rule 167 and Chapter 42 of the Texas Civil Practice and Remedies Code;

(3) identify the party or parties making the offer and the party or parties to whom the offer is made;

(4) state the terms by which all monetary claims — including any attorney fees, interest, and costs that would be recoverable up to the time of the offer — between the offeror or offerors on the one hand and the offeree or offerees on the other may be settled;

(5) state a deadline — no sooner than 14 days after the offer is served — by which the offer must be accepted;

(6) be served on all parties to whom the offer is made.

(c) *Conditions of offer.* An offer may be made subject to reasonable conditions, including the execution of appropriate releases, indemnities, and other documents. An offeree may object to a condition by written notice served on the offeror before the deadline stated in the offer. A condition to which no such objection is made is presumed to have been reasonable. Rejection of an offer made subject to a condition determined by the trial court to have been unreasonable cannot be the basis for an award of litigation costs under this rule.

(d) *Non-monetary and excepted claims not included.* An offer must not include non-monetary claims and other claims to which this rule does not apply.

(e) *Time limitations.* An offer may not be made:

(1) before a defendant's declaration is filed;

(2) within 60 days after the appearance in the case of the offeror or offeree, whichever is later;

(3) within 14 days before the date the case is set for a conventional trial on the merits, except that an offer may be made within that period if it is in response to, and within seven days of, a prior offer.

(f) *Successive offers.* A party may make an offer after having made or rejected a prior offer. A rejection of an offer is subject to imposition of litigation costs under this rule only if the offer is more favorable to the offeree than any prior offer.

167.3. Withdrawal, Acceptance, and Rejection of Offer.

(a) *Withdrawal of offer.* An offer can be withdrawn before it is accepted. Withdrawal is effective when written notice of the withdrawal is served on the offeree. Once an unaccepted offer has been withdrawn, it cannot be accepted or be the basis for awarding litigation costs under this rule.

(b) *Acceptance of offer.* An offer that has not been withdrawn can be accepted only by written notice served on the offeror by the deadline stated in the offer. When an offer is accepted, the offeror or offeree may file the offer and acceptance and may move the court to enforce the settlement.

(c) *Rejection of offer.* An offer that is not withdrawn or accepted is rejected. An offer may also be rejected by written notice served on the offeror by the deadline stated in the offer.

(d) *Objection to offer made before an offeror's joinder or designation of responsible third party.* An offer made before an offeror joins another party or designates a responsible third party may not be the basis for awarding litigation costs under this rule against an offeree who files an objection to the offer within 15 days after service of the offeror's pleading or designation.

167.4. Awarding Litigation Costs.

(a) *Generally.* If a settlement offer made under this rule is rejected, and the judgment to be awarded on the monetary claims covered by the offer is significantly less favorable to the offeree than was the offer, the court must award the offeror litigation costs against the offeree from the time the offer was rejected to the time of judgment.

(b) *"Significantly less favorable" defined.* A judgment award on monetary claims is significantly less favorable than an offer to settle those claims if:

(1) the offeree is a claimant and the judgment would be less than 80 percent of the offer; or

(2) the offeree is a defendant and the judgment would be more than 120 percent of the offer.

(c) *Litigation costs.* Litigation costs are the expenditures actually made and the obligations actually incurred — directly in relation to the claims covered by a settlement offer under this rule — for the following:

(1) court costs;

(2) reasonable deposition costs, in cases filed on or after September1, 2011;

(3) reasonable fees for not more than two testifying expert witnesses; and

(3) reasonable fees for not more than two testifying witnesses; and

(4) reasonable attorney fees.

(d) *Limits on litigation costs.*

(1) In cases filed before September 1, 2011, the litigation costs that may be awarded under this rule must not exceed the following amount:

(A) the sum of the noneconomic damages, the exemplary or additional damages, and one-half of the economic damages to be awarded to the claimant in the judgment; minus

(B) the amount of any statutory or contractual liens in connection with the occurrences or incidents giving rise to the claim.

(2) In cases filed on or after September I, 2011, the litigation costs that may be awarded to any party under this rule must not exceed the total amount that the claimant recovers or would recover before adding an award of litigation costs under this rule in favor of the claimant or subtracting as an offset an award of litigation costs under this rule in favor of the defendant.

(e) *No double recovery permitted.* A party who is entitled to recover attorney fees and costs under another law may not recover those same attorney fees and costs as litigation costs under this rule.

(f) *Limitation on attorney fees and costs recovered by a party against whom litigation costs are awarded.* A party against whom litigation costs are awarded may not recover attorney fees and costs under another law incurred after the date the party rejected the settlement offer made the basis of the award.

(g) *Litigation costs to be awarded to defendant as a setoff.* Litigation costs awarded to a defendant must be made a setoff to the claimant's judgment against the defendant.

167.5. Procedures.

(a) *Modification of time limits.* On motion, and for good cause shown, the court may — by written order made before commencement of trial on the merits — modify the time limits for filing a declaration under Rule 167.2(a) or for making an offer.

(b) *Discovery permitted.* On motion, and for good cause shown, a party against whom litigation costs are to be awarded may conduct discovery to ascertain the reasonableness of the costs requested. If the court determines the costs to be reasonable, it must order the party requesting discovery to pay all attorney fees and expenses incurred by other parties in responding to such discovery.

(c) *Hearing required.* The court must, upon request, conduct a hearing on a request for an award of litigation costs, at which the affected parties may present evidence.

167.6. Evidence Not Admissible.

Evidence relating to an offer made under this rule is not admissible except for purposes of enforcing a settlement agreement or obtaining litigation costs. The provisions of this rule may not be made known to the jury by any means.

167.7. Other Settlement Offers Not Affected.

This rule does not apply to any offer made in a mediation or arbitration proceeding. A settlement offer not made in compliance with this rule, or a settlement offer not made under this rule, or made in an action to which this rule does not apply, cannot be the basis for awarding litigation costs under this rule as to any party. This rule does not limit or affect a party's right to make a settlement offer that does not comply with this rule, or in an action to which this rule does not apply.

(Adopted Oct. 9, 2003, eff. Jan. 1, 2004, only in cases filed on or after effective date. Amended by Order Aug. 31, 2011, eff. Sept. 1, 2011; Sept. 9, 2011, eff. Sept. 9, 2011.)

Rule 168. Permission to Appeal.

On a party's motion or on its own initiative, a trial court may permit an appeal from an interlocutory order that is not otherwise appealable, as provided by statute. Permission must be stated in the order to be appealed. An order previously issued may be amended to include such permission. The permission must identify the controlling question of law as to which there is a substantial ground for difference of opinion, and must state why an immediate appeal may materially advance the ultimate termination of the litigation.

(Adopted by Order Aug. 31, 2011, eff. Sept. 1, 2011. Amended by Order Sept. 9, 2011, eff. Sept. 9, 2011.)

Comment to 2011 change: Rule 168 is a new rule, added to implement amendments to section 51.0 14(d)-(f) of the Texas Civil Practice and Remedies Code. Rule 168 applies only to cases filed on or after September 1, 2011. Rule 168 clarifies that the trial court's permission to appeal should be included in the order to be appealed rather than in a separate order. Rule of Appellate Procedure 28.3 sets out the corollary requirements for permissive appeals in the courts of appeals.

RULE 166B to 169. [REPEALED]

(Repealed by Order Aug. 5, 1998, and Nov. 9, 1998, eff. Jan. 1, 1999.)

Rule 169. Expedited Actions.

(a) *Application.*

(1) The expedited actions process in this rule applies to a suit in which all claimants, other than counter-claimants, affirmatively plead that they seek only monetary relief aggregating $100,000 or less, including damages of any kind, penalties, costs, expenses, pre-judgment interest, and attorney fees.

(2) The expedited actions process does not apply to a suit in which a party has filed a claim governed by the Family Code, the Property Code, the Tax Code, or Chapter 74 of the Civil Practice & Remedies Code.

(b) *Recovery.* In no event may a party who prosecutes a suit under this rule recover a judgment in excess of $ 100,000, excluding post-judgment interest.

(c) *Removal from Process.*

(1) A court must remove a suit from the expedited actions process:

(A) on motion and a showing of good cause by any party; or

(B) if any claimant, other than a counter-claimant, files a pleading or an amended or supplemental pleading that seeks any relief other than the monetary relief allowed by (a)(l).

(2) A pleading, amended pleading, or supplemental pleading that removes a suit from the expedited actions process may not be filed without leave of court unless it is filed before the earlier of 30 days after the discovery period is closed or 30 days before the date set for trial. Leave to amend may be granted only if good cause for filing the pleading outweighs any prejudice to an opposing party.

(3) If a suit is removed from the expedited actions process, the court must reopen discovery under Rule 190.2(c).

(d) *Expedited Actions Process.*

(1) Discovery. Discovery is governed by Rule 190.2.

(2) Trial Setting; Continuances. On any party's request, the court must set the case for a trial date that is within 90 days after the discovery period in Rule 190.2(b)(l) ends. The court may continue the case twice, not to exceed a total of 60 days.

(3) Time Limits for Trial. Each side is allowed no more than eight hours to complete jury selection, opening statements, presentation of evidence, examination and cross-examination of witnesses, and closing arguments. On motion and a showing of good cause by any party, the court may extend the time limit to no more than twelve hours per side.

(A) The term "side" has the same definition set out in Rule 233.

(B) Time spent on objections, bench conferences, bills of exception, and challenges for cause to a juror under Rule 228 are not included in the time limit.

(4) Alternative Dispute Resolution.

(A) Unless the parties have agreed not to engage in alternative dispute resolution, the court may refer the case to an alternative dispute resolution procedure once, and the procedure must:

(i) not exceed a half-day in duration, excluding scheduling time;

(ii) not exceed a total cost of twice the amount of applicable civil filing fees; and

(iii) be completed no later than 60 days before the initial trial setting.

(B) The court must consider objections to the referral unless prohibited by statute.

(C) The parties may agree to engage in alternative dispute resolution other than that provided for in (A).

(5) Expert Testimony. Unless requested by the party sponsoring the expert, a party may only challenge the admissibility of expert testimony as an objection to summary judgment evidence under Rule 166a or during the trial on the merits. This paragraph does not apply to a motion to strike for late designation.

(Adopted by Order Nov. 13, 2012, eff. March 1, 2013. Amended by Order Feb 12, 2013, eff. March 1, 2013. (Applies to cases filed on or after March 1, 2013, except those filed in justice court.))

Comments to 2013 change:

1. Rule 169 is a new rule implementing section 22.004(h) of the Texas Government Code, which was added in 2011 and calls for rules to promote the prompt, efficient, and cost-effective resolution of civil actions when the amount in controversy does not exceed $100,000.

2. The expedited actions process created by Rule 169 is mandatory; any suit that falls within the definition of 169(a)(l) is subject to the provisions of the rule.

3. In determining whether there is good cause to remove the case from the process or extend the time limit for trial, the court should consider factors such as whether the damages sought by multiple claimants against the same defendant exceed in the aggregate the relief allowed under 169(a)(l), whether a defendant has filed a compulsory counterclaim in good faith that seeks relief other than that allowed under 169(a)(l), the number of parties and witnesses, the complexity of the legal and factual issues, and whether an interpreter is necessary.

4. Rule 169(b) specifies that a party who prosecutes a suit under this rule cannot recover a judgment in excess of $100,000. Thus, the rule in *Greenhalgh v. Service Lloyds Ins. Co.*, 787 S.W.2d 938 (Tex. 1990), does not apply if a jury awards damages in excess of $100,000 to the party. The limitation in 169(b) does not apply to a counter-claimant that seeks relief other than that allowed under 5. The discovery limitations for expedited actions are set out in Rule 190.2, which is also amended to implement section 22.004(h) of the Texas Government Code.

RULE 170. [REPEALED]

(Repealed by Order Dec. 5, 1983, eff. April 1, 1984.)

RULE 171. MASTER IN CHANCERY.

The court may, in exceptional cases, for good cause appoint a master in chancery, who shall be a citizen of this State, and not an attorney for either party to the action, nor related to either party, who shall perform all of the duties required of him by the court, and shall be under orders of the court, and have such power as the master of chancery has in a court of equity.

The order of reference to the master may specify or limit his powers, and may direct him to report only upon particular issues, or to do or perform particular acts, or to receive and report evidence only and may fix the time and place for beginning and closing the hearings, and for the filing of the master's report. Subject to the limitations and specifications stated in the order, the master has and shall exercise the power to regulate all proceedings in every hearing before him and to do all acts and take all measures necessary or proper for the efficient performance of his duties under the order. He may require the production before him of evidence upon all matters embraced in the reference, including the production of books, papers, vouchers, documents and other writings applicable thereto. He may rule upon the admissibility of evidence, unless otherwise directed by the order of reference and has the authority to put witnesses on oath, and may, himself, examine them, and may call the parties to the action and examine them upon oath. When a party so requests, the master shall make a record of the evidence offered and excluded in the same manner as provided for a court sitting in the trial of a case.

The clerk of the court shall forthwith furnish the master with a copy of the order of reference.

The parties may procure the attendance of witnesses before the master by the issuance and service of process as provided by law and these rules.

The court may confirm, modify, correct, reject, reverse or recommit the report, after it is filed, as the court may deem proper and necessary in the particular circumstances of the case. The court shall award reasonable compensation to such master to be taxed as costs of suit.

(Amended by Order Sept. 20, 1941, eff. Dec. 31, 1941.)

RULE 172. AUDIT.

When an investigation of accounts or examination of vouchers appears necessary for the purpose of justice between the parties to any suit, the court shall appoint an auditor or auditors to state the accounts between the parties and to make report thereof to the court as soon as possible. The auditor shall verify his report by his affidavit stating that he has carefully examined the state of the account between the parties, and that his report contains a true statement thereof, so far as the same has come within his knowledge. Exceptions to such report or of any item thereof must be filed within 30 days of the filing of such report. The court shall award reasonable compensation to such auditor to be taxed as costs of suit.

(Amended by Order July 15, 1987, eff. Jan. 1, 1988.)

RULE 173. GUARDIAN AD LITEM.

173.1. Appointment Governed by Statute or Other Rules.

This rule does not apply to an appointment of a guardian ad litem governed by statute or other rules.

173.2. Appointment of Guardian Ad Litem.

(a) ***When Appointment Required or Prohibited.*** The court must appoint a guardian ad litem for a party represented by a next friend or guardian only if:

(1) the next friend or guardian appears to the court to have an interest adverse to the party, or

(2) the parties agree.

(b) ***Appointment of the Same Person for Different Parties.*** The court must appoint the same guardian ad litem for similarly situated parties unless the court finds that the appointment of different guardians ad litem is necessary.

173.3. Procedure.

(a) ***Motion Permitted But Not Required.*** The court may appoint a guardian ad litem on the motion of any party or on its own initiative.

(b) ***Written Order Required.*** An appointment must be made by written order.

(c) ***Objection.*** Any party may object to the appointment of a guardian ad litem.

173.4. Role of Guardian Ad Litem.

(a) ***Court Officer and Advisor.*** A guardian ad litem acts as an officer and advisor to the court.

(b) ***Determination of Adverse Interest.*** A guardian ad litem must determine and advise the court whether a party's next friend or guardian has an interest adverse to the party.

(c) ***When Settlement Proposed.*** When an offer has been made to settle the claim of a party represented by a next friend or guardian, a guardian ad litem has the limited duty to determine and advise the court whether the settlement is in the party's best interest.

(d) ***Participation in Litigation Limited.*** A guardian ad litem:

- **(1)** may participate in mediation or a similar proceeding to attempt to reach a settlement;
- **(2)** must participate in any proceeding before the court whose purpose is to determine whether a party's next friend or guardian has an interest adverse to the party, or whether a settlement of the party's claim is in the party's best interest;
- **(3)** must not participate in discovery, trial, or any other part of the litigation unless:
  - **(A)** further participation is necessary to protect the party's interest that is adverse to the next friend's or guardian's, and
  - **(B)** the participation is directed by the court in a written order stating sufficient reasons.

173.5. Communications Privileged.

Communications between the guardian ad litem and the party, the next friend or guardian, or their attorney are privileged as if the guardian ad litem were the attorney for the party.

173.6. Compensation.

(a) ***Amount.*** If a guardian ad litem requests compensation, he or she may be reimbursed for reasonable and necessary expenses incurred and may be paid a reasonable hourly fee for necessary services performed.

(b) ***Procedure.*** At the conclusion of the appointment, a guardian ad litem may file an application for compensation. The application must be verified and must detail the basis for the compensation requested. Unless all parties agree to the application, the court must conduct an evidentiary hearing to determine the total amount of fees and expenses that are reasonable and necessary. In making this determination, the court must not consider compensation as a percentage of any judgment or settlement.

(c) ***Taxation as Costs.*** The court may tax a guardian ad litem's compensation as costs of court.

(d) ***Other Benefit Prohibited.*** A guardian ad litem may not receive, directly or indirectly, anything of value in consideration of the appointment other than as provided by this rule.

173.7. Review.

(a) ***Right of Appeal.*** Any party may seek mandamus review of an order appointing a guardian ad litem or directing a guardian ad litem's participation in the litigation. Any party and a guardian ad litem may appeal an order awarding the guardian ad litem compensation.

(b) ***Severance.*** On motion of the guardian ad litem or any party, the court must sever any order awarding a guardian ad litem compensation to create a final, appealable order.

(c) ***No Effect on Finality of Settlement or Judgment.*** Appellate proceedings to review an order pertaining to a guardian ad litem do not affect the finality of a settlement or judgment.

(Amended by Order June 16, 1943, eff. Dec. 31, 1943; Jan. 27, 2005, eff. Feb. 1, 2005 in all pending cases.)

Comment - 2005

1. The rule is completely revised.

2. This rule does not apply when the procedures and purposes for appointment of guardians ad litem (as well as attorneys ad litem) are prescribed by statutes, such as the Family Code and the Probate Code, or by other rules, such as the Parental Notification Rules.

3. The rule contemplates that a guardian ad litem will be appointed when a party's next friend or guardian appears to have an interest adverse to the party because of the division of settlement proceeds. In those situations, the responsibility of the guardian ad litem as prescribed by the rule is very limited, and no reason exists for the guardian ad litem to participate in the conduct of the litigation in any other way or to review the discovery or the litigation file except to the limited extent that it may bear on the division of settlement proceeds. *See Jocson v. Crabb*, 133 S.W.3d 268 (Tex. 2004)(per curiam). A guardian ad litem may, of course,

choose to review the file or attend proceedings when it is unnecessary, but the guardian ad litem may not be compensated for unnecessary expenses or services.

4. Only in extraordinary circumstances does the rule contemplate that a guardian ad litem will have a broader role. Even then, the role is limited to determining whether a party's next friend or guardian has an interest adverse to the party that should be considered by the court under Rule 44. In no event may a guardian ad litem supervise or supplant the next friend or undertake to represent the party while serving as guardian ad litem.

5. As an officer and advisor to the court, a guardian ad litem should have qualified judicial immunity.

6. Though an officer and adviser to the court, a guardian ad litem must not have *ex parte* communications with the court. *See* TEX. CODE JUD. CONDUCT, Canon 3.

7. Because the role of guardian ad litem is limited in all but extraordinary situations, and any risk that might result from services performed is also limited, compensation, if any is sought, should ordinarily be limited.

8. A violation of this rule is subject to appropriate sanction.

RULE 174. CONSOLIDATION; SEPARATE TRIALS.

(a) *Consolidation.* When actions involving a common question of law or fact are pending before the court, it may order a joint hearing or trial of any or all the matters in issue in the actions; it may order all the actions consolidated; and it may make such orders concerning proceedings therein as may tend to avoid unnecessary costs or delay.

(b) *Separate Trials.* The court in furtherance of convenience or to avoid prejudice may order a separate trial of any claim, cross-claim, counterclaim, or third-party claim, or of any separate issue or of any number of claims, cross-claims, counterclaims, third-party claims, or issues.

RULE 175. ISSUE OF LAW AND DILATORY PLEAS.

When a case is called for trial in which there has been no pretrial hearing as provided by Rule 166, the issues of law arising on the pleadings, all pleas in abatement and other dilatory pleas remaining undisposed of shall be determined; and it shall be no cause for postponement of a trial of the issues of law that a party is not prepared to try the issues of fact.

SECTION 9.
EVIDENCE AND DISCOVERY

EXPLANATORY STATEMENT ACCOMPANYING THE 1999 AMENDMENTS TO THE RULES OF CIVIL PROCEDURE GOVERNING DISCOVERY.

The rules pertaining to discovery have been substantively revised and reorganized to clarify and streamline discovery procedures and to reduce costs and delays associated with discovery practice. The notes and comments appended to the rules, unlike most other notes and comments in the Rules of Civil Procedure, are intended to inform their construction and application by both courts and practitioners.

Discovery in civil cases is founded on the principle that justice is best served when litigants may obtain information not in their possession to prosecute and defend claims. Discovery provides access to that information, but at a price. Recent years' experience has shown that discovery may be misused to deny justice to parties by driving up the costs of litigation until it is unaffordable and stalling resolution of cases. As any litigant on a budget knows, the benefits to be gained by discovery in a particular case must be weighed against its costs. The rules of procedure must provide both adequate access to information and effective means of curbing discovery when appropriate to preserve litigation as a viable, affordable, and expeditious dispute resolution mechanism.

These revisions recognize the importance of discovery as well as the necessity for reasonable limits. The scope of discovery, always broad, is unchanged. All the forms of discovery under the prior rules are retained, and a new one—disclosure—is added. Disclosure is not required unless requested and thus does not burden cases in which it is not sought. When requested, it provides ready access to basic information without objection. At the same time, the necessity of a discovery control plan in each case, whether by rule or by order, is intended to focus courts and parties on both the need for discovery and its costs in each case. The Level 1 plan allows a party seeking recovery of no more than $60,000 to insist that discovery be minimal. The Level 2 plan will provide adequate discovery in most cases, and Level 3 is available for cases needing special attention. No single set of rules can address so diverse and changing a practice as discovery, and thus the rules maintain the ability of parties by agreement and courts by order to tailor discovery to individual cases.

Presentation of objections and assertions of privilege are streamlined under these rules. A party who objects to only part of a discovery request must usually comply with the rest of the request. Assertions of privilege are not to be made prophylactically against the threat of waiver, but only when information is actually withheld. Documents produced in discovery are now presumed to be authentic for use against the party producing them, thus avoiding the cost of proving authentication when there is no dispute. Procedures for oral depositions are revised to encourage focused examination by imposing time limits and to discourage colloquy between counsel.

An important aspect of these revisions has been the regrouping of provisions in a more logical sequence and the elimination of archaic and confusing language.

A.
EVIDENCE

RULE 176. SUBPOENAS

176.1. Form.

Every subpoena must be issued in the name of "The State of Texas" and must:

(a) state the style of the suit and its cause number;

(b) state the court in which the suit is pending;

(c) state the date on which the subpoena is issued;

(d) identify the person to whom the subpoena is directed;

(e) state the time, place, and nature of the action required by the person to whom the subpoena is directed, as provided in Rule 176.2;

(f) identify the party at whose instance the subpoena is issued, and the party's attorney of record, if any;

(g) state the text of Rule 176.8(a); and

(h) be signed by the person issuing the subpoena.

176.2. Required Actions.

A subpoena must command the person to whom it is directed to do either or both of the following:

(a) attend and give testimony at a deposition, hearing, or trial;

(b) produce and permit inspection and copying of designated documents or tangible things in the possession, custody, or control of that person.

176.3. Limitations.

(a) **Range**. A person may not be required by subpoena to appear or produce documents or other things in a county that is more than 150 miles from where the person resides or is served. However, a person whose appearance or production at a deposition may be compelled by notice alone under Rules 199.3 or 200.2 may be required to appear and produce documents or other things at any location permitted under Rules 199.2(b)(2).

(b) **Use for discovery.** A subpoena may not be used for discovery to an extent, in a manner, or at a time other than as provided by the rules governing discovery.

176.4. Who May Issue.

A subpoena may be issued by:

(a) the clerk of the appropriate district, county, or justice court, who must provide the party requesting the subpoena with an original and a copy for each witness to be completed by the party;

(b) an attorney authorized to practice in the State of Texas, as an officer of the court; or

(c) an officer authorized to take depositions in this State, who must issue the subpoena immediately on a request accompanied by a notice to take a deposition under Rules 199 or 200, or a notice under Rule 205.3, and who may also serve the notice with the subpoena.

176.5. Service.

(a) **Manner of service.** A subpoena may be served at any place within the State of Texas by any sheriff or constable of the State of Texas, or any person who is not a party and is 18 years of age or older. A subpoena must be served by delivering a copy to the witness and tendering to that person any fees required by law. If the witness is a party and is represented by an attorney of record in the proceeding, the subpoena may be served on the witness's attorney of record.

(b) **Proof of service.** Proof of service must be made by filing either:

(1) the witness's signed written memorandum attached to the subpoena showing that the witness accepted the subpoena; or

(2) a statement by the person who made the service stating the date, time, and manner of service, and the name of the person served.

176.6. Response.

(a) **Compliance required**. Except as provided in this subdivision, a person served with a subpoena must comply with the command stated therein unless discharged by the court or by the party summoning such witness. A person commanded to appear and give testimony must remain at the place of deposition hearing, or trial from day to day until discharged by the court or by the party summoning the witness.

(b) **Organizations**. If a subpoena commanding testimony is directed to a corporation, partnership, association, governmental agency, or other organization, and the matters on which examination is requested are described with reasonable particularity, the organization must designate one or more persons to testify on its behalf as to matters known or reasonably available to the organization.

(c) **Production of documents or tangible things**. A person commanded to produce documents or tangible things need not appear in person at the time and place of production unless the person is also commanded to attend and give testimony, either in the same subpoena or a separate one. A person must produce documents as they are kept in the usual course of business or must organize and label them to correspond with the categories in the demand. A person may withhold material or information claimed to be privileged but must comply with Rule 193.3. A nonparty's production of a document authenticates the document for use against the nonparty to the same extent as a party's production of a document is authenticated for use against the party under Rule 193.7.

(d) **Objections**. A person commanded to produce and permit inspection or copying of designated documents and things may serve on the party requesting issuance of the subpoena—before the time specified for compliance—written objections to producing any or all of the designated materials. A person need not comply with the part of a subpoena to which objection is made as provided in this paragraph unless ordered to do so by the court. The party requesting the subpoena may move for such an order at any time after an objection is made.

(e) **Protective orders**. A person commanded to appear at a deposition, hearing, or trial, or to produce and permit inspection and copying of designated documents and things, and any other person affected by the subpoena, may move for a protective order under Rule 192.6(b)—before the time specified for compliance—either in the court in which the action is pending or in a district court in the county where the subpoena was served. The person must serve the motion on all parties in accordance with Rule 21a. A person need not comply with the part of a subpoena from which protection is sought under this paragraph unless ordered to do so by the court. The party requesting the subpoena may seek such an order at any time after the motion for protection is filed.

(f) **Trial subpoenas**. A person commanded to attend and give testimony, or to produce documents or things, at a hearing or trial, may object or move for protective order before the court at the time and place specified for compliance, rather than under paragraphs (d) and (e).

176.7. Protection of Person from Undue Burden and Expense.

A party causing a subpoena to issue must take reasonable steps to avoid imposing undue burden or expense on the person served. In ruling on objections or motions for protection, the court must provide a person served with a subpoena an adequate time for compliance, protection from disclosure of privileged material or information, and protection from undue burden or expense. The court may impose reasonable conditions on compliance with a subpoena, including compensating the witness for undue hardship.

176.8. Enforcement of Subpoena.

(a) **Contempt**. Failure by any person without adequate excuse to obey a subpoena served upon that person may be deemed a contempt of the court from which the subpoena is issued or a district court in the county in which the subpoena is served, and may be punished by fine or confinement, or both.

(b) **Proof of payment of fees required for fine or attachment**. A fine may not be imposed, nor a person served with a subpoena attached, for failure to comply with a subpoena without proof by affidavit of the party requesting the subpoena or the party's attorney of record that all fees due the witness by law were paid or tendered.

(Added Aug. 5, 1998. Amended Nov. 9, 1998, eff. Jan. 1, 1999.)

Comments to 1999 change:

1. This rule combines the former rules governing subpoenas for trial and discovery. When a subpoena is used for discovery, the protections from undue burden and expense apply, just as with any discovery.

2. Rule 176.3(b) prohibits the use of a subpoena to circumvent the discovery rules. Thus, for example, a deposition subpoena to a party is subject to the procedures of Rules 196, 199, and 200, and a deposition subpoena to a nonparty is subject to the procedures of Rule 205.

[No change in Rules 180-185.]

RULES 177, 178, and 179. [REPEALED]

(Repealed by Order Aug. 5, 1998, and Nov. 9, 1998, eff. Jan. 1, 1999.)

RULE 180. REFUSAL TO TESTIFY.

Any witness refusing to give evidence may be committed to jail, there to remain without bail until such witness shall consent to give evidence.

RULE 181. PARTY AS WITNESS.

Either party to a suit may examine the opposing party as a witness, and shall have the same process to compel his attendance as in the case of any other witness.

RULE 182 and 182a. [REPEALED]

(Repealed by Order July 15, 1987, eff. Jan. 1, 1988.)

RULE 183. INTERPRETERS.

The court may appoint an interpreter of its own selection and may fix the interpreter's reasonable compensation. The compensation shall be paid out of funds provided by law or by one or more of the parties as the court may direct, and may be taxed ultimately as costs, in the discretion of the court.

(Amended by Order April 24, 1990, eff. Sept. 1, 1990.)

RULE 184 and 184a. [REPEALED]

(Repealed by Order April 24, 1990, eff. Sept. 1, 1990.)

RULE 185. SUIT ON ACCOUNT.

When any action or defense is founded upon an open account or other claim for goods, wares and merchandise, including any claim for a liquidated money demand based upon written contract or founded on business dealings between the parties, or is for personal service rendered, or labor done or labor or materials furnished, on which a systematic record has been kept, and is supported by the affidavit of the party, his agent or attorney taken before some officer authorized to administer oaths, to the effect that such claim is, within the knowledge of affiant, just and true, that it is due, and that all just and lawful offsets, payments and credits have been allowed, the same shall be taken as prima facie evidence thereof, unless the party resisting such claim shall file a written denial, under oath. A party resisting such a sworn claim shall comply with the rules of pleading as are required in any other kind of suit, provided, however, that if he does not timely file a written denial, under oath, he shall not be permitted to deny the claim, or any item therein, as the case may be. No particularization or description of the nature of the component parts of the account or claim is necessary unless the trial court sustains special exceptions to the pleadings.

(Amended by Order Oct. 12, 1949, eff. March 1, 1950; July 21, 1970, eff. Jan. 1, 1971; Dec. 5, 1983, eff. April 1, 1984.)

B.
DISCOVERY

RULES 186, 187, 188, and 189. [REPEALED]

(Rules 186 and 189 repealed Dec. 5, 1983, eff. April 1, 1984; Rules 187 and 188 repealed Aug. 5, 1998, and Nov. 9, 1998, eff. Jan. 1, 1999.)

RULE 190. DISCOVERY LIMITATIONS

190.1. Discovery Control Plan Required.

Every case must be governed by a discovery control plan as provided in this Rule. A plaintiff must allege in the first numbered paragraph of the original petition whether discovery is intended to be conducted under Level 1, 2, or 3 of this Rule.

190.2. Discovery Control Plan—Expedited Actions and Divorces Involving $50,000 or Less (Level 1).

(a) **Application**. This subdivision applies to:
   (1) any suit that is governed by the expedited actions process in Rule 169; and
   (2) unless the parties agree that Rule 190.3 should apply or the court orders a discovery control plan under Rule 190.4, any suit for divorce not involving children in which a party pleads that the value of the marital estate is more than zero but not more than $50,000.

(b) **Limitations**. Discovery is subject to the limitations provided elsewhere in these rules and to the following additional limitations:

(1) **Discovery Period**. All discovery must be conducted during the discovery period, which begins when the suit is filed and continues until 180 days after the date the first request for discovery of any kind is served on a party.

(2) **Total Time for Oral Depositions**. Each party may have no more than six hours in total to examine and cross-examine all witnesses in oral depositions. The parties may agree to expand this limit up to ten hours in total, but not more except by court order. The court may modify the deposition hours so that no party is given unfair advantage.

(3) **Interrogatories**. Any party may serve on any other party no more than 15 written interrogatories, excluding interrogatories asking a party only to identify or authenticate specific documents. Each discrete subpart of an interrogatory is considered a separate interrogatory.

(4) **Requests for Production**. Any party may serve on any other party no more than 15 written requests for production. Each discrete subpart of a request for production is considered a separate request for production.

(5) **Requests for Admissions**. Any party may serve on any other party no more than 15 written requests for admissions. Each discrete subpart of a request for admission is considered a separate request for admission.

(6) **Requests for Disclosure**. In addition to the content subject to disclosure under Rule 194.2. a party may request disclosure of all documents, electronic information, and tangible items that the disclosing party has in its possession, custody, or control and may use to support its claims or defenses. A request for disclosure made pursuant to this paragraph is not considered a request for production.

(c) **Reopening Discovery**. If a suit is removed from the expedited actions process in Rule 169 or. in a divorce, the filing of a pleading renders this subdivision no longer applicable, the discovery period reopens, and discovery must be completed within the limitations provided in Rules 190.3 or 190.4, whichever is applicable. Any person previously deposed may be redeposed. On motion of any party, the court should continue the trial date if necessary to permit completion of discovery.

(Amended by Order Nov. 13, 2012, eff. March 1, 2013; Feb 12, 2013, eff. March 1, 2013 (Applies to cases filed on or after March 1, 2013, except those filed in justice court.).)

190.3. Discovery Control Plan—By Rule (Level 2).

(a) **Application**. Unless a suit is governed by a discovery control plan under Rules 190.2 or 190.4 discovery must be conducted in accordance with this subdivision.

(b) **Limitations**. Discovery is subject to the limitations provided elsewhere in these rules and to the following additional limitations:

(1) **Discovery period**. All discovery must be conducted during the discovery period, which begins when suit is filed and continues until:

(A) 30 days before the date set for trial, in cases under the Family Code; or

(B) in other cases, the earlier of

(i) 30 days before the date set for trial, or

(ii) nine months after the earlier of the date of the first oral deposition or the due date of the first response to written discovery.

(2) **Total time for oral depositions**. Each side may have no more than 50 hours in oral depositions to examine and cross-examine parties on the opposing side, experts designated by those parties, and persons who are subject to those parties' control. "Side" refers to all the litigants with generally common interests in the litigation. If one side designates more than two experts, the opposing side may have an additional six hours of total deposition time for each additional expert designated. The court may modify the deposition hours and must do so when a side or party would be given unfair advantage.

(3) **Interrogatories**. Any party may serve on any other party no more than 25 written interrogatories, excluding interrogatories asking a party only to identify or authenticate specific documents. Each discrete subpart of an interrogatory is considered a separate interrogatory.

190.4. Discovery Control Plan—By Order (Level 3).

(a) **Application**. The court must, on a party's motion, and may, on its own initiative, order that discovery be conducted in accordance with a discovery control plan tailored to the circumstances of the specific suit. The parties may submit an agreed order to the court for its consideration. The court should act on a party's motion or agreed order under this subdivision as promptly as reasonably possible.

(b) **Limitations**. The discovery control plan ordered by the court may address any issue concerning discovery or the matters listed in Rule 166, and may change any limitation on the time for or amount of discovery set forth in these rules. The discovery limitations of Rule 190.2, if applicable, or otherwise of Rule 190.3 apply unless specifically changed in the discovery control plan ordered by the court. The plan must include:

(1) a date for trial or for a conference to determine a trial setting;

(2) a discovery period during which either all discovery must be conducted or all discovery requests must be sent, for the entire case or an appropriate phase of it;

(3) appropriate limits on the amount of discovery; and

(4) deadlines for joining additional parties, amending or supplementing pleadings, and designating expert witnesses.

190.5. Modification of Discovery Control Plan.

The court may modify a discovery control plan at any time and must do so when the interest of justice requires. Unless a suit is governed by the expedited actions process in Rule 169, the court must allow additional discovery:

(a) related to new, amended or supplemental pleadings, or new information disclosed in a discovery response or in an amended or supplemental response, if:

  (1) the pleadings or responses were made after the deadline for completion of discovery or so nearly before that deadline that an adverse party does not have an adequate opportunity to conduct discovery related to the new matters, and

  (2) the adverse party would be unfairly prejudiced without such additional discovery;

(b) regarding matters that have changed materially after the discovery cutoff if trial is set or postponed so that the trial date is more than three months after the discovery period ends.

(Amended by Order Nov. 13, 2012, eff. March 1, 2013; Feb 12, 2013, eff. March 1, 2013.)

Comment to 2013 change: Rule 190 is amended to implement section 22.004(h) of the Texas Government Code, which calls for rules to promote the prompt, efficient, and cost-effective resolution of civil actions when the amount in controversy does not exceed $100,000. Rule 190.2 now applies to expedited actions, as defined by Rule 169. Rule 190.2 continues to apply to divorces not involving children in which the value of the marital estate is not more than $50,000, which are otherwise exempt from the expedited actions process. Amended Rule 190.2(b) ends the discovery period 180 days after the date the first discovery request is served; imposes a fifteen limit maximum on interrogatories, requests for production, and requests for admission; and allows for additional disclosures. Although expedited actions are not subject to mandatory additional discovery under amended Rule 190.5, the court may still allow additional discovery if the conditions of Rule 190(a) are met.

190.6. Certain Types of Discovery Excepted.

This rule's limitations on discovery do not apply to or include discovery conducted under Rule 202 ("Depositions Before Suit or to Investigate Claims"), or Rule 621a ("Discovery and Enforcement of Judgment"). But Rule 202 cannot be used to circumvent the limitations of this rule.

(Added Aug. 5, 1998, and amended Nov. 9, 1998 and Dec. 31, 1998, to apply to all cases filed on or after Jan. 1, 1999, but a court may adopt an appropriate discovery control plan in previously filed cases.)

Comments to 1999 change:

1. This rule establishes three tiers of discovery plans and requires that every case be in one at all times. A case is in Level 1 if it is pleaded by the plaintiff so as to invoke application of Level 1, as provided by Rule 190.2(a). If a plaintiff does not or cannot plead the case in compliance with Rule 190.2(a) so as to invoke the application of Level 1, the case is automatically in Level 2. A case remains in Level 1 or Level 2, as determined by the pleadings, unless and until it is moved to Level 3. To be in Level 3, the court must order a specific plan for the case, either on a party's motion or on the court's own initiative. The plan may be one agreed to by the parties and submitted as an agreed order. A Level 3 plan may simply adopt Level 1 or Level 2 restrictions. Separate Level 3 plans for phases of the case may be appropriate. The initial pleading required by Rule 190.1 is merely to notify the court and other parties of the plaintiff's intention; it does not determine the applicable discovery level or bind the court or other parties. Thus, a plaintiff's failure to state in the initial pleading that the case should be in Level 1, as provided in Rule 190.1, does not alone make the case subject to Level 2 because the discovery level is determined by Rule 190.2. Likewise, a plaintiff's statement in the initial paragraph of the petition that the case is to be governed by Level 3 does not make Level 3 applicable, as a case can be in Level 3 only by court order. A plaintiff's failure to plead as required by Rule 190.1 is subject to special exception.

2. Rule 190.2 does not apply to suits for injunctive relief or divorces involving children. The requirement of an affirmative pleading of limited relief (*e.g.*: "Plaintiff affirmatively pleads that he seeks only monetary relief aggregating $50,000 or less, excluding costs, pre-judgment interest and attorneys' fees") does not conflict with other pleading requirements, such as Rule 47 and TEX. REV. CIV. STAT. ANN. art. 4590i, § 5.01. In a suit to which Rule 190.2 applies, the relief awarded cannot exceed the limitations of Level 1 because the purpose of the rule, unlike Rule 47, is to bind the pleader to a maximum claim. To this extent, the rule in *Greenhalgh v. Service Lloyds Ins. Co.*, 787 S.W.2d 938 (Tex. 1990), does not apply.

3. "Discrete subparts" of interrogatories are counted as single interrogatories, but not every separate factual inquiry is a discrete subpart. *See* FED. R. CIV. P. 33(a). While not susceptible of precise definition, *see Braden v. Downey*, 811 S.W.2d 922, 927-928 (Tex. 1991), a "discrete subpart" is, in general, one that calls for information that is not logically or factually related to the primary interrogatory. The number of sets of interrogatories is no longer limited to two.

4. As other rules make clear, unless otherwise ordered or agreed, parties seeking discovery must serve requests sufficiently far in advance of the end of the discovery period that the deadline for responding will be within the discovery period. The court may order a deadline for sending discovery requests in lieu of or in addition to a deadline for completing discovery.

5. Use of forms of discovery other than depositions and interrogatories, such as requests for disclosure, admissions, or production of documents, are not restricted in Levels 1 and 2. But depositions on written questions cannot be used to circumvent the limits on interrogatories.

6. The concept of "side" in Rule 190.3(b)(2) borrows from Rule 233, which governs the allocation of peremptory strikes, and from FED. R. CIV. P. 30(a)(2). In most cases there are only two sides—plaintiffs and defendants. In complex cases, however, there may be more than two sides, such as when defendants have sued third parties not named by plaintiffs, or when defendants have sued each other. As an example, if P1 and P2 sue D1, D2, and D3, and D1 sues D2 and D3, Ps would together be entitled to depose Ds and others permitted by the rule (*i.e.*, Ds' experts and persons subject to Ds' control) for 50 hours, and Ds would together be entitled to depose Ps and others for 50 hours. D1 would also be entitled to depose D2 and D3 and others for 50 hours on matters in controversy among them, and D2 and D3 would together be entitled to depose D1 and others for 50 hours.

7. Any matter listed in Rule 166 may be addressed in an order issued under Rule 190.4. A pretrial order under Rule 166 may be used in individual cases regardless of the discovery level.

8. For purposes of defining discovery periods, "trial" does not include summary judgment.

RULE 191. MODIFYING DISCOVERY PROCEDURES AND LIMITATIONS; CONFERENCE REQUIREMENT; SIGNING DISCLOSURES, DISCOVERY REQUESTS, RESPONSES, AND OBJECTIONS; FILING REQUIREMENTS.

191.1. Modification of Procedures.

Except where specifically prohibited, the procedures and limitations set forth in the rules pertaining to discovery may be modified in any suit by the agreement of the parties or by court order for good cause. An agreement of the parties is enforceable if it complies with Rule 11 or, as it affects an oral deposition, if it is made a part of the record of the deposition.

191.2. Conference.

Parties and their attorneys are expected to cooperate in discovery and to make any agreements reasonably necessary for the efficient disposition of the case. All discovery motions or requests for hearings relating to discovery must contain a certificate by the party filing the motion or request that a reasonable effort has been made to resolve the dispute without the necessity of court intervention and the effort failed.

191.3. Signing of Disclosures, Discovery Requests, Notices, Responses, and Objections.

(a) **Signature required**. Every disclosure, discovery request, notice, response, and objection must be signed:

(1) by an attorney, if the party is represented by an attorney, and must show the attorney's State Bar of Texas identification number, address, telephone number, and fax number, if any; or

(2) by the party, if the party is not represented by an attorney, and must show the party's address, telephone number, and fax number, if any.

(b) **Effect of signature on disclosure**. The signature of an attorney or party on a disclosure constitutes a certification that to the best of the signer's knowledge, information, and belief, formed after a reasonable inquiry, the disclosure is complete and correct as of the time it is made.

(c) **Effect of signature of discovery request, notice, response, or objection**. The signature of an attorney or party on a discovery request, notice, response, or objection constitutes a certification that to the best of the signer's knowledge, information, and belief, formed after a reasonable inquiry, the request, notice, response, or objection:

(1) is consistent with the rules of civil procedure and these discovery rules and warranted by existing law or a good faith argument for the extension, modification, or reversal of existing law;

(2) has a good faith factual basis;

(3) is not interposed for any improper purpose, such as to harass or to cause unnecessary delay or needless increase in the cost of litigation; and

(4) is not unreasonable or unduly burdensome or expensive, given the needs of the case, the discovery already had in the case, the amount in controversy, and the importance of the issues at stake in the litigation.

(d) **Effect of failure to sign**. If a request, notice, response, or objection is not signed, it must be stricken unless it is signed promptly after the omission is called to the attention of the party making the request, notice, response, or objection. A party is not required to take any action with respect to a request or notice that is not signed.

(e) **Sanctions**. If the certification is false without substantial justification, the court may, upon motion or its own initiative, impose on the person who made the certification, or the party on whose behalf the request, notice, response, or objection was made, or both, an appropriate sanction as for a frivolous pleading or motion under Chapter 10 of the Civil Practice and Remedies Code.

191.4. Filing of Discovery Materials.

(a) **Discovery materials not to be filed**. The following discovery materials must not be filed:

(1) discovery requests, deposition notices, and subpoenas required to be served only on parties;

(2) responses and objections to discovery requests and deposition notices, regardless on whom the requests or notices were served;

(3) documents and tangible things produced in discovery; and

(4) statements prepared in compliance with Rule 193.3 (b) or (d).

(b) **Discovery materials to be filed**. The following discovery materials must be filed:

(1) discovery requests, deposition notices, and subpoenas required to be served on nonparties;

(2) motions and responses to motions pertaining to discovery matters; and

(3) agreements concerning discovery matters, to the extent necessary to comply with Rule 11.

(c) **Exceptions**. Notwithstanding paragraph (a)—

(1) the court may order discovery materials to be filed;

(2) a person may file discovery materials in support of or in opposition to a motion or for other use in a court proceeding; and

(3) a person may file discovery materials necessary for a proceeding in an appellate court.

(d) **Retention requirement for persons**. Any person required to serve discovery materials not required to be filed must retain the original or exact copy of the materials during the pendency of the case and any related appellate proceedings begun within six months after judgment is signed, unless otherwise provided by the trial court.

(e) **Retention requirement for courts**. The clerk of the court shall retain and dispose of deposition transcripts and depositions upon written questions as directed by the Supreme Court. [See Misc. Docket No. 05-9025, Order Relating to Retention and Disposition of Deposition Transcripts in Civil Cases, Jan. 27, 2005, eff. June 1, 2005.]

191.5. Service of Discovery Materials.

Every disclosure, discovery request, notice, response, and objection required to be served on a party or person must be served on all parties of record.

(Added Aug. 5, 1998, and amended Nov. 9, 1998, eff. Jan. 1, 1999, except that Rules 191.3 and 191.4 apply only to discovery conducted on or after that date.)

Comments to 1999 change:

1. Rule 191.1 preserves the ability of parties by agreement and trial courts by order to adapt discovery to different circumstances. That ability is broad but not unbounded. Parties cannot merely by agreement modify a court order without the court's concurrence. Trial courts cannot simply "opt out" of these rules by form orders or approve or order a discovery control plan that does not contain the matters specified in Rule 190.4, but trial courts may use standard or form orders for providing discovery plans, scheduling, and other pretrial matters. In individual instances, courts may order, or parties may agree, to use discovery methods other than those prescribed in these rules if appropriate. Because the general rule is stated here, it is not repeated in each context in which it applies. Thus, for example, parties can agree to enlarge or shorten the time permitted for a deposition and to change the manner in which a deposition is conducted, notwithstanding Rule 199.5, although parties could not agree to be abusive toward a witness.

2. Rule 191.2 expressly states the obligation of parties and their attorneys to cooperate in conducting discovery.

3. The requirement that discovery requests, notices, responses, and objections be signed also applies to documents used to satisfy the purposes of such instruments. An example is a statement that privileged material or information has been withheld, which may be separate from a response to the discovery request but is nevertheless part of the response.

RULE 192. PERMISSIBLE DISCOVERY: FORMS AND SCOPE; WORK PRODUCT; PROTECTIVE ORDERS; DEFINITIONS.

192.1. Forms of Discovery.

Permissible forms of discovery are:

(a) requests for disclosure;

(b) requests for production and inspection of documents and tangible things;

(c) requests and motions for entry upon and examination of real property;

(d) interrogatories to a party;

(e) requests for admission;

(f) oral or written depositions; and

(g) motions for mental or physical examinations.

192.2. Sequence of Discovery.

The permissible forms of discovery may be combined in the same document and may be taken in any order or sequence.

192.3. Scope of Discovery.

(a) **Generally**. In general, a party may obtain discovery regarding any matter that is not privileged and is relevant to the subject matter of the pending action, whether it relates to the claim or defense of the party seeking discovery or the claim or defense of any other party. It is not a ground for objection that the information sought will be inadmissible at trial if the information sought appears reasonably calculated to lead to the discovery of admissible evidence.

(b) **Documents and tangible things**. A party may obtain discovery of the existence, description, nature, custody, condition, location, and contents of documents and tangible things (including papers, books, accounts, drawings, graphs, charts, photographs, electronic or videotape recordings, data, and data compilations) that constitute or contain matters relevant to the subject matter of the action. A person is required to produce a document or tangible thing that is within the person's possession, custody, or control.

(c) **Persons with knowledge of relevant facts**. A party may obtain discovery of the name, address, and telephone number of persons having knowledge of relevant facts, and a brief statement of each identified person's connection with the case. A person has knowledge of relevant facts when that person has or may have knowledge of any discoverable matter. The person need not have admissible information or personal knowledge of the facts. An expert is "a person with knowledge of relevant facts" only if that knowledge was obtained first-hand or if it was not obtained in preparation for trial or in anticipation of litigation.

(d) **Trial witnesses**. A party may obtain discovery of the name, address, and telephone number of any person who is expected to be called to testify at trial. This paragraph does not apply to rebuttal or impeaching witnesses the necessity of whose testimony cannot reasonably be anticipated before trial.

(e) **Testifying and consulting experts**. The identity, mental impressions, and opinions of a consulting expert whose mental impressions and opinions have not been reviewed by a testifying expert are not discoverable. A party may discover the following information regarding a testifying expert or regarding a consulting expert whose mental impressions or opinions have been reviewed by a testifying expert:

   (1) the expert's name, address, and telephone number;

   (2) the subject matter on which a testifying expert will testify;

   (3) the facts known by the expert that relate to or form the basis of the expert's mental impressions and opinions formed or made in connection with the case in which the discovery is sought, regardless of when and how the factual information was acquired;

   (4) the expert's mental impressions and opinions formed or made in connection with the case in which discovery is sought, and any methods used to derive them;

   (5) any bias of the witness;

   (6) all documents, tangible things, reports, models, or data compilations that have been provided to, reviewed by, or prepared by or for the expert in anticipation of a testifying expert's testimony;

   (7) the expert's current resume and bibliography.

(f) **Indemnity and insuring agreements**. Except as otherwise provided by law, a party may obtain discovery of the existence and contents of any indemnity or insurance agreement under which any person may be liable to satisfy part or all of a judgment rendered in the action or to indemnify or reimburse for payments made to satisfy the judgment. Information concerning the indemnity or insurance agreement is not by reason of disclosure admissible in evidence at trial.

(g) **Settlement agreements**. A party may obtain discovery of the existence and contents of any relevant portions of a settlement agreement. Information concerning a settlement agreement is not by reason of disclosure admissible in evidence at trial.

(h) **Statements of persons with knowledge of relevant facts**. A party may obtain discovery of the statement of any person with knowledge of relevant facts—a "witness statement"—regardless of when the statement was made. A witness statement is

   (1) a written statement signed or otherwise adopted or approved in writing by the person making it, or

   (2) a stenographic, mechanical, electrical, or other type of recording of a witness's oral statement, or any substantially verbatim transcription of such a recording. Notes taken during a conversation or interview with a witness are not a witness statement. Any person may obtain, upon written request, his or her own statement concerning the lawsuit, which is in the possession custody or control of any party.

(i) **Potential parties**. A party may obtain discovery of the name, address, and telephone number of any potential party.

(j) **Contentions**. A party may obtain discovery of any other party's legal contentions and the factual bases for those contentions.

192.4. Limitations on Scope of Discovery.

The discovery methods permitted by these rules should be limited by the court if it determines, on motion or on its own initiative and on reasonable notice, that:

(a) the discovery sought is unreasonably cumulative or duplicative, or is obtainable from some other source that is more convenient, less burdensome, or less expensive; or

(b) the burden or expense of the proposed discovery outweighs its likely benefit, taking into account the needs of the case, the amount in controversy, the parties' resources, the importance of the issues at stake in the litigation, and the importance of the proposed discovery in resolving the issues.

192.5. Work Product.

(a) **Work product defined**. Work product comprises:

(1) material prepared or mental impressions developed in anticipation of litigation or for trial by or for a party or a party's representatives, including the party's attorneys, consultants, sureties, indemnitors, insurers, employees, or agents; or

(2) a communication made in anticipation of litigation or for trial between a party and the party's representatives or among a party's representatives, including the party's attorneys, consultants, sureties, indemnitors, insurers, employees, or agents.

(b) **Protection of work product**.

(1) **Protection of core work product-attorney mental processes**. Core work product—the work product of an attorney or an attorney's representative that contains the attorney's or the attorney's representative's mental impressions, opinions, conclusions, or legal theories—is not discoverable.

(2) **Protection of other work product**. Any other work product is discoverable only upon a showing that the party seeking discovery has substantial need of the materials in the preparation of the party's case and that the party is unable without undue hardship to obtain the substantial equivalent of the material by other means.

(3) **Incidental disclosure of attorney mental processes**. It is not a violation of subparagraph (1) if disclosure ordered pursuant to subparagraph (2) incidentally discloses by inference attorney mental processes otherwise protected under subparagraph (1).

(4) **Limiting disclosure of mental processes**. If a court orders discovery of work product pursuant to subparagraph (2), the court must—insofar as possible—protect against disclosure of the mental impressions, opinions, conclusions, or legal theories not otherwise discoverable.

(c) **Exceptions**. Even if made or prepared in anticipation of litigation or for trial, the following is not work product protected from discovery:

(1) information discoverable under Rule 192.3 concerning experts, trial witnesses, witness statements, and contentions;

(2) trial exhibits ordered disclosed under Rule 166 or Rule 190.4;

(3) the name, address, and telephone number of any potential party or any person with knowledge of relevant facts;

(4) any photograph or electronic image of underlying facts (e.g., a photograph of the accident scene) or a photograph or electronic image of any sort that a party intends to offer into evidence; and

(5) any work product created under circumstances within an exception to the attorney-client privilege in Rule 503 (d) of the Rules of Evidence.

(d) **Privilege**. For purposes of these rules, an assertion that material or information is work product is an assertion of privilege.

192.6. Protective Orders.

(a) **Motion**. A person from whom discovery is sought, and any other person affected by the discovery request, may move within the time permitted for response to the discovery request for an order protecting that person from the discovery sought. A person should not move for protection when an objection to written discovery or an assertion of privilege is appropriate, but a motion does not waive the objection or assertion of privilege. If a person seeks protection regarding the time or place of discovery, the person must state a reasonable time and place for discovery with which the person will comply. A person must comply with a request to the extent protection is not sought unless it is unreasonable under the circumstances to do so before obtaining a ruling on the motion.

(b) **Order**. To protect the movant from undue burden, unnecessary expense, harassment, annoyance, or invasion of personal, constitutional, or property rights, the court may make any order in the interest of justice and may—among other things—order that:

(1) the requested discovery not be sought in whole or in part;

(2) the extent or subject matter of discovery be limited;

(3) the discovery not be undertaken at the time or place specified;

(4) the discovery be undertaken only by such method or upon such terms and conditions or at the time and place directed by the court;

(5) the results of discovery be sealed or otherwise protected, subject to the provisions of Rule 76a.

192.7. Definitions.

As used in these rules—

(a) Written discovery means requests for disclosure, requests for production and inspection of documents and tangible things, requests for entry onto property, interrogatories, and requests for admission.

(b) Possession, custody, or control of an item means that the person either has physical possession of the item or has a right to possession of the item that is equal or superior to the person who has physical possession of the item.

(c) A testifying expert is an expert who may be called to testify as an expert witness at trial.

(d) A consulting expert is an expert who has been consulted, retained, or specially employed by a party in anticipation of litigation or in-preparation for trial, but who is not a testifying expert.

(Added Aug. 5, 1998, and amended Nov. 9, 1998, eff. Jan. 1, 1999.)

Comments to 1999 change:

1. While the scope of discovery is quite broad, it is nevertheless confined by the subject matter of the case and reasonable expectations of obtaining information that will aid resolution of the dispute. The rule must be read and applied in that context. *See In re American Optical Corp.*, ___ S.W.2d ___ (Tex. 1998) (per curiam); *K-Mart v. Sanderson*, 937 S.W.2d 429 (Tex. 1996) (per curiam); *Dillard Dept. Stores v. Hall*, 909 S.W.2d 491 (Tex. 1995) (per curiam); *Texaco, Inc. v. Sanderson*, 898 S.W.2d 813 (Tex. 1995) (per curiam); *Loftin v. Martin*, 776 S.W.2d 145, 148 (Tex. 1989).

2. The definition of documents and tangible things has been revised to clarify that things relevant to the subject matter of the action are within the scope of discovery regardless of their form.

3. Rule 192.3(c) makes discoverable a "brief statement of each identified person's connection with the case." This provision does not contemplate a narrative statement of the facts the person knows, but at most a few words describing the person's identity as relevant to the lawsuit. For instance: "treating physician," "eyewitness," "chief financial officer," "director," "plaintiff's mother and eyewitness to accident." The rule is intended to be consistent with *Axelson v. McIlhany*, 798 S.W.2d 550 (Tex. 1990).

4. Rule 192.3(g) does not suggest that settlement agreements in other cases are relevant or irrelevant.

5. Rule 192.3(j) makes a party's legal and factual contentions discoverable but does not require more than a basic statement of those contentions and does not require a marshaling of evidence.

6. The sections in former Rule 166b concerning land and medical records are not included in this rule. They remain within the scope of discovery and are discussed in other rules.

7. The court's power to limit discovery based on the needs and circumstances of the case is expressly stated in Rule 192.4. The provision is taken from Rule 26(b)(2) of the Federal Rules of Civil Procedure. Courts should limit discovery under this rule only to prevent unwarranted delay and expense as stated more fully in the rule. A court abuses its discretion in unreasonably restricting a party's access to information through discovery.

8. Work product is defined for the first time, and its exceptions stated. Work product replaces the "attorney work product" and "party communication" discovery exemptions from former Rule 166b.

9. Elimination of the "witness statement" exemption does not render all witness statements automatically discoverable but subjects them to the same rules concerning the scope of discovery and privileges applicable to other documents or tangible things.

RULE 193. WRITTEN DISCOVERY: RESPONSE; OBJECTION; ASSERTION OF PRIVILEGE; SUPPLEMENTATION AND AMENDMENT; FAILURE TO TIMELY RESPOND; PRESUMPTION OF AUTHENTICITY.

193.1. Responding to Written Discovery; Duty to Make Complete Response.

A party must respond to written discovery in writing within the time provided by court order or these rules. When responding to written discovery, a party must make a complete response, based on all information reasonably available to the responding party or its attorney at the time the response is made. The responding party's answers, objections, and other responses must be preceded by the request to which they apply.

193.2. Objecting to Written Discovery.

(a) **Form and time for objections**. A party must make any objection to written discovery in writing—either in the response or in a separate document—within the time for response. The party must state specifically the legal or factual basis for the objection and the extent to which the party is refusing to comply with the request.

(b) **Duty to respond when partially objecting objection to time or place of production**. A party must comply with as much of the request to which the party has made no objection unless it is unreasonable under the circumstances to do so before obtaining a ruling on the objection. If the responding party objects to the requested time or place of production, the responding party must state a reasonable time and place for complying with the request and must comply at that time and place without further request or order.

(c) **Good faith basis for objection**. A party may object to written discovery only if a good faith factual and legal basis for the objection exists at the time the objection is made.

(d) **Amendment**. An objection or response to written discovery may be amended or supplemented to state an objection or basis that, at the time the objection or response initially was made, either was inapplicable or was unknown after reasonable inquiry.

(e) **Waiver of objection**. An objection that is not made within the time required, or that is obscured by numerous unfounded objections, is waived unless the court excuses the waiver for good cause shown.

(f) **No objection to preserve privilege**. A party should not object to a request for written discovery on the grounds that it calls for production of material or information that is privileged but should instead comply with Rule 193.3. A party who objects to production of privileged material or information does not waive the privilege but must comply with Rule 193.3 when the error is pointed out.

193.3. Asserting a Privilege.

A party may preserve a privilege from written discovery in accordance with this subdivision.

(a) **Withholding privileged material or information**. A party who claims that material or information responsive to written discovery is privileged may withhold the privileged material or information from the response. The party must state—in the response (or an amended or supplemental response) or in a separate document—that:

(1) information or material responsive to the request has been withheld,

(2) the request to which the information or material relates, and

(3) the privilege or privileges asserted.

(b) **Description of withheld material or information**. After receiving a response indicating that material or information has been withheld from production, the party seeking discovery may serve a written request that the withholding party identify the information and material withheld. Within 15 days of service of that request, the withholding party must serve a response that:

(1) describes the information or materials withheld that, without revealing the privileged information itself or otherwise waiving the privilege, enables other parties to assess the applicability of the privilege, and

(2) asserts a specific privilege for each item or group of items withheld.

(c) **Exemption**. Without complying with paragraphs (a) and (b), a party may withhold a privileged communication to or from a lawyer or lawyer's representative or a privileged document of a lawyer or lawyer's representative—

(1) created or made from the point at which a party consults a lawyer with a view to obtaining professional legal services from the lawyer in the prosecution or defense of a specific claim in the litigation in which discovery is requested, and

(2) concerning the litigation in which the discovery is requested.

(d) **Privilege not waived by production**. A party who produces material or information without intending to waive a claim of privilege does not waive that claim under these rules or the Rules of Evidence if—within ten days or a shorter time ordered by the court, after the producing party actually discovers that such production was made—the producing party amends the response, identifying the material or information produced and stating the privilege asserted. If the producing party thus amends the response to assert a privilege, the requesting party must promptly return the specified material or information and any copies pending any ruling by the court denying the privilege.

193.4. Hearing and Ruling on Objections and Assertions of Privilege.

(a) **Hearing**. Any party may at any reasonable time request a hearing on an objection or claim of privilege asserted under this rule. The party making the objection or asserting the privilege must present any evidence necessary to support the objection or privilege. The evidence may be testimony presented at the hearing or affidavits served at least seven days before the hearing or at such other reasonable time as the court permits. If the court determines that an in camera review of some or all of the requested discovery is necessary, that material or information must be segregated and produced to the court in a sealed wrapper within a reasonable time following the hearing.

(b) **Ruling**. To the extent the court sustains the objection or claim of privilege, the responding party has no further duty to respond to that request. To the extent the court overrules the objection or claim of privilege, the responding party must produce the requested material or information within 30 days after the court's ruling or at such time as the court orders. A party need not request a ruling on that party's own objection or assertion of privilege to preserve the objection or privilege.

(c) **Use of material or information withheld under claim of privilege**. A party may not use—at any hearing or trial—material or information withheld from discovery under a claim of privilege, including a claim sustained by the court, without timely amending or supplementing the party's response to that discovery.

193.5. Amending or Supplementing Responses to Written Discovery.

(a) **Duty to amend or supplement**. If a party learns that the party's response to written discovery was incomplete or incorrect when made, or, although complete and correct when made, is no longer complete and correct, the party must amend or supplement the response:

(1) to the extent that the written discovery sought the identification of persons with knowledge of relevant facts, trial witnesses, or expert witnesses, and

(2) to the extent that the written discovery sought other information, unless the additional or corrective information has been made known to the other parties in writing, on the record at a deposition, or through other discovery responses.

(b) **Time and form of amended or supplemental response**. An amended or supplemental response must be made reasonably promptly after the party discovers the necessity for such a response. Except as otherwise provided by these rules, it is presumed that an amended or supplemental response made less than 30 days before trial was not made reasonably promptly. An amended or supplemental response must be in the same form as the initial response and must be verified by the party if the original response was required to be verified by the party, but the failure to comply with this requirement does not make the amended or supplemental response untimely unless the party making the response refuses to correct the defect within a reasonable time after it is pointed out.

193.6. Failing to Timely Respond—Effect on Trial.

(a) **Exclusion of evidence and exceptions**. A party who fails to make, amend, or supplement a discovery response in a timely manner may not introduce in evidence the material or information that was not timely disclosed, or offer the testimony of a witness (other than a named party) who was not timely identified, unless the court finds that:

(1) there was good cause for the failure to timely make, amend, or supplement the discovery response; or

(2) the failure to timely make, amend, or supplement the discovery response will not unfairly surprise or unfairly prejudice the other parties.

(b) **Burden of establishing exception**. The burden of establishing good cause or the lack of unfair surprise or unfair prejudice is on the party seeking to introduce the evidence or call the witness. A finding of good cause or of the lack of unfair surprise or unfair prejudice must be supported by the record.

(c) **Continuance.** Even if the party seeking to introduce the evidence or call the witness fails to carry the burden under paragraph (b), the court may grant a continuance or temporarily postpone the trial to allow a response to be made, amended, or supplemented, and to allow opposing parties to conduct discovery regarding any new information presented by that response.

193.7. Production of Documents Self-Authenticating.

A party's production of a document in response to written discovery authenticates the document for use against that party in any pretrial proceeding or at trial unless—within ten days or a longer or shorter time ordered by the court, after the producing party has actual notice that the document will be used—the party objects to the authenticity of the document, or any part of it, stating the specific basis for objection. An objection must be either on the record or in writing and must have a good faith factual and legal basis. An objection made to the authenticity of only part of a document does not affect the authenticity of the remainder. If objection is made, the party attempting to use the document should be given a reasonable opportunity to establish its authenticity.

(Added Aug. 5, 1998, and amended Nov. 9, 1998 and Dec. 31, 1998, eff. Jan. 1, 1999, except that a response to a discovery request, an objection to a discovery request, an assertion of privilege, or an amendment or supplementation to a discovery response made before that date need not comply with the new rule.)

Comments to 1999 change:

1. This rule imposes a duty upon parties to make a complete response to written discovery based upon all information reasonably available, subject to objections and privileges.

2. An objection to written discovery does not excuse the responding party from complying with the request to the extent no objection is made. But a party may object to a request for "all documents relevant to the lawsuit" as overly broad and not in compliance with the rule requiring specific requests for documents and refuse to comply with it entirely. *See Loftin v. Martin*, 776 S.W.2d 145 (Tex. 1989). A party may also object to a request for a litigation file on the ground that it is overly broad and may assert that on its face the request seeks only materials protected by privilege. *See National Union Fire Ins. Co. v. Valdez*, 863 S.W.2d 458 (Tex. 1993). A party who objects to production of documents from a remote time period should produce documents from a more recent period unless that production would be burdensome and duplicative should the objection be overruled.

3. This rule governs the presentation of all privileges including work product. It dispenses with objections to written discovery requests on the basis that responsive information or materials are protected by a specific privilege from discovery. Instead, the rule requires parties to state that information or materials have been withheld and to identify the privilege upon which the party relies. The statement should not be made prophylactically, but only when specific information and materials have been withheld. The party must amend or supplement the statement if additional privileged information or material is found subsequent to the initial response. Thus, when large numbers of documents are being produced, a party may amend the initial response when documents are found as to which the party claims privilege. A party need not state that material created by or for lawyers for the litigation has been withheld as it can be assumed that such material will be withheld from virtually any request on the grounds of attorney-client privilege or work product. However, the rule does not prohibit a party from specifically requesting the material or information if the party has a good faith basis for asserting that it is discoverable. An example would be material or information described by Rule 503(d)(1) of the Rules of Evidence.

4. Rule 193.3(d) is a new provision that allows a party to assert a claim of privilege to material or information produced inadvertently without intending to waive the privilege. The provision is commonly used in complex cases to reduce costs and risks in large document productions. The focus is on the intent to waive the privilege, not the intent to produce the material or infor-

mation. A party who fails to diligently screen documents before producing them does not waive a claim of privilege. This rule is thus broader than TEX. R. EVID. 511 and overturns *Granada Corp. v. First Court of Appeals*, 844 S.W.2d 223 (Tex. 1992), to the extent the two conflict. The ten-day period (which may be shortened by the court) allowed for an amended response does not run from the production of the material or information but from the party's first awareness of the mistake. To avoid complications at trial, a party may identify prior to trial the documents intended to be offered, thereby triggering the obligation to assert any overlooked privilege under this rule. A trial court may also order this procedure.

5. This rule imposes no duty to supplement or amend deposition testimony. The only duty to supplement deposition testimony is provided in Rule 195.6.

6. Any party can request a hearing in which the court will resolve issues brought up in objections or withholding statements. The party seeking to avoid discovery has the burden of proving the objection or privilege.

7. The self-authenticating provision is new. Authentication is, of course, but a condition precedent to admissibility and does not establish admissibility. *See* TEX. R. EVID. 901(a). The ten-day period allowed for objection to authenticity (which period may be altered by the court in appropriate circumstances) does not run from the production of the material or information but from the party's actual awareness that the document will be used. To avoid complications at trial, a party may identify prior to trial the documents intended to be offered, thereby triggering the obligation to object to authenticity. A trial court may also order this procedure. An objection to authenticity must be made in good faith.

RULE 194. REQUESTS FOR DISCLOSURE.

194.1. Request.

A party may obtain disclosure from another party of the information or material listed in Rule 194.2 by serving the other party—no later than 30 days before the end of any applicable discovery period—the following request: "Pursuant to Rule 194, you are requested to disclose, within 30 days of service of this request, the information or material described in Rule [state rule, e.g., 194.2, or 194.2 (a), (c), and (f), or 194.2 (d)-(g)]."

194.2. Content.

A party may request disclosure of any or all of the following:

(a) the correct names of the parties to the lawsuit;

(b) the name, address, and telephone number of any potential parties;

(c) the legal theories and, in general, the factual bases of the responding party's claims or defenses (the responding party need not marshal all evidence that may be offered at trial);

(d) the amount and any method of calculating economic damages;

(e) the name, address, and telephone number of persons having knowledge of relevant facts, and a brief statement of each identified person's connection with the case;

(f) for any testifying expert:

  (1) the expert's name, address, and telephone number;

  (2) the subject matter on which the expert will testify;

  (3) the general substance of the expert's mental impressions and opinions and a brief summary of the basis for them, or if the expert is not retained by, employed by, or otherwise subject to the control of the responding party, documents reflecting such information;

  (4) if the expert is retained by, employed by, or otherwise subject to the control of the responding party:

    (A) all documents, tangible things, reports, models, or data compilations that have been provided to, reviewed by, or prepared by or for the expert in anticipation of the expert's testimony; and

    (B) the expert's current resume and biography;

(g) any indemnity and insuring agreements described in Rule 192.3 (f);

(h) any settlement agreements described in Rule 192.3 (g);

(i) any witness statements described in Rule 192.3 (h);

(j) in a suit alleging physical or mental injury and damages from the occurrence that is the subject of the case, all medical records and bills that are reasonably related to the injuries or damages asserted or, in lieu thereof, an authorization permitting the disclosure of such medical records and bills;

(k) in a suit alleging physical or mental injury and damages from the occurrence that is the subject of the case, all medical records and bills obtained by the responding party by virtue of an authorization furnished by the requesting party;

(l) the name, address, and telephone number of any person who may be designated as a responsible party.

(Amended by Order Mar. 3, 2004, effective in cases filed on or after July 1, 2003, in which a request for disclosure under Rule 194.1 is made on or after May 1, 2004.)

2004 Amendment: Rule 194.2(l) is added as required by changes in chapter 33 of the Texas Civil Practice and Remedies Code. The amendment applies in all cases filed on or after July 1, 2003, in which a request under Rule 194.1 is made after May 1, 2004.

194.3. Response.

The responding party must serve a written response on the requesting party within 30 days after service of the request, except that:

(a) a defendant served with a request before the defendant's answer is due need not respond until 50 days after service of the request, and

(b) a response to a request under Rule 194.2(f) is governed by Rule 195.

194.4. Production.

Copies of documents and other tangible items ordinarily must be served with the response. But if the responsive documents are voluminous, the response must state a reasonable time and place for the production of documents. The responding party must produce the documents at the time and place stated, unless otherwise agreed by the parties or ordered by the court, and must provide the requesting party a reasonable opportunity to inspect them.

194.5. No Objection or Assertion of Work Product.

No objection or assertion of work product is permitted to a request under this rule.

194.6. Certain Responses Not Admissible.

A response to requests under Rule 194.2 (c) and (d) that has been changed by an amended or supplemental response is not admissible and may not be used for impeachment.

(Added Aug. 5, 1998 and Nov. 9, 1998, and amended Dec. 31, 1998, eff. Jan. 1, 1999. Rule 194.2 amended Mar. 3, 2004.)

Comments to 1999 change:

1. Disclosure is designed to afford parties basic discovery of specific categories of information, not automatically in every case, but upon request, without preparation of a lengthy inquiry, and without objection or assertion of work product. In those extremely rare cases when information ordinarily discoverable should be protected, such as when revealing a person's residence might result in harm to the person, a party may move for protection. A party may assert any applicable privileges other than work product using the procedures of Rule 193.3 applicable to other written discovery. Otherwise, to fail to respond fully to a request for disclosure would be an abuse of the discovery process.

2. Rule 194.2(c) and (d) permit a party further inquiry into another's legal theories and factual claims than is often provided in notice pleadings. So-called "contention interrogatories" are used for the same purpose. Such interrogatories are not properly used to require a party to marshal evidence or brief legal issues. Paragraphs (c) and (d) are intended to require disclosure of a party's basic assertions, whether in prosecution of claims or in defense. Thus, for example, a plaintiff would be required to disclose that he or she claimed damages suffered in a car wreck caused by defendant's negligence in speeding, and would be required to state how loss of past earnings and future earning capacity was calculated, but would not be required to state the speed at which defendant was allegedly driving. Paragraph (d) does not require a party, either a plaintiff or a defendant, to state a method of calculating non-economic damages, such as for mental anguish. In the same example, defendant would be required to disclose his or her denial of the speeding allegation and any basis for contesting the damage calculations.

3. Responses under Rule 194.2(c) and (d) that have been amended or supplemented are inadmissible and cannot be used for impeachment, but other evidence of changes in position is not likewise barred.

RULE 195. DISCOVERY REGARDING TESTIFYING EXPERT WITNESSES.

195.1. Permissible Discovery Tools.

A party may request another party to designate and disclose information concerning testifying expert witnesses only through a request for disclosure under Rule 194 and through depositions and reports as permitted by this rule.

195.2. Schedule for Designating Experts.

Unless otherwise ordered by the court, a party must designate experts—that is, furnish information requested under Rule 194.2 (f)—by the later of the following two dates: 30 days after the request is served, or—

(a) with regard to all experts testifying for a party seeking affirmative relief, 90 days before the end of the discovery period;

(b) with regard to all other experts, 60 days before the end of the discovery period.

195.3. Scheduling Depositions.

(a) **Experts for party seeking affirmative relief**. A party seeking affirmative relief must make an expert retained by, employed by, or otherwise in the control of the party available for deposition as follows:

(1) **If no report furnished**. If a report of the expert's factual observations, tests, supporting data, calculations, photographs, and opinions is not produced when the expert is designated, then the party must make the expert available for deposition reasonably promptly after the expert is designated. If the deposition cannot—due to the actions of the tendering party—reasonably be concluded more than 15 days before the deadline for designating other experts, that deadline must be extended for other experts testifying on the same subject.

(2) **If report furnished**. If a report of the expert's factual observations, tests, supporting data, calculations, photographs, and opinions is produced when the expert is designated, then the party need not make the expert available for deposition until reasonably promptly after all other experts have been designated.

(b) **Other experts**. A party not seeking affirmative relief must make an expert retained by, employed by, or otherwise in the control of the party available for deposition reasonably promptly after the expert is designated and the experts testifying on the same subject for the party seeking affirmative relief have been deposed.

195.4. Oral Deposition.

In addition to disclosure under Rule 194, a party may obtain discovery concerning the subject matter on which the expert is expected to testify, the expert's mental impressions and opinions, the facts known to the expert (regardless of when the factual information was acquired) that relate to or form the basis of the testifying expert's mental impressions and opinions, and other discoverable matters, including documents not produced in disclosure, only by oral deposition of the expert and by a report prepared by the expert under this rule.

195.5. Court-Ordered Reports.

If the discoverable factual observations, tests, supporting data, calculations, photographs, or opinions of an expert have not been recorded and reduced to tangible form, the court may order these matters reduced to tangible form and produced in addition to the deposition.

195.6. Amendment and Supplementation.

A party's duty to amend and supplement written discovery regarding a testifying expert is governed by Rule 193.5. If an expert witness is retained by, employed by, or otherwise under the control of a party, that party must also amend or supplement any deposition testimony or written report by the expert, but only with regard to the expert's mental impressions or opinions and the basis for them.

195.7. Cost of Expert Witnesses.

When a party takes the oral deposition of an expert witness retained by the opposing party, all reasonable fees charged by the expert for time spent in preparing for, giving, reviewing, and correcting the deposition must be paid by the party that retained the expert.

(Added Aug. 5, 1998, and amended Nov. 9, 1998 and Dec. 31, 1998, eff. Jan. 1, 1999, except that interrogatories that have been served but not answered as of that date and request information pertaining to experts should be answered; and the rule should not be applied to disrupt expert discovery that is in progress or impending, or that has been scheduled by order or by agreement of the parties.)

Comments to 1999 change:

1. This rule does not limit the permissible methods of discovery concerning consulting experts whose mental impressions or opinions have been reviewed by a testifying expert. *See* Rule 192.3(e). Information concerning purely consulting experts, of course, is not discoverable.

2. This rule and Rule 194 do not address depositions of testifying experts who are not retained by, employed by, or otherwise subject to the control of the responding party, nor the production of the materials identified in Rule 192.3(e)(5) and (6) relating to such experts. Parties may obtain this discovery, however, through Rules 176 and 205.

3. In scheduling the designations and depositions of expert witnesses, the rule attempts to minimize unfair surprise and undue expense. A party seeking affirmative relief must either produce an expert's report or tender the expert for deposition before an opposing party is required to designate experts. A party who does not wish to incur the expense of a report may simply tender the expert for deposition, but a party who wishes an expert to have the benefit of an opposing party's expert's opinions before being deposed may trigger designation by providing a report. Rule 191.1 permits a trial court, for good cause, to modify the order or deadlines for designating and deposing experts and the allocation of fees and expenses.

RULE 196. REQUESTS FOR PRODUCTION AND INSPECTION TO PARTIES; REQUESTS AND MOTIONS FOR ENTRY UPON PROPERTY.

196.1. Request for Production and Inspection to Parties.

(a) **Request**. A party may serve on another party—no later than 30 days before the end of the discovery period—a request for production or for inspection, to inspect, sample, test, photograph and copy documents or tangible things within the scope of discovery.

(b) **Contests of request**. The request must specify the items to be produced or inspected, either by individual item or by category, and describe with reasonable particularity each item and category. The request must specify a reasonable time (on or after the date on which the response is due) and place for production. If the requesting party will sample or test the requested items, the means, manner and procedure for testing or sampling must be described with sufficient specificity to inform the producing party of the means, manner, and procedure for testing or sampling.

(c) **Requests for production of medical or mental health records regarding nonparties**.

(1) **Service of request on nonparty**. If a party requests another party to produce medical or mental health records regarding a nonparty, the requesting party must serve the nonparty with the request for production under Rule 21a.

(2) **Exceptions**. A party is not required to serve the request for production on a nonparty whose medical records are sought if:

(A) the nonparty signs a release of the records that is effective as to the requesting party;

(B) the identity of the nonparty whose records are sought will not directly or indirectly be disclosed by production of the records; or

(C) the court, upon a showing of good cause by the party seeking the records, orders that service is not required.

(3) **Confidentiality**. Nothing in this rule excuses compliance with laws concerning the confidentiality of medical or mental health records.

196.2. Response to Request for Production and Inspection.

(a) **Time for response**. The responding party must serve a written response on the requesting party within 30 days after service of the request, except that a defendant served with a request before the defendant's answer is due need not respond until 50 days after service of the request.

(b) **Content of response**. With respect to each item or category of items, the responding party must state objections and assert privileges as required by these rules, and state, as appropriate, that:

(1) production, inspection, or other requested action will be permitted as requested,

(2) the requested items are being served on the requesting party with the response;

(3) production, inspection, or other requested action will take place at a specified time and place, if the responding party is objecting to the time and place of production; or

(4) no items have been identified—after a diligent search—that are responsive to the request.

196.3. Production.

(a) **Time and place of production**. Subject to any objections stated in the response, the responding party must produce the requested documents or tangible things within the person's possession, custody or control at either the time and place requested or the time and place stated in the response, unless otherwise agreed by the parties or ordered by the court, and must provide the requesting party a reasonable opportunity to inspect them.

(b) **Copies**. The responding party may produce copies in lieu of originals unless a question is raised as to the authenticity of the original or in the circumstances it would be unfair to produce copies in lieu of originals. If originals are produced, the responding party is entitled to retain the originals while the requesting party inspects and copies them.

(c) **Organization**. The responding party must either produce documents and tangible things as they are kept in the usual course of business or organize and label them to correspond with the categories in the request.

196.4. Electronic or Magnetic Data.

To obtain discovery of data or information that exists in electronic or magnetic form, the requesting party must specifically request production of electronic or magnetic data and specify the form in which the requesting party wants it produced. The responding party must produce the electronic or magnetic data that is responsive to the request and is reasonably available to the responding party in its ordinary course of business. If the responding party cannot—through reasonable efforts—retrieve the data or information requested or produce it in the form requested, the responding party must state an objection complying with these rules. If the court orders the responding party to comply with the request, the court must also order that the requesting party pay the reasonable expenses of any extraordinary steps required to retrieve and produce the information.

196.5. Destruction or Alteration.

Testing, sampling or examination of an item may not destroy or materially alter an item unless previously authorized by the court.

196.6. Expenses of Production.

Unless otherwise ordered by the court for good cause, the expense of producing items will be borne by the responding party and the expense of inspecting, sampling, testing, photographing, and copying items produced will be borne by the requesting party.

196.7. Request or Motion for Entry Upon Property.

(a) **Request or motion**. A party may gain entry on designated land or other property to inspect, measure, survey, photograph, test, or sample the property or any designated object or operation thereon by serving—no later than 30 days before the end of any applicable discovery period -

(1) a request on all parties if the land or property belongs to a party, or

(2) a motion and notice of hearing on all parties and the nonparty if the land or property belongs to a nonparty. If the identity or address of the nonparty is unknown and cannot be obtained through reasonable diligence, the court must permit service by means other than those specified in Rule 21a that are reasonably calculated to give the nonparty notice of the motion and hearing.

(b) **Time, place, and other conditions**. The request for entry upon a party's property, or the order for entry upon a nonparty's property, must state the time, place, manner, conditions, and scope of the inspection, and must specifically describe any desired means, manner, and procedure for testing or sampling, and the person or persons by whom the inspection, testing, or sampling is to be made.

(c) **Response to request for entry**.

(1) **Time to Respond**. The responding party must serve a written response on the requesting party within 30 days after service of the request, except that a defendant served with a request before the defendant's answer is due need not respond until 50 days after service of the request.

(2) **Content of response**. The responding party must state objections and assert privileges as required by these rules, and state, as appropriate, that:

(A) entry or other requested action will be permitted as requested;

(B) entry or other requested action will take place at a specified time and place, if the responding party is objecting to the time and place of production; or

(C) entry or other requested action cannot be permitted for reasons stated in the response.

(d) **Requirements for order for entry on nonparty's property**. An order for entry on a nonparty's property may issue only for good cause shown and only if the land, property, or object thereon as to which discovery is sought is relevant to the subject matter of the action.

(Added Aug. 5, 1998, and amended Nov. 9, 1998 and Dec. 31, 1998, eff. Jan. 1, 1999.)

Comments to 1999 change:

1. "Document and tangible things" are defined in Rule 192.3(b).
2. A party requesting sampling or testing must describe the procedure with sufficient specificity to enable the responding party to make any appropriate objections.
3. A party requesting production of magnetic or electronic data must specifically request the data, specify the form in which it wants the data produced, and specify any extraordinary steps for retrieval and translation. Unless ordered otherwise, the responding party need only produce the data reasonably available in the ordinary course of business in reasonably usable form.
4. The rule clarifies how the expenses of production are to be allocated absent a court order to the contrary.
5. The obligation of parties to produce documents within their possession, custody or control is explained in Rule 192.3(b).
6. Parties may request production and inspection of documents and tangible things from nonparties under Rule 205.3.
7. Rule 196.3(b) is based on TEX. R. EVID. 1003.
8. Rule 196.1(c) is merely a notice requirement and does not expand the scope of discovery of a nonparty's medical records.

RULE 197. INTERROGATORIER TO PARTIES.

197.1. Interrogatories.

A party may serve on another party—no later than 30 days before the end of the discovery period—written interrogatories to inquire about any matter within the scope of discovery except matters covered by Rule 195. An interrogatory may inquire whether a party makes a specific legal or factual contention and may ask the responding party to state the legal theories and to describe in general the factual bases for the party's claims or defenses, but interrogatories may not be used to require the responding party to marshal all of its available proof or the proof the party intends to offer at trial.

197.2. Response to Interrogatories.

(a) **Time for response**. The responding party must serve a written response on the requesting party within 30 days after service of the interrogatories, except that a defendant served with interrogatories before the defendant's answer is due need not respond until 50 days after service of the interrogatories.

(b) **Content of response**. A response must include the party's answers to the interrogatories and may include objections and assertions of privilege as required under these rules.

(c) **Option to produce records**. If the answer to an interrogatory may be derived or ascertained from public records, from the responding party's business records, or from a compilation, abstract or summary of the responding party's business records, and the burden of deriving or ascertaining the answer is substantially the same for the requesting party as for the responding party, the responding party may answer the interrogatory by specifying and, if applicable, producing the records or compilation, abstract or summary of the records. The records from which the answer may be derived or ascertained must be specified in sufficient detail to permit the requesting party to locate and identify them as readily as can the responding party. If the responding party has specified business records, the responding party must state a reasonable time and place for examination of the documents. The responding party must produce the documents at the time and place stated, unless otherwise agreed by the parties or ordered by the court, and must provide the requesting party a reasonable opportunity to inspect them.

(d) **Verification required, exceptions**. A responding party—not an agent or attorney as otherwise permitted by Rule 14—must sign the answers under oath except that:

(1) when answers are based on information obtained from other persons, the party may so state, and

(2) a party need not sign answers to interrogatories about persons with knowledge of relevant facts, trial witnesses, and legal contentions.

197.3. Use.

Answers to interrogatories may be used only against the responding party. An answer to an interrogatory inquiring about matters described in Rule 194.2 (c) and (d) that has been amended or supplemented is not admissible and may not be used for impeachment.

(Added Aug. 5, 1998, and amended Nov. 9, 1998 and Dec. 31, 1998, eff. Jan. 1, 1999.)

Comments to 1999 change:

1. Interrogatories about specific legal or factual assertions—such as, whether a party claims a breach of implied warranty, or when a party contends that limitations began to run—are proper, but interrogatories that ask a party to state all legal and factual assertions are improper. As with requests for disclosure, interrogatories may be used to ascertain basic legal and factual claims and defenses but may not be used to force a party to marshal evidence. Use of the answers to such interrogatories is limited, just as the use of similar disclosures under Rule 194.6 is.

2. Rule 191's requirement that a party's attorney sign all discovery responses and objections applies to interrogatory responses and objections. In addition, the responding party must sign some interrogatory answers under oath, as specified by the rule. Answers in amended and supplemental responses must be signed by the party under oath only if the original answers were required to be signed under oath. The failure to sign or verify answers is only a formal defect that does not otherwise impair the answers unless the party refuses to sign or verify the answers after the defect is pointed out.

RULE 198. REQUESTS FOR ADMISSIONS.

198.1. Request for Admissions.

A party may serve on another party—no later than 30 days before the end of the discovery period—written requests that the other party admit the truth of any matter within the scope of discovery, including statements of opinion or of fact or of the application of law to fact, or the genuineness of any documents served with the request or otherwise made available for inspection and copying. Each matter for which an admission is requested must be stated separately.

198.2. Response to Requests for Admissions.

(a) **Time for response**. The responding party must serve a written response on the requesting party within 30 days after service of the request, except that a defendant served with a request before the defendant's answer is due need not respond until 50 days after service of the request.

(b) **Content of response**. Unless the responding party states an objection or asserts a privilege, the responding party must specifically admit or deny the request or explain in detail the reasons that the responding party cannot admit or deny the request. A response must fairly meet the substance of the request. The responding party may qualify an answer, or deny a request in part, only when good faith requires. Lack of information or knowledge is not a proper response unless the responding party states that a reasonable inquiry was made but that the information known or easily obtainable is insufficient to enable the responding party to admit or deny. An assertion that the request presents an issue for trial is not; a proper response.

(c) **Effect of failure to respond**. If a response is not timely served, the request is considered admitted without the necessity of a court order.

198.3. Effect of Admissions; Withdrawal or Amendment.

Any admission made by a party under this rule may be used solely in the pending action and not in any other proceeding. A matter admitted under this rule is conclusively established as to the party making the admission unless the court permits the party to withdraw or amend the admission. The court may permit the party to withdraw or amend the admission if:

(a) the party shows good cause for the withdrawal or amendment; and

(b) the court finds that the parties relying upon the responses and deemed admissions will not be unduly prejudiced and that the presentation of the merits of the action will be subserved by permitting the party to amend or withdraw the admission.

(Added Aug. 5, 1998, and Nov. 9, 1998, eff. Jan. 1, 1999.)

RULE 199. DEPOSITIONS UPON ORAL EXAMINATION.

199.1. Oral Examination; Alternative Methods of Conducting or Recording.

(a) **Generally**. A party may take the testimony of any person or entity by deposition on oral examination before any officer authorized by law to take depositions. The testimony, objections, and any other statements during the deposition must be recorded at the time they are given or made.

(b) **Depositions by telephone or other remote electronic means**. A party may take an oral deposition by telephone or other remote electronic means if the party gives reasonable prior written notice of intent to do so. For the purposes of these rules, an oral deposition taken by telephone or other remote electronic means is considered as having been taken in the district and at the place where the witness is located when answering the questions. The officer taking the deposition may be located with the party noticing the deposition instead of with the witness if the witness is placed under oath by a person who is present with the witness and authorized to administer oaths in that jurisdiction.

(c) **Nonstenographic recording**. Any party may cause a deposition upon oral examination to be recorded by other than stenographic means, including videotape recording. The party requesting the nonstenographic recording will be responsible for obtaining a person authorized by law to administer the oath and for assuring that the recording will be intelligible, accurate, and trustworthy. At least five days prior to the deposition, the party must serve on the witness and all parties a notice, either in the notice of deposition or separately, that the deposition will be recorded by other than stenographic means. This notice must state the method of nonstenographic recording to be used and whether the deposition will also be recorded stenographically. Any other party may then serve written notice designating another method of recording in addition to the method specified, at the expense of such other party unless the court orders otherwise.

199.2. Procedure for Noticing Oral Deposition.

(a) **Time to notice deposition**. A notice of intent to take an oral deposition must be served on the witness and all parties a reasonable time before the deposition is taken. An oral deposition may be taken outside the discovery period only by agreement of the parties or with leave of court.

(b) **Content of notice**.

(1) **Identity of witness; organizations**. The notice must state the name of the witness, which may be either an individual or a public or private corporation, partnership, association, governmental agency, or other organization. If an organization is named as the witness, the notice must describe with reasonable particularity the matters on which examination is requested. In response, the organization named in the notice must—a reasonable time before the deposition—designate one or more individuals to testify on its behalf and set forth, for each individual designated, the matters on which the individual will testify. Each individual designated must testify as to matters that are known or reasonably available to the organization. This subdivision does not preclude taking a deposition by any other procedure authorized by these rules.

(2) **Time and Place**. The notice must state a reasonable time and place for the oral deposition. The place may be in:

(A) the county of the witness's residence;

(B) the county where the witness is employed or regularly transacts business in person;

(C) the county of suit, if the witness is a party or a person designated by a party under Rule 199.2 (b)(1);

(D) the county where the witness was served with the subpoena, or within 150 miles of the place of service, if the witness is not a resident of Texas or is a transient person; or

(E) subject to the foregoing, at any other convenient place directed by the court in which the cause is pending.

(3) **Alternative means of conducting and recording**. The notice must state whether the deposition is to be taken by telephone or other remote electronic means and identify the means. If the deposition is to be recorded by nonstenographic means, the notice may include the notice required by Rule 199.1 (c).

(4) **Additional attendees**. The notice may include the notice concerning additional attendees required by Rule 199.5 (a)(3).

(5) **Request for production of documents**. A notice may include a request that the witness produce at the deposition documents or tangible things within the scope of discovery and within the witness's possession, custody, or control. If the witness is a nonparty, the request must comply with Rule 205 and the designation of materials required to be identified in the subpoena must be attached to, or included in, the notice. The nonparty's response to the request is governed by Rules 176 and 205. When the witness is a party or subject to the control of a party, document requests under this subdivision are governed by Rules 193 and 196.

199.3. Compelling Witness to Attend.

A party may compel the witness to attend the oral deposition by serving the witness with a subpoena under Rule 176. If the witness is a party or is retained by, employed by, or otherwise subject to the control of a party, however, service of the notice of oral deposition upon the party's attorney has the same effect as a subpoena served on the witness.

199.4. Objections to Time and Place of Oral Deposition.

A party or witness may object to the time and place designated for an oral deposition by motion for protective order or by motion to quash the notice of deposition. If the motion is filed by the third business day after service of the notice of deposition an objection to the time and place of a deposition stays the oral deposition until the motion can be determined.

199.5. Examination, Objection, and Conduct During Oral Depositions.

(a) Attendance.

(1) **Witness**. The witness must remain in attendance from day to day until the deposition is begun and completed.

(2) **Attendance by party**. A party may attend an oral deposition in person, even if the deposition is taken by telephone or other remote electronic means. If a deposition is taken by telephone or other remote electronic means, the party noticing the deposition must make arrangements for all persons to attend by the same means. If the party noticing the deposition appears in person, any other party may appear by telephone or other remote electronic means if that party makes the necessary arrangements with the deposition officer and the party noticing the deposition.

(3) **Other attendees**. If any party intends to have in attendance any persons other than the witness, parties, spouses of parties, counsel, employees of counsel, and the officer taking the oral deposition, that party must give reasonable notice to all parties, either in the notice of deposition or separately, of the identity of the other persons.

(b) **Oath; examination**. Every person whose deposition is taken by oral examination must first be placed under oath. The parties may examine and cross-examine the witness. Any party, in lieu of participating in the examination, may serve written questions in a sealed envelope on the party noticing the oral deposition, who must deliver them to the deposition officer, who must open the envelope and propound them to the witness.

(c) **Time limitation**. No side may examine or cross-examine an individual witness for more than six hours. Breaks during depositions do not count against this limitation.

(d) **Conduct during the oral deposition, conferences**. The oral deposition must be conducted in the same manner as if the testimony were being obtained in court during trial. Counsel should cooperate with and be courteous to each other and to the witness. The witness should not be evasive and should not unduly delay the examination. Private conferences between the witness and the witness's attorney during the actual taking of the deposition are improper except for the purpose of determining whether a privilege should be asserted. Private conferences may be held, however, during agreed recesses and adjournments. If the lawyers and witnesses do not comply with this rule, the court may allow in evidence at trial statements, objections, discussions, and other occurrences during the oral deposition that reflect upon the credibility of the witness or the testimony.

(e) **Objections**. Objections to questions during the oral deposition are limited to "Objection, leading" and "Objection, form." Objections to testimony during the oral deposition are limited to "Objection, nonresponsive." These objections are waived if not stated as phrased during the oral deposition. All other objections need not be made or recorded during the oral deposition to be later raised with the court. The objecting party must give a clear and concise explanation of an objection if requested by the party taking the oral deposition, or the objection is waived. Argumentative or suggestive objections or explanations waive objection and may be grounds for terminating the oral deposition or assessing costs or other sanctions. The officer taking the oral deposition will not rule on objections but must record them for ruling by the court. The officer taking the oral deposition must not fail to record testimony because an objection has been made.

(f) **Instructions not to answer**. An attorney may instruct a witness not to answer a question during an oral deposition only if necessary to preserve a privilege, comply with a court order or these rules, protect a witness from an abusive question or one for which any answer would be misleading, or secure a ruling pursuant to paragraph (g). The attorney instructing the witness not to answer must give a concise, nonargumentative, nonsuggestive explanation of the grounds for the instruction if requested by the party who asked the question.

(g) **Suspending the deposition**. If the time limitations for the deposition have expired or the deposition is being conducted or defended in violation of these rules, a party or witness may suspend the oral deposition for the time necessary to obtain a ruling.

(h) **Good faith required**. An attorney must not ask a question at an oral deposition solely to harass or mislead the witness, for any other improper purpose, or without a good faith legal basis at the time. An attorney must not object to a question at an oral deposition, instruct the witness not to answer a question, or suspend the deposition unless there is a good faith factual and legal basis for doing so at the time.

199.6. Hearing on Objections.

Any party may, at any reasonable time, request a hearing on an objection or privilege asserted by an instruction not to answer or suspension of the deposition; provided the failure of a party to obtain a ruling prior to trial does not waive any objection or privilege. The party seeking to avoid discovery must present any evidence necessary to support the objection or privilege either by testimony at the hearing or by affidavits served on opposing parties at least seven days before the hearing If the court determines that an in camera review of some or all of the requested discovery is necessary to rule, answers to the deposition questions may be made *in camera*, to be transcribed and sealed in the event the privilege is sustained, or made in an affidavit produced to the court in a sealed wrapper.

(Added Aug. 5, 1998, and amended Nov. 9, 1998, eff. Jan. 1, 1999.)

Comments to 1999 change:

1. Rule 199.2(b)(5) incorporates the procedures and limitations applicable to requests for production or inspection under Rule 196, including the 30-day deadline for responses, as well as the procedures and duties imposed by Rule 193.

2. For purposes of Rule 199.5(c), each person designated by an organization under Rule 199.2(b)(1) is a separate witness.

3. The requirement of Rule 199.5(d) that depositions be conducted in the same manner as if the testimony were being obtained in court is a limit on the conduct of the lawyers and witnesses in the deposition, not on the scope of the interrogation permitted by Rule 192.

4. An objection to the form of a question includes objections that the question calls for speculation, calls for a narrative answer, is vague, is confusing, or is ambiguous. Ordinarily, a witness must answer a question at a deposition subject to the objection. An objection may therefore be inadequate if a question incorporates such unfair assumptions or is worded so that any answer would necessarily be misleading. A witness should not be required to answer whether he has yet ceased conduct he denies ever doing, subject to an objection to form (*i.e.*, that the question is confusing or assumes facts not in evidence) because any answer would necessarily be misleading on account of the way in which the question is put. The witness may be instructed not to answer. Abusive questions include questions that inquire into matters clearly beyond the scope of discovery or that are argumentative, repetitious, or harassing.

RULE 200. DEPOSITIONS UPON WRITTEN QUESTIONS.

200.1. Procedure for Noticing Deposition Upon Written Questions.

(a) **Who may be noticed, when**. A party may take the testimony of any person or entity by deposition on written questions before any person authorized by law to take depositions on written questions. A notice of intent to take the deposition must be served on the witness and all parties at least 20 days before the deposition is taken. A deposition on written questions may be taken outside the discovery period only by agreement of the parties or with leave of court. The party noticing the deposition must also deliver to the deposition officer a copy of the notice and of all written questions to be asked during the deposition.

(b) **Content of notice**. The notice must comply with Rules 199.1 (b), 199.2 (b), and 199.5 (a)(3). If the witness is an organization, the organization must comply with the requirements of that provision. The notice also may include a request for production of documents as permitted by Rule 199.2 (b)(5), the provisions of which will govern the request, service, and response.

200.2. Compelling Witness to Attend.

A party may compel the witness to attend the deposition on written questions by serving the witness with a subpoena under Rule 176. If the witness is a party or is retained by, employed by, or otherwise subject to the control of a party, however, service of the deposition notice upon the party's attorney has the same effect as a subpoena served on the witness.

200.3. Questions and Objections.

(a) **Direct questions**. The direct questions to be propounded to the witness must be attached to the notice.

(b) **Objections and additional questions**. Within ten days after the notice and direct questions are served, any party may object to the direct questions and serve cross-questions on all other parties. Within five days after cross-questions are served, any party may object to the cross-questions and serve redirect questions on all other parties. Within three days after redirect questions are served, any party may object to the redirect questions and serve recross questions on all other parties. Objections to recross questions must be served within five days after the earlier of when recross questions are served or the time of the deposition on written questions.

(c) **Objections to form of questions**. Objections to the form of a question are waived unless asserted in accordance with this subdivision.

200.4. Conducting the Deposition Upon Written Questions.

The deposition officer must: take the deposition on written questions at the time and place designated; record the testimony of the witness under oath in response to the questions; and prepare, certify, and deliver the deposition transcript in accordance with Rule 203. The deposition officer has authority when necessary to summon and swear an interpreter to facilitate the taking of the deposition.

(Added Aug. 5 1998 and Nov. 9, 1998, and amended Dec. 31, 1998, eff. Jan. 1, 1999.)

Comments to 1999 change:

1. The procedures for asserting objections during oral depositions under Rule 199.5(e) do not apply to depositions on written questions.

2. Section 20.001 of the Civil Practice and Remedies Code provides that a deposition on written questions of a witness who is alleged to reside or to be in this state may be taken by a clerk of a district court, a judge or clerk of a county court, or a notary public of this state.

RULE 201. DEPOSITIONS IN FOREIGN JURISDICTIONS FOR USE IN TEXAS PROCEEDINGS; DEPOSITIONS IN TEXAS FOR USE IN FOREIGN PROCEEDINGS.

201.1. Depositions in Foreign Jurisdictions for Use in Texas Proceedings.

(a) **Generally**. A party may take a deposition on oral examination or written questions of any person or entity located in another state or a foreign country for use in proceedings in this State. The deposition may be taken by:

(1) notice;

(2) letter rogatory, letter of request, or other such device;

(3) agreement of the parties; or

(4) court order.

(b) **By notice**. A party may take the deposition by notice in accordance with these rules as if the deposition were taken in this State, except that the deposition officer may be a person authorized to administer oaths in the place where the deposition is taken.

(c) **By letter rogatory**. On motion by a party, the court in which an action is pending must issue a letter rogatory on terms that are just and appropriate, regardless of whether any other manner of obtaining the deposition is impractical or inconvenient. The letter must:

(1) be addressed to the appropriate authority in the jurisdiction in which the deposition is to be taken;

(2) request and authorize that authority to summon the witness before the authority at a time and place stated in the letter for examination on oral or written questions; and

(3) request and authorize that authority to cause the witness's testimony to be reduced to writing and returned, together with any items marked as exhibits, to the party requesting the letter rogatory.

(d) **By letter of request or other such device**. On motion by a party, the court in which an action is pending, or the clerk of that court, must issue a letter of request or other such device in accordance with an applicable treaty or international convention on terms that are just and appropriate. The letter or other device must be issued regardless of whether any other manner of obtaining the deposition is impractical or inconvenient. The letter or other device must:

(1) be in the form prescribed by the treaty or convention under which it is issued, as presented by the movant to the court or clerk; and

(2) must state the time, place, and manner of the examination of the witness.

(e) **Objections to form of letter rogatory, letter of request, or other such device**. In issuing a letter rogatory, letter of request, or other such device, the court must set a time for objecting to the form of the device. A party must make any objection to the form of the device in writing and serve it on all other parties by the time set by the court, or the objection is waived.

(f) **Admissibility of evidence**. Evidence obtained in response to a letter rogatory, letter of request, or other such device is not inadmissible merely because it is not a verbatim transcript, or the testimony was not taken under oath, or for any similar departure from the requirements for depositions taken within this State under these rules.

(g) **Deposition by electronic means**. A deposition in another jurisdiction may be taken by telephone, videoconference, teleconference, or other electronic means under the provisions of Rule 199.

201.2. Depositions in Texas for Use in Proceedings in Foreign Jurisdictions.

If a court of record of any other state or foreign jurisdiction issues a mandate, writ, or commission that requires a witness's oral or written deposition testimony in this State, the witness may be compelled to appear and testify in the same manner and by the same process used for taking testimony in a proceeding pending in this State.

(Added Aug. 5, 1998 and Nov. 9, 1998, eff. Jan. 1, 1999.)

Comments to 1999 change:

1. Rule 201.1 sets forth procedures for obtaining deposition testimony of a witness in another state or foreign jurisdiction for use in Texas court proceedings. It does not, however, address whether any of the procedures listed are, in fact, permitted or recognized by the law of the state or foreign jurisdiction where the witness is located. A party must first determine what procedures are permitted by the jurisdiction where the witness is located before using this rule.

2. Section 20.001 of the Civil Practice and Remedies Code provides a nonexclusive list of persons who are qualified to take a written deposition in Texas and who may take depositions (oral or written) in another state or outside the United States.

3. Rule 201.2 is based on Section 20.002 of the Civil Practice and Remedies Code.

RULE 202. DEPOSITIONS BEFORE SUIT OR TO INVESTIGATE CLAIMS.

202.1. Generally.

A person may petition the court for an order authorizing the taking of a deposition on oral examination or written questions either:

(a) to perpetuate or obtain the person's own testimony or that of any other person for use in an anticipated suit; or

(b) to investigate a potential claim or suit.

202.2. Petition.

The petition must:

(a) be verified;

(b) be filed in a proper court of any county:

(1) where venue of the anticipated suit may lie, if suit is anticipated; or

(2) where the witness resides, if no suit is yet anticipated;

(c) be in the name of the petitioner;

(d) state either:

(1) that the petitioner anticipates the institution of a suit in which the petitioner may be a party; or

(2) that the petitioner seeks to investigate a potential claim by or against petitioner;

(e) state the subject matter of the anticipated action, if any, and the petitioner's interest therein;

(f) if suit is anticipated, either:

(1) state the names of the persons petitioner expects to have interests adverse to petitioner's in the anticipated suit, and the addresses and telephone numbers for such persons; or

(2) state that the names, addresses, and telephone numbers of persons petitioner expects to have interests adverse to petitioner's in the anticipated suit cannot be ascertained through diligent inquiry, and describe those persons;

(g) state the names, addresses and telephone numbers of the persons to be deposed, the substance of the testimony that the petitioner expects to elicit from each, and the petitioner's reasons for desiring to obtain the testimony of each; and

(h) request an order authorizing the petitioner to take the depositions of the persons named in the petition.

202.3. Notice and Service.

(a) **Personal service on witnesses and persons named**. At least 15 days before the date of the hearing on the petition, the petitioner must serve the petition and a notice of the hearing—in accordance with Rule 21a—on all persons petitioner seeks to depose and, if suit is anticipated, on all persons petitioner expects to have interests adverse to petitioner's in the anticipated suit.

(b) **Service by publication on persons not named**.

(1) **Manner**. Unnamed persons described in the petition whom the petitioner expects to have interests adverse to petitioner's in the anticipated suit if any, may be served by publication with the petition and notice of the hearing. The notice must state the place for the hearing and the time it will be held, which must be more than 14 days after the first publication of the notice. The petition and notice must be published once each week for two consecutive weeks in the newspaper of broadest circulation in the county in which the petition is filed, or if no such newspaper exists, in the newspaper of broadest circulation in the nearest county where a newspaper is published.

(2) **Objection to depositions taken on notice by publication**. Any interested party may move, in the proceeding or by bill of review, to suppress any deposition, in whole or in part, taken on notice by publication, and may also attack or oppose the deposition by any other means available.

(c) **Service in probate cases**. A petition to take a deposition in anticipation of an application for probate of a will, and notice of the hearing on the petition, may be served by posting as prescribed by Section 33(f)(2) of the Probate Code. The notice and petition must be directed to all parties interested in the testator's estate and must comply with the requirements of Section 33(c) of the Probate Code insofar as they may be applicable.

(d) **Modification by order**. As justice or necessity may require, the court may shorten or lengthen the notice periods under this rule and may extend the notice period to permit service on any expected adverse party.

202.4. Order.

(a) **Required findings**. The court must order a deposition to be taken if, but only if, it finds that:

(1) allowing the petitioner to take the requested deposition may prevent a failure or delay of justice in an anticipated suit: or

(2) the likely benefit of allowing the petitioner to take the requested deposition to investigate a potential claim outweighs the burden or expense of the procedure.

(b) **Contents**. The order must state whether a deposition will be taken an oral examination or written questions. The order may also state the time and place at which a deposition will be taken. If the order does not state the time and place at which a deposition will be taken, the petitioner must notice the deposition as required by Rules 199 or 200. The order must contain any protections the court finds necessary or appropriate to protect the witness or any person who may be affected by the procedure.

202.5. Manner of Taking and Use.

Except as otherwise provided in this rule, depositions authorized by this rule are governed by the rules applicable to depositions of nonparties in a pending suit. The scope of discovery in depositions authorized by this rule is the same as if the anticipated suit or potential claim had been filed. A court may restrict or prohibit the use of a deposition taken under this rule in a subsequent suit to protect a person who was not served with notice of the deposition from any unfair prejudice or to prevent abuse of this rule.

(Added Aug. 5. 1998 and Nov. 8, 1998, to apply to proceedings filed on or after Jan. 1, 1999, but a court may use the rule for guidance in previously filed proceedings.)

Comments to 1999 change:

1. This rule applies to all discovery before suit covered by former rules governing depositions to perpetuate testimony and bills of discovery.

2. A deposition taken under this rule may be used in a subsequent suit as permitted by the rules of evidence, except that a court may restrict or prohibit its use to prevent taking unfair advantage of a witness or others. The bill of discovery procedure, which Rule 202 incorporates, is equitable in nature, and a court must not permit it to be used inequitably.

RULE 203. SIGNING, CERTIFICATION AND USE OF ORAL AND WRITTEN DEPOSITIONS.

203.1. Signature and Changes.

(a) **Deposition transcript to be provided to witness**. The deposition officer must provide the original deposition transcript to the witness for examination and signature. If the witness is represented by an attorney at the deposition, the deposition officer must provide the transcript to the attorney instead of the witness.

(b) **Changes by witness; signature**. The witness may change responses as reflected in the deposition transcript by indicating the desired changes, in writing, on a separate sheet of paper, together with a statement of the reasons for making the changes. No erasures or obliterations of any kind may be made to the original deposition transcript. The witness must then sign the transcript under oath and return it to the deposition officer. If the witness does not return the transcript to the deposition officer within 20 days of the date the transcript was provided to the witness or the witness's attorney, the witness may be deemed to have waived the right to make the changes.

(c) **Exceptions**. The requirements of presentation and signature under this subdivision do not apply:

(1) if the witness and all parties waive the signature requirement;

(2) to depositions on written questions; or

(3) to nonstenographic recordings of oral depositions.

203.2. Certification.

The deposition officer must file with the court, serve on all parties, and attach as part of the deposition transcript or nonstenographic recording of an oral deposition a certificate duly sworn by the officer stating:

(a) that the witness was duly sworn by the officer and that the transcript or nonstenographic recording of the oral deposition is a true record of the testimony given by the witness;
(b) that the deposition transcript, if any, was submitted to the witness or to the attorney for the witness for examination and signature, the date on which the transcript was submitted, whether the witness returned the transcript, and if so, the date on which it was returned.
(c) that changes, if any, made by the witness are attached to the deposition transcript;
(d) that the deposition officer delivered the deposition transcript or nonstenographic recording of an oral deposition in accordance with Rule 203.3;
(e) the amount of time used by each party at the deposition;
(f) the amount of the deposition officer's charges for preparing the original deposition transcript, which the clerk of the court must tax as costs; and
(g) that a copy of the certificate was served on all parties and the date of service.

203.3. Delivery.

(a) **Endorsement, to whom delivered**. The deposition officer must endorse the title of the action and "Deposition of (name of witness)" on the original deposition transcript (or a copy, if the original was not returned) or the original nonstenographic recording of an oral deposition, and must return:
   (1) the transcript to the party who asked the first question appearing in the transcript, or
   (2) the recording to the party who requested it.
(b) **Notice**. The deposition officer must serve notice of delivery on all other parties.
(c) **Inspection and copying; copies**. The party receiving the original deposition transcript or nonstenographic recording must make it available upon reasonable request for inspection and copying by any other party. Any party or the witness is entitled to obtain a copy of the deposition transcript or nonstenographic recording from the deposition officer upon payment of a reasonable fee.

203.4. Exhibits.

At the request of a party, the original documents and things produced for inspection during the examination of the witness must be marked for identification by the deposition officer and annexed to the deposition transcript or nonstenographic recording. The person producing the materials may produce copies instead of originals if the party gives all other parties fair opportunity at the deposition to compare the copies with the originals. If the person offers originals rather than copies, the deposition officer must, after the conclusion of the deposition, make copies to be attached to the original deposition transcript or nonstenographic recording, and then return the originals to the person who produced them. The person who produced the originals must preserve them for hearing or trial and make them available for inspection or copying by any other party upon seven days' notice. Copies annexed to the original deposition transcript or nonstenographic recording may be used for all purposes.

203.5. Motion to Suppress.

A party may object to any errors and irregularities in the manner in which the testimony is transcribed, signed, delivered, or otherwise dealt with by the deposition officer by filing a motion to suppress all or part of the deposition. If the deposition officer complies with Rule 203.3 at least one day before the case is called to trial, with regard to a deposition transcript, or 30 days before the case is called to trial, with regard to a nonstenographic recording, the party must file and serve a motion to suppress before trial commences to preserve the objections.

203.6. Use.

(a) **Nonstenographic recording; transcription**. A nonstenographic recording of an oral deposition, or a written transcription of all or part of such a recording, may be used to the same extent as a deposition taken by stenographic means. However, the court, for good cause shown, may require that the party seeking to use a nonstenographic recording or written transcription first obtain a complete transcript of the deposition recording from a certified court reporter. The court reporter's transcription must be made from the original or a certified copy of the deposition recording. The court reporter must, to the extent applicable, comply with the provisions of this rule, except that the court reporter must deliver the original transcript to the attorney requesting the transcript, and the court reporter's certificate must include a statement that the transcript is a true record of the nonstenographic recording. The party to whom the court reporter delivers the original transcript must make the transcript available, upon reasonable request, for inspection and copying by the witness or any party.
(b) **Same proceeding**. All or part of a deposition may be used for any purpose in the same proceeding in which it was taken. If the original is not filed, a certified copy may be used. "Same proceeding" includes a proceeding in a different

court but involving the same subject matter and the same parties or their representatives or successors in interest. A deposition is admissible against a party joined after the deposition was taken if:

(1) the deposition is admissible pursuant to Rule 804 (b)(1) of the Rules of Evidence, or

(2) that party has had a reasonable opportunity to redepose the witness and has failed to do so.

(c) **Different proceeding**. Depositions taken in different proceedings may be used as permitted by the Rules of Evidence.

(Added Aug. 5, 1998 and Nov. 9, 1998, eff. Jan. 1, 1999.)

RULE 204. PHYSICAL AND MENTAL EXAMINATIONS.

204.1. Motion and Order Required.

(a) **Motion**. A party may—no later than 30 days before the end of any applicable discovery period—move for an order compelling another party to:

(1) submit to a physical or mental examination by a qualified physician or a mental examination by a qualified psychologist; or

(2) produce for such examination a person in the other party's custody, conservatorship or legal control.

(b) **Service**. The motion and notice of hearing must be served on the person to be examined and all parties.

(c) **Requirements for obtaining order**. The court may issue an order for examination only for good cause shown and only in the following circumstances:

(1) when the mental or physical condition (including the blood group) of a party, or of a person in the custody, conservatorship or under the legal control of a party, is in controversy; or

(2) except as provided in Rule 204.4, an examination by a psychologist may be ordered when the party responding to the motion has designated a psychologist as a testifying expert or has disclosed a psychologist's records for possible use at trial.

(d) **Requirements of order**. The order must be in writing and must specify the time, place, manner, conditions, and scope of the examination and the person or persons by whom it is to be made.

204.2. Report of Examining Physician or Psychologist.

(a) **Right to report**. Upon request of the person ordered to be examined, the party causing the examination to be made must deliver to the person a copy of a detailed written report of the examining physician or psychologist setting out the findings, including results of all tests made, diagnoses and conclusions, together with like reports of all earlier examinations of the same condition. After delivery of the report, upon request of the party causing the examination, the party against whom the order is made must produce a like report of any examination made before or after the ordered examination of the same condition, unless the person examined is not a party and the party shows that the party is unable to obtain it. The court on motion may limit delivery of a report on such terms as are just. If a physician or psychologist fails or refuses to make a report the court may exclude the testimony if offered at the trial.

(b) **Agreements; relationship to other rules**. This subdivision applies to examinations made by agreement of the parties, unless the agreement expressly provides otherwise. This subdivision does not preclude discovery of a report of an examining physician or psychologist or the taking of a deposition of the physician or psychologist in accordance with the provisions of any other rule.

204.3. Effect of No Examination.

If no examination is sought either by agreement or under this subdivision, the party whose physical or mental condition is in controversy must not comment to the court or jury concerning the party's willingness to submit to an examination, or on the right or failure of any other party to seek an examination.

204.4. Cases Arising Under Titles II or V, Family Code.

In cases arising under Family Code Titles II or V, the court may—on its own initiative or on motion of a party—appoint:

(a) one or more psychologists or psychiatrists to make any and all appropriate mental examinations of the children who are the subject of the suit or of any other parties, and may make such appointment irrespective of whether a psychologist or psychiatrist has been designated by any party as a testifying expert;

(b) one or more experts who are qualified in paternity testing to take blood, body fluid, or tissue samples to conduct paternity tests as ordered by the court.

204.5. Definition.

For the purpose of this rule, a psychologist is a person licensed or certified by a state or the District of Columbia as a psychologist.

(Added Aug. 5, 1998 and Nov. 9, 1998, eff. Jan. 1, 1999.)

RULE 205. DISCOVERY FROM NONPARTIES.

205.1. Forms of Discovery; Subpoena Requirement.

A party may compel discovery from a nonparty—that is, a person who is not a party or subject to a party's control—only by obtaining a court order under Rules 196.7, 202, or 204, or by serving a subpoena compelling:

(a) an oral deposition;

(b) a deposition on written questions;

(c) a request for production of documents or tangible things, pursuant to Rule 199.2(b)(5) or Rule 200.1(b), served with a notice of deposition on oral examination or written questions; and

(d) a request for production of documents and tangible things under this rule.

205.2. Notice.

A party seeking discovery by subpoena from a nonparty must serve, on the nonparty and all parties, a copy of the form of notice required under the rules governing the applicable form of discovery. A notice of oral or written deposition must be served before or at the same time that a subpoena compelling attendance or production under the notice is served. A notice to produce documents or tangible things under Rule 205.3 must be served at least 10 days before the subpoena compelling production is served.

205.3. Production of Documents and Tangible Things Without Deposition.

(a) **Notice; subpoena**. A party may compel production of documents and tangible things from a nonparty by serving—a reasonable time before the response is due but no later than 30 days before the end of any applicable discovery period—the notice required in Rule 205.2 and a subpoena compelling production or inspection of documents or tangible things.

(b) **Contents of notice**. The notice must state:

(1) the name of the person from whom production or inspection is sought to be compelled;

(2) a reasonable time and place for the production or inspection; and

(3) the items to be produced or inspected, either by individual item or by category, describing each item and category with reasonable particularity, and, if applicable, describing the desired testing and sampling with sufficient specificity to inform the nonparty of the means, manner, and procedure for testing or sampling.

(c) **Requests for production of medical or mental health records of other nonparties**. If a party requests a nonparty to produce medical or mental health records of another nonparty, the requesting party must serve the nonparty whose records are sought with the notice required under this rule. This requirement does not apply under the circumstances set forth in Rule 196.1 (c)(2).

(d) **Response**. The nonparty must respond to the notice and subpoena in accordance with Rule 176.6.

(e) **Custody, inspection and copying**. The party obtaining the production must make all materials produced available for inspection by any other party on reasonable notice, and must furnish copies to any party who requests at that party's expense.

(f) **Cost of production**. A party requiring production of documents by a nonparty must reimburse the nonparty's reasonable costs of production.

(Added Aug. 5, 1998 and Nov. 9, 1998, and amended Dec. 31, 1998, eff. Jan. 1, 1999.)

Comments to 1999 change: Under this rule, a party may subpoena production of documents and tangible things from nonparties without need for a motion or oral or written deposition.

RULES 206, 207, 208, 208a, 209, 210, 211, 212, 213, and 214. [REPEALED]

(Rules 206 to 209 repealed Aug. 5, 1998 and Nov. 9, 1998, eff. Jan. 1, 1999; Rules 210 to 214 repealed Dec. 5, 1983, eff. April 1, 1984.)

RULE 215. ABUSE OF DISCOVERY; SANCTIONS.

215.1. Motion for Sanctions or Order Compelling Discovery.

A party, upon reasonable notice to other parties and all other persons affected thereby, may apply for sanctions or an order compelling discovery as follows:

(a) **Appropriate court**. On matters relating to a deposition, an application for an order to a party may be made to the court in which the action is pending, or to any district court in the district where the deposition is being taken. An application for an order to a deponent who is not a party shall be made to the court in the district where the deposition is being taken. As to all other discovery matters, an application for an order will be made to the court in which the action is pending.

(b) **Motion**.

(1) If a party or other deponent which is a corporation or other entity fails to make a designation under Rules 199.2 (b)(1) or 200.1 (b); or

(2) If a party, or other deponent, or a person designated to testify on behalf of a party or other deponent fails:

(A) to appear before the officer who is to take his deposition, after being served with a proper notice; or

(B) to answer a question propounded or submitted upon oral examination or upon written questions; or

(3) if a party fails:

(A) to serve answers or objections to interrogatories submitted under Rule 197, after proper service of the interrogatories; or

(B) to answer an interrogatory submitted under Rule 197; or

(C) to serve a written response to a request for inspection submitted under Rule 196, after proper service of the request; or

(D) to respond that discovery will be permitted as requested or fails to permit discovery as requested in response to a request for inspection submitted under Rule 196; the discovering party may move for an order compelling a designation, an appearance, an answer or answers, or inspection or production in accordance with the request, or apply to the court in which the action is pending for the imposition of any sanction authorized by Rule 215.2 (b) without the necessity of first having obtained a court order compelling such discovery. When taking a deposition on oral examination, the proponent of the question may complete or adjourn the examination before he applies for an order. If the court denies the motion in whole or in part, it may make such protective order as it would have been empowered to make on a motion pursuant to Rule 192.6.

(c) **Evasive or incomplete answer**. For purposes of this subdivision an evasive or incomplete answer is to be treated as a failure to answer.

(d) **Disposition of motion to compel: award of expenses**. If the motion is granted, the court shall, after opportunity for hearing, require a party or deponent whose conduct necessitated the motion or the party or attorney advising such conduct or both of them to pay, at such time as ordered by the court, the moving party the reasonable expenses incurred in obtaining the order, including attorney fees, unless the court finds that the opposition to the motion was substantially justified or that other circumstances make an award of expenses unjust. Such an order shall be subject to review on appeal from the final judgment. If the motion is denied, the court may, after opportunity for hearing, require the moving party or attorney advising such motion to pay to the party or deponent who opposed the motion the reasonable expenses incurred in opposing the motion, including attorney fees, unless the court finds that the making of the motion was substantially justified or that other circumstances make an award of expenses unjust. If the motion is granted in part and denied in part, the court may apportion the reasonable expenses incurred in relation to the motion among the parties and persons in a just manner. In determining the amount of reasonable expenses, including attorney fees, to be awarded in connection with a motion, the trial court shall award expenses which are reasonable in relation to the amount of work reasonably expended in obtaining an order compelling compliance or in opposing a motion which is denied.

(e) **Providing person's own statement**. If a party fails to comply with any person's written request for the person's own statement as provided in Rule 192.3(h), the person who made the request may move for an order compelling compliance. If the motion is granted, the movant may recover the expenses incurred in obtaining the order, including attorney fees, which are reasonable in relation to the amount of work reasonably expended in obtaining the order.

215.2. Failure to Comply with Order or with Discovery Request.

(a) **Sanctions by court in district where deposition is taken**. If a deponent fails to appear or to be sworn or to answer a question after being directed to do so by a district court in the district in which the deposition is being taken, the failure may be considered a contempt of that court.

(b) **Sanctions by court in which action is pending**. If a party or an officer, director, or managing agent of a party or a person designated under Rules 199.2 (b)(1) or 200.1 (b) to testify on behalf of a party fails to comply with proper discovery requests or to obey an order to provide or permit discovery, including an order made under Rules 204 or 215.1, the court in which the action is pending may, after notice and hearing, make such orders in regard to the failure as are just, and among others the following:
   (1) an order disallowing any further discovery or any kind or of a particular kind by the disobedient party;
   (2) an order charging all or any portion of the expenses of discovery or taxable court costs or both against the disobedient party or the attorney advising him;
   (3) an order that the matters regarding which the order was made or any other designated facts shall be taken to be established for the purposes of the action in accordance with the claim of the party obtaining the order;
   (4) an order refusing to allow the disobedient party to support or oppose designated claims or defenses, or prohibiting him from introducing designated matters in evidence;
   (5) an order striking out pleadings or parts thereof, or staying further proceedings until the order is obeyed, or dismissing with or without prejudice the action or proceedings or any part thereof, or rendering a judgment by default against the disobedient party;
   (6) in lieu of any of the foregoing orders or in addition thereto, an order treating as a contempt of court the failure to obey any orders except an order to submit to a physical or mental examination;
   (7) when a party has failed to comply with an order under Rule 204 requiring him to appear or produce another for examination, such orders as are listed in paragraphs (1), (2), (3), (4) or (5) of this subdivision, unless the person failing to comply shows that he is unable to appear or to produce such person for examination.
   (8) In lieu of any of the foregoing orders or in addition thereto, the court shall require the party failing to obey the order or the attorney advising him, or both, to pay, at such time as ordered by the court, the reasonable expenses, including attorney fees, caused by the failure, unless the court finds that the failure was substantially justified or that other circumstances make an award of expenses unjust. Such an order shall be subject to review on appeal from the final judgment.

(c) **Sanction against nonparty for violation of Rules 196.7 or 205.3**. If a nonparty fails to comply with an order under Rules 196.7 or 205.3, the court which made the order may treat the failure to obey as contempt of court.

215.3. Abuse of Discovery Process in Seeking, Making, or Resisting Discovery.

If the court finds a party is abusing the discovery process in seeking, making or resisting discovery or if the court finds that any interrogatory or request for inspection or production is unreasonably frivolous, oppressive, or harassing, or that a response or answer is unreasonably frivolous or made for purposes of delay, then the court in which the action is pending may, after notice and hearing, impose any appropriate sanction authorized by paragraphs (1), (2), (3), (4), (5), and (8) of Rule 215.2(b). Such order of sanction shall be subject to review on appeal from the final judgment.

215.4. Failure to Comply with Rule 198.

(a) **Motion**. A party who has requested an admission under Rule 198 may move to determine the sufficiency of the answer or objection. For purposes of this subdivision an evasive or incomplete answer may be treated as a failure to answer. Unless the court determines that an objection is justified, it shall order that an answer be served. If the court determines that an answer does not comply with the requirements of Rule 198, it may order either that the matter is admitted or that an amended answer be served. The provisions of Rule 215.1 (d) apply to the award of expenses incurred in relation to the motion.

(b) **Expenses on failure to admit**. If a party fails to admit the genuineness of any document or the truth of any matter as requested under Rule 198 and if the party requesting the admissions thereafter proves the genuineness of the document or the truth of the matter, he may apply to the court for an order requiring the other party to pay him the reasonable expenses incurred in making that proof, including reasonable attorney fees. The court shall make the order unless it finds that
   (1) the request was held objectionable pursuant to Rule 193, or
   (2) the admission sought was of no substantial importance, or
   (3) the party failing to admit had a reasonable ground to believe that he might prevail on the matter, or
   (4) there was other good reason for the failure to admit.

215.5. Failure of Party or Witness to Attend or to Serve Subpoena; Expenses.

(a) **Failure of party giving notice to attend**. If the party giving the notice of the taking of an oral deposition fails to attend and proceed therewith and another party attends in person or by attorney pursuant to the notice, the court may order the party giving the notice to pay such other party the reasonable expenses incurred by him and his attorney in attending, including reasonable attorney fees.

(b) **Failure of witness to attend**. If a party gives notice of the taking of an oral deposition of a witness and the witness does not attend because of the fault of the party giving the notice, if another party attends in person or by attorney because he expects the deposition of that witness to be taken, the court may order the party giving the notice to pay such other party the reasonable expenses incurred by him and his attorney in attending, including reasonable attorney fees.

215.6. Exhibits to Motions and Responses.

Motions or responses made under this rule may have exhibits attached including affidavits, discovery pleadings, or any other documents.

(Amended by Order Aug. 5, 1998, and Nov. 9, 1998, eff. Jan. 1, 1999.)

Comments to 1999 change: The references in this rule to other discovery rules are changed to reflect the revisions in those rules, and former Rule 203 is added as Rule 215.5 in place of the former provision, which is superseded by Rule 193.6.

SECTION 10.
THE JURY IN COURT

RULE 216. REQUEST AND FEE FOR JURY TRIAL.

a. **Request**. No jury trial shall be had in any civil suit, unless a written request for a jury trial is filed with the clerk of the court a reasonable time before the date set for trial of the cause on the non-jury docket, but not less than thirty days in advance.

b. **Jury Fee**. Unless otherwise provided by law, a fee of ten dollars if in the district court and five dollars if in the county court must be deposited with the clerk of the court within the time for making a written request for a jury trial. The clerk shall promptly enter a notation of the payment of such fee upon the court's docket sheet.

(Amended by Order March 31, 1941, eff. Sept. 1, 1941; Sept. 20, 1941, eff. Dec. 31, 1941; Oct. 12, 1949, eff. March 1, 1950; July 15, 1987, eff. Jan. 1, 1988; April 24, 1990, eff. Sept. 1, 1990.)

RULE 217. OATH OF INABILITY.

The deposit for a jury fee shall not be required when the party shall within the time for making such deposit, file with the clerk his affidavit to the effect that he is unable to make such deposit, and that he can not, by the pledge of property or otherwise, obtain the money necessary for that purpose; and the court shall then order the clerk to enter the suit on the jury docket.

RULE 218. JURY DOCKET.

The clerks of the district and county courts shall each keep a docket, styled, "The Jury Docket," in which shall be entered in their order the cases in which jury fees have been paid or affidavit in lieu thereof has been filed as provided in the two preceding rules.

RULE 219. JURY TRIAL DAY.

The court shall designate the days for taking up the jury docket and the trial of jury cases. Such order may be revoked or changed in the court's discretion.

(Amended by Order Dec. 5, 1983, eff. April 1, 1984.)

RULE 220. WITHDRAWING CAUSE FROM JURY DOCKET.

When any party has paid the fee for a jury trial, he shall not be permitted to withdraw the cause from the jury docket over the objection of the parties adversely interested. If so permitted, the court in its discretion may by an order permit him to withdraw also his jury fee deposit. Failure of a party to appear for trial shall be deemed a waiver by him of the right to trial by jury.

(Amended by Order Aug. 18, 1947, eff. Dec. 31, 1947; July 21, 1970, eff. Jan. 1, 1971.)

RULE 221. CHALLENGE TO THE ARRAY.

When the jurors summoned have not been selected by jury commissioners or by drawing the names from a jury wheel, any party to a suit which is to be tried by a jury may, before the jury is drawn challenge the array upon the ground that the officer summoning the jury has acted corruptly, and has wilfully summoned jurors known to be prejudiced against the party challenging or biased in favor of the adverse party. All such challenges must be in writing setting forth distinctly the grounds of such challenge and supported by the affidavit of the party or some other credible person. When such challenge is made, the court shall hear evidence and decide without delay whether or not the challenge shall be sustained.

RULE 222. WHEN CHALLENGE IS SUSTAINED.

If the challenge be sustained, the array of jurors summoned shall be discharged, and the court shall order other jurors summoned in their stead, and shall direct that the officer who summoned the persons so discharged, and on account of whose misconduct the challenge has been sustained, shall not summon any other jurors in the case.

RULE 223. JURY LIST IN CERTAIN COUNTIES.

In counties governed as to juries by the laws providing for interchangeable juries, the names of the jurors shall be placed upon the general panel in the order in which they are randomly selected, and jurors shall be assigned for service from the top thereof, in the order in which they shall be needed, and jurors returned to the general panel after service in any of such courts shall be enrolled at the bottom of the list in the order of their respective return; provided, however, after such assignment to a particular court, the trial judge of such court, upon the demand prior to voir dire examination by any party or attorney in the case reached for trial in such court, shall cause the names of all members of such assigned jury panel in such case to be placed in a receptacle, shuffled, and drawn, and such names shall be transcribed in the order drawn on the jury list from which the jury is to be selected to try such case. There shall be only one shuffle and drawing by the trial judge in each case.

(Amended by Order April 24, 1990, eff. Sept. 1, 1990.)

RULE 224. PREPARING JURY LIST.

In counties not governed as to juries by the laws providing for interchangeable juries, when the parties have announced ready for trial the clerk shall write the name of each regular juror entered of record for that week on separate slips of paper, as near the same size and appearance as may be, and shall place the slips in a box and mix them well. The clerk shall draw from the box, in the presence of the court, the names of twenty-four jurors, if in the district court, or so many as there may be, if there be a less number in the box; and the names of twelve jurors if in the county court, or so many as there may be, and write the names as drawn upon two slips of paper and deliver one slip to each party to the suit or his attorney.

RULE 225. SUMMONING TALESMAN.

When there are not as many as twenty-four names drawn from the box, if in the district court, or as many as twelve, if in the county court, the court shall direct the sheriff to summon such number of qualified persons as the court deems necessary to complete the panel. The names of those thus summoned shall be placed in the box and drawn and entered upon the slips as provided in the preceding rules.

RULE 226. OATH TO JURY PANEL.

Before the parties or their attorneys begin the examination of the jurors whose names have thus been listed, the jurors shall be sworn by the court or under its direction, as follows: "You, and each of you, do solemnly swear that you will true answers give to all questions propounded to you concerning your qualifications as a juror, so help you God."

RULE 226a. INSTRUCTIONS TO JURY PANEL AND JURY.

The court must give instructions to the jury panel and the jury as prescribed by order of the Supreme Court under this rule.

(Added July 20, 1966, eff. Jan. 1, 1967. Amended by Order July 15, 1987, eff. Jan. 1, 1988; Jan. 27, 2005, eff. Feb. 1, 2005 in all pending cases.)

Comment – 2005:

The rule is clarified. With these amendments, the Supreme Court has ordered changes in the prescribed jury instructions consistent with Act of June 2, 2003, 78th Leg., R.S., c. 204, § 13.04, 2003 Tex. Gen. Laws 847, 888, codified as TEX. CIV. PRAC. & REM. CODE § 41.003.

AMENDMENTS TO JURY INSTRUCTIONS
UNDER RULE 226a, TEXAS RULES OF CIVIL PROCEDURE

To implement Act of June 2, 2003, 78th Leg., R.S., c. 204, § 13.04, 2003 Tex. Gen. Laws 847, 888, codified as TEX. CIV. PRAC. & REM. CODE § 41.003, Part III of the jury instructions prescribed under Rule 226a, Texas Rules of Civil Procedure, by orders dated July 20, 1966 (effective January 1, 1967), July 21, 1970 (effective January 1, 1971), October 3, 1972 (effective February 1, 1973), December 5, 1983 (effective April 1, 1984), March 10, 1987 (effective January 1, 1988), December 16, 1987 (effective January 1, 1988), and January 28, 1988 (effective January 1, 1988), and March 15, 2011 (effective April 1, 2011), and April 13, 2011 (effective April 13, 2011) is amended as follows.

Jury Instructions Prescribed by Order Under Rule 226a

I.

That the following oral instructions, with such modifications as the circumstances of the particular case may require, shall be given by the court to the members of the jury panel after they have been sworn in as provided in Rule 226 and before the voir dire examination:

Members of the Jury Panel [or Ladies and Gentlemen of the Jury Panel]:

Thank you for being here. We are here to select a jury. Twelve [six] of you will be chosen for the jury. Even if you are not chosen for the jury, you are performing a valuable service that is your right and duty as a citizen of a free country.

Before we begin: Turn off all phones and other electronic devices. While you are in the courtroom, do not communicate with anyone through any electronic device. [For example, do not communicate by phone, text message, email message, chat room, blog, or social networking websites such as Facebook, Twitter, or Myspace.] [I will give you a number where others may contact you in case of an emergency.] Do not record or photograph any part of these court proceedings, because it is prohibited by law.

If you are chosen for the jury, your role as jurors will be to decide the disputed facts in this case. My role will be to ensure that this case is tried in accordance with the rules of law.

Here is some background about this case. This is a civil case. It is a lawsuit that is not a criminal case. The parties are as follows: The plaintiff is __________, and the defendant is __________. Representing the plaintiff is __________, and representing the defendant is __________. They will ask you some questions during jury selection. But before their questions begin, I must give you some instructions for jury selection.

Every juror must obey these instructions. You may be called into court to testify about any violations of these instructions. If you do not follow these instructions, you will be guilty of juror misconduct, and I might have to order a new trial and start this process over again. This would waste your time and the parties' money, and would require the taxpayers of this county to pay for another trial.

These are the instructions.

1. To avoid looking like you are friendly with one side of the case, do not mingle or talk with the lawyers, witnesses, parties, or anyone else involved in the case. You may exchange casual greetings like "hello" and "good morning." Other than that, do not talk with them at all. They have to follow these instructions too, so you should not be offended when they follow the instructions.

2. Do not accept any favors from the lawyers, witnesses, parties, or anyone else involved in the case, and do not do any favors for them. This includes favors such as giving rides and food.

3. Do not discuss this case with anyone, even your spouse or a friend, either in person or by any other means [including by phone, text message, email message, chat room, blog, or social networking websites such as Facebook, Twitter, or Myspace]. Do not allow anyone to discuss the case with you or in your hearing. If anyone tries to discuss the case with you or in your hearing, tell me immediately. We do not want you to be influenced by something other than the evidence admitted in court.

4. The parties, through their attorneys, have the right to ask you questions about your background, experiences, and attitudes. They are not trying to meddle in your affairs. They are just being thorough and trying to choose fair jurors who do not have any bias or prejudice in this particular case.

5. Remember that you took an oath that you will tell the truth, so be truthful when the lawyers ask you questions, and always give complete answers. If you do not answer a question that applies to you, that violates your oath. Sometimes a lawyer will ask a question of the whole panel instead of just one person. If the question applies to you, raise your hand and keep it raised until you are called on.

Do you understand these instructions? If you do not, please tell me now.

The lawyers will now begin to ask their questions.

II.

That the following oral and written instructions, with such modifications as the circumstances of the particular case may require, shall be given by the court to the jury immediately after the jurors are selected for the case:

Members of the Jury [or Ladies and Gentlemen]:

You have been chosen to serve on this jury. Because of the oath you have taken and your selection for the jury, you become officials of this court and active participants in our justice system.

[Hand out the written instructions.]

You have each received a set of written instructions. I am going to read them with you now. Some of them you have heard before and some are new.

1. Turn off all phones and other electronic devices. While you are in the courtroom and while you are deliberating, do not communicate with anyone through any electronic device. [For example, do not communicate by phone, text message, email message, chat room, blog, or social networking websites such as Facebook, Twitter, or Myspace.] [I will give you a number where others may contact you in case of an emergency.] Do not post information about the case on the Internet before these court proceedings end and you are released from jury duty. Do not record or photograph any part of these court proceedings, because it is prohibited by law.

2. To avoid looking like you are friendly with one side of the case, do not mingle or talk with the lawyers, witnesses, parties, or anyone else involved in the case. You may exchange casual greetings like "hello" and "good morning." Other than that, do not talk with them at all. They have to follow these instructions too, so you should not be offended when they follow the instructions.

3. Do not accept any favors from the lawyers, witnesses, parties, or anyone else involved in the case, and do not do any favors for them. This includes favors such as giving rides and food.

4. Do not discuss this case with anyone, even your spouse or a friend, either in person or by any other means [including by phone, text message, email message, chat room, blog, or social networking websites such as Facebook, Twitter, or Myspace]. Do not allow anyone to discuss the case with you or in your hearing. If anyone tries to discuss the case with you or in your hearing, tell me immediately. We do not want you to be influenced by something other than the evidence admitted in court.

5. Do not discuss this case with anyone during the trial, not even with the other jurors, until the end of the trial. You should not discuss the case with your fellow jurors until the end of the trial so that you do not form opinions about the case before you have heard everything. After you have heard all the evidence, received all of my instructions, and heard all of the lawyers' arguments, you will then go to the jury room to discuss the case with the other jurors and reach a verdict.

6. Do not investigate this case on your own. For example, do not:

   a. try to get information about the case, lawyers, witnesses, or issues from outside this courtroom;
   b. go to places mentioned in the case to inspect the places;
   c. inspect items mentioned in this case unless they are presented as evidence in court;
   d. look anything up in a law book, dictionary, or public record to try to learn more about the case;
   e. look anything up on the Internet to try to learn more about the case; or
   f. let anyone else do any of these things for you.

This rule is very important because we want a trial based only on evidence admitted in open court. Your conclusions about this case must be based only on what you see and hear in this courtroom because the law does not permit you to base your conclusions on information that has not been presented to you in open court. All the information must be presented in open court so the parties and their lawyers can test it and object to it. Information from other sources, like the Internet, will not go through this important process in the courtroom. In addition, information from other sources could be completely unreliable. As a result, if you investigate this case on your own, you could compromise the fairness to all parties in this case and jeopardize the results of this trial.

7. Do not tell other jurors about your own experiences or other people's experiences. For example, you may have special knowledge of something in the case, such as business, technical, or professional information. You may even have expert knowledge or opinions, or you may know what happened in this case or another similar case. Do not tell the other jurors about it. Telling other jurors about it is wrong because it means the jury will be considering things that were not admitted in court.

8. Do not consider attorneys' fees unless I tell you to. Do not guess about attorneys' fees.

9. Do not consider or guess whether any party is covered by insurance unless I tell you to.

10. During the trial, if taking notes will help focus your attention on the evidence, you may take notes using the materials the court has provided. Do not use any personal electronic devices to take notes. If taking notes will distract your attention from the evidence, you should not take notes. Your notes are for your own personal use. They are not evidence. Do not show or read your notes to anyone, including other jurors.

You must leave your notes in the jury room or with the bailiff. The bailiff is instructed not to read your notes and to give your notes to me promptly after collecting them from you. I will make sure your notes are kept in a safe, secure location and not disclosed to anyone.

[You may take your notes back into the jury room and consult them during deliberations. But keep in mind that your notes are not evidence. When you deliberate, each of you should rely on your independent recollection of the evidence and not be influenced by the fact that another juror has or has not taken notes. After you complete your deliberations, the bailiff will collect your notes.]

When you are released from jury duty, the bailiff will promptly destroy your notes so that nobody can read what you wrote.

11. I will decide matters of law in this case. It is your duty to listen to and consider the evidence and to determine fact issues that I may submit to you at the end of the trial. After you have heard all the evidence, I will give you instructions to follow as you make your decision. The instructions also will have questions for you to answer. You will not be asked and you should not consider which side will win. Instead, you will need to answer the specific questions I give you.

Every juror must obey my instructions. If you do not follow these instructions, you will be guilty of juror misconduct, and I may have to order a new trial and start this process over again. This would waste your time and the parties' money, and would require the taxpayers of this county to pay for another trial.

Do you understand these instructions? If you do not, please tell me now.

Please keep these instructions and review them as we go through this case. If anyone does not follow these instructions, tell me.

III.
Court's Charge

Before closing arguments begin, the court must give to each member of the jury a copy of the charge, which must include the following written instructions, with such modifications as the circumstances of the particular case may require:

Members of the Jury [or Ladies & Gentlemen of the Jury]:

After the closing arguments, you will go to the jury room to decide the case, answer the questions that are attached, and reach a verdict. You may discuss the case with other jurors only when you are all together in the jury room.

Remember my previous instructions: Do not discuss the case with anyone else, either in person or by any other means. Do not do any independent investigation about the case or conduct any research. Do not look up any words in dictionaries or on the Internet. Do not post information about the case on the Internet. Do not share any special knowledge or experiences with the other jurors. Do not use your phone or any other electronic device during your deliberations for any reason. [I will give you a number where others may contact you in case of an emergency.]

[Any notes you have taken are for your own personal use. You may take your notes back into the jury room and consult them during deliberations, but do not show or read your notes to your fellow jurors during your deliberations. Your notes are not evidence. Each of you should rely on your independent recollection of the evidence and not be influenced by the fact that another juror has or has not taken notes.]

[You must leave your notes with the bailiff when you are not deliberating. The bailiff will give your notes to me promptly after collecting them from you. I will make sure your notes are kept in a safe, secure location and not disclosed to anyone. After you complete your deliberations, the bailiff will collect your notes. When you are released from jury duty, the bailiff will promptly destroy your notes so that nobody can read what you wrote.]

Here are the instructions for answering the questions.

1. Do not let bias, prejudice, or sympathy play any part in your decision.
2. Base your answers only on the evidence admitted in court and on the law that is in these instructions and questions. Do not consider or discuss any evidence that was not admitted in the courtroom.
3. You are to make up your own minds about the facts. You are the sole judges of the credibility of the witnesses and the weight to give their testimony. But on matters of law, you must follow all of my instructions.
4. If my instructions use a word in a way that is different from its ordinary meaning, use the meaning I give you, which will be a proper legal definition.
5. All the questions and answers are important. No one should say that any question or answer is not important.
6. Answer "yes" or "no" to all questions unless you are told otherwise. A "yes" answer must be based on a preponderance of the evidence [unless you are told otherwise]. Whenever a question requires an answer other than "yes" or "no," your answer must be based on a preponderance of the evidence [unless you are told otherwise].

   The term "preponderance of the evidence" means the greater weight of credible evidence presented in this case. If you do not find that a preponderance of the evidence supports a "yes" answer, then answer "no." A preponderance of the evidence is not measured by the number of witnesses or by the number of documents admitted in evidence. For a fact to be proved by a preponderance of the evidence, you must find that the fact is more likely true than not true.
7. Do not decide who you think should win before you answer the questions and then just answer the questions to match your decision. Answer each question carefully without considering who will win. Do not discuss or consider the effect your answers will have.
8. Do not answer questions by drawing straws or by any method of chance.
9. Some questions might ask you for a dollar amount. Do not agree in advance to decide on a dollar amount by adding up each juror's amount and then figuring the average.
10. Do not trade your answers. For example, do not say, "I will answer this question your way if you answer another question my way."
11. [Unless otherwise instructed] The answers to the questions must be based on the decision of at least 10 of the 12 [5 of the 6] jurors. The same 10 [5] jurors must agree on every answer. Do not agree to be bound by a vote of anything less than 10 [5] jurors, even if it would be a majority.

As I have said before, if you do not follow these instructions, you will be guilty of juror misconduct, and I might have to order a new trial and start this process over again. This would waste your time and the parties' money, and would require the taxpayers of this county to pay for another trial. If a juror breaks any of these rules, tell that person to stop and report it to me immediately.

[Definitions, questions, and special instructions given to the jury will be transcribed here. If exemplary damages are sought against a defendant, the jury must unanimously find, with respect to that defendant, (i) liability on at least one claim for actual damages that will support an award of exemplary damages, (ii) any additional conduct, such as malice or gross negligence, required for an award of exemplary damages, and (iii) the amount of exemplary damages to be awarded. The jury's answers to questions regarding (ii) and (iii) must be conditioned on a unanimous finding regarding (i), except in an extraordinary circumstance when the conditioning instruction would be erroneous. The jury need not be unanimous in finding the amount of actual damages. Thus, if questions regarding (ii) and (iii) are submitted to the jury for defendants D1 and D2, instructions in substantially the following form must immediately precede such questions:

Preceding question (ii):
Answer Question (ii) for D1 only if you unanimously answered "Yes" to Question[s] (i) regarding D1. Otherwise, do not answer Question (ii) for D1. [Repeat for D2.]
You are instructed that in order to answer "Yes" to [any part of] Question (ii), your answer must be unanimous. You may answer "No" to [any part of] Question (ii) only upon a vote of 10 [5] or more jurors. Otherwise, you must not answer [that part of] Question (ii).
Preceding question (iii):
Answer Question (iii) for D1 only if you answered "Yes" to Question (ii) for D1. Otherwise, do not answer Question (iii) for D1. [Repeat for D2.]
You are instructed that you must unanimously agree on the amount of any award of exemplary damages.
These examples are given by way of illustration.]

Presiding Juror:

1. When you go into the jury room to answer the questions, the first thing you will need to do is choose a presiding juror.
2. The presiding juror has these duties:
    a. have the complete charge read aloud if it will be helpful to your deliberations;
    b. preside over your deliberations, meaning manage the discussions, and see that you follow these instructions;
    c. give written questions or comments to the bailiff who will give them to the judge;
    d. write down the answers you agree on;
    e. get the signatures for the verdict certificate; and
    f. notify the bailiff that you have reached a verdict.

Do you understand the duties of the presiding juror? If you do not, please tell me now.

Instructions for Signing the Verdict Certificate:

1. [Unless otherwise instructed] You may answer the questions on a vote of 10 [5] jurors. The same 10 [5] jurors must agree on every answer in the charge. This means you may not have one group of 10 [5] jurors agree on one answer and a different group of 10 [5] jurors agree on another answer.
2. If 10 [5] jurors agree on every answer, those 10 [5] jurors sign the verdict.
    If 11 jurors agree on every answer, those 11 jurors sign the verdict.
    If all 12 [6] of you agree on every answer, you are unanimous and only the presiding juror signs the verdict.
3. All jurors should deliberate on every question. You may end up with all 12 [6] of you agreeing on some answers, while only 10 [5] or 11 of you agree on other answers. But when you sign the verdict, only those 10 [5] who agree on every answer will sign the verdict.
4. [Added if the charge requires some unanimity] There are some special instructions before Questions _______ explaining how to answer those questions. Please follow the instructions. If all 12 [6] of you answer those questions, you will need to complete a second verdict certificate for those questions.

Do you understand these instructions? If you do not, please tell me now.

____
Judge Presiding

Verdict Certificate

Check one:
_____ Our verdict is unanimous. All 12 [6] of us have agreed to each and every answer. The presiding juror has signed the certificate for all 12 [6] of us.

_________________________ _________________________
Signature of Presiding Juror Printed Name of Presiding Juror

_____ Our verdict is not unanimous. Eleven of us have agreed to each and every answer and have signed the certificate below.

_____ Our verdict is not unanimous. Ten [Five] of us have agreed to each and every answer and have signed the certificate below.

SIGNATURE	NAME PRINTED
1. ______________________	______________________
2. ______________________	______________________
3. ______________________	______________________
4. ______________________	______________________
5. ______________________	______________________

6. ____________________ ____________________
7. ____________________ ____________________
8. ____________________ ____________________
9. ____________________ ____________________
10. ____________________ ____________________
11. ____________________ ____________________

If you have answered Question No. ________ [the exemplary damages amount], then you must sign this certificate also.

Additional Certificate

[Used when some questions require unanimous answers]

I certify that the jury was unanimous in answering the following questions. All 12 [6] of us agreed to each of the answers. The presiding juror has signed the certificate for all 12 [6] of us.

[Judge to list questions that require a unanimous answer, including the predicate liability question.]

____________________ ____________________
Signature of Presiding Juror Printed Name of Presiding Juror

IV.

That the following oral instructions shall be given by the court to the jury after the verdict has been accepted by the court and before the jurors are released from jury duty:

Thank you for your verdict.

I have told you that the only time you may discuss the case is with the other jurors in the jury room. I now release you from jury duty. Now you may discuss the case with anyone. But you may also choose not to discuss the case; that is your right.

After you are released from jury duty, the lawyers and others may ask you questions to see if the jury followed the instructions, and they may ask you to give a sworn statement. You are free to discuss the case with them and to give a sworn statement. But you may choose not to discuss the case and not to give a sworn statement; that is your right.

Instructions adopted by orders dated July 20, 1966 (eff. Jan. 1, 1967). Amended by Orders July 21, 1970 (eff. Jan. 1, 1971); Oct. 3, 1972 (eff. Feb. 1, 1973); Dec. 5, 1983 (eff. April 1, 1984); March 10, 1987 (eff. Jan. 1, 1988); Dec. 16, 1987 (eff. Jan. 1, 1988); Jan. 28, 1988 (eff. Jan. 1, 1988); Jan. 27, 2005 (eff. Feb. 1, 2005, in all cases filed on or after Sept. 1, 2003); March 15, 2011 (effective April 1, 2011); April 13, 2011 (effective April 13, 2011).

RULE 227. CHALLENGE TO JUROR.

A challenge to a particular juror is either a challenge for cause or a peremptory challenge. The court shall decide without delay any such challenge, and if sustained, the juror shall be discharged from the particular case. Either such challenge may be made orally on the formation of a jury to try the case.

RULE 228. "CHALLENGE FOR CAUSE" DEFINED.

A challenge for cause is an objection made to a juror, alleging some fact which by law disqualifies him to serve as a juror in the case or in any case, or which in the opinion of the court, renders him an unfit person to sit on the jury. Upon such challenge the examination is not confined to the answers of the juror, but other evidence may be heard for or against the challenge.

RULE 229. CHALLENGE FOR CAUSE.

When twenty-four or more jurors, if in the district court, or twelve or more, if in the county court, are drawn, and the lists of their names delivered to the parties, if either party desires to challenge any juror for cause, the challenge shall then be made. The name of a juror challenged and set aside for cause shall be erased from such lists.

RULE 230. CERTAIN QUESTIONS NOT TO BE ASKED.

In examining a juror, he shall not be asked a question the answer to which may show that he has been convicted of an offense which disqualifies him, or that he stands charged by some legal accusation with theft or any felony.

RULE 231. NUMBER REDUCED BY CHALLENGES.

If the challenges reduce the number of jurors to less than twenty-four, if in the district court, or to less than twelve, if in the county court, the court shall order other jurors to be drawn from the wheel or from the central jury panel or summoned, as the practice may be in the particular county, and their names written upon the list instead of those set aside for cause. Such jurors so summoned may likewise be challenged for cause.

RULE 232. MAKING PEREMPTORY CHALLENGES.

If there remain on such lists not subject to challenge for cause, twenty-four names, if in the district court, or twelve names, if in the county court, the parties shall proceed to make their peremptory challenges. A peremptory challenge is made to a juror without assigning any reason therefor.

RULE 233. NUMBER OF PEREMPTORY CHALLENGES.

Except as provided below, each party to a civil action is entitled to six peremptory challenges in a case tried in the district court, and to three in the county court.

Alignment of the Parties. In multiple party cases, it shall be the duty of the trial judge to decide whether any of the litigants aligned on the same side of the docket are antagonistic with respect to any issued to be submitted to the jury, before the exercise of peremptory challenges.

Definition of Side. The term "side" as used in this rule is not synonymous with "party," "litigant," or "person." Rather, "side" means one or more litigants who have common interests on the matters with which the jury is concerned.

Motion to Equalize. In multiple party cases, upon motion of any litigant made prior to the exercise of peremptory challenges, it shall be the duty of the trial judge to equalize the number of peremptory challenges so that no litigant or side is given unfair advantage as a result of the alignment of the litigants and the award of peremptory challenges to each litigant or side. In determining how the challenges should be allocated the court shall consider any matter brought to the attention of the trial judge concerning the ends of justice and the elimination of an unfair advantage.

(Amended by Order Dec. 5, 1983, eff. April 1, 1984.)

RULE 234. LISTS RETURNED TO THE CLERK.

When the parties have made or declined to make their peremptory challenges, they shall deliver their lists to the clerk. The clerk shall, if the case be in the district court, call off the first twelve names on the lists that have not been erased; and if the case be in the county court, he shall call off the first six names on the lists that have not been erased; those whose names are called shall be the jury.

RULE 235. IF JURY IS INCOMPLETE.

When by peremptory challenges the jury is left incomplete, the court shall direct other jurors to be drawn or summoned to complete the jury; and such other jurors shall be impaneled as in the first instance.

RULE 236. OATH TO JURY.

The jury shall be sworn by the court or under its direction, in substance as follows: "You, and each of you, do solemnly swear that in all cases between parties which shall be to you submitted, you will a true verdict render, according to the law, as it may be given you in charge by the court, and to the evidence submitted to you under the rulings of the court. So help you God."

SECTION 11.
TRIAL OF CAUSES

A.
APPEARANCE AND PROCEDURE

RULE 237. APPEARANCE DAY.

If a defendant, who has been duly cited, is by the citation required to answer on a day which is in term time, such day is appearance day as to him. If he is so required to answer on a day in vacation, he shall plead or answer accordingly, and the first day of the next term is appearance day as to him.

(Amended by Order March 31, 1941, eff. Sept. 1, 1941; July 20, 1954, eff. Jan. 1, 1955.)

RULE 237a. CASES REMANDED FROM FEDERAL COURT.

When any cause is removed to the Federal Court and is afterwards remanded to the state court, the plaintiff shall file a certified copy of the order of remand with the clerk of the state court and shall forthwith give written notice of such filing to the attorneys of record for all adverse parties. All such adverse parties shall have fifteen days from the receipt of such notice within which to file an answer. No default judgment shall be rendered against a party in a removed action remanded from federal court if that party filed an answer in federal court during removal.

(Added July 20, 1954, eff. Jan. 1, 1955. Amended by Order Dec. 5, 1983, eff. April 1, 1984; caption amended by order of July 15, 1987, eff. Jan. 1, 1988; April 24, 1990, eff. Sept. 1, 1990.)

RULE 238. CALL OF APPEARANCE DOCKET.

On the appearance day of a particular defendant and at the hour named in the citation, or as soon thereafter as may be practicable, the court or clerk in open court shall call, in their order, all the cases on the docket in which such day is appearance day as to any defendant, or, the court or clerk failing therein, any such case shall be so called on request of the plaintiff's attorney.

RULE 239. JUDGMENT BY DEFAULT.

Upon such call of the docket, or at any time after a defendant is required to answer, the plaintiff may in term time take judgment by default against such defendant if he has not previously filed an answer, and provided that return of service shall have been on file with the clerk for the length of time required by Rule 107.

(Amended by Order April 12, 1962, eff. Sept. 1, 1962; Oct. 17, 2011, eff. Jan. 1, 2012.)

RULE 239a. NOTICE OF DEFAULT JUDGMENT.

At or immediately prior to the time in interlocutory or final default judgment is rendered, the party taking the same or his attorney shall certify to the clerk in writing the last known mailing address of the party against whom the judgment is taken, which certificate shall be filed among the papers in the cause. Immediately upon the signing of the judgment, the clerk shall mail written notice thereof to the party against whom the judgment was rendered at the address shown in the certificate, and note the fact of such mailing on the docket. The notice shall state the number and style of the case, the court in which the case is pending, the names of the parties in whose favor and against whom the judgment was rendered, and the date of the signing of the judgment. Failure to comply with the provisions of this rule shall not affect the finality of the judgment.

(Added July 20, 1966, eff. Jan. 1, 1967. Amended by Order July 15, 1987, eff. Jan. 1, 1988.)

RULE 240. WHERE ONLY SOME ANSWER.

Where there are several defendants, some of whom have answered or have not been duly served and some of whom have been duly served and have made default, an interlocutory judgment by default may be entered against those who have made default, and the cause may proceed or be postponed as to the others.

RULE 241. ASSESSING DAMAGES ON LIQUIDATED DEMANDS.

When a judgment by default is rendered against the defendant, or all of several defendants, if the claim is liquidated and proved by an instrument in writing, the damages shall be assessed by the court, or under its direction, and final judgment shall be rendered therefor, unless the defendant shall demand and be entitled to a trial by jury.

(Amended by Order Dec. 5, 1983, eff. April 1, 1984.)

RULE 242. [REPEALED]

(Repealed by Order Sept. 20, 1941, eff. Dec. 31, 1941.)

RULE 243. UNLIQUIDATED DEMANDS.

If the cause of action is unliquidated or be not proved by an instrument in writing, the court shall hear evidence as to damages and shall render judgment therefor, unless the defendant shall demand and be entitled to a trial by jury in which case the judgment by default shall be noted, a writ of inquiry awarded, and the cause entered on the jury docket.

(Amended by Order March 31, 1941, eff. Sept. 1, 1941.)

RULE 244. ON SERVICE BY PUBLICATION.

Where service has been made by publication, and no answer has been filed nor appearance entered within the prescribed time, the court shall appoint an attorney to defend the suit in behalf of the defendant, and judgment shall be rendered as in other cases; but, in every such case a statement of the evidence, approved and signed by the judge, shall be filed with the papers of the cause as a part of the record thereof The court shall allow such attorney a reasonable fee for his services, to be taxed as part of the costs.

RULE 245. ASSIGNMENT OF CASES FOR TRIAL.

The court may set contested cases on written request of any party, or on the court's own motion, with reasonable notice of not less than forty-five days to the parties of a first setting for trial, or by agreement of the parties; provided, however, that when a case previously has been set for trial, the Court may reset said contested case to a later date on any reasonable notice to the parties or by agreement of the parties. Noncontested cases may be tried or disposed of at any time whether set or not, and may be set at any time for any other time.

A request for trial setting constitutes a representation that the requesting party reasonably and in good faith expects to be ready for trial by the date requested, but no additional representation concerning the completion of pretrial proceedings or of current readiness for trial shall be required in order to obtain a trial setting in a contested case.

(Amended by Order July 22, 1975, eff. Jan. 1, 1976; Dec. 5, 1983, eff. April 1, 1984; April 24, 1990, eff. Sept. 1, 1990.)

RULE 246. CLERK TO GIVE NOTICE OF SETTINGS.

The clerk shall keep a record in his office of all cases set for trial, and it shall be his duty to inform any non-resident attorney of the date of setting of any case upon request by mail from such attorney, accompanied by a return envelope properly addressed and stamped. Failure of the clerk to furnish such information on proper request shall be sufficient ground for continuance or for a new trial when it appears to the court that such failure has prevented the attorney from preparing or presenting his claim or defense.

RULE 247. TRIED WHEN SET.

Every suit shall be tried when it is called, unless continued or postponed to a future day or placed at the end of the docket to be called again for trial in its regular order. No cause which has been set upon the trial docket of the court shall be taken from the trial docket for the date set except by agreement of the parties or for good cause upon motion and notice to the opposing party.

(Amended by Order Dec. 5, 1983, eff. April 1, 1984.)

RULE 248. JURY CASES.

When a jury has been demanded, questions of law, motions, exceptions to pleadings, and other unresolved pending matters shall, as far as practicable, be heard and determined by the court before the trial commences, and jurors shall be summoned to appear on the day so designated.

(Amended by Order Dec. 5, 1983, eff. April 1, 1984; April 24, 1990, eff. Sept. 1, 1990.)

RULE 249. CALL OF NONJURY DOCKET.

The nonjury docket shall be taken up at such times as not unnecessarily to interfere with the dispatch of business on the jury docket.

RULE 250. [REPEALED]

(Repealed by Order Sept. 20, 1941, eff. Dec. 31, 1941.)

B.
CONTINUANCE AND CHANGE OF VENUE

RULE 251. CONTINUANCE.

No application for a continuance shall be heard before the defendant files his defense, nor shall any continuance be granted except for sufficient cause supported by affidavit, or by consent of the parties, or by operation of law.

RULE 252. APPLICATION FOR CONTINUANCE.

If the ground of such application be the want of testimony, the party applying therefor shall make affidavit that such testimony is material, showing the materiality thereof, and that he has used due diligence to procure such testimony, stating such diligence, and the cause of failure, if known; that such testimony cannot be procured from any other source; and, if it be for the absence of a witness, he shall state the name and residence of the witness, and what he expects to prove by him; and also state that the continuance is not sought for delay only, but that justice may be done; provided that, on a first application for a continuance, it shall not be necessary to show that the absent testimony cannot be procured from any other source.

The failure to obtain the deposition of any witness residing within 100 miles of the courthouse of the county in which the suit is pending shall not be regarded as want of diligence when diligence has been used to secure the personal attendance of such witness under the rules of law, unless by reason of age, infirmity or sickness, or official duty, the witness will be unable to attend the court, or unless such witness is about to leave, or has left, the State or county in which the suit is pending and will not probably be present at the trial.

(Amended by Order Dec. 5, 1983, eff. April 1, 1984.)

RULE 253. ABSENCE OF COUNSEL AS GROUND FOR CONTINUANCE.

Except as provided elsewhere in these rules, absence of counsel will not be good cause for a continuance or postponement of the cause when called for trial, except it be allowed in the discretion of the court, upon cause shown or upon matters within the knowledge or information of the judge to be stated on the record.

RULE 254. ATTENDANCE ON LEGISLATURE.

In all civil actions, including matters of probate, and in all matters ancillary to such suits which require action by or the attendance of an attorney, including appeals but excluding temporary restraining orders, at any time within thirty days of a date when the legislature is to be in session, or at any time the legislature is in session, or when the legislature sits as a Constitutional Convention, it shall be mandatory that the court continue the cause if it shall appear to the court, by affidavit, that any party applying for continuance, or any attorney for any party to the cause, is a member of either branch of the legislature, and will be or is in actual attendance on a session of the same. If the member of the legislature is an attorney for a party to the cause, his affidavit shall contain a declaration that it is his intention to participate actively in the preparation and/or presentation of the case. Where a party to any cause, or an attorney for any party to a cause, is a member of the legislature, his affidavit need not be corroborated. On the filing of such affidavit, the court shall continue the cause until thirty days after adjournment of the legislature and the affidavit shall be proof of the necessity for the continuance, and the continuance shall be deemed one of right and shall not be charged against the movant upon any subsequent application for continuance.

The right to a continuance shall be mandatory, except only where the attorney was employed within ten days of the date the suit is set for trial, the right to continuance shall be discretionary.

(Amended by Order June 10, 1980, eff. Jan. 1, 1981.)

RULE 255. CHANGE OF VENUE BY CONSENT.

Upon the written consent of the parties filed with the papers of the cause, the court, by an order entered on the minutes, may transfer the same for trial to the court of any other county having jurisdiction of the subject matter of such suit.

RULE 256. [REPEALED]

(Repealed by Order March 31, 1941, eff. Sept. 1, 1941.)

RULE 257. GRANTED ON MOTION.

A change of venue may be granted in civil causes upon motion of either party, supported by his own affidavit and the affidavit of at least three credible persons, residents of the county in which the suit is pending, for any following cause:

(a) That there exists in the county where the suit is pending so great a prejudice against him that he cannot obtain a fair and impartial trial.

(b) That there is a combination against him instigated by influential persons, by reason of which he cannot expect a fair and impartial trial.

(c) That an impartial trial cannot be had in the county where the action is pending.

(d) For other sufficient cause to be determined by the court.

(Amended by Order June 15, 1983, eff. Sept. 1, 1983.)

RULE 258. SHALL BE GRANTED.

Where such motion to transfer venue is duly made, it shall be granted, unless the credibility of those making such application, or their means of knowledge or the truth of the facts set out in the said application are attacked by the affidavit of a credible person; when thus attacked, the issue thus formed shall be tried by the judge; and the application either granted or refused. Reasonable discovery in support of, or in opposition to, the application shall be permitted, and such discovery as is relevant, including deposition testimony on file, may be attached to, or incorporated by reference in, the affidavit of a party, a witness, or an attorney who has knowledge of such discovery.

(Amended by Order June 15, 1983, eff. Sept. 1, 1983.)

RULE 259. TO WHAT COUNTY.

If the motion under Rule 257 is granted, the cause shall be removed:

(a) If from a district court, to any county of proper venue in the same or an adjoining district;

(b) If from a county court, to any adjoining county of proper venue;

(c) If (a) or (b) are not applicable, to any county of proper venue;

(d) If a county of proper venue (other than the county of suit) cannot be found, then if from

(1) A district court, to any county in the same or an adjoining district or to any district where an impartial trial can be had;

(2) A county court, to any adjoining county or to any district where an impartial trial can be had; but the parties may agree that venue shall be changed to some other county, and the order of the court shall conform to such agreement.

(Amended by Order June 15, 1983, eff. Sept. 1, 1983.)

RULE 260. [REPEALED]

(Repealed by Order April 24, 1990, eff. Sept. 1, 1990.)

RULE 261. TRANSCRIPT ON CHANGE.

When a change of venue has been granted, the clerk shall immediately make out a correct transcript of all the orders made in said cause, certifying thereto officially under the seal of the court, and send the same, with the original papers in the cause, to the clerk of the court to which the venue has been changed.

C.
THE TRIAL

RULE 262. TRIAL BY THE COURT.

The rules governing the trial of causes before a jury shall govern in trials by the court in so far as applicable.

RULE 263. AGREED CASE.

Parties may submit matters in controversy to the court upon an agreed statement of facts filed with the clerk, upon which judgment shall be rendered as in other cases; and such agreed statement signed and certified by the court to be correct and the judgment rendered thereon shall constitute the record of the cause.

RULE 264. VIDEOTAPE TRIAL.

By agreement of the parties, the trial court may allow that all testimony and such other evidence as may be appropriate be presented at trial by videotape. The expenses of such videotape recordings shall be taxed as costs. If any party withdraws agreement to a videotape trial, the videotape costs that have accrued will be taxed against the party withdrawing from the agreement.

(Added July 15, 1987, eff. Jan. 1, 1988.)

RULE 265. ORDER OF PROCEEDINGS ON TRIAL BY JURY.

The trial of cases before a jury shall proceed in the following order unless the court should, for good cause stated in the record, otherwise direct:

(a) The party upon whom rests the burden of proof on the whole case shall state to the jury briefly the nature of his claim or defense and what said party expects to prove and the relief sought. Immediately thereafter, the adverse party may make a similar statement, and intervenors and other parties will be accorded similar rights in the order determined by the court.

(b) The party upon whom rests the burden of proof on the whole case shall then introduce his evidence.

(c) The adverse party shall briefly state the nature of his claim or defense and what said party expects to prove and the relief sought unless he has already done so.

(d) He shall then introduce his evidence.

(e) The intervenor and other parties shall make their statement, unless they have already done so, and shall introduce their evidence.

(f) The parties shall then be confined to rebutting testimony on each side.

(g) But one counsel on each side shall examine and cross-examine the same witness, except on leave granted.

(Amended by Order March 31, 1941, eff. Sept. 1, 1941; July 20, 1966, eff. Jan. 1, 1967; July 11, 1977, eff. Jan. 1, 1978.)

RULE 266. OPEN AND CLOSE—ADMISSION.

Except as provided in Rule 269 the plaintiff shall have the right to open and conclude both in adducing his evidence and in the argument, unless the burden of proof on the whole case under the pleadings rests upon the defendant, or unless the defendant or all of the defendants, if there should be more than one, shall, after the issues of fact are settled and before the trial commences, admit that the plaintiff is entitled to recover as set forth in the petition, except so far as he may be defeated, in whole or in part, by the allegations of the answer constituting a good defense, which may be established on the trial; which admission shall be entered of record, whereupon the defendant, or the defendants, if more than one, shall have the right to open and conclude in adducing the evidence and in the argument of the cause. The admission shall not serve to admit any allegation which is inconsistent with such defense, which defense shall be one that defendant has the burden of establishing, as for example, and without excluding other defenses: accord and satisfaction, adverse possession, arbitration and award, contributory negligence, discharge in bankruptcy, duress, estoppel, failure of consideration, fraud, release, res judicata, statute of frauds, statute of limitations, waiver, and the like.

RULE 267. WITNESSES PLACED UNDER RULE.

(a) At the request of either party, in a civil case, the witnesses on both sides shall be sworn and removed out of the courtroom to some place where they cannot hear the testimony as delivered by any other witness in the cause. This is termed placing witnesses under the rule.

(b) This rule does not authorize exclusion of (1) a party who is a natural person or the spouse of such natural person, or (2) an officer or employee of a party that is not a natural person and who is designated as its representative by its attorney, or (3) a person whose presence is shown by a party to be essential to the presentation of the cause.

(c) If any party be absent, the court in its discretion may exempt from the rule a representative of such party.

(d) Witnesses, when placed under Rule 614 of the Texas Rules of Civil Evidence, shall be instructed by the court that they are not to converse with each other or with any other person about the case other than the attorneys in the case, except by permission of the court, and that they are not to read any report of or comment upon the testimony in the case while under the rule.

(e) Any witness or other person violating such instructions may be punished for contempt of court.

(Amended by Order July 15, 1987, eff. Jan. 1, 1988.)

RULE 268. MOTION FOR INSTRUCTED VERDICT.

A motion for directed verdict shall state the specific grounds therefor.

RULE 269. ARGUMENT.

(a) After the evidence is concluded and the charge is read, the parties may argue the case to the jury. The party having the burden of proof on the whole case, or on all matters which are submitted by the charge, shall be entitled to open and conclude the argument; where there are several parties having separate claims or defenses, the court shall prescribe the order of argument between them.

(b) In all arguments, and especially in arguments on the trial of the case, the counsel opening shall present his whole case as he relies on it, both of law and facts, and shall be heard in the concluding argument only in reply to the counsel on the other side.

(c) Counsel for an intervenor shall occupy the position in the argument assigned by the court according to the nature of the claim.

(d) Arguments on questions of law shall be addressed to the court, and counsel should state the substance of the authorities referred to without reading more from books than may be necessary to verify the statement. On a question on motions, exceptions to the evidence, and other incidental matters, the counsel will be allowed only such argument as may be necessary to present clearly the question raised and refer to authorities on it, unless further discussion is invited by the court.

(e) Arguments on the facts should be addressed to the jury, when one is impaneled in a case that is being tried, under the supervision of the court. Counsel shall be required to confine the argument strictly to the evidence and to the arguments of opposing counsel. Mere personal criticism by counsel upon each other shall be avoided, and when indulged in shall be promptly corrected as a contempt of court.

(f) Side-bar remarks, and remarks by counsel of one side, not addressed to the court, while the counsel on the other side is examining a witness or arguing any question to the court, or addressing the jury, will be rigidly repressed by the court.

(g) The court will not be required to wait for objections to be made when the rules as to arguments are violated; but should they not be noticed and corrected by the court, opposing counsel may ask leave of the court to rise and present his point of objection. But the court shall protect counsel from any unnecessary interruption made on frivolous and unimportant grounds.

(h) It shall be the duty of every counsel to address the court from his place at the bar, and in addressing the court to rise to his feet; and while engaged in the trial of a case he shall remain at his place in the bar.

(Amended by Order March 31, 1941, eff. Sept. 1, 1941; April 24, 1990, eff. Sept. 1, 1990.)

RULE 270. ADDITIONAL TESTIMONY.

When it clearly appears to be necessary to the due administration of justice, the court may permit additional evidence to be offered at any time; provided that in a jury case no evidence on a controversial matter shall be received after the verdict of the jury.

(Amended by Order Dec. 5, 1983, eff. April 1, 1984.)

D.
CHARGE TO THE JURY

RULE 271. CHARGE TO THE JURY.

Unless expressly waived by the parties, the trial court shall prepare and in open court deliver a written charge to the jury.

(Amended by Order May 25, 1973, eff. Sept. 1, 1973; July 15, 1987, eff. Jan. 1, 1988.)

RULE 272. REQUISITES.

The charge shall be in writing, signed by the court, and filed with the clerk, and shall be a part of the record of the cause. It shall be submitted to the respective parties or their attorneys for their inspection, and a reasonable time given them in which to examine and present objections thereto outside the presence of the jury, which objections shall in every instance be presented to the court in writing, or be dictated to the court reporter in the presence of the court and opposing counsel, before the charge is read to the jury. All objections not so presented shall be considered as waived. The court shall announce its rulings thereon before reading the charge to the jury and shall endorse the rulings on the objections if written or dictate same to the court reporter in the presence of counsel. Objections to the charge and the court's rulings thereon may be included as a part of any transcript or statement of facts on appeal and, when so included in either, shall constitute a sufficient bill of exception to the rulings of the court thereon. It shall be presumed, unless otherwise noted in the record, that the party making such objections presented the same at the proper time and excepted to the ruling thereon.

(Amended by Order Sept. 20, 1941, eff. Dec. 31, 1941; May 25, 1973, eff. Sept. 1, 1973; July 22, 1975, eff. Jan. 1, 1976; July 15, 1987, eff. Jan. 1, 1988.)

RULE 273. JURY SUBMISSIONS.

Either party may present to the court and request written questions, definitions, and instructions to be given to the jury; and the court may give them or a part thereof, or may refuse to give them, as may be proper. Such requests shall be prepared and presented to the court and submitted to opposing counsel for examination and objection within a reasonable time after the charge is given to the parties or their attorneys for examination. A request by either party for any questions, definitions, or instructions shall be made separate and apart from such party's objections to the court's charge.

(Amended by Order Oct. 12, 1949, eff. March 1, 1950; July 15, 1987, eff. Jan. 1, 1988.)

RULE 274. OBJECTIONS AND REQUESTS.

A party objecting to a charge must point out distinctly the objectionable matter and the grounds of the objection. Any complaint as to a question, definition, or instruction, on account of any defect, omission, or fault in pleading, is waived unless specifically included in the objections. When the complaining party's objection, or requested question, definition, or instruction is, in the opinion of the appellate court, obscured or concealed by voluminous unfounded objections, minute differentiations or numerous unnecessary requests, such objection or request shall be untenable. No objection to one part of the charge may be adopted and applied to any other part of the charge by reference only.

(Amended by Order Sept. 20, 1941, eff. Dec. 31, 1941; July 15, 1987, eff. Jan. 1, 1988.)

RULE 275. CHARGE READ BEFORE ARGUMENT.

Before the argument is begun, the trial court shall read the charge to the jury in the precise words in which it was written, including all questions, definitions, and instructions which the court may give.

(Amended by Order July 15, 1987, eff. Jan. 1, 1988.)

RULE 276. REFUSAL OR MODIFICATION.

When an instruction, question, or definition is requested and the provisions of the law have been complied with and the trial judge refuses the same, the judge shall endorse thereon "Refused," and sign the same officially. If the trial judge modifies the same the judge shall endorse thereon "Modified as follows: (stating in what particular the judge has modified the same) and given, and exception allowed" and sign the same officially. Such refused or modified instruction, question, or definition, when so endorsed shall constitute a bill of exceptions, and it shall be conclusively presumed that the party asking the same presented it at the proper time, excepted to its refusal or modification, and that all the requirements of law have been observed, and such procedure shall entitle the party requesting the same to have the action of the trial judge thereon reviewed without preparing a formal bill of exceptions.

(Amended by Order July 15, 1987, eff. Jan. 1, 1988.)

RULE 277. SUBMISSION TO THE JURY.

In all jury cases the court shall, whenever feasible, submit the cause upon broad-form questions. The court shall submit such instructions and definitions as shall be proper to enable the jury to render a verdict.

Inferential rebuttal questions shall not be submitted in the charge. The placing of the burden of proof may be accomplished by instructions rather than by inclusion in the question.

In any cause in which the jury is required to apportion the loss among the parties the court shall submit a question or questions inquiring what percentage, if any, of the negligence or causation, as the case may be, that caused the occurrence or injury in question is attributable to each of the persons found to have been culpable. The court shall also instruct the jury to answer the damage question or questions without any reduction because of the percentage of negligence or causation, if any, of the person injured. The court may predicate the damage question or questions upon affirmative findings of liability.

The court may submit a question disjunctively when it is apparent from the evidence that one or the other of the conditions or facts inquired about necessarily exists.

The court shall not in its charge comment directly on the weight of the evidence or advise the jury of the effect of their answers, but the court's charge shall not be objectionable on the ground that it incidentally constitutes a comment on the weight of the evidence or advises the jury of the effect of their answers when it is properly a part of an instruction or definition.

(Amended by Order March 31, 1941, eff. Sept. 1, 1941; May 25, 1973, eff. Sept. 1, 1973; Dec. 5, 1983, eff. April 1, 1984; July 15, 1987, eff. Jan. 1, 1988.)

RULE 278. SUBMISSION OF QUESTIONS, DEFINITIONS, AND INSTRUCTIONS.

The court shall submit the questions, instructions and definitions in the form provided by Rule 277, which are raised by the written pleadings and the evidence. Except in trespass to try title, statutory partition proceedings, and other special proceedings in which the pleadings are specially defined by statutes or procedural rules, a party shall not be entitled to any submission of any question raised only by a general denial and not raised by affirmative written pleading by that party. Nothing herein shall change the burden of proof from what it would have been under a general denial. A judgment shall not be reversed because of the failure to submit other and various phases or different shades of the same question. Failure to submit a question shall not be deemed a ground for reversal of the judgment, unless its submission, in substantially correct wording, has been requested in writing and tendered by the party complaining of the judgment; provided, however, that objection to such failure shall suffice in such respect if the question is one relied upon by the opposing party. Failure to submit a definition or instruction shall not be deemed a ground for reversal of the judgment unless a substantially correct definition or instruction has been requested in writing and tendered by the party complaining of the judgment.

(Added July 15, 1987, eff. Jan. 1, 1988.)

RULE 279. OMISSIONS FROM THE CHARGE.

Upon appeal all independent grounds of recovery or of defense not conclusively established under the evidence and no element of which is submitted or requested are waived. When a ground of recovery or defense consists of more than one element, if one or more of such elements necessary to sustain such ground of recovery or defense, and necessarily referable thereto, are submitted to and found by the jury, and one or more of such elements are omitted from the charge, without request or objection, and there is factually sufficient evidence to support a finding thereon, the trial court, at the request of either party, may after notice and hearing and at any time before the judgment is rendered, make and file written findings on such omitted element or elements in support of the judgment. If no such written findings are made, such omitted element or elements shall be deemed found by the court in such manner as to support the judgment. A claim that the evidence was legally or factually insufficient to warrant the submission of any question may be made for the first time after verdict, regardless of whether the submission of such question was requested by the complainant.

(Amended by Order March 31, 1941, eff. Sept. 1, 1941; July 15, 1987, eff. Jan. 1, 1988.)

E.
CASE TO THE JURY

RULE 280. PRESIDING JUROR OF JURY.

Each jury shall appoint one of their body presiding juror.

(Amended by Order Dec. 5, 1983, eff. April 1, 1984.)

RULE 281. PAPERS TAKEN TO JURY ROOM.

With the court's permission, the jury may take with them to the jury room any notes they took during the trial. In addition, the jury may, and on request shall, take with them in their retirement the charges and instructions, general or special, which were given and read to them, and any written evidence, except the depositions of witnesses, but shall not take with them any special charges which have been refused. Where only part of a paper has been read in evidence, the jury shall not take the same with them, unless the part so read to them is detached from that which was excluded.

(Amended by Order Dec. 5, 1983, eff. April 1, 1984; March 15, 2011, eff. April 1, 2011.)

RULE 282. JURY KEPT TOGETHER.

The jury may either decide a case in court or retire for deliberation. If they retire, they shall be kept together in some convenient place, under the charge of an officer, until they agree upon a verdict or are discharged by the court; but the court in its discretion may permit them to separate temporarily for the night and at their meals, and for other proper purposes.

RULE 283. DUTY OF OFFICER ATTENDING JURY.

The officer in charge of the jury shall not make nor permit any communication to be made to them, except to inquire if they have agreed upon a verdict, unless by order of the court; and he shall not before their verdict is rendered communicate to any person the state of their deliberations or the verdict agreed upon.

RULE 284. JUDGE TO CAUTION JURY.

Immediately after jurors are selected for a case, the court must instruct them to turn off their phones and other electronic devices and not to communicate with anyone through any electronic device while they are in the courtroom or while they are deliberating. The court must also instruct them that, while they are serving as jurors, they must not post any information about the case on the Internet or search for any information outside of the courtroom, including on the Internet, to try to learn more about the case.

If jurors are permitted to separate before they are released from jury duty, either during the trial or after the case is submitted to them, the court must instruct them that it is their duty not to communicate with, or permit themselves to be addressed by, any other person about any subject relating to the case.

(Amended by Order March 15, 2011, eff. April 1, 2011.)

RULE 285. JURY MAY COMMUNICATE WITH COURT.

The jury may communicate with the court by making their wish known to the officer in charge, who shall inform the court, and they may then in open court, and through their presiding juror, communicate with the court, either verbally or in writing. If the communication is to request further instructions, Rule 286 shall be followed.

(Amended by Order Dec. 5, 1983, eff. April 1, 1984.)

RULE 286. JURY MAY RECEIVE FURTHER INSTRUCTIONS.

After having retired, the jury may receive further instructions from the court touching any matter of law, either at their request or upon the court's own motion. For this purpose they shall appear before the judge in open court in a body, and if the instruction is being given at their request, they shall through their presiding juror state to the court, in writing, the particular question of law upon which they desire further instruction. The court shall give such instruction in writing, but no instruction shall be given except in conformity with the rules relating to the charge. Additional argument may be allowed in the discretion of the court.

(Amended by Order Dec. 5, 1983, eff. April 1, 1984; July 15, 1987, eff. Jan. 1, 1988.)

RULE 287. DISAGREEMENT AS TO EVIDENCE.

If the jury disagree as to the statement of any witness, they may, upon applying to the court, have read to them from the court reporter's notes that part of such witness' testimony on the point in dispute; but, if there be no such reporter, or if his notes cannot be read to the jury, the court may cause such witness to be again brought upon the stand and the judge shall direct him to repeat his testimony as to the point in dispute, and no other, as nearly as he can in the language used on the trial; and on their notifying the court that they disagree as to any portion of a deposition or other paper not permitted to be carried with them in their retirement, the court may, in like manner, permit such portion of said deposition or paper to be again read to the jury.

RULE 288. COURT OPEN FOR JURY.

The court, during the deliberations of the jury, may proceed with other business or recess from time to time, but shall be deemed open for all purposes connected with the case before the jury.

RULE 289. DISCHARGE OF JURY.

The jury to whom a case has been submitted may be discharged by the court when they cannot agree and the parties consent to their discharge, or when they have been kept together for such time as to render it altogether improbable that they can agree, or when any calamity or accident may, in the opinion of the court, require it, or when by sickness or other cause their number is reduced below the number constituting the jury in such court.

The cause shall again be placed on the jury docket and shall again be set for trial as the court directs.

(Amended by Order Dec. 5, 1983, eff. April 1, 1984.)

F.
VERDICT

RULE 290. DEFINITION AND SUBSTANCE.

A verdict is a written declaration by a jury of its decision, comprehending the whole or all the issues submitted to the jury, and shall be either a general or special verdict, as directed, which shall be signed by the presiding juror of the jury.

A general verdict is one whereby the jury pronounces generally in favor of one or more parties to the suit upon all or any of the issues submitted to it. A special verdict is one wherein the jury finds the facts only on issues made up and submitted to them under the direction of the court.

A special verdict shall, as between the parties, be conclusive as to the facts found.

(Amended by Order Dec. 5, 1983, eff. April 1, 1984.)

RULE 291. FORM OF VERDICT.

No special form of verdict is required, and the judgment shall not be arrested or reversed for mere want of form therein if there has been substantial compliance with the requirements of the law in rendering a verdict.

(Amended by Order Oct. 3, 1972, eff. Feb. 1, 1973.)

RULE 292. VERDICT BY PORTION OF ORIGINAL JURY.

(a) Except as provided in subsection (b), a verdict may be rendered in any cause by the concurrence, as to each and all answers made, of the same ten or more members of an original jury of twelve or of the same five or more members of an original jury of six. However, where as many as three jurors die or be disabled from sitting and there are only nine of the jurors remaining of an original jury of twelve, those remaining may render and return a verdict. If less than the original twelve or six jurors render a verdict, the verdict must be signed by each juror concurring therein.

(b) A verdict may be rendered awarding exemplary damages only if the jury was unanimous in finding liability for and the amount of exemplary damages.

(Amended by Order Oct. 3, 1972, eff. Feb. 1, 1973; Jan. 27, 2005, eff. Feb. 1, 2005 in all cases filed on or after Sept. 1, 2003.)

Comment - 2005

The rule is divided into two subsections. Subsection (a) is clarified. Subsection (b) is added to make the rule consistent with Act of June 2, 2003, 78th Leg., R.S., c. 204, § 13.04, 2003 Tex. Gen. Laws 847, 888, codified as TEX. CIV. PRAC. & REM. CODE § 41.003.

RULE 293. WHEN THE JURY AGREE.

When the jury agree upon a verdict, they shall be brought into court by the proper officer, and they shall deliver their verdict to the clerk; and if they state that they have agreed, the verdict shall be read aloud by the clerk. If the verdict is in proper form, no juror objects to its accuracy, no juror represented as agreeing thereto dissents therefrom, and neither party requests a poll of the jury, the verdict shall be entered upon the minutes of the court.

(Amended by Order Oct. 3, 1972, eff. Feb. 1, 1973.)

RULE 294. POLLING THE JURY.

Any party shall have the right to have the jury polled. A jury is polled by reading once to the jury collectively the general verdict, or the questions and answers thereto consecutively, and then calling the name of each juror separately and asking the juror if it is the juror's verdict. If any juror answers in the negative when the verdict is returned signed only by the presiding juror as a unanimous verdict, or if any juror shown by the juror's signature to agree to the verdict should answer in the negative, the jury shall be retired for further deliberation.

(Amended by Order Oct. 3, 1972, eff. Feb. 1, 1973; Dec. 5, 1983, eff. April 1, 1984; April 24, 1990, eff. Sept. 1, 1990.)

RULE 295. CORRECTION OF VERDICT.

If the purported verdict is defective, the court may direct it to be reformed. If it is incomplete, or not responsive to the questions contained in the court's charge, or the answers to the questions are in conflict, the court shall in writing instruct the jury in open court of the nature of the incompleteness, unresponsiveness, or conflict, provide the jury such additional instructions as may be proper, and retire the jury for further deliberations.

(Amended by Order July 15, 1987, eff. Jan. 1, 1988.)

G.
FINDINGS BY COURT

RULE 296. REQUESTS FOR FINDINGS OF FACTS AND CONCLUSIONS OF LAW.

In any case tried in the district or county court without a jury, any party may request the court to state in writing its findings of fact and conclusions of law. Such request shall be entitled "Request for Findings of Fact and Conclusions of Law" and shall be filed within twenty days after judgment is signed with the clerk of the court, who shall immediately call such request to the attention of the judge who tried the case. The party making the request shall serve it on all other parties in accordance with Rule 21a.

(Amended by Order March 19, 1957, eff. Sept. 1, 1957; June 10, 1980, eff. Jan. 1, 1981; Dec. 5, 1983, eff. April 1, 1984; April 24, 1990, eff. Sept. 1, 1990.)

RULE 297. TIME TO FILE FINDINGS OF FACT AND CONCLUSIONS OF LAW.

The court shall file its findings of fact and conclusions of law within twenty days after a timely request is filed. The court shall cause a copy of its findings and conclusions to be mailed to each party in the suit.

If the court fails to file timely findings of fact and conclusions of law, the party making the request shall, within thirty days after filing the original request, file with the clerk and serve on all other parties in accordance with Rule 21a a "Notice of Past Due Findings of Fact and Conclusions of Law" which shall be immediately called to the attention of the court by the clerk. Such notice shall state the date the original request was filed and the date the findings and conclusions were due. Upon filing this notice, the time for the court to file findings of fact and conclusions of law is extended to forty days from the date the original request was filed.

(Amended by Order June 10, 1980, eff. Jan. 1, 1981; Dec. 5, 1983, eff. April 1, 1984; April 24, 1990, eff. Sept. 1, 1990.)

RULE 298. ADDITIONAL OR AMENDED FINDINGS OF FACT AND CONCLUSIONS OF LAW.

After the court files original findings of fact and conclusions of law, any party may file with the clerk of the court a request for specified additional or amended findings or conclusions. The request for these findings shall be made within ten days after the filing of the original findings and conclusions by the court. Each request made pursuant to this rule shall be served on each party to the suit in accordance with Rule 21a.

The court shall file any additional or amended findings and conclusions that are appropriate within ten days after such request is filed, and cause a copy to be mailed to each party to the suit. No findings or conclusions shall be deemed or presumed by any failure of the court to make any additional findings or conclusions.

(Amended by Order March 19, 1957, eff. Sept. 1. 1957; April 24, 1990, eff. Sept. 1, 1990.)

RULE 299. OMITTED FINDINGS.

When findings of fact are filed by the trial court they shall form the basis of the judgment upon all grounds of recovery and of defense embraced therein. The judgment may not be supported upon appeal by a presumed finding upon any ground of recovery or defense, no element of which has been included in the findings of fact; but when one or more elements thereof have been found by the trial court, omitted unrequested elements, when supported by evidence, will be supplied by presumption in support of the judgment. Refusal of the court to make a finding requested shall be reviewable on appeal.

(Amended by Order Sept. 20, 1941, eff. Dec. 31, 1941; April 24, 1990, eff. Sept. 1, 1990.)

RULE 299a. FINDINGS OF FACT TO BE SEPARATELY FILED AND NOT RECITED IN A JUDGMENT.

Findings of fact shall not be recited in a judgment. If there is a conflict between findings of fact recited in a judgment in violation of this rule and findings of fact made pursuant to Rules 297 and 298, the latter findings will control for appellate purposes. Findings of fact shall be filed with the clerk of the court as a document or documents separate and apart from the judgment.

(Added by Order April 24, 1990, eff. Sept. 1, 1990.)

H. JUDGMENTS

RULE 300. COURT TO RENDER JUDGMENT.

Where a special verdict is rendered, or the conclusions of fact found by the judge are separately stated the court shall render judgment thereon unless set aside or a new trial is granted, or judgment is rendered notwithstanding verdict or jury finding under these rules.

RULE 301. JUDGMENTS.

The judgment of the court shall conform to the pleadings, the nature of the case proved and the verdict, if any, and shall be so framed as to give the party all the relief to which he may be entitled either in law or equity. Provided, that upon motion and reasonable notice the court may render judgment non obstante veredicto if a directed verdict would have been proper, and provided further that the court may upon like motion and notice, disregard any jury finding on a question that has no support in the evidence. Only one final judgment shall be rendered in any cause except where it is otherwise specially provided by law. Judgment may, in a proper case, be given for or against one or more of several plaintiffs, and for or against one or more of several defendants or intervenors.

(Amended by Order July 15, 1987, eff. Jan. 1, 1988; April 24, 1990, eff. Sept. 1, 1990; amendment withdrawn Sept. 4, 1990, eff. retroactively to Sept. 1, 1990.)

RULE 302. ON COUNTERCLAIM.

If the defendant establishes a demand against the plaintiff upon a counterclaim exceeding that established against him by the plaintiff, the court shall render judgment for defendant for such excess.

(Amended by Order Dec. 5, 1983, eff. April 1, 1984.)

RULE 303. ON COUNTERCLAIM FOR COSTS.

When a counterclaim is pleaded, the party in whose favor final judgment is rendered shall also recover the costs, unless it be made to appear on the trial that the counterclaim of the defendant was acquired after the commencement of the suit, in which case, if the plaintiff establishes a claim existing at the commencement of the suit, he shall recover his costs.

(Amended by Order Dec. 5, 1983, eff. April 1, 1984.)

RULE 304. JUDGMENT UPON RECORD.

Judgments rendered upon questions raised upon citations, pleadings, and all other proceedings, constituting the record proper as known at common law, must be entered at the date of each term when pronounced.

RULE 305. PROPOSED JUDGMENT.

Any party may prepare and submit a proposed judgment to the court for signature.

Each party who submits a proposed judgment for signature shall serve the proposed judgment on all other parties to the suit who have appeared and remain in the case, in accordance with Rule 21a.

Failure to comply with this rule shall not affect the time for perfecting an appeal.

(Amended by Order April 24, 1990, eff. Sept. 1, 1990.)

RULE 306. RECITATION OF JUDGMENT.

The entry of the judgment shall contain the full names of the parties, as stated in the pleadings, for and against whom the judgment is rendered. In a suit for termination of the parent-child relationship or a suit affecting the parent-child relationship filed by a governmental entity for managing conservatorship. the judgment must state the specific grounds for termination or for appointment of the managing conservator.

(Amended by Order July 21, 1970, eff. Jan. 1, 1971; Order Dec. 12, 2011, eff. March 1, 2012; Order Feb. 13, 2012, eff. March 1, 2012.)

RULE 306a. PERIODS TO RUN FROM SIGNING OF JUDGMENT.

1. **Beginning of Periods**. The date of judgment or order is signed as shown of record shall determine the beginning of the periods prescribed by these rules for the court's plenary power to grant a new trial or to vacate, modify, correct or reform a judgment or order and for filing in the trial court the various documents that these rules authorize a party to file within such periods including, but not limited to, motions for new trial, motions to modify judgment, motions to reinstate a case dismissed for want of prosecution, motions to vacate judgment and requests for findings of fact and conclusions of law; but this rule shall not determine what constitutes rendition of a judgment or order for any other purpose.
2. **Date to Be Shown**. Judges, attorneys and clerks are directed to use their best efforts to cause all judgments, decisions and orders of any kind to be reduced to writing and signed by the trial judge with the date of signing stated therein. If the date of signing is not recited in the judgment or order, it may be shown in the record by a certificate of the judge or otherwise; provided, however, that the absence of a showing of the date in the record shall not invalidate any judgment or order.
3. **Notice of Judgment**. When the final judgment or other appealable order is signed, the clerk of the court shall immediately give notice to the parties or their attorneys of record by first-class mail advising that the judgment or order was signed. Failure to comply with the provisions of this rule shall not affect the periods mentioned in paragraph (1) of this rule, except as provided in paragraph (4).
4. **No Notice of Judgment**. If within twenty days after the judgment or other appealable order is signed, a party adversely affected by it or his attorney has neither received the notice required by paragraph (3) of this rule nor acquired actual knowledge of the order, then with respect to that party all the periods mentioned in paragraph (1) shall begin on the date that such party or his attorney received such notice or acquired actual knowledge of the signing, whichever occurred first, but in no event shall such periods begin more than ninety days after the original judgment or other appealable order was signed.
5. **Motion, Notice and Hearing**. In order to establish the application of paragraph (4) of this rule, the party adversely affected is required to prove in the trial court, on sworn motion and notice, the date on which the party or his attorney first either received a notice of the judgment or acquired actual knowledge of the signing and that this date was more than twenty days after the judgment was signed.
6. **Nunc Pro Tunc Order**. When a collected judgment has been signed after expiration of the court's plenary power pursuant to Rule 316, the periods mentioned in paragraph (1) of this rule shall run from the date of signing the corrected judgment with respect to any complaint that would not be applicable to the original document.
7. **When Process Served by Publication**. With respect to a motion for new trial filed more than thirty days after the judgment was signed pursuant to Rule 329 when process has been served by publication, the periods provided by paragraph (1) shall be computed as if the judgment were signed on the date of filing the motion.

(Added by Order June 16, 1943, eff. Dec. 31, 1943. Amended by Order Oct. 10, 1945, eff. Feb. 1, 1946; June 10, 1980, eff. Jan. 1, 1981; Dec. 5, 1983, eff. April 1, 1984; April 10, 1986, eff. Sept. 1, 1986; July 15, 1987, eff. Jan. 1, 1988.)

RULE 306b. [REPEALED]

(Repealed by Order Dec. 5, 1983, eff. April 1, 1984.)

RULE 306c. PREMATURELY FILED DOCUMENTS.

No motion for new trial or request for findings of fact and conclusions of law shall be held ineffective because prematurely filed; but every such motion shall be deemed to have been filed on the date of but subsequent to the time of signing of the judgment the motion assails, and every such request for findings of fact and conclusions of law shall be deemed to have been filed on the date of but subsequent to the time of signing of the judgment.

(Added by Order Oct. 10, 1945, eff. Feb. 1, 1946. Amended by Order April 12, 1962, eff. Sept. 1, 1962; July 22, 1975, eff. Jan. 1, 1976; Dec. 5, 1983, eff. April 1, 1984; April 10, 1986, eff. Sept. 1, 1986; April 24, 1990, eff. Sept. 1, 1990.)

RULE 306d. [REPEALED]

(Repealed by Order Dec. 5, 1983, eff. April 1, 1984.)

RULE 307. EXCEPTIONS, ETC., TRANSCRIPT.

In non-jury cases, where findings of fact and conclusions of law are requested and filed, and in jury cases, where a special verdict is returned, any party claiming that the findings of the court or the jury, as the case may be, do not support the judgment, may have noted in the record an exception to said judgment and thereupon take an appeal or writ of error, where such writ is allowed, without a statement of facts or further exceptions in the transcript, but the transcript in such cases shall contain the conclusions of law and fact or the special verdict and the judgment rendered thereon.

RULE 308. COURT SHALL ENFORCE ITS DECREES.

The court shall cause its judgments and decrees to be carried into execution; and where the judgment is for personal property, and it is shown by the pleadings and evidence and the verdict, if any, that such property has an especial value to the plaintiff, the court may award a special writ for the seizure and delivery of such property to the plaintiff; and in such case may enforce its judgment by attachment, fine and imprisonment.

RULE 308a. IN SUITS AFFECTING THE PARENT-CHILD RELATIONSHIP.

When the court has ordered child support or possession of or access to a child and it is claimed that the order has been violated, the person claiming that a violation has occurred shall make this known to the court. The court may appoint a member of the bar to investigate the claim to determine whether there is reason to believe that the court order has been violated. If the attorney in good faith believes that the order has been violated, the attorney shall take the necessary action as provided under Chapter 14, Family Code. On a finding of a violation, the court may enforce its order as provided in Chapter 14, Family Code.

Except by order of the court, no fee shall be charged by or paid to the attorney representing the claimant. If the court determines that an attorney's fee should be paid, the fee shall be adjudged against the party who violated the court's order. The fee may be assessed as costs of court, or awarded by judgment, or both.

(Added by Order Oct. 12, 1949, eff. March 1, 1950. Amended by Order Oct. 10, 1951, eff. March 1, 1952; July 15, 1987, eff. Jan. 1, 1988; April 24, 1990, eff. Sept. 1, 1990.)

Rule 308B. determining the enforceability of a judgement or arbitration award based on foreign law in certain Suits under the family code.

(a) *Definitions.* In this rule:

(1) *Comity* means the recognition by a court of one jurisdiction of the laws and judicial decisions of another jurisdiction.

(2) *Foreign law* means a law, rule, or code of a jurisdiction outside of the states and territories of the United States.

(b) *Applicability of This Rule.*

(1) Except as provided in (2) and (3), this rule applies to the recognition or enforcement of a judgment or arbitration award based on foreign law in a suit involving a marriage relationship or a parent-child relationship under the Family Code.

(2) This rule does not apply to an action brought under the International Child Abduction Remedies Act (22 U.S.C. § 9001 *et seq.*) concerning rights under the Hague Convention on the Civil Aspects of International Child Abduction.

(3) In the event of a conflict between this rule and any federal or state law, the federal or state law will prevail.

(c) *Applicability of Texas Rule of Evidence 203.*

(1) Paragraphs (c) and (d) of Rule 203, Texas Rules of Evidence, apply to an action under this rule.

(2) Paragraphs (a) and (b) of Rule 203, Texas Rules of Evidence, do not apply to an action under this rule.

(d) *Notice.*

(1) *Party Seeking Enforcement of a Judgment or Arbitration Award Based on Foreign Law.* Within 60 days of filing an original pleading, the party seeking enforcement must give written notice to the court and all parties that describes the court's authority to enforce or decide to enforce the judgment or award.

(2) *Party Opposing Enforcement of a Judgment or Arbitration Award Based on Foreign Law.* Within 30 days of the date that a notice under (1) is served, a party opposing enforcement must give written notice to the court and all parties that explains the basis for the party's opposition and states whether the party asserts that the judgment or award violates constitutional rights or public policy.

(e) *Pretrial Conference.* Within 75 days of the date that a notice under (d)(1) is served, the court must conduct a pretrial conference to set deadlines and make other appropriate orders regarding:

(1) the submission of materials for the court to consider in determining foreign law;

(2) the translation of foreign-language documents; and

(3) the designation of expert witnesses.

(f) *Determination Hearing and Order.*

(1) At least 30 days before trial, the court must conduct a hearing on the record to determine whether to enforce the judgment or award. The parties must have timely notice of the hearing.

(2) Within 15 days of the hearing, the Court must issue a written order on the determination that includes findings of fact and conclusions of law. This deadline must not be altered absent extraordinary circumstances.

(3) The court may issue any order necessary to preserve the principles of comity or the freedom to contract for arbitration while protecting against violations of constitutional rights and public policy.

(4) The court must comply with all requirements of this paragraph and make an independent determination whether to enforce the judgment or award even if no party opposes enforcement of the judgment or award.

(g) *Temporary Orders*. Notwithstanding any other provision of this rule, the court may set filing deadlines and conduct the determination hearing to accommodate the circumstances of the case in connection with issuing temporary orders.

(Adopted by Tex. Sup. Ct. Misc. Docket No. 16-9018 Dec. 28, 2017, eff. Jan. 1, 2018.)

RULE 309. IN FORECLOSURE PROCEEDINGS.

Judgments for the foreclosure of mortgages and other liens shall be that the plaintiff recover his debt, damages and costs, with a foreclosure of the plaintiff's lien on the property subject thereto, and, except in judgments against executors, administrators and guardians, that an order of sale shall issue to any sheriff or any constable within the State of Texas, directing him to seize and sell the same as under execution, in satisfaction of the judgment; and, if the property cannot be found, or if the proceeds of such sale be insufficient to satisfy the judgment, then to take the money or any balance thereof remaining unpaid, out of any other property of the defendant, as in case of ordinary executions.

(Amended by Order July 20, 1966, eff. Jan. 1, 1967.)

RULE 310. WRIT OF POSSESSION.

When an order foreclosing a lien upon real estate is made in a suit having for its object the foreclosure of such lien, such order shall have all the force and effect of a writ of possession as between the parties to the foreclosure suit and any person claiming under the defendant to such suit by any right acquired pending such suit; and the court shall so direct in the judgment providing for the issuance of such order. The sheriff or other officer executing such order of sale shall proceed by virtue of such order of sale to place the purchaser of the property sold thereunder in possession thereof within thirty days after the day of sale.

RULE 311. ON APPEAL FROM PROBATE COURT.

Judgment on appeal or certiorari from any county court sitting in probate shall be certified to such county court for observance.

RULE 312. ON APPEAL FROM JUSTICE COURT.

Judgment on appeal or certiorari from a justice court shall be enforced by the county or district court rendering the judgment.

RULE 313. AGAINST EXECUTORS, ETC.

A judgment for the recovery of money against an executor, administrator or guardian, as such, shall state that it is to be paid in the due course of administration. No execution shall issue thereon, but it shall be certified to the county court, sitting in matters of probate, to be there enforced in accordance with law, but judgment against an executor appointed and acting under a will dispensing with the action of the county court in reference to such estate shall be enforced against the property of the testator in the hands of such executor, by execution, as in other cases.

RULE 314. CONFESSION OF JUDGMENT.

Any person against whom a cause of action exists may, without process, appear in person or by attorney, and confess judgment therefor in open court as follows:

(a) A petition shall be filed and the justness of the debt or cause of action be sworn to by the person in whose favor the judgment is confessed.

(b) If the judgment is confessed by attorney, the power of attorney shall be filed and its contents be recited in the judgment.

(c) Every such judgment duly made shall operate as a release of all errors in the record thereof, but such judgment may be impeached for fraud or other equitable cause.

I.
REMITTITUR AND CORRECTION

RULE 315. REMITTITUR.

Any party in whose favor a judgment has been rendered may remit any part thereof in open court, or by executing and filing with the clerk a written remittitur signed by the party or the party's attorney of record, and duly acknowledged by the party or the party's attorney. Such remittitur shall be a part of the record of the cause. Execution shall issue for the balance only of such judgment.

(Amended by Order July 15, 1987, eff. Jan. 1, 1988.)

RULE 316. CORRECTION OF CLERICAL MISTAKES IN JUDGMENT RECORD.

Clerical mistakes in the record of any judgment may be corrected by the judge in open court according to the truth or justice of the case after notice of the motion therefor has been given to the parties interested in such judgment, as provided in Rule 21a, and thereafter the execution shall conform to the judgment as amended.

(Amended by Order June 16, 1943, eff. Dec. 31, 1943; July 15, 1987, eff. Jan. 1, 1988.)

RULES 317 TO 319. [REPEALED]

(Repealed by Order July 15, 1987, eff. Jan. 1, 1988.)

J.
NEW TRIALS

RULE 320. MOTION AND ACTION OF COURT THEREON.

New trials may be granted and judgment set aside for good cause, on motion or on the court's own motion on such terms as the court shall direct. New trials may be granted when the damages are manifestly too small or too large. When it appears to the court that a new trial should be granted on a point or points that affect only a part of the matters in controversy and that such part is clearly separable without unfairness to the parties, the court may grant a new trial as to that part only, provided that a separate trial on unliquidated damages alone shall not be ordered if liability issues are contested. Each motion for new trial shall be in writing and signed by the party of his attorney.

(Amended by Order July 20, 1964, eff. Jan. 1, 1955; July 22, 1975, eff. Jan. 1, 1976; July 11, 1977, eff. Jan. 1, 1978, June 10, 1980, eff. Jan. 1, 1981; Dec. 5, 1983, eff. April 1, 1984; July 15, 1987, eff. Jan. 1, 1988.)

RULE 321. FORM.

Each point relied upon in a motion for new trial or in arrest of judgment shall briefly refer to that part of the ruling of the court, charge given to the jury, or charge refused, admission or rejection of evidence, or other proceedings which are designated to be complained of, in such a way that the objection can be clearly identified and understood by the court.

(Amended by Order June 10, 1980, eff. Jan. 1, 1981.)

RULE 322. GENERALITY TO BE AVOIDED.

Grounds of objections couched in general terms—as that the court erred in its charge, in sustaining or overruling exceptions to the pleadings, and in excluding or admitting evidence, the verdict of the jury is contrary to law, and the like—shall not be considered by the court.

RULE 323. [REPEALED]

(Repealed by Order July 11, 1977, eff. Jan. 1, 1978.)

RULE 324. PREREQUISITES OF APPEAL.

(a) **Motion for New Trial Not Required**. A point in a motion for new trial is not a prerequisite to a complaint on appeal in either a jury or a nonjury case, except as provided in subdivision (b).

(b) **Motion for New Trial Required**. A point in a motion for new trial is a prerequisite to the following complaints on appeal:

  (1) A complaint on which evidence must be heard such as one of jury misconduct or newly discovered evidence or failure to set aside a judgment by default;

  (2) A complaint of factual insufficiency of the evidence to support a jury finding;

  (3) A complaint that a jury finding is against the overwhelming weight of the evidence;

  (4) A complaint of inadequacy or excessiveness of the damages found by the jury; or

  (5) Incurable jury argument if not otherwise ruled on by the trial court.

(c) **Judgment Notwithstanding Findings; Cross-Points**. When judgment is rendered non obstante veredicto or notwithstanding the findings of a jury on one or more questions, the appellee may bring forward by cross-point contained in his brief filed in the Court of Appeals any ground which would have vitiated the verdict or would have prevented an affirmance of the judgment had one been rendered by the trial court in harmony with the verdict, including although not limited to the ground that one or more of the jury's findings have insufficient support in the evidence or are against the overwhelming preponderance of the evidence as a matter of fact, and the ground that the verdict and judgment based thereon should be set aside because of improper argument of counsel. The failure to bring forward by cross-points such grounds as would vitiate the verdict shall be deemed a waiver thereof; provided, however, that if a cross-point is upon a ground which requires the taking of evidence in addition to that adduced upon the trial of the cause, it is not necessary that the evidentiary hearing be held until after the appellate court determines that the cause be remanded to consider such a cross-point.

(Amended by Order March 31, 1941, eff. Sept. 1, 1941; Sept. 20, 1941, eff. Dec. 31, 1941; July 20, 1954, eff. Jan. 1, 1955; March 19, 1957, eff. Sept. 1, 1957; April 12, 1962, eff. Sept. 1, 1962; July 11, 1977, eff. Jan. 1, 1978; June 10, 1980, eff. Jan. 1, 1981; Dec. 5, 1983, eff. April 1, 1984; July 15, 1987, eff. Jan. 1, 1988.)

RULE 325. [REPEALED]

(Repealed by Order July 11, 1977, eff. Jan. 1, 1978.)

RULE 326. NOT MORE THAN TWO.

Not more than two new trials shall be granted either party in the same cause because of insufficiency or weight of the evidence.

RULE 327. FOR JURY MISCONDUCT.

a. When the ground of a motion for new trial, supported by affidavit, is misconduct of the jury or of the officer in charge of them, or because of any communication made to the jury, or that a juror gave an erroneous or incorrect answer on voir dire examination, the court shall hear evidence thereof from the jury or others in open court, and may grant a new trial if such misconduct proved, or the communication made, or the erroneous or incorrect answer on voir dire examination, be material, and if it reasonably appears from the evidence both on the hearing of the motion and the trial of the case and from the record as a whole that injury probably resulted to the complaining party.

b. A juror may not testify as to any matter or statement occurring during the course of the jury's deliberations or to the effect of anything upon his or any other juror's mind or emotions as influencing him to assent to or dissent from the verdict concerning his mental processes in connection therewith, except that a juror may testify whether any outside influence was improperly brought to bear upon any juror. Nor may his affidavit or evidence of any statement by him concerning a matter about which he would be precluded from testifying be received for these purposes.

(Amended by Order July 20, 1954, eff. Jan. 1, 1955; Dec. 5, 1983, eff. April 1, 1984.)

RULE 328. [REPEALED]

(Repealed by Order July 15, 1987, eff. Jan. 1, 1988.)

RULE 329. MOTION FOR NEW TRIAL ON JUDGMENT FOLLOWING CITATION BY PUBLICATION

In cases in which judgment has been rendered on service of process by publication, when the defendant has not appeared in person or by attorney of his own selection:

(a) The court may grant a new trial upon petition of the defendant showing good cause, supported by affidavit, filed within two years after such judgment was signed. The parties adversely interested in such judgment shall be cited as in other cases.

(b) Execution of such judgment shall not be suspended unless the party applying therefor shall give a good and sufficient bond payable to the plaintiff in the judgment, in an amount fixed in accordance with Appellate Rule 47 relating to supersedeas bonds, to be approved by the clerk, and conditioned that the party will prosecute his petition for new trial to effect and will perform such judgment as may be rendered by the court should its decision be against him.

(c) If property has been sold under the judgment and execution before the process was suspended, the defendant shall not recover the property so sold, but shall have judgment against the plaintiff in the judgment for the proceeds of such sale.

(d) If the motion is filed more than thirty days after the judgment was signed, the time period shall be computed pursuant to Rule 306a(7).

(Amended by Order June 10, 1980, eff. Jan. 1, 1981; Dec. 5, 1983, eff. April 1, 1984; July 15, 1987, eff. Jan. 1, 1988.)

RULE 329a. COUNTY COURT CASES.

If a case or other matter is on trial or in the process of hearing when the term of the county court expires, such trial, hearing or other matter may be proceeded with at the next or any subsequent term of court and no motion or plea shall be considered as waived or overruled, because not acted upon at the term of court at which it was filed, but may be acted upon at any time the judge may fix or at which it may have been postponed or continued by agreement of the parties with leave of the court. This subdivision is not applicable to original or amended motions for new trial which are governed by Rule 329b.

(Added by Order July 20, 1954 eff. Jan. 1, 1955. Amended by Order March 19, 1957, eff. Sept. 1, 1957; July 26, 1960, eff. Jan. 1, 1961.)

RULE 329b. TIME FOR FILING MOTIONS.

The following rules shall be applicable to motions for new trial and motions to modify, correct, or reform judgments (other than motions to correct the record under Rule 316) in all district and county courts:

(a) A motion for new trial, if filed, shall be filed prior to or within thirty days after the judgment or other order complained of is signed.

(b) One or more amended motions for new trial may be filed without leave of court before any preceding motion for new trial filed by the movant is overruled and within thirty days after the judgment or other order complained of is signed.

(c) In the event an original or amended motion for new trial or a motion to modify, correct or reform a judgment is not determined by written order signed within seventy-five days after the judgment was signed, it shall be considered overruled by operation of law on expiration of that period.

(d) The trial court, regardless of whether an appeal has been perfected, has plenary power to grant a new trial or to vacate, modify, correct, or reform the judgment within thirty days after the judgment is signed.

(e) If a motion for new trial is timely filed by any party, the trial court, regardless of whether an appeal has been perfected, has plenary power to grant a new trial or to vacate, modify, correct, or reform the judgment until thirty days after all such timely-filed motions are overruled, either by a written and signed order or by operation of law, whichever occurs first.

(f) On expiration of the time within which the trial court has plenary power, a judgment cannot be set aside by the trial court except by bill of review for sufficient cause, filed within the time allowed by law; provided that the court may at any time correct a clerical error in the record of a judgment and render judgment nunc pro tunc under Rule 316, and may also sign an order declaring a previous judgment or order to be void because signed after the court's plenary power had expired.

(g) A motion to modify, correct, or reform a judgment (as distinguished from motion to correct the record of a judgment under Rule 316), if filed, shall be filed and determined within the time prescribed by this rule for a motion for new trial and shall extend the trial court's plenary power and the time for perfecting an appeal in the same manner as a motion for new trial. Each such motion shall be in writing and signed by the party or his attorney and shall specify the respects in which the judgment should be modified, corrected, or reformed. The overruling of such a motion shall not preclude the filing of a motion for new trial, nor shall the overruling of a motion for new trial preclude the filing of a motion to modify, correct, or reform.

(h) If a judgment is modified, corrected or reformed in any respect, the time for appeal shall run from the time the modified, corrected, or reformed judgment is signed, but if a correction is made pursuant to Rule 316 after expiration of the period of plenary power provided by this rule, no complaint shall be heard on appeal that could have been presented in an appeal from the original judgment.

(Added by Order July 20, 1954, eff. Jan. 1, 1955. Amended by Order July 26, 1960), eff. Jan. 1, 1961; July 20, 1966, eff. Jan. 1, 1967; Oct. 3, 1972, eff. Feb. 1, 1973; July 11, 1977, eff. Jan. 1, 1978; June 10, 1980, eff. Jan. 1, 1981; Dec. 5, 1983, eff. April 1, 1984; July 15, 1987, eff. Jan. 1, 1988.)

K.
CERTAIN DISTRICT COURTS

RULE 330. RULES OF PRACTICE AND PROCEDURE IN CERTAIN DISTRICT COURTS.

The following rules of practice and procedure shall govern and be followed in all civil actions in district courts in counties where the only district court of said county vested with civil jurisdiction, or all the district courts thereof having civil jurisdiction, have successive terms in said county throughout the year, without more than two days intervening between any of such terms, whether or not any one or more of such district courts include one or more other counties within its jurisdiction.

(a) **Appealed Cases**. In cases appealed to said district courts from inferior courts, the appeal, including transcript, shall be filed in the district court within thirty (30) days after the rendition of the judgment or order appealed from, and the appellee shall enter his appearance on the docket or answer to said appeal on or before ten o'clock a.m. of the Monday next after the expiration of twenty (20) days from the date the appeal is filed in the district court.

(b) Repealed by order of July 22, 1975, eff. Jan. 1, 1976.

(c) **Postponement or Continuance**. Cases may be postponed or continued by agreement with the approval of the court, or upon the court's own motion or for cause. When a case is called for trial and only one party is ready, the court may for good cause either continue the case for the term or postpone and reset it for a later day in the same or succeeding term.

(d) **Cases May Be Reset**. A case that is set and reached for trial may be postponed for a later day in the term or continued and reset for a day certain in the succeeding term on the same grounds as an application for continuance would be granted in other district courts. After any case has been set and reached in its due order and called for trial two (2) or more times and not tried, the court may dismiss the same unless the parties agree to a postponement or continuance but the court shall respect written agreements of counsel for postponement and continuance if filed in the case when or before it is called for trial unless to do so will unreasonably delay or interfere with other business of the court.

(e) **Exchange and Transfer**. Where in such county there are two or more district courts having civil jurisdiction, the judges of such courts may, in their discretion, exchange benches or districts from time to time, and may transfer cases and other proceedings from one court to another, and any of them may in his own courtroom try and determine any case or proceeding pending in another court without having the case transferred, or may sit in any other of said courts and there hear and determine any case there pending, and every judgment and order shall be entered in the minutes of the court in which the case is pending and at the time the judgment or order is rendered, and two (2) or more judges may try different cases in the same court at the same time, and each may occupy his own courtroom or the room of any other court. The judge of any such court may issue restraining orders and injunctions returnable to any other judge or court, and any judge may transfer any case or proceeding pending in his court to any other of said courts, and the judge of any court to which a case or proceeding is transferred shall receive and try the same, and in turn shall have power in his discretion to transfer any such case to any other of said courts and any other judge may in his courtroom try any case pending in any other of such courts.

(f) **Cases Transferred to Judges Not Occupied**. Where in such counties there are two or more district courts having civil jurisdiction, when the judge of any such court shall become disengaged, he shall notify the presiding judge, and the presiding judge shall transfer to the court of the disengaged judge the next case which is ready for trial in any of said courts. Any judge not engaged in his own court may try any case in any other court.

(g) **Judge May Hear Only Part of Case**. Where in such counties there are two or more district courts having civil jurisdiction, any judge may hear any part of any case or proceeding pending in any of said courts and determine the same, or may hear and determine any question in any case, and any other judge may complete the hearing and render judgment in the case.

(h) **Any Judge May Hear Dilatory Pleas**. Where in such county there are two or more district courts having civil jurisdiction, any judge may hear and determine motions, petitions for injunction, applications for appointment of receivers, interventions, pleas of privilege, pleas in abatement, all dilatory pleas and special exceptions, motions for a new trial and all preliminary matters, questions and proceedings and may enter judgment or order thereon in the court in which the case is pending without having the case transferred to the court of the judge acting, and the judge in whose court the case is pending may thereafter proceed to hear, complete and determine the case or other matter, or any part thereof, and render final judgment therein. Any judgment rendered or action taken by any judge in any of said courts in the county shall be valid and binding.

(i) **Acts in Succeeding Terms**. If a case or other matter is on trial, or in the process of hearing when the term of court expires, such trial, hearing or other matter may be proceeded with at the next or any subsequent term of court and no motion or plea shall be considered as waived or overruled, because not acted upon at the term of court at which it was filed, but may be acted upon at any time the judge may fix or at which it may have been postponed or continued by agreement of the parties with leave of the court. This subdivision is not applicable to original or amended motions for new trial which are governed by Rule 329b.

(Amended by Order July 20, 1954, eff. Jan. 1, 1955; July 26, 1960, eff. Jan. 1, 1961; Oct. 3, 1972, eff. Feb. 1, 1973; July 22, 1975, eff. Jan. 1, 1976.)

RULE 331. [REPEALED]

(Repealed by Order July 15, 1987, eff. Jan. 1, 1988.)

SECTION 12.
REVIEW BY DISTRICT COURTS OF COUNTY COURT RULINGS

RULES 332 TO 351. [REPEALED]

(Repealed by Order July 22, 1975, eff. Jan. 1, 1976.)

PART III.
RULES OF PROCEDURE FOR THE COURTS OF APPEALS

RULES 352 TO 358. [REPEALED]

(Repealed by Order April 10, 1986, eff. Sept. 1, 1986.)

RULE 359. [REPEALED]

(Repealed by Order Dec. 5, 1983, eff. April 1, 1984.)

RULE 360. [REPEALED]

(Repealed by Order April 10, 1986, eff. Sept. 1, 1986.)

RULES 361 AND 362. [REPEALED]

(Repealed by Order Dec. 5, 1983, eff. April 1, 1984.)

RULES 363 TO 369a. [REPEALED]

(Repealed by Order April 10, 1986, eff. Sept. 1, 1986.)

RULE 370. [REPEALED]

(Repealed by Order June 10, 1980, eff. Jan. 1, 1981.)

RULES 371 TO 373. [REPEALED]

(Repealed by Order April 10, 1986, eff. Sept. 1, 1986.)

RULE 374. [REPEALED]

(Repealed by Order July 11, 1977, eff. Jan. 1, 1978.)

RULES 375 AND 376. [REPEALED]

(Repealed by Order April 10, 1986, eff. Sept. 1, 1986.)

RULE 376a TO 389a. [REPEALED]

(Repealed by Order April 10, 1986, eff. Sept. 1, 1986.)

RULE 390. [REPEALED]

(Repealed by Order Dec. 5, 1983, eff. April 1, 1984.)

RULE 391. [REPEALED]

(Repealed by Order Oct. 12, 1949, eff. March 1, 1950.)

RULE 392. [REPEALED]

(Repealed by Order Dec. 5, 1983, eff. April 1, 1984.)

RULES 393 TO 414. [REPEALED]

(Repealed by Order April 10, 1986, eff. Sept. 1, 1986.)

RULES 415 TO 417. [REPEALED]

(Repealed by Order Dec. 5, 1983, eff. April 4, 1984.)

RULES 418 TO 420. [REPEALED]

(Repealed by Order April 10, 1986, eff. Sept. 1, 1986.)

RULE 421. [REPEALED]

(Repealed by Order June 10, 1980, eff. Jan. 1, 1981.)

RULE 422. [REPEALED]

(Repealed by Order April 10, 1986, eff. Sept. 1, 1986.)

RULE 423. [REPEALED]

(Repealed by Order April 10, 1986, eff. Sept. 1, 1986.)

RULES 424 TO 427. [REPEALED]

(Repealed by Order Dec. 5, 1983, eff. April 1, 1984.)

RULES 428 AND 429. [REPEALED]

(Repealed by Order April 10, 1986, eff. Sept. 1, 1986.)

RULES 430 TO 432. [REPEALED]

(Repealed by Order Dec. 5, 1983, eff. April 1, 1984.)

RULES 433 TO 442. [REPEALED]

(Repealed by Order April 10, 1986, eff. Sept. 1, 1986.)

RULES 443 AND 444. [REPEALED]

(Repealed by Order Dec. 5, 1983, eff. April 1, 1984.)

RULE 445. [REPEALED]

(Repealed by Order July 11, 1977, eff. Jan. 1, 1978.)

RULES 446 TO 448. [REPEALED]

(Repealed by Order April 10, 1986, eff. Sept. 1, 1986.)

RULES 449 AND 450. [REPEALED]

(Repealed by Order Dec. 5, 1983, eff. April 1, 1984.)

RULES 451 AND 452. [REPEALED]

(Repealed by Order April 10, 1986, eff. Sept. 1, 1986.)

RULES 453 TO 455. [REPEALED]

(Repealed by Order Dec. 5, 1983, eff. April 1, 1984.)

RULES 456 TO 458. [REPEALED]

(Repealed by Order April 10, 1986, eff. Sept. 1, 1986.)

RULE 459. [REPEALED]

(Repealed by Order Sept. 20, 1941, eff. Dec. 31, 1941.)

RULES 460 TO 462. [REPEALED]

(Repealed by Order April 10, 1986, eff. Sept. 1, 1986.)

RULES 463 AND 464. [REPEALED]

(Repealed by Order Dec. 5, 1983, eff. April 1, 1984.)

RULES 465 AND 466. [REPEALED]

(Repealed by Order April 10, 1986, eff. Sept. 1, 1986.)

RULE 467. [REPEALED]

(Repealed by Order Dec. 5, 1983, eff. April 1, 1984.)

RULES 468 TO 470. [REPEALED]

(Repealed by Order April 10, 1986, eff. Sept. 1, 1986.)

RULE 471. [REPEALED]

(Repealed by Order Dec. 5, 1983, eff. April 1, 1984.)

RULE 472. [REPEALED]

(Repealed by Order April 10, 1986, eff. Sept. 1, 1986.)

RULE 473. [REPEALED]

(Repealed by Order Dec. 5, 1983, eff. April 1, 1984.)

PART IV.
RULES OF PRACTICE FOR THE SUPREME COURT

RULES 474 TO 481. [REPEALED]

(Repealed by Order April 10, 1986, eff. Sept. 1, 1986)

RULE 482. [REPEALED]

(Repealed by Order Dec. 5, 1983, eff. April 1, 1984.)

RULES 483 TO 486. [REPEALED]

(Repealed by Order April 10, 1986, eff. Sept. 1, 1986.)

RULE 487. [REPEALED]

(Repealed by Order Oct. 10, 1945, eff. Feb. 1, 1946.)

RULES 488 TO 491. [REPEALED]

(Repealed by Order April 10, 1986, eff. Sept. 1, 1986.)

RULE 492. [REPEALED]

(Repealed by Order April 10, 1986, eff. Sept. 1, 1986.)

RULE 493. [REPEALED]

(Repealed by Order April 10, 1986, eff. Sept. 1, 1986.)

RULE 494. [REPEALED]

(Repealed by Order Oct. 10, 1945, eff. Feb. 1, 1946.)

RULE 495. [REPEALED]

(Repealed by Order April 10, 1986, eff. Sept. 1, 1986.)

RULE 496. [REPEALED]

(Repealed by Order April 10, 1986, eff. Sept. 1, 1986.)

RULES 497 TO 505. [REPEALED]

(Repealed by Order April 10, 1986, eff. Sept., 1, 1986.)

RULE 506. [REPEALED]

(Repealed by Order Dec. 5, 1983, eff. April 1, 1984.)

RULE 507. [REPEALED]

(Repealed by Order April 10, 1986, eff. Sept. 1, 1986.)

RULE 508. [REPEALED]

(Repealed by Order Dec. 5, 1983, eff. April 1, 1984.)

RULE 509. [REPEALED]

(Repealed by Order July 11, 1977, eff. Jan. 1, 1978.)

RULE 510. [REPEALED]

(Repealed by Order April 10, 1986, eff. Sept. 1, 1986.)

RULES 511 TO 513. [REPEALED]

(Repealed by Order Dec. 5, 1983, eff. April 1, 1984.)

RULES 514 AND 515. [REPEALED]

(Repealed by Order April 10, 1986, eff. Sept. 1, 1986.)

RULES 516 AND 517. [REPEALED]

(Repealed by Order Dec. 5, 1983, eff. April 1, 1984.)

RULES 518 TO 522. [REPEALED]

(Repealed by Order Oct. 10, 1945, eff. Feb. 1, 1946.)

PART V.
IN RULES OF PRACTICE IN JUSTICE COURTS

[Rules of Civil Procedure 500-510 govern cases filed on or after August 31 , 2013, and cases pending on August 31 , 2013, except to the extent that in the opinion of the court their application in a case pending on August 31 , 2013, would not be feasible or would work injustice, in which event the formerly applicable procedure applies. An action taken before August 31 , 2013, in a case pending on August 31, 2013, that was done pursuant to any previously applicable procedure must be treated as valid. Where citation or other process was issued or served prior to August 31, 2013 , in compliance with any previously applicable procedure, the party served has the time provided for under the previously applicable procedure to answer or otherwise respond.]

RULE 500. GENERAL RULES.

RULE 500.1. CONSTRUCTION OF RULES.

Unless otherwise expressly provided, in Part V of these Rules of Civil Procedure:

(a) the past, present, and future tense each includes the other;

(b) the term "it" includes a person of either gender or an entity; and

(c) the singular and plural each includes the other.

RULE 500.2. DEFINITIONS.

In Part V of these Rules of Civil Procedure:

(a) "Answer" is the written response that a party who is sued must file with the court after being served with a citation.

(b) "Citation" is the court-issued document required to be served upon a party to inform the party that it has been sued.

(c) "Claim" is the legal theory and alleged facts that, if proven, entitle a party to relief against another party in court.

(d) "Clerk" is a person designated by the judge as a justice court clerk, or the judge if there is no clerk available.

(e) "Counterclaim" is a claim brought by a party who has been sued against the party who filed the lawsuit, for example, a defendant suing a plaintiff.

(f) "County court" is the county court, statutory county court, or district court in a particular county with jurisdiction over appeals of civil cases from justice court.

(g) "Cross-claim" is a claim brought by one party against another party on the same side of a lawsuit. For example, if a plaintiff sues two defendants, the defendants can seek relief against each other by means of a cross-claim.

(h) "Default judgment" is a judgment awarded to a plaintiff when the defendant fails to answer and dispute the plaintiff s claims in the lawsuit.

(i) "Defendant" is a party who is sued, including a plaintiff against whom a counterclaim is filed.

(j) "Defense" is an assertion by a defendant that the plaintiff is not entitled to relief from the court.

(k) "Discovery" is the process through which parties obtain information from each other in order to prepare for trial or enforce a judgment. The term does not refer to any information that a party is entitled to under applicable law.

(l) "Dismissed without prejudice" means a case has been dismissed but has not been finally decided and may be refiled.

(m) "Dismissed with prejudice" means a case has been dismissed and finally decided and may not be refiled.

(n) "Judge" is a justice of the peace.

(o) "Judgment" is a final order by the court that states the relief, if any, a party is entitled to or must provide.

(p) "Jurisdiction" is the authority of the court to hear and decide a case.

(q) "Motion" is a request that the court make a specified ruling or order.

(r) "Notice" is a document prepared and delivered by the court or a party stating that something is required of the party receiving the notice.

(s) "Party" is a person or entity involved in the case that is either suing or being sued, including all plaintiffs, defendants, and third parties that have been joined in the case.

(t) "Petition" is a formal written application stating a party's claims and requesting relief from the court. It is the first document filed with the court to begin a lawsuit.

(u) "Plaintiff' is a party who sues, including a defendant who files a counterclaim.

(v) "Pleading" is a written document filed by a party, including a petition and an answer, that states a claim or defense and outlines the relief sought.

(w) "Relief' is the remedy a party requests from the court, such as the recovery of money or the return of property.

(x) "Serve" and "service" are delivery of citation as required by Rule 50 1 .2, or of a document as required by Rule 501 .4.

(y) "Sworn" means signed in front of someone authorized to take oaths, such as a notary, or signed under penalty of perjury. Filing a false sworn document can result in criminal prosecution.

(z) "Third party claim" is a claim brought by a party being sued against someone who is not yet a party to the case.

RULE 500.3. APPLICATION OF RULES IN JUSTICE COURT CASES.

(a) *Small Claims Case.* A small claims case is a lawsuit brought for the recovery of money damages, civil penalties, personal property, or other relief allowed by law. The claim can be for no more than $ 1 0,000, excluding statutory interest and court costs but including attorney fees, if any. Small claims cases are governed by Rules 500-507 of Part V of the Rules of Civil Procedure.

(b) *Debt Claim Case.* A debt claim case is a lawsuit brought to recover a debt by an assignee of a claim, a debt collector or collection agency, a financial institution, or a person or entity primarily engaged in the business of lending money at interest. The claim can be for no more than $ 1 0,000, excluding statutory interest and court costs but including attorney fees, if any. Debt claim cases injustice court are governed by Rules 500-507 and 508 of Part V of the Rules of Civil Procedure. To the extent of any conflict between Rule 508 and the rest of Part V, Rule 508 applies.

(c) *Repair and Remedy Case.* A repair and remedy case is a lawsuit filed by a residential tenant under Chapter 92, Subchapter B of the Texas Property Code to enforce the landlord's duty to repair or remedy a condition materially affecting the physical health or safety of an ordinary tenant. The relief sought can be for no more than $ 1 0,000, excluding statutory interest and court costs but including attorney fees, if any. Repair and remedy cases are governed by Rules 500-507 and 509 of Part V of the Rules of Civil Procedure. To the extent of any conflict between Rule 509 and the rest of Part V, Rule 509 applies.

(d) *Eviction Case.* An eviction case is a lawsuit brought to recover possession of real property under Chapter 24 of the Texas Property Code, often by a landlord against a tenant. A claim for rent may be joined with an eviction case if the amount of rent due and unpaid is not more than $10,000, excluding statutory interest and court costs but including attorney fees, if any. Eviction cases are governed by Rules 500-507 and 5 1 0 of Part V of the Rules of Civil Procedure. To the extent of any conflict between Rule 5 1 0 and the rest of Part V, Rule 510 applies.

(e) *Application of Other Rules.* The other Rules of Civil Procedure and the Rules of Evidence do not apply except:
  (1) when the judge hearing the case determines that a particular rule must be followed to ensure that the proceedings are fair to all parties; or
  (2) when otherwise specifically provided by law or these rules.

(f) *Examination of Rules.* The court must make the Rules of Civil Procedure and the Rules of Evidence available for examination, either in paper form or electronically, during the court's business hours.

RULE 500.4. REPRESENTATION IN JUSTICE COURT CASES.

(a) *Representation of an Individual.* An individual may:
  (1) represent himself or herself;
  (2) be represented by an authorized agent in an eviction case; or
  (3) be represented by an attorney.

(b) *Representation of a Corporation or Other Entity.* A corporation or other entity may:
  (1) be represented by an employee, owner, officer, or partner of the entity who is not an attorney;
  (2) be represented by a property manager or other authorized agent in an eviction case; or
  (3) be represented by an attorney.

(c) *Assisted Representation.* The court may, for good cause, allow an individual representing himself or herself to be assisted in court by a family member or other individual who is not being compensated.

RULE 500.5. COMPUTATION OF TIME; TIMELY FILING.

(a) *Computation of Time.* To compute a time period in these rules:
  (1) exclude the day of the event that triggers the period;
  (2) count every day, including Saturdays, Sundays, and legal holidays; and
  (3) include the last day of the period, but
    (A) if the last day is a Saturday, Sunday, or legal holiday, the time period is extended to the next day that is not a Saturday, Sunday, or legal holiday; and
    (B) if the last day for filing falls on a day during which the court is closed before 5:00p.m., the time period is extended to the court's next business day.

(b) *Timely Filing by Mail.* Any document required to be filed by a given date is considered timely filed if deposited in the U.S. mail on or before that date, and received within 10 days of the due date. A legible postmark affixed by the United States Postal Service is evidence of the date of mailing.

(c) *Extensions.* The judge may, for good cause shown, extend any time period under these rules except those relating to new trial and appeal.

RULE 500.6. JUDGE TO DEVELOP THE CASE.

In order to develop the facts of the case, a judge may question a witness or party and may summon any person or party to appear as a witness when the judge considers it necessary to ensure a correct judgment and a speedy disposition.

RULE 500.7. EXCLUSION OF WITNESSES.

The court must, on a party's request, or may, on its own initiative, order witnesses excluded so that they cannot hear the testimony of other witnesses. This rule does not authorize the exclusion of:

(a) a party who is a natural person or the spouse of such natural person;

(b) an officer or employee designated as a representative of a party who is not a natural person; or

(c) a person whose presence is shown by a party to be essential to the presentation of the party's case.

RULE 500.8. SUBPOENAS.

(a) *Use.* A subpoena may be used by a party or the judge to command a person or entity to attend and give testimony at a hearing or trial. A person may not be required by subpoena to appear in a county that is more than ISO miles from where the person resides or is served.

(b) *Who Can Issue.* A subpoena may be issued by the clerk of the justice court or an attorney authorized to practice in the State of Texas, as an officer of the court.

(c) *Form.* Every subpoena must be issued in the name of the "State of Texas" and must:

(1) state the style of the suit and its case number;

(2) state the court in which the suit is pending;

(3) state the date on which the subpoena is issued;

(4) identify the person to whom the subpoena is directed;

(5) state the date, time, place, and nature of the action required by the person to whom the subpoena is directed;

(6) identify the party at whose instance the subpoena is issued, and the party's attorney of record, if any;

(7) state that "Failure by any person without adequate excuse to obey a subpoena served upon that person may be deemed a contempt of court from which the subpoena is issued and may be punished by fine or confinement, or both"; and

(8) be signed by the person issuing the subpoena.

(d) *Service: Where, By Whom, How.* A subpoena may be served at any place within the State of Texas by any sheriff or constable of the State of Texas, or by any person who is not a party and is 18 years of age or older. A subpoena must be served by delivering a copy to the witness and tendering to that person any fees required by law. If the witness is a party and is represented by an attorney of record in the proceeding, the subpoena may be served on the witness's attorney of record. Proof of service must be made by filing either:

(1) the witness's signed written memorandum attached to the subpoena showing that the witness accepted the subpoena; or

(2) a statement by the person who made the service stating the date, time, and manner of service, and the name of the person served.

(e) *Compliance Required.* A person commanded by subpoena to appear and give testimony must remain at the hearing or trial from day to day until discharged by the court or by the party summoning the witness. If a subpoena commanding testimony is directed to a corporation, partnership, association, governmental agency, or other organization, and the matters on which examination is requested are described with reasonable particularity, the organization must designate one or more persons to testify on its behalf as to matters known or reasonably available to the organization.

(f) *Objection.* A person commanded to attend and give testimony at a hearing or trial may object or move for a protective order before the court at or before the time and place specified for compliance. A party causing a subpoena to issue must take reasonable steps to avoid imposing undue burden or expense on the person served. In ruling on objections or motions for protection, the court must provide a person served with a subpoena an adequate time for compliance and protection from undue burden or expense. The court may impose reasonable conditions on compliance with a subpoena, including compensating the witness for undue hardship.

(g) *Enforcement.* Failure by any person without adequate excuse to obey a subpoena served upon that person may be deemed a contempt of the court from which the subpoena is issued or of a district court in the county in which the subpoena is served, and may be punished by fine or confinement, or both. A fine may not be imposed, nor a person served with a subpoena attached, for failure to comply with a subpoena without proof of service and proof by affidavit of the party requesting the subpoena or the party's attorney of record that all fees due the witness by law were paid or tendered.

RULE 500.9. DISCOVERY.

(a) *Pretrial Discovery*. Pretrial discovery is limited to that which the judge considers reasonable and necessary. Any requests for pretrial discovery must be presented to the court for approval by written motion. The motion must be served on the responding party. Unless a hearing is requested, the judge may rule on the motion without a hearing. The discovery request must not be served on the responding party unless the judge issues a signed order approving the request. Failure to comply with a discovery order can result in sanctions, including dismissal of the case or an order to pay the other party's discovery expenses.

(b) *Post-judgment Discovery*. Post-judgment discovery is not required to be filed with the court. The party requesting discovery must give the responding party at least 3 0 days to respond to a post-judgment discovery request. The responding party may file a written objection with the court within 30 days of receiving the request. If an objection is filed, the judge must hold a hearing to determine if the request is valid. If the objection is denied, the judge must order the party to respond to the request. If the objection is upheld, the judge may reform the request or dismiss it entirely.

(Adopted by Order Feb 12, 2013 and Order April 15, 2013, eff. Aug. 31, 2013.)

Rules of Civil Procedure 500-510 govern cases filed on or after August 31 , 2013, and cases pending on August 31 , 2013, except to the extent that in the opinion of the court their application in a case pending on August 31 , 2013, would not be feasible or would work injustice, in which event the formerly applicable procedure applies. An action taken before August 31 , 2013, in a case pending on August 31, 2013, that was done pursuant to any previously applicable procedure must be treated as valid. Where citation or other process was issued or served prior to August 31, 2013 , in compliance with any previously applicable procedure, the party served has the time provided for under the previously applicable procedure to answer or otherwise respond.

RULE 501. CITATION AND SERVICE.

RULE 501.1. CITATION.

(a) *Issuance*. When a petition is tiled with a justice court to initiate a suit, the clerk must promptly issue a citation and deliver the citation as directed by the plaintiff. The plaintiff is responsible for obtaining service on the defendant of the citation and a copy of the petition with any documents filed with the petition. Upon request, separate or additional citations must be issued by the clerk. The clerk must retain a copy of the citation in the court's file.

(b) *Form*. The citation must:

(1) be styled "The State of Texas";

(2) be signed by the clerk under seal of court or by the judge;

(3) contain the name, location, and address of the court;

(4) show the date of filing of the petition;

(5) show the date of issuance of the citation;

(6) show the file number and names of parties;

(7) be directed to the defendant;

(8) show the name and address of attorney for plaintiff, or if the plaintiff does not have an attorney, the address of plaintiff; and

(9) notify defendant that if the defendant fails to file an answer, judgment by default may be rendered for the relief demanded in the petition.

(c) *Notice*. The citation must include the following notice to the defendant in boldface type:

"You have been sued. You may employ an attorney to help you in defending against this lawsuit. But you are not required to employ an attorney. You or your attorney must file an answer with the court. Your answer is due by the end of the 14th day after the day you were served with these papers. If the 14th day is a Saturday, Sunday, or legal holiday, your answer is due by the end of the first day following the 14th day that is not a Saturday, Sunday, or legal holiday. Do not ignore these papers. If you do not file an answer by the due date, a default judgment may be taken against you. For further information, consult Part V of the Texas Rules of Civil Procedure, which is available online and also at the court listed on this citation."

(d) *Copies*. The plaintiff must provide enough copies to be served on each defendant. If the plaintiff fails to do so, the clerk may make copies and charge the plaintiff the allowable copying cost.

RULE 501.2. SERVICE OF CITATION.

(a) *Who May Serve*. No person who is a party to or interested in the outcome of the suit may serve citation in that suit, and, unless otherwise authorized by written court order, only a sheriff or constable may serve a citation in an eviction case, a writ that requires the actual taking of possession of a person, property or thing, or process requiring that an enforcement action be physically enforced by the person delivering the process. Other citations may be served by:

(1) a sheriff or constable;

(2) a process server certified under order of the Supreme Court;

(3) the clerk of the court, if the citation is served by registered or certified mail; or

(4) a person authorized by court order who is 18 years of age or older.

(b) *Method of Service.* Citation must be served by:

(1) delivering a copy of the citation with a copy of the petition attached to the defendant in person, after endorsing the date of delivery on the citation; or

(2) mailing a copy of the citation with a copy of the petition attached to the defendant by registered or certified mail, restricted delivery, with return receipt or electronic return receipt requested.

(c) *Service Fees.* A plaintiff must pay all fees for service unless the plaintiff has filed a Statement of Inability to Afford Payment of Court Costs with the court. If the plaintiff has filed a Statement, the plaintiff must arrange for the citation to be served by a sheriff, constable, or court clerk.

(d) *Service on Sunday.* A citation cannot be served on a Sunday except in attachment, garnishment, sequestration, or distress proceedings.

(e) *Alternative Service of Citation.* If the methods under (b) are insufficient to serve the defendant, the plaintiff, or the constable, sheriff, process server certified under order of the Supreme Court, or other person authorized to serve process, may make a request for alternative service. This request must include a sworn statement describing the methods attempted under (b) and stating the defendant's usual place of business or residence, or other place where the defendant can probably be found. The court may authorize the following types of alternative service:

(1) mailing a copy of the citation with a copy of the petition attached by first class mail to the defendant at a specified address, and also leaving a copy of the citation with petition attached at the defendant's residence or other place where the defendant can probably be found with any person found there who is at least 16 years of age; or

(2) mailing a copy of the citation with a copy of the petition attached by first class mail to the defendant at a specified address, and also serving by any other method that the court finds is reasonably likely to provide the defendant with notice of the suit.

(f) *Service by Publication.* In the event that service of citation by publication is necessary, the process is governed by the rules in county and district court.

(Amended by Tex. Sup. Ct. Misc. Docket No. 16-9122, eff. Sept. 1, 2016.)

[Statement of Inability to Afford Payment of Court Costs as provided in Tex. Sup. Ct. Misc. Docket No. 16-9122, eff. Sept. 1, 2016 and applies to any contest of, or challenge to, a claim of inability to afford payment of court costs that is pending on September 1, 2016.]

RULE 501.3. DUTIES OF OFFICER OR PERSON RECEIVING CITATION; RETURN OF SERVICE.

(a) *Endorsement; Execution; Return.* The officer or authorized person to whom process is delivered must:

(1) endorse on the process the date and hour on which he or she received it;

(2) execute and return the same without delay; and

(3) complete a return of service, which may, but need not, be endorsed on or attached to the citation.

(b) *Contents of Return.* The return, together with any document to which it is attached, must include the following information:

(1) the case number and case name;

(2) the court in which the case is filed;

(3) a description of what was served;

(4) the date and time the process was received for service;

(5) the person or entity served;

(6) the address served;

(7) the date of service or attempted service;

(8) the manner of delivery of service or attempted service;

(9) the name of the person who served or attempted service;

(10) if the person named in (9) is a process server certified under Supreme Court Order, his or her identification number and the expiration date of his or her certification; and

(11) any other information required by rule or law.

(c) *Citation by Mail.* When the citation is served by registered or certified mail as authorized by Rule 501.2(b)(2), the return by the officer or authorized person must also contain the receipt with the addressee's signature.

(d) *Failure to Serve.* When the officer or authorized person has not served the citation, the return must show the diligence used by the officer or authorized person to execute the same and the cause of failure to execute it, and where the defendant is to be found, if ascertainable.

(e) *Signature.* The officer or authorized person who serves or attempts to serve a citation must sign the return. If the return is signed by a person other than a sheriff; constable, or clerk of the court, the return must either be verified or be signed under penalty of perjury. A return signed under penalty of perjury must contain the statement below in substantially the following form:

> "My name is (First) (Middle) (Last), my date of birth is (Month) (Day), (Year), and my address is (Street), (City), (State) (Zip Code), (Country). I declare under penalty of perjury that the foregoing is true and correct.
> Executed in ________________ County, State of ____________, on the _______ day of (Month), (Year).
>
> ____
>
> Declarant"

(f) *Alternative Service.* Where citation is executed by an alternative method as authorized by 501.2(e), proof of service must be made in the manner ordered by the court.

(g) *Filing Return.* The return and any document to which it is attached must be filed with the court and may be filed electronically or by fax, if those methods of filing are available.

(h) *Prerequisite for Default Judgment.* No default judgment may be granted in any case until proof of service as provided by this rule, or as ordered by the court in the event citation is executed by an alternative method under 501.2(e), has been on tile with the clerk of the court 3 days, exclusive of the day of filing and the day of judgment.

RULE 501.4. SERVICE OF PAPERS OTHER THAN CITATION.

(a) *Method of Service.* Other than a citation or oral motions made during trial or when all parties are present, every notice required by these rules, and every pleading, plea, motion, application to the court for an order, or other form of request, must be served on all other parties in one of the following ways:
   (1) In person. A copy may be delivered to the party to be served, or the party's duly authorized agent or attorney of record, in person or by agent.
   (2) Mail or courier. A copy may be sent by courier-receipted delivery or by certified or registered mail, to the party's last known address. Service by certified or registered mail is complete when the document is properly addressed and deposited in the United States mail, postage prepaid.
   (3) Fax. A copy may be faxed to the recipient's current fax number. Service by fax after 5:00 p.m. local time of the recipient will be deemed to have been served on the following day.
   (4) Email. A copy may be sent to an email address expressly provided by the receiving party, if the party has consented to email service in writing. Service by email after 5:00 p.m. local time of the recipient will be deemed to have been served on the following day.
   (5) Other. A copy may be delivered in any other manner directed by the court.

(b) *Timing.* If a document is served by mail, 3 days will be added to the length of time a party has to respond to the document. Notice of any hearing requested by a party must be served on all other parties not less than 3 days before the time specified for the hearing.

(c) *Who May Serve.* Documents other than a citation may be served by a party to the suit, an attorney of record, a sheriff or constable, or by any other person competent to testify.

(d) *Certificate of Service.* The party or the party's attorney of record must include in writing on all documents filed a signed statement describing the manner in which the document was served on the other party or parties and the date of service. A certificate by a party or the party's attorney of record, or the return of the officer, or the sworn statement of any other person showing service of a notice is proof of service.

(e) *Failure to Serve.* A party may offer evidence or testimony that a notice or document was not received, or, if service was by mail, that it was not received within 3 days from the date of mailing, and upon so finding, the court may extend the time for taking the action required of the party or grant other relief as it deems just.

(Adopted by Order Feb 12, 2013 and Order April 15, 2013, eff. Aug. 31, 2013.)

Rules of Civil Procedure 500-510 govern cases filed on or after August 31 , 2013, and cases pending on August 31 , 2013, except to the extent that in the opinion of the court their application in a case pending on August 31 , 2013, would not be feasible or would work injustice, in which event the formerly applicable procedure applies. An action taken before August 31 , 2013, in a case pending on August 31, 2013, that was done pursuant to any previously applicable procedure must be treated as valid. Where citation or other process was issued or served prior to August 31, 2013 , in compliance with any previously applicable procedure, the party served has the time provided for under the previously applicable procedure to answer or otherwise respond.

RULE 502. INSTITUTION OF SUIT.

RULE 502.1. PLEADINGS AND MOTIONS MUST BE WRITTEN, SIGNED, AND FILED.

Except for oral motions made during trial or when all parties are present, every pleading, plea, motion, application to the court for an order, or other form of request must be written and signed by the party or its attorney and must be filed with the court. A document may be filed with the court by personal or commercial delivery, by mail, or electronically, if the court allows electronic filing. Electronic filing is governed by Rule 21.

(Amended by Order Aug. 16, 2013, eff. Jan. 1, 2014; Dec. 13, 2013, eff. Jan. 1, 2013.)

RULE 502.2. PETITION.

(a) *Contents*. To initiate a lawsuit, a petition must be filed with the court. A petition must contain:
  (1) the name of the plaintiff;
  (2) the name, address, telephone number, and fax number, if any, of the plaintiff's attorney, if applicable, or the address, telephone number, and fax number, if any, of the plaintiff;
  (3) the name, address, and telephone number, if known, of the defendant;
  (4) the amount of money, if any, the plaintiff seeks;
  (5) a description and claimed value of any personal property the plaintiff seeks;
  (6) a description of any other relief requested;
  (7) the basis for the plaintiff's claim against the defendant; and
  (8) if the plaintiff consents to email service of the answer and any other motions or pleadings, a statement consenting to email service and email contact information.

(b) *Justice Court Civil Case Information Sheet*. A justice court civil case information sheet, in the form promulgated by the Supreme Court of Texas, must accompany the filing of a petition and must be signed by the plaintiff or the plaintiff's attorney. The justice court civil case information sheet is for data collection for statistical and administrative purposes and does not affect any substantive right. The court may not reject a pleading because the pleading is not accompanied by a justice court civil case information sheet.

[Justice Court Civil Case Information Sheet as provided in Misc. Docket No. 13-9049, Feb. 12, 2013, eff Aug. 31, 2013; April 15, 2013, eff. Aug. 31, 2013 and applies to all cases filed on or after Aug. 31, 2013.]

RULE 502.3. FEES; INABILITY TO AFFORD FEES.

(a) *Fees and Statement of Inability to Afford Payment of Court Costs*. On filing the petition, the plaintiff must pay the appropriate filing fee and service fees, if any, with the court. A plaintiff who is unable to afford to pay the fees must file a Statement of Inability to Afford Payment of Court Costs. The Statement must either be sworn to before a notary or made under penalty of perjury. Upon filing the Statement, the clerk must docket the action, issue citation, and provide any other customary serv1ces.

(b) *Supreme Court Form*; *Contents of Statement*. The plaintiff must use the form Statement approved by the Supreme Court, or the Statement must include the information required by the Court-approved form. The clerk must make the form available to all persons without charge or request.

(c) *Certificate of Legal-Aid Provider*. If the party is represented by an attorney who is providing free legal services because of the party's indigence, without contingency, and the attorney is providing services either directly or by referral from legal-aid provider described in Rule 145(e)(2), the attorney may file a certificate confirming that the provider screened the party for eligibility under the income and asset guidelines established by the provider. A Statement that is accompanied by the certificate of a legal-aid provider may not be contested under (d).

(d) *Contest*. Unless a certificate is filed under (c), the defendant may file a contest of the Statement at any time within 7 days after the day the defendant's answer is due. If the Statement attests to receipt of government entitlement based on indigence, the Statement may only be contested with regard to the veracity of the attestation. If contested, the judge must hold a hearing to determine the plaintiffs ability to afford the fees. At the hearing, the burden is on the plaintiff to prove the inability to afford fees. The judge may, regardless of whether the defendant contests the Statement, examine the Statement and conduct a hearing to determine the plaintiffs ability to afford fees. If the judge determines that the plaintiff is able to afford the fees, the judge must enter a written order listing the reasons for the determination, and the plaintiff must pay the fees in the time specified in the order or the case will be dismissed without prejudice.

(Amended by Tex. Sup. Ct. Misc. Docket No. 16-9056 and Tex. Sup. Ct. Misc. Docket No. 16-9122, eff. Sept. 1, 2016.)

[Statement of Inability to Afford Payment of Court Costs as provided in Tex. Sup. Ct. Misc. Docket No. 16-9122, eff. Sept. 1, 2016 and applies to any contest of, or challenge to, a claim of inability to afford payment of court costs that is pending on September 1, 2016.]

RULE 502.4. VENUE—WHERE A LAWSUIT MAY BE BROUGHT.

(a) *Applicable Law*. Laws specifying the venue—the county and precinct where a lawsuit may be brought—are found in Chapter 15, Subchapter E of the Texas Civil Practice and Remedies Code, which is available online and for examination during the court's business hours.

(b) *General Rule.* Generally, a defendant in a small claims case as described in Rule 500.3(a) or a debt claim case as described in Rule 500.3(b) is entitled to be sued in one of the following venues:

   (1) the county and precinct where the defendant resides;

   (2) the county and precinct where the incident, or the majority of incidents, that gave rise to the claim occurred;

   (3) the county and precinct where the contract or agreement, if any, that gave rise to the claim was to be performed; or

   (4) the county and precinct where the property is located, in a suit to recover personal property.

(c) *Non-Resident Defendant; Defendant's Residence Unknown.* If the defendant is a non-resident of Texas, or if defendant's residence is unknown, the plaintiff may file the suit in the county and precinct where the plaintiff resides.

(d) *Motion to Transfer Venue.* If a plaintiff files suit in an improper venue, a defendant may challenge the venue selected by filing a motion to transfer venue. The motion must be filed before trial, no later than 21 days after the day the defendant's answer is filed, and must contain a sworn statement that the venue chosen by the plaintiff is improper and a specific county and precinct of proper venue to which transfer is sought. If the defendant fails to name a county and precinct, the court must instruct the defendant to do so and allow the defendant 7 days to cure the defect. If the defendant fails to correct the defect, the motion will be denied, and the case will proceed in the county and precinct where it was originally filed.

   (1) *Procedure.*

      (A) Judge to Set Hearing. If a defendant files a motion to transfer venue, the judge must set a hearing on the motion.

      (B) Response. A plaintiff may file a response to a defendant's motion to transfer venue.

      (C) Hearing. The parties may present evidence at the hearing. A witness may testify at a hearing, either in person or, with permission of the court, by means of telephone or an electronic communication system.

      (D) Judge's Decision. If the motion is granted, the judge must sign an order designating the court to which the case will be transferred. If the motion is denied, the case will be heard in the court in which the plaintiff initially filed suit.

      (E) Review. Motions for rehearing and interlocutory appeals of the judge's ruling on venue are not permitted.

      (F) Time for Trial of the Case. No trial may be held until at least the 14th day after the judge's ruling on the motion to transfer venue.

      (G) Order. An order granting a motion to transfer venue must state the reason for the transfer and the name of the court to which the transfer is made. When such an order of transfer is made, the judge who issued the order must immediately make out a true and correct transcript of all the entries made on the docket in the case, certify the transcript, and send the transcript, with a certified copy of the bill of costs and the original papers in the case, to the court in the precinct to which the case has been transferred. The court receiving the case must then notify the plaintiff that the case has been received and, if the case is transferred to a different county, that the plaintiff has 14 days after receiving the notice to pay the filing fee in the new court, or file a Statement of Inability to Afford Payment of Court Costs. The plaintiff is not entitled to a refund of any fees already paid. Failure to pay the fee or file a Statement will result in dismissal of the case without prejudice.

(e) *Fair Trial Venue Change.* If a party believes it cannot get a fair trial in a specific precinct or before a specific judge, the party may file a sworn motion stating such, supported by the sworn statements of two other credible persons, and specifying if the party is requesting a change of location or a change of judge. Except for good cause shown, this motion must be filed no less than 7 days before trial. If the party seeks a change of judge, the judge must exchange benches with another qualified justice of the peace, or if no judge is available to exchange benches, the county judge must appoint a visiting judge to hear the case. If the party seeks a change in location, the case must be transferred to the nearest justice court in the county that is not subject to the same or some other disqualification. If there is only one justice of the peace precinct in the county, then the judge must exchange benches with another qualified justice of the peace, or if no judge is available to exchange benches, the county judge must appoint a visiting judge to hear the case. In cases where exclusive jurisdiction is within a specific precinct, as in eviction cases, the only remedy available is a change of judge. A party may apply for relief under this rule only one time in any given lawsuit.

(f) *Transfer of Venue by Consent.* On the written consent of all parties or their attorneys, filed with the court, venue must be transferred to the court of any other justice of the peace of the county, or any other county.

(Amended by Tex. Sup. Ct. Misc. Docket No. 16-9122, eff. Sept. 1, 2016.)

[Statement of Inability to Afford Payment of Court Costs as provided in Tex. Sup. Ct. Misc. Docket No. 16-9122, eff. Sept. 1, 2016 and applies to any contest of, or challenge to, a claim of inability to afford payment of court costs that is pending on September 1, 2016.]

RULE 502.5. ANSWER.

(a) *Requirements.* A defendant must file with the court a written answer to a lawsuit as directed by the citation and must also serve a copy of the answer on the plaintiff. The answer must contain:

(1) the name of the defendant;

(2) the name, address, telephone number, and fax number, if any, of the defendant's attorney, if applicable, or the address, telephone number, and fax number, if any, of the defendant; and

(3) if the defendant consents to email service, a statement consenting to email service and email contact information.

(b) *General Denial.* An answer that denies all of the plaintiffs allegations without specifying the reasons is sufficient to constitute an answer or appearance and does not bar the defendant from raising any defense at trial.

(c) *Answer Docketed.* The defendant' s appearance must be noted on the court's docket.

(d) *Due Date.* Unless the defendant is served by publication, the defendant's answer is due by the end of the 1 4th day after the day the defendant was served with the citation and petition, but

(1) if the 14th day is a Saturday, Sunday, or legal holiday, the answer is due on the next day that is not a Saturday, Sunday, or legal holiday; and

(2) if the 14th day falls on a day during which the court is closed before 5:00 p.m., the answer is due on the court' s next business day.

(e) *Due Date When Defendant Served by Publication.* If a defendant is served by publication, the defendant' s answer is due by the end of the 42nd day after the day the citation was issued, but

(1) if the 42nd day is a Saturday, Sunday, or legal holiday, the answer is due on the next day that is not a Saturday, Sunday, or legal holiday; and

(2) if the 42nd day falls on a day during which the court is closed before 5:00 p.m., the answer is due on the court's next business day.

RULE 502.6. COUNTERCLAIM; CROSS-CLAIM; THIRD PARTY CLAIM.

(a) *Counterclaim.* A defendant may file a petition stating as a counterclaim any claim against a plaintiff that is within the jurisdiction of the justice court, whether or not related to the claims in the plaintiff s petition. The defendant must file a counterclaim petition as provided in Rule 502.2, and must pay a filing fee or provide a Statement of Inability to Afford Payment of Court Costs. The court need not generate a citation for a counterclaim and no answer to the counterclaim need be filed. The defendant must serve a copy of the counterclaim as provided by Rule 501.4.

(b) *Cross-Claim.* A plaintiff seeking relief against another plaintiff, or a defendant seeking relief against another defendant may file a cross-claim. The filing party must file a cross-claim petition as provided in Rule 502.2, and must pay a filing fee or provide a Statement of Inability to Afford Payment of Court Costs. A citation must be issued and served as provided by Rule 501.2 on any party that has not yet filed a petition or an answer, as appropriate. If the party filed against has filed a petition or an answer, the filing party must serve the cross-claim as provided by Rule 501.4.

(c) *Third Party Claim.* A defendant seeking to bring another party into a lawsuit who may be liable for all or part of the plaintiffs claim against the defendant may file a petition as provided in Rule 502.2, and must pay a filing fee or provide a Statement of Inability to Afford Payment of Court Costs. A citation must be issued and served as provided by Rule 501.2.

(Amended by Tex. Sup. Ct. Misc. Docket No. 16-9122, eff. Sept. 1, 2016.)

[Statement of Inability to Afford Payment of Court Costs as provided in Tex. Sup. Ct. Misc. Docket No. 16-9122, eff. Sept. 1, 2016 and applies to any contest of, or challenge to, a claim of inability to afford payment of court costs that is pending on September 1, 2016.]

RULE 502.7. AMENDING AND CLARIFYING PLEADINGS.

(a) *Amending Pleadings.* A party may withdraw something from or add something to a pleading, as long as the amended pleading is filed and served as provided by Rule 501.4 not less than 7 days before trial. The court may allow a pleading to be amended less than 7 days before trial if the amendment will not operate as a surprise to the opposing party.

(b) *Insufficient Pleadings.* A party may file a motion with the court asking that another party be required to clarify a pleading. The court must determine if the pleading is sufficient to place all parties on notice of the issues in the lawsuit, and may hold a hearing to make that determination. If the court determines a pleading is insufficient, the court must order the party to amend the pleading and set a date by which the party must amend. If a party fails to comply with the court's order, the pleading may be stricken.

(Adopted by Order Feb 12, 2013 and Order April 15, 2013, eff. Aug. 31, 2013.)

Rules of Civil Procedure 500-510 govern cases filed on or after August 31 , 2013, and cases pending on August 31 , 2013, except to the extent that in the opinion of the court their application in a case pending on August 31 , 2013, would not be feasible or would work injustice, in which event the formerly applicable procedure applies. An action taken before August 31 , 2013, in a case pending on August 31, 2013, that was done pursuant to any previously applicable procedure must be treated as valid. Where citation or other process was issued or served prior to August 31, 2013 , in compliance with any previously applicable procedure, the party served has the time provided for under the previously applicable procedure to answer or otherwise respond.

RULE 503. DEFAULT JUDGMENT; PRE-TRIAL MATTERS; TRIAL.

RULE 503.1. IF DEFENDANT FAILS TO ANSWER.

(a) *Default Judgment.* If the defendant fails to file an answer by the date stated in Rule 502.5, the judge must ensure that service was proper, and may hold a hearing for this purpose. If it is determined that service was proper, the judge must render a default judgment in the following manner:

(1) *Claim Based on Written Document.* If the claim is based on a written document signed by the defendant, and a copy of the document has been filed with the court and served on the defendant, along with a sworn statement from the plaintiff that this is a true and accurate copy of the document and the relief sought is owed, and all payments, offsets or credits due to the defendant have been accounted for, the judge must render judgment for the plaintiff in the requested amount, without any necessity for a hearing. The plaintiff's attorney may also submit affidavits supporting an award of attorney fees to which the plaintiff is entitled, if any.

(2) *Other Cases.* Except as provided in (1), a plaintiff who seeks a default judgment against a defendant must request a hearing, orally or in writing. The plaintiff must appear at the hearing and provide evidence of its damages. If the plaintiff proves its damages, the judge must render judgment for the plaintiff in the amount proven. If the plaintiff is unable to prove its damages, the judge must render judgment in favor of the defendant. With the permission of the court, a party may appear at a hearing by means of telephone or an electronic communication system.

(b) *Appearance.* If a defendant files an answer or otherwise appears in a case before a default judgment is signed by the judge, the judge must not enter a default judgment and the case must be set for trial as described in Rule 503.3.

(c) *Post-Answer Default.* If a defendant who has answered fails to appear for tria!, the court may proceed to hear evidence on liability and damages and render judgment accordingly.

(d) *Notice.* The plaintiff requesting a default judgment must provide to the clerk in writing the last known mailing address of the defendant at or before the time the judgment is signed. When a default judgment is signed, the clerk must immediately mail written notice of the judgment to the defendant at the address provided by the plaintiff, and note the fact of such mailing on the docket. The notice must state the number and style of the case, the court in which the case is pending, the names of the parties in whose favor and against whom the judgment was rendered, and the date the judgment was signed. Failure to comply with the provisions of this rule does not affect the finality of the judgment.

RULE 503.2. SUMMARY DISPOSITION.

(a) *Motion.* A party may file a sworn motion for summary disposition of all or part of a claim or defense without a trial. The motion must set out all supporting facts. All documents on which the motion relies must be attached. The motion must be granted if it shows that:

(1) there are no genuinely disputed facts that would prevent a judgment in favor of the party;

(2) there is no evidence of one or more essential elements of a defense which the defendant must prove to defeat the plaintiff s claim; or

(3) there is no evidence of one or more essential elements of the plaintiffs claim.

(b) *Response.* The party opposing the motion may tile a sworn written response to the motion.

(c) *Hearing.* The court must not consider a motion for summary disposition until it has been on file for at least 14 days. The judge may consider evidence offered by the parties at the hearing. By agreement of the parties, the judge may decide the motion and response without a hearing.

(d) *Order.* The judge may enter judgment as to the entire case or may specify the facts that are established and direct such further proceedings in the case as are just.

RULE 503.3. SETTINGS AND NOTICE; POSTPONING TRIAL.

(a) *Settings and Notice.* After the defendant answers, the case will be set on a trial docket at the discretion of the judge. The court must send a notice of the date, time, and place of this setting to all parties at their address of record no less than 45 days before the setting date, unless the judge determines that an earlier setting is required in the interest of justice. Reasonable notice of all subsequent settings must be sent to all parties at their addresses of record.

(b) *Postponing Trial.* A party may file a motion requesting that the trial be postponed. The motion must state why a postponement is necessary. The judge, for good cause, may postpone any trial for a reasonable time.

RULE 503.4. PRETRIAL CONFERENCE.

(a) *Conference Set; Issues.* If all parties have appeared in a lawsuit, the court, at any party's request or on its own, may set a case for a pretrial conference. Reasonable notice must be sent to all parties at their addresses of record. Appropriate issues for the pretrial conference include:

(1) discovery;

(2) the amendment or clarification of pleadings;
(3) the admission of facts and documents to streamline the trial process;
(4) a limitation on the number of witnesses at trial;
(5) the identification of facts, if any, which are not in dispute between the parties;
(6) mediation or other alternative dispute resolution services;
(7) the possibility of settlement;
(8) trial setting dates that are amenable to the court and all parties;
(9) the appointment of interpreters, if needed;
(10) the application of a Rule of Civil Procedure not in Part V or a Rule of Evidence; and
(11) any other issue that the court deems appropriate.

(b) *Eviction Cases.* The court must not schedule a pretrial conference in an eviction case if it would delay trial.

RULE 503.5. ALTERNATIVE DISPUTE RESOLUTION.

(a) *State Policy.* The policy of this state is to encourage the peaceable resolution of disputes through alternative dispute resolution, including mediation, and the early settlement of pending litigation through voluntary settlement procedures. For that purpose, the judge may order any case to mediation or another appropriate and generally accepted alternative dispute resolution process.

(b) *Eviction Cases.* The court must not order mediation or any other alternative dispute resolution process in an eviction case if it would delay trial.

RULE 503.6. TRIAL.

(a) *Docket Called.* On the day of the trial setting, the judge must call all of the cases set for trial that day.

(b) *If Plaintiff Fails to Appear.* If the plaintiff fails to appear when the case is called for trial, the judge may postpone or dismiss the suit.

(c) *If Defendant Fails to Appear.* If the defendant fails to appear when the case is called for trial, the judge may postpone the case, or may proceed to take evidence. If the plaintiff proves its case, judgment must be awarded for the relief proven. If the plaintiff fails to prove its case, judgment must be rendered against the plaintiff.

(Adopted by Order Feb 12, 2013 and Order April 15, 2013, eff. Aug. 31, 2013.)

Rules of Civil Procedure 500-510 govern cases filed on or after August 31 , 2013, and cases pending on August 31 , 2013, except to the extent that in the opinion of the court their application in a case pending on August 31 , 2013, would not be feasible or would work injustice, in which event the formerly applicable procedure applies. An action taken before August 31 , 2013, in a case pending on August 31, 2013, that was done pursuant to any previously applicable procedure must be treated as valid. Where citation or other process was issued or served prior to August 31, 2013 , in compliance with any previously applicable procedure, the party served has the time provided for under the previously applicable procedure to answer or otherwise respond.

RULE 504. JURY.

RULE 504.1. JURY TRIAL DEMANDED.

(a) *Demand.* Any party is entitled to a trial by jury. A written demand for a jury must be filed no later than 14 days before the date a case is set for trial. If the demand is not timely, the right to a jury is waived unless the late filing is excused by the judge for good cause.

(b) *Jury Fee.* Unless otherwise provided by law, a party demanding a jury must pay a fee of $22.00 or must file a Statement of Inability to Afford Payment of Court Costs at or before the time the party files a written request for a jury.

(c) *Withdrawal of Demand.* If a party who demands a jury and pays the fee withdraws the demand, the case will remain on the jury docket unless all other parties present agree to try the case without a jury. A party that withdraws its jury demand is not entitled to a refund of the jury fee.

(d) *No Demand.* If no party timely demands a jury and pays the fee, the judge will try the case without a jury.

(Amended by Tex. Sup. Ct. Misc. Docket No. 16-9122, eff. Sept. 1, 2016.)

[Statement of Inability to Afford Payment of Court Costs as provided in Tex. Sup. Ct. Misc. Docket No. 16-9122, eff. Sept. 1, 2016 and applies to any contest of, or challenge to, a claim of inability to afford payment of court costs that is pending on September 1, 2016.]

RULE 504.2. EMPANELING THE JURY.

(a) *Drawing Jury and Oath.* If no method of electronic draw has been implemented, the judge must write the names of all prospective jurors present on separate slips of paper as nearly alike as may be, place them in a box, mix them well, and then draw the names one by one from the box. The judge must list the names drawn and deliver a copy to each of the parties or their attorneys.

(b) *Oath.* After the draw, the judge must swear the panel as follows: "You solemnly swear or affirm that you will give true and correct answers to all questions asked of you concerning your qualifications as a juror."

(c) *Questioning the Jury.* The judge, the parties, or their attorneys will be allowed to question jurors as to their ability to serve impartially in the trial but may not ask the jurors how they will rule in the case. The judge will have discretion to allow or disallow specific questions and determine the amount of time each side will have for this process.

(d) *Challenge for Cause.* A party may challenge any juror for cause. A challenge for cause is an objection made to a juror alleging some fact, such as a bias or prejudice, that disqualifies the juror from serving in the case or that renders the juror unfit to sit on the jury. The challenge must be made during jury questioning. The party must explain to the judge why the juror should be excluded from the jury. The judge must evaluate the questions and answers given and either grant or deny the challenge. When a challenge for cause has been sustained, the juror must be excused.

(e) *Challenges Not for Cause.* After the judge determines any challenges for cause, each party may select up to 3 jurors to excuse for any reason or no reason at all. But no prospective juror may be excused for membership in a constitutionally protected class.

(f) *The Jury.* After all challenges, the first 6 prospective jurors remaining on the list constitute the jury to try the case.

(g) *If Jury Is Incomplete.* If challenges reduce the number of prospective jurors below 6, the judge may direct the sheriff or constable to summon others and allow them to be questioned and challenged by the parties as before, until at least 6 remain.

(h) *Jury Sworn.* When the jury has been selected, the judge must require them to take substantially the following oath: "You solemnly swear or affirm that you will render a true verdict according to the law and the evidence presented."

RULE 504.3. JURY NOT CHARGED.

The judge must not charge the jury.

RULE 504.4. JURY VERDICT FOR SPECIFIC ARTICLES.

When the suit is for the recovery of specific articles and the jury finds for the plaintiff, the jury must assess the value of each article separately, according to the evidence presented at trial.

RULE 505. JUDGMENT; NEW TRIAL.

RULE 505.1. JUDGMENT.

(a) *Judgment Upon Jury Verdict.* Where a jury has returned a verdict, the judge must announce the verdict in open court, note it in the court's docket, and render judgment accordingly. The judge may render judgment on the verdict or, if the verdict is contrary to the law or the evidence, judgment notwithstanding the verdict.

(b) *Case Tried by Judge.* When a case has been tried before the judge without a jury, the judge must announce the decision in open court, note the decision in the court's docket, and render judgment accordingly.

(c) *Form.* A judgment must:

  (1) clearly state the determination of the rights of the parties in the case;

  (2) state who must pay the costs;

  (3) be signed by the judge; and

  (4) be dated the date of the judge's signature.

(d) *Costs.* The judge must award costs allowed by law to the successful party.

(e) *Judgment for Specific Articles.* Where the judgment is for the recovery of specific articles, the judgment must order that the plaintiff recover such specific articles, if they can be found, and if not, then their value as assessed by the judge or jury with interest at the prevailing post-judgment interest rate.

RULE 505.2. ENFORCEMENT OF JUDGMENT.

Justice court judgments are enforceable in the same method as in county and district court, except as provided by law. When the judgment is for personal property, the court may award a special writ for the seizure and delivery of such property to the plaintiff, and may, in addition to the other relief granted in such cases, enforce its judgment by attachment or fine.

RULE 505.3. MOTION TO SET ASIDE; MOTION TO REINSTATE; MOTION FOR NEW TRIAL.

(a) *Motion to Reinstate after Dismissal.* A plaintiff whose case is dismissed may file a motion to reinstate the case no later than 1 4 days after the dismissal order is signed. The plaintiff must serve the defendant with a copy of the motion no later than the next business day using a method approved under Rule 50 1 .4. The court may reinstate the case for good cause shown.

(b) *Motion to Set Aside Default.* A defendant against whom a default judgment is granted may file a motion to set aside the judgment no later than 1 4 days after the judgment is signed. The defendant must serve the plaintiff with a copy of the motion no later than the next business day using a method approved under Rule 501.4. The court may set aside the judgment and set the case for trial for good cause shown.

(c) *Motion for New Trial.* A party may file a motion for a new trial no later than 1 4 days after the judgment is signed. The party must serve all other parties with a copy of the motion no later than the next business day using a method approved under Rule 50 1 .4. The judge may grant a new trial upon a showing that justice was not done in the trial of the case. Only one new trial may be granted to either party.

(d) *Motion Not Required.* Failure to file a motion under this rule does not affect a party's right to appeal the underlying judgment.

(e) *Motion Denied as a Matter of Law.* If the judge has not ruled on a motion to set aside, motion to reinstate, or motion for new trial, the motion is automatically denied at 5:00 p.m. on the 21st day after the day the judgment was signed.

(Adopted by Order Feb 12, 2013 and Order April 15, 2013, eff. Aug. 31, 2013.)

Rules of Civil Procedure 500-510 govern cases filed on or after August 31 , 2013, and cases pending on August 31 , 2013, except to the extent that in the opinion of the court their application in a case pending on August 31 , 2013, would not be feasible or would work injustice, in which event the formerly applicable procedure applies. An action taken before August 31 , 2013, in a case pending on August 31, 2013, that was done pursuant to any previously applicable procedure must be treated as valid. Where citation or other process was issued or served prior to August 31, 2013 , in compliance with any previously applicable procedure, the party served has the time provided for under the previously applicable procedure to answer or otherwise respond.

RULE 506. APPEAL.

RULE 506.1. APPEAL.

(a) *How Taken; Time.* A party may appeal a judgment by filing a bond, making a cash deposit, or filing a Statement of Inability to Afford Payment of Court Costs with the justice court within 2 1 days after the judgment is signed or the motion to reinstate, motion to set aside, or motion for new trial, if any, is denied.

(b) *Amount of Bond; Sureties; Terms.* A plaintiff must file a $500 bond. A defendant must file a bond in an amount equal to twice the amount of the judgment. The bond must be supported by a surety or sureties approved by the judge. The bond must be payable to the appellee and must be conditioned on the appellant's prosecution of its appeal to effect and payment of any judgment and all costs rendered against it on appeal.

(c) *Cash Deposit in Lieu of Bond.* In lieu of filing a bond, an appellant may deposit with the clerk of the court cash in the amount required of the bond. The deposit must be payable to the appellee and must be conditioned on the appellant's prosecution of its appeal to effect and payment of any judgment and all costs rendered against it on appeal.

(d) *Statement of Inability to Afford Payment of Court Costs.*

(1) Filing. An appellant who cannot furnish a bond or pay a cash deposit in the amount required may instead file a Statement of Inability to Afford Payment of Court Costs. The Statement must be on the form approved by the Supreme Court or include the information required by the Court-approved for and may be the same one that was filed with the petition.

(2) Contest. The Statement may be contested as provided in Rule 502.3(d) within 7 days after the opposing party receives notice that the Statement was filed.

(3) Appeal If Contest Sustained. If the contest is sustained, the appellant may appeal that decision by filing notice with the justice court within 7 days of that court's written order. The justice court must then forward all related documents to the county court for resolution. The county court must set the matter for hearing within 1 4 days and hear the contest de novo, as if there had been no previous hearing, and if the appeal is granted, must direct the justice court to transmit to the clerk of the county court the transcript, records, and papers of the case, as provided in these rules.

(4) If No Appeal or If Appeal Overruled. If the appellant does not appeal the ruling sustaining the contest, or if the county court denies the appeal, the appellant may, within five days, post an appeal bond or make a cash deposit in compliance with this rule.

(e) *Notice to Other Parties Required.* If a Statement of Inability to Afford Payment of Court Costs is filed, the court must provide notice to all other parties that the statement was filed no later than the next business day. Within 7 days of filing a bond or making a cash deposit, an appellant must serve written notice of the appeal on all other parties using a method approved under Rule 501.4.

(f) *No Default on Appeal Without Compliance With Rule.* The county court to which an appeal is taken must not render default judgment against any party without first determining that the appellant has fully complied with this rule.

(g) *No Dismissal of Appeal Without Opportunity for Correction.* An appeal must not be dismissed for defects or irregularities in procedure, either of form or substance, without allowing the appellant, after 7 days' notice from the court, the opportunity to correct such defect.

(h) *Appeal Perfected.* An appeal is perfected when a bond, cash deposit, or Statement of Inability to Afford Payment of Court Costs is filed in accordance with this rule.

(i) *Costs.* The appellant must pay the costs on appeal to a county court in accordance with Rule 1 43a.

(Amended by Tex. Sup. Ct. Misc. Docket No. 16-9122, eff. Sept. 1, 2016.)

[Statement of Inability to Afford Payment of Court Costs as provided in Tex. Sup. Ct. Misc. Docket No. 16-9122, eff. Sept. 1, 2016 and applies to any contest of, or challenge to, a claim of inability to afford payment of court costs that is pending on September 1, 2016.]

RULE 506.2. RECORD ON APPEAL.

When an appeal has been perfected from the justice court, the judge must immediately send to the clerk of the county court a certified copy of all docket entries, a certified copy of the bill of costs, and the original papers in the case.

RULE 506.3. TRIAL DE NOVO.

The case must be tried de novo in the county court. A trial de novo is a new trial in which the entire case is presented as if there had been no previous trial.

RULE 506.4. WRIT OF CERTIORARI.

(a) *Application.* Except in eviction cases, after final judgment in a case tried in justice court, a party may apply to the county court for a writ of certiorari.

(b) *Grounds.* An application must be granted only if it contains a sworn statement setting forth facts showing that either:

  (1) the justice court did not have jurisdiction; or

  (2) the final determination of the suit worked an injustice to the applicant that was not caused by the applicant's own inexcusable neglect.

(c) *Bond, Cash Deposit, or Sworn Statement of Indigency to Pay Required.* If the application is granted, a writ of certiorari must not issue until the applicant has filed a bond, made a cash deposit, or filed a Statement of Inability to Afford Payment of Court Costs that complies with Rule 145.

(d) *Time for Filing.* An application for writ of certiorari must be filed within 90 days after the date the final judgment is signed.

(e) *Contents of Writ.* The writ of certiorari must command the justice court to immediately make and certify a copy of the entries in the case on the docket, and immediately transmit the transcript of the proceedings in the justice court, together with the original papers and a bill of costs, to the proper court.

(f) *Clerk to Issue Writ and Citation.* When the application is granted and the bond, cash deposit, or sworn Statement of Inability to Afford Payment of Court Costs has been filed, the clerk must issue a writ of certiorari to the justice court and citation to the adverse party.

(g) *Stay of Proceedings.* When the writ of certiorari is served on the justice court, the court must stay further proceedings on the judgment and comply with the writ.

(h) *Cause Docketed.* The action must be docketed in the name of the original plaintiff, as plaintiff, and of the original defendant, as defendant.

(i) *Motion to Dismiss.* Within 30 days after the service of citation on the writ of certiorari, the adverse party may move to dismiss the certiorari for want of sufficient cause appearing in the affidavit, or for want of sufficient bond. If the certiorari is dismissed, the judgment must direct the justice court to proceed with the execution of the judgment below.

(j) *Amendment of Bond or Oath.* The affidavit or bond may be amended at the discretion of the court in which it is filed.

(k) *Trial De Novo.* The case must be tried de novo in the county court and judgment must be rendered as in cases appealed from justice courts. A trial de novo is a new trial in which the entire case is presented as if there had been no previous trial.

(Adopted by Order Feb 12, 2013 and Order April 15, 2013, eff. Aug. 31, 2013. Amended by Tex. Sup. Ct. Misc. Docket No. 16-9122, eff. Sept. 1, 2016.)

Rules of Civil Procedure 500-510 govern cases filed on or after August 31 , 2013, and cases pending on August 31 , 2013, except to the extent that in the opinion of the court their application in a case pending on August 31 , 2013, would not be feasible or would work injustice, in which event the formerly applicable procedure applies. An action taken before August 31 , 2013, in a case pending on August 31, 2013, that was done pursuant to any previously applicable procedure must be treated as valid. Where citation or other process was issued or served prior to August 31, 2013 , in compliance with any previously applicable procedure, the party served has the time provided for under the previously applicable procedure to answer or otherwise respond.

[Statement of Inability to Afford Payment of Court Costs as provided in Tex. Sup. Ct. Misc. Docket No. 16-9122, eff. Sept. 1, 2016 and applies to any contest of, or challenge to, a claim of inability to afford payment of court costs that is pending on September 1, 2016.]

RULE 507. ADMINISTRATIVE RULES FOR JUDGES AND COURT PERSONNEL.

RULE 507.1. PLENARY POWER.

A justice court loses plenary power over a case when an appeal is perfected or if no appeal is perfected, 21 days after the later of the date judgment is signed or the date a motion to set aside, motion to reinstate, or motion for new trial, if any, is denied.

RULE 507.2. FORMS.

The court may provide forms to enable a party to file documents that comply with these rules. No party may be forced to use the court's forms.

RULE 507.3. DOCKET AND OTHER RECORDS.

(a) *Docket.* Each judge must keep a civil docket in a permanent record containing the following information:
   (1) the title of all suits commenced before the court;
   (2) the date when the first process was issued against the defendant, when returnable, and the nature of that process;
   (3) the date when the parties, or either of them, appeared before the court, either with or without a citation;
   (4) a description of the petition and any documents filed with the petition;
   (5) every adjournment, stating at whose request and to what time;
   (6) the date of the trial, stating whether the same was by a jury or by the judge;
   (7) the verdict of the jury, if any;
   (8) the judgment signed by the judge and the date the judgment was signed;
   (9) all applications for setting aside judgments or granting new trials and the orders of the judge thereon, with the date;
   (10) the date of issuing execution, to whom directed and delivered, and the amount of debt, damages and costs and, when any execution is returned, the date of the return and the manner in which it was executed; and
   (11) all stays and appeals that may be taken, and the date when taken, the amount of the bond and the names of the sureties.

(b) *Other Records.* The judge must also keep copies of all documents filed; other dockets, books, and records as may be required by law or these rules; and a fee book in which all costs accruing in every suit commenced before the court are taxed.

(c) *Form of Records.* All records required to be kept under this rule may be maintained electronically.

RULE 507.4. ISSUANCE OF WRITS.

Every writ from the justice courts must be in writing and be issued and signed by the judge officially. The style thereof must be "The State of Texas." It must, except where otherwise specially provided by law or these rules, be directed to the person or party upon whom it is to be served, be made returnable to the court, and note the date of its issuance.

(Adopted by Order Feb 12, 2013 and Order April 15, 2013, eff. Aug. 31, 2013.)

Rules of Civil Procedure 500-510 govern cases filed on or after August 31, 2013, and cases pending on August 31, 2013, except to the extent that in the opinion of the court their application in a case pending on August 31, 2013, would not be feasible or would work injustice, in which event the formerly applicable procedure applies. An action taken before August 31, 2013, in a case pending on August 31, 2013, that was done pursuant to any previously applicable procedure must be treated as valid. Where citation or other process was issued or served prior to August 31, 2013, in compliance with any previously applicable procedure, the party served has the time provided for under the previously applicable procedure to answer or otherwise respond.

RULE 508. DEBT CLAIM CASES.

RULE 508.1. APPLICATION.

Rule 508 applies to a claim for the recovery of a debt brought by an assignee of a claim, a financial institution, a debt collector or collection agency, or a person or entity primarily engaged in the business of lending money at interest.

RULE 508.2. PETITION.

(a) *Contents.* In addition to the information required by Rule 502.2, a petition filed in a lawsuit governed by this rule must contain the following information:

(1) Credit Accounts. In a claim based upon a credit card, revolving credit, or open account, the petition must state:
   (A) the account name or credit card name;
   (B) the account number (which may be masked);
   (C) the date of issue or origination of the account, if known;
   (D) the date of charge-off or breach of the account, if known;
   (E) the amount owed as of a date certain; and
   (F) whether the plaintiff seeks ongoing interest.
(2) Personal and Business Loans. In a claim based upon a promissory note or other promise to pay a specific amount as of a date certain, the petition must state:
   (A) the date and amount of the original loan;
   (B) whether the repayment of the debt was accelerated, if known;
   (C) the date final payment was due;
   (D) the amount due as of the final payment date;
   (E) the amount owed as of a date certain; and
   (F) whether plaintiff seeks ongoing interest.
(3) Ongoing Interest. If a plaintiff seeks ongoing interest, the petition must state:
   (A) the effective interest rate claimed;
   (B) whether the interest rate is based upon contract or statute; and
   (C) the dollar amount of interest claimed as of a date certain.
(4) Assigned Debt. If the debt that is the subject of the claim has been assigned or transferred, the petition must state:
   (A) that the debt claim has been transferred or assigned;
   (B) the date of the transfer or assignment;
   (C) the name of any prior holders of the debt; and
   (D) the name or a description of the original creditor.

RULE 508.3. DEFAULT JUDGMENT.

(a) *Generally.* If the defendant does not file an answer to a claim by the answer date or otherwise appear in the case, the judge must promptly render a default judgment upon the plaintiffs proof of the amount of damages.
(b) *Proof of the Amount of Damages.*
   (1) Evidence Must Be Served or Submitted. Evidence of plaintiff's damages must either be attached to the petition and served on the defendant or submitted to the court after defendant's failure to answer by the answer date.
   (2) Form of Evidence. Evidence of plaintiff's damages may be offered in a sworn statement or in live testimony. The evidence offered may include documentary evidence.
   (3) Establishment of the Amount of Damages. The amount of damages is established by evidence:
      (A) that the account or loan was issued to the defendant and the defendant is obligated to pay it;
      (B) that the account was closed or the defendant breached the terms of the account or loan agreement;
      (C) of the amount due on the account or loan as of a date certain after all payment credits and offsets have been applied; and
      (D) that the plaintiff owns the account or loan and, if applicable, how the plaintiff acquired the account or loan.
   (4) Documentary Evidence Offered By Sworn Statement. Documentary evidence may be considered if it is attached to a sworn statement made by the plaintiff or its representative, a prior holder of the debt or its representative, or the original creditor or its representative, that attests to the following:
      (A) the documents were kept in the regular course of business;
      (B) it was the regular course of business for an employee or representative with knowledge of the act recorded to make the record or to transmit information to be included in such record;
      (C) the documents were created at or near the time or reasonably soon thereafter; and
      (D) the documents attached are the original or exact duplicates of the original.
   (5) Consideration of Sworn Statement. A judge is not required to accept a sworn statement if the source of information or the method or circumstances of preparation indicate lack of trustworthiness. But a judge may not reject a sworn statement only because it is not made by the original creditor or because the documents attested to were created by a third party and subsequently incorporated into and relied upon by the business of the plaintiff.
(c) *Hearing.* The judge may enter a default judgment without a hearing if the plaintiff submits sufficient written evidence of its damages and should do so to avoid undue expense and delay. Otherwise, the plaintiff may request a default judgment hearing at which the plaintiff must appear, in person or by telephonic or electronic means, and prove its damages.

If the plaintiff proves its damages, the judge must render judgment for the plaintiff in the amount proven. If the plaintiff is unable to prove its damages, the judge must render judgment in favor of the defendant.

(d) *Appearance.* If the defendant files an answer or otherwise appears in a case before a default judgment is signed by the judge, the judge must not render a default judgment and must set the case for trial.

(e) *Post-Answer Default.* If a defendant who has answered fails to appear for trial, the court may proceed to hear evidence on liability and damages and render judgment accordingly.

(Adopted by Order Feb 12, 2013 and Order April 15, 2013, eff. Aug. 31, 2013.)

Rules of Civil Procedure 500-510 govern cases filed on or after August 31 , 2013, and cases pending on August 31 , 2013, except to the extent that in the opinion of the court their application in a case pending on August 31 , 2013, would not be feasible or would work injustice, in which event the formerly applicable procedure applies. An action taken before August 31 , 2013, in a case pending on August 31, 2013, that was done pursuant to any previously applicable procedure must be treated as valid. Where citation or other process was issued or served prior to August 31, 2013 , in compliance with any previously applicable procedure, the party served has the time provided for under the previously applicable procedure to answer or otherwise respond.

RULE 509. REPAIR AND REMEDY CASES.

RULE 509.1. APPLICABILITY OF RULE.

Rule 509 applies to a lawsuit filed in a justice court by a residential tenant under Chapter 92, Subchapter B of the Texas Property Code to enforce the landlord' s duty to repair or remedy a condition materially affecting the physical health or safety of an ordinary tenant.

RULE 509.2. CONTENTS OF PETITION; COPIES; FORMS AND AMENDMENTS.

(a) *Contents of Petition.* The petition must be in writing and must include the following:

   (1) the street address of the residential rental property;

   (2) a statement indicating whether the tenant has received in writing the name and business street address of the landlord and landlord's management company;

   (3) to the extent known and applicable, the name, business street address, and telephone number of the landlord and the landlord's management company, on-premises manager, and rent collector serving the residential rental property;

   (4) for all notices the tenant gave to the landlord requesting that the condition be repaired or remedied:

      (A) the date of the notice;

      (B) the name of the person to whom the notice was given or the place where the notice was given;

      (C) whether the tenant' s lease is in writing and requires written notice;

      (D) whether the notice was in writing or oral;

      (E) whether any written notice was given by certified mail, return receipt requested, or by registered mail; and

      (F) whether the rent was current or had been timely tendered at the time notice was given;

   (5) a description of the property condition materially affecting the physical health or safety of an ordinary tenant that the tenant seeks to have repaired or remedied;

   (6) a statement of the relief requested by the tenant, including an order to repair or remedy a condition, a reduction in rent, actual damages, civil penalties, attorney's fees, and court costs;

   (7) if the petition includes a request to reduce the rent:

      (A) the amount of rent paid by the tenant, the amount of rent paid by the government, if known, the rental period, and when the rent is due; and

      (B) the amount of the requested rent reduction and the date it should begin;

   (8) a statement that the total relief requested does not exceed $ 1 0,000, excluding interest and court costs but including attorney's fees; and

   (9) the tenant's name, address, and telephone number.

(b) *Copies.* The tenant must provide the court with copies of the petition and any attachments to the petition for service on the landlord.

(c) *Forms and Amendments.* A petition substantially in the form promulgated by the Supreme Court is sufficient. A suit may not be dismissed for a defect in the petition unless the tenant is given an opportunity to correct the defect and does not promptly correct it.

RULE 509.3. CITATION: ISSUANCE; APPEARANCE DATE; ANSWER.

(a) *Issuance.* When the tenant files a written petition with a justice court, the judge must immediately issue citation directed to the landlord, commanding the landlord to appear before such judge at the time and place named in the citation.

(b) *Appearance Date; Answer.* The appearance date on the citation must not be less than 10 days nor more than 21 days after the petition is filed. For purposes of this rule, the appearance date on the citation is the trial date. The landlord may, but is not required to, file a written answer on or before the appearance date.

RULE 509.4. SERVICE AND RETURN OF CITATION; ALTERNATIVE SERVICE OF CITATION.

(a) *Service and Return of Citation.* The sheriff, constable, or other person authorized by Rule 50 1 .2 who receives the citation must serve the citation by delivering a copy of it, along with a copy of the petition and any attachments, to the landlord at least 6 days before the appearance date. At least one day before the appearance date, the person serving the citation must file a return of service with the court that issued the citation. The citation must be issued, served, and returned in like manner as ordinary citations issued from a justice court.

(b) *Alternative Service of Citation.*

(1) If the petition does not include the landlord's name and business street address, or if, after making diligent efforts on at least two occasions, the officer or authorized person is unsuccessful in serving the citation on the landlord under (a), the officer or authorized person must serve the citation by delivering a copy of the citation, petition, and any attachments to:

(A) the landlord's management company if the tenant has received written notice of the name and business street address of the landlord's management company; or

(B) if (b)(I)(A) does not apply and the tenant has not received the landlord's name and business street address in writing, the landlord's authorized agent for service of process, which may be the landlord's management company, on-premise manager, or rent collector serving the residential rental property.

(2) If the officer or authorized person is unsuccessful in serving citation under (b)(1) after making diligent efforts on at least two occasions at either the business street address of the landlord's management company, if (b)(l)(A) applies, or at each available business street address of the landlord's authorized agent for service of process, if (b)(I)(B) applies, the officer or authorized person must execute and file in the justice court a sworn statement that the officer or authorized person made diligent efforts to serve the citation on at least two occasions at all available business street addresses of the landlord and, to the extent applicable, the landlord's management company, on-premises manager, and rent collector serving the residential rental property, providing the times, dates, and places of each attempted service. The judge may then authorize the officer or authorized person to serve citation by:

(A) delivering a copy of the citation, petition, and any attachments to someone over the age of 1 6 years, at any business street address listed in the petition, or, if nobody answers the door at a business street address, either placing the citation, petition, and any attachments through a door mail chute or slipping them under the front door, and if neither of these latter methods is practical, affixing the citation, petition, and any attachments to the front door or main entry to the business street address;

(B) within 24 hours of complying with (b)(2)(A), sending by first class mail a true copy of the citation, petition, and any attachments addressed to the landlord at the landlord's business street address provided in the petition; and

(C) noting on the return of the citation the date of delivery under (b)(2)(A) and the date of mailing under (b)(2)(B).

The delivery and mailing to the business street address under (b)(2)(A)-(B) must occur at least 6 days before the appearance date. At least one day before the appearance date, a return of service must be completed and filed in accordance with Rule 50 1 .3 with the court that issued the citation. It is not necessary for the tenant to request the alternative service authorized by this rule.

RULE 509.5. DOCKETING AND TRIAL; FAILURE TO APPEAR.

(a) *Docketing and Trial.* The case must be docketed and tried as other cases. The judge may develop the facts of the case in order to ensure justice.

(b) *Failure to Appear.*

(1) If the tenant appears at trial and the landlord has been duly served and fails to appear at trial, the judge may proceed to hear evidence. If the tenant establishes that the tenant is entitled to recover, the judge must render judgment against the landlord in accordance with the evidence.

(2) If the tenant fails to appear for trial, the judge may dismiss the lawsuit.

RULE 509.6. JUDGMENT: AMOUNT; FORM AND CONTENT; ISSUANCE AND SERVICE; FAILURE TO COMPLY.

(a) *Amount.* Judgment may be rendered against the landlord for failure to repair or remedy a condition at the residential rental property if the total judgment does not exceed $ 10,000, excluding interest and court costs but including attorney's fees. Any party who prevails in a lawsuit brought under these rules may recover the party's court costs and reasonable attorney's fees as allowed by law.

(b) *Form and Content.*

(1) The judgment must be in writing, signed, and dated and must include the names of the parties to the proceeding and the street address of the residential rental property where the condition is to be repaired or remedied.

(2) In the judgment, the judge may:

(A) order the landlord to take reasonable action to repair or remedy the condition;

(B) order a reduction in the tenant's rent, from the date of the first repair notice, in proportion to the reduced rental value resulting from the condition until the condition is repaired or remedied;

(C) award a civil penalty of one month's rent plus $500;

(D) award the tenant's actual damages; and

(E) award court costs and attorney's fees, excluding any attorney's fees for a claim for damages relating to a personal injury.

(3) If the judge orders the landlord to repair or remedy a condition, the judgment must include in reasonable detail the actions the landlord must take to repair or remedy the condition and the date when the repair or remedy must be completed.

(4) If the judge orders a reduction in the tenant's rent, the judgment must state:

(A) the amount of the rent the tenant must pay, if any;

(B) the frequency with which the tenant must pay the rent;

(C) the condition justifying the reduction of rent;

(D) the effective date of the order reducing rent;

(E) that the order reducing rent will terminate on the date the condition is repaired or remedied; and

(F) that on the day the condition is repaired or remedied, the landlord must give the tenant written notice, served in accordance with Rule 501.4, that the condition justifying the reduction of rent has been repaired or remedied and the rent will revert to the rent amount specified in the lease.

(c) *Issuance and Service.* The judge must issue the judgment. The judgment may be served on the landlord in open court or by any means provided in Rule 501 .4 at an address listed in the citation, the address listed on any answer, or such other address the landlord furnishes to the court in writing. Unless the judge serves the landlord in open court or by other means provided in Rule 50 1 .4, the sheriff, constable, or other authorized person who serves the landlord must promptly file a return of service in the justice court.

(d) *Failure to Comply.* If the landlord fails to comply with an order to repair or remedy a condition or reduce the tenant's rent, the failure is grounds for citing the landlord for contempt of court under Section 2 1 .002 of the Texas Government Code.

RULE 509.7. COUNTERCLAIMS.

Counterclaims and the joinder of suits against third parties are not permitted in suits under these rules. Compulsory counterclaims may be brought in a separate suit. Any potential causes of action, including a compulsory counterclaim, that are not asserted because of this rule are not precluded.

RULE 509.8. APPEAL: TIME AND MANNER; PERFECTION; EFFECT; COSTS; TRIAL ON APPEAL.

(a) *Time and Manner.* Either party may appeal the decision of the justice court to a statutory county court or, if there is no statutory county court with jurisdiction, a county court or district court with jurisdiction by filing a written notice of appeal with the justice court within 2 1 days after the date the judge signs the judgment. If the judgment is amended in any respect, any party has the right to appeal within 2 1 days after the date the judge signs the new judgment, in the same manner set out in this rule.

(b) *Perfection.* The posting of an appeal bond is not required for an appeal under this rule, and the appeal is considered perfected with the filing of a notice of appeal. Otherwise, the appeal is in the manner provided by law for appeal from a justice court.

(c) *Effect.* The timely filing of a notice of appeal stays the enforcement of any order to repair or remedy a condition or reduce the tenant's rent, as well as any other actions.

(d) *Costs.* The appellant must pay the costs on appeal to a county court in accordance with Rule 143a.

(e) *Trial on Appeal.* On appeal, the parties are entitled to a trial de novo. A trial de novo is a new trial in which the entire case is presented as if there had been no previous trial. Either party is entitled to trial by jury on timely request and payment of a fee, if required. An appeal of a judgment of a justice court under these rules takes precedence in the county court and may be held at any time after the eighth day after the date the transcript is filed in the county court.

RULE 509.9. EFFECT OF WRIT OF POSSESSION.

If a judgment for the landlord for possession of the residential rental property becomes final, any order to repair or remedy a condition is vacated and unenforceable.

(Adopted by Order Feb 12, 2013 and Order April 15, 2013, eff. Aug. 31, 2013.)

Rules of Civil Procedure 500-510 govern cases filed on or after August 31 , 2013, and cases pending on August 31 , 2013, except to the extent that in the opinion of the court their application in a case pending on August 31 , 2013, would not be feasible or would work injustice, in which event the formerly applicable procedure applies. An action taken before August 31 , 2013, in a case pending on August 31, 2013, that was done pursuant to any previously applicable procedure must be treated as valid. Where citation or other process was issued or served prior to August 31, 2013 , in compliance with any previously applicable procedure, the party served has the time provided for under the previously applicable procedure to answer or otherwise respond.

RULE 510. EVICTION CASES.

RULE 510.1. APPLICATION.

Rule 510 applies to a lawsuit to recover possession of real property under Chapter 24 of the Texas Property Code.

RULE 510.2. COMPUTATION OF TIME FOR EVICTION CASES.

Rule 500.5 applies to the computation of time in an eviction case. But if a document is filed by mail and not received by the court by the due date, the court may take any action authorized by these rules, including issuing a writ of possession requiring a tenant to leave the property.

RULE 510.3. PETITION.

(a) *Contents.* In addition to the requirements of Rule 502.2, a petition in an eviction case must be sworn to by the plaintiff and must contain:

(1) a description, including the address, if any, of the premises that the plaintiff seeks possession of;

(2) a description of the facts and the grounds for eviction;

(3) a description of when and how notice to vacate was delivered;

(4) the total amount of rent due and unpaid at the time of filing, if any; and

(5) a statement that attorney fees are being sought, if applicable.

(b) *Where Filed.* The petition must be filed in the precinct where the premises is located. If it is filed elsewhere, the judge must dismiss the case. The plaintiff will not be entitled to a refund of the filing fee, but will be refunded any service fees paid if the case is dismissed before service is attempted.

(c) *Defendants Named.* If the eviction is based on a written residential lease, the plaintiff must name as defendants all tenants obligated under the lease residing at the premises whom plaintiff seeks to evict. No judgment or writ of possession may issue or be executed against a tenant obligated under a lease and residing at the premises who is not named in the petition and served with citation.

(d) *Claim for Rent.* A claim for rent within the justice court's jurisdiction may be asserted in an eviction case.

(e) *Only Issue.* The court must adjudicate the right to actual possession and not title.

Counterclaims and the joinder of suits against third parties are not permitted in eviction cases. A claim that is not asserted because of this rule can be brought in a separate suit in a court of proper jurisdiction.

RULE 510.4. ISSUANCE, SERVICE, AND RETURN OF CITATION.

(a) *Issuance of Citation; Contents.* When a petition is filed, the court must immediately issue citation directed to each defendant. The citation must:

(1) be styled "The State of Texas";

(2) be signed by the clerk under seal of court or by the judge;

(3) contain the name, location, and address of the court;

(4) state the date of filing of the petition;

(5) state the date of issuance of the citation;

(6) state the file number and names of parties;

(7) state the plaintiffs cause of action and relief sought;

(8) be directed to the defendant;

(9) state the name and address of attorney for plaintiff, or if the plaintiff does not have an attorney, the address of plaintiff;

(10) state the day the defendant must appear in person for trial at the court issuing citation, which must not be less than 10 days nor more than 21 days after the petition is filed;

(11) notify the defendant that if the defendant fails to appear in person for trial, judgment by default may be rendered for the relief demanded in the petition;

(12) inform the defendant that, upon timely request and payment of a jury fee no later than 3 days before the day set for trial, the case will be heard by a jury;

(13) contain all warnings required by Chapter 24 of the Texas Property Code; and

(14) include the following statement: "For further information, consult Part V of the Texas Rules of Civil Procedure, which is available online and also at the court listed on this citation."

(b) *Service and Return of Citation.*

(1) Who May Serve. Unless otherwise authorized by written court order, citation must be served by a sheriff or constable.

(2) Method of Service. The constable, sheriff, or other person authorized by written court order receiving the citation must execute it by delivering a copy with a copy of the petition attached to the defendant, or by leaving a copy with a copy of the petition attached with some person, other than the plaintiff, over the age of 1 6 years, at the defendant's usual place of residence, at least 6 days before the day set for trial.

(3) Return of Service. At least one day before the day set for trial, the constable, sheriff, or other person authorized by written court order must complete and file a return of service in accordance with Rule 501.3 with the court that issued the citation.

(c) *Alternative Service by Delivery to the Premises.*

(1) When Allowed. The citation may be served by delivery to the premises if:

(A) the constable, sheriff, or other person authorized by written court order is unsuccessful in serving the citation under (b);

(B) the petition lists all home and work addresses of the defendant that are known to the plaintiff and states that the plaintiff knows of no other home or work addresses of the defendant in the county where the premises are located; and

(C) the constable, sheriff, or other person authorized files a sworn statement that it has made diligent efforts to serve such citation on at least two occasions at all addresses of the defendant in the county where the premises are located, stating the times and places of attempted service.

(2) Authorization. The judge must promptly consider a sworn statement filed under (1)(C) and determine whether citation may be served by delivery to the premises. The plaintiff is not required to make a request or motion for alternative service.

(3) Method. If the judge authorizes service by delivery to the premises, the constable, sheriff, or other person authorized by written court order must, at least 6 days before the day set for trial:

(A) deliver a copy of the citation with a copy of the petition attached to the premises by placing it through a door mail chute or slipping it under the front door; if neither method is possible, the officer may securely affix the citation to the front door or main entry to the premises; and

(B) deposit in the mail a copy of the citation with a copy of the petition attached, addressed to defendant at the premises and sent by first class mail.

(4) Notation on Return. The constable, sheriff, or other person authorized by written court order must note on the return of service the date the citation was delivered and the date it was deposited in the mail.

RULE 510.5. REQUEST FOR IMMEDIATE POSSESSION.

(a) *Immediate Possession Bond.* The plaintiff may, at the time of filing the petition or at any time prior to final judgment, file a possession bond to be approved by the judge in the probable amount of costs of suit and damages that may result to defendant in the event that the suit has been improperly instituted, and conditioned that the plaintiff will pay defendant all such costs and damages that are adjudged against plaintiff.

(b) *Notice to Defendant.* The court must notify a defendant that the plaintiff has filed a possession bond. The notice must be served in the same manner as service of citation and must inform the defendant that if the defendant does not file an answer or appear for trial, and judgment for possession is granted by default, an officer will place the plaintiff in possession of the property on or after the 7th day after the date defendant is served with the notice.

(c) *Time for Issuance and Execution of Writ.* If judgment for possession is rendered by default and a possession bond has been filed, approved, and served under this rule, a writ of possession must issue immediately upon demand and payment of any required fees. The writ must not be executed before the 7th day after the date defendant is served with notice under (b).

(d) *Effect of Appearance.* If the defendant files an answer or appears at trial, no writ of possession may issue before the 6th day after the date a judgment for possession is signed or the day following the deadline for the defendant to appeal the judgment, whichever is later.

RULE 510.6. TRIAL DATE; ANSWER; DEFAULT JUDGMENT.

(a) *Trial Date and Answer.* The defendant must appear for trial on the day set for trial in the citation. The defendant may, but is not required to, file a written answer with the court on or before the day set for trial in the citation.

(b) *Default Judgment.* If the defendant fails to appear at trial and fails to file an answer before the case is called for trial, and proof of service has been filed in accordance with Rule 510.4, the allegations of the complaint must be taken as admitted and judgment by default rendered accordingly. If a defendant who has answered fails to appear for trial, the court may proceed to hear evidence and render judgment accordingly.

(c) *Notice of Default.* When a default judgment is signed, the clerk must immediately mail written notice of the judgment by first class mail to the defendant at the address of the premises.

RULE 510.7. TRIAL.

(a) *Trial.* An eviction case will be docketed and tried as other cases. No eviction trial may be held less than 6 days after service under Rule 5 1 0.4 has been obtained.

(b) *Jury Trial Demanded.* Any party may file a written demand for trial by jury by making a request to the court at least 3 days before the trial date. The demand must be accompanied by payment of a jury fee or by filing a Statement of Inability to Afford Payment of Court Costs. If a jury is demanded by either party, the jury will be impaneled and sworn as in other cases; and after hearing the evidence it will return its verdict in favor of the plaintiff or the defendant. If no jury is timely demanded by either party, the judge will try the case.

(c) *Limit on Postponement.* Trial in an eviction case must not be postponed for more than 7 days total unless both parties agree in writing.

(Amended by Tex. Sup. Ct. Misc. Docket No. 16-9122, eff. Sept. 1, 2016.)

[Statement of Inability to Afford Payment of Court Costs as provided in Tex. Sup. Ct. Misc. Docket No. 16-9122, eff. Sept. 1, 2016 and applies to any contest of, or challenge to, a claim of inability to afford payment of court costs that is pending on September 1, 2016.]

RULE 510.8. JUDGMENT; WRIT; NO NEW TRIAL.

(a) *Judgment Upon Jury Verdict.* Where a jury has returned a verdict, the judge may render judgment on the verdict or, if the verdict is contrary to the law or the evidence, judgment notwithstanding the verdict.

(b) *Judgment for Plaintiff.* If the judgment is in favor of the plaintiff, the judge must render judgment for plaintiff or possession of the premises, costs, delinquent rent as of the date of entry of judgment, if any, and attorney fees if recoverable by law.

(c) *Judgment for Defendant.* If the judgment is in favor of the defendant, the judge must render judgment for defendant against the plaintiff for costs and attorney fees if recoverable by law.

(d) *Writ.* If the judgment or verdict is in favor of the plaintiff, the judge must award a writ of possession upon demand of the plaintiff and payment of any required fees.

   (1) Time to Issue. Except as provided by Rule 510.5, no writ of possession may issue before the 6th day after the date a judgment for possession is signed or the day following the deadline for the defendant to appeal the judgment, whichever is later. A writ of possession may not issue more than 60 days after a judgment for possession is signed. For good cause, the court may extend the deadline for issuance to 90 days after a judgment for possession is signed.

   (2) Time to Execute. A writ of possession may not be executed after the 90th day after a judgment for possession is signed.

   (3) Effect of Appeal. A writ of possession must not issue if an appeal is perfected and, if applicable, rent is paid into the registry, as required by these rules.

(e) *No Motion For New Trial.* No motion for new trial may be filed.

RULE 510.9. APPEAL.

(a) *How Taken; Time.* A party may appeal a judgment in an eviction case by filing a bond, making a cash deposit, or Statement of Inability to Afford Payment of Court Costs with the justice court within 5 days after the judgment is signed.

(b) *Amount of Security; Terms.* The justice court judge will set the amount of the bond or cash deposit to include the items enumerated in Rule 510.11. The bond or cash deposit must be payable to the appellee and must be conditioned on the appellant's prosecution of its appeal to effect and payment of any judgment and all costs rendered against it on appeal.

(c) *Statement of Inability to Afford Payment of Court Costs.*

(1) Filing. An appellant who cannot furnish a bond or pay a cash deposit in the amount required may instead Statement of Inability to Afford Payment of Court Costs. The Statement must be on a form approved by the Supreme Court or include the information required by the Court-approved form.

(2) Contest. The Statement may be contested as provided in Rule 502.3(d) within 5 days after the opposing party receives notice that the Statement was filed.

(3) Appeal If Contest Sustained. If the contest is sustained, the appellant may appeal that decision by filing notice with the justice court within 5 days of that court's written order. The justice court must then forward all related documents to the county court for resolution. The county court must set the matter for hearing within 5 days and hear the contest de novo, as if there had been no previous hearing, and, if the appeal is granted, must direct the justice court to transmit to the clerk of the county court the transcript, records, and papers of the case, as provided in these rules.

(4) If No Appeal or If Appeal Overruled. If the appellant does not appeal the ruling sustaining the contest, or if the county court denies the appeal, the appellant may, within one business day, post an appeal bond or make a cash deposit in compliance with this rule.

(5) Payment of Rent in Nonpayment of Rent Appeals.

(A) Notice. If a defendant appeals an eviction for nonpayment of rent by filing a Statement of Inability to Afford Payment of Court Costs, the justice court must provide to the defendant a written notice at the time the Statement is filed that contains the following information in bold or conspicuous type:

(i) the amount of the initial deposit of rent, equal to one rental period's rent under the terms of the rental agreement, that the defendant must pay into the justice court registry;

(ii) whether the initial deposit must be paid in cash, cashier's check, or money order, and to whom the cashier's check or money order, if applicable, must be made payable;

(iii) the calendar date by which the initial deposit must be paid into the justice court registry, which must be within 5 days of the date the Statement of Inability to Afford Payment of Court Costs is filed; and

(iv) a statement that failure to pay the required amount into the justice court registry by the required date may result in the court issuing a writ of possession without hearing.

(B) Defendant May Remain in Possession. A defendant who appeals an eviction for nonpayment of rent by filing a Statement of Inability to Afford Payment of Court Costs is entitled to stay in possession of the premises during the pendency of the appeal by complying with the following procedure:

(i) Within 5 days of the date that the defendant files a Statement of Inability to Afford Payment of Court Costs, it must pay into the justice court registry the amount set forth in the notice provided at the time the defendant filed the Statement. If the defendant was provided with notice and fails to pay the designated amount into the justice court registry within 5 days, and the transcript has not been transmitted to the county clerk, the plaintiff is entitled, upon request and payment of the applicable fee, to a writ of possession, which the justice court must issue immediately and without hearing.

(ii) During the appeal process as rent becomes due under the rental agreement, the defendant must pay the designated amount into the county court registry within 5 days of the rental due date under the terms of the rental agreement.

(iii) If a government agency is responsible for all or a portion of the rent, the defendant must pay only that portion of the rent determined by the justice court to be paid during appeal. Either party may contest the portion of the rent that the justice court determines must be paid into the county court registry by filing a contest within 5 days after the judgment is signed. If a contest is filed, the justice court must notify the parties and hold a hearing on the contest within 5 days. If the defendant objects to the justice court's ruling at the hearing, the defendant is required to pay only the portion claimed to be owed by the defendant until the issue is tried in county court.

(iv) If the defendant fails to pay the designated amount into the court registry within the time limits prescribed by these rules, the plaintiff may file a sworn motion that the defendant is in default in county court. The plaintiff must notify the defendant of the motion and the hearing date. Upon a showing that the defendant is in default, the court must issue a writ of possession.

(v) The plaintiff may withdraw any or all rent in the county court registry upon sworn motion and hearing, prior to final determination of the case, showing just cause; dismissal of the appeal; or order of the court after final hearing.

(vi) All hearings and motions under this subparagraph are entitled to precedence in the county court.

(d) *Notice to Other Parties Required.* If a Statement of Inability to Afford Payment of Court Costs is filed, the court must provide notice to all other parties that the Statement was filed no later than the next business day. Within 5 days of filing a bond or making a cash deposit, an appellant must serve written notice of the appeal on all other parties using a method approved under Rule 501.4.

(e) *No Default on Appeal Without Compliance With Rule.* No judgment may be taken by default against the adverse party in the court to which the case has been appealed without first showing substantial compliance with this rule.

(f) *Appeal Perfected.* An appeal is perfected when a bond, cash deposit, or Statement of Inability to Afford Payment of Court Costs is filed in accordance with this rule.

(Amended by Tex. Sup. Ct. Misc. Docket No. 16-9122, eff. Sept. 1, 2016.)

[Statement of Inability to Afford Payment of Court Costs as provided in Tex. Sup. Ct. Misc. Docket No. 16-9122, eff. Sept. 1, 2016 and applies to any contest of, or challenge to, a claim of inability to afford payment of court costs that is pending on September 1, 2016.]

RULE 510.10. RECORD ON APPEAL; DOCKETING; TRIAL DE NOVO.

(a) *Preparation and Transmission of Record.* Unless otherwise provided by law or these rules, when an appeal has been perfected, the judge must stay all further proceedings on the judgment and must immediately send to the clerk of the county court a certified copy of all docket entries, a certified copy of the bill of costs, and the original papers in the case together with any money in the court registry, including sums tendered pursuant to Rule 510.9(c)(5)(B).

(b) *Docketing; Notice.* The county clerk must docket the case and must immediately notify the parties of the date of receipt of the transcript and the docket number of the case. The notice must advise the defendant that it must file a written answer in the county court within 8 days if one was not filed in the justice court.

(c) *Trial De Novo.* The case must be tried de novo in the county court. A trial de novo is a new trial in which the entire case is presented as if there had been no previous trial. The trial, as well as any hearings and motions, is entitled to precedence in the county court.

RULE 510.11. DAMAGES ON APPEAL.

On the trial of the case in the county court the appellant or appellee will be permitted to plead, prove and recover his damages, if any, suffered for withholding or defending possession of the premises during the pendency of the appeal. Damages may include but are not limited to loss of rentals during the pendency of the appeal and attorney fees in the justice and county courts provided, as to attorney fees, that the requirements of Section 24.006 of the Texas Property Code have been met. Only the party prevailing in the county court will be entitled to recover damages against the adverse party. The prevailing party will also be entitled to recover court costs and to recover against the sureties on the appeal bond in cases where the adverse party has executed an appeal bond.

RULE 510.12. JUDGMENT BY DEFAULT ON APPEAL.

An eviction case appealed to county court will be subject to trial at any time after the expiration of 8 days after the date the transcript is filed in the county court. If the defendant has filed a written answer in the justice court, it must be taken to constitute his appearance and answer in the county court and may be amended as in other cases. If the defendant made no answer in writing in the justice court and fails to file a written answer within 8 days after the transcript is filed in the county court, the allegations of the complaint may be taken as admitted and judgment by default may be entered accordingly.

RULE 510.13. WRIT OF POSSESSION ON APPEAL.

The writ of possession, or execution, or both, will be issued by the clerk of the county court according to the judgment rendered, and the same will be executed by the sheriff or constable, as in other cases. The judgment of the county court may not be stayed unless within 10 days from the judgment the appellant files a supersedeas bond in an amount set by the county court pursuant to Section 24.007 of the Texas Property Code.

(Adopted by Order Feb 12, 2013 and Order April 15, 2013, eff. Aug. 31, 2013.)

Rules of Civil Procedure 500-510 govern cases filed on or after August 31 , 2013, and cases pending on August 31 , 2013, except to the extent that in the opinion of the court their application in a case pending on August 31 , 2013, would not be feasible or would work injustice, in which event the formerly applicable procedure applies. An action taken before August 31 , 2013, in a case pending on August 31, 2013, that was done pursuant to any previously applicable procedure must be treated as valid. Where citation or other process was issued or served prior to August 31, 2013 , in compliance with any previously applicable procedure, the party served has the time provided for under the previously applicable procedure to answer or otherwise respond.

PART V.
IN RULES OF PRACTICE JUSTICE COURTS

RULES 523-591. [Repealed.]

(Repealed by Order Feb 12, 2013 and Order April 15, 2013, eff. Aug. 31, 2013.)

PART VI.
RULES RELATING TO ANCILLARY PROCEEDINGS

SECTION 1.
ATTACHMENT

RULE 592. APPLICATION FOR WRIT OF ATTACHMENT AND ORDER.

Either at the commencement of a suit or at any time during its progress the plaintiff may file an application for the issuance of a writ of attachment. Such application shall be supported by affidavits of the plaintiff, his agent, his attorney, or other persons having knowledge of relevant facts. The application shall comply with all statutory requirements and shall state the grounds for issuing the writ and the specific facts relied upon by the plaintiff to warrant the required findings by the court. The writ shall not be quashed because two or more grounds are stated conjunctively or disjunctively. The application and any affidavits shall be made on personal knowledge and shall set forth such facts as would be admissible in evidence; provided that facts may be stated based upon information and belief if the grounds of such belief are specifically stated.

No writ shall issue except upon written order of the court after a hearing, which may be ex parte. The court, in its order granting the application, shall make specific findings of facts to support the statutory grounds found to exist, and shall specify the maximum value of property that may be attached, and the amount of bond required of plaintiff, and, further shall command that the attached property be kept safe and preserved subject to further orders of the court. Such bond shall be in an amount which, in the opinion of the court, will adequately compensate the defendant in the event plaintiff fails to prosecute his suit to effect, and to pay all damages and costs which may be adjudged against him for wrongfully suing out the writ of attachment. The court shall further find in its order the amount of bond required of defendant to replevy, which, unless the defendant chooses to exercise his option as provided in Rule 599, shall be the amount of plaintiff's claim, one year's accrual of interest if allowed by law on the claim, and the estimated costs of court. The order may direct the issuance of several writs at the same time, or in succession, to be sent to different counties.

(Amended by Order July 11, 1977, eff. Jan. 1, 1978.)

RULE 592a. BOND FOR ATTACHMENT.

No writ of attachment shall issue until the party applying therefor has filed with the officer authorized to issue such writ a bond payable to the defendant in the amount fixed by the court's order, with sufficient surety or sureties as provided by statute to be approved by such officer, conditioned that the plaintiff will prosecute his suit to effect and pay to the extent of the penal amount of the bond all damages and costs as may be adjudged against him for wrongfully suing out such writ of attachment.

After notice to the opposite party, either before or after the issuance of the writ, the defendant or plaintiff may file a motion to increase or reduce the amount of such bond, or to question the sufficiency of the sureties thereon, in the court in which such suit is pending. Upon hearing, the court shall enter its order with respect to such bond and sufficiency of the sureties.

(Added July 11, 1977, eff. Jan. 1, 1978.)

RULE 592b. FORM OF ATTACHMENT BOND.

The following form of bond may be used:

"The State of Texas,
"County of ________________,

"We, the undersigned, ______________________________ as principal, and ______________________________ and ______________________ as sureties, acknowledge ourselves bound to pay to C.D. the sum of ______________________ dollars, conditioned that the above bound plaintiff in attachment against the said C.D., defendant, will prosecute his said suit to effect, and that he will pay all such damages and costs to the extent of the penal amount of this bond as shall be adjudged against him for wrongfully suing out such attachment. Witness our hands this _______ day of ________, 19__."

(Renumbered from Rule 592 and amended by Order July 11, 1977, eff. Jan. 1, 1978.)

RULE 593. REQUISITES FOR WRIT.

A writ of attachment shall be directed to the sheriff or any constable within the State of Texas. It shall command him to attach and hold, unless replevied, subject to the further order of the court, so much of the property of the defendant, of a reasonable value in approximately the amount fixed by the court, as shall be found within his county.

(Amended by Order July 11, 1977, eff. Jan. 1, 1978.)

RULE 594. FORM OF WRIT.

The following form of writ may be issued:

"The State of Texas. "To the Sheriff or any Constable of any County of the State of Texas, greeting:
"We command you that you attach forthwith so much of the property of C.D., if it be found in your county, repleviable on security, as shall be of value sufficient to make the sum of ________ dollars, and the probable costs of suit, to satisfy the demand of A.B., and that you keep and secure in your hands the property so attached, unless replevied, that the same may be liable to further proceedings thereon to be had before our court in ____________, County of _________________. You will true return make of this writ on or before 10 a.m. of Monday, the _______ day of _______, 19__, showing how you have executed the same."

RULE 595. SEVERAL WRITS.

Several writs of attachment may, at the option of the plaintiff, be issued at the same time, or in succession and sent to different counties, until sufficient property shall be attached to satisfy the writ.

RULE 596. DELIVERY OF WRIT.

The writ of attachment shall be dated and tested as other writs, and may be delivered to the sheriff or constable by the officer issuing it, or he may deliver it to the plaintiff, his agent or attorney, for that purpose.

RULE 597. DUTY OF OFFICER.

The sheriff or constable receiving the writ shall immediately proceed to execute the same by levying upon so much of the property of the defendant subject to the writ, and found within his county, as may be sufficient to satisfy the command of the writ.

RULE 598. LEVY, HOW MADE.

The writ of attachment shall be levied in the same manner as is, or may be, the writ of execution upon similar property.

RULE 598a. SERVICE OF WRIT ON DEFENDANT.

The defendant shall be served in any manner prescribed for service of citation, or as provided in Rule 21a, with a copy of the writ of attachment, the application, accompanying affidavits, and orders of the court as soon as practicable following the levy of the writ. There shall be prominently displayed on the face of the copy of the writ served on the defendant, in ten-point type and in a manner calculated to advise a reasonably attentive person of its contents, the following:

"To _________________________, Defendant:
"You are hereby notified that certain properties alleged to be owned by you have been attached. If you claim any rights in such property, you are advised:
"YOU HAVE A RIGHT TO REGAIN POSSESSION OF THE PROPERTY BY FILING A REPLEVY BOND. YOU HAVE A RIGHT TO SEEK TO REGAIN POSSESSION OF THE PROPERTY BY FILING WITH THE COURT A MOTION TO DISSOLVE THIS WRIT."

(Added by Order July 11, 1977, eff. Jan. 1, 1978.)

RULE 599. DEFENDANT MAY REPLEVY.

At any time before judgment, should the attached property not have been previously claimed or sold, the defendant may replevy the same, or any part thereof, or the proceeds from the sale of the property if it has been sold under order of the court, by giving bond with sufficient surety or sureties as provided by statute, to be approved by the officer who levied the writ, payable to plaintiff, in the amount fixed by the court's order, or, at the defendant's option, for the value of the property sought to be replevied (to be estimated by the officer), plus one year's interest thereon at the legal rate from the date of the bond, conditioned that the defendant shall satisfy, to the extent of the penal amount of the bond, any judgment which may be rendered against him in such action.

On reasonable notice to the opposing party (which may be less than three days) either party shall have the right to prompt judicial review of the amount of bond required, denial of bond, sufficiency of sureties, and estimated value of the property, by the court which authorized issuance of the writ. The court's determination may be made upon the basis of affidavits, if uncontroverted, setting forth such facts as would be admissible in evidence; otherwise, the parties shall submit evidence. The court shall forthwith enter its order either approving or modifying the requirements of the officer or of the court's prior order, and such order of the court shall supersede and control with respect to such matters.

On reasonable notice to the opposing party (which may be less than three days) the defendant shall have the right to move the court for a substitution of property, of equal value as that attached, for the property attached. Provided that there has been located sufficient property of the defendants to satisfy the order of attachment, the court may authorize substitution of one or more items of defendant's property for all or for part of the property attached. The court shall first make findings as to the value of the property to be substituted. If property is substituted, the property released from attachment shall be delivered to defendant, if such property is personal property, and all liens upon such property from the original order of attachment or modification thereof shall be terminated. Attachment of substituted property shall be deemed to have existed from the date of levy on the original property attached, and no property on which liens have become affixed since the date of levy on the original property may be substituted.

(Amended by Order July 11, 1977, eff. Jan. 1, 1978.)

RULE 600. SALE OF PERISHABLE PROPERTY.

Whenever personal property which has been attached shall not have been claimed or replevied, the judge, or justice of the peace, out of whose court the writ was issued, may, either in term time or in vacation, order the same to be sold, when it shall be made to appear that such property is in danger of serious and immediate waste or decay, or that the keeping of the same until the trial will necessarily be attended with such expense or deterioration in value as greatly to lessen the amount likely to be realized therefrom.

RULE 601. TO PROTECT INTERESTS.

In determining whether the property attached is perishable, and the necessity or advantage of ordering a sale thereof, the judge or justice of the peace may act upon affidavits in writing or oral testimony, and may by a preliminary order entered of record, with or without notice to the parties as the urgency of the case in his opinion requires, direct the sheriff or constable to sell such property at public auction for cash, and thereupon the officer shall sell it accordingly.

RULE 602. BOND OF APPLICANT FOR SALE.

If the application for an order of sale be filed by any person or party other than the defendant from whose possession the property was taken by levy, the court shall not grant such order unless the applicant shall file with such court a bond payable to such defendant with two or more good and sufficient sureties, to be approved by said court, conditioned that they will be responsible to the defendant for such damages as he may sustain in case such sale be illegally and unjustly applied for, or be illegally and unjustly made.

RULE 603. PROCEDURE FOR SALE.

Such sale of attached perishable personal property shall be conducted in the same manner as sales of personal property under execution; provided, however, that the time of the sale, and at the time of advertisement thereof, may be fixed by the judge or justice of the peace at a time earlier than ten days according to the exigency of the case, and in such event notice thereof shall be given in such manner as directed by the order.

RULE 604. RETURN OF SALE.

The officer making such sale of perishable property shall promptly pay the proceeds of such sale to the clerk of such court or justice of the peace, as the case may be, and shall make written return of the order of sale signed by him officially, stating the time and place of the sale, the name of the purchaser, and the amount of money received, with an itemized account of the expenses attending the sale. Such return shall be filed with the papers of the case.

RULE 605. JUDGE MAY MAKE NECESSARY ORDERS.

When the perishable personal property levied on under the attachment writ has not been claimed or replevied, the judge or justice of the peace may make such orders, either in term time or vacation, as may be necessary for its preservation or use.

RULE 606. RETURN OF WRIT.

The officer executing the writ of attachment shall return the writ, with his action endorsed thereon, or attached thereto, signed by him officially, to the court from which it issued, at or before 10 o'clock a.m. of the Monday next after the expiration of fifteen days from the date of issuance of the writ. Such return shall describe the property attached with sufficient certainty to identify it, and state when the same was attached, and whether any personal property attached remains still in his hands, and, if not, the disposition made of the same. When property has been replevied he shall deliver the replevy bond to the clerk or justice of the peace to be filed with the papers of the cause.

RULE 607. REPORT OF DISPOSITION OF PROPERTY.

When the property levied on is claimed, replevied or sold, or otherwise disposed of after the writ has been returned, the officer having the custody of the same shall immediately make a report in writing, signed by him officially, to the clerk, or justice of the peace, as the case may be, showing such disposition of the property. Such report shall be filed among the papers of the cause.

RULE 608. DISSOLUTION OR MODIFICATION OF WRIT OF ATTACHMENT.

A defendant whose property has been attached or any intervening party who claims an interest in such property, may by sworn written motion, seek to vacate, dissolve, or modify the writ, and the order directing its issuance, for any grounds or cause, extrinsic or intrinsic. Such motion shall admit or deny each finding of the order directing the issuance of the writ except where the movant is unable to admit or deny the finding, in which case movant shall set forth the reasons why he cannot admit or deny. Unless the parties agree to an extension of time, the motion shall be heard promptly, after reasonable notice to the plaintiff (which may be less than three days), and the issue shall be determined not later than ten days after the motion is filed. The filing of the motion shall stay any further proceedings under the writ, except for any orders concerning the care, preservation, or sale of perishable property, until a hearing is had and the issue is determined. The writ shall be dissolved unless at such hearing, the plaintiff shall prove the grounds relied upon for its issuance, but the court may modify its previous order granting the writ and the writ issued pursuant thereto. The movant shall, however, have the burden to prove that the reasonable value of the property attached exceeds the amount necessary to secure the debt, interest for one year, and probable costs. He shall also have the burden to prove the facts to justify substitution of property.

The court's determination may be made upon the basis of affidavits, if uncontroverted, setting forth such facts as would be admissible in evidence; otherwise, the parties shall submit evidence. The court may make all such orders, including orders concerning the care, preservation, or disposition of the property (or the proceeds therefrom if the same has been sold), as justice may require. If the movant has given a replevy bond, an order to vacate or dissolve the writ shall vacate the replevy bond and discharge the sureties thereon, and if the court modifies its order or the writ issued pursuant thereto, it shall make such further orders with respect to the bond as may be consistent with its modification.

(Amended by Order July 11, 1977, eff. Jan. 1, 1978.)

RULE 609. AMENDMENT.

Clerical errors in the affidavit, bond, or writ of attachment, or the officer's return thereof, may upon application in writing to the judge or justice of the court in which the suit is filed, and after notice to the opponent, be amended in such manner and on such terms as the judge or justice shall authorize by an order entered in the minutes of the court or noted on the docket of the justice of the peace, provided the amendment does not change or add to the grounds of such attachment as stated in the affidavit, and provided such amendment appears to the judge or justice to be in furtherance of justice.

SECTION 2.
DISTRESS WARRANT

RULE 610. APPLICATION FOR DISTRESS WARRANT AND ORDER.

Either at the commencement of a suit or at any time during its progress the plaintiff may file an application for the issuance of a distress warrant with the justice of the peace. Such application may be supported by affidavits of the plaintiff, his agent, his attorney, or other persons having knowledge of relevant facts, but shall include a statement that the amount sued for is rent, or advances described by statute, or shall produce a writing signed by the tenant to that effect, and shall further swear that such warrant is not sued out for the purpose of vexing and harassing the defendant. The application shall comply with all statutory requirements and shall state the grounds for issuing the warrant and the specific facts relied upon by the plaintiff to warrant the required findings by the justice of the peace. The warrant shall not be quashed because two or more grounds are stated conjunctively or disjunctively. The application and any affidavits shall be made on personal knowledge and shall set forth such facts as would be admissible in evidence provided that facts may be stated based upon information and belief if the grounds of such belief are specifically stated.

No warrant shall issue before final judgment except on written order of the justice of the peace after a hearing, which may be ex parte. Such warrant shall be made returnable to a court having jurisdiction of the amount in controversy. The justice of the peace in his order granting the application shall make specific findings of fact to support the statutory grounds found to exist, and shall specify the maximum value of property that may be seized, and the amount of bond required of plaintiff, and, further shall command that property be kept safe and preserved subject to further orders of the court having jurisdiction. Such bond shall be in an amount which, in the opinion of the court, shall adequately compensate defendant in the event plaintiff fails to prosecute his suit to effect, and pay all damages and costs as shall be adjudged against him for wrongfully suing out the warrant. The justice of the peace shall further find in his order the amount of bond required to replevy, which, unless the defendant chooses to exercise his option as provided in Rule 614, shall be the amount of plaintiff's claim, one year's accrual of interest if allowed by law on the claim, and the estimated costs of court. The order may direct the issuance of several warrants at the same time, or in succession, to be sent to different counties.

(Added by Order June 10, 1980, eff. Jan. 1, 1981.)

RULE 611. BOND FOR DISTRESS WARRANT.

No distress warrant shall issue before final judgment until the party applying therefor has filed with the justice of the peace authorized to issue such warrant a bond payable to the defendant in an amount approved by the justice of the peace, with sufficient surety or sureties as provided by statute, conditioned that the plaintiff will prosecute his suit to effect and pay all damages and costs as may be adjudged against him for wrongfully suing out such warrant.

After notice to the opposite party, either before or after the issuance of the warrant, the defendant or plaintiff may file a motion to increase or reduce the amount of such bond, or to question the sufficiency of the sureties thereon, in a court having jurisdiction of the subject matter. Upon hearing, the court shall enter its order with respect to such bond and sufficiency of the sureties.

(Added by Order June 10, 1980, eff. Jan. 1, 1981.)

RULE 612. REQUISITES FOR WARRANT.

A distress warrant shall be directed to the sheriff or any constable within the State of Texas. It shall command him to attach and hold, unless replevied, subject to the further orders of the court having jurisdiction, so much of the property of the defendant, not exempt by statute, of reasonable value in approximately the amount fixed by the justice of the peace, as shall be found within his county.

(Added by Order June 10, 1980, eff. Jan. 1, 1981.)

RULE 613. SERVICE OF WARRANT ON DEFENDANT.

The defendant shall be served in any manner prescribed for service of citation, or as provided in Rule 21a, with a copy of the distress warrant, the application, accompanying affidavits, and orders of the justice of the peace as soon as practicable following the levy of the warrant. There shall be prominently displayed on the face of the copy of the warrant served on the defendant, in 10-point type and in a manner calculated to advise a reasonably attentive person of its contents, the following:

To _________________, Defendant:

You are hereby notified that certain properties alleged to be owned by you have been seized. If you claim any rights in such property, you are advised: "YOU HAVE A RIGHT TO REGAIN POSSESSION OF THE PROPERTY BY FILING A REPLEVY BOND. YOU HAVE A RIGHT TO SEEK TO REGAIN POSSESSION OF THE PROPERTY BY FILING WITH THE COURT A MOTION TO DISSOLVE THIS WARRANT."

(Added by Order June 10, 1980, eff. Jan. 1, 1981.)

RULE 614. DEFENDANT MAY REPLEVY.

At any time before judgment, should the seized property not have been previously claimed or sold, the defendant may replevy the same, or any part thereof, or the proceeds from the sale of the property if it has been sold under order of the court, by giving bond with sufficient surety or sureties as provided by statute, to be approved by a court having jurisdiction of the amount in controversy payable to plaintiff in double the amount of the plaintiff's debt, or, at the defendant's option for not less than the value of the property sought to be replevied, plus one year's interest thereon at the legal rate from the date of the bond conditioned that the defendant shall satisfy to the extent of the penal amount of the bond any judgment which may be rendered against him in such action.

On reasonable notice to the opposing party (which may be less than three days) either party shall have the right to prompt judicial review of the amount of bond required, denial of bond, sufficiency of sureties and estimated value of the property, by a court having jurisdiction of the amount in controversy. The court's determination may be made upon the basis of affidavits if uncontroverted setting forth such facts as would be admissible in evidence, otherwise the parties shall submit evidence. The court shall forthwith enter its order either approving or modifying the requirements of the order of the justice of the peace, and such order of the court shall supersede and control with respect to such matters.

On reasonable notice to the opposing party (which may be less than three days) the defendant shall have the right to move the court for a substitution of property, of equal value as that attached, for the property seized. Provided that there has been located sufficient property of the defendant's to satisfy the order of seizure, the court may authorize substitution of one or more items of defendant's property for all or part of the property seized. The court shall first make findings as to the value of the property to be substituted. If property is substituted, the property released from seizure shall be delivered to defendant, if such property is personal property, and all liens upon such property from the original order of seizure or modification thereof shall be terminated. Seizure of substituted property shall be deemed to have existed from the date of levy on the original property seized, and no property on which liens have become affixed since the date of levy on the original property may be substituted.

(Added by Order June 10, 1980, eff. Jan. 1, 1981.)

RULE 614a. DISSOLUTION OR MODIFICATION OF DISTRESS WARRANT.

A defendant whose property has been seized or any intervening claimant who claims an interest in such property, may by sworn written motion, seek to vacate, dissolve, or modify the seizure, and the order directing its issuance, for any grounds or cause, extrinsic or intrinsic. Such motion shall admit or deny each finding of the order directing the issuance of the warrant except where the movant is unable to admit or deny the finding, in which case movant shall set forth the reasons why he cannot admit or deny. Unless the parties agree to an extension of time, the motion shall be heard promptly, after reasonable notice to the plaintiff (which may be less than three days), and the issue shall be determined not later than 10 days after the motion is filed. The filing of the motion shall stay any further proceedings under the warrant, except for any orders concerning the care, preservation, or sale of any perishable property, until a hearing is had, and the issue is determined. The warrant shall be dissolved unless, at such hearing, the plaintiff shall prove the specific facts alleged and the grounds relied upon for its issuance, but the court may modify the order of the justice of the peace granting the warrant and the warrant issued pursuant thereto. The movant shall however have the burden to prove that the reasonable value of the property seized exceeds the amount necessary to secure the debt, interest for one year, and probable costs. He shall also have the burden to prove the facts to justify substitution of property.

The court's determination may be made upon the basis of affidavits setting forth such facts as would be admissible in evidence, but additional evidence, if tendered by either party shall be received and considered. The court may make all such orders, including orders concerning the care, preservation, or disposition of the property (or the proceeds therefrom if the same has been sold), as justice may require. If the movant has given a replevy bond, an order to vacate or dissolve the warrant shall vacate the replevy bond and discharge the sureties thereon, and if the court modifies the order of the justice of the peace of the warrant issued pursuant thereto, it shall make such further orders with respect to the bond as may be consistent with its modification.

(Added by Order June 10, 1980, eff. Jan. 1, 1981.)

RULE 615. SALE OF PERISHABLE PROPERTY.

Whenever personal property which has been levied on under a distress warrant shall not have been claimed or replevied, the judge, or justice of the peace, to whose court such writ is made returnable may, either in term time or in vacation, order the same to be sold, when it shall be made to appear that such property is in danger of serious and immediate waste or decay, or that the keeping of the same until the trial will necessarily be attended with such expense or deterioration in value as greatly to lessen the amount likely to be realized therefrom.

RULE 616. TO PROTECT INTERESTS.

In determining whether the property levied upon is perishable, and the necessity or advantage of ordering a sale thereof, the judge or justice of the peace may act upon affidavits in writing or oral testimony, and may by a preliminary order entered of record with or without notice to the parties as the urgency of the case in his opinion requires, direct the sheriff or constable to sell such property at public auction for cash, and thereupon the sheriff or constable shall sell it accordingly. If the application for an order of sale be filed by any person or party other than the defendant from whose possession the property was taken by levy, the court shall not grant such order, unless the applicant shall file with such court a bond payable to such defendant, with two or more good and sufficient sureties, to be approved by said court, conditioned that they will be responsible to the defendant for such damages as he may sustain in case such sale be illegally and unjustly applied for, or be illegally and unjustly made.

RULE 617. PROCEDURE FOR SALE.

Such sale of perishable personal property shall be conducted in the same manner as sales of personal property under execution; provided, however, that the time of the sale, and the time of advertisement thereof, may be fixed by the judge or justice of the peace at a time earlier than ten days, according to the exigency of the case, and in such event notice thereof shall be given in such manner as directed by the order.

RULE 618. RETURN OF SALE.

The officer making such sale of perishable property shall promptly pay the proceeds of such sale to the clerk of such court or to the justice of the peace, as the case may be, and shall make written return of the order of sale, signed by him officially, stating the time and place of the sale, the name of the purchaser, and the amount of money received, with an itemized account of the expenses attending the sale. Such return shall be filed with the papers of the case.

RULE 619. CITATION FOR DEFENDANT.

The justice at the time he issues the warrant shall issue a citation to the defendant requiring him to answer before such justice at the first day of the next succeeding term of court, stating the time and place of holding the same, if he has jurisdiction to finally try the cause, and upon its being returned served, to proceed to judgment as in ordinary cases; and, if he has not such jurisdiction, the citation shall require the defendant to answer before the court to which the warrant was made returnable at or before ten o'clock a.m. of the Monday next after the expiration of twenty days from the date of service thereof, stating the place of holding the court, and shall be returned with the other papers to such court. If the defendant has removed from the county without service, the proper officer shall state this fact in his return on the citation; and the court shall proceed to try the case ex parte, and may enter judgment.

RULE 620. PETITION.

When the warrant is made returnable to the district or county court, the plaintiff shall file his petition within ten days from the date of the issuance of the writ.

SECTION 3.
EXECUTIONS

RULE 621. ENFORCEMENT OF JUDGMENT.

The judgments of the district, county, and justice courts shall be enforced by execution or other appropriate process. Such execution or other process shall be returnable in thirty, sixty, or ninety days as requested by the plaintiff, his agent or attorney.

RULE 621a. DISCOVERY AND ENFORCEMENT OF JUDGMENT.

At any time after rendition of judgment, and so long as said judgment has not been suspended by a supersedeas bond or by order of a proper court and has not become dormant as provided by Article 3773, V.A.T.S., the successful party may, for the purpose of obtaining information to aid in the enforcement of such judgment, initiate and maintain in the trial court in the same suit in which said judgment was rendered any discovery proceeding authorized by these rules for pre-trial matters. Also, at any time after rendition of judgment, either party may, for the purpose of obtaining information relevant to motions allowed by Texas Rules of Appellate Procedure 47 and 49 initiate and maintain in the trial court in the same suit in which said judgment was rendered any discovery proceeding authorized by these rules for pre-trial matters. The rules governing and related to such pre-trial discovery proceedings shall apply in like manner to discovery proceedings after judgment. The rights herein granted to the parties shall inure to their successors or assignees, in whole or in part. Judicial supervision of such discovery proceedings after judgment shall be the same as that provided by law or these rules for pre-trial discovery and proceedings insofar as applicable.

(Added by Order July 21, 1970, eff. Jan. 1, 1971. Amended by Order July 15, 1987, eff. Jan. 1, 1988.)

RULE 622. EXECUTION.

An execution is a process of the court from which it is issued. The clerk of the district or county court or the justice of the peace, as the case may be, shall tax the costs in every case in which a final judgment has been rendered and shall issue execution to enforce such judgment and collect such costs. The execution and subsequent executions shall not be addressed to a particular county, but shall be addressed to any sheriff or any constable within the State of Texas.

(Amended by Order Sept. 20, 1941, eff. Dec. 31, 1941.)

RULE 623. ON DEATH OF EXECUTOR.

When an executor, administrator, guardian or trustee of an express trust dies, or ceases to be such executor, administrator, guardian or trustee after judgment, execution shall issue on such judgment in the name of his successor, upon an affidavit of such death or termination being filed with the clerk of the court or the justice of the peace, as the case may be, together with the certificate of the appointment of such successor under the hand and seal of the clerk of the court wherein the appointment was made.

RULE 624. ON DEATH OF NOMINAL PLAINTIFF.

When a person in whose favor a judgment is rendered for the use of another dies after judgment, execution shall issue in the name of the party for whose use the suit was brought upon an affidavit of such death being filed with the clerk of the court or the justice of the peace.

RULE 625. ON MONEY OF DECEASED.

If a sole defendant dies after judgment for money against him, execution shall not issue thereon, but the judgment may be proved up and paid in due course of administration.

RULE 626. ON PROPERTY OF DECEASED.

In any case of judgment other than a money judgment, where the sole defendant, or one or more of several joint defendants, shall die after judgment, upon an affidavit of such death being filed with the clerk, together with the certificate of the appointment of a representative of such decedent under the hand and seal of the clerk of the court wherein such appointment was made, the proper process on such judgment shall issue against such representative.

RULE 627. TIME FOR ISSUANCE.

If no supersedeas bond or notice of appeal, as required of agencies exempt from filing bonds, has been filed and approved, the clerk of the court or justice of the peace shall issue the execution upon such judgment upon application of the successful party or his attorney after the expiration of thirty days from the time a final judgment is signed. If a timely motion for new trial or in arrest of judgment is filed, the clerk shall issue the execution upon the judgment on application of the party or his attorney after the expiration of thirty days from the time the order overruling the motion is signed or from the time the motion is overruled by operation of law.

(Amended by Order July 22, 1975, eff. Jan. 1, 1976; June 10, 1980, eff. Jan. 1, 1981; Dec. 5, 1983, eff. April 1, 1984.)

RULE 628. EXECUTION WITHIN THIRTY DAYS.

Such execution may be issued at any time before the thirtieth day upon the filing of an affidavit by the plaintiff in the judgment or his agent or attorney that the defendant is about to remove his personal property subject to execution by law out of the county, or is about to transfer or secrete such personal property for the purpose of defrauding his creditors.

(Amended by Order July 22, 1976, eff. Jan. 1, 1976.)

RULE 629. REQUISITES OF EXECUTION.

The style of the execution shall be "The State of Texas." It shall be directed to any sheriff or any constable within the State of Texas. It shall be signed by the clerk or justice officially, and bear the seal of the court, if issued out of the district or county court, and shall require the officer to execute it according to its terms, and to make the costs which have been adjudged against the defendant in execution and the further costs of executing the writ. It shall describe the judgment, stating the court in which, and the time when, rendered, and the names of the parties in whose favor and against whom the judgment was rendered. A correct copy of the bill of costs taxed against the defendant in execution shall be attached to the writ. It shall require the officer to return it within thirty, sixty, or ninety days, as directed by the plaintiff or his attorney.

(Amended by Order Sept. 20, 1941, eff. Dec. 2, 1941.)

RULE 630. EXECUTION ON JUDGMENT FOR MONEY.

When an execution is issued upon a judgment for a sum of money, or directing the payment simply of a sum of money, it must specify in the body thereof the sum recovered or directed to be paid and the sum actually due when it is issued and the rate of interest upon the sum due. It must require the officer to satisfy the judgment and costs out of the property of the judgment debtor subject to execution by law.

RULE 631. EXECUTION FOR SALE OF PARTICULAR PROPERTY.

An execution issued upon a judgment for the sale of particular estates or personal property or real estate, must particularly describe the property, and shall direct the officer to make the sale by previously giving the public notice of the time and place of sale required by law and these rules.

RULE 632. EXECUTION FOR DELIVERY OF CERTAIN PROPERTY.

An execution issued upon a judgment for the delivery of the possession of a chattel or personal property, or for the delivery of the possession of real property, shall particularly describe the property, and designate the party to whom the judgment awards the possession. The writ shall require the officer to deliver the possession of the property to the party entitled thereto.

RULE 633. EXECUTION FOR POSSESSION OR VALUE OF PERSONAL PROPERTY.

If the judgment be for the recovery of personal property or its value, the writ shall command the officer, in case a delivery thereof cannot be had, to levy and collect the value thereof for which the judgment was recovered, to be specified therein, out of any property of the party against whom judgment was rendered, liable to execution.

RULE 634. EXECUTION SUPERSEDED.

The clerk or justice of the peace shall immediately issue a writ of supersedeas suspending all further proceedings under any execution previously issued when a supersedeas bond is afterward filed and approved within the time prescribed by law or these rules.

RULE 635. STAY OF EXECUTION IN JUSTICE COURT.

At any time within ten days after the rendition of any judgment in a justice court, the justice may grant a stay of execution thereof for three months from the date of such judgment, if the person against whom such judgment was rendered shall, with one or more good and sufficient sureties, to be approved by the justice, appear before him and acknowledge themselves and each of them bound to the successful party in such judgment for the full amount thereof, with interest and costs, which acknowledgment shall be entered in writing on the docket, and signed by the persons binding themselves as sureties; provided, no such stay of execution shall be granted unless the party applying therefor shall first file an affidavit with the justice that he has not the money with which to pay such judgment, and that the enforcement of same by execution prior to three months would be a hardship upon him and would cause a sacrifice of his property which would not likely be caused should said execution be stayed. Such acknowledgment shall be entered by the justice on his docket and shall constitute a judgment against the defendant and such sureties, upon which execution shall issue in case the same is not paid on or before the expiration of such day.

RULE 636. INDORSEMENTS BY OFFICER.

The officer receiving the execution shall indorse thereon the exact hour and day when he received it. If he receives more than one on the same day against the same person he shall number them as received.

RULE 637. LEVY OF EXECUTION.

When an execution is delivered to an officer he shall proceed without delay to levy the same upon the property of the defendant found within his county not exempt from execution, unless otherwise directed by the plaintiff, his agent or attorney. The officer shall first call upon the defendant, if he can be found, or, if absent, upon his agent within the county, if known, to point out property to be levied upon, and the levy shall first be made upon the property designated by the defendant, or his agent. If in the opinion of the officer the property so designated will not sell for enough to satisfy the execution and costs of sale, he shall require an additional designation by the defendant. If no property be thus designated by the defendant, the officer shall levy the execution upon any property of the defendant subject to execution.

RULE 638. PROPERTY NOT TO BE DESIGNATED.

A defendant in execution shall not point out property which he has sold, mortgaged or conveyed in trust, or property exempt from forced sale.

RULE 639. LEVY.

In order to make a levy on real estate, it shall not be necessary for the officer to go upon the ground but it shall be sufficient for him to indorse such levy on the writ. Levy upon personal property is made by taking possession thereof, when the defendant in execution is entitled to the possession. Where the defendant in execution has an interest in personal property, but is not entitled to the possession thereof, a levy is made thereon by giving notice thereof to the person who is entitled to the possession, or one of them where there are several.

RULE 640. LEVY ON STOCK RUNNING AT LARGE.

A levy upon livestock running at large in a range, and which cannot be herded and penned without great inconvenience and expense, may be made by designating by reasonable estimate the number of animals and describing them by their marks and brands, or either; such levy shall be made in the presence of two or more credible persons, and notice thereof shall be given in writing to the owner or his herder or agent, if residing within the county and known to the officer.

RULE 641. LEVY ON SHARES OF STOCK.

A levy upon shares of stock of any corporation or joint stock company for which a certificate is outstanding is made by the officer seizing and taking possession of such certificate. Provided, however, that nothing herein shall be construed as restricting any rights granted under Section 8.317 of the Texas Uniform Commercial Code.

(Amended by Order Aug. 18, 1947, eff. Dec. 31, 1947; July 21, 1970, eff. Jan. 1, 1971.)

RULE 642. [REPEALED]

(Repealed by Order July 22, 1975, eff. Jan. 1, 1976.)

RULE 643. LEVY ON GOODS PLEDGED OR MORTGAGED.

Goods and chattels pledged, assigned or mortgaged as security for any debt or contract, may be levied upon and sold on execution against the person making the pledge, assignment or mortgage subject thereto; and the purchaser shall be entitled to the possession when it is held by the pledgee, assignee or mortgagee, on complying with the conditions of the pledge, assignment or mortgage.

RULE 644. MAY GIVE DELIVERY BOND.

Any personal property taken in execution may be returned to the defendant by the officer upon the delivery by the defendant to him of a bond, payable to the plaintiff, with two or more good and sufficient sureties, to be approved by the officer, conditioned that the property shall be delivered to the officer at the time and place named in the bond, to be sold according to law, or for the payment to the officer of a fair value thereof, which shall be stated in the bond.

RULE 645. PROPERTY MAY BE SOLD BY DEFENDANT.

Where property has been replevied, as provided in the preceding rule, the defendant may sell or dispose of the same, paying the officer the stipulated value thereof.

RULE 646. FORFEITED DELIVERY BOND.

In case of the non-delivery of the property according to the terms of the delivery bond, and nonpayment of the value thereof, the officer shall forthwith indorse the bond "Forfeited" and return the same to the clerk of the court or the justice of the peace from which the execution issued; whereupon, if the judgment remain unsatisfied in whole or in part, the clerk or justice shall issue execution against the principal debtor and the sureties on the bond for the amount due, not exceeding the stipulated value of the property, upon which execution no delivery bond shall be taken, which instruction shall be indorsed by the clerk or justice on the execution.

RULE 646a. SALE OF REAL PROPERTY.

Real property taken by virtue of any execution shall be sold at public auction, at the courthouse door of the county, unless the court orders that such sale be at the place where the real property is situated, on the first Tuesday of the month, between the hours of ten o'clock, a.m. and four o'clock, p.m.

(Added by Order July 26, 1960, eff. Jan. 1, 1961.)

RULE 647. NOTICE OF SALE OF REAL ESTATE.

The time and place of sale of real estate under execution, order of sale, or venditioni exponas, shall be advertised by the officer by having the notice thereof published in the English language once a week for three consecutive weeks preceding such sale, in some newspaper published in said county. The first of said publications shall appear not less than twenty days immediately preceding the day of sale. Said notice shall contain a statement of the authority by virtue of which the sale is to be made, the time of levy, and the time and place of sale, it shall also contain a brief description of the property to be sold, and shall give the number of acres, original survey, locality in the county, and the name by which the land is most generally known, but it shall not be necessary for it to contain field notes. Publishers of newspapers shall charge the legal rate of Two (2) Cents per word for the first insertion of such publication and One (1) Cent per word for such subsequent insertions, or such newspapers shall be entitled to charge for such publication at a rate equal to but not in excess of the published word or line rate of that newspaper for such class of advertising. If there be no newspaper published in the county, or none which will publish the notice of sale for the compensation herein fixed, the officer shall then post such notice in writing in three public places in the county, one of which shall be at the courthouse door of such county, for at least twenty days successively next before the day of sale. The officer making the levy shall give the defendant, or his attorney, written notice of such sale, either in person or by mail, which notice shall substantially conform to the foregoing requirements.

(Amended by Order Sept. 20, 1941, eff. Dec. 31, 1941.)

RULE 648. "COURTHOUSE DOOR" DEFINED.

By the term "courthouse door" of a county is meant either of the principal entrances to the house provided by the proper authority for the holding of the district court. If from any cause there is no such house, the door of the house where the district court was last held in that county shall be deemed to be the courthouse door. Where the courthouse, or house used by the court, has been destroyed by fire or other cause, and another has not been designated by the proper authority, the place where such house stood shall be deemed to be the courthouse door.

RULE 649. SALE OF PERSONAL PROPERTY.

Personal property levied on under execution shall be offered for sale on the premises where it is taken in execution, or at the courthouse door of the county, or at some other place if, owing to the nature of the property, it is more convenient to exhibit it to purchasers at such place. Personal property susceptible of being exhibited shall not be sold unless the same be present and subject to the view of those attending the sale, except shares of stock in joint stock or incorporated companies, and in cases where the defendant in execution has merely an interest without right to the exclusive possession in which case the interest of defendant may be sold and conveyed without the presence or delivery of the property. When a levy is made upon livestock running at large on the range, it is not necessary that such stock, or any part thereof, be present at the place of sale, and the purchaser at such sale is authorized to gather and pen such stock and select therefrom the number purchased by him.

RULE 650. NOTICE OF SALE OF PERSONAL PROPERTY.

Previous notice of the time and place of the sale of any personal property levied on under execution shall be given by posting notice thereof for ten days successively immediately prior to the day of sale at the courthouse door of any county and at the place where the sale is to be made.

RULE 651. WHEN EXECUTION NOT SATISFIED.

When the property levied upon does not sell for enough to satisfy the execution, the officer shall proceed anew, as in the first instance, to make the residue.

RULE 652. PURCHASER FAILING TO COMPLY.

If any person shall bid off property at any sale made by virtue of an execution, and shall fail to comply with the terms of the sale, he shall be liable to pay the plaintiff in execution twenty per cent on the value of the property thus bid off, besides costs, to be recovered on motion, five days notice of such motion being given to such purchaser; and should the property on a second sale bring less than on the former, he shall be liable to pay to the defendant in execution all loss which he sustains thereby, to be recovered on motion as above provided.

RULE 653. RESALE OF PROPERTY.

When the terms of the sale shall not be complied with by the bidder the levying officer shall proceed to sell the same property again on the same day, if there be sufficient time, but if not, he shall readvertise and sell the same as in the first instance.

RULE 654. RETURN OF EXECUTION.

The levying officer shall make due return of the execution, in writing and signed by him officially, stating concisely what such officer has done in pursuance of the requirements of the writ and of the law. The return shall be filed with the clerk of the court or the justice of the peace as the case may be. The execution shall be returned forthwith if satisfied by the collection of the money or if ordered by the plaintiff or his attorney indorsed thereon.

RULE 655. RETURN OF EXECUTION BY MAIL.

When an execution is placed in the hands of an officer of a county other than the one in which the judgment is rendered, return may be made by mail; but money cannot be thus sent except by direction of the party entitled to receive the same or his attorney of record.

RULE 656. EXECUTION DOCKET.

The clerk of each court shall keep an execution docket in which he shall enter a statement of all executions as they are issued by him, specifying the names of the parties, the amount of the judgment, the amount due thereon, the rate of interest when it exceeds six per cent, the costs, the date of issuing the execution, to whom delivered, and the return of the officer thereon, with the date of such return. Such docket entries shall be taken and deemed to be a record. The clerk shall keep an index and cross-index to the execution docket. When execution is in favor or against several persons, it shall be indexed in the name of each person. Any clerk who shall fail to keep said execution docket and index thereto, or shall neglect to make the entries therein, shall be liable upon his official bond to any person injured for the amount of damages sustained by such neglect.

SECTION 4.
GARNISHMENT

RULE 657. JUDGMENT FINAL FOR GARNISHMENT.

In the case mentioned in subsection 3, section 63.001, Civil Practice and Remedies Code, the judgment whether based upon a liquidated demand or an unliquidated demand, shall be deemed final and subsisting for the purpose of garnishment from and after the date it is signed, unless a supersedeas bond shall have been approved and filed in accordance with Texas Rule of Appellate Procedure 47.

(Amended by Order June 10, 1980, eff. Jan. 1, 1981; July 15, 1987, eff. Jan. 1, 1988.)

RULE 658. APPLICATION FOR WRIT OF GARNISHMENT AND ORDER.

Either at the commencement of a suit or at any time during its progress the plaintiff may file an application for a writ of garnishment. Such application shall be supported by affidavits of the plaintiff, his agent, his attorney, or other person having knowledge of relevant facts. The application shall comply with all statutory requirements and shall state the grounds for issuing the writ and the specific facts relied upon by the plaintiff to warrant the required findings by the court. The writ shall not be quashed because two or more grounds are stated conjunctively or disjunctively. The application and any affidavits shall be made on personal knowledge and shall set forth such facts as would be admissible in evidence; provided that facts may be stated based upon information and belief if the grounds of such belief are specifically stated.

No writ shall issue before final judgment except upon written order of the court after a hearing, which may be ex parte. The court in its order granting the application shall make specific findings of facts to support the statutory grounds found to exist, and shall specify the maximum value of property or indebtedness that may be garnished and the amount of bond required of plaintiff. Such bond shall be in an amount which, in the opinion of the court, shall adequately compensate defendant in the event plaintiff fails to prosecute his suit to effect, and pay all damages and costs as shall be adjudged against him for wrongfully suing out the writ of garnishment. The court shall further find in its order the amount of bond required of defendant to replevy, which, unless defendant exercises his option as provided under Rule 664, shall be the amount of plaintiff's claim, one year's accrual of interest if allowed by law on the claim, and the estimated costs of court. The order may direct the issuance of several writs at the same time, or in succession, to be sent to different counties.

(Amended by Order Aug. 18, 1947, eff. Dec. 31, 1947; July 11, 1977, eff. Jan. 1, 1978.)

RULE 658a. BOND FOR GARNISHMENT.

No writ of garnishment shall issue before final judgment until the party applying therefor has filed with the officer authorized to issue such writ a bond payable to the defendant in the amount fixed by the court's order, with sufficient surety or sureties as provided by statute, conditioned that the plaintiff will prosecute his suit to effect and pay to the extent of the penal amount of the bond all damages and costs as may be adjudged against him for wrongfully suing out such writ of garnishment.

After notice to the opposite party, either before or after the issuance of the writ, the defendant or plaintiff may file a motion to increase or reduce the amount of such bond, or to question the sufficiency of the sureties. Upon hearing, the court shall enter its order with respect to such bond and the sufficiency of the sureties.

Should it be determined from the garnishee's answer if such is not controverted that the garnishee is indebted to the defendant, or has in his hands effects belonging to the defendant, in an amount or value less than the amount of the debt claimed by the plaintiff, then after notice to the defendant the court in which such garnishment is pending upon hearing may reduce the required amount of such bond to double the sum of the garnishee's indebtedness to the defendant plus the value of the effects in his hands belonging to the defendant.

(Added by Order July 26, 1960, eff. Jan. 1, 1961. Amended by Order July 11, 1977, eff. Jan. 1, 1978.)

RULE 659. CASE DOCKETED.

When the foregoing requirements of these rules have been complied with, the judge, or clerk, or justice of the peace, as the case may be, shall docket the case in the name of the plaintiff as plaintiff and of the garnishee as defendant; and shall immediately issue a writ of garnishment directed to the garnishee commanding him to appear before the court out of which the same is issued at or before 10 o'clock a.m. of the Monday next following the expiration of twenty days from the date the writ was served, if the writ is issued out of the district or county court, or the Monday next after the expiration of ten days from the date the writ was served, if the writ is issued out of the justice court. The writ shall command the garnishee to answer under oath upon such return date what, if anything, he is indebted to the defendant, and was when the writ was served, and what effects, if any, of the defendant he has in his possession, and had when such writ was served, and what other persons, if any, within his knowledge, are indebted to the defendant or have effects belonging to him in their possession.

(Amended by Order Sept. 20, 1941, eff. Dec. 31, 1941; Aug. 18, 1947, eff. Dec. 31, 1947; July 11, 1977, eff. Jan. 1, 1978.)

RULE 660. [REPEALED]

(Repealed by Order Aug. 18, 1947, eff. Dec. 31, 1947.)

RULE 661. FORM OF WRIT.

The following form of writ may be used:

"The State of Texas.

"To E.F., Garnishee, greeting:

"Whereas, in the ________________ Court of ______________ County (if a justice court, state also the number of the precinct), in a certain cause wherein A.B. is plaintiff and C.D. is defendant, the plaintiff, claiming an indebtedness against the said C.D. of _________ dollars, besides interest and costs of suit, has applied for a writ of garnishment against you, E.F.; therefore you are hereby commanded to be and appear before said court at _______________ in said county (if the writ is issued from the county or district court, here proceed: 'at 10 o'clock a.m. on the Monday next following the expiration of twenty days from the date of service hereof.' If the writ is issued from a justice of the peace court, here proceed: 'at or before 10 o'clock a.m. on the Monday next after the expiration of ten days from the date of service hereof.' In either event, proceed as follows:) then and there to answer upon oath what, if anything, you are indebted to the said C.D., and were when this writ was served upon you, and what effects, if any, of the said C.D. you have in your possession, and had when this writ was served, and what other persons, if any, within your knowledge, are indebted to the said C.D. or have effects belonging to him in their possession. You are further commanded NOT to pay to defendant any debt or to deliver to him any effects, pending further order of this court. Herein fail not, but make due answer as the law directs."

(Amended by Order Sept. 20, 1941, eff. Dec. 31, 1941; Aug. 18, 1947 eff. Dec. 31, 1947: July 11, 1977. eff. Jan. 1, 1978.)

RULE 662. DELIVERY OF WRIT.

The writ of garnishment shall be dated and tested as other writs, and may be delivered to the sheriff or constable by the officer who issued it, or he may deliver it to the plaintiff, his agent or attorney, for that purpose.

RULE 663. EXECUTION AND RETURN OF WRIT.

The sheriff or constable receiving the writ of garnishment shall immediately proceed to execute the same by delivering a copy thereof to the garnishee, and shall make return thereof as of other citations.

RULE 663a. SERVICE OF WRIT ON DEFENDANT.

The defendant shall be served in any manner prescribed for service of citation or as provided in Rule 21a with a copy of the writ of garnishment, the application, accompanying affidavits and orders of the court as soon as practicable following the service of the writ. There shall be prominently displayed on the face of the copy of the writ served on the defendant, in ten-point type and in a manner calculated to advise a reasonably attentive person of its contents, the following:

"To ______________________, Defendant:

"You are hereby notified that certain properties alleged to be owned by you have been garnished. If you claim any rights in such property, you are advised:

"YOU HAVE A RIGHT TO REGAIN POSSESSION OF THE PROPERTY BY FILING A REPLEVY BOND. YOU HAVE A RIGHT TO SEEK TO REGAIN POSSESSION OF THE PROPERTY BY FILING WITH THE COURT A MOTION TO DISSOLVE THIS WRIT."

(Added by Order July 11, 1977, eff. Jan. 1, 1978.)

RULE 664. DEFENDANT MAY REPLEVY.

At any time before judgment, should the garnished property not have been previously claimed or sold, the defendant may replevy the same, or any part thereof, or the proceeds from the sale of the property if it has been sold under order of the court, by giving bond with sufficient surety or sureties as provided by statute, to be approved by the officer who levied the writ, payable to plaintiff, in the amount fixed by the court's order, or, at the defendant's option, for the value of the property or indebtedness sought to be replevied (to be estimated by the officer), plus one year's interest thereon at the legal rate from the date of the bond, conditioned that the defendant, garnishee, shall satisfy, to the extent of the penal amount of the bond, any judgment which may be rendered against him in such action.

On reasonable notice to the opposing party (which may be less than three days) either party shall have the right to prompt judicial review of the amount of bond required, denial of bond, sufficiency of sureties, and estimated value of the property, by the court which authorized issuance of the writ. The court's determination may be made upon the basis of affidavits, if uncontroverted, setting forth such facts as would be admissible in evidence; otherwise, the parties shall submit evidence. The court shall forthwith enter its order either approving or modifying the requirements of the officer or of the court's prior order, and such order of the court shall supersede and control with respect to such matters.

On reasonable notice to the opposing party (which may be less than three days) the defendant shall have the right to move the court for a substitution of property, of equal value as that garnished, for the property garnished. Provided that there has been located sufficient property of the defendant's to satisfy the order of garnishment, the court may authorize substitution of one or more items of defendant's property for all or for part of the property garnished. The court shall first make findings as to the value of the property to be substituted. If property is substituted, the property released from garnishment shall be delivered to defendant, if such property is personal property, and all liens upon such property from the original order of garnishment or modification thereof shall be terminated. Garnishment of substituted property shall be deemed to have existed from date of garnishment on the original property garnished, and no property on which liens have become affixed since the date of garnishment of the original property may be substituted.

(Amended by Order July 11, 1977, eff. Jan. 1, 1978.)

RULE 664a. DISSOLUTION OR MODIFICATION OF WRIT OF GARNISHMENT.

A defendant whose property or account has been garnished or any intervening party who claims an interest in such property or account, may by sworn written motion, seek to vacate, dissolve or modify the writ of garnishment, and the order directing its issuance, for any grounds or cause, extrinsic or intrinsic. Such motion shall admit or deny each finding of the order directing the issuance of the writ except where the movant is unable to admit or deny the finding, in which case movant shall set forth the reasons why he cannot admit or deny. Unless the parties agree to an extension of time, the motion shall be heard promptly, after reasonable notice to the plaintiff (which may be less than three days), and the issue shall be determined not later than ten days after the motion is filed. The filing of the motion shall stay any further proceedings under the writ, except for any orders concerning the care, preservation or sale of any perishable property, until a hearing is had, and the issue is determined. The writ shall be dissolved unless, at such hearing, the plaintiff shall prove the grounds relied upon for its issuance, but the court may modify its previous order granting the writ and the writ issued pursuant thereto. The movant shall, however, have the burden to prove that the reasonable value of the property garnished exceeds the amount necessary to secure the debt, interest for one year, and probable costs. He shall also have the burden to prove facts to justify substitution of property.

The court's determination may be made upon the basis of affidavits, if uncontroverted, setting forth such facts as would be admissible in evidence; otherwise, the parties shall submit evidence. The court may make all such orders including orders concerning the care, preservation or disposition of the property (or the proceeds therefrom if the same has been sold), as justice may require. If the movant has given a replevy bond, an order to vacate or dissolve the writ shall vacate the replevy bond and discharge the sureties thereon, and if the court modifies its order or the writ issued pursuant thereto, it shall make such further orders with respect to the bond as may be consistent with its modification.

(Added by Order July 11, 1977, eff. Jan. 1, 1978.)

RULE 665. ANSWER TO WRIT.

The answer of the garnishee shall be under oath, in writing and signed by him, and shall make true answers to the several matters inquired of in the writ of garnishment.

RULE 666. GARNISHEE DISCHARGED.

If it appears from the answer of the garnishee that he is not indebted to the defendant, and was not so indebted when the writ of garnishment was served upon him, and that he has not in his possession any effects of the defendant and had not when the writ was served, and if he has either denied that any other persons within his knowledge are indebted to the defendant or have in their possession effects belonging to the defendant, or else has named such persons, should the answer of the garnishee not be controverted as hereinafter provided, the court shall enter judgment discharging the garnishee.

(Amended by Order Aug. 18, 1947, eff. Dec. 31, 1947.)

RULE 667. JUDGMENT BY DEFAULT.

If the garnishee fails to file an answer to the writ of garnishment at or before the time directed in the writ, it shall be lawful for the court, at any time after judgment shall have been rendered against the defendant, and on or after appearance day, to render judgment by default, as in other civil cases, against such garnishee for the full amount of such judgment against the defendant together with all interest and costs that may have accrued in the main case and also in the garnishment proceedings. The answer of the garnishee may be filed as in any other civil case at any time before such default judgment is rendered.

RULE 668. JUDGMENT WHEN GARNISHEE IS INDEBTED.

Should it appear from the answer of the garnishee or should it be otherwise made to appear and be found by the court that the garnishee is indebted to the defendant in any amount, or was so indebted when the writ of garnishment was served, the court shall render judgment for the plaintiff against the garnishee for the amount so admitted or found to be due to the defendant from the garnishee, unless such amount is in excess of the amount of the plaintiff's judgment against the defendant with interest and costs, in which case, judgment shall be rendered against the garnishee for the full amount of the judgment already rendered against the defendant, together with interest and costs of the suit in the original case and also in the garnishment proceedings. If the garnishee fail or refuse to pay such judgment rendered against him, execution shall issue thereon in the same manner and under the same conditions as is or may be provided for the issuance of execution in other cases.

RULE 669. JUDGMENT FOR EFFECTS.

Should it appear from the garnishee's answer, or otherwise, that the garnishee has in his possession, or had when the writ was served, any effects of the defendant liable to execution, including any certificates of stock in any corporation or joint stock company, the court shall render a decree ordering sale of such effects under execution in satisfaction of plaintiff's judgment and directing the garnishee to deliver them, or so much thereof as shall be necessary to satisfy plaintiff's judgment, to the proper officer for that purpose.

(Amended by Order Aug. 18, 1947, eff. Dec. 31, 1947.)

RULE 670. REFUSAL TO DELIVER EFFECTS.

Should the garnishee adjudged to have effects of the defendant in his possession, as provided in the preceding rule, fail or refuse to deliver them to the sheriff or constable on such demand, the officer shall immediately make return of such failure or refusal, whereupon on motion of the plaintiff, the garnishee shall be cited to show cause upon a date to be fixed by the court why he should not be attached for contempt of court for such failure or refusal. If the garnishee fails to show some good and sufficient excuse for such failure or refusal, he shall be fined for such contempt and imprisoned until he shall deliver such effects.

RULE 671. [REPEALED]

(Repealed by Order Aug. 18, 1947, eff. Dec. 31, 1947.)

RULE 672. SALE OF EFFECTS.

The sale so ordered shall be conducted in all respects as other sales of personal property under execution; and the officer making such sale shall execute a transfer of such effects or interest to the purchaser, with a brief recital of the judgment of the court under which the same was sold.

(Amended by Order Aug. 18, 1947, eff. Dec. 31, 1947.)

RULE 673. MAY TRAVERSE ANSWER.

If the plaintiff should not be satisfied with the answer of any garnishee, he may controvert the same by his affidavit stating that he has good reason to believe, and does believe, that the answer of the garnishee is incorrect, stating in what particular he believes the same to be incorrect. The defendant may also, in like manner, controvert the answer of the garnishee.

RULE 674. TRIAL OF ISSUE.

If the garnishee whose answer is controverted, is a resident of the county in which the proceeding is pending, an issue shall be formed under the direction of the court and tried as in other cases.

RULE 675. DOCKET AND NOTICE.

The clerk of the court or the justice of the peace, on receiving certified copies filed in the county of the garnishee's residence under the provisions of the statutes, shall docket the case in the name of the plaintiff as plaintiff, and of the garnishee as defendant, and issue a notice to the garnishee, stating that his answer has been so controverted, and that such issue will stand for trial on the docket of such court. Such notice shall be directed to the garnishee, be dated and tested as other process from such court, and served by delivering a copy thereof to the garnishee. It shall be returnable, if issued from the district or county court, at ten o'clock a.m. of the Monday next after the expiration of twenty days from the date of its service; and if issued from the justice court, to the next term of such court convening after the expiration of twenty days after the service of such notice.

(Amended by Order Sept. 20, 1941, eff. Dec. 31, 1941.)

RULE 676. ISSUE TRIED AS IN OTHER CASES.

Upon the return of such notice served, an issue shall be formed under the direction of the court and tried as in other cases.

RULE 677. COSTS.

Where the garnishee is discharged upon his answer, the costs of the proceeding, including a reasonable compensation to the garnishee, shall be taxed against the plaintiff; where the answer of the garnishee has not been controverted and the garnishee is held thereon, such costs shall be taxed against the defendant and included in the execution provided for in this section; where the answer is contested, the costs shall abide the issue of such contest.

RULE 678. GARNISHEE DISCHARGED ON PROOF.

It shall be a sufficient answer to any claim of the defendant against the garnishee founded on an indebtedness of such garnishee, or on the possession by him of any effects, for the garnishee to show that such indebtedness has been paid, or such effects, including any certificates of stock in any incorporated or joint stock company, have been delivered to any sheriff or constable as provided for in Rule 669.

(Amended by Order Aug. 18, 1947, eff. Dec. 31, 1947.)

RULE 679. AMENDMENT.

Clerical errors in the affidavit, bond, or writ of garnishment or the officer's return thereof, may upon application in writing to the judge or justice of the court in which the suit is filed, and after notice to the opponent, be amended in such manner and on such terms as the judge or justice shall authorize by an order entered in the minutes of the court (or noted on the docket of the justice of the peace), provided such amendment appears to the judge or justice to be in furtherance of justice.

SECTION 5.
INJUNCTIONS

RULE 680. TEMPORARY RESTRAINING ORDER.

No temporary restraining order shall be granted without notice to the adverse party unless it clearly appears from specific facts shown by affidavit or by the verified complaint that immediate and irreparable injury, loss, or damage will result to the applicant before notice can be served and a hearing had thereon. Every temporary restraining order granted without notice shall be endorsed with the date and hour of issuance; shall be filed forthwith in the clerk's office and entered of record; shall define the injury and state why it is irreparable and why the order was granted without notice, and shall expire by its terms within such time after signing, not to exceed fourteen days, as the court fixes, unless within the time so fixed the order, for good cause shown, is extended for a like period or unless the party against whom the order is directed consents that it may be extended for a longer period. The reasons for the extension shall be entered of record. No more than one extension may be granted unless subsequent extensions are unopposed. In case a temporary restraining order is granted without notice, the application for a temporary injunction shall be set down for hearing at the earliest possible date and takes precedence of all matters except older matters of the same character; and when the application comes on for hearing the party who obtained the temporary restraining order shall proceed with the application for a temporary injunction and, if he does not do so, the court shall dissolve the temporary restraining order. On two days' notice to the party who obtained the temporary restraining order without notice or on such shorter notice to that party as the court may prescribe, the adverse party may appear and move its dissolution or modification and in that event the court shall proceed to hear and determine such motion as expeditiously as the ends of justice require.

Every restraining order shall include an order setting a certain date for hearing on the temporary or permanent injunction sought.

(Amended by Order Dec. 5, 1983, eff. April 1, 1984; July 15, 1987, eff. Jan. 1, 1988.)

RULE 681. TEMPORARY INJUNCTIONS: NOTICE.

No temporary injunction shall be issued without notice to the adverse party.

RULE 682. SWORN PETITION.

No writ of injunction shall be granted unless the applicant therefor shall present his petition to the judge verified by his affidavit and containing a plain and intelligible statement of the grounds for such relief.

(Amended by Order March 31, 1941, eff. Sept. 1, 1941.)

RULE 683. FORM AND SCOPE OF INJUNCTION OR RESTRAINING ORDER.

Every order granting an injunction and every restraining order shall set forth the reasons for its issuance, shall be specific in terms shall describe in reasonable detail and not by reference to the complaint or other document, the act or acts sought to be restrained; and is binding only upon the parties to the action, their officers, agents, servants, employees, and attorneys, and upon those persons in active concert or participation with them who receive actual notice of the order by personal service or otherwise.

Every order granting a temporary injunction shall include an order setting the cause for trial on the merits with respect to the ultimate relief sought. The appeal of a temporary injunction shall constitute no cause for delay of the trial.

(Amended by Order Dec. 5, 1983, eff. April 1, 1984.)

RULE 684. APPLICANT'S BOND.

In the order granting any temporary restraining order or temporary injunction, the court shall fix the amount of security to be given by the applicant. Before the issuance of the temporary restraining order or temporary injunction the applicant shall execute and file with the clerk a bond to the adverse party, with two or more good and sufficient sureties, to be approved by the clerk, in the sum fixed by the judge, conditioned that the applicant will abide the decision which may be made in the cause, and that he will pay all sums of money and costs that may be adjudged against him if the restraining order or temporary injunction shall be dissolved in whole or in part.

Where the temporary restraining order or temporary injunction is against the State, a municipality, a State agency, or a subdivision of the State in its governmental capacity, and is such that the State, municipality, State agency, or subdivision of the State in its governmental capacity, has no pecuniary interest in the suit and no monetary damages can be shown, the bond shall be allowed in the sum fixed by the judge, and the liability of the applicant shall be for its face amount if the restraining order or temporary injunction shall be dissolved in whole or in part. The discretion of the trial court in fixing the amount of the bond shall be subject to review. Provided that under equitable circumstances and for good cause shown by affidavit or otherwise the court rendering judgment on the bond may allow recovery for less than its full face amount, the action of the court to be subject to review.

(Amended by Order June 16, 1943, eff. Dec. 31, 1943; Oct. 12, 1949, eff. March 1, 1950; June 10, 1980, eff. Jan. 1, 1981.)

RULE 685. FILING AND DOCKETING.

Upon the grant of a temporary restraining order or an order fixing a time for hearing upon an application for a temporary injunction, the party to whom the same is granted shall file his petition therefor, together with the order of the judge, with the clerk of the proper court; and, if such orders do not pertain to a pending suit in said court, the cause shall be entered on the docket of the court in its regular order in the name of the party applying for the writ as plaintiff and of the opposite party as defendant.

RULE 686. CITATION.

Upon the filing of such petition and order not pertaining to a suit pending in the court, the clerk of such court shall issue a citation to the defendant as in other civil cases, which shall be served and returned in like manner as ordinary citations issued from said court; provided, however, that when a temporary restraining order is issued and is accompanied with a true copy of plaintiff's petition, it shall not be necessary for the citation in the original suit to be accompanied with a copy of plaintiffs petition, nor contain a statement of the nature of plaintiffs demand, but it shall be sufficient for said citation to refer to plaintiff's claim as set forth in a true copy of plaintiffs petition which accompanies the temporary restraining order; and provided further that the court may have a hearing upon an application for a temporary restraining order or temporary injunction at such time and upon such reasonable notice given in such manner as the court may direct.

(Amended by Order June 16, 1943, eff. Dec. 31, 1943; Aug. 18, 1947, eff. Dec. 31, 1947.)

RULE 687. REQUISITES OF WRIT.

The writ of injunction shall be sufficient if it contains substantially the following requisites:

(a) Its style shall be, "The State of Texas."

(b) It shall be directed to the person or persons enjoined.

(c) It must state the names of the parties to the proceedings, plaintiff and defendant, and the nature of the plaintiff's application, with the action of the judge thereon.

(d) It must command the person or persons to whom it is directed to desist and refrain from the commission or continuance of the act enjoined, or to obey and execute such order as the judge has seen proper to make.

(e) If it is a temporary restraining order, it shall state the day and time set for hearing, which shall not exceed fourteen days from the date of the court's order granting such temporary restraining order; but if it is a temporary injunction, issued after notice, it shall be made returnable at or before ten o'clock a.m. of the Monday next after the expiration of twenty days from the date of service thereof, as in the case of ordinary citations.

(f) It shall be dated and signed by the clerk officially and attested with the seal of his office and the date of its issuance must be indorsed thereon.

(Amended by Order April 24, 1990, eff. Sept. 1, 1990.)

RULE 688. CLERK TO ISSUE WRIT.

When the petition, order of the judge and bond have been filed, the clerk shall issue the temporary restraining order or temporary injunction, as the case may be, in conformity with the terms of the order, and deliver the same to the sheriff or any constable of the county of the residence of the person enjoined, or to the applicant, as the latter shall direct. If several persons are enjoined, residing in different counties, the clerk shall issue such additional copies of the writ as shall be requested by the applicant. The clerk must retain a copy of the temporary restraining order or temporary injunction in the court's file.

(Amended by Order Oct. 17, 2011, eff. Jan. 1, 2012; Order Dec. 12, 2011, eff. Jan. 1, 2012.)

RULE 689. SERVICE AND RETURN.

The officer receiving a writ of injunction shall indorse thereon the date of its receipt by him, and shall forthwith execute the same by delivering to the party enjoined a true copy thereof. The officer must complete and file a return in accordance with Rule 107.

(Amended by Order Oct. 17, 2011, eff. Jan. 1, 2012; Order Dec. 12, 2011, eff. Jan. 1, 2012.)

RULE 690. THE ANSWER.

The defendant to an injunction proceeding may answer as in other civil actions; but no injunction shall be dissolved before final hearing because of the denial of the material allegations of the plaintiff's petition, unless the answer denying the same is verified by the oath of the defendant.

RULE 691. BOND ON DISSOLUTION.

Upon the dissolution of an injunction restraining the collection of money, by an interlocutory order of the court or judge, made in term time or vacation, if the petition be continued over for trial, the court or judge shall require of the defendant in such injunction proceedings a bond, with two or more good and sufficient sureties, to be approved by the clerk of the court, payable to the complainant in double the amount of the sum enjoined, and conditioned to refund to the complainant the amount of money, interest and costs which may be collected of him in the suit or proceeding enjoined if such injunction is made perpetual on final hearing. If such injunction is so perpetuated, the court, on motion of the complainant, may enter judgment against the principal and sureties in such bond for such amount as may be shown to have been collected from such defendant.

RULE 692. DISOBEDIENCE.

Disobedience of an injunction may be punished by the court or judge, in term time or in vacation, as a contempt. In case of such disobedience, the complainant, his agent or attorney, may file in the court in which such injunction is pending or with the judge in vacation, his affidavit stating what person is guilty of such disobedience and describing the acts constituting the same; and thereupon the court or judge shall cause to be issued an attachment for such person, directed to the sheriff or any constable of any county, and requiring such officer to arrest the person therein named if found within his county and have him before the court or judge at the time and place named in such writ; or said court or judge may issue a show cause order, directing and requiring such person to appear on such date as may be designated and show cause why he should not be adjudged in contempt of court. On return of such attachment or show cause order, the judge shall proceed to hear proof; and if satisfied that such person has disobeyed the injunction, either directly or indirectly, may commit such person to jail without bail until he purges himself of such contempt, in such manner and form as the court or judge may direct.

(Amended by Order June 16, 1943, eff. Dec. 31, 1943.)

RULE 693. PRINCIPLES OF EQUITY APPLICABLE.

The principles, practice and procedure governing courts of equity shall govern proceedings in injunctions when the same are not in conflict with these rules or the provisions of the statutes.

RULE 693a. BOND IN DIVORCE CASE.

In a divorce case the court in its discretion may dispense with the necessity of a bond in connection with an ancillary injunction in behalf of one spouse against the other.

(Added by Order June 16, 1943, eff. Dec. 31, 1943.)

SECTION 6.
MANDAMUS

RULE 694. NO MANDAMUS WITHOUT NOTICE.

No mandamus shall be granted by the district or county court on ex parte hearing, and any peremptory mandamus granted without notice shall be abated on motion.

SECTION 7.
RECEIVERS

RULE 695. NO RECEIVER OF IMMOVABLE PROPERTY APPOINTED WITHOUT NOTICE.

Except where otherwise provided by statute, no receiver shall be appointed without notice to take charge of property which is fixed and immovable. When an application for appointment of a receiver to take possession of property of this type is filed, the judge or court shall set the same down for hearing and notice of such hearing shall be given to the adverse party by serving notice thereof not less than three days prior to such hearing. If the order finds that the defendant is a nonresident or that his whereabouts is unknown, the notice may be served by affixing the same in a conspicuous manner and place upon the property or if that is impracticable it may be served in such other manner as the court or judge may require.

(Amended by Order June 16, 1943, eff. Dec. 31, 1943.)

RULE 695a. BOND, AND BOND IN DIVORCE CASE.

No receiver shall be appointed with authority to take charge of property until the party applying therefor has filed with the clerk of the court a good and sufficient bond, to be approved by such clerk, payable to the defendant in the amount fixed by the court, conditioned for the payment of all damages and cost in such suit, in case it should be decided that such receiver was wrongfully appointed to take charge of such property. The amount of such bond shall be fixed at a sum sufficient to cover all such probable damages and costs. In a divorce case the court or judge, as a matter of discretion, may dispense with the necessity of a bond.

(Added by Order June 16, 1940, eff. Dec. 31, 1943.)

SECTION 8.
SEQUESTRATION

RULE 696. APPLICATION FOR WRIT OF SEQUESTRATION AND ORDER.

Either at the commencement of a suit or at any time during its progress the plaintiff may file an application for a writ of sequestration. The application shall be supported by affidavits of the plaintiff, his agent, his attorney, or other persons having knowledge of relevant facts. The application shall comply with all statutory requirements and shall state the grounds for issuing the writ, including the description of the property to be sequestered with such certainty that it may be identified and distinguished from property of a like kind, giving the value of each article of the property and the county in which it is located, and the specific facts relied upon by the plaintiff to warrant the required findings by the court. The writ shall not be quashed because two or more grounds are stated conjunctively or disjunctively. The application and any affidavits shall be made on personal knowledge and shall set forth such facts as would be admissible in evidence, provided that facts may be stated based upon information and belief if the grounds of such belief are specifically stated.

No writ shall issue except upon written order of the court after a hearing, which may be ex parte. The court, in its order granting the application, shall make specific findings of facts to support the statutory grounds found to exist, and shall describe the property to be sequestered with such certainty that it may be identified and distinguished from property of a like kind, giving the value of each article of the property and the county in which it is located. Such order shall further specify the amount of bond required of plaintiff which shall be in an amount which, in the opinion of the court, shall adequately compensate defendant in the event plaintiff fails to prosecute his suit to effect and pay all damages and costs as shall be adjudged against him for wrongfully suing out the writ of sequestration including the elements of damages stated in Sections 62.044 and 62.045, Civil Practice and Remedies Code. The court shall further find in its order the amount of bond required of defendant to replevy, which shall be in an amount equivalent to the value of the property sequestered or to the amount of plaintiff's claim and one year's accrual of interest if allowed by law on the claim, whichever is the lesser amount, and the estimated costs of court. The order may direct the issuance of several writs at the same time, or in succession, to be sent to different counties.

(Amended by Order July 11, 1977, eff. Jan. 1, 1978; July 15, 1987, eff. Jan. 1, 1988.)

RULE 697. PETITION.

If the suit be in the district or county court, no writ of sequestration shall issue, unless a petition shall have been first filed therein, as in other suits in said courts.

RULE 698. BOND FOR SEQUESTRATION.

No writ of sequestration shall issue until the party applying therefor has filed with the officer authorized to issue such writ a bond payable to the defendant in the amount fixed by the court's order, with sufficient surety or sureties as provided by statute to be approved by such officer, conditioned that the plaintiff will prosecute his suit to effect and pay to the extent of the penal amount of the bond all damages and costs as may be adjudged against him for wrongfully suing out such writ of sequestration, and plaintiff may further condition the bond pursuant to the provisions of Rule 708, in which case he shall not be required to give additional bond to replevy unless so ordered by the court.

After notice to the opposite party, either before or after the issuance of the writ, the defendant or plaintiff may file a motion to increase or reduce the amount of such bond, or to question the sufficiency of the sureties thereon, in the court in which such suit is pending. Upon hearing, the court shall enter its order with respect to such bond and sufficiency of the sureties as justice may require.

(Amended by Order July 11, 1977, eff. Jan. 1, 1978.)

RULE 699. REQUISITES OF WRIT.

The writ of sequestration shall be directed "To the Sheriff or any Constable within the State of Texas" (not naming a specific county) and shall command him to take into his possession the property, describing the same as it is described in the application or affidavits, if to be found in his county, and to keep the same subject to further orders of the court, unless the same is replevied. There shall be prominently displayed on the face of the writ, in ten-point type and in a manner calculated to advise a reasonably attentive person of its contents, the following:

"YOU HAVE A RIGHT TO REGAIN POSSESSION OF THE PROPERTY BY FILING A REPLEVY BOND. YOU HAVE A RIGHT TO SEEK TO REGAIN POSSESSION OF THE PROPERTY BY FILING WITH THE COURT A MOTION TO DISSOLVE THIS WRIT."

(Amended by Order July 11, 1977, eff. Jan. 1, 1978.)

RULE 700. AMENDMENT.

Clerical errors in the affidavit, bond, or writ of sequestration or the officer's return thereof may upon application in writing to the judge of the court in which the suit is filed and after notice to the opponent, be amended in such manner and on such terms as the judge shall authorize by an order entered in the minutes of the court, provided the amendment does not change or add to the grounds of such sequestration as stated in the affidavit, and provided such amendment appears to the judge to be in furtherance of justice.

RULE 700a. SERVICE OF WRIT ON DEFENDANT.

The defendant shall be served in any manner provided for service of citation or as provided in Rule 21a, with a copy of the writ of sequestration, the application, accompanying affidavits, and orders of the court as soon as practicable following the levy of the writ. There shall also be prominently displayed on the face of the copy of the writ served on defendant, in ten-point type and in a manner calculated to advise a reasonably attentive person of its contents, the following:

"To ____________________, Defendant:
"You are hereby notified that certain properties alleged to be claimed by you have been sequestered. If you claim any rights in such property, you are advised:
"YOU HAVE A RIGHT TO REGAIN POSSESSION OF THE PROPERTY BY FILING A REPLEVY BOND. YOU HAVE A RIGHT TO SEEK TO REGAIN POSSESSION OF THE PROPERTY BY FILING WITH THE COURT A MOTION TO DISSOLVE THIS WRIT."

(Added by Order July 11, 1977, eff. Jan. 1, 1978.)

RULE 701. DEFENDANT MAY REPLEVY.

At any time before judgment, should the sequestered property not have been previously claimed, replevied, or sold, the defendant may replevy the same, or any part thereof, or the proceeds from the sale of the property if it has been sold under order of the court, by giving bond, with sufficient surety or sureties as provided by statute, to be approved by the officer who levied the writ, payable to plaintiff in the amount fixed by the court's order, conditioned as provided in Rule 702 or Rule 703.

On reasonable notice to the opposing party (which may be less than three days) either party shall have the right to prompt judicial review of the amount of bond required, denial of bond, sufficiency of sureties, and estimated value of the property, by the court which authorized issuance of the writ. The court's determination may be made upon the basis of affidavits, if uncontroverted, setting forth such facts as would be admissible in evidence; otherwise, the parties shall submit evidence. The court shall forthwith enter its order either approving or modifying the requirements of the officer or of the court's prior order, and such order of the court shall supersede and control with respect to such matters.

(Amended by Order July 11, 1977, eff. Jan. 1, 1978.)

RULE 702. BOND FOR PERSONAL PROPERTY.

If the property to be replevied be personal property, the condition of the bond shall be that the defendant will not remove the same out of the county, or that he will not waste, ill-treat, injure, destroy, or dispose of the same, according to the plaintiff's affidavit, and that he will have such property, in the same condition as when it is replevied, together with the value of the fruits, hire or revenue thereof, forthcoming to abide the decision of the court, or that he will pay the value thereof, or the difference between its value at the time of replevy and the time of judgment and of the fruits, hire or revenue of the same in case he shall be condemned to do so.

RULE 703. BOND FOR REAL ESTATE.

If the property be real estate, the condition of such bond shall be that the defendant will not injure the property, and that he will pay the value of the rents of the same in case he shall be condemned so to do.

RULE 704. RETURN OF BOND AND ENTRY OF JUDGMENT.

The bond provided for in the three preceding rules shall be returned with the writ to the court from whence the writ issued. In case the suit is decided against the defendant, final judgment shall be rendered against all the obligors in such bond, jointly and severally, for the value of the property replevied as of the date of the execution of the replevy bond, and the value of the fruits, hire, revenue, or rent thereof, as the case may be.

(Amended by Order June 10, 1980, eff. Jan. 1, 1981.)

RULE 705. DEFENDANT MAY RETURN SEQUESTERED PROPERTY.

Within ten days after final judgment for personal property the defendant may deliver to the plaintiff, or to the officer who levied the sequestration or to his successor in office the personal property in question, and such officer shall deliver same to plaintiff upon his demand therefor; or such defendant shall deliver such property to the officer demanding same under execution issued therefor upon a judgment for the title or possession of the same; and such officer shall receipt the defendant for such property; provided, however, that such delivery to the plaintiff or to such officer shall be without prejudice to any rights of the plaintiff under the replevy bond given by the defendant. Where a mortgage or other lien of any kind is foreclosed upon personal property sequestered and replevied, the defendant shall deliver such property to the officer calling for same under order of sale issued upon a judgment foreclosing such mortgage or other lien, either in the county of defendant's residence or in the county where sequestered, as demanded by such officer; provided, however, that such delivery by the defendant shall be without prejudice to any rights of the plaintiff under the replevy bond given by the defendant.

(Amended by Order Sept. 20, 1941, eff. Dec. 31, 1941.)

RULE 706. DISPOSITION OF THE PROPERTY BY OFFICER.

When the property is tendered back by the defendant to the officer who sequestered the same or to the officer calling for same under an order of sale, such officer shall receive said property and hold or dispose of the same as ordered by the court; provided, however, that such return to and receipt of same by the officer and any sale or disposition of said property by the officer under order or judgment of the court shall not affect or limit any rights of the plaintiff under the bond provided for in Rule 702.

(Amended by Order Sept. 20, 1941, eff. Dec. 31, 1941.)

RULE 707. EXECUTION.

If the property be not returned and received, as provided in the two preceding rules, execution shall issue upon said judgment for the amount due thereon, as in other cases.

RULE 708. PLAINTIFF MAY REPLEVY.

When the defendant fails to replevy the property within ten days after the levy of the writ and service of notice on defendant, the officer having the property in possession shall at any time thereafter and before final judgment, deliver the same to the plaintiff upon his giving bond payable to defendant in a sum of money not less than the amount fixed by the court's order, with sufficient surety or sureties as provided by statute to be approved by such officer. If the property to be replevied be personal property, the condition of the bond shall be that he will have such property, in the same condition as when it is replevied, together with the value of the fruits, hire or revenue thereof, forthcoming to abide the decision of the court, or that he will pay the value thereof, or the difference between its value at the time of replevy and the time of judgment (regardless of the cause of such difference in value, and of the fruits, hire or revenue of the same in case he shall be condemned to do so). If the property be real estate, the condition of such bond shall be that the plaintiff will not injure the property, and that he will pay the value of the rents of the same in case he shall be condemned to do so.

On reasonable notice to the opposing party (which may be less than three days) either party shall have the right to prompt judicial review of the amount of bond required, denial of bond, sufficiency of sureties, and estimated value of the property, by the court which authorized issuance of the writ. The court's determination may be made upon the basis of affidavits, if uncontroverted, setting forth such facts as would be admissible in evidence, otherwise, the parties shall submit evidence. The court shall forthwith enter its order either approving or modifying the requirements of the officer or of the court's prior order, and such order of the court shall supersede and control with respect to such matters.

(Amended by Order July 11, 1977, eff. Jan. 1, 1978; Dec. 5, 1983, eff. April 1, 1984.)

RULE 709. WHEN BOND FORFEITED.

The bond provided for in the preceding rule shall be returned by the officer to the court issuing the writ immediately after he has approved same, and in case the suit is decided against the plaintiff, final judgment shall be entered against all the obligors in such bond, jointly and severally for the value of the property replevied as of the date of the execution of the replevy bond, and the value of the fruits, hire, revenue or rent thereof as the case may be. The same rules which govern the discharge or enforcement of a judgment against the obligors in the defendant's replevy bond shall be applicable to and govern in case of a judgment against the obligors in the plaintiff's replevy bond.

RULE 710. SALE OF PERISHABLE GOODS.

If after the expiration of ten days from the levy of a writ of sequestration the defendant has failed to replevy the same, if the plaintiff or defendant shall make affidavit in writing that the property levied upon, or any portion thereof, is likely to be wasted or destroyed or greatly depreciated in value by keeping, and if the officer having possession of such property shall certify to the truth of such affidavit, it shall be the duty of the judge or justice of the peace to whose court the writ is returnable, upon the presentation of such affidavit and certificate, either in term time or vacation, to order the sale of said property or so much thereof as is likely to be so wasted, destroyed or depreciated in value by keeping, but either party may replevy the property at any time before such sale.

RULE 711. ORDER OF SALE FOR.

The judge or justice granting the order provided for in the preceding rule shall issue an order directed to the officer having such property in possession, commending such officer to sell such property in the same manner as under execution.

RULE 712. RETURN OF ORDER.

The officer making such sale shall, within five days thereafter, return the order of sale to the court from whence the same issued, with his proceedings thereon, and shall, at the time of making such return, pay over to the clerk or justice of the peace the proceeds of such sale.

RULE 712a. DISSOLUTION OR MODIFICATION OF WRIT OF SEQUESTRATION.

A defendant whose property has been sequestered or any intervening party who claims an interest in such property, may by sworn written motion, seek to vacate, dissolve, or modify the writ and the order directing its issuance, for any grounds or cause, extrinsic or intrinsic, including a motion to reduce the amount of property sequestered when the total amount described and authorized by such order exceeds the amount necessary to secure the plaintiffs claim, one year's interest if allowed by law on the claim, and costs. Such motion shall admit or deny each finding of the order directing the issuance of the writ except where the movant is unable to admit or deny the finding, in which case movant shall set forth the reasons why he cannot admit or deny. Unless the parties agree to an extension of time, the motion shall be heard promptly, after reasonable notice to the plaintiff (which may be less than three days), and the issue shall be determined not later than ten days after the motion is filed. The filing of the motion shall stay any further proceedings under the writ, except for any orders concerning the care, preservation, or sale of any perishable property, until a hearing is had, and the issue is determined. The writ shall be dissolved unless, at such hearing, the plaintiff shall prove the grounds relied upon for its issuance, but the court may modify its previous order granting the writ and the writ issued pursuant thereto. The movant shall, however, have the burden to prove that the reasonable value of the property sequestered exceeds the amount necessary to secure the debt, interest for one year, and probable costs.

The court's determination may be made upon the basis of affidavits, if uncontroverted, setting forth such facts as would be admissible in evidence; otherwise, the parties shall submit evidence. The court may make all such orders, including orders concerning the care, preservation, or disposition of the property (or the proceeds therefrom if the same has been sold) as justice may require. If the movant has given a replevy bond, an order to vacate or dissolve the writ shall vacate the replevy bond and discharge the sureties thereon, and if the court modifies its order or the writ issued pursuant thereto, it shall make such further orders with respect to the bond as may be consistent with its modification.

(Added by Order July 11, 1977, eff. Jan. 1, 1978.)

RULE 713. SALE ON DEBT NOT DUE.

If the suit in which the sequestration issued be for a debt or demand not yet due, and the property sequestered be likely to be wasted, destroyed or greatly depreciated in value by keeping, the judge or justice of the peace shall, under the regulations hereinbefore provided, order the same to be sold, giving credit on such sale until such debt or demand shall become due.

RULE 714. PURCHASER'S BOND.

In the case of a sale as provided for in the preceding rule, the purchaser of the property shall execute his bond, with two or more good and sufficient sureties, to be approved by the officer making the sale, and payable to such officer, in a sum not less than double the amount of the purchase money, conditioned that such purchaser shall pay such purchase money at the expiration of the time given.

RULE 715. RETURN OF BOND.

The bond provided for in the preceding rule shall be returned by the officer taking the same to the clerk or justice of the peace from whose court the order of sale issued, with such order, and shall be filed among the papers in the cause.

RULE 716. RECOVERY ON BOND.

In case the purchaser does not pay the purchase money at the expiration of the time given, judgment shall be rendered against all the obligors in such bond for the amount of such purchase money, interest thereon and all costs incurred in the enforcement and collection of the same; and execution shall issue thereon in the name of the plaintiff in the suit, as in other cases, and the money when collected shall be paid to the clerk or justice of the peace to abide the final decision of the cause.

SECTION 9.
TRIAL OF THE RIGHT OF PROPERTY

RULE 717. CLAIMANT MUST MAKE AFFIDAVIT.

Whenever a distress warrant, writ of execution, sequestration, attachment, or other like writ is levied upon personal property, and such property, or any part thereof, shall be claimed by any claimant who is not a party to such writ, such claimant may make application that such claim is made in good faith, and file such application with the court in which such suit is pending. Such application may be supported by affidavits of the claimant, his agent, his attorney, or other persons having knowledge of relevant facts. The application shall comply with all statutory requirements and shall state the grounds for such claim and the specific facts relied upon by the claimant to warrant the required findings by the court.

The claim shall not be quashed because two or more grounds are stated conjunctively or disjunctively. The application and any affidavits shall be made on personal knowledge and shall set forth such facts as would be admissible in evidence provided that facts may be stated based upon information and belief if the grounds of such belief are specifically stated.

No property shall be delivered to the claimant except on written order of the court after a hearing pursuant to Rule 718. The court in its order granting the application shall make specific findings of facts to support the statutory grounds found to exist and shall specify the amount of the bond required of the claimant.

(Added by Order June 10, 1980, eff. Jan. 1, 1981.)

RULE 718. PROPERTY DELIVERED TO CLAIMANT.

Any claimant who claims an interest in property on which a writ has been levied may, by sworn written motion, seek to obtain possession of such property. Such motion shall admit or deny each finding of the order directing the issuance of the writ except where the claimant is unable to admit or deny the finding, in which case claimant shall set forth the reasons why he cannot admit or deny. Such motion shall also contain the reasons why the claimant has superior right or title to the property claimed as against the plaintiff in the writ. Unless the parties agree to an extension of time, the motion shall be heard promptly, after reasonable notice to the plaintiff (which may be less than three days), and the issue shall be determined not later than 10 days after the motion is filed. The filing of the motion shall stay any further proceedings under the writ, except for any orders concerning the care, preservation, or sale of any perishable property, until a hearing is had, and the issue is determined. The claimant shall have the burden to show superior right or title to the property claimed as against the plaintiff and defendant in the writ.

The court's determination may be made upon the basis of affidavits, if uncontroverted, setting forth such facts as would be admissible in evidence, but additional evidence, if tendered by either party shall be received and considered. The court may make all such orders, including orders concerning the care, preservation, or disposition of the property, or the proceeds therefrom if the same has been sold, as justice may require, and if the court modifies its order or the writ issued pursuant thereto, it shall make such further orders with respect to the bond as may be consistent with its modification.

(Added by Order June 10, 1980, eff. Jan. 1, 1981.)

RULE 719. BOND.

No property shall be put in the custody of the claimant until the claimant has filed with the officer who made the levy, a bond in an amount fixed by the court's order equal to double the value of the property so claimed, payable to the plaintiff in the writ, with sufficient surety or sureties as provided by statute to be approved by such officer, conditioned that the claimant will return the same to the officer making the levy, or his successor, in as good condition as he received it, and shall also pay the reasonable value of the use, hire, increase and fruits thereof from the date of said bond, or, in case he fails so to return said property and pay for the use of the same, that he shall pay the plaintiff the value of said property, with legal interest thereon from the date of the bond, and shall also pay all damages and costs that may be awarded against him for wrongfully suing out such claim.

The plaintiff or claimant may file a motion to increase or reduce the amount of such bond, or to question the sufficiency of the sureties thereon, in the court in which such suit is pending. Upon hearing, the court shall enter its order with respect to such bond and sufficiency of the sureties.

(Added by Order June 10, 1980, eff. Jan. 1, 1981.)

RULE 720. RETURN OF BOND.

Whenever any person shall claim property and shall duly make the application and give the bond, if the writ under which the levy was made was issued by a justice of the peace or a court of the county where such levy was made, the officer receiving such application and bond shall endorse on the writ that such claim has been made and application and bond given, and by whom; and shall also endorse on such bond the value of the property as assessed by himself, and shall forthwith return such bond with a copy of the writ to the proper court having jurisdiction to try such claim.

(Added by Order June 10, 1980, eff. Jan. 1, 1981.)

RULE 721. OUT-COUNTY LEVY.

Whenever any person shall claim property and shall make the application and give the bond as provided for herein, if the writ under which such levy was made was issued by a justice of the peace or a court of another county than that in which such levy was made, then the officer receiving such bond shall endorse on such bond the value of the property as assessed by himself. and shall forthwith return such bond with a copy of the writ, to the proper court having jurisdiction to try such claim.

(Added by Order June 10, 1980, eff. Jan. 1, 1981.)

RULE 722. RETURN OF ORIGINAL WRIT.

The officer taking such bond shall also endorse on the original writ, if in his possession, that such claim has been made and application and bond given, stating by whom, the names of the surety or sureties, and to what justice or court the bond has been returned; and he shall forthwith return such original writ to the tribunal from which it issued.

(Added by Order June 10, 1980, eff. Jan 1, 1981.)

RULE 723. DOCKETING CAUSE.

Whenever any bond for the trial of the right of property shall be returned, the clerk of the court, or such justice of the peace, shall docket the same in the original writ proceeding in the name of the plaintiff in the writ as the plaintiff, and the claimant of the property as intervening claimant.

(Added by Order June 10, 1980, eff. Jan. 1, 1981.)

RULE 724. ISSUE MADE UP.

After the claim proceedings have been docketed, and on the hearing day set by the court, then the court, or the justice of the peace, as the case may be shall enter an order directing the making and joinder of issues by the parties. Such issues shall be in writing and signed by each party or his attorney. The plaintiff shall make a brief statement of the authority and right by which he seeks to subject the property levied on to the process, and it shall be sufficient for the claimant and other parties to make brief statements of the nature of their claims thereto.

(Added by Order June 10, 1980, eff. Jan. 1, 1981.)

RULE 725. JUDGMENT BY DEFAULT.

If the plaintiff appears and the claimant fails to appear or neglects or refuses to join issue under the direction of the court or justice within the time prescribed for pleading, the plaintiff shall have judgment by default.

(Added by Order June 10, 1980, eff. Jan. 1, 1981.)

RULE 726. JUDGMENT OF NON-SUIT.

If the plaintiff does not appear, he shall be nonsuited.

(Amended by Order June 10, 1980, eff. Jan. 1, 1981.)

RULE 727. PROCEEDINGS.

The proceedings and practice on the trial shall be as nearly as may be the same as in other cases before such court or justice.

(Amended by Order June 10, 1980, eff. Jan. 1, 1981.)

RULE 728. BURDEN OF PROOF.

If the property was taken from the possession of the claimant pursuant to the original writ, the burden of proof shall be on the plaintiff in the writ. If it was taken from the possession of the defendant in such writ, or any other person than the claimant, the burden of proof shall be on the claimant.

(Added by Order June 10, 1980, eff. Jan. 1, 1981.)

RULE 729. COPY OF WRIT EVIDENCE.

In all trials of the right of property, under the provisions of this section in any county other than that in which the writ issued under which the levy was made, the copy of the writ herein required to be returned by the officer making the levy shall be received in evidence in like manner as the original could be.

(Amended by Order June 10, 1980, eff. Jan. 1, 1981.)

RULE 730. FAILURE TO ESTABLISH TITLE.

Where any claimant has obtained possession of property, and shall ultimately fail to establish his right thereto, judgment may be rendered against him and his sureties for the value of the property, with legal interest thereon from the date of such bond. Such judgment shall be rendered in favor of the plaintiff or defendant in the writ, or of the several plaintiffs or defendants, if more than one, and shall fix the amount of the claim of each.

(Added by Order June 10, 1980, eff. Jan. 1, 1981.)

RULE 731. EXECUTION SHALL ISSUE.

If such judgment should not be satisfied by a return of the property, then after the expiration of ten days from the date of the judgment, execution shall issue thereon in the name of the plaintiff or defendant for the amount of the claim, or of all the plaintiffs or defendants for the sum of their several claims, provided the amount of such judgment shall inure to the benefit of any person who shall show superior right or title to the property claimed as against the claimant; but if such judgment be for a less amount than the sum of the several plaintiffs' or defendants' claims, then the respective rights and priorities of the several plaintiffs or defendants shall be fixed and adjusted in the judgment.

(Amended by Order June 10, 1980, eff. Jan. 1, 1981.)

RULE 732. RETURN OF PROPERTY BY CLAIMANT.

If, within ten days from the rendition of said judgment, the claimant shall return such property in as good condition as he received it, and pay for the use of the same together with the damages and costs, such delivery and payment shall operate as a satisfaction of such judgment.

(Added by Order June 10, 1980, eff. Jan. 1, 1981.)

RULE 733. CLAIM IS A RELEASE OF DAMAGES.

A claim made to the property, under the provisions of this section, shall operate as a release of all damages by the claimant against the officer who levied upon said property.

(Added by Order June 10, 1980, eff. Jan. 1, 1981.)

RULE 734. LEVY ON OTHER PROPERTY.

Proceedings for the trial of right of property under these rules shall in no case prevent the plaintiff in the writ from having a levy made upon any other property of the defendant.

(Amended by Order June 10, 1980, eff. Jan. 1, 1981.)

PART VII.
RULES RELATING SPECIAL PROCEEDINGS

SECTION 1.
PROCEDURES RELATED TO FORECLOSURES OF CERTAIN LIENS

RULE 735. FORECLOSURES REQUIRING A COURT ORDER.

735.1. Liens Affected.

Rule 736 provides the procedure for obtaining a court order, when required, to allow foreclosure of a lien containing a power of sale in the security instrument, dedicatory instrument, or declaration creating the lien, including a lien securing any of the following:

(a) a home equity loan, reverse mortgage, or home equity line of credit under article XVI, sections 50(a)(6), 50(k), and 50(t) of the Texas Constitution;

(b) a tax lien transfer or property tax loan under sections 32.06 and 32.065 of the Tax Code; or

(c) a property owners' association assessment under section 209.0092 of the Property Code.

735.2. Other Statutory and Contractual Foreclosure Provisions Unaltered.

A Rule 736 order does not alter any foreclosure requirement or duty imposed under applicable law or the terms of the loan agreement, contract, or lien sought to be foreclosed. The only issue to be determined in a Rule 736 proceeding is whether a party may obtain an order under Rule 736 to proceed with foreclosure under applicable law and the terms of the loan agreement, contract, or lien sought to be foreclosed.

735.3. Judicial Foreclosure Unaffected.

A Rule 736 order is not a substitute for a judgment for judicial foreclosure, but any loan agreement, contract, or lien that may be foreclosed using Rule 736 procedures may also be foreclosed by judgment in an action for judicial foreclosure.

(Adopted by Order Oct. 17, 2011, eff. Jan. 1, 2012; Order Dec. 30, 2011, eff. Jan 1, 2012.)

RULE 736. EXPEDITED ORDER PROCEEDING.

736.1. Application.

(a) *Where Filed.* An application for an expedited order allowing the foreclosure of a lien listed in Rule 735 to proceed must be filed in a county where all or part of the real property encumbered by the loan agreement, contract, or lien sought to be foreclosed is located or in a probate court with jurisdiction over proceedings involving the property.

(b) *Style.* An application must be styled "In re: Order for Foreclosure Concerning [state: property's mailing address] under Tex. R. Civ. P. 736."

(c) *When Filed.* An application may not be filed until the opportunity to cure has expired under applicable law and the loan agreement, contract, or lien sought to be foreclosed.

(d) *Contents.* The application must:

(1) Identify by name and last known address each of the following parties:

(A) "Petitioner" - any person legally authorized to prosecute the foreclosure;

(B) "Respondent" - according to the records of the holder or servicer of the loan agreement, contract, or lien sought to be foreclosed;

(i) for a home equity loan, reverse mortgage, or home equity line of credit, each person obligated to pay the loan agreement, contract, or lien sought to be foreclosed and each mortgagor, if any, of the loan agreement, contract, or lien sought to be foreclosed;

(ii) for a tax lien transfer or property tax loan, each person obligated to pay the loan agreement, contract, or lien sought to be foreclosed, each mortgagor, if any, of the loan agreement, contract, or lien sought to be foreclosed, each owner of the property, and the holder of any recorded preexisting first lien secured by the property;

(iii) for a property owners' association assessment, each person obligated to pay the loan agreement, contract, or lien sought to be foreclosed who has a current ownership interest in the property.

(2) Identify the property encumbered by the loan agreement, contract, or lien sought to be foreclosed by its commonly known street address and legal description.

(3) Describe or state:

(A) the type of lien listed in Rule 735 sought to be foreclosed and its constitutional or statutory reference;

(B) the authority of the party seeking foreclosure, whether as the servicer, beneficiary, lender, investor, property owners' association, or other person with authority to prosecute the foreclosure;

(C) each person obligated to pay the loan agreement, contract, or lien sought to be foreclosed;

(D) each mortgagor, if any, of the loan agreement, contract, or lien sought to be foreclosed who is not a maker or assumer of the underlying debt;

(E) as of a date that is not more than sixty days prior to the date the application is filed:

(i) if the default is monetary, the number of unpaid scheduled payments,

(ii) if the default is monetary, the amount required to cure the default,

(iii) if the default is non-monetary, the facts creating the default, and

(iv) if applicable, the total amount required to pay off the loan agreement, contract or lien;

(F) that the requisite notice or notices to cure the default has or have been mailed to each person as required under applicable law and the loan agreement, contract, or lien sought to be foreclosed and that the opportunity to cure has expired; and

(G) that before the application was filed, any other action required under applicable law and the loan agreement, contract, or lien sought to be foreclosed was performed.

(4) For a tax lien transfer or property tax loan, state all allegations required to be contained in the application in accordance with section 32.06(c-1)(1) of the Tax Code.

(5) Conspicuously state:

(A) that legal action is not being sought against the occupant of the property unless the occupant is also names as a respondent in the application; and

(B) that if the petitioner obtains a court order, the petitioner will proceed with a foreclosure of the property in accordance with applicable law and the terms of the loan agreement, contract, or lien sought to be foreclosed.

(6) Include an affidavit of material facts in accordance with Rule 166a(f) signed by the petitioner or the servicer describing the basis for foreclosure and, depending on the type of lien sought to be foreclosed, attach a legible copy of:

(A) the note, original recorded lien, or pertinent part of a property owners' association declaration or dedicatory instrument establishing the lien, and current assignment of the lien, if assigned;

(B) each notice required to be mailed to any person under applicable law and the loan agreement, contract, or lien sought to be foreclosed before the application was filed and proof of mailing of each notice; and

(C) for a tax lien transfer or property tax loan:

(i) the property owner's sworn document required under section 32.06(-1) of the Tax Code; and

(ii) the taxing authority's certified statement attesting to the transfer of the lien, required under section 32.06(b) of the Tax Code.

736.2. Costs.

All filing, citation, mailing, service, and other court costs and fees are costs of court and must be paid by petitioner at the time of filing an application with the clerk of the court.

736.3. Citation.

(a) *Issuance.*

(1) When the application is filed, the clerk must issue a separate citation for each respondent named in the application and one additional citation for the occupant of the property sought to be foreclosed.

(2) Each citation that is directed to a respondent must state that any response to the application is due the first Monday after the expiration of 38 days from the date the citation was placed in the custody of the U.S. Postal Service in accordance with the clerk's standard mailing procedures and state the date that the citation was placed in the custody of the U.S. Postal Service by the clerk.

(b) *Service and Return.*

(1) The clerk of the court must serve each citation, with a copy of the application attached, by both first class mail and certified mail. A citation directed to a respondent must be mailed to the respondent's last known address that is stated in the application. A citation directed to the occupant of the property sought to be foreclosed must be mailed to Occupant of [state: property's mailing address] at the address of the property sought to be foreclosed that is stated in the application.

(2) Concurrently with service, the clerk must complete a return of service in accordance with Rule 107, except that the return of service need not contain a return receipt. For a citation mailed by the clerk in accordance with (b)(1), the date of service is the date and time the citation was placed in the custody of the U.S. Postal Service in a properly addressed, postage prepaid envelope in accordance with the clerk's standard mailing procedures.

(3) The clerk must only charge one fee per respondent or occupant served under this rule.

736.4. Discovery.

No discovery is permitted in a Rule 736 proceeding.

736.5. Response.

(a) *Generally.* A respondent may file a response contesting the application.

(b) *Due Date.* Any response to the application is due the first Monday after the expiration of 38 days from the date the citation was placed in the custody of the U.S. Postal Service in accordance with the clerk's standard mailing procedures, as stated on the citation.

(c) *Form.* A response must be signed in accordance with Rule 57 and may be in the form of a general denial under Rule 92, except that a respondent must affirmatively plead:

(1) why the respondent believes a respondent did not sign a loan agreement document, if applicable, that is specifically identified by the respondent;

(2) why the respondent is not obligated for payment of the lien;

(3) why the number of months of alleged default or the reinstatement or pay off amounts are materially incorrect;

(4) why any document attached to the application is not a true and correct copy of the original; or

(5) proof of payment in accordance with Rule 95.

(d) *Other Claims.* A response may not state an independent claim for relief. The court must, without a hearing, strike and dismiss any counterclaim, cross claim, third party claim, intervention, or cause of action filed by any person in a Rule 736 proceeding.

736.6. Hearing Required When Response Filed.

The court must not conduct a hearing under this rule unless a response is filed. If a response is filed, the court must hold a hearing after reasonable notice to the parties. The hearing on the application must not be held earlier than 20 days or later than 30 days after a request for a hearing is made by any party. At the hearing, the petitioner has the burden to prove by affidavits on file or evidence presented the grounds for granting the order sought in the application.

736.7. Default When No Response Filed.

(a) If no response to the application is filed by the due date, the petitioner may file a motion and proposed order to obtain a default order. For the purposes of obtaining a default order, all facts alleged in the application and supported by the affidavit of material facts constitute prima facie evidence of the truth of the matters alleged.
(b) The court must grant the application by default order no later than 30 days after a motion is filed under (a) if the application complies with the requirements of Rule 736.1 and was properly served in accordance with Rule 736.3. The petitioner need not appear in court to obtain a default order.
(c) The return of service must be on file with the clerk of the court for at least 10 days before the court may grant the application by default.

736.8. Order.

(a) The court must issue an order granting the application if the petitioner establishes the basis for the foreclosure. Otherwise, the court must deny the application.
(b) An order granting the application must describe:
    (1) the material facts establishing the basis for foreclosure;
    (2) the property to be foreclosed by commonly known mailing address and legal description;
    (3) the name and last known address of each respondent subject to the order; and
    (4) the recording or indexing information of each lien to be foreclosed.
(c) An order granting or denying the application is not subject to a motion for rehearing, new trial, bill of review, or appeal. Any challenge to a Rule 736 order must be made in a suit filed in a separate, independent, original proceeding in a court of competent jurisdiction.

736.9. Effect of the Order.

An order is without prejudice and has no res judicata, collateral estoppel, estoppel by judgment, or other effect in any other judicial proceeding. After an order is obtained, a person may proceed with the foreclosure process under applicable law and the terms of the lien sought to be foreclosed.

736.10. Bankruptcy.

If a respondent provides proof to the clerk of the court that respondent filed bankruptcy before an order is signed, the proceeding under this rule must be abated so long as the automatic stay is effective.

736.11. Automatic Stay and Dismissal if Independent Suit Filed.

(a) A proceeding or order under this rule is automatically stayed if a respondent files a separate, original proceeding in a court of competent jurisdiction that puts in issue any matter related to the origination, servicing, or enforcement of the loan agreement, contract, or lien sought to be foreclosed prior to 5:00 p.m. on the Monday before the scheduled foreclosure sale.
(b) Respondent must give prompt notice of the filing of the suit to petitioner or petitioner's attorney and the foreclosure trustee or substitute trustee by any reasonable means necessary to stop the scheduled foreclosure sale.
(c) Within ten days of filing suit, the respondent must file a motion and proposed order to dismiss or vacate with the clerk of the court in which the application was filed giving notice that respondent has filed an original proceeding contesting the right to foreclose in a court of competent jurisdiction. If no order has been signed, the court must dismiss a pending proceeding. If an order has been signed, the court must vacate the Rule 736 order.
(d) If the automatic stay under this rule is in effect, any foreclosure sale of the property is void. Within 10 business days of notice that the foreclosure sale was void, the trustee or substitute trustee must return to the buyer of the foreclosed property the purchase price paid by the buyer.
(e) The court may enforce the Rule 736 process under chapters 9 and 10 of the Civil Practices and Remedies Code.

736.12. Attachment of Order to Trustee's Deed.

A conformed copy of the order must be attached to the trustee or substitute trustee's foreclosure deed.

736.13. Promulgated Forms.

The Supreme Court of Texas may promulgate forms that conform to this rule.

(Added by Order Jan. 27, 1998. Amended by Order May 15, 1998, eff. May 15, 1998; Order effective April 15, 2000; Order Oct. 17, 2011, eff. Jan. 1, 2012; Order Dec. 30, 2011, eff. Jan 1, 2012.)

Comment to 2011 change

Rules 735 and 736 have been rewritten and expanded to cover property owners' associations' assessment liens, in accordance with amendments to chapter 209 of the Property Code. Rule 735.1 makes the expedited procedures of Rule 736 available only when the lienholder has a power of sale but a court order is nevertheless required by law to foreclose the lien. Rule 735.2 makes clear that Rule 736 is procedural only and does not affect other contractual or legal rights or duties. Any lien which can be foreclosed under Rule 736 may also be foreclosed in an action for judicial foreclosure, as Rule 735.3 states, but no lienholder is required to obtain both a Rule 736 order and a judgment for judicial foreclosure. The requirement of conspicuousness in Rule 736.1(d)(5) has reference to section 1.201(b)(10) of the Business and Commerce Code.

Forms for Expedited Foreclosure Proceedings (Pursuant to the Act of May 27, 2013, 83rd Leg., R.S., c. 1044 (HB 2978) and section 22.018 of the Texas Government Code, the Supreme Court of Texas approves the following set of forms for use in expedited foreclosure proceedings under Texas Rule of Civil Procedure 736.)

RULES 737-755. [REPEALED.]

(Repealed by Order Feb 12, 2013, eff. Aug. 31, 2013; Order April 15, 2013, eff. Aug. 31, 2013.)

SECTION 4.
PARTITION REAL ESTATE

RULE 756. PETITION.

The plaintiff's petition shall state:

(a) The names and residence, if known, of each of the other joint owners, or joint claimants, of such property.

(b) The share or interest which the plaintiff and the other joint owners, or joint claimants, of same own or claim so far as known to the plaintiff.

(c) The land sought to be partitioned shall be so described as that the same may be distinguished from any other and the estimated value thereof stated.

RULE 757. CITATION AND SERVICE.

Upon the filing of a petition for partition, the clerk shall issue citation for each of the joint owners, or joint claimants, named therein, as in other cases, and such citations shall be served in the manner and for the time provided for the service of citations in other cases.

RULE 758. WHERE DEFENDANT IS UNKNOWN OR RESIDENCE IS UNKNOWN.

If the plaintiff, his agent or attorney, at the commencement of any suit, or during the progress thereof, for the partition of land, shall make affidavit that an undivided portion of the land described in plaintiff's petition in said suit is owned by some person unknown to affiant, or that the place of residence of any known party owning an interest in land sought to be partitioned is unknown to affiant, the Clerk of the Court shall issue citation for publication, conforming to the requirements of Rules 114 and 115, and served in accordance with the directions of Rule 116. In case of unknown residence or party, the affidavit shall include a statement that after due diligence plaintiff and the affiant have been unable to ascertain the name or locate the residence of such party, as the case may be, and in such case it shall be the duty of the court trying the action to inquire into the sufficiency of the diligence so stated before granting any judgment.

(Amended by Order July 20, 1954, eff. Jan. 1, 1955; Dec. 19, 1984, eff. April 1, 1985.)

RULE 759. JUDGMENT WHERE DEFENDANT CITED BY PUBLICATION.

When the defendant has been duly cited by publication in accordance with the preceding rule, and no appearance is entered within the time prescribed for pleadings, the court shall appoint an attorney to defend in behalf of such owner or owners, and proceed as in other causes where service is made by publication. It shall be the special duty of the court in all cases to see that its decree protects the rights of the unknown parties thereto. The judge of the court shall fix the fee of the attorney so appointed, which shall be entered and collected as costs against said unknown owner or owners.

RULE 760. COURT SHALL DETERMINE, WHAT.

Upon the hearing of the cause, the court shall determine the share or interest of each of the joint owners or claimants in the real estate sought to be divided, and all questions of law or equity affecting the title to such land which may arise.

RULE 761. APPOINTMENT OF COMMISSIONERS.

The court shall determine before entering the decree of partition whether the property, or any part thereof, is susceptible of partition; and, if the court determines that the whole, or any part of such property is susceptible of partition, then the court for that part of such property held to be susceptible of partition shall enter a decree directing the partition of such real estate, describing the same, to be made in accordance with the respective shares or interests of each of such parties entitled thereto, specify in such decree the share or interest of each party, and shall appoint three or more competent and disinterested persons as commissioners to make such partition in accordance with such decree and the law, a majority of which commissioners may act.

RULE 762. WRIT OF PARTITION.

The clerk shall issue a writ a partition, directed to the sheriff or any constable of the county, commanding such sheriff or constable to notify each of the commissioners of their appointment as such, and shall accompany such writ with a certified copy of the decree of the court directing the partition.

RULE 763. SERVICE OF WRIT OF PARTITION.

The writ of partition shall be served by reading the same to each of the persons named therein as commissioners, and by delivering to any one of them the accompanying certified copy of the decree of the court.

RULE 764. MAY APPOINT SURVEYOR.

The court may, should it be deemed necessary, appoint a surveyor to assist the commissioners in making the partition, in which case the writ of partition shall name such surveyor, and shall be served upon him by reading the same to him.

RULE 765. RETURN OF WRIT.

A writ of partition, unless otherwise directed by the court, shall be made returnable twenty days from date of service on the commissioner last served; and the officer serving it shall endorse thereon the time and manner of such service.

RULE 766. SHALL PROCEED TO PARTITION.

The commissioners, or a majority of them, shall proceed to partition the real estate described in the decree of the court, in accordance with the directions contained in such decree and with the provisions of law and these rules.

RULE 767. MAY CAUSE SURVEY.

If the commissioners deem it necessary, they may cause to be surveyed the real estate to be partitioned into several tracts or parcels.

RULE 768. SHALL DIVIDE REAL ESTATE.

The commissioners shall divide the real estate to be partitioned into as many shares as there are persons entitled thereto, as determined by the court, each share to contain one or more tracts or parcels, as the commissioners may think proper, having due regard in the division to the situation, quantity and advantages of each share, so that the shares may be equal in value, as nearly as may be, in proportion to the respective interests of the parties entitled. The commissioners shall then proceed by lot to set apart to each of the parties entitled one of said shares, as determined by the decrees of the court.

RULE 769. REPORT OF COMMISSIONERS.

When the commissioners have completed the partition, they shall report the same in writing and under oath to the court, which report shall show:

(a) The property divided, describing the same.

(b) The several tracts or parcels into which the same was divided by them, describing each particularly

(c) The number of shares and the land which constitutes each share, and the estimated value of each share.

(d) The allotment of each share.

(e) The report shall be accompanied by such field notes and maps as may be necessary to make the same intelligible. The clerk shall immediately mail written notice of the filing of the report to all parties.

(Amended by Order April 24, 1990, eff. Sept. 1, 1990.)

RULE 770. PROPERTY INCAPABLE OF DIVISION.

Should the court be of the opinion that a fair and equitable division of the real estate, or any part thereof, cannot be made, it shall order a sale of so much as is incapable of partition, which sale shall be for cash, or upon such other terms as the court may direct, and shall be made as under execution or by private or public sale through a receiver, if the court so order, and the proceeds thereof shall be returned into court and be partitioned among the persons entitled thereto, according to their respective interests.

(Amended by Order Oct. 12, 1949, eff. March 1, 1950.)

RULE 771. OBJECTIONS TO REPORT.

Either party to the suit may file objections to any report of the commissioners in partition within thirty days of the date the report is filed, and in such case a trial of the issues thereon shall be had as in other cases. If the report be found to be erroneous in any material respect, or unequal and unjust, the same shall be rejected, and other commissioners shall be appointed by the Court, and the same proceedings had as in the first instance.

(Amended by Order April 24, 1990, eff. Sept. 1, 1990.)

SECTION 5.
PARTITION OF PERSONAL PROPERTY

RULE 772. PROCEDURE.

An action seeking partition of personal property as authorized by Section 23.001, Texas Property Code, shall be commenced in the same manner as other civil suits, and the several owners or claimants of such property shall be cited as in other cases.

(Amended by Order July 15, 1987, eff. Jan. 1, 1988.)

RULE 773. VALUE ASCERTAINED.

The separate value of each article of such personal property, and the allotment in kind to which each owner is entitled, shall be ascertained by the court, with or without a jury.

RULE 774. DECREE OF COURT EXECUTED.

When partition in kind of personal property is ordered by the judgment of the court, a writ shall be issued in accordance with such judgment, commanding the sheriff or constable of the county where the property may be to put the parties forthwith in possession of the property allotted to each respectively.

RULE 775. PROPERTY SOLD.

When personal property will not admit of a fair and equitable partition, the court shall ascertain the proportion to which each owner thereof is entitled, and order the property to be sold, and execution shall be issued to the sheriff or any constable of the county where the property may be describing such property and commanding such officer to sell the same as in other cases of execution, and pay over the proceeds of sale to the parties entitled thereto, in the proportion ascertained by the judgment of the court.

SECTION 6. PARTITION:
MISCELLANEOUS PROVISIONS

RULE 776. CONSTRUCTION.

No provision of the statutes or rules relating to partition shall affect the mode of proceeding prescribed by law for the partition of estates of decedents among the heirs and legatees, nor preclude partition in any other manner authorized by the rules of equity, which rules shall govern in proceedings for partition in all respects not provided for by law or these rules.

RULE 777. PLEADING AND PRACTICE.

The same rules of pleading, practice and evidence which govern in other civil actions shall govern in suits for partition, when not in conflict with any provisions of the law or these rules relating to partition.

RULE 778. COSTS.

The court shall adjudge the costs in a partition suit to be paid by each party to whom a share has been allotted in proportion to the value of such share.

SECTION 7.
QUO WARRANTO

RULE 779. JOINDER OF PARTIES.

When it appears to the court or judge that the several rights of divers parties to the same office or franchise may properly be determined on one information, the court or judge may give leave to join all such persons in the same information in order to try their respective rights to such office or franchise.

RULE 780. CITATION TO ISSUE.

When such information is filed, the clerk shall issue citation as in civil actions, commanding the defendant to appear and answer the relator in an information in the nature of a quo warranto.

RULE 781. PROCEEDINGS AS IN CIVIL CASES.

Every person or corporation who shall be cited as hereinbefore provided shall be entitled to all the rights in the trial and investigation of the matters alleged against him, as in cases of trial of civil cases in this State. Either party may prosecute an appeal or writ of error from any judgment rendered, as in other civil cases, subject, however, to the provisions of Rule 42, Texas Rules of Appellate Procedure, and the appellate court shall give preference to such case, and hear and determine the same as early as practicable.

(Amended by Order Aug. 18, 1947, eff. Dec. 31, 1947; April 24, 1990, eff. Sept. 1, 1990.)

RULE 782. REMEDY CUMULATIVE.

The remedy and mode of procedure hereby prescribed shall be construed to be cumulative of any now existing.

SECTION 8.
TRESPASS TO TRY TITLE

RULE 783. REQUISITES OF PETITION.

The petition shall state:

(a) The real names of the plaintiff and defendant and their residences, if known.

(b) A description of the premises by metes and bounds, or with sufficient certainty to identify the same, so that from such description possession thereof may be delivered, and state the county or counties in which the same are situated.

(c) The interest which the plaintiff claims in the premises, whether it be a fee simple or other estate; and, if he claims an undivided interest, the petition shall state the same and the amount thereof.

(d) That the plaintiff was in possession of the premises or entitled to such possession.

(e) That the defendant afterward unlawfully entered upon and dispossessed him of such premises, stating the date, and withholds from him the possession thereof.

(f) If rents and profits or damages are claimed, such facts as show the plaintiff to be entitled thereto and the amount thereof.

(g) It shall conclude with a prayer for the relief sought.

RULE 784. THE POSSESSOR SHALL BE DEFENDANT.

The defendant in the action shall be the person in possession if the premises are occupied, or some person claiming title thereto in case they are unoccupied.

RULE 785. MAY JOIN AS DEFENDANTS, WHEN.

The plaintiff may join as a defendant with the person in possession, any other person who, as landlord, remainderman, reversioner or otherwise, may claim title to the premises, or any part thereof, adversely to the plaintiff.

RULE 786. WARRANTOR, ETC., MAY BE MADE A PARTY.

When a party is sued for lands, the real owner or warrantor may make himself, or may be made, a party defendant in the suit, and shall be entitled to make such defense as if he had been the original defendant in the action.

RULE 787. LANDLORD MAY BECOME DEFENDANT.

When such action shall be commenced against a tenant in possession, the landlord may enter himself as the defendant, or he may be made a party on motion of such tenant; and he shall be entitled to make the same defense as if the suit had been originally commenced against him.

RULE 788. MAY FILE PLEA OF "NOT GUILTY" ONLY.

The defendant in such action may file only the plea of "not guilty," which shall state in substance that he is not guilty of the injury complained of in the petition filed by the plaintiff against him, except that if he claims an allowance for improvements, he shall state the facts entitling him to the same.

RULE 789. PROOF UNDER SUCH PLEA.

Under such plea of "not guilty" the defendant may give in evidence any lawful defense to the action except the defense of limitations, which shall be specially pleaded.

RULE 790. ANSWER TAKEN AS ADMITTING POSSESSION.

Such plea or any other answer to the merits shall be an admission by the defendant, for the purpose of that action, that he was in possession of the premises sued for, or that he claimed title thereto at the time of commencing the action, unless he states distinctly in his answer the extent of his possession or claim, in which case it shall be an admission to such extent only.

RULE 791. MAY DEMAND ABSTRACT OF TITLE.

After answer filed, either party may, by notice in writing, duly served on the opposite party or his attorney of record, not less than ten days before the trial of the cause, demand an abstract in writing of the claim or title to the premises in question upon which he relies.

RULE 792. TIME TO FILE ABSTRACT.

Such abstract of title shall be filed with the papers of the cause that within thirty days after the service of the notice, or within such further time that the court on good cause shown may grant; and in default thereof, the court may, after notice and hearing prior to the beginning of trial, order that no written instruments which are evidence of the claim or title of such opposite party be given on trial.

(Amended by Order July 15, 1987, eff. Jan. 1, 1988; April 24, 1990, eff. Sept. 1, 1990.)

RULE 793. ABSTRACT SHALL STATE, WHAT.

The abstract mentioned in the two preceding rules shall state:

(a) The nature of each document or written instrument intended to be used as evidence and its date;

(b) If a contract or conveyance, its date, the parties thereto and the date of the proof of acknowledgment, and before what officer the same was made; and

(c) Where recorded, stating the book and page of the record.

(d) If not recorded in the county when the trial is had, copies of such instrument, with the names of the subscribing witnesses, shall be included. If such unrecorded instrument be lost or destroyed it shall be sufficient to state the nature of such instrument and its loss or destruction.

RULE 794. AMENDED ABSTRACT.

The court may allow either party to file an amended abstract of title, under the same rules, which authorize the amendment of pleadings so far as they are applicable; but in all cases the documentary evidence of title shall at the trial be confined to the matters contained in the abstract of title.

RULE 795. RULES IN OTHER CASES OBSERVED.

The trial shall be conducted according to the rules of pleading, practice and evidence in other cases in the district court and conformable to the principles of trial by ejectment, except as otherwise provided by these rules.

RULE 796. SURVEYOR APPOINTED, ETC.

The judge of the court may, either in term time or in vacation, at his own discretion, or on motion of either party to the action appoint a surveyor, who shall survey the premises in controversy pursuant to the order of the court, and report his action under oath to such court. If said report be not rejected for good cause shown, the same shall be admitted as evidence on the trial.

RULE 797. SURVEY UNNECESSARY, WHEN.

Where there is no dispute as to the lines or boundaries of the land in controversy, or where the defendant admits that he is in possession of the lands or tenements included in the plaintiff's claim, or title, an order of survey shall be unnecessary.

RULE 798. COMMON SOURCE OF TITLE.

It shall not be necessary for the plaintiff to deraign title beyond a common source. Proof of a common source may be made by the plaintiff by certified copies of the deeds showing a chain of title to the defendant emanating from and under such common source. Before any such certified copies shall be read in evidence, they shall be filed with the papers of the suit three days before the trial, and the adverse party served with notice of such filing as in other cases. Such certified copies shall not be evidence of title in the defendant unless offered in evidence by him. The plaintiff may make any legal objection to such certified copies, or the originals thereof, when introduced by the defendant.

RULE 799. JUDGMENT BY DEFAULT.

If the defendant, who has been personally served with citation according to law or these rules fails to appear and answer by himself or attorney within the time prescribed by law or these rules for other actions in the district court, then judgment by default may be entered against him and in favor of the plaintiff for the title to the premises, or the possession thereof, or for both, according to the petition, and for all costs, without any proof of title by the plaintiff.

RULE 800. PROOF EX PARTE.

If the defendant has been cited only by publication, and fails to appear and answer by himself, or by attorney of his own selection, or if any defendant, having answered, fails to appear by himself or attorney when the case is called for trial on its merits, the plaintiff shall make such proof as will entitle him prima facie to recover, whereupon the proper judgment shall be entered.

RULE 801. WHEN DEFENDANT CLAIMS PART ONLY.

Where the defendant claims part of the premises only, the answer shall be equivalent to a disclaimer of the balance.

RULE 802. WHEN PLAINTIFF PROVES PART.

Where the defendant claims the whole premises, and the plaintiff shows himself entitled to recover part, the plaintiff shall recover such part and costs.

RULE 803. MAY RECOVER A PART.

When there are two or more plaintiffs or defendants any one or more of the plaintiffs may recover against one or more of the defendants the premises, or any part thereof, or any interest therein, or damages, according to the rights of the parties.

RULE 804. THE JUDGMENT.

Upon the finding of the jury, or of the court where the case is tried by the court, in favor of the plaintiff for the whole or any part of the premises in controversy, the judgment shall be that the plaintiff recover of the defendant the title or possession, or both, as the case may be, of such premises, describing them, and where he recovers the possession, that he have his writ of possession.

RULE 805. DAMAGES.

Where it is alleged and proved that one of the parties is in possession of the premises, the court or jury, if they find for the adverse party, shall assess the damages for the use and occupation of the premises. If special injury to the property be alleged and proved, the damages for such injury shall also be assessed, and the proper judgment shall be entered therefor, on which execution may issue.

RULE 806. CLAIM FOR IMPROVEMENTS.

When the defendant or person in possession has claimed an allowance for improvements in accordance with Sections 22.021-22.024, Texas Property Code, the claim for use and occupation and damages mentioned in the preceding rule shall be considered and acted on in connection with such claim by the defendant or person in possession.

(Amended by Order Dec. 5, 1983, eff. April 1, 1984; July 15, 1987, eff. Jan. 1, 1988.)

RULE 807. JUDGMENT WHEN CLAIM FOR IMPROVEMENTS IS MADE.

When a claim for improvements is successfully made under Sections 22.021 PROP.-22.024, Texas Property Code, the judgment shall recite the estimated value of the premises without the improvements, and shall also include the conditions, stipulations and directions contained in Sections 22.021-22.024., Texas Property Code so far as applicable to the case before the court.

(Amended by Order Dec. 5, 1983, eff. April 1, 1984; July 15, 1987, eff. Jan. 1, 1988.)

RULE 808. THESE RULES SHALL NOT GOVERN, WHEN.

Nothing in Sections 22.001-22.045, Texas Property Code, shall be so construed as to alter, impair or take away the rights of parties, as arising under the laws in force before the introduction of the common law, but the same shall be decided by the principles of the law under which the same accrued, or by which the same were regulated or in any manner affected.

(Amended by Order Dec. 5, 1983, eff. April 1, 1984; July 15, 1987, eff. Jan. 1, 1988.)

RULE 809. THESE RULES SHALL NOT GOVERN, WHEN.

Nothing in these rules relating to trespass to try title shall be so construed as to alter, impair or take away the rights of parties, as arising under the laws in force before the introduction of the common law, but the same shall be decided by the principles of the law under which the same accrued, or by which the same were regulated or in any manner affected.

SECTION 9.
SUITS AGAINST NON-RESIDENTS

RULE 810. REQUISITES OF PLEADINGS.

The petition in actions authorized by section 17.003, Civil Practice and Remedies Code, shall state the real names of the plaintiff and defendant, and shall describe the property involved with sufficient certainty to identify the same, the interest which the plaintiff claims, and such proceedings shall be had in such action as may be necessary to fully settle and determine the question of right or title in and to said property between the parties to said suit, and to decree the title or right of the party entitled thereto; and the court may issue the appropriate order to carry such decree, judgment or order into effect; and whenever such petition has been duly filed and citation thereon has been duly served by publication as required by Rules 114-116, the plaintiff may, at any time prior to entering the decree by leave of court first had and obtained, file amended and supplemental pleadings that do not subject additional property to said suit without the necessity of reciting the defendants so cited as aforesaid.

(Amended by Order Dec. 5, 1983, eff. April 1, 1984; July 15, 1987, eff. Jan. 1, 1988.)

RULE 811. SERVICE BY PUBLICATION IN ACTIONS UNDER SECTION 17.003 CIV. PRAC. & REM, CIVIL PRACTICE AND REMEDIES CODE.

In actions authorized by Section 17.003, Civil Practice and Remedies Code, service on the defendant or defendants may be made by publication as is provided by Rules 114-116 or by service of notice of the character and in the manner provided by Rule 108.

(Amended by Order Dec. 5, 1983, eff. April 1, 1984; July 15, 1987, eff. Jan. 1, 1988.)

RULE 812. NO JUDGMENT BY DEFAULT.

No judgment by default shall be taken in such case when service has been had by publication, but in such case the facts entitling the plaintiff to judgment shall be exhibited to the court on the trial; and a statement of facts shall be filed as provided by law and these rules in suits against nonresidents of this State served by publication, where no appearance has been made by them.

(Amended by Order Oct. 12, 1949, eff. March 1, 1950.)

RULE 813. SUIT TO EXTINGUISH LIEN.

If said suit shall be for the extinguishment of a lien or claim for money on said property that may be held by the defendant, the amount thereof, with interest, shall be ascertained by the court; and the same deposited in the registry of the court, subject to the drawn by the parties entitled thereto; but in such case no decree shall be entered until said sum is deposited; which fact shall be noted in said decree.

PART VIII.
CLOSING RULES

RULE 814. EFFECTIVE DATE.

These rules shall take effect on September 1st, 1941. They shall govern all proceedings in actions brought after they take effect, and also all further proceedings in actions then pending, except to the extent that in the opinion of the court their application in a particular action pending when the rules take effect would not be feasible or would work injustice, in which event the former procedure shall apply. All things properly done under any previously existing rule or statutes prior to the taking effect of these rules shall be treated as valid. Where citation or other process is issued and served in compliance with existing rules or laws prior to the taking effect of these rules, the party upon whom such citation or other process has been served shall have the time provided for under such previously existing rules or laws in which to comply therewith.

RULE 815. SUBSTANTIVE RIGHTS UNAFFECTED.

These rules shall not be construed to enlarge or diminish any substantive rights or obligations of any parties to any civil action.

RULE 816. JURISDICTION AND VENUE UNAFFECTED.

These rules shall not be construed to extend or limit the jurisdiction of the courts of the State of Texas nor the venue of actions therein.

RULE 817. [RENUMBERED]

(Renumbered as rule 3a Dec. 5, 1983, eff. April 1, 1984.)

RULE 818. REFERENCE TO FORMER STATUTES.

Wherever any statute or rule refers to any practice or procedure in any law, laws, statute or statutes, or to a title, chapter, section, or article of the statutes, or contains any reference of any such nature, and the matter referred to has been supplanted in whole or in part by these rules, every such reference shall be deemed to be to the pertinent part or parts of these rules.

RULE 819. PROCEDURE CONTINUED.

All procedure prescribed by statutes of the State of Texas not specifically listed in the accompanying enumeration of repealed articles shall, insofar as the same is not inconsistent with the provisions of these rules, continue in accordance with the provisions of such statutes as rules of court. In case of inconsistency between the provisions of these rules and any statutory procedure not specifically listed as repealed, these rules shall apply.

RULE 820. WORKERS' COMPENSATION LAW.

All portions of the Workers' Compensation Law, Articles 8306-8309-1, Revised Civil Statutes, and amendments thereto, which relate to matters of practice and procedure are hereby adopted and retained in force and effect as rules of court.

(Amended by Order Dec. 5, 1983, eff. April 1, 1984.)

RULE 821. PRIOR COURT RULES REPEALED.

These rules shall supersede all Court Rules heretofore promulgated for any court; and all of said prior Court Rules are hereby repealed; provided, however, any rules of procedure heretofore adopted by a particular county or district court or by any Court of Appeals which were not of general application but were solely to regulate procedure in the particular court promulgating such rules are to remain in force and effect insofar as they are not inconsistent with these rules.

(Amended by Order Dec. 5, 1983, eff. April 1, 1984.)

RULE 822. TITLE.

These rules may be known and cited as the Texas Rules of Civil Procedure.

Texas Rules of Appellate Procedure

Adopted effective Sept. 1, 1997 including amendments received through January 1, 2019.

SECTION ONE.
GENERAL PROVISIONS

RULE 1. SCOPE OF RULES; LOCAL RULES OF COURTS OF APPEALS

1.1. Scope.

These rules govern procedure in appellate courts and before appellate judges and post-trial procedure in trial courts in criminal cases.

1.2. Local Rules.

(a) Promulgation. A court of appeals may promulgate rules governing its practice that are not inconsistent with these rules. Local rules governing civil cases must first be approved by the Supreme Court. Local rules governing criminal cases must first be approved by the Court of Criminal Appeals.

(b) Copies. The clerk must provide a copy of the court's local rules to anyone who requests it.

(c) Party's Noncompliance. A court must not dismiss an appeal for noncompliance with a local rule without giving the noncomplying party notice and a reasonable opportunity to cure the noncompliance.

(Adopted by Order eff. Sept. 1, 1997.)

Comment to 1997 change: Subdivision 1.1 is simplified without substantive change. Subdivision 1.2 is amended to make clear that any person is entitled to a copy of local rules. Paragraph 1.2(c), restricting dismissal of a case for noncompliance with a local rule, is added.

RULE 2. SUSPENSION OF RULES.

On a party's motion or on its own initiative an appellate court may—to expedite a decision or for other good cause—suspend a rule's operation in a particular case and order a different procedure; but a court must not construe this rule to suspend any provision in the Code of Criminal Procedure or to alter the time for perfecting an appeal in a civil case.

Comment to 1997 change: Former subdivision (a) regarding appellate court jurisdiction is deleted. The power to suspend rules is extended to civil cases. Other nonsubstantive changes are made.

RULE 3. DEFINITIONS; UNIFORM TERMINOLOGY

3.1. Definitions.

(a) Appellant means a party taking an appeal to an appellate court.

(b) Appellate court means the courts of appeals, the Court of Criminal Appeals, and the Supreme Court.

(c) Appellee means a party adverse to an appellant.

(d) Applicant means a person seeking relief by a habeas corpus in a criminal case.

(e) Petitioner means a party petitioning the Supreme Court or the Court of Criminal Appeals for review.

(f) Relator means a person seeking relief in an original proceeding in an appellate court other than by habeas corpus in a criminal case.

(g) Reporter or court reporter means the court reporter or court recorder.

(h) Respondent means:

(1) a party adverse to a petitioner in the Supreme Court or the Court of Criminal Appeals; or

(2) a party against whom relief is sought in an original proceeding in an appellate court.

3.2. Uniform Terminology in Criminal Cases.

In documents filed in criminal appeals, the parties are the State and the appellant. But if the State has appealed under **Article 44.01 of the Code of Criminal Procedure**, the defendant is the appellee. Otherwise, papers should use real names for parties, and such labels as appellee, petitioner, respondent, and movant should be avoided unless necessary for clarity. In habeas corpus proceedings, the person for whose relief the writ is requested is the applicant; **Code of Criminal Procedure article 11.13.**

(Adopted by Order eff. Sept. 1, 1997.)

Comment to 1997 change: The definition of court below and the reference to "suing out a writ of error to the court of appeals," are deleted as those terms are no longer used in these rules. Other changes are made.

RULE 4. TIME AND NOTICE PROVISIONS

4.1. Computing Time.

(a) In General. The day of an act, event, or default after which a designated period begins to run is not included when computing a period prescribed or allowed by these rules, by court order, or by statute. The last day of the period is included, but if that day is a Saturday, Sunday, or legal holiday, the period extends to the end of the next day that is not a Saturday, Sunday, or legal holiday.

(b) Clerk's Office Closed or Inaccessible. If the act to be done is filing a document, and if the clerk's office where the document is to be filed is closed or inaccessible during regular hours on the last day for filing the document, the period for filing the document extends to the end of the next day when the clerk's office is open and accessible. The closing or inaccessibility of the clerk's office may be proved by a certificate of the clerk or counsel, by a party's affidavit, or by other satisfactory proof, and may be controverted in the same manner.

4.2. No Notice of Trial Court's Judgment in Civil Case.

(a) Additional Time to File Documents.

(1) In general. If a party affected by a judgment or other appealable order has not—within 20 days after the judgment or order was signed—either received the notice required by Texas Rule of Civil Procedure 306a.3 or acquired actual knowledge of the signing, then a period that, under these rules, runs from the signing will begin for that party on the earlier of the date when the party receives notice or acquires actual knowledge of the signing. But in no event may the periods begin more than 90 days after the judgment or order was signed.

(2) Exception for restricted appeal. Subparagraph (1) does not extend the time for perfecting a restricted appeal.

(b) Procedure to Gain Additional Time. The procedure to gain additional time is governed by Texas Rule of Civil Procedure 306a.5.

(c) The Court's Order. After hearing the motion, the trial court must sign a written order that finds the date when the party or the party's attorney first either received notice or acquired actual knowledge that the judgment or order was signed.

4.3. Periods Affected by Modified Judgment in Civil Case.

(a) During Plenary-Power Period. If a judgment is modified in any respect while the trial court retains plenary power, a period that, under these rules, runs from the date when the judgment is signed will run from the date when the modified judgment is signed.

(b) After Plenary Power Expires. If the trial court corrects or reforms the judgment under > Texas Rule of Civil Procedure 316 after expiration of the trial court's plenary power, all periods provided in these rules that run from the date the judgment is signed run from the date the corrected judgment is signed for complaints that would not apply to the original judgment.

4.4. Periods Affected When Process Served by Publication.

If process was served by publication and if a motion for new trial was filed under Texas Rule of Civil Procedure 329 more than 30 days after the judgment was signed, a period that, under these rules, runs from the date when the judgment is signed will be computed as if the judgment were signed on the date when the motion for new trial was filed.

4.5. No Notice of Judgment or Order of Appellate Court; Effect on Time to File Certain Documents.

(a) Additional Time to File Documents. A party may move for additional time to file a motion for rehearing or en banc reconsideration in the court of appeals, a petition for review, or a petition for discretionary review, if the party did not—until after the time expired for filing the document—either receive notice of the judgment or order from the clerk or acquire actual knowledge of the rendition of the judgment or order.

(b) Procedure to Gain Additional Time. The motion must state the earliest date when the party or the party's attorney received notice or acquired actual knowledge that the judgment or order had been rendered. The motion must be filed within 15 days of that date but in no event more than 90 days after the date of the judgment or order.

(c) Where to File.

(1) A motion for additional time to file a motion for rehearing or en banc reconsideration in the court of appeals must be filed in and ruled on by the court of appeals in which the case is pending.

(2) A motion for additional time to file a petition for review must be filed in and ruled on by the Supreme Court.

(3) A motion for additional time to file a petition for discretionary review must be filed in and ruled on by the Court of Criminal Appeals.

(d) Order of the Court. If the court finds that the motion for additional time was timely filed and the party did not—within the time for filing the motion for rehearing or en banc reconsideration, petition for review, or petition for discretionary review, as the case may be—receive the notice or have actual knowledge of the judgment or order, the court must grant the motion. If the court grants the motion, the time for filing the document will begin to run on the date when the court grants the motion.

(Adopted by Order eff. Sept. 1, 1997. Amended by Order Dec. 23, 2002 eff. Jan. 1, 2003; Order Aug. 20, 2008, eff. Sept. 1, 2008.)

Comment to 2002 change: Subdivision 4.5 is amended to clarify that a party may obtain additional time to file documents when the party fails to receive notice not only of an appellate court judgment, but of an appellate court order—such as one denying a motion for rehearing—that triggers the appeal period.

Comment to 2008 change: Subdivision 4.5 is changed, consistent with other changes in the rules, to specifically address a motion for en banc reconsideration and treat it as a motion for rehearing.

Rule 4.6. No Notice of Trial Court's Order on Motion for Forensic DNA Testing

(a) *Additional Time to File Notice of Appeal.* Notwithstanding Rules 26.2 and 26.3, a defendant may move for additional time to file a notice of appeal under Code of Criminal Procedure chapter 64 (Motion for Forensic DNA Testing) if the defendant neither received notice nor acquired actual knowledge that the trial judge signed an appealable order before the time for filing a notice of appeal had expired.

(b) *Contents of Motion for Additional Time.* The motion must be in writing and sworn, state the earliest date when the defendant first received notice or acquired actual knowledge that the appealable order had been signed, and comply with Rule 10.5(b)(2).

(c) *When and Where to File.*

(1) The motion must be filed within 30 days of the date upon which the defendant first received notice or acquired actual knowledge of the trial court's signing of the appealable order. But in no event may the motion be filed more than 120 days after the date the appealable order was signed.

(2) The motion must be filed in the proper court of appeals.

(d) *Order of the Court.* The court of appeals must grant a motion for additional time if it finds that the defendant neither received notice nor acquired actual knowledge of the trial judge's signing of an appealable order before the time for filing a notice of appeal had expired and that the defendant timely filed the motion for additional time. The time for filing the document will begin to run on the date when the court grants the motion.

(Adopted by Tex. Sup. Ct. Misc. Docket No. 16-9061 June 13, 2017, eff. Sept. 1, 2017.)

RULE 5. FEES IN CIVIL CASES

A party who is not excused by statute or these rules from paying costs must pay—at the time an item is presented for filing—whatever fees are required by statute or Supreme Court order. The appellate court may enforce this rule by any order that is just.

(Adopted by Order eff. Sept. 1, 1997.)

Comment to 1997 change: This is former Rule 13. The rule is simplified. The fees an appellate court may charge in a civil case are now specified by Supreme Court order.

RULE 6. REPRESENTATION BY COUNSEL

6.1. Lead Counsel.

(a) For Appellant. Unless another attorney is designated, lead counsel for an appellant is the attorney whose signature first appears on the notice of appeal.

(b) For a Party Other Than Appellant. Unless another attorney is designated, lead counsel for a party other than an appellant is the attorney whose signature first appears on the first document filed in the appellate court on that party's behalf.

(c) How to Designate. The original or a new lead counsel may be designated by filing a notice stating that attorney's name, mailing address, telephone number, fax number, if any, email address, and State Bar of Texas identification number. If a new lead counsel is being designated, both the new attorney and either the party or the former lead counsel must sign the notice.

(Amended by Order Aug. 16, 2013, eff. Jan. 1, 2014; Order Dec. 13, 2013, eff. Jan. 1, 2014.)

6.2. Appearance of Other Attorneys.

An attorney other than lead counsel may file a notice stating that the attorney represents a specified party to the proceeding and giving that attorney's name, mailing address, telephone number, fax number, if any, email address, and State Bar of Texas identification number. The clerk will note on the docket the attorney's appearance. When a brief or motion is filed, the clerk will note on the docket the name of each attorney, if not already noted, who appears on the document.

(Amended by Order Aug. 16, 2013, eff. Jan. 1, 2014; Order Dec. 13, 2013, eff. Jan. 1, 2014.)

6.3. To Whom Communications Sent.

Any notice, copies of documents filed in an appellate court, or other communications must be sent to:

(a) each party's lead counsel on appeal;

(b) a party's lead counsel in the trial court if:

(1) that party was represented by counsel in the trial court;

(2) lead counsel on appeal has not yet been designated for that party; and

(3) lead counsel in the trial court has not filed a nonrepresentation notice or been allowed to withdraw;

(c) a party if the party is not represented by counsel.

6.4. Nonrepresentation Notice.

(a) In General. If, in accordance with paragraph 6.3(b), the lead counsel in the trial court is being sent notices, copies of documents, or other communications, that attorney may file a nonrepresentation notice in the appellate court. The notice must:

(1) state that the attorney is not representing the party on appeal;

(2) state that the court and other counsel should communicate directly with the party in the future;

(3) give the party's name and last known address and telephone number; and

(4) be signed by the party.

(b) Appointed Counsel. In a criminal case, an attorney appointed by the trial court to represent an indigent party cannot file a nonrepresentation notice.

6.5. Withdrawal.

An appellate court may, on appropriate terms and conditions, permit an attorney to withdraw from representing a party in the appellate court.

(a) Contents of Motion. A motion for leave to withdraw must contain the following:

(1) a list of current deadlines and settings in the case;

(2) the party's name and last known address and telephone number;

(3) a statement that a copy of the motion was delivered to the party; and

(4) a statement that the party was notified in writing of the right to object to the motion.

(b) Delivery to Party. The motion must be delivered to the party in person or mailed—both by certified and by first-class mail—to the party at the party's last known address.

(c) If Motion Granted. If the court grants the motion, the withdrawing attorney must immediately notify the party, in writing, of any deadlines or settings that the attorney knows about at the time of withdrawal but that were not previously disclosed to the party. The withdrawing attorney must file a copy of that notice with the court clerk.

(d) Exception for Substitution of Counsel. If an attorney substitutes for a withdrawing attorney, the motion to withdraw need not comply with (a) but must state only the substitute attorney's name, mailing address, telephone number, fax number, if any, and State Bar of Texas identification number. The withdrawing attorney must comply with (b) but not (c).

6.6. Agreements of Parties or Counsel.

To be enforceable, an agreement of parties or their counsel concerning an appellate court proceeding must be in writing and signed by the parties or their counsel. Such an agreement is subject to any appellate court order necessary to ensure that the case is properly presented.

(Adopted by Order eff. Sept. 1, 1997.)

Comment to 1997 change: Former Rules 7 and 57 are merged and substantially revised. Former Rule 8 regarding agreements of counsel is included here as subdivision 6.6 and the requirement that an agreement be filed and included in the record is deleted.

RULE 7. SUBSTITUTING PARTIES

7.1. Parties Who Are Not Public Officers.

(a) Death of a Party.

(1) Civil Cases. If a party to a civil case dies after the trial court renders judgment but before the case has been finally disposed of on appeal, the appeal may be perfected, and the appellate court will proceed to adjudicate the appeal as if all parties were alive. The appellate court's judgment will have the same force and effect as if rendered when all parties were living. The decedent party's name may be used on all papers.

(2) Criminal Cases. If the appellant in a criminal case dies after an appeal is perfected but before the appellate court issues the mandate, the appeal will be permanently abated.

(b) Substitution for Other Reasons. If substitution of a party in the appellate court is necessary for a reason other than death, the appellate court may order substitution on any party's motion at any time.

7.2. Public Officers.

(a) Automatic Substitution of Officer. When a public officer is a party in an official capacity to an appeal or original proceeding, and if that person ceases to hold office before the appeal or original proceeding is finally disposed of, the public officer's successor is automatically substituted as a party if appropriate. Proceedings following substitution are to be in the name of the substituted party, but any misnomer that does not affect the substantial rights of the parties may be disregarded. Substitution may be ordered at any time, but failure to order substitution of the successor does not affect the substitution.

(b) Abatement. If the case is an original proceeding under Rule 52, the court must abate the proceeding to allow the successor to reconsider the original party's decision. In all other cases, the suit will not abate, and the successor will be bound by the appellate court's judgment or order as if the successor were the original party.

(Adopted by Order eff. Sept. 1, 1997.)

Comment to 1997 change: This is former Rule 9. Former subdivision (a) regarding death of a party in a civil case is now subparagraph 7.1(a)(1). Former subdivision (b) regarding death of a party in a criminal case is now subparagraph 7.1(a)(2). Former subdivision (c) regarding separation of office by public officers is now subdivision 7.2. Former paragraph (c)(3) regarding a successor's liability for costs is omitted as unnecessary. Former subdivision (d) regarding substitution for other causes is now paragraph 7.1(b). Subdivision 7.2 is revised to make it applicable to all cases in which a public officer is a party, and to make substitution automatic if appropriate.

RULE 8. BANKRUPTCY IN CIVIL CASES

8.1. Notice of Bankruptcy.

Any party may file a notice that a party is in bankruptcy. The notice must contain:

(a) the bankrupt party's name;

(b) the court in which the bankruptcy proceeding is pending;

(c) the bankruptcy proceeding's style and case number; and

(d) the date when the bankruptcy petition was filed.

(Amended by Order March 10, 2008 eff. Sept. 1, 2008; Order Aug. 20, 2008, eff. Sept. 1, 2008.)

Comment to 2008 change: The amendment eliminates the former requirement that the bankruptcy notice contain certain pages of the bankruptcy petition, in recognition that electronic filing is now prevale28.1.nt in bankruptcy courts and access to bankruptcy petitions is widely available through the federal PACER system.

8.2. Effect of Bankruptcy.

A bankruptcy suspends the appeal and all periods in these rules from the date when the bankruptcy petition is filed until the appellate court reinstates or severs the appeal in accordance with federal law. A period that began to run and had not expired at the time the proceeding was suspended begins anew when the proceeding is reinstated or severed under 8.3. A document filed by a party while the proceeding is suspended will be deemed filed on the same day, but after, the court reinstates or severs the appeal and will not be considered ineffective because it was filed while the proceeding was suspended.

8.3. Motion to Reinstate or Sever Appeal Suspended by Bankruptcy.

(a) Motion to Reinstate. If a case has been suspended by a bankruptcy filing, a party may move that the appellate court reinstate the appeal if permitted by federal law or the bankruptcy court. If the bankruptcy court has lifted or terminated the stay, a certified copy of the order must be attached to the motion.

(b) Motion to Sever. A party may move to sever the appeal with respect to the bankrupt party and to reinstate the appeal with respect to the other parties. The motion must show that the case is severable and must comply with applicable federal law regarding severance of a bankrupt party. The court may proceed under this paragraph on its own initiative.

(Adopted by Order eff. Sept. 1, 1997.)

Comment to 1997 change: This is a new rule.

RULE 9. DOCUMENTS GENERALLY

9.1. Signing.

(a) Represented Parties. If a party is represented by counsel, a document filed on that party's behalf must be signed by at least one of the party's attorneys. For each attorney whose name appears on a document as representing that party, the document must contain that attorney's State Bar of Texas identification number, mailing address, telephone number, fax number, if any, and email address.

(b) Unrepresented Parties. A party not represented by counsel must sign any document that the party files and give the party's mailing address, telephone number, and fax number, if any, and email address.

(c) Electronic Signatures. A document that is electronically served, filed, or issued by a court or clerk is considered signed if the document includes:

(1) a "/s/" and name typed in the space where the signature would otherwise appear, unless the document is notarized or sworn; or

(2) an electronic image or scanned image of the signature.

(Amended by Order Aug. 16, 2013, eff. Jan. 1, 2014; Order Dec. 13, 2013, eff. Jan. 1, 2014.)

9.2. Filing.

(a) With Whom. A document is filed in an appellate court by delivering it to:

(1) the clerk of the court in which the document is to be filed; or

(2) a justice or judge of that court who is willing to accept delivery. A justice or judge who accepts delivery must note on the document the date and time of delivery, which will be considered the time of filing, and must promptly send it to the clerk.

(b) Filing by Mail.

(1) Timely Filing. A document received within ten days after the filing deadline is considered timely filed if:

(A) it was sent to the proper clerk by United States Postal Service first class, express, registered, or certified mail or a commercial delivery service;

(B) it was placed in an envelope or wrapper properly addressed and stamped; and

(C) it was deposited in the mail or delivered to a commercial delivery service on or before the last day for filing.

(2) Proof of Mailing. Though it may consider other proof, the appellate court will accept the following as conclusive proof of the date of mailing:

(A) a legible postmark affixed by the United States Postal Service;

(B) a receipt for registered or certified mail if the receipt is endorsed by the United States Postal Service;

(C) a certificate of mailing by the United States Postal Service;

(D) a receipt endorsed by the commercial delivery service.

(c) Electronic Filing.

(1) Requirement. Attorneys in civil cases must electronically file documents. Attorneys in criminal cases must electronically file documents except for good cause shown in a motion filed in the appellate court. Unrepresented parties in civil and criminal cases may electronically file documents, but it is not required.

(2) Mechanism. Electronic filing must be done through the electronic filing manager established by the Office of Court Administration and an electronic filing service provider certified by the Office of Court Administration.

(3) Exceptions. Documents filed under seal, subject to a pending motion to seal, or to which access is otherwise restricted by law or court order must not be electronically filed. For good cause, an appellate court may permit a party to file other documents in paper form in a particular case.

(4) Timely Filing. Unless a document must be filed by a certain time of day, a document is considered timely filed if it is electronically filed at any time before midnight (in the court's time zone) on the filing deadline. An electronically filed document is deemed filed when transmitted to the filing party's electronic filing service provider, except:

(A) if a document is transmitted on a Saturday, Sunday, or legal holiday, it is deemed filed on the next day that is not a Saturday, Sunday, or legal holiday; and

(B) if a document requires a motion and an order allowing its filing, the document is deemed filed on the date the motion is granted.

(5) Technical Failure. If a document is untimely due to a technical failure or a system outage, the filing party may seek appropriate relief from the court.

(6) Confirmation of Filing. The electronic filing manager will send a filing confirmation notice to the filing party.

(7) Electronic Notices From the Court. The clerk may send notices, orders, or other communications about the case to the party electronically. A court seal may be electronic.

(Amended by Order June 27, 2011, eff. June 30, 2011; Order Aug. 16, 2013, eff. Jan. 1, 2014; Order Dec. 13, 2013, eff. Jan. 1, 2014.)

9.3. Number of Copies.

(a) Courts of Appeals.

(1) Document Filed in Paper Form. If a document is not electronically filed, a party must file the original and one unbound copy of the document unless otherwise required by local rule. The unbound copy of an appendix must contain a separate page before each document and must not include tabs that extend beyond the edge of the page.

(2) Electronically Filed Document. Unless required by local rule, a party need not file a paper copy of an electronically filed document.

(b) Supreme Court and Court of Criminal Appeals.

(1) Document Filed in Paper Form. If a document is not electronically filed, a party must file the original and 11 copies of any document addressed to either the Supreme Court or the Court of Criminal Appeals, except that in the Supreme Court only an original and one copy must be filed of any motion, response to the motion, and reply in support of the motion, and in the Court of Criminal Appeals, only the original must be filed of a motion for extension of time or a response to the motion, or a pleading under Code of Criminal Procedure article 11.07.

(2) Electronically Filed Document. Paper copies of each document that is electronically filed with the Supreme Court or the Court of Criminal Appeals must be mailed or hand-delivered to the Supreme Court or the Court of Criminal Appeals, as appropriate, within three business days after the document is electronically filed. The number of paper copies required shall be determined, respectively, by order of the Supreme Court or the Court of Criminal Appeals.

(c) Exception for Record. Only the original record need be filed in any proceeding.

(Amended by Order March 10, 2008, eff. Sept. 1, 2008; Order Aug. 20, 2008, eff. Sept. 1, 2008; Order June 27, 2011, eff. June 30, 2011; Order Aug. 16, 2013, eff. Jan. 1, 2014; Order Dec. 13, 2013, eff. Jan. 1, 2014.)

APPENDIX A

Local Rule _____. Electronic Copies of Documents Filed in Paper Form.

(a) Electronic copies of documents required. For the convenience of the court, attorneys, parties, and the public, an attorney for a party must email to the court an electronic copy of every document filed with the court, except a document under seal or subject to a motion to seal. A party who is not represented by an attorney is encouraged to email to the court an electronic copy of every document filed with the court, except a document under seal or subject to a motion to seal. [Courts may add exceptions for attorneys and unrepresented parties.]

(b) Filing required. An electronic copy does not constitute a filing. Documents must continue to be filed as provided by the Texas Rules of Appellate Procedure[, except that only the original and [insert number] copies must be filed of any document other than a petition for discretionary review. A party must file the original and 11 copies of a petition for discretionary review].

(c) Time to email electronic copy. The electronic copy must be emailed to the court at [insert applicable email address] on the same day the original document is filed. Also on that day, the electronic copy must be emailed to each other party's lead counsel for whom the filing attorney has an email address.

(d) Identification of document. The email subject line must identify the document by case number and by name. The electronic copy must be named as follows: [insert court's desired naming conventions here].

(e) Redaction of electronic copies. An electronic copy must be substantively identical to the original document filed with the court, except it must not contain a social security number; a birth date; a home address; the name of any person who was a minor when the underlying suit was filed; a driver's license number, passport number, tax identification number, or similar government issued personal identification number; or a bank account number, credit card number, or other financial account number. The attorney emailing the electronic copy must redact all such information in accordance with the redaction guidelines posted by the Supreme Court's Clerk on the Supreme Court's website; however, the electronic copy may contain a reference to this information as long as the reference does not include any part of the actual information (e.g., "passport number"). For good cause, the court may order redaction of additional information.

(f) Certification of counsel. The submission of an electronic copy constitutes a certification by all attorneys of record for the party filing the document that the electronic copy complies with paragraph (e).

(g) Posting of electronic copies. The clerk may post electronic copies of documents in a case on the court's website. By letter to the clerk, a party to the case may request that electronic copies posted on the court's website be redacted further or removed altogether. The request must identify with particularity the document(s) to be removed or the information to be redacted and state specific reasons for the request. If the request is for further redaction, the party must email a copy of the requested version of the document.

(h) Format of electronic copies. An electronic copy must be formatted as follows:

(1) An electronic copy must be in text-searchable portable document format (PDF) compatible with the latest version of Adobe Reader.

(2) Except as otherwise provided by this rule, an electronic copy of a document created by a word processing program must not be a scan of the original but must instead be converted from the original directly into a PDF file using Adobe Acrobat, a word processing program's PDF conversion utility, or another software program.

(3) Records filed in original proceedings and appendix materials may be scanned if necessary, but scanning creates larger file sizes with images of lesser quality and should be avoided when possible. An appendix must be combined into one computer file with the document it is associated with, unless the resulting computer file would exceed the size limits in paragraph (i). If a record filed in an original proceeding or an appendix contains more than one item, it should include a table of contents and either bookmarks to assist in locating each item or separator pages with the title of the item immediately following and any number or letter associated with the item in the table of contents.

(4) A scanned document must be made searchable using optical-character-recognition software, such as Adobe Acrobat, and have a resolution of 300 dots per inch (dpi).

(5) An electronic copy may contain hyperlinks to another part of the same document, an external source cited in the document, an appendix item associated with the document, an embedded case, or a record cite. Hyperlinks within an appendix item are also permitted.

(6) An electronic copy must not contain a virus or malware. The submission of an electronic copy constitutes a certification by all attorneys of record for the party filing the document that the electronic copy has been checked for viruses and malware.

(7) An electronic copy need not be signed.

(i) Size of electronic copies. A electronic copy must not exceed 20 megabytes. Electronic copies larger than 20 megabytes must be divided into smaller files.

(j) Communications with the clerk. An attorney who emails an electronic copy of a document must supply the clerk with an email address to which the clerk may send notices or other communications about the case in lieu of mailing paper documents. If the attorney's email address changes, the attorney must provide the clerk with the new email address within one business day of the change. Lead counsel must register for Casemail and follow the instructions for receiving notices for cases in which they represent a party.

APPENDIX B

Local Rule _____. Electronic Filings of Documents.

(a) Electronic filing permitted. A party may electronically file (e-file) any document that may be filed with the court in paper form, except a document under seal or subject to a motion to seal.

(b) E-filing mechanism. E-filing must be done through Texas.gov, the portal established by the Texas Legislature. Directions for its use may be found on its website. This is a summary. A person must first register with an Electronic Filing Service Provider (EFSP). A list of approved EFSPs is on the Texas.gov website. The EFSP will provide the registrant with a confidential, secure username and password to use when e-filing a document. This username and password will also function as a signature on each e-filed document, and will authorize payment of all filing fees and service fees. A document to be e-filed must be transmitted to the EFSP, which will send the document to Texas.gov, which in turn will send the document to the clerk. The e-filer will receive by email an immediate acknowledgment of the e-filing, a confirmation of the clerk's acceptance of the filing, and a file-stamped copy of the document. Fees charged by Texas.gov for the e-filing of a document are in addition to any filing fees and are costs of court.

(c) Electronic service. A party who has registered to e-file documents through an EFSP may electronically serve (e-serve) documents through that EFSP on any other party who has consented to e-service by registering for the e-service option with an EFSP or by setting up a complimentary account with Texas.gov. Directions may be found on the Texas.gov website.

(1) Service through an EFSP is complete on transmission to the e-served person's EFSP or complimentary Texas.gov account. The e-filer's EFSP will send proof of service to the e-filer. Fees that an EFSP charges for e-service are not costs of court.

(2) If an e-filer must serve a copy of a document on a party who has not consented to eservice, the e-filer must comply with the service requirements in Texas Rule of Appellate Procedure 9.5 and, on the same day the document is e-filed, must send the document to:

(A) the party's lead counsel by email if the e-filer has an email address for the lead counsel; or

(B) if the party is not represented by counsel, to the party by email if the e-filer has the party's email address.

(d) Redaction of information in e-filed document.

(1) Unless the court orders otherwise, an e-filed document must not contain a social security number; a birth date; a home address; the name of any person who was a minor when the underlying suit was filed; a driver's license number, passport number, tax identification number, or similar government-issued personal identification number; or a bank account number, credit card number, or other financial account number. The e-filer must redact all of this information in accordance with the redaction guidelines posted by the Supreme Court's Clerk on the Supreme Court's website; however, the e-filed document may contain a reference to this information as long as the reference does not include any part of the actual information (e.g., "passport number"). For good cause, the court may order redaction of additional information.

(2) The e-filing of a document constitutes a certification by all attorneys of record for the party filing the document that the document complies with paragraph (1) of this rule.

(3) If an e-filer believes any information described in paragraph (1) of this rule is essential to an e-filed document or that the e-filed document would be confusing without the information, the e-filer may submit the information to the court in a reference list that is in paper form and under seal. The reference list must specify an appropriate identifier that corresponds uniquely to each item listed. Any reference in the e-filed document to a listed identifier will be construed to refer to the corresponding item of information. If the e-filer provides a reference list pursuant to this rule, the front page of the e-filed document must indicate that the reference list has been, or will be, provided.

(4) On its own initiative, the court may order a sealed reference list in any case. The court may also order that a document be filed under seal in paper form, without redaction. The court may later unseal the document or order the filer to provide a redacted version of the document for the public record.

(e) Format of e-filed document. An e-filed document must be formatted as follows:

(1) An e-filed document must be formatted in accordance with Texas Rule of Appellate Procedure 9.4(b)-(e). The "paper" requirements in Rule 9.4(b)-(c) apply equally to a "page" of the e-filed document.

(2) An e-filed document must be in text-searchable portable document format (PDF) compatible with the latest version of Adobe Reader. An EFSP will convert each e-filed document from its original form into a PDF file that complies with this rule.

(3) Records filed in original proceedings and appendix materials may be scanned if necessary, but scanning creates larger file sizes with images of lesser quality and should be avoided when possible. An appendix must be combined into one computer file with the document it is associated with, unless the resulting computer file would exceed Texas.gov's size limits for the document. If a record filed in an original proceeding or an appendix contains more than one item, it should include a table of contents and either bookmarks to assist in locating each item or separator pages with the title of the item immediately following and any number or letter associated with the item in the table of contents.

(4) A scanned document must be made searchable using optical-character-recognition software, such as Adobe Acrobat, and have a resolution of 300 dots per inch (dpi).

(5) An e-filed document may contain hyperlinks to another part of the same document, an external source cited in the document, an appendix item associated with the document, an embedded case, or a record cite. Hyperlinks within an appendix item are also permitted.

(6) An e-filed document must not contain a virus or malware. The e-filing of a document constitutes a certification by the e-filer that the document has been checked for viruses and malware.

(7) The court may strike an e-filed document for nonconformance with this rule.

(f) Signatures on e-filed documents.

(1) Except as otherwise provided by this rule, the confidential, secure username and password that the e-filer must use to e-file a document constitute the e-filer's signature on the document, in compliance with signature requirements in the Texas Rules of Appellate Procedure. When a signature is provided in this manner, the e-filer must also include either an "/s/" and the e-filer's name typed in the space where the e-filer's signature would otherwise appear or an electronic image of the e-filer's signature, which may take the form of a public key-based digital signature or a scanned image of the e-filer's signature. The efiler must not allow the e-filer's username or password to be used by anyone other than an agent who is authorized by the e-filer.

(2) If a document must be notarized, sworn to, or made under oath, the e-filer must e-file the document as a scanned image containing the necessary signature(s).

(3) If a document requires the signature of an opposing party, the e-filer must e-file the document as a scanned image containing the opposing party's signature.

(4) When an e-filer e-files a scanned image of a document pursuant to paragraph (2) or (3) of this rule, the e-filer must retain the original document from which the scanned image was made until the case in which the document was filed is resolved. If the original document is in another party's possession, that party must retain the original document until the case in which the document was filed is resolved.

(5) If an e-served document was also e-filed and the person who completes a certificate of service under Texas Rule of Appellate Procedure 9.5(e) is different from the person who e-filed the document, the person who completes the certificate of service must sign the certificate by including either an'Vs/" and his or her name typed in the space where his or her signature would otherwise appear or an electronic image of his or her signature.

(g) Time of e-filing. A document will be considered filed timely if it is e-filed at any time before midnight (in the court's time zone) on the date on which the document is due.

(1) An e-filed document is deemed filed when the e-filer transmits the document to the e-filer's EFSP, unless the document is transmitted on a Saturday, Sunday, or legal holiday or requires a motion and an order allowing its filing.

(2) If a document is transmitted on a Saturday, Sunday, or legal holiday, it will be deemed filed on the next day that is not a Saturday, Sunday, or legal holiday.

(3) If a document requires a motion and an order allowing its filing, it will be deemed filed on the date the motion is granted.

(4) If an e-filed document is untimely due to a technical failure or a system outage, the e-filer may seek appropriate relief from the court.

(h) Paper copies.

OPTION 1: An e-filer is not required to file any paper copies of an e-filed document, except that paper copies of a petition for discretionary review must still be filed in accordance with Rule 9 of the Texas Rules of Appellate Procedure within one business day after the petition is e-filed.

OPTION 2: An e-filer must file 11 paper copies of an e-filed petition for discretionary review and [insert number] paper copies of any other e-filed document in accordance with Rule 9 of the Texas Rules of Appellate Procedure within one business day after the document is e-filed.

(i) Email address requirements and communications with the clerk. An e-filed document must include the e-filer's email address, in addition to any other information required by the Texas Rules of Appellate Procedure. If the e-filer's email address changes, the e-filer must provide the clerk and the e-filer's EFSP with the new email address within one business day of the change. If there is a change in the email address of a party who has consented to receive e-service, the party must provide Texas.gov or, if applicable, the party's EFSP with the new email address within one business day of the change. The clerk may send notices or other communications about a case to an attorney's email address in lieu of mailing paper documents.

(j) Casemail registration. Lead counsel must register for Casemail and follow the instructions for receiving notices for cases in which they represent a party.

(k) Construction of rules. This rule must be liberally construed so as to avoid undue prejudice to any person who makes a good-faith effort to comply with requirements in this rule.

9.4. Form.

Except for the record, a document filed with an appellate court, including a paper copy of an electronically filed document, must—unless the court accepts another form in the interest of justice—be in the following form:

(a) Printing. A document may be produced by standard typographic printing or by any duplicating process that produces a distinct black image. For a paper document, printing may be on both sides of the paper.

(b) Paper Type and Size. The paper on which a document is produced must 8½ by 11 inches, white or nearly white, and opaque.

(c) Margins. Documents must have at least one-inch margins on both sides and at the top and bottom.

(d) Spacing. Text must be double-spaced, but footnotes, block quotations, short lists, and issues or points of error may be single-spaced.

(e) Typeface. A document produced on a computer must be printed in a conventional typeface no smaller than 14-point except for footnotes, which must be no smaller than 12-point. A typewritten document must be printed in standard 10-character-per-inch (cpi) monospaced typeface.

(f) Binding and Covering. A paper document must be bound so as to ensure that it will not lose its cover or fall apart in regular use. A paper document should be stapled once in the top left-hand corner or be bound so that it will lie flat when open. A paper petition or brief should have durable front and back covers which must not be plastic or be red, black, or dark blue.

(g) Contents of Cover. A document's front cover, if any, must contain the case style, the case number, the title of the document being filed, the name of the party filing the document, and the name, mailing address, telephone number, fax number, if any, email address, and State Bar of Texas identification number of the lead counsel for the filing party. If a party requests oral argument in the court of appeals, the request must appear on the front cover of that party's first brief.

(h) Appendix and Original Proceeding Record. A paper appendix may be bound either with the document to which it is related or separately. If separately bound, the appendix must comply with paragraph (f). A paper record in an original proceeding or a paper appendix must be tabbed and indexed. An electronically filed record in an original proceeding or an electronically filed appendix that includes more than one item must contain bookmarks to assist in locating each item.

(i) Length.

(1) Contents Included and Excluded. In calculating the length of a document, every word and every part of the document, including headings, footnotes, and quotations, must be counted except the following: caption, identity of parties and counsel, statement regarding oral argument, table of contents, index of authorities, statement of the case, statement of issues presented, statement of jurisdiction, statement of procedural history, signature, proof of service, certification, certificate of compliance, and appendix.

(2) Maximum Length. The documents listed below must not exceed the following limits:

(A) A brief and response in a direct appeal to the Court of Criminal Appeals in a case in which the death penalty has been assessed: 37.500 words if computer-generated, and 125 pages if not.

(B) A brief and response in an appellate court (other than a brief under subparagraph (A)) and a petition and response in an original proceeding in the court of appeals: 15.000 words if computer generated, and 50 pages if not. In a civil case in the court of appeals, the aggregate of all briefs filed by a party must not exceed 27,000 words if computer-generated, and 90 pages if not.

(C) A reply brief in an appellate court and a reply to a response to a petition in an original proceeding in the court of appeals: 7,500 words if computer-generated, and 25 pages if not.

(D) A petition and response in an original proceeding in the Supreme Court, a petition for review and response in the Supreme Court, a petition for discretionary review and response in the Court of Criminal Appeals, and a motion for rehearing and response in an appellate court: 4,500 words if computer-generated, and 15 pages if not.

(E) A reply to a response to a petition for review in the Supreme Court, a reply to a response to a petition in an original proceeding in the Supreme Court, and a reply to a response to a petition for discretionary review in the Court of Criminal Appeals: 2.400 words if computer-generated, and 8 pages if not.

(3) Certificate of Compliance. A computer-generated document that is subject to a word limit under this rule must include a certificate by counsel or an unrepresented party stating the number of words in the document. The person certifying may rely on the word count of the computer program used to prepare the document.

(4) Extensions. A court may, on motion, permit a document that exceeds the prescribed limit.

(j) Electronically Filed Documents. An electronically filed document must:

(1) be in text-searchable portable document format (PDF);

(2) be directly converted to PDF rather than scanned, if possible;

(3) not be locked;

(4) be combined with any appendix into one computer file, unless that file would exceed the size limit prescribed by the electronic file manager; and

(5) otherwise comply with the Technology Standards promulgated by the Judicial Committee on Information Technology and approved by the Supreme Court.

(k) Nonconforming Documents. If a document fails to conform with these rules, the court may strike the document or identify the error and permit the party to resubmit the document in a conforming format by a specified deadline.

(Amended by Order Aug. 10, 2012, eff. Dec. 1, 2012; Order Nov. 13, 2012, eff. Dec. 1, 2012; Order March 4, 2013, eff. March 4, 2013; Order Aug. 16, 2013, eff. Jan. 1, 2014; Order Dec. 13, 2013, eff. Jan. 1, 2014; Order March 4, 2013, eff. March 4, 2013.)

Comment to 2012 Change: Rule 9 is revised to consolidate all length limits and establish word limits for documents produced on a computer. All documents produced on a computer must comply with the word limits. Page limits are retained for documents that are typewritten or otherwise not produced on a computer.

9.5. Service.

(a) Service of All Documents Required. At or before the time of a document's filing, the filing party must serve a copy on all parties to the proceeding. Service on a party represented by counsel must be made on that party's lead counsel. Except in original proceedings, a party need not serve a copy of the record.

(b) Manner of Service.

(1) Documents Filed Electronically. A document filed electronically under Rule 9.2 must be served electronically through the electronic filing manager if the email address of the party or attorney to be served is on file with the electronic filing manager. If the email address of the party or attorney to be served is not on file with the electronic filing manager, the document may be served on that party or attorney under subparagraph (2).

(2) Documents Not Filed Electronically. A document that is not filed electronically may be served in person, by mail, by commercial delivery service, by fax, or by email. Personal service includes delivery to any responsible person at the office of the lead counsel for the party served.

(c) When Complete.

(1) Service by mail is complete on mailing.

(2) Service by commercial delivery service is complete when the document is placed in the control of the delivery service.

(3) Service by fax is complete on receipt.

(4) Electronic service is complete on transmission of the document to the serving party's electronic filing service provider. The electronic filing manager will send confirmation of service to the serving party.

(d) Proof of Service. A document presented for filing must contain a proof of service in the form of either an acknowledgment of service by the person served or a certificate of service. Proof of service may appear on or be affixed to the filed document. The clerk may permit a document to be filed without proof of service, but will require the proof to be filed promptly.

(e) Certificate Requirements. A certificate of service must be signed by the person who made the service and must state:

(1) the date and manner of service;

(2) the name and address of each person served; and

(3) if the person served is a party's attorney, the name of the party represented by that attorney.

(Amended by Order Dec. 23, 2002, eff. Jan. 1, 2003; Order Aug. 16, 2013, eff. Jan. 1, 2014; Order Dec. 13, 2013, eff. Jan. 1, 2014.)

Comment to 2002 change: The change clarifies that the filing party must serve a copy of the document filed on all other parties, not only in an appeal or review, but in original proceedings as well. The rule applies only to filing *parties*. Thus, when the clerk or court reporter is responsible for filing the record, as in cases on appeal, a copy need not be served on the parties. The rule for original civil proceedings, in which a party is responsible for filing the record, is stated in subdivision 52.7.

9.6. Communications With the Court.

Parties and counsel may communicate with the appellate court about a case only through the clerk.

(Adopted by Order eff. Sept. 1, 1997.)

Comment to 1997 change: This is former Rule 4. Subdivision 9.4, prescribing the form of documents filed in the appellate courts, is changed and the form to be used is stated in significantly more detail. Former subdivisions (f) and (g), regarding service of documents, are merged into subdivision 9.5. Former Rule 6 is included as subdivision 9.6, but no substantive change is made. Other changes are made throughout the rule. Electronic filing is authorized by §§ 51.801-.807 of the Government Code.

9.7. Adoption by Reference.

Any party may join in or adopt by reference all or any part of a brief, petition, response, motion, or other document filed in an appellate court by another party in the same case.

(Amended by Order Dec. 23, 2002 eff. Jan. 1, 2003.)

Comment to 2002 change: Subdivision 9.7 is added to provide express authorization for the practice of adopting by reference all or part of another party's filing.

9.8. Protection of Minor's identity in parental-rights termination cases or juvenile court cases.

(a) Alias Defined. For purposes of this rule, an alias means one or more of a person's initials or fictitious name, used to refer to the person.

(b) Parental-Rights Termination Cases.

(1) except for a docketing statement, in all papers submitted to the court, including all appendix items submitted with a brief, petition, or motion:

(A) a minor must be identified only by an alias unless the court orders otherwise;

(B) the court may order that a minor's parent or other family member be identified only by an alias if necessary to protect a minor's identity; and

(C) all documents must be redacted accordingly;

(2) the court must, in its opinion, use an alias to refer to a minor, and if necessary to protect the minor's identity, to the minor's parent or other family member.

(c) Juvenile Court Cases. In an appeal or an original proceeding in an appellate court, including all appendix items submitted with a brief, petition, or motion;

(1) except for a docketing statement, in all papers submitted to the court, including all appendix items submitted with a brief, petition, or motion:

(A) a minor must be identified only by an alias;

(B) a minor's parent of other family member must be identified only by an alias; and

(C) all documents must be redacted accordingly;

(2) the court must, in its opinion, use an alias to refer to a minor and to the minor's parent or other family member.

(d) No Alteration of Appellate Record. Nothing in this rule permits alteration of the original appellate record except as specifically authorized by court order.

(Adopted by Order March 10, 2008 eff. Sept. 1, 2008; Order Aug. 20, 2008, eff. Sept. 1, 2008.)

9.9. Privacy Protection for Documents Filed in Civil Cases.

(a) Sensitive Data Defined. Sensitive data consists of:

(1) a driver's license number, passport number, social security number, tax identification number or similar government-issued personal identification number;

(2) a bank account number, credit card number, or other financial account number; and

(3) a birth date, home address, and the name of any person who was a minor when the underlying suit was filed.

(b) Filing of Documents Containing Sensitive Data Prohibited. Unless the inclusion of sensitive data is specifically required by a statute, court rule, or administrative regulation, an electronic or paper document containing sensitive data may not be filed with a court unless the sensitive data is redacted, except for the record in an appeal under Section Two.

(c) Redaction of Sensitive Data; Retention Requirement. Sensitive data must be redacted by using the letter "X" in place of each omitted digit or character or by removing the sensitive data in a manner indicating that the data has been redacted. The filing party must retain an unredacted version of the filed document during the pendency of the appeal and any related proceedings filed within six months of the date the judgment is signed.

(d) Notice to Clerk. If a document must contain sensitive data, the filing party must notify the clerk by:

(1) designating the document as containing sensitive data when the document is electronically filed; or

(2) if the document is not electronically filed, by including, on the upper lefthand side of the first page, the phrase: "NOTICE: THIS DOCUMENT CONTAINS SENSITIVE DATA."

(e) Restriction on Remote Access. Documents that contain unredacted sensitive data in violation of this rule must not be posted on the Internet.

(Adopted by Order Aug. 16, 2013, eff. Jan. 1, 2014; Order Dec. 13, 2013, eff. Jan. 1, 2014.)

Comment to 1997 change: This is former Rule 4. Subdivision 9.4, prescribing the form of documents filed in the appellate courts, is changed and the form to be used is stated in significantly more detail. Former subdivisions (f) and (g), regarding service of documents, are merged into subdivision 9.5. Former Rule 6 is included as subdivision 9.6, but no substantive change is made. Other changes are made throughout the rule. Electronic filing is authorized by §§ 51.801-.807 of the Government Code.

Comment to 2002 change: The change [to Rule 9.5(a)] clarifies that the filing party must serve a copy of the document filed on all other parties, not only in an appeal or review, but in original proceedings as well. The rule applies only to filing parties. Thus, when the clerk or court reporter is responsible for filing the record, as in cases on appeal, a copy need not be served on the parties. The rule for original civil proceedings, in which a party is responsible for filing the record, is stated in subdivision 52.7. Subdivision 9.7 is added to provide express authorization for the practice of adopting by reference all or part of another party's filing.

Comment to 2008 change: Subdivision 9.3 is amended to reduce the number of copies of a motion for extension of time or response filed in the Supreme Court. Subdivision 9.8 is new. To protect the privacy of minors in suits affecting the parent-child relationship (SAPCR), including suits to terminate parental rights, Section 109.002(d) of the Family Code authorizes appellate courts, in their opinions, to identify parties only by fictitious names or by initials. Similarly, Section 56.01(j) of the Family Code prohibits identification of a minor or a minor's family in an appellate opinion related to juvenile court proceedings. But as appellate briefing becomes more widely available through electronic media sources, appellate courts' efforts to protect minors' privacy by disguising their identities in appellate opinions may be defeated if the same children are fully identified in briefs and other court papers available to the public. The rule provides protection from such disclosures. Any fictitious name should not be pejorative or suggest the person's true identity. The rule does not limit an appellate court's authority to disguise parties' identities in appropriate circumstances in other cases. Although appellate courts are authorized to enforce the rule's provisions requiring redaction, parties and amici curiae are responsible for ensuring that briefs and other papers submitted to the court fully comply with the rule.

Comment to 2012 Change: Rule 9 is revised to consolidate all length limits and establish word limits for documents produced on a computer. All documents produced on a computer must comply with the word limits. Page limits are retained for documents that are typewritten or otherwise not produced on a computer.

Comment to 2013 Change: Rule 9 is revised to incorporate rules for electronic filing, in accordance with the Supreme Court's order—Misc. Docket No. 12-9206, amended by Misc. Docket Nos. 13-9092 and 13-9164—mandating electronic filing in civil cases in appellate courts, effective January 1, 2014. In addition, Rule 9.9 is added to provide privacy protection for all documents, both paper and electronic, filed in civil cases in appellate courts.

Technology Standards (These standards apply to documents filed electronically under Texas Rule of Civil Procedure 21 and Texas Rule of Appellate Procedure 9.)

9.10. Privacy Protection for Documents Filed in Criminal Cases

(a) Sensitive Data Defined. Sensitive data consists of:

(1) a driver's license number, passport number, social security number, tax identification number or similar government-issued personal identification number;

(2) bank account number, credit card number, and other financial account number;

(3) a birth date, a home address, and the name of any person who was a minor at the time the offense was committed.

(b) Redacted Filings. Unless a court orders otherwise, an electronic or paper filing with the court, including the contents of any appendices, must not contain sensitive data.

(c) Redaction procedures. Sensitive data must be redacted by using the letter "X" in place of each omitted digit or character or by removing the sensitive data in a manner indicating that the data has been redacted. The filer must retain an unredacted version of the filed document during the pendency of the appeal and any related proceedings filed within three years of the date the judgment is signed. If a district court clerk or appellate court clerk discovers unredacted sensitive data in the record, the clerk shall notify the parties and seek a ruling from the court.

(d) Certification. The filing of a document constitutes a certification by the filer that the document complies with paragraphs (a) and (b) of this rule.

(e) Reference List. If a filer believes any information described in paragraph (a) of this rule is essential to a document or that the document would be confusing without the information, the filer may submit the information to the court in a reference list that is in paper form and under seal. The reference list must specify an appropriate identifier that corresponds uniquely to each item listed. Any reference in the document to a listed identifier will be construed to refer to the corresponding item of information. If the filer provides a reference list pursuant to this rule, the front page of the document containing the redacted information must indicate that the reference list has been, or will be, provided. On its own initiative, the court may order a sealed reference list in any case.

(f) Sealed materials. Materials that are required by statute to be sealed, redacted, or kept confidential, such as the items set out in Articles 35.29 (Personal Information About Jurors), 38.45 (Evidence Depicting or Describing Abuse of or Sexual Conduct by Child or Minor), and 42.12, § 9(j), must be treated in accordance with the pertinent statutes and shall not be publicly available on the Internet. A court may also order that a document be filed under seal in paper form or electronic form, without redaction. The court may later unseal the document or order the filer to provide a redacted version of the document for the public record. If a court orders material sealed, whether it be sensitive data or other materials, the court's sealing order must be affixed to the outside of the sealed container if the sealed material is filed in paper form, or be the first document that appears if filed in electronic form. Sealed portions of the clerk's and reporter's records should be clearly marked and separated from unsealed portions and tendered as separate records, whether in paper form or electronic form. Sealed material shall not be available either on the Internet or in other form without court order.

(Adopted by Order Dec. 13, 2013, eff. Jan. 1, 2014.)

RULE 10. MOTIONS IN THE APPELLATE COURTS.

10.1. Contents of Motions; Response.

(a) Motion. Unless these rules prescribe another form, a party must apply by motion for an order or other relief. The motion must:

(1) contain or be accompanied by any matter specifically required by a rule governing such a motion;

(2) state with particularity the grounds on which it is based;

(3) set forth the order or relief sought;

(4) be served and filed with any brief, affidavit, or other paper filed in support of the motion; and

(5) in civil cases, except for motions for rehearing and motions for en banc reconsideration, contain or be accompanied by a certificate stating that the filing party conferred, or made a reasonable attempt to confer, with all other parties about the merits of the motion and whether those parties oppose the motion.

(b) Response. A party may file a response to a motion at any time before the court rules on the motion or by any deadline set by the court. The court may determine a motion before a response is filed.

(Amended by Order March 10, 2008 eff. Sept. 1, 2008; Order Aug. 20, 2008, eff. Sept. 1, 2008.)

Comment to 2008 change: It is presumed that non-movants will oppose the relief sought in motions for rehearing and motions for en banc reconsideration. To encourage consistent application of the certificate-of-conference requirement, Rule 10.1(a)(5) is amended—and Rule 49.11 is added—to exempt those motions from the certificate requirement.

10.2. Evidence on Motions.

A motion need not be verified unless it depends on the following types of facts, in which case the motion must be supported by affidavit or other satisfactory evidence. The types of facts requiring proof are those that are:

(a) not in the record;

(b) not within the court's knowledge in its official capacity; and

(c) not within the personal knowledge of the attorney signing the motion.

(Amended by Order March 10, 2008 eff. Sept. 1, 2008; Order Aug. 20, 2008, eff. Sept. 1, 2008.)

10.3. Determining Motions.

(a) Time for Determination. A court should not hear or determine a motion until 10 days after the motion was filed, unless:

(1) the motion is to extend time to file a brief, a petition for review, or a petition for discretionary review;

(2) the motion states that the parties have conferred and that no party opposes the motion; or

(3) the motion is an emergency.

(b) Reconsideration. If a motion is determined prematurely, any party adversely affected may request the court to reconsider its order.

10.4. Power of Panel or Single Justice or Judge to Entertain Motions.

(a) Single Justice. In addition to the authority expressly conferred by these rules or by law, a single justice or judge of an appellate court may grant or deny a request for relief that these rules allow to be sought by motion. But in a civil case, a single justice should not do the following:

(1) act on a petition for an extraordinary writ; or

(2) dismiss or otherwise determine an appeal or a motion for rehearing.

(b) Panel. An appellate court may provide, by order or rule, that a panel or the full court must act on any motion or class of motions.

10.5. Particular Motions.

(a) Motions Relating to Informalities in the Record. A motion relating to informalities in the manner of bringing a case into court must be filed within 30 days after the record is filed in the court of appeals. The objection, if waivable, will otherwise be deemed waived.

(b) Motions to Extend Time.

(1) Contents of Motion in General. All motions to extend time, except a motion to extend time for filing a notice of appeal, must state:

(A) the deadline for filing the item in question;

(B) the length of the extension sought;

(C) the facts relied on to reasonably explain the need for an extension; and

(D) the number of previous extensions granted regarding the item in question.

(2) Contents of Motion to Extend Time to File Notice of appeal. A motion to extend the time for filing a notice of appeal must:

(A) comply with (1)(A) and (C);

(B) identify the trial court;

(C) state the date of the trial court's judgment or appealable order; and

(D) state the case number and style of the case in the trial court.

(3) Contents of Motion to Extend Time to File Petition for Review or Petition for Discretionary Review. A motion to extend time to file a petition for review or petition for discretionary review must also specify:

(A) the court of appeals;

(B) the date of the court of appeals' judgment; and

(C) the case number and style of the case in the court of appeals; and

(D) the date every motion for rehearing or en banc reconsideration was filed, and either the date and nature of the court of appeals' ruling on the motion, or that if remains pending.

(c) Motions to Postpone Argument. Unless all parties agree, or unless sufficient cause is apparent to the court, a motion to postpone argument of a case must be supported by sufficient cause.

(Adopted by Order eff. Sept. 1, 1997. Amended by Order Aug. 20, 2008, eff. Sept. 1, 2008)

Comment to 1997 change: This is former Rule 19. Under subdivision 10.1, a response may be filed at any time before the court rules on the motion. The provision of former subdivision (b) regarding docketing motions is incorporated in Rule 12.2. The provision of former subdivision (b) for noting attorneys' names on the docket is incorporated in Rule 6.2. Former subdivision (c), requiring the clerk to send notices of the filing of motions is deleted as unnecessary because the parties must serve all motions under Rule 9.5. Subdivision 10.2 is amended to eliminate the requirement of an oath where the facts are within the personal knowledge of the attorney. Subdivision 10.5 is new and incorporates the provisions of other rules concerning motions, as follows: 10.5(a) from former Rule 71; 10.5(b) from former Rules 73, 130(d), and 160; and 10.5(c) from former Rule 70. Other changes are made.

Comment to 2008 change: It happens so infrequently that a non-movant does not oppose a motion for rehearing on en banc reconsideration that such motions are excepted from the certificate-of-conference requirement in Subdivision 10.1(a)(5). Subdivision 10.2 is revised to clarify that facts supporting a motion need not be verified by the filer if supporting evidence is in the record, the facts are known to the court, or the filer has personal knowledge of them. Subdivision 10.5(b)(3)(D) is added.

RULE 11. AMICUS CURIAE BRIEFS.

An appellate clerk may receive, but not file, an amicus curiae brief. But the court for good cause may refuse to consider the brief and order that it be returned. An amicus curiae brief must:

(a) comply with the briefing rules for parties;

(b) identify the person or entity on whose behalf the brief is tendered;

(c) disclose the source of any fee paid or to be paid for preparing the brief; and

(d) certify that copies have been served on all parties.

(Amended by Order Dec. 23, 2002 eff. Jan. 1, 2003.)

Comment to 2002 change: The change expressly recognizes that a court may refuse to consider an amicus curiae brief for good cause.

RULE 12. DUTIES OF APPELLATE CLERK.

12.1. Docketing the Case.

On receiving a copy of the notice of appeal, the petition for review, the petition for discretionary review, the petition in an original proceeding, or a certified question, the appellate clerk must:

(a) endorse on the document the date of receipt;

(b) collect any filing fee;

(c) docket the case;

(d) notify all parties of the receipt of the document; and

(e) if the document filed is a petition for review filed in the Supreme Court, notify the court of appeals clerk of the filing of the petition.

12.2. Docket Numbers.

The clerk must put the case's docket number on each item received in connection with the case and must put the docket number on the envelope in which the record is stored.

(a) Numbering System. Each case filed in a court of appeals must be assigned a docket number consisting of the following four parts, separated by hyphens:

(1) the number of the court of appeals district;

(2) the last two digits of the year in which the case is filed;

(3) the number assigned to the case; and

(4) the designation "CV" for a civil case or "CR" for a criminal case.

(b) Numbering Order. Each case must be docketed in the order of its filing.

(c) Multiple Notices of Appeal. All notices of appeal filed in the same case must be given the same docket number.

(d) Appeals Not Yet Filed. A motion relating to an appeal that has been perfected but not yet filed must be docketed and assigned a docket number that will also be assigned to the appeal when it is filed.

12.3. Custody of Papers.

The clerk must safeguard the record and every other item filed in a case. If the record or any part of it or any other item is missing, the court will make an order for the replacement of the record or item that is just under the circumstances.

12.4. Withdrawing Papers.

The clerk may permit the record or other filed item to be taken from the clerk's office at any time, on the following conditions:

(a) the clerk must have a receipt for the record or item;

(b) the clerk should make reasonable conditions to ensure that the withdrawn record or item is preserved and returned;

(c) the clerk may demand the return of the record or item at any time;

(d) after the case is submitted to the court and before the court's decision, the record cannot be withdrawn;

(e) after the court's decision, the losing party must be given priority in withdrawing the record;

(f) the clerk may not allow original documents filed under Rule 34.5(f) or original exhibits filed under Rule 34.6(g) to be taken from the clerk's office;

(g) if the court allows an original document or exhibit to be taken by a party and it is not returned, the court may accept the opposing party's statement concerning the document's or exhibit's nature and contents;

(h) withdrawn material must not be removed from the court's jurisdiction; and

(i) the court may, on the motion of any party or its own initiative, modify any of these conditions.

12.5. Clerk's Duty to Account.

The clerk of an appellate court who receives money due another court must promptly pay the money to the court to whom it is due. This rule is enforceable by the Supreme Court.

12.6. Notices of Court's Judgments and Orders.

In any proceeding, the clerk of an appellate court must promptly send a notice of any judgment, mandate, or other court order to all parties to the proceeding.

(Adopted by Order eff. Sept. 1, 1997. Amended by Order Dec. 23, 2002, eff. Jan. 1, 2003.)

Comment to 2002 change: Subdivision 12.6 is amended to require the clerk to notify the parties of all of the court's rulings, including the mandate.

RULE 13. COURT REPORTERS AND COURT RECORDERS.

13.1. Duties of Court Reporters and Recorders.

The official court reporter or court recorder must:

(a) unless excused by agreement of the parties, attend court sessions and make a full record of the proceedings;

(b) take all exhibits offered in evidence during a proceeding and ensure that they are marked;

(c) file all exhibits with the trial court clerk after a proceeding ends;

(d) perform the duties prescribed by Rules 34.6 and 35; and

(e) perform other acts relating to the reporter's or recorder's official duties, as the trial court directs.

(Amended by Order Dec. 23, 2002, eff. Jan. 1, 2003.)

Comment to 2002 change: Subdivision 13.1(a) is amended merely for clarification.

13.2. Additional Duties of Court Recorder.

The official court recorder must also:

(a) ensure that the recording system functions properly throughout the proceeding and that a complete, clear, and transcribable recording is made;

(b) make a detailed, legible log of all proceedings being recorded, showing:

(1) the number and style of the case before the court;

(2) the name of each person speaking;

(3) the event being recorded such as the voir dire, the opening statement, direct and cross-examinations, and bench conferences;

(4) each exhibit offered, admitted, or excluded;

(5) the time of day of each event; and

(6) the index number on the recording device showing where each event is recorded;

(c) after a proceeding ends, file with the clerk the original log;

(d) have the original recording stored to ensure that it is preserved and is accessible; and

(e) ensure that no one gains access to the original recording without the court's written order.

13.3. Priorities of Reporters.

The trial court must help ensure that the court reporter's work is timely accomplished by setting work priorities. The reporter's duties relating to proceedings before the court take preference over other work.

13.4. Report of Reporters.

To aid the trial court in setting priorities under 13.3, each court reporter must give the trial court a monthly written report showing the amount and nature of the business pending in the reporter's office. A copy of this report must be filed with the appellate clerk of each district in which the court sits.

13.5 Appointing Deputy Reporter.

When the official court reporter is unable to perform the duties in 13.1 or 13.2 because of illness, press of official work, or unavoidable absence or disability, the trial court may designate a deputy reporter. If the court appoints a deputy reporter, that person must file with the trial court clerk a document stating:

(a) the date the deputy worked;

(b) the court in which the deputy worked; and

(c) the number and style of the case on which the deputy worked.

13.6. Filing of Notes in a Criminal Case.

When a defendant is convicted and sentenced, or is granted deferred adjudication for a felony other than a state jail felony, and does not appeal, the court reporter must—within 20 days after the time to perfect the appeal has expired—file the untranscribed notes or the original recording of the proceeding with the trial court clerk. The trial court clerk need not retain the notes beyond 15 years of their filing date.

(Adopted by Order eff. Sept. 1, 1997.)

Comment to 1997 change: Former Rules 11 and 12 are merged. Former Rules 11(a), (c) and (d) now appear as subdivisions 13.1, 13.5 and 13.6. Former Rule 11(b) is omitted as unnecessary. The provisions of former Rule 12(a) are moved to Rule 35.3. Former Rules 12(b) and (c) now appear as subdivisions 13.3 and 13.4. The rule is made to apply to court recorders as well as court reporters. Paragraph 13.1(a) merges paragraphs (a)(1) and (2) of former Rule 11, and now requires the reporter to make a record of voir dire and closing argument unless excused by agreement of the parties. Paragraph 13.1(b) is new, but codifies current practice. Subdivision 13.2 is new and specifies rules for electronic recording of proceedings. A provision requiring a deputy court reporter to file with the trial court clerk a document identifying the proceedings in which the reporter worked is included in paragraph 13.5. Other changes are made.

RULE 14. RECORDING AND BROADCASTING COURT PROCEEDINGS.

14.1. Recording and Broadcasting Permitted.

An appellate court may permit courtroom proceedings to be broadcast, televised, recorded, or photographed in accordance with this rule.

14.2. Procedure.

(a) Request to Cover Court Proceeding.

(1) A person wishing to broadcast, televise, record, or photograph a court proceeding must file with the court clerk a request to cover the proceeding. The request must state:

(A) the case style and number;

(B) the date and time when the proceeding is to begin;

(C) the name of the requesting person or organization;

(D) the type of coverage requested (for example, televising or photographing); and

(E) the type and extent of equipment to be used.

(2) A request to cover argument of a case must be filed no later than five days before the date the case is set for argument and must be served on all parties to the case. A request to cover any other proceeding must be filed no later than two days before the date when the proceeding is to begin.

(b) Response. Any party may file a response to the request. If the request is to cover argument, the response must be filed no later than two days before the date set for argument. If a party objects to coverage of the argument, the response should state the injury that will allegedly result from coverage.

(c) Court May Shorten Time. The court may, in the interest of justice, shorten the time for filing a document under this rule if no party or interested person would be unduly prejudiced.

(d) Decision of Court. In deciding whether to allow coverage, the court may consider information known ex parte to the court. The court may allow, deny, limit, or terminate coverage for any reason the court considers necessary or appropriate, such as protecting the parties' rights or the dignity of the court and ensuring the orderly conduct of the proceedings.

14.3. Equipment and Personnel.

The court may, among other things:

(a) require that a person seeking to cover a proceeding demonstrate or display the equipment that will be used;
(b) prohibit equipment that produces distracting sound or light;
(c) prohibit signal lights or devices showing when equipment is operating, or require their concealment;
(d) prohibit moving lights, flash attachments, or sudden lighting changes;
(e) require the use of the courtroom's existing video, audio, and lighting systems, if any;
(f) specify the placement of personnel and equipment;
(g) determine the number of cameras to be allowed in the courtroom; and
(h) require pooling of equipment if more than one person wishes to cover a proceeding.

14.4. Enforcement.

The court may sanction a violation of this rule by measures that include barring a person or organization from access to future coverage of proceedings in that court for a defined period.

(Adopted by Order eff. Sept. 1, 1997.)

Comment to 1997 change: This is former Rule 21. The rule is rewritten and now allows recording and broadcasting of court proceedings at the discretion of the court and subject to the stated guidelines.

RULE 15. ISSUANCE OF WRIT OR PROCESS BY APPELLATE COURT.

15.1. In General.

(a) Signature Under Seal. A writ or process issuing from an appellate court must bear the court's seal and be signed by the clerk.

(b) To Whom Directed; by Whom Served. Unless a rule or statute provides otherwise, the writ or process must be directed to the person or court to be served. The writ or process may be served by the sheriff, constable, or other peace officer whose jurisdiction includes the county in which the person or court to be served may be found.

(c) Return; Lack of Execution; Simultaneous Writs. The writ or process must be returned to the issuing court according to the writ's direction. If the writ or process is not executed, the clerk may issue another writ or process if requested by the party who requested the former writ or process. At a party's request, the clerk may issue two or more writs simultaneously.

15.2. Appearance Without Service; Actual Knowledge.

A party who appears in person or by attorney in an appellate court proceeding—or who has actual knowledge of the court's opinion, judgment, or order related to a writ or process—is bound by the opinion, judgment, or order to the same extent as if personally served under 15.1.

(Adopted by Order eff. Sept. 1, 1997.)

Comment to 1997 change: This is former Rule 17. Nonsubstantive changes are made.

RULE 16. DISQUALIFICATION OR RECUSAL OF APPELLATE JUDGES.

16.1. Grounds for Disqualification.

The grounds for disqualification of an appellate court justice or judge are determined by the Constitution and laws of Texas.

16.2. Grounds for Recusal.

The grounds for recusal of an appellate court justice or judge are the same as those provided in the Rules of Civil Procedure. In addition, a justice or judge must recuse in a proceeding if it presents a material issue which the justice or judge participated in deciding while serving on another court in which the proceeding was pending.

16.3. Procedure for Recusal.

(a) Motion. A party may file a motion to recuse a justice or judge before whom the case is pending. The motion must be filed promptly after the party has reason to believe that the justice or judge should not participate in deciding the case.

(b) Decision. Before any further proceeding in the case, the challenged justice or judge must either remove himself or herself from all participation in the case or certify the matter to the entire court, which will decide the motion by a majority of the remaining judges sitting en banc. The challenged justice or judge must not sit with the remainder of the court to consider the motion as to him or her.

(c) Appeal. An order of recusal is not reviewable, but the denial of a recusal motion is reviewable.

(Adopted by Order eff. Sept. 1, 1997.)

Comment to 1997 change: Former Rules 15 and 15a are merged. Former Rule 15a appears as subdivision 16.2. For grounds for disqualification, reference is made to the Constitution and statutes rather than the Rules of Civil Procedure. The procedure for disqualification is not specified. The nature of prior participation in a proceeding that requires recusal is clarified. Former subdivision (b) of Rule 15, requiring service of the motion, is omitted as unnecessary. The remaining subdivisions of former Rule 15 are contained in subdivision 16.3. Other changes are made.

RULE 17. COURT OF APPEALS UNABLE TO TAKE IMMEDIATE ACTION.

17.1. Inability to Act.

A court of appeals is unable to take immediate action if it cannot—within the time when action must be taken—assemble a panel because members of the court are ill, absent, or unavailable. A justice who is disqualified or recused is unavailable. A court of appeals' inability to act immediately may be established by certificate of the clerk, a member of the court, or a party's counsel, or by affidavit of a party.

17.2. Nearest Available Court of Appeals.

If a court of appeals is unable to take immediate action, the nearest court of appeals that is able to take immediate action may do so with the same effect as the other court. The nearest court of appeals is the one whose courthouse is nearest—measured by a straight line—the courthouse of the trial court.

17.3. Further Proceedings.

After acting or refusing to act, the nearest court of appeals must promptly send a copy of its order, and the original or a copy of any document presented to it, to the other court, which will conduct any further proceedings in the matter.

(Adopted by Order eff. Sept. 1, 1997.)

Comment to 1997 change: This is former Rule 16. The rule is rewritten and simplified.

RULE 18. MANDATE.

18.1. Issuance.

The clerk of the appellate court that rendered the judgment must issue a mandate in accordance with the judgment and send it to the clerk of the court to which it is directed and to all parties to the proceeding when one of the following periods expires:

(a) In the Court of Appeals.

(1) Ten days after the time has expired for filing a motion to extend time to file a petition for review or a petition for discretionary review if:

(A) no timely petition for review or petition for discretionary review has been filed;

(B) no timely filed motion to extend time to file a petition for review or petition for discretionary review is pending; and

(C) in a criminal case, the Court of Criminal Appeals has not granted review on its own initiative.

(2) Ten days after the time has expired for filing a motion to extend time to file a motion for rehearing of a denial, refusal, or dismissal of a petition for review, or a refusal or dismissal of a petition for discretionary review, if no timely filed motion for rehearing or motion to extend time is pending.

(b) In the Supreme Court and the Court of Criminal Appeals. Ten days after the time has expired for filing a motion to extend time to file a motion for rehearing if no timely filed motion for rehearing or motion to extend time is pending.

(c) Agreement to Issue. The mandate may be issued earlier if the parties so agree, or for good cause on the motion of a party.

(Amended by Order Dec. 23, 2002, eff. Jan. 1, 2003.)

Comment to 2002 change: Subdivision 18.1 is amended consistent with the change in subdivision 12.6.

18.2. Stay of Mandate.

A party may move to stay issuance of the mandate pending the United States Supreme Court's disposition of a petition for writ of certiorari. The motion must state the grounds for the petition and the circumstances requiring the stay. The appellate court authorized to issue the mandate may grant a stay if it finds that the grounds are substantial and that the petitioner or others would incur serious hardship from the mandate's issuance if the United States Supreme Court were later to reverse the judgment. In a criminal case, the stay will last for no more than 90 days, to permit the timely filing of a petition for writ of certiorari. After that period and others mentioned in this rule expire, the mandate will issue.

18.3. Trial Court Case Number.

The mandate must state the trial court case number.

18.4. Filing of Mandate.

The clerk receiving the mandate will file it with the case's other papers and note it on the docket.

18.5. Costs.

The mandate will be issued without waiting for costs to be paid. If the Supreme Court declines to grant review, Supreme Court costs must be included in the court of appeals' mandate.

18.6. Mandate in Accelerated Appeals.

The appellate court's judgment on an appeal from an interlocutory order takes effect when the mandate is issued. The court may issue the mandate with its judgment or delay the mandate until the appeal is finally disposed of. If the mandate is issued, any further proceeding in the trial court must conform to the mandate.

18.7. Recall of Mandate.

If an appellate court vacates or modifies its judgment or order after issuing its mandate, the appellate clerk must promptly notify the clerk of the court to which the mandate was directed and all parties. The mandate will have no effect and a new mandate may be issued.

(Adopted by Order eff. Sept. 1, 1997.)

Comment to 1997 change: This is a new rule that combines the provisions of former Rules 43(g), 86, 186, 231, and 232.

RULE 19. PLENARY POWER OF THE COURTS OF APPEALS AND EXPIRATION OF TERM.

19.1. Plenary Power of Courts of Appeals.

A court of appeals' plenary power over its judgment expires:

(a) 60 days after judgment if no timely filed motion for rehearing or timely filed motion en banc reconsideration, or timely filed motion to extend time to file such a motion, is then pending; or

(b) 30 days after the court overrules all timely filed motions for rehearing or en banc reconsideration, and all timely filed motions to extend time to file such a motion.

(Amended by Order Dec. 23, 2002, eff. Jan. 1, 2003; Order March 10, 2008, eff. Sept. 1, 2008.)

Comment to 2002 change: Subdivision 19.1 is changed, consistent with other changes in the rules, to specifically address a motion for en banc reconsideration and treat it as a motion for rehearing.

Comment to 2008 change: The provisions of Rule 19 governing the courts of appeals' plenary power are revised in conjunction with the amendments to Rules 49 and 53.7 concerning motions for en banc reconsideration.

19.2. Plenary Power Continues After Petition Filed.

In a civil case, the court of appeals retains plenary power to vacate or modify its judgment during the periods prescribed in 19.1 even if a party has filed a petition for review in the Supreme Court.

19.3. Proceedings After Plenary Power Expires.

After its plenary power expires, the court cannot vacate or modify its judgment. But the court may:

(a) correct a clerical error in its judgment or opinion;

(b) issue and recall its mandate as these rules provide;

(c) enforce or suspend enforcement of its judgment as these rules or applicable law provide;

(d) order or modify the amount and type of security required to suspend a judgment, and decide the sufficiency of the sureties, under Rule 24; and

(e) order its opinion published in accordance with Rule 47.

19.4. Expiration of Term.

The expiration of the appellate court's term does not affect the court's plenary power or its jurisdiction over a case that is pending when the court's term expires.

(Adopted by Order eff. Sept. 1, 1997.)

Comment to 1997 change: This is a new rule except the provisions of former Rule 234 are incorporated in subdivision 19.4.

RULE 20. WHEN PARTY IS INDIGENT.

20.1. Civil Cases.

(a) *Costs Defined.* In this rule, "costs" mean filing fees charged by the appellate court. Fees charged for preparation of the appellate record are governed by Texas Rule of Civil Procedure 145.

(b) *When a Statement Was Filed in the Trial Court.*

(1) *General Rule; Status in Trial Court Carries Forward.* A party who filed a Statement of Inability to Afford Payment of Court Costs in the trial court is not required to pay costs in the appellate court unless the trial court overruled the party's claim of indigence in an order that complies with Texas Rule of Civil Procedure 145. A party is not required to pay costs in the appellate court if the trial court ordered the party to pay partial costs or to pay costs in installments.

(2) *Establishing the Right to Proceed Under the General Rule.* To establish the right to proceed without payment of costs under (1), a party must communicate to the appellate court clerk in writing that the party is presumed indigent under this rule. In an appeal under Section Two of these rules, the applicability of the presumption should be stated in the notice of appeal and in the docketing statement.

(3) *Exception; Material Change in Circumstances.* An appellate court may permit a party who is not entitled to proceed under (1) to proceed without payment of costs if the party establishes that the party's financial circumstances have materially changed since the date of the trial court's order under Texas Rule of Civil Procedure 145.

(A) *Requirements.* The party must file a motion in the appellate court alleging that the party's financial circumstances have materially changed since the date of the trial court's order and a current Statement of Inability to Afford Payment of Court Costs that complies with Texas Rule of Civil Procedure 145. The Statement that was filed in the trial court does not meet the requirements of this rule.

(B) *Action by Appellate Court.* The appellate court may decide the motion based on the record or refer the motion to the trial court with instructions to hear evidence and issue findings of fact. If a motion is referred to the trial court, the appellate court must review the trial court's findings and the record of the hearing before ruling on the motion.

(c) *When No Statement Was Filed in the Trial Court.* An appellate court may permit a party who did not file a Statement of Inability to Afford Payment of Court Costs in the trial court to proceed without payment of costs. The court may require the party to file a Statement in the appellate court. If the court denies the party's request to proceed without payment of costs, it must do so in a written order.

(Amended by Order March 10, 2008 eff. Sept. 1, 2008; Order Aug. 20, 2008, eff. Sept. 1, 2008; Order Aug. 31, 2011, eff. Sept. 1, 2011; Order Dec. 12, 2011, eff. March 1, 2012; Order Feb. 13, 2012, eff. March 1, 2012; Tex. Sup. Ct. Misc. Docket No. 16-9056, eff. Sept. 1, 2016; Tex. Sup. Ct. Misc. Docket No. 16-9122, eff. Sept. 1, 2016.)

[Statement of Inability to Afford Payment of Court Costs as provided in Tex. Sup. Ct. Misc. Docket No. 16-9122, eff. Sept. 1, 2016 and applies to any contest of, or challenge to, a claim of inability to afford payment of court costs that is pending on September 1, 2016.]

Comment to 2016 Change: The rule has been rewritten so that it only governs filing fees and any other fee charged by the appellate court. Texas Rule of Civil Procedure 145 governs a party's claim that the party is unable to afford costs for preparation of the appellate record.

Because appellate filing fees are minimal, a party that filed a Statement of Inability to Afford Payment of Court Costs in the trial court is not required to file a new Statement in the appellate court unless the trial court made affirmative findings under Texas Rule of Civil Procedure 145 that the party is able to afford all court costs and to pay those costs as they are incurred. Furthermore, because a determination of indigence by the trial court carries forward to appeal in all cases, Family Code section 107.013 is satisfied.

Experience has shown that, in most cases, a party's financial circumstances do not change substantially between the trial court proceedings and the appellate court proceedings. Nonetheless, (b)(3) permits a party whom the trial court determined is able to afford all costs to demonstrate to the appellate court that the party's circumstances have changed since the trial court's ruling and that the party is unable to afford appellate filing fees.

Comment to 2008 change: Subdivision 20.1(a) is added to provide, as in Texas Rule of Civil Procedure 145, that an affidavit of indigence accompanied by an IOLTA or other Texas Access to Justice Foundation certificate cannot be challenged. Subdivision 20.1(c)(1) is revised to clarify that an affidavit of indigence filed to proceed in the trial court without advance payment of costs is insufficient to establish indigence on appeal; a separate affidavit must be filed with or before the notice of appeal. Subdivision 20.1(c)(3) is revised to provide that an appellate court must give an appellant who fails to file a proper appellate indigence affidavit notice of the defect and an opportunity to cure it before dismissing the appeal or affirming the judgment on that basis. *See Higgins v. Randall County Sheriff's Office*, 193 S.W .3d 898 (Tex. 2006). The limiting phrase "under (c)(2)" in Subdivision 20.1(d)(2) is deleted to clarify that the appellate clerk's duty to forward copies of the affidavit to the trial court clerk and the court reporter, along with a notice setting a deadline to contest the affidavit, applies to affidavits on appeal erroneously filed in the appellate court, not only to affidavits in other appellate proceedings properly filed in the appellate court under subdivision 20.1(c)(2). Although Subdivision 3.1(g) defines "court reporter" to include court recorder, subdivision 20.1(e) is amended to make clear that a court recorder can contest an affidavit.

20.2. Criminal Cases.

Within the time for perfecting the appeal, an appellant who is unable to pay for the appellate record may, by motion and affidavit, ask the trial court to have the appellate record furnished without charge. If after hearing the motion the court finds that the appellant cannot pay or give security for the appellate record, the court must order the reporter to transcribe the proceedings. When the court certifies that the appellate record has been furnished to the appellant, the reporter must be paid from the general funds of the county in which the offense was committed, in the amount set by the trial court.

(Adopted by Order eff. Sept. 1, 1997.)

Comment to 1997 change: The rule is new and combines the provisions of former Rules 13(k), 40(a)(3), and 53(j). The procedure for proceeding in civil cases in an appellate court without advance payment of costs, in both appeals and original proceedings, is stated. The information that must be given in the affidavit is prescribed. An extension of time to file the affidavit is now available. The indigent party is no longer required to serve the court reporter, but must file the affidavit with the appropriate clerk who is to notify the court reporter. A contest need not be under oath. Provision is made for later ability to pay the costs. Nonsubstantive changes are made to the rule for criminal cases.

Reference

See also: Civil Practice and Remedies Code § 13.003.

SECTION TWO.
APPEALS FROM TRIAL COURT JUDGMENTS AND ORDERS

RULE 21. NEW TRIALS IN CRIMINAL CASES.

21.1. Definitions.

(a) *New trial* means the rehearing of a criminal action after the trial court has, on the defendant's motion, set aside a finding or verdict of guilt.

(b) *New trial on punishment* means a new hearing of the punishment stage of a criminal action after the trial court has, on the defendant's motion, set aside an assessment of punishment without setting aside a finding or verdict of guilt.

21.2. When Motion for New Trial Required.

A motion for new trial is a prerequisite to presenting a point of error on appeal only when necessary to adduce facts not in the record.

21.3. Grounds.

The defendant must be granted a new trial, or a new trial on punishment, for any of the following reasons:

(a) except in a misdemeanor case in which the maximum possible punishment is a fine, when the defendant has been unlawfully tried in absentia or has been denied counsel;

(b) when the court has misdirected the jury about the law or has committed some other material error likely to injure the defendant's rights;

(c) when the verdict has been decided by lot or in any manner other than a fair expression of the jurors' opinion;

(d) when a juror has been bribed to convict or has been guilty of any other corrupt conduct;

(e) when a material defense witness has been kept from court by force, threats, or fraud, or when evidence tending to establish the defendant's innocence has been intentionally destroyed or withheld, thus preventing its production at trial;

(f) when, after retiring to deliberate, the jury has received other evidence; when a juror has talked with anyone about the case; or when a juror became so intoxicated that his or her vote was probably influenced as a result;

(g) when the jury has engaged in such misconduct that the defendant did not receive a fair and impartial trial; or

(h) when the verdict is contrary to the law and the evidence.

21.4. Time to File and Amend Motion.

(a) To File. The defendant may file a motion for new trial before, but no later than 30 days after, the date when the trial court imposes or suspends sentence in open court.

(b) To Amend. Within 30 days after the date when the trial court imposes or suspends sentence in open court but before the court overrules any preceding motion for new trial, a defendant may, without leave of court, file one or more amended motions for new trial.

21.5. State May Controvert; Effect.

The State may oppose in writing any reason the defendant sets forth in the motion for new trial. The State's having opposed a motion for new trial does not affect a defendant's responsibilities under 21.6.

21.6. Time to Present.

The defendant must present the motion for new trial to the trial court within 10 days of filing it, unless the trial court in its discretion permits it to be presented and heard within 75 days from the date when the court imposes or suspends sentence in open court.

21.7. Types of Evidence Allowed at Hearing.

The court may receive evidence by affidavit or otherwise.

21.8. Court's Ruling.

(a) Time to Rule. The court must rule on a motion for new trial within 75 days after imposing or suspending sentence in open court.

(b) Ruling. In ruling on a motion for new trial, the court may make oral or written findings of fact. The granting of a motion for new trial must be accomplished by written order. A docket entry does not constitute a written order.

(c) Failure to Rule. A motion not timely ruled on by written order will be deemed denied when the period prescribed in (a) expires.

21.9. Granting a new trial.

(a) A court must grant a new trial when it has found a meritorious ground for new trial, but a court must grant only a new trial on punishment when it has found a ground that affected only the assessment of punishment.

(b) Granting a new trial restores the case to its position before the former trial, including, at any party's option, arraignment or pretrial proceedings initiated by that party.

(c) Granting a new trial on punishment restores the case to its position after the defendant was found guilty. Unless the defendant, State, and trial court all agree to a change, punishment in a new trial shall be assessed in accordance with the defendant's original election under article 37.07, § 2(b) of the Code of Criminal Procedure.

(d) A finding or verdict of guilt in the former trial must not be regarded as a presumption of guilt, nor may it be alluded to in the presence of the jury that hears the case on retrial of guilt. A finding of fact or an assessment of punishment in the former trial may not be alluded to in the presence of the jury that hears the case on retrial of punishment.

(Adopted by Order eff. Sept. 1, 1997. Amended by Order Dec. 13, 2006 eff. Jan. 1, 2007.)

Comment to 1997 change: Former Rules 30, 31, and 32 are merged. Paragraph (b)(6) of former Rule 30 is deleted because the rule-making authority of the Court of Criminal Appeals was withdrawn. *See* Code of Criminal Procedure article 40.001. Other nonsubstantive changes are made.

RULE 22. ARREST OF JUDGMENT IN CRIMINAL CASES.

22.1. Definition.

Motion in arrest of judgment means a defendant's oral or written suggestion that, for reasons stated in the motion, the judgment rendered against the defendant was contrary to law. Such a motion is made in the trial court.

22.2. Grounds.

The motion may be based on any of the following grounds:

(a) that the indictment or information is subject to an exception on substantive grounds;

(b) that in relation to the indictment or information a verdict is substantively defective; or

(c) that the judgment is invalid for some other reason.

22.3. Time to File Motion.

A defendant may file a motion in arrest of judgment before, but no later than 30 days after, the date when the trial court imposes or suspends sentence in open court.

22.4. Court's Ruling.

(a) Time to Rule; Form of Ruling. The court must rule on a motion in arrest of judgment within 75 days after imposing or suspending sentence in open court. The ruling may be oral or in writing.

(b) Failure to Rule. A motion not timely ruled on will be deemed denied when the period prescribed in (a) expires.

22.5. Effect of Denying.

For purposes of the defendant's giving notice of appeal, an order denying a motion in arrest of judgment will be considered an order denying a motion for new trial.

22.6. Effect of Granting.

(a) Defendant Restored. If judgment is arrested, the defendant is restored to the position that he or she had before the indictment or information was presented.

(b) Defendant Discharged or Remanded. If the judgment is arrested, the defendant will be discharged. But the trial court may remand the defendant to custody or fix bail if the court determines, from the evidence adduced at trial, that the defendant may be convicted on a proper indictment or information, or on a proper verdict in relation to the indictment or information.

(Adopted by Order eff. Sept. 1, 1997.)

Comment to 1997 change: Former Rules 33, 34, and 35 are merged without substantive change.

RULE 23. NUNC PRO TUNC PROCEEDINGS IN CRIMINAL CASES.

23.1. Judgment and Sentence.

Unless the trial court has granted a new trial or arrested the judgment, or unless the defendant has appealed, a failure to render judgment and pronounce sentence may be corrected at any time by the court's doing so.

23.2. Credit on Sentence.

When sentence is pronounced, the trial court must give the defendant credit on that sentence for:

(a) all time the defendant has been confined since the time when judgment and sentence should have been entered and pronounced; and

(b) all time between the defendant's arrest and confinement to the time when judgment and sentence should have been entered and pronounced.

(Adopted by Order eff. Sept. 1, 1997.)

Comment to 1997 change: This is former Rule 36. The rule is amended without substantive change.

RULE 24. SUSPENSION OF ENFORCEMENT OF JUDGMENT PENDING APPEAL IN CIVIL CASES.

24.1. Suspension of Enforcement.

(a) Methods. Unless the law or these rules provide otherwise, a judgment debtor may supersede the judgment by:

(1) filing with the trial court clerk a written agreement with the judgment creditor for suspending enforcement of the judgment;

(2) filing with the trial court clerk a good and sufficient bond;

(3) making a deposit with the trial court clerk in lieu of a bond; or

(4) providing alternate security ordered by the court.

(b) Bonds.

(1) A bond must be:

(A) in the amount required by 24.2;

(B) payable to the judgment creditor;

(C) signed by the judgment debtor or the debtor's agent;

(D) signed by a sufficient surety or sureties as obligors; and

(E) conditioned as required by (d).

(2) To be effective a bond must be approved by the trial court clerk. On motion of any party, the trial court will review the bond.

(c) Deposit in Lieu of Bond.

(1) Types of Deposits. Instead of filing a surety bond, a party may deposit with the trial court clerk:

(A) cash;

(B) a cashier's check payable to the clerk, drawn on any federally insured and federally or state-chartered bank or savings-and-loan association; or

(C) with leave of court, a negotiable obligation of the federal government or of any federally insured and federally or state-chartered bank or savings-and-loan association.

(2) Amount of Deposit. The deposit must be in the amount required by 24.2.

(3) Clerk's Duties. The clerk must promptly deposit any cash or a cashier's check in accordance with law. The clerk must hold the deposit until the conditions of liability in (d) are extinguished. The clerk must then release any remaining funds in the deposit to the judgment debtor.

(d) Conditions of Liability. The surety or sureties on a bond, any deposit in lieu of a bond, or any alternate security ordered by the court is subject to liability for all damages and costs that may be awarded against the debtor—up to the amount of the bond, deposit, or security—if:

(1) the debtor does not perfect an appeal or the debtor's appeal is dismissed, and the debtor does not perform the trial court's judgment;

(2) the debtor does not perform an adverse judgment final on appeal; or

(3) the judgment is for the recovery of an interest in real or personal property, and the debtor does not pay the creditor the value of the property interest's rent or revenue during the pendency of the appeal.

(e) Orders of Trial Court. The trial court may make any order necessary to adequately protect the judgment creditor against loss or damage that the appeal might cause.

(f) Effect of Supersedeas. Enforcement of a judgment must be suspended if the judgment is superseded. Enforcement begun before the judgment is superseded must cease when the judgment is superseded. If execution has been issued, the clerk will promptly issue a writ of supersedeas.

24.2. Amount of Bond, Deposit or Security.

(a) Type of Judgment.

(1) For Recovery of Money. When the judgment is for money, the amount of the bond, deposit, or security must equal the sum of compensatory damages awarded in the judgment, interest for the estimated duration of the appeal, and costs awarded in the judgment. But the amount must not exceed the lesser of:

(A) 50 percent of the judgment debtor's current net worth; or

(B) 25 million dollars.

(2) For Recovery of Property. When the judgment is for the recovery of an interest in real or personal property, the trial court will determine the type of security that the judgment debtor must post. The amount of that security must be at least:

(A) the value of the property interest's rent or revenue, if the property interest is real; or

(B) the value of the property interest on the date when the court rendered judgment, if the property interest is personal.

(3) Other Judgment. When the judgment is for something other than money or an interest in property, the trial court must set the amount and type of security that the judgment debtor must post. The security must adequately protect the judgment creditor against loss or damage that the appeal might cause. But the trial court may decline to permit the judgment to be superseded if the judgment creditor posts security ordered by the trial court in an amount and type that will secure the judgment debtor against any loss or damage caused by the relief granted the judgment creditor if an appellate court determines, on final disposition, that that relief was improper. When the judgment debtor is the state, a department of this state, or the head of a department of this state, the trial court must permit a judgment to be superseded except in a matter arising from a contested case in an administrative enforcement action.

(4) Conservatorship or Custody. When the judgment involves the conservatorship or custody of a minor or other person under legal disability, enforcement of the judgment will not be suspended, with or without security, unless ordered by the trial court. But upon a proper showing, the appellate court may suspend enforcement of the judgment with or without security.

(5) For a Governmental Entity. When a judgment in favor of a governmental entity in its governmental capacity is one in which the entity has no pecuniary interest, the trial court must determine whether to suspend enforcement, with or without security, taking into account the harm that is likely to result to the judgment debtor if enforcement is not suspended, and the harm that is likely to result to others if enforcement is suspended. The appellate court may review the trial court's determination and suspend enforcement of the judgment, with or without security, or refuse to suspend the judgment. If security is required, recovery is limited to the governmental entity's actual damages resulting from suspension of the judgment.

(b) Lesser Amount. The trial court must lower the amount of security required by (a) to an amount that will not cause the judgment debtor substantial economic harm if, after notice to all parties and a hearing, the court finds that posting a bond, deposit, or security in the amount required by (a) is likely to cause the judgment debtor substantial economic harm.

(c) Determination of Net Worth.

(1) Judgment Debtor's Affidavit Required; Contents; Prima Facie Evidence. A judgment debtor who provides a bond, deposit, or security under (a)(1)(2) in an amount based on the debtor's net worth must simultaneously file with the trial court clerk an affidavit that states the debtor's net worth and states complete, detailed information concerning the debtor's assets and liabilities from which net worth can be ascertained. An affidavit that meets these requirements is prima facie evidence of the debtor's net worth for the purpose of establishing the amount of the bond, deposit, or security required to suspend enforcement of the judgment. A trial court clerk must receive and file a net worth affidavit tendered for filing by a judgment debtor.

(2) Contest; Discovery. A judgment creditor may file a contest to the debtor's claimed net worth. The contest need not be sworn. The creditor may conduct reasonable discovery concerning the judgment debtor's net worth.

(3) Hearing; Burden of Proof; Findings; Additional Security. The trial court must hear a judgment creditor's contest of the judgment debtor's claimed net worth promptly after any discovery has been completed. The judgment debtor has the burden of proving net worth. The trial court must issue an order that states the debtor's net worth and states with particularity the factual basis for that determination. If the trial court orders additional or other security to supercede the judgment, the enforcement of the judgment will be suspended for twenty days after the trial court's order. If the judgment debtor does not comply with the order within that period, the judgment may be enforced against the judgment debtor.

(d) Injunction. The trial court may enjoin the judgment debtor from dissipating or transferring assets to avoid satisfaction of the judgment, but the trial court may not make any order that interferes with the judgment debtor's use, transfer, conveyance, or dissipation of assets in the normal course of business.

(Amended by Order August 29, 2003, effective in all cases in which a final judgment is signed on or after Sept. 1. 2003; Order March 10, 2008, eff. Sept. 1, 2008; Order Aug. 20, 2008, eff. Sept. 1, 2008; Misc. Docket No. 18-9061 April 2, 2018, eff May 1, 2018..)

24.3. Continuing Trial Court Jurisdiction; Duties of Judgment Debtor.

(a) Continuing Jurisdiction. Even after the trial court's plenary power expires, the trial court has continuing jurisdiction to do the following:

(1) order the amount and type of security and decide the sufficiency of sureties; and

(2) if circumstances change, modify the amount or type of security required to continue the suspension of a judgment's execution.

(b) Duties of Judgment Debtor. If, after jurisdiction attaches in an appellate court, the trial court orders or modifies the security or decides the sufficiency of sureties, the judgment debtor must notify the appellate court of the trial court's action.

24.4. Appellate Review.

(a) Motions; Review. A party may seek review of the trial court's ruling by motion filed in the court of appeals with jurisdiction or potential jurisdiction over the appeal from the judgment in the case. A party may seek review of the court of appeals' ruling on the motion by petition for writ of mandamus in the Supreme Court. The appellate court may review:

(1) the sufficiency or excessiveness of the amount of security, but when the judgment is for money, the appellate court must not modify the amount of security to exceed the limits imposed by rule 24.2(a)(1);

(2) the sureties on any bond;

(3) the type of security;

(4) the determination whether to permit suspension of enforcement; and

(5) the trial court's exercise of discretion under Rule 24.3(a).

(b) Grounds of Review. Review may be based both on conditions as they existed at the time the trial court signed an order, and on changes in those conditions afterward.

(c) Temporary Orders. The appellate court may issue any temporary orders necessary to preserve the parties' rights.

(d) Filing in Appellate Court. A motion filed under paragraph (a) should be filed in the court of appeals having potential appellate jurisdiction over the underlying judgment. The court of appeals' ruling is subject to review on petition for writ of mandamus to the Texas Supreme Court.

(e) Action by Appellate Court. The motion must be heard at the earliest practicable time. The appellate court may require that the amount of a bond, deposit, or other security be increased or decreased, and that another bond, deposit, or security be provided and approved by the trial court clerk. The appellate court may require other changes in the trial court order. The appellate court may remand to the trial court for entry of findings of fact or for the taking of evidence.

(f) Effect of Ruling. If the appellate court orders additional or other security to supersede the judgment, enforcement will be suspended for 20 days after the appellate court's order. If the judgment debtor does not comply with the order within that period, the judgment may be enforced. When any additional bond, deposit, or security has been filed, the trial court clerk must notify the appellate court. The posting of additional security will not release the previously posted security or affect any alternative security arrangements that the judgment debtor previously made unless specifically ordered by the appellate court.

(Adopted by Order eff. Sept. 1, 1997. Amended by Order Aug. 29, 2003, eff. Sept. 1, 2003; Order March 10, 2008 eff. Sept. 1, 2008; Order Aug. 20, 2008, eff. Sept. 1, 2008.)

Comment to 1997 change: Former Rules 47, 48, and 49 are merged. The rule is substantially revised. Paragraph 24.1(a) now provides for superseding the judgment by agreement. Paragraph 24.1(c) is taken from former Rule 48 and provides for a deposit in lieu of the bond, including specific provisions for the release of the deposit. Paragraph 24.1(d) provides the conditions for the surety to honor the bond and for the deposit to be paid to the judgment creditor. In subdivision 24.2, the provisions for determining the amount of the bond or deposit are simplified. All provisions regarding superseding a judgment for an interest in property are merged into subparagraph 24.2(a)(2). The procedure for allowing security in a lesser amount is moved to paragraph 24.2(b) and is made applicable to all judgments. Subdivision 24.4 is taken from former Rule 49. The procedure for appellate review is more precisely stated.

Comment to 2008 changes: Subdivision 24.2(c) is amended to clarify the procedure in determining net worth. A debtor's affidavit of net worth must be detailed, but the clerk must file what is tendered without determining whether it complies with the rule. If the trial court orders that additional or other security be given, the debtor is afforded time to comply. Subdivision 24.4(a) is revised to clarify that a party seeking relief from a supersedeas ruling should file a motion in the court of appeals that has or presumably will have jurisdiction of the appeal. After the court of appeals has ruled, a party may seek review by filing a petition for writ of mandamus in the Supreme Court. *See In re Smith/In re Main Place Custom Homes, Inc.*, 192 S.W.3d 564, 568 (Tex. 2006) (per curiam).

RULE 25. PERFECTING APPEALs.

25.1. Civil Cases.

(a) Notice of Appeal. An appeal is perfected when a written notice of appeal is filed with the trial court clerk. If a notice of appeal is mistakenly filed with the appellate court, the notice is deemed to have been filed the same day with the trial court clerk, and the appellate clerk must immediately send the trial court clerk a copy of the notice.

(b) Jurisdiction of Appellate Court. The filing of a notice of appeal by any party invokes the appellate court's jurisdiction over all parties to the trial court's judgment or order appealed from. Any party's failure to take any other step required by these rules, including the failure of another party to perfect an appeal under (c), does not deprive the appellate court of jurisdiction but is ground only for the appellate court to act appropriately, including dismissing the appeal.

(c) Who Must File Notice. A party who seeks to alter the trial court's judgment or other appealable order must file a notice of appeal. Parties whose interests are aligned may file a joint notice of appeal. The appellate court may not grant a party who does not file a notice of appeal more favorable relief than did the trial court except for just cause.

(d) Contents of Notice. The notice of appeal must:

(1) identify the trial court and state the case's trial court number and style;

(2) state the date of the judgment or order appealed from;

(3) state that the party desires to appeal;

(4) state the court to which the appeal is taken unless the appeal is to either the First or Fourteenth Court of Appeals, in which case the notice must state that the appeal is to either of those courts;

(5) state the name of each party filing the notice;

(6) n an accelerated appeal, state that the appeal is accelerated and state whether it is a parental termination or child protection case, as defined in Rule 28.4;

(7) in a restricted appeal:

(A) state that the appellant is a party affected by the trial court's judgment but did not participate—either in person or through counsel—in the hearing that resulted in the judgment complained of;

(B) state that the appellant did not timely file either a postjudgment motion, request for findings of fact and conclusions of law, or notice of appeal; and

(C) be verified by the appellant if the appellant does not have counsel.

(8) state, if applicable, that the appellant is presumed indigent and may proceed without paying costs under Rule 20.1.

(e) Service of Notice. The notice of appeal must be served on all parties to the trial court's final judgment or, in an interlocutory appeal, on all parties to the trial court proceeding.

(f) Clerk's Duties. The trial court clerk must immediately send a copy of the notice of appeal to the appellate court clerk and to the court reporter or court reporters responsible for preparing the reporter's record.

(g) Amending the Notice. An amended notice of appeal correcting a defect or omission in an earlier filed notice may be filed in the appellate court at any time before the appellant's brief is filed. The amended notice is subject to being struck for cause on the motion of any party affected by the amended notice. After the appellant's brief is filed, the notice may be amended only on leave of the appellate court and on such terms as the court may prescribe.

(h) Enforcement of Judgment Not Suspended by Appeal. The filing of a notice of appeal does not suspend enforcement of the judgment. Enforcement of the judgment may proceed unless:

(1) the judgment is superseded in accordance with Rule 24, or

(2) the appellant is entitled to supersede the judgment without security by filing a notice of appeal.

(Amended by Order Aug. 31, 2011, eff. Sept. 1, 2011; Order Dec. 12, 2011, eff. March 1, 2012; Order Feb. 13, 2012, eff. March 1, 2012; Tex. Sup. Ct. Misc. Docket No. 16-9056, eff. Sept. 1, 2016; Amended by Tex. Sup. Ct. Misc. Docket No. 16-9122, eff. Sept. 1, 2016.)

[Statement of Inability to Afford Payment of Court Costs as provided in Tex. Sup. Ct. Misc. Docket No. 16-9122, eff. Sept. 1, 2016 and applies to any contest of, or challenge to, a claim of inability to afford payment of court costs that is pending on September 1, 2016.]

25.2. Criminal Cases.

(a) Rights to Appeal.

(1) Of the State. The State is entitled to appeal a court's order in a criminal case as provided by Code of Criminal Procedure article 44.01.

(2) Of the Defendant. A defendant in a criminal case has the right of appeal under Code of Criminal Procedure article 44.02 and these rules. The trial court shall enter a certification of the defendant's right of appeal each time it enters a judgment of guilt or other appealable order other than an order appealable under Code of Criminal Procedure Chapter 64. In a plea bargain case—that is, a case in which a defendant's plea was guilty or nolo contendere and the punishment did not exceed the punishment recommended by the prosecutor and agreed to by the defendant—a defendant may appeal only:

(A) those matters that were raised by written motion filed and ruled on before trial,

(B) after getting the trial court's permission to appeal, or

(C) where the specific appeal is expressly authorized by statute.

(b) Perfection of Appeal. In a criminal case, appeal is perfected by timely filing a sufficient notice of appeal. In a death-penalty case it is unnecessary to file a notice of appeal, but, in every death-penalty case, the clerk of the trial court shall file a notice of conviction with the Court of Criminal Appeals within thirty days after the defendant is sentenced to death.

(c) Form and Sufficiency of Notice.

(1) Notice must be given in writing and filed with the trial court clerk. If the notice of appeal is received in the court of appeals, the clerk of that court shall immediately record on the notice the date that it was received and send the notice to the trial court clerk.

(2) Notice is sufficient if it shows the party's desire to appeal from the judgment or other appealable order, and, if the State is the appellant, the notice complies with Code of Criminal Procedure article 44.01.

(d) Certification of Defendant's Right of Appeal. If the defendant is the appellant, the record must include the trial court's certification of the defendant's right of appeal under Rule 25.2(a)(2). The certification shall include a notice that the defendant has been informed of his rights concerning an appeal, as well as any right to file a *pro se* petition for discretionary review. This notification shall be signed by the defendant, with a copy given to him. The certification should be part of the record when notice is filed, but may be added by timely amendment or supplementation under this rule or Rule 34.5(c)(1) or Rule 37.1 or by order of the appellate court under Rule 34.5(c)(2). The appeal must be dismissed if a certification that shows the defendant has the right of appeal has not been made part of the record under these rules.

(e) Clerk's Duties. The trial court clerk must note on the copies of the notice of appeal and the trial court's certification of the defendant's right of appeal the case number and the date when each was filed. The clerk must then immediately send one copy to the clerk of the appropriate court of appeals and, if the defendant is the appellant, one copy of each to the State's attorney.

(f) Amending the Notice or Certification. An amended notice of appeal or trial court's certification of the defendant's right of appeal correcting a defect or omission in an earlier filed notice or certification, including a defect in the notification of the defendant's appellate rights, may be filed in the appellate court in accordance with Rule 37.1, or at any time before the appealing party's brief is filed if the court of appeals has not used Rule 37.1. The amended notice or certification is subject to being struck for cause on the motion of any party affected by the amended notice or certification. After the appealing party's brief is filed, the notice or certification may be amended only on leave of the appellate court and on such terms as the court may prescribe.

(g) Effect of Appeal. Once the record has been filed in the appellate court, all further proceedings in the trial court—except as provided otherwise by law or by these rules—will be suspended until the trial court receives the appellate-court mandate.

(h) Advice of Right of Appeal. When a court enters a judgment or other appealable order and the defendant has a right of appeal, the court (orally or in writing) shall advise the defendant of his right of appeal and of the requirements for timely filing a sufficient notice of appeal.

(Amended by Order Dec. 23, 2002, eff. Jan. 1, 2003; Order Dec. 13, 2006, eff. Jan. 1, 2007; Order May 2, 2007, eff. Sept. 1, 2007; Order Aug. 20, 2008, eff. Sept. 1, 2008; Order Nov. 5, 2018 eff. Dec. 1, 20018.)

Comment on 2002 change: Rule 25.2, for criminal cases, is amended. Subdivision 25.2(a) states the parties' right of appeal that are established by Code of Criminal Procedure article 44.01 and by article 44.02, the proviso of which was repealed when rulemaking power was given to the Court of Criminal Appeals. Subdivision 25.2(b) is given the requirement that a notice of appeal be in "sufficient" form, which codifies the decisional law. The requirement in former subdivision 25.2(b)(3) that a plea-bargain appellant's notice of appeal specify the right of appeal is replaced by a requirement in subdivision 25.2(d) that the trial court certify the defendant's right of appeal in every case in which a judgment or other appealable order is entered. The certificate should be signed at the time of judgment or other appealable order is pronounced. The form of certification of the defendant's right of appeal is provided in an appendix [see below] to these rules. If the record does not include the trial court's certification that the defendant has the right of appeal, the appeal must be dismissed. If a sufficient notice of appeal or certification is not filed after the appellate court deals with the defect (*See* Rules 34.5(c) and 37.1), preparation of an appellate record and representation by an appointed attorney may cease.

[Form to be included in Appendix and is omitted.]

RULE 26. TIME TO PERFECT APPEAL.

26.1. Civil Cases.

The notice of appeal must be filed within 30 days after the judgment is signed, except as follows:

(a) the notice of appeal must be filed within 90 days after the judgment is signed if any party timely files:

(1) a motion for new trial;

(2) a motion to modify the judgment;

(3) a motion to reinstate under Texas Rule of Civil Procedure 165a; or

(4) a request for findings of fact and conclusions of law if findings and conclusions either are required by the Rules of Civil Procedure or, if not required, could properly be considered by the appellate court;

(b) in an accelerated appeal, the notice of appeal must be filed within 20 days after the judgment or order is signed;

(c) in a restricted appeal, the notice of appeal must be filed within six months after the judgment or order is signed; and

(d) if any party timely files a notice of appeal, another party may file a notice of appeal within the applicable period stated above or 14 days after the first filed notice of appeal, whichever is later.

26.2. Criminal Cases.

(a) By the Defendant. The notice of appeal must be filed:

(1) within 30 days after the day sentence is imposed or suspended in open court, or after the day the trial court enters an appealable order; or

(2) within 90 days after the day sentence is imposed or suspended in open court if the defendant timely files a motion for new trial.

(b) By the State. The notice of appeal must be filed within 20 days after the day the trial court enters the order, ruling, or sentence to be appealed.

(Amended by Order March 10, 2008, eff. Sept. 1, 2008; Order Aug. 20, 2008, eff. Sept. 1, 2008.)

26.3. Extension of Time.

The appellate court may extend the time to file the notice of appeal if, within 15 days after the deadline for filing the notice of appeal, the party:

(a) files in the trial court the notice of appeal; and

(b) files in the appellate court a motion complying with Rule 10.5(b).

(Adopted by Order eff. Sept. 1, 1997.)

Comment to 1997 change: This is former Rule 41. All times for perfecting appeal in civil cases—including the time for perfecting a restricted appeal—are stated. An extension of time is available for all appeals. The provisions of former Rule 41(c) regarding prematurely filed documents are moved to Rule 27. Nonsubstantive changes are made in the rule for criminal cases.

RULE 27. PREMATURE FILINGS.

27.1. Prematurely Filed Notice of Appeal.

(a) Civil Cases. In a civil case, a prematurely filed notice of appeal is effective and deemed filed on the day of, but after, the event that begins the period for perfecting the appeal.

(b) Criminal Cases. In a criminal case, a prematurely filed notice of appeal is effective and deemed filed on the same day, but after, sentence is imposed or suspended in open court, or the appealable order is signed by the trial court. But a notice of appeal is not effective if filed before the trial court makes a finding of guilt or receives a jury verdict.

27.2. Other Premature Actions.

The appellate court may treat actions taken before an appealable order is signed as relating to an appeal of that order and give them effect as if they had been taken after the order was signed. The appellate court may allow an appealed order that is not final to be modified so as to be made final and may allow the modified order and all proceedings relating to it to be included in a supplemental record.

27.3. If Appealed Order Modified or Vacated.

After an order or judgment in a civil case has been appealed, if the trial court modifies the order or judgment, or if the trial court vacates the order or judgment and replaces it with another appealable order or judgment, the appellate court must treat the appeal as from the subsequent order or judgment and may treat actions relating to the appeal of the first order or judgment as relating to the appeal of the subsequent order or judgment. The subsequent order or judgment and actions relating to it may be included in the original or supplemental record. Any party may nonetheless appeal from the subsequent order or judgment.

(Adopted by Order eff. Sept. 1, 1997.)

Comment to 1997 change: This rule is new and combines the provisions of former Rules 41(c) and 58.

RULE 28. ACCELERATED, Agreed, and Permissive APPEALS IN CIVIL CASES.

28.1. Civil cases—Appeal as of Right.

(a) Types of Accelerated Appeals. Appeals from interlocutory orders (when allowed by statute), appeals in quo warranto proceedings, appeals required by statute to be accelerated or expedited, and appeals required by law to be filed or perfected within less than 30 days after the date of the order or judgment being appealed are accelerated appeals.

(b) Perfection of Accelerated Appeal. Unless otherwise provided by statute, an accelerated appeal is perfected by filing a notice of appeal in compliance with Rule 25.1 within the time allowed by Rule 26.1(b) or as extended by Rule 26.3. Filing a motion for new trial, any other post-trial motion, or a request for findings of fact will not extend the time to perfect an accelerated appeal.

(c) Appeals of Interlocutory Orders. The trial court need not file findings of fact and conclusions of law but may do so within 30 days after the order is signed.

(d) Quo Warranto Appeals. The trial court may grant a motion for new trial timely filed under Texas Rule of Civil Procedure 329b(a)-(b) until 50 days after the trial court's final judgment is signed. If not determined by signed written order within that period, the motion will be deemed overruled by operation of law on expiration of that period.

(e) Record and Briefs. In lieu of the clerk's record, the appellate court may hear an accelerated appeal on the original papers forwarded by the trial court or on sworn and uncontroverted copies of those papers. The appellate court may allow the case to be submitted without briefs. The deadlines and procedures for filing the record and briefs in an accelerated appeal are provided in Rules 35.1 and 38.6.

(Amended by Order March 10, 2008, eff. Sept. 1, 2008; Order Aug. 20, 2008, eff. Sept. 1, 2008; Order Aug. 20, 2008, eff. Sept. 1, 2008; Order Aug. 25, 2008, eff. Sept. 1, 2008.)

28.2. Agreed Interlocutory Appeals in Civil Cases.

(a) Perfecting Appeal. An agreed appeal of an interlocutory order permitted by statute must be perfected as provided in Rule 25.1. The notice of appeal must be filed no later than the 20th day after the date the trial court signs a written order granting permission to appeal, unless the court of appeals extends the time for filing pursuant to Rule 26.3.

(b) Other Requirements. In addition to perfecting appeal, the appellant must file with the clerk of the appellate court a docketing statement as provided in Rule 32.1 and pay to the clerk of the appellate court all required fees authorized to be collected by the clerk.

(c) Contents of Notice. The notice of accelerated appeal must contain, in addition to the items required by Rule 25.1(d), the following:

(1) a list of the names of all parties to the trial court proceeding and the names, addresses, and telefax numbers of all trial and appellate counsel;

(2) a copy of the trial court's order granting permission to appeal;

(3) a copy of the trial court order appealed from;

(4) a statement that all parties to the trial court proceeding agreed to the trial court's order granting permission to appeal;

(5) a statement that all parties to the trial court proceeding agreed that the order granting permission to appeal involves a controlling question of law as to which there is a substantial ground for difference of opinion;

(6) a brief statement of the issues or points presented; and

(7) a concise explanation of how an immediate appeal may materially advance the ultimate termination of litigation.

(d) Determination of Jurisdiction. If the court of appeals determines that a notice of appeal filed under this rule does not demonstrate the court's jurisdiction, it may order the appellant to file an amended notice of appeal. On a party's motion or its own initiative, the court of appeals may also order the appellant or any other party to file briefing addressing whether the appeal meets the statutory requirements, and may direct the parties to file supporting evidence. If, after providing an opportunity to file an amended notice of appeal or briefing addressing potential jurisdictional defects, the court of appeals concludes that a jurisdictional defect exists, it may dismiss the appeal for want of jurisdiction at any stage of the appeal.

(e) Record; Briefs. The rules governing the filing of the appellate record and briefs in accelerated appeals apply. A party may address in its brief any issues related to the court of appeals' jurisdiction, including whether the appeal meets the statutory requirements.

(f) No Automatic Stay of Proceedings in Trial Court. An agreed appeal of an interlocutory order permitted by statute does not stay proceedings in the trial court except as agreed by the parties and ordered by the trial court or the court of appeals.

28.3. Permissive Appeals in Civil Cases.

(a) Petition Required. When a trial court has permitted an appeal from an interlocutory order that would not otherwise be appealable, a party seeking to appeal must petition the court of appeals for permission to appeal.

(b) Where Filed. The petition must be filed with the clerk of the court of appeals having appellate jurisdiction over the action in which the order to be appealed is issued. The First and Fourteenth Courts of Appeals must determine in which of those two courts a petition will be filed.

(c) When Filed. The petition must be filed within 15 days after the order to be appealed is signed. If the order is amended by the trial court, either on its own or in response to a party's motion, to include the court's permission to appeal, the time to petition the court of appeals runs from the date the amended order is signed.

(d) Extension of Time to File Petition. The court of appeals may extend the time to file the petition if the party;

(1) files the petition within 15 days after the deadline, and

(2) files a motion complying with Rule 10.5(b).

(e) Contents. The petition must:

(1) contain the information required by Rule 25.1 (d) to be included in a notice of appeal:

(2) attach a copy of the order from which appeal is sought;

(3) contain a table of contents, index of authorities, issues presented, and a statement of facts; and

(4) argue clearly and concisely why the order to be appealed involves a controlling question of law as to which there is a substantial ground for difference of opinion and how an immediate appeal from the order may materially advance the ultimate termination of the litigation.

(f) Response; Reply; Cross-Petition; Time for Filing. If any party timely files a petition, any other party may file a response or a cross-petition within 10 days. A party may file a response to a cross-petition within 10 days of the date the cross-petition is filed. A petitioner or cross-petitioner may reply to any matter in a response within 7 days of the date the response is filed. The court of appeals may extend the time to file a response, reply, and cross-petition.

(g) Length of Petition. Cross-Petition, Response, and Reply. A petition, cross-petition, response, and reply must comply with the page limitations in Rule 9.4(i)(2)(D)-(E).

(h) Service. A petition, cross-petition, response, and reply must be served on all parties to the trial court proceeding.

(i) Docketing Statement. Upon filing the petition, the petitioner must file the docketing statement required by Rule 32.1.

(j) Time for Determination. Unless the court of appeals orders otherwise, a petition, and any cross-petition, response, and reply, will be determined without oral argument, no earlier than 10 days after the petition is filed.

(k) When Petition Granted. If the petition is granted, a notice of appeal is deemed to have been filed under Rule 26. Kb) on that date, and the appeal is governed by the rules for accelerated appeals. A separate notice of appeal need not be filed. A copy of the order granting the petition must be filed with the trial court clerk.

(Amended by Order March 4, 2013, eff. March 4, 2013.)

28.4. Accelerated Appeals in Parental Termination and Child Protection Cases

(a) Application and Definitions.

(1) Appeals in parental termination and child protection cases are governed by the rules of appellate procedure for accelerated appeals, except as otherwise provided in Rule 28.4.

(2) In Rule 28.4:

(A) a "parental termination case" means a suit in which termination of the parent-child relationship is at issue.

(B) a "child protection case" means a suit affecting the parent-child relationship filed by a governmental entity for managing conservatorship.

(b) Appellate Record.

(1) Responsibility for Preparation of Reporter's Record. In addition to the responsibility imposed on the trial court in Rule 35.3(c), when the reporter's responsibility to prepare, certify and timely file the reporter s record arises under Rule 35.3(b), the trial court must direct the official or deputy reporter to immediately commence the preparation of the reporter's record. The trial court must arrange for a substitute reporter, if necessary.

(2) Extension of Time. The appellate court may grant an extension of time to file a record under Rule 35.3(c); however, the extension or extensions granted must not exceed 30 days cumulatively, absent extraordinary circumstances.

(3) Restriction on Preparation Inapplicable. Section 13.003 of the Civil Practice & Remedies Code does not apply to an appeal from a parental termination or child protection case.

(c) Remand for New Trial. If the judgment of the appellate court reverses and remands a parental termination or child protection case for a new trial, the judgment must instruct the trial court to commence the new trial no later than 180 days after the mandate is issued by the appellate court.

(Adopted by Order eff. Sept. 1, 1997. Amended by Order March 10, 2008 eff. Sept. 1, 2008; Order Aug. 20, 2008, eff. Sept. 1, 2008; Order Aug. 31, 2011, eff. Sept. 1, 2011; Order Sept. 9, 2011, eff. Sept. 9, 2011; Order Dec. 12, 2011, eff. March 1, 2012; Order Feb. 13, 2012, eff. March 1, 2012.)

Comment to 1997 change: This is former Rule 42. A motion for new trial is now permitted in an appeal from an interlocutory order, but it does not extend the time to perfect appeal. The deadlines for filing items in an accelerated appeal are moved to other rules. *See* Rules 26.1, 35.1 and 38.6. Former Rule 42(b), regarding discretionary acceleration, is omitted as unnecessary. *See* Rule 40.1. The provision in former Rule 42(c) allowing the court to shorten the time to file briefs is omitted as unnecessary. *See* Rule 38.6.

Comment to 2008 changes: Rule 28 is rewritten. Subdivision 28.1 more clearly defines accelerated appeals and provides a uniform appellate timetable. But many statutes that provide for accelerated or expedited appeals also set appellate timetables, and statutory deadlines govern over deadlines provided in the rule. Subdivision 28.2 provides procedures for an agreed appeal of an interlocutory order permitted by statute. Such appeals are now permitted under Section 51.014(d) of the Civil Practice and Remedies Code. The requirements for perfecting appeal are generally set out in Rule 25.1, and as provided there, only the notice of appeal is jurisdictional.

Comment to 2011 Change: Section 51.014(d)-(f) of the Texas Civil Practice and Remedies Code, as amended in 2011, provides for appeals of orders not otherwise appealable when permitted by the trial court. The 2011 amendments, which explicitly apply only to cases commenced on or after September 1, 2011, eliminated the prior requirement that the parties agree to the appeal and reinstated a requirement that the court of appeals also permit the appeal. Act of May 25, 2011, 82nd Leg., R.S., ch. 203, §§ 3.01, 6.01 [HB 274], amending Act of May 27, 2005, 79th Leg. R.S., ch. 1051 [HB 1294], §§ 1-2, 2005 Tex. Gen. Laws 3512, 3512-3513 and Act of May 17, 2001, 77th Leg., R.S., ch. 1389 [HB 978], § 1, 2001 Tex. Gen. Laws 3575. The amendments necessitated the addition of Rule 28.3 and the adoption of Rule of Civil Procedure 168, which governs the procedure for obtaining permission to appeal from the trial court.

New Rule 28.3 applies only to appeals in cases that were filed in the trial court on or after September I, 2011. Rule 28.2 applies only to appeals in cases that were filed in the trial court before September 1, 2011.

Rule of Civil Procedure 168 clarifies that the trial court's permission to appeal should be included in the order to be appealed rather than in a separate order. As stated in Rule 28.3(c), if a prior order containing the trial court's ruling is amended to include such permission, the time for appeal runs from the amended order. Rule 28.3(k) further clarifies that if the petition is granted, appeal is thereby perfected, and the appeal proceeds as an accelerated appeal, with all deadlines-including deadlines and obligations for preparing the record-running from the date the petition was granted. A separate notice of appeal need not be filed. The petition procedure in Rule 28.3 is intended to be similar to the Rule 53 procedure governing petitions for review in the Supreme Court.

RULE 29. ORDERS PENDING INTERLOCUTORY APPEAL IN CIVIL CASES.

29.1. Effect of Appeal.

Perfecting an appeal from an order granting interlocutory relief does not suspend the order appealed from unless:

(a) the order is superseded in accordance with 29.2; or

(b) the appellant is entitled to supersede the order without security by filing a notice of appeal.

29.2. Security.

The trial court may permit an order granting interlocutory relief to be superseded pending an appeal from the order, in which event the appellant may supersede the order in accordance with Rule 24. If the trial court refuses to permit the appellant to supersede the order, the appellant may move the appellate court to review that decision for abuse of discretion.

29.3. Temporary Orders of Appellate Court.

When an appeal from an interlocutory order is perfected, the appellate court may make any temporary orders necessary to preserve the parties' rights until disposition of the appeal and may require appropriate security. But the appellate court must not suspend the trial court's order if the appellant's rights would be adequately protected by supersedeas or another order made under Rule 24.

29.4. Enforcement of Temporary Orders.

While an appeal from an interlocutory order is pending, only the appellate court in which the appeal is pending may enforce the order. But the appellate court may refer any enforcement proceeding to the trial court with instructions to:

(a) hear evidence and grant appropriate relief; or

(b) make findings and recommendations and report them to the appellate court.

29.5. Further Proceedings in Trial Court.

While an appeal from an interlocutory order is pending, the trial court retains jurisdiction of the case and unless prohibited by statute may make further orders, including one dissolving the order complained of on appeal. If permitted by law, the trial court may proceed with a trial on the merits. But the court must not make an order that:

(a) is inconsistent with any appellate court temporary order; or

(b) interferes with or impairs the jurisdiction of the appellate court or effectiveness of any relief sought or that may be granted on appeal.

(Amended by Order Dec. 23, 2002 eff. Jan. 1, 2003. Amended by Order March 10, 2008 eff. Sept. 1, 2008; Order Aug. 20, 2008, eff. Sept. 1, 2008.)

Comment to 2002 change: Rule 29.5 is amended to acknowledge that a trial court may be prohibited by law from proceeding to trial during the pendency of an interlocutory appeal, as for example by section 51.014(b) of the Texas Civil Practice and Remedies Code.

Comment to 2008 changes: Rule 29.5 is amended to be consistent with § 51.014(b) of the Civil Practice and Remedies Code, as amended in 2003, staying all proceedings in the trial court pending resolution of interlocutory appeals of class certification orders, denials of summary judgments based on assertions of immunity by governmental officers or employees, and orders granting or denying a governmental unit's plea to the jurisdiction.

29.6. Review of Further Orders.

(a) Motion to Review Further Orders. While an appeal from an interlocutory order is pending, on a party's motion or on the appellate court's own initiative, the appellate court may review the following:

(1) a further appealable interlocutory order concerning the same subject matter; and

(2) any interlocutory order that interferes with or impairs the effectiveness of the relief sought or that may be granted on appeal.

(b) Record. The party filing the motion may rely on the original record or may file a supplemental record with the motion.

(Adopted by Order eff. Sept. 1, 1997.)

Comment to 1997 change: This is former Rule 43. The provision in the former rule that an appeal from an order certifying a class suspends the order is repealed. The provision in the former rule that an order denying interlocutory relief cannot be suspended is omitted as unnecessary because the rule provides for superseding only orders granting relief. No substantive change is intended. The provision in former Rule 43(d) prohibiting the trial court from making an order granting substantially the same relief as the order appealed is repealed as being too broad. The provisions of former Rule 43(g) regarding the mandate are moved to Rule 18.6 and 18.7. The provision of former Rule 43(h) regarding rehearings is moved to Rule 49.4.

RULE 30. RESTRICTED APPEAL TO COURT OF APPEALS IN CIVIL CASES.

A party who did not participate—either in person or through counsel—in the hearing that resulted in the judgment complained of and who did not timely file a postjudgment motion or request for findings of fact and conclusions of law, or a notice of appeal within the time permitted by Rule 26.1(a), may file a notice of appeal within the time permitted by Rule 26.1(c). Restricted appeals replace writ of error appeals to the court of appeals. Statutes pertaining to writ of error appeals to the court of appeals apply equally to restricted appeals.

(Adopted by Order eff. Sept. 1, 1997.)

Comment to 1997 change: This is former Rule 45. The appeal by writ of error procedure is repealed. A procedure for an appeal filed within 6 months—called a restricted appeal—is substituted. This rule sets out who may take a restricted appeal. Rules 25.1 and 26.1 set out the method of perfection and the time for perfecting the appeal.

RULE 31. APPEALS IN HABEAS CORPUS, BAIL, AND EXTRADITION PROCEEDINGS IN CRIMINAL CASES.

31.1. Filing the Record and Briefs.

When written notice of appeal from a judgment or order in a habeas corpus or bail proceeding is filed, the trial court clerk must prepare and certify the clerk's record and, if the appellant requests, the court reporter must prepare and certify a reporter's record. The clerk must send the clerk's record and the court reporter must send the reporter's record to the appellate court within 15 days after the notice of appeal is filed. On reasonable explanation, the appellate court may shorten or extend the time to file the records.

(a) For an appeal from a habeas corpus proceeding challenging a conviction or an order placing the defendant on community supervision—but not challenging any particular condition of community supervision—the appellate court should use the same briefing rules, deadlines, and schedule that apply to direct appeals from criminal cases. On motion of any party, or on its own initiative, the appellate court may impose a more expedited timeline or submit the case without briefing, if necessary to do substantial justice to the parties.

(b) For an appeal from a bail proceeding or any other habeas corpus proceeding, including one that challenges a particular condition of community supervision, the court will—if it desires briefs—set the time for filing briefs.

(Amended by Order Nov. 5, 2018, eff. Dec. 1, 2018)

31.2. Submission; Hearing.

The applicant need not personally appear. The appellate court will not review any incidental question that might have arisen on the hearing of the application before the trial court. The sole purpose of the appeal is to do substantial justice to the parties.

(a) In an appeal from a habeas corpus proceeding challenging a conviction or an order placing the defendant on community supervision—but not challenging a particular condition of community supervision—the appellate court should use the same submission and hearing schedules that apply to direct appeals from criminal cases. On motion of any party, or on its own initiative, the appellate court may impose a more expedited timeline or submit the case without briefing, if necessary to do substantial justice to the parties.

(b) An appeal in any other habeas corpus or bail proceeding, including a challenge to a particular condition of community supervision, shall be submitted and heard at the earliest practicable time.

(Amended by Order Nov. 5, 2018, eff. Dec. 1, 2018)

31.3. Orders on Appeal.

The appellate court will render whatever judgment and make whatever orders the law and the nature of the case require. The court may make an appropriate order relating to costs, whether allowing costs and fixing the amount, or allowing no costs.

31.4. Stay of Mandate.

(a) When Motion for Stay Required. Despite Rule 18 or any other of these rules, in the following circumstances a party who in good faith intends to seek discretionary review must—within 15 days after the court of appeals renders judgment—file with the court of appeals clerk a motion for stay of mandate, to which is appended the party's petition for discretionary review showing reasons why the Court of Criminal Appeals should review the appellate court judgment:

(1) when a court of appeals affirms the judgment of the trial court in an extradition matter and thereby sanctions a defendant's extradition; or

(2) when a court of appeals reverses the trial court's judgment in a bail matter—including bail pending appeal under > Code of Criminal Procedure article 44.04(g)—and thereby grants or reduces the amount of bail.

(b) Determination of the Motion. The clerk must promptly submit the motion and appendix to the court of appeals, or to one or more judges as the court deems appropriate, for immediate consideration and determination.

(1) If the motion for stay is granted, the clerk will file the petition for discretionary review and process the case in accordance with Rule 68.7.

(2) If the motion is denied, the clerk will issue a mandate in accordance with the court of appeals' judgment.

(c) Denial of Stay. If the motion for stay is denied under 31.4(b)(2), the losing party may then present the motion and appendix to the clerk of the Court of Criminal Appeals, who will promptly submit them to the Court, or to one or more judges as the Court deems appropriate, for immediate consideration and determination. The Court of Criminal Appeals may deny the motion or stay or recall the mandate. If the mandate is stayed or recalled, the court of appeals clerk will file the petition for discretionary review and process the case in accordance with Rule 68.7.

31.5. Judgment Conclusive.

The court of appeals' judgment is final and conclusive if the Court of Criminal Appeals does not grant discretionary review. If the Court of Criminal Appeals grants discretionary review, that court's judgment is final and conclusive. In either case, no further application in the same case can be made for the writ unless the law provides otherwise.

31.6. Defendant Detained by Other Than Officer.

If the defendant is held by a person other than an officer, the sheriff receiving the appellate court mandate so ordering must immediately cause the defendant to be discharged, for which discharge the mandate is sufficient authority.

31.7. Judgment to Be Certified.

The appellate court clerk will certify the court's judgment to the officer holding the defendant in custody or, if the defendant is held by a person other than an officer, to the appropriate sheriff.

(Adopted by Order eff. Sept. 1, 1997.)

Comment to 1997 change: This is former Rule 44. Since the purpose of the appeal is to do substantial justice, it is extended to both parties in recognition that both parties now have the right to appeal. Other nonsubstantive changes are made.

RULE 32. DOCKETING STATEMENT.

32.1. Civil Cases.

Promptly upon filing the notice of appeal in a civil case, the appellant must file in the appellate court a docketing statement that includes the following information:

(a)(1) if the appellant filing the statement has counsel, the name of that appellant and the name, address, telephone number, fax number, if any, and State Bar of Texas identification number of the appellant's lead counsel; or

(2) if the appellant filing the statement is not represented by an attorney, that party's name, address, telephone number, and fax number, if any;

(b) the date the notice of appeal was filed in the trial court and, if mailed to the trial court clerk, the date of mailing;

(c) the trial court's name and county, the name of the judge who tried the case, and the date the judgment or order appealed from was signed;

(d) the date of filing of any motion for new trial, motion to modify the judgment, request for findings of fact, motion to reinstate, or other filing that affects the time for perfecting the appeal;

(e) the names of all other parties to the trial court's judgment or the order appealed from, and:

(1) if represented by counsel, their lead counsel's names, addresses, telephone numbers, and fax numbers, if any; or

(2) if not represented by counsel, the name, address, and telephone number of the party, or a statement that the appellant diligently inquired but could not discover that information;

(f) the general nature of the case—for example, personal injury, breach of contract, or temporary injunction;

(g) whether the appeal's submission should be given priority, whether the appeal is an accelerated one under Rule 28 or another rule or statute and whether it is a parental termination or child protection case, as defined in Rule 28.4;

(h) whether the appellant has requested or will request a reporter's record, and whether the trial was electronically recorded;

(i) the name of the court reporter;

(j) whether the appellant intends to seek temporary or ancillary relief while the appeal is pending;

(k) if the appellant filed a Statement of Inability to Afford Payment of Court Costs in the trial court:

(1) the date the Statement was filed;

(2) the date of filing of any motion challenging the Statement;

(3) the date of any hearing on the appellant's ability to afford costs; and

(4) if the trial court signed an order under Texas Rule of Civil Procedure 145, the court's findings regarding the appellant's ability to afford costs and the date that the order was signed.

(l) whether the appellant has filed or will file a supersedeas bond; and

(m) any other information the appellate court requires.

(Amended by Order Dec. 12, 2011, eff. March 1, 2012; Order Feb. 13, 2012, eff. March 1, 2012; Tex. Sup. Ct. Misc. Docket No. 16-9056, eff. Sept. 1, 2016; Amended by Tex. Sup. Ct. Misc. Docket No. 16-9122, eff. Sept. 1, 2016.)

[Statement of Inability to Afford Payment of Court Costs as provided in Tex. Sup. Ct. Misc. Docket No. 16-9122, eff. Sept. 1, 2016 and applies to any contest of, or challenge to, a claim of inability to afford payment of court costs that is pending on September 1, 2016.]

32.2. Criminal Cases.

Upon perfecting the appeal in a criminal case, the appellant must file in the appellate court a docketing statement that includes the following information:

(a)(1) if the appellant has counsel, the name of the appellant and the name, address, telephone number, fax number, if any, and State Bar of Texas identification number of the appellant's counsel, and whether the counsel is appointed or retained; or

(2) if the appellant is not represented by an attorney, that party's name, address, telephone number, and fax number, if any;

(b) the date the notice of appeal was filed in the trial court and, if mailed to the trial court clerk, the date of mailing;

(c) the trial court's name and county, and the name of the judge who tried the case;

(d) the date the trial court imposed or suspended sentence in open court, or the date the judgment or order appealed from was signed;

(e) the date of filing any motion for new trial, motion in arrest of judgment, or any other filing that affects the time for perfecting the appeal;

(f) the offense charged and the date of the offense;

(g) the defendant's plea;

(h) whether the trial was jury or nonjury;

(i) the punishment assessed;

(j) whether the appeal is from a pretrial order;

(k) whether the appeal involves the validity of a statute, ordinance, or rule;

(l) whether a reporter's record has been or will be requested, and whether the trial was electronically recorded;

(m) the name of the court reporter;

(n)(1) the dates of filing of any motion and affidavit of indigence;

(2) the date of any hearing;

(3) the date of any order; and

(4) whether the motion was granted or denied; and

(o) any other information the appellate court requires.

32.3. Supplemental Statements.

Any party may file a statement supplementing or correcting the docketing statement.

32.4. Purpose of Statement.

The docketing statement is for administrative purposes and does not affect the appellate court's jurisdiction.

(Adopted by Order eff. Sept. 1, 1997.)

Comment to 1997 change: The rule is new.

RULE 33. PRESERVATION OF APPELLATE COMPLAINTS

33.1. Preservation; How Shown.

(a) In General. As a prerequisite to presenting a complaint for appellate review, the record must show that:

(1) the complaint was made to the trial court by a timely request, objection, or motion that:

(A) stated the grounds for the ruling that the complaining party sought from the trial court with sufficient specificity to make the trial court aware of the complaint, unless the specific grounds were apparent from the context; and

(B) complied with the requirements of the Texas Rules of Evidence or the Texas Rules of Civil or Appellate Procedure; and

(2) the trial court:

(A) ruled on the request, objection, or motion, either expressly or implicitly; or

(B) refused to rule on the request, objection, or motion, and the complaining party objected to the refusal.

(b) Ruling by Operation of Law. In a civil case, the overruling by operation of law of a motion for new trial or a motion to modify the judgment preserves for appellate review a complaint properly made in the motion, unless taking evidence was necessary to properly present the complaint in the trial court.

(c) Formal Exception and Separate Order Not Required. Neither a formal exception to a trial court ruling or order nor a signed, separate order is required to preserve a complaint for appeal.

(d) Sufficiency of Evidence Complaints in Civil Nonjury Cases. In a civil nonjury case, a complaint regarding the legal or factual insufficiency of the evidence—including a complaint that the damages found by the court are excessive or inadequate, as distinguished from a complaint that the trial court erred in refusing to amend a fact finding or to make an additional finding of fact—may be made for the first time on appeal in the complaining party's brief.

(Amended by Order Dec. 23, 2002, eff. Jan. 1, 2003; Order Tex. Sup. Ct. Misc. Docket No. 16-9018 and Final Order Misc. Docket No. 17-9067, eff. July 1, 2017.)

Comment to 2002 change: The last sentence of former Rule 52(d) of the Rules of Appellate Procedure has been reinstated in substance.

Comment to 2017 change: The 2017 amendment is intended only to clarify, and not to change existing law.

33.2. Formal Bills of Exception.

To complain on appeal about a matter that would not otherwise appear in the record, a party must file a formal bill of exception.

(a) Form. No particular form of words is required in a bill of exception. But the objection to the court's ruling or action, and the ruling complained of, must be stated with sufficient specificity to make the trial court aware of the complaint.

(b) Evidence. When the appellate record contains the evidence needed to explain a bill of exception, the bill itself need not repeat the evidence, and a party may attach and incorporate a transcription of the evidence certified by the court reporter.

(c) Procedure.

(1) The complaining party must first present a formal bill of exception to the trial court.

(2) If the parties agree on the contents of the bill of exception, the judge must sign the bill and file it with the trial court clerk. If the parties do not agree on the contents of the bill, the trial judge must—after notice and hearing—do one of the following things:

(A) sign the bill of exception and file it with the trial court clerk if the judge finds that it is correct;

(B) suggest to the complaining party those corrections to the bill that the judge believes are necessary to make it accurately reflect the proceedings in the trial court, and if the party agrees to the corrections, have the corrections made, sign the bill, and file it with the trial court clerk; or

(C) if the complaining party will not agree to the corrections suggested by the judge, return the bill to the complaining party with the judge's refusal written on it, and prepare, sign, and file with the trial court clerk such bill as will, in the judge's opinion, accurately reflect the proceedings in the trial court.

(3) If the complaining party is dissatisfied with the bill of exception filed by the judge under (2)(C), the party may file with the trial court clerk the bill that was rejected by the judge. That party must also file the affidavits of at least three people who observed the matter to which the bill of exception is addressed. The affidavits must attest to the correctness of the bill as presented by the party. The matters contained in that bill of exception may be controverted and maintained by additional affidavits filed by any party within ten days after the filing of that bill. The truth of the bill of exception will be determined by the appellate court.

(d) Conflict. If a formal bill of exception conflicts with the reporter's record, the bill controls.

(e) Time to File.

(1) Civil Cases. In a civil case, a formal bill of exception must be filed no later than 30 days after the filing party's notice of appeal is filed.

(2) Criminal Cases. In a criminal case, a formal bill of exception must be filed:

(A) no later than 60 days after the trial court pronounces or suspends sentence in open court; or

(B) if a motion for new trial has been timely filed, no later than 90 days after the trial court pronounces or suspends sentence in open court.

(3) Extension of Time. The appellate court may extend the time to file a formal bill of exception if, within 15 days after the deadline for filing the bill, the party files in the appellate court a motion complying with Rule 10.5(b).

(f) Inclusion in Clerk's Record. When filed, a formal bill of exception should be included in the appellate record.

(Adopted by Order eff. Sept. 1, 1997.)

Comment to 1997 change: This is former Rule 52. Subdivision 33.1 is rewritten. Former Rule 52(b), regarding offers of proof, is omitted as unnecessary. *See* TEX. R. CIV. EVID. 103; TEX. R. CRIM. EVID. 103. Subdivision 33.2 is also rewritten and the procedure is more definitely stated. Former Rule 52(d), regarding motions for new trial, is omitted as unnecessary. *See* TEX. R. CIV. P. 324(a) & (b).

RULE 34. APPELLATE RECORD.

34.1. Contents.

The appellate record consists of the clerk's record and, if necessary to the appeal, the reporter's record. Even if more than one notice of appeal is filed, there should be only one appellate record in a case.

34.2. Agreed Record.

By written stipulation filed with the trial court clerk, the parties may agree on the contents of the appellate record. An agreed record will be presumed to contain all evidence and filings relevant to the appeal. To request matter to be included in the agreed record, the parties must comply with the procedures in Rules 34.5 and 34.6.

34.3. Agreed Statement of the Case.

In lieu of a reporter's record, the parties may agree on a brief statement of the case. The statement must be filed with the trial court clerk and included in the appellate record.

34.4. Form.

The Supreme Court and Court of Criminal Appeals will prescribe the form of the appellate record.

APPENDIX C
IN THE SUPREME COURT OF TEXAS
ORDER DIRECTING
THE FORM OF THE APPELLATE RECORD IN CIVIL CASES

ORDERED that:

Pursuant to Texas Rule of Appellate Procedure 34.4, the Supreme Court orders that the appellate record in civil cases be in the form specified below:

RULE 1. CLERK'S RECORD

1.1. Preparation of Electronic or Paper Clerk's Record.

The trial court clerk must prepare and file the clerk's record in accordance with Rules of Appellate Procedure 34.5 and 35. Even if more than one notice of appeal or request for inclusion of items is filed, the clerk should prepare only one consolidated record in a case. To prepare the clerk's record, the trial court clerk must:

(a) gather the documents required by Rule of Appellate Procedure 34.5(a) and those requested by a party under Rule of Appellate Procedure 34.5(b);

(b) start each document on a new page;

(c) include the date of filing on each document;

(d) arrange the documents in ascending chronological order, by date of filing or occurrence;

(e) start the page numbering on the front cover of the first volume of the clerk's record and continue to number all pages consecutively—including the front and back covers, tables of contents, certification page, and separator pages, if any—until the final page of the clerk's record, without regard for the number of volumes in the clerk's record, and place each page number at the bottom of each page;

(f) prepare, label, and certify the clerk's record as required by this rule;

(g) as far as practicable, include the date of signing by the judge on each order and judgment;

(h) include on the front cover of the first volume, and any subsequent volumes, of the clerk's record, whether filed in paper or electronic form, the following information, in substantially the following form:

CLERK'S RECORD
VOLUME ____ of ____
Trial Court Cause No. ______________________
In the ______ (District or County) Court
of __________ County, Texas,
Honorable ______________, Judge Presiding

__________________, Plaintiff(s)
vs.
__________________, Defendant(s)

Appealed to the
(Supreme Court of Texas at Austin, Texas,
or Court of Criminal Appeals of Texas at Austin, Texas,
or Court of Appeals for the _____ District of Texas, at ______________, Texas).

Attorney for Appellant(s):
Name ____
Address ____
Telephone no.: __________________________
Fax no.: ________________________________
E-mail address: __________________________
SBOT no.: _______________________________
Attorney for: ___________________________, Appellant(s)
____
Name of clerk preparing the clerk's record: _______________________________

(i) prepare and include after the front cover of the clerk's record a detailed table of contents identifying each document in the entire record (including sealed documents), the date each document was filed, and, except for sealed documents, the page on which each document begins. The table of contents must be double-spaced and conform to the order in which documents appear in the clerk's record, rather than in alphabetical order. If the clerk's record consists of multiple volumes, the table of contents must indicate the page on which each volume begins. If the clerk's record is filed in electronic form, the clerk must use bookmarks to link each document description in the table of contents, except descriptions of sealed documents, to the page on which each document begins; and

(j) conclude the clerk's record with a certificate in substantially the following form:

The State of Texas)
County of _____________)

I, ___________, Clerk of the ______ Court of _________ County, Texas do hereby certify that the documents contained in this record to which this certification is attached are all of the documents specified by Texas Rule of Appellate Procedure 34.5(a) and all other documents timely requested by a party to this proceeding under Texas Rule of Appellate Procedure 34.5(b).

GIVEN UNDER MY HAND AND SEAL at my office in ________, County, Texas this ___ day of ____________.

signature of clerk ______________________
name of clerk ______________________
title ______________________

If the clerk's record is filed in electronic form, the trial court clerk must include either a scanned image of the clerk's signature or "/s/" and the clerk's name typed in the space where the signature would otherwise appear.

1.2. Filing an Electronic Clerk's Record.

The clerk of a court subject to mandatory civil electronic filing must file the record electronically. The clerk of any other court must file the record electronically, if possible. When filing a clerk's record in electronic form, the trial court clerk must:

(a) file each computer file in text-searchable Portable Document Format (PDF);

(b) create electronic bookmarks to mark the first page of each document in the clerk's record;

(c) limit the size of each computer file to 100 MB or less, if possible;

(d) directly convert, rather than scan, the record to PDF, if possible;

(e) comply with the Technology Standards promulgated by the Judicial Committee on Information Technology;

(f) include the following elements in the computer file name, exemplified as CR (01 of 02).pdf:

(1) "CR";

(2) the volume number, using at least two digits, with leading zeroes if needed; "of"; and the total number of volumes;

(3) a period; and

(4) "pdf";

(g) file each sealed document separately from the remainder of the clerk's record and include the word "sealed" in the computer file name;

(h) if filing a supplement to the clerk's record, include the number of the supplement and "Supp";

(i) if filing a supplement to the clerk's record, include a hyphen, the number of the supplement, the term "Supp," and another hyphen after the term "CLR" in the computer file name (e.g., FortBend-DC-09-29-CLR-1Supp-Vol001.pdf, FortBend-DC-09-29-CLR-2Supp-Vol001.pdf);

(j) submit each computer file to the Texas Appeals Management and E-filing System (TAMES) web portal using the instructions provided on the appellate court's website; and

(k) not lock any document that is part of the record.

1.3. Filing a Paper Clerk's Record.

When filing a paper record with the appellate court, the trial court clerk must:

(a) bind the documents together in one or more volumes with a top bound, two-inch capacity, two-and-three-quarter-inch, center-to-center removable fastener and no other binding materials, like wax, ribbon, glue, staples, tape, etc.;

(b) include no more than 500 pages in each volume, or limit the thickness of each volume to a maximum of two inches;

(c) include only one-sided copies in the clerk's record;

(d) number the first volume "1" and each succeeding volume sequentially;

(e) if practicable, make a legible copy of the documents on opaque, white, 8½ x 11 inch paper; and

(f) place each sealed document in a securely sealed, manila envelope that is not bound with the other documents in the clerk's record.

1.4. Non-Conforming Records and Supplements.

In the event of a material violation of this rule in the preparation or filing of the clerk's record, on motion of a party or on its own initiative, the appellate court may require the trial court clerk to amend the clerk's record or to prepare a new clerk's record in proper form—and provide it to any party who has previously made a copy of the original, defective clerk's record—at the trial clerk's expense. A supplement to a clerk's record must also be prepared in conformity with this rule.

RULE 2. ELECTRONIC REPORTER'S RECORD.

(a) The court reporter or court recorder must prepare and file the reporter's record in accordance with Rules of Appellate Procedure 34.6 and 35 and the Uniform Format Manual for Texas Reporters' Records, and the court's local rules. Even if more than one notice of appeal or request for preparation of the record is filed, the court reporter or court recorder should prepare only one consolidated record in the case.

(b) If proceedings were recorded stenographically, the court reporter or recorder must file the reporter's record in an electronic format via the Texas Appeals Management and E-filing System (TAMES) web portal and in accordance with Section 8 of the Uniform Format Manual for Texas Reporters' Records, the court's local rules, and any guidelines posted on the appellate court's website.

(c) If the record is filed in electronic format, the court reporter or recorder must include either a scanned image of any required signature or "/s/" and name typed in the space where the signature would otherwise appear.

(d) A court reporter or recorder must not lock any document that is part of the record.

(e) In exhibit volumes, the court reporter or recorder must create bookmarks to mark the first page of each exhibit document.

(f) In the event of a material violation of this rule in the preparation of a reporter's record, on motion of a party or on the court's own initiative, the appellate court may require the court reporter or court recorder to amend the reporter's record or to prepare a new reporter's record in proper form - and provide it to any party who has previously made a copy of the original, defective reporter's record - at the reporter's or recorder's expense. A court reporter who fails to comply with the requirements of the Uniform Format Manual for Texas Reporters' Records is also subject to discipline by the Court Reporters Certification Board.

(Appendix C adopted by Order Aug. 16, 2013, eff. Jan. 1, 2014; Dec. 13, 2013, eff. Jan. 1, 2014.)

34.5. Clerk's Record.

(a) Contents. Unless the parties designate the filings in the appellate record by agreement under Rule 34.2, the record must include copies of the following:

(1) in civil cases, all pleadings on which the trial was held;

(2) in criminal cases, the indictment or information, any special plea or defense motion that was presented to the court and overruled, any written waiver, any written stipulation, and, in cases in which a plea of guilty or nolo contendere has been entered, any documents executed for the plea;

(3) the court's docket sheet;

(4) the court's charge and the jury's verdict, or the court's findings of fact and conclusions of law;

(5) the court's judgment or other order that is being appealed;

(6) any request for findings of fact and conclusions of law, any post-judgment motion, and the court's order on the motion;

(7) the notice of appeal;

(8) any formal bill of exception;

(9) any request for a reporter's record, including any statement of points or issues under Rule 34.6(c);

(10) any request for preparation of the clerk's record;

(11) in civil cases, a certified bill of costs including the cost of preparing the clerk's record, showing credits for payments made;

(12) in criminal cases, the trial court's certification of the defendant's right of appeal under Rule 25.2; and

(13) subject to (b), any filing that a party designates to have included in the record.

(b) Request for Additional Items.

(1) Time for Request. At any time before the clerk's record is prepared, any party may file with the trial court clerk a written designation specifying items to be included in the record.

(2) Request Must Be Specific. A party requesting that an item be included in the clerk's record must specifically describe the item so that the clerk can readily identify it. The clerk will disregard a general designation, such as one for "all papers filed in the case."

(3) Requesting Unnecessary Items. In a civil case, if a party requests that more items than necessary be included in the clerk's record or any supplement, the appellate court may—regardless of the appeal's outcome—require that party to pay the costs for the preparation of the unnecessary portion.

(4) Failure to Timely Request. An appellate court must not refuse to file the clerk's record or a supplemental clerk's record because of a failure to timely request items to be included in the clerk's record.

(c) Supplementation.

(1) If a relevant item has been omitted from the clerk's record, the trial court, the appellate court, or any party may by letter direct the trial court clerk to prepare, certify, and file in the appellate court a supplement containing the omitted item.

(2) If the appellate court in a criminal case orders the trial court to prepare and file findings of fact and conclusions of law as required by law, or certification of the defendant's right of appeal as required by these rules, the trial court clerk must prepare, certify, and file in the appellate court a supplemental clerk's record containing those findings and conclusions.

(3) Any supplemental clerk's record will be part of the appellate record.

(d) Defects or Inaccuracies. If the clerk's record is defective or inaccurate, the appellate clerk must inform the trial court clerk of the defect or inaccuracy and instruct the clerk to make the correction.

(e) Clerk's Record Lost or Destroyed. If a filing designated for inclusion in the clerk's record has been lost or destroyed, the parties may, by written stipulation, deliver a copy of that item to the trial court clerk for inclusion in the clerk's record or a supplement. If the parties cannot agree, the trial court must—on any party's motion or at the appellate court's request—determine what constitutes an accurate copy of the missing item and order it to be included in the clerk's record or a supplement.

(f) Original Documents. If the trial court determines that original documents filed with the trial court clerk should be inspected by the appellate court or sent to that court in lieu of copies, the trial court must make an order for the safekeeping, transportation, and return of those original documents. The order must list the original documents and briefly describe them. All the documents must be arranged in their listed sequence and bound firmly together. On any party's motion or its own initiative, the appellate court may direct the trial court clerk to send it any original document.

(g) Additional Copies of Clerk's Record in Criminal Cases. In a criminal case, the clerk's record must be made in duplicate, and in a case in which the death penalty was assessed, in triplicate. The trial court clerk must retain the copy or copies for the parties to use with the court's permission.

(h) Clerk May Consult With Parties. The clerk may consult with the parties concerning the contents of the clerk's record.

(Amended by Order Dec. 23, 2002 eff. Jan. 1, 2003.)

Comment to 2002 change: Rule 34.5(a) is amended to require that the record in a criminal case include the certification of defendant's right of appeal; *see* Rule 25.2(d). Rule 34.5(c) is amended to make clear that an appellate court may order the trial court to make such a certification for inclusion in a supplemental clerk's record.

34.6. Reporter's Record.

(a) Contents.

(1) Stenographic Recording. If the proceedings were stenographically recorded, the reporter's record consists of the court reporter's transcription of so much of the proceedings, and any of the exhibits, that the parties to the appeal designate.

(2) Electronic Recording. If the proceedings were electronically recorded, the reporter's record consists of certified copies of all tapes or other audio-storage devices on which the proceedings were recorded, any of the exhibits that the parties to the appeal designate, and certified copies of the logs prepared by the court recorder under Rule 13.2.

(b) Request for Preparation.

(1) Request to Court Reporter. At or before the time for perfecting the appeal, the appellant must request in writing that the official reporter prepare the reporter's record. The request must designate the exhibits to be included. A request to the court reporter—but not the court recorder—must also designate the portions of the proceedings to be included.

(2) Filing. The appellant must file a copy of the request with the trial court clerk.

(3) Failure to Timely Request. An appellate court must not refuse to file a reporter's record or a supplemental reporter's record because of a failure to timely request it.

(c) Partial Reporter's Record.

(1) Effect on Appellate Points or Issues. If the appellant requests a partial reporter's record, the appellant must include in the request a statement of the points or issues to be presented on appeal and will then be limited to those points or issues.

(2) Other Parties May Designate Additions. Any other party may designate additional exhibits and portions of the testimony to be included in the reporter's record.

(3) Costs; Requesting Unnecessary Matter. Additions requested by another party must be included in the reporter's record at the appellant's cost. But if the trial court finds that all or part of the designated additions are unnecessary to the appeal, the trial court may order the other party to pay the costs for the preparation of the unnecessary additions. This paragraph does not affect the appellate court's power to tax costs differently.

(4) Presumptions. The appellate court must presume that the partial reporter's record designated by the parties constitutes the entire record for purposes of reviewing the stated points or issues. This presumption applies even if the statement includes a point or issue complaining of the legal or factual insufficiency of the evidence to support a specific factual finding identified in that point or issue.

(5) Criminal Cases. In a criminal case, if the statement contains a point complaining that the evidence is insufficient to support a finding of guilt, the record must include all the evidence admitted at the trial on the issue of guilt or innocence and punishment.

(d) Supplementation. If anything relevant is omitted from the reporter's record, the trial court, the appellate court, or any party may by letter direct the official court reporter to prepare, certify, and file in the appellate court a supplemental reporter's record containing the omitted items. Any supplemental reporter's record is part of the appellate record.

(e) Inaccuracies in the Reporter's Record.

(1) Correction of Inaccuracies by Agreement. The parties may agree to correct an inaccuracy in the reporter's record, including an exhibit, without the court reporter's recertification.

(2) Correction of Inaccuracies by Trial Court. If the parties cannot agree on whether or not to correct the reporter's record so that the text accurately discloses what occurred in the trial court and the exhibits are accurate, the trial court must—after notice and hearing—settle the dispute. If the court finds any inaccuracy, it must order the court reporter to conform the reporter's record (including text and any exhibits) to what occurred in the trial court, and to file certified corrections in the appellate court.

(3) Correction After Filing in Appellate Court. If the dispute arises after the reporter's record has been filed in the appellate court, that court may submit the dispute to the trial court for resolution. The trial court must then proceed as under subparagraph (e)(2).

(f) Reporter's Record Lost or Destroyed. An appellant is entitled to a new trial under the following circumstances:

(1) if the appellant has timely requested a reporter's record;

(2) if, without the appellant's fault, a significant exhibit or a significant portion of the court reporter's notes and records has been lost or destroyed or—if the proceedings were electronically recorded—a significant portion of the recording has been lost or destroyed or is inaudible;

(3) if the lost, destroyed, or inaudible portion of the reporter's record, or the lost or destroyed exhibit, is necessary to the appeal's resolution; and

(4) if the lost, destroyed or inaudible portion of the reporter's record cannot be replaced by agreement of the parties, or the lost or destroyed exhibit cannot be replaced either by agreement of the parties or with a copy determined by the trial court to accurately duplicate with reasonable certainty the original exhibit.

(g) Original Exhibits.

(1) Reporter May Use in Preparing Reporter's Record. At the court reporter's request, the trial court clerk must give all original exhibits to the reporter for use in preparing the reporter's record. Unless ordered to include original exhibits in the reporter's record, the court reporter must return the original exhibits to the clerk after copying them for inclusion in the reporter's record. If someone other than the trial court clerk possesses an original exhibit, either the trial court or the appellate court may order that person to deliver the exhibit to the trial court clerk.

(2) Use of Original Exhibits by Appellate Court. If the trial court determines that original exhibits should be inspected by the appellate court or sent to that court in lieu of copies, the trial court must make an order for the safekeeping, transportation, and return of those exhibits. The order must list the exhibits and briefly describe them. To the extent practicable, all the exhibits must be arranged in their listed order and bound firmly together before being sent to the appellate clerk. On any party's motion or its own initiative, the appellate court may direct the trial court clerk to send it any original exhibit.

(h) Additional Copies of Reporter's Record in Criminal Cases. In a criminal case in which a party requests a reporter's record, the court reporter must prepare a duplicate of the reporter's record and file it with the trial court clerk. In a case where the death penalty was assessed, the court reporter must prepare two duplicates of the reporter's record.

(i) Supreme Court and Court of Criminal Appeals May Set Fee. From time to time, the Supreme Court and the Court of Criminal Appeals may set the fee that the court reporters may charge for preparing the reporter's record.

(Amended by Order Dec. 23, 2002 eff. Jan. 1, 2003.)

Comment to 2002 change: Subparagraphs 34.6(e) and (f) are amended to clarify the application to exhibits. The language in subparagraph (e)(2) referring to the text of the record is simplified without substantive change. Subparagraph (e)(3) incorporates the procedures specified in (e)(2). The language in subparagraph (f) is clarified to require agreement only as to the portion of the text at issue, and to provide that the trial court may determine that a copy of an exhibit should be used even if the parties cannot agree.

RULE 35. TIME TO FILE RECORD; RESPONSIBILITY FOR FILING RECORD.

35.1. Civil Cases.

The appellate record must be filed in the appellate court within 60 days after the judgment is signed, except as follows:

(a) if Rule 26.1(a) applies, within 120 days after the judgment is signed;

(b) if Rule 26.1(b) applies, within 10 days after the notice of appeal is filed; or

(c) if Rule 26.1(c) applies, within 30 days after the notice of appeal is filed.

35.2. Criminal Cases.

The appellate record must be filed in the appellate court:

(a) if a motion for new trial is not filed, within 60 days after the date the sentence is imposed or suspended in open court or the order appealed from is signed;

(b) if a timely motion for new trial is filed and denied, within 120 days after the date the sentence is imposed or suspended in open court; or

(c) if a motion for new trial is granted, within 60 days after the order granting the motion is signed.

35.3. Responsibility for Filing Record.

(a) Clerk's Record. The trial court clerk is responsible for preparing, certifying, and timely filing the clerk's record if:

(1) a notice of appeal has been filed, and in criminal proceedings, the trial court has certified the defendant's right of appeal, as required by Rule 25.2(d); and

(2) the party responsible for paying for the preparation of the clerk's record has paid the clerk's fee, has made satisfactory arrangements with the clerk to pay the fee, or is entitled to appeal without paying the fee.

(b) Reporter's Record. The official or deputy reporter is responsible for preparing, certifying, and timely filing the reporter's record if:

(1) a notice of appeal has been filed;

(2) the appellant has requested that the reporter's record be prepared; and

(3) the party responsible for paying for the preparation of the reporter's record has paid the reporter's fee, or has made satisfactory arrangements with the reporter to pay the fee, or is entitled to appeal without paying the fee.

(c) Courts to Ensure Record Timely Filed. The trial and appellate courts are jointly responsible for ensuring that the appellate record is timely filed. The appellate court may extend the deadline to file the record if requested by the clerk or reporter. Each extension must not exceed 30 days in an ordinary or restricted appeal, or 10 days in an accelerated appeal. The appellate court must allow the record to be filed late when the delay is not the appellant's fault, and may do so when the delay is the appellant's fault. The appellate court may enter any order necessary to ensure the timely filing of the appellate record.

(Adopted by Order eff. Sept. 1, 1997. Amended by Order Dec. 13, 2006, eff. Jan. 1, 2007; Order Dec. 12, 2011, eff. March 1, 2012; Order Feb. 13, 2012, eff. March 1, 2012.)

Comment to 1997 change: This is former Rule 54. In subdivision 35.1, the time to file the record in civil cases is based on the date the judgment is signed except in accelerated and restricted appeals, in which the time to file the record is based on the date the notice of appeal is filed. Subdivision 35.3 is new and makes it the responsibility of the trial court clerk and court reporter to file the record. Former Rule 54(c), providing for an extension of time to file the record, is repealed as unnecessary. The trial court clerk and court reporter should make arrangements with the court of appeals if additional time is required to file the record, as suggested in Rule 37.3.

RULE 36. AGENCY RECORD IN ADMINISTRATIVE APPEALS.

36.1. Scope.

This rule applies only to cases involving judicial review of state agency decisions in contested cases under the Administrative Procedure Act.

36.2. Inclusion in Appellate Record.

The record of an agency proceeding filed in the trial court may be included in either the clerk's record or the reporter's record.

36.3. Correcting the Record.

(a) Correction by Agreement. At any stage of the proceeding, the parties may agree to correct an agency record filed under Section 2001.175(b) of the Government Code to ensure that the agency record accurately reflects the contested case proceedings before the agency. The court reporter need not recertify the agency record.

(b) Correction by Trial Court. If the parties cannot agree to a correction to the agency record, the appellate court must—on any party's motion or its own incentive—send the question to the trial court. After notice and hearing, the trial court must determine what constitutes an accurate copy of the agency record and order the agency to send an accurate copy to the clerk of the court in which the case is pending.

(Adopted by Order eff. Sept. 1, 1997.)

Comment to 1997 change: The rule is new.

RULE 37. DUTIES OF THE APPELLATE CLERK ON RECEIVING THE NOTICE OF APPEAL AND RECORD.

37.1. On Receiving the Notice of Appeal.

If the appellate clerk determines that the notice of appeal or certification of defendant's rights of appeal in a criminal case is defective, the clerk must notify the parties of the defect so that it can be remedied, if possible. If a proper notice of appeal or certification of a criminal defendant's right of appeal is not filed in the trial court within 30 days of the date of the clerk's notice, the clerk must refer the matter to the appellate court, which will make an appropriate order under this rule or Rule 34.5(c)(2).

(Amended by Order Dec. 23, 2002, eff. Jan. 1, 2003.)

37.2. On Receiving the Record.

On receiving the clerk's record or the reporter's record, the appellate clerk must determine whether each complies with the Supreme Court's and Court of Criminal Appeals' order on preparation of the record. If so, the clerk must endorse on each the date of receipt, file it, and notify the parties of the filing and the date. If not, the clerk must endorse on the clerk's record or reporter's record—whichever is defective—the date of receipt and return it to the official responsible for filing it. The appellate court clerk must specify the defects and instruct the official to correct the defects and return the record to the appellate court by a specified date. In a criminal case, the record must not be posted on the Internet.

(Amended by Order Dec. 13, 2013, eff. Jan. 1, 2014.)

37.3. If No Record Filed.

(a) Notice of Late Record.

(1) Civil Cases. If the clerk's record or reporter's record has not been timely filed, the appellate clerk must send notice to the official responsible for filing it, stating that the record is late and requesting that the record be filed within 30 days if an ordinary or restricted appeal, or 10 days if an accelerated appeal. The appellate clerk must send a copy of this notice to the parties and the trial court. If the clerk does not receive the record within the stated period, the clerk must refer the matter to the appellate court. The court must make whatever order is appropriate to avoid further delay and to preserve the parties' rights.

(2) Criminal Cases. If the clerk's record or reporter's record has not been timely filed, the appellate court clerk must refer the matter to the appellate court. The court must make whatever order is appropriate to avoid further delay and to preserve the parties' rights.

(b) If No Clerk's Record Filed Due to Appellant's Fault. If the trial court clerk failed to file the clerk's record because the appellant failed to pay or make arrangements to pay the clerk's fee for preparing the clerk's record, the appellate court may—on a party's motion or its own initiative—dismiss the appeal for want of prosecution unless the appellant was entitled to proceed without payment of costs. The court must give the appellant a reasonable opportunity to cure before dismissal.

(c) If No Reporter's Record Filed Due to Appellant's Fault. Under the following circumstances, and if the clerk's record has been filed, the appellate court may—after first giving the appellant notice and a reasonable opportunity to cure—consider and decide those issues or points that do not require a reporter's record for a decision. The court may do this if no reporter's record has been filed because:

(1) the appellant failed to request a reporter's record; or

(2)(A) appellant failed to pay or make arrangements to pay the reporter's fee to prepare the reporter's record; and

(B) the appellant is not entitled to proceed without payment of costs.

(Adopted by Order eff. Sept. 1, 1997.)

Comment to 1997 change: Former Rules 56 and 57(a) are merged. Subdivisions 37.2 and 37.3 are new.

RULE 38. REQUISITES OF BRIEFS.

38.1. Appellant's Brief.

The appellant's brief must, under appropriate headings and in the order here indicated, contain the following:

(a) Identity of Parties and Counsel. The brief must give a complete list of all parties to the trial court's judgment or order appealed from, and the names and addresses of all trial and appellate counsel, except as otherwise provided in Rule 9.8.

(b) Table of Contents. The brief must have a table of contents with references to the pages of the brief. The table of contents must indicate the subject matter of each issue or point, or group of issues or points.

(c) Index of Authorities. The brief must have an index of authorities arranged alphabetically and indicating the pages of the brief where the authorities are cited.

(d) Statement of the Case. The brief must state concisely the nature of the case (e.g., whether it is a suit for damages, on a note, or involving a murder prosecution), the course of proceedings, and the trial court's disposition of the case. The statement should be supported by record references, should seldom exceed one-half page, and should not discuss the facts.

(e) Any Statement Regarding Oral Argument. The brief may include a statement explaining why oral argument should, or should not, be permitted. Any such statement must not exceed one page and should not address how the court's decisional process would, or would not, be aided by oral argument. As required by Rule 39.7, any party requesting oral argument must note that request on the front cover of its brief.

(f) Issues Presented. The brief must state concisely all issues or points presented for review. The statement of an issue or point will be treated as covering every subsidiary question that is fairly included.

(g) Statement of Facts. The brief must state concisely and without argument the facts pertinent to the issues or points presented. In a civil case, the court will accept as true the facts stated unless another party contradicts them. The statement must be supported by record references.

(h) Summary of the Argument. The brief must contain a succinct, clear, and accurate statement of the arguments made in the body of the brief. This summary must not merely repeat the issues or points presented for review.

(i) Argument. The brief must contain a clear and concise argument for the contentions made, with appropriate citations to authorities and to the record.

(j) Prayer. The brief must contain a short conclusion that clearly states the nature of the relief sought.

(k) Appendix in Civil Cases.

(1) Necessary Contents. Unless voluminous or impracticable, the appendix must contain a copy of:

(A) the trial court's judgment or other appealable order from which relief is sought;

(B) the jury charge and verdict, if any, or the trial court's findings of fact and conclusions of law, if any; and

(C) the text of any rule, regulation, ordinance, statute, constitutional provision, or other law (excluding case law) on which the argument is based, and the text of any contract or other document that is central to the argument.

(2) Optional Contents. The appendix may contain any other item pertinent to the issues or points presented for review, including copies or excerpts of relevant court opinions, laws, documents on which the suit was based, pleadings, excerpts from the reporter's record, and similar material. Items should not be included in the appendix to attempt to avoid the page limits for the brief.

(Amended by Order March 10, 2008, eff. Sept. 1, 2008; Order Aug. 20, 2008, eff. Sept. 1, 2008.)

Comment to 2008 change: A party may choose to include a statement in the brief regarding oral argument.

38.2. Appellee's Brief.

(a) Form of Brief.

(1) An appellee's brief must conform to the requirements of Rule 38.1, except that:

(A) the list of parties and counsel is not required unless necessary to supplement or correct the appellant's list;

(B) the appellee's brief need not include a statement of the case, a statement of the issues presented, or a statement of facts, unless the appellee is dissatisfied with that portion of the appellant's brief; and

(C) the appendix to the appellee's brief need not contain any item already contained in an appendix filed by the appellant.

(2) When practicable, the appellee's brief should respond to the appellant's issues or points in the order the appellant presented those issues or points.

(b) Cross-Points.

(1) Judgment Notwithstanding the Verdict. When the trial court renders judgment notwithstanding the verdict on one or more questions, the appellee must bring forward by cross-point any issue or point that would have vitiated the verdict or that would have prevented an affirmance of the judgment if the trial court had rendered judgment on the verdict. Failure to bring forward by cross-point an issue or point that would vitiate the verdict or prevent an affirmance of the judgment waives that complaint. Included in this requirement is a point that:

(A) the verdict or one or more jury findings have insufficient evidentiary support or are against the overwhelming preponderance of the evidence as a matter of fact; or

(B) the verdict should be set aside because of improper argument of counsel.

(2) When Evidentiary Hearing Needed. The appellate court must remand a case to the trial court to take evidence if:

(A) the appellate court has sustained a point raised by the appellant; and

(B) the appellee raised a cross-point that requires the taking of additional evidence.

(Amended by Order Dec. 23, 2002, eff. Jan. 1, 2003.)

38.3. Reply Brief.

The appellant may file a reply brief addressing any matter in the appellee's brief. However, the appellate court may consider and decide the case before a reply brief is filed.

38.4. Repealed by Order Nov. 13, 2012, eff. Dec. 1, 2012.

38.5. Appendix for Cases Recorded Electronically.

In cases where the proceedings were electronically recorded, the following rules apply:

(a) Appendix.

(1) In General. At or before the time a party's brief is due, the party must file one copy of an appendix containing a transcription of all portions of the recording that the party considers relevant to the appellate issues or points. Unless another party objects, the transcription will be presumed accurate.

(2) Repetition Not Required. A party's appendix need not repeat evidence included in any previously filed appendix.

(3) Form. The form of the appendix and transcription must conform to any specifications of the Supreme Court and Court of Criminal Appeals concerning the form of the reporter's record except that it need not have the reporter's certificate.

(4) Notice. At the time the appendix is filed, the party must give written notice of the filing to all parties to the trial court's judgment or order. The notice must specify, by referring to the index numbers in the court recorder's logs, those parts of the recording that are included in the appendix. The filing party need not serve a copy of the appendix but must make a copy available to all parties for inspection and copying.

(b) Presumptions. The same presumptions that apply to a partial reporter's record under Rule 34.6(c)(4) apply to the parties' appendixes. The appellate court need not review any part of the electronic recording.

(c) Supplemental Appendix. The appellate court may direct or allow a party to file a supplemental appendix containing a transcription of additional portions of the recording.

(d) Inability to Pay. A party who cannot pay the cost of an appendix must file the affidavit provided for by Rule 20. The party must also state in the affidavit or a supplemental affidavit that the party has neither the access to the equipment necessary nor the skill necessary to prepare the appendix. If a contest to the affidavit is not sustained by written order, the court recorder must transcribe or have transcribed those portions of the recording that the party designates and must file the transcription as that party's appendix, along with all exhibits.

(e) Inaccuracies.

(1) Correction by Agreement. The parties may agree to correct an inaccuracy in the transcription of the recording.

(2) Correction by Appellate or Trial Court. If the parties dispute whether an electronic recording or transcription accurately discloses what occurred in the trial court but cannot agree on corrections, the appellate court may:

(A) settle the dispute by reviewing the recording; or

(B) submit the dispute to the trial court, which must—after notice and hearing—settle the dispute and ensure that the recording or transcription is made to conform to what occurred in the trial court.

(f) Costs. The actual expense of preparing the appendixes or the amount prescribed for official reporters, whichever is less, is taxed as costs. The appellate court may disallow the cost of any portion of the appendixes that it considers surplusage or that does not conform to any specifications prescribed by the Supreme Court or Court of Criminal Appeals.

38.6. Time to File Briefs.

(a) Appellant's Filing Date. Except in a habeas corpus or bail appeal, which is governed by Rule 31, an appellant must file a brief within 30 days—20 days in an accelerated appeal—after the later of:

(1) the date the clerk's record was filed; or

(2) the date the reporter's record was filed.

(b) Appellee's Filing Date. The appellee's brief must be filed within 30 days—20 days in an accelerated appeal—after the date the appellant's brief was filed. In a civil case, if the appellant has not filed a brief as provided in this rule, an appellee may file a brief within 30 days—20 days in an accelerated appeal—after the date the appellant's brief was due.

(c) Filing Date for Reply Brief. A reply brief, if any, must be filed within 20 days after the date the appellee's brief was filed.

(d) Modifications of Filing Time. On motion complying with Rule 10.5(b), the appellate court may extend the time for filing a brief and may postpone submission of the case. A motion to extend the time to file a brief may be filed before or after the date the brief is due. The court may also, in the interests of justice, shorten the time for filing briefs and for submission of the case.

(Amended by Order Dec. 23, 2002, eff. Jan. 1, 2003.)

Comment to 2002 change: Rule 38.6(d) is amended to clarify that an appellate court may postpone the filing of any brief, not just the appellant's brief.

38.7. Amendment or Supplementation.

A brief may be amended or supplemented whenever justice requires, on whatever reasonable terms the court may prescribe.

38.8. Failure of Appellant to File Brief.

(a) Civil Cases. If an appellant fails to timely file a brief, the appellate court may:

(1) dismiss the appeal for want of prosecution, unless the appellant reasonably explains the failure and the appellee is not significantly injured by the appellant's failure to timely file a brief;

(2) decline to dismiss the appeal and give further direction to the case as it considers proper; or

(3) if an appellee's brief is filed, the court may regard that brief as correctly presenting the case and may affirm the trial court's judgment upon that brief without examining the record.

(b) Criminal Cases.

(1) Effect. An appellant's failure to timely file a brief does not authorize either dismissal of the appeal or, except as provided in (4), consideration of the appeal without briefs.

(2) Notice. If the appellant's brief is not timely filed, the appellate clerk must notify counsel for the parties and the trial court of that fact. If the appellate court does not receive a satisfactory response within ten days, the court must order the trial court to immediately conduct a hearing to determine whether the appellant desires to prosecute his appeal, whether the appellant is indigent, or, if not indigent, whether retained counsel has abandoned the appeal, and to make appropriate findings and recommendations.

(3) Hearing. In accordance with (2), the trial court must conduct any necessary hearings, make appropriate findings and recommendations, and have a record of the proceedings prepared, which record—including any order and findings—must be sent to the appellate court.

(4) Appellate Court Action. Based on the trial court's record, the appellate court may act appropriately to ensure that the appellant's rights are protected, including initiating contempt proceedings against appellant's counsel. If the trial court has found that the appellant no longer desires to prosecute the appeal, or that the appellant is not indigent but has not made the necessary arrangements for filing a brief, the appellate court may consider the appeal without briefs, as justice may require.

38.9. Briefing Rules to Be Construed Liberally.

Because briefs are meant to acquaint the court with the issues in a case and to present argument that will enable the court to decide the case, substantial compliance with this rule is sufficient, subject to the following.

(a) Formal Defects. If the court determines that this rule has been flagrantly violated, it may require a brief to be amended, supplemented, or redrawn. If another brief that does not comply with this rule is filed, the court may strike the brief, prohibit the party from filing another, and proceed as if the party had failed to file a brief.

(b) Substantive Defects. If the court determines, either before or after submission, that the case has not been properly presented in the briefs, or that the law and authorities have not been properly cited in the briefs, the court may postpone submission, require additional briefing, and make any other order necessary for a satisfactory submission of the case.

(Adopted by Order eff. Sept. 1, 1997.)

Comment to 1997 change: This is former Rule 74. The rule is substantially rewritten. Paragraph 38.1(e) now specifically allows a party to either present issues or points of error. Paragraphs 38.1(f) and (g) are new and require a brief to include a statement of facts and summary of the argument. Paragraph 38.2(b) is new and gives specific requirements for cross-points. *See also* TEX. R. CIV. P. 324(c). Subdivision 38.3 is new and provides for a reply brief. Subdivision 38.4 imposes a total brief limit of 90 pages on each party. Thus, if more than one party has filed a notice of appeal, there will be multiple appellant's, appellee's, and reply briefs, but each party is limited to a total of 90 pages. Subdivision 38.5 is new and provides for an appendix in cases recorded electronically in the trial court. Paragraph 38.6(b) now provides that the appellee has 30—rather than 25—days to file a brief. The provisions of former Rules 74(i) (Number of Copies), (j) (Briefs Typewritten or Printed), and (q) (Service of Briefs) are omitted as unnecessary. *See* Rule 9.

RULE 39. ORAL ARGUMENT; DECISION WITHOUT ARGUMENT.

39.1. Right to Oral Argument.

Any party who has filed a brief and who has timely requested oral argument may argue the case to the court unless the court, after examining the briefs, decides that oral argument is unnecessary for any of the following reasons:

(1) the appeal is frivolous;

(2) the dispostive issue or issues have been authoritatively decided;

(3) the facts and legal arguments are adequately presented in the briefs and record; or

(4) the decisional process would not be significantly aided by oral argument.

(Amended by Order March 10, 2008, eff. Sept. 1, 2008; Order Aug. 20, 2008, eff. Sept. 1, 2008.)

39.2. Purpose of Argument.

Oral argument should emphasize and clarify the written arguments in the briefs. Counsel should not merely read from prepared text. Counsel should assume that all members of the court have read the briefs before oral argument and counsel should be prepared to respond to questions. A party should not refer to or comment on matters not involved in or pertaining to what is in the record.

39.3 Time Allowed.

The court will set the time that will be allowed for argument. Counsel must complete argument in the time allotted and may continue after the expiration of the allotted time only with permission of the court. Counsel is not required to use all the allotted time. The appellant must be allowed to conclude the argument.

39.4. Number of Counsel.

Generally, only one counsel should argue for each side. Except on leave of court, no more than two counsel on each side may argue. Only one counsel may argue in rebuttal.

39.5. Argument by Amicus.

With leave of court obtained before the argument and with a party's consent, an amicus curiae may share allotted time with that party. Otherwise, counsel for amicus may not argue.

39.6. When Only One Party Files a Brief.

If counsel for only one party has filed a brief, the court may allow that party to argue.

39.7. Request and Waiver.

A party desiring oral argument must note that request on the front cover of the party's brief. A party's failure to request oral argument waives the party's right to argue. But even if a party has waived oral argument, the court may direct the party to appear and argue.

39.8 Clerk's Notice.

The clerk must send to the parties—at least 21 days before the date the case is set for argument or submission without argument—a notice telling the parties:

(a) whether the court will allow oral argument or will submit the case without argument;

(b) the date of argument or submission without argument;

(c) if argument is allowed, the time allotted for argument; and.

(d) the names of the members of the panel to which the case will be argued or submitted, subject to change by the court.

A party's failure to receive the notice does not prevent a case's argument or submission on the scheduled date.

(Adopted by Order eff. Sept. 1, 1997. Amended by Order March 10, 2008 eff. Sept. 1, 2008; Order Aug. 20, 2008, eff. Sept. 1, 2008.)

Comment to 1997 change: This is former Rule 75. Technical and nonsubstantive changes are made.

Comment to 2008 change: Subdivision 39.1 is amended to provide for oral argument unless the court determines it is unnecessary and to set out the reasons why argument may be unnecessary. The appellate court must evaluate these reasons in view of the traditional importance of oral argument. The court need not agree on, and generally should not announce, a specific reason or reasons for declining oral argument.

RULE 40. ORDER OF DECISION.

40.1. Civil Cases.

The court of appeals may determine the order in which civil cases will be decided. But the following types of cases have precedence over all others:

(a) a case given precedence by law;

(b) an accelerated appeal; and

(c) a case that the court determines should be given precedence in the interest of justice.

40.2. Criminal Cases.

In cases not otherwise given precedence by law, the court of appeals must hear and determine a criminal appeal at the earliest possible time, having due regard for the parties' rights and for the proper administration of justice.

(Adopted by Order eff. Sept. 1, 1997.)

Reference

See Code of Criminal Procedure article 44.01(f).

Comment on 1997 change: The provisions of former Rules 76, 77 and 78 are merged. Civil cases involving the Railroad Commission, the State, and "cases submitted on oral argument for all parties" are no longer given preference unless given preference by law.

RULE 41. PANEL AND EN BANC DECISION.

41.1. Decision by Panel.

(a) Constitution of Panel. Unless a court of appeals with more than three justices votes to decide a case en banc, a case must be assigned for decision to a panel of the court consisting of three justices, although not every member of the panel must be present for argument. If the case is decided without argument, three justices must participate in the decision. A majority of the panel, which constitutes a quorum, must agree on the judgment. Except as otherwise provided in these rules, a panel's opinion constitutes the court's opinion, and the court must render a judgment in accordance with the panel opinion.

(b) When Panel Cannot Agree on Judgment. After argument, if for any reason a member of the panel cannot participate in deciding a case, the case may be decided by the two remaining justices. If they cannot agree on a judgment, the chief justice of the court of appeals must:

(1) designate another justice of the court to sit on the panel to consider the case;

(2) request the Chief Justice of Supreme Court to temporarily assign an eligible justice of judge to sit on the panel to consider the case; or

(3) or convene the court en banc to consider the case.

The reconstituted panel or the en banc court may order the case reargued.

(c) When Court Cannot Agree on Judgment. After argument, if for any reason a member of a court consisting of only three justices cannot participate in deciding a case, the case may be decided by the two remaining justices. If they cannot agree on a judgment, that fact must be certified to the Chief Justice of the Supreme Court. The Chief Justice may then temporarily assign an eligible justice or judge to sit with the court of appeals to consider the case. The reconstituted court may order the case reargued.

(Amended by Order March 10, 2008, eff. Sept. 1, 2008; Order Aug. 20, 2008, eff. Sept. 1, 2008.)

41.2. Decision by En Banc Court.

(a) Constitution of En Banc Court. An en banc court consists of all members of the court who are not disqualified or recused and—if the case was originally argued before or decided by a panel—any members of the panel who are not members of the court but remain eligible for assignment to the court. A majority of the en banc court constitutes a quorum. A majority of the en banc court must agree on a judgment.

(b) When En Banc Court Cannot Agree on Judgment. If a majority of an en banc court cannot agree on a judgment, that fact must be certified to the Chief Justice of the Supreme Court. The Chief Justice may then temporarily assign an eligible justice or judge to sit with the court of appeals to consider the case. The reconstituted court may order the case reargued.

(c) En Banc Consideration Disfavored. En banc consideration of a case is not favored and should not be ordered unless necessary to secure or maintain uniformity of the court's decisions or unless extraordinary circumstances require en banc consideration. A vote to determine whether a case will be heard or reheard en banc need not be taken unless a justice of the court requests a vote. If a vote is requested and a majority of the court's members vote to hear or rehear the case en banc, the en banc court will hear or rehear the case. Otherwise, a panel of the court will consider the case.

(Adopted by Order eff. Sept. 1, 1997. Amended by Order March 10, 2008, eff. Sept. 1, 2008 ; Order Aug. 20, 2008, eff. Sept. 1, 2008.)

41.3. Precedent in Transferred Cases.

In cases transferred by the Supreme Court from on court of appeals to another, the court of appeals to which the case is transferred must decide the case in accordance with the precedent of the transferor court under principles of stare decisis if the transferee court's decision otherwise would have been inconsistent with the precedent of the transferor court. The court's opinion may state whether the outcome would have been different had the transferee court not been required to decide the case in accordance with the transferor court's precedent.

(Amended by Order March 10, 2008, eff. Sept. 1, 2008; Order Aug. 20, 2008, eff. Sept. 1, 2008.)

Comment to 1997 change: This is former Rule 79. The rule is reorganized. Paragraphs 41.1(b) and (c) are amended to make clear that a three judge panel must hear the case. Therefore, only if a member of a panel is lost after argument do the provisions for appointment of another justice to break a deadlock come into play. Paragraph 41.2(a) is amended to define an en banc court.

Comment to 2008 changes: Subdivisions 41.1 and 41.2 are amended to acknowledge the full authority of the Chief Justice of the Supreme Court to temporarily assign a justice or judge to hear a matter pending in an appellate court. The statutory provisions governing the assignment of judges to appellate courts are located in Chapters 74 and 75 of the Government Code. Other minor changes are made for consistency. Subdivision 41.3 is added to require, in appellate cases transferred by the Supreme Court under Section 73.001 of the Government Code for docket equalization or other purposes, that the transferee court must generally resolve any conflict between the precedent of the transferor court and the precedent of the transferee court—or that of any other intermediate appellate court the transferee court otherwise would have followed—by following the precedent of the transferor court, unless it appears that the transferor court itself would not be bound by that precedent. The rule requires the transferee court to "stand in the shoes" of the transferor court so that an appellate transfer will not produce a different outcome, based on application of substantive law, than would have resulted had the case not been transferred. The transferee court is not expected to follow the transferor courts local rules or otherwise supplant its own local procedures with those of the transferor court.

RULE 42. DISMISSAL; SETTLEMENT.

42.1. Voluntary Dismissal and Settlement in Civil Cases.

(a) On Motion or By Agreement. The appellate court may dispose of an appeal as follows:

(1) On Motion of Appellant. In accordance with a motion of appellant, the court may dismiss the appeal of affirm the appealed judgment or order unless such disposition would prevent a party from seeking relief to which it would otherwise be entitled.

(2) By Agreement. In accordance with an agreement signed by the parties or their attorneys and filed with the clerk, the court may:

(A) render judgment effectuating the parties' agreement;

(B) set aside the trial court's judgment without regard to the merits and remand the case to the trial court for rendition of judgment in accordance with the agreement; or

(C) abate the appeal and permit proceedings in the trial court to effectuate the agreement.

(b) Partial Disposition. A severable portion of the proceeding may be disposed of under (a) if it will not prejudice the remaining parties.

(c) Effect on Court's Opinion. In dismissing a proceeding, the appellate court will determine whether to withdraw any opinion it has already issued. An agreement or motion for dismissal cannot be conditioned on withdrawal of the opinion.

(d) Costs. Absent agreement of the parties, the court will tax costs against the appellant.

(Amended by Order Dec. 23, 2002, eff. Jan. 1, 2003.)

Comment to 2002 change: Rule 42.1 is amended to clarify the procedures for implementing settlements on appeal and to expressly give courts flexibility in effectuating settlements. The rule is also clarified to expressly permit the dismissal of an appeal without dismissal of the action itself. The rule does not permit an appellate court to order a new trial merely on the agreement of the parties absent reversible error, or to vacate a trial court's judgment absent reversible error or a settlement.

42.2. Voluntary Dismissal in Criminal Cases.

(a) At any time before the appellate court's decision, the appellate court may dismiss the appeal upon the appellant's motion. The appellant and his or her attorney must sign the written motion to dismiss and file it in duplicate with the appellate clerk, who must immediately send the duplicate copy to the trial court clerk.

(b) After the court of appeals hands down its opinion, it may not grant a appellant's motion to dismiss the appeal unless the other parties consent. It the other parties consent and the court of appeals grants the appellant's motion to dismiss the appeal, the appellate opinion must be withdrawn and the appeal dismissed. The appellate clerk must send notice of the dismissal to the trial court clerk.

(Amended by Order Oct. 16, 2000, eff. Jan. 1, 2001. Amended by Order Dec. 13, 2006, eff. Jan. 1, 2007.)

Comment to 2000 change: In the first sentence of Rule 42.2(a) "appellant" is replaced by "party that appealed," to make it clear that the rule applies to the State when it is the appealing party. *See State v. Miles*, 994 S.W.2d 410 (Tex.App.—Waco 1999). The requirement that the appellant's attorney must sign the withdrawal is deleted, and the last sentence is added, to remove any implication that the attorney may veto the appellant's decision to withdraw the notice of appeal. The word "personally" is added to emphasize that the appellant must participate in the withdrawal of his or her appeal. The provisions of Rule 9.1(a) do not restrict the appellant's ability to withdraw the notice of appeal.

42.3. Involuntary Dismissal in Civil Cases.

Under the following circumstances, on any party's motion—or on its own initiative after giving ten days' notice to all parties—the appellate court may dismiss the appeal or affirm the appealed judgment or order. Dismissal or affirmance may occur if the appeal is subject to dismissal:

(a) for want of jurisdiction;

(b) for want of prosecution; or

(c) because the appellant has failed to comply with a requirement of these rules, a court order, or a notice from the clerk requiring a response or other action within a specified time.

42.4. Involuntary Dismissal in Criminal Cases.

The appellate court must dismiss an appeal on the State's motion, supported by affidavit, showing that the appellant has escaped from custody pending the appeal and that to the affiant's knowledge, the appellant has not, within ten days after escaping, voluntarily returned to lawful custody within the state.

(a) Timely Return to Custody; Reinstatement. The appeal may not be dismissed—or, if dismissed, must be reinstated—if an affidavit of an officer or other credible person is filed showing that the appellant, within ten days after escaping, voluntarily returned to lawful custody within the state.

(b) Life Sentence. The appellate court may overrule the motion to dismiss—or, if the motion was granted, may reinstate the appeal—if:

(1) the appellant received a life sentence; and

(2) the appellant is recaptured or voluntarily surrenders within 30 days after escaping.

(Adopted by Order eff. Sept. 1, 1997.)

Comment to 1997 change: Former Rules 59 and 60 are merged. Paragraph 42.1(c), allowing a court of appeals to withdraw its opinion, is new. Provision is made in paragraph 42.3(c) for dismissal of an appeal for failure to comply with a notice from the clerk. Other changes are made.

RULE 43. JUDGMENT OF THE COURT OF APPEALS.

43.1. Time.

The court of appeals should render its judgment promptly after submission of a case.

43.2. Types of Judgment.

The court of appeals may:

(a) affirm the trial court's judgment in whole or in part;

(b) modify the trial court's judgment and affirm it as modified;

(c) reverse the trial court's judgment in whole or in part and render the judgment that the trial court should have rendered;

(d) reverse the trial court's judgment and remand the case for further proceedings;

(e) vacate the trial court's judgment and dismiss the case; or

(f) dismiss the appeal.

43.3. Rendition Appropriate Unless Remand Necessary.

When reversing a trial court's judgment, the court must render the judgment that the trial court should have rendered, except when:

(a) a remand is necessary for further proceedings; or

(b) the interests of justice require a remand for another trial.

43.4. Judgment for Costs in Civil Cases.

The court of appeals' judgment should award to the prevailing party costs incurred by that party related to the appeal, including filing fees in the court of appeals and costs for preparation of the record. The court of appeals may tax costs otherwise as required by law or for good cause. But the judgment must not require the payment of costs by a party who was entitled to proceed without payment of costs under Rule 20.1, and a provision in the judgment purporting to do so is void.

(Amended by Tex. Sup. Ct. Misc. Docket No. 16-9122, eff. Sept. 1, 2016.)

[Statement of Inability to Afford Payment of Court Costs as provided in Tex. Sup. Ct. Misc. Docket No. 16-9122, eff. Sept. 1, 2016 and applies to any contest of, or challenge to, a claim of inability to afford payment of court costs that is pending on September 1, 2016.]

43.5. Judgment Against Sureties in Civil Cases.

When a court of appeals affirms the trial court judgment, or modifies that judgment and renders judgment against the appellant, the court of appeals must render judgment against the sureties on the appellant's supersedeas bond, if any, for the performance of the judgment and for any costs taxed against the appellant.

43.6. Other Orders.

The court of appeals may make any other appropriate order that the law and the nature of the case require.

(Adopted by Order eff. Sept. 1, 1997.)

Comment to 1997 changes: Former Rules 80(a)-(c) and 82 are merged. Paragraph 43.2(e) allows the court of appeals to vacate the trial court's judgment and dismiss the case; paragraph 43.2(f) allows the court of appeals to dismiss the appeal. Both provisions are new but codify current practice. Paragraph 43.3(a) is moved here from former Rule 81(c). Paragraph 43.3(b), allowing a remand in the interest of justice, is new. Subdivisions 43.4 and 43.5 are from former Rule 82.

RULE 44. REVERSIBLE ERROR.

44.1. Reversible Error in Civil Cases.

(a) Standard for Reversible Error. No judgment may be reversed on appeal on the ground that the trial court made an error of law unless the court of appeals concludes that the error complained of:

(1) probably caused the rendition of an improper judgment; or

(2) probably prevented the appellant from properly presenting the case to the court of appeals.

(b) Error Affecting Only Part of Case. If the error affects part of, but not all, the matter in controversy and that part is separable without unfairness to the parties, the judgment must be reversed and a new trial ordered only as to the part affected by the error. The court may not order a separate trial solely on unliquidated damages if liability is contested.

44.2. Reversible Error in Criminal Cases.

(a) Constitutional Error. If the appellate record in a criminal case reveals constitutional error that is subject to harmless error review, the court of appeals must reverse a judgment of conviction or punishment unless the court determines beyond a reasonable doubt that the error did not contribute to the conviction or punishment.

(b) Other Errors. Any other error, defect, irregularity, or variance that does not affect substantial rights must be disregarded.

(c) Presumptions. Unless the following matters were disputed in the trial court, or unless the record affirmatively shows the contrary, the court of appeals must presume:

(1) that venue was proved in the trial court;

(2) that the jury was properly impaneled and sworn;

(3) that the defendant was arraigned;

(4) that the defendant pleaded to the indictment or other charging instrument; and

(5) that the court's charge was certified by the trial court and filed by the clerk before it was read to the jury.

44.3. Defects in Procedure.

A court of appeals must not affirm or reverse a judgment or dismiss an appeal for formal defects or irregularities in appellate procedure without allowing a reasonable time to correct or amend the defects or irregularities.

44.4. Remediable Error of the Trial Court.

(a) Generally. A court of appeals must not affirm or reverse a judgment or dismiss an appeal if:

(1) the trial court's erroneous action or failure or refusal to act prevents the proper presentation of a case to the court of appeals; and

(2) the trial court can correct its action or failure to act.

(b) Court of Appeals Direction if Error Remediable. If the circumstances described in (a) exist, the court of appeals must direct the trial court to correct the error. The court of appeals will then proceed as if the erroneous action or failure to act had not occurred.

(Adopted by Order eff. Sept. 1, 1997.)

Comment to 1997 change: Former Rules 80(d), 81 and 83 are merged. The reversible error standard in subdivision 44.1 is amended to omit the reference to an action "reasonably calculated to cause" an improper judgment, but no substantive change is intended. Paragraph 44.2(a) is amended to limit its standard of review to constitutional errors that are subject to harmless error review. Paragraph 44.2(b) is new and is taken from Federal Rule of Criminal Procedure 52(a) without substantive change. Paragraph 44.2(c) is former Rule 80(d) without substantive change. Subdivision 44.3 is amended to delete the reference to defects of "substance" and to delete the provisions regarding the late filing of the record.

RULE 45. DAMAGES FOR FRIVOLOUS APPEALS IN CIVIL CASES.

If the court of appeals determines that an appeal is frivolous, it may—on motion of any party or on its own initiative, after notice and a reasonable opportunity for response—award each prevailing party just damages. In determining whether to award damages, the court must not consider any matter that does not appear in the record, briefs, or other papers filed in the court of appeals.

(Adopted by Order eff. Sept. 1, 1997.)

Comment to 1997 change: This is former Rule 84. The limit on the amount of the sanction that may be imposed is repealed. A requirement of notice and opportunity to respond is added.

RULE 46. REMITTITUR IN CIVIL CASES.

46.1. Remittitur After Appeal Perfected.

If the trial court suggests a remittitur but the case is appealed before the remittitur is filed, the party who would make the remittitur may do so in the court of appeals in the same manner as in the trial court. The court of appeals must then render the judgment that the trial court should have rendered if the remittitur had been made in the trial court.

46.2. Appeal on Remittitur.

If a party makes the remittitur at the trial judge's suggestion and the party benefiting from the remittitur appeals, the remitting party is not barred from contending in the court of appeals that all or part of the remittitur should not have been required, but the remitting party must perfect an appeal to raise that point. If the court of appeals sustains the remitting party's contention that remittitur should not have been required, the court must render the judgment that the trial court should have rendered.

46.3. Suggestion of Remittitur by Court of Appeals.

The court of appeals may suggest a remittitur. If the remittitur is timely filed, the court must reform and affirm the trial court's judgment in accordance with the remittitur. If the remittitur is not timely filed, the court must reverse the trial court's judgment.

46.4. Refusal to Remit Must Not Be Mentioned in Later Trial.

If the court of appeals suggests a remittitur, but no remittitur is filed, evidence of the court's determination regarding remittitur is inadmissible in a later trial of the case.

46.5. Voluntary Remittitur.

If a court of appeals reverses the trial court's judgment because of a legal error that affects only part of the damages awarded by the judgment, the affected party may—within 15 days after the court of appeals' judgment—voluntarily remit the amount that the affected party believes will cure the reversible error. A party may include in a motion for rehearing—without waiving any complaint that the court of appeals erred—a conditional request that the court accept the remittitur and affirm the trial court's judgment as reduced. If the court of appeals determines that the voluntary remittitur is not sufficient to cure the reversible error, but that remittitur is appropriate, the court must suggest a remittitur in accordance with Rule 46.3. If the remittitur is timely filed and the court of appeals determines that the voluntary remittitur cures the reversible error, then the court must accept the remittitur and reform and affirm the trial court judgment in accordance with the remittitur.

(Amended by Order Dec. 23, 2002 eff. Jan. 1, 2003.)

Comment to 2002 change: Subdivision 46.5 is amended to clarify the procedure for offering a voluntary remittitur. The offer may be made in a motion for rehearing without waiving any complaint that the court of appeals erred, thereby extending the deadlines for further appeal.

RULE 47. OPINIONS, DISTRIBUTION, PUBLICATION, AND CITATION.

47.1. Written Opinions.

The court of appeals must hand down a written opinion that is as brief as practicable but that addresses every issue raised and necessary to final disposition of the appeal.

(Amended by Order Dec. 23, 2002 eff. Jan. 1, 2003.)

47.2. Designation and Signing of Opinions; Participating Justices.

(a) Civil and Criminal Cases. Each opinion of the court must be designated either an "Opinion" or a "Memorandum Opinion." A majority of the justices who participate in considering the case must determine whether the opinion will be signed by a justice or will be per curiam and whether it will be designated an opinion or memorandum opinion. The names of the participating justices must be noted on all written opinions or orders of the court or a panel of the court.

(b) Criminal Cases. In addition, each opinion and memorandum opinion in a criminal case must bear the notation "publish" or "do not publish" as determined—before the opinion is handed down—by a majority of the justices who participate in considering the case. Any party may move the appellate court to change the notation, but the court of appeals must not change the notation after the Court of Criminal Appeals has acted on any party's petition for discretionary review or other request for relief. The Court of Criminal Appeals may, at any time, order that a "do not publish" notation be changed to "publish."

(c) Civil Cases. Opinions and memorandum opinions in civil cases issued on or after January 1, 2003 shall not be designated "do not publish."

(Amended by Order Dec. 23, 2002, eff. Jan. 1, 2003. Amended by Order March 10, 2008, eff. Sept. 1, 2008; Order Aug. 20, 2008, eff. Sept. 1, 2008.)

47.3. Distribution of Opinions.

All opinions of the courts of appeals are open to the public and must be made available to public reporting services, print or electronic.

(Amended by Order Dec. 23, 2002, eff. Jan. 1, 2003.)

47.4. Memorandum Opinions.

If the issues are settled, the court should write a brief memorandum opinion no longer than necessary to advise the parties of the court's decision and the basic reasons for it. An opinion may not be designated a memorandum opinion if the author of a concurrence or dissent opposes that designation. An opinion must be designated a memorandum opinion unless it does any of the following:

(a) establishes a new rule of law, alters or modifies an existing rule, or applies an existing rule to a novel fact situation likely to recur in future cases;

(b) involves issues of constitutional law or other legal issues important to the jurisprudence of Texas;

(c) criticizes existing law; or

(d) resolves an apparent conflict of authority.

(Amended by Order Dec. 23, 2002, eff. Jan. 1, 2003.)

47.5. Concurring and Dissenting Opinions.

Only a justice who participated in the decision of a case may file or join in an opinion concurring in or dissenting from the judgment of the court of appeals. Any justice on the court may file an opinion in connection with a denial of a hearing or rehearing en banc.

(Amended by Order Dec. 23, 2002 eff. Jan. 1, 2003.)

47.6. Change in Designation by En Banc Court.

A court en banc may change a panel's designation of an opinion.

(Amended by Order Dec. 23, 2002, eff. Jan. 1, 2003.)

47.7. Citation of Unpublished Opinions.

(a) Criminal Cases. Opinions and memorandum opinions not designated for publication by the court of appeals under these or prior rules have no precedential value but may be cited with the notation, "(not designated for publication)."

(b) Civil Cases. Opinions and memorandum opinions designated "do not publish" under these rules by the court of appeals prior to January 1, 2003 have no precedential value but may be cited with the notation, "(not designated for publication)." If an opinion or memorandum opinion issued on or after that date is erroneously designated "do not publish," the erroneous designation will not affect the precedential value of the decision.

(Amended by Order Dec. 23, 2002, eff. Jan. 1, 2003. Amended by Order March 10, 2008, eff. Sept. 1, 2008; Order Aug. 20, 2008, eff. Sept. 1, 2008.)

Comment to 2002 change: The rule is substantively changed to discontinue the use of the "do no publish" designation in civil cases, to require that all opinions of the court of appeals be made available to public reporting services, and to remove prospectively any prohibition against the citation of opinions as authority in civil cases. The rule favors the use of "memorandum opinions" designated as such except in certain types of cases but does not change other requirements, such as those in *Pool v. Ford Motor Co.*, 715 S.W.2d 629, 635-636 (Tex. 1986). An opinion previously designated "do not publish" has no precedential value but may be cited. The citation must include the notation, "(not designated for publication)." Of course, whenever an opinion not readily available is cited, copies should be furnished to the court and opposing counsel.

Comment to 2008 changes: Effective January 1, 2003, Rule 47 was amended to discontinue in civil cases, on a prospective basis, the practice of allowing courts of appeals to designate opinions as either "published" or "unpublished." Rule 47.7 is revised to clarify that, with respect to civil cases, only opinions issued prior to the 2003 amendment and affirmatively designated "do not publish" should be considered "unpublished" cases lacking precedential value. All opinions and memorandum opinions in civil cases issued after the 2003 amendment have precedential value. The provisions governing citation of unpublished opinions in criminal cases are substantively unchanged. Rules 47.2 and 47.7 are amended to clarify that memorandum opinions are subject to those rules.

RULE 48. COPY OF OPINION AND JUDGMENT TO INTERESTED PARTIES AND OTHER COURTS.

48.1. recipients of Opinion and Judgment in All Cases.

On the date when an appellate court's opinion is handed down, the appellate clerk must send or deliver copies of the opinion and judgment to the following persons:

(a) the trial judge;
(b) the trial court clerk;
(c) the regional administrative judge; and
(d) all parties to the appeal.

(Amended by Order Dec. 13, 2013, eff. Jan. 1, 2014.)

48.2. Additional Recipients in Criminal Cases.

In criminal cases, copies of the opinion and judgment will also be mailed or delivered to the State Prosecuting Attorney.

48.3. Filing Opinion and Judgment.

The trial court clerk must file a copy of the opinion and judgment among the papers of the case in that court.

48.4. Opinion Sent to Criminal Defendant.

In criminal cases, the attorney representing the defendant on appeal shall, within five days after the opinion is handed down, send his client a copy of the opinion and judgment, along with notification of the defendant's right to file a *pro se* petition for discretionary review under Rule 68. This notification shall be sent certified mail, return receipt requested, to the defendant at his last known address. The attorney shall also send the court of appeals a letter certifying his compliance with this rule and attaching a copy of the return receipt within the time for filing a motion for rehearing. The court of appeals shall file this letter in its record of the appeal.

(Adopted by Order eff. Sept. 1, 1997. Amended by Order May 2, 2007, eff. Sept. 1, 2007.)

Comment to 1997 change: This is former Rule 91 with changes.

RULE 49. MOTION FOR REHEARING AND EN BANC RECONSIDERATION.

49.1. Motion for Rehearing.

A motion for rehearing may be filed within 15 days after the court of appeals' judgment or order is rendered. The motion must clearly state the points relied on for the rehearing. After a motion for rehearing is decided, another motion for rehearing may be filed within 15 days of the court's action only if the court:

(a) modifies its judgment;
(b) vacates its judgment and renders a new judgment; or
(c) issues an opinion in overruling a motion for rehearing.

(Amended by Order March 10, 2008, eff. Sept. 1, 2008.)

49.2. Response.

No response to a motion for rehearing need be filed unless the court so requests. A motion will not be granted unless a response has been filed or requested by the court.

49.3. Decision on Motion.

A motion for rehearing may be granted by a majority of the justices who participated in the decision of the case. Otherwise, it must be denied. If rehearing is granted, the court or panel may dispose of the case with or without rebriefing and oral argument.

49.4. Accelerated Appeals.

In an accelerated appeal, the appellate court may deny the right to file a motion for rehearing or shorten the time to file such a motion.

49.5. Further motion for rehearing.

After a motion for rehearing is decided, a further motion for rehearing may be filed within 15 days of the court's action if the court:

(a) modifies its judgment;

(b) vacates its judgment and renders a new judgment; or

(c) issues a different opinion.

(Adopted by Order Aug. 20, 2008, eff. Sept. 1, 2008.)

49.6. Amendments.

A motion for rehearing or a motion for en banc reconsideration may be amended as a matter of right anytime before the 15-day period allowed for filing the motion expires, and with leave of the court, anytime before the court of appeals decides the motion.

(Amended by Order March 10, 2008, eff. Sept. 1, 2008; Order Aug. 20, 2008, eff. Sept. 1, 2008.)

49.7. En Banc Reconsideration.

A party may file a motion for en banc reconsideration as a separate motion, with or without filing a motion for rehearing. The motion must be filed within 15 days after the court of appeals' judgment or order, or when permitted, within 15 days after the court of appeals' denial of the party's last timely filed motion for rehearing or en banc reconsideration. While the court has plenary power a majority of the en banc court may, with or without a motion, order en banc reconsideration of a panel's decision. If a majority orders reconsideration, the panel's judgment or order does not become final, and the case will be resubmitted to the court for en banc review and disposition.

(Amended by Order March 10, 2008, eff. Sept. 1, 2008; Order Aug. 20, 2008, eff. Sept. 1, 2008; Order Aug. 25, 2008, eff. Sept. 1, 2008.)

49.8. Extensions of Time.

A court of appeals may extend the time for filing a motion for rehearing or a motion for en banc reconsideration if a party files a motion complying with Rule 10.5(b) no later than 15 days after the last date for filing the motion for rehearing.

(Amended by Order March 10, 2008, eff. Sept. 1, 2008; Order Aug. 20, 2008, eff. Sept. 1, 2008.)

49.9. Not Required for Review.

A motion for rehearing is not required to preserve error and is not a prerequisite to filing:

(a) a motion for en banc reconsideration as provided by Rule 49.6;

(b) a petition for review in the Supreme Court; or

(c) a petition for discretionary review to the Court of Criminal Appeals.

(Amended by Order March 10, 2008, eff. Sept. 1, 2008; Order Aug. 20, 2008, eff. Sept. 1, 2008.)

49.10. Repealed by Order Nov. 13, 2012, Eff. Dec. 1, 2012.

49.11. Relationship to Petition for Review.

A party may not file a motion for rehearing in the court of appeals after that party has filed a petition for review in the Supreme Court unless the court of appeals modifies its opinion or judgment after the petition for review is filed. The filing of a petition for review does not preclude another party from filing a motion for rehearing or the court of appeals from ruling on the motion. If a motion for rehearing in timely filed after a petition for review is filed, the petitioner must immediately notify the Supreme Court clerk of the filing of the motion, and must notify the clerk when the last timely filed motion is overruled by the court of appeals.

(Adopted by Order March 10, 2008, eff. Sept. 1, 2008; Order Aug. 20, 2008, eff. Sept. 1, 2008.)

49.12. Certificate of Conference Not Required.

A certificate of conference is not required for a motion for rehearing or for a motion for en banc reconsideration of a panel's decision.

(Amended by Order March 10, 2008, eff. Sept. 1, 2008; Order Aug. 20, 2008, eff. Sept. 1, 2008.)

Comment to 1997 change: This is former Rule 100. Subdivision 49.4 is moved here from former Rule 43(h). Subdivisions 49.9 and 49.10 are added.

Comment to 2008 changes: Rule 49 is revised to treat a motion for en banc reconsideration as a motion for rehearing and to include procedures governing the filing of a motion for en banc reconsideration. Subdivision 49.5(c) is amended to clarify that a further motion for rehearing may be filed if the court issues a different opinion, irrespective of whether the opinion is issued in connection with the overruling of a prior motion for rehearing. Issuance of a new opinion that is not substantially different should not occasion a further motion for rehearing, but a motion's lack of merit does not affect appellate deadlines. The provisions of former Rule 53.7(b) that address motions for rehearing are moved to new subdivision 49.11 without change, leaving the provisions of Rule 53.7(b) that address petitions for review undisturbed. Subdivision 49.12 mirrors Rule 10.1(a)(5) in excepting motions for rehearing and motions for en banc reconsideration from the certificate-of-conference requirement.

RULE 50. RECONSIDERATION ON PETITION FOR DISCRETIONARY REVIEW.

Within 60 days after a petition for discretionary review is filed with the clerk of the court of appeals that delivered the decision, the justices who participated in the decision may, as provided by subsection (a), reconsider and correct or modify the court's opinion or judgment. Within the same period of time, any of the justices who participated in the decision may issue a concurring of dissenting opinion.

(a) If the court's original opinion or judgment is corrected or modified, that opinion or judgment is withdrawn and the modified or corrected opinion or judgment is substituted as the opinion or judgment of the court. No further opinions may be issued by the court of appeals. The original petition for discretionary review is not dismissed by operation of law, unless the filing party files a new petition in the court of appeals. In the alternative, the petitioning party shall submit to the court of appeals copies of the corrected or modified opinion or judgment as an amendment to the original petition.

(b) Any party may then file with the court of appeals a new petition for discretionary review seeking review of the corrected or modified opinion or judgment, including any dissents or concurrences, under Rule 68.2.

(Adopted by Order eff. Sept. 1, 1997. Amended by Order March 10, 2008, eff. Sept. 1, 2008; Order Aug. 20, 2008, eff. Sept. 1, 2008.)

Comment to 1997 change: This is former Rule 101. The rule is amended to allow 30 days for the court of appeals to review the petition for discretionary review and to require the withdrawal of the prior opinion and judgment if the court of appeals renders a new judgment or hands down a new opinion.

RULE 51. ENFORCEMENT OF JUDGMENTS AFTER MANDATE.

51.1. Civil Cases.

(a) Statement of Costs. The appellate clerk must prepare, and send to the trial court clerk with the mandate, a statement of costs showing:

(1) the preparation costs for the appellate record, and any court of appeals filing fees, with a notation of those items that have been paid and those that are owing; and

(2) the party or parties against whom costs have been adjudged.

(b) Enforcement of Judgment. When the trial court clerk receives the mandate, the appellate court's judgment must be enforced. Appellate court costs must be included with the trial court costs in any process to enforce the judgment. If all or part of the costs are collected, the trial court clerk must immediately remit to the appellate court clerk any amount due to that clerk. The trial court need not make any further order in the case, and the appellate court's judgment may be enforced as in other cases, when the appellate judgment:

(1) affirms the trial court's judgment;

(2) modifies the trial court's judgment and, as so modified, affirms that judgment; or

(3) renders the judgment the trial court should have rendered.

51.2. Criminal Cases.

When the trial court clerk receives the mandate, the appellate court's judgment must be enforced as follows:

(a) Clerk's Duties. The trial court clerk must:

(1) send an acknowledgment to the appellate clerk of the mandate's receipt; and

(2) immediately file the mandate.

(b) Judgment of Affirmance; Defendant Not in Custody.

(1) Capias to Be Issued. If the judgment contains a sentence of confinement or imprisonment that has not been suspended, the trial court must promptly issue a capias for the defendant's arrest so that the court's sentence can be executed.

(2) Contents of Capias. The capias may issue to any county of this state and must be executed and returned as in felony cases, except that no bail may be taken. The capias must:

(A) recite the fact of conviction;

(B) set forth the offense and the court's judgment and sentence;

(C) state that the judgment was appealed from and affirmed, and that the mandate has been filed; and

(D) command the sheriff to arrest and take the defendant into his custody, and to place and keep the defendant in custody until delivered to the proper authorities as directed by the sentence.

(3) Sheriff's Duties. The sheriff must promptly execute the capias as directed. The sheriff must notify the trial court clerk and the appellate clerk when the mandate has been carried out and executed.

(c) Judgment of Reversal.

(1) When New Trial Ordered. When the appellate court reverses the trial court's judgment and grants the defendant a new trial, the procedure is governed by Code of Criminal Procedure article 44.29. If the defendant is in custody and entitled to bail, the defendant must be released upon giving bail.

(2) When Case Dismissed. When the appellate court reverses the trial court's judgment and orders the case to be dismissed, the defendant—if in custody—must be discharged.

(d) Judgment of Acquittal. When the appellate court reverses a judgment and orders the defendant's acquittal, the defendant—if in custody—must be discharged, and no further order or judgment of the trial court is necessary.

(Adopted by Order eff. Sept. 1, 1997.)

Comment to 1997 change: Former Rules 87 and 88 are merged. The reference to costs in tax suits is deleted.

SECTION THREE.
ORIGINAL PROCEEDINGS IN THE SUPREME COURT AND THE COURTS OF APPEALS

RULE 52. ORIGINAL PROCEEDINGS.

52.1. Commencement.

An original appellate proceeding seeking extraordinary relief—such as a writ of habeas corpus, mandamus, prohibition, injunction, or quo warranto—is commenced by filing a petition with the clerk of the appropriate appellate court. The petition must be captioned "In re [name of relator]."

52.2. Designation of Parties.

The party seeking the relief is the relator. In original proceedings other than habeas corpus, the person against whom relief is sought—whether a judge, court, tribunal, officer, or other person—is the respondent. A person whose interest would be directly affected by the relief sought is a real party in interest and a party to the case.

52.3. Form and Contents of Petition.

The petition must, under appropriate headings and in the order here indicated, contain the following:

(a) Identity of Parties and Counsel. The petition must give a complete list of all parties, and the names, and addresses of all counsel.

(b) Table of Contents. The petition must include a table of contents with references to the pages of the petition. The table of contents must indicate the subject matter of each issue or point, or group of issues or points.

(c) Index of Authorities. The petition must include an index of authorities arranged alphabetically and indicating the pages of the petition where the authorities are cited.

(d) Statement of the Case. The petition must contain a statement of the case that should seldom exceed one page and should not discuss the facts. The statement must contain the following:

(1) a concise description of the nature of any underlying proceeding (e.g., a suit for damages, a contempt proceeding for failure to pay child support, or the certification of a candidate for inclusion on an election ballot);

(2) if the respondent is a judge, the name of the judge, the designation of the court in which the judge was sitting, and the county in which the court is located; and if the respondent is an official other than a judge, the designation and location of the office held by the respondent;

(3) a concise description of the respondent's action from which the relator seeks relief;

(4) if the relator seeks a writ of habeas corpus, a statement describing how and where the relator is being deprived of liberty;

(5) if the petition is filed in the Supreme Court after a petition requesting the same relief was filed in the court of appeals:

(A) the date the petition was filed in the court of appeals;

(B) the district of the court of appeals and the names of the justices who participated in the decision;

(C) the author of any opinion for the court of appeals and the author of any separate opinion;

(D) the citation of the court's opinion;

(E) the disposition of the case by the court of appeals, and the date of the court of appeals' order.

(e) Statement of Jurisdiction. The petition must state, without argument, the basis of the court's jurisdiction. If the Supreme Court and the court of appeals have concurrent jurisdiction, the petition must be presented first to the court of appeals unless there is a compelling reason not to do so. If the petition is filed in the Supreme Court without first being presented to the court of appeals, the petition must state the compelling reason why the petition was not first presented to the court of appeals.

(f) Issues Presented. The petition must state concisely all issues or points presented for relief. The statement of an issue or point will be treated as covering every subsidiary question that is fairly included.

(g) Statement of Facts. The petition must state concisely and without argument the facts pertinent to the issues or points presented. Every statement of fact in the petition must be supported by citation to competent evidence included in the appendix or record.

(h) Argument. The petition must contain a clear and concise argument for the contentions made, with appropriate citations to authorities and to the appendix or record.

(i) Prayer. The petition must contain a short conclusion that clearly states the nature of the relief sought.

(j) Certification. The person filing the petition must certify that he or she has reviewed the petition and concluded that every factual statement in the petition is supported by competent evidence included in the appendix or record.

(k) Appendix.

(1) Necessary Contents. The appendix must contain:

(A) a certified or sworn copy of any order complained of, or any other document showing the matter complained of;

(B) any order or opinion of the court of appeals, if the petition is filed in the Supreme Court;

(C) unless voluminous or impracticable, the text of any rule, regulation, ordinance, statute, constitutional provision, or other law (excluding case law) on which the argument is based; and

(D) if a writ of habeas corpus is sought, proof that the relator is being restrained.

(2) Optional Contents. The appendix may contain any other item pertinent to the issues or points presented for review, including copies or excerpts of relevant court opinions, statutes, constitutional provisions, documents on which the suit was based, pleadings, and similar material. Items should not be included in the appendix to attempt to avoid the page limits for the petition. The appendix should not contain any evidence or other item that is not necessary for a decision.

(Amended by Order March 10, 2008, eff. Sept. 1, 2008 ; Order Aug. 20, 2008, eff. Sept. 1, 2008.)

Comment to 2008 changes: The reference to "unpublished" opinions in Subdivision 52.3(d)(5)(D) is deleted. The filer should provide the best cite available for the court of appeals' opinion, which may be a LEXIS, Westlaw, or other citation to an electronic medium. Subdivision 52.3 is further amended to delete the requirement that all factual statements be verified by affidavit. Instead, the filer—in the usual case of a party with legal representation, the lead counsel—must include a statement certifying that all factual statements are supported by competent evidence in the appendix or record to which the petition has cited. The certification required by subdivision 52.3(j) does not count against the page limitations.

52.4. Response.

Any party may file a response to the petition, but it is not mandatory. The court must not grant relief—other than temporary relief—before a response has been filed or requested by the court. The response must conform to the requirements of 52.3, except that:

(a) the list of parties and counsel is not required unless necessary to supplement or correct the list contained in the petition;

(b) the response need not include a statement of the case, a statement of the issues presented, or a statement of the facts unless the responding party is dissatisfied with that portion of the petition;

(c) a statement of jurisdiction should be omitted unless the petition fails to assert valid grounds for jurisdiction, in which case the reasons why the court lacks jurisdiction must be concisely stated;

(d) the argument must be confined to the issues or points presented in the petition; and

(e) the appendix to the response need not contain any item already contained in an appendix filed by the relator.

52.5. Relator's Reply to Response.

The relator may file a reply addressing any matter in the response. However, the court may consider and decide the case before a reply brief is filed.

52.6. Repealed by Order Nov. 13, 2012, Eff. Dec. 1, 2012.

52.7. Record.

(a) Filing by Relator Required. Relator must file with the petition:

(1) a certified or sworn copy of every document that is material to the relator's claim for relief and that was filed in any underlying proceeding; and

(2) a properly authenticated transcript of any relevant testimony from any underlying proceeding, including any exhibits offered in evidence, or a statement that no testimony was adduced in connection with the matter complained.

(b) Supplementation Permitted. After the record is filed, relator or any other party to the proceeding may file additional materials for inclusion in the record.

(c) Service of Record on All Parties. Relator and any party who files materials for inclusion in the record must—at the same time—serve on each party:

(1) those materials not previously served on that party as part of the record in another original appellate proceeding in the same or another court; and

(2) an index listing the materials filed and describing them in sufficient detail to identify them.

(Amended by Order Dec. 23, 2002, eff. Jan. 1, 2003.)

Comment to 2002 change: Subdivision 52.7(c) is added to specify how record materials in original proceedings are to be served. Ordinarily, a party must serve record materials and an index of those materials on all other parties. But when materials have already been served in related original proceedings, they need not be served again. Examples are when original proceedings raising the same issues are brought in both the court of appeals and the Supreme Court, or when separate original proceedings are filed arising out of the same underlying lawsuit. The purpose of this procedure is to ensure that all parties have record materials readily available without requiring unnecessary duplication.

52.8. Action on Petition.

(a) Relief Denied. If the court determines from the petition and any response and reply that the relator is not entitled to the relief sought, the court must deny the petition. If the relator in a habeas corpus proceeding has been released on bond, the court must remand the relator to custody and issue an order of commitment. If the relator is not returned to custody, the court may declare the bond to be forfeited and render judgment against the surety.

(b) Interim Action. If the court is of the tentative opinion that relator is entitled to the relief sought or that a serious question concerning the relief requires further consideration:

(1) the court must request a response if one has not been filed;

(2) the Supreme Court may request full briefing under Rule 55;

(3) in a habeas corpus proceeding, the court may order that relator be discharged on execution and filing of a bond in an amount set by the court; and

(4) the court may set the case for oral argument.

(c) Relief Granted. If the court determines that relator is entitled to relief, it must make an appropriate order. The court may grant relief without hearing oral argument.

(d) Opinion. When denying relief, the court may hand down an opinion but is not required to do so. When granting relief, the court must hand down an opinion as in any other case. Rule 47 is applicable to an order or opinion by a court of appeals except that the court of appeals may not order an unpublished opinion published after the Supreme Court or Court of Criminal Appeals has acted on any party's petition for extraordinary relief addressing the same issues.

52.9. Motion for Rehearing.

Any party may file a motion for rehearing within 15 days after the final order is rendered. The motion must clearly state the points relied on for the rehearing. No response to a motion for rehearing need be filed unless the court so requests. The court will not grant a motion for rehearing unless a response has been filed or requested.

(Amended by Order March 4, 2013, eff. March 4, 2013.)

52.10. Temporary Relief.

(a) Motion for Temporary Relief; Certificate of Compliance. The relator may file a motion to stay any underlying proceedings or for any other temporary relief pending the court's action on the petition. The relator must notify or make a diligent effort to notify all parties by expedited means (such as by telephone or fax) that a motion for temporary relief has been or will be filed and must certify to the court that the relator has complied with this paragraph before temporary relief will be granted.

(b) Grant of Temporary Relief. The court—on motion of any party or on its own initiative—may without notice grant any just relief pending the court's action on the petition. As a condition of granting temporary relief, the court may require a bond to protect the parties who will be affected by the relief. Unless vacated or modified, an order granting temporary relief is effective until the case is finally decided.

(c) Motion to Reconsider. Any party may move the court at any time to reconsider a grant of temporary relief.

52.11. Groundless Petition or Misleading Statement or Record.

On motion of any party or on its own initiative, the court may—after notice and a reasonable opportunity to respond—impose just sanctions on a party or attorney who is not acting in good faith as indicated by any of the following:

(a) filing a petition that is clearly groundless;

(b) bringing the petition solely for delay of an underlying proceeding;

(c) grossly misstating or omitting an obviously important and material fact in the petition or response; or

(d) filing an appendix or record that is clearly misleading because of the omission of obviously important and material evidence or documents.

(Adopted by Order eff. Sept. 1, 1997.)

Comment to 1997 change: Former Rules 120, 121, and 122 are merged into this rule. The requirement of a motion for leave in original proceedings is repealed. The form of the petition and response, contents of the appendix and record, page limits, and relief that may be granted are specifically stated. Specific provision is now made for a motion for rehearing. A provision for sanctions is added.

SECTION FOUR. PROCEEDINGS IN THE SUPREME COURT

RULE 53. PETITION FOR REVIEW.

53.1. Method of Review.

The Supreme Court may review a court of appeals' final judgment on a petition for review addressed to "The Supreme Court of Texas." A party who seeks to alter the court of appeals' judgment must file a petition for review. The petition for review procedure replaces the writ of error procedure. Statutes pertaining to the writ of error in the Supreme Court apply equally to the petition for review.

53.2. Contents of Petition.

The petition for review must, under appropriate headings and in the order here indicated, contain the following items:

(a) Identity of Parties and Counsel. The petition must give a complete list of all parties to the trial court's final judgment, and the names and addresses of all trial and appellate counsel.

(b) Table of Contents. The petition must have a table of contents with references to the pages of the petition. The table of contents must indicate the subject matter of each issue or point, or group of issues or points.

(c) Index of Authorities. The petition must have an index of authorities arranged alphabetically and indicating the pages of the petition where the authorities are cited.

(d) Statement of the Case. The petition must contain a statement of the case that should seldom exceed one page and should not discuss the facts. The statement must contain the following:

(1) a concise description of the nature of the case (e.g., whether it is a suit for damages, on a note, or in trespass to try title);

(2) the name of the judge who signed the order or judgment appealed from;

(3) the designation of the trial court and the county in which it is located;

(4) the disposition of the case by the trial court;

(5) the parties in the court of appeals;

(6) the district of the court of appeals;

(7) the names of the justices who participated in the decision in the court of appeals, the author of the opinion for the court, and the author of any separate opinion;

(8) the citation for the court of appeals' opinion; and

(9) the disposition of the case by the court of appeals, including the court's disposition of any motions for rehearing or motions for en banc reconsideration and whether any motions for rehearing or motions for en banc reconsideration are pending in the court of appeals at the time the petition for review is filed.

(e) Statement of Jurisdiction. The petition must state, without argument, the basis of the Court's jurisdiction.

(f) Issues Presented. The petition must state concisely all issues or points presented for review. The statement of an issue or point will be treated as covering every subsidiary question that is fairly included. If the matter complained of originated in the trial court, it should have been preserved for appellate review in the trial court and assigned as error in the court of appeals.

(g) Statement of Facts. The petition must affirm that the court of appeals correctly stated the nature of the case, except in any particulars pointed out. The petition must state concisely and without argument the facts and procedural background pertinent to the issues or points presented. The statement must be supported by record references.

(h) Summary of the Argument. The petition must contain a succinct, clear, and accurate statement of the arguments made in the body of the petition. This summary must not merely repeat the issues or points presented for review.

(i) Argument. The petition must contain a clear and concise argument for the contentions made, with appropriate citations to authorities and to the record. The argument need not address every issue or point included in the statement of issues or points. Any issue or point not addressed may be addressed in the brief on the merits if one is requested by the Court. The argument should state the reasons why the Supreme Court should exercise jurisdiction to hear the case with specific reference to the factors listed in Rule 56.1(a). The petition need not quote at length from a matter included in the appendix; a reference to the appendix is sufficient. The Court will consider the court of appeals' opinion along with the petition, so statements in that opinion need not be repeated.

(j) Prayer. The petition must contain a short conclusion that clearly states the nature of the relief sought.

(k) Appendix.

(1) Necessary Contents. Unless voluminous or impracticable, the appendix must contain a copy of:

(A) the judgment or other appealable order of the trial court from which relief in the court of appeals was sought;

(B) the jury charge and verdict, if any, or the trial court's findings of fact and conclusions of law, if any;

(C) the opinion and judgment of the court of appeals; and

(D) the text of any rule, regulation, ordinance, statute, constitutional provision, or other law on which the argument is based (excluding case law), and the text of any contract or other document that is central to the argument.

(2) Optional Contents. The appendix may contain any other item pertinent to the issues or points presented for review, including copies or excerpts of relevant court opinions, statutes, constitutional provisions, documents on which the suit was based, pleadings, and similar material. Items should not be included in the appendix to attempt to avoid the page limits for the petition.

(Amended by Order March 10, 2008, eff. Sept. 1, 2008; Order Aug. 20, 2008, eff. Sept. 1, 2008.)

53.3. Response to Petition for Review.

Any other party to the appeal may file a response to the petition for review, but it is not mandatory. If no response is timely filed, or if a party files a waiver of response, the Court will consider the petition without a response. A petition will not be granted before a response has been filed or requested by the Court. The response must conform to the requirements of 53.2, except that:

(a) the list of parties and counsel is not required unless necessary to supplement or correct the list contained in the petition;

(b) a statement of the case and a statement of the facts need not be made unless the respondent is dissatisfied with that portion of the petition;

(c) a statement of the issues presented need not be made unless:

(1) the respondent is dissatisfied with the statement made in the petition;

(2) the respondent is asserting independent grounds for affirmance of the court of appeals' judgment; or

(3) the respondent is asserting grounds that establish the respondent's right to a judgment that is less favorable to the respondent than the judgment rendered by the court of appeals but more favorable to the respondent than the judgment that might be awarded to the petitioner (e.g., a remand for a new trial rather than a rendition of judgment in favor of the petitioner);

(d) a statement of jurisdiction should be omitted unless the petition fails to assert valid grounds for jurisdiction, in which case the reasons why the Supreme Court lacks jurisdiction must be concisely stated;

(e) the respondent's argument must be confined to the issues or points presented in the petition or asserted by the respondent in the respondent's statement of issues; and

(f) the appendix to the response need not contain any item already contained in an appendix filed by the petitioner.

53.4. Points Not Considered in Court of Appeals.

To obtain a remand to the court of appeals for consideration of issues or points briefed in that court but not decided by that court, or to request that the Supreme Court consider such issues or points, a party may raise those issues or points in the petition, the response, the reply, any brief, or a motion for rehearing.

53.5. Petitioner's Reply to Response.

The petitioner may file a reply addressing any matter in the response. However, the Court may consider and decide the case before a reply brief is filed.

53.6. Repealed by Order Nov. 13, 2012, Eff. Dec. 1, 2012.

53.7. Time and Place of Filing.

(a) Petition. Unless the Supreme Court for good cause orders an earlier filing deadline, the petition must be filed with the Supreme Court clerk within 45 days after the following:

(1) the date the court of appeals rendered judgment, if no motion for rehearing or motion for enbanc reconsideration is timely filed; or

(2) the date of the court of appeals' last ruling on all timely filed motions for rehearing or en banc reconsideration.

(b) Premature Filing. A petition filed before the last ruling on all timely filed motions for rehearing and en banc reconsideration is treated as having been filed on the date of, but after, the last ruling on any such motion. If a party files a petition for review while a motion for rehearing or en banc reconsideration is pending in the court of appeals, the party must include that information in its petition for review.

(c) Petitions Filed by Other Parties. If a party files a petition for review within the time specified in 53.7(a)—or within the time specified by the Supreme Court in an order granting an extension of time to file a petition—any other party required to file a petition may do so within 45 days after the last timely motion for rehearing is overruled or within 30 days after any preceding petition is filed, whichever date is later.

(d) Response. Any response must be filed with the Supreme Court clerk within 30 days after the petition is filed.

(e) Reply. Any reply must be filed with the Supreme Court clerk within 15 days after the response is filed.

(f) Extension of Time. The Supreme Court may extend the time to file a petition for review if a party files a motion complying with Rule 10.5(b) no later than 15 days after the last day for filing the petition. The Supreme Court may extend the time to file a response or reply if a party files a motion complying with Rule 10.5(b) either before or after the response or reply is due.

(g) Petition Filed in Court of Appeals. If a petition is mistakenly filed in the court of appeals, the petition is deemed to have been filed the same day with the Supreme Court clerk, and the court of appeals clerk must immediately send the petition to the Supreme Court clerk.

(Amended by Order March 10, 2008, eff. Sept. 1, 2008; Order Aug. 20, 2008, eff. Sept. 1, 2008.)

53.8. Amendment.

On motion showing good cause, the Court may allow the petition, response, or reply to be amended on such reasonable terms as the Court may prescribe.

53.9. Court May Require Revision.

If a petition, response, or reply does not conform with these rules, the Supreme Court may require the document to be revised or may return the document to the party who filed it and consider the case without allowing the document to be revised.

(Adopted by Order eff. Sept. 1, 1997.)

Comment to 1997 change: Former Rules 130 and 131 are merged. The 50-page application for writ of error is replaced by a 15-page petition for review, which is filed in the Supreme Court and should concentrate on the reasons the Court should exercise jurisdiction to hear the case. The contents of the petition and response, the length of the documents, the time for filing are all specifically stated.

Comment to 2008 change: Subdivision 53.7(a)is amended to clarify that the Supreme Court may shorten the time for filing a petition for review and that the timely filing of a motion for en banc reconsideration tolls the commencement of the 45-day period for filing a petition for review until the motion is overruled. Subdivision 53.2(d)(8) is amended to delete the reference to unpublished opinions in civil cases. Subdivision 53.2(d)(9) is amended to require a party that prematurely files a petition for review to notify the Supreme Court of any panel rehearing or en banc reconsideration motions still pending in the court of appeals. Subdivision 53.7(b) is revised to reference this new requirement and to relocate to new Rule 49.11 those provisions governing motions for rehearing.

RULE 54. FILING THE RECORD.

54.1. Request for Record.

With or without granting the petition for review, the Supreme Court may request that the record from the court of appeals be filed with the clerk of the Supreme Court.

54.2. Duty of Court of Appeals Clerk.

(a) Request for Record. The court of appeals clerk must not send the record to the Supreme Court unless it is requested. Upon receiving the Supreme Court clerk's request for the record, the court of appeals clerk must promptly send to the Supreme Court clerk all of the following:

(1) the original record;
(2) any motion filed in the court of appeals;
(3) copies of all orders of the court of appeals; and
(4) copies of all opinions and the judgment of the court of appeals.

(b) Nondocumentary Exhibits. The clerk should not send any nondocumentary exhibits unless the Supreme Court specifically requests.

54.3. Expenses.

The petitioner must pay to the court of appeals clerk a sum sufficient to pay the cost of mailing or shipping the record to and from the Supreme Court clerk.

54.4. Duty of Supreme Court Clerk.

Upon receiving the record, the Supreme Court clerk must file it and enter the filing on the docket. The clerk may refuse the record if the charges for mailing or shipping have not been paid.

(Adopted by Order eff. Sept. 1, 1997.)

Comment to 1997 change: This is former Rule 132. Subdivision 54.1 is new and provides for the Supreme Court to request the filing of the record. Other changes are made.

RULE 55. BRIEFS ON THE MERITS.

55.1. Request by Court.

A brief on the merits must not be filed unless requested by the Court. With or without granting the petition for review, the Court may request the parties to file briefs on the merits. In appropriate cases, the Court may realign parties and direct that parties file consolidated briefs.

(Amended by Order Dec. 23, 2002 eff. Jan. 1, 2003.)

Comment to 2002 change: Subdivision 55.1 is clarified to provide that the Court may realign parties require consolidated briefing for a clearer and more efficient presentation of the case.

55.2. Petitioner's Brief on the Merits.

The petitioner's brief on the merits must be confined to the issues or points stated in the petition for review and must, under appropriate headings and in the order here indicated, contain the following items:

(a) Identity of Parties and Counsel. The brief must give a complete list of all parties to the trial court's final judgment, and the names and addresses of all trial and appellate counsel.

(b) Table of Contents. The brief must have a table of contents with references to the pages of the brief. The table of contents must indicate the subject matter of each issue or point, or group of issues or points.

(c) Index of Authorities. The brief must have an index of authorities arranged alphabetically and indicating the pages of the brief where the authorities are cited.

(d) Statement of the Case. The brief must contain a statement of the case that should seldom exceed one page and should not discuss the facts. The statement must contain the following:

(1) a concise description of the nature of the case (e.g., whether it is a suit for damages, on a note, or in trespass to try title);
(2) the name of the judge who signed the order or judgment appealed from;
(3) the designation of the trial court and the county in which it is located;
(4) the disposition of the case by the trial court;
(5) the parties in the court of appeals;
(6) the district of the court of appeals;
(7) the names of the justices who participated in the decision in the court of appeals, the author of the opinion for the court, and the author of any separate opinion;
(8) the citation for the court of appeals' opinion, if available, or a statement that the opinion was unpublished; and
(9) the disposition of the case by the court of appeals;

(e) Statement of Jurisdiction. The brief must state, without argument, the basis of the Court's jurisdiction.

(f) Issues Presented. The brief must state concisely all issues or points presented for review. The statement of an issue or point will be treated as covering every subsidiary question that is fairly included. The phrasing of the issues or points need not be identical to the statement of issues or points in the petition for review, but the brief may not raise additional issues or points or change the substance of the issues or points presented in the petition.

(g) Statement of Facts. The brief must affirm that the court of appeals correctly stated the nature of the case, except in any particulars pointed out. The brief must state concisely and without argument the facts and procedural background pertinent to the issues or points presented. The statement must be supported by record references.

(h) Summary of the Argument. The brief must contain a succinct, clear, and accurate statement of the arguments made in the body of the brief. This summary must not merely repeat the issues or points presented for review.

(i) Argument. The brief must contain a clear and concise argument for the contentions made, with appropriate citations to authorities and to the record.

(j) Prayer. The brief must contain a short conclusion that clearly states the nature of the relief sought.

(Amended by Order Dec. 23, 2002, eff. Jan. 1, 2003.)

55.3. Respondent's Brief.

If the petitioner files a brief on the merits, any other party to the appeal may file a brief in response, which must conform to 55.2, except that:

(a) the list of parties and counsel is not required unless necessary to supplement or correct the list contained in the petitioner's brief;

(b) a statement of the case and a statement of the facts need not be made unless the respondent is dissatisfied with that portion of the petitioner's brief; and

(c) a statement of the issues presented need not be made unless:

(1) the respondent is dissatisfied with the statement made in the petitioner's brief;

(2) the respondent is asserting independent grounds for affirmance of the court of appeals' judgment; or

(3) the respondent is asserting grounds that establish the respondent's right to a judgment that is less favorable to the respondent than the judgment rendered by the court of appeals but more favorable to the respondent than the judgment that might be awarded to the petitioner (e.g., a remand for a new trial rather than a rendition of judgment in favor of the petitioner);

(d) a statement of jurisdiction should be omitted unless the petition fails to assert valid grounds for jurisdiction; and

(e) the respondent's argument must be confined to the issues or points presented in the petitioner's brief or asserted by the respondent in the respondent's statement of issues.

55.4. Petitioner's Brief in Reply.

The petitioner may file a reply brief addressing any matter in the brief in response. However, the Court may consider and decide the case before a reply brief is filed.

55.5. Reliance on Prior Brief.

As a brief on the merits or a brief in response, a party may file the brief that the party filed in the court of appeals.

55.6. Repealed by Order Nov. 13, 2012, eff. Dec. 1, 2012.

55.7. Time and Place of Filing; Extension of Time.

Briefs must be filed with the Supreme Court clerk in accordance with the schedule stated in the clerk's notice that the Court has requested briefs on the merits. If no schedule is stated in the notice, petitioner must file a brief on the merits within 30 days after the date of the notice, respondent must file a brief in response within 20 days after receiving petitioner's brief, and petitioner must file any reply brief within 15 days after receiving respondent's brief. On motion complying with Rule 10.5(b) either before or after the brief is due, the Supreme Court may extend the time to file a brief.

55.8. Amendment.

On motion showing good cause, the Court may allow a party to amend a brief on such reasonable terms as the Court may prescribe.

55.9. Court May Require Revision.

If a brief does not conform with these rules, the Supreme Court may require the brief to be revised or may return it to the party who filed it and consider the case without further briefing by that party.

(Adopted by Order eff. Sept. 1, 1997.)

Comment to 1997 change: The rule is new and provides for a 50 page brief on the merits if requested by the Supreme Court.

RULE 56. ORDERS ON PETITION FOR REVIEW.

56.1. Orders on Petition for Review.

(a) Considerations in Granting Review. Whether to grant review is a matter of judicial discretion. Among the factors the Supreme Court considers in deciding whether to grant a petition for review are the following:

(1) whether the justices of the court of appeals disagree on an important point of law;

(2) whether there is a conflict between the courts of appeals on an important point of law;

(3) whether a case involves the construction or validity of a statute;

(4) whether a case involves constitutional issues;

(5) whether the court of appeals appears to have committed an error of law of such importance to the state's jurisprudence that it should be corrected; and

(6) whether the court of appeals has decided an important question of state law that should be, but has not been, resolved by the Supreme Court.

(b) Petition Denied or Dismissed. When the petition has been on file in the Supreme Court for 30 days, the Court may deny or dismiss the petition—whether or not a response has been filed—with one of the following notations:

(1) "Denied." If the Supreme Court is not satisfied that the opinion of the court of appeals has correctly declared the law in all respects, but determines that the petition presents no error that requires reversal or that is of such importance to the jurisprudence of the state as to require correction, the Court will deny the petition with the notation "Denied."

(2) "Dismissed w.o.j." If the Supreme Court lacks jurisdiction, the Court will dismiss the petition with the notation "Dismissed for Want of Jurisdiction."

(c) Petition Refused. If the Supreme Court determines—after a response has been filed or requested—that the court of appeals' judgment is correct and that the legal principles announced in the opinion are likewise correct, the Court will refuse the petition with the notation "Refused." The court of appeals' opinion in the case has the same precedential value as an opinion of the Supreme Court.

(d) Improvident Grant. If the Court has granted review but later decides that review should not have been granted, the Court may, without opinion, set aside the order granting review and dismiss the petition or deny or refuse review as though review had never been granted.

56.2. Moot Cases.

If a case is moot, the Supreme Court may, after notice to the parties, grant the petition and, without hearing argument, dismiss the case or the appealable portion of it without addressing the merits of the appeal.

56.3. Settled Cases.

If a case is settled by agreement of the parties and all parties so move, the Supreme Court may grant the petition if it has not already been granted and, without hearing argument or considering the merits, render a judgment to effectuate the agreement. The Supreme Court's action may include setting aside the judgment of the court of appeals or the trial court without regard to the merits and remanding the case to the trial court for rendition of a judgment in accordance with the agreement. The Supreme Court may abate the case until the lower court's proceedings to effectuate the agreement are complete. A severable portion of the proceeding may be disposed of if it will not prejudice the remaining parties. In any event, the Supreme Court's order does not vacate the court of appeals' opinion unless the order specifically provides otherwise. An agreement or motion cannot be conditioned on vacating the court of appeals' opinion.

(Amended by Order Dec. 23, 2002, eff. Jan. 1, 2003.)

Comment to 2002 change: Subdivision 56.3 is clarified to provide for partial settlements.

56.4. Notice to Parties.

When the Supreme Court grants, denies, refuses, or dismisses a petition for review, the Supreme Court clerk must send a written notice of the disposition to the court of appeals, the trial court, and all parties to the appeal.

56.5. Return of Documents to Court of Appeals.

When the Supreme Court denies, refuses, or dismisses a petition for review, the clerk will retain the petition, together with the record and accompanying papers, for 30 days after the order is rendered. If no motion for rehearing has been filed by the end of that period or when any motion for rehearing of the order has been overruled, the clerk must send a certified copy of its order to the court of appeals and return the record and all papers (except for documents filed in the Supreme Court) to the court of appeals clerk.

(Adopted by Order eff. Sept. 1, 1997.)

Comment to 1997 change: The rule is from former Rule 133. Subdivision 56.3 regarding settled cases is added.

RULE 57. DIRECT APPEALS TO THE SUPREME COURT.

57.1. Application.

This rule governs direct appeals to the Supreme Court that are authorized by the Constitution and by statute. Except when inconsistent with a statute or this rule, the rules governing appeals to courts of appeals also apply to direct appeals to the Supreme Court.

57.2. Jurisdiction.

The Supreme Court may not take jurisdiction over a direct appeal from the decision of any court other than a district court or county court, or over any question of fact. The Supreme Court may decline to exercise jurisdiction over a direct appeal of an interlocutory order if the record is not adequately developed, or if its decision would be advisory, or if the case is not of such importance to the jurisprudence of the state that a direct appeal should be allowed.

57.3. Statement of Jurisdiction.

Appellant must file with the record a statement fully but plainly setting out the basis asserted for exercise of the Supreme Court's jurisdiction. Appellee may file a response to appellant's statement of jurisdiction within ten days after the statement is filed.

57.4. Preliminary Ruling on Jurisdiction.

If the Supreme Court notes probable jurisdiction over a direct appeal, the parties must file briefs under Rule 38 as in any other case. If the Supreme Court does not note probable jurisdiction over a direct appeal, the appeal will be dismissed.

57.5. Direct Appeal Exclusive While Pending.

If a direct appeal to the Supreme Court is filed, the parties to the appeal must not, while that appeal is pending, pursue an appeal to the court of appeals. But if the direct appeal is dismissed, any party may pursue any other appeal available at the time when the direct appeal was filed. The other appeal must be perfected within ten days after dismissal of the direct appeal.

(Adopted by Order eff. Sept. 1, 1997.)

Comment to 1997 change: This is former Rule 140. The rule is amended without substantive change except subdivision 57.5 is amended to make clear that no party to the direct appeal may pursue the appeal in the court of appeals while the direct appeal is pending, but allowing 10 days to perfect a subsequent appeal.

RULE 58. CERTIFICATION OF QUESTIONS OF LAW BY UNITED STATES COURTS.

58.1. Certification.

The Supreme Court of Texas may answer questions of law certified to it by any federal appellate court if the certifying court is presented with determinative questions of Texas law having no controlling Supreme Court precedent. The Supreme Court may decline to answer the questions certified to it.

58.2. Contents of the Certification Order.

An order from the certifying court must set forth:

(a) the questions of law to be answered; and

(b) a stipulated statement of all facts relevant to the questions certified, showing fully the nature of the controversy in which the questions arose.

58.3. Transmission of Certification Order.

The clerk of the certifying court must send to the clerk of the Supreme Court of Texas the following:

(a) the certification order under the certifying court's official seal;

(b) a list of the names of all parties to the pending case, giving the address and telephone number, if known, of any party not represented by counsel; and

(c) a list of the names, addresses, and telephone numbers of counsel for each party.

58.4. Transmission of Record.

The certifying court should not send the Supreme Court of Texas the record in the pending case with the certification order. The Supreme Court may later require the original or copies of all or part of the record before the certifying court to be filed with the Supreme Court clerk.

58.5. Fees and Costs.

Unless the certifying court orders otherwise in its certification order, the parties must bear equally the fees under Rule 5.

58.6. Notice.

If the Supreme Court agrees to answer the questions certified to it, the Court will notify all parties and the certifying court. The Supreme Court clerk must also send a notice to the Attorney General of Texas if:

(a) the constitutionality of a Texas statute is the subject of a certified question that the Supreme Court has agreed to answer; and

(b) the State of Texas or an officer, agency, or employee of the state is not a party to the proceeding in the certifying court.

58.7. Briefs and Oral Argument.

(a) Briefs. The appealing party in the certifying court must file a brief with the Supreme Court clerk within 30 days after the date of the notice. Opposing parties must file an answering brief within 20 days after receiving the opening brief. Briefs must comply with Rule 55 to the extent its provisions apply. On motion complying with Rule 10.5(b), either before or after the brief is due, the Supreme Court may extend the time to file a brief.

(b) Oral Argument. Oral argument may be granted either on a party's request or on the Court's own initiative. Argument is governed by Rule 59.

58.8. Intervention by the State.

If the constitutionality of a Texas statute is the subject of a certified question that the Supreme Court has agreed to answer the State of Texas may intervene at any reasonable time for briefing and oral argument (if argument is allowed), on the question of constitutionality.

58.9. Opinion on Certified Questions.

If the Supreme Court has agreed to answer a certified question, it will hand down an opinion as in any other case.

58.10. Answering Certified Questions.

After all motions for rehearing have been overruled, the Supreme Court clerk must send to the certifying court the written opinion on the certified questions. The opinion must be under the Supreme Court's seal.

(Adopted by Order eff. Sept. 1, 1997.)

Comment to 1997 change: This is former Rule 114. The rule is substantially revised, but no substantive change in procedure is intended.

RULE 59. SUBMISSION AND ARGUMENT.

59.1. Submission Without Argument.

If at least six members of the Court so vote, a petition may be granted and an opinion handed down without oral argument.

59.2. Submission With Argument.

If the Supreme Court decides that oral argument would aid the Court, the Court will set the case for argument. The clerk will notify all parties of the submission date.

59.3. Purpose of Argument.

Oral argument should emphasize and clarify the written arguments in the briefs. Counsel should not merely read from a prepared text. Counsel should assume that all Justices have read the briefs before oral argument and should be prepared to respond to the Justices' questions.

59.4. Time for Argument.

Each side is allowed only as much time as the Court orders. Counsel is not required to use all the allotted time. On motion filed before the day of argument, the Court may extend the time for argument. The Court may also align the parties for purposes of presenting argument.

59.5. Number of Counsel.

Generally, only one counsel should argue for each side. Except on leave of court, no more than two counsel on each side may argue. Only one counsel may argue in rebuttal.

59.6. Argument by Amicus Curiae.

With leave of court obtained before the argument and with a party's consent, an amicus may share allotted time with that party. Otherwise, counsel for amicus curiae may not argue.

(Adopted by Order eff. Sept. 1, 1997.)

Comment to 1997 change: Former Rules 170, 171, and 172 are merged. Subdivisions 59.2 and 59.3 are new. Other changes are made.

RULE 60. JUDGMENTS IN THE SUPREME COURT.

60.1. Announcement of Judgments.

The Court's judgments will be announced by the clerk.

60.2. Types of Judgment.

The Supreme Court may:

(a) affirm the lower court's judgment in whole or in part;

(b) modify the lower court's judgment and affirm it as modified;

(c) reverse the lower court's judgment in whole or in part and render the judgment that the lower court should have rendered;

(d) reverse the lower court's judgment and remand the case for further proceedings;

(e) vacate the judgments of the lower courts and dismiss the case; or

(f) vacate the lower court's judgment and remand the case for further proceedings in light of changes in the law.

60.3. Remand in the Interest of Justice.

When reversing the court of appeals' judgment, the Supreme Court may, in the interest of justice, remand the case to the trial court even if a rendition of judgment is otherwise appropriate.

60.4. Judgment for Costs.

The Supreme Court's judgment will award to the prevailing party the costs incurred by that party in the Supreme Court. If appropriate, the judgment may also award the prevailing party the costs—including preparation costs for the record—incurred by that party in the court of appeals and in the trial court. But the Court may tax costs otherwise as required by law or for good cause.

60.5. Judgment Against Sureties.

When affirming, modifying, or rendering a judgment against the party who was the appellant in the court of appeals, the Supreme Court must render judgment against the sureties on that party's supersedeas bond, if any, for the performance of the judgment. If the Supreme Court taxes costs against the party who was the appellant in the court of appeals, the Court must render judgment for those costs against the sureties on that party's supersedeas bond, if any.

60.6. Other Orders.

The Supreme Court may make any other appropriate order required by the law and the nature of the case.

(Adopted by Order eff. Sept. 1, 1997.)

Comment to 1997 change: Former Rules 180 and 182(a) are merged. Subdivision 60.1 is from former Rule 181. Paragraphs 60.2(b), (e), and (f) are new but codify current practice. Subdivision 60.6 is new. Other changes are made.

RULE 61. REVERSIBLE ERROR.

61.1. Standard for Reversible Error.

No judgment may be reversed on appeal on the ground that the trial court made an error of law unless the Supreme Court concludes that the error complained of:

(a) probably caused the rendition of an improper judgment; or

(b) probably prevented the petitioner from properly presenting the case to the appellate courts.

61.2. Error Affecting Only Part of the Case.

If the error affects a part, but not all, of the matter in controversy, and that part is separable without unfairness to the parties, the judgment must be reversed and a new trial ordered only as to the part affected by the error. The Court may not order a separate trial solely on unliquidated damages if liability is contested.

61.3. Defects in Procedure.

The Supreme Court will not affirm or reverse a judgment or dismiss a petition for review for formal defects or irregularities in appellate procedure without allowing a reasonable time to correct or amend the defects or irregularities.

61.4. Remediable Error of the Trial Court or Court of Appeals.

(a) Generally. The Supreme Court will not affirm or reverse a judgment or dismiss a petition for review if:

(1) the trial court's or court of appeals' erroneous action or failure or refusal to act prevents the proper presentation of a case to the Supreme Court; and

(2) the trial court or court of appeals can correct its action or failure to act.

(b) Supreme Court Direction if Error Remediable. If the circumstances described in (a) exist, the Supreme Court will direct the trial court or court of appeals to correct the error. The Supreme Court will then proceed as if the error had not occurred.

(Adopted by Order eff. Sept. 1, 1997.)

Comment to 1997 change: Former Rules 184 and 185 are merged. The reversible error standard is amended to omit the reference to an action "reasonably calculated to cause" an improper judgment, but no substantive change is intended. Subdivision 61.3 is amended to delete the reference to defects of "substance."

RULE 62. DAMAGES FOR FRIVOLOUS APPEALS.

If the Supreme Court determines that a direct appeal or a petition for review is frivolous, it may—on motion of any party or on its own initiative, after notice and a reasonable opportunity for response—award to each prevailing party just damages. In determining whether to award damages, the Court must not consider any matter that does not appear in the record, briefs, or other papers filed in the court of appeals or the Supreme Court.

(Adopted by Order eff. Sept. 1, 1997.)

Comment to 1997 change: This is former Rule 182(b). The rule is changed from allowing a sanction when an appeal "filed for delay and without sufficient cause" to allowing a sanction when the appeal is "frivolous." A requirement for notice and an opportunity to respond is included.

RULE 63. OPINIONS; COPY OF OPINION AND JUDGMENT TO INTERESTED PARTIES AND OTHER COURTS.

The Supreme Court will hand down a written opinion in all cases in which it renders a judgment. The clerk will send a copy of the opinion and judgment to the court of appeals clerk, the trial court clerk, the regional administrative judge, and all parties to the appeal.

(Adopted by Order eff. Sept. 1, 1997.)

Comment to 1997 change: This is former Rule 181 with changes.

RULE 64. MOTION FOR REHEARING.

64.1. Time for Filing.

A motion for rehearing may be filed with the Supreme Court clerk within 15 days from the date when the Court renders judgment or makes an order disposing of a petition for review. In exceptional cases, if justice requires, the Court may shorten the time within which the motion may be filed or even deny the right to file it altogether.

64.2. Contents.

The motion must specify the points relied on for the rehearing.

64.3. Response and Decision.

No response to a motion for rehearing need be filed unless the Court so requests. A motion will not be granted unless a response has been filed or requested by the Court. But in exceptional cases, if justice so requires, the Court may deny the right to file a response and act on a motion any time after it is filed.

64.4. Second Motion.

The Court will not consider a second motion for rehearing unless the Court modifies its judgment, vacates its judgment and renders a new judgment, or issues a different opinion.

(Amended by Order Aug. 20, 2008, eff. Sept. 1, 2008.)

Comment to 2008 change: Subdivision 64.4 is amended to reflect the Court's practice of considering a second motion for rehearing after modifying its judgment or opinion in response to a prior motion for rehearing. When the Court modifies its opinion without modifying its judgment, the Court will ordinarily deny a second motion for rehearing unless the new opinion is substantially different from the original opinion.

64.5. Extensions of Time.

The Court may extend the time to file a motion for rehearing in the Supreme Court, if a motion complying with Rule 10.5(b) is filed with the Court no later than 15 days after the last date for filing a motion for rehearing.

64.6. Repealed by Order Nov. 13, 2012, eff. Dec. 1, 2012.

Comment to 1997 change: This is former Rule 190. The service and notice provisions of former subdivisions (b) and (c) are deleted. *See* Rule 9.5. Other changes are made.

RULE 65. ENFORCEMENT OF JUDGMENT AFTER MANDATE.

65.1. Statement of Costs.

The Supreme Court clerk will prepare, and send to the clerk to whom the mandate is directed, a statement of costs showing:

(a) the costs that were incurred in the Supreme Court, with a notation of those items that have been paid and those that are owing; and

(b) the party or parties against whom costs have been adjudged.

65.2. Enforcement of Judgment.

If the Supreme Court renders judgment, the trial court need not make any further order. Upon receiving the Supreme Court's mandate, the trial court clerk must proceed to enforce the judgment of the Supreme Court's as in any other case. Appellate court costs must be included with the trial court costs in any process to enforce the judgment. If all or part of the costs are collected, the trial court clerk must immediately remit to the appellate court clerk any amount due to that clerk.

(Adopted by Order eff. Sept. 1, 1997.)

Comment to 1997 change: Subdivision 65.1 is new. Subdivision 65.2 is from former Rule 183.

SECTION FIVE.
PROCEEDINGS IN THE COURT OF CRIMINAL APPEALS

RULE 66. DISCRETIONARY REVIEW IN GENERAL.

66.1. With or Without Petition.

The Court of Criminal Appeals may review a court of appeals' decision in a criminal case on its own initiative under Rule 67 or on the petition of a party under Rule 68.

66.2. Not a Matter of Right.

Discretionary review by the Court of Criminal Appeals is not a matter of right, but of the Court's discretion.

66.3. Reasons for Granting Review.

While neither controlling nor fully measuring the Court of Criminal Appeals' discretion, the following will be considered by the Court in deciding whether to grant discretionary review:

(a) whether a court of appeals' decision conflicts with another court of appeals' decision on the same issue;

(b) whether a court of appeals has decided an important question of state or federal law that has not been, but should be, settled by the Court of Criminal Appeals;

(c) whether a court of appeals has decided an important question of state or federal law in a way that conflicts with the applicable decisions of the Court of Criminal Appeals or the Supreme Court of the United States;

(d) whether a court of appeals has declared a statute, rule, regulation, or ordinance unconstitutional, or appears to have misconstrued a statute, rule, regulation, or ordinance;

(e) whether the justices of a court of appeals have disagreed on a material question of law necessary to the court's decision; and

(f) whether a court of appeals has so far departed from the accepted and usual course of judicial proceedings, or so far sanctioned such a departure by a lower court, as to call for an exercise of the Court of Criminal Appeals' power of supervision.

66.4. Documents to Aid Decision.

(a) Acquiring Documents. The Court of Criminal Appeals—or any judge of the Court—may order the court of appeals clerk to promptly send the following items to the Court in order to aid it in deciding whether to grant discretionary review:

(1) the appellate record;

(2) a copy of the opinions of the court of appeals;

(3) a copy of the motions filed in the court of appeals; and

(4) certified copies of any judgment or order of the court of appeals.

(b) Return of Documents. If discretionary review is not granted, the clerk of the Court of Criminal Appeals will return the appellate record to the court of appeals clerk.

(Adopted by Order eff. Sept. 1, 1997.)

Comment to 1997 change: This is former Rule 200. The former rule's reference to motions for rehearing now appears in Rule 49.9. The rule is otherwise amended without substantive change.

RULE 67. DISCRETIONARY REVIEW WITHOUT PETITION.

67.1. Four Judges' Vote.

By a vote of at least four judges, the Court of Criminal Appeals may grant review of a court of appeals' decision in a criminal case at any time before the mandate of the court of appeals issues. An order granting review will be filed with the clerk of the Court of Criminal Appeals, who must send a copy to the court of appeals clerk.

(Amended by Order Oct. 16, 2000 eff. Jan. 1, 2003.)

Comment to 2000 change: Language which was in the catchline of former Rule 201 has been deleted from Rule 67.1, to restore the substance of the rule, and to remove any implication that the court may not grant review on its own motion when a petition for discretionary review has been filed.

67.2. Order Staying Mandate.

To provide enough time for the Court of Criminal Appeals to decide whether to grant discretionary review under 67.1, the Court—or any judge of the Court—may file with the clerk of the court of appeals an order staying the court of appeals' mandate. The order must be signed by a judge of the Court of Criminal Appeals. The clerk of the Court of Criminal Appeals must immediately send a copy of the order to the court of appeals clerk.

67.3. Time to Issue Mandate Extended.

Unless otherwise limited in the order itself, an order staying the court of appeals' mandate under 67.2 will extend for an additional 45 days the time before issuance of the court of appeals' mandate. An order granting review prevents the issuance of the court of appeals' mandate pending the further order of the Court of Criminal Appeals. If four judges do not agree to grant review within that time the court of appeals clerk must issue the mandate.

(Adopted by Order eff. Sept. 1, 1997.)

Comment to 1997 change: This is former Rule 201. The rule is amended without substantive change.

RULE 68. DISCRETIONARY REVIEW WITH PETITION.

68.1. Generally.

On petition by any party, the Court of Criminal Appeals may review a court of appeals' decision in a criminal case.

68.2. Time to File Petition.

(a) First Petition. The petition must be filed within 30 days after either the day the court of appeals' judgment was rendered or the day the last timely motion for rehearing was overruled by the court of appeals.

(b) Subsequent Petition. Even if the time specified in (a) has expired, a party who otherwise may file a petition may do so within 10 days after the timely filing of another party's petition.

(c) Extension of Time. The Court of Criminal Appeals may extend the time to file a petition for discretionary review if a party files a motion complying with Rule 10.5(b) no later than 15 days after the last day for filing the petition. The Court of

Criminal Appeals may extend the time to file a response or reply if a party files a motion complying with Rule 10.5(b) either before or after the response or reply is due.

68.3. Where to File Petition.

The petition and all copies of the petition must be filed with the clerk of the court of appeals, but if the State's Prosecuting Attorney files a petition, the State's Prosecuting Attorney may file the copies of the petition—but not the original—with the clerk of the Court of Criminal Appeals instead of with the court of appeals clerk.

68.4. Contents of Petition.

A petition for discretionary review must be as brief as possible. It must be addressed to the "Court of Criminal Appeals of Texas" and must state the name of the party or parties applying for review. The petition must contain the following items:

(a) Identity of Judge, Parties, and Counsel. The petition must list the trial court judge, all parties to the judgment or order appealed from, and the names and addresses of all trial and appellate counsel.

(b) Table of Contents. The petition must include a table of contents with references to the pages of the petition. The table of contents must indicate the subject matter of each ground or question presented for review.

(c) Index of Authorities. The petition must include an index of authorities arranged alphabetically and indicating the pages of the petition where the authorities are cited.

(d Statement Regarding Oral Argument. The petition must include a short statement of why oral argument would be helpful, or a statement that oral argument is waived. If a reply or cross-petition is filed, it likewise must include a statement of why oral argument should or should not be heard.

(e) Statement of the Case. The petition must state briefly the nature of the case. This statement should seldom exceed half a page. The details of the case should be reserved and stated with the pertinent grounds or questions.

(f) Statement of Procedural History. The petition must state:

(1) the date any opinion of the court of appeals was handed down, or the date of any order of the court of appeals disposing of the case without an opinion;

(2) the date any motion for rehearing was filed (or a statement that none was filed); and

(3) the date the motion for rehearing was overruled or otherwise disposed of.

(g) Grounds for Review. The petition must state briefly, without argument, the grounds on which the petition is based. The grounds must be separately numbered. If the petitioner has access to the record, the petitioner must (after each ground) refer to the page of the record where the matter complained of is found. Instead of listing grounds for review, the petition may contain the questions presented for review, expressed in the terms and circumstances of the case but without unnecessary detail. The statement of questions should be short and concise, not argumentative or repetitious.

(h) Argument. The petition must contain a direct and concise argument, with supporting authorities, amplifying the reasons for granting review. *See* Rule 66.3. The court of appeals' opinions will be considered with the petition, and statements in those opinions need not be repeated if counsel accepts them as correct.

(i) Prayer for Relief. The petition must state clearly the nature of the relief sought.

(j) Appendix. The petition must contain a copy of any opinion of the court of appeals.

(Amended by Order Dec. 23, 2002, eff. Jan. 1, 2003; Dec. 13, 2013, eff. Jan. 1, 2014.)

Comment to 2002 change: The original catchline of subdivision 68.4(g) was "Reasons for Review," which caused confusion because of its similarity to the catch line in subdivision 66.3 ("Reasons for Granting Review"). It is changed to "Argument."

68.5. Repealed by Order Nov. 13, 2012, eff. Dec. 1, 2012.

68.6. Nonconforming Petition.

The Court may strike, order redrawn, or summarily refuse a petition for discretionary review that is unnecessarily lengthy or that does not conform to these rules.

68.7. Court of Appeals Clerk's Duties.

(a) On Filing of the Petition. Upon receiving the petition, the court of appeals clerk must file the original petition and note the filing on the docket.

(b) Reply. The opposing party has 30 days after the timely filing of the petition in the court of appeals to file a reply to the petition with the clerk of the court of appeals. Upon receiving a reply to the petition, the clerk for the court of appeals must file the reply and note the filing on the docket.

(c) Sending Petition and Reply to Court of Criminal Appeals. Unless a petition for discretionary review is dismissed under Rule 50, the clerk of the court of appeals must, within 60 days after the petition is filed, send to the clerk of the Court of Criminal Appeals the petition and any copies furnished by counsel, the reply, if any, and any copies furnished by counsel, together with the record, copies of the motions filed in the case, and copies of any judgments, opinions, and orders of the court of appeals. The clerk need not forward any nondocumentary exhibits unless ordered to do so by the Court of Criminal Appeals.

(Amended by Order March 10, 2008, eff. Sept. 1, 2008; Order Aug. 20, 2008, eff. Sept. 1, 2008.)

68.8. Court of Criminal Appeals Clerk's Duties on Receipt of Petition.

The clerk of the Court of Criminal Appeals will receive a petition for discretionary review, file the petition and the accompanying record from the court of appeals, note the filing of the petition and record on the docket, and notify the parties by U.S. Mail of the filing. The Court may dispense with notice and grant or refuse the petition immediately upon its filing.

68.9. Amendment.

The petition or a reply may be amended or supplemented within 30 days after the original petition was filed in the court of appeals or at any time when justice requires. The record may be amended in the Court of Criminal Appeals under the same circumstances and in the same manner as in the court of appeals.

68.10. Service on State Prosecuting Attorney.

In addition to the service required by Rule 9.5, service of the petition, the reply, and any amendment or supplementation of a petition or reply must be made on the State Prosecuting Attorney, P.O. Box 12405, Austin, Texas 78711.

(Adopted by Order eff. Sept. 1, 1997.)

Comment to 1997 change: This is former Rule 202. Subdivisions (k) and (l) of the former rule have been relocated to Rule 69. The new rule limits the length of a petition and reply. The time for amendment of a petition or reply is increased to conform with the amendment in Rule 50. The rule is otherwise amended without substantive change.

RULE 69. ACTION OF COURT ON PETITION FOR DISCRETIONARY REVIEW AND AFTER GRANTING REVIEW.

69.1. Granting or Refusal.

If four judges do not vote to grant a petition for discretionary review, the Court will enter a docket notation that the petition is refused. If four judges vote to grant a petition, the Court will enter a docket notation that discretionary review is granted.

69.2. Setting Case for Submission.

If discretionary review is granted, either on the petition of a party or by the Court on its own initiative, the case will be set for submission.

69.3. Improvident Grant of Review.

If, after granting discretionary review, five judges are of the opinion that discretionary review should not have been granted, the case will be dismissed.

69.4. Clerk's Duties.

(a) On Refusal or Dismissal. When the Court refuses or dismisses a petition, the clerk will send to the parties and the State Prosecuting Attorney a notice informing them that the petition was refused or dismissed. The clerk will retain the petition and all other items filed in the case for at least 15 days from the date of the refusal or dismissal. At the end of that time, if no motion for rehearing has been timely filed, or upon the overruling or dismissal of such a motion, the clerk will send to the court of appeals clerk a certified copy of the order refusing or dismissing the petition (as well as any order overruling a motion for rehearing). The clerk of the Court of Criminal Appeals will return the appellate record to the court of appeals clerk but will retain the petition, and other documents filed in the Court of Criminal Appeals.

(b) On Granting Review. If the Court grants discretionary review, the clerk will send to the parties and the State Prosecuting Attorney a notice informing them that discretionary review was granted.

(Adopted by Order eff. Sept. 1, 1997.)

Comment to 1997 change: This is former subdivisions (k) and (l) of Rule 202. Internal procedures of the Court are deleted. Provisions are added in 69.4(a) and (b) for the clerk to send notice of the granting, refusal, or dismissal of a petition for discretionary review. Other nonsubstantive changes are made.

RULE 70. BRIEF ON THE MERITS.

70.1. Initial Brief.

If review is granted, the petitioner—or, if there was no petition, the party who lost in the court of appeals—must file a brief within 30 days after review is granted.

70.2. Respondent's Brief.

The opposing party must file a brief within 30 days after the petitioner's brief is filed.

(Amended by Order Dec. 13, 2013, eff. Jan. 1, 2014.)

70.3. Brief Contents and Form.

Briefs must comply with the requirements of Rules 9 and 38, except that they need not contain the appendix (Rule 38.1(k)). Copies must be served as required by Rule 68.11.

(Amended by Order March 10, 2008, eff. Sept. 1, 2008; Order Aug. 20, 2008, eff. Sept. 1, 2008; Order Aug. 10, 2012, eff. Dec. 1, 2012; Order Nov. 13, 2012, eff. Dec. 1, 2012.)

70.4. Other Briefs.

The Court of Criminal Appeals may direct that a party file a brief, or an additional brief, in a particular case. Additionally, upon motion by a party the Court may permit the filing of additional briefs.

(Adopted by Order eff. Sept. 1, 1997. Amended by Order Dec. 13, 2013, eff. Jan. 1, 2014.)

Comment to 1997 change: This is former Rule 203. The rule is amended without substantive change.

RULE 71. DIRECT APPEALS.

71.1. Direct Appeal.

Cases in which the death penalty has been assessed under Code of Criminal Procedure article 37.071, and cases in which bail has been denied in non-capital cases under Article I, Section 11a of the Constitution, are appealed directly to the Court of Criminal Appeals.

(Amended by Order Dec. 23, 2002 eff. Jan. 1, 2003.)

71.2. Record.

The appellate record should be prepared and filed in accordance with Rules 31, 32, 34, 35 and 37, except that the record must be filed in the Court of Criminal Appeals. After disposition of the appeal, the Court may discard copies of juror information cards or other portions of the clerk's record that are not relevant to an issue on appeal.

(Amended by Order Dec. 23, 2002 eff. Jan. 1, 2003.)

71.3. Briefs.

Briefs in a direct appeal should be prepared and filed in accordance with Rule 38, except that the brief need not contain an appendix (Rule 38.1(k)). All briefs must be filed in the Court of Criminal Appeals. The brief must include a short statement of why oral argument would be helpful, or a statement that oral argument is waived.

(Amended by Order Dec. 23, 2002, eff. Jan. 1, 2003; Order March 10, 2008, eff. Sept. 1, 2008; Order Aug. 20, 2008, eff. Sept. 1, 2008; Order Aug. 10, 2012, eff. Dec. 1, 2012; Order Nov. 13, 2012, eff. Dec. 1, 2012.)

Comment to 2002 change: A requirement that briefs include a statement regarding oral argument is added.

71.4. Additional briefs.

Upon motion by a party the Court may permit the filing of additional briefs other than those provided for in Rule 38.

(Adopted by Order Dec. 13, 2013, eff. Jan. 1, 2014.)

RULE 72. EXTRAORDINARY MATTERS.

72.1. Leave to File.

A motion for leave to file must accompany an original petition for writ of habeas corpus, mandamus, procedendo, prohibition, certiorari, or other extraordinary writ, or any other motion not otherwise provided for in these rules.

72.2. Disposition.

If five judges tentatively believe that the case should be filed and set for submission, the motion for leave will be granted and the case will then be handled and disposed of in accordance with Rule 52.7. If the motion for leave is denied, no motions for rehearing or reconsideration will be entertained. But the Court may, on its own initiative, reconsider a denial of a motion for leave.

(Adopted by Order eff. Sept. 1, 1997.)

Comment to 1997 change: This is former Rule 211. The rule is amended to include all the Court's jurisdiction of extraordinary matters. Internal procedures of the Court are deleted. Other nonsubstantive changes are made.

RULE 73. POSTCONVICTION APPLICATIONS FOR WRITS OF HABEAS CORPUS.

73.1. Form for Application Filed Under Article 11.07 of the Code of Criminal Procedure.

(a) Prescribed Form. An application filed under Article 11.07 must be on the form prescribed by the Court of Criminal Appeals.

(b) Availability of Form. The district clerk of the county of conviction shall make the forms available to applicants on request, without charge.

(c) Contents. The applicant or petitioner must provide all information required by the form. The form must include all grounds for relief and set forth in summary fashion the facts supporting each ground. Any ground not raised on the form will not be considered. Legal citations and arguments may be made in a separate memorandum. The form must be computer-generated, typewritten, or legibly handwritten.

(d) Length. Each ground for relief and supporting facts raised on the form shall not exceed the two pages provided for each ground in the form. The applicant or petitioner may file a separate memorandum. This memorandum shall comply with these rules and shall not exceed 15,000 words if computer-generated or 50 pages if not. If the total number of pages, including those in the original and any additional memoranda, exceed the word or page limits, an application may be dismissed unless the convicting court for good cause shown grants leave to exceed the prescribed limits. The prescribed limits do not include appendices, exhibits, cover page, table of contents, table of authorities, and certificate of compliance.

(e) Typeface. A computer-generated memorandum must be printed in a conventional typeface no smaller than 14-point except for footnotes, which must be no smaller than 12-point. A typewritten document must be printed in standard 10-character-per-inch (cpi) monospaced typeface.

(f) Certificate of Compliance. A computer-generated memorandum, including any additional memoranda, must include a certificate by the applicant or petitioner stating the number of words in the document. The person certifying may rely on the word count of the computer program used to prepare the document.

(g) Verification. The application must be verified by either:

(1) oath made before a notary public or other officer authorized to administer oaths; or

(2) an unsworn declaration in substantially the form required by Civil Practice and Remedies Code chapter 132 as set out in the verification section of the application form.

(Adopted by Order Oct. 16, 2000, eff. Jan. 1, 2001. Amended by Order Dec. 13, 2013, eff. Jan. 1, 2014; Order Nov. 5, 2018, eff. Dec. 1, 2018.)

73.2. Noncompliant Applications.

The Court of Criminal Appeals may dismiss an application that does not comply with these rules.

(Adopted by Order Oct. 16, 2000, eff. Jan. 1, 2001. Amended by Order Dec. 13, 2013, eff. Jan. 1, 2014.)

73.3. State's Response.

Any response by the State must comply with length, typeface, and certificate of compliance requirements set out in rule 73.1 (d),(e) and (f).

(Adopted by Order Dec. 13, 2013, eff. Jan. 1, 2014.)

73.4. Filing and Transmission of Habeas Record.

(a) The district clerk of the county of conviction shall accept and file all Code of Criminal Procedure article 11.07 applications.

(b) In addition to the duties set out in Article 11.07, the clerk shall do the following:

(1) If the convicting court enters an order designating issues, the clerk shall immediately transmit to the Court of Criminal Appeals a copy of that order and proof of the date the district attorney received the habeas application.

(2) When any pleadings, objections, motions, affidavits, exhibits, proposed or entered findings of fact and conclusions of law, or other orders are filed or made a part of the record, the district clerk shall immediately send a copy to all parties in the case. A party has ten days from the date he receives the trial court's findings of fact and conclusions of law to file objections, but the trial court may, nevertheless, order the district clerk to transmit the record to the Court of Criminal Appeals before the expiration of the ten days. Upon transmission of the record, the district clerk shall immediately notify all parties in the case.

(3) When a district clerk transmits the record in a postconviction application for a writ of habeas corpus under Code of Criminal Procedure articles 11.07 or 11.071, the district clerk must prepare and transmit a summary sheet that includes the following information:

(A) the convicting court's name and county, and the name of the judge who tried the case;

(B) the applicant's name, the offense, the plea, the cause number, the sentence, and the date of sentence, as shown in the judgment of conviction;

(C) the cause number of any appeal from the conviction and the citation to any published report;

(D) whether a hearing was held on the application, whether findings of fact were made, any recommendation of the convicting court, and the name of the judge who presided over the application;

(E) the name of counsel if applicant is represented; and

(F) the following certification:

I certify that all applicable requirements of Texas Rule of Appellate Procedure 73.4 have been complied with in this habeas proceeding, including the requirement to serve on all the parties in the case any objections, motions, affidavits, exhibits, proposed findings of fact and conclusions of law, findings of fact and conclusions of law, and any other orders entered or pleadings filed in the habeas case.

________________________________ ______________
Signature of District Clerk or Clerk's Representative Date Signed.

The Court of Criminal Appeals may by order adopt a form of summary sheet that the district clerks must use.

(4) The district clerk shall also include in the record transmitted to the Court of Criminal Appeals, among any other pertinent papers or supplements, the indictment or information, any plea papers, the court's docket sheet, the court's charge and the jury's verdict, any proposed findings of fact and conclusions of law, the court's findings of fact and conclusions of law, any objections to the court's findings of fact and conclusions of law filed by either party, and the transcript of any hearings held.

(5) On the 181st day from the date of receipt of the application by the State of a postconviction application for writ of habeas corpus under Article 11.07, the district clerk shall forward the writ record to this Court unless the district court has received an extension of time from the Court of Criminal Appeals pursuant to Rule 73.5.

(Adopted by Order eff. Sept. 1, 1997. Amended by Order Nov. 8, 2000, eff. Jan. 1, 2001; Dec. 13, 2013, eff. Jan. 1, 2014; Tex. Sup. Ct. Misc. Docket No. 15-006 Dec. 7, 2015, eff. Jan. 1, 2016; Tex. Sup. Ct. Misc. Docket No. 16-9012 Feb. 29, 2016, eff. Jan. 1, 2016; Order Nov. 5, 2018, eff. Dec. 1, 2018; Order Nov. 5, 2018, eff. Dec. 1, 2018.)

Comment to 2018 change: Rules 73.1 and 73.4 are amended in conjunction with amendments to the form for applications filed under Article 11.07 of the Code of Criminal Procedure (Appendix E to these rules) and the Clerk's Summary Sheet (Appendix F to these rules). The amendments clarify terminology and procedures for filing Article 11.07 writ applications and update the Article 11.07 writ application form to incorporate current technologies and filing procedures. The application form will be made available on the internet through the Court of Criminal Appeals' website. In addition, the amendments bring the application and filing procedures into conformity with Civil Practice and Remedies Code chapter 132, which permits both inmates and non-inmates to file unsworn declarations in lieu of notarized oaths. Further, the rules amendments and changes to the clerk's summary sheet clarify the information that district clerks must provide to the Court of Criminal Appeals and add a new requirement that clerks certify that they have complied with all the requirements of Rule 73.4, including the requirement to serve on all parties in the case all objections, motions, affidavits, exhibits, proposed findings of fact and conclusions of law, findings of fact and conclusions of law, and any other orders entered or pleadings filed in the habeas case. The phrase "all parties in the case" as used in Rule 73.4 includes: the attorney representing the State; the applicant (including pro se and inmate applicants); and, if the applicant is represented by counsel, applicant's attorney.

73.5. Time Frame for Resolution of Claims Raised in Application.

Within 180 days from the date of receipt of the application by the State, the convicting court shall resolve any issues that the court has timely designated for resolution. Any motion for extension of time must be filed in the Court of Criminal Appeals before the expiration of the 180-day period.

(Adopted by Order Dec. 13, 2013, eff. Jan. 1, 2014.)

73.6. Action on Application.

The Court may deny relief based upon its own review of the application or may issue such other instructions or orders as may be appropriate.

(Adopted by Order eff. Sept. 1, 1997. Amended by Order Nov. 8, 2000, eff. Jan. 1, 2001.)

Comment to 1997 change: This is former Rule 4 of the Appendix for Criminal Cases. The rule is amended without substantive change.

Comment to 2000 change: Rules 73.1 and 73.2 are added, and a form is added in an appendix. [Appendix is omitted.]

RULE 74. REVIEW OF CERTIFIED STATE CRIMINAL-LAW QUESTIONS.

74.1. Certification.

The Court of Criminal Appeals may answer questions of Texas criminal law certified to it by any federal appellate court if the certifying court is presented with determinative questions of Texas criminal law having no controlling Court of Criminal Appeals precedent. The Court may decline to answer the questions certified to it.

74.2. Contents of the Certification Order.

An order from the certifying court must set forth:

(a) the questions of law to be answered; and

(b) a stipulated statement of all facts relevant to the questions certified, showing fully the nature of the controversy in which the questions arose.

74.3. Transmission of Certification Order.

The clerk of the certifying court must send to the clerk of the Court of Criminal Appeals the following:

(a) the certification order under the certifying court's official seal;

(b) a list of the names of each party to the pending case, giving the address and telephone number, if known, of any party not represented by counsel; and

(c) a list of the names and addresses of counsel for each party.

74.4. Transmission of Record.

The certifying court should not send to the Court of Criminal Appeals the record in the pending case with the certification order. The Court of Criminal Appeals may later require the original or copies of all or part of the record before the certifying court to be filed with the Court of Criminal Appeals clerk.

74.5. Notice.

If the Court of Criminal Appeals agrees to answer the questions certified to it, the Court will notify all parties and the certifying court. The Court of Criminal Appeals clerk must also send a notice to the Attorney General of Texas if:

(a) the constitutionality of a Texas statute is the subject of a certified question that the Court of Criminal Appeals has agreed to answer; and

(b) the State of Texas or an officer, agency, or employee of the State is not a party to the proceeding in the certifying court.

74.6. Briefs and Oral Argument.

(a) Briefs. The appealing party in the certifying court must file a brief with the clerk of the Court of Criminal Appeals within 30 days after the date of the notice. Opposing parties must file an answering brief within 15 days of receiving the opening brief. Briefs must comply with Rule 38 to the extent that its provisions apply.

(b) Oral Argument. Oral argument may be granted either on a party's request or on the Court's own initiative. Argument is governed by Rule 39.

74.7. Intervention by the State.

If the constitutionality of a Texas statute is the subject of a certified question that the Court of Criminal Appeals has agreed to answer, the State of Texas may intervene at any reasonable time for briefing and oral argument (if argument is allowed) on the question of constitutionality.

74.8. Opinion on Certified Question.

If the Court of Criminal Appeals has agreed to answer a certified question, it will hand down an opinion as in any other case.

74.9. Motion for Rehearing.

Any party may file a motion for rehearing within 15 days after the opinion is handed down. The motion must clearly state the points relied on for the rehearing. No reply to a motion for rehearing need be filed unless the Court so requests. The Court will not grant a motion for rehearing unless a response has been filed or requested.

74.10. Answering Certified Questions.

After all motions for rehearing have been overruled, the clerk of the Court of Criminal Appeals must send to the certifying court the written opinion on the certified questions. The opinion must be under the Court of Criminal Appeals' seal.

(Adopted by Order eff. Sept. 1, 1997.)

Comment to 1997 change: This is former Rule 214. The rule is amended without substantive change.

RULE 75. NOTIFICATION; ORAL ARGUMENT.

75.1. Notification of Argument or Submission.

Oral argument will be permitted only in cases designated by the Court of Criminal Appeals. If the Court permits argument in a case, the clerk will notify the parties of the date set for argument. If a case will be submitted without argument, the clerk will notify the parties of the date of submission. The clerk must use all reasonable diligence to notify counsel of settings, but counsel's failure to receive notice will not necessarily prevent argument or submission of the case on the day it is set.

75.2. Request for Argument.

If a case is not designated for oral argument but counsel desires oral argument, counsel may—within 30 days of the date of the clerk's notice—petition the Court to allow oral argument. This petition must contain specific reasons why oral argument is desired.

75.3. Oral Argument.

Unless extended in a special case, the total maximum time for oral argument is 20 minutes per side. Counsel for the appellant or petitioner is entitled to open and conclude the argument. Counsel should not read at length from the briefs, records, or authorities. Counsel may orally correct a brief, but multiple additional citations should not be given orally; instead, these citations should be filed in writing with the clerk.

(Adopted by Order eff. Sept. 1, 1997.)

Comment to 1997 change: This is former Rule 220. The rule is amended without substantive change.

RULE 76. SUBMISSIONS EN BANC.

The Court will sit en banc to consider the following types of cases:

(a) direct appeals;
(b) cases of discretionary review;
(c) cases in which leave to file was granted under Rule 72;
(d) cases that were docketed under Code of Criminal Procedure articles 11.07 or 11.071;
(e) certified questions; and
(f) rehearings under Rule 79.

(Adopted by Order eff. Sept. 1, 1997.)

Comment to 1997 change: This is former Rule 222. The rule is expanded to include other kinds of cases. Internal procedures of the Court are deleted. Other nonsubstantive changes are made.

RULE 77. OPINIONS.

77.1. Generally.

In each case that is argued or submitted without argument to the Court of Criminal Appeals, the Court will hand down a written opinion setting forth the reasons for its decision and any germane precedent. Any judge may file an opinion dissenting from or concurring in the Court's judgment.

77.2. Signing; Publication.

A majority of the judges will determine whether an opinion will be signed by a judge or issued per curiam, and whether the opinion (or a portion of the opinion) will be published.

77.3. Unpublished Opinions.

Unpublished opinions have no precedential value and must not be cited as authority by counsel or by a court.

77.4. Copies.

On the date when an opinion is handed down or an order rendered, the clerk of the Court of Criminal Appeals must mail copies of the opinion or order to:

(a) the parties;

(b) the State Prosecuting Attorney;

(c) the trial court clerk; and

(d) if the case is of discretionary review, the court of appeals clerk.

(Adopted by Order eff. Sept. 1, 1997.)

Comment to 1997 change: This is former Rule 223. The rule is amended without substantive change.

RULE 78. JUDGMENTS IN THE COURT OF CRIMINAL APPEALS.

78.1. Types of Judgment.

The Court of Criminal Appeals may:

(a) affirm the lower court's judgment in whole or in part;

(b) modify the lower court's judgment and affirm it as modified;

(c) reverse the court's judgment in whole or in part and render the judgment that the lower court should have rendered;

(d) reverse the lower court's judgment and remand the case for further proceedings;

(e) vacate the judgments of the lower courts and dismiss the case;

(f) vacate the lower court's judgment and remand the case for further proceedings in light of changes in the law; or

(g) dismiss the appeal.

78.2. Remand in the Interests of Justice.

When reversing the court of appeals' judgment, the Court of Criminal Appeals may, in the interests of justice, remand the case to the trial court even if a rendition of judgment is otherwise appropriate.

78.3. Other Orders.

The Court of Criminal Appeals may make any other appropriate order required by the law and the nature of the case.

(Adopted by Order eff. Sept. 1, 1997.)

Comment to 1997 change: The rule is new.

RULE 79. REHEARINGS.

79.1. Motion for Rehearing.

A motion for rehearing may be filed with the Court of Criminal Appeals clerk within 15 days from the date of the judgment or order. In exceptional cases, if justice requires, the Court may shorten the time within which the motion may be filed or even deny the right to file it altogether.

79.2. Contents.

(a) The motion must briefly and distinctly state the grounds and arguments relied on for rehearing.

(b) A motion for rehearing an order that grants discretionary review may not be filed.

(c) A motion for rehearing an order that refuses a petition for discretionary review may be grounded only on substantial intervening circumstances or on other significant circumstances which are specified in the motion. Counsel must certify that the motion is so grounded and that the motion is made in good faith and not for delay.

(d) A motion for rehearing an order that denies habeas corpus relief or dismisses a habeas corpus application under Code of Criminal Procedure, articles 11.07 or 11.071, may not be filed. The Court may on its own initiative reconsider the case.

(Amended by Tex. Sup. Ct. Misc. Docket No. 15-006 Dec. 7, 2015, eff. Jan. 1, 2016; Tex. Sup. Ct. Misc. Docket No. 16-9012 Feb. 29, 2016, eff. Jan. 1, 2016.)

79.3. Amendments.

A motion for rehearing may be amended anytime before the period allowed for filing the motion expires, and with leave of the court, anytime before the Court decides the motion.

79.4. Decision.

If the Court grants rehearing, the case will be set for submission. Oral argument may, but normally will not, be permitted.

79.5. Further Motion for Rehearing.

The Court will not consider a second motion for rehearing after rehearing is denied. If rehearing is granted and the Court delivers an opinion on rehearing, a party may file a further motion for rehearing.

79.6. Extension of Time.

The Court may extend the time for filing a motion or a further motion for rehearing if a party files a motion complying with Rule 10.5(b) within the time for filing a motion or further motion for rehearing.

79.7. Service.

The requirements of Rule 68.11 apply.

(Adopted by Order eff. Sept. 1, 1997.)

Comment to 1997 change: This is former Rule 230, and the portion of former Rule 213 that prohibited motions for rehearing. The Court may now permit oral argument after granting rehearing, although it is disfavored. A further motion for rehearing may now be filed by any party, rather than only the losing party. Other nonsubstantive changes are made.

Table of Cases

-E-

-F-

-G-

-H-

-I-

-J-

-K-

-L-

-M-

-N-

-O-

-P-

-R-

-S-

-T-

-U-

-V-

-W-